lonely planet

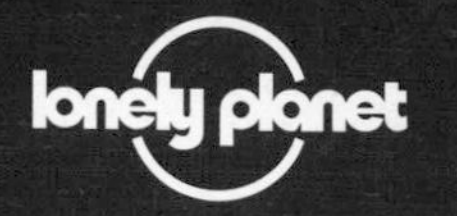

Indonesia

Justine Vaisutis
Neal Bedford, Mark Elliott, Nick Ray, Iain Stewart, Ryan Ver Berkmoes,
China Williams, Patrick Witton, Wendy Yanagihara

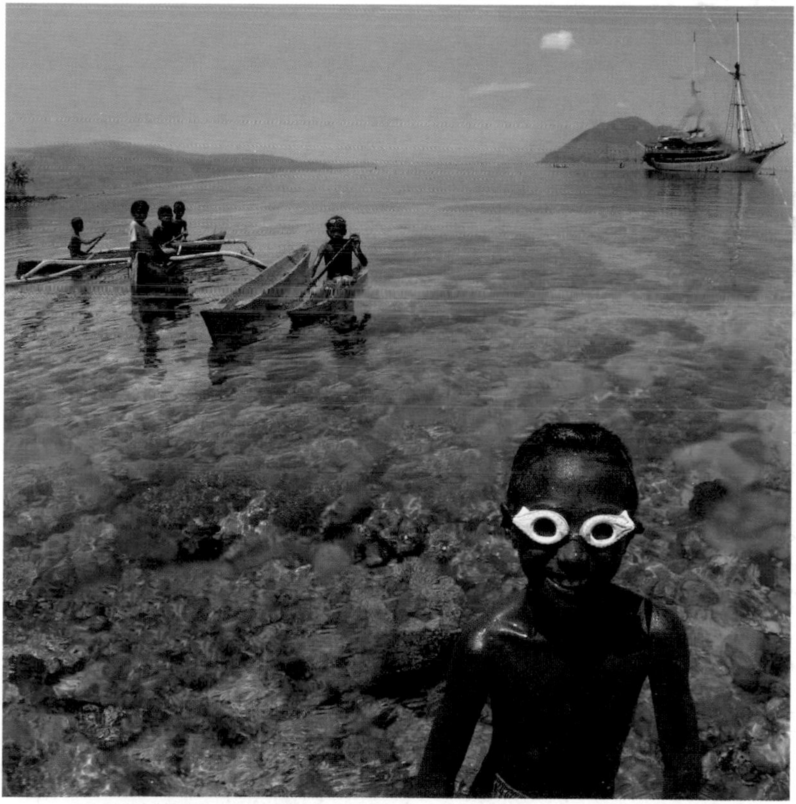

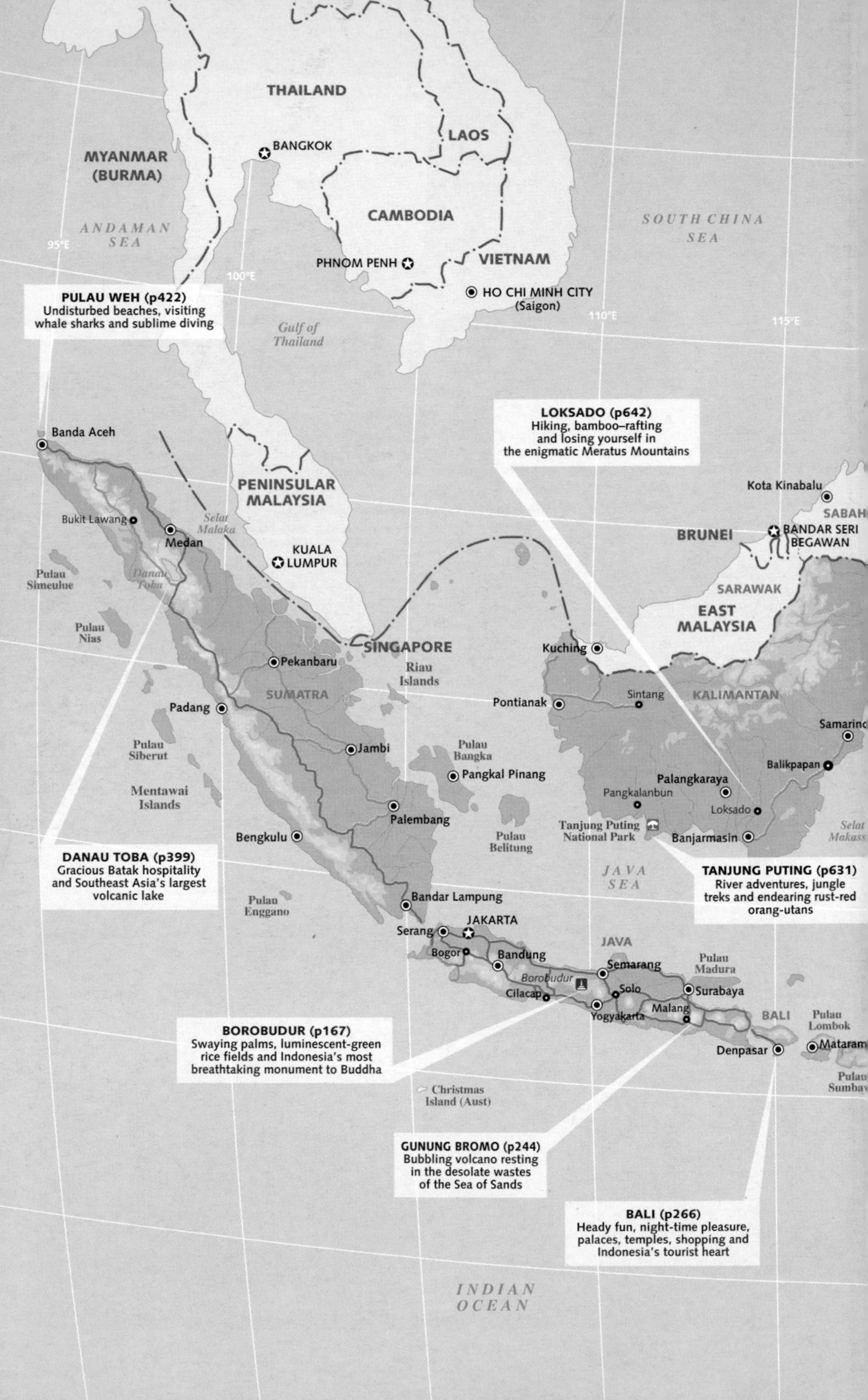

THAILAND
LAOS
BANGKOK
MYANMAR (BURMA)
CAMBODIA
ANDAMAN SEA
SOUTH CHINA SEA
95°E
100°E
110°E
115°E
PHNOM PENH
VIETNAM
HO CHI MINH CITY (Saigon)
PULAU WEH (p422)
Undisturbed beaches, visiting whale sharks and sublime diving
Gulf of Thailand
LOKSADO (p642)
Hiking, bamboo–rafting and losing yourself in the enigmatic Meratus Mountains
Banda Aceh
PENINSULAR MALAYSIA
Kota Kinabalu
SABAH
Bukit Lawang
Medan
Selat Malaka
BRUNEI
BANDAR SERI BEGAWAN
Pulau Simeulue
Danau Toba
KUALA LUMPUR
SARAWAK
EAST MALAYSIA
Pulau Nias
SINGAPORE
Kuching
Pekanbaru
Riau Islands
SUMATRA
Sintang
KALIMANTAN
Padang
Pontianak
Samarinda
Pulau Siberut
Jambi
Pulau Bangka
Balikpapan
Mentawai Islands
Pangkal Pinang
Palangkaraya
Pangkalanbun
Palembang
Loksado
Tanjung Puting National Park
Bengkulu
Pulau Belitung
Banjarmasin
Selat Makassar
DANAU TOBA (p399)
Gracious Batak hospitality and Southeast Asia's largest volcanic lake
JAVA SEA
TANJUNG PUTING (p631)
River adventures, jungle treks and endearing rust-red orang-utans
Pulau Enggano
Bandar Lampung
JAKARTA
Serang
JAVA
Bogor
Bandung
Semarang
Pulau Madura
Borobudur
Solo
Surabaya
Cilacap
Yogyakarta
Malang
BALI
Pulau Lombok
BOROBUDUR (p167)
Swaying palms, luminescent-green rice fields and Indonesia's most breathtaking monument to Buddha
Denpasar
Mataram
Pulau Sumbawa
Christmas Island (Aust)
GUNUNG BROMO (p244)
Bubbling volcano resting in the desolate wastes of the Sea of Sands
BALI (p266)
Heady fun, night-time pleasure, palaces, temples, shopping and Indonesia's tourist heart
INDIAN OCEAN

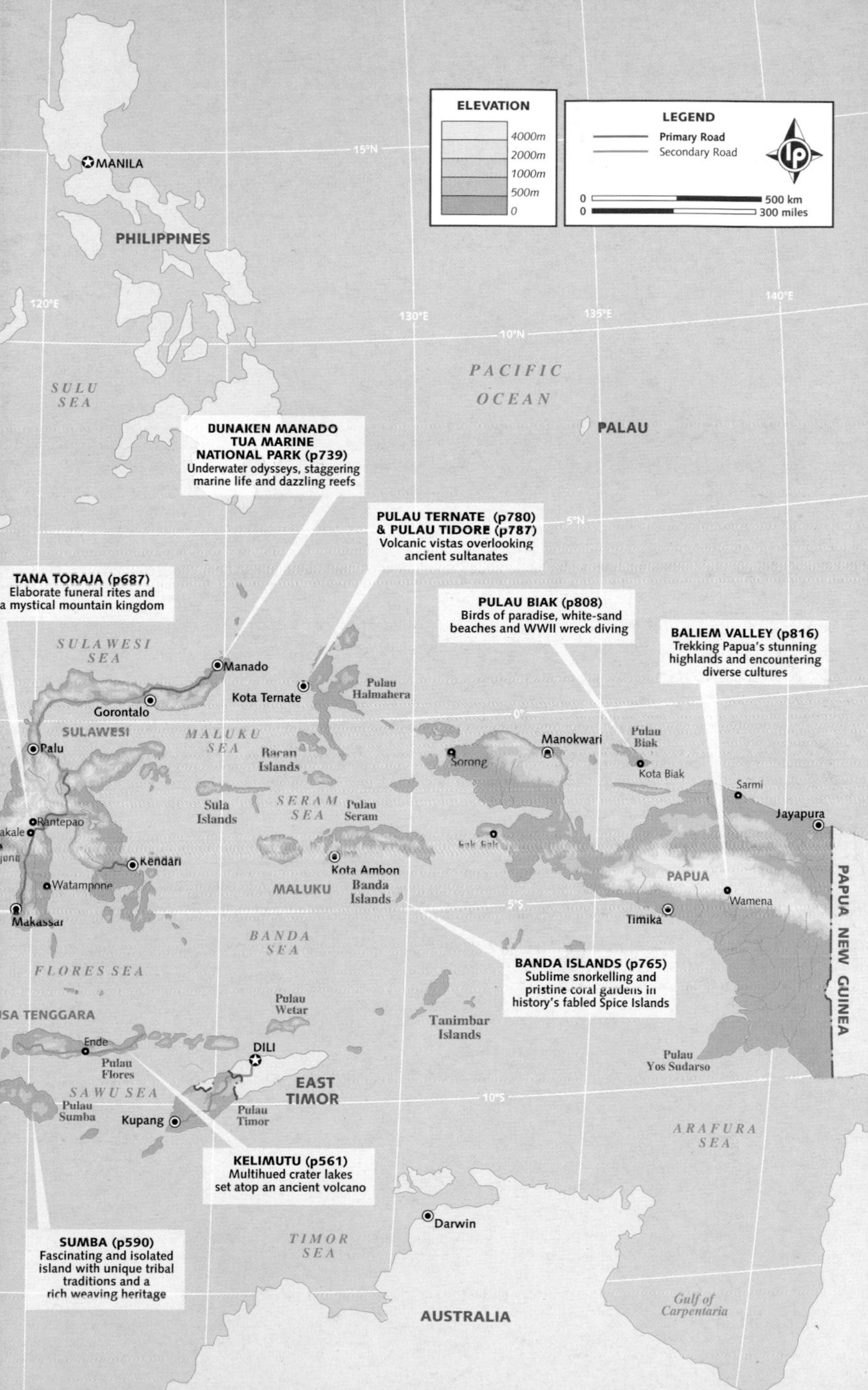

ELEVATION
4000m
2000m
1000m
500m
0
LEGEND
Primary Road
Secondary Road
0 500 km
0 300 miles
MANILA
PHILIPPINES
15°N
120°E
130°E
135°E
140°E
10°N
5°N
0°
5°S
10°S
PACIFIC OCEAN
PALAU
SULU SEA
DUNAKEN MANADO TUA MARINE NATIONAL PARK (p739)
Underwater odysseys, staggering marine life and dazzling reefs
PULAU TERNATE (p780) & PULAU TIDORE (p787)
Volcanic vistas overlooking ancient sultanates
TANA TORAJA (p687)
Elaborate funeral rites and a mystical mountain kingdom
PULAU BIAK (p808)
Birds of paradise, white-sand beaches and WWII wreck diving
BALIEM VALLEY (p816)
Trekking Papua's stunning highlands and encountering diverse cultures
SULAWESI SEA
Manado
Kota Ternate
Pulau Halmahera
Gorontalo
SULAWESI
MALUKU SEA
Palu
Bacan Islands
Sorong
Manokwari
Pulau Biak
Kota Biak
Sarmi
Jayapura
Sula Islands
SERAM SEA
Pulau Seram
Rantepao
Makale
Kendari
Kota Ambon
Banda Islands
MALUKU
Watampone
Makassar
PAPUA
Wamena
Timika
PAPUA NEW GUINEA
BANDA SEA
FLORES SEA
BANDA ISLANDS (p765)
Sublime snorkelling and pristine coral gardens in history's fabled Spice Islands
NUSA TENGGARA
Pulau Wetar
Tanimbar Islands
Ende
Pulau Flores
DILI
EAST TIMOR
Pulau Yos Sudarso
SAWU SEA
Pulau Sumba
Kupang
Pulau Timor
ARAFURA SEA
KELIMUTU (p561)
Multihued crater lakes set atop an ancient volcano
Darwin
SUMBA (p590)
Fascinating and isolated island with unique tribal traditions and a rich weaving heritage
TIMOR SEA
Gulf of Carpentaria
AUSTRALIA

Destination Indonesia

Adventure looms large in this vast and steamy archipelago, where the best of Southeast Asia's spicy melange simmers tantalisingly. Heady scents, vivid colours, dramatic vistas and diverse cultures spin and multiply to the point of exhaustion, their potent brew leaving your senses reeling.

Rippling across the equator for nearly 5000km, Indonesia encompasses more than 17,000 islands, two-thirds of which are inhabited and richly layered with character. The elaborate funeral ceremonies and timeless tradition of Sulawesi's Toraja are light years from the surfing culture of Lombok. But so too are the mighty saddle-backed Batak mansions and volcanic lakes of Sumatra's Danua Toba from the mummies and deeply etched gorges of Papua's Baliem Valley. Bali's resorts and restaurants pamper precocious style cats, while at the same moment threadbare backpackers are adopted by homestays in Kalimantan.

Indonesia's cities are in a constant state of urban evolution, where dense populations, technology and construction live in hectic symbiosis. But most of the archipelago's territory remains unexplored, concealing a wealth of cultures and a myriad of landscapes. Oceanic rice fields and ancient sultanates in Java are humbled by haunting volcanic cones. Maluku's alabaster beaches and desert islands remain pristine while the tourist trail heads elsewhere. The jungles of Sumatra, Kalimantan and Papua are zoological wonders, revealing impish monkeys, stoic sun bears, leopards, orang-utans and remarkable marsupials.

And then there are the micromoments, equally exquisite but entirely unexpected; impromptu English lessons with school children, instant friendships in crammed bemos, lending an ear to your becak rider... In Indonesia there is plenty of cause to pause, except when dodging hurtling traffic – but that's all part of the adventure.

ERIC L WHEA

Culture

PETER PTSCHELINZEW

Ikat (p70) being woven on a hand loom

LEE FOSTER

Watch a performance of gamelan (p66) – a form of ancient Indonesian music

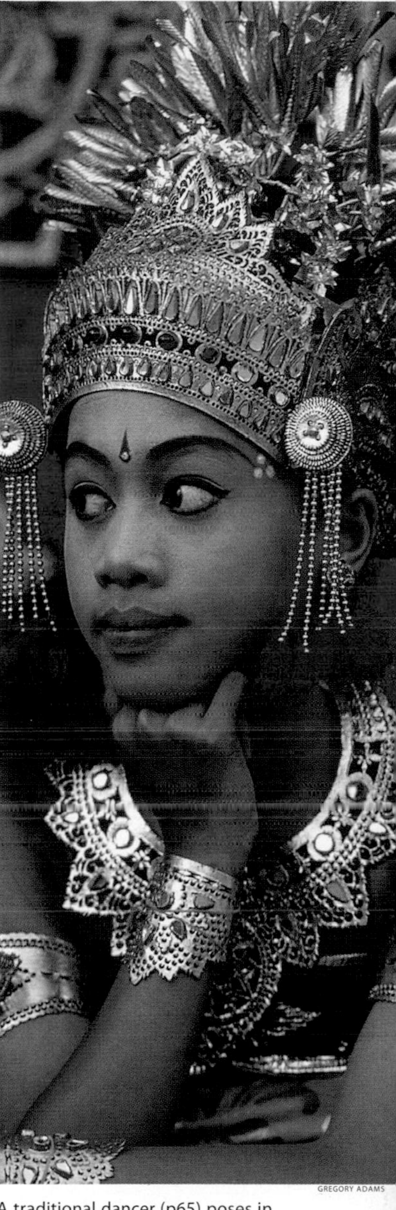

GREGORY ADAMS

A traditional dancer (p65) poses in spectacular costume

Beaches & Islands

PAUL KENNEDY

Explore the beaches of picturesque Teluk Lagundri (p409)

Enjoy snorkelling off Sangalaki Island (p663)

MICHAEL AW

Discover the pristines beaches of Pulau Derawan (p663)

PETER PTSCHELINZ

PAUL KENNEDY

Surf the world-famous waves of the Indonesian archipelago (p846)

PAUL BEINSSEN

Soak it up on Kuta Beach (p281)

National Parks & Wildlife

KRAIG LIEB

Experience a close encounter with the amazing Komodo dragon (p542)

Say 'hello' to a cockatoo at Taman Burung Bali Bird Park (p327)

PAUL BEINSSEN

MICHAEL AW

Turtles (p78) are among the rich variety of marine life living in Indonesian waters

MARK NEWMAN

Witness adorable orang-utans (p77) in their natural habitat

RICHARD I'ANSON

Look out for cheeky monkeys along roadsides in Lombok (p488)

Iguanas can be found in parks such as Taman Nasional Bali Barat (p356)

JANE SWEENEY

Ancient Wonders

BERNARD NAPTHINE

Marvel at the spectacular Prambanan temples (p190) in Java

A Buddha statue sits in contemplation at the magnificent Borobudur temple (p167)

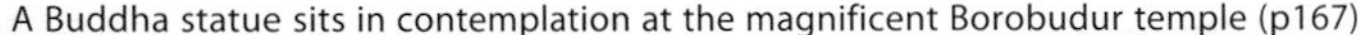

MICK EL

Shopping

JOHN BANAGAN

Weaving is displayed in Sukarara (p524) on Lombok

Colourful masks are sold along Monkey Forest Rd (p323) in Ubud

PAUL BEINSSEN

There's plenty of souvenir shopping to do along Monkey Forest Rd (p323) in Ubud

RICHARD I'ANSON

Activities

CHRISTINE OSBORNE

If you're feeling adventurous, take a white-water rafting trip (p314) near Ubud in Bali

Go parasailing (p294) while you're hanging around in Bali

NICHOLAS REUSS

Indonesia has many great spots for trying out your diving skills (p842)

TIM

Contents

Regional Map Contents

The Authors

JUSTINE VAISUTIS

Coordinating Author, Kalimantan

A desperate yen for the tropics landed Justine in deepest, darkest Borneo for this guide, where she trekked, bused, ferried, cycled, flew, canoed and marvelled her way around Kalimantan. Once there she developed a crush on the local population and invented new and creative forms of sign language. Justine has selflessly donned the travel-writer's hat in the Queensland, Southern African and Fijian tropics, and this is her eighth title for Lonely Planet. She lives in Melbourne, where a distinct lack of wild beasties and tropical weather keeps her feet well and truly itchy. Justine also wrote Destination Indonesia, Getting Started, Itineraries, Snapshot, Directory, Transport and the Glossary.

My Favourite Trip

In this dizzying archipelago my favourite trip would last about a year, but if pressed I'd start with Bali's hypnotic sunshine, dosing up on culture in Ubud (p307). The humbling architecture of Borobudur (p167) would be high on my list of things to do, but I'd soon make it back to the beach in Sumatra's Mentawai Islands (p437).

I'd skip over to Kalimantan and marvel at the orang-utans in Tanjung Puting National Park (p631). Next I'd hightail it to Sulawesi for more wildlife in Lore Lindu National Park (p718) and a good week of diving in the Bunaken Manado Tua Marine National Park (p739), before finishing up on a remote beach in Maluku's Banda Islands (p765).

NEAL BEDFORD

Java

Neal put Indonesia on his authoring wish list, thinking it was a staggeringly exotic place of jungle and beaches, Asian culture and temples. Little did he know that by accepting the Java gig on *Indonesia* 8 he'd get all this and more, including bursting cities, manic streets, thick bus smoke, crazy becak (bicycle-rickshaw) drivers, even crazier bus drivers, fiery volcanoes and enough rice for, well, Indonesia. Before he knew it he was thriving in the magic of Java and wondering why so few people ever visit the place. As soon as he gets the time, he'll be back to take another bite of the durian and explore the rest of this life-changing country.

LONELY PLANET AUTHORS

Why is our travel information the best in the world? It's simple: our authors are independent, dedicated travellers. They don't research using just the internet or phone, and they don't take freebies in exchange for positive coverage. They travel widely, to all the popular spots and off the beaten track. They personally visit thousands of hotels, restaurants, cafés, bars, galleries, palaces, museums and more – and they take pride in getting all the details right, and telling it how it is. For more, see the authors section on www.lonelyplanet.com.

MARK ELLIOTT

Maluku

Since his first trip in 1987, Mark has visited virtually every corner of Indonesia, with trips ranging from relaxing holidays in blissful Bali to leech-infested upriver treks with Kalimantan Dayaks. He's jammed on the harmonica in end-of-Ramadan festivities aboard a Pelni liner, survived an appallingly storm-battered sea crossing in a Bugis fishing boat and escaped from a Solo hotel shortly before it was burnt down by anti-Soeharto rioters. Mark remains fascinated by Indonesia's smorgasbord of cultures and considers the Maluku spice islands to be among the greatest undiscovered travel gems in Asia.

NICK RAY

Sulawesi

A Londoner of sorts, Nick comes from Watford, the sort of town that makes you want to travel. Soon after completing a degree in history and politics, he began roaming around Indonesia, boarding bad, bad buses for more than two days at a time to travel between places like Padang and Jakarta. Needless to say, he applauds the arrival of budget airlines in the country. In this edition he covered the irregular contours of Sulawesi, a place he fell for when working in Tana Toraja on the BBC series *Around the World in 80 Treasures*. He currently lives in Phnom Penh, Cambodia and has contributed to more than 20 Lonely Planet titles.

IAIN STEWART

Nusa Tenggara

Iain first visited Indonesia and the glorious islands of Nusa Tenggara in 1992, when he travelled between Sumatra and Timor. He's returned several times to different parts of the archipelago: diving the reefs of Pulau Bunaken off Sulawesi, hiking volcanoes and clubbing in Bali. Iain has been writing guidebooks for a decade, and for *Indonesia* he racked up the kilometres on rusty boats, dodgy prop planes and bemos (minibuses), fuelled by a fortifying combination of lethal *sambal* (chilli sauce) and almost cool Bintang.

RYAN VER BERKMOES

Bali

Ryan first visited Bali in 1993. On his visits since he has explored almost every corner of the island – along with side trips to Nusa Lembongan, Nusa Penida and Lombok. Just when he thinks Bali holds no more surprises, he rounds a corner and is struck, for example, by the fabulous vistas from Munduk. A frequent visitor, he's at times amazed that his social calendar is even fuller on island than off it. Most of the time he lives in Portland, Oregon, where it rains as often as it does on Bali's tropical peaks but rarely gets as hot.

CHINA WILLIAMS

Sumatra

Ever since her first cup of Sumatra Mandheling coffee, China had dreamed of the cool highlands and hibernating volcanoes of this exotic island, but the country's bad luck leading up to the turn of the millennium spooked her enough to reroute an Indonesian trip through mainland Southeast Asia. Just shy of a decade later, China entered the Sumatran spin cycle, which carved out a few extra travel wrinkles with long bus rides that turned muscle tone to veal and thunderstorms that soaked notes and short-circuited electronics. She is now recuperating, with her husband Matt, amid the toothy mountains and long vistas of Montana.

PATRICK WITTON

History, The Culture, Indonesian Crafts, Environment and Food & Drink

Patrick Witton first visited Indonesia at the age of 13. He has returned numerous times – for study, for work and for the sheer thrill. He has worked on numerous Indonesia-focused titles for Lonely Planet, including as coordinating author for the previous edition of this guide, as author of the *Indonesian Phrasebook* and as author of *World Food Indonesia*. For this edition he trawled through books, papers and reports, harangued academics, and hassled locals and other people obsessed with this startling and spectacular archipelago. He lives large in Victoria.

WENDY YANAGIHARA

Papua

Wendy grew up in bucolic coastal California, raised on white rice and wanderlust. Childhood trips led to study abroad and then onto a brief expat life. Occupational stints have included psychology-and-art student, farmer's marketer, espresso puller, jewellery pusher, graphic designer and, more recently, Lonely Planet author on titles including *Southeast Asia on a Shoestring*. Papua altered her mind with its elections and riots, rock stars and penis gourds, and the amazing diversity of wordless landscape and raw humanity. When not roaming such locations, she circulates around the San Francisco Bay Area.

CONTRIBUTING AUTHORS

John Martinkus first began working as a freelance reporter in East Timor in the mid-'90s. He was based in Dili from mid-'98 until 2000, working for AAP, AP, the *Bulletin* and Fairfax. He wrote an account of the period in *A Dirty Little War* (2001). He has extensively covered the conflicts in Aceh and West Papua, resulting in the publication of *Quarterly Essay 7: Paradise Betrayed, West Papua's struggle for independence* (2002) and the book *Indonesia's Secret War in Aceh* (2004). He has since worked for SBS Dateline in Iraq, Aceh, the Philippines, Timor, Afghanistan and on the Thailand–Burma border. John wrote the Indonesia's Separatist Conflicts boxed text (p54).

Dr Trish Batchelor is a general practitioner and travel medicine specialist who works at the CIWEC Clinic in Kathmandu, Nepal. She is also a medical advisor to the Travel Doctor New Zealand clinics. Trish teaches travel medicine through the University of Otago, and is interested in underwater and high-altitude medicine, and in the impact of tourism on host countries. She has travelled extensively through Southeast Asia. Trish wrote the Health chapter (p879).

Getting Started

Indonesia is big, cheap, rough and effortless. It's everything to everyone, a choose-your-own-adventure travel destination. With little more than a passport, sunscreen and a day's notice, urban-fatigue victims arrive dazed at Denpasar to recover in comfortable Balinese resorts. With a bit of planning and preparation, explorers can put packs to their backs and chart six-month rugged routes in which time, energy and a keen sense of adventure are the chief companions.

WHEN TO GO

Straddling the equator, Indonesia tends to have a fairly even climate year-round. Rather than four seasons, Indonesia has two – wet and dry – and there are no extremes of winter and summer.

In most parts of Indonesia, the wet season falls between October and April (low season), and the dry season between May and September (high season). Rain tends to come in sudden tropical downpours, but it can also rain nonstop for days. In some parts of the country, such as Kalimantan, the difference between the seasons is slight – the dry season just seems to be slightly hotter and slightly drier than the wet season. In other areas, such as Nusa Tenggara, the differences are very pronounced, with droughts in the dry season and floods in the wet.

Though travel in the wet season is not usually a major problem in most parts of Indonesia, mud-clogged back roads can be a deterrent. The best time to visit is in the dry season. The 'wet' starts to descend in October and varies in intensity across the archipelago. The December to February rains can make travel prohibitive in Nusa Tenggara, when rough seas either cancel (or sink) ferries, and roads on Flores are washed out. Parts of Papua are also inaccessible. The rains shift in Sumatra, peaking from October to January in the north, and from January to February in the south. But seasonal change makes little difference in Bali, and in Kalimantan higher water levels from December to February improve access to rivers and small tributaries.

See Climate Charts (p848) for more information.

In most cases, experiencing an Indonesian festival is reason enough to head to a destination. Some are so significant, however, that they can generate difficult conditions for travellers. Tana Toraja's funeral season boosts Rantepao's population, and hotel prices, substantially during July and August. In Java it's a good idea to avoid the final days of Idul Fitri (p856), when public transport is mayhem and some businesses close.

A tragic drop in tourist hordes (see p34) means that Indonesia's 'high season' no longer presents the same kind of bother it once did. The December–January Christmas holiday period and the school holidays still brings a wave of migratory Australians, and Europeans head to Bali, Java, Sumatra and Sulawesi in July and August. But climatic impediments aside, pretty much any time is a good time to head to Indonesia at the moment.

The main Indonesian holiday periods are the end of Ramadan (p855), when domestic tourists fill resorts and prices escalate; Christmas; and mid-June to mid-July, when graduating high-school students take off by the busload to various tourist attractions, mainly in Java and Bali.

COSTS & MONEY

Costs vary depending on where you go, but Indonesia remains one of the cheapest travel destinations in Asia. Hotels, food and transport are all inexpensive in US dollar terms.

Accommodation is usually the greatest expense of Indonesian travel, followed by 'luxury' foreign articles such as electronics. A stream of price hikes in petrol during 2005 increased the cost of bus travel, although it's still inexpensive by any standard. Three square warung (food stall) meals can cost you as little as US$2 (less than 10,000Rp per meal), but even if you dine in decent local restaurants, you still won't be spending much more than US$10 per day (around 30,000Rp per meal) on food.

If you confine yourself to Sumatra, Java and Nusa Tenggara, a shoestring traveller can spend as little as US$15 per day. A midrange budget starts at about US$40 per day, which will get you an air-conditioned hotel room, an occasional tour and car hire. Midrange accommodation is more expensive in Balinese resorts, so budget for around US$50 per day there. Top-end travellers will end up spending anything between US$50 and US$250 per day, although if you stick to the best of the luxury resorts, that figure can blow out to US$2000 a day.

Travellers' centres with lots of competition, such as Danau Toba, Yogyakarta and Bali, can be superb value for accommodation and food. Sulawesi and Nusa Tenggara are also good budget options.

Elsewhere, budget accommodation can be limited and prices are higher because competition is less fierce. Accommodation prices in Maluku and Papua can be twice as high as in tourist towns, and transport costs on Kalimantan are relatively high.

Transport expenses also increase once you get into the outer provinces. In Bali, Sumatra, Java and Nusa Tenggara there's very little need to take to the air, but in the interior of Papua you have no choice but to fly. Flying is much more expensive than other forms of transport, though still cheap in dollar terms.

HOW MUCH?

Snorkel hire 20,000-50,000Rp

Bike hire 15,000-30,000Rp

Ikat (hand-dyed cloth) 500,000Rp, and up

Internet access per hr 6000Rp

Cup of fresh coffee 2000-5000Rp

See also Lonely Planet Index, inside front cover

TRAVEL LITERATURE

Wrapping your head around Indonesian culture can be a daunting task, as the country's history, economics, politics and culture have been widely interpreted and documented by a host of writers. Literature

DON'T LEAVE HOME WITHOUT...

- checking the visa situation (p862) – it's constantly changing and constantly frustrating
- an emergency stash of cash for remote or isolated areas
- a hat, sunglasses and sunscreen – the Indonesian sun is relentless
- sturdy boots and sandals (such as Reefs) or thongs
- locks for your luggage – it's better to be safe than sorry (p851)
- an empty bag to haul your shopping home
- a fantastic set of earplugs for the mosque and traffic wake-up calls
- a snorkel and mask
- dental floss, tampons and shaving cream – they're harder to come by than your average toiletries
- waterproof jacket – it's the tropics, it rains…a lot
- antimalarial tablets and DEET repellent (see p882)
- thick skin and a sense of humour
- a mental note to purchase a sarong once you're in Indonesia – it's a fashion statement, blanket, beach mat, top sheet, mattress cover, towel and shade from the pounding sun.

TOP TENS

Adventures

- Sampling the deserted islands, volcanoes and jungle of untouristed Maluku (p747).
- Taking in the mummies, markets and culture of Papua's Baliem Valley (p816).
- Snorkelling and diving the psychedelic reefs of the Banda Islands (p765).
- Braving the elements, sun bears and jungle in Kalimantan's Kayan Mentarang National Park (p660) or Apokayan Highlands (p659) .
- Surfing the legendary Desert Point (p499) in southwest Lombok.
- Tramping through coffee plantations and waterfalls around Bali's Munduk (p364).
- Marvelling at the 6km-wide crater lake and summit views of Lombok's Gunung Rinjani (p519).
- Spotting orang-utans, gibbons, macaques and kingfishers in Tanjung Puting National Park (p631).
- Getting a bird's-eye view of Sumatra's smoking guns, Gunung Sinabung (p396) and Gunung Sibayak (p395).
- Discovering pristine wilderness and beaches in Java's remote Ujung Kulon National Park (p128).

Indonesian Experiences

- A beaming Indonesian smile – locals here are unfailingly happy and warm .
- Spontaneous guitar-strumming sessions on street corners, warung, Pelni boats….
- Dancing Poco Poco (Indonesian line dancing) at a Maluku village disco.
- Taking your becak (bicycle-rickshaw) driver for a ride instead of the other way around.
- Sharing your rambutans and rupiah during impromptu card games on overnight ferries.
- Catching a bus when school's out and responding to a dozen kids practising their five English questions.
- Starring in countless strangers' holiday pictures.
- Helmet-less *ojek* (motorcycle) trips.
- Coffee, cigarettes and conversations at 2am bus stops.
- Learning how to sleep through the morning call to prayer.

Festivals

- Nyale Fishing Festival, February or March (p525) – Hundreds flock to catch a glimpse of Lombok's first *nyale* (wormlike fish) at this huge fishing festival.
- Pasola, February or March (p603) – ritual warfare marks Nusa Tenggara's harvest festival.
- Waisak, May (p170) – Buddha's birth and enlightenment are celebrated by thousands of monks and pilgrims in Borobudur.
- Festival Teluk Kendari, April (p711) – partying and dragon-boat races in Sulawesi's Kendari Bay.
- Yogya arts festival, June to July (p177) – A month-long smorgasbord of shows and exhibitions in Java's cultural capital.
- Bali Arts Festival, June to July (p303) – A celebration of Bali's enigmatic dance, music and crafts.
- Tana Toraja funeral festival, July to September (p690) – Toraja from all over Indonesia return to Sulawesi to celebrate these annual funeral rituals.
- *Bidar* race, August (p473) – Dozens of vivid *bidar* (canoes) race on Sumatra's Sungai Musi.
- Baliem Festival, August (p826) – A rich celebration of the Baliem Valley's diverse indigenous cultures .
- Ubud Writers & Readers Festival, October (p315) – An internationally acclaimed writers' festival.

about Java and Bali is relatively common, but anything about the other islands can be hard to find. The following provide general scratch-beneath-the-surface accounts of some of the experiences Indonesia has to offer.

Lyall Watson's *Gifts of Unknown Things* observes the symbiotic relationship of a community and its environment on unnamed Indonesian island. The value of the natural world features highly in the book, and fans describe it as life affirming.

Hard Bargaining in Sumatra: Western Travelers and Toba Bataks in the Marketplace of Souvenirs, by Andrew Causey, describes the narrator's sabbatical with the Toba Bataks of northern Sumatra, and humbly captures the sensual and physical landscape of the region.

Tim Flannery's *Throwim Way Leg* is a must for Papuan inspiration. The author recounts his scientific expeditions to the province, where he discovered new species in Indiana Jones–style adventures. And it's all true!

Indonesian history is detailed in Simon Winchester's *Krakatoa – The Day the World Exploded*, which melds history, geology and politics, all centred on the 1888 eruption of Krakatoa – the world's biggest bang.

In Search of Moby Dick, by Tim Severin, is an engagingly written search for the globe's last whale-hunters that includes an extended stay in the whaling village of Lamalera, Nusa Tenggara.

Couched in an academic title, Adrian Vickers' *A History of Modern Indonesia* is based around the writings of Pramoedya Ananta Toer, and summons the culture, turbulence and emotion of everyday Indonesian life.

Bali enthusiasts will love *Dancing Out of Bali* by John Coast, which invokes the people, life, music, and dance of Bali, told through the eyes of a young Englishman and his Javanese wife.

If you think travel's rugged now, delve into Helen and Frank Schreider's *Drums of Tonkin*, which documents their 1963 journey from Sumatra to Timor in an amphibious jeep: landslides, gun-toting soldiers and sea voyages galore.

'If you think travel's rugged now, delve into Helen and Frank Schreider's Drums of Tonkin'

INTERNET RESOURCES

The internet is a rich resource for all types of travellers – before you jump on a plane jump online to get accurate and current information.

Some interesting sites:

Antara (www.antara.co.id/en) This is the site for the official Indonesian news agency; it has a searchable database.

Bali Discovery (www.balidiscovery.com) Although run by a tour company, this excellent site is the best source for Bali news and features.

Central Java Tourism (www.central-java-tourism.com) Tourism website for Central Java.

EastJava.com (www.eastjava.com) Excellent site for tourism and business in East Java, with information on everything from hospitals to moneychangers.

Indahnesia.com (http://indahnesia.com) Good site for news, features, online forums, events and other links.

Indonesia: Society & Culture (coombs.anu.edu.au/WWWVLPages/IndonPages/WWWVL-Indonesia.html) Australian National University's links site, this is the 'granddaddy' of links to everything Indonesian.

Indonesian Homepage (http://indonesia.elga.net.id/) A good general introduction to Indonesia, with a range of links.

Indonesia Tourism (www.indonesia-tourism.com) Useful site for general information about tourism and holiday destinations in Indonesia.

Jakarta Post (www.thejakartapost.com) The extensive website of Indonesia's English-language daily.

Living in Indonesia: A Site for Expatriates (www.expat.or.id) Information, advice and links aimed at the expatriate community, but useful for all visitors.

Lombok Network (www.lombok-network.com) A very comprehensive site bringing together huge amounts of current information on Lombok.

Lombok Times (www.lomboktimes.com) Useful website on all things touristy on Lombok – restaurants, features, accommodation and more.

LonelyPlanet.com (www.lonelyplanet.com) Share knowledge and experiences with other travellers about islands that have been Lonely Planet favourites from the start.

Tempo Interactive (www.tempointeractive.com) One of Indonesia's most respected magazines, offering good news articles in Indonesian and English.

Thorn Tree (http://thorntree.lonelyplanet.com) Lonely Planet's bulletin board, with travel news, updates, forums and links to useful travel resources.

Tourism Indonesia (www.tourismindonesia.com) The website for Indonesia's national tourist organisation is general but informative.

Itineraries

CLASSIC ROUTES

BEACHES, BARS, BODIES & BLISS

Three Weeks/Bali to the Gilis

Start in Bali, where you can acclimatise in the resorts, clubs and shops of **Kuta** (p276). Dose up on sun at the beach, then feast on fabulous food and sling back cocktails in **Seminyak's** (p287) trendy haunts.

Head north to immerse yourself in the 'other' Bali – the culture, temples and rich history of **Ubud** (p307). Visit **Goa Gajah** (p325) and the nearby craft villages. Take a cooking course or learn batik, woodcarving or silver-smithing. Once you've exhausted your yen for culture, escape civilisation altogether – in a volcanic crater. Take yourself to **Gunung Agung** (p333) and **Gunung Batur** (p358).

Next on the agenda is Lombok; make a beeline for **Padangbai** (p334) and jump on a ferry to **Lembar** (p499), the island's launching pad. Potter through the rice fields and Hindu temples around **Mataram** (p497), then head to **Senggigi** (p500) for indulgent resorts, fine beaches and uninterrupted R&R.

From Senggigi take a ferry to the deservedly celebrated **Gili Islands** (p504), where seamless beaches, translucent water and vivid reefs beg for snorkel-clad swimmers.

Bali and Lombok are the heart of Indonesia's tourist industry. This well-trodden 160km-long path starts in Kuta, snakes north through Bali to Ubud and skips over to Lombok before ending in the Gili Islands.

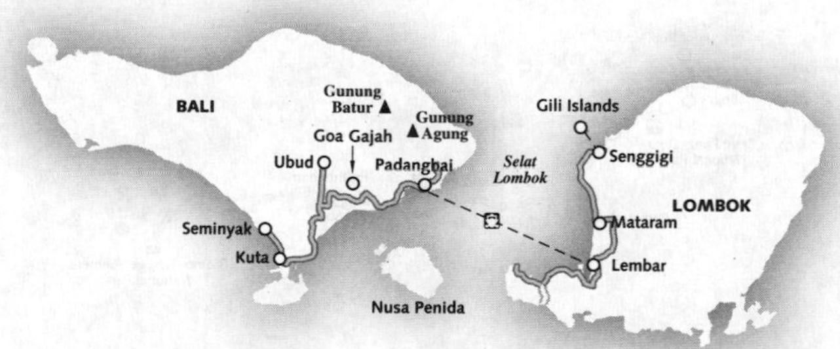

THE JAVA JAUNT

Three Weeks to Three Months/Jakarta to Bromo-Tengger-Semeru National Park

Start your journey in **Jakarta** (p99) and wrap your senses around the dizzying smells, sounds, sights and people of Indonesia's teeming capital. Linger long enough to binge on Bintang beer and shopping, then head to **Bogor** (p129) to lose yourself in the sublime Kebun Raya Botanic Gardens.

From Bogor set a course east through Java's centre, traversing the tea plantations, waterfalls and dramatic scenery of the **Puncak Pass area** (p136). Visit **Gede Pangrango National Park** (p138) and take a day to reach the summit of Gunung Gede for jaw-dropping views. Continue your journey for a stint in the urban jungle of **Bandung** (p138). Satiate yearnings for the modern world in this city's hotels and restaurants, then make a quick exit from the chaos.

It's time to hit the coast, ditch the boots for a while and camp out in some well-earned calm – and that's where **Pangandaran** (p151), Java's premier beach resort, comes in. The national park, wide shorelines and a coastal party buzz dominate the visual and social landscapes here, and the accommodation is kind to all budgets.

After you've worshipped the sun for a week or so, pack the bags and head to **Yogyakarta** (p171), Java's cultural capital. Dabble in batik, amble through the *kraton* (walled city palace) and part with your rupiah at the vibrant markets. A day trip to majestic **Borobudur** (p167) is a must. From Yogyakarta make your way to the laid-back city of **Solo** (p194), via the enigmatic temples of **Prambanan** (p190). Finish your Java expedition with a visit to the awesome **Bromo-Tengger-Semeru National Park** (p244), spending your last night on the lip of Tengger crater.

Positively churning with life, Java has the lion's share of Indonesia's population, and a wealth of culture and landscapes to match. This 800km route takes in the highlights, beginning in the teeming capital Jakarta and ending in the awe-inspiring peaks of Bromo-Tengger-Semeru National Park.

SULTRY SUMATRA

One Month/Medan to Padang

Dominated by wild and chaotic jungle peppered with urban centres, Sumatra has its own beaten path to accommodate the inquisitive traveller.

All roads lead to **Medan** (p382), which is the perfect point to stock up on necessities and creature comforts. Satisfy your craving for Dutch pottery, dazzle the taste buds with a Malay or Indian curry and down a Bintang at sunset.

But you didn't come for the air-con, so hit the road and make your way north to **Bukit Lawang** (p389), home to Sumatra's most adored natural attraction – the orang-utan. Feeding sessions for semideprived primates offers unparalleled viewing of these graceful creatures. If you fancy roughing it, you can test your survivor skills on a two-day trek through the park, with the potential reward of seeing orang-utans in the wild.

From Bukit Lawang, bus your way down south to **Danau Toba** (p399) for Batak culture, a gorgeous volcanic lake and a languid ambience. Trekking is the traditional lure to this area, but there are rambling markets, handicraft villages and gargantuan orchids to behold as well.

The route then takes a dive south to **Bukittinggi** (p441), a busy market town dwarfed by more volcanic peaks. The town itself is a pleasant spot to amble about for a few days but the attractions lie just outside in the handicraft village of **Koto Gadang** (p445), the terraced rice fields, and the nearby **Batang Palupah Nature Reserve** (p446) and **Lembah Anai Nature Reserve** (p446).

Your journey ends in **Padang** (p431), one of Sumatra's busiest cities. Keep yourself occupied with museums and festivals, or use the city as a launching pad to escape to the **Mentawai Islands** (p437).

This 900km journey takes in the cities of Medan and Padang, orang-utans in Bukit Lawang and the majestic volcanic lake of Danua Toba. There are markets, handicraft villages and nature reserves on the schedule, and a laze on the gorgeous Mentawai Islands.

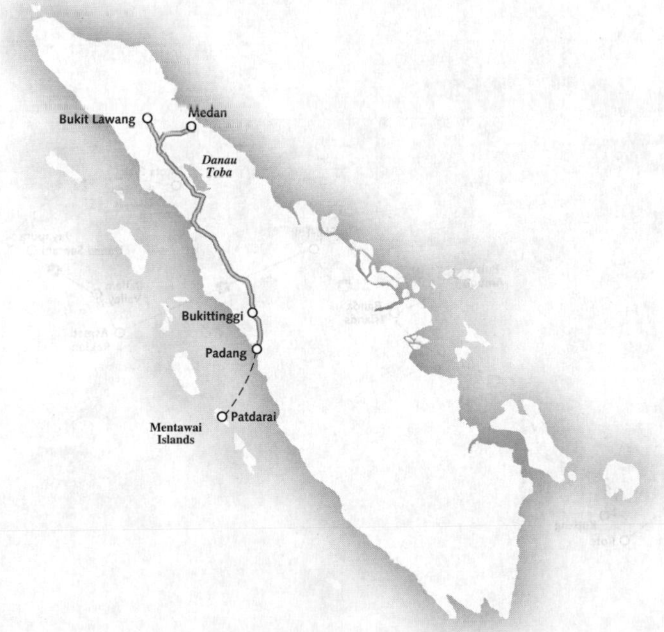

ROADS LESS TRAVELLED

This 3000km off-the-radar adventure takes in the picturesque islands around Papua's Kota Biak before heading to the sublime Danau Sentani and the beguiling Baliem Valley. Maluku's Pulau Ambon and Banda Island provide a change of scene before the route heads south to West Timor and Flores.

THE TRAIL THAT TIME FORGOT

Two Months/Papua to Flores

Papua is the launching pad for this route, starting at **Kota Biak** (p808). A relaxed and pleasant town, Biak is most useful as a base for trips to the beauty beyond. Pack a tent and make for the exquisite reefs and beaches of the **Padaido Islands** (p813) and the unspoilt, ethereal **Pulau Numfor** (p813).

Next on the itinerary is a quick plane ride from Kota Biak to **Jayapura** (p828). But you'll only be stopping long enough to charter a boat to visit the magnificent **Danau Sentani** (p835), a 96.5-sq-km lake with 19 islands.

Back on dry land the route heads inland to the beautiful **Baliem Valley** (p816), rich in culture and dramatic mountain scenery. From here the truly intrepid (and wealthy) can embark on an expedition into the pristine but seemingly impenetrable **Asmat region** (p837).

Heading further afield requires a flight to **Fak-Fak** (p803) before another flight or a ferry to Kota Ambon on Maluku's **Pulau Ambon** (p752). Dose up on urban comfort and culture, then take a ferry or plane to the crystalline seas, multicoloured reefs and empty beaches of the **Banda Islands** (p765).

After indulging in sun and isolation, pack your gear up and board a Pelni ferry for **Kupang** (p580) in West Timor. Visit villages in the surrounding areas, then jump over to **Rote** (p588) for relaxed coastal vibes. For a perfect ending, make your way to **Flores** (p543), a rugged volcanic island with fishing villages, thriving culture and dramatic terrain.

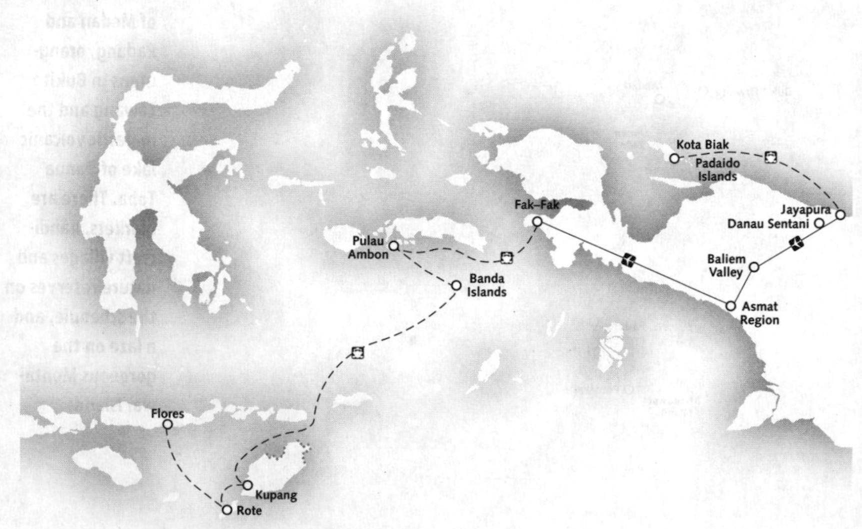

THE CULTURAL QUEST

Six to Eight Weeks/Kalimantan to Sulawesi

Unassuming **Pangkalan Bun** (p628) is the entry point to this excursion – it's the launching pad for trips into glorious **Tanjung Puting National Park** (p631), one of Indonesia's best orang-utan haunts. Scan the canopy for their amber bodies from the top of a houseboat as it ambles down the beautiful Sungai Kumai, then fly back to reality in colourful **Banjarmasin** (p635). Dabble in the best of Kalimantan's urban culture – brave a 5am call for the animated floating markets, then cruise the canals and meet the locals at dusk.

From Banjarmasin travel overland to **Samarinda** (p649) and make an expedition along **Sungai Mahakam** (p654). Several days upstream will land you in the river's western reaches, which are peppered with semitraditional Dayak villages and preserved forests.

From Samarinda catch the weekly Pelni ferry to **Makassar** (p671) to marvel at colonial Dutch architecture and gorge on some of Indonesia's best seafood. Chart a course due north for vast and mesmerising **Tana Toraja** (p687), home to Sulawesi's most fascinating indigenous culture. Take part in the elaborate funeral ceremonies, hop through remote villages, raft the Sungai Sa'dan's rapids, and scale spectacular summits.

Continue north and settle in Central Sulawesi for hiking around Indonesia's third largest lake, **Danau Poso** (p716). From here escape the 'mainland' and plant yourself on the blissful **Togean Islands** (p725), which are laden in marine life and culture. After snorkelling and diving the vivid reefs head into Northern Sulawesi and the laid-back port of **Gorontalo** (p731), where you can get busy with the camera on some of the finest Dutch architecture in the country.

One for the wildlife and culture junkies, this 2700-odd-kilometre route takes in the orang-utans of magical Tanjung Puting National Park and the Dayaks of Kalimantan's interior, before skipping over to Sulawesi for Toraja funeral ceremonies, river rapids, mountain treks and marine life.

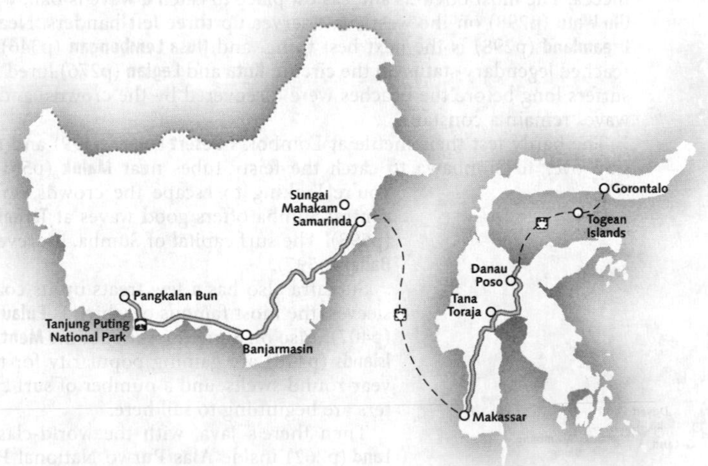

TAILORED TRIPS

BEGUILING BEASTIES

Indonesia's natural world is so vast and diverse that scientists seem to discover new species at the drop of a hat.

High on the list of must-sees are the enigmatic orang-utans, best viewed at Sumatra's **Bukit Lawang** (p389) and Kalimantan's **Kutai National Park** (p652) and **Tanjung Puting National Park** (p631). This last conservation area is also populated by gibbons, macaques, proboscis monkeys, sun bears, clouded leopards and a whole host more. In East Kalimantan the wetlands of **Danau Jempang** (p657) are home to over 90 species of bird and the tiny Irrawaddy dolphin.

Papua is flavour of the zoologist month: a 2006 expedition into the remote **Foja Mountains** (see p797) uncovered a teeming community of unknown frogs, birds and even a kangaroo. You can catch a glimpse of Australianesque fauna in **Wasur National Park** (p837), or you can try spotting the rare *cenderawasih* (bird of paradise) in the islands around **Pulau Biak** (p808).

In Nusa Tenggara the gargantuan Komodo dragon dwells in the depths of **Komodo** (p540).

For butterflies bigger than your hand and exquisite birdlife, head to Sulawesi's **Lore Lindu National Park** (p718). The island is also home to **Morowali Nature Reserve** (p723), which is equally rich in birdlife and other fauna.

SURF'S UP

With a dizzying array of coastlines and beaches, Indonesia is a surfing mecca. The most obvious and easiest place to catch a wave is Bali, where **Ulu Watu** (p298) on the west coast serves up three left-handers. Nearby, **Dreamland** (p298) is the next best thing, and **Nusa Lembongan** (p346) has reached legendary status on the circuit. **Kuta** and **Legian** (p276) lured avid surfers long before the beaches were discovered by the crowds, and the waves remain a constant.

The hardy test their mettle at Lombok's **Desert Point** (p499) and then skip over to Sumbawa to catch the feisty tubes near **Maluk** (p531). If you're looking to escape the crowds, south-central Sumba offers good waves at **Tarimbang** (p598). The surf capital of Sumba, however, is **Baing** (p597).

Sumatra also has a few treats up its coastal sleeves, the most famous of which is **Pulau Nias** (p407). Also on Sumatra, the sublime **Mentawai Islands** (p440) are gaining popularity for their year-round swells, and a number of surf charters are beginning to sail here.

Then there's Java, with the world-class **G-Land** (p262) inside Alas Purwo National Park, and superlative reef breaks near **Pelabuhan Ratu** (p134). Beginners can find their balance on the friendly surf at **Batu Karas** (p156).

UNDERWATER ODYSSEYS

With more than 17,500 islands under its archipelago belt, Indonesia boggles the minds of divers and snorkellers with a feast of underwater adventures.

Maluku's **Banda Islands** (p765) are encircled by dense coral gardens, cascading drop-offs and superb marine life. Best of all, they're so remote you may score this underwater vista all to yourself.

Oversized fish, sleepy sea fans and gaping canyons lounge beneath the ocean's surface near Sumatra's **Pulau Weh** (p422). The pick of the destinations here are the 20 dive sites around **Long Angen** (p424), the stomping ground for majestic manta rays, lion fish and morays.

Sulawesi's spectacular **Pulau Bunaken** (p739) simmers with more than 300 species of fish and coral types. Countless drop-offs, caves and valleys provide ample viewing for days of diving, and turtles, rays, sharks and dolphins are common visitors. Then there's the renowned **Lembeh Strait** (p743), an underwater universe of otherworldly and utterly photogenic marine life.

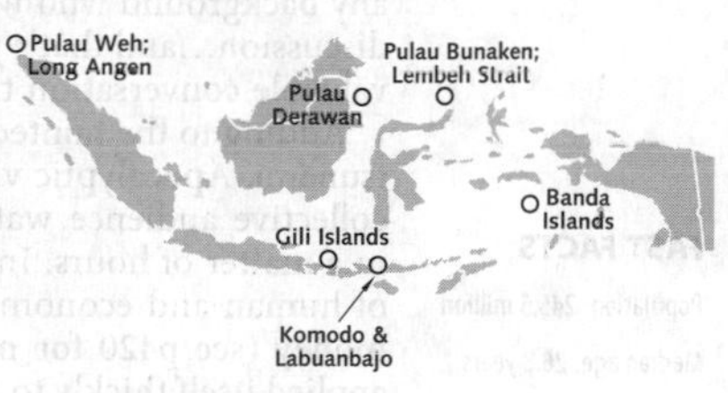

Off Kalimantan's northeast corner, **Pulau Derawan** (p663) is the best base for the Sangalaki Archipelago, as indicated by the turtles who nest here regularly and the schools of tuna who shimmy offshore.

In Nusa Tenggara, a diverse range of marine life simmers underwater in the **Gili Islands** (p511), and around **Komodo** and **Labuanbajo** (see p546).

GUNUNG BAGGING

Indonesia's undulating landscapes encompass enough peaks and troughs to keep even marathon trekkers happy.

There's good tramping to be found around Sumatra's **Gunung Sinabung** (p396) and **Gunung Sibayak** (p395), but serious explorers can brave the jungle beasties in the interior of **Gunung Leuser National Park** (p427).

Java's Unesco World Heritage–listed **Ujung Kulon National Park** (p128) is a remote outpost of untouched wilderness, and a three-day hike through the park reveals pristine forest and diverse wildlife. At the island's southeast tip, the **Ijen Plateau** (p249) is peppered with volcanic cones and offers a spectacular day trek to a sulphur lake.

The cascading rice fields around Sulawesi's **Tana Toraja** (p687) give way to excellent highland trekking, with soaring summits and cool-water swimming pools. Treks last anywhere from several hours to several days – highlights include the 2150m-high **Gunung Sesean** (p704). You can also mingle with the wildlife on organised treks in **Lore Lindu National Park** (p718).

Intrepid hikers should head to Papua's sublime **Baliem Valley** (p816) or test their mettle amid the mighty rivers and mangroves of the undeveloped **Asmat region** (p837).

Kalimantan's interior also provides excellent opportunities for hikers with time and experience, particularly around **Loksado** (p642) in Pegunungan Meratus (Meratus Mountains) and in the **Apokayan Highlands** (p659).

Snapshot

Indonesia has held top billing in the international press in recent years, but sadly for all the wrong reasons. The Jakarta and Bali bombings of 2002 and 2005, coupled with high-profile media coverage of Islamic radicals, have exacted their malevolent toll and the locals are suffering as a consequence. Indonesians are terrified that the world has abandoned them out of security concerns and Islamophobia; fast joining 'Hello Mister' in the mod-Indo vocab is a mournful 'Where are the tourists?'. Islamic devotion is incredibly varied in this massive archipelago (see p62 to get the full picture) and Muslims from Medan to Kupang go to great pains to express sorrow and despair that their faith has been hijacked and misconstrued. They are also eager to swap religious, cultural and ethnic similarities with foreigners. In fact it's difficult to find a local of any background who *won't* readily engage you in personal and complex discussion…and that's just at the bus stop. See the boxed text on p65 for valuable conversation tips.

Adding to the tainted picture is the aftermath of the 2004 Boxing Day tsunami. Apocalyptic visions pummelled the globe's TV screens and the collective audience watched whole cities and holiday Edens disappear in a matter of hours. In Indonesia, Sumatra bore the brunt, and the tide of human and economic aid that followed gave the ocean a run for its money (see p420 for more information). But the image of destruction applied itself thickly to Indonesia as a whole, and tour operators far from the tsunami's reach find themselves suffering by proxy.

The recently introduced one-month visa rule adds yet another snag for both locals and foreigners. Restricting exploratory travels for long haulers, it amplifies the frustration and anguish of an industry battling to survive. The wheels of bureaucracy churn in Jakarta, and meanwhile hotels, restaurants and everyone else in the service industry are suffering from a 40% plummet in visitor numbers. Island-hopping routes that were destined to become the next big trail remain untrodden and the first sign of foreign activity is received with such gratitude and warmth you'd think it was the Second Coming.

The political hot topics of the moment are peace deals and disputed provinces. After 29 years of guerrilla war, it took a devastating sleight of nature to catalyse cohesion in Aceh. The 2004 tsunami wreaked unheralded destruction in the isolated region, but its one positive legacy has been the resulting peace deal between the Free Aceh Movement (GAM – Gerakan Aceh Merdeka) and the Indonesian military. More than 12 months on and the deal is sticking; locals are optimistic and this is one area where travellers are beginning to turn up.

Another province once plagued by internal conflict, Maluku is also experiencing a sanguine renaissance thanks to a massive injection of recovery money and feverish development. Ambon and Ternate in particular seem to be aiming for the gold-medal podium in the global construction stakes, with a bevy of buildings on the make.

On the other hand, bombs in Palu and Tentena on Sulawesi and the gruesome beheading of schoolgirls around Poso are tragic proof that central Sulawesi remains volatile. And in Papua, separatist violence is flaring loudly. Many protests are ostensibly about the foreign exploitation, but the underlying tensions are rooted in Papua's lack of autonomy, the oppressive Indonesian military presence, and human rights violations

FAST FACTS

Population: 245.5 million

Median age: 26.8 years

GDP per capita: US$3,700

Inflation: 10.4%

Unemployment: 10.9%

Number of islands: 17,508

Number of mobile phones in use: 30 million

Number of airports: 668

Number of airports with paved runways: 161

against native Papuans. The US-owned Freeport Mine has become a target of violence, and the death of five Indonesian policemen in riots in March 2006 highlighted the extent of local frustrations. Alleged reprisal deaths and arrests at the hands of the Indonesian military followed. In the same month, the Australian government granted asylum to 42 Papuan refugees. The move infuriated Jakarta and fragile relations between the two countries dominated headlines and conversations in both countries. Diplomatic tensions were soon abated, but the conflict in Papua continues; see the boxed text on p54 for a greater insight into the issue.

Far less polarising than politics, but just as fervently discussed, is the state of the economy. Shattered tourist industry aside, for most Indonesians things were looking up following the October 2004 elections. Folk were happy with President Susilo Bambang Yudhoyono's reform rhetoric, and his move to furnish provincial governments with greater autonomy promised greater political and economic equality. But the hope and confidence are waning with the sneaking realisation that anticorruption efforts are either futile or empty. An even greater blow to national morale arrived in the form of consecutive hikes in fuel prices during 2005, amounting to a whopping 126%. The fallout has touched every corner of the archipelago and bitter laments can be heard in warung, bemo, buses, street corners and restaurants throughout. Some pockets of Java even wax lyrical about the good old Soeharto days; when 'tummies were full, crime was nonexistent and the country was stable' (give or take the odd violent protest and dire social disintegration in his latter years). Fear of future price hikes easily surpasses those of an avian flu epidemic, which registers only slightly higher than the fear of a banana shortage in most places. See p51 for greater details about Indonesia's political climate.

'Overriding all the complexities of life in Indonesia is the resilient national optimism'

Overriding all the complexities of life in Indonesia is the resilient national optimism. Middle-class school kids and businessmen in Jakarta gleefully parade the latest mobile technology; traditional Balinese dancers bewitch abridged audiences and karaoke is still king on Java. Despite economic and environmental hardships, little has changed on Sumatra in the past 15 to 20 years. They do know about Kurt Cobain though, and are equally enthusiastic about discussing him as any other topic under the sun.

History

IN THE BEGINNING

The life of Indonesia is a tale of discovery, oppression and liberation, so it's both impressive and perplexing to see the nation's history displayed in a hokey diorama at Jakarta's National Monument (p107). The exhibit even includes Indonesia's first inhabitant, Java Man *(Pithecanthropus erectus),* who crossed land bridges to Java over one million years ago. Java Man then became extinct or mingled with later migrations. Indonesians today are, like Malaysians and Filipinos, of Malay origin and are the descendants of migrants that arrived around 4000 BC. The discovery in 2003 of a small skeleton, nicknamed 'the hobbit', in Flores added a new piece to Indonesia's – and, indeed, the world's – evolutionary jigsaw (p552).

The Dongson culture, which originated in Vietnam and southern China around 1000 BC, spread to Indonesia, bringing irrigated rice-growing techniques, husbandry skills, buffalo sacrifice rituals, bronze casting, the custom of erecting megaliths, and ikat weaving methods. Some of these practices survive today in the Batak areas of Sumatra, Tana Toraja in Sulawesi, parts of Kalimantan, and Nusa Tenggara. By 700 BC, Indonesia was dotted with permanent villages where life was linked to rice production.

These early Indonesians were animists, believing all objects had a life force or soul. The spirits of the dead had to be honoured, as they could still help the living and influence natural events, while evil spirits had to be placated with offerings and ceremonies. As there was a belief in the afterlife, weapons and utensils were left in tombs for use in the next world.

By the 1st century AD, small kingdoms, little more than collections of villages subservient to petty chieftains, evolved in Java. The island's constant hot temperature, plentiful rainfall and volcanic soil was ideal for wet-field rice cultivation. The organisation this required may explain why the Javanese developed a seemingly more feudal society than the other islands. (Dry-field rice cultivation is much simpler, requiring no elaborate social structure to support it.)

How Hinduism and Buddhism arrived in Indonesia is not certain. The oldest works of Hindu art in Indonesia (statues from the 3rd century AD) were found in Sulawesi and Sumatra. One theory suggests that the developing courts invited Brahman priests from India to advise on spirituality and ritual, thereby providing occult status to those in control.

Tempo Interactive (www.tempointeractive.com) is one of Indonesia's most respected magazines and provides good news-articles in English.

Trade, established by south Indians, was another likely religious inroad. By the 1st century AD, Indonesia's location on the sea routes between India and China was proving integral to trade development between these two civilisations. Though Indonesia had its own products to trade, such as spices, gold and benzoin (an aromatic gum valued by the Chinese), it owed its importance to its geographical position at the crossroads of sea trade.

TIMELINE

1 million BC	4000 BC
Indonesian archipelago already inhabited by 'Java Man'	Malay people begin to migrate from Southeast Asia

THE GOLDEN YEARS

The reign of King Hayam Wuruk (literally meaning 'Rotting Chicken') and Prime Minister Gajah Mada (literally 'Rutting Elephant') of the Majapahit kingdom is usually referred to as a 'golden age' of Indonesia. As well as controlling strategic regions of the archipelago, the kingdom is said to have maintained relations internationally. One account, by the court poet Prapanca, claims the kingdom maintained regular relations with China, Cambodia, Annam (now part of Vietnam) and Siam (now Thailand).

EARLY KINGDOMS

The Hindu-Buddhist kingdom of Sriwijaya rose in Sumatra during the 7th century AD. It was the first major Indonesian commercial sea power able to control much of the trade in Southeast Asia by virtue of being located on the Strait of Melaka. Merchants from Arabia, Persia and India brought goods to Sriwijaya's coastal cities in exchange for goods from China and local products.

The Buddhist Sailendra dynasty and the Hindu Mataram dynasty flourished in Central Java between the 8th and 10th centuries. While Sriwijaya's wealth came from trade, Javanese kingdoms like Mataram (in the region of what is now Solo) had far more human labour at their disposal and developed as agrarian societies. These kingdoms absorbed Indian influences and left magnificent structures such as the Buddhist monument at Borobudur (p167) and the Hindu temples of Prambanan (p190).

At the end of the 10th century, the Mataram kingdom mysteriously declined. The centre of power shifted from Central to East Java and it was a period when Hinduism and Buddhism were syncretised and when Javanese culture began to come into its own. A series of kingdoms held sway until the 1294 rise of the Majapahit kingdom, which grew to prominence during the reign of Hayam Wuruk from 1350 to 1389. Its territorial expansion can be credited to brilliant military commander Gajah Mada, who helped the kingdom claim control over much of the archipelago, exerting suzerainty over smaller kingdoms and extracting trading rights from them (see boxed text, above). After Hayam Wuruk's death in 1389, the kingdom began a steady decline.

ISLAM

The first Islamic inscriptions found in Indonesia date from the 11th century, and there may have been Muslims in the Majapahit court. Islam really first took hold in northern Sumatra, where Arab traders had settled by the 13th century.

From the 15th and 16th centuries, Indonesian rulers made Islam the state religion. It was, however, superimposed on the prevailing mix of Hinduism and animism to produce the hybrid religion that is followed in much of Indonesia today.

In 1292, Marco Polo visited Aceh and noted that the inhabitants had already converted to Islam.

By the 15th century, the trading kingdom of Melaka (on the Malay Peninsula) was reaching the height of its power and had embraced Islam. Its influence strengthened the spread of Islam through the archipelago.

By the time of the collapse of the Majapahit kingdom in the early 1500s, many of its satellite kingdoms had already declared themselves

1st century AD

Small kingdoms established in Java

7th century

Sumatran Hindu-Buddhist kingdom of Sriwijaya begins its rise independent Islamic states. Much of their wealth came from being transhipment points for the spice trade, and Islam followed the trade routes across the archipelago.

By the end of the 16th century, a new sea power had emerged on Sulawesi: the twin principalities of Makassar and Gowa, which had been settled by Malay traders and whose commercial realm spread well beyond the region. In 1607, the explorer Torres met Makassar Muslims on New Guinea.

Makassar fleets visited the northern Australian coast over centuries, introducing Aborigines in the area to metal tools, pottery and tobacco. This legacy is acknowledged in Makassar's Museum Balla Lompoa.

PORTUGUESE ARRIVAL

Marco Polo and a few early missionary travellers aside, the first Europeans to visit Indonesia were the Portuguese, who sought to dominate the valuable spice trade in the spice islands of Maluku. Vasco da Gama had led the first European ships around the Cape of Good Hope to Asia in 1498. The Portuguese had captured Goa in India by 1510, Melaka in 1511, and the following year they arrived in Maluku. Their fortified bases and superior firepower at sea won the Portuguese strategic trading ports stretching from Angola to Maluku.

Soon the Spanish, Dutch and English sent ships to the region in search of wealth. Although they had taken Melaka, the Portuguese soon could not control the growing volume of trade. Banten in West Java became the main port of the region, attracting merchants away from Melaka.

Nathaniel's Nutmeg by Giles Milton offers a fascinating account of the battle to control trade from the Spice Islands.

DUTCH DAYS

Of the newcomers, it was the Dutch who would eventually lay the foundations of the Indonesian state, though their initial efforts were pretty shoddy: an expedition of four ships led by Cornelius de Houtman in 1596 lost half its crew, killed a Javanese prince and lost a ship in the process. Nevertheless, it returned to Holland with enough spices to turn a profit.

Recognising the great potential of East Indies trade, the Dutch government amalgamated competing merchant companies into the Vereenigde Oost-Indische Compagnie (VOC; United East India Company). This government-run monopoly soon became the main competitor in the spice trade.

The government's intention was to bring military pressure to bear on the Portuguese and Spanish. VOC trading ships were replaced with armed fleets instructed to attack Portuguese bases. By 1605 the VOC had defeated the Portuguese at Tidore and Ambon and occupied the heart of the Spice Islands.

The VOC then looked for a base closer to the shipping lanes of the Melaka and Sunda Straits. The ruler of Jayakarta (now Jakarta) in West Java granted the VOC permission to build a warehouse in 1610, but he also granted the English trading rights. The VOC warehouse became a fort, relations between the VOC and English deteriorated, and skirmishes resulted in a siege of the fort by the English and the Jayakartans. The VOC retaliated, razing the town in 1619. They renamed their new headquarters Batavia.

The founder of this corner of the empire was the imaginative but ruthless Jan Pieterszoon Coen. Among his 'achievements' was the near total extermination of the indigenous population of the Banda Islands

800–1000
Buddhist Sailendra and Hindu Mataram dynasties flourish in Central Java; Borobudur and Prambanan temples are built

1294
Majapahit, the last great Hindu kingdom, founded in East Java

in Maluku. Coen developed plans to make Batavia the centre of intra-Asian trade from Japan to Persia, and to develop spice plantations using Burmese, Madagascan and Chinese labourers.

Although these more grandiose plans failed, he was instrumental in obtaining a VOC monopoly on the spice trade. In 1607 an alliance with the sultan of Ternate in Maluku gave the VOC control over the production of cloves, and the occupation of the Bandas from 1609 to 1621 gave them control of the nutmeg trade.

VOC control grew rapidly: it took Melaka from the Portuguese in 1641, quelled attacks from within Java, secured the Sumatran ports and defeated Makassar in 1667. The VOC policy at this stage was to keep control of trade while avoiding expensive territorial conquests. An accord was established with the king of Mataram, the dominant kingdom in Java. (Despite having the same name, this Islamic kingdom had nothing to do with the Hindu Mataram dynasty.) This accord allowed only VOC ships (or those with permission) to trade with the Spice Islands.

The British, keen to profit from the spice trade, kept control of Pulau Run until 1667. Then they swapped it for a Dutch-controlled island: Manhattan.

Unwillingly at first, but later in leaps and bounds, the VOC progressed from being a trading company to being a colonial master. From the late 1600s Java was beset by wars as the Mataram kingdom fragmented. The VOC was only too willing to lend military support to contenders for the throne, in return for compensation and land concessions. The Third Javanese War of Succession (1746–57) saw Prince Mangkubumi and Mas Said contest the throne of Mataram's King Pakubuwono II. This spelled the end for Mataram, largely because of Pakubuwono II's concessions and capitulation to VOC demands.

In 1755 the VOC divided the Mataram kingdom into two states: Yogyakarta and Surakarta (Solo). These and other smaller Javanese states were only nominally sovereign; in reality they were dominated by the VOC. Fighting among the princes was halted, and peace was brought to East Java by the forced cessation of invasions and raids from Bali. Thus Java was finally united under a foreign trading company whose army comprised only 1000 Europeans and 2000 Asians.

Despite these dramatic successes, the fortunes of the VOC were soon to decline. After the Dutch–English War of 1780, the VOC spice-trade monopoly was finally broken by the Treaty of Paris which permitted free trade in the East. In addition, trade shifted from spices to Chinese silk and Japanese copper, as well as coffee, tea and sugar, over which it was impossible to establish a monopoly.

An Empire of the East by Norman Lewis visits Indonesia's hot spots (past and present) in travelogue form.

Dutch trading interests gradually centred more on Batavia. The Batavian government became increasingly dependent on customs dues and tolls charged for goods coming into Batavia, and on taxes from the local Javanese population.

Smuggling, illicit trade by company employees, the mounting expense of wars in Java and the cost of administering additional territory acquired after each new treaty all played a part in the decline of the VOC. The company turned to the Dutch government at home for support, and the subsequent investigation of VOC affairs revealed corruption, mismanagement and bankruptcy. In 1799 the VOC was formally wound up, its territorial possessions seized by the Dutch government, and the trading empire became a colonial empire.

16th century

Traders from Portugal start trade in the Spice Islands

1596

Dutch arrive, then return to Holland with lucrative spices

Around 1830, Dutch control was at a crossroads. Trade profits were in decline, the cost of controlling conflicts continued, and when the Dutch lost Belgium in 1830, the home country itself faced bankruptcy. Any government investment in the East Indies now *had* to make quick returns, so the exploitation of Indonesian resources began.

A new governor general, Johannes van den Bosch, fresh from experiences with slave labour in the West Indies, was appointed to make the East Indies pay their way. He succeeded by introducing an agricultural policy called the Culture System. This was a system of government-controlled agriculture or, as Indonesian historians refer to it, Tanam Paksa (Compulsory Planting). Instead of paying land taxes, peasants had to either cultivate government-owned crops on 20% of their land or work in government plantations for nearly 60 days of the year. Much of Java became a Dutch plantation, generating great wealth for the Netherlands. For the Javanese peasantry, this forced-labour system brought hardship and resentment. They were forced to grow crops such as indigo and sugar instead of rice, and famine and epidemics swept through Java in the 1840s. In strong contrast, the Culture System was a boon for the Dutch and the Javanese aristocracy. In the ensuing years, Indonesia supplied most of the world's quinine and pepper, over a third of its rubber, a quarter of its coconut products and almost a fifth of its tea, sugar, coffee and oil. The profits made Java a self-sufficient colony and saved the Netherlands from bankruptcy.

Indonesian farmers were forced to cultivate the indigo plant so the Dutch could sell the extracted dye in Europe, where it fetched a high price.

Public opinion in the Netherlands began to decry the deplorable treatment of Indonesians under the colonial government. In response, the Liberal Period was initiated. From 1870, farmers no longer had to provide export crops, and the Indies were opened to private enterprise, which developed large plantations. As the population increased, less land was available for rice production, thereby bringing further hardship. Meanwhile, Dutch profits grew dramatically. New products such as oil became a valuable export due to Europe's industrial demands. As Dutch commercial interests expanded throughout the archipelago, so did the need to protect them. More and more territory was taken under direct control of the Dutch government.

During the 1800s, the Dutch set up plantations of the Cinchona tree, the bark of which contains quinine: the most effective antimalarial of the time.

A new approach to colonial government, known as the Ethical Period, was introduced in 1901. Under this policy it was the Dutch government's duty to further programmes of health, education and other societal initia-

BATTLEGROUND INDONESIA

From the time the first Dutch ships arrived in 1596 to the declaration of independence in 1945, Dutch rule was tenuous. Fighting continuously flared up in both Java and Sumatra, as well as elsewhere in the archipelago. Between 1846 and 1849, expeditions were sent to Bali in the first attempts to subjugate the island. In southeastern Borneo, the violent Banjarmasin War (1859–63) saw the Dutch defeat the reigning sultan. The longest and most devastating war was in Aceh, lasting 35 years from the Dutch invasion in 1873 until Aceh's guerrilla leaders surrendered in 1908. Even into the 20th century, Dutch control remained incomplete. They only took control of southwestern Sulawesi and Bali in 1906, and Bird's Head Peninsula of West New Guinea didn't come under Dutch administration until 1920 (see Indonesia's Separatist Conflicts, p54).

1746–57

Third Javanese War of Succession brings an end to Mataram dynasty

1799

Dutch government establishes colonial power over Indonesia

tives. Direct government control was exerted on the outer islands. Minor rebellions broke out everywhere, from Sumatra to Timor, but these were easily crushed and the Dutch took control from traditional leaders, thus establishing a true Indies empire for the first time.

New policies were implemented, including the *transmigrasi* (transmigration) of farmers from heavily populated Java to lightly populated islands. There were also plans for improved communications, agriculture, industrialisation and the protection of native industry. Other policies aimed to give greater autonomy to the colonial government and lessen control from the Netherlands, as well as give more power to local governments within the archipelago.

These humanitarian policies were laudable but ultimately inadequate: public health funding was simply not enough, and while education opportunities for some upper and middle class Indonesians increased, the vast majority remained illiterate. Though primary schools were established and education was theoretically open to all, by 1930 only 8% of school-age children received an education. Industrialisation was never seriously implemented and Indonesia remained an agricultural colony.

'By 1930 only 8% of school-age children received an education'

BRITISH OCCUPATION & THE JAVA WAR

France occupied Holland during the Napoleonic Wars and in 1811 the British occupied parts of the Dutch East Indies, including Java. Control was restored to the Dutch in 1816 and a treaty was signed in 1824 under which the British exchanged Bengkulu in Sumatra for Dutch-controlled Melaka on the Malay Peninsula. While the two European powers may have settled their differences, the Indonesians were far from happy with European control. There were a number of wars and insurrections during this time; the most prolonged struggles were the Paderi War in Sumatra (1821–38) and the Java War (1825–30) led by Pangeran (Prince) Diponegoro. The eldest son of the sultan of Yogyakarta, Diponegoro had recently been passed over for succession to the throne, in favour of a younger claimant. Having bided his time, Diponegoro eventually vanished from court and in 1825 launched a guerrilla war against the Dutch. The courts of Yogyakarta and Solo largely remained loyal to the Dutch, but many members of the Javanese aristocracy supported the rebellion. Diponegoro had received mystical signs that convinced him he was the divinely appointed future king of Java. News spread among the people that he was the long-prophesied Ratu Adil (the Just King) who would free them from colonial oppression.

The rebellion ended in 1830 when the Dutch tricked Diponegoro into a peace negotiation, arrested him and then exiled him to Sulawesi. The five-year war had cost the lives of 8000 European and 7000 Indonesian soldiers of the Dutch army. At least 200,000 Javanese died, most from famine and disease. Diponegoro is commemorated throughout Indonesia by having a major street in most cities and towns named after him.

INDONESIAN NATIONALISM

Although the Ethical Period failed to deliver widespread education, it did provide a Dutch education for the children of the Indonesian elite, and with that came Western political ideas of freedom and democracy.

1821–38
Paderi War fought in Sumatra

1825–30
Java War fought by Diponegoro

However, the first seeds of Indonesian nationalism were sown by Islamic movements.

Sarekat Islam (SI), an early nationalist movement founded in 1909 by Islamic traders, rallied Indonesian Muslims under the banner of Islam, initially to combat Chinese influence in the batik trade but soon widening its agenda to take a more radical anticolonial stance.

The Indonesian Communist Party (Partai Komunis Indonesia; PKI) began as a splinter group within SI. However, its members were expelled by SI and soon developed the PKI into Indonesia's first fully fledged pro-independence party inspired by European politics. It was formed in 1920 and found support among workers in the industrial cities. In 1926 the PKI attempted an uprising, carrying out isolated insurrections across Java and West Sumatra. The outraged Dutch government arrested and exiled thousands of communists, effectively putting them out of action for the rest of the Dutch occupation.

'The first seeds of Indonesian nationalism were sown by Islamic movements'

Despite Dutch repression, the nationalist movement was finding a unified voice. In a historic announcement in 1928, the All Indonesia Youth Congress proclaimed its Youth Pledge, adopting the notions of one national identity (Indonesian), one country (Indonesia) and one language (Bahasa Indonesia). In Bandung in 1929, Soekarno founded the Partai Nasional Indonesia (PNI). It became the most significant nationalist organisation and was the first secular party devoted primarily to independence.

Soekarno was educated in East Java and Europe before studying at the Bandung Institute of Technology. Bandung was a hotbed of political intellectualism and Soekarno was widely influenced by Javanese, Western, Islamic and socialist ideals. He blended these influences towards a national ideology.

Soekarno was soon arrested and a virtual ban placed on the PNI. Nationalist sentiment remained high during the 1930s, but with many nationalist leaders in jail or exiled, independence seemed a long way off. Even when Germany invaded the Netherlands in May 1940, the colonial government in exile was determined to hold fast.

All was to change when the Japanese forces stormed through Southeast Asia. Following the fall of Singapore, many Europeans fled to Australia, and the Dutch colonial government abandoned their colony.

JAPANESE OCCUPATION & THE BATTLE FOR INDEPENDENCE

The Japanese Imperial Army marched into Batavia on 5 March 1942, carrying the red and white Indonesian flag alongside that of the Japanese rising sun. The city's name was changed to Jakarta, Europeans were arrested and all signs of the former Dutch masters eliminated.

Though the Japanese were greeted as liberators, public opinion turned against them as the war wore on and Indonesians were expected to endure more hardships for the war effort.

The Japanese gained a reputation as cruel masters, but they also gave Indonesians more responsibility and – for the first time – participation in government. The Japanese also gave prominence to nationalist leaders, such as Soekarno and Mohammed Hatta, and trained youth militias to defend the country. Apart from instilling in Indonesia a military psyche

1840s
Famine and epidemics sweep Java

1883
Krakatau erupts 26 August

STREET NAMES & INDONESIAN HEROES

In every city, town and village in Indonesia, streets are named after Indonesian heroes who helped fight the Dutch. Here are some of the more well known:

Bonjol, Imam (1772–1864) An important West Sumatran Islamic leader, he inspired resistance against the Dutch in the Paderi War of 1821–38.

Diponegoro, Pangeran (1785–1855) This prince from Yogyakarta was a leader in the Java War (1825–30) against the Dutch.

Gajah Mada (d 1364) Prime minister in the Javanese Majapahit kingdom in the 14th century, Gajah Mada was also a brilliant military commander. He helped defeat rebels who fought King Jayanegara (but later arranged the king's murder because he took Gajah Mada's wife!).

Hatta, Mohammed (1902–80) A Sumatran, Hatta was arrested in 1927 for promoting resistance against the Dutch. On 17 August 1945 he declared Indonesian independence with Soekarno and served as vice president and/or prime minister from 1945 to 1956.

Monginsidi, Wolter (1925–49) During the revolution, the Dutch captured and shot 24-year-old Monginsidi who had inspired the youth of Sulawesi to fight the colonialists.

Sisingamangaraja (1849–1907) The last of a long line of Batak kings who had ruled since the 16th century; Sisingamangaraja's ancestors were spiritual leaders, but he became a leader of the resistance against the Dutch, which cost him his life.

Subroto, Gatot (1907–62) This hero fought for Indonesian independence in the 1940s and helped quell communist rebels in 1948. He became military governor of Surakarta, then a general, and later helped found Indonesia's national defence academy.

Sudarso, Yos (1925–62) A senior naval officer, Sudarso died when his ship was sunk by the Dutch during the 'liberation' of Irian Jaya (now Papua).

Sudirman (1916–50) Between 1945 and 1950 General Sudirman led the resistance against the Dutch and was Indonesia's first commander in chief.

Syahrir, Sutan (1909–66) Syahrir was a leading nationalist leader against the Dutch in Java in the 1930s. During WWII he refused to cooperate with the Japanese. He served as prime minister from 1945 to 1947 and led Indonesia's delegation in negotiating independence from the Dutch.

Thamrin, Mohammed (1894–1941) This hero was a nationalist leader and politician in the 1920s and '30s.

that has endured in Indonesian politics, these militias gave rise to the *pemuda* (youth groups) of the independence movement, many of whom would later join the Republican army.

As the war ended, Soekarno and Hatta were by far the most popular nationalist leaders. In August 1945 they were kidnapped and pressured by radical *pemuda* to declare independence before the Dutch could return. On 17 August 1945, with tacit Japanese backing, Soekarno proclaimed the independence of the Republic of Indonesia, from his Jakarta home.

Indonesians rejoiced, but the Netherlands refused to accept the proclamation and still claimed sovereignty over Indonesia. British troops entered Java in October 1945 to accept the surrender of the Japanese. Under British auspices, Dutch troops gradually returned to Indonesia and it became obvious that independence would have to be fought for.

Clashes broke out with the new Republican army and came to a head in the bloody Battle for Surabaya. The situation deteriorated when British Indian troops landed in the city. When General Mallaby, leader of the British forces, was killed by a bomb, the British launched a bloody retribution. On 10 November (now celebrated as Heroes Day) the British

Revolt In Paradise by Scottish-American author K'tut Tantri is a gripping portrayal of her involvement in Indonesia's fight for independence. Timothy Lindsey's *The Romance of K'tut Tantri and Indonesia* offers great background to the original.

1920

The Indonesian Communist Party (Partai Komunis Indonesia; PKI) is formed

1942

Japanese Imperial Army marches into Batavia on 5 March

PANCASILA – THE FIVE PRINCIPLES

In government buildings, on highway markers, at the end of TV broadcasts and on school uniforms you'll see the *garuda,* Indonesia's mythical bird and national symbol. On its breast are the five symbols of the Pancasila (five principles), the philosophical doctrine of Indonesia, which was first expounded by Soekarno in 1945:

Star Represents faith in God, whether Islamic, Christian, Buddhist, Hindu or any other religion.
Chain Represents humanity within Indonesia and its links to humankind as a whole.
Banyan tree Represents nationalism and promoting unity between Indonesia's many ethnic groups.
Buffalo Symbolises representative government.
Rice and cotton Represents social justice.

began to take the city under cover of air attacks. Thousands of Indonesians died, the population fled to the countryside, and the poorly armed Republican forces fought a pitched battle for three weeks. The brutal retaliation of the British and the spirited defence of Surabaya by Republicans galvanised Indonesian support and helped turn world opinion.

The Dutch dream of easy reoccupation was shattered, while the British were keen to extricate themselves from military action and broker a peace agreement. The last British troops left in November 1946, by which time 55,000 Dutch troops had landed in Java. Indonesian Republican officials were imprisoned, and bombing raids on Palembang and Medan in Sumatra prepared the way for the Dutch occupation of these cities. In southern Sulawesi, Dutch Captain Westerling was accused of pacifying the region – by murdering 40,000 Indonesians in a few weeks. Elsewhere, the Dutch were attempting to form puppet states among the more amenable ethnic groups.

In Jakarta the Republican government, with Soekarno as president and Hatta as vice president, tried to maintain calm. Meanwhile, *pemuda* advocating armed struggle saw the old leadership as prevaricating and betraying the revolution.

Outbreaks occurred across the country, and Soekarno and Hatta were outmanoeuvred in the Republican government. A Sumatran socialist, Sultan Syahrir, became prime minister and, as the Dutch assumed control in Jakarta, the Republicans moved their capital to Yogyakarta. Sultan Hamengkubuwono IX, who was to become Yogyakarta's most revered and able sultan, played a leading role in the revolution.

Inside Indonesia (www.insideindonesia.org) provides excellent articles covering everything from power plays within the army to art-house films.

The battle for independence wavered between warfare and diplomacy. Under the Linggarjati Agreement of November 1946, the Dutch recognised the Republican government and both sides agreed to work towards an Indonesian federation under a Dutch commonwealth. The agreement was soon swept aside as war escalated. The Dutch mounted a large offensive in July 1947, causing the UN to step in.

During these uncertain times, the main forces in Indonesian politics regrouped: the communist PKI, Soekarno's PNI, and the Islamic parties of Masyumi and Nahdatul Ulama. The army also emerged as a force, though it was split by many factions. The Republicans were far from united, and in Java civil war threatened to erupt when in 1948 the PKI staged rebellions in Surakarta (Solo) and Madiun. In a tense threat to the

1945
Soekarno proclaims independence of the Republic of Indonesia on 17 August

1949
Indonesian flag raised at Jakarta's Istana Merdeka; power officially handed over

revolution, Soekarno galvanised opposition to the communists, who were massacred by army forces.

In February 1948 the Dutch launched another full-scale attack on the Republicans, breaking the UN agreement and turning world opinion. Under pressure from the USA, which threatened to withdraw its postwar aid to the Netherlands, and a growing realisation at home that this was an unwinnable war, the Dutch negotiated for independence. On 27 December 1949 the Indonesian flag was raised at Jakarta's Istana Merdeka (Freedom Palace) as power was officially handed over.

ECONOMIC DEPRESSION & DISUNITY

In the first years of independence, the threat of external attacks by the Dutch helped keep the nationalists united. However, with the Dutch gone, divisions in Indonesian society began to appear. Soekarno had tried to hammer out the principles of Indonesian unity in his Pancasila speech of 1945 (see opposite) but while these, as he said, may have been 'the highest common factor and the lowest common multiple of Indonesian thought', divisions could not be swept away by a single speech. Regional differences in customs, morals, traditions and religion, the impact of Christianity and Marxism, and fears of political domination by the Javanese all contributed to disunity.

At the entrance to a neighbourhood or village you may see an arch with the words 'Dirgahayu RI' painted across it. This translates as 'Long live the Republic of Indonesia' and the arch has been built to celebrate Independence Day.

Various separatist movements battled the new republic. They included the militant Darul Islam (Islamic Domain), which proclaimed an Islamic State of Indonesia and waged guerrilla warfare in West Java and south Sulawesi from 1948 to 1962. In Maluku, Ambonese members of the former Royal Dutch Indies Army tried to establish an independent republic.

Against this background lay the sorry state of the conflict-battered economy and divisions in the leadership. The population was increasing but food production was low and the export economy was damaged, as many plantations had been destroyed during the war. Illiteracy was high and there was a dearth of skilled workers. Inflation was chronic and smuggling was costing the government badly needed foreign currency.

On top of this, political parties proliferated and there were continuous deals brokered between parties for a share of cabinet seats. This resulted in a rapid turnover of coalition governments: 17 cabinets over 13 years.

GRASS ROOTS GOVERNANCE

Below the president, Indonesia's government hierarchy involves governors, district heads and sub-district heads. But for many Indonesians the most relevant government representation is at the village level. Here, local affairs are handled by an elected *lurah* or *kepala desa* (both words mean 'village chief'), though often the position of *lurah* is hereditary. The *lurah* is the person to see if you wander into a village and need to spend the night, or resolve a problem.

The village is the main social unit, providing welfare, support and guidance. If fire destroys a house, or a village needs a new well, then everyone pitches in. This grass-roots system of mutual help is called *gotong-royong*. The main local community organisation is the *rukun tetangga* (neighbourhood association). Among other tasks, it registers families and organises neighbourhood security. A *pos kamling* (security post), which doubles as an informal meeting point, can be found at the centre of most villages – just look for a raised platform and wooden drum.

1958

Rebellions, backed by the CIA, UK and Australia, break out in Sumatra and Sulawesi

1963

Irian Jaya (Papua) formally made a province of Indonesia

Frequently postponed national elections were finally held in 1955 and the PNI – regarded as Soekarno's party – narrowly topped the poll. There was a dramatic increase in support for the PKI but no party managed more than a quarter of the votes, and so short-lived coalitions continued.

SOEKARNO'S RULE

By 1956 President Soekarno was openly criticising parliamentary democracy, stating that it was 'based upon inherent conflict'. He sought a system based on the traditional Indonesian village system of discussion and consensus, which occurred under the guidance of village elders. He proposed the threefold division – *nasionalisme* (nationalism), *agama* (religion) and *komunisme* (communism) – be blended into a cooperative Nas-A-Kom government, thereby appeasing the main factions of Indonesian politics: the army, Islamic groups and the communists.

In February 1957, with military support, Soekarno proclaimed 'guided democracy' and proposed a cabinet representing all the political parties of importance (including the PKI). For the next 40 years, Western-style, party-based democracy was finished in Indonesia, though the parties were not abolished.

Peter Weir's *The Year of Living Dangerously* (1982), starring Mel Gibson and Sigourney Weaver, is set in Jakarta during the tumultuous Soekarno years.

In 1958, rebellions backed by the CIA, with support from the UK and Australian governments, broke out in Sumatra and Sulawesi. These were a reaction against Soekarno's usurpation of power, the growing influence of the PKI and the corruption and mismanagement of the central government. They were also a reaction against Java, whose leaders and interests dominated Indonesia despite the fact that other islands provided most of the country's export income.

The rebellions were put down by mid-1958, though guerrilla activity continued for three years. Rebel leaders were granted amnesty but their political parties were banned. Some of the early nationalist leaders, such as former prime minister Syahrir, were discredited or arrested.

Soekarno now set about reorganising the political system to give himself *real* power. In 1960 the elected parliament was dissolved and replaced by a parliament appointed by, and subject to the will of, the president. The Supreme Advisory Council, another non-elected body, became the chief policy-making body. A national front, set up to 'mobilise the revolutionary forces of the people', was presided over by the president and became a useful adjunct to government in organising 'demonstrations'.

Soekarno had set Indonesia on a course of stormy nationalism. His speeches were those of a romantic revolutionary, which held his people spellbound. He united them against a common external threat, and *konfrontasi* became the buzz word as Indonesia confronted Malaysia (and its imperialist backer, the UK), the USA and, indeed, the whole Western world.

Soekarno believed that Asia had been humiliated by the West and that Indonesia remained threatened by the remnants of Western imperialism: the British and their new client-state of Malaysia, the hated Dutch who continued to occupy Irian Jaya (now Papua) and the Americans and their military bases in the Philippines.

First on the agenda was Irian Jaya, which Indonesia had always claimed on the basis that it had been part of the Dutch East Indies. An arms agree-

1965

Six generals executed in an attempted coup; hundreds of thousands of communists and sympathisers are slaughtered or imprisoned

1968

Soeharto 'elected' as president

SOEKARNO'S CULT OF PERSONALITY

Soekarno, popularly referred to as '*bung* (older brother) Karno', was a man of the people who carried the dreams and aspirations of his nation and dared to take on the West. Soekarno is best remembered for his flamboyance and his contradictions. He was a noted womaniser, a practising Muslim and a Marxist, yet he was also very much a mystic in the Javanese tradition. He somehow held these elements together, as well as Indonesia's inherent cultural differences, through the force of his oratory and personality.

Soekarno often spoke as if he held absolute power, but his position depended on his ability to maintain a balance between the nation's main political players, primarily the army and the PKI.

ment with the Soviet Union in 1960 enabled the Indonesians to begin a diplomatic and military confrontation with the Dutch over the disputed territory, though it was US pressure on the Dutch that finally led to the Indonesian takeover in 1963.

In the same year, Indonesia embarked on *konfrontasi* with the new nation of Malaysia. The northern states in Borneo, which bordered on Indonesian Kalimantan, wavered in their desire to join Malaysia. Indonesia saw itself as the rightful leader of the Malay peoples and supported an attempted revolution in Brunei. The Indonesian army mounted offensives along the Kalimantan–Malaysia border and the PKI demonstrated in the streets in Jakarta.

The West became increasingly alarmed at Indonesia's foreign policy. Foreign aid dried up after the USA withdrew its assistance because of *konfrontasi*. The cash strapped government abolished many subsidies, leading to massive increases in public transport, electricity, water and postal charges. Economic plans had failed miserably and inflation was running at 500%.

Despite achieving national unity, Soekarno could not create a viable economic system to lift Indonesia out of poverty. What's more, great funds were spent on symbols designed to celebrate Indonesia's identity, including Jakarta's National Monument and the massive Mesjid Istiqlal. Unable to advance from revolution to rebuilding, Soekarno's monuments became substitutes for real development.

As *konfrontasi* alienated Western nations, Indonesia came to depend more on support from the Soviet Union, and, to a lesser extent, from communist China. Meanwhile, tensions grew between the Indonesian Army and the PKI.

In 1965, Indonesia's PKI was the largest communist party in the world outside the Soviet Union and China.

With the PKI and its affiliate organisations claiming membership of 20 million, Soekarno realised he had to give the communists recognition in his government. Increasingly, the PKI gained influence ahead of the army, which had been the main power base of Indonesian politics since independence.

'Guided Democracy' under Soekarno was marked by an effort to give peasants better social conditions, but attempts to give tenant farmers a fairer share of their rice crops and to redistribute land led to more class conflict. The PKI pushed for reforms and encouraged peasants to seize land without waiting for decisions from land reform committees. In 1964 these tactics led to violent clashes in Central and East Java and Bali.

1969
Papua becomes part of Indonesia after a controversial UN-certified referendum

1970
Soekarno dies

Tension continued to grow between the PKI and the army. In a visit to Jakarta in April 1965, Zhou Enlai (premier of China) proposed the government build an armed people's militia, independent of the armed forces. Soekarno supported this proposal to arm the communists, the army opposed it, and rumours of an army takeover became rife.

On the night of 30 September 1965, six of Indonesia's top generals were taken from their Jakarta homes and executed in an attempted coup. Led by Colonel Untung of the palace guard and backed by elements of the armed forces, the insurgents took up positions around the presidential palace and later seized the national radio station. The group claimed they had acted against a plot organised by the generals to overthrow the president.

This exercise appears to have had little or no coordination in the rest of the country. Within a few hours of the coup, General Soeharto, head of the army's Strategic Reserve, was able to mobilise army forces to undertake counteraction. By the following evening it was clear the coup had failed.

Exactly who had organised the coup or what it had set out to achieve remains shrouded in mystery. The Indonesian army asserted that the PKI plotted the coup and used discontented army officers to carry it out. Another theory claims it was an internal army affair led by younger officers against the older leadership. Certainly, civilians from the PKI's People's Youth organisation accompanied the army battalions that seized the generals, but whatever the PKI's real role in the coup, the effect on its fortunes was devastating.

Soeharto orchestrated a countercoup, and an anticommunism purge swept Indonesia. Hundreds of thousands of communists and their sympathisers were slaughtered or imprisoned, primarily in Java and Bali. The party and its affiliates were banned and its leaders were killed, imprisoned or went into hiding.

Following the army's lead, anticommunist civilians went on the rampage. In Java, where long-simmering tensions between pro-Islamic and pro-communist factions erupted in the villages, both sides believed that their opponents had drawn up death lists to be carried out when they achieved power. The anticommunists, with encouragement from the government and even Western embassies, carried out their list of executions. On top of this uncontrolled slaughter there were violent demonstrations in Jakarta by pro- and anti-Soekarno groups. Also, perhaps as many as 250,000 people were arrested and sent without trial to prison camps for alleged involvement in the coup.

There are two great history books with the same name: *A History of Modern Indonesia*. One is by MC Ricklefs and offers a very readable account with extra focus on Java. The other, by Adrian Vickers, draws on the life of Pramoedya to tell the nation's story.

Estimates of the post-coup death toll vary widely. Adam Malik, who was to become Soeharto's foreign minister, said that a 'fair figure' was 160,000. Independent commentators estimate the figure to be closer to 500,000.

Soeharto took over leadership of the armed forces and set about manoeuvring Soekarno from power. Despite the chaos, Soekarno continued as president, and as he still had supporters in the armed forces it seemed unlikely that he would voluntarily resign. However, on 11 March 1966, after troops loyal to Soeharto surrounded the Presidential Palace, Soekarno signed the 11 March Order giving Soeharto the power to restore

1975
Indonesia invades East Timor

1975
Taman Mini Indonesia (Jakarta's leisure park) opens

order. While always deferring to the name of Soekarno, Soeharto rapidly consolidated his power. The PKI was officially banned. Pro-Soekarno soldiers and a number of cabinet ministers were arrested. A new six-man inner cabinet, which included Soeharto and two of his nominees, Adam Malik and Sultan Hamengkubuwono of Yogyakarta, was formed.

Soeharto then launched a campaign of intimidation to blunt any grass-roots opposition. Thousands of public servants were dismissed as PKI sympathisers, putting thousands more in fear of losing their jobs.

By 1967 Soeharto was firmly enough entrenched to finally cut Soekarno adrift. The People's Consultative Congress, following the arrest of many of its members and an infusion of Soeharto appointees, relieved Soekarno of all power and, on 27 March 1968, it 'elected' Soeharto as president.

SOEHARTO & THE NEW ORDER

With Soekarno's 'Guided Democracy' no more; the governing label became 'The New Order'. Soeharto set to mending rifts with the West by changing tack on foreign policy and attracting foreign investment. Democracy was paid lip service in the 1971 general elections with Soeharto's Golkar Party a sure bet: other parties were banned, candidates disqualified and voters disenfranchised. Predictably, Golkar swept to power. The new People's Consultative Congress included 207 Soeharto appointments and 276 officers from the armed forces.

Soeharto then enforced the merger of other political parties. The four Islamic parties were amalgamated into the Development Unity Party (PPP) and the other parties were formed into the Indonesian Democratic Party (PDI).

With the elimination of the communists and the establishment of a more repressive government, political stability returned to Indonesia. A determined effort to promote national rather than regional identity was largely successful, but often it was at considerable cost to the population. Infamous examples were the 1975 invasion of East Timor and the brutal treatment of separatist guerrillas in Aceh and Irian Jaya. Smaller scale dissent was also managed through a culture of intimidation and imprisonment.

Thanks mainly to an oil boom and new strains of rice ('the Green Revolution'), the lot of many Indonesians improved considerably under Soeharto. But while life became more tolerable for the poor, the rich became much richer. Corruption was rife at all levels of society, and Indonesian business culture came to revolve around kickbacks and bribes. The most obvious recipients of the new wealth were Soeharto's business associates and his family. They acquired huge business empires, along with prime government contracts.

Grass-roots grumblings increased along with disparity of wealth. The political opposition, particularly the PDI, grew in stature and popularity. So much so that in 1996 the government helped engineer a split in the PDI, resulting in its popular leader Megawati Soekarnoputri (Soekarno's daughter) being dumped. PDI supporters rioted in Jakarta, but it was only a taste of things to come.

An ageing Soeharto made noises about retirement, but without an obvious successor (and with the local and international business community

The English-language press is limited mostly to the daily *Jakarta Post*. Coverage can be a little thin, but it does give a useful rundown of events in Jakarta.

The Invisible Palace by Jose Manuel Tesoro is a investigative account of the 1996 murder of a journalist. The gripping novel also examines ancient Javanese belief systems that are still prevalent today.

1983–84
Nearly 10,000 killed as part of the government's anticrime initiative

1991–93
Demonstrators killed in Dili; Xanana Gusmao captured; Irian Jaya rebel leader Marthen Luther Prawar killed

ARMED FORCES

Whether celebrated or abhorred, Indonesia's military has played in integral part in forging Indonesia's identity. The military's psyche developed during WWII, when the Japanese organised village militias to fight in the event of reoccupation. When the Dutch returned, independence was gained only after a bloody war waged by these village armies united under the banner of the new republic.

The leaders of Indonesia's new army became heroes: their achievements are endlessly retold in schools and their names now adorn Indonesian streets (p43). Indonesia's history has become a military one, and even obscure leaders of ancient, easily crushed peasant rebellions have become national heroes. The military has been a part of the political process since independence, and it hardly regards itself as having usurped power that somehow 'rightfully' belongs to civilians.

Under Soekarno, powers and aspirations of the military intensified. In 1958 General Nasution expounded the doctrine of *dwifungsi* (dual function) to justify an expanded military role in government. This stated that it not only played a security role, it also had a social and political role as 'one of the many forces in society'.

Following the 1965 coup, the military became not just one of many forces in society, but a dominant one. Its support was now necessary for power. As well as having automatic representation in parliament, the military was involved in local government right down to the village level.

The military may now have lost political representation, nevertheless political leaders continue to show it deference. Criticism of military influence continues, especially from student groups who have often borne the brunt of the military's law-and-order campaigns. Others consider it the only force that can keep Indonesia together in the face of disintegration. It's a position the military has been seen to exploit: evidence often arises implicating the military in inciting (then quelling) violence so as to justify its prominent position.

so used to Indonesia's brand of crony capitalism) the government reaffirmed his leadership.

THE FALL OF SOEHARTO

All was to change when the 1997 Asian currency crisis spilled over into Indonesia, savaging the country's economy. The International Monetary Fund (IMF) pledged financial backing in return for reforms such as the abolition of government subsidies on food and fuel, the deregulation of monopolies (such as the clove monopoly controlled by Soeharto's son, Tommy) and the abandonment of grandiose government-sponsored industries, many of which were also controlled by 'Soeharto Family Inc'.

Rising prices resulted in sporadic riots as the people, already hard hit by the monetary crisis, looted shops owned by the minority ethnic Chinese, a significant business class that became the scapegoat for this sudden loss of faith in the economy.

Foreign debt and inflation continued to skyrocket, many banks collapsed, companies faced bankruptcy and millions lost their jobs. The swiftness and scope of the human tragedy is difficult to comprehend. Substantial progress in reducing poverty – for so long the pride and excuse of authoritarian government – was rapidly reversed. In just one year the number of Indonesians living below the poverty line jumped from 20 million to 100 million (nearly 50% of the populace).

1997
Financial markets savage the rupiah during Asian currency crisis

1998
Soeharto re-elected as president; antigovernment rallies resume; Soeharto resigns; Habibie becomes third president

At the same time, Soeharto was up for re-election. This was a foregone conclusion but, as never before, critics from the Islamic parties, opposition groups and especially student demonstrators demanded that he step down.

Soeharto's re-election in February 1998 seemed to at least promise political certainty, and the government moved towards fulfilling IMF demands. The rupiah stabilised but demands for political reform continued as students demonstrated across the country. Initially, these demonstrations were confined to campuses, but in April violent rioting erupted in the streets of Medan, then other cities. Adding to the hardship and furthering unrest, the government announced fuel and electricity price rises, as demanded by the IMF.

The word *sembako* refers to Indonesia's nine essential ingredients: rice, sugar, eggs, meat, flour, corn, fuel, cooking oil and salt. When any of these become unavailable or more costly, repercussions can be felt right through to the presidency.

Throughout the turmoil the army reiterated its support for the government. Tanks and army trucks appeared on the streets, but demands for Soeharto's resignation increased. Student demonstrations would not go away and on 12 May, with Soeharto away on a visit to Cairo, soldiers swapped rubber bullets for live ammunition and shot dead four students at Trisakti University in Jakarta.

Jakarta erupted – in three days of rioting and looting, over 6000 buildings in the city were damaged or destroyed and an estimated 1200 people died. Law and order collapsed. The army was often ineffectual as soldiers looked on, trying to portray the army as the people's ally. Hardest hit were the Chinese, whose businesses were looted and destroyed – shocking tales of rape and murder emerged after the riots. Mounting evidence pointed to General Prabowo, Soeharto's son-in-law, as having used military goon squads to spearhead attacks on Chinese shops and Chinese women. He did this to create a situation where Soeharto could once more 'save the nation'. However, Prabowo's plan backfired and, following Soeharto's fall, he was dismissed from the army and sent into exile for a few years.

Sidelines by *Tempo* editor Goenawan Mohamad offers readers intriguing vignettes of daily life in an often tumultuous country.

The riots subsided but anti-Soeharto demonstrations increased while the army threatened to shoot on sight. The country looked on, fearing massive bloodshed. Still Soeharto clung to the presidency, but with the writing on the wall, some of his own ministers called for his resignation. Soeharto finally stepped down on 21 May, ending 32 years of rule.

THE ROAD TO DEMOCRACY

In May 1998 Vice President BJ Habibie was sworn in, and quickly set about making the right noises on reform by releasing political prisoners and promising elections. Habibie tried to cultivate an image of himself as a man of the people, but as a long-standing minister and close friend of Soeharto, his credentials were always going to be questioned.

The economy was still in tatters and the rupiah plumbed new depths, but Indonesia embraced a new era of political openness. The government talked about *reformasi* (reform), but at the same time tried to ban demonstrations and reaffirmed the role of the army in Indonesian politics.

The army's reputation was severely tarnished. Not only had it started the riots by shooting students, then failed to contain the rioting, evidence emerged that military factions had indeed incited the rioting. The newly vocal press also exposed army killings in Aceh and the abduction and murder of opposition activists.

1999
Indonesian government relinquishes claim to East Timor after referendum and violence

1999
Abdurrahman Wahid named as president, Megawati as vice president

IMF money flowed into Indonesia but hardship ensued. Some people sold their meagre possessions to buy food while others simply stole what they needed. Old grudges resurfaced during these uncertain times and the Chinese continued to suffer as scapegoats.

In November 1998 the Indonesian parliament met to discuss a new election. Student demands for immediate elections and the abolition of military appointees to parliament were ignored. Three days of skirmishes peaked on 13 November when students marched on parliament. Clashes with the army left 12 dead and hundreds injured. Then disturbances took on an even more worrying trend: a local dispute involving Christians and Muslims resulted in churches being burned in Jakarta. Throughout Indonesia Christians were outraged, and in eastern Indonesia Christians attacked mosques and the minority Islamic community. Riots in West

SOEHARTO'S GREATEST HITS (1968–98)

In many ways Indonesia is still reeling from Soeharto's 30 years of rule. His culture of collusion, corruption and nepotism reached deep into the nation's fabric. Here are some memorable Soeharto moments:

1968 Soeharto 'elected' as president.

1969 Government officials banned from joining any political party other than Soeharto's Golkar party. Flour mills part-owned by Ibu Tien (Soeharto's wife) are granted a milling and distribution monopoly.

1978 Bandung Institute of Technology students criticise the government. Troops occupy the campus.

1982 Security forces fire on antigovernment rallies. Press coverage of the incident is banned. Censorship laws are increased, widening the power to shut down not only publications that criticise the government but also any businesses affiliated with those publications.

1983–4 Nearly 10,000 killed as part of government's anticrime initiative.

1984 Jakarta's Soekarno-Hatta International Airport opens. Soeharto's son allegedly skims more than US$75 million from the construction budget.

1985 Crackdown on alleged PKI (Indonesian communist party) members. Many members already serving prison sentences are executed.

1987 Tutut (Soeharto's daughter) wins bid to build Jakarta toll road.

1989 Government founds publication censorship board, with intelligence officers included as members. Cigarette companies forced to buy cloves from distributor run by Soeharto's son, Tommy.

1991 Tutut starts up TV station without incurring fees for using state-owned telecommunication infrastructure.

1993 New 50,000 rupiah banknote minted, depicting image of Soeharto.

1994 Tommy Soeharto opens supermarket chain with a massive loan that is never repaid. *Tempo* magazine's publishing licence is revoked by the government, who claimed the magazine's reports would cause national instability.

1996 Politician Sri Bintang Pamungkas sentenced to jail for nearly three years for insulting the president.

1997 Ari Sigit Soeharto (Soeharto's grandson) plans a project whereby all school students would be required to buy shoes manufactured by his company.

1998 Soeharto re-elected as president; antigovernment rallies resume; Soeharto resigns; Habibie becomes third president.

2001
Wahid ousted from presidency, Megawati sworn in as fifth president

2002
Two bombs explode in Kuta, Bali, killing over 200 people

Timor were followed by prolonged Muslim-Christian violence in Maluku and Kalimantan. Instability was also renewed in the separatist-minded regions of Aceh, Irian Jaya and East Timor.

In early 1999, after continuous refusal to grant East Timor autonomy or independence, President Habibie did an about-turn and prepared a ballot. Despite such a laudable move, pro-Indonesian militia launched a bloody campaign of intimidation, with the tacit backing of the army. Nevertheless, 78.5% of East Timorese voted in favour of independence. Celebrations soon turned to despair as militia groups, orchestrated by elements of the Indonesian military, unleashed a reign of terror that killed up to 2000 unarmed civilians, displaced much of the population and devastated 80% of the country's infrastructure. Three weeks later, an international peacekeeping force entered East Timor to restore order. Thousands of expatriate advisers and soldiers were flown in on massive salaries and allowances while the poverty-stricken Timorese looked on. The United Nations Transitional Administration in East Timor (UNTAET) did bring stability to East Timor, and independence was officially celebrated on 20 May 2002.

One of Pramoedya's earlier books, *Tales from Djakarta*, gives readers a backstreet view of the capital during the rocky early days of independence and the rise of military control. Many of his other books draw on Javanese culture to tell stories with contemporary relevance, such as *The King, the Witch and the Priest*.

Despite the ongoing instability, Indonesia's June 1999 elections were largely a joyous celebration of democracy. In the first free election in over 40 years, Megawati Soekarnoputri was the popular choice for president, but her PDI-P (Indonesian Democratic Party for Struggle) could muster only a third of the vote. The Golkar party, without the benefit of a rigged electoral system, had its vote slashed from over 70% to just over 20%.

Although Megawati received more votes, a coalition of other parties had the numbers to deny her the presidency, so on 20 October the People's Consultative Assembly voted in Abdurrahman Wahid as the new president and Megawati as vice president. As head of Nahdatul Ulama (Indonesia's largest Islamic organisation), Wahid already commanded widespread support. However, his moves to reform the government, address corruption and quell conflict in outlying provinces were continually hamstrung by those who opposed such reform. Wahid's effort to bring Soeharto to justice were hindered by a corrupt and timid judiciary, and claims that Soeharto was too ill to stand trial. Wahid's effort to bring peace to such areas as Aceh, Irian Jaya (which he renamed Papua) and Maluku were not helped by an army that seemed to use the conflict as a justification of a continuation of their influence and political presence. Not helped by his failing health, Wahid's 21-month presidency may be seen as a time when the wheels of reform began to turn, but were too often punctured by the powerful few who were set to lose so much as a consequence.

With a unanimous vote in parliament, Megawati Soekarnoputri was sworn in as the fifth president on 23 July 2001. Although stability was restored at the presidential level, her strategy of not rocking the boat meant corruption, human rights abuses and abuse of military power remained widespread. This, along with the threat to security reflected in the Bali, Marriott, and Embassy bombings hindered the prospect of foreign support and investment.

Indonesia's first direct presidential elections were held in October 2004. Candidates continued to promise political reform and a crackdown

2003
Martial law imposed in Aceh after peace talks reach an impasse

2004
Susilo Bambang Yudhoyono wins first direct presidential election

INDONESIA'S SEPARATIST CONFLICTS *John Martinkus*

To the people of Aceh and Papua, Indonesia has, since independence from the Dutch, been a Javanese empire. The exploitation of resources – gold from Papua and natural gas and oil from Aceh – by the bureaucracy in Jakarta, backed up by a repressive military, has been the major factor in keeping these separatist conflicts continuing into the 21st century.

In Aceh it's no coincidence that the declaration of Acehnese independence in 1976 came just as the Exxon Mobil Arun plant was reaching full production. It was this declaration that led to the establishment of the Free Aceh Movement (Gerakan Aceh Merdeka; GAM) and to the guerrilla war and the brutal Indonesian military response that ensured GAM recruits for the next 29 years of conflict. It is well reported that Exxon-Mobil pays the Indonesian military to protect the plant. In 2001, 11 Acehnese took the company to court in the US for the 'abuses including genocide, murder, torture, crimes against humanity and sexual violence' that had been conducted by troops in the employ of Exxon-Mobil. The US state department eventually had the case thrown out of court.

In Papua is the world's largest gold mine and Indonesia's largest single taxpayer, the US owned Freeport-McMoran mine in Tembagapura. It is the reason why Papuan independence will never be considered by the Indonesians. The concession for the mine was granted two years before the 1969 UN-sponsored 'Act of Free Choice' officially handed over sovereignty of Papua from the Dutch to the Indonesians. That said a lot about the Indonesians' confidence in predicting the outcome of a plebiscite in which 1026 delegates selected by themselves voted on behalf of the 814,000 Papuans registered. In 2001 one of the UN staffers involved told Associated Press, 'It was just a whitewash.' Whitewash though it was, the Act of Free Choice did put the UN stamp of approval on the integration of Papua into Indonesia and, unlike East Timor, whose 1975 takeover was never recognised by the UN, the plebiscite set back the cause of independence for West Papua and is still quoted by Indonesian authorities as the legitimisation for their often brutal rule. Internal Freeport documents reveal annual payments of US$11 million to the Indonesian military. The first recorded Indonesian military killing of civilians in the area was in 1972. In 1977 the Organisasi Papua Merdeka (OPM) sabotaged Freeport, forcing a halt in production; attacks on local communities increased. No human rights investigators have ever been allowed into the area.

When Soeharto was finally removed from power in May 1998, East Timor, Aceh and Papua all began to campaign for independence. Demonstrations in East Timor and international pressure led President Habibie to allow the UN to enter the country and conduct a referendum. The Indonesian military responded by forming militias and conducting its own campaign of killing. The territory voted for independence – but not before the Indonesian military had burnt and looted all major towns and driven the population to the mountains or across the border into

on corruption, as well as making new promises to stamp out terrorism. The election became a battle between Megawati and Susilo Bambang Yudhoyono (SBY), the latter winning the final vote and becoming the sixth president of Indonesia. Although fronting the newly formed Democratic Party, SBY was already well known to voters. As a long-serving general, he had been regarded as a military reformist, but was also directly involved in the East Timor occupation. He was also Minister for Security and Political Affairs in both the Wahid and Megawati governments.

During Indonesia's first direct presidential election (20 October 2004) over 115 million people cast their vote, making it the world's largest ever one-day election.

Under SBY, corruption remains endemic, terrorism remains a threat and the military, although no longer having automatic representation in government, still holds great sway over society. Despite some reforms and freedoms, political activism and dissent remains a risky pursuit as was

2004
Over 200,000 die across Sumatra in December tsunami

2005
October suicide bombings in Bali kill 23

West Timor, killing thousands. In Aceh the calls for a referendum led a million people onto the streets of the capital in 1999. The Indonesians responded with more troops, more operations, more massacres and, finally, martial law in 2003 that closed the province to journalists and aid workers entirely; they conducted operations and widespread arrests.

Again, thousands were killed away from view, until the 2004 Boxing Day tsunami devastated the province and forced the Indonesian government to allow foreign aid back in and to resume the peace process with GAM. The Indonesian military, which had been profiting from the implementation of martial law in Aceh since May 2003, realised there was more money to be made in allowing the aid dollars to flow into Aceh rather than continue the war against GAM. For its part, GAM was simply exhausted from the struggle (particularly the harsh martial-law period from May 2003 to Boxing Day 2004) and agreed to disarm and transform itself into a peaceful political movement. At the time of writing, the peace process was on track but the Indonesian military's decision to redeploy 10,000 extra troops to the province for 'reconstruction' was greeted with suspicion by Acehnese who had experienced many well publicised but phoney troop withdrawals as ceasefires have come and gone in the past.

In Papua the foundation of the Papuan Presidium Council led by Theys Eluay promised a broad-based coalition to push for independence. The Indonesian Special Forces responded by killing him in November 2001. Independence supporters, human rights workers, indeed anyone connected with the brief exercise of free speech in Papua, was either arrested or killed or forced into exile. Foreign journalists were once again banned and the most senior posts in the military and police in Papua taken up by the very same officers who carried out the violence in East Timor and Aceh. Despite detailed investigations by the UN and a host of human rights organisations, no senior officers have been punished for crimes in Indonesia's three separatist wars and the perpetrators are still in business in Papua. East Timor could separate from Indonesia – it was, after all, the poorest province in the country. Unfortunately, for the Papuans and the Acehnese that option is not so easy. Their abundance of natural resources means the Indonesian military, once again supported by the US and Australia, will continue to commit human rights abuses to ensure their access to these resources. That is why to the people in Aceh and Papua the Indonesian nation is still the Javanese empire.

John Martinkus began working as a freelance reporter in East Timor in the mid-'90s. He has extensively covered the conflicts in Aceh and West Papua, and has worked in Iraq, the Philippines, Afghanistan and on the Thailand–Burma border.

shown when Munir, a human rights activist, was poisoned on a Garuda flight in 2005.

After the 2003 tsunami, SBY won favour by making sure foreign aid could get to the affected areas (including Aceh, which was still under martial law). He also took the initiative to restart talks with Acehnese rebels, which resulted in a peace deal in 2005. Whether these efforts have a lasting effect is uncertain (see boxed text, opposite).

But even almost 10 years after his downfall, it's still apparent that Soeharto's network of corruption, collusion and nepotism still lingers. Attempts to bring corrupt officials to justice have rarely eventuated in convictions, often because the implications of a serious crackdown would reach far into the current power structure. A 35-year, multibillion dollar web of state-supported corruption is a hard thing to untangle.

2005
Acehnese rebels and Indonesian government sign peace deal

2006
Bantul, near Yogyakarta, Central Java, is hit by an earthquake on 27 May – 6000 die and 200,000 are left homeless across the region

The Culture

THE NATIONAL PSYCHE

Indonesia comprises a massively diverse range of societies and cultures; the differences between, say, the Sumbanese and Sundanese are as marked as those between the Swedes and Sicilians. Even so, a national Indonesian identity has emerged, originally through the struggle for independence and, following that, through education programmes and the promotion of Bahasa Indonesia as a national language. This is despite the fact that Indonesia continues to be stretched by opposing forces: 'strict' Islam versus 'moderate' Islam, Islam versus Christianity versus Hinduism, country versus city, modern versus traditional, rich versus poor.

These differences may challenge social cohesion and have at times been used as an excuse to incite conflict, but the nation still prevails. And, with notable exceptions like Papua, the bonds have grown stronger, with the notion of an Indonesian identity overlapping rather than supplanting the nation's many pre-existing regional cultures. The national slogan, Bhinneka Tunggal Ika (Unity in Diversity), has been widely adopted by Indonesians, who function across widely varying ethnic and social standpoints. Perhaps this is why Indonesians are often keen to strike up a conversation with a traveller: everyone has their own story and perspective.

A cultural element that bridges both the regional and the national is religion – the Pancasila principle of belief in a god holds firm. Though Indonesia is predominantly Islamic, in many places Islam is interwoven with traditional customs, giving it unique qualities and characteristics. In terms of area rather than population, most of Indonesia is, in fact, Christian or animist. And to leaven the mix, Bali has its own unique brand of Hinduism. Religion plays a role in the everyday: mosques and *musholla* (prayer rooms) are in constant use, and the vibrant Hindu ceremonies of Bali are a daily occurrence, to the delight of many visitors.

Mobile phones and other facets of modernity have found purchase in Indonesia. But while Java and Bali can appear technologically rich, other areas remain untouched by the mod cons many city dwellers take for granted. But even where modernisation has taken hold, it's clear that Indonesians have a very traditionalist heart. As well as adherence to religious and ethnic traditions, social customs are maintained. For example, elders are accorded great respect. When visiting someone's home, elders are always greeted first, and often customary permission to depart is also offered. This can occur whether in a high-rise in Medan or a hut in Merauke.

Jakarta Inside Out by Daniel Ziv is a candid and colourful profile of the megalopolis.

LIFESTYLE

Daily life for Indonesians has changed rapidly over the years. These days, many people live away from their home region and the role of women has extended well beyond domestic duties to include career and study (see p64). Nevertheless, the role of the family remains strong. This is evident during such festivals as Lebaran (the end of the Islamic fasting month), when highways become gridlocked with those returning home to loved ones. Even at weekends, many travel for hours to spend a day with their relatives. In many ways, the notion of family or regional identity has become more pronounced: as people move away from small-scale communities and enter the milieu of the cities, the sense of belonging becomes more valued.

Beyond family, the main social unit is the village. This is obvious in rural areas but can also be seen in the cities: the backstreets of Jakarta, for example, are home to tightknit neighbourhoods where kids run from house to house and everyone knows who owns which chicken. A sense of community may also evolve in a *kos* (apartment with shared facilities), where tenants, far from their families, come together for meals and companionship.

Villages can also act as something of a welfare system during tough times. But as more and more people move to large cities, this social safety net has thinned, which, in turn, has increased the prevalence of begging or crime.

For the many Indonesians who still live in their home region, customs and traditions remain a part of the everyday: the Toraja of Sulawesi continue to build traditional houses due to their social importance (see p690); the focus of a Sumbanese village remains the gravestones of their ancestors due to the influence they are believed to have in daily happenings (see p590). These aren't customs offered attention once a year – they are a part of life. And even where modernity has found purchase, age-old traditions can still underpin the everyday: in Bali, for example, you'll see flashy buses blessed in the Hindu tradition before they hurtle down the highway.

POPULATION

Indonesia, with over 242 million people, is the world's fourth most populous nation after China, India and the USA, and Java alone has a population of over 130 million. Yet population growth has slowed to 1.45% as a result of family-planning programmes such as the appointment of coordinators in villages who advise on contraception, monitor birth rates and promote such national campaigns as *Dua Anak Cukup* (Two Children is Enough). In rural areas, large families are still common, as children are seen as 'insurance' for the parents' old age.

Indonesia: An Introduction to Contemporary Traditions by Ian Chalmers covers everything from language to the struggle for democracy.

Overpopulation is largely a Javanese problem. The total area of Java, including Madura, is 132,000 sq km (which is just over half the area of the UK), while Java's population density is over 1000 people per sq km (four times that of the UK).

Population in Indonesia is very unevenly distributed and the national population density figure is 126 people per sq km (in Papua, it drops to under 10). A programme of transmigration tried to alleviate the population density issue, with mixed results (see p60). Meanwhile, Jakarta and other cities continue to grow, as people move in to try their luck in these commercial hubs.

MULTICULTURALISM

Indonesia's rugged, mountainous terrain, and the fact that the country is made up of many islands, has separated groups of people from each other, resulting in an extraordinary differentiation of language and culture across the archipelago.

Ethnic Groups

MALAYS & MELANESIANS

Most Indonesians are Malays, descended from peoples who originated in China and Indochina and spread into Indonesia over several thousand years. The other major grouping is the darker skinned, fuzzy-haired Melanesians who inhabit much of easternmost Indonesia.

Despite the Malay predominance, the languages and customs of Indonesians vary widely. Some more distinct groups include the Kubu tribe of

South Sumatra, thought to be descendants of settlers from Sri Lanka, who were barely known to outsiders until guerrillas fighting the Dutch came into contact with them. There are also the Dani people of the Baliem Valley in Papua, and the inhabitants of Borneo's interior, who are collectively known as the Dayaks but comprise many ethnic groupings. Even

TRAVELLER TACT

Tourism provides much-needed income and on the whole it's encouraged; however, it can have a negative impact that you can help lessen. If you respect Indonesia's culture, customs, environment and, most importantly, the people you meet, not only will your own travels be more rewarding, so will the experience of your hosts.

Customs & Culture

Learn something of Indonesia's religious, family and social values, and avoid behaviour that contradicts those values. Brief beach attire, public displays of affection and aggressive behaviour are considered poor form in Indonesia. They may be tolerated in tourist resorts such as Kuta in Bali, but that doesn't mean they are acceptable.

Tourist Economy

Staying in family-owned hotels, eating at food stalls and travelling on local transport means your money flows more directly into the local economy. You'll also meet locals and gain a wider knowledge of Indonesian society. That said, staying in swanky hotels, travelling 1st class or taking tours contributes just as much, if not more, to the economy.

Bargaining is an essential social skill and you'll gain more respect if you're aware of local prices and can bargain for goods. At the same time, while overcharging becomes annoying after a while, remember that tourism is a luxury item that attracts a premium – for rich Indonesians as well as foreign tourists.

Visiting Villages

Some villages receive bus-loads of visitors and are almost tourist theme parks, but in general wandering into a village is like wandering into someone's home, and a few rules of etiquette apply. It's polite to first introduce yourself to the *kepala desa* (village head) or another senior person.

Those villages that are used to visitors often have a visitors book, where you sign in and make a donation – 10,000Rp is usually sufficient. In more remote villages, bring a guide, especially if language difficulty is likely. A guide can make the introductions, teach you protocol and explain points of interest.

Making Contact

For a visitor to Indonesia, many customs are not initially evident; it's everyday behaviour that's most apparent. Probably the most noticeable Indonesian characteristic is their forwardness. Whether they want to practise English, sell you some Chanel No 5, chat about politics or invite you for a meal, most Indonesians won't think twice about breaking the ice. Many travellers tire of such attention, so it's worth remembering that 99% of the time an Indonesian's interest comes with genuine friendliness.

Indonesians are generally extremely courteous; criticisms are not spoken directly and they'll often agree with you rather than offend. They may also prefer to say something rather than appear as if they don't know the answer. They mean well, but when you ask for directions, you may find yourself being sent off in the wrong direction.

The other habit which may take visitors by surprise is touching between those of the same gender. Indonesians may hold your knee for balance as they get into a bemo (and basically sit on you so more can squeeze in), or reach out and touch your arm while making a point in conversation. All this is considered friendly; in a nation of over 200 million people, there's sometimes not much personal space.

STOPPING CHILD-SEX TOURISM IN INDONESIA

Unfortunately, Indonesia has become a destination for foreigners seeking to sexually exploit local children. A range of socio-economic factors render many children and young people vulnerable to such abuse and some individuals prey upon this vulnerability. The sexual abuse and exploitation of children has serious, life-long and even life-threatening consequences for the victims. Strong laws exist in Indonesia to prosecute offenders and many countries also have extraterritorial legislation which allows nationals to be prosecuted in their own country for these intolerable crimes.

Travellers can help stop child-sex tourism by reporting suspicious behaviour. In Bali, call the **Women and Children Care Unit** (☎ 0361-226 783 ext 127) of the Bali police. Elsewhere in Indonesia, reports can be made to the **Anti-Human Trafficking Unit** (☎ 021 721 8309) of the Indonesian police. If you know the nationality of the individual, you can contact their embassy directly.

For more information, contact the following organisations:

ECPAT (End Child Prostitution and Trafficking; www.ecpat.org) A global network working on these issues, with over 70 affiliate organisations around the world. Child Wise (www.childwise.net) is the Australian member of ECPAT.

PKPA (Center for Study and Child Protection; ☎ 061 663 7821 in Medan, Sumatra) An organisation committed to the protection of Indonesia's children and the prevention of child-sex tourism.

in densely populated Java there are distinct groups, such as the Badui of West Java, who withdrew to the highlands as Islam spread through the island and have had little contact with outsiders. Other groups, like the Balinese and Javanese, have preserved their traditions despite intense contact with other cultures.

Indonesia's population currently increases by about 3.5 million people per year.

CHINESE

Of all the ethnic minorities in Indonesia, none has had a larger impact on the country than the Chinese. Although comprising less than 3% of the population, the Chinese are the wealthiest ethnic group in the country, leading to much anti-Chinese resentment (even though only a small percentage of the Chinese population holds great wealth and there are many wealthy non-Chinese Indonesians).

The Chinese in Indonesia have long suffered repression and even slaughter. Under Dutch rule, the role of the Chinese in society was predominantly entrepreneurial – their roles included running businesses and working as intermediaries in trade – but colonial authorities restricted Chinese settlement and land ownership. As far back as 1740, anti-Chinese sentiment erupted in a massacre of the Chinese in Batavia. In the early 20th century, frustration with colonialism often resulted in attacks, not on the Dutch but on the Chinese. After independence, the Chinese were seen as a privileged group and their culture was discriminated against by law: written Chinese was banned, Chinese schooling forbidden and noncitizen Chinese repatriated to China. Whenever there's unrest in Indonesia, the Chinese are often singled out. In 1965 they were killed for being communists; more recently, during the 1998 riots, it was because they were capitalists.

Indonesians comprise approximately 300 ethnic groups that speak some 365 languages and dialects.

Though many Chinese fled Indonesia after 1998, the majority stayed and many have returned. Indonesia is home to them, as it has been for many generations, and even if they wanted to leave, many Chinese Indonesians cannot afford to, and have nowhere else, to go.

The current government has taken steps to eradicate anti-Chinese discrimination, and Chinese Indonesians are now represented in government. The ban on Chinese-language press has been lifted and cities such as Jakarta have Chinese-language TV, radio and printed media. Imlek (Chinese New Year), banned under Soeharto, is now held openly and has been proclaimed a national holiday.

Transmigration

Throughout Indonesia's history, no other factor has changed the nation's cultural make-up more than *transmigrasi*, a programme aimed at taking pressure off heavily populated areas, particularly Java and Bali, by moving people out to less populated islands like Sumatra, Kalimantan, Papua and Maluku.

Transmigrasi was initiated in 1905 by the Dutch, who moved some 650,000 people, mostly from Java, to Sumatra. Since the peak period of 1984 to 1989, when approximately 3.2 million people were resettled, *transmigrasi* has slowed. Birth control programmes proved to be much more effective at reducing population growth.

Most government-sponsored transmigrants are not experienced farmers; two-thirds of transmigrants are landless peasants and another 10% are homeless city dwellers. Up until 1973, Jakarta's urban poor were often virtually press-ganged into moving out of Java – they turned out to be the least successful transmigrants, often returning to the towns they came from. Inexperienced farmers tended to attempt wet-rice cultivation in unsuitable areas and ended up as subsistence farmers no better off than they were before.

Nationalism and Ethnic Conflict in Indonesia by Jacques Bertrand investigates the reasons behind the violence in areas like Maluku and Kalimantan.

Transmigration also takes its toll on the natural environment, through destruction of forest, loss of topsoil and degradation of water supplies. Also, tension has arisen due to what has been seen as a 'Javanisation' of other regions. Horrific violence has erupted between transmigrants and the local community, as was the case in Kalimantan in 1997, when conflict between Madurese transmigrants and the Dayaks resulted in hundreds being killed and many more displaced.

Transmigration from South Sulawesi to Ambon had a similar result. Religious differences were cited as the catalyst for conflict, but other factors such as economic stresses and military influence could not be ignored as triggers.

Mass transmigration is all but over in Indonesia. The government still supports population mobility and there's now more sensitivity to agricultural suitability, employment growth, demographic balance and the rights of locals, but the programme has been markedly reduced.

MEDIA

The freedoms experienced by the press after Soeharto's fall were one sign that reform was taking place. They were, however, short-lived. Although the press remains much freer than it was before 1998, the government and influential individuals are now able to use the Criminal Code against the media. In one case, the editor of *Rakyat Merdeka* newspaper was given a six-month suspended sentence for 'intentionally insulting' the then president Megawati. The application of this law, which was used by Soeharto, does not bode well for press freedom, as those convicted more than once can be barred from practising journalism. The English-language *Tempo* magazine and its affiliated publications have been hit hard by similar lawsuits. Other press-stymieing actions have included barring journalists from Aceh during the 2004 conflicts, and international journalists and academics being refused entry visas.

RELIGION

The early Indonesians were animists who practised ancestor and spirit worship. When Hinduism and Buddhism spread into the archipelago, they were layered onto this spiritual base, and there are areas where animism survives, including West Sumba and parts of Papua.

AMAZING GRAIN

Indonesia's verdant rice fields create a landscape of exceptional beauty. But behind the beautiful terraces is a rich history, complex production and a lot of hard work. Indonesia's most fertile soils are in Bali and most of Java as well as a few small patches across the archipelago.

In the less fertile, sparsely populated areas of Sumatra, Kalimantan, Sulawesi and West Java, where the peasants moved from one place to another, a form of shifting cultivation known as *ladang* developed. In *ladang,* the jungle is burned off to speed up the process of decomposition and to enrich the soil in preparation for planting, but the soil quickly loses fertility. Farmers must move to another site, as settled agriculture is impossible without the continuous addition of fertilisers.

On the other hand, the rich volcanic soils of most of Java, Bali and western Lombok are suitable for *sawah* (wet-rice) cultivation in flooded rice fields. Rice cultivation in terraced fields has been practised for over 2000 years. The system has continually been refined and developed and is widely seen as a contributing factor to the development of civilisations in Java and Bali. The development of the fields required great organisation, either at a cooperative village level or through the suppression of a peasant workforce. The wonder of this method of agriculture is that *sawah* fields can produce two or even three crops a year, year after year, with little or no drop in soil fertility. This is due not solely to the fertility of the soil; this astonishing ecosystem depends on water to provide nutrients and bacteria. Other nutrients are provided by the remains of previous crops and by adding extra organic material.

After each rice harvest, the stubble from the crop is ploughed back into the field. Small carpets of the best rice seed are planted and, when ready, seedlings are prised apart and laboriously transplanted in rows across a flooded field. The level of the water is crucial in the life cycle of the rice plant – the water depth is increased as the plant grows, and is reduced in increments until the field is dry at harvest time. The field may also be drained during the growing period in order to weed the field or aerate the soil.

Rice production requires both gruelling effort and constant fine tuning, but the result of this toil fuels a nation – according to the majority of Indonesians, a meal isn't complete without the humble grain.

Islam is the predominant religion, with followers making up 88% of the population. Nevertheless, old beliefs persist: in Java there are hundreds of holy places where spiritual energy is said to be concentrated. Pilgrims flock to these areas and to the graves of saints, despite the proscription of saint worship by Islam.

Indonesia's eastern regions and the Kalimantan interior are inhabited mostly by Christians, who make up 8% of the population, and animists (1%). Bali's Hindus comprise 2% of the population, and Buddhists make up the remaining 1%.

Hinduism & Buddhism

HINDUISM

Hinduism is a complex religion, but its core principle is the belief that the physical world is an illusion and until this is realised through enlightenment, the individual is condemned to a cycle of reincarnations. Brahma is the ultimate god and universal spirit, though Hinduism has a vast pantheon of gods. The two main gods after Brahma are Shiva the destroyer and Vishnu the preserver. Shivaism, which represents a more esoteric and ascetic path, generally found greater acceptance in Indonesia, perhaps because it was closer to existing fertility worship and the appeasement of malevolent spirits. Vishnuism places greater emphasis on devotion and duty, and Vishnu's incarnations, Krishna and Rama, feature heavily in Indonesian art and culture.

BUDDHISM

Siddhartha Gautama, an Indian prince, founded Buddhism in the 6th century BC. His message is that the cause of life's suffering is desire, and that by overcoming desire we can free ourselves from suffering. The ultimate goal is nirvana: escape from the cycle of birth and rebirth.

Buddhism is essentially a Hindu reform movement. The big difference is that Buddhism shunned the Hindu pantheon of gods and the caste system. It was initially not so much a religion but a philosophy, free from the priestly Brahman hierarchy.

HINDUISM & BUDDHISM IN INDONESIA

Many ancient Hindu and Buddhist shrines, statues and inscriptions have been found across the archipelago, the oldest dating back to the 5th century AD. The two religions were often intertwined and fused with older religious beliefs.

Historically, both religions have greatly influenced Indonesia's royal courts and governments. One theory is the emerging kingdoms of Indonesia invited Brahman priests from India to assist in creating a religion-based power structure, so that royal rule would have 'divine' justification.

Outside India, Hindus predominate only in Nepal and Bali, yet the Hinduism of Bali is far removed from that of India.

The Sumatran-based Sriwijaya kingdom, which arose in the 7th century, was the centre of Buddhism in Indonesia. Indonesia adapted Hinduism and Buddhism to its needs, and events recorded in epics like the Ramayana have even been shifted out of India to Java.

Bali's establishment as a Hindu enclave dates from the 17th century, when the Javanese Hindu kingdom of Majapahit, in the face of Islam, evacuated to the neighbouring island (a few pockets of Hinduism remain, notably the Tengger people around Gunung Bromo). The Balinese probably already had strong religious beliefs and an active cultural life and the new influences were simply overlaid on the existing practices.

Most Buddhists in Indonesia are Chinese, though their version of Buddhism also acknowledges tenets of Taoism, Confucianism and ancestor worship.

Islam

In the early 7th century in Mecca, the Prophet Muhammed received the word of Allah (God) and called on the people to submit to the one true God ('Islam' is the Arabic word for submission). This profession of faith is the first of the Five Pillars of Islam, the tenets that guide Muslims in daily life. The other four advocate praying five times a day, giving alms to the poor, fasting during the month of Ramadan and making the pilgrimage to Mecca at least once in a lifetime.

In its early days, Islam suffered a major schism resulting in two branches – the Sunni (or Sunnite) and Shiite – after a struggle to take over the caliphate. The Sunni comprises the majority of Muslims today, including most Muslims in Indonesia.

ISLAM IN INDONESIA

Indonesia's first contact with Islam came through Muslim traders, primarily from India, who introduced a less orthodox form of Islam than in Arabia. The region of Aceh adopted Islam near the end of the 13th century, then it spread through to Java and further east in the 16th and 17th centuries.

Centres of Islamic studies along the northern coast of Java played an important role in disseminating the new religion. Javanese tradition holds that the first propagators of Islam in Java were nine holy men, the *wali songo,* who possessed a deep knowledge of Islamic teaching as well as exceptional supernatural powers. Another theory holds that Islam was adopted by the rulers of trading ports, who broke with the Hindu kingdoms of the interior that claimed suzerainty over the north. The common people followed suit in much the same way as Europeans adopted the religions of their kings, and these Islamic kingdoms supplanted the Hindu centres of power.

Customs in Indonesia often differ from those of other Islamic countries. Muslim women in Indonesia are not segregated, nor do they have to wear head coverings (although recently they have become more popular). Muslim men are allowed to marry two women but must have the consent of their first wife. Even so, polygamy in Indonesia is very rare. Many pre-Islamic traditions and customs remain in place. The Minangkabau society of Sumatra, for example, is strongly Islamic but remains matrilineal according to tradition.

Islam requires that all boys be circumcised, and in Indonesia this is usually done between the ages of six and 11. They also observe the fasting month of Ramadan, a time when visitors should be sensitive about eating in public during the day. Also, travel can become difficult at the end of this month when Muslims journey home to celebrate Lebaran. In accordance with Islamic teaching, millions of Indonesians have made the pilgrimage to Mecca.

Islam not only influences routine daily living but also Indonesian politics. It was with the Diponegoro revolt in the 19th century that Islam first became a rallying point. Early in the 20th century, Sarekat Islam became the first mass political party. Its philosophy was derived from Islam and its support from the Muslim population. In post-independence Indonesia it was an Islamic organisation, Darul Islam, that launched a separatist movement in West Java. Former president Wahid headed Nahdatul Ulama, Indonesia's – and, indeed, the world's – largest Islamic organisation.

Likely upcoming Ramadan periods:

13 Sep-12 Oct 2007

2 Sep-1 Oct 2008

22 Aug-20 Sep 2009

11 Aug-9 Sep 2010

Christianity in Indonesia

The Portuguese introduced Christianity to Indonesia in the 16th century. Although they dabbled in religious conversion in Maluku and sent Dominican friars to Timor and Flores, their influence was never strong. For the Dutch, trade was paramount and interference in religion was avoided. Missionary efforts came only when the Dutch set about establishing direct colonial rule in the rest of Indonesia at the end of the 19th century. Animist areas were up for grabs and missionaries set about their work with zeal in east Nusa Tenggara, Maluku, Kalimantan, Papua and parts of Sumatra and Sulawesi. Thus Christianity is a relatively new religion in Indonesia. Protestants form a slight majority because of the work of Dutch Calvanist and Lutheran missions, but Catholics are also numerous, especially in Flores.

Religious Conflict

Indonesia's religious communities generally coexist in harmony and religious leaders from all faiths persistently stress tolerance, but violence continues to flare up in pockets of Indonesia, recently in Kalimantan, Maluku and Central Sulawesi. Although violence has been defined as playing along religious lines, there are other catalysts that cannot be ignored: ill-conceived transmigration policies, unequal distribution of wealth and even deliberate provocation by the government have all been cited as the real sparks behind the violence.

INDONESIAN MOSQUES

As Indonesia has the world's largest Muslim population, it's no surprise that the country is home to literally thousands of *mesjid* (mosques). Although all mosques are primarily places of prayer, they can be differentiated according to specific function: the *jami mesjid* is used for Friday prayer meetings; the *musalla* is used for prayer meetings Sunday to Thursday; the 'memorial mosque' is for the commemoration of victorious events in Islamic history; and the *mashad* is found in a tomb compound. There are also prayer houses that are used by only one person at a time, often found in large hotels and transport hubs.

The oldest mosques in Indonesia – such as those in Cirebon and Palembang – have rooms with two, three or five storeys. It's thought these multistorey rooms were based on Hindu shrines, similar to those in Bali.

Today's mosques are often built with a high dome over a prayer hall. Inside are five main features: the *mihrab* (a niche in a wall marking the direction to Mecca); the *mimbar* (a raised pulpit, often canopied, with a staircase); a stand to hold the Koran; a screen to provide privacy for important worshippers; and a water-source for ablutions. Outside the building there is often a *menara* (minaret) from which the muezzin summons the community to prayer. Apart from these items, the interior of the mosque is empty. There are no seats and no decorations. If there is any ornamentation at all, it will be quotations of verses from the Koran.

Friday afternoons are officially set aside for believers to worship, and all government offices and many businesses are closed as a result. All over Indonesia you'll hear the call to prayer from the mosques, but the muezzin of Indonesia are now a dying breed – the wailing is now usually pre-recorded and broadcast – as many visitors soon discover – at significant volume.

There's usually no problem with visiting a mosque, as long as appropriately modest clothing is worn – there is usually a place to leave shoes, and headscarves are often available for hire. As well as providing a chance to see an intrinsic part of Indonesian culture, visiting a mosque can provide welcome relief from the tropical heat – on a hot afternoon, a contemplative rest in a cool, quiet mosque can reinvigorate both body and soul.

Militant Islamic groups exist in Indonesia, as do fanatics on the fringes of many religions across the world. But despite what is reflected in the media, such extremism in Indonesia remains in the absolute minority. Most Indonesians, Muslim and non-Muslim, are very suspicious of extremist groups, and see their activities as counterproductive, to say the very least. This is especially the case since many Indonesians have suffered directly from the Bali bombings and other acts of violence. Calls to ban such groups, notably Jemaah Islamiyah, are often considered ineffective, as such action may simply push militant organisations further underground, making their nefarious plans harder to monitor.

In the Shadow of Swords by Sally Neighbour investigates the rise of terrorism in Indonesia and beyond, from an Australian perspective.

WOMEN IN INDONESIA

For Indonesian women, the challenge of balancing traditional roles and the responsibilities of the modern era have been most pronounced. Some women may have the same work and study opportunities as men – all the way to the presidency – yet many still see roles such as housekeeping and child rearing as their domain.

Indonesia is a predominantly Islamic society and is very male oriented. However, women are not cloistered or required to observe purdah, although head coverings have become more common in recent years. Whatever one's opinion of the *jilbab* (head covering), it does not automatically mean the women who choose to wear it have a subservient, passive personality. Female circumcision does occur in some Islamic areas. In Java, it's typically done soon after birth; a small incision is made, the intention being to draw a few drops of blood, not to remove the clitoris.

Sexual politics are rarely on the agenda. However, there are a number of organisations whose agenda is to promote the role of women, both in the workplace and in general society.

Many Indonesian women still undertake traditional roles but are also well educated and gainfully employed; two-income households are increasingly common and often a necessity. Women are widely represented in the bureaucracy and industry. In traditional rural societies, the divisions of labour are very well defined and social organisation is male dominated, but women are not excluded and some societies are matriarchal, notably the Minangkabau of Sumatra.

Women and the State in Modern Indonesia by Susan Blackburn explores the role women take in the nation and the changes they have achieved.

ARTS

Indonesian art is impossible to ignore: you'll see it in wood carvings lining the shops of Ubud; you'll stumble over piles of batik sarongs in a Yogyakarta market. And no travel documentary on Indonesia is complete without scenes of a Balinese dance or a shadow-puppet performance, performed to the mesmerising gongs of a Javanese or Balinese gamelan orchestra. Yet Java and Bali offer only part of Indonesia's vast range of dance, music and crafts (p68).

Claire Holt's *Art in Indonesia: Continuities and Change* is an excellent introduction to the arts of Indonesia, focusing on traditional dance, *wayang* and literature.

Theatre

Javanese *wayang* (plays), performed by people, shadow puppets or wooden marionettes, have their origins in the Hindu epics, the Ramayana and the Mahabharata. Although condensed versions are performed for tourists, traditional *wayang* can go for hours and it's not expected that the audience sit silent for the whole show (see p94).

Dance

If you spend much time in Jakarta or Kuta, you could be forgiven for thinking disco was Indonesia's traditional folk dance. But beyond the clubs throbbing to Madonna remixes, you'll find Indonesia has a rich heritage of traditional dance styles. Java is home to *wayang* dance

SMALL TALK

Dari mana? (Where do you come from?) You'll be asked this question frequently, along with many other things like *Sudah kawin?* (Are you married?) and *Mau kemana?* (Where are you going?). Visitors can find these questions intrusive, irritating and even infuriating, but Indonesians regard them as polite conversation; a way to start a chat or simply acknowledge someone walking through their village. Indonesians may ask foreign visitors such questions in English (it may be their only English) and you should not get annoyed – a smile, a hello, or an Indonesian greeting is a polite and adequate response.

If the questions continue, which is likely, you'll need to take a different approach, as one new arrival in Indonesia found out. The newcomer met a young man who immediately began asking her many personal questions: Where did she come from? Was she married? Where was she staying? Did she like Indonesia? Anxious to be friendly and polite, she tried to answer every question, while becoming increasingly dubious about his motives. But he never seemed to be satisfied with her responses and he seemed to become more morose with each exchange. Finally, and with utter despondency in his voice, the young man announced, 'I have five children.'

The message is that you don't really have to answer every question, but you should ask some questions yourself to show a polite interest in the other person. If the questioning becomes too nosy, try responding with an equally nosy question and you might be surprised at the warmth of the response. When you've had enough chatter, you can answer the question 'Where are you going?' even if it wasn't asked.

dramas. Yogyakarta has dance academies and is a good place to see performances of the Ramayana. Solo is also a centre of dance study. Wonosobo (Central Java) has its Lengger dance, in which masked men dress as women. Jaipongan, a modern dance from West Java, is a dynamic style that features swift movements to rhythms complicated enough to dumbfound an audience of musicologists. Central Kalimantan is home to the Manasai, a friendly dance in which tourists are welcome to participate. Kalimantan also has the Mandau dance, performed with knives and shields. Some of the most colourful performances of all, including the Barong, Kecak, Topeng, Legong and Baris dances, are found in Bali (see p272).

Author Djenar Maesa Ayu rocked Indonesia's literary scene with her candid portrayal of the injustices tackled by women. Her books include *They Say I'm a Monkey* and *Nyala*.

Literature

Probably the best place to find books by Indonesian authors is at the Gramedia bookstore chain, however English translations are sometimes hard to come by.

The late Pramoedya Ananta Toer, a Javanese author, is Indonesia's most well-known novelist. Toer spent more than 14 years in jail because of his political affiliations and criticism of the government. His famous quartet of novels set in the colonial era includes *This Earth of Mankind, Child of All Nations, Footsteps* and *House of Glass*. The quartet charts the life of Minke, a Javanese intellectual who must reconcile his Javanese beliefs with the colonial world around him.

Other Indonesian authors translated into English include the cutting and courageous Djenar Maesa Ayu, and Ayu Utami, who explores touchy issues including sex, politics and religion in her two books *Saman* and *Larung*.

The annual Ubud Writers & Readers Festival, held around September/October, showcases both local and international writers. Its website (www.ubudwritersfestival.com) offers information about local authors.

Cinema & TV

Despite the pressures of a fragile economy and the popularity of Hollywood and Bollywood blockbusters, Indonesia still produces a healthy amount of its own films. Many horror films (including *Bangsal 13*) and a swag of romance flicks (like *Arisan* and *Brownies*) have been churned out recently and are eagerly received by local audiences. But there's also a steady stream of films that portray contemporary social themes such as peer pressure and social tussles.

Director Riri Reza and other film-makers started their careers by directly approaching cinemas themselves and bypassing a reluctant distribution system. Indonesian films rarely have English subtitles but can still offer travellers an insight into Indonesian culture (and the audience reactions can be entertaining).

Riri Reza's *GIE*, the story of Soe Hok Gie, a Chinese Indonesian national activist, was submitted for consideration in the Best Foreign Film category of the 2006 Academy Awards.

Peter Weir's *The Year of Living Dangerously* (1982) remains the most well-known film based in Indonesia. It was recently televised in Indonesia, but with scenes of the military killing civilians edited out.

Indonesian TV is dominated by live sitcoms, game shows and current-affairs programmes. Locally made *sinetron* (soap dramas), complete with love affairs and zoom-ins on expressions of incredulity, are churned out.

Music

Indonesian music spans everything from thousand-year-old traditional music to high-powered punk pop.

Probably the best-known Indonesian music form is gamelan. Traditional gamelan orchestras are found primarily in Java and Bali. The orchestras are composed mainly of percussion instruments, including drums, gongs, xylophones and *angklung*, bamboo tubes shaken to produce a note (see p96).

Other traditional music forms include *kacapi suling:* serene music featuring the *kacapi* (harplike instrument) and *suling* (wooden flute) as well as singing.

Indonesia has a massive contemporary music market that spans all genres, from indie rock to schlock. MTV broadcasts to much of Asia from Indonesia, regularly featuring local acts, reflecting the strength of the scene. As is the case anywhere, bands come and go, but some of the more popular recent outfits include Peterpan and Radja.

Dangdut music is a melange of traditional and modern music that originated in Indonesia but it features instruments such as Indian tablas and flute. The result is sexy, love-drunk songs sung by heartbroken women or cheesy men, accompanied by straight-faced musicians in matching suits. *Dangdut* music is like no other – the beats are gutsy, the singing evocative and the emotion high.

Love it or hate it, karaoke remains a part of Indonesia's aural landscape. From beachside dives to blinging bars, you'll find folk eager to belt out their best Whitney Houston.

The Jakarta International Film Festival, held around December, features local and international movies. Its website (www.jiffest.org) lists the schedule and gives information about local films.

Rock legend Iwan Fals has been around for decades but still packs stadiums. His anti-establishment bent has caused him to be arrested several times.

SPORT

Soccer and badminton are the national sporting obsessions. Indonesians regularly hold the world badminton titles, and you'll see courts set up anywhere there's space. The Football Association of Indonesia (PSSI) comprises teams from across the country, each with their own fanatic followers. The schedule *(jadwal)* can be viewed at www.pssi-online.com.

Volleyball is played in villages everywhere, and you may also see people playing *sepak takraw* (also known as *sepak raga*). Played with a rattan ball, it's a cross between volleyball and soccer and, except when serving, only the feet are used, resulting in amazing acrobatics.

Pencak silat, Indonesia's own form of martial arts, is most popular in West Java and West Sumatra. This form of fighting uses not only hands and feet but also some weapons, including sticks and swords. Many regions, particularly those with a history of tribal warfare, also stage traditional contests to accompany weddings, harvest festivals and other ceremonial events. Mock fighting ceremonies are sometimes staged in Papua; *caci* whip fights are a speciality in Flores; men fight with sticks and shields in Lombok; but the most spectacular ceremonial fight is Sumba's *pasola,* where every February and March horse riders in traditional dress hurl spears at each other.

Other sports are male oriented and often associated with illegal gambling. You may see cockfighting in Bali and Kalimantan. Bull racing, horse racing and even ram head-butting are staged around the country and are usually designed to improve the breed.

Indonesian Crafts

History, religion, custom and modern influences are all reflected in Indonesia's vastly diverse range of craftwork. Broadly speaking, there are three major craft groupings.

The first is that of 'outer' Indonesia – Sumatra, Kalimantan, Sulawesi, Nusa Tenggara, Maluku and Papua – which has strong animist traditions. Crafts such as carving, weaving and pottery have developed from the tribal art of this region.

For an overall guide to Indonesian crafts, *Arts and Crafts of Indonesia,* by Anne Richter, is detailed and beautifully illustrated.

The second grouping is that of 'inner' Indonesia – Java and Bali – which has been the most influenced by Hindu-Buddhist tradition. The techniques and styles used to create the Borobudur temple, Hindu epics such as the Mahabharata, and that form the basis for *wayang* (traditional Javanese theatre) are still a major influence on arts and crafts.

The third influence is Islam, which not so much introduced its own artistic tradition as modified existing traditions. Its more rigid style and ban on human and animal representation led to existing artistic traditions becoming more stylised, evident today in the woodcarvings of Jepara in Java.

These days the religious significance or practical function of many traditional objects is disappearing. For example, the *sahan* (Batak medicine holders made from buffalo horn) in craft shops around Danau Toba are now crafted simply for their sale value. While traditional meaning and methods are diminishing, the tourist trade is not destroying traditional crafts. The sophistication and innovation of the craft industry is growing. Batak carvers now produce bigger, more intricately carved *sahan* – designs have changed to suit the market because small, simple *sahan* just don't sell.

Made in Indonesia: A Tribute to the Country's Craftspeople, by Warwick Purser, provides great photos and background information on the crafts of the country.

Many trinkets made for the tourist trade are of poor quality and there's an increasing cross-fertilisation of craft styles: the 'primitive' Kalimantan statues, so in vogue in Balinese art shops, may well have been carved just up the road in Peliatan. On the other hand, Javanese woodcarvers are turning out magnificent traditional panels and innovative furniture commissioned by large hotels, and Balinese jewellers influenced by Western designs are producing works of stunning quality.

WOODCARVING

In what was such a heavily forested nation, it's no surprise woodcarving took hold across the archipelago, with each culture developing its own style. Often woodcarving is interwoven with practical skills such as house building. In some regions, a house not only provides protection, but also repels unwanted spirits. Artistic evidence of this can be seen in the horned lion heads that protect Batak houses, the water buffalo representations that signify prosperity on Toraja houses, and the serpent carvings

TOPENG – MASKS

Although carved masks exist throughout the archipelago, the most readily identifiable form of mask is the *topeng,* used in *wayang topeng,* the masked dance-dramas of Java and Bali. Dancers perform local tales or adaptations of Hindu epics such as the Mahabharata, with the masks used to represent different characters. Masks vary from the stylised but plain masks of Central and West Java to the heavily carved masks of East Java. Balinese masks are less stylised and more naturalistic than in Java – the Balinese save their love of colour and detail for the masks of the Barong dance, starring a mythical lion-dog creature who fights tirelessly against evil.

Detail of traditional woodcarvings
JOHN BANAGAN

on Dayak houses. The serpent is a spirit that will protect the house. An offering is often given to this spirit so that it remains benevolent.

On the outer islands, woodcarvings and statues are crafted to represent the spirit world and the ancestors who live there. Woodcarving is an intrinsic part of the Toraja's famed funerals: the deceased is represented by a *tau-tau* (a life-sized wooden statue), and their coffin is adorned with carved animal heads. In the Ngaju and Dusun Dayak villages in Kalimantan, *temadu* (giant carved ancestor totems) also depict the dead.

There are *mbis* on permanent display at New York's Metropolitan Museum of Art.

Perhaps Indonesia's most famous woodcarvers are the Asmat of south west Papua. Shields, canoes, spears and drums are carved, but the most distinctive Asmat woodcarvings are *mbis* (ancestor poles). These poles show the dead, one above the other, and the open carved 'wing' at the top of the pole is a phallic symbol representing fertility and power. The poles are also an expression of revenge, and were traditionally carved to accompany a feast following a head hunting raid.

In many regions, everyday objects are intricately carved. These include baby carriers and stools from Kalimantan, lacquered bowls from South Sumatra, bamboo containers from Sulawesi, doors from West Timor and horse effigies from Sumba.

Balinese woodcarving is the most ornamental and intricate in Indonesia. Statues, temple doors and relief panels are intricately decorated with the gods and demons of Balinese cosmology. Western influence and demand for art and souvenirs has seen a revolution in woodcarving akin to that in Balinese painting (see p271). Balinese woodcarvers began by producing simpler, elongated statues of purely ornamental design with a natural finish. Nowadays Bali produces its own interpretations of Asmat totems or Kalimantan fertility statues, as well as unique modern statues.

Bali Style, by Barbara Walker & Rio Helmi, is a lavishly photographed look at Balinese design, architecture and interior decoration. In the same series is *Java Style*.

In Java, the centre for woodcarving is Jepara. The intricate crafts produced here are of the same tradition as the Balinese, but Islamic influence has seen human representation replaced by carved and stylised motifs. Carved furniture is the main business in Jepara. Another Javanese woodcarving centre is Kudus, where intricate panels for traditional houses are produced.

The most favoured and durable wood in Indonesia is *jati* (teak), though this is getting increasingly expensive. Sandalwood is occasionally seen in Balinese carvings, as is mahogany and ebony (imported from Sulawesi and Kalimantan). Jackfruit is a common, cheap wood, though it tends to warp and split. Generally, local carvers use woods at hand: heavy ironwood and *meranti* (a hard wood) in Kalimantan, and *belalu* (a light wood) in Bali.

TEXTILES

Ikat

The Indonesian word ikat means to tie or bind, but is also the name for the intricately patterned cloth of threads that are painstakingly tie-dyed before being woven together. Ikat is made in many regions, from Sumatra to West Timor, but it's in Nusa Tenggara that this ancient art form thrives.

Ikat garments come in an incredible diversity of colours and patterns: the spectacular ikat of Sumba and the intricately patterned work of Flores (including *kapita*, used to wrap the dead) are the best known.

MAKING IKAT

Although some factory-made threads are utilised, ikat is usually made of cotton, and hand-spun. The whole process of ikat production – from planting the cotton to folding the finished product – is performed by women. Once the cotton is harvested, it is spun with a spindle. The thread is strengthened by immersing it in baths of crushed cassava, rice or maize, then threaded onto a winder.

Traditional dyes are made from natural sources. The most complex processes result in a rusty colour known as *kombu* (it's produced from the bark and roots of the *kombu* tree). Blue dyes come from the indigo plant, and purple or brown can be produced by dyeing the cloth deep blue and then dyeing it again with *kombu*.

Any sections that are not coloured are bound together with dye-resistant fibre. Each colour requires a separate tying-and-dyeing process. The sequence of colouring takes into consideration the effect of each application of dye. This stage requires great skill, as the dyer has to work out – before the threads are woven – exactly which parts of the thread are to receive which colour in order to create the pattern of the final cloth. After the thread has been dyed, the cloth is woven on a simple hand loom.

In Tenganan (Bali) a cloth called *gringsing* is woven using a rare method of double ikat in which both warp and weft threads are pre-dyed.

ORIGINS & MEANING OF IKAT

The technique for making ikat was probably brought to Indonesia over 2000 years ago by migrants, who were of the Dongson culture, from southern China and Vietnam.

Ikat styles vary according to the village and the gender of the wearer, and some styles are reserved for special purposes. In parts of Nusa Tenggara, high-quality ikat is part of a bride's dowry. Until recently on Sumba, only members of the highest clans could make and wear ikat textiles. Certain motifs were traditionally reserved for noble families (as on Sumba and Rote) or members of a specific tribe or clan (as on Sabu or among the Atoni of West Timor). The function of ikat as an indicator of its wearer's role or rank has since declined.

MOTIFS & PATTERNS

Some experts believe that motifs found on Sumba, such as front views of people, animals and birds, stem from an artistic tradition even older

IKAT SEASONS

There are traditional times for the production of ikat. On Sumba the thread is spun between July and October, and the patterns bound between September and December. After the rains end in April, the dyeing is carried out. In August the weaving starts – more than a year after work on the thread began.

CHOOSING IKAT

Not so easy! Books on the subject aren't much use when you're confronted with a market trader telling you that yes, this cloth is definitely hand-spun and yes, of course the dyes are natural. Taking a look at the process is informative: you can see women weaving in many places, and at the right time of year you may see dye-making, thread-spinning or tie-dyeing. Ikat made in villages is nearly always hand-spun and hand-woven. Here are some tips on recognising the traditional product:

- Thread – hand-spun cotton has a less perfect 'twist' to it than factory cloth.
- Weave – hand-woven cloth, whether made from hand-spun or factory thread, feels rougher and, when new, stiffer than machine-woven cloth. It will probably have minor imperfections in the weave.
- Dyes – until you've seen enough ikat to get a feel for whether colours are natural or chemical, you often have to rely on your instincts as to whether they are 'earthy' enough. Some cloths contain both natural and artificial dyes.
- Dyeing method – the patterns on cloths which have been individually tie-dyed using the traditional method are rarely perfectly defined, but they're unlikely to have the detached specks of colour that often appear on mass-dyed cloth.
- Age – no matter what anybody tells you, there are very few antique cloths around. There are several processes to make cloth look old.

than Dongson, whose influence was geometric motifs like diamond and key shapes (which often go together), meanders and spirals.

One strong influence was *patola* cloth from Gujarat in India. In the 16th and 17th centuries these became highly prized in Indonesia, and one characteristic motif – a hexagon framing a four pronged star – was copied by local ikat weavers. On the best *patola* and geometric ikat, repeated small patterns combine to form larger patterns, like a mandala. Over the past century, European styles have influenced the motifs used in ikat.

Songket

Songket is silk cloth with gold or silver threads woven into it, although these days imitation silver or gold is often used. *Songket* is most commonly found where Islam has had the most impact, such as Aceh and among the Malays of coastal Kalimantan, but can also be seen in parts of Bali.

Batik

The technique of applying wax or other dye-resistant substances (like rice paste) to cloth to produce a design is found in many parts of the world, but none is as famous as the batik of Java. The Javanese were making batik as early as the 12th century, but its origins are hard to trace. Some think the craft was brought from India, others that the Javanese developed the technique themselves. The word 'batik' is an old Javanese word meaning 'to dot'.

The tradition of wearing gaudy garb at Asia-Pacific Economic Cooperation (APEC) meetings began when Bill Clinton and cohorts donned batik shirts in Bogor in 1994.

Batik's development is usually associated with the flowering of the creative arts around the royal courts – it's likely that certain motifs were the preserve of the aristocracy. The rise of Islam probably contributed to the stylisation of batik patterns and to the absence of representations of living things.

The oldest method of making batik is known as *batik tulis* (hand-painted or literally 'written' batik). Designs are first traced out onto cloth, then patterns are drawn in hot wax with a pen-like instrument.

The wax-covered areas resist colour change when immersed in a dye bath. The waxing and dyeing, with increasingly darker shades, continues until the final colours are achieved. Wax is added to protect previously dyed areas or scraped off to expose new areas to the dye. Finally, all the wax is scraped off and the cloth boiled to remove all traces of wax.

From the mid-19th century, batik production was increased by applying the wax with a metal stamp called a *cap*. The *cap* technique can usually be identified by the repetition of identical patterns, whereas in *batik tulis*, even repeated geometric motifs vary. Some batik combine the two techniques with *batik tulis* used for fine detail. It's worth noting that *batik cap* is true batik; don't confuse it with screen-printed cloth which completely bypasses the waxing process and is often passed off as batik.

Traditional batik clothing, Sumbawa Besar, Nusa Tenggara

JERRY ALEXANDER

Java is the home of batik and each district produces its own style. The court cities of Yogyakarta and Solo are major batik centres, and Solo is also a major textile centre. Traditional court designs are dominated by brown, yellow and indigo blue. These days both cities produce a wide range of modern and traditional batik.

Batik from the north coast of Java has always been more colourful and innovative in design – as the trading region of Java, the north coast came in contact with many influences. Pekalongan is the other major north-coast batik centre, producing traditional floral designs which are brightly coloured and show a Chinese influence. Some of Indonesia's most interesting batik, including that which incorporates bird motifs, comes from Pekalongan. Cirebon also produces very colourful and fine traditional *batik tulis*.

CERAMICS

Indonesia's position on the trade routes saw the import of large amounts of ceramics from China, making it a fertile hunting ground for antique Chinese ceramics dating back to the Han dynasty. The best examples of truly indigenous ceramics are the terracottas from the Majapahit kingdom of East Java.

Indonesian pottery is usually unglazed and handworked, although the wheel is also used. It may be painted, but is more often left natural. Potters around Mojokerto, close to the original Majapahit capital, still produce terracottas, but the best known pottery centre in Java is just outside Yogyakarta at Kasongan, where intricate, large figurines and pots are produced.

In the Singkawang area of west Kalimantan, the descendants of Chinese potters produce a unique style of utilitarian pottery.

Lombok pottery has an earthy, primitive look, with subtle colouring. Balinese ceramics show a stronger Western influence and are more inclined to be glazed.

BASKETWORK & BEADWORK

Some of the finest basketwork in Indonesia comes from Lombok. The spiral woven rattan work is very fine and large baskets are woven using this method; smaller receptacles topped with wooden carvings are also popular.

In Java, Tasikmalaya is a major cane-weaving centre, often adapting baskets and vessels to modern uses with the introduction of zips and plastic linings. The Minangkabau people, centred around Bukittinggi, also produce interesting palm leaf bags and purses, while the lontar palm is used extensively in weaving on West Timor, Rote and other outer eastern islands. The Dayak of Kalimantan produce some superb woven baskets and string bags.

Some of the most colourful and attractive beadwork is made by the Toraja of Sulawesi. Beadwork can be found all over Nusa Tenggara and in the Dayak region of Kalimantan. Small, highly prized cowrie shells are used like beads and are found on Dayak and Lombok works, though the best application of these shells is as intricate beading in Sumbanese tapestries.

KRIS

The kris (wavy-bladed traditional dagger) is no ordinary knife. In Java it is said to be endowed with supernatural powers. *Adat* (traditional law) requires that every father furnish his son with a kris upon his reaching manhood – preferably an heirloom kris enabling his son to draw on the powers of his ancestors (which are stored in the sacred weapon).

Some think the Javanese kris (from iris, meaning 'to cut') is derived from the bronze daggers produced by the Dongson around the 1st century AD. Bas-reliefs of a kris appear in the 14th-century Panataran temple complex in East Java, and the carrying of the kris as a custom in Java was noted in 15th-century Chinese records. Today, the kris is still an integral part of men's formal dress on ceremonial and festive occasions.

Before the arrival of Islam, Hindu-inspired images were quite often used to decorate the wooden hilts – the *garuda* (mythological man-bird) was a popular figure. After the spread of Islam such motifs were discouraged, but were often preserved in stylised forms – the origins and symbolism of the kris lay too deep in Javanese mysticism to be eradicated completely.

Distinctive features, the number of curves in the blade and the damascene design on the blade are read to indicate good or bad fortune for its owner. The number of curves in the blade has symbolic meaning: five curves symbolise the five Pandava brothers of the Mahabharata epic; three represents fire, ardour and passion. Although the blade is the most important part of the kris, the hilt and scabbard are also beautifully decorated.

Although the kris is mostly associated with Java and Bali, larger and less-ornate variations are found in Sumatra, Kalimantan and Sulawesi.

Indonesia's first president, Soekarno, was often described as the great *dalang* (puppet master) due to his ability to keep opposing forces in check, like a *dalang* does in a Javanese shadow-puppet show.

PUPPETS

The most famous puppets of Indonesia are the carved leather *wayang kulit* puppets. These intricate lace figures are cut from buffalo hide with a sharp, chisel-like stylus, and then painted. They are produced in Bali and Java, particularly in Central Java. The leaf-shaped *kayon* representing the 'tree' or 'mountain of life' is also made of leather and is used to end scenes during a performance.

Silhouette of the Pandava brothers, characters in a traditional *wayang kulit* play
GREGORY ADAMS

Wayang golek are three-dimensional wooden puppets found in Central and West Java. The *wayang klitik* puppets are the rarer flat wooden puppets of East Java.

METALWORK

The bronze age in Indonesia began when metalwork was introduced by the Dongson culture, and it peaked with the Hindu-Buddhist empires of Java. Brassware was mostly of Indian and Islamic influence. Today, some of the best brass workmanship is that of the Minangkabau in Sumatra, but brassware is also produced in Java, South Kalimantan and Sulawesi.

The most important ironwork objects are knives and swords such as the Javanese kris and the *parang* of Kalimantan. *Parang* are sacred weapons used in everything from clearing jungle to – at one time – head-hunting. Scabbards for ceremonial *parang* are intricately decorated with beads, shells and feathers.

JEWELLERY

The ubiquitous *toko mas* (gold shop) found in every Indonesian city is mostly an investment house selling gold jewellery by weight – design and workmanship take a back seat. However, gold and silverwork does have a long history in Indonesia. Some of the best gold jewellery comes from Aceh, where fine filigree work is produced, while chunky bracelets and earrings are produced in the Batak region.

The best-known jewellery is the silverwork of both Bali and the ancient city of Kota Gede within the city boundaries of Yogyakarta.

Balinese jewellery is nearly always handworked and rarely involves casting techniques. Balinese work is innovative, employing both traditional designs and those adapted from jewellery presented by Western buyers. The traditional centre for Balinese jewellery is Cleek.

Kota Gede in Yogyakarta is famous for its fine filigree work. Silverware from here tends to be more traditional, but new designs are also being adapted. As well as jewellery, Kota Gede produces a wide range of silver tableware.

Environment

THE LAND

It makes sense that Indonesians call their country Tanah Air (literally, 'Earth and Water') as it is the world's most expansive archipelago. Indonesia's land area of 1,920,000 sq km is speckled along the equator for 5000km, from Sabang off the northern tip of Sumatra, to a little beyond Merauke in Papua. It's so extensive that the actual number of islands making up Indonesia is contentious. Officially the number is 17,508, but others estimate the number to be above 18,000 (perhaps when the tide's out).

Indonesia's landscape is a crumpled terrain of peaks and valleys – in Papua there are mountains so high they're snowcapped year-round – and in most other parts of Indonesia volcanoes dominate the skyline. They dot down the western coast of Sumatra, continue through Java, Bali and Nusa Tenggara, and then loop around through Maluku to Sulawesi.

Some of these volcanoes have erupted with such force it's no wonder they hold such a strong place in Indonesian culture: to many Balinese people the 1963 eruption of Gunung Agung was a sign of the wrath of the gods; in East Java the Tenggerese people still offer a propitiatory sacrifice to the smoking Bromo crater, which dominates the local landscape.

Indonesia is home to no fewer than 129 active volcanoes, the most of any nation.

High rainfall and year-round humidity mean that nearly two-thirds of Indonesia is covered in tropical rainforest – most of it in Sumatra, Kalimantan, Sulawesi and Papua. Most of the forests of Java disappeared centuries ago as land was cleared for agriculture. Today the rest of Indonesia's rainforest, which in terms of area is second only to Brazil's, is disappearing at an alarming rate as local and foreign timber, agricultural and mining companies continue to plunder the region's resources (see p79).

Along the east coast of Sumatra, the southern coast of Kalimantan and Papua, and much of the northern coast of Java, there is swampy, low-lying land often covered in mangroves. There are also a few areas of Sulawesi and some of the islands closer to Australia – notably Sumba and Timor – that are considerably drier.

Indonesia's diverse vegetation, mountainous terrain and widely scattered islands have been integral in shaping the nation's history and astoundingly diverse culture. Looking at the big picture, this country has served as a crossroad between India, China and beyond – it was a convenient midway point where cultures crossed over, and merchants met and exchanged goods. However, difficult travel *within* Indonesia, due to seas and rough terrain, resulted in the nation's distinct cultural entities.

The regular climate in most of the country means that the rhythm of life for many Indonesian farmers is based less on the annual fluctuations of the seasons than on the growth patterns of their crops. In areas with heavy rainfall and terraced rice-field cultivation, there is no set planting season or harvest season but a continuous flow of activity, where at any one time one hillside may demonstrate the whole cycle of rice cultivation, from ploughing to harvesting. Such intense agricultural activity has fuelled kingdoms and continues to feed the densely populated regions.

GUNUNG API – FIRE MOUNTAINS

If you have the urge to ascend spectacular peaks, watch the sun rise through the haze of steaming craters and peer into the earth's bubbling core, you've come to the right place. Indonesia is *the* destination for volcano enthusiasts. This is thanks to the fact that it lies on a significant segment of the Pacific 'Ring of Fire', where two large crustal plates (the Indian Ocean and western Pacific) are forced under the massive Eurasian plate, where they melt at approximately 100km beneath the surface. Some of the magma rises and erupts to form the string of volcanic islands across Indonesia. Indonesia's volcanoes do erupt, sometimes with shocking consequences (see Krakatau p127). With tectonic activity comes devastating earthquakes and tsunamis, as happened so tragically on Boxing Day in 2004.

TOP VOLCANOES

Java

- Gunung Bromo (p244) – journey to Bromo, a sacred and eerie peak surrounded by the desolate Sea of Sands
- Gunung Merapi (p188) – tackle the lush, jungle-covered slopes of Merapi, an almost-perfect conical volcano dominating the cultural heartland of Java
- Gunung Krakatau (p126) – take a boat trip to see the remnants, and new beginnings, of one of the world's A-list volcanoes
- Kawah Ijen (p249) – spend the night at a peaceful coffee plantation before climbing this volcano to view its remarkable turquoise sulphur lake

Bali

- Gunung Agung (p333) – take one of the numerous routes up and down Bali's tallest and most sacred mountain; include seldom-visited temples in your journey

Sumatra

- Gunung Sibayak (p395) – enjoy an easy and rewarding day hike a few hours' bus ride from Medan
- Gunung Merapi (p446) – climb Sumatra's most restless volcano in the middle of the night for a sunrise view from the top
- Gunung Kerinci (p451) – brave this challenging ascent up into the heavens on Sumatra's highest peak

Nusa Tenggara

- Gunung Rinjani (p519) – join pilgrims at the summit of this sacred peak, which has a huge crater lake overlooked by the active cone of Gunung Baru
- Kelimutu (p561) – wonder at the ethereal scenery atop this volcano, with its three differently coloured crater lakes and lunaesque landscape
- Wawo Muda (p557) – climb the summit of this cone in Flores, which only emerged in 2001, and view several small lakes of a rusty-red hue

Maluku

- Gunung Api Gamalama (p783) – catch the view from Ternate of lovely Tidore and its string of offshore volcanoes
- Gunung Api (p770) – scramble up this volcano in the Banda Islands to experience the awesome sunrise views

WILDLIFE

From tiny tarsiers to massive stinking flowers, the range of natural attractions in Indonesia is phenomenal. In 2006, the discovery of never-before-seen species of wildlife in Papua's Pegunungan Foja (the Foja mountain range) highlighted just how rich Indonesia's natural environment is. It also emphasised the value of what is being destroyed for limited gain (see p79).

Animals

The fact that Sumatra, Java, Kalimantan and Bali (all part of the Sunda shelf) were once linked to the Asian mainland is reflected in the animals roaming the region. Some large Asian land animals still survive in this area, including tigers, rhinoceroses, leopards and the sun bear. A few places in Java claim to be the last refuge of the tiger, but tigers in Indonesia are now only known to exist in Sumatra. Leopards (the black leopard, or panther, is more common in Southeast Asia) are rare but still live in Sumatra and in Java's Ujung Kulon National Park. This park is also home to the rare, almost extinct, one-horned Javan rhinoceros. Rhinos have not fared well in Indonesia and the two-horned variety, found in Sumatra, is also on the endangered list.

Two good illustrated books on Indonesian wildlife are *The Wildlife of Indonesia* by Kathy MacKinnon and *Wild Indonesia* by Tony and Jane Whitten.

Perhaps the most famous Indonesian animal is the orang-utan (literally, 'forest man'), the long-haired red apes found only in Sumatra and Kalimantan. The Bohorok Orang-utan Viewing Centre in North Sumatra provides easy access to orang-utans in their natural setting, as does the centre at the Tanjung Puting National Park in Kalimantan. Kalimantan is also home to the proboscis monkey, named for its pendulous nose. Various species of the graceful gibbon also exist throughout the region, as do other primate species.

Elephants are not numerous, but they still exist in the wild in Sumatra and can be seen at the Way Kambas National Park in Sumatra's Lampung province. Kalimantan also has a few wild elephants in the northeast, but they are very rare and the species is most probably introduced.

The Birds of Java and Bali by Derek Holmes and Stephen Nash is one of the best birding guides available. *The Birds of Sulawesi* by Derek Holmes and Karen Phillipps is also worthwhile.

Wildlife at the eastern end of the nation has a closer connection to that which scurries around Australia, as Papua and the Aru Islands were both once part of the Australian landmass and lie on the Sahul shelf. Papua is the only part of Indonesia to have marsupials such as tree kangaroos, bandicoots and ring-tailed possums, all marsupials found in Australia.

A long-beaked echidna and a golden-mantled tree kangaroo were just two of the discoveries in Papua's Pegunungan Foja. There are also Aussie reptiles including crocodiles and frilled lizards. Then there's Papua's extraordinary birdlife: the area is home to over 600 species, the most well known being the cassowary and bird of paradise.

Lying across the centre of Indonesia are the islands of Sulawesi, Nusa Tenggara and Maluku, all of which have long been isolated from the continental land mass. Endemic to Sulawesi is the *anoa* (dwarf buffalo), a wallowing animal that looks like a cross between a deer and a cow and stands only about 80cm high. The *babi rusa* (deer pig) has great curving tusks that come out the side of the mouth and through the top of the snout. The bulbous beaked hornbills are found across west Indonesia, but the *enggang Sulawesi* (Buton hornbill), with its brightly coloured beak and neck, is one of the most spectacular of the species. One hard-to-see animal is the tarsier, a tiny, nocturnal primate of North Sulawesi.

The Malay Archipelago by Alfred Russel Wallace is an 1869 classic account of this famous naturalist's wanderings throughout the Indonesian islands.

Maluku shows similarities with Sulawesi, but with fewer wildlife species. The *babi rusa* and smaller mammals are here, as are some primates, but it seems most of the migratory waves bypassed Maluku. However, it is noted for its butterflies – Pulau Seram (Seram Island) has reported some enormous species – and bird life, particularly the *nuri raja* (Amboina king parrot), a large, magnificently coloured bird.

From Lombok eastwards, beyond the Wallace Line, the fauna of Nusa Tenggara reflects the more arid conditions of these islands (see p670). Large Asian mammals are nonexistent and mammal species in general are smaller and less diverse. Asian bird species diminish further east and Australian birds are found on the eastern islands. Nusa Tenggara has one astonishing and famous animal, the Komodo dragon, the world's largest lizard, found only on Komodo Island and a few neighbouring islands.

Stick insects measuring 546mm have been found in Kalimantan.

And of course Indonesia's waterways are home to a kaleidoscopic array of sea creatures. Sea horses, dolphins, turtles and stretches of coral attract snorkellers and divers to popular spots like Sulawesi's Bunaken and Togean Islands, and the wrecks and reefs off Bali.

Plants

What makes Indonesia's rapid clearing of rainforest areas all the more disheartening is that these areas are home to more types of flora than could be listed in this guide – from tiny moss species and spectacular orchids, to massive mangrove systems and the world's tallest flower (with the testosterone-charged name *amorphohallus titanium).* Then there's one of the world's most infamous plants: the rafflesia (see below). Environmental degradation may be severe, but Sumatra and Kalimantan still present some of the best opportunities in the world to explore rainforest environments.

NATIONAL PARKS & PROTECTED AREAS

Although environmentalists have been critical of Indonesia's government for its history of environmental neglect, it's only fair to mention that the past decade has seen a rapid increase in the number of national parks, nature reserves and historical sites. While it's true that loggers, farmers and hunters ignore national park boundaries, there has been a sincere effort to enforce the rules – no easy task in a country with so much sparsely inhabited jungle. Local opinion on land protection of course varies widely. Many appreciate their country's natural beauty, many make a living indirectly or directly from its demise, and many have more pressing issues to contend with, such as abject poverty.

Indonesian national parks are managed by the Directorate General of Forest Protection and Nature Conservation (PHKA or KSDA). Many new national parks have been proclaimed in recent years. National parks receive greater international recognition and funding than nature, wildlife and marine reserves, of which there are also many in Indonesia.

Most of Indonesia's national parks are very isolated and have minimal facilities. Exploring the country's magnificent wilderness areas requires time, endurance and usually a guide. Some parks have huts where visitors

BLOOMIN' STINKY

Of all Indonesia's flora, the most spectacular is the *rafflesia arnoldi*. Considered the world's largest flower (it's actually a parasite) the rafflesia grows up to 1m in diameter, weighs as much as 7kg and unfurls inch-thick petals. The plant blooms between August and November, and in doing so emits a perfume of rotting flesh to attract insects necessary for pollination – it's not recommended for a romantic gift. The rafflesia is found primarily in Sumatra, but smaller versions are found in Kalimantan and Java.

TOP 10 NATIONAL PARKS & RESERVES

Park	Location	Features	Activities	Best time to visit	Page
Gunung Leuser	Sumatra	biologically diverse conservation area, rivers, rainforest, mountains; tigers, rhinoceroses, elephants, orang-utans, primates such as the white-breasted Thomas Leaf monkey	orang-utan viewing, wildlife spotting, bird watching; trekking, rafting	Dec-Mar	p427
Tanjung Puting	Kalimantan	tropical rainforest, mangrove forest, wetlands; macaques, proboscis monkeys, diverse wildlife	orang-utan viewing, bird-watching	May-Sep	p631
Kelimutu	Nusa Tenggara	coloured lakes	volcanology, short walks	Apr-Sep	p561
Gunung Rinjani	Nusa Tenggara	volcano	trekking, volcano climbing	Apr-Sep	p519
Ujung Kulon	Java	lowland rainforest, scrub, grassy plains, swamps, sandy beaches; one-horned rhinoceroses, otters, squirrels, leaf monkeys, gibbons	wildlife spotting, jungle walks	Apr-Oct	p128
Gunung Bromo	Java	volcanic landscape	crater climbing	Apr-Oct	p244
Pulau Bunaken	Sulawesi	coral fringed islands	snorkelling, diving, island lazing	Jun-Jan	p739
Kerinci Seblat	Sumatra	mountainous rainforest, one of Sumatra's highest peaks	wildlife spotting, bird-watching; trekking	Dec-Mar	p451
Komodo	Nusa Tenggara	Komodo dragon	being chased by wildlife; snorkelling, diving	Apr-Sep	p541
West Bali	Bali	grasslands, coral fringed coasts	wildlife spotting; snorkelling, diving	year round	p356

can stay, but most have no visitor facilities. If the wilderness is your main reason for visiting Indonesia, bring a good tent, sleeping bag and kerosene stove. As a general rule, park staff spend little time in the parks and more time in the office, which will be located in the nearest town or city. Call into these offices before heading to the park to check the latest conditions.

ENVIRONMENTAL ISSUES

Indonesia's environmental record is a sorry read. Years of unregulated logging, waste mismanagement and rampant development have all left their scars and continue to create new ones. Even when environmental protection programs are put in place they are often poorly funded and enforcement, when attempted at all, is difficult.

Forest continues to be cleared at an horrific rate, and with much of it done on the sly, it could be well above 3 million hectares per year. Over 70% of Indonesia's forests have been destroyed, and the impact on flora and fauna has been catastrophic – there are more endangered species in Indonesia than anywhere else in the world.

The side effects of deforestation is felt across the nation and beyond: floods and landslides wash away valuable topsoil, rivers are used as dumping grounds for mine tailings and smoke from burning off is so severe it cloaks Malaysia and Singapore on an annual basis (around August). The government blames shifting 'slash-and-burn' cultivators, but

TRAVELLER TACT: ENVIRONMENTAL CONCERNS

Environmental issues often seem to be alien in Indonesia, and Indonesians are wont to say to Europeans: 'We are a poor country that needs to exploit our natural resources. How can you tell us not to cut down our forests when you have already cut down all your own?' That said, Indonesia has a growing environmental awareness and environmental laws, even if they are poorly enforced. You can lecture all you like and even report violations to the local authorities, but the best you can hope for is to avoid adding to environmental degradation.

Hikers should follow the maxim that is posted in every Indonesian national park: 'take nothing but photos, leave nothing but footprints'. Minimise disposable waste and take it with you, even if the trails are already littered.

Avoid buying goods with excess packaging – go for food wrapped in banana leaf rather than polystyrene.

Re-use water bottles – many hotels let you refill bottles with *air putih* (drinking water).

Snorkellers and divers should never stand on coral and should avoid touching or otherwise disturbing living marine organisms (see p843).

There are laws to protect endangered species, but you still see such creatures for sale in local bird markets. Many souvenirs are made from threatened species: turtle shell products, sea shells, snakeskin, stuffed birds and framed butterflies are readily available in Indonesia. Not only does buying them encourage ecological damage, but import into most countries is banned and they will be confiscated by customs. See the **Convention on International Trade in Endangered Species** (CITES; www.cites.org) for more information.

outside experts say the fires are triggered by the waste wood and debris left by loggers, setting off peat and coal fires beneath the ground which burn for months. The problems flow right through to Indonesia's coastline and seas, where over 80% of reef habitat is considered to be at risk.

Of course the people most affected are those who live closest to, or within, the forested areas. Evictions from, restricted access to, and loss of land has seen many local communities lose their lifeline and spill into ever-spreading urban areas with ever-increasing populations living below the poverty line.

Walhi, the Indonesian Forum for Environment, is working to protect Indonesia's environment. Find out more and offer your support at www.walhi.or.id.

As Indonesia becomes more urbanised – over 30% of Indonesians now live in cities compared with 15% in 1970 – more strains are put on the urban environment. Although it stalled during the economic crisis, the wealth of the middle classes continues to grow, as does the number of new motor vehicles which add to the haze that hangs over the cities. Waste removal services have difficulty coping with household and industrial garbage, but the worst threat to living standards is the lack of decent sewerage systems. Very few cities have sewerage systems and so rely on septic tanks, or dispose effluent through the canals and river systems. This is a major source of pollution of water resources: most Indonesians are not supplied with safe drinking water and must boil it before use.

Food & Drink

By eating in Indonesia you imbibe the essence of the country, as no other nation is so well represented by its cuisine. The abundance of rice reflects Indonesia's fertile landscape, the spices are reminiscent of a time of trade and invasion, and the fiery chilli echoes the passion of the people. Indonesian cuisine is really one big food swap. Chinese, Portuguese, colonists and traders have all influenced the ingredients that appear at the Indonesian table and the cuisine has been shaped over time by the archipelago's diverse landscape, people and culture.

Indonesians eat simple but delicious meals. Eating only becomes grand at celebrations. For everyday eating, in the morning most households prepare plain rice, three or four dishes and *sambal* (chilli sauce), which are left covered on the table and can be eaten throughout the day. The dishes on the table constitute the entire meal, as Indonesian meals aren't served in courses.

Apart from rice, which is kept warm, most meals are eaten at room temperature. This may be disconcerting if you feel food is only safe to eat if it's cooked in front of you, but the cooking methods help keep food edible for the day. It's important to remember that rice (or another staple such as sago) is the filler while the accompanying dishes provide the flavour. Filling up on rice also helps to keep down the cost of feeding a family, or guest.

Rice in the field is called *padi;* rice grain at the market is called *beras;* cooked rice on your plate is called *nasi.*

STAPLES & SPECIALITIES

Indonesian cooking is not complex and the tastes stay separate. Coriander, cumin, chilli, lemon grass, coconut, soy sauce and palm sugar are all important flavourings; *sambal* is a crucial condiment. Fish is a favourite and the seafood restaurants are often of a good standard. Indonesians traditionally eat with their fingers, hence the stickiness of the rice. Sate (skewered meat), *nasi goreng* (fried rice) and *gado gado* (vegetables with peanut sauce) are some of Indonesia's most famous dishes.

Jajanan (snacks) are sold everywhere – there are thousands of varieties of sweet and savoury snacks made from almost anything and everything: peanuts, coconuts, bananas, sweet potato etc.

Queen Victoria once offered a reward to anyone able to transport a still-edible mangosteen fruit back to England.

REGIONAL VARIATIONS

Java

The cuisine of the Betawi (original inhabitants of the Jakarta region) is known for its richness. *Gado gado* is a Betawi original, as is *ketoprak* (noodles, bean sprouts and tofu with soy and peanut sauce; named after a musical style, as it resembles the sound of ingredients being chopped). *Soto Betawi* (beef soup) is made creamy with coconut milk. There's also *nasi uduk* (rice cooked in coconut milk, served with meat, tofu and/or vegetables).

In West Java, the Sundanese love their greens. Their specialities include *karedok* (salad of long beans, bean sprouts and cucumber with spicy sauce), *soto Bandung* (beef-and-vegetable soup with lemon grass) and *ketupat tahu* (pressed rice, bean sprouts and tofu with soy and peanut sauce). The West Javan town of Sumedang is home to the world's best tofu. Sundanese sweet specialities include *colenak* (roasted cassava with coconut sauce) and *ulen* (roasted sticky rice with peanut sauce), both best eaten warm. *Dodol,* a toffee-like sweet, is the culinary offering of Garut. Bandung's cooler hills are the place for *bandrek* (ginger tea with coconut and pepper) and *bajigur* (spiced coffee with coconut milk). Cirebon's offerings include *empal genton* (beef and turmeric soup) and *tahu gejrot* (tofu swimming in spiced soy sauce).

Central Javan food is sweet, even the curries, like *gudeg* (jackfruit curry). Yogyakarta specialities include *ayam goreng* (fried chicken) and *kelepon* (green rice-flour balls with a palm-sugar filling). In Solo, specialities include *nasi liwet* (rice with coconut milk, unripe papaya, garlic and shallots, served with chicken or egg) and *serabi* (coconut-milk pancakes topped with chocolate, banana or jackfruit). Other Javanese specialities include *pecel* (peanut sauce with spinach and bean sprouts), *lotek* (peanut sauce with vegetable and pressed rice), *opor ayam* (chicken in pepper and coconut curry) and *rawon* (dark beef stew).

There's a lot of crossover between Central and East Javan cuisine. Fish is popular, especially *pecel lele* (deep-fried catfish served with rice and *pecel*). The best *pecel* comes from the town of Madiun.

Two very popular Madurese dishes are *soto Madura* (beef soup with lime, pepper, peanuts, chilli and ginger) and *sate Madura* (skewered meat with sweet soy sauce).

Bali

Balinese specialities are hard to find as many tourists don't seem to like spicy, fleshy dishes like *lawar* (salad of chopped coconut, garlic and chilli with pork or chicken meat and blood). More popular is *bebek betutu* (duck stuffed with spices, wrapped in banana leaves and coconut husks and cooked in embers). The local sate, *sate lilit*, is made with minced, spiced meat pressed onto skewers. The grandest Balinese dish is *babi guling* (spit-roast pig stuffed with chilli, turmeric, garlic and ginger).

Indonesian Regional Food & Cookery by Sri Owen interweaves recipes with cultural insight.

Sumatra

In North Sumatra, the Acehnese love their *kare* or *gulai* (curry). The Bataks have a taste for pig and, to a lesser extent, dog (see boxed text, p84). Pork features in *babi panggang* (pork boiled in vinegar and pig blood then roasted). Another bloody delicacy is *ayam namargota* (chicken cooked in spices and blood). Bataks often use a local, mouth-numbing pepper called *lada rimba*.

FRUITY DELIGHTS

It's worth making a trip to Indonesia just to sample the tropical fruits:

- *Belimbing* (star fruit) is cool and crisp; slice one to see how it gets its name.
- Durian is the spiky fruit people either love or hate (see boxed text, p84).
- *Jambu air* (water apple) is a pink bell-shaped fruit with crisp and refreshing flesh.
- *Manggis* (mangosteen) is a small purple fruit with white fleshy segments and fantastic flavour.
- *Nangka* (jackfruit) is an enormous, spiky fruit that can weigh over 20kg. Inside are segments of yellow, moist, sweet flesh with a slightly rubbery texture. The flesh can be eaten fresh or cooked in a curry.
- Rambutan is a bright red fruit covered in soft spines; the name means 'hairy'. Break it open to reveal a delicious white fruit similar to lychee.
- *Salak* is recognisable by its brown 'snakeskin' covering. Peel it off to reveal segments that resemble something between an apple and a walnut.
- *Sirsak* (soursop, or zurzak) is a warty, green-skinned fruit with a white, pulpy interior that has a slightly lemonish taste.

In West Sumatra, the buffalo, a symbol of the region, is used in *rendang* (buffalo coconut curry). The region is the home of Padang cuisine (see p435), and the market in Bukittinggi is a great place to sample *nasi Kapau* (cuisine from the village of Kapau). It's similar to Padang food but uses more vegetables. There's also *sate Padang* (skewered meat with pressed rice and a smooth peanut sauce), *ampiang dadiah* (buffalo yogurt with palm-sugar syrup, coconut and rice) and *bubur kampiun* (mung-bean porridge with banana and rice yogurt).

The culinary capital of South Sumatra is Palembang, famous for *pempek* (deep-fried fish and sago dumpling; also called *empek-empek*). South Sumatra is also home to *pindang* (spicy fish soup with soy and tamarind), *ikan brengkes* (fish in a spicy, durian-based sauce), *tempoyak* (sauce of shrimp paste, lime juice, chilli and fermented durian) and *sambal buah* (chilli sauce made with fruit). Palembang's sweetie is *srikaya* (green custard of sticky rice, sugar, coconut milk and egg).

Nusa Tenggara

In dry East Nusa Tenggara you'll eat less rice and more sago, corn, cassava and taro. Fish remains popular and one local dish is Sumbawa's *sepat* (shredded fish in coconut and mango sauce). The Sasak people of Lombok like spicy *ayam Taliwang* (roasted chicken served with a peanut, tomato, chilli and lime dip) and *pelecing* sauce (made with chilli, shrimp paste and tomato). Nonmeat dishes include *kelor* (soup with vegetables), *serebuk* (vegetables mixed with coconut) and *timun urap* (cucumber with coconut, onion and garlic).

Kalimantan

Dayak food varies, but you may sample *rembang*, a sour fruit that's made into *sayur asem rembang* (sour vegetable soup). In Banjarmasin, the Banjar make *pepes ikan* (spiced fish cooked in banana leaves with tamarind and lemon grass). Kandangan town is famous for *ketupat Kandangan* (fish and pressed rice with lime-infused coconut sauce). The regional soup, *soto Banjar*, is a chicken broth made creamy by mashing boiled eggs into the stock. Chicken also goes into *ayam masak habang*, cooked with large red chillies. Sugar freaks will love Banjarmasin's many little sweeties, known as *ampar tatak* (literally meaning 'cut plate').

Sulawesi

South Sulawesi locals love seafood, especially *ikan bakar* (grilled fish). Another local dish is *coto Makassar* (soup of beef innards, pepper, cumin and lemon grass). For sugar cravers, there's *es pallubutun* (coconut custard and banana in coconut milk and syrup).

The Toraja people have their own distinct cuisine (see p692).

If a North Sulawesi dish has the name *rica-rica*, it's prepared with a paste of chilli, shallots, ginger and lime. Fish and chicken are two versions (also look out for dog). Things get very fishy with *bakasang* (flavouring paste made with fermented fish), sometimes used in *bubur tinotuan* (porridge made with corn, cassava, rice, pumpkin, fish paste and chilli). Minahasans have a few surprises: are you up for some *kawaok* (fried forest rat) or *keluang* (fruit bat)?

Maluku

A typical Maluku meal is tuna and *dabu-dabu* (raw vegetables with a chilli and fish-paste sauce). Sometimes fish is made into *kohu kohu* (fish salad with citrus fruit and chilli). Sago pith is used to make porridge,

WE DARE YOU

Everyday eating in Indonesia can be strange and there are some specialities that make for a real culture shock:

- It's not a staple, but dog is eaten in North Sulawesi and the Batak region of Sumatra. They are, however, surreptitious about canine consumption and you'll never see the word *anjing* (dog) advertised. The Bataks call dog *B1* (pronounced beh *sah*-tuh), as dog in the local language is *biang,* which has one 'b'. They call *babi* (pig) *B2*. In North Sulawesi, Fido is known as *rw* (pronounced *err*-weh), in which 'r' stands for *rintek* (soft) and 'w' stands for *wu'uk* (fur).
- The durian has a serious public image problem. This fruit's spiky skin looks like a Spanish Inquisition torture tool; opening it releases the fruit's odorous power. Many hotels ban the fruit from their premises so as to avoid offending guests with its 'aroma'. If you can keep close you'll see five segments of custard-like flesh surrounding large seeds. These are the jewels in the king's crown. Some say the glorious taste overrides the stench; others say 'Run away!' Yes, durian is an acquired taste.
- Balinese specialities are often difficult to find, but ask around and you might find *lawar* (salad of chopped coconut, garlic and chilli with pork or chicken meat and blood) or *siobak* (minced pig's head, stomach, tongue and skin cooked with spices).
- Avocado juice: take an avocado, blend with ice and condensed milk (or chocolate syrup) and serve. Indonesians don't consider this strange, as the avocado is just another sweet fruit.

bread and *mutiara* (small, jelly-like 'beans' that are added to desserts and sweet drinks).

Papua

In the highlands of Papua the sweet potato is king. The Dani people grow around 60 varieties, some of which can only be eaten by the elders. Other plants, such as sago palms, are also cultivated. The locals eat the pith of the sago palm and also leave the plant to rot so they can collect and eat beetle grubs. On special occasions, chickens and pigs are cooked in earth ovens.

Lonely Planet's *World Food Indonesia,* by Patrick Witton, looks at the history and culture of Indonesian cuisine.

DRINKS

Tea

Indonesia's most popular brew is black with sugar. If you don't want sugar ask for *teh pahit* (bitter tea), and if you want milk buy yourself a cow. Bandung's hills are the place for *bandrek* (ginger tea with coconut and pepper).

Coffee

Indonesian coffee, especially from Sulawesi, is of exceptional quality. Indonesians drink a chewy concoction called *kopi tubruk* (ground coffee with sugar and boiling water).

Ice & Fruit Drinks

Indonesia's *es* (ice drinks) are not only refreshing, they are visually stimulating, made with syrups, fruit and jellies. There are plenty of places serving *es jus* (iced fruit juice) or cordial-spiked *kelapa muda* (young coconut juice).

Alcoholic Drinks

Islam may be the predominant religion in Indonesia, but there's a range of alcohol available, including *tuak* (palm-sap wine), *arak* (rice or palm-sap wine) and Balinese *brem* (rice wine). Two domestic breweries, Bintang and Anker, produce a clean, slightly sweet brew.

CELEBRATIONS

Whether a marriage, funeral or party with friends, food – and lots of it – is essential. Celebratory meals can include any combination of dishes, but for special occasions a *tumpeng* is the centrepiece: a pyramid of yellow rice, the tip of which is cut off and offered to the VIP. Meat is always served, often a speciality such as Sumatran *rendang* or Balinese *babi guling.* Once formalities are over (Indonesians love speeches) it's time for guests to dig in.

Eat Smart in Indonesia, by J & D Peterson and SV Medaris, is a good, well-illustrated introduction to Indonesian dishes and their ingredients.

For Muslims, the largest celebrations are Ramadan (the fasting month, which ends with the Lebaran holiday) and Idul Adha. Each day of Ramadan, Muslims rise before sunrise to eat the only meal before sunset. It may sound like a bad time to be in Indonesia – you may have to plan meals and go without lunch – but when sunset comes, the locals' appreciation of a good meal is contagious. The first thing Indonesians eat after fasting is *kolak* (fruit in coconut milk) as a gentle way to re-acquaint the body with food. Then, after prayers, the evening meal begins with aplomb. In some areas, such as in Bukittinggi, cooks set out food on the street. People gather to savour and enjoy their food as a community.

After Ramadan, many travel to celebrate Lebaran with their families. During Lebaran, *ketupat* (rice steamed in packets of woven coconut fronds) are hung everywhere, like Christmas bells and holly.

Seventy days after Lebaran is Idul Adha, the festival commemorating Abraham's devotion. Allah ordered Abraham to sacrifice his son, but ended up sparing him as Abraham's devotion to him was soon obvious. In the boy's place, a ram was sacrificed. This is repeated across the Islamic world; in Indonesia a sheep or goat is the victim, and you'll know it's close to Idul Adha when you see the unfortunate animals sold everywhere.

The Balinese calendar is peppered with festivals including Kedaso (the 10th full-moon festival) and Penampahan (a purification festival). Such celebrations are always observed with a communal meal, sometimes eaten together from one massive banana leaf piled with dishes.

Festivals aside, every day in Bali you'll see food used to symbolise devotion: rice in woven banana-leaf pockets are placed in doorways, beside rice fields, at bus terminals – wherever a god or spirit may reside. Larger offerings studded with whole chickens and produce are made to mark special occasions such as *odalan* (birthday of a temple). You'll see processions of women gracefully balancing offerings on their heads as they make their way to temple. Bali's offerings are made by female-only collectives called *anyaman,* which also have a social aspect. At an *odalan*, men may prepare an *ebat* (five-dish feast).

The Javanese Mitoni celebration marks the seventh month of pregnancy. Mitoni involves a feast that includes a *tumpeng* surrounded by six smaller dishes, and seven hard-boiled eggs. If the feast looks beautiful, it's a girl. If it looks ordinary, a boy's in the making.

Another celebration occurs when a child is 35 days old: their head is shaved and a meal is prepared with dishes of beef (representing the child's ability to walk), fish (to swim) and chicken (to fly).

With so many cultures, there's a wide variety of ways Indonesians celebrate marriage. Some Indonesian weddings include an animal sacrifice, others include karaoke. Some probably have both. But there's always a massive meal. At Javanese weddings, the bride feeds the groom by hand, symbolising her responsibilities. At the reception, the food served can be anything, as long as there's lots of it.

A funeral is another celebration that varies depending on where you are. In some areas, such as Tana Toraja and Sumba, funerals are massive occasions involving the whole community, as well as some unlucky animals.

WHERE TO EAT & DRINK

There are a few choices for dining out in Indonesia. Warungs are simple, open-air eateries providing a small range of dishes. Often their success comes from cooking one dish better than anyone else. *Rumah makan* (eating house) or *restoran* refers to anything that is a step above a warung. Offerings may be as simple as from a warung but usually include more choices of meat and vegetable dishes, and spicy accompaniments.

Indonesia's markets are wonderful examples of how food feeds both the soul and the stomach. There's no refrigeration, so freshness is dependent on quick turnover. You'll also find a huge range of sweet and savoury snacks. Supermarkets are also common.

'Indonesia's markets are wonderful examples of how food feeds both the soul and the stomach'

For information on business hours see p845.

Quick Eats

As many Indonesians can't afford fine service and surrounds, the most authentic food is found at street level. Even high rollers know this, so everyone dines at stalls or gets their noodle fix from roving vendors who carry their victuals in two bundles connected by a stick over their shoulders: a stove and wok on one side; ready-to-fry ingredients on the other. Then there's *kaki lima* (roving vendors) whose carts hold a work bench, stove and cabinet. *Kaki lima* means 'five legs', for the three wheels of the cart and the two legs of the vendor. You'll find any and every type of dish, drink and snack sold from a *kaki lima*. Some have a permanent spot, others roam the streets, calling out what they are selling or making a signature sound, such as the 'tock' of a wooden *bakso* bell. In some places, sate sellers operate from a boat-shaped cart, with bells jingling to attract the hungry.

VEGETARIANS & VEGANS

Vegetarians will be pleased to know that *tempe* and *tahu* (tofu) are in abundance, sold as chunky slabs of *tempe penyet* (deep-fried *tempe*), *tempe kering* (diced *tempe* stir-fried with sweet soy sauce) and *tahu isi* (deep-fried stuffed tofu). Finding fresh vegies requires more effort. Look for Chinese establishments; they can whip up *cap cai* (mixed vegetables). Vegetarian fried rice or noodles can be found at many other eateries. A huge number of places, including Padang restaurants, offer *nasi campur* (rice with a choice of side dishes). Here you can avoid meat and go for things like tofu, *tempe*, jackfruit dishes, egg dishes and leafy vegies. If meat is in a dish it's usually pretty obvious, but ask about hidden things like *terasi* (fish paste), often used in *sambal* (chilli sauce). Vegans should be wary of condensed milk – often added to juices and pancakes. Vendors with blenders mix up some fine fresh fruit concoctions. And there's fantastic fruit available at the local market (see p82).

EATING WITH KIDS

There's always the fear that a hidden chilli is going to make your child explode. But most Indonesian children dread chilli attacks, so a proprietor will often warn you if a dish is spicy. In any case, you can always ask *'Pedas tidak?'* ('Is it spicy?') or *'Makanan tidak pedas ada?'* ('Are there nonspicy dishes?').

INDONESIA'S TOP FIVE

- Horizontal Bar & Lounge (p515) is so stylish it gives the Med a run for its money. This sophisticated lounge bar on Gili Trawangan serves superior tapas, mod-Oz cuisine and Indonesian favourites with a contemporary twist. It all goes down much better with a dishy cocktail.
- Jimbaran (p182), a pagoda-style restaurant in a languid setting just north of Yogyakarta, dishes up spectacular seafood, all sold by the ounce. Sound tough? Wait till you have to choose between the couldn't-be-fresher-unless-it-was-swimming crab, lobster and prawns.
- Floridas (p786) on Maluku is a modest terraced eatery that serves some of the finest seafood in Indonesia, particularly the *ikan woku kenari* (fish in hot almond sauce roasted in a banana leaf), all in front of a sublime panorama.
- Deli Cat (p320), a Balinese deli in Ubud, is laden with character, delightfully cheap vino and delectable comfort grub.
- Lae Lae (p677) is where Makassar's freshest seafood is barbecued in fragrant and spicy sauces (get a load of the *cobek-cobek* sauce made with chilli, lime and shrimp paste) and served in modest and friendly surrounds. The bonus is it's cheap enough to eat there three times a day.

Children may enjoy *nasi goreng* (fried rice), *mie goreng* (fried noodles), *bakso* (meatball soup), *mie rebus* (noodle soup), *perkedel* (fritters), *pisang goreng* (banana fritters), sate, *bubur* (rice porridge), fruit and fruit drinks. Indonesia's sugar-rich iced drinks are useful secret weapons for when energy levels are low. All of these are available at street stalls and restaurants. Not available, however, are highchairs and kiddy menus. That's not to say children aren't welcome; in fact, they'll probably get more attention than they can handle.

If your little fella yearns for familiar tastes, supermarkets stock Western foods; and fast food places are around, if that's really what your child wants. Be warned that heat can hit hard, so make sure children are getting enough fluids.

HABITS & CUSTOMS

With a population of over 215 million, you'd expect a little variety in Indonesia's culinary customs. There will be no surprises if you are eating at a restaurant, apart from the lack of a menu. Things may change, however, if you are invited to a home. Often dishes for a meal will be prepared earlier and set out buffet style, and you'll be implored to help yourself. Be sure not to engorge yourself – take a little of everything, and fill up on rice.

COOKING COURSES

If you want to learn some local kitchen tricks, Ubud in Bali has a number of cooking schools ready to take you through the finer points of curry creation and sate sizzling. If you have a favourite dish, they'll teach you to make that, too.

At **Bumbu Bali** (☎ 0361-774502; www.balifoods.com; Jl Pratama) long-time resident and cookbook author Heinz von Holzen runs a cooking school from his excellent South Bali restaurant (p302). Classes start at US$65.

Another option is the Balinese cooking courses held by creative cuisine pioneer Janet De Neefe at the **Casa Luna Cooking School** (www.casalunabali.com). The half-day courses (250,000Rp) are held five days a week at the Honeymoon Guesthouse (p319) and are highly recommended. They cover ingredients, cooking techniques and the cultural background of the

TRAVELLER TACT – DINING

In Indonesia hospitality is highly regarded. If you're invited to someone's home for a meal, you'll be treated warmly and social hiccups will be ignored. Nevertheless, here are some tips to make the experience more enjoyable for everyone:

- When food or drink is presented, wait until your host invites you to eat.
- Indonesians rarely eat at the table, preferring to sit on a mat or around the lounge room.
- Don't be surprised if, when invited to a home, you're the only one eating. This is your host's way of showing you're special, and you should have choice pickings. But don't eat huge amounts, as these dishes will feed others later. Fill up on rice and take a spoonful from each other dish.
- Indonesia isn't a nation of chopstick users; this is fork and spoon country. Many prefer eating with their hands (if you're worried about hygiene, remember that only you can be sure where your fingers have been). Only use your right hand (ie for eating, passing things, anything); the left hand is for 'other duties'.
- Your host will implore you to eat more than is humanly possible, but the best approach is to eat as much as a restaurant would serve. And – not that you'll need prompting – be sure to praise the food.
- In Islamic areas, be sure not to eat and drink in public during Ramadan. Restaurants do stay open, though they usually cover the door so as not to cause offence.
- Smoking seems to be acceptable everywhere, anytime. But perhaps wait until after a meal before lighting up, unless everyone else is puffing away.
- Men and women dining together is the norm. An invitation to a meal from (or for) the opposite sex may be considered an 'expression of interest', as it is in most countries.

Balinese kitchen. Excellent gourmet tours are also held on the weekend (300,000Rp).

EAT YOUR WORDS

Want to buy mangoes at a market or eat *rendang* at a restaurant? Don't be left speechless; check out the Language chapter. For pronunciation guidelines see p888.

Useful Phrases

Knowing these basic phrases will help make ordering a meal easier.

Where is a (cheap) restaurant? *Di mana ada rumah makan (murah)?*

I want ... *Saya mau ...*
- **to eat** *makan*
- **to drink** *minum*

Can you please bring me ...? *Bisa minta ...?*
- **a knife** *pisau*
- **a fork** *garpu*
- **a spoon** *sendok*
- **(some) water** *air minum (lagi)*

I can't eat ... *Saya tidak mau makan ...*
- **eggs** *telur*
- **meat** *daging*
- **peanuts** *kacang tanah*

Not too spicy, please.	*Jangan terlalu pedas.*
What's that?	*Apa itu?*
What are they eating?	*Mereka makan apa?*
That was delicious!	*Ini enak sekali!*

Food Glossary

acar pickle; cucumber or other vegetables in a mixture of vinegar, salt, sugar and water
air water
arak rice wine; also known as *brem*
ayam chicken; fried chicken is *ayam goreng*
babi pork; since most Indonesians are Muslim, pork is generally only found in market stalls and restaurants run by the Chinese, and in areas where there are non-Muslim populations, such as Bali, Papua and Tana Toraja on Sulawesi
bakar barbecued, roasted
bakso/ba'so meatball soup
bubur rice porridge
cassava known as tapioca in English; a long, thin, dark brown root which looks something like a shrivelled turnip
daging kambing goat or mutton
daging sapi beef
es buah combination of crushed ice, condensed milk, shaved coconut, syrup, jelly and fruit
gado gado very popular Indonesian dish of steamed bean sprouts and various vegetables, served with a spicy peanut sauce
ikan fish
kopi coffee
krupuk shrimp with cassava flour, or fish flakes with rice dough, cut into slices and fried to a crisp
lombok chilli
lontong rice steamed in a banana leaf
martabak a pancake-like dish stuffed with meat, egg and vegetables
mie goreng fried wheat-flour noodles, served with vegetables or meat
nasi rice
nasi campur steamed rice topped with a little bit of everything – some vegetables, some meat, a bit of fish, a *krupuk* or two; usually a tasty and filling meal
nasi goreng fried rice
nasi putih white (*putih*) rice, usually steamed
pempek (empek-empek) deep fried/grilled fish and sago balls (from Palembang)
pisang goreng fried banana fritters
roti bread; nearly always white and sweet
sambal a hot, spicy chilli sauce served as an accompaniment with most meals
sate small pieces of various types of meat grilled on a skewer and served with peanut sauce
sayur vegetables
soto meat and vegetable broth; soup
tahu tofu or soybean curd
teh tea; tea without sugar is *teh pahit*
telur egg
tempe made from whole soybeans which are fermented into a cake
udang prawns or shrimps

Java

Of all the 17,000 islands that make up Indonesia, Java is king. It may not have the beaches of Bali, the jungles of Kalimantan, or the remoteness of Papua, but it's the heart of the country, a heart with more drive and energy than any other island in this vast archipelago. With 120 million people crammed into an area half the size of Great Britain, Java is one populated place. And with such unfathomable human resources, it's no wonder that the nation's political and economic past, present and future are decided within its shores. For many, Indonesia quite simply begins and ends with Java.

Jakarta, the capital, is a colossal metropolis with all the problems of a city vastly overstretched; it won't grab your attention for long unless you're a mad shopper or über-urbanite. But the rest of the island has offerings that shouldn't be ignored.

A string of volcanoes lace the island like fiery rubies. Some are docile giants, while others blow their top at the drop of a Javanese fez; Gunung Bromo is a must for any visitor. Pounding the southern coast is the Indian Ocean; a magical sight, but it can be dangerous for swimming. There are, however, some fine beach enclaves, such as Pangandaran, Java's premier beach resort, and world-class surf breaks at Ujung Kulon and Alas Purwo National Parks. Java's calmer northern side hides less-developed tropical islands. Inspired by such natural beauty, and influenced by Hindu-Buddhist, Muslim and Western invaders, the Javanese have over the centuries created temples and *kraton* (palaces) of unique splendour. The Buddhist temple Borobudur is an architectural wonder and its nearby Hindu counterpart, Prambanan, shines almost as brightly. Cultural Yogyakarta and Solo are perfect places to sample Javanese art.

HIGHLIGHTS

- Catching the sunrise at **Borobudur** (p167), Indonesia's eternal Buddhist temple
- Climbing 253 steps to **Bromo's** (p244) summit for unearthly vistas
- Overnighting at a coffee plantation before climbing sulphur-belching **Kawah Ijen** (p249)
- Time-travelling to Java's golden age in the cultural capitals of **Yogyakarta** (p171) and **Solo** (p194)
- Discovering Java's untouched corners at **Ujung Kulon** (p128), **Meru Betiri** (p252), **Alas Purwo** (p261) and **Baluran** (p264) National Parks

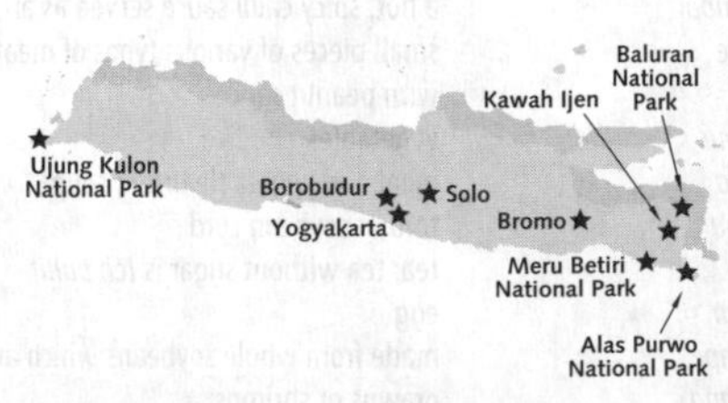

POPULATION: 120 MILLION	LAND AREA: 132,007 SQ KM	HIGHEST PEAK: GUNUNG SEMERU (3676M)

HISTORY

Java has a history of epic proportions and a record of human habitation that extends back 1.7 million years to when 'Java Man' (p204) roamed the river banks of Sungai Bengawan Solo in Central Java. Waves of migrants followed, moving down through Southeast Asia.

Early Javanese Kingdoms

The island's exceptional fertility allowed the development of an intensive *sawah* (wet rice) agriculture, which in turn required close cooperation between villages. Out of village alliances, small kingdoms developed, including that of King Purnawarman of Taruma (p134), but the first major principality was that of King Sanjaya, who founded the Mataram kingdom at the beginning of the 8th century. Mataram's religion centred on the Hindu god Shiva, and produced some of Java's earliest Hindu temples on the Dieng Plateau (p165).

The Sailendra dynasty followed, overseeing Buddhism's heyday and the building of Borobudur (p167). But Hinduism and Buddhism continued to coexist and the massive Hindu Prambanan complex (p190) was constructed within a century of Borobudur.

Mataram eventually fell, perhaps at the hands of the Sumatra-based Sriwijaya kingdom, which invaded Java in the 11th century. However, Javanese power began its revival in 1019 under King Airlangga, a semi-legendary figure who formed the first royal link between the island and Bali. Despite his role as a unifier, Airlangga later split the kingdom between his two sons, creating Janggala to the east and Kediri to the west.

It was only a matter of time before the balance of power was to change once again. Early in the 13th century the commoner Ken Angrok usurped the throne of Singosari (a part of the Janggala kingdom), defeated Kediri and brought Janggala under his control. The new kingdom ended in 1292 with the murder of its last king, Kertanegara, but in its short 70 years Javanese culture flourished and some of the island's most striking temples were built (p236). Shivaism and Buddhism evolved during this time into the new religion Shiva-Buddhism, which is still worshipped in Java and Bali today.

Majapahit Kingdom

The fall of the Singosari kingdom made room for one of Java's most famous early kingdoms, the Majapahit kingdom. Ruling from its capital at Trowulan (p226), it established the first Javanese commercial empire by taking control of ports and shipping lanes. Its rulers skilfully brokered trading relations with Cambodia, Siam, Burma and Vietnam – and even sent missions to China – and claimed sovereignty over the entire Indonesian archipelago (which probably amounted to Java, Madura and Bali).

As the Majapahit kingdom went into decline in the late 1300s, Islam moved to fill the vacuum.

Islamic Kingdoms

Islam broke over Java like a wave, converting many among the island's elite, and by the 15th and 16th centuries the Islamic kingdoms such as Demak (p213), Cirebon (p157) and Banten (p121) were on the ascent.

The Muslim state of Demak was the first to make military inroads into Java, raiding much of East Java and forcing many Hindu-Buddhists eastwards to Bali. Some, however, stayed put; the Tenggerese people of Bromo (p246) can trace their history back to Majapahit. Soon Demak was flexing its muscles in West Java, and in 1524 it took the port of Banten and then Sunda Kelapa (now Jakarta), before later overrunning Cirebon.

Demak's rule was not to last long. By the end of the 16th century the Muslim kingdom of Mataram (p176) had risen to take control of huge swathes of Central and East Java. Banten still remained independent, however, and grew to become a powerful maritime capital holding sway over much of West Java. By the 17th century, Mataram and Banten were the only two powers in Java left to face the arrival of the Dutch.

Dutch Period

The arrival of the Dutch and their eventual domination of Java is summarised in the History chapter (p38); a snapshot of Javanese resistance to the new invaders (and the royal houses' internal bickering) follows.

As the Dutch set up camp in what was to become Jakarta, Banten remained a powerful ruling house and a harbour for foreign competitors. An impressive trading network was set up under Banten's greatest

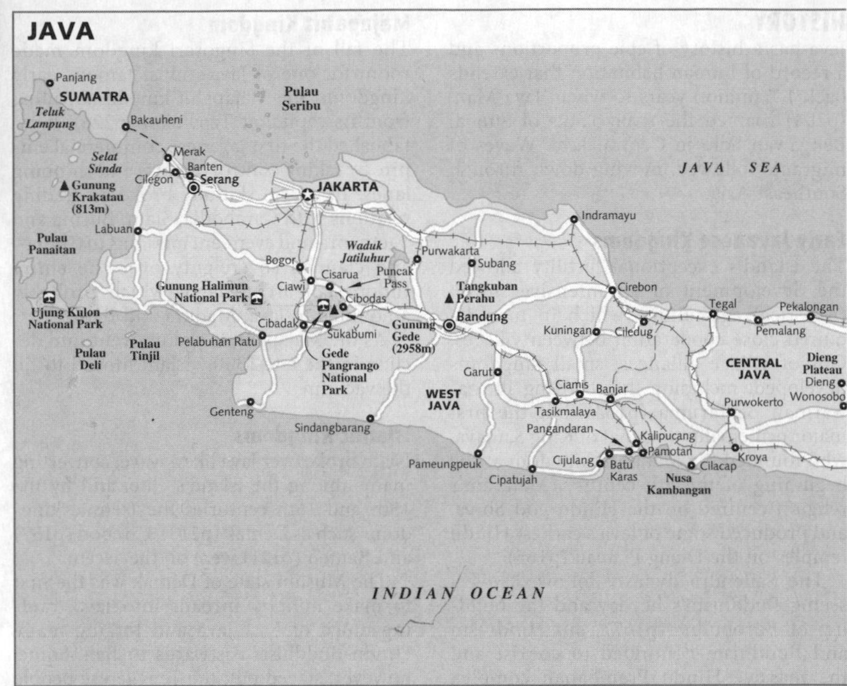

ruler, Sultan Agung, but unfortunately civil war within the house led to Dutch intervention and its eventual collapse.

The Mataram kingdom was another matter. As the power of the Dutch grew, the empire began to disintegrate, and by the 18th century infighting was taking its toll. The first two Javanese Wars of Succession were fought but fortunately resolved by the treaty of 1743; the ruler Pakubuwono II was restored to his battered court, but the price of concessions to the colonial power was high.

Obviously needing a fresh start, Pakubuwono II abandoned his old capital at Kartosuro and established a new court at Solo (Surakarta; p194). However, rivalry within the court soon reared its ugly head again, resulting in the Third Javanese War of Succession in 1746. The Dutch rapidly lost patience and split the kingdom in three, creating the royal houses of Solo and Yogyakarta (p172), and the smaller domain of Mangkunegaran (p197) within Solo.

Yogyakarta's founder, Hamengkubuwono I, was a most able ruler, but within 40 years of his death his successor had all but soured relations with the Dutch and his rivals in Solo. In 1812 European troops, supported by the sultan's ambitious brother and Mangkunegara, plundered the court of Yogyakarta and the sultan was exiled to Penang, to be replaced by his son.

Into this turbulent picture stepped one of the most famous figures of Indonesian history, Prince Pangeran Diponegoro, who subsequently launched the anti-Dutch Java War of 1825–30. At the end of this guerrilla war, the Dutch held sway over all the royal courts, which soon became ritual establishments with a Dutch *residen* (head of a residency during colonial administration) exercising control. With no real room or will for political manoeuvre, the courts turned their energies to traditional court ceremonies and artistic patronage, thus creating the rich cultural cities we see today.

Java Today

For Java's, and Indonesia's, struggle for independence from the Dutch and its subsequent growing pains, see the History chapter (p38).

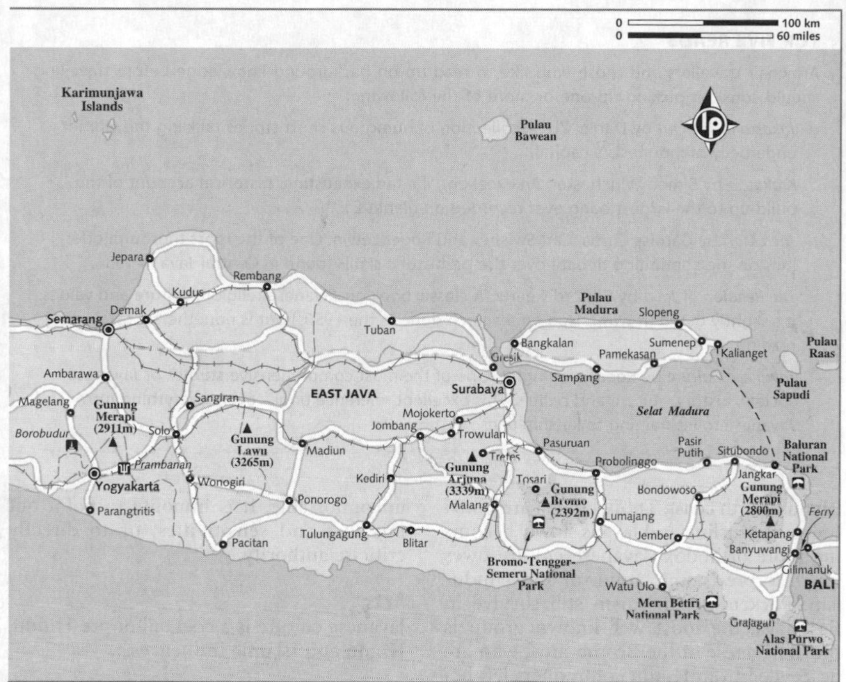

Java still rules the roost when it comes to political and economic life in Indonesia. It has the bulk of the country's industry, is easily the most developed island in Indonesia, and has over the years received the lion's share of foreign investment.

That doesn't mean it comes up smelling of roses, though. The economic crisis of the late '90s hit hard, and huge numbers of urban workers lost their jobs. Rising prices have caused unrest across the island, and disturbances, although sporadic, have remained a constant threat. The year 1998 saw the worst riots in the country's recent history, with Chinese communities targeted in Solo (p194) and Jakarta (p99).

In the current century, terrorist targeting of foreign investments in Jakarta (p99) and the Bali bombings of 2002 and 2005 have left Indonesia's leading island reeling. Tourism is struggling to survive, and the capture of suspected terrorist Muslim cleric Abu Bakar Ba'asyir from a Solo hospital in 2002, and the killing of Jemaah Islamiah member Azahari Husin in Batu in 2005, has raised questions about the island's links with radical Islam.

But as the seat of government and with the bulk of the nation's resources behind it, Java will also be one of the first islands to recover.

CULTURE

Java has three main ethnic groups, each speaking their own language: the Javanese of Central and East Java; the Sundanese of West Java; and the Madurese from Pulau Madura. In general the Central and East Javanese are more refined than their Maduran cousins, who are known for their blunt, proud demeanour. The Sundanese are a more relaxed people. The divisions, however, are blurred – the Madurese have settled across East Java and further afield, and Indonesians from all over the archipelago have come to seek work in the cities. Smaller pockets of pre-Islamic peoples also remain, and even metropolitan Jakarta identifies its own polyglot tradition in the Betawi, the name for the original inhabitants of the city.

Today, the Javanese are Muslim, and the stronghold of Islam can be found along the

TOP FIVE READS

Armchair travellers and those who like to read up on background knowledge before travelling should consider picking up one or more of the following:

- *Jakarta Inside Out* by Daniel Ziv. A collection of humorous short stories tackling the vibrant underbelly of Indonesia's capital.
- *Krakatoa* by Simon Winchester. An excellent, if a tad exhausting, historical account of the build-up to the largest bang ever recorded on planet Earth.
- *Java Man* by Garniss Curtis, Carl Swisher and Roger Lewin. One of the most thorough offerings on the continuing debate over the prehistoric skulls found in Central Java in 1936.
- *The Religion of Java* by Clifford Geertz. A classic book on Javanese religion, culture and values. It's slightly dated (it was based on research done in the 1950s) but is nonetheless fascinating reading.
- *Javanese Culture* by Koentjaraningrat. One of the most comprehensive studies of Javanese society, history, culture and beliefs. This excellent reference book covers everything from Javanese toilet training to kinship lines.

island's north coast. Though most are *santri* (devout) Muslim, and Java is slowly becoming more orthodox, Javanese culture owes much to pre-Islamic animism and Hinduism. Pockets of Hinduism still survive in East Java; the most well-known group is the Tenggerese of the Bromo area, who are descended from Hindu commoners left behind when the Majapahit elite fled to Bali.

The Javanese cosmos is composed of different levels of belief stemming from older and more accommodating mysticism, the Hindu court culture and a very real belief in ghosts and numerous benevolent and malevolent spirits. Underneath the unifying code of Islam, magic power is concentrated in amulets and heirlooms (especially the Javanese dagger known as the kris), in parts of the human body, such as the nails and the hair, and in sacred musical instruments. The *dukun* (faith healer and herbal doctor or mystic) is still consulted when illness strikes.

Halus (refined) Javanese is part of the Hindu court tradition, which still exists in the heartland of Central Java. In contrast to Islam, the court tradition has a hierarchical world-view, based on privilege and often guided by the gods or nature spirits. Refinement and politeness are highly regarded, and loud displays of emotion and flamboyant behaviour are considered *kasar* (bad manners).

Indirectness is a Javanese trait that stems from an unwillingness to make others feel uncomfortable. It is impolite to point out mistakes and sensitivities, or to directly criticise authority.

Arts

Javanese culture is a cocktail of pre-Hindu, Hindu and Islamic influences.

WAYANG

Javanese *wayang* (puppet) theatre has been a major way of preserving the Hindu-Buddhist heritage in Java.

Wayang Kulit

Wayang kulit is the art of theatre performances using shadow puppets. Perforated leather figures are manipulated behind an illuminated cotton screen to retell stories, usually based on the Hindu epics the Ramayana and Mahabharata. Unsurprisingly, *wayang kulit* owes much to Indian tradition.

In a traditional performance, a whole night might be devoted to just one *lakon* (drama). Many *wayang kulit* figures and stories have a specific mystical function; certain stories are performed to protect a crop, a village or even individuals.

By the 11th century, *wayang* performances with leather puppets flourished in Java, and by the end of the 18th century *wayang kulit* had developed most of the details we see today. The standardisation of the puppet designs is traditionally attributed to King Raden Patah of Demak, a 16th-century Islamic king.

The creation of a puppet is an art form in itself. First, an outline is cut using a knife, then the fine details are carved out using small chisels and a hammer. When the carving is finished, the movable arms are attached and the puppet is painted. Lines are drawn in and accentuated with black ink before the *cempurit*, the stick of horn used to hold the puppet upright, is attached.

The leaf-shaped *kayon* represents the 'tree' or 'mountain of life', and is used to end scenes or to symbolise wind, mountains, obstacles, clouds or the sea.

The characters in *wayang* are brought to life by a single *dalang* (puppeteer), who might manipulate dozens of figures during a performance. The *dalang* must be a linguist, capable of speaking both the language of the audience and the ancient Kawi language of the aristocratic protagonists of the play. He must also be able to reproduce the different voices of the characters, and direct the accompanying gamelan orchestra.

Wayang Golek

Three-dimensional wooden puppets, *wayang golek* have movable heads and arms, and are manipulated in the same way as shadow puppets. They are most popular in West Java.

First used in north-coast towns for Muslim propaganda, *wayang golek* was Islamic in nature and a popular, robust parody of the stylised aristocratic *wayang kulit* play.

MAHABHARATA & RAMAYANA

Ancient India, like ancient Greece, produced two great epics. The Ramayana describes the adventures of a banished prince who wanders for many years in the wilderness, while the Mahabharata is based on the legends of a great war. The first story is reminiscent of *The Odyssey*, which relates the adventures of Ulysses as he struggles to return home from Troy; the second has much in common with *The Iliad*, which deals with the mythical clash between Greeks and Trojans.

When Hinduism came to Java, so did the Ramayana and Mahabharata. The Javanese shifted the locale to Java, Javanese children were named after the protagonists, and the kings of Java became the descendants of the epic heroes.

The Mahabharata and the Ramayana are the basis of the most important *wayang* stories in Java and Bali. Both are essentially morality tales and have played a large part in establishing traditional Javanese values.

Mahabharata

The great war portrayed in the Mahabharata is believed to have been fought in northern India around the 13th or 14th century BC. The war became the focus of legends, songs and poems, which were finally brought together in the 'Epic of the Bharata Nation (India)' – the Mahabharata. Over the following centuries it grew to become seven times the size of *The Iliad* and *The Odyssey* combined.

The central theme of the Mahabharata is the power struggle between the Kaurava brothers and their cousins, the Pandavas. After years of intrigue, infighting and exile, the Pandavas conclude that there is no alternative but war and the blood-letting begins.

It is at this time that the Pandava warrior Arjuna becomes despondent at the thought of fighting his own kin, prompting Krishna, his charioteer, to explain the duties of the warrior in the well-known song known as the 'Bhagavad Gita'.

During the course of the war, many of the great heroes from both sides are slain, but it is the Pandavas who prevail as the curtains fall.

Ramayana

The Ramayana, the story of Prince Rama, is thought to have been written after the Mahabharata. Rama is an incarnation of the god Vishnu, and it is his destiny to kill the ogre king Rawana.

Due to scheming in the palace, Rama and his beautiful wife Sita are exiled to the forest, where Sita is abducted by Rawana and carried off to his island kingdom of Lanka.

Rama begins his search for Sita and is joined by the monkey god Hanuman and the monkey king Sugriwa. Eventually a full-scale assault is launched on the evil king and Sita is rescued.

In the early 19th century, a Sundanese prince of Sumedang had a set of wooden puppets made to correspond exactly to the *wayang kulit* puppets of the Javanese courts and was therefore able to perform the Hindu epics.

Wayang golek uses the same stories as the *wayang kulit*, but also has its own set, inspired by Islamic myths.

Sometimes a *wayang golek* puppet is used at the end of a *wayang kulit* play to symbolise the transition back from the world of two dimensions.

Other Wayang

Wayang klitik or *kerucil* is popular in East Java and uses flat wooden puppets carved in low relief. This type of *wayang* is performed without a shadow screen. *Wayang orang* (also known as *wayang wong*) is a dance-drama in which real people dance the part of the *wayang* characters.

Wayang topeng is similar to *wayang orang*, only dancers don masks.

GAMELAN

A gamelan is a traditional orchestra of some 60 to 80 musical instruments, consisting of a large percussion section – which includes bronze 'kettle drums', xylophones, and gongs – accompanied by spike fiddles and bamboo flutes.

The sound produced by a gamelan can range from harmonious to eerie (but always hypnotic), with the tempo and intensity of sound undulating on a regular basis. Expect to hear powerful waves of music one minute and a single instrument holding court the next.

More often than not gamelan music can be heard at *wayang* performances, but gamelan concerts are also quite common throughout Java.

GETTING THERE & AWAY

Air

Jakarta (p116) is Indonesia's busiest entrance point for international airlines and is the best place to shop around for cheap air tickets. Two of the most popular short-hop international connections are the Jakarta–Singapore and Jakarta–Kuala Lumpur runs, which can cost as little as US$75. Surabaya (p225) has a few international flights, as does Solo (p201).

Sea

Jakarta is the main hub for Pelni passenger ships (see p116) that run all over Indonesia, but no international connections exist. The most direct connection from Singapore is to take a ferry from Singapore to Tanjung Pinang on Pulau Bintan in the Riau archipelago off the Sumatran coast and then take a ship to Jakarta (see p379).

BALI

Ferries run round the clock between Banyuwangi/Ketapang harbour in East Java (p263) and Gilimanuk in Bali. From Ketapang, numerous buses and trains travel to the rest of Java. An easier alternative is to take a through-bus from Denpasar to any major city in Java – these buses include the ferry journey.

SUMATRA

Ferries shuttle between the Javanese port of Merak (p123) and Bakauheni in southern Sumatra, 24 hours a day. From both ports, regular buses head for the main centres of their respective islands. The easy options are the long-distance buses that run from Jakarta (p117) straight through to the main Sumatran destinations such as Medan (48 hours).

The long bus journeys in Sumatra can take their toll, and as most points of interest are in North Sumatra, many travellers prefer to take a Pelni boat.

GETTING AROUND

Most travellers going through Java follow the well-worn route of Jakarta–Bogor–Bandung–Pangandaran–Yogyakarta–Solo–Surabaya–Gunung Bromo, and on to Bali, with short diversions from points along that route.

Air

If time is short, domestic flights can be a good option, but Java is small enough to get around using trains and buses. Plus, by taking land or sea transport you'll be minimising damage to the environment through carbon emission. Flight information is listed throughout the chapter and in the Transport chapter (p869).

Note that Jakarta (p116) is the hub of the domestic airline network.

WAYANG CHARACTERS

The *wayang* characters are often based on figures from the Mahabharata and Ramayana. In the Mahabharata, the Kauravas are essentially the forces of greed and evil, while the Pandavas represent refinement and enlightenment.

At a *wayang* or dance performance the *halus* (refined) characters tend to be smaller and more elegant in proportion; their legs are slender, and their heads are tilted downwards, representing humility. The *kasar* (coarse) characters are often muscular and hairy, with upturned heads.

Colour is also of great significance. Red often indicates aggressiveness, greed or anger. Black and blue indicate calm, spiritual awareness and maturity. Gold and yellow are reserved for the highest nobles and white symbolises virtue.

Mahabharata Characters

Bima is the second-eldest of the Pandavas. He is big, burly and aggressive. He is able to fly and is the most powerful warrior on the battlefield, but he also has infinite kindness and a firm adherence to principle.

The svelte figure of Arjuna is a fitting representative of the noble class, with good looks and a keen sense of virtue. He can be fickle, but he remains *halus* – refined in manner. Arjuna's charioteer is Krishna, an incarnation of the god Vishnu, who plays the dual role of spiritual adviser and ruthless, Machiavellian politician.

The dwarf clown Semar is an incarnation of a god. He is a great source of wisdom and advice to Arjuna – but his body is squat with an enormous posterior, bulging belly and a predisposition for explosive farting.

Gareng, Petruk and Bagong are Semar's three sons and are awkward, comic figures. Despite their ungainly appearances, they are the mouthpieces of truth and wisdom.

On the Kaurava side, Duryudana is the handsome, powerful leader, too easily influenced by the evil designs of his uncle, Sangkuni. Karna is actually a Pandava, brought up by the rival family but, adhering to the code of the warrior, he stands by his king and so dies tragically at the hands of Arjuna.

Ramayana Characters

The characters of the Ramayana are a little more clear-cut. Like Arjuna, Rama is the ideal man and his wife Sita (or sometimes Shinta) is the ideal wife. Rawana's warrior brother, Kumbakarna, however, is more complex. He knows that Rawana is evil but is bound by the ethics of the Ksatria warrior to support his brother to the extremely grisly end.

Boat

Ferries ply the water between Java and Madura (p231) and to the island groups Pulau Seribu (p120) and Karimunjawa (p217). There is also a ferry linking Cilacap and Majingklak (p155), and a few random excursion spots, such as Krakatau (p126), can be reached by boat.

Bus

Buses are the main form of transport in Java. The normal practice is simply to front up at a bus terminal and catch the first one out; you shouldn't have to wait more than half an hour for services between cities and towns. Services range from public, economy-class buses to super-luxury coaches.

Tickets for buses are purchased on board, although tickets for *patas* (express) and luxury buses can be bought in advance at bus terminals, bus agents in the city centres, and sometimes hotels.

Small minibuses that cover shorter routes and back runs are commonly called Colts (after the Mitsubishi Colt) and shouldn't be confused with door-to-door minibuses *(travel)*. The latter are (usually) air-con minibuses that travel all over Java and pick you up at your hotel and drop you off wherever you want to go in the destination city.

Note that many terminals (in Jakarta, Surabaya and Bandung for instance) are located a long way from the centre of town. In these cities, the train is a better alternative.

JAVA AIRFARES

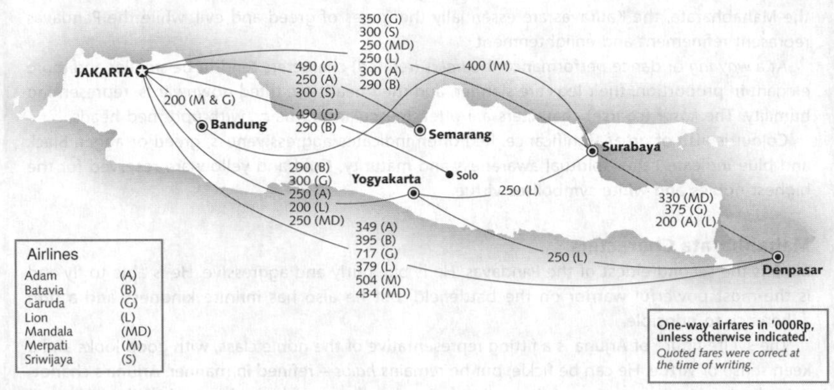

Car & Motorcycle

Driving in Java is not for the faint-hearted; most big cities are constantly *macet* (gridlocked) and main routes can be hellishly clogged. Accidents often result in large pay-offs or pricey lawsuits and a number of drivers are killed every year by angry crowds exacting mob justice following an accident.

If you're still keen, self-drive cars can be hired in most of the major cities, with rates hovering around 930,000Rp per day. Another option is to hire a car and driver, which can save a lot of headache and money. Private operators can be as low as 350,000Rp per day, but the average price is 500,000Rp (petrol may or may not be included). This is also a good option for taking in the best of a city in one day.

Scooters are the favoured mode of transport for the Javanese, and hiring one yourself can be a good idea for the island's quieter corners. Rental prices start at around 30,000Rp per day, and should include a proper helmet (not the illegal horse-riding variety normally handed out). Note that Java's roads are no place to try your hand at riding for the first time.

Train

Java has a good rail service running right across the island. It connects with the ferry to Bali (Ketapang/Banyuwangi) and with the ferry to Sumatra (Merak). The service is well maintained and while long overruns do occur, they're fast becoming a thing of the past.

A complete train timetable to Java, the *InfoKA*, is supposedly available from the larger train stations, but we've never seen one. A better option is to check timetables online at www.infoka.kereta-api.com (Bahasa Indonesia only). Timetables are displayed on boards at stations and printed *jadwal* (timetables) are available at main stations (for that station).

It's an idea to select a train that begins in the city you are departing from, thus guaranteeing a seat; obtaining a seat on through-trains can sometimes prove difficult.

CLASSES

Java's most popular class with the masses is economy *(ekonomi)*. Cheap, basic, slow, excessively crowded, and a riot of livestock, hawkers, musicians and all manner of produce, these chicken trains move the country around and halt at *every* stop (except, quite often, a city's central one). Seats on these trains are hard (literally) to get and cannot be booked. Some, however, have been upgraded – designated 'economy plus'– and are limited express with padded seats that can be booked.

One giant step up from economy are the express trains, which offer business-class *(bisnis)* and executive-class *(eksekutif)* carriages. Comfortable seats with plenty of leg room are guaranteed in both, but while business class has fans, executive class offers air-con, reclining seats, video (maybe) and a snack.

Top of the range are the fast luxury trains that operate from Jakarta. Usually indicated by *Argo* at the head of the name, they have everything an executive-class carriage offers, plus business services.

RESERVATIONS

Purchasing tickets at ticket windows is usually straightforward, but sometimes queues become mosh pits, especially for economy trains. The bigger cities have helpful information desks; otherwise, information is usually handed out with authority by the *kepala stasiun* (station master) or one of his cohorts.

For basic economy-class trains, tickets go on sale an hour before departure – just front up, buy a ticket and hope that you can get a seat. The better economy-class services can be booked up to a week in advance for a small extra fee.

Business- and executive-class trains can be booked weeks in advance at the appropriate ticket window, and a few travel agencies and hotels may also buy tickets for you.

Note that though it's often possible to get a ticket in any class on the day of departure, seats are hard to get on weekends and during holiday periods when enterprising *calo* (scalpers) buy large numbers of tickets and fob them off to desperate passengers at a hefty mark-up. It's best to book a few days in advance during these times. Avoid planning a trip during the Idul Fitri public holiday, when the entire island is on the move and tickets are as rare as an honest Yogya batik seller.

JAKARTA

☎ 021 / pop 8.75 million

Whether you love it or hate it, there is no escaping Jakarta, Indonesia's overweight capital. This 'Big Durian' is filled with all the good and bad of Indonesian life.

At first glance, this hot, smoggy city, which sprawls for miles over a featureless plain, feels like nothing more than a waiting lounge for the millions queuing up to make their fortune. Jakarta's infamous *macet* chokes its freeways, town planning is anathema and all attempts to forge a central focal point for the city have stuttered and ultimately failed. The first – or only – thought on most travellers' minds is how quickly the city and its polluted streets can be left behind.

Beneath the veneer of glass fascias, concrete slabs and shabby slums, however, this is a city of surprises and a city of many faces. From the steamy, richly scented streets of Chinatown to the city's thumping, decadent nightlife, Jakarta is a Pandora's box, filled with unexpected gems. Here it's possible to rub shoulders with Indonesia's future leaders, artists, thinkers, movers and shakers, and to see first hand the deep-seated desire so many Indonesians have to rise above the poverty they were born into. Populated by Bataks from Sumatra, Ambonese from Maluku, Balinese, Madurese and Timorese, Jakarta is also a vast cultural melting pot in which the larger Indonesian identity is forged; it is Indonesia in a nutshell.

Jakarta certainly isn't a primary tourist destination, but parts of the old city (Kota) offer an interesting insight into the capital's long history, and there are a handful of good museums scattered about. But if you want to get under the skin of Indonesia, a visit to this mammoth city is an absolute must.

HISTORY

Jakarta's earliest history centres on the port of Sunda Kelapa, in the north of the modern city. When the Portuguese arrived in 1522, Sunda Kelapa was a bustling port of the Pajajaran dynasty, the last Hindu kingdom of West Java. By 1527 the Portuguese had gained a foothold in the city, but were driven out by Sunan Gunungjati, the Muslim saint and leader of Demak. He renamed the city Jayakarta, meaning 'victorious city', and it became a fiefdom of the Banten sultanate.

At the beginning of the 17th century the Dutch and English jostled for power in the city, and in late 1618 the Jayakartans, backed by the British, besieged the Vereenigde Oost-Indische Compagnie (VOC) fortress. The Dutch managed to fend off the attackers until May 1619 when, under the command of Jan Pieterszoon Coen, reinforcements stormed the town and reduced it to ashes. A stronger shoreline fortress was built and the town was renamed

JAKARTA

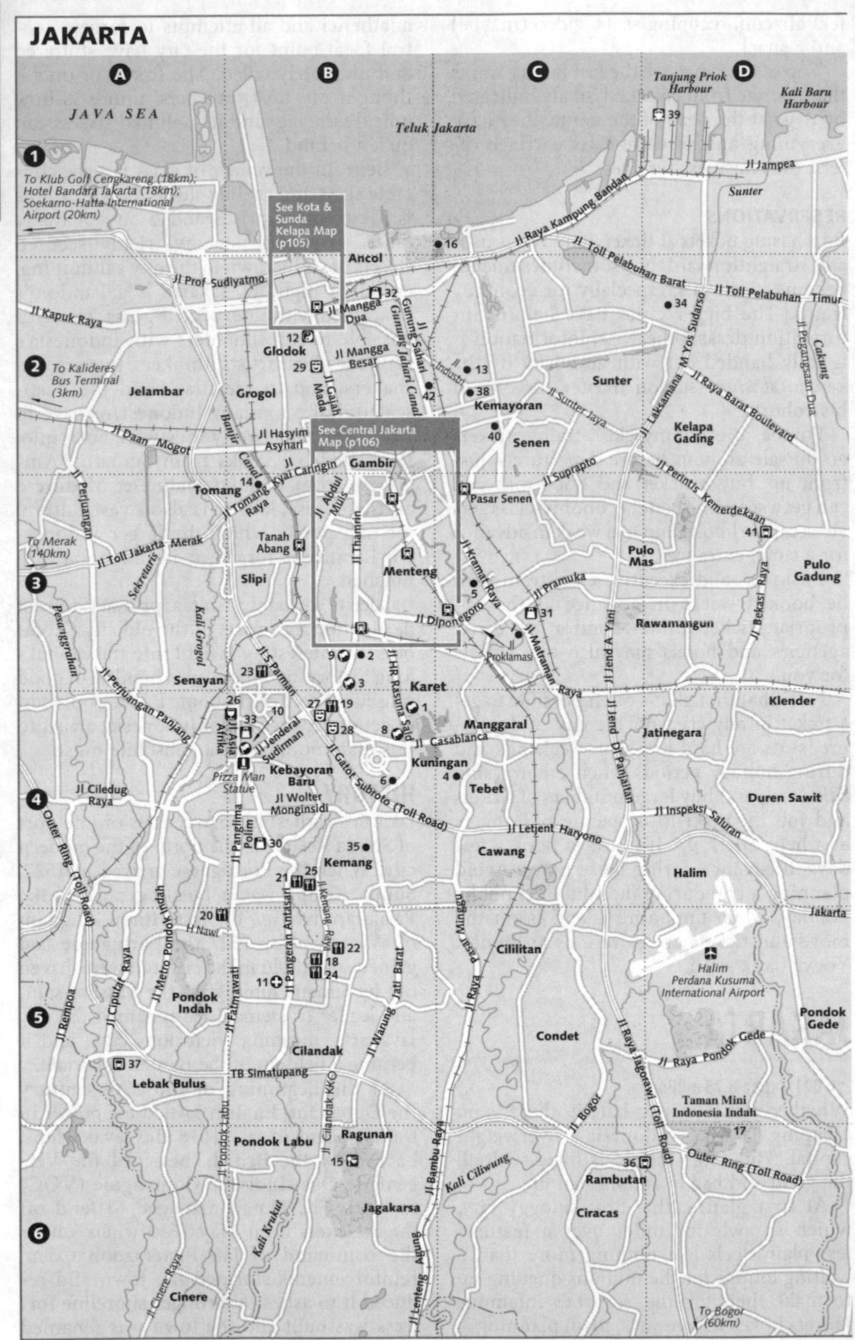

JAVA SEA
Teluk Jakarta
Tanjung Priok Harbour
Kali Baru Harbour
To Klub Golf Cengkareng (18km); Hotel Bandara Jakarta (18km); Soekarno-Hatta International Airport (20km)
See Kota & Sunda Kelapa Map (p105)
See Central Jakarta Map (p106)
To Kalideres Bus Terminal (3km)
To Merak (140km)
To Bogor (60km)
Ancol
Glodok
Jelambar
Grogol
Kemayoran
Sunter
Senen
Kelapa Gading
Gambir
Tomang
Pasar Senen
Tanah Abang
Pulo Mas
Pulo Gadung
Slipi
Menteng
Rawamangun
Senayan
Karet
Klender
Manggarai
Jatinegara
Kebayoran Baru
Kuningan
Tebet
Pizza Man Statue
Duren Sawit
Cawang
Kemang
Halim
Cililitan
Halim Perdana Kusuma International Airport
Pondok Indah
Pondok Gede
Condet
Cilandak
Lebak Bulus
TB Simatupang
Taman Mini Indonesia Indah
Pondok Labu
Ragunan
Rambutan
Jagakarsa
Ciracas
Cinere
Jl Jampea
Jl Raya Kampung Bandan
Jl Toll Pelabuhan Barat
Jl Toll Pelabuhan Timur
Jl Prof Sudiyatmo
Jl Kapuk Raya
Jl Mangga Dua
Jl Mangga Besar
Jl Gunung Sahari
Gunung Jahari Canal
Jl Industri
Jl Gajah Mada
Jl Hasyim Asyhari
Banjir Canal
Jl Daan Mogot
Jl Sunter Jaya
Jl Laksamana M Yos Sudarso
Jl Raya Barat Boulevard
Jl Pegangsaan Dua
Cakung
Jl Suprapto
Jl Perintis Kemerdekaan
Jl Kyai Caringin
Jl Tomang Raya
Jl Abdul Muis
Jl Thamrin
Jl Perjuangan
Jl Toll Jakarta Merak
Sekretaris
Jl Kramat Raya
Jl Pramuka
Jl Bekasi Raya
Pesanggrahan
Kali Grogol
Jl Diponegoro
Jl Proklamasi
Jl Matraman Raya
Jl Jend A Yani
Jl S Parman
Jl HR Rasuna Said
Jl Perjuangan Panjang
Jl Asia Afrika
Jl Jenderal Sudirman
Jl Casablanca
Jl Gatot Subroto (Toll Road)
Jl Jend DI Panjaitan
Jl Ciledug Raya
Jl Wolter Monginsidi
Outer Ring (Toll Road)
Jl Inspeksi Saluran
Jl Letjent Haryono
Jl Panglima Polim
Jl Kemang Raya
Jl Metro Pondok Indah
H Nawi
Jl Pasar Minggu
Jakarta
Jl Pangeran Antasari
Jl Warung Jati Barat
Jl Raya
Jl Ciputat Raya
Jl Rempoa
Jl Fatmawati
Jl Raya Pondok Gede
Jl Raya Jagorawi (Toll Road)
Jl Cilandak KKO
Jl Bogor
Jl Pondok Labu
Jl Bambu Raya
Kali Ciliwung
Outer Ring (Toll Road)
Kali Krukut
Jl Cinere Raya
Jl Lenteng Agung

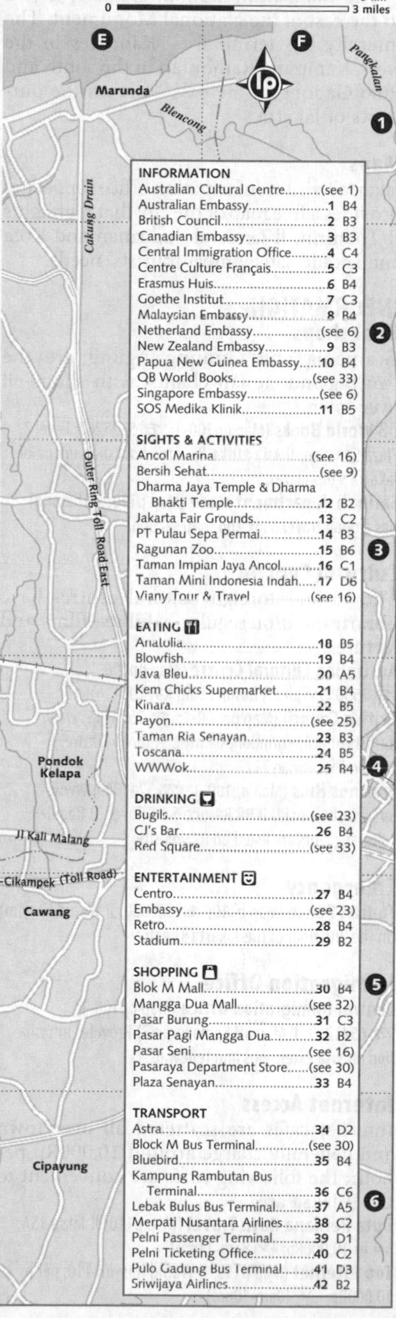

'Batavia' after a tribe that once occupied parts of the Netherlands in Roman times. It soon became the capital of the Dutch East Indies.

Within the walls of Batavia the prosperous Dutch built tall houses and pestilential canals in an attempt to create an Amsterdam in the tropics. By the early 18th century, the city's population had swelled, boosted by both Indonesians and Chinese eager to take advantage of Batavia's commercial prospects.

By 1740 ethnic unrest in the Chinese quarters had grown to dangerous levels and on 9 October violence broke out on Batavia's streets; around 5000 Chinese were massacred. A year later Chinese inhabitants were moved to Glodok, outside the city walls. Other Batavians, discouraged by the severe epidemics between 1735 and 1780, also moved, and the city began to spread far south of the port.

Dutch colonial rule came to an end with the Japanese occupation in 1942 and the name 'Jakarta' was restored, but it wasn't until 1950 that Jakarta officially became the capital of the new republic.

Over the next four decades, the capital struggled under the weight of an ever-increasing population of poor migrants, but by the 1990s Jakarta's economic situation had turned around. This all changed, however, with the start of an economic collapse at the end of 1997. The capital quickly became a political battleground and protests demanding longtime leader Soeharto's resignation increased in intensity in early 1998.

After months of tension the floodgates opened on 12 May 1998 when the army fired live ammunition into a group of students at Trisakti University; four were killed. Jakarta erupted in three days of rioting as thousands took to the streets. The Chinese were hardest hit, with shocking tales of rape and murder emerging after the riots.

Over the past few years Jakarta has braved a spate of natural and unnatural disasters. In August 2003 the US-owned Marriott Hotel was bombed and in September 2004 Australia's embassy experienced a similar fate; both nations were targeted for their involvement in the Afghanistan and Iraq occupations. Flooding disabled many parts of the city in 2002, 2003 and 2006, causing massive damage to homes and public services, and bringing more misery to the abject poor.

However, the biggest problem facing the city may still be its ability to handle protesters. A proposed increase in fuel and utility prices in January 2003 caused thousands to hit the streets and forced the government to backtrack on its plans. However in October 2005 it went through with fuel increases amid widespread protests; fortunately military intervention was not required to maintain calm, but if fuel prices are raised once more violence could easily erupt on the streets of the capital.

ORIENTATION

Jakarta sprawls more than 25km from the docks to the suburbs of south Jakarta, covering 661 sq km. The city centre fans out from around Merdeka Sq, which contains the central landmark of Soekarno's towering gold-tipped National Monument. Merdeka Sq, however, isn't really the city's central focal point; rather it has a number of centres, separated by vast traffic jams and sweltering heat.

For most visitors, Jakarta revolves around the modern part of the city to the south of the monument. Jl Thamrin runs from the southwestern corner of Merdeka Sq down to the Welcome Monument roundabout and is the main thoroughfare, containing many of the big hotels and a couple of major shopping centres.

To the south, Jl Thamrin becomes Jl Jenderal Sudirman, which is home to more hotels, large banks and office blocks. Further south are the affluent suburban areas of Kebayoran Baru, Pondok Indah and Kemang, with their own centres and busy shopping districts. Kemang, in particular, is swamped with top-notch bars, restaurants and shops, but accommodation options are limited.

Just east of Jl Thamrin and south of the National Monument is Jl Jaksa, the main backpacker centre.

North of the National Monument, you will find the old city of Kota, Jakarta's main tourist attraction, while nearby is the schooner harbour of Sunda Kelapa. The modern harbour, Tanjung Priok, is several kilometres along the coast to the east, past the Taman Impian Jaya Ancol recreation park.

The main train station, Gambir, is just to the east of the National Monument. The intercity bus terminals – Kalideres in the west, Kampung Rambutan in the south and Pulo Gadung in the east – are on the outskirts of Jakarta.

Maps

Jakarta's visitor information office (opposite) provides a free map of the city that highlights Jl Thamrin, Jl Jenderal Sudirman and Kota and should satisfy most tourists' needs.

INFORMATION

Bookshops

Gramedia and Gunung Agung are the two big Indonesian chains, with shops all over town.

QB World Books (Map pp100-1; ☎ 5725267; Level 3, Plaza Senayan, Jl Asia Afrika 8) Large bookshop in one of Jakarta's top plazas.

Sarinah department store (Map p110; Jl Thamrin) Has a good travel book and map section.

Cultural Centres

The various foreign cultural centres have libraries and/or regular exhibits, films and lectures:

Australian Cultural Centre (Map pp100-1; ☎ 25505555; Jl HR Rasuna Said Kav C15-16)

British Council (Map pp100-1; ☎ 2524115; www.britishcouncil.org/indonesia.htm; Widjoyo Centre, Jl Jenderal Sudirman 71)

Erasmus Huis (Map pp100-1; ☎ 5241069; www.erasmushuis.or.id; Jl HR Rasuna Said Kav S-3) Regular cultural events are listed on its website.

Emergency

Tourist Police (Map p110; ☎ 566000; Jl Wahid Hasyim) On the 2nd floor of the Jakarta Theatre.

Immigration Office

Central Immigration Office (Map pp100-1; ☎ 6541209; Jl Merpati Kemayoran 3) Provides information on visa extensions and renewals.

Internet Access

Internet cafés are scattered all over town and generally charge around 10,000Rp per hour; the following cafés are convenient to the Jl Jaksa area:

Duta Perdana Raya Travel (Map p110; Jl Jaksa 15A; per hr 10,000Rp; 🕙 8am-11pm)

Top Internet (Map p110; Jl Wahid Hasyim 110; per hr 10,000Rp; 🕙 10am-10pm)

Internet Resources

www.expat.or.id Caters to longer-term visitors and boasts everything from language guides to chatrooms.

www.jakarta.go.id The Jakarta City Government Tourism Office's official site; offers a host of info on where to go and what to see – when it loads.

www.jakweb.com Lists cultural events in the capital and provides links to international newspaper articles on Indonesia.

Media

Djakarta! (20,000Rp) Published monthly and with youth-oriented stories in English and Bahasa Indonesia, as well as an invaluable restaurant and entertainment reviews section.

Jakarta Kini (www.jakartajavakini.com; 20,000Rp) Monthly English publication that features restaurant and entertainment reviews alongside lifestyle articles; usually free in many of the bigger hotels.

Jakarta Post (www.thejakartapost.com; from street vendors 5000Rp) Excellent English-language daily with news, views and cultural happenings.

Medical Services

Cikini Hospital (Map p106; ☎ 23550180; Jl Raden Saleh Raya) Caters to foreigners.

SOS Medika Klinik (Map pp100-1; ☎ 7505973; Jl Puri Sakti 10, Kemang; 🕓 24hr) Offers English-speaking GP appointments, as well as the full range of emergency and specialist healthcare services.

Money

Jakarta is crawling with banks offering the best exchange rates nesia, although it usually pays to shop around. There are ATMs galore at the main post office near the National Monument and at Plaza Indonesia.

BCA bank ATM (Bank Central Asia; Map p110; Jl Haji Agus Salim) A stone's throw from the Jakarta Visitor Information Office.

BII bank (Bank Internasional Indonesia; Map p106; Jl Thamrin) With ATM; in the basement level of Plaza Indonesia.

BNI bank (Bank Negara Indonesia; Map p110; Jl Kebon Sirih Raya) Near Jl Jaksa, with ATM for MasterCard withdrawals.

Lippo Bank (Map p110; Jl Kebon Sirih Raya) Also with ATM for MasterCard withdrawals.

Post

Main post office (Map p106; Jl Gedung Kesenian 1; 🕓 8am-7pm Mon-Fri, 8am-1pm Sat) Occupying an octagonal building near Lapangan Banteng. Also offers a poste restante service.

Telephone & Fax

Faxes can be sent from most wartel and all major hotels. Wartel are found throughout the city and are usually open daily from around 7am until midnight, but are sometimes open 24 hours. As a rule, wartel don't offer a collect-call service. Convenient ones for those staying around Jl Jaksa include the following:

Duta Perdana Raya Travel (opposite)

Top Internet (opposite)

Tourist Information

Jakarta Visitor Information Office (Map p110; ☎ 3154094, 3161293; www.jakarta.go.id; Jl Wahid Hasyim 9; 🕓 9am-5pm Mon-Fri, 9am-1pm Sat) In the Jakarta Theatre building opposite the Sarinah department store. Staff can answer most queries and hand out a number of excellent leaflets and publications. It also has a desk at the airport.

Travel Agencies

Travel agencies on Jl Jaksa are convenient places to start looking for international flights and long-haul bus tickets. Domestic air tickets usually cost the same from a travel agency as from the airline, but discounts are sometimes available.

Global Travel Service (Map p110; ☎ 3143932; globalid@indo.net.id; Jl Jaksa 49) One of the most professional outfits in the Jl Jaksa area.

Indotel (☎ 5502787) In the arrivals terminal of Soekarno-Hatta international airport; can sometimes slash as much as a third off posted rates.

Robertu Kencana Travel (Map p110; ☎ 3142926; Jl Jaksa 20B) Good deals available.

Smailing Tours (www.mysmailing.com) Jl Majapahit 28 (Map p106; ☎ 3800022; Jl Majapahit 28); Jl Thamrin 9 (Map p110; ☎ 31931994; Jl Thamrin 9) Offices all over town. The Jl Majapahit branch is one of Jakarta's biggest travel agencies and the Jl Thamrin office is in the Skyline building just next to the tourist office.

DANGERS & ANNOYANCES

For such a huge city with obvious social problems and an unhealthy reputation, Jakarta is surprisingly safe. It does, however, remain the most crime-prone city in Indonesia. Violent crime is not unknown, but tourists are rarely targeted. It's best to take the usual precautions though – avoid disreputable areas (Glodok and Kota can be unsafe in the early hours of the morning), don't walk the streets alone at night and move out of the way quickly if violence does break out. Attacks by taxi drivers have been known to take place, so always opt for reputable firms at night, such as the citywide Bluebird group.

Jakarta's buses and trains tend to be hopelessly crowded, particularly during rush hours. Pickpockets are notoriously adept and many locals will warn you against such thieves.

Following the Bali and Jakarta bombings, many foreign embassies have warned against travel to Indonesia and especially Jakarta. Attacks against foreign interests have occurred and protests, although often peaceful, may still become violent with little warning. Continued conflict in the Middle East, or developments in the case against those responsible for the bombings, may provoke further unrest. While such warnings are often manically overcautious, once you're in the country, it's always wise to check the current situation with your embassy.

SIGHTS

Kota

The old town of Batavia, now known as Kota, was once the hub of Dutch colonial Indonesia. Much of the one-time grandeur has now rotted, crumbled or been bulldozed away, but **Taman Fatahillah**, Kota's central cobblestone square, is still reminiscent of the area's heyday.

A block west of the square is **Kali Besar**, the great canal along Sungai Ciliwung. This was once a high-class residential area and on the west bank of the river are the last of the homes that date from the early 18th century. **Toko Merah** (Red Shop; Map p105; Jl Kali Besar Barat) was formerly the home of Governor General van Imhoff and at the northern end of Kali Besar is the last remaining Dutch drawbridge, the **Chicken Market Bridge**, which dates from the 17th century.

To reach Taman Fatahillah, you can either take the Korridor I bus from Blok M or Jl Thamrin to Kota train station and walk, or take a city train from Gondangdia, near Jl Jaksa, to the train station. A taxi will cost around 15,000Rp from Jl Thamrin.

MUSEUM WAYANG

This **Puppet Museum** (Map p105; ☎ 6929560; Taman Fatahillah; admission 2000Rp; 🕑 9am-1.30pm Tue-Fri & Sun, 9am-12.30pm Sat) has one of the best collections of *wayang* puppets in Java and its dusty cabinets are lined with a multitude of characters once used for performances. The collection not only includes puppets from Indonesia but also China, Malaysia, India and Cambodia.

Formerly the Museum of Old Batavia, the building itself dates from 1912. In the downstairs courtyard, there are memorials to Dutch governors general who were once buried here, including Jan Pieterszoon Coen, founder of Batavia, who died of cholera in 1629 during the siege by Mataram.

MUSEUM SEJARAH JAKARTA

The **Jakarta History Museum** (Map p105; Taman Fatahillah; admission 2000Rp; 🕑 9am-3pm Tue-Sun) is housed in the old town hall of Batavia, and is probably one of the most solid reminders of Dutch rule within Indonesia. This bell-towered hall, built in 1627, served the administration of the city. It was also used by the city law courts, and its dungeons were the main prison compound of Batavia.

Today it contains lots of heavy, carved furniture and other memorabilia from the Dutch period. Among the more interesting exhibits are early pictures of Batavia and a series of dour portraits of Dutch governors general.

In the back courtyard is a strange memorial stone to Pieter Erbervelt, put to death in 1722 for allegedly conspiring to massacre the Dutch inhabitants of Batavia, and the huge bronze **Cannon Si Jagur** that once graced Taman Fatahillah. This Portuguese cannon, brought to Batavia as a trophy of war after the fall of Melaka in 1641, tapers at one end into a large clenched fist, with the thumb protruding between the index and middle fingers. This suggestive fist is a sexual symbol in Indonesia, and childless women would offer flowers and sit astride the cannon in the hope of gaining children.

BALAI SENI RUPA

Built between 1866 and 1870, the former Palace of Justice building is now a **Fine Arts Museum** (Map p105; Taman Fatahillah; admission 2000Rp; 🕑 9am-1.30pm Tue-Fri & Sun, 9am-12.30pm Sat). It houses contemporary paintings with works by prominent painters, including Affandi, Raden Saleh and Ida Bagus Made. Part of the building is also a ceramics museum, with Chinese ceramics and Majapahit terracottas.

GEREJA SION

Near the Kota train station, this **church** (Map p105; Jl Pangeran Jayakarta) dates from 1695 and is the oldest remaining church in Jakarta. Also known as Gereja Portugis (Portuguese Church), it was built just outside the old city walls for the so-called 'black Portuguese' – the Eurasians and natives captured from Portuguese trading ports in India and Malaya and brought to Batavia as slaves.

The exterior of the church is very plain, but inside there are copper chandeliers, a baroque pulpit and the original organ. Although more than 2000 people were buried in the graveyard during 1790 alone, very few tombs remain.

Sunda Kelapa

Just a 10-minute walk north of Taman Fatahillah, the old port of **Sunda Kelapa** (Map p105; admission 1000Rp) has many magnificent Makassar schooners *(pinisi)*. These brightly painted sailing ships are one of Jakarta's more unusual sights, although the port itself is run down and a good deal less photogenic.

MUSEUM BAHARI

Near the entrance to Sunda Kelapa, an old VOC warehouse built in 1645 is now a **Maritime Museum** (Map p105; admission 2000Rp; 9am-1.30pm Tue-Fri & Sun, 9am-2.30pm Sat). It exhibits crafts from around Indonesia and has an interesting collection of old photographs re-creating the voyage to Jakarta from Europe via Aden, Ceylon and Singapore. The building itself is worth a visit and the sentry posts outside are part of the old city wall.

Just before the entrance to the museum is the old **watchtower** (Map p105; admission 2000Rp). It was built in 1839 to sight and direct traffic to the port. There are good views over the harbour, but opening hours are haphazard – ask for the caretaker if it is closed.

Further along the same street from the museum is the early-morning **Pasar Ikan** (fish market; Map p105). It's an intense, colourful scene of busy crowds around dawn, when the day's catch is sold. Later in the day it sells household items and a growing collection of souvenirs.

Glodok

The neighbourhood of Glodok, the traditional enclave of the Chinese, is a bustling, rundown part of town with fading markets and a decadent nightlife (it's wise to be careful here after dark). It was also the sight of the terrible riots of May and November 1998, which reduced huge swathes of the area to ash and rubble. Much of the legislation that had discriminated against the Chinese and their language for decades was lifted in 2000, but it will be years before the scars are fully erased and the last of the burnt buildings rebuilt.

Glodok is bounded to the east by Jl Gajah Mada, a busy commercial thoroughfare, but if you walk in from Jl Pancoran, old Glodok still consists of winding lanes, narrow crooked houses with balconies, slanting red-tiled roofs and tiny obscure shops. There is also a market here selling

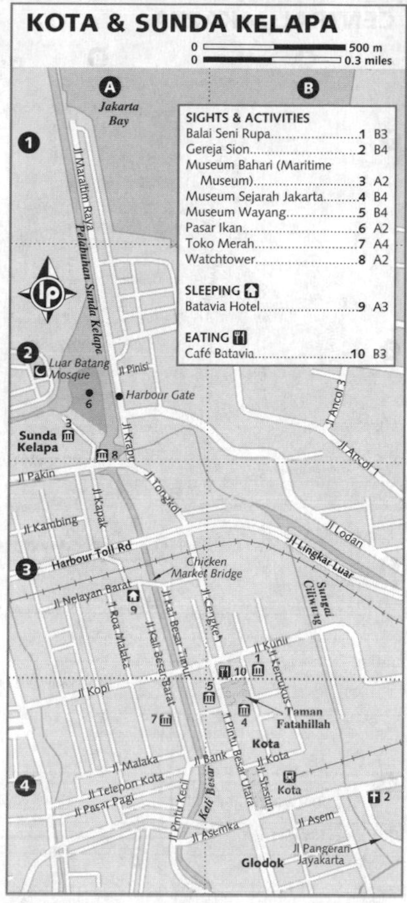

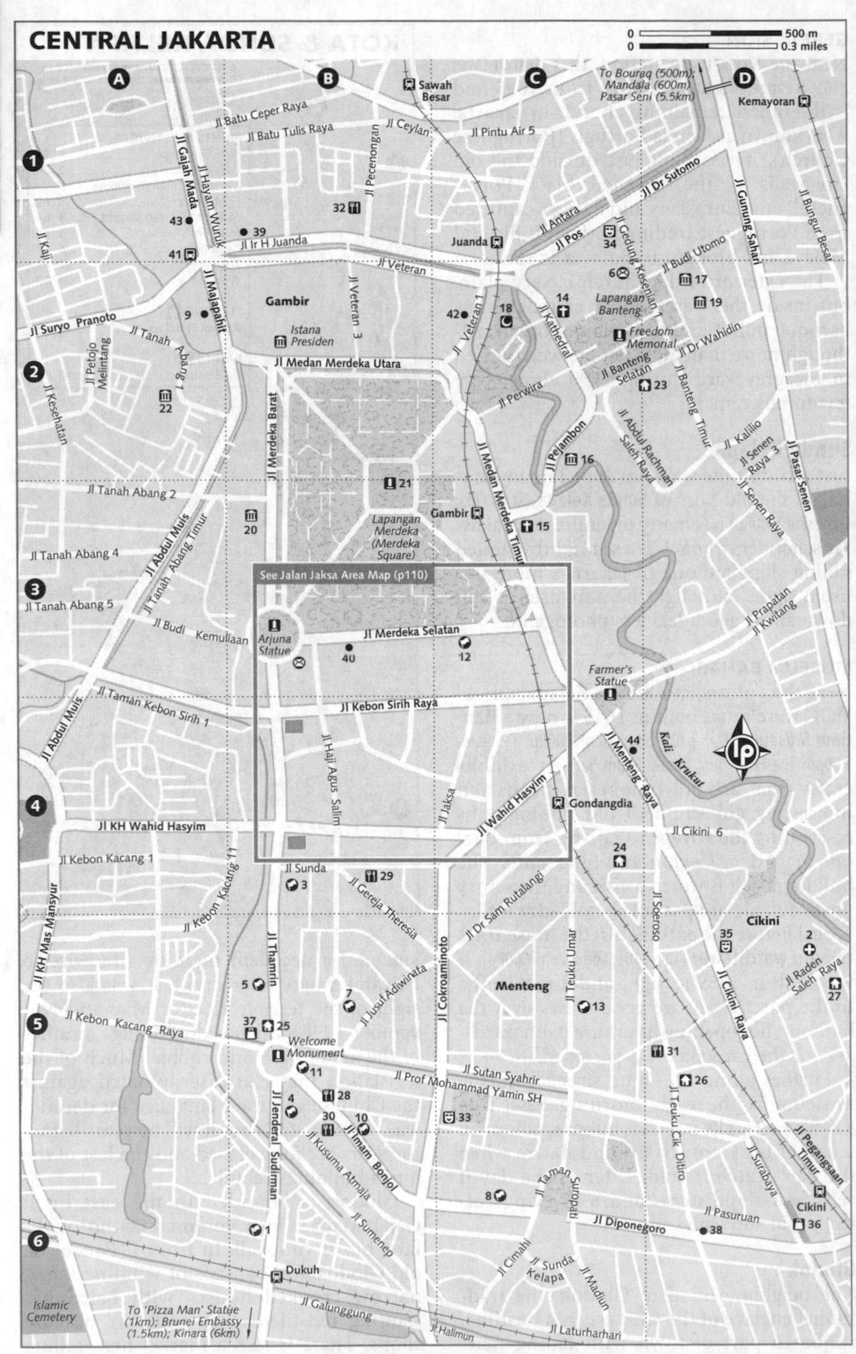
CENTRAL JAKARTA
0 500 m
0 0.3 miles
A
B
C
D
1
2
3
4
5
6
Sawah Besar
To Bouraq (500m); Mandala (600m) Pasar Seni (5.5km)
Kemayoran
Jl Batu Ceper Raya
Jl Batu Tulis Raya
Jl Ceylan
Jl Pintu Air 5
Jl Pecenongan
Jl Gajah Mada
Jl Hayam Wuruk
Jl Dr Sutomo
Jl Gunung Sahari
Jl Bungur Besar
Jl Antara
Jl Pos
Jl Gedung Kesenian 1
Jl Budi Utomo
Jl Kaji
Jl Ir H Juanda
Juanda
Jl Veteran
Jl Majapahit
Gambir
Jl Veteran 3
Jl Veteran 1
Jl Kathedral
Lapangan Banteng
Freedom Memorial
Jl Dr Wahidin
Jl Suryo Pranoto
Jl Tanah Abang 1
Jl Petojo Melintang
Istana Presiden
Jl Medan Merdeka Utara
Jl Banteng Selatan
Jl Perwira
Jl Kesehatan
Jl Banteng Timur
Jl Abdul Rachman Saleh Raya
Jl Kalilio
Jl Senen Raya 3
Jl Pasar Senen
Jl Merdeka Barat
Jl Pejambon
Jl Medan Merdeka Timur
Jl Tanah Abang 2
Gambir
Jl Senen Raya
Lapangan Merdeka (Merdeka Square)
Jl Tanah Abang 4
Jl Abdul Muis
Jl Tanah Abang Timur
See Jalan Jaksa Area Map (p110)
Jl Tanah Abang 5
Jl Budi Kemuliaan
Arjuna Statue
Jl Merdeka Selatan
Jl Prapatan
Jl Kwitang
Farmer's Statue
Jl Taman Kebon Sirih 1
Jl Kebon Sirih Raya
Jl Haji Agus Salim
Jl Menteng Raya
Kali Krukut
Jl Jaksa
Jl Wahid Hasyim
Gondangdia
Jl KH Wahid Hasyim
Jl Cikini 6
Jl Kebon Kacang 1
Jl Sunda
Jl Gereja Theresia
Jl Dr Sam Rutalangi
Jl Soeroso
Jl Kebon Kacang 11
Jl KH Mas Mansyur
Cikini
Jl Thamrin
Jl Cokroaminoto
Jl Teuku Umar
Jl Jusuf Adiwinata
Menteng
Jl Cikini Raya
Jl Raden Saleh Raya
Jl Kebon Kacang Raya
Welcome Monument
Jl Sutan Syahrir
Jl Prof Mohammad Yamin SH
Jl Teuku Cik Ditiro
Jl Kusuma Atmaja
Jl Imam Bonjol
Jl Surabaya
Jl Pegangsaan Timur
Jl Jenderal Sudirman
Jl Taman Suropati
Jl Sumenep
Jl Diponegoro
Jl Pasuruan
Cikini
Jl Cimahi
Jl Sunda Kelapa
Jl Madiun
Dukuh
Islamic Cemetery
To 'Pizza Man' Statue (1km); Brunei Embassy (1.5km); Kinara (6km)
Jl Galunggung
Jl Halimun
Jl Laturharhari
1
2
3
4
5
6
7
8
9
10
11
12
13
14
15
16
17
18
19
20
21
22
23
24
25
26
27
28
29
30
31
32
33
34
35
36
37
38
39
40
41
42
43
44

INFORMATION

BII Bank	(see 37)
Brunei Embassy	1 B6
Cikini Hospital	2 D5
French Embassy	3 B4
German Embassy	4 B5
Japanese Embassy	5 B5
Main Post Office	6 C2
Myanmar Embassy	7 B5
Philippines Embassy	8 C6
Smailing Tours	9 A2
Thailand Embassy	10 B5
UK Embassy	11 B5
US Embassy	12 C3
Vietnamese Embassy	13 C5
SIGHTS & ACTIVITIES	
Catholic Cathedral	14 C2
Emanuel Church	15 C3
Gedung Pancasila	16 C2
Mahkamah Agung	17 D2
Mesjid Istiqlal	18 C2
Ministry of Finance Building	19 D2
Museum Nasional	20 B3
National Monument (Monas)	21 B3
Taman Prasasti Museum	22 A2
SLEEPING	
Borobudur Inter-Continental Jakarta	23 D2
Gondia International Guesthouse	24 C4
Grand Hyatt Jakarta	25 B5
Hotel Marcopolo	26 D5
Yannie International Guesthouse	27 D5
EATING	
Cinnabar	28 B5
Hazara	(see 30)
Kafe Pisa	29 B4
Lan Na Thai	30 B5
Lara Djonggrang	31 D5
Night Warung	32 B1
DRINKING	
Burgundy	(see 25)
Face Bar	(see 30)
ENTERTAINMENT	
BB's	33 C5
Gedung Kesenian Jakarta	34 C1
Taman Ismail Marzuki (TIM)	35 D5
SHOPPING	
Flea Market	36 D6
Plaza Indonesia	37 B5
TRANSPORT	
Avis	38 D6
Batavia Air	39 B1
Garuda Indonesia	40 B3
Harmoni Bus Terminal	41 A1
Kerta Jaya	42 C2
Lion Air	43 A1
Menara Buana Surya	44 C4

everything from live bugs to pirate CDs. Just south of Jl Pancoran are the Chinese **Dharma Jaya Temple** and **Dharma Bhakti Temple**, from the 17th century.

Central Jakarta

If a centre for this sprawling city had to be chosen, then Lapangan Merdeka (Merdeka Sq) would be it. This huge, almost barren square is home to Soekarno's monument to the nation, and is surrounded by a couple of the capital's more inviting museums and colonial buildings.

MUSEUM NASIONAL

On the western side of Merdeka Sq, the **National Museum** (Map p106; adult/child 750/250Rp; 8.30am-2.30pm Tue-Thu & Sun, 8.30-11.30am Fri, 8.30-11.30am Sat), built in 1862, is the best of its kind in Indonesia and one of the finest in Southeast Asia.

It has an enormous collection of cultural objects of the various ethnic groups around the country – costumes, musical instruments, model houses and so on – and numerous fine bronzes from the Hindu-Javanese period, as well as many interesting stone pieces salvaged from the Central Javanese and other temples. There's also a superb display of Chinese ceramics dating back to the Han dynasty (300 BC to AD 220), which was almost entirely amassed in Indonesia.

Just outside the museum is a bronze elephant that was presented by the King of Thailand in 1871; thus the museum building is popularly known as the Gedung Gajah (Elephant House). Next door is the museum's sleek new building, used for temporary exhibitions; entry is included in the admission fee.

The **Indonesian Heritage Society** (5725870) organises free English tours of the museum at 9.30am every Tuesday and Thursday and 10.30am every second Saturday and last Sunday in the month; French tours take place at 9.30am every third Wednesday of the month.

MONAS

Ingloriously dubbed 'Soekarno's final erection', this 132m-high **National Monument** (Monumen Nasional or Monas; Map p106; 8.30am-5pm, closed last Mon of every month), towering over Merdeka Sq, is both Jakarta's principal landmark and the most famous architectural extravagance of the former dictator. Begun in 1961, this typically masculine column was not completed until 1975, when it was officially opened by Soeharto. The

National Monument is allegedly constructed 'entirely of Italian marble', and is topped with a sculpted flame, gilded with 35kg of gold leaf.

In the base of the National Monument, the **National History Museum** (adult/child 1500/500Rp) tells the story of Indonesia's independence struggle in 48 dioramas using *Thunderbird*-like models. The numerous uprisings against the Dutch are overstated but interesting; Soekarno is barely mentioned and the events surrounding the 1965 coup are a whitewash.

The highlight of a visit are the smoggy views of Jakarta from the top of the monument (adult/child 5000/2500Rp). Avoid Sunday and holidays, when the queues for the lift are long.

TAMAN PRASASTI

To the northwest of the National Museum is the so-called **Park of Inscription** (Map p106; Jl Tanah Abang; admission 2000Rp; 9am-3pm Tue-Thu & Sun, 9am-2.30pm Fri, 9am-12.30pm Sat), which is actually the Kebon Jahe Cemetery; important figures from the colonial era are buried here.

LAPANGAN BANTENG

Just east of Merdeka Sq, in front of the Borobudur Inter-Continental Jakarta hotel, **Lapangan Banteng** (Banteng Square, formerly the Waterlooplein; Map p106) was laid out by the Dutch in the 19th century, and the area has some of Jakarta's best colonial architecture.

The **Catholic cathedral** (Map p106) has twin spires and was built in 1901 to replace an earlier church. Facing the cathedral is Jakarta's principal place of Muslim worship, the modernistic **Mesjid Istiqlal** (Map p106), which was constructed under Soekarno and is reputedly the largest mosque in Southeast Asia.

To the east of Lapangan Banteng is the **Mahkamah Agung** (Supreme Court; Map p106), built in 1848, and next door is the **Ministry of Finance Building** (Map p106), formerly the Witte Huis (White House). This grand government complex was built by Daendels in 1809 as the administrative centre for the Dutch government.

To the southwest is **Gedung Pancasila** (Map p106; Jl Pejambon), which is an imposing neoclassical building built in 1830 as the Dutch army commander's residence. It later became the meeting hall of the Volksraad (People's Council), but is best known as the place where Soekarno made his famous Pancasila speech in 1945, laying the foundation for Indonesia's constitution. Just west along Jl Pejambon from Gedung Pancasila is the **Emanuel Church** (Map p106), another classic building dating from 1893.

Southern Jakarta

In the southern reaches of the city reside a couple of attractions that require a day trip to fully enjoy.

TAMAN MINI INDONESIA INDAH

In the city's southeast, near Kampung Rambutan, **Taman Mini Indonesia Indah** (Map pp100-1; ☎ 5454545; Jl Raya Pondok Gede; adult/child 6000/4000Rp; 8am-5pm) is one of those 'whole country in one park' collections popular in Asia. Conceived by Madame Tien Soeharto in 1971, the park was opened in 1975 after the families inhabiting the land were cleared out and an estimated US$26 million was spent on the project.

This 100-hectare park has a full-scale traditional house for each of Indonesia's provinces, with displays of regional handicrafts and clothing, and even a mini-scale Borobudur. Museums, theatres and restaurants are scattered throughout, and free cultural performances are staged in selected regional houses (usually around 10am); Sunday is the big day for cultural events but shows are also held during the week.

You can walk or drive your own car around Taman Mini. Free shuttle buses operate regularly, or you can take the monorail or the cable car that goes from one end of the park to the other. Taman Mini is about 18km from the city centre; allow about 1½ hours to get there and at least three hours to look around. Take any bus to the Kampung Rambutan terminal (air-con, *patas* buses 9, 10 and 11 run from Jl Thamrin) and then a T15 metro-mini to the park entrance. A taxi is much quicker and will cost around 35,000Rp from central Jakarta, plus the tolls.

RAGUNAN ZOO

Jakarta's **Ragunan Zoo** (Map pp100-1; ☎ 7806623; Jl Harsono RM 1; adult/child 4000/3000Rp; 7.30am-6pm) is 16km south of the city centre in the Pasar Minggu area. As home to 4000 animals, this large zoo has a good collection of Indonesian wildlife including Komodo dragons. It's not world class (some of the enclosures are depressingly small), but this is by far the best zoo in Indonesia, and its new primate enclosure, featuring orang-utans and gorillas, is a highlight. From Jl Thamrin take bus 19.

ACTIVITIES

Golf

Jakarta has some of the best-value golf in Asia, with 38 courses within and around the city. **Klub Golf Cengkareng** (☎ 5591111; Taman Niaga Soewarna G, Lot 1-2), near the airport, is one of the priciest, but remains the residents' favourite, with stunning fairways and a top-notch bar at the 19th. It is members only at the weekend, but 18 holes during the week costs 300,000Rp.

Massage

Jakarta has an abundance of massage establishments, some of which are simply fronts for brothels. **Bersih Sehat** (Map pp100-1; ☎ 5704444; Hotel Sahid Jaya, Jl Jenderal Sudirman 86; 1hr massage 100,000Rp) certainly doesn't fall into that category, but rather has a reputation for quality, expertise and professionalism.

JAKARTA FOR CHILDREN

Taman Impian Jaya Ancol

Along the bay front, between Kota and Tanjung Priok, the people's **'Dreamland'** (Map pp100-1; ☎ 64710497; basic admission 10,000Rp, includes entry to Pasar Seni; ⏲ 24hr) is built on land reclaimed in 1962. This 300-hectare landscaped recreation park, providing nonstop entertainment, has hotels, nightclubs, theatres and a variety of sporting facilities. It's easily the city's best entertainment for kids in the city.

Taman Impian Jaya Ancol's prime attractions include **Pasar Seni** (Art Market), which has sidewalk cafés, a host of craft shops, art exhibitions, and live music every Friday and Saturday night, and the water-themed **Seaworld** aquarium and **Gelanggang Samudra** (☎ 6406677; admission Mon-Fri/Sat & Sun 35,000/45,000Rp; ⏲ 11am-6pm Mon-Thu, 2-8pm Fri, 11am 8pm Sat & Sun), with a boat ride and dolphin shows.

Swimmers have the option of the **Gelanggang Renang** (☎ 6406677; Mon-Fri 40,000Rp, Sat & Sun 50,000Rp; ⏲ 11am-6pm Mon-Thu, 2-8pm Fri, 11am-8pm Sat & Sun) complex, which includes a wave pool and slide pool, or **Ancol Beach**; the latter isn't the greatest place to swim, but boat trips to some of the Pulau Seribu islands (p120) leave from here.

The biggest draw card in the larger Ancol recreation park is **Dunia Fantasi** (Fantasy Land; ☎ 64712000; Mon-Fri 60,000Rp, Sat & Sun 80,000Rp; ⏲ 11am-6pm Mon-Thu, 2-8pm Fri, 11am-8pm Sat & Sun), a fun park that must have raised eyebrows at the Disney legal department. Similarities to Disneyland start at the 'main street' entrance and extend to the Puppet Castle, a straight 'it's a small world' replica.

The park can be very crowded on weekends, but on weekdays it's fairly quiet. Take a bus or city train to Kota train station, then bus 64, 65, 125 or *mikrolet* (small taxi) 51. A taxi will cost around 30,000Rp from Jl Thamrin.

TOURS

Numerous travel agencies offer daily tours of Jakarta. Bookings can be made through the tourist office and major hotels.

Gray Line (☎ 630 8105) Offers a 24-hour booking line for tours to Batavia (US$20), Bogor's Kebun Raya (Botanical Gardens), Puncak and Taman Safari Indonesia (US$40) and both day (US$60) and overnight (US$110 including accommodation) trips to Pulau Seribu.

Indonesian Heritage Society Located at Museum Nasional. Offers city tours for 100,000Rp; see p107.

Wanawisata Alamhayati (☎ 5710392) Has tours to Krakatau (p126) and Ujung Kulon National Park (p128).

FESTIVALS & EVENTS

June/July

Jakarta Anniversary On 22 June, this marks the establishment of the city by Gunungjati back in 1527, and is celebrated with fireworks and the Jakarta Fair (fairground event held at the Jakarta Fairgrounds, Map pp100-1, from late June until mid-July).

August

Independence Day Indonesia's independence is celebrated on 17 August and the parades in Jakarta are the biggest in the country.

Jalan Jaksa Street Fair Features Betawi dance, theatre and music, as well as popular modern performances. Street stalls sell food and souvenirs, and art and photography exhibits are also staged. It is held for one week in August.

December

JiFFest (Jakarta International Film Festival; www.jiffest.org) Indonesia's only film festival takes place in the second week of December; check the website for details, as lack of funding may force it out of business.

SLEEPING

Jakarta is the most expensive city in Indonesia for hotels, but economic meltdown and a drop in tourism have seen big discounts, especially at midrange and top-end hotels. Conversely, falling visitor numbers have seen standards slip in many of the traditional backpacker haunts, and while hostels remain cheap, few have much character.

Jalan Jaksa Area

Cheap hotels and restaurants are the mainstay of this budget accommodation area, but it also has a smattering of midrange options. It's conveniently located near Jakarta's main drag, Jl Thamrin, and is a 10- to 15-minute walk from Gambir train station.

BUDGET

Bloem Steen Homestay (Map p110; ☎ 31925389; Gang 1 173; r 30,000Rp, with mandi 50,000Rp; 💻) With a quiet, mellow ambience, simple yet good clean rooms, a small library of English novels and welcoming staff, Bloem Steen rates as one of Jakarta's best budget options.

Kresna Homestay (Map p110; ☎ 31925403; Gang 1 175; r 40,000Rp, with mandi 50,000Rp) For budget options in Jl Jaksa, Kresna plays second fiddle only to Bloem Steen next door. Rooms are cramped, but as clean and as cosy as you'll get for 40,000Rp, and the owner is amiable.

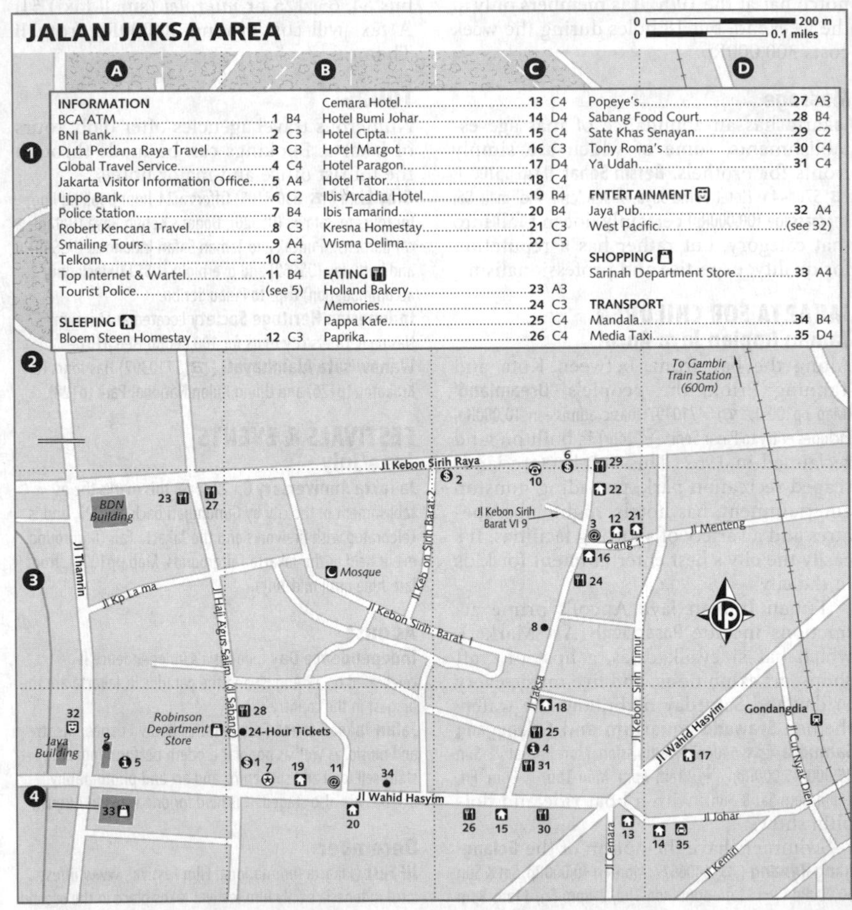

Wisma Delima (Map p110; ☎ 3923850; Jl Jaksa 5; r with mandi 40,000Rp) The original guesthouse on Jl Jaksa, Delima is now rather scruffy and has very basic rooms, but the entire place exudes a homely feel.

Hotel Tator (Map p110; ☎ 31923940; Jl Jaksa 37; r with shower & toilet 70,000Rp, r with hot water/air-con & telephone 85,000-100,000Rp; ❄) Tator is perched on the cusp of budget and midrange, but is let down by dim light bulbs and spartan rooms (rooms on the top floor are your best bet). It does have the advantage of a good little café, though, and breakfast is included with the more expensive rooms.

Hotel Margot (Map p110; ☎ 3913830; Jl Jaksa 15; r from 150,000Rp; ❄) This hotel has slightly scruffy rooms with weak air con but they're reasonably clean and staff are willing and able. There's also a café-bar downstairs that attracts backpackers.

MIDRANGE

Hotel Bumi Johar (Map p110; ☎ 3145746; Jl Johar 17-19; r 270,000-305,000Rp; ❄) This is a small hotel with a Japanese restaurant; rooms have a subdued air due to lack of strong light bulbs, but they're in good shape and discounts are readily available.

Hotel Cipta (Map p110; ☎ 31930424; cipta1@cbn.net.id; Jl Wahid Hasyim 53; r 275,000-330,000Rp plus 21% tax; ❄) Rooms at the Cipta are plain but cosy, and considerably brighter than most hotels. There's a restaurant on the ground floor and staff will often drop the 21% service tax to snag your business.

Hotel Paragon (Map p110; ☎ 3917070; Jl Wahid Hasyim 29; r from 295,000Rp; ❄) Paragon is a strangely designed, multistorey hotel with rooms fronting onto open corridors. Rooms are, however, immaculate – if slightly musty – and very quiet.

Cemara Hotel (Map p110; ☎ 3908215; cemara@centrin.net.id; Jl Cemara 1; r 350,000-550,000Rp plus 21% tax; ❄ 💻) On the corner of busy Jl Wahid Hasyim, Cemara is a glossy and well-maintained hotel with attentive staff and rooms that are spacious, though a little dark.

Jl Wahid Hasyim has a string of midrange options, including two Ibis hotels, **Ibis Arcadia** (Map p110; ☎ 2300050; hotelarcadia@speed.net.Id; Jl Wahid Hasyim 114; r from 333,000Rp; ❄ 💻) and **Ibis Tamarind** (Map p110; ☎ 3912323; ibistam@indosat.net.id; Jl Wahid Hasyim 77; r 350,000Rp; ❄ 🏊). Both have comfortable rooms, but Arcadia comes up trumps with more stylish décor.

Cikini

Cikini is east of Jl Thamrin and has a selection of midrange hotels and good guesthouses, but doesn't have the travellers resources of Jl Jaksa.

BUDGET

Gondia International Guesthouse (Map p106; ☎ 3909221; gondia@rad.net.id; Jl Gondangdia Kecil 22; r with breakfast 120,000Rp; ❄) In a quiet side street off Jl Soeroso, Gondia is just like granny's house, with comfortable rooms, a homy ambience and a small garden area.

Yannie International Guesthouse (Map p106; ☎ 3140012; ygh@cbn.net.id; Jl Raden Saleh Raya 35; s/d 120,000/150,000Rp; ❄) Yanni is a good-value and deservedly popular guesthouse, with clean rooms, hot water and friendly staff. There is no sign, just a 'Y' out front.

MIDRANGE

our pick **Hotel Marcopolo** (Map p106; ☎ 2301777; mcopolojkt@telkom.net; Jl Teuku Cik Ditiro 19; r from 240,000Rp plus 21% tax; ❄ 🏊) Marcopolo may not be the most salubrious hotel in the city, but it is great value for money. This high-rise hotel in the heart of suburbia offers a range of enormous rooms (all of which are kept in top condition), with sport baths and balconies. A fine buffet breakfast is available in its ground-floor restaurant, and staff couldn't be more friendly or helpful.

Airport

BUDGET

Hotel Bandara Jakarta (☎ 6191964; Jl Jurumudi, Km 2.5, Cengkareng; s/d with air-con & bath from 180,000/200,000Rp; ❄) This is the cheapest hotel near the airport. While there's nothing fancy about it, it does have a 24-hour coffee shop and usually has a representative at the airport hotel booths offering free transport.

TOP END

Quality Hotel Aspac (☎ 5590008; fax 5590018; r from US$80; ❄ 💻) For transit visitors, Aspac is handily located right in the international terminal at the airport, upstairs in the departure area. It has a small bar and restaurant, but no other facilities.

Other Areas

MIDRANGE

Batavia Hotel (Map p105; ☎ 6904118; www.batavia-hotel.com; Jl Kali Besar Barat 44-46; r 363,000-510,000Rp;

) The Batavia may be in the middle of nowhere in the north of Kota, but its rooms, which are surprisingly plush, make up for it. Service is excellent, and it's also a lot closer to the airport than most hotels. Discounts are available for 12-hour stays.

TOP END

Borobudur Inter-Continental Jakarta (Map p106; ☎ 3805555; www.hotelborobudur.com; Jl Banteng Selatan; r from US$130;) This is one of the older generation of luxury hotels, with style, grace, refurbished rooms and a large range of sporting facilities. It's on the southern side of Lapangan Banteng.

Grand Hyatt Jakarta (Map p106; ☎ 3901234; http://jakarta.grand.hyatt.com; Jl Thamrin; r from US$160 plus 21% tax;) The Hyatt is the city centre's most salubrious hotel, rising above Plaza Indonesia. It attracts the great, the good and the just plain beautiful to its top-notch bars and restaurants. You'll find it with its high-rise friends overlooking Welcome Monument on Jl Thamrin.

EATING

Jakarta has the best selection of restaurants in Indonesia, offering everything from top international restaurants to street fare and monkey meat on the streets of Glodok. Eateries are expensive by Indonesian standards, though.

Jalan Jaksa Area

Jl Jaksa's cafés are convivial meeting places dishing out standard travellers fare. They are certainly cheap and the breakfasts are very good value. Food is quasi-European or bland Indonesian.

BUDGET

Holland Bakery (Map p110; Jl Hali Agus Salim; cakes & cookies from 2000Rp; breakfast & lunch) Just across the road from Popeye's, Holland Bakery sells a menagerie of sticky buns and cakes from beneath its trademark rotating windmill.

Sabang Food Court (Map p110; Jl Hali Agus Salim 49; mains around 15,000Rp; lunch & dinner) Sabang is a stripped-back food court popular with locals for its wide selection of regional Indonesian cuisine.

Pappa Kafe (Map p110; Jl Jaksa 41; mains 20,000Rp; breakfast, lunch & dinner) Most travellers holed up in Jl Jaksa tend to gravitate to Pappa at least once during their stay, which creates a lively and convivial place to be. The food isn't the best, but there are outdoor tables and a varied menu.

Memories (Map p110; Jl Jaksa 17; mains 20,000Rp; breakfast, lunch & dinner) Memories is another of Jl Jaksa's backpacker and expat haunts, with a remarkably similar menu to the Pappa Kafe and plenty of folk willing to swap a story or two.

Popeye's (Map p110; cnr Jl Hali Agus Salim & Jl Kebon Sirih Raya; mains 20,000Rp; lunch & dinner) At the northern end of Jl Sabang, this place flies the flag for junk-food fetishists, serving an assortment of deep-fried fish and chicken.

Ya Udah (Map p110; ☎ 3144121; Jl Jaksa 49; mains 20,000-40,000Rp; breakfast, lunch & dinner) This popular airy hang-out serves breakfasts, Western dishes and even a wide selection of pies. It's by far the best place in the Jl Jaksa area for a cheap bite to eat.

MIDRANGE

Sate Khas Senayan (Map p110; Jl Kebon Sirih Raya 31A; mains 20,000-50,000Rp; lunch & dinner) At the northern end of Jl Jaksa, this smarter air-con restaurant serves a variety of superb sate, *gado gado*, *rawon buntut* (oxtail stew) and other classic Indonesian dishes.

At the southern end of Jl Jaksa, Jl Wahid Hasyim is home to a number of midrange restaurants:

Paprika (Map p110; ☎ 3144113; Jl Wahid Hasyim 55; mains 40,000-80,000Rp; lunch & dinner) The best of the bunch here, with a varied menu, sparkling glassware and a decent wine list.

Tony Roma's (Map p110; Jl Wahid Hasyim 49; mains 50,000-90,000Rp; lunch & dinner) Has belly-extending, melt-in-the-mouth ribs for 165,000Rp, or half portions.

Other Areas

Quality restaurants are scattered the length and breadth of this busy city, which is great for choice, but it may mean travelling an hour just to dine.

There are, however, areas where fine restaurants like company: Jl Kemang Raya, the main drag of the affluent, southern suburb of Kemang, is inundated with top-notch Western-style eateries and bars, and the Menteng neighbourhood, just south of Jl Jaksa, chimes in with its fair share of top-notch eating options.

BUDGET

Street food is found throughout the city, but is particularly plentiful on Jl Pecenongan (Map p106), about 500m north of the National Monument, where numerous night warungs set up shop.

MIDRANGE

Payon (Map pp100-1; ☎ 7194826; Jl Kemang Raya 17; mains 30,000-80,000Rp; lunch & dinner) With its open pagoda setting, calming ambience, army of attentive staff and excellent authentic Indonesian cuisine, Payon is an inviting option. Just remember to bring some bug spray.

WWWok (Map pp100-1; ☎ 7193928; Jl Kemang Raya 9 J-K; mains 30,000-100,000Rp; lunch & dinner) WWWok is the place to mix dining and internet surfing; it offers plenty of internet terminals and oodles of noodles in hip, lively surroundings.

Kinara (Map pp100-1; ☎ 7192677; Jl Kemang Raya 78B; mains 40,000-100,000Rp; lunch & dinner) The mock medieval doors guarding Kinara lead to a stylish and sophisticated interior populated with some of the finest Indian dishes in Jakarta. Watch as Jakartans alternate between mouthfuls of hot curry and cooling gulps of water.

our pick Lara Djonggrang (Map p106; ☎ 3153252; Jl Teuku Cik Ditiro 4; mains 40,000-150,000Rp; lunch & dinner) An attractive selection of dishes from around the archipelago, a stunning décor that mixes traditional Indonesian flair with North African charm, subdued lighting, and lazy to uplifting tunes all make Lara Djonggrang one of the most pleasant spots to dine in the city.

Café Batavia (Map p105; ☎ 6915531; Jl Pintu Besar Utara 14; mains 50,000Rp; breakfast, lunch dinner) In the heart of historic Kota on Taman Fatahillah is Batavia, an establishment barely changed since Dutch traders sipped coffee here in white linen suits. The restaurant is housed in a tastefully renovated Dutch building. The food is a triumph of form over content, but there is no better place to spend cocktail hour.

Cinnabar (Map p106; ☎ 3903615; Plaza Gani Djemat, Jl Imam Bonjol 76-78; mains 50,000-150,000Rp; dinner) Cinnabar serves excellent West-meets-East fusion food and cocktails in elegant, contemporary Asian surrounds.

Anatolia (Map pp100-1; ☎ 7194658; Jl Kemang Raya 110A; mains 50,000-150,000Rp; dinner) At the southern end of Kemang Raya this is one of the most authentic Turkish restaurants in the city, with a menu featuring kebabs and excellent coffee and *chai* (spiced tea).

Also worth trying:

Kem Chicks Supermarket (Map pp100-1; Jl Kemang Raya 3-5; breakfast & lunch) The place to find everything, including the ever-elusive Marmite, Vegemite and peanut butter.

Kafe Pisa (Map p106; ☎ 3100149; Jl Gereja Theresia 1; mains 40,000-120,000Rp; lunch & dinner) Rustic Mediterranean décor, an outside area, and decent pasta, pizza and ice cream.

TOP END

Lan Na Thai/Hazara (Map p106; ☎ 3150424; Jl Kusuma Atmaja 85; mains 60,000-100,000Rp; lunch & dinner) This three-in-one place (Face Bar, p114, is also located here) is for those who just can't make a decision; upstairs, Lan Na Thai offers exquisite Thai, while downstairs Hazara's kitchen produces divine North Indian cuisine.

Blowfish (Map pp100-1; ☎ 57991678; Menara Bank Danamon Penthouse 29-F, Jl Prof Dr Satrio; mains 60,000-200,000Rp; dinner) This slick Japanese restaurant has one of the best views of smoggy Jakarta; it resides on the 35th floor of the Menara Bank Danamon tower. The food is also highly rated and it's a grand spot for a cocktail.

Toscana (Map pp100-1; ☎ 7181216; Jl Kemang Raya 120; mains 70,000-150,000Rp; dinner) Toscana is an overly upmarket pizzeria (something you'll never see in Tuscany) that saves itself with lovely pizzas, a romantic atmosphere and a good selection of Tuscan wines.

Java Bleu (Map pp100-1; ☎ 7697291; Kompleks D'Best, Jl Fatmawati 15, Blok E31; dinner for 2 400,000-600,000Rp; dinner Tue-Sat) Java Bleu is arguably one of Jakarta's finest restaurants. It only opens for three hours a day and it only has space for 20, but the French menu, incorporating Indonesia's finest foie gras, is excellent. Bookings are essential.

DRINKING

Like so many other aspects of this gigantic city, Jakarta's bar scene is spread far and wide. You'll find plenty of places to drop in for a drink (and a quick karaoke). Only a handful of the more established drinking holes are listed here. If you're looking for a concentration of bars, however, try in and around Blok M; www.jakartablokm.com can provide you with a list of places favoured by expats and locals alike.

Note that most bars stay open till around 1am or 2am, sometimes later on weekends, and all establishments listed under Live Music (right) rank highly as drinking spots.

Bugils (Map pp100-1; ☎ 5747777; www.bartele.com; Taman Ria Senayan, Jl Gatot Subroto) Bugils is one of the most famous bars among expats, and everyone has heard of its owner, Bartele. The bar itself appears modelled on an Amsterdam brown café, and the atmosphere is generally relaxed and convivial, except on weekends when it's rowdy and good natured.

Red Square (Map pp100-1; ☎ 57901281; PT Segiempat Merah Prima Plaza Senayan Arcadia, Unit X-105; Jl New Delhi, Pintu I Senayan) If you love vodka, you'll love this place. Dubbed Jakarta's first vodka bar, Red Square has more of Russia's standard drink than you can drown your sorrows in; it even has a walk-in freezer for knocking back slammers. The interior is modern and chic, as is the clientele.

Burgundy (Map p106; ☎ 3901234; Grand Hyatt Hotel, Jl Thamrin) This is Jakarta's most salubrious drinking haunt, with spectacularly expensive cocktails, avant-garde décor, a ceiling-high cigar humidor and more beautiful people than you can shake a daiquiri at.

Restaurants can also be perfect places for a drink only:

Blowfish (Map pp100-1; ☎ 57991678; Menara Bank Danamon Penthouse 29-F, Jl Prof Dr Satrio) Attracts a 'too cool for school' crowd eager to sip cocktails from such an elevated position.

Cinnabar (Map p106; ☎ 3903615; Plaza Gani Djemat, Jl Imam Bonjol 76-78) Another restaurant-bar frequented by Jakarta's upwardly mobile crowd; great cocktails.

Café Batavia (Map p105; ☎ 6915531; Jl Pintu Besar Utara 14) Historic spot with a touch of colonial living in modern Jakarta.

Face Bar (p113) Modern Southeast Asian bar with plenty of subdued reds and dark woods.

ENTERTAINMENT

Jakarta is Indonesia's most broad-minded, sophisticated and decadent city, with the nightlife to match. Hundreds of bars, discos, karaoke lounges and nightclubs fill the city, and range from sleazy to refined. Some sections of Jakarta still have plenty of money and people partying till dawn in spite of, or perhaps because of, the ongoing economic uncertainty. Bands start around 10pm or 11pm, and continue until 2am or 3am, sometimes later on weekends. During the week many places close at 1am.

Many venues don't have cover charges, though sometimes a first drink cover charge applies in the discos. A beer or a mixed drink costs from 30,000Rp, more in exclusive hotel bars.

Check the entertainment pages of the *Jakarta Post* or *Jakarta Kini* for films, concerts and special events.

Cultural Performances

Taman Ismail Marzuki (TIM; Map p106; ☎ 31937325; pkj_tim@cbn.net.id; Jl Cikini Raya 73) TIM is Jakarta's cultural showcase; there is a performance almost every night and you might see anything from Balinese dancing to poetry readings and gamelan concerts. The TIM monthly programme is available from the tourist office, the TIM office and major hotels. Events are also listed in the *Jakarta Post*.

Gedung Kesenian Jakarta (Map p106; ☎ 3808282; Jl Gedung Kesenian 1) Gedung Kesenian has a regular programme of traditional dance and theatre, as well as European classical music and dance. The Jakarta Visitor Information Office (p103) can provide further information.

Museum Wayang (Map p105; ☎ 6929560; Taman Fatahillah; admission 2000Rp) *Wayang kulit* and *golek* performances are regularly held on Sunday between 10am and 2pm at this museum (p104).

Erasmus Huis (Map pp100-1; ☎ 5241069; www.erasmushuis.or.id; Jl HR Rasuna Said Kav S-3) This cultural centre, along with others in the city, holds regular events; consult its website for more information.

Live Music

West Pacific (Map p110; ☎ 3912025; Jl Thamrin 12) West Pacific is a haunt for those with a thirst for indie/alternative music but are not interested in getting all grunged up. It's also a fine spot to mingle with Jakarta's young movers and shakers.

BB's (Map p106; Jl Cokroaminoto) This blues bar in the heart of Menteng is a good place to catch live bands and meet local students and expats. Drinks are marginally cheaper here than most places.

Jaya Pub (Map p110; Jl Thamrin 12) This Jakarta institution has been around for more than 30 years and isn't showing signs of slowing down. Expect an older crowd and live performers most evenings.

Kafe Pisa (Map p106; ☎ 3100149; Jl Gereja Theresia 1) This eatery-bar has 'daggy' bands (as one expat put it) on weekends, which only add to its lively atmosphere. See also p113.

Nightclubs

Jakarta has some of the biggest clubs in Southeast Asia, with high-tech lighting, massive sound systems and pumping dance music. The clubs open around 9pm, but they don't really get going until midnight, when the bars close. On weekends they are open to 4am or later. Cover charges range from 25,000Rp to 60,000Rp and Wednesday is Ladies' Night, when ladies gain free entry.

Embassy (Map pp100-1; ☎ 5742047; Taman Ria Senayan, Jl Gatot Subroto) Embassy is one of the biggest clubs in the city, with a massive dance floor and plenty of fashionable Jakartans grooving the night away.

Centro (Map pp100-1; ☎ 72780800; Jl Dharmawangsa IX) Another of Jakarta's huge clubs, and one that attracts international DJs on a regular basis.

Retro (Map pp100-1; ☎ 52962828; Crown Plaza Hotel, Jl Gatot Subroto Kav 2-3) This hotel club draws a young, hip crowd at the weekends with a superb sound and light show.

Stadium (Map pp100-1; ☎ 6263323; Jl Hayum Waruk 111 FF-JJ) Glodok's Stadium represents the seediest side of Jakartan clubbing, with sex and dark corners aplenty – most weekends the music pumps nonstop from Friday night until Sunday afternoon.

SHOPPING

Shopping is one of Jakarta's biggest attractions. Clothes, shoes, bags and electrical goods (including DVDs) are very cheap, especially those that are locally made. Brand-name goods are available in profusion, but the genuine ones are rarely any cheaper than you could get them at home. Jakarta has handicrafts from almost everywhere in Indonesia, and while prices are higher than in the places of origin, it's a good opportunity to get an idea of prices if you have just arrived, or to make last-minute purchases if you are just leaving.

Arts & Handicrafts

Flea market (Map p106; Jl Surabaya) Jakarta's famous flea market is in Menteng. It has woodcarvings, furniture, brassware, jewellery, batik, oddities such as old typewriters and many (often instant) antiques. It is always fun to browse, but bargain like crazy – prices may be up to 10 times the value of the goods.

Jl Kebon Sirih Timur (Map p110), the street east of Jl Jaksa, has a number of shops that sell antiques and curios. The quality is high, but so are the prices. Jl Palatehan 1 is just to the north of the Blok M bus terminal (Map pp100–1), and has some interesting antique and craft shops.

Pasar Seni (Map pp100-1; Taman Impian Jaya Ancol) In north Jakarta, this is a good place to look for regional handicrafts and to see many of them being made.

Pasaraya department store (Map pp100-1; Jl Iskandarsyah II/2) Opposite Blok M Mall, Pasaraya has two huge floors that seem to go on forever and are devoted to batik and handicrafts from throughout the archipelago.

Sarinah department store (Map p110; Jl Thamrin) The 3rd floor of this store has a similar range of batik and handicrafts as Pasaraya.

Shopping Centres

Jakarta has more shopping centres than you could spend a month of Sundays in, and the general rule in the capital is, the bigger, the better.

Pasar Pagi Mangga Dua (Map pp100-1; Jl Mangga Dua) This is an enormous wholesale market with some of Jakarta's cheapest clothes, accessories and shoes, as well as a host of other goods. Quality can be a problem, though.

Mangga Dua Mall (Map pp100-1; Jl Mangga Dua) Across the road from Pasar Pagi Mangga Dua, this is the place for computers, electronics and super-cheap DVDs and CDs. The surrounding area has other shopping centres, making it Southeast Asia's biggest shopping precinct.

Blok M (Map pp100-1; Kebayoran Baru) The Blok M Mall, above the large bus terminal, has scores of small, reasonably priced shops offering clothes, shoes, CDs and DVDs. Most goods are of a better standard than those found in Mangga Dua, but only just.

Plaza Indonesia (Map p106; Jl Thamrin) Exclusive and expensive, Plaza Indonesia tops Jakarta's A list for shopping centres, with dozens of designer stores.

Plaza Senayan (Map pp100 1; Jl Asia Afrika) Number two in the shopping centre popularity stakes, this huge plaza has everything from Marks & Spencer to Starbucks. Unfortunately, its designer stores are even more expensive than back home.

GETTING THERE & AWAY

Jakarta is the main international gateway to Indonesia; for details on arriving here from overseas, see Transport (p865). Jakarta is also a major centre for domestic travel, with extensive bus, train, air and boat connections.

Air

International and domestic flights operate from the modern, efficient Soekarno-Hatta international airport; only domestic flights are handled out of the little-used Halim airport. For information on departure tax and international airlines, see p866 and p865 respectively.

Domestic airline offices in Jakarta include the following:

Adam Air (☎ 5507505, 6909999; www.adamair.co.id; Soekarno-Hatta international airport)

Batavia Air (Map p106; ☎ 3840888; www.batavia-air.co.id, in Indonesian only; Jl Ir H Juanda 15)

Garuda (Map p106; ☎ 2311801, 0807 1807807; www.garuda-indonesia.com; Garuda Bldg, Jl Merdeka Selatan 13)

Lion Air (Map p106; ☎ 6326039; www.lionair.co.id; Jl Gajah Mada 7)

Mandala (Map p110; ☎ 3144838; www.mandalaair.com; Jl Wahid Hasyim 84-88)

Merpati Nusantara Airlines (Map pp100-1; ☎ 6548888; www.merpati.co.id; Jl Angkasa Blok B/15 Kav 2-3, Kemayoran)

Sriwijaya Airlines (Map pp100-1; ☎ 6405566; Jl Gunung Sahari)

For information on prices, see the Java Airfares map (p98).

Boat

See p872 for information on the Pelni shipping services that operate on a regular two-week schedule to ports all over the archipelago. The **Pelni ticketing office** (Map pp100-1; ☎ 4212893; www.pelni.com; Jl Angkasa 18) is northeast of the city centre in Kemayoran. Tickets plus commission can also be bought from designated Pelni agents: **Menara Buana Surya** (Map p106; ☎ 3142464; Jl Menteng Raya 29), in the Tedja Buana building, 500m east of Jl Jaksa; or **Kerta Jaya** (Map p106; ☎ 3451518; Jl Veteran I 27), opposite Mesjid Istiqlal.

Direct Pelni destinations from Jakarta include Padang, Tanjung Pandan (Pulau Belitung), Surabaya, Semarang, Muntok (Pulau Bangka), Belawan, Kijang (Pulau Bintan) and Batam. Services on the *Lambelu* to Padang and the *Kelud* to Batam (near Singapore) are of most interest to travellers. To Kalimantan, the *Lawit* goes via Tanjung Pandan to Pontianak. A number of Pelni boats go to Makassar (Sulawesi) via Semarang or Surabaya, but there are no direct services.

Pelni ships all arrive at and depart from Pelabuhan Satu (Dock No 1) at Tanjung Priok, 13km northeast of the city centre. Take bus 1 from Jl Thamrin, opposite Sarinah department store (Map p110); allow at least an hour. The bus terminal is at the old Tanjung Priok train station, from where it is a 1km walk to the dock or 5000Rp by *ojek* (motorcycle that takes passengers). A taxi to Jl Jaksa will cost around 35,000Rp. The **information centre** (☎ 4367487) at the front of the Dock No 1 arrival hall can be helpful, or try the nearby **Pelni Information Office** (Map pp100-1; ☎ 4301260; Jl Palmas 2), though you can't buy tickets here!

Other passenger ships also go from Dock No 1 to Pulau Bintan and Pulau Batam, from where it is just a short ferry ride to Singapore. The *Samudera Jaya* is a small but reasonably comfortable air-con hydrofoil that seats up to 300 passengers. It leaves Tanjung Priok on Saturday at noon and sails to Tanjung Pandan (150,000Rp, 12 hours) on Pulau Belitung, before continuing on to Tanjung Pinang (200,000Rp) and Batam (200,000Rp). Count on a 24-hour trip to Batam. In the reverse direction it leaves Thursday.

Bus

Jakarta's four major bus terminals – Kalideres, Kampung Rambutan, Pulo Gadung and Lebak Bulus – are all a long way from the city centre. In some cases it can take longer getting to the bus terminal than the bus journey itself, making the trains a better alternative for arriving in or leaving Jakarta.

Tickets (some including travel to the terminals) for the better buses can be bought from agencies (p103).

KALIDERES

Buses to the west of Jakarta go from here, about 15km northwest of Merdeka Sq. Frequent buses run to Merak (11,000Rp, three hours) and Labuan (35,000Rp, 3½ hours). A few buses go through to Sumatra from Kalideres, but most Sumatra buses leave from Pulo Gadung bus terminal.

KAMPUNG RAMBUTAN

Buses that travel to areas south and southwest of Jakarta leave from this big bus terminal (Map pp100–1), some 18km south of the centre. It was designed to carry much of Jakarta's intercity bus traffic, but it mostly handles buses to West Java, including Bogor (normal/air-con 7000/10,000Rp, 40 minutes) and Bandung (20,000Rp to 45,000Rp, 4½ hours). Note that it is quicker to take the train to Bogor or Bandung.

PULO GADUNG

Twelve kilometres east of the city centre, Pulo Gadung (Map pp100–1) has buses to Cirebon, Central and East Java, Sumatra and Bali. Many of the air-con, deluxe buses operate from here. This wild bus terminal is the busiest in Indonesia.

The terminal is divided into two sections: one for buses to Sumatra and the other for all buses to the east. Most buses to Sumatra leave between 10am and 3pm, and you can catch a bus right through to Aceh if you are crazy enough. Destinations and fares from here include Bengkulu (150,000Rp to 200,000Rp), Palembang (140,000Rp to 180,000Rp) and also Padang and Bukittinggi (155,000Rp to 220,000Rp). Prices listed are for air-con deluxe buses with reclining seats and toilets – well worth it for those long hauls through Sumatra.

To the east, frequent buses go to Central and East Java and on to Bali. Destinations include Cirebon (23,000Rp to 35,000Rp, four hours) and Yogyakarta (85,000Rp to 115,000Rp, 12 hours).

LEBAK BULUS

This terminal (Map pp100–1) is 16km south of the city centre, and is another departure point for the long-distance deluxe buses to Yogyakarta, Surabaya and Bali. Most bus departures are scheduled for the late afternoon or evening.

Car & Motorcycle

See p119 for details on car hire in Jakarta.

Minibus

Door-to-door *travel* minibuses are not a good option in Jakarta because it can take hours to pick up or drop off passengers in the traffic jams. Some travel agencies book them, but you may have to go to a depot on the city outskirts.

Global Travel Service (Map p110; ☎ 3143932; globalid@indo.net.id; Jl Jaksa 49) Operates direct minibuses to Yogyakarta (150,000Rp).

Media Taxis (Map p110; ☎ 3909010; Jl Johar 15) Has minibuses to Bandung (60,000Rp).

Train

Jakarta's four main train stations are quite central, making trains the easiest way out of the city into Java. The most convenient and important is Gambir station (Map p106), on the eastern side of Merdeka Sq, a 15-minute walk from Jl Jaksa. Gambir handles express trains to Bogor, Bandung, Yogyakarta, Solo, Semarang and Surabaya. Some Gambir trains also stop at Kota (Map p105), the train station in the old city area in the north. The Pasar Senen train station (Map pp100–1) is to the east and mostly has economy-class trains. Tanah Abang (Map pp100–1) train station has economy trains to the west.

For express trains, tickets can be bought in advance at the booking offices at the northern end of Gambir train station, while the ticket windows at the southern end are for tickets bought on the day of departure. You can call for schedules and departure times (☎ 3842777, 3523790) or consult the helpful staff at the station's **information office** (☎ 6929194; 🕑 24hr).

To get to Jl Jaksa, avoid the taxi booking desk inside Gambir station and head outside to the long line of taxis, or make your way to the main road and hail a *bajaj* (motorised three-wheeler taxi); the fare will be around 20,000Rp or 10,000Rp respectively.

If you need a hotel, there is an **Indohotel** (☎ 345080) desk inside the station.

BOGOR

No-frills, economy-class trains from Gambir to Bogor are part of the city rail network and can be horribly crowded during rush hours (watch your gear), but at other times they are quite tolerable and provide an efficient service. They can also be boarded at Gondangdia train station (Map p110), only a short stroll from Jl Jaksa. They leave Gondangdia every 20 minutes from 7am until 9.13pm and cost 2500Rp for the 90-minute journey. Better *Pakuan Express* trains (10,000Rp, one hour) leave from Gambir much more infrequently.

BANDUNG

The easiest way to get to Bandung is by train. The journey is very scenic as the train climbs into the hills before Bandung. It is best to book in advance and essential on weekends and public holidays.

The efficient and comfortable *Parahyangan* service departs from Gambir train station heading for Bandung (business/executive 45,000/65,000Rp, three hours) roughly every hour between 4.40am and 10.15pm. The more luxurious *Argo Gede* (executive 75,000Rp, 2½ hours) departs approximately every two hours from 6.20am to 7.30pm.

CIREBON

Most trains that run along the north coast or to Yogyakarta go through Cirebon. One of the best services is the *Cirebon Express* (business/executive 50,000/65,000Rp, 3½ hours) departing from Gambir train station at 5.55am, 9.40am, 10.45am, 1.45pm and 6.15pm.

YOGYAKARTA & SOLO

The most luxurious trains are the *Argo Lawu* (210,000Rp, seven hours) departing at 8pm, and the *Argo Dwipangga* (210,000Rp, eight hours) departing at 8am. These trains go to Solo and stop at Yogyakarta, 45 minutes before Solo, but cost the same to either destination.

Cheaper services from the Pasar Senen train station to Yogyakarta are the *Fajar Utama Yogya* (business 100,000Rp, eight hours), departing at 6.20am; and the *Senja Utama Yogya* (100,000Rp, nine hours) at 7.30pm. The *Senja Utama Solo* goes to Solo (100,000Rp, 10 hours) at 8.25pm and also stops in Yogyakarta.

SURABAYA

Most trains between Jakarta and Surabaya take the shorter northern route via Semarang, though a few take the longer southern route via Yogyakarta. Express trains range from the *Jayabaya Selatan* (business 120,000Rp, 12 hours), that departs from Kota at 2pm and travels via Yogyakarta and Solo, to the luxurious *Argo Bromo Anggrek* (special executive class from 200,000Rp, nine hours), which departs from Gambir at 8.05am, 9.15am, 3.50pm and 9.15pm.

GETTING AROUND

To/From the Airport

Jakarta's Soekarno-Hatta international airport is 35km west of the city centre. A toll road links the airport to the city and the journey takes about an hour (longer during rush hours).

Damri (☎ 4603708, 5501290) airport buses (15,000Rp) depart every 30 minutes starting around 5am and continuing till 6.30pm between the airport and Gambir train station (near Jl Jaksa) in central Jakarta. From Gambir train station to Jl Jaksa, take a *bajaj* (10,000Rp or less with bargaining) or taxi (25,000Rp from the overpriced taxi desk), or walk (it is just under 1km).

Taxis from the airport to Jl Thamrin/Jl Jaksa cost about 150,000Rp if booked from one of the taxi desks or 100,000Rp on the meter. On top of the metered fare, you have to pay around 10,000Rp in toll-road charges. Take metered taxis from the booth outside the arrival area, *not* the private drivers that assail you.

Bajaj & Other Local Transport

Bajaj (pronounced 'ba-jai') are nothing more than Indian auto-rickshaws: orange three-wheelers that carry two passengers (three if you're tiny) and sputter around on noisy two-stroke engines. They are pretty much open to the elements – locals joke that they also offer *AC alam* (natural air-con) as standard. Short trips such as Jl Jaksa to the main post office will cost about 10,000Rp. They're good value, especially during rush hours, but hard bargaining is required. Always agree on the price beforehand. *Bajaj* are not allowed along main streets such as Jl Thamrin, so make sure they don't simply drop you off at the border.

Jakarta has some other weird and wonderful means of getting around. Bemos are the original three-wheelers from the 1960s that still operate around Glodok and other parts of Jakarta. In the back streets of Kota, pushbikes with a padded 'kiddy carrier' on the back will take you for a ride!

The *helicak*, cousin to the *bajaj*, is a green motorcycle contraption with a passenger car mounted on the front. Jakarta also has *ojeks*, which are motorcycles that take pillion passengers. Weaving in and out of Jakarta's traffic on the back of an *ojek* is decidedly risky. Becak (bicycle-rickshaws) have been banned from the city and only a few tourist becak remain at Ancol.

Bus

Jakarta has a comprehensive city bus network. Around town at least a dozen bus companies run a knot of routes. Big, regular city buses charge a fixed 2000Rp fare. The big express *patas* buses also charge 2000Rp and the air-con *transjakarta* buses cost 3500Rp; these are usually less crowded and are the best option. At the time of writing, only three *transjakarta* lines were in operation but another 15 were planned for the coming years.

These services are supplemented by orange toy-sized buses and, in a few areas, by pale-blue *mikrolet* buses that cost 2000Rp. The main terminal for *mikrolet* and the numerous red and blue Metro Mini buses is at the Pasar Senen station. Note that the crowded buses have their fair share of pickpockets and bag slashers; the more expensive buses are generally safer, as well as being more comfortable.

The tourist office can provide a little information on buses around Jakarta. Some useful buses:

ACB1 Blok M to Kota via Jl Sudirman and Jl Thamrin.
Korridor I Blok M to Kota via Jl Sudirman and Jl Thamrin.
Korridor II Harmoni bus terminal to Pulo Gadung.
Korridor III Harmoni to Kalideres bus terminal.
P38 Blok M to Tanjung Priok via Jl Gatot Subroto.
P125 Blok M to Tanjung Priok via Jl Jenderal Sudirman.
S77 Blok M to Ragunan via Kemang.

Car

Jakarta has branches of the major car-rental operators, including **Avis** (Map p106; ☎ 3142900; Jl Diponegoro 25), **Bluebird** (Map pp100-1; ☎ 7941234; Jl Mampang Prapatan Raya 6) and **Astra** (Map pp100-1; ☎ 6508919; Jl Gaya Motor 1/10). Alternatively, inquire at the cheaper travel agencies, as a vehicle with driver may be the most economical option.

A number of the 'transport' guys who hang out on Jl Jaksa can offer some of the best deals if you negotiate directly with them, avoiding hotel or travel agency commission.

The big operators charge about 500,000Rp per day with a driver (400,000Rp without), while private operators may ask for around 10% less.

Taxi

Taxis in Jakarta are metered and cost 5000Rp for the first kilometre and 250Rp for each subsequent 100m. Make sure the meter *(argo)* is used. Many taxi drivers provide a good service, but Jakarta has enough rogues to give its taxis a bad reputation and a number of travellers have complained about pushy drivers. Tipping is expected, if not demanded, but not obligatory. It is customary to round the fare up to the next 1000Rp. Carry plenty of small notes – Jakarta taxi drivers rarely give change.

Bluebird cabs (☎ 7941234, 7981001) are pale blue, and have the best reputation; a minimum of 20,000Rp is charged for ordered taxis. Any toll road charges and parking fees – there are lots of them – are extra and paid by the passenger.

AROUND JAKARTA

Pulau Seribu

☎ 021 / pop 15,000

A popular destination for locals and expats alike lies only kilometres from the polluted harbour of Jakarta. Pulau Seribu (Thousand Islands), a string of islands in the Bay of Jakarta, is the perfect respite for those stuck in the capital too long, or those who simply want a taste of island life without hopping on a bus, train or plane.

Despite the misleading name, there are actually only 130 islands in the group, and of these, 37 have been used for commercial purposes. **Pulau Pramuka** is the group's district centre, but most people live on **Pulau Kelapa**, which is about 15km north of Jakarta. Near Pulau Kelapa, **Pulau Panjang** has the only airstrip on the islands.

While many of those accessible to tourists have been developed by resorts, the beaches remain white, the seas calm and clean (aside from the islands close to the mainland), and the pace of life unhurried.

All the resorts have individual bungalows with attached bathrooms and provide water sports facilities, including diving. While comfortable, none are international-standard resorts, despite the prices. Most resorts offer packages that also include buffet-only meals and transport. Weekends are up to 50% more expensive than prices quoted here and hefty single supplements apply (quotes are usually per person, based on two sharing). Most resorts also charge inflated rates for the first night, offering discounts of up to 30% for additional nights. The resorts have offices in Jakarta or at the **Ancol Marina** (Map pp100-1; ☎ 64711822; Taman Impian Jaya Ancol) for bookings. As well as booking through their respective offices, you can make reservations through the **Jakarta Visitor Information Office** (Map p110; ☎ 3154094, 3161293; www.jakarta.go.id; Jl Wahid Hasyim 9; 9am-5pm Mon-Fri, 9am-1pm Sat), allowing for better comparisons.

Getting There & Around

The resorts have daily speedboats from Jakarta's Ancol Marina for guests and day-trippers, usually leaving around 8am and returning around 2pm. Even the furthest islands take only a little over two hours to reach. Return day-trip rates to the resorts with lunch include Pulau Bidadari (125,000Rp), Pulau Ayer (230,000Rp), Pulau Kotok (550,000Rp), Pulau Putri (455,000Rp) and Pulau Sepa (438,000Rp). Gray Line also offers day trips to the islands (p109).

You should have little problem finding someone to ferry you from one island to the next (but prices vary widely, depending on where you want to go) and most islands are small enough to easily explore on foot.

PULAU BIDADARI

This is the closest resort island and is popular with Jakarta residents for day trips. It is one of the least interesting resorts, but you can use it to visit other islands such as **Pulau Kahyangan**; **Pulau Kelor**, which has the ruins of an old Dutch fort; or **Pulau Onrust**, where the remains of an 18th-century shipyard can be explored. Boats can be hired for the short trip from Pulau Bidadari for 30,000Rp per hour.

The island's **resort** (per person with full board from 446,000Rp) has a variety of simple cottages and sports facilities, and can be booked at **Ancol Marina** (Map pp100-1; ☎ 64711822; Taman Impian Jaya Ancol).

PULAU AYER

Pulau Ayer is a little further north and is another popular day-trip destination. Its **resort** (☎ 3852004; www.pulauayer.com/cottages.htm; packages with full board 1st/additional night from 540,000/440,000Rp) has comfortable cottages and a small stretch of good beach with cloudy water.

PULAU KOTOK

Near the islands' administrative centre is Pulau Kotok, an island with reputedly some of the best reef for snorkelling and diving around.

On the western side of Kotok, **Kul Kul Kotok Island Resort** (bungalows with fan/air-con from 600,000/625,000Rp, with full board & transfers 900,000/925,000Rp;) is about the quietest and most traditional option, scoring high marks in the deserted tropical island stakes. It also offers diving from the resort, or direct from Ancol (two boat dives, lunch and transport for 1,400,000Rp). The resort can be booked through its **Jakarta office** (☎ 53675634; www.alamresorts.com/lang-en/kotok; Jl Bima 14).

PULAU PUTRI

About 4km north of Pulau Kelapa is Pulau Putri, which is notable for its aquariums and restaurants. Its **resort** (packages 1st/additional night from 1,100,000/880,000Rp;), which consists of rustic yet charming cottages, has an idyllic setting at the north of the island; it can be booked through **PT Buana Bintang Samudra** (☎ 8281093; Jl Sultan Agung 21).

PULAU SEPA

Pulau Sepa is another island near Pulau Putri; it's quite small (by foot, it takes about 10 minutes to circumnavigate) and is surrounded by wide stretches of pristine white sand.

Rooms at **Pulau Sepa Resort** (full-board packages 1st/additional night from 688,000/448,000Rp;) have hot water but are really just a better class of losmen, while bungalows are also simple but have more character. Book through **PT Pulau Sepa Permai** (Map pp100-1; ☎ 63863477; Jl Kyai Caringin 20).

PULAU BIRA

Pulau Bira is a more developed island, with good beaches and the added advantage of a golf course.

Bira Resort (bungalows with full board 1st/additional night 1,235,000/718,000Rp;) has spacious, well-equipped bungalows and the island's golf course; book through **PT Buana Bintang Samudra** (☎ 8281093; Jl Sultan Agung 21).

PULAU ANTUK TIMUR & ANTUK BARAT

Pulau Antuk Timur and Pulau Antuk Barat are some of the most northerly islands and are separated by a small channel. Both of them are home to Pulau Seribu's fanciest resort.

The upmarket **Pulau Seribu Marine Resort** (packages with full board 1,600,000Rp;) has very comfortable bungalows and a range of facilities considerably better than other islands. Full-board packages cost 200,000Rp more at weekends. This, along with other resorts, can be booked through **Viany Tour & Travel** (Map pp100-1; ☎ 6453377; www.vianytravel.com; Jl Lodan Timur 7, Taman Impian Jaya Ancol).

WEST JAVA

Many tourists experience the lush, volcanic panoramas of West Java (Jawa Barat) through the murky window of a speeding bus. In the rush to get to Yogyakarta and the high-profile attractions of Central Java, those with limited time make a beeline through the province, stopping for breath only in the regional capital, Bandung. But this dramatic, diverse region, historically known as Sunda and still home to the Sundanese people, has a fair few marvels of its own. Many of these marvels are off the beaten track, but while they will take some extra time to get to, they are well worth searching out.

Covering 46,229 sq km, West Java stretches from the remote islands of the Ujung Kulon National Park (last Javan home of the one-horned rhino) in the west to the waterways, sweeping beaches and bars of the beach resort of Pangandaran in the east. In between, you can also visit the infamous offshore volcano of Krakatau, kick back in the chilled coastal resorts of the west coast and stroll through Bogor's lush botanical gardens.

JAKARTA TO MERAK

Most visitors just head straight from Jakarta to Merak on their way to (or from) Sumatra, simply because there's not a lot in this area to attract your attention. From here it is possible to head for the west coast though, and the historic town of Banten can be an intriguing diversion if you have time to kill.

Banten

On the coast due north of Serang, the dusty fishing village of Banten was once a great maritime capital, where the Dutch and English first landed in Java to secure trade and struggle for economic supremacy.

Banten reached its peak during the reign of Sultan Agung (1651–83), and in 1680 he declared war on the Dutch, but internal conflict within the royal house ultimately led to his downfall. Agung fled Banten but finally surrendered in 1683, and his defeat marked the real beginning of Dutch territorial expansion in Java.

The chief landmark of a prosperous era, the 16th-century mosque **Mesjid Agung** dominates the village. This is a good example of early Islamic architecture, though its great white minaret was reputedly designed by a Chinese Muslim.

Next to the mosque is an **archaeological museum** (admission 2000Rp; 9am-4pm Tue-Sun), which has a modest collection of local clay artefacts, and a few of the long iron chained spikes for which the 'Debus players' are famous. Banten has long been a centre for practitioners of the Debus tradition, which is supposed to have come from India. These Islamic ascetics engage in masochistic activities such as plunging sharp weapons into their bodies (without drawing blood!) and are able to control the pain by the strength of their faith.

Directly across from the mosque is the large grass-covered site of Hasanuddin's fortified palace, the **Surosowan**, which was wrecked in the bloody civil war during the reign of Sultan Agung. It was rebuilt, only to be razed to the ground by the Dutch in 1832. Hasanuddin was a powerful ruler in the early 1500s who spread Banten's authority to the pepper-producing district of Lampung in southern Sumatra.

Other points of interest around the mosque include the massive ruins of **Fort Speelwijk** to the northwest; opposite the entrance to the fort is a **Chinese temple**, dating from the 18th century, which is still in use. Back along the road to Serang are the huge crumbling walls and archways of the **Kaibon** palace, and nearby is the **tomb of Maulana Yusuf**, who died in 1580.

GETTING THERE & AWAY

Take a bus from Jakarta's Kalideres bus terminal to Serang (12,000Rp, 1½ hours),

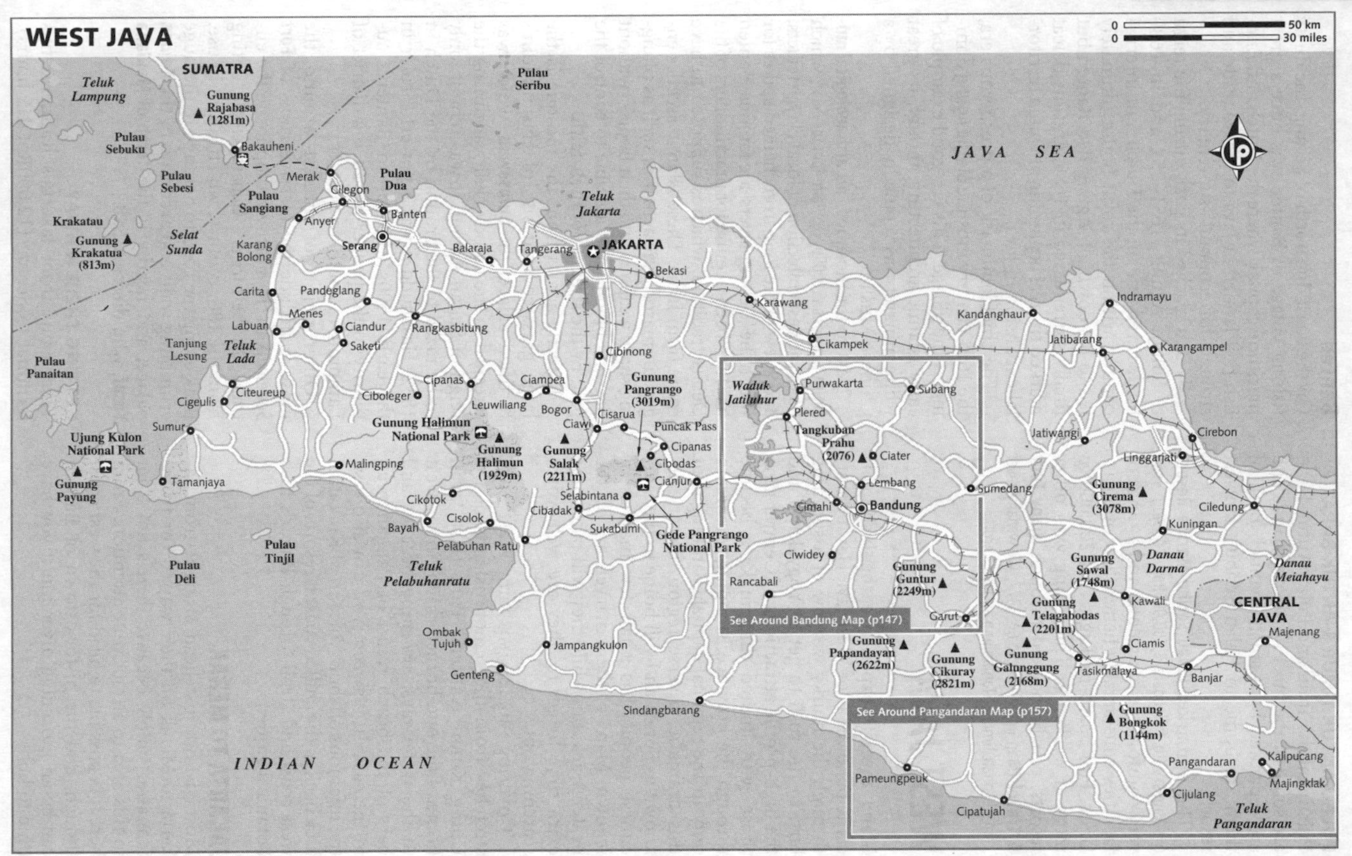
WEST JAVA
0 50 km
0 30 miles
JAVA SEA
INDIAN OCEAN
SUMATRA
Teluk Lampung
Gunung Rajabasa (1281m)
Pulau Seribu
Pulau Sebuku
Bakauheni
Pulau Sebesi
Merak
Pulau Dua
Cilegon
Pulau Sangiang
Banten
Anyer
Teluk Jakarta
Krakatau
Gunung Krakatua (813m)
Selat Sunda
Serang
Karang Bolong
Balaraja
Tangerang
JAKARTA
Bekasi
Carita
Pandeglang
Menes
Labuan
Ciandur
Saketi
Rangkasbitung
Karawang
Indramayu
Kandanghaur
Cikampek
Jatibarang
Karangampel
Tanjung Lesung
Teluk Lada
Cibinong
Pulau Panaitan
Citeureup
Cigeulis
Cipanas
Ciboleger
Ciampea
Leuwiliang
Bogor
Gunung Pangrango (3019m)
Cisarua
Waduk Jatiluhur
Purwakarta
Subang
Plered
Tangkuban Prahu (2076)
Ciater
Lembang
Bandung
Cimahi
Sumur
Ujung Kulon National Park
Gunung Payung
Tamanjaya
Gunung Halimun National Park
Gunung Halimun (1929m)
Ciawi
Gunung Salak (2211m)
Puncak Pass
Cipanas
Cibodas
Cianjur
Malingping
Selabintana
Cibadak
Sukabumi
Gede Pangrango National Park
Cikotok
Cisolok
Bayah
Pelabuhan Ratu
Pulau Tinjil
Pulau Deli
Teluk Pelabuhanratu
Ciwidey
Rancabali
Gunung Guntur (2249m)
See Around Bandung Map (p147)
Garut
Jatiwangi
Cirebon
Linggarjati
Sumedang
Gunung Cirema (3078m)
Ciledung
Kuningan
Gunung Sawal (1748m)
Danau Darma
Danau Meiahayu
Kawali
CENTRAL JAVA
Gunung Telagabodas (2201m)
Majenang
Ciamis
Gunung Galunggung (2168m)
Tasikmalaya
Banjar
Gunung Papandayan (2622m)
Gunung Cikuray (2821m)
Ombak Tujuh
Jampangkulon
Genteng
Sindangbarang
See Around Pangandaran Map (p157)
Gunung Bongkok (1144m)
Pameungpeuk
Cipatujah
Pangandaran
Kalipucang
Majingklak
Cijulang
Teluk Pangandaran

SUNDANESE MUSIC & DANCE

Sundanese instrument makers are highly innovative and are capable of producing a sweet sound from just about anything. Of their better-known designs, the *kecapi* (a type of plucked lute) is the most idiosyncratic and is often accompanied by the *suling*, a soft-toned bamboo flute that fades in and out of the long vibrating notes of the *kecapi*. The *angklung* is less gainly in appearance and consists of a series of bamboo pieces of differing length and diameter, loosely suspended from a bamboo frame. When shaken, it produces an unlikely echoing sound.

Another traditional form is *gamelan degung*. This is played like Central Javanese gamelan, by a small ensemble, but with the addition of a set of small, suspended gongs *(degung)* and an accompanying *suling*. The music produced exists in the hinterland and has a sound somewhere between the soporific Central Javan and livelier Balinese styles of gamelan.

The best-known, contemporary West Javan dance form, Jaipongan, is a whirlwind of fast drumming and erotic movement, interspersed with a good dose of *pencak silat* (Indonesian martial arts) and a flick of New York–style break dancing. Jaipongan dance/music is a recent mutation of a more traditional Sundanese form called Ketuktilu, in which a group of professional female dancers (sometimes prostitutes) dance for male spectators.

Other dance forms include Longser, Joker and Ogel. Longser and Joker involve the passing of a sash between two couples. Ogel is a slow and exhaustive form, featuring measured movements and a rehearsal regime that many young performers simply lack the time or patience for.

10km south of Banten, from where a minibus (2000Rp, 30 minutes) will drop you near the Mesjid Agung.

Pulau Dua Bird Sanctuary

Off the north coast at Banten, Pulau Dua is one of Indonesia's major bird sanctuaries. The island has a large resident population – mainly herons, storks and cormorants – but the peak time is between March and July, when great numbers of migratory birds flock here for the breeding season.

It's a half-hour trip by chartered boat from the Karanghantu harbour in Banten, but you can walk across the fish ponds (via bridges) to the island. From Banten, take an *angkot* (minibus) 5km east to Sawahluhur village. The trail to the island starts 100m or so before the village and then it's a hot 1km walk, weaving between the fish ponds – just keep heading for the trees on the horizon. There is a Perlindungan Hutan dan Konservasi Alam (PHKA) post with a derelict hut that has bare wooden beds and not much else. If you are planning to stay bring food and water.

MERAK

☎ 0254

Right on the northwestern tip of Java, 140km from Jakarta, Merak is the terminus for ferries shuttling to and from Bakauheni on the southern end of Sumatra. Think of it only as an arrival and departure point, and you won't be disappointed by this rough-and-ready town.

Hotel Anda (☎ 571041; Jl Raya Pulorida 4; r from 45,000Rp, with air-con from 85,000Rp; ❄) will do if you're stuck; rooms are basic but staff are friendly and it's right opposite the ferry terminal.

Getting There & Away

The bus terminal and train station are at the ferry dock.

BOAT

Ferries to Bakauheni in Sumatra depart every 30 minutes, 24 hours a day (see also p379). Ferries cost 8000/10,000Rp in economy/business class and take two hours. Alternatively, the slightly less-frequent Dermaga is a fast, passenger-only ferry to Bagoni, taking 45 minutes and costing 30,000Rp. The through-buses to Bandarlampung are the easiest option.

BUS

There are frequent buses making the run between Merak and Jakarta (economy 11,000Rp, three hours; express 20,000Rp, two hours). Most terminate at Jakarta's Kalideres bus terminal, but buses also run to/from Pulo Gadung and Kampung Rambutan. Other buses run all over Java, including Bogor (20,000Rp) and Bandung (normal/air-con 30,000/45,000Rp).

Buses leave from the front of the Merak bus terminal for Serang (5000Rp) and Cilegon (4000Rp); for Labuan (8000Rp), a change at Cilegon is required.

TRAIN

A business train to Jakarta (16,500Rp, three hours) departs at 12.30pm, but is sometimes cancelled; a slower economy-class train (6500Rp, five hours) leaves at 6am and 2pm.

WEST-COAST BEACHES

The west-coast beaches of Java are some of the best on the island; good surf, calm swimming spots and sparkling white sand. It's not Bali, but it makes a pleasant break from Jakarta, which, if you turn up on a weekend, you'll notice is common knowledge to many Jakartans.

Apart from the multiplying resorts, the area is sparsely populated. The main place of interest is Carita, for arranging tours to Krakatau (p126), visible on the horizon from most of the resorts, and Ujung Kulon National Park (p128). Strangely, this area is also notorious for motorcycle theft; if you bring your own vehicle, keep a close eye on it.

Anyer & Karang Bolong

☎ 0254

Anyer, some 14km to the southwest of Cilegon, is easily the most upmarket village along the west coast. Here you'll find the west coast's semi-luxurious resorts and decent beaches. Anyer was once the biggest Dutch port on Selat Sunda before being totally destroyed by the tidal waves generated by the eruption of Krakatau. The **Anyer lighthouse** was built by the Dutch at the instigation of King Willem III in 1885.

Karang Bolong, 11km south of Anyer and 30km north of Labuan, also has a good beach. A huge stand of rock forms a natural archway from the land to the sea.

SLEEPING

The resorts along this stretch of coast are expensive, but the standards are generally high. They are spaced out over a 5km stretch and start just south of the Anyer market; the better places are past the Anyer lighthouse.

At weekends the hotels fill up and prices are 20% to 30% more than the weekday rates quoted here. Discounts are sometimes available during the week.

Hotel Mambruk Anyer (☎ 601602; www.mambruk.co.id; r from 560,000Rp plus 21% tax; ❄) Mambruk is the first place south of the lighthouse; it is hacienda style and has a good range of facilities and decent rooms, but only a ribbon of beach.

Anyer Cottage (☎ 601556; r from 750,000Rp, traditional bungalows 1,500,000Rp plus 21% tax; ❄ 🏊) At the 21km mark heading to Carita is Anyer Cottage, with an inviting yellow-sand beach and a relaxed, beachy atmosphere. Rooms, cottages and bungalows are a little worn around the edges on the outside, but indoors they're comfy and cool. Expect heavy discounts on weekdays.

Sol Elite Marbella (☎ 602345; www.solelitemarbella.com; r from 1,080,000Rp plus 21% tax; ❄ 🏊) Owned by a Spaniard, this 580-room giant is more than a little reminiscent of the super-resorts of the Iberian Costas. Half hotel, half shopping mall, this has it all, with swimming pools, shops, restaurants and a host of activities. The beach is also appealing, as long as it isn't in the hotel's enormous shadow.

Pondok Tubagus Resort (☎ 601776; tropical tents 1,250,000Rp, cottages from 2,750,000Rp; ❄ 🏊) This is one of the classiest resorts on the coast. It looks more like a tidy village than an expensive hotel. Cottages are in excellent condition, and the breezier 'tents' are right on the beach.

EATING

Marina Anyer Kafe (mains 20,000-50,000Rp; 🕑 lunch & dinner) A little further south of Sol Elite Marbella and just before Karang Bolong is the marina housing the Anyer Kafe. It faces the waterfront and is a fashionable spot for a drink or light meal. Bands play on the weekend.

Griya Anyer Spa (☎ 602577; Jl Griya Anyer, Km 127; mains around 50,000Rp; 🕑 lunch & dinner) On the very northern edge of Anyer, 2.5km before the Hotel Mambruk Anyer, is Griya, a top-notch Japanese and seafood restaurant in pleasant, airy surrounds. If you want to make a day of it, there is also a full complement of massage and spa treatments available.

Sol Elite Marbella (mains around 50,000Rp; 🕑 lunch & dinner) This offers good dining options. You can get a good paella, among other things, here.

Seafood warungs are scattered along the coast from Anyer to Karang Bolong and provide the only cheap dining.

GETTING THERE & AWAY

Most visitors to Anyer go by car from Jakarta – 2½ to three hours via the toll road (turn off at Cilegon). By bus from Jakarta, take a Merak bus (11,000Rp) and get off at Cilegon, from where infrequent buses and frequent minibuses run to Labuan via Anyer (5000Rp) and Karang Bolong.

Carita

☎ 0253

Carita has a more rustic and laidback feel than Anyer, with a wide beach that's good for swimming and wandering. It's the most popular beach for travellers because it has moderately priced accommodation and is the best place to arrange visits to Krakatau (p126) and Ujung Kulon National Park (p128).

A new tourist information office was under construction at the time of research; look for it around 500m north of Rakata Hotel. Heading north from Labuan port, the usual access point, Carita proper starts around the Km 8 mark.

SIGHTS

About 2km from Carita over the rice paddies you can see the village of **Sindanglaut** (End of the Sea), which is where the giant tsunami of 1883 ended its destructive run. **Hutan Wisata Carita** is a forest reserve with walks through the hills and jungle. **Curug Gendang** waterfall is a three-hour return hike through the reserve.

ACTIVITIES

The big hotels or travel agencies such as **Black Rhino** (☎ 802818; blackrhinojva@yahoo.com), next to the Sunset View hotel, can arrange diving. Boats and diving equipment can also be hired through **Marina Lippo Carita** (☎ 801525); Rakata Hotel is another contact point for diving tours. Equipment rental starts at 250,000Rp, while a boat to Krakatau starts at 1,800,000Rp (maximum six). The best diving is in Ujung Kulon National Park, but Krakatau and Pulau Sanghiang are also of interest.

TOURS

In Carita, a number of operators offer tours to Krakatau and Ujung Kulon. Their rates tend to be better than those offered by the big hotels. Black Rhino (left) and Rakata Hotel (below) can help out with tours. All operators offer almost identical tours to Krakatau and Ujung Kulon (from US$225 per person for four days and three nights), as well as Badui villages (one-day/overnight trip US$90/140).

SLEEPING

Carita is the place to find budget to midrange hotels.

Sunset View (☎ 801075; r 60,000Rp, with air-con 120,000Rp;) Sunset View is close to the cheapest place on the coast, and it shows; rooms are small, dark and pokey, but if you're going to spend the day on the beach or diving, it probably won't matter much.

Rakata Hotel (☎ 801171; r 65,000Rp, with air-con & TV 140,000Rp;) Rakata is situated in the middle of Carita, and is a solid bet for those looking for a clean room and a soft bed. It has a good restaurant and can organise tours to Ujung Kulon and Krakatau. The bright rooms are a reasonable deal in Carita. All rates are pricier at the weekend.

Niguadharma Hotel (☎ 803288; economy/air-con r 100,000/220,000R;) Not far from the Km 10 mark, this used to be a very attractive boutique hotel, but sparrow droppings and sea air have taken their toll. The central pool looks very inviting, and rooms are set back from the busy road.

Carita Baka Baka (☎ 801126; r from 100,000Rp, 10-person bungalows from 300,000Rp;) Like many of the hotels and resorts along the west coast, Carita Baka Baka is looking battered by the sea air, but it has an idyllic spot right on the beach and is surrounded by palm trees. Rates are more than double on the weekends.

Krakatau Surf Carita (☎ 803848; villas from 600,000Rp plus 21% tax;) Perched on the beach with a view of the crashing surf and Krakatau in the background, this small place has a superb location. It's also one of the most luxurious spots in Carita.

Mutiara Carita (☎ 801069; www.mutiara-carita.com; cottages from 300,000Rp, beach-front cottages from 1,050,000Rp;) This large complex of cottages and bungalows occupies the southern point of Carita Bay. Its cottages are spacious and immaculate, there's a private beach, and activities are organised to entertain the kids on a regular basis.

EATING

Carita has plenty of warungs and *rumah makan* (restaurants) lining the beach and main drag, along with a couple of good restaurants.

Diminati (mains 5000-15,000Rp; breakfast, lunch & dinner) Opposite Carita marina is this simple place, with 'Mama' at the helm and homemade Indonesian dishes on the menu. It's a good place to hang out and swap stories with fellow backpackers, if there are any around.

Carita Baka Baka (mains 30,000-70,000Rp; lunch & dinner) At the hotel of the same name, this open restaurant occupies a perfect spot right on the beach, but the food can be hit and miss.

Valentine Restaurant (mains 35,000-70,000Rp; lunch & dinner) Opposite the Krakatau Surf, Valentine is the most upmarket eating option in Carita, with a pleasant, airy ambience and a plethora of fish dishes. You could always try the frog specialities if you so desire.

GETTING THERE & AWAY

To get to Carita from Jakarta, take a bus to Labuan and then a Colt or *angkot* to Carita (4000Rp). Overcharging is common.

To Anyer, an *angkot* costs around 6000Rp.

LABUAN

☎ 0253

The dreary little port of Labuan is merely a jumping-off point for Carita or for Ujung Kulon National Park (p128), but it is home to the **Labuan PHKA office** (☎ 801731; 8am-4pm Mon-Fri). This office is 2km north of town towards Carita and is a helpful spot for travellers wishing to visit Ujung Kulon independently.

Carita is so close that it's not even worth considering an overnight stay in this dumpy town.

Frequent buses depart from Kalideres bus terminal in Jakarta for Labuan (35,000Rp, 3½ hours) via Serang and Pandeglang. Frequent buses also operate between Labuan and Bogor (20,000Rp, four hours), while the only bus to Bandung (30,000Rp, seven hours) leaves at 6am.

Angkot for Carita (4000Rp, 30 minutes) leave from the market, 100m from the Labuan bus terminal.

TANJUNG LESUNG

☎ 0253

Tanjung Lesung, 30km southwest of Labuan, is a quiet and unspoilt peninsula with beautiful beaches and untouched Sundanese villages. Accommodation is limited to a couple of relatively upmarket resorts.

Near the resort hotel, **Tanjung Lesung Sailing Club** (☎ 802904; cottages weekdays/weekends from 200,000/250,000Rp plus 21% tax) has boat rental and pleasant, but more basic, cottage accommodation. It also has a bar and restaurant.

Tanjung Lesung Resort Hotel (☎ 802900, in Jakarta 021-5727270; www.tanjunglesung.com; cottages weekdays/weekends from 756,000/1,500,000Rp plus 21% tax;) may be having an identity crisis (is it a resort or hotel?), but either way you look at it, the four-star comfort and peaceful surroundings offered are very welcome. It has a spa and restaurant, and the price includes breakfast and dinner.

From Labuan, you can take an *angkot* to Citeureup (12,000Rp, 45 minutes) and then hire an *ojek* (5000Rp, 10 minutes) to the resort or sailing club.

GUNUNG KRAKATAU

The legendary peak of Krakatau, the most famous of the world's famous volcanoes, is a name almost everyone knows – but few actually know of its location (take the film makers of *Krakatoa, East of Java*, for instance). Resting in relative peace some 50km from the West Java coast and 40km from Sumatra, the volcano is nowadays a shadow of its former self – a small group of disconnected islands centred on **Anak Krakatau** (Child of Krakatau), a volcanic mass that has been on the boil since 1928.

The highlight of any trip to Krakatau is rounding Pulau Rakata and first glimpsing the menacing peak of Krakatau's child.

Information

Labuan PHKA office (☎ 801731; 8am-4pm Mon-Fri) has information on the volcano; otherwise consult your hotel reception for information on tours and Anak Krakatau's current activity status.

Activities

Boat trips are the only way to visit Krakatau. It's sometimes possible to land on the eastern side of Anak Krakatau. At the time of writing, organised tours were taking visitors about 150m up the side of Anak Krakatau, and on walking and snorkelling tours to neighbouring islands. Walking to the edge of the caldera is never advisable, and you should seek qualified advice before making any trip to the volcano.

Getting There & Away

Most visitors to Krakatau come from Carita or the other beach resorts on the west coast of Java. However, Krakatau officially lies in Sumatra's Lampung province, and it is slightly quicker and cheaper to reach Krakatau from the small port of Kalianda, 30km north of the ferry terminal at Bakauheni (p482).

Tour operators out of Carita (see p125) will take down the names of interested travellers wanting to share a ride, but usually the numbers just aren't available and you will have to charter.

Prices vary depending on the quality of the boat, but always charter the best boat you can afford. During the rainy season (November to March) there are strong currents and rough seas, but even during the dry season strong southeast winds can whip up the swells and make a crossing inadvisable. When weather conditions are fine it's a long one-day trip, but it's definitely worth the effort – *if* you can hire a safe boat.

Small fishing boats may be cheap, but so are the tales of travellers who spent the night, or longer, adrift in high swells. Reliable boats with radios and life jackets cost

THE WORLD'S LOUDEST RECORDED BANG

Few volcanoes have as explosive a place in history as Krakatau, the island that blew itself apart in 1883 with the loudest bang ever recorded on earth. Turning day into night and hurling devastating tsunamis against the shores of Java and Sumatra, Krakatau quickly became volcanology's A-list celebrity.

Few would have guessed that Krakatau would have snuffed itself out with such a devastating swan song. It had been dormant since 1680 and was regarded as little more than a familiar nautical landmark for maritime traffic passing through the narrow Selat Sunda.

But from May through to early August in 1883, passing ships reported moderate activity, and by 26 August Krakatau was raging.

At 10am on 27 August 1883, Krakatau erupted so explosively that on the island of Rodriguez, more than 4600km to the southwest, a police chief reported hearing the booming of 'heavy guns from eastward'.

With its cataclysmic eruptions, Krakatau sent up a record column of ash 80km high and threw into the air nearly 20 cu kilometres of rock. Ash fell on Singapore 840km to the north and on ships as far as 6000km away; darkness covered Selat Sunda from 10am on 27 August until dawn the next day.

Far more destructive were the great ocean waves that were triggered by the collapse of Krakatau's cones into its empty belly. A giant tsunami, more than 40m high, swept over the nearby shores of Java and Sumatra, and the sea wave's passage was recorded far from Krakatau, reaching Aden (on the Arabian Peninsula) in 12 hours over a distance 'travelled by a good steamer in 12 days'. Measurable wave effects were even said to have reached the English Channel. Coastal Java and Sumatra were devastated: 165 villages were destroyed and more than 36,000 people were killed.

The following day a telegram sent to Singapore from Batavia (160km east of Krakatau) reported odd details such as 'fish dizzy and caught with glee by natives', and for three years, ash clouds circled the earth, creating strange and spectacular sunsets.

The astonishing return of life to the devastated islands has been the subject of scientific study ever since. Not a single plant was found on Krakatau a few months after the event; 100 years later – although the only fauna are snakes, insects, rats, bats and birds – it seems almost as though the vegetation was never disturbed.

Krakatau may have blown itself to smithereens but it is currently being replaced by Anak Krakatau, which has been on the ascendant ever since its first appearance nearly 80 years ago. It has a restless and uncertain temperament, sending out showers of glowing rocks and belching smoke and ashes.

from 1,800,000Rp for a small utility boat (maximum of six people) to 3,000,000Rp for a faster boats (eight to 10 people). These can be organised through Carita agents or **Marina Lippo** (☎ 0253-801525) in Carita.

Wanawisata Alamhayati (☎ 5710392) also arranges expensive tours to Krakatau from Jakarta.

UJUNG KULON NATIONAL PARK

On the remote southwestern tip of Java, the Unesco World Heritage–listed **Ujung Kulon National Park** (admission 59,500Rp) covers about 760 sq km of land, including the large Pulau Panaitan. Because of its isolation and difficult access, Ujung Kulon has remained an outpost of primeval forest and untouched wilderness in heavily developed Java; alongside some fine opportunities for hiking, it also has some good beaches with intact coral reefs. Few people visit the park, but despite its remoteness, it is one of the most rewarding national parks in Java.

Ujung Kulon is best known as the last refuge in Java for the once plentiful one-horned rhinoceros, now numbering only around 55. The shy Javan rhino is an extremely rare sight and you are far more likely to come across *banteng* (wild cattle), wild pigs, otters, squirrels, leaf monkeys and gibbons. Panthers also live in the forest and crocodiles in the river estuaries, but these are also rare. Green turtles nest in some of the bays and Ujung Kulon also has a wide variety of bird life. On Pulau Peucang, sambar deer, long-tailed macaques and big monitor lizards are common, and there is good snorkelling around coral reefs.

The main park area is on the peninsula but it also includes the nearby island of Panaitan and the smaller offshore islands of Peucang and Handeuleum. Much of the peninsula is dense lowland rainforest and a mixture of scrub, grassy plains, swamps, pandanus palms and long stretches of sandy beach on the west and south coasts. Walking trails follow the coast around much of the peninsula and loop around Gunung Payung on the western tip.

Information

The **Labuan PHKA office** (☎ 801731; ⏰ 8am-4pm Mon-Fri) is a useful source of information, but you pay your entry fee when you enter the park at the park office in Tamanjaya or on the islands. Try to pick up a copy of the excellent, but rarely available, *Visitor's Guidebook to the Trails of Ujung Kulon National Park* (25,000Rp) from the park office. The **Jakarta Visitor Information Office** (Map p110; ☎ 3154094, 3161293; www.jakarta.go.id; Jl Wahid Hasyim 9; ⏰ 9am-5pm Mon-Fri, 9am-1pm Sat) also has information and can organise tours.

The best time to visit Ujung Kulon is in the dry season (April to October), when the sea is generally calm and the reserve less boggy. Be aware that malaria has been reported in Ujung Kulon.

Guides must be hired for hiking in the park and cost around 250,000Rp per day. Bring along lightweight food, such as packaged noodles, and drinking water if you are trekking; otherwise food can be organised by tour operators or the park wardens. Supplies are available in Tamanjaya, but in Sumur and Labuan there is more choice.

Activities

Tamanjaya village, the entry point to the park, has accommodation and can arrange guides for the three-day hike across to the west coast and on to Pulau Peucang. This is the most rewarding way to explore the park and its diversity. It can be tackled by anyone of reasonable fitness, but is not a stroll.

Conditions on the trail are basic – there are rough shelters, but some are almost derelict. If you have a tent, bring it. The trail heads to the south coast and the hut near Pantai Cibandawoh. The second day is a five-hour walk along the beach to the hut at Sungai Cibunar – rivers have to be waded through. On the third day, most hikers cross over the hills to the west coast at Cidaon, opposite Peucang. An alternative and longer trail with good coastal scenery goes from Cibunar via Sanghiang Sirah and the lighthouse at Tanjung Layar, the westernmost tip of mainland Java.

Pulau Peucang is the other main entry into the park but can only be reached by chartered boat. Good but expensive accommodation and a restaurant are run by a private tour company, **Wanawisata Alamhayati** (☎ 5710392). Peucang also has beautiful white-sand beaches and coral reefs on the sheltered eastern coast. Hikers might be able to hitch a lift on a boat out of Peucang, but don't count on it.

There is also comfortable but simple accommodation at **Pulau Handeuleum**, which is ringed by mangroves and doesn't have Peucang's attractions. Boats or canoes can be hired for the short crossing to Cigenter, on the mainland opposite Pulau Handeuleum, and other trails can be explored on this side of the park.

Large **Pulau Panaitan** is more expensive to reach, but has some fine beaches and hiking opportunities. Panaitan is also popular with surfers (see p847). It is a day's walk between the PHKA posts at Legon Butun and Legon Haji, or you can walk to the top of Gunung Raksa, topped by a Hindu statue of Ganesh, from Citambuyung on the east coast.

Tours

A typical tour from Carita, as offered by travel agencies such as **Black Rhino** (☎ 802818; blackrhinojva@yahoo.com), is four days/three nights with a transfer by car to Sumur, then a boat to Handeuleum (about seven to eight hours) where you camp. Then you trek to Jamang and camp overnight at the ranger's post. The next day you can explore around Tanjung Alang Alang and the nearby beaches, then return. The all-inclusive tours cost US$225 per person for a minimum of four.

Boat hire from Labuan or Carita can also be arranged. A three-day return trip to Pulau Peucang costs US$300 in a speedboat (2½ hours, maximum six persons). The park office in Tamanjaya can arrange boat transfers to the islands for around 1,800,000Rp.

Wanawisata Alamhayati (☎ 5710392) has all-inclusive, two-day/three-night tours to Pulau Peucang for around US$300 per person, depending on accommodation, for a minimum of two people.

Sleeping & Eating

Advance bookings through the tourist office and tour operators in Carita (p125) are recommended for Pulau Peucang and Handeuleum, particularly at weekends.

Umang Resort & Spa (☎ 0253-803331, in Jakarta 021-563 9023; www.pulau-umang.com; packages for 2 from 3,500,000Rp; ⊠ ⊠) This stunning new resort takes up the entire island of Umang, close to Sumur. The spacious, stylish cottages are decked out in dark-wood furniture, and many come with a private terrace facing the sea. Its seclusion and romantic ambience make it popular with honeymooners and love-struck couples.

Tamanjaya, a sleepy, rural village with a few shops and warungs, also has homestays. Here you'll find **Wisma Wisata Alam** (☎ 0253-802224; Jl Dermaga; r 40,000-50,000Rp), with reasonable rooms and good views of Krakatau, and **Sunda Jaya homestay** (r per person 40,000Rp), a basic place that also offers meals.

On Pulau Peucang there are double rooms in the old **guesthouse** (d 400,000Rp), and the much more luxurious **Flora A & B bungalows** (d US$80; ⊠) has hot water and fridges. Add 15% tax to all rates, including meals in the very good restaurant.

Not to be outdone, Pulau Handeuleum has a reasonably good **guesthouse** (r 110,000Rp plus 15% tax) in pleasant surroundings. It has a kitchen but you need to bring your own food, as the island has no other dining options.

Within the park you can camp or stay at the primitive huts for a small fee. Bring food for yourself and your guide.

Getting There & Away

The cheapest way to get to the park is by minibus from Labuan to Sumur (30,000Rp, 3½ hours), and then an *ojek* to Tamanjaya (50,000Rp, 1½ hours) along a badly rutted road.

The only other way to reach the park is to charter a boat. Given the long stretch of open sea, which is often subject to large swells, make sure you take a good boat.

BOGOR

☎ 0251 / pop 715,000

'A romantic little village' is how Sir Stamford Raffles described Bogor when he made it his country home during the British interregnum. As an oasis of unpredictable European weather – it is credited with 322 thunderstorms a year – cool, quiet Bogor was long the chosen retreat of starch-collared colonials escaping the stifling and crowded capital.

Today, the long arm of Jakarta reaches almost the whole way to Bogor, and while a ribbon of green still just about survives between the two, the city is already choked with the overspill of the capital's perennial traffic problem.

But while Bogor's transformation into a distant Jakartan suburb continues apace, the real oasis remains untouched. Planted in the very centre of the city, with the traffic passing idly by, Bogor's botanical gardens are truly world class.

The gardens can be visited as a day trip from Jakarta, or since the capital is only an hour away, Bogor can be used as a cooler and more manageable base from which to visit Jakarta. From Bogor you can venture to the nearby mountains that surround the city or continue on to Bandung or Pelabuhan Ratu.

Though Bogor stands at a height of only 290m, it's appreciably cooler than Jakarta. Visitors in the wet season should bear in mind the town's 'City of Rain' moniker. Bogor has probably the highest annual rainfall in Java, so bring an umbrella and be prepared for wet feet.

Information

INTERNET ACCESS & TELEPHONE

Wartels can be found next to the post office and at the entrance to the botanical gardens.

Hotel Salak (☎ 350400; Jl Ir H Juanda 8; per hr 5000Rp; 🕒 8am-10pm)

Warnet and Wartel Paledang (Jl Paledang; per hr 10,000Rp; 🕒 8am-9pm) Next to Pensione Firman.

MONEY

Bogor has plenty of banks. Both the following banks have ATMs:

BCA bank (Bank Central Asia; Jl Ir H Juanda 28)

BII bank (Bank Internasional Indonesia; Jl Dewi Sartika)

POST

Post office (🕒 8am-5pm) Just south of the western entrance to the gardens; also has internet access.

TOURIST INFORMATION

PHKA Headquarters (Jl Ir H Juanda 15; 🕒 7am-2pm Mon-Thu, 7-11am Fri) The official body for administration of all of Indonesia's wildlife reserves and national parks; located next to the main garden gates.

Tourist office (☎ 081 1110347; Jl Ir H Juanda 10; 🕒 8am-4pm) On the western side of the gardens, the office has hotel information, a rough map of the town, and can organise guides and tours (p132).

Sights

KEBUN RAYA

At the heart of Bogor are the huge botanical gardens, known as the **Kebun Raya** (Great Garden; admission 5500Rp Sat & Sun, 7500Rp Mon-Fri; 🕒 8am-5pm), covering an area of around 80 hectares. They are said to be the inspiration of Governor General Raffles, but the spacious grounds of the Istana Bogor (Presidential Palace) were converted to botanical gardens by the Dutch botanist Professor Reinwardt, with assistance from Kew Gardens, and officially opened by the Dutch in 1817. It was from these gardens that various colonial cash crops, such as tea, cassava, tobacco and cinchona, were developed by early Dutch researchers during the infamous Cultivation Period in the 19th century. The park is still a major centre for botanical research in Indonesia.

The gardens contain streams and lotus ponds, and more than 15,000 species of trees and plants, including 400 types of magnificent palms. The orchid houses are reputed to contain more than 3000 orchid varieties. Near the main entrance of the gardens is a small **monument**, erected in memory of Olivia Raffles, who died in 1814 and was buried in Batavia. There is also a **cemetery** near the palace with Dutch headstones.

Crowds flock to here on Sunday, but the gardens are quiet at most other times. The southern gate is the main entrance and is home to Bogor's only touts; other gates are only open on Sunday and holidays.

ZOOLOGICAL MUSEUM

Near the entrance to the botanical gardens, this **museum** (admission 2000Rp; 🕒 8am-4pm Sat-Thu, 8am-noon Fri) has a motley but interesting collection of zoological oddities, including the skeleton of a blue whale. If you have heard about Flores having a rat problem, one glance at the stuffed Flores version in the showcase of Indonesian rats will explain why.

ISTANA BOGOR

In the northwestern corner of the botanical gardens, the summer palace of the president was formerly the opulent official residence of the Dutch governors general from 1870 to 1942.

Today, herds of white-spotted deer roam the immaculate lawns and the building contains Soekarno's huge art collection, which largely focuses on the female figure. The palace is only open to groups (minimum 10) by prior arrangement, and children are not allowed inside. Contact the tourist office for more information.

OTHER SIGHTS

The **Batutulis** is an inscribed stone dedicated to Sri Baduga Maharaja (1482–1521), a Pa-

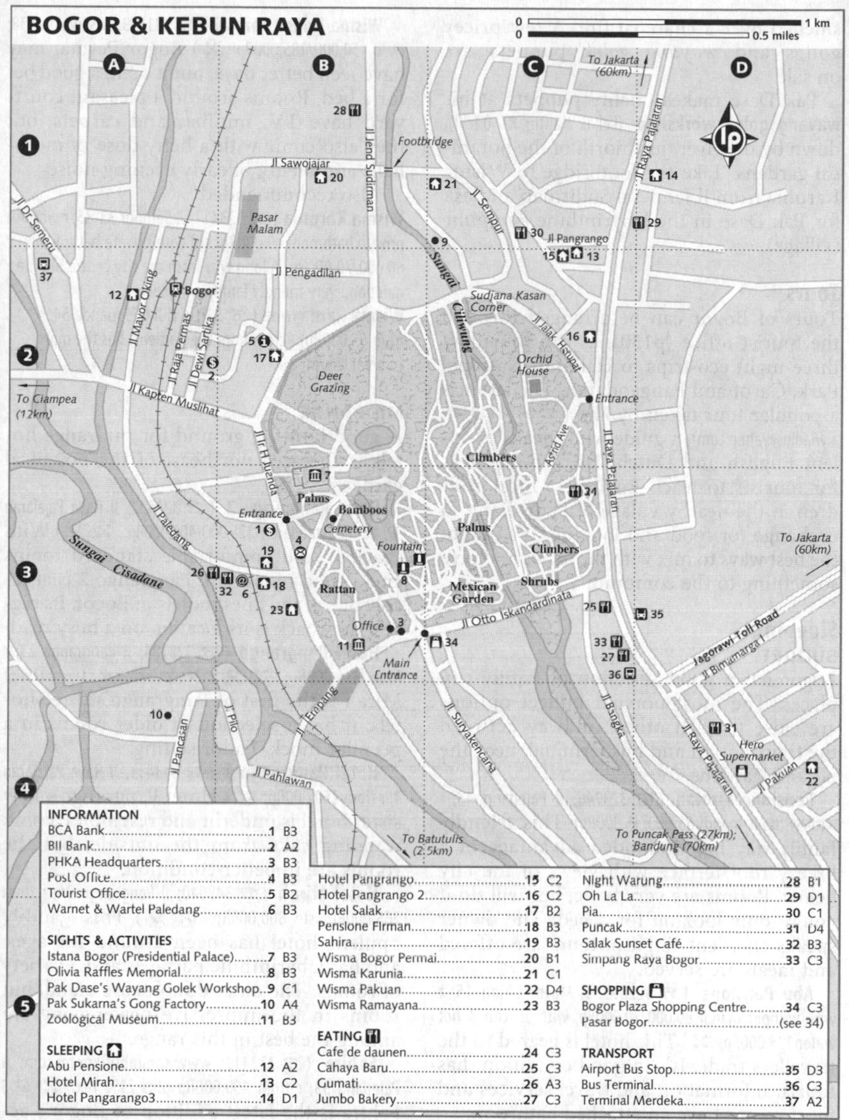

jajaran king credited with great mystical power. The stone is housed in a small shrine visited by pilgrims – remove your shoes and pay a small donation before entering. Batutulis is 2.5km south of the botanical gardens, on Jl Batutulis. It's almost opposite the former home of Soekarno, who was attracted by the stone's mystical power. His request to be buried here was ignored by Soeharto, who wanted the former president's grave as far away from the capital as possible.

One of the few remaining gongsmiths in West Java is Pak Sukarna, and you can visit his **gong factory** (☎ 324132; Jl Pancasan 17), where gongs and other gamelan instruments are smelted over a charcoal fire. A few pricey gongs and *wayang golek* puppets are on sale.

Pak Dase makes quality puppets at his **wayang golek workshop** (Lebak Kantin RT 02/VI), down by the river, just north of the botanical gardens. Take the footbridge to Wisma Karunia from Jl Jenderal Sudirman and ask for Pak Dase in the labyrinthine *kampung* (village).

Tours

Tours of Bogor can be arranged through the tourist office (p130), as can four-day/three-night eco-trips to Halimun National Park, Garut and Pangandaran. The latter is a popular tour taken by **Alwi** (☎ 081 1110347; alwiadin@yahoo.com), a guide who speaks excellent English and Dutch. He also arranges for tourists to teach English to local children in the nearby village of Leuwiliang in exchange for food and lodging. It's one of the best ways to mix with the locals and give something to the community.

Sleeping

BUDGET

Bogor has a good selection of family-run places. The most popular budget options are close to each other, midway between the train station and bus terminal, near the botanic gardens.

Pensione Firman (☎ 323246; Jl Paledang 48; r with/without mandi 55,000/45,000Rp) This friendly family-stay has the added advantage of a breezy roof terrace with views of the city below. Rooms are very basic, but will do if you're only looking for a bed. The owner speaks excellent English, tours are offered and meals are served.

Abu Pensione (☎ 322893; Jl Mayor Oking 15; r with/without mandi 80,000/70,000Rp, with air-con & hot water 135,000Rp;) This hotel is geared to the travellers trade. It's in good condition, has tourist information and travel services and most rooms have an attached bathroom.

Wisma Pakuan (☎ 319430; Jl Pakuan 12; r with balcony 110,000Rp, with air-con 175,000Rp;) Pakuan occupies the upper floor of a large, modern family home southeast of the bus terminal. Rooms are in excellent condition and the owners are more than happy to share their knowledge of town and the surrounding area. It's on a busy street, so ask for a room at the back.

Wisma Bogor Permai (☎ 381633; Jl Sawojajar 38; tw/d 150,000/185,000Rp;) Bogor Permai may have seen better days, but it's still a good bet for a bed. Rooms around a pleasant courtyard have TV, minibar and carpets, but they also come with a hefty dose of mothballs and plenty of early evening noise.

Also recommended:

Wisma Karunia (☎ 323411; Jl Sempur 33-35; r without private bathroom 40,000Rp, s/d with private bathroom 60,000/70,000Rp) A long way from the city centre but is a quiet and very friendly family-run place.

Wisma Ramayana (☎ 320364; Jl Ir H Juanda 54; r from 65,000Rp) Across from the gardens; has the most colonial charm.

MIDRANGE

A good hunting ground for midrange hotels is the area northeast of the botanical gardens.

Hotel Pangrango 2 (☎ 321482; Jl Raya Pajajaran 32; budget/standard r 125,000/400,000Rp;) With spacious and comfortable standard rooms and a good restaurant, Pangrango 2 is arguably one of the finest hotels in Bogor. Its biggest drawback is its location on a busy road.

Hotel Pangrango (☎ 328284; Jl Pangrango 23; r from 236,000Rp;) Next door to Hotel Mirah is the first of Pangrango's three hotels; it has a selection of older rooms in a peculiar mock-Tudor setting.

Hotel Pangrango 3 (☎ 343433; Jl Raya Pajajaran 1; r from 250,000Rp;) Hotel Pangrango's new sister hotel is underlit and resembles a pink wedding cake from the outside, but the rooms are in better condition.

Hotel Mirah (☎ 348040; Jl Pangrango 9A; r from 265,000Rp, ste 800,000Rp;) This gaudily opulent hotel has been around for ages, and has labyrinthine passages and a variety of rooms. The older doubles are bland, but rooms in the impressive newer wing are among the best in this range.

Sahira (☎ 322413; www.sahirabutikhotel.com; Jl Paledang 53; r from 460,000Rp plus 21% tax;) Sahira is the latest addition to Bogor's accommodation scene; rooms sparkle in their newness and face an inner courtyard taken up by the hotel's pool.

Hotel Salak (☎ 350400; www.hotelsalek.co.id; Jl Juanda 8; r from 510,000Rp plus 21% tax;) Salak is a large hotel with plenty of business facilities and comfy rooms. It's within easy walking distance of the train station and the gardens.

Eating

Cheap warungs appear at night along Jl Dewi Sartika and Jl Jenderal Sudirman. During the day, you'll find plenty of food stalls and good fruit at **Pasar Bogor** (breakfast & lunch), the market close to the main garden gates. In the late afternoon along Jl Raja Permas next to the train station, street vendors cook up delicious snacks, such as deep-fried *tahu* (tofu) and *pisang goreng* (fried banana fritters).

Jumbo Bakery (Jl Raya Pajajaran; cakes 2000Rp; breakfast & lunch) This simple diner-style bakery has been needing new light bulbs for years, but the lack of light doesn't seem to affect the bakers, who produce some fine cakes.

Pia (329765; Jl Pangrango 10; pies around 3000Rp; breakfast & lunch) Just across from the Hotel Pangrango, Pia would surely snatch a place on the podium if Java were ever to host an apple-pie contest. As well as apple pastries, expect apple salad, apple and ice cream and even apple sauce spaghetti.

Simpang Raya Bogor (Jl Raya Pajajaran; mains from 10,000Rp; lunch & dinner) This sprawling *masakan Padang* (Padang dish) heaves with customers by early evening; stroll on in and find a seat wherever there is room.

Café de daunen (350023; mains 20,000-50,000Rp; lunch & dinner) This may unashamedly be a tourist eatery in the botanical gardens, but it has lovely views across an open meadow, an international menu, and an open terrace that attracts a cool breeze. Plus, it's the perfect spot to watch (and avoid) the rainstorms that roll in.

Cahaya Baru (Jl Raya Pajajaran 7; mains around 30,000Rp; lunch & dinner) This air-con restaurant is a good bet for Chinese food, but a better bet for seafood.

Gumati (Jl Palendang 28; mains 30,000-50,000Rp; lunch & dinner) Gumati is a hip café-bar with plenty of wood and wicker, a large open balcony with valley vistas, and a big East-meets-West menu. Most of the fresh produce is on view, including piles of chillis big enough to bring tears to the eyes of even the spiciest boys and girls.

Puncak (Jl Kantor Pos 6; mains 30,000-50,000Rp; dinner) Puncak is on a quiet back street near Wisma Pakuan. It serves up some steaming Thai and Chinese feasts in a lazy, bamboo setting; problem is, the 'lazy' setting also extends to the waitresses.

You can also test your tastebuds at the following:

Oh La La (Jl Raya Pajajaran 7; cakes 2000Rp; breakfast & lunch) Specialises in cappuccino and croissants.

Salak Sunset Café (Jl Paledang 38; mains 20,000Rp; lunch & dinner) Chic, cheap little place with river views. Juices, pizzas, spaghetti and Indonesian favourites are featured.

Getting There & Away

BUS

Every 15 minutes or so, buses depart from Jakarta's Kampung Rambutan bus terminal (normal/air-con 7000/10,000Rp), and can do the trip in a little over half an hour via the Jagorawi toll road. The only problem is that it takes at least double that time to travel between Kampung Rambutan and central Jakarta.

A Damri bus goes to Jakarta's Soekarno-Hatta international airport (16,000Rp) hourly from 4am to 6pm. It leaves from opposite KFC on Jl Raya Pajajaran.

Buses depart frequently from Bogor for Bandung (15,900/25,000Rp, three hours). At weekends the buses are not allowed to go via the scenic Puncak Pass and therefore travel via Sukabumi. Other bus destinations from Bogor include Pelabuhan Ratu (18,000/24,000Rp, three hours) and Labuan (20,000Rp, four hours).

Air-con, door-to-door minibuses go to Bandung for 75,000Rp. **Dimas Dewa** (653671) has the best buses. Phone for a pick-up.

CAR

Bogor is a good place to hire a car and driver. Bargaining is essential. Bogor has a number of private operators who are used to taking tourists on day trips or extended trips further afield. Many speak English, and some speak Dutch. Prices start at around 400,000Rp. This price includes a driver, and if you've booked through a hotel, expect it to add on a large commission.

TRAIN

The easiest way of reaching central Jakarta is to take the trains, which run every 20 minutes from around 4am to 8pm and take 1½ hours. The economy-class trains (2500Rp) are reasonably efficient but best avoided during peak hours when they can be crowded to bursting point. Much more comfortable *Pakuan* express trains

(10,000Rp) leave Bogor for the capital at least once an hour from 6.10am till 6pm.

Getting Around

Green *angkot* minibuses (2000Rp) shuttle around town, particularly between the bus terminal and train station. Blue *angkot* run to outlying districts and terminate at Terminal Merdeka. From the bus terminal, *angkot* leave from the street behind, Jl Bangka. *Angkot* 03 does an anticlockwise loop of the botanical gardens on its way to Jl Kapten Muslihat, near the train station. To the bus terminal from the tourist office take 06.

Becak are banned from the main road encircling the gardens. Metered taxis are few and far between, although some Jakartan taxi drivers do hang out by the airport bus stop by the Jagorawi toll road. You can also haggle with the minivan drivers who hang out near the entrance to the botanical gardens.

AROUND BOGOR

Batutulis (Purnawarman Stone)

Those in need of reminding that all great empires come to an end can head for Batutulis, where sits the large black boulder on which King Purnawarman inscribed his name and footprint around AD 450. His rather immodest inscription, in the Palawa script of South India, is uncannily reminiscent of Percy Shelley's *Ozymandias*, and reads: 'This is the footstep of King Purnawarman of Tarumanegara kingdom, the great conqueror of the world'.

The Ciampea boulder has been raised from its original place and embedded in the shallow water of Sungai Ciaruteun. The inscription on the stone is still remarkably clear after more than 1500 years.

Colts make the run to Batutulis from the village of Ciampea, about 12km northwest of Bogor.

Gunung Halimun National Park

This national park is home to some primary rainforest, but the park has mixed usage and also includes plantations such as the Nirmala Tea Estate. The dominant feature of the park is the rich montane forest in the highland regions around **Gunung Halimun** (1929m), which is the highest peak.

Visitor facilities at the park are undeveloped and park administration is handled by the Gede Pangrango National Park (p138) at Cibodas some distance away. The most-visited attractions in the park are the waterfalls near Cikidang and those near the Nirmala estate, but the big draw card is **white-water rafting. Pt Lintas Seram Nusantara** (☎ 021-8355885) in Jakarta organises white-water rafting on the Class II to IV (depending on season) Sungai Citarak on the southeastern edge of the park. Prices start at 165,000Rp for a 1½-hour trip and end at 245,000Rp for a three-hour trip.

The usual access (you need your own transport) is through Cibadak on the Bogor to Pelabuhan Ratu road, from where you turn off to Cikadang and then on to the Nirmala Tea Estate. Rainfall in the park is between 4000mm and 6000mm per year, most of which falls from October to May, when a visit is more or less out of the question.

SUKABUMI & SELABINTANA

☎ 0266

Sukabumi is a thriving commercial town of 120,000 people at the foot of Pangrango and Gede volcanoes. The main reason to visit is for bus connections to Bandung and Pelabuhan Ratu or to visit Selabintana, a small hill resort 7km north of town.

Selabintana is much less developed than the Puncak Pass resort area to the north of Gunung Gede, which means fewer people. It is possible to walk up the hillside to **Sawer Waterfall** and on to **Gunung Gede**, but there is no PHKA post in Selabintana. Selabintana has a golf course, swimming pools and a good selection of midrange hotels. Otherwise it is simply a quiet place to relax.

The old-fashioned, slightly faded **Hotel Selabintana** (☎ 221501; Jl Selabintana, Km 7; r from 200,000Rp, VIP bungalows 348,000Rp plus 21% tax; 🏊) is for sport junkies; it has a golf course, tennis and volleyball courts, two swimming pools and a bar-restaurant for afterwards. There are rooms or huge bungalows with antique furniture. Minibuses from Sukabumi (take a 10 from the Yogyakarta department store) to Selabintana run straight up to the foot of Gunung Gede and terminate at the hotel.

PELABUHAN RATU

☎ 0266

About 90km south of Bogor on Java's southern coast is Pelabuhan Ratu, a small fishing village that moonlights as a seaside resort. The town itself is loud and fairly ugly – saved only by its long black beach and the colourful outrigger fishing boats crowding the harbour – and most people come here for the beaches to the west.

Legend has it that Pelabuhan Ratu (which translates as 'Harbour of the Queen') actually witnessed the creation of Nyai Loro Kidul, the malevolent goddess who takes fishermen and swimmers off to her watery kingdom. Don't wear green on the beach or in the water (it's *her* colour), and in the Hotel Indonesia Samudra a room is set aside for meditating mystics wishing to contact the Queen of the South Seas.

Information

The **tourist office** (☎ 433544; Jl Kidang Kencana; 🕑 9am-4pm Mon-Fri) is within easy walking distance of the bus terminal – just head for the water. You'll find a wartel next door and another in the bus terminal. The **BCA bank** (Bank Central Asia; Jl Siliwangi) will change US dollars and travellers cheques, and cash only for other currencies, but the rates are low. The ATM accepts Visa cards.

Sights & Activities

Swimming is possible up and down the coast when the sea is quiet, but like most of Java's south coast, the crashing surf can be treacherous. Drownings do occur in spite of the warning signs.

Aside from its **fish market**, Pelabuhan Ratu won't hold your interest for long – it's best to head west once you've got your bearings. **Cimaja**, 8km west of Pelabuhan Ratu, has a pebble beach and a lively surfing community that flocks here to catch some of the south coast's best waves at the **Ombak Tujuh** (Seven Waves) surf break. This is also the place to arrange diving or motorcycling trips.

Pantai Karang Hawu, 13km west of Pelabuhan Ratu, is a towering cliff with caves, rocks and pools created by a large lava flow. According to legend, it was from the rocks of Karang Hawu that Nyai Loro Kidul leapt into the mighty ocean to regain her lost beauty and never returned. Stairs lead up to a small *kramat* (shrine) at the top.

Further west, about 2km past Cisolok, are the **Cipanas hot springs**. Boiling water sprays into the river, and you can soak downstream where the hot and cold waters mingle. It is a very scenic area; you can walk a few kilometres upstream through the lush forest to a waterfall. Cipanas has changing sheds, warungs and crowds on the weekend.

Goa Lalay is a bat cave that's about 4km southeast of Pelabuhan Ratu. It's of limited interest except at sunset, when thousands of small bats fly out.

Sleeping & Eating

Though quiet during the week, Pelabuhan Ratu can be crowded at weekends and holidays, and accommodation reflects Jakarta prices.

PELABUHAN RATU

Pelabuhan Ratu has its fair share of accommodation options, but you're better off heading west – even if it's only for 1km or so – than staying in town.

Bayu Amrta (☎ 431031; fax 431344; bayu_amrta@cbn.net.id; Jl Karang Pamuland; r with air-con from 210,000Rp plus 21% tax; ❄ 🍴) About 1.5km from town on a headland, Bayu is perched on precipitous cliffs, with good views of crashing surf and whirling gulls. The restaurant is perfect for sunset tipples.

Queen Restaurant (Jl Kidang Kencana; mains 30,000-60,000Rp; 🕑 lunch & dinner) Just west of the tourist office, this is the pick of Pelabuhan Ratu's excellent Chinese seafood restaurants.

CITEPUS

Citepus is a tiny village 3km from Pelabu han Ratu. As well as the places listed here, it has a number of homestays.

Padi Padi (☎ 432124; padi2@dnet.net.id; standard r from 350,000Rp, penthouse 690,000Rp) With Santa Fe architecture, rustic Asian furnishings and a good restaurant, Padi Padi is an above average choice. It is dead during the week, but superb rooms have all the mod cons and back onto a fish-pond maze.

Hotel Inna Samudra (☎ 431200; s/d from 470,000/560,000Rp plus 21% tax) Another 2km further west from Padi Padi is one of Soekarno's original 1960s luxury hotels, with a rather bleak Stalin-on-the-South-Seas look. It has its own beach, but it's starting to look past its use-by date. Room 308 is said to be the haunt of the Queen of the South Seas.

CIMAJA

The surfing beach of Cimaja has the best breaks around, friendly, good-quality accommodation, a relaxed vibe and three surf shops.

Pondok Kencana (☎ 431465; lms@cbn.net.id; dm 30,000Rp, bungalows from 200,000Rp plus 15% tax;) Perched up above the main road, this surfer hang-out features good, comfortable villa-style accommodation and the Ombak 7 pub, with surf flicks and other diversions. The Kencana's Australian expat owner is an endless source of information about the area and can organise just about everything from diving excursions to fishing trips for black marlin.

Green Room (☎ 432608; s/d 40,000/60,000Rp) This is one of the coast's simpler surfer haunts, with stripped-back rooms that are fan-cooled and, as the name states, green. The bar downstairs is small but lively and inviting.

Rumah Makan Mirasa (☎ 436337; r 40,000-60,000Rp; breakfast, lunch & dinner) Almost opposite the Green Room is this perennial favourite with surfers, with simple, adequate rooms and hearty portions of Indonesian fare (mains around 15,000Rp) .

Hotel Daun Daun (☎ 431501; r from 60,000Rp;) Daun Daun is a simple place with a range of clean, YHA-style rooms.

Didesa (☎ 433288; www.didesa.co.id; Jl Raya Cisolok 23; r from 390,000Rp;) Also known as *Cek Ombak* ('check the waves' in Bahasa Indonesia), this hotel is an excellent option for those looking for some comfort. There are plush bungalows on stilts, a sun terrace, a surf shop/repair service, a tower for checking surf conditions, and live reggae every Saturday night.

Any's Tavern (☎ 431184; mains around 15,000Rp; breakfast, lunch & dinner) Any's Tavern is a legend in these parts and even features in Jakarta-based magazines. It's popular with surfers for its lively bar and good, cheap food. Arrangements for motorcycling trips can be made here. It's between Cimaja and Cisolok.

Getting There & Away

By car, Pelabuhan Ratu can be reached in four hours from Jakarta. Local buses run throughout the day from Bogor (24,000Rp, three hours) and Sukabumi (15,000Rp, 2½ hours). Buses from Sukabumi continue on to Cisolok from Pelabuhan Ratu, and it is possible to continue right along the south coast by a variety of connections.

Getting Around

Angkot run between Pelabuhan Ratu and Cisolok (5000Rp) and occasionally continue on to Cipanas; otherwise, charter them from Cisolok to Cipanas for around 10,000Rp. *Ojek* at the Pelabuhan Ratu and Cisolok bus terminals can be hired for around 20,000Rp per hour for sightseeing. Motorbikes (65,000Rp per day) can be hired at the Bayu Amrta (p135).

BOGOR TO BANDUNG (PUNCAK PASS AREA)

Snaking through sleepy tea plantations and terraced fields, the road over the 1500m-high Puncak Pass between Bogor and Bandung tips and rises through some of West Java's most sensational scenery. The climate is cool, there are some fantastic walking opportunities and the resort towns that line the route offer a wide range of accommodation.

But while the vistas are a worthwhile addition to any photo album, the Puncak area has also fallen victim to its own beauty. Inundated with tourists who are hoping to escape the push-and-shove of Jakarta, Bogor and Bandung, the region's narrow roads are often a chaotic knot of gridlocked traffic, blaring karaoke lounges and pricey motels. Weekends can bring pandemonium.

Almost the whole highway is a resort strip that's crammed with hotels and villas starting about 10km out of Bogor at Ciawi and continuing up through Cibogo, Cipayung and Cisarua to the Puncak Pass and over the other side to Cipanas. Crowds quickly evaporate away from the highway, however, and peace and quiet is never too far away.

From Jakarta's Kampung Rambutan bus terminal, any Bandung bus can drop you off at any of the resort towns on the highway (but not on Sunday, when they aren't allowed to use this highway). From Bogor, frequent buses and Colts (which travel on Sunday) also ply the highway.

When heading to Bandung from Puncak, buses can be flagged down on the main road. Be sure to check that the bus is going into Bandung itself though, as buses going to other destinations will often drop you on the ring road, miles from the city centre.

The best way to see the area in a day is to hire a car in Bogor (500,000Rp per day) and make your visit during the week.

Cisarua

☎ 0251

Ten kilometres from Bogor on the slopes of the Puncak, Cisarua has budget accommodation and walks to picnic spots and waterfalls.

SIGHTS

Curug Cilember, the town's most scenic waterfall, is about a 30-minute walk from Cisarua. Just east of Cisarua is the turn-off to **Taman Safari Indonesia** (☎ 250000; adult/child under 6 60,000/55,000Rp, car 15,000Rp; 9am-5pm). This spacious drive-through game park has well-tended indigenous and African 'safari' animals, a bird park, white tiger pavilion, red pandas, children's rides and animal shows. It also has a night safari (35,000Rp) on Saturday night for viewing nocturnal animals. The park is best explored by car, but a park bus does tours of the safari park for those without a car. Park facilities include a swimming pool, restaurants and accommodation (rooms from 325,000Rp).

In the foothills, 7km before the Puncak summit, you finally leave the over-development behind and pass through the tea-carpeted hills of **Gunung Mas Tea Estate** (9am-5pm Tue-Sun). You can tour the tea factory (5000Rp), which is a couple of kilometres from the highway, or combine it with a guided walk through the plantation itself (50,000Rp). Accommodation is available on site.

Almost at the top of the pass, the **Rindu Alam Restaurant** is a must on all tour itineraries and either has fine views of the surrounding tea estates or is surrounded by ethereal mist. Set just below the restaurant is **Telaga Warna**, a small 'lake of many colours'. The colours require sunlight; otherwise the lake is not as exciting as the patch of montane forest surrounding it.

SLEEPING

Scores of midrange hotels and villas are spread out along the highway from Ciawi to Cipanas.

Wisma Dirga Cibulan (☎ 254056; r/bungalows from 44,000/228,000Rp;) This is a large place with OK rooms. It's a good bet if everything else if full.

Gunung Mas Guesthouse (☎ 252501; basic r 160,000Rp, deluxe r 209,000Rp, bungalows from 500,000Rp) In the grounds of the tea estate, Gunung Mas oozes soporific, colonial charm and is one of the best places around to kick back and relax. Add 50,000Rp to all rates on weekends.

Puncak Pass Hotel (☎ 0263-512503; www.puncakpassresort.com; r/bungalows from 350,000/500,000Rp;) On the Bandung side of the pass, this is the most salubrious choice in these parts. It has dreamy vistas and bungalows hugging the hillsides.

GETTING THERE & AWAY

From Bogor take a bus or Colt to Cisarua (5000Rp, 45 minutes).

Cibodas

☎ 0263

Cibodas, the next village over the Puncak Pass, is home to billions of pot plants for sale and the beautiful high-altitude extension of the Bogor botanical gardens, the **Kebun Raya Cibodas** (admission per person/per car 4000/6500Rp; 8am-6pm). It's surrounded by thick tropical jungle on the slopes of the twin volcanoes of Gunung Gede and Gunung Pangrango. The gardens, which are bigger than Bogor's, were originally planted in 1860 and now contain 1014 species. Beside the entrance to the gardens is the entrance to the Gede Pangrango National Park.

Cibodas has limited facilities and gets far fewer visitors than Cisarua, but it has fine scenery and excellent walks. Visitors must pay 2000Rp on entering the village.

SLEEPING & EATING

Freddy's Homestay (☎ 515473; r without mandi 75,000Rp) Located down a tight alleyway beside Wartel Resimi, 500m before the gardens, Freddy's has cheerful rooms and can organise guides for walking and birdwatching. Meals are available.

Cibodas Guest House (☎ 512051; r from 100,000Rp) Cibodas is a fair way below the gardens and is an unusual place to spend the night. It is quirky and chaotic, with lots of greenery, a menagerie of pet dogs, goats, horses and birds, and a tip-top restaurant overlooking the valley. Ask for a discount.

Wisma Tamu (☎ 517776; lodge 1,000,000Rp) Right inside the gardens, a 1km walk uphill from the gate, Wisma Tamu has one of the best settings of any hotel in Java. It's a colonial place, with five faded but large rattan-style rooms with loads of character, that sleeps up to 10 persons. There is a kitchen, but individual rooms are not available for rent; bookings are essential.

There's cheap food at warungs near the gardens and in the village, 500m down the hill.

GETTING THERE & AWAY

The turn-off to Cibodas is on the Bogor–Bandung Hwy, a few kilometres west of Cipanas. The gardens are 5km off the main road. *Angkot* run from Cipanas (3000Rp, 30 minutes).

Gede Pangrango National Park

The Cibodas gardens are right next to the main entrance to Gede Pangrango National Park, the highlight of which is the climb to the 2958m peak of the volcanically active Gunung Gede. From the top of Gede on a clear day you can see Jakarta, Cirebon and even Pelabuhan Ratu on the south coast – well, Raffles reported that he could.

Register for the climb and obtain your permit (4000Rp, 2500Rp for Cibeureum Falls only) from the **PHKA office** just outside the gardens' entrance. The office has an information centre and pamphlets on the park, which is noted for its alpine forest and bird life, including the rare Javan eagle. Guides to the summit can also be hired here for 300,000Rp at the office, or for 400,000Rp at Freddy's (p137).

From Cibodas, the trail passes **Telaga Biru** (15 minutes), which is a blue/green lake. **Cibeureum Falls** (one hour away) lies just off the main trail. Most picnickers only go this far, though some continue on to the **hot springs**, 2½ hours from the gate. The trail continues to climb another 1½ hours to **Kandang Badak**, where a hut has been built on the saddle between the peaks of Gunung Gede and Gunung Pangrango (3019m). Take the trail to the right for a hard three-hour climb to Pangrango. Most hikers turn left for the easier, but still steep, 1½-hour climb to Gede, which has more spectacular views. The **Gede Crater** lies below the summit, and you can continue on to the **Suryakencana Meadow**.

The 10km hike right to the top of Gunung Gede takes at least 10 hours there and back, so you should start as early as possible and take warm clothes (night temperatures can drop to 5°C), food, water and a torch (flashlight). Most hikers leave by 2am to reach the summit in the early morning before the mists roll in. Register at the park office the day before. The main trails are easy to follow. The hike should only be undertaken in the dry season from May to October.

BANDUNG

☎ 022 / pop 2 million

After the bottle-green hills of the Puncak Pass, the sprawling bulk of Bandung hits you like a baseball bat across the back of the head. Once the 'Paris of Java', the city is now a twisting throng of congested streets and endless suburbs, and any romantic notions of colonial glamour have long disappeared. This is Indonesia's fourth-largest city and West Java's capital, and it likes everyone to know it.

But not everything has gone to pot. Among the shopping malls and business hotels you'll find a dynamic, major city that's on the move. It attracts workers, intellectuals and artisans from across the archipelago, and its industries, bars and restaurants throb with life. Today, grandiose Art Deco buildings, heaving market stalls, becak and multiplexes jostle for space in a city where past, present and future effortlessly coexist. It's also the centre of Sundanese culture, which plays a supporting role in the city's identity.

Bandung was originally established in the late 19th century as a colonial garrison town, but it rapidly acquired importance as a commercial and educational centre. Because of its pleasant climate – it stands at 750m above sea level – the Dutch even had plans to make it the capital prior to WWII. Bandung's most notable entry in the history books was as host of the Asia-Africa conference in 1955, which finally placed it in the world spotlight.

The main attraction of Bandung is its proximity to sights; high volcanic peaks, hot springs and enormous tea plantations are all easy day trips from the city. But with its cool climate and a handful of its own attractions, Bandung is worth a day or two of your time. This is the place to dip into Sundanese culture and, with street after street of shopping options, explore the depths of your shopping desires.

Orientation

Bandung spreads out over the northern foothills of a huge plateau surrounded by high mountain ridges. The main part of the city lies south of the train line, and is centred around Jl Asia Afrika and the *alun-alun* (main public square). Along Jl Asia Afrika are the tourist office, post office and most of the banks, airline offices, restaurants and top-end hotels. Jl Braga was the ritzy shopping area in Dutch times, but is now the hub of Bandung's after-dark activity.

In colonial times, the train tracks divided the riffraff in the south from the Dutch city in the north, and the social divide still rings true. The gracious residential areas in the north are studded with tree-lined streets and parks, and bordered on the northernmost edge by the hills of Dago.

Information

BOOKSHOPS

Gramedia (Jl Merdeka; 9am-5pm Mon-Sat) Small selection of English books and maps.

INTERNET ACCESS

X-net (Jl Lengkong Kecil 38; 8am-10pm) Access for 5000Rp per hour; smiles and 'Hello, Misters' thrown in for free.

MEDICAL SERVICES

Adventist Hospital (2034386; Jl Cihampelas 161) A missionary hospital with English-speaking staff.

MONEY

Banks with ATMs are scattered across Bandung.

Golden Megah moneychanger (Jl Asia Afrika 142) Some of the best rates in town.

POST

Main post office (cnr Jl Banceuy & Jl Asia Afrika; 8am-7pm) Opposite the *alun-alun*.

TELEPHONE

Wartel aplenty can be found just south of the train station.

TOURIST INFORMATION

Bandung Tourist Information Centre (4206644; Jl Asia Afrika; 9am-5pm Mon-Sat, 9am-2pm Sun) While the *alun-alun* receives a facelift, the city's tourist office can be found in the Masjid Agung next door. It offers excellent free booklets, maps and information on cultural events.

Sights

CITY CENTRE

If you're interested in learning more about the Asia-Africa conference of 1955, visit the **Museum Konperensi** (Conference Museum; Jl Asia Afrika; admission by donation; 9am-3pm Mon-Fri) in Gedung Merdeka (Freedom Building). Exhibits and photos detail the meeting between Soekarno, Chou En-Lai, Ho Chi Minh, Nasser and other Third World leaders of the 1950s.

Not far north of Gedung Merdeka is the **Museum Mandala Wangsit** (Army Museum; Jl Lembong 38; admission free; 9am-3pm Mon-Fri), which devotes itself to the history and exploits of the West Java Siliwangi Division (based in Bandung).

For a bird's-eye view of central Bandung, climb the easterly tower of **Masjid Agung** (Jl Jenderal Sudirman; admission 2000Rp; 9am-5pm Sat & Sun), next to the *alun-alun*.

NORTH OF THE CENTRE

North across the railway tracks, the **Museum Geologi** (Geological Museum; Jl Diponegoro 57; adult/child 2000/1500Rp; 9am-3.30pm Mon-Thu, 9am-1.30pm Sat & Sun) is housed in the massive old headquarters of the Dutch Geological Service. It has excellent volcano exhibits and an array of fossils, including a model skull of Java Man. From the train station you can take an *angkot* bound for 'Sadang Serang' and get off at the Gedung Sate (Regional Government) complex, about 300m from the museum.

While you're in the neighbourhood, dip into the **Museum Prangko** (Stamp Museum; Jl Diponegoro; admission free; 9am-3pm Mon-Fri) in the northeastern corner of the Gedung Sate complex. As well as thousands of stamps from around the world, the museum has everything from post boxes to pushcarts used since colonial times.

BANDUNG INSTITUTE OF TECHNOLOGY

Further north of Gedung Sate is the Bandung Institute of Technology (ITB; Jl Ganeca), built at the beginning of the 20th century. The university has large grounds and gardens, and the main campus complex is notable for its 'Indo European' architecture, featuring Minangkabau-style roofs atop colonial-style buildings.

Opened in 1920, ITB was the first Dutch-founded university open to Indonesians. It

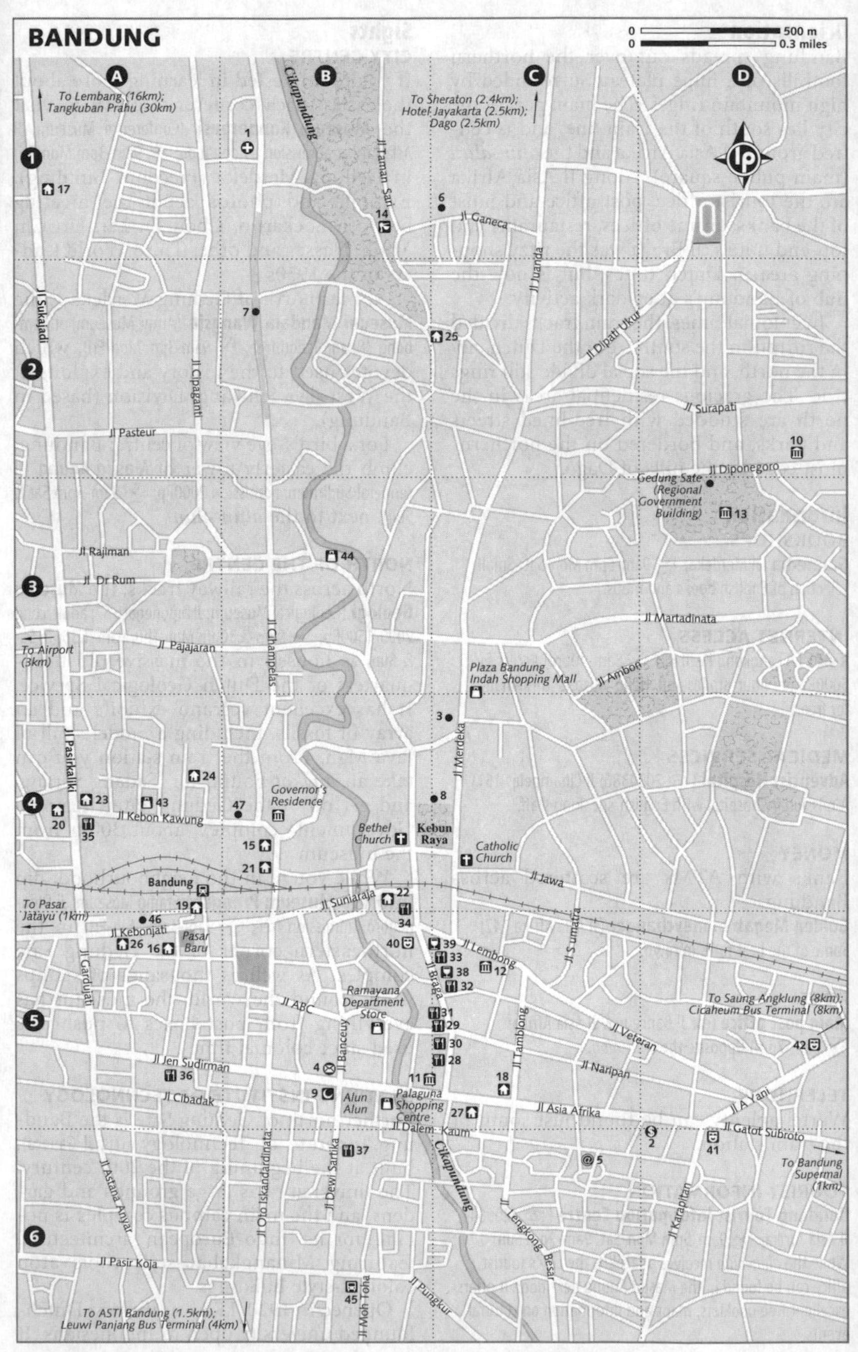
BANDUNG
0 500 m
0 0.3 miles
A
B
C
D
1
2
3
4
5
6
To Lembang (16km); Tangkuban Prahu (30km)
To Sheraton (2.4km); Hotel Jayakarta (2.5km); Dago (2.5km)
Cikapundung
Jl Taman Sari
Jl Ganeca
Jl Juanda
Jl Dipati Ukur
Jl Surapati
Jl Diponegoro
Gedung Sate (Regional Government Building)
Jl Sukajadi
Jl Cipaganti
Jl Pasteur
Jl Rajiman
Jl Dr Rum
To Airport (3km)
Jl Pajajaran
Jl Champelas
Jl Martadinata
Plaza Bandung Indah Shopping Mall
Jl Ambon
Jl Merdeka
Jl Pasirkaliki
Jl Kebon Kawung
Governor's Residence
Bethel Church
Kebun Raya
Catholic Church
Jl Jawa
Bandung
To Pasar Jatayu (1km)
Jl Suniaraja
Jl Kebonjati
Pasar Baru
Jl Gardujati
Jl Lembong
Jl Braga
Jl Sumatra
Ramayana Department Store
Jl ABC
Jl Tamblong
Jl Veteran
To Saung Angklung (8km); Cicaheum Bus Terminal (8km)
Jl Jen Sudirman
Jl Banceuy
Jl Naripan
Jl Cibadak
Alun Alun
Palaguna Shopping Centre
Jl Dalem Kaum
Jl Asia Afrika
Jl A Yani
Jl Gatot Subroto
To Bandung Supermal (1km)
Jl Oto Iskandardinata
Jl Dewi Sartika
Jl Astana Anyar
Jl Lengkong Besar
Jl Karapitan
Jl Pasir Koja
Jl Moh Toha
Jl Pungkur
To ASTI Bandung (1.5km); Leuwi Panjang Bus Terminal (4km)
1
2
3
4
5
6
7
8
9
10
11
12
13
14
15
16
17
18
19
20
21
22
23
24
25
26
27
28
29
30
31
32
33
34
35
36
37
38
39
40
41
42
43
44
45
46
47

INFORMATION		
Adventist Hospital	1	B1
Golden Megah Moneychanger	2	D6
Gramedia	3	C4
Main Post Office	4	B5
Tourist Information Centre	(see 9)	
X-net	5	C6
SIGHTS & ACTIVITIES		
ITB (Bandung Institute of Technology)	6	C1
Jeans Street	7	B2
Kantor Walikota (City Hall)	8	C4
Masjid Agung	9	B5
Museum Geologi	10	D2
Museum Konperensi	11	B5
Museum Mandala Wangsit	12	C5
Museum Prangko	13	D3
Zoo	14	B1
SLEEPING		
Arion Swiss-Belhotel	15	B4
By Moritz	16	A5
Edelweiss	17	A1
Grand Hotel Preanger	18	C5
Hotel Arimbi	19	A4
Hotel Cemerlang	20	A4
Hotel Gunter	21	B4
Hotel Kedaton	22	B4
Hotel Mutiara	23	A4
Hotel Patradissa	24	A4
Hotel Sawunggaling	25	C2
Hotel Surabaya	26	A5
Savoy Homann Hotel	27	C5
EATING		
Braga Café	28	C5
French Bakery	29	C5
Kartika Sari	(see 43)	
Kyooki	30	C5
London Bakery	31	C5
Momiji	32	C5
Roempoet	33	C5
Royal Siam	34	B4
Rumah Makan Mandarin	35	A4
Rumah Makan Sari Sunda	36	A5
Warung Nasi Mang Udju	37	B6
DRINKING		
Amsterdam Café	38	C5
Downtown	(see 38)	
North Sea Bar	39	C5
ENTERTAINMENT		
Braga Disco	40	B5
Fame Station	41	D6
Rumentang Siang	42	D5
SHOPPING		
Cupu Manik Puppet Factory	43	A4
Flower Market	44	B3
TRANSPORT		
Abd Muis Angkot Terminal	45	B6
Garuda	(see 18)	
Kramatdjati	46	A5
Merpati	47	B4
Pahala Kencana	(see 46)	

was here that Soekarno studied civil engineering (1920–25) and helped to found the Bandung Study Club, whose members formed a political party that grew into the Indonesian Nationalist Party (Partai Nasional Indonesia; PNI), with independence as its goal. The institute's students have maintained their reputation for outspokenness and political activism, and in 1978 they published the *White Book of the 1978 Students' Struggle*, which alleged corruption in high places. In 1998, in the lead-up to Soeharto's downfall, up to 100,000 students rallied daily, but in keeping with Bandung's laid-back reputation, there were no riots in the city.

The ITB is the foremost scientific university in the country, but it also has one of the best fine-arts schools, and its **art gallery** (admission free; 🕒 on request) can be visited. Across from the main gate is a useful canteen in the *asrama mahasiswa* (student dorm complex), where many of the students congregate.

To reach the ITB, take a Lembang or Dago *angkot* from the train station and then walk down Jl Ganeca.

ZOO

The Bandung **zoo** (Jl Taman Sari; admission 5000Rp; 🕒 8am-4pm) has spacious, beautifully landscaped gardens, which are very attractive, but there are few animals and most are housed in typically cramped conditions. The zoo is a few minutes' walk from the ITB – the entrance is down the steps past the toy stalls opposite Jl Ganeca.

DAGO

At the end of Jl Merdeka, Jl Juanda climbs up to Dago Hill to the north, overlooking the city. The famous, but faded, **Dago Thee Huis** (Dago Tea House; ☎ 2505364; admission 1000Rp) offers views through the forest of power lines and radio towers and is a fine place to catch the sunset. The complex has an outdoor theatre and an indoor theatre further down the hill where cultural events are sometimes held.

On the main road, 100m past the teahouse turn-off, a path leads down to **Curug Dago** (Dago Waterfall). From here you can walk along the river to **Taman Hutan Raya Ir H Juanda**, which is a pleasant forest park with another waterfall, 'caves' and walking paths. By road, the park entrance is 2km past the Dago bemo terminal.

Gua Pakar is in fact an ammunition store hacked out by the Japanese during the war. Further north is **Gua Belanda**, which is the same deal but built by the Dutch. A tunnel leads right through the mountain to the start of the trail that leads all the way to **Maribaya** (p145) along Sungai Cikapundung.

'JEANS' STREET

Advertising is one thing, but a 20ft-high plaster statue of Rambo? Bandung's celebrated 'Jeans' Street, Jl Cihampelas, is the place where seeing is believing. Traditionally the home of the city's thriving textile industry, this congested drag, in the affluent northern suburbs of Bandung, is now a menagerie of kitsch plaster giants, looming over shops competing with one another for the top spot in the city's booming denim trade. The jeans are definitely cheap; just don't expect to look like a Dean or a Monroe when you slip them on.

ABU DOMBA

These noisy ram-butting fights, held most Sundays between 9am and 1pm, are a favourite pastime of the Bandung populace. Animal lovers won't like it a bit, but, like Spain's bullfights, they're a sight to behold, and at least the rams only walk away with a sore head. Consult the tourist information centre (p139) for more details.

Tours & Courses

Many of Bandung's budget hotels, such as By Moritz (below) and Hotel Patradissa (right), offer **one-day tours** (300,000Rp per person) of the sights to the north and south of the city, and also two-day trips to Garut and Pangandaran (750,000Rp).

Bahasa Indonesia courses can be taken at the Institute of Technology; contact the Tourist Information Centre (p139) for details.

Sleeping

BUDGET

Many of Bandung's budget options are close to the train station and city centre.

Hotel Arimbi (☎ 4202734; Jl Station Selatan 5; dm 27,500Rp, s/d with shared mandi 40,000/47,500Rp) Arimbi is a rough-and-ready place a stone's throw from the train station. Staff are exceptionally friendly, but the throng of hangers-on crowding the foyer is a little off-putting.

By Moritz (☎ 4205788; Kompleks Luxor Permai 35, Jl Kebonjati; s/d with breakfast & shared bathroom 35,000/45,000Rp) Even though the walls are thin, cleaning doesn't seem a priority and rooms are Spartan, By Moritz still gets more than its fair share of readers' recommendations. It's also a good place to swap stories with other travellers and arrange trips to outlying attractions.

Hotel Surabaya (☎ 436791; Jl Kebonjati 71; s/d/q 35,000/45,000/65,000Rp) Surabaya is an unusual beast, even by Javan standards. Housed in a beautiful, colonial lodge, this could be a fabulous hotel if someone gave it a good make-over. But with its yellowed 1920s photographs, Moulin Rouge prints and authentic layer of dusts, it still has plenty of charm; just don't expect too much in the way of comfort.

Hotel Patradissa (☎ 4206680; Jl H Moch Iskat 8; s/d 75,000/90,000Rp, with TV from 100,000Rp, with air-con from 130,000Rp; ❄) Patradissa is looking a bit worse for wear these days and fails to attract many travellers, but staff are welcoming and rooms are in better condition than most of its contemporaries.

Hotel Gunter (☎ 4203763; Jl Oto Iskandardinata 20; r with/without air-con 160,000/135,000Rp; ❄) Gunter is an old-fashioned hotel lacking character, but its rooms are in very good condition and quite spacious. Fortunately, it's set back from busy Jl Oto Iskandardinata, making it a quiet option.

Edelweiss (☎ 2032369; Jl Sukajadi 206; r with air-con & TV from 188,000Rp; ❄) This quiet and clean guesthouse is a fair trip from the centre, but handy for a quick escape to Tangkuban Prahu. Rooms are in very good nick, and if you can't find any staff members, try the factory outlet store out front.

MIDRANGE

Bandung has plenty of midrange hotels, especially north of the train station and along Jl Gardujati, but most are old and faded.

Hotel Cemerlang (☎ 6071383; Jl Pasirkaliki 45; r from 250,000Rp; ❄) Near Hotel Mutiara, this midrange hotel has above-average rooms that lose out on the charm factor, but it's still a good bet all round. Add 30,000Rp at weekends.

Hotel Sawunggaling (☎ 4218254; Jl Sawunggaling 13; r from 250,000Rp; ❄) This attractive and pleasant hotel, out near ITB, oozes colonial style. It occupies a quiet corner and rooms are big and comfy.

Hotel Mutiara (☎ 4200333; fax 4200111; www.mutiarahotel.com; Jl Kebon Kawung 60; r from 330,000Rp, ste 550,000Rp; ❄ 🏊) Mutiara is a polished, motel-style place, with a range of rooms around a busy courtyard. All rooms come with hot water, TV and air-con. It also has a restaurant and bar, so you won't need to go far to fill up. Ask for a room away from the extremely loud street.

Hotel Kedaton (☎ 4219898; kedaton@indosat.net.id; Jl Suniaraja 14; r from 338,000Rp; ❄ 🏊) Towering over a busy intersection in shades of pale pink and yellow is this rather opulent hotel. Rooms are well kept and of a high standard, and discounts may be available if you ask nicely.

Savoy Homann Hotel (☎ 4232244; www.savoyhomann-hotel.com; Jl Asia Afrika 112; s/d from 475,000/500,000Rp;) This temple to Art Deco style is looking as good as ever, and is Bandung's most famous hotel. Rooms are plush, and come with buckets of style and character.

Arion Swiss-Belhotel (☎ 4240000; www.swiss-belhotel.com; Jl Oto Iskandardinata 16; r from 495,000Rp plus 21% tax;) This hotel is so new it looked as though the plastic wrapping was removed five minutes before we walked in. Rooms are long, spacious and immaculate (some even have carpeted walls), and the top floor is given over to the pool and fitness centre.

Hotel Jayakarta (☎ 2505888; rsvo_bdg@jayakartahotelresorts.com; Jl Juanda 381; r from 568,000Rp;) Right near the Dago Tea House at the top of Jl Juanda is this boutique hotel. Views from top-floor rooms are extensive, there's aromatherapy on site, and discounts may be available.

TOP END

Like any big city, Bandung has a glut of luxury hotels, all with swimming pools. Most offer good discounts, so ring around.

Sheraton (☎ 2500303; www.sheraton.com/bandung; Jl Juanda 390; r from 700,000Rp;) Smaller but slicker than Grand Hotel Preanger, Bandung's Sheraton is a small oasis of calm on the crowded and busy road to Dago. Needless to say, rooms and facilities are of the highest standard.

Grand Hotel Preanger (☎ 4231631; www.preanger.aerowisata.com; Jl Asia Afrika 181; r from 756,000Rp, ste from 2,000,000Rp;) Built in 1928, the Grand lives up to its name, with Art Deco charm coupled with modern luxury. Its suites are as plush as anything you'll find in the city.

Eating

Jl Braga is the city's quasi-European strip, featuring a plethora of coffee shops, quality restaurants and bakeries. The best night warungs are on Jl Cikapundung Barat, across from the *alun-alun* near the Ramayana department store. Stalls sell a bit of everything – try the *soto jeroan*, intestine soup with various medicinal properties, mostly designed to stimulate male libido.

Warung Nasi Mang Udju (Jl Dewi Sartika; mains from 15,000Rp; lunch & dinner) Just south of the *alun-alun*, this Spartan place is a good spot to sample some traditional Sundanese food.

Rumah Makan Sari Sunda (Jl Jenderal Sudirman 103-107; mains 20,000Rp; lunch & dinner) Sari Sunda is a more salubrious eatery, with rattan décor, a not-so-tasteful artificial waterfall, and huts in the garden for dining on mats. The Sundanese food, however, is of the same standard as Nasi Mang Udju – delicious.

Rumah Makan Mandarin (Jl Kebon Kawung; mains 20,000Rp; lunch & dinner) Mandarin is a very simple eatery with seafood specialities and a loyal band of Chinese regulars.

Roempoet (Jl Braga 80; mains around 20,000Rp; dinner) Roempoet is a stripped-back eatery-bar popular with a young crowd. You'll find regular live bands and simple but tasty Indonesian fare cooked on an open barbecue.

Kyooki (☎ 4204188; Jl Braga 21; mains 25,000-50,000Rp; dinner) This minimalist restaurant attracts Bandung's bright young things with a range of Japanese favourites and some of the city's best cocktails.

Momiji (☎ 4203786; Jl Braga 64; mains 25,000-65,000Rp; lunch & dinner) Another of Jl Braga's Japanese restaurants, Momiji is a more traditional place, with a serene atmosphere and even a small library of Japanese books. Expect plenty of fresh sushi, maki and sashimi.

Royal Siam (☎ 4241459; Jl Braga 121; mains 30,000-50,000Rp; lunch & dinner) This top-notch Thai restaurant has formal service, authentic wooden décor and huge dishes of *gai pad pid* (red curry). Sit at tables or sprawl out Asian style and soak up the atmosphere.

Bandung Supermal (Jl Gatot Subroto 289; mains 10,000Rp; breakfast, lunch & dinner) In the east of the city, this shopping mall has all the usual food court favourites.

Bandung has a surprisingly large number of excellent bakeries, and probably an excessive amount of dentists too. The following are all worth visiting (bakeries, not dentists):

Kartika Sari (Jl Haji Akbar 4; cakes around 2000Rp; breakfast & lunch) Next door to the Cupu Manik puppet factory; has an incredible array of sweets and a steady flow of customers.

London Bakery (Jl Braga 37; cakes 2000Rp; ⌚ breakfast & lunch) Serves sweet cakes and strong coffees alongside burgers; try the brownies.

French Bakery (Jl Braga 35; cakes 2000Rp; ⌚ breakfast & lunch) Has more of the same, just the name is different.

Braga Café (Jl Braga 19; cakes 2000Rp; ⌚ breakfast & lunch) Yet another Bandung bakery excelling in providing the population with sweet treats; this time the pastries are the best bet.

Drinking

For a night out on the turps in Bandung, head for Jl Braga, where you'll find a string of bars, including the following:

Downtown (Jl Braga 70) Big bright pool hall filled with a local rather than expat atmosphere.

North Sea Bar (Jl Braga 82) The beer flows into the wee small hours at this expat and bar-girl hangout.

Amsterdam Café (Jl Braga 74) Offers a heady mix of loud music, bar girls and booze; North Sea Bar's rival for the expat crowd.

Entertainment

CULTURAL PERFORMANCES

Bandung is the place to see Sundanese performing arts; however, performance times are haphazard – check with the Tourist Information Centre for the latest schedules.

Rumentang Siang (☎ 4233562; Jl Baranangsiang 1) This is Bandung's performing arts centre, where *wayang golek*, Jaipongan (West Javanese dance), *pencak silat* (the art of self-defence), Sandiwara (traditional Javanese theatre) and *ketoprak* (popular Javanese folk theatre) performances are held.

ASTI-Bandung (☎ 7314982; Jl Buah Batu 212) In the southern part of the city, this is a school for traditional Sundanese arts – music, dancing and *pencak silat*.

Saung Angklung (☎ 7271714; Jl Padasuka 118; performances 35,000Rp; ⌚ 10.30am-5pm) *Angklung* (bamboo musical instrument) performances take place at Pak Ujo's Saung Angklung, east of the city on the way to the Cicaheum bus terminal. You can also see the instruments being made here. Performances are held most afternoons at 3.30pm.

LIVE MUSIC

A mix of bar and restaurant, **Roempoet** (Jl Braga 80) has a relaxed, informal air and lives bands most evenings.

NIGHTCLUBS

Like anywhere in the world, Bandung's youth love to get out on the dance floor and shake it up. Just off Jl Braga, Braga Disco is a safe bet for loud music, dark corners and people-watching, as is **Fame Station** (Jl Gatot Subroto 2), a busy dance club on the 11th floor of the Lippo Centre Building.

Shopping

Shopping centres dominate the town these days, but Bandung isn't all about glitzy stores and mall fever. Jl Cibaduyut, in southwest Bandung, is to shoes what Jl Cihampelas is to jeans, but without the gaudy statues. Shop after shop sells everything from Puma to Bata, but if you've big feet, you may have trouble finding the right size.

Bandung Supermal (Jl Gatot Subroto 289) This is Bandung's latest addition to its plethora of shopping centres; it has the largest Hero Supermarket in Indonesia, a bowling alley, a couple of cinemas, and more than 200 shops.

Pak Ruhiyat (No 78/17B; ⌚ 7am-5pm) Down a small, unnamed alley behind Jl Pangarang 22, this small shop produces *wayang golek* puppets and masks.

Cupu Manik puppet factory (Jl Haji Akbar 10; ⌚ 8am-4pm Mon-Sat) This is another puppet maker, with a range of styles for sale.

Saung Angklung (☎ 7271714; Jl Padasuka 118; ⌚ 10.30am-5pm) Traditional Sundanese musical instruments can be bought here at this bamboo workshop.

Markets to explore in Bandung include the following:

Pasar Baru (Jl Kebonjati; ⌚ 8am-5pm) Somewhat grotty central market, with fruit, vegetables and assorted paraphernalia.

Pasar Jatayu (Jl Arjuna; ⌚ 9am-5pm) One kilometre west of the train station, this flea market is where a few collectables hide in piles of junk.

Flower market (Jl Wastukencana; ⌚ 7am-3pm) On the way to the zoo.

For everyday purchases, the liveliest shopping district is on Jl Dalem Kaum and in the nearby streets, just east of the *alun-alun*. Supermarkets can be found in the Ramayana department stores on Jl Cikapundung Barat and Jl Dalem Kaum, and in the Plaza Bandung Indah.

Getting There & Away

AIR

You can book your flight to Jakarta and Surabaya with **Merpati** (☎ 4260253; Jl Kebon Kawung 16); **Garuda** (☎ 4209468) is in the Grand Hotel Preanger (p143). Consult the Java Airfares map (p98) for prices.

BUS

Five kilometres south of the city centre, **Leuwi Panjang bus terminal** (Jl Soekarno Hatta) has buses west to places such as Bogor (normal/air-con 15,900/25,000Rp, three hours), Sukabumi (15,000Rp, three hours) and Jakarta's Kampung Rambutan bus terminal (20,000Rp to 45,000Rp, 4½ hours). Buses to Bogor are not allowed to take the scenic Puncak Pass route during weekends.

Buses to the east leave from the Cicaheum bus terminal on the eastern outskirts of the city. They include Cirebon (normal/air-con 20,000/33,000Rp, 3½ hours), Garut (10,000Rp, two hours) and Pangandaran (32,000Rp, six hours).

Sari Harum (☎ 6077065) has air-con minibuses to Pangandaran (60,000Rp, five hours) at 6am and 2pm. Both **Kramatdjati** (☎ 4239860; Jl Kebonjati 96) and **Pahala Kencana** (☎ 4232911; Jl Kebonjati 90) run luxury buses to long-distance destinations, such as Yogyakarta (81,000Rp).

TRAIN

The best train service for Jakarata is the *Parahyangan* (business/executive 45,000/60,000Rp, three hours), with departures roughly every hour from 4am to 8.25pm.

Several trains operate on the Bandung–Banjar–Yogyakarta route, most continuing on to Surabaya. Most are night expresses, such as the business-class *Mutiara Selatan*, which passes through Bandung at 5.05pm on its way to Yogyakarta (80,000Rp) and Surabaya (120,000Rp). The *Lodaya* leaves Bandung at 8am for Yogyakarta and Solo (business/executive 90,000/150,000Rp).

Getting Around

TO/FROM THE AIRPORT

Bandung's Husein Sastranegara airport is 4km northwest of town; it costs 60,000Rp to get there by taxi.

BUS, ANGKOT & TAXI

Bandung has a fairly good, if crowded, Damri city bus service that charges a fixed 2000Rp. Buses 9 and 11 run from west to east down Jl Asia Afrika to Cicaheum bus terminal.

Angkot run over set routes all over town between numerous stations. From Stasiun Hall (St Hall), on the southern side of the train station, *angkot* go to Dago, Ledeng and other stations. When returning, catch any *angkot* displaying 'St Hall'. Abdul Muis (Abd Muis), south of the *alun-alun* on Jl Dewi Sartika, and Cicaheum are the other main *angkot* terminals. *Angkot* cost from 2000Rp to 3000Rp.

Becak have all but disappeared from central Bandung. Taxis, both private and metered, are numerous, but meters are rarely used – drivers will ask for a minimum of 10,000Rp.

NORTH OF BANDUNG

Lembang

☎ 022

The town of Lembang was once a noted hill resort but is now a busy little market town. Most visitors keep heading further up the hills, but if you're looking for a quick break from Bandung, 16km to the south, then it's a decent option.

The old-fashioned and comfortable **Grand Hotel Lembang** (☎ 2786671; ghl@bdg.centrin.net.id; Jl Raya Lembang 272; weekday/weekend r from 279,000/410,000Rp; 🏊) harks back to the days when Lembang was a fashionable resort for Bandung's Dutch colonial community. It's a sprawling place with dated but comfortable rooms, beautiful gardens and tennis courts.

Maribaya Hot Springs

Maribaya, 5km east of Lembang, has a thermal spa, landscaped gardens and a thundering waterfall (admission to waterfall is 5000Rp). It's another tourist spot, crowded on Sunday, but worth visiting. You can extend your Tangkuban Prahu (below) trip by walking from the bottom end of the gardens down through a brilliant, deep and wooded river gorge all the way to Dago. There's a good track, and if you allow about two hours for the walk (6km), you can be at a Dago vantage point for sunset. From there it's only a short trip by Colt back into Bandung.

Tangkuban Prahu

The 'overturned *perahu*' volcano crater is 30km north of Bandung. Years ago the centre

THE LEGEND OF TANGKUBAN PRAHU

Like so many of Java's unusual geographical features, there is a legend behind Tangkuban Prahu.

An estranged young prince returned home and unwittingly fell in love with his own mother. When the queen discovered the terrible truth of her lover's identity, she challenged him to build a dam and a huge boat during a single night before she would agree to marry him. Seeing that the young man was about to complete this impossible task, she called on the gods to bring the sun up early, and as the cocks began to crow, the boat builder turned his nearly completed boat over in a fit of anger.

of Tangkuban Prahu collapsed under the weight of built-up ash and, instead of the usual conical volcano shape, it has a flat, elongated summit with a huge caldera.

At 2076m Tangkuban Prahu can be quite cool, and around noon the mist starts to roll in through the trees, so try to go early. The crater is easily accessible by car, so it's very much a tourist trap.

At the crater is an **information centre** (7am-5pm), warungs and a parade of peddlers hustling postcards, souvenirs and other junk. It's a tacky jumble that detracts from the scenery, but you can escape this bedlam of activity.

The huge **crater** is an impressive sight. Tangkuban Prahu still emits sulphur fumes but is not particularly active – its last serious eruption was in 1969. It's possible to circumnavigate the crater in around two hours.

Kawah Ratu is the huge 'Queen Crater' at the top. Walk around the rim of the main crater for about 20 minutes for views of the secondary crater, **Kawah Upas**. The trail leads further along a ridge between the two craters and returns to the car park, but it is steep and slippery in parts – exercise caution. A better and less-crowded walk is to **Kawah Domas**, a volcanic area of steaming and bubbling geysers that can be reached by a side trail to the top. You can also head off across country towards Ciater or Lembang; guides can be hired for 50,000Rp per hour.

Surrounded by forest just north of the town of Cikole, the outdoor centre **Taman Wisata Alam** (☎ 022-91150480; camping 5000Rp, bungalows 150,000Rp) has camp sites and basic wooden bungalows that sleep up to four. Cooking facilities are available, or there's a tiny restaurant for meals. Tours and treks to the mountain are offered by staff. Bookings are advisable.

GETTING THERE & AWAY

From Bandung's minibus terminal in front of the train station, take a Subang Colt (10,000Rp) via Lembang to the park entrance.

Entry is 20,000Rp per person. Minibuses to the top officially cost 10,000Rp per person, but the drivers will probably ask for more; if there are not enough people to share, you will have to charter – bargain hard.

Alternatively, you can walk from the gate at the main road. It's 4.5km along the road or you can take the more interesting side trail that goes via Kawah Domas. It is a very steep one-hour walk through the jungle and better tackled from the top down. It starts just behind the information centre and is very easy to follow.

Drivers in Bandung will charge around 300,000Rp for a visit to Tangkuban Prahu, depending on the time spent at the crater, or 150,000Rp to 180,000Rp for a motorbike; prices include petrol but exclude entry (6000Rp extra for a car, 2000Rp for a bike).

Ciater Hot Springs

Eight kilometres northeast of Tangkuban Prahu, Ciater is a pretty little place in the middle of huge tea and clove estates. The area has good walks, and a tea factory on the south side of Ciater can be visited.

At the end of the road through the village, Ciater's main attraction is the **Sari Ater Hot Spring Resort** (☎ 0260-471700; admission 10,000Rp, pools extra 20,000Rp; 24hr). Although they're quite commercialised, the pools are probably the best of all the hot springs around Bandung. If you've been climbing around the volcano on a cool, rainy day there's no better way to get warm. Rooms (from 250,000Rp) and rustic bungalows are also available.

Ciater has plenty of small *penginapan* (lodging houses) with rooms starting at around 30,000Rp – those on the main road are cheaper.

You can walk to Ciater – about 12km across country – from Tangkuban Prahu, or flag down a Colt at the entrance point to Tangkuban Prahu; the road that leads up to Tangkuban from the main road.

SOUTH OF BANDUNG

☎ 022

Less developed than the resorts to the north, the mountains south of Bandung have fewer facilities, but are quieter. The road south of Bandung leads to **Ciwidey**, a town where every second house has a strawberry patch.

From there, the road winds through the hills to the turn-off to **Kawah Putih** (admission per person 5500Rp, plus motorbike/car 1000/3000Rp; 7am-5pm), a volcanic crater with a beautiful turquoise lake. The turn-off is 6km before Rancabali, and then it is 8km to the small crater lake just below Gunung Patuha (2334m). Although it is only a small crater, Kawah Putih is exceptionally beautiful and eerily quiet when the mists roll in.

Back on the road a few kilometres further south from the turn-off to Kawah Putih are two developed hot springs at **Cimanggu**; the newer **Walini** complex has big hot pools and a few bungalows.

Rancabali, 42km from Bandung, is basically one big tea estate surrounded by rolling green hills of tea plantations. Just 2km south of the town is **Situ Patengan**, a pretty

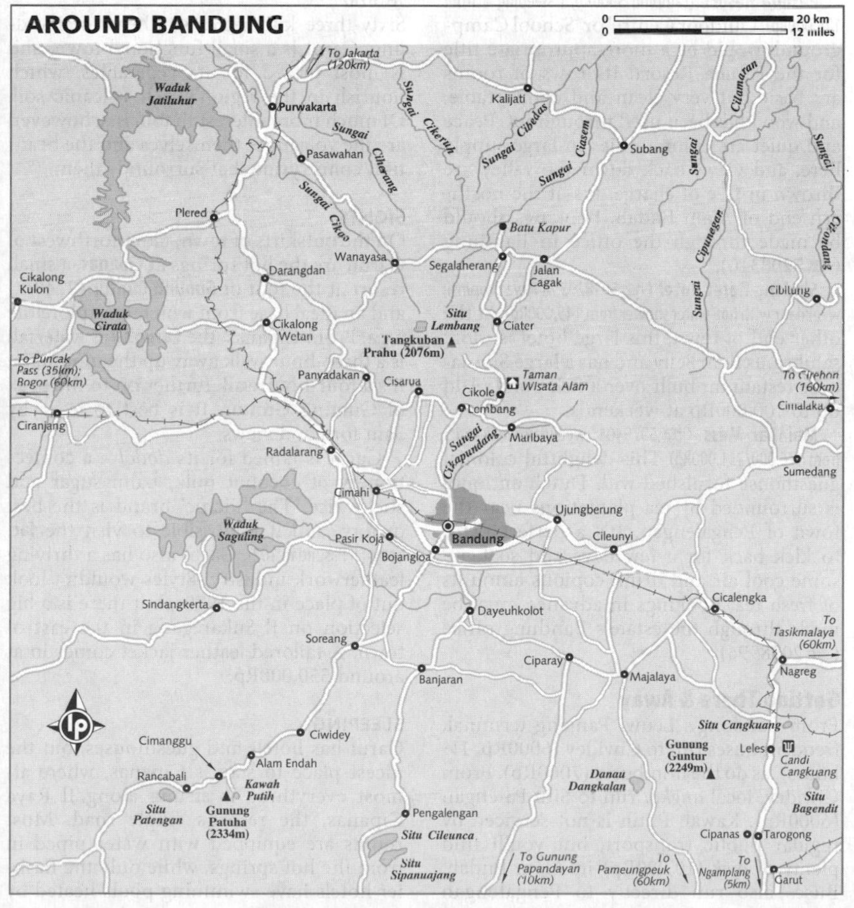

lake with tea rooms and boats catering to the Sunday crowds.

The area's main attraction is the **Malabar Tea Estate**, 5km from Pengalengan, where you can tour the plantations and stay at the wonderful guesthouse, the Malabar Mess (below).

Sleeping

Accommodation is limited to a couple of places in Ciwidey, Alam Endah and Pengalengan, plus the Malabar Tea Estate. Generally they're all empty during the week.

Hotel Selly (☎ 5928261; Jl Raya Rancabali, Km 1; r from 60,000Rp) This pink place has spotless rooms and is on the southern edge of Ciwidey. It's also on the busy main road.

Patuha Resort (camping 5000Rp, r sleeping 4 from 125,000Rp) 'Outdoor Centre' or 'School Campground' would be a more appropriate title for the Patuha Resort. Its rows of rooms are basic but very clean and comfortable, and wood has been used throughout. Peace and quiet are commodities in large supply here, and views back down the valley are thrown in free of charge. It's at the northern end of Alam Endah. Bookings should be made through the office in Bandung (☎ 7208310).

Sindang Reret Hotel (☎ 5928205; Jl Raya Propinsi; weekday r with hot-water shower from 145,000Rp) At the other end of town, this large hotel is more salubrious than Selly and has a large Sundanese restaurant built over a fish pond. Add up to 100,000Rp at weekends.

Malabar Mess (☎ 5979401; weekday/weekend r from 176,000/231,000Rp) This delightful colonial guesthouse furnished with Dutch antiques is surrounded by tea plantations near the town of Pengalengan. It's a perfect place to kick back for a few days and soak up some cool air and drink copious amounts of fresh tea. Bookings in advance must be made through the estate's Bandung office (☎ 2038996).

Getting There & Away

From Bandung's Leuwi Panjang terminal, frequent buses run to Ciwidey (6000Rp, 1½ hours), as do the minibuses (7000Rp). From Ciwidey, local *angkot* run to Situ Patengan (6000Rp). Kawah Putih is not serviced by regular public transport, but you'll find plenty of *ojek* (10,000Rp) in Alam Endah. Buses also run directly to Pengalengan (7000Rp), where *ojek* hang out at the bus terminal.

BANDUNG TO PANGANDARAN

Heading southeast from Bandung, the road passes through rolling hills and stunning volcanic peaks skirting – at a safe distance – the particularly explosive **Gunung Papandayan** (2622m). This is the Bandung–Yogyakarta road as far as Banjar; the Bandung to Yogyakarta train line passes through Tasikmalaya and Banjar, but not Garut. After the choked roads of Jakarta and Bandung, driving on these quieter Javan roads is a pleasure.

Garut & Cipanas

☎ 0262

Sixty-three kilometres southeast of Bandung, Garut is a small functional town, and is most prized for its vegetables, which flourish in the region's rich volcanic soil. Of much more interest to tourists, however, are the volcanoes themselves and the beautiful countryside that surrounds them.

SIGHTS

On the outskirts of town, 6km northwest of Garut, are the hot springs at **Cipanas**, a small resort at the foot of **Gunung Guntur** (2249m) and an ideal base from which to explore the area. From Cipanas, the **Curug Citiis** waterfall is a three-hour walk away up the mountain; it's a four-hour walk further on to the peak of Gunung Guntur. It is best to leave by 5am for good views.

Garut is famed for its *dodol* – a confectionery of coconut milk, palm sugar and sticky rice. The 'Picnic' brand is the best quality, and it is possible to visit the **factory** (Jl Pasundan 102). Garut also has a thriving leatherwork industry. Styles wouldn't look out of place in the 1970s, but there is a big selection on Jl Sukaregang in the east of town. A tailored leather jacket comes in at around 550,000Rp.

SLEEPING

Garut has hotels and guesthouses, but the nicest place to stay is Cipanas, where almost everything is strung along Jl Raya Cipanas, the resort's single road. Most rooms are equipped with water piped in from the hot springs, while only the flashier hotels have swimming pools heated by the springs; if you're staying at a cheaper option, it's possible to use the pools for a minimal fee (adult/child 4000/2000Rp). Prices quoted here are weekly rates; expect anything between a 15% and 40% increase on weekends.

Hotel Tirta Merta (☎ 231112; r from 75,000Rp) This simple place has clean rooms, cheerful staff and plenty of decorative concrete tree stumps.

Hotel Tirta Alam (☎ 241556; r/bungalows 90,000/300,000Rp) This hotel is popular with drivers, who can park directly outside their plain rooms; bungalows sit inches above thermal pools.

Hotel Nurgraha (☎ 234829; r 100,000Rp, ste from 175,000Rp) The pick of the cheap/midrange options, Nurgraha has rooms with balconies overlooking the road, and sunset views of a thermal pond and coconut trees.

Cipanas Indah (☎ 233736; r from 100,000Rp, VIP r 200,000Rp;) With simple, clean rooms centred on a pool, Cipanas Indah supplies a nice holiday atmosphere for its guests.

Sumber Alam (☎ 238000; www.kampungsumberalam.com; r 250,000-1,000,000Rp;) Alam is the most attractive hotel in Cipanas, with wooden bungalows built over the water; it's a popular family hang-out, particularly on weekends.

Tirtagangga Hotel (☎ 232549; r/ste from 265,000/735,000Rp;) Easily the town's second best hotel, Tirtagangga comes complete with tasteful rooms, a quality restaurant and information on the area.

GETTING THERE & AWAY

Buses and *angkot* leave from the Guntur terminal in Garut, in the north of the town. Garut is easily reached by bus from Bandung (10,000Rp, two hours) and also from Tasikmalaya (12,000Rp, two hours). For Pangandaran, take another bus from Tasikmalaya.

Regular *angkot* run around town and to Cipanas (*angkot* 4, 2000Rp).

A car or minibus with driver can be rented in Cipanas – ask around the hotels. A trip to Papandayan will cost 300,000Rp to 400,000Rp, depending on the quality of the car.

Around Garut

Near Leles, about 10km north of Garut, is **Candi Cangkuang**, which is one of the few stone Hindu temples found in West Java. Dating from the 8th century, some of its stones were found to have been carved into tombstones for a nearby Islamic cemetery. The small, restored temple lies on the edge of Situ Cangkuang, a small lake. It has become something of a tourist trap, but it's a peaceful and beautiful trip. From Garut take a green *angkot* to Leles (3000Rp) on the highway and then another *angkot* or horse-drawn *dilman* (two-wheeled buggy, 2500Rp per person) for the 3km to Candi Cangkuang. Rafts across the lake to the temple cost 25,000Rp.

Twenty-eight kilometres to the southwest of Garut, **Gunung Papandayan** (2622m) is one of the most active volcanoes in West Java. Papandayan first became active in 1772, when a large piece of the mountain exploded sideways in a catastrophe that killed more than 3000 people. It was active again in the closing months of 2002 and thousands of villagers were forced to evacuate their homes as plumes of smoke and ash were spewed thousands of feet into the air. Papandayan is once again open to visitors, but check with locals before setting out on what could be a wild goose chase, or something far more dangerous.

The bubbling yellow crater (Kawah Papandayan) just below the peak is an impressive sight and clearly visible from the Garut Valley on clear mornings. To get there, take a Cikajang minibus and get off at the turn-off on the outskirts of Cisurupan (5000Rp), where you can catch a waiting *ojek* (25,000Rp one way, 13km).

From the car park area it is an easy half-hour walk to the crater, which is riddled with bubbling mud pools, steam vents and crumbling sulphur deposits. Take care – keep well to the right when ascending through the crater; it may pay to hire a guide (250,000Rp per day; from the PHKA office, as the car park area is generally full of cowboys) for closer inspection. For fine views, go very early in the morning before the clouds roll in. Gunung Papandayan's summit is a two-hour walk beyond the crater, and there are fields of Javan edelweiss near the top. PHKA staff can arrange a camping permit.

To the east of Garut town, **Gunung Telagabodas** (2201m) has a bubbling bright-green crater lake that's alive with sulphur.

To get to Telagabodas, take an *angkot* to Wanaraja (4000Rp), an *ojek* (10,000Rp) to the parking area and then walk to the crater. Craters to the west of Garut that can be visited are **Kawah Darajat**, 26km away, and **Kawah Kamojang**, 23km away, the site of a geothermal plant that has defused the once spectacular geyser activity and replaced it with huge pipes.

Halfway between Garut and Tasikmalaya is **Kampung Naga**, a traditional village and a museum piece of Sundanese architecture and village life. It is home to 110 families, who preserve the old ways of life despite the crowds of tourists that pass through here during the peak season. Kampung Naga, with its thatched-roof houses, is a photographer's dream, nestled next to a river and surrounded by precipitous hillsides – there are 360 steps up to the car park on the main highway. Guides (50,000Rp) can be found next to the warungs by the car park.

Tasikmalaya

☎ 0265

Sixty kilometres east of Garut, Tasikmalaya is the centre for the district of the same name. For travellers, it is merely a transit town on the way to Pangandaran. The surrounding area has a few points of interest and Tasik has plenty of hotels; the **Crown Mahkota Graha** (☎ 332282; Jl Martadinata 45; r 225,000-395,000Rp;), with its restaurant and tidy rooms, is the best.

From Tasikmalaya, buses operate to Bandung (20,000Rp, four hours), Garut (12,000Rp, two hours) and Pangandaran (30,000Rp, three hours). Overcharging from here to Pangandaran is common, so bargain hard. The main bus terminal is 4km from the town centre on the eastern outskirts. Tasikmalaya is also on the main train line.

Around Tasikmalaya

For cheap rattan crafts, for which the area is famous, visit the village of **Rajapolah** (12km north of Tasikmalaya on the road to Bandung), where many of the weavers work.

Cipanas Galunggung is 20km northwest and is a hot spring at the foot of **Gunung Galunggung** (2168m), a volcano that exploded dramatically in 1982. From the hot springs recreation park, a trail leads to a small waterfall and then on to Galunggung crater, 3km away. A steep road to the crater is an easier walk but less interesting. From Tasikmalaya's main bus terminal take an *angkot* to Bantar on the highway. From there, an *ojek* can take you 14km along a rough road.

Situ Lengkong is about 40km north of Tasikmalaya and 500m from the village of Panjalu. It's a serene lake that was formed when the Hindu ruler of Panjalu dammed the valley. There is a forested island in the middle and boats can be hired to take you around the island. Panjalu village has a small **museum** containing the heirlooms of the kings of Panjalu. Situ Lengkong can be reached by bus from Tasikmalaya or from Kawali terminal, where *angkot* run the 20km to Ciamis.

On the highway to Banjar and Pangandaran, 16km southeast of Ciamis, **Karang Komulyan** is the excavated site of the ancient Galuh kingdom. Local guides and tourist literature give a glorified account of the Galuh kingdom as both the first Hindu and the first Muslim kingdom in Java, but this Neolithic settlement dating from around the 5th century points to the pre-Hindu period. Only a few stone walls and foundations remain of the 'palace', store, prayer and bathing areas, but it is a beautiful walk through the jungle and bamboo groves down to the confluence of the swift Ciliwung and Citanduy Rivers. A large car park and government-built cottages next to the park are attempts to make it a major tourist stop.

Banjar

Banjar, 42km east of Tasikmalaya, is the junction point where the Pangandaran road branches from the Bandung to Yogyakarta road and rail route. It has some basic hotels if you get stuck en route to Pangandaran.

The bus terminal is 4km west of town on the highway. Many buses can be caught as they come through the centre of town near the train station. From Banjar the buses go to Pangandaran (12,000Rp, 1½ hours), Bandung, Purwokerto and Jakarta. Buses also go from the Banjarsari bus terminal, half an hour south of Banjar, to Jakarta.

Banjar is not a good place to catch trains, since most are crowded through-trains. To Yogyakarta and Solo, the best option is the *Lodaya* (business 60,000Rp), which heads east at 11.07am. On its way back to Bandung, the *Lodaya* passes through Banjar just after midnight. The economy-class *Pasun-*

dan II (35,000Rp) leaves Banjar for Surabaya at 10.35am.

PANGANDARAN

☎ 0265

Situated on a narrow isthmus, with a broad sweep of sand on either side and a thickly forested national park on the nearby headland, Pangandaran is Java's premier beach resort. While it can never compete with Bali's pristine white sands or party atmosphere, it is nevertheless an attractive, friendly and peaceful – or lively, if you're here during Indonesia's school holidays – spot to recuperate before pushing onto sights inland.

As well as days of sun-worshipping on Pangandaran's volcanic black-sand beaches, the town and its surrounds offer up coastal walks, forest treks and seafood so fresh it's still sparkling. And with an army of hotels covering every budget base, you should have no problem finding something to suit.

Like Bali, Pangandaran has been hard hit by the fallout of the recent bombings. Usually catering to thousands of tourists each year, Pangandaran saw the perennial flood of new arrivals become a trickle following the attacks. The resulting discounts offered by hotels are great for travellers, but terrible for the local economy.

Orientation

Pangandaran extends for about 2km from the bus terminal and *pasar* (market) to the national park boundary in the south. The town is flanked by the west and east beaches, and bisected by the main street, Jl Kidang Pananjung. The west beach is a wide sweep of sand and the main resort strip. The east beach is a quieter, fishing beach, and not much sand remains since a retaining wall was built.

Information

A 2500Rp admission charge is levied at the gates on entering Pangandaran.

BNI ATM (Bank Negara Indonesia; Jl Bulak Laut; 🕓 24hr)

PANGANDARAN'S TSUNAMI

Pangandaran was devastated by a tsunami on 17 July 2006. See the boxed text on p265 for further information.

BRI bank (Bank Rakyat Indonesia; Jl Kidang Pananjung; 🕓 8am-2.30pm Mon-Fri) Changes most currencies and major brands of travellers cheques, but at poor rates.

CV Sawargi (☎ 639180; Jl Kidang Pananjung 123; 🕓 9am-11pm) Has internet access (per hr 18,000Rp), can book onward travel and tours, and is very knowledgeable about Pangandaran.

Magic Mushroom Books (Jl Pasanggrahan; 🕓 8.30am-8.30pm) Sells Western titles from a psychedelic shack.

Main post office (Jl Kidang Pananjung; 🕓 7.30am-3pm Mon-Thu, 7.30am-1.30pm Sat) On the main street.

PT Lotus Wisata (☎ 639635; lotus_wisata@yahoo.com; Jl Bulak Laut; 🕓 6am-midnight) Very helpful travel agent with plenty of local experience.

Telkom office (Jl Kidang Pananjung; 🕓 6am-midnight) Near the main post office; has a Home Country Direct phone.

Sights & Activities

The **Taman Nasional Pangandaran** (Pangandaran National Park; admission 2500Rp; 🕓 dawn-dusk), which takes up the entire southern end of Pangandaran, is a wild expanse of dense jungle. Within its boundaries live banteng, *kijang* (barking deer), hornbills and monkeys, including Javan gibbons, and small bays within the park enclose tree-fringed beaches. Occasionally, the park is even used as a temporary home for elephants being transported around the archipelago. The park is divided into two sections: the recreation park and the jungle. Due to environmental degradation, the jungle is now off limits, but some guides still offer illegal tours.

It's possible to follow the **stone path** in the recreation park, which has a few nondescript caves and a couple of nice beaches on the eastern side, but in general trails are very muddy and not easy to follow – don't enter alone. Guides can be hired for around 50,000Rp. The best walk is the **Boundary Trail**, which is a natural trail that skirts the jungle. Starting at the eastern entrance, take the trail along the coast past Wisma Cirengganis; the Boundary Trail starts 150m before Goa Cirengganis cave. It leads uphill and then down along the river for 30 minutes to the Wisma Cikumal and the western entrance.

Like most south-coast beaches, Pangandaran has black sand. The surf can be treacherous, particularly the northern end of the west beach, where people still drown regularly. South from Bumi Nusantara Hotel, the beach is patrolled (sometimes) and is sheltered by the headland, so swimming

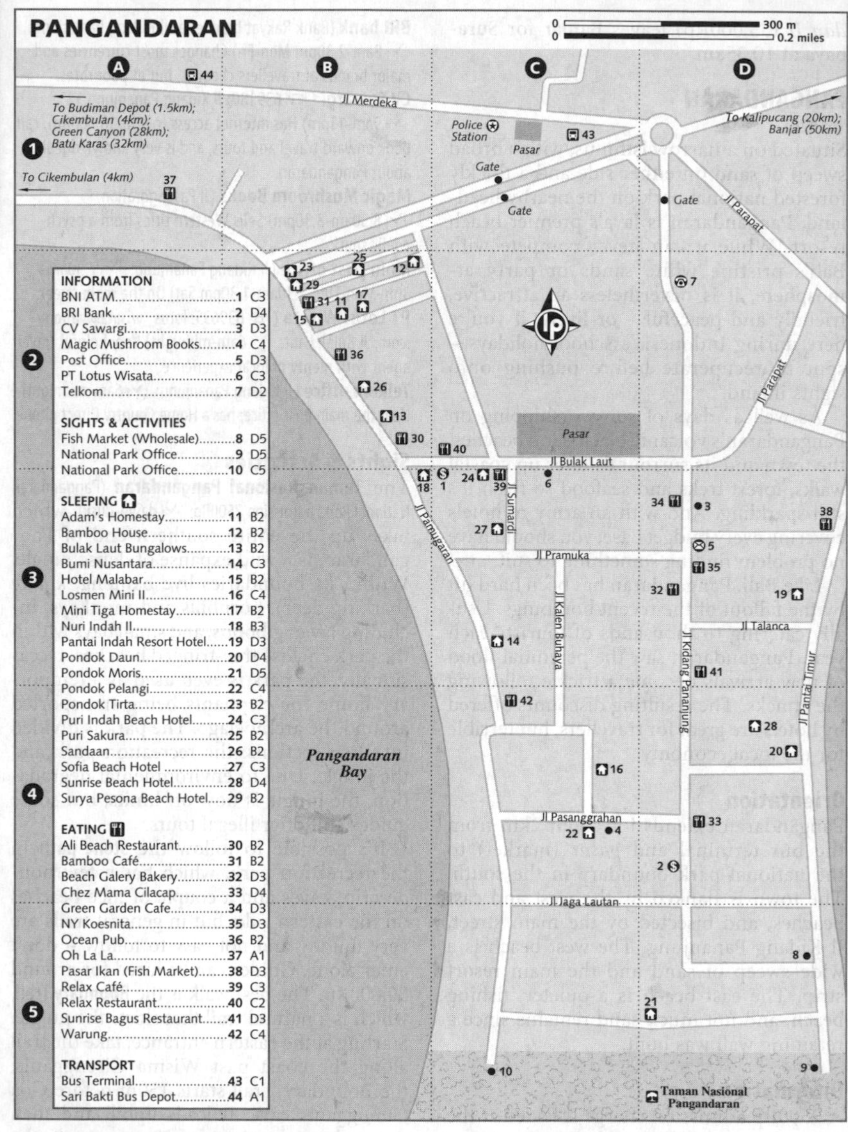

is safer. Pangandaran's best beach, Pasir Putih, on the western side of the national park, is now off limits to stop the hordes that have destroyed the reef.

Tours

The most popular tours run to the Green Canyon (100,000Rp per person), see p156, but also widely available are the 'countryside' or 'home industry' tours (100,000Rp), which take you to plantations and local industries to see the making of *tahu* and *krupuk* (prawn crackers), as well as a *wayang golek* maker.

There are also tours to **Paradise Island**, an uninhabited nearby island with good beaches (including a 5km white-sand beach) and surfing. Day trips cost 300,000Rp per person (minimum four persons); for food, make an early-morning trip to Pangandaran's fish market and fire up a barbecue when you get to the island.

There are also cycling, boating, and walking tours to just about anywhere within a 50km radius of Pangandaran.

To organise tours, try **CV Sawargi** (p151), or ask in your hotel.

Sleeping

Pangandaran has more than 100 sleeping options. During the Christmas and Lebaran (the end of Ramadan) holidays, Pangandaran is crowded and prices skyrocket. Prices are very seasonal and in busy periods may be higher than quoted here.

BUDGET

Many of Pangandaran's best homestays and losmen are crowded along the northern stretch of the town's western beach.

Pondok Moris (☎ 639490; Gang Moris 3; r 50,000Rp) Occupying a quiet spot on a back alley, this is one of Pangandaran's best cheap options. Rooms are simple and clean, with a porch facing a green garden/jungle. It would be a veritable oasis, if it wasn't so close to the mosque.

Losmen Mini II (☎ 639298; Jl Kalen Buhaya 14; r 50,000Rp) Mini II has rather empty rooms, but they're still quite pleasant and the sheets are clean. The setting is tranquil and staff are eager to please.

Mini Tiga Homestay (☎ 639436; r 50,000Rp) Mini Tiga is more than a solid bet, with its cheery and colourful rooms that are both large and cool. The owner has been running the place for the past 20 years and knows how to make guests feel at home. You'll find it down an alleyway off Jl Pamugaran.

Bamboo House (☎ 639419; r with fan/air-con 50,000/85,000Rp;) Don't be put off by the shabby frontage of Bamboo House; rooms out back are in tip-top condition and graced with touches of art. The air-con rooms are enormous although characterless compared to the fan rooms, which are darker, warmer and come with open-air bathrooms.

Puri Sakura (☎ 630552; r with fan/air-con 55,000/85,000Rp;) Puri Sakura keeps its standards very high with immaculate and stylish rooms filled with solid wood furniture and local art; if you're exceedingly claustrophobic, you may want to look elsewhere, though. The owner will treat you like a long-lost friend, and tea and coffee is available all day.

Bulak Laut Bungalows (☎ 639377; Jl Pamugaran; r from 65,000Rp, bungalows 80,000-185,000Rp, with air-con 185,000-275,000Rp;) This unusual place directly opposite the beach has reasonable rooms, colourful, spacious bungalows with bamboo floors, and plenty of concrete relief. Unfortunately one of the town's mosques is so close you'll be wanting the best earplugs money can buy.

Pondok Tirta (☎ 639235; Jl Pamugaran 140; r with fan 70,000Rp) The plethora of bright white tiles give Pondok Tirta an almost sterile gleam, but its huge, clean rooms save the day, as does the friendly, family atmosphere.

Sandaan (☎ 639165; Jl Pamugaran; r from 75,000Rp;) This business-style hotel has very good value standard rooms complete with fan, bathroom and terrace. Better VIP rooms have all the trimmings. Motorbike hire and tours can be arranged at the front desk.

Adam's Homestay (☎ 639164; Jl Pamugaran; r from 100,000Rp;) For a long time Adam's Homestay has been the pick of Pangandaran's budget accommodation, but at the time of writing it was receiving a major overhaul. If the past is anything to go by, expect lovely new rooms and plenty of atmosphere.

MIDRANGE & TOP END

Pangandaran's midrange and top-end hotels are spread the length and breadth of the town; hunt around to discover which area suits you best.

Surya Pesona Beach Hotel (☎ 639428; Jl Pamugaran; economy r 122,000Rp, 'deluxe' r from 344,000Rp;) This is one of Pangandaran's bigger resort hotels, but it's starting to look a little mouldy. It has a restaurant and decent rooms, ranging from very basic to borderline plush.

Pondok Daun (☎ 630681; Jl Pantai Timur; r from 250,000Rp;) Pondok Daun is a stylish hotel on Pangandaran's eastern beach. The rooms are spotless, the bathrooms exceptionally large and the dark wood décor has real class.

Bumi Nusantara (☎ 639032; Jl Pamugaran; nusantarahotel@yahoo.com; cottages 300,000-700,000Rp;)

Facing Pangandaran's sandy western beach is this large resort, with a range of spacious and charming cottages featuring plenty of bamboo fittings. There's also a restaurant on site.

Pantai Indah Resort Hotel (☎ 63219004; www.pantaiindah.com; Jl Pantai Timur; r 324,000-720,000Rp;) This large resort won't charm you with its character, but it will win you over with its super-clean rooms (the more expensive come with sea views), professional service and modern facilities.

Pondok Pelangi (☎ 639023; Jl Pasanggrahan 7; r 50,000Rp, 2-/3-bedroom bungalows 350,000/450,000Rp) Pelangi is an excellent choice for families, with self-contained bungalows in an attractive garden. The bungalows are old but well kept, while the cheaper rooms could do with a bit of TLC (the bathrooms are quite clean, though).

Hotel Malabar (☎ 639969; Jl Pamugaran 128; r from 350,000Rp;) The impressive bamboo façade of Malabar unfortunately hides a mass of fairly plain rooms, but management had just begun a major overhaul of the hotel at the time of writing, so hopefully things will improve tenfold.

Sunrise Beach Hotel (☎ 639220; Jl Kidang Pananjung 185; r 450,000-550,000Rp, ste 700,000-1,700,000Rp;) Sunrise Beach is arguably Pangandaran's best hotel. Even its standard rooms are well above average, with sea views, a terrace, air-con and not a spot of dirt in sight. Privacy and seclusion are thrown in free of charge.

Nuri Indah II (☎ 639415; Jl Bulak Laut; r from 496,000Rp;) Nuri Indah II (there's a I and III, but they're not up to scratch) is a small resort-style hotel with quality rooms in excellent condition. There are plenty of secluded corners for those wishing to spend a lazy day in a book, and a fine restaurant on site if you don't want to wander far.

Also recommended:

Sofia Beach Hotel (☎ 639329; Jl Sumardi; r 250,000Rp;) Spotless, if a little Spartan, new rooms; popular with families.

Puri Indah Beach Hotel (☎ 639194; Jl Bulak Laut 12; r from 310,000Rp;) A glossy hotel with fruit trees and well-equipped rooms centred on a pool.

Eating

Pangandaran is famous for its excellent seafood. For cheap Indonesian food, the town has many warungs. The **main pasar** (market; Jl Merdeka), near the bus terminal, is the place to stock up on fruit and groceries.

Pasar Ikan (Fish Market; Jl Talanca; breakfast, lunch & dinner) On the east beach is Pangandaran's fish market, and arguably the best place for fresh seafood. Pick out what you want from the selection of fresh seafood at the front of the warungs here and pay according to weight. The market is to the north, near the post office (not the wholesale fish market to the south).

Relax Restaurant (☎ 630377; Jl Bulak Laut 74; mains 20,000Rp; breakfast, lunch & dinner) This is truly a relaxed spot for a bite to eat, a mango lassi, some ice cream or simply a game of dominoes. The menu covers both Western and Indonesian fare, and the Swiss owner can recommend excellent guides and drivers.

Sunshine Bagus (☎ 639220; Jl Kidang Pananjung 177; mains 30,000Rp; lunch & dinner) This is Pangandaran's most chichi offering, with traditional décor, plenty of greenery and water features galore. The enormous menu spans just about every continent and will satisfy just about any craving.

Ali Beach Restaurant (Jl Bulak Laut 92; mains around 12,000Rp; breakfast, lunch & dinner) Ali Beach is a relaxed and welcoming restaurant with natural air-conditioning (there are basically no walls) and a menu filled with standard traveller fare. There's also the option of a massage if you're feeling tuckered out.

Chez Mama Cilacap (Jl Kidang Pananjung 187; mains 30,000Rp; breakfast, lunch & dinner) This is one of Pangandaran's best restaurants and specialises in seafood fresh from the market. The menu is extensive and the atmosphere relaxed without being too sleepy.

Green Garden Cafe (Jl Kidang Pananjung 116; mains around 20,000Rp; lunch & dinner) This bamboo hut far from the beach has a delightful garden setting, and its Indonesian dishes, steak, seafood and salads are served with some style.

NY Koesnita (Jl Kidang Pananjung; mains 15,000-20,000Rp; breakfast, lunch & dinner) On the main drag near the post office, NY Koesnita has a scrumptious selection of Sundanese and Padang dishes in cheerful surrounds.

Oh La La (Jl Pamugaran; mains from 10,000Rp; breakfast, lunch & dinner) On the road to Cikembulan is this quiet bamboo-style haunt. The Indonesian menu is cheaper than most, and the convivial English-teacher owner will tell you all you need to know about Pangandaran.

Ocean Pub (☎ 630083; Jl Pamugaran; mains around 20,000Rp; breakfast, lunch & dinner) A favoured haunt of many of the town's expat residents, Ocean Pub is a good place to chow down on steaks, Indonesian dishes and some hearty breakfasts while making new friends. The beer also comes ice cold, and there's a pool table.

Bamboo Café (Jl Pamugaran; mains 20,000Rp; breakfast, lunch & dinner) Bamboo Café is a few doors up from Ocean Pub and follows the same formula, with plenty of rattan and mellow sea views.

Also recommended:

Nuri Indah II (Jl Bulak Laut; mains 30,000Rp; breakfast, lunch & dinner) Restaurant in the hotel of the same name, with some of the best Chinese seafood around.

Beach 'Galery' Bakery (Jl Kidang Pananjung 146; pastries around 3000Rp; breakfast & lunch) Sells a smorgasbord of pies, puffs and pastries.

Relax Café (Jl Bulak Laut; mains 15,000Rp; lunch & dinner) Simple eats and beer in yet another bamboo-style haunt.

Getting There & Away

Pangandaran lies halfway between Bandung and Yogyakarta. Coming from Yogyakarta by bus or rail, Banjar is the transit point. An alternative way of reaching Pangandaran is via the pleasant boat trip from Cilacap to Kalipucang or Majingklak. From Bandung, plenty of direct buses go to Pangandaran, or it's possible to change for connections in Tasikmalaya.

Due to falling tourist numbers, Pangandaran's transport options have been scaled back, and in some cases even stopped. Therefore it's a good idea to check with Pangandaran's travel agencies for the most up-to-date information on buses and boats.

BOAT

An alternative way of getting to/away from Pangandaran is the interesting backwater trip between Cilacap and Majingklak (this may change to the Kalipucang harbour in the near future; check with local travel agencies). From Pangandaran it starts with a 17km bus trip to Majingklak (5000Rp, 40 minutes), where *compreng* (wooden boats) can be chartered for the trip across the wide expanse of Segara Anakan and along the waterway sheltered by the island of Nusa Kambangan. The boats hold eight people (minimum six required) and cost 250,000Rp each way.

At the time of writing, this was the only option for boat travel between Pangandaran and Cilacap. Normally car ferries operate between Majingklak and Cilacap, but due to dwindling tourist numbers and lack of local interest, they have been cancelled. This is not to say they won't start up again in the near future; once again, check with travel agencies or your hotel in Pangandaran for more up-to-date information.

From the Cilacap harbour it is about 1km to the main road (5000Rp by becak), from where bemos go to the Cilacap bus terminal (2000Rp). A becak all the way to the terminal costs around 10,000Rp.

Door-to-door services between Pangandaran and Yogyakarta are also a good option. Bus-ferry-bus services (125,000Rp, 10 hours) are sold all around Pangandaran (minimum six people) and will drop you at your hotel in Yogyakarta. Connections to Wonosobo are also advertised, but these are on Yogyakarta buses that will drop you in Kebumen, from where you are put on a public bus to Wonosobo.

See Cilacap (p163) for information on transport to Yogyakarta and Wonosobo.

BUS

Local buses run from Pangandaran's bus terminal to Tasikmalaya (30,000Rp, three hours), Ciamis (20,000Rp, 2½ hours), Banjar (12,000Rp, 1½ hours), Kalipucang or Majingklak (5000Rp, 40 minutes) and to Cilacap (25,000Rp, 2½ hours). Buses also run along the west coast as far as Cijulang (7000Rp, 40 minutes).

The large *patas* buses generally leave from the Sari Bakti Utama depot, just north of town, and Budiman bus company depot, about 2km west of Pangandaran along Jl Merdeka. Frequent normal buses go to Bandung (32,000Rp, six hours) between 6am and 9pm.

However, the most comfortable way to travel to Bandung is with the **Sari Harum** (☎ 639276) door-to-door minibus for 50,000Rp. **Perkasa Jaya minibuses** (☎ 639607) pick up from hotels for the trip to Jakarta's

Kampung Rambutan terminal (normal/air-con 55,000/75,000Rp, nine hours). Travel agencies can also book tickets for most buses and minibuses for a premium, but transport to the depots is usually included.

CAR

Most travel agencies rent minibuses with drivers for about 500,000Rp per day including driver and petrol. Put together your own tour and you may be able to negotiate a better rate. The most popular trip is a three-day tour to Yogyakarta. The usual route will take you as far as Wonosobo for the first night. The second day goes to Dieng for the sunrise, then on to Borobudur for the night. The final day is to Yogyakarta via Prambanan.

Getting Around

Pangandaran's brightly painted becak start at around 5000Rp and require heavy negotiation. Bicycles can be rented for 25,000Rp per day, and motorcycles cost around 40,000Rp per day, excluding petrol.

AROUND PANGANDARAN

The scenic coast road west from Pangandaran to Cipatujah skirts along surf-pounded beaches and runs through small villages and paddy fields. **Cikembulan**, a sleepy stretch of huts and houses, is 4km from Pangandaran and has accommodation and local industries that can be visited, including the *krupuk* factory and a *wayang golek* workshop.

Karang Tirta is a lagoon set back from the beach with *bagang* (fishing platforms). It's 16km from Pangandaran and 2km from the highway. **Batu Hiu** (Shark Rock) is 23km from Pangandaran and 1km from the highway, and has a recreational park atop the cliffs with views along the coast.

Inland from Parigi, near Cigugur, **Gunung Tilu** has fine views and is included in some of the tour itineraries. **Sungai Citumang** is reached by a rough and hard-to-find inland road from Karang Benda, and has a small dam from where you can walk upstream to a beautiful gorge – 'Green Canyon II' in Pangandaran tour parlance.

SLEEPING & EATING

The following two places occupy a peaceful setting in Cikembulan. Note that there isn't much in the way of eating options in this part of the world.

our pick **Delta Gecko** (☎ 630886; bungalows with breakfast 75,000Rp) About 5km from Pangandaran central, this current manifestation of Delta Gecko is a retreat for those wanting earthy surroundings accompanied by peace and quiet. The bungalows are by no means flash (there's plenty of gaps in the bamboo walls for the mosquitoes to zip through, but nets are provided) but they have oodles of beachy charm and partial views of the ocean. Meals are available, and the owner is happy to show you his tribal art.

Stella Guesthouse (r 75,000Rp) In a pleasant bamboo-style building with a large terrace overlooking the sea, Stella has stripped-back but clean rooms, and is a fine option if Delta (which is directly behind it) is full.

Green Canyon

The number one tour from Pangandaran is to Green Canyon (Cujang Taneuh). Many tour operators in Pangandaran run trips here for about 100,000Rp and include 'countryside' excursions to make a full-day tour. To get there yourself, hire a boat from the Green Canyon river harbour on the highway, 1km before the turn-off to Batu Karas. Boats cost 70,000Rp for five people and operate daily from 7.30am to 4pm (Friday 1.30pm to 4pm). They travel up the emerald-green river through the forest to a waterfall and a canyon, and stop for swimming (during the rainy season the water may be murky and uninviting). Count on about 1½ hours for this excellent trip. Go as early as possible at peak times to avoid the crush, although the canyon has been quieter since the Bali blast.

Batu Karas

This small fishing village 32km from Pangandaran is one of the most relaxed places to kick back in Java and has one of the coast's best surf beaches, sheltered by a rocky promontory. Accommodation favoured by surfers can be found 1km beyond the fishing village at the headland beach. Surfboards can be rented for 35,000Rp per day and lessons are available; entry to the town costs 1500Rp.

SLEEPING & EATING

Hotel Melati Murni (☎ 633683; r with fan 50,000Rp) Simple clean rooms can be found at this

laid-back establishment, where staff are happy to hang out and chat.

Teratai (☎ 633681; r with fan 75,000Rp, bungalows 100,000Rp;) Large, basic rooms and better-quality bungalows are surrounded by coconut trees at this family-friendly place. You may have to fight for the one hammock, though.

Hotel Pondok Putri (☎ 633315; r from 100,000Rp;) Facing a beach cluttered with outrigger fishing boats, Putri is a standard midrange hotel with the added advantage of a pet monkey called Wendy.

Reef Hotel (☎ 631108; s/d 150,000/200,000Rp;) Frequented by surfers eager to take advantage of the break outside its front door, Reef caters to wave lovers with clean, simple rooms, hammocks, and stacks of surfing mags. The pool remains unused and uncleaned.

Batu Karas Beach Bungalows (☎ 631111; batukarasbungalows@yahoo.com; bungalows 200,000Rp;) At the very eastern end of town, this resort-style place is looking a bit worse for wear. The rooms could do with a good airing, but it's a very secluded spot and an option for those wanting some privacy. The beach is not good for swimming.

Inviting spots to catch a bite to eat while watching the surfers catch waves are two places side by side near the point: **Kang Ayi** (mains 10,000-20,000Rp) and **Sederhana** (mains 10,000-20,000Rp).

GETTING THERE & AWAY

Batu Karas can be reached from Pangandaran by taking a bus to Cijulang (7000Rp) and then an *ojek* over the pretty bamboo bridge for 5000Rp.

Cipatujah

The coast road ends at the village of Cipatujah, which has a wide but uninspiring beach with dangerous swimming and a couple of cheap hotels. Five kilometres before Cipatujah is a small PHKA post that monitors the green turtles that lay their eggs at **Sindangkerta** beach. The post welcomes visitors who are interested in their work.

From Cijulang, buses run as far as Cimanuk (6000Rp), from where *ojek* will take you the extra stretch to Cipatujah (7000Rp). However, the best way to see this stretch of coast is to hire a motorcycle in Pangandaran.

Karang Nini

To the east of Pangandaran, Karang Nini is a recreational park perched high on the cliffs. Trails lead down the cliff face to the beach and crashing surf below.

For Karang Nini, take any Kalipucang-bound bus to the Karang Nini turn-off, 5km east of Pangandaran on the highway. It is then a 3km walk to the park.

CIREBON

☎ 0231

Well off the tourist trail, on the sunburnt north coast, Cirebon is a cultural melting pot, blending the scattered remains of the ancient Islamic kingdom that once had its base here, with a more contemporary cocktail of Javanese, Sundanese and Chinese culture.

But compared to many of Java's cities, Cirebon is refreshingly laid-back. And with a string of venerable *kraton*, a thriving batik industry and one of the north coast's biggest fishing fleets, it's a worthwhile stopover for seafood lovers and inquisitive travellers alike. Cirebon is famous for its batik; its *tari topeng*, a type of masked dance; and *tarling*, music blending guitar, *suling* (bamboo flute) and voice.

Cirebon was one of the independent sultanates founded by Sunan Gunungjati of Demak in the early 16th century. Later the powerful kingdoms of Banten and Mataram fought over the town, which declared its allegiance to Sultan Agung of Mataram but was finally ceded to the Dutch in 1677. By a further treaty signed in 1705, Cirebon became a Dutch protectorate, jointly administered by three sultans whose courts at that time rivalled those of Central Java in opulence and splendour.

Information

Banks and ATMs can be found all over town; a branch of BII Bank is located at the northern end of Jl Siliwangi.

Centralnet (Ruko Grand Centre B/9; internet per hr 5500Rp; 9am-8pm)

Elganet (Ruko Grand Centre B/4; internet per hr 5500Rp; 9am-8pm)

Main post office (Jl Yos Sudarso) Near the harbour.

Telkom office (Jl Yos Sudarso) For international telephone calls and faxes; this is also near the harbour and has a Home Country Direct phone.

Tourist office (486856; Jl Dharsono 5; 7am-3pm Mon-Fri) Lies 5km out of town on the bypass road, near Gua Sunyaragi; it has helpful, English-speaking staff and one English brochure.

Sights

KRATON KESEPUHAN

At the southern end of Jl Lemah Wungkuk, **Kraton Kesepuhan** (admission 3000Rp; 8am-4pm Mon-Thu & Sat, 8-11am & 2-4pm Fri, 8am-4pm Sun) is the oldest and best preserved of Cirebon's *kraton*. Built in 1527, its architectural style is a curious blend of Sundanese, Javanese, Islamic, Chinese and Dutch. Although this is the home of the sultan of Kesepuhan, part of the building is open to visitors. Inside is a pavilion with whitewashed walls dotted with blue-and-white Delft tiles, a marble floor and a ceiling hung with glittering French chandeliers.

The *kraton* museum has an interesting, if somewhat rundown, collection of *wayang* puppets, kris, cannons, furniture, Portuguese armour (weighing in at an impressive 45kg) and ancient royal clothes. The *pièce de résistance* of the collection is the Kereta Singa Barong, a 17th-century gilded chariot with the trunk of an elephant (Hindu), the body and head of a dragon (Chinese-Buddhist), and wings (Islamic). It was traditionally pulled by four white buffaloes and the suspension apparently flapped the wings and waggled the creature's tongue. It is quite possibly the weirdest carriage you'll ever see.

Entry to the *kraton* includes a guided tour (payment at your discretion), which may finish at the Museum Kereta Singa Barong. Behind in the large grounds of the palace is a dance pavilion where practice is sometimes held. There's also a pleasure palace, Gua Sunyaragi, in the same style as Kraton Kesepuhan.

KRATON KANOMAN

A short walk from Kraton Kesepuhan, Kraton Kanoman was constructed in 1588. The Kanoman dynasty was founded by Sultan Badaruddin, who broke away from the main sultanate after a lineage dispute with the sixth sultan's heir. Outside the *kraton* is a red-brick, Balinese-style compound and a massive banyan tree. Further on past the white stone lions is the *kraton*, a smaller, neglected cousin of Kraton Kesepuhan.

Head to the right past the lions, look lost and someone might – they don't always – come and unlock the museum. It's worth it, because among the museum's small holdings of mostly carved doors and layers of dust is a stunning sultan's chariot in the same style as the one in the Kraton Kesepuhan. It's claimed that the chariot in the Kraton Kesepuhan is a newer copy – the rivalry for the sultanate still exists, it seems. You can also visit the *pendopo* (large open-sided pavilion) and its inner altar. Antique European plates, some with Dutch Reformist scenes from the Bible, can be seen before entering. Opening hours are haphazard to say the least, and the entry fee is by donation.

The colourful **Pasar Kanoman**, just in front of the *kraton*, is at its most vibrant in the morning and is worth a visit in its own right.

KRATON KECIREBONAN

Although it's classed as a *kraton*, this is really only a house occupied by members of the current royal family, descendants of Raja Kanomin, who broke away from the 10th Kesepuhan sultanate. Wander in, knock on the door and someone will be happy to show you around. Built in 1839, the house has fine colonial architecture and a small collection of swords, documents and other royal memorabilia. A donation is expected.

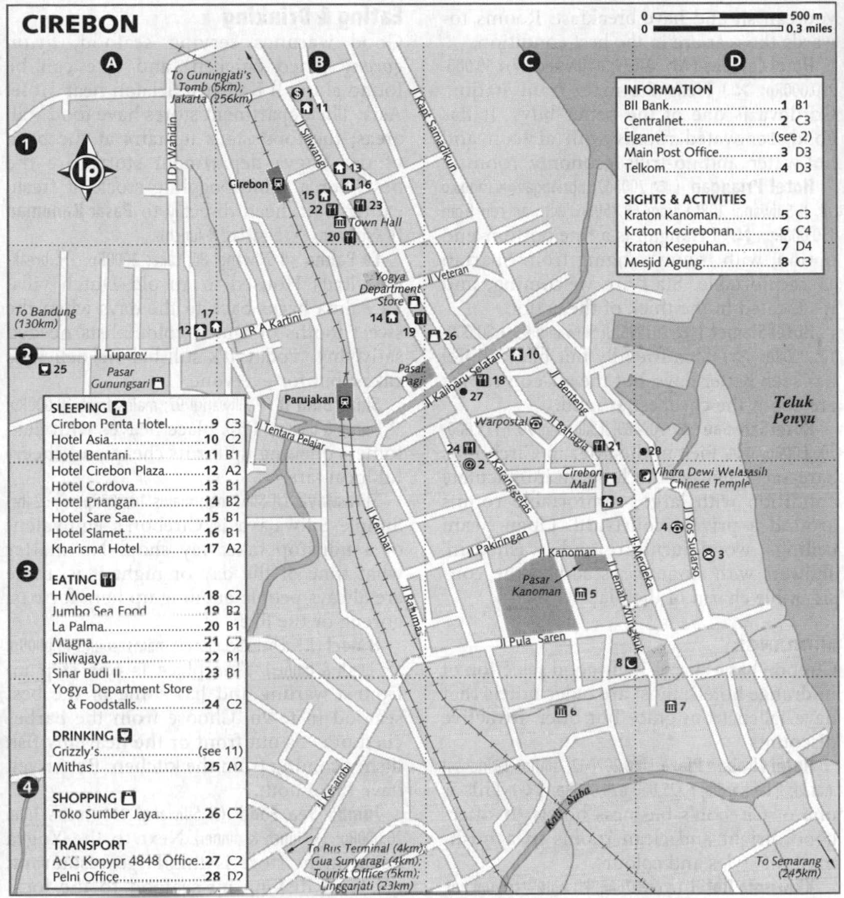

MESJID AGUNG

On the western side of the field in front of Kraton Kesepuhan is Mesjid Agung. It has a tiered roof, is one of the oldest mosques in Java and is similar in style to the Mesjid Agung in Banten.

GUA SUNYARAGI

Approximately 4km southwest of town is this bizarre ruined 'cave' – a grotto of rocks, red brick and plaster, honeycombed with secret chambers, tiny doors and staircases that lead nowhere. It was originally a water palace for a sultan of Cirebon in the early 18th century and owes its present shape to a Chinese architect who had a go at it in 1852. It's often frequented by local students who, at the sight of a tourist, are more than happy to practise their English, even from 50m away.

Sleeping

BUDGET

Inexpensive hotels can be found directly opposite the main train station and along Jl Siliwangi, but conditions are prisonlike and premises are often patrolled by prostitutes; you might be better off forking out a little extra for a midrange option.

Hotel Asia (☎ 204905; Jl Kalibaru Selatan 11A; r 45,000-75,000Rp; ❄) Located alongside the tree-lined canal near Pasar Pagi, this fine old Dutch-Indonesian inn has seen better days, but it does have a terraced courtyard where you can sit and have breakfast. Rooms towards the rear are in the best condition.

Hotel Cordova (☎ 204677; Jl Siliwangi 87; r 50,000-220,000Rp;) Near the main train station, Cordova is one of the better buys. It has good, renovated rooms with air-con and hot water, and no-frills 'economy' rooms.

Hotel Priangan (☎ 200862; hpriangan@yahoo.co.id; Jl Siliwangi 108; r from 68,750Rp, with air-con from 150,000Rp;) Priangan is a fine bottom-end option, with rooms ranging from Spartan to comfortable. Staff are welcoming, and it's located in the thick of the action.

Hotel Slamet (☎ 203296; Jl Siliwangi 95; r 80,000-125,000Rp;) This friendly but bland hotel has seen better days, but the air-con rooms are about the cheapest around.

Hotel Sare Sae (☎ 209489; Jl Siliwangi 70; r 175,000-200,000Rp;) Pick of the litter in Cirebon is Sare Sae, a newly built hotel in immaculate condition with large, comfortable rooms around a private courtyard. Open beam ceilings, wood furniture and 'washbasin' showers with stone bases add to the considerable charm of the place.

MIDRANGE

Cirebon has a surprisingly good selection of midrange hotels; most are older hotels that have fallen from grace but offer attractive discounts.

Hotel Cirebon Plaza (☎ 202062; cphhotel@indosat.net.id; Jl RA Kartini; r 225,000-625,000Rp;) This is one of Cirebon's business hotels. It offers good, bright and clean rooms in a mishmash of styles and colours.

Kharisma Hotel (☎ 207668; kh-hotel@telkom.net; Jl RA Kartini 60; r from 326,000Rp;) Despite its midrange pricing, Kharisma is one of Cirebon's plushest hotels. Rooms in its new section are very spacious, and there are a couple of bars for late-night drinks.

Hotel Bentani (☎ 203246; bentani@cirebon.wasantara.net.id; Jl Siliwangi 69; s/d from 375,000/425,000Rp;) Despite its orientation towards business clients, Bentani exudes plenty of style, with lots of colour, good facilities, and well-appointed rooms.

Cirebon Penta Hotel (☎ 203328; Jl Syarif Abdurrahman 159; r from 450,000Rp;) What Penta lacks in soul, it makes up for in location. It's in the bustling heart of the city and has dated yet comfy rooms, a rooftop garden and a health centre. Very basic rooms are also available.

Eating & Drinking

Good warungs serving seafood, *ayam goreng* (fried chicken) and sate can be found along Jl Kalibaru Selatan near Hotel Asia. The department stores have food stall areas; the food stalls upstairs at the back of the Yogya department stores are the best. For a mind-boggling stock of fresh, exotic fruit, head directly to **Pasar Kanoman** (Jl Kanoman; breakfast & lunch).

La Palma (Jl Siliwangi 86; cakes 2000Rp; breakfast & lunch) Housed in an old Dutch villa, La Palma harks back to the days when the sweet tooths of Dutch colonialists needed satisfying. Today it's still baking delicious cakes, but for everyone.

Sinar Budi II (Jl Siliwangi 97; mains from 10,000Rp; lunch & dinner) This place heaves with customers queuing up for its cheap and cheerful local fare.

Siliwajaya (Jl Siliwangi; mains 10,000Rp; 24hr) Simple Siliwajaya is Cirebon's equivalent of a nonstop takeaway shop. No matter what time of the day or night it is, there are always people queuing up here for nasi goreng or the like.

H Moel (Jl Kalibaru Selatan 69; mains around 15,000Rp; lunch & dinner) This place is one step up from a warung and has some of the best seafood in town. Choose from the barbecued prawns out front or the heavenly fish dishes coming from the kitchen. Better yet, have them both.

Jumbo Sea Food (Jl Siliwangi 191; mains from 20,000Rp; lunch & dinner) Next to the Yogya department store is this large restaurant; it's been dishing up seafood to the local populace for years and serves big seafood grills.

Magna (☎ 208045; Jl Bahagia 45; mains 40,000Rp; lunch & dinner) Despite a name change, Magna is still one of Cirebon's best Chinese seafood restaurants. Shrimp and crab dishes are specialities, but don't expect an intimate feel at this cavernous place,

For a drink try the following:

Grizzly's (Jl Siliwangi 69) In the Hotel Bentani, this is the place to mingle with Cirebon's tiny expat community and business types over drinks and a live band.

Mithas (Jl Tuparev 323) Pub-style atmosphere attracts locals rather than fleeting visitors to town.

Shopping

Toko Sumber Jaya (Jl Siliwangi 211 & 229) The two branches of this store stock all sorts of *oleh-*

oleh (souvenirs) from Cirebon. Most *oleh-oleh* are of the syrup, dried prawn and *krupuk* variety, but pottery, bamboo crafts and other interesting knick-knacks are also on sale.

Getting There & Away

BOAT

At the harbour, the **Pelni office** (☎ 204300) is past the entrance. The *Lawit* stops in Cirebon every two weeks when travelling to/from Pontianak in Kalimantan (economy/VIP 160,000/550,000Rp).

BUS

The Cirebon bus terminal is 4km southwest of the centre of town.

Normal/air-con buses run between Cirebon and Jakarta (23,000/35,000Rp, five hours), Bandung (20,000/33,000Rp, 3½ hours), Pekalongan (18,000/25,000Rp, four hours); and Semarang (30,000/42,000Rp, seven hours), as well as many of Java's main cities.

For express minibuses from Cirebon, the **ACC Kopyor 4848 office** (☎ 204343; Jl Karanggetas 9) can accommodate. It has air-con minibuses to Bandung (55,000Rp, 3½ hours), Semarang (90,000Rp, six hours) and Yogyakarta (85,000Rp, eight hours).

TRAIN

Cirebon is serviced by frequent trains that run on both the main northern Jakarta Semarang–Surabaya train line and the southern Jakarta–Yogyakarta–Surabaya line. The better services leave from Cirebon's main train station, just off Jl Siliwangi. Crowded economy-class trains leave from the Parujakan train station further south.

For Jakarta's Gambir station, the *Cirebon Express* (business/executive 50,000/65,000Rp, three hours) departs from Cirebon at 6.15am, 10.15am, 2.50pm and 6pm. To Yogyakarta, the *Fajar Yogya* (100,000Rp, 4½ hours) departs at 8.57am. To Semarang, via Tegal and Pekalongan, the *Fajur Semarang* (10,000Rp business, four hours) departs at 9pm.

Getting Around

Cirebon's city minibus *(angkutan kota)* service operates from behind the main bus terminal; a fixed 2000Rp fare is charged.

Cirebon has legions of becak, and a ride from the train station to Pasar Pagi costs around 10,000Rp. There are also taxis, but meters are seemingly reserved for family members and royalty.

AROUND CIREBON

In the royal cemetery, 5km north of Cirebon, is the **tomb of Sunan Gunungjati**, who died in 1570. The most revered of Cirebon's kings, Gunungjati was also one of the nine *wali songo* (holy men who spread Islam throughout Java), and his tomb is one of the holiest places in the country. The inner tombs are only open once a month on Kliwon Thursday of the Javanese calendar (the calendar is a combination of the normal seven-day week and the five-day Javanese market week), and at Idul Fitri and Maulud Nabi Muhammed (see p856). Pilgrims sit in contemplation and pray outside the doors on other days. Along from Sunan Gunungjati's tomb is the tomb of his first wife, who was Chinese – this tomb attracts Chinese worshippers.

Linggarjati, a small mountain resort 23km south of Cirebon, was assured of its place in the history books when, in 1946, representatives of the Republican government and the returning Dutch occupying forces met to negotiate a British-sponsored co-operation agreement. Terms were thrashed out in a colonial hotel at the foot of **Gunung Cirema** (3078m), once a retreat from the heat for Cirebon's Dutch residents. Soekarno briefly attended, but the Linggarjati Agreement was soon swept aside as the war for independence escalated. The hotel is now **Gedung Naksa**, a museum re-creating the events.

To reach Linggarjati, take a Kuningan bus from Cirebon to Cilimus (5000Rp) and then a Colt (2000Rp) or horse-drawn *andong* to either resort.

CENTRAL JAVA

Jakarta may be the nation's capital, but the Javan identity is at its strongest here, in the island's historic heartlands. As the seat of Java's first major Indianised civilisation, as well as the great Islamic sultanates centred on the *kraton* of Yogyakarta and Solo, Central Java (Jawa Tengah) remains the province in which the island's cultural pulse beats loudest.

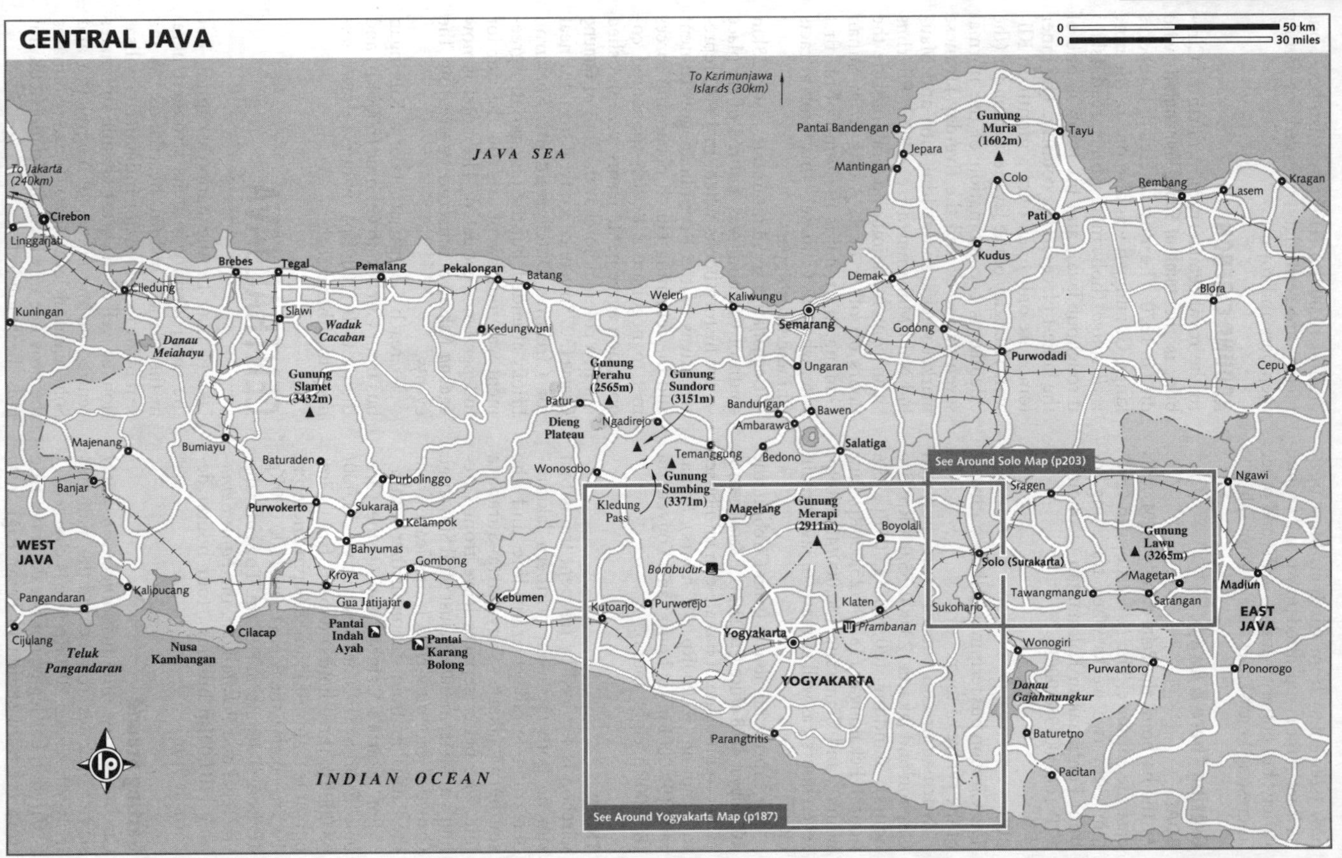
CENTRAL JAVA
0 50 km
0 30 miles
To Karimunjawa Islands (30km)
JAVA SEA
To Jakarta (240km)
Cirebon
Linggarjati
Kuningan
Ciledug
Brebes
Tegal
Slawi
Pemalang
Pekalongan
Batang
Kedungwuni
Waduk Cacaban
Danau Meiahayu
Gunung Slamet (3432m)
Weleri
Kaliwungu
Semarang
Demak
Pantai Bandengan
Jepara
Mantingan
Gunung Muria (1602m)
Colo
Tayu
Pati
Kudus
Rembang
Lasem
Kragan
Blora
Godong
Purwodadi
Cepu
Ungaran
Gunung Perahu (2565m)
Gunung Sundoro (3151m)
Batur
Dieng Plateau
Ngadirejo
Bandungan
Bawen
Ambarawa
Salatiga
Temanggung
Bedono
Wonosobo
Gunung Sumbing (3371m)
Majenang
Bumiayu
Baturaden
Purbolinggo
Banjar
Purwokerto
Sukaraja
Kelampok
Bahyumas
WEST JAVA
Gombong
Kroya
Kalipucang
Pangandaran
Gua Jatijajar
Kebumen
Cijulang
Teluk Pangandaran
Nusa Kambangan
Cilacap
Pantai Indah Ayah
Pantai Karang Bolong
Kledung Pass
Magelang
Gunung Merapi (2911m)
Boyolali
Borobudur
Kutoarjo
Purworejo
Klaten
Yogyakarta
Prambanan
YOGYAKARTA
Parangtritis
See Around Solo Map (p203)
Sragen
Ngawi
Gunung Lawu (3265m)
Solo (Surakarta)
Magetan
Madiun
Tawangmangu
Sarangan
Sukoharjo
EAST JAVA
Wonogiri
Purwantoro
Ponorogo
Danau Gajahmungkur
Baturetno
Pacitan
INDIAN OCEAN
See Around Yogyakarta Map (p187)

Even though Central Java has a reputation for a short fuse when dealing with religious and political sentiments, it's a relaxed, easygoing province for tourists. Yogyakarta, at the centre of its own quasi-independent 'special region' stretching from the south coast to Gunung Merapi, and Solo, just 65km to the northeast of Yogyakarta, are Java's most interesting cities by far. But even Semarang, the province's busy, maritime capital, has its fair share of charm and is, like its more bombastic tourist centres, an intriguing fusion of Java's past and future. Most, though, will find the intricate Borobudur and Prambanan temples the highlight of any trip to the centre of this stunning island.

CILACAP

☎ 0282

Over the border from West Java, Cilacap is an unhurried city of wide boulevards and usable footpaths, and it has the only natural harbour with deep-water berthing facilities on Java's south coast. It's a pleasant enough town, but the main reason to visit is to make the backwater trip to Pangandaran.

The **tourist office** (☎ 534481; Jl A Yani 8; 7.30am-3.30pm Mon Fri, 7.30am-1pm Sat) is opposite the Hotel Wijayakusuma.

Sights & Activities

Built between 1861 and 1879, **Benteng Pendem** (admission 2000Rp; 8am-4pm) is an impressive Dutch fort complex at the entrance to the old harbour. It has intact barracks (bring a torch to explore properly, as they're rather dark) and massive ramparts, and is one of the best-preserved forts in Java.

The fort overlooks a long stretch of dirty sand, **Pantai Teluk Penyu**. This popular local beach has souvenir stalls that sell an array of shells and trinkets.

For better beaches – complete with white sand – head to **Nusa Kambangan**, an island south of the port. While there isn't a lot to do here (swimming is not safe), it does make a pleasant break from the town. Ferries sail at 7am (30,000Rp).

Sleeping & Eating

Hotel Anggrek (☎ 533835; Jl Anggrek 16; r with shared mandi/air-con 30,000/65,000Rp;) At the low end of the scale, Anggrek has Spartan and reasonably clean rooms. It's about a five-minute walk to Jl Yani, the main drag.

Hotel Wijayakusuma (☎ 534871; www.wijayakusumahotel.com; Jl A Yani 12A; r 300,000-550,000Rp;) At the southern end of town, this is the top hotel in Cilacap. It has a range of rooms in good order, helpful staff and a quiet restaurant.

Sahabat 64 (mains 20,000-40,000Rp) In the very centre of town, next door to Perapatan, Sahabat 64 is a little cheaper on quality and price.

Restaurant Perapatan/Sien Hieng (Jl A Yani 62; mains around 30,000Rp) This place has been an institution for years – possibly since the '50s looking at the retro décor – and serves top-rate Chinese.

Getting There & Away

BOAT

At the time of writing, only charter boats were plying the backwaters from Cilacap to Majingklak. See p155 for more information on trips. The jetty is near the big Pertamina installations.

BUS

The Cilacap **bus terminal** (Jl Gatot Subroto) is 3km north of the city centre. Buses run between Cilacap and Pangandaran (25,000Rp, three hours), Yogyakarta (34,000Rp, five hours) and Purwokerto (10,000Rp, 1½ hours), where you'll need to change for Wonosobo.

For door-to-door minibuses to Yogyakarta (60,000Rp), Bandung (80,000Rp) and Wonosobo (65,000Rp), call **Toko Djadi** (☎ 533490; Jl A Yani 72) and **Travel Rejeki** (☎ 533371; Jl A Yani 68).

TRAIN

Cilacap's central train station is just off Jl A Yani and close to the tourist office. Only a handful of trains operate from here. The *Purwojaya* leaves for Jakarta (executive/business 100,000/50,000Rp) at 6.30pm and the economy-class *Logawa* departs at 5.30am for Solo (23,000Rp, five hours), Surabaya (33,000Rp, 10 hours) and Jember (44,000Rp, 15 hours).

PURWOKERTO

A surprisingly clean city with some architectural reminders of the Dutch colonial era, Purwokerto is a crossroads for travellers heading to Wonosobo from Cilacap. There are hotels in the town, but you're better off staying at the mountain resort of Baturaden, 14km north of town.

The train station is close to the city centre and the bus terminal is about 2km south. Buses run to all major centres, including Cilacap (10,000Rp, 1½ hours), Wonosobo (13,000Rp, three hours), Banjar and Yogyakarta. Infrequent direct buses go to Baturaden (6000Rp), or catch an *angkot* from Pasar Wage (6000Rp) in town.

WONOSOBO

☎ 0286 / pop 25,000

Wonosobo is the main gateway to the Dieng Plateau. At 900m above sea level in the central mountain range, it has a comfortable climate and is a typical country town with a busy market. On national holidays it comes alive as people from surrounding villages gather for festivities in the main square. You might see the Kuda Kepang dance from nearby Temanggung, or the local Lengger dance, in which men cross-dress and wear masks.

Information

Bina (Jl Veteran 36; 24 hrs) Internet access for 5000Rp per hour.

BNI bank (Bank Negara Indonesia; Jl A Yani) Changes cash and travellers cheques at low rates, and has an ATM for credit-card withdrawals; better rates can be found in Yogyakarta.

Telkom office (Jl A Yani) Near the *alun-alun* and has Home Country Direct telephones.

Tourist office (☎ 321194; Jl Kartini 3; 8am-3pm Mon-Fri) Has maps and brochures of Wonosobo and the Dieng Plateau, and contact details for tour operators in the area.

Sleeping

Citra Homestay (☎ 321880; Jl Angkatan 45; r 50,000Rp) Citra is a simple homestay above a carpenter's with very basic rooms and tours of the Dieng Plateau on offer. Light sleepers should note that it's close to a mosque.

Hotel Sri Kencono (☎ 321522; Jl A Yani 81; r 50,000-250,000Rp) Sri Kencono nicely spans the gap between budget and midrange, with well-kept economy rooms with *mandis* (common Indonesian form of bath, consisting of a large water tank from which water is ladled over the body) and a larger, comfier variety sporting hot showers and TVs.

Wisma Duta Homestay (☎ 321674; Jl Rumah Sakit 3; r with/without shower 250,000/50,000Rp) Duta offers rooms at two extremes: the basic rooms are faded but still a good budget option, while the pricier versions are brand spanking new, with plenty of attractive stonework, thick mattresses and bathroom floors clean enough to eat off.

Hotel Nirwana (☎ 321066; Jl Resimen 18 No 34; r from 150,000Rp) Right in the thick of the market goings-on, this midrange option still manages to provide quiet and secure rooms.

Hotel Surya Asia (☎ 322992; www.suryaasia.com; Jl A Yani 137; r from 230,000Rp) This medium-sized hotel has large rooms and attentive service, and fills up quickly on weekends. There's also a decent restaurant on site.

Gallery Hotel Kresna (☎ 324111; www.galleryhotelkresnawonosobo.com; Jl Pasukan Ronggolawe 30; r 385,000-1,430,000Rp plus 21% tax;) Kresna dates from 1921 when it was a retreat for Dutch planters. It still retains oodles of colonial charm while providing stylish and new rooms. Its restaurant is top-notch, and comes complete with an airy veranda and excellent service.

Eating

Dieng Restaurant (☎ 21266-21433; Jl Mayjend Bambang; mains 20,000-60,000Rp) A top spot near the bus terminal, Dieng has good Indonesian, Chinese and European food served buffet-style. Mr Argus, the owner, can arrange tours of Dieng Plateau (150,000Rp).

Asia (Jl Kawedanan 43; mains 20,000-50,000Rp; lunch & dinner) One of central Wonosobo's best Chinese restaurants, Asia has been around in one form or another since 1933. It has frog legs and pigeon alongside normal offerings.

Getting There & Away

Wonosobo's bus terminal is 3km out of town on the Magelang road.

From Yogyakarta take a bus to Magelang (12,0000Rp, one hour) and then another bus to Wonosobo (12,000Rp, two hours). **Rahayu Travel** (☎ 321217; Jl A Yani 95) has door-to-door minibuses to Yogyakarta (36,000Rp, three hours). Hotels can arrange pick-up.

Hourly buses go to Semarang (15,000Rp, four hours), passing through Secang and Ambarawa (10,000Rp) en route.

For Cilacap (four hours), a change at Purwokerto (13,000Rp, three hours) is required. Leave early in the morning to catch the ferry to Majingklak and on to Pangandaran.

Frequent buses to Dieng (7000Rp, one hour) leave throughout the day and continue on to Batur.

DIENG PLATEAU

☎ 0286

The lofty plateau of Dieng (2093m above sea level) is home to the oldest Hindu temples in Java. Its name comes from Di-Hyang (Abode of the Gods), and it's thought that this was once the site of a flourishing temple-city of priests.

More than 400 temples, most of which were built between the 8th and 9th centuries, covered the highland plain, but with the mysterious depopulation of Central Java, this site, like Borobudur, was abandoned and forgotten. It was not until 1856 that the archaeologist Van Kinsbergen drained the flooded valley around the temples and catalogued the ruins. The eight remaining temples are characteristic of early Central Javanese architecture – stark, squat and boxlike.

These simple temples, while of great archaeological importance, are not stunning. Rather, Dieng's beautiful landscape is the main reason to make the long journey to this isolated region. Steep mountainsides terraced with vegetable plots enclose the huge volcanically active plateau, a marshy caldera of a collapsed volcano. Any number of walks to mineral lakes, steaming craters or other lonely places can be made around Dieng, including a walk to the highest village in Java, Sembungan.

To really appreciate Dieng, it's best to stay in Dieng village, although Wonosobo has better facilities and can be used as a base. The temples and the main 'natural' sights can be seen in one day on foot – arrive in Dieng in the morning before the afternoon mists roll in.

It is a pleasant three- or four-hour loop south from Dieng village to Telaga Warna (Coloured Lake), Candi Bima (Bima Temple), Kawah Sikidang (Sikidang Crater), and then back to Candi Gatutkaca, the Arjuna Complex and the village. Many other lakes and craters around Dieng are scattered over a large area and are difficult to reach.

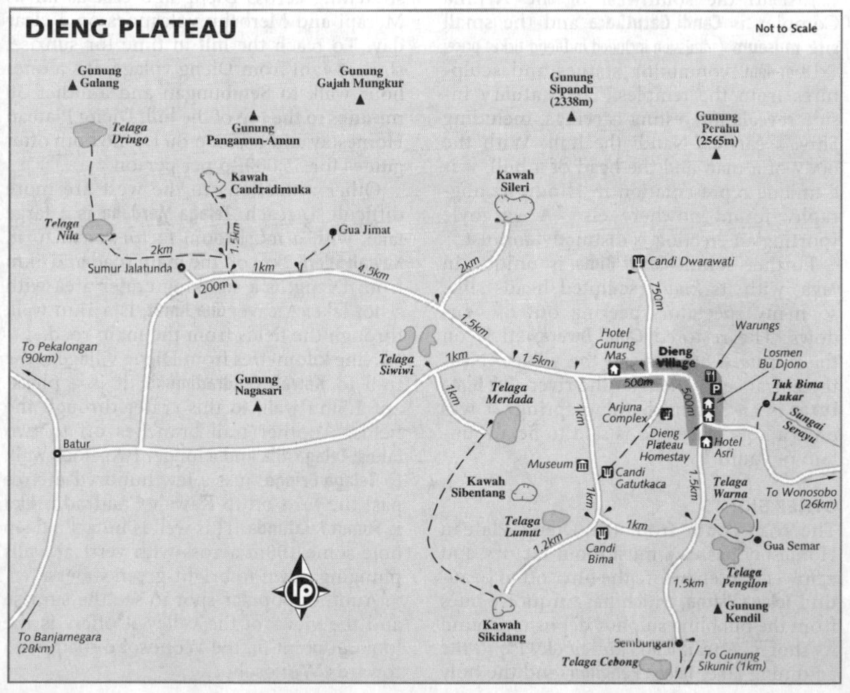

Information

In Dieng village a kiosk sells tickets to most of the Dieng sights for 12,000Rp, and hands out basic maps of the area. It costs a further 7000Rp for Telaga Warna and Telaga Pengilon, and another 3000Rp if touring the temples by car.

BRI bank (Bank Rakyat Indonesia; 8am-2pm Mon-Fri) Near Hotel Gunung Mas; changes US dollars at poor rates.

Kios Telephone Dian (8am-6pm) This wartel is on the main street, just before Hotel Gunung Mas.

Sights

TEMPLES

The five main temples that form the **Arjuna Complex** are clustered together on the central plain. They are Shiva temples, but like the other Dieng temples they have been named after the heroes of the *wayang* stories of the Mahabharata epic: Arjuna, Puntadewa, Srikandi, Sembadra and Semar. Raised walkways link the temples (as most of this land is waterlogged), but you can see the remains of ancient underground tunnels, which once drained the marshy flatlands.

Just to the southwest of the Arjuna Complex is **Candi Gatutkaca** and the small site **museum** (admission included in Dieng ticket price; 8am-4pm) containing statues and sculptures from the temples. The statuary inside reveals interesting carvings, including Shiva's carrier, Nandi the bull. With the body of a man and the head of a bull, it is a unique representation in Hindu iconography found nowhere else. A gargoyle sporting an erection is distinctly animist.

Further south, **Candi Bima** is unique in Java, with its *kudu* (sculpted heads) like so many spectators peering out of windows. The restored **Candi Dwarawati** is on the northern outskirts of the village. Near the entrance to Dieng at the river, **Tuk Bima Lukar** is an ancient bathing spring. It was once a holy place and is said to be a fountain of youth.

OTHER SIGHTS

The road south from the Dieng Plateau Homestay passes a mushroom factory and a flower garden before the turn-off to beautiful **Telaga Warna**, which has turquoise hues from the bubbling sulphur deposits around its shores. A trail leads anticlockwise to the adjoining lake, **Telaga Pengilon**, and the holy **Gua Semar**, a renowned meditation cave. Return to the main road via the indistinct trail that leads around Telaga Pengilon and up the terraced hillside. The colours of the lakes are better viewed from up high.

From Telaga Warna it's about 1km along the main road to Candi Bima, and then another 1.2km to **Kawah Sikidang**, a volcanic crater with steaming vents and frantically bubbling mud ponds. Exercise extreme caution here – there are no guard rails to keep you from slipping off the sometimes muddy trails into the scalding-hot waters. **Kawah Sibentang** is a less spectacular crater nearby, and **Telaga Lumut** is another small lake.

South of the geothermal station, the paved road leads on to **Sembungan**, said to be the highest village in Java, at 2300m. Potato farming has made this large village relatively wealthy – it sends an inordinate number of pilgrims to Mecca.

Gunung Sikunir, 1km past Sembungan, and the shallow lake of **Telaga Cebong**, just beyond the village, are the main attractions in this area. Views from Sikunir are spectacular, stretching across Dieng and east as far as Merapi and Merbabu volcanoes on a clear day. To reach the hill in time for sunrise, start at 4am from Dieng village. It's a one-hour walk to Sembungan and another 30 minutes to the top of the hill. Dieng Plateau Homestay and Losmen Bu Djono both offer guides for 35,000Rp per person.

Other attractions to the west are more difficult to reach. **Telaga Merdada** is a large lake, with a mushroom factory next to it. **Kawah Sileri**, 2km off the main road and 6km from Dieng, is a smoking crater area with a hot lake. A cave, **Gua Jimat**, is a 1km walk through the fields from the main road.

Nine kilometres from Dieng village is the trail to **Kawah Candradimuka**; it is a pleasant 1.5km walk to this crater through the fields. Another trail branches off to two lakes: **Telaga Nila** and a longer two-hour walk to **Telaga Dringo**. Just a few hundred metres past the turn-off to Kawah Candradimuka is **Sumur Jalatunda**. This well is in fact a deep hole some 100m across with vertical walls plunging down to bright-green waters.

Another popular spot to see the sunrise and the views of the valley it offers is the lookout point on the Wonosobo road, 5km towards Wonosobo.

Sleeping & Eating

Dieng has a handful of Spartan hotels to choose from if you are on a budget, but beware: hot water is not always forthcoming.

Hotel Asri (☎ 642034; r 30,000-40,000Rp) Asri is about as cheap as you get in Dieng, but don't expect much for the price; there's no hot water and only shared *mandis*.

Losmen Bu Djono (☎ 642046; Jl Raya, Km 27; r 30,000-40,000Rp, 'VIP' room with hot water 70,000-80,000Rp) Bu Djono is a very basic losmen in poor – yet charming – condition. Staff are incredibly friendly and can supply you with information on the area, and there's hot water – yippee!

Dieng Plateau Homestay (Jl Raya, Km 27; r 50,000Rp) This place is similar in look and atmosphere to Bu Djono, its perennial competitor. You may have trouble tracking down the owner, though.

Hotel Gunung Mas (☎ 592417; r 80,000, with hot water 100,000Rp) This is the most 'upmarket' hotel in town, but that's not saying much. It looks quite dilapidated from the outside, but rooms are in reasonable condition and the beds don't sag (much).

Food is not Dieng's strong suit. Losmen Bu Djono wins back a few points from the Dieng Plateau Homestay in the eats department, and it has cold beer.

Warungs next to the Losmen Bu Djono are a pittance cheaper, but chilly after dark.

Getting There & Away

Dieng is 26km from Wonosobo (7000Rp, one hour), which is the usual access point. Buses continue on to Batur (3000Rp from Dieng), where it's possible to catch a further bus to Pekalongan (12,000Rp, three hours, 90km). The road is steep and bumpy but paved.

It's possible to reach Dieng from Yogyakarta in one day (including a stop at Borobudur) by public bus provided you leave early enough to make the connection; the route is Yogyakarta–Magelang–Wonosobo–Dieng. Travel agents in Yogyakarta offer day trips that include Borobudur, but you'll spend most of your time on a bus and generally end up seeing Dieng clouded in mist.

BOROBUDUR

☎ 0293

Like Angkor Wat in Cambodia and Bagan in Myanmar, Java's Borobudur makes the rest of Southeast Asia's spectacular sites seem almost incidental. Looming out of a patchwork of bottle-green paddies and swaying palm tops, this colossal Buddhist relic is one of Southeast Asia's marvels, surviving Gunung Merapi's ash flows, terrorist bombs, and the wear and tear of a million pairs of tourist flip-flops (thongs) to remain as enigmatic and beautiful as it must have been 1200 years ago.

History

Rulers of the Sailendra dynasty built Borobudur some time between AD 750 and AD 850. Little else is known about Borobudur's early history, but the Sailendras must have recruited a huge workforce, as some 60,000 cubic metres of stone had to be hewn, transported and carved during its construction. The name Borobudur is possibly derived from the Sanskrit words 'Vihara Buddha Uhr', which mean 'Buddhist Monastery on the Hill'.

With the decline of Buddhism and the shift of power to East Java, Borobudur was abandoned soon after completion and for centuries lay forgotten, buried under layers of volcanic ash. It was only in 1815, when Sir Thomas Stamford Raffles governed Java, that the site was cleared and the sheer magnitude of the builders' imagination and technical skill was revealed. Early in the 20th century the Dutch began to tackle the restoration of Borobudur, but over the years the supporting hill had become waterlogged and the whole immense stone mass started to subside. A mammoth US$25 million restoration project was undertaken between 1973 and 1983 to finally finish the job.

On 21 January 1985, bombs planted by opponents of Soeharto exploded on the upper layers of Borobudur. Many of the smaller stupas were damaged, but it has once again been fully restored, demonstrating the structure's timeless resilience. In 1991 Borobudur gained the status of a World Heritage site.

Orientation & Information

The small, bustling village of Borobudur consists of several warungs, souvenir stalls and a few hotels that face the monument. The bus terminal is less than 10-minutes' walk from the monument.

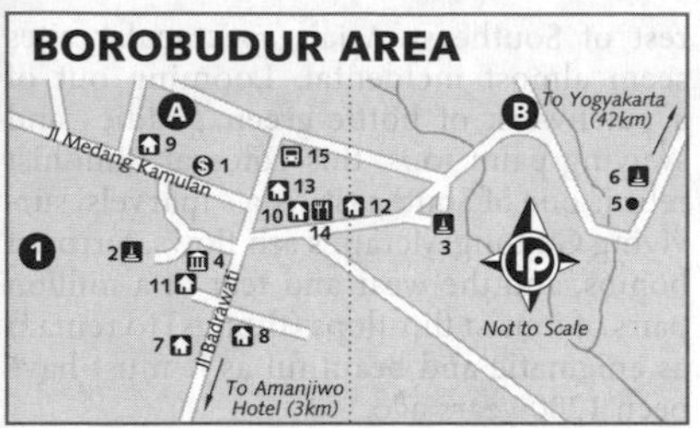

INFORMATION
BNI ATM.......1 A1

SIGHTS & ACTIVITIES
Borobudur Temple.......2 A1
Candi Pawon.......3 B1
Karmawibhangga Archaeological Museum.......4 A1
Mendut Buddhist Monastery.......5 B1
Mendut Temple.......6 B1

SLEEPING
Homestay Rajasa.......7 A1
Hotel Bhumisambhara.......8 A1
Lotus Guest House.......9 A1
Lotus II.......10 A1
Manohara Hotel.......11 A1
Pondok Tinggal Hotel & Restaurant.......12 B1
Pondok Wisata Bunga Rose.......13 A1

EATING
Borobudur Restaurant.......14 A1

TRANSPORT
Bus Terminal.......15 A1

Information can be gathered from the **information office** (☎ 788266; www.borobudurpark.com; admission to temple US$11; 🕑 6am-5pm) at the temple's entrance, and from hotels in town. Official guides are available at the information office for 40,000Rp (up to 20 persons). There's a **BNI ATM** (Bank Negara Indonesia; Jl Medang Kamulan; 🕑 24hr) near the temple's entrance.

Sights

BOROBUDUR TEMPLE

Borobudur is built from two million block stones in the form of a massive symmetrical stupa, literally wrapped around a small hill. It stands solidly on its 118m x 118m base. Six square terraces are topped by three circular ones, with four stairways leading up through finely carved gateways to the top. The paintwork is long gone, but it's thought that the grey stone of Borobudur was at one time washed with a colour to catch the sun.

Viewed from the air, the structure resembles a colossal three-dimensional tantric mandala. It has been suggested, in fact, that the people of the Buddhist community that once supported Borobudur were early Vajrayana or Tantric Buddhists who used it as a walk-through mandala.

The monument was conceived as a Buddhist vision of the cosmos in stone, starting in the everyday world and spiralling up to nirvana, the Buddhist heaven. At the base of the monument is a series of reliefs representing a world dominated by passion and desire, where the good are rewarded by reincarnation as a higher form of life, while the evil are punished by a lowlier reincarnation. These carvings and their carnal scenes are covered by stone to hide them from view, but they are partly visible on the south side.

Starting at the main eastern gateway, go clockwise (as one should around all Buddhist monuments) around the galleries of the stupa. Although Borobudur is impressive for its sheer bulk, the delicate sculptural work when viewed close up is exquisite. The pilgrim's walk is about 5km long and takes you along narrow corridors past nearly 1460 richly decorated narrative panels and 1212 decorative panels in which the sculptors have carved a virtual textbook of Buddhist doctrines as well as many aspects of Javanese life 1000 years ago – a continual procession of ships and elephants, musicians and dancing girls, warriors and kings. Some 432 serene-faced Buddha images stare out from open chambers above the galleries, while 72 more Buddha images sit only partly visible in latticed stupas on the top three terraces. Reaching in through the stupa to touch the fingers or foot of the Buddha inside is believed to bring good luck.

Admission to the temple includes entrance to **Karmawibhangga archaeological museum**, which is just east of the monument and contains 4000 original stones and carvings from Borobudur, an exhibition of tools and chemicals used in its restoration and some interesting photographs, including some recording the damage caused by the 1985 bomb. An audiovisual show at the Manohara Hotel (p170) costs 5000Rp, and there are a few other attractions at Borobudur, including a children's playground and tacky magic museum.

Borobudur is Indonesia's single most popular tourist attraction, and despite a recent drop-off in tourist numbers since the Bali bombings, it can be crowded and noisy, especially on weekends. Hawkers both outside and inside the archaeological park are becoming increasingly aggressive, but are sometimes put off if you tell them in Bahasa Indonesia that you are a resident of Yogyakarta *(saya tinggal di Yogyakarta)*. The finest time to see Borobudur and capture something of the spirit of the temple is at dawn or sunset, but you won't have it to yourself. These are popular times for the bus loads of tour groups to visit Borobudur. The temple is usually at its quietest during Ramadan.

It is, however, possible to beat the crowds at sunrise; for 230,000Rp (90,000Rp if you stay at the hotel) Manohara Hotel (p170) lets visitors enter the temple's grounds before 6am. A passport is required for entry.

MENDUT TEMPLE

This **temple** (admission 3000Rp; 6am-5pm) is around 3.5km east of Borobudur, back towards Muntilan. It may be small and insignificant compared with its mighty neighbour Borobudur, but it houses the most outstanding statue in its original setting of any temple in Java. The magnificent 3m-high figure of Buddha is flanked by Bodhisattvas: Lokesvara on the left and Vairapana on the right. The Buddha is also notable for his posture: instead of the usual lotus position, he sits Western-style with both feet on the ground.

BOROBUDUR TEMPLE PLAN

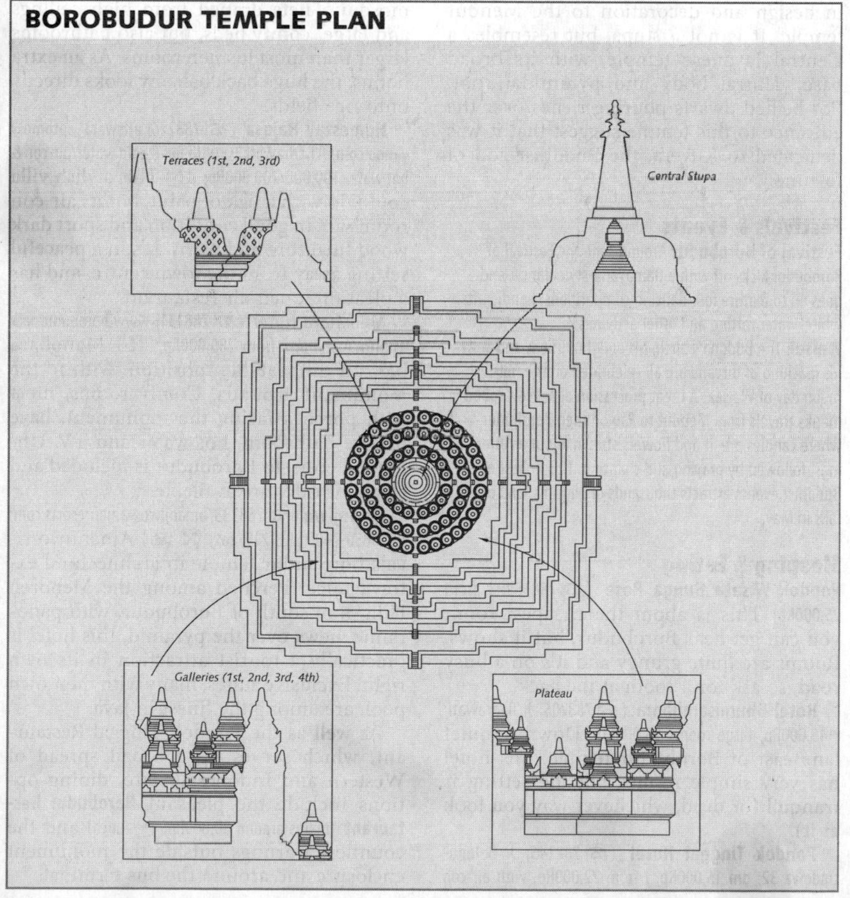

The Mendut temple, also called Venu Vana Mandira (Temple in the Bamboo Grove), was discovered in 1836, and restoration attempts were made by the Dutch between 1897 and 1904. Although parts of the roof and entrance remain unfinished, it is nevertheless a fine temple and the gracefully carved relief panels on its outer walls are among the finest and largest examples of Hindu-Javanese art in the country.

Next to the temple is the **Mendut Buddhist Monastery**. Meditation courses are often held here around December.

CANDI PAWON

Around 1.5km east of Borobudur, this tiny **temple** (admission 3000Rp; 6am-5pm) is similar in design and decoration to the Mendut temple. It is not a stupa, but resembles a Central Javanese temple, with its broad base, central body and pyramidal roof. Pot-bellied dwarfs pouring riches over the entrance to this temple suggest that it was dedicated to Kuvera, the Buddhist god of fortune.

Festivals & Events

Festival of Borobudur Around June the Festival of Borobudur kicks off with a Ramayana-style dance, and goes on to feature folk-dancing competitions, handicrafts, white-water rafting and other activities.

Waisak The Buddha's birth, his enlightenment and his reaching of nirvana are all celebrated on the full-moon day of Waisak. A great procession of saffron-robed monks travels from Mendut to Pawon then Borobudur, where candles are lit and flowers strewn about as offerings, followed by praying and chanting. This holiest of Buddhist events attracts thousands of pilgrims, and usually falls in May.

Sleeping & Eating

Pondok Wisata Bunga Rose (☎ 788362; r from 25,000Rp) This is about the cheapest room you can get near Borobudur, but it shows. Rooms are quite grungy and it's on a busy road, so ask for a room at the back.

Hotel Bhumisambhara (☎ 788205; Jl Badrawati; r 45,000Rp, large rooms 55,000Rp) Down a quiet lane east of Borobudur temple, this hotel has very simple rooms, but the setting is tranquil (or dead, whichever way you look at it).

Pondok Tinggal Hotel (☎ 788145; Jl Balaputradewa 32; dm 15,000Rp, r from 72,000Rp, with air-con from 120,000Rp;) With flash rooms around an attractive garden, this is a good bet 1km from Borobudur. The dorms are often empty and the better rooms are excellent value. The hotel also has a decent **restaurant** (mains around 30,000Rp; 6am-10pm).

Lotus Guest House (☎ 788281; Jl Medang Kamulan 2; s/d with breakfast from 60,000/80,000Rp) To the north of the temple, near the main parking area, Lotus is a super-friendly and homely guesthouse. Conditions can be a little rough-and-ready, but many rooms are quite large. It has a small café and plenty of local info.

Lotus II (☎ 788845; Jl Balaputradewa 54; r 100,000Rp) The newly renovated rooms at this guesthouse are stylish in their simplicity. Expect to find not only tiled floors, bamboo mats, mosquito nets draped from high ceilings and large, comfy beds, but also bathrooms larger than most losmen rooms. As an extra bonus, the huge back balcony looks directly onto rice fields.

Homestay Rajasa (☎ 788276; ariswara_sutomo@yahoo.com; Jl Badrawati 2; r with fan & cold water/air-con & hot water 100,000/200,000Rp;) This stylish villa could do with a lick of paint, but its air-con rooms are in good condition and sport dark wood furniture and baths. It's in a peaceful setting away from the town centre, and has a pleasant, open-air restaurant.

Manohara Hotel (☎ 788131; www.borobudurpark.com/manohara; r from 285,000Rp;) Manohara has an unbeatable position within the monument grounds. Comfy rooms, most with porches facing the monument, have private bathroom, hot water and TV. Unlimited entry to Borobudur is included and elephant rides are available.

Amanjiwo (☎ 788333; amanjiwo@amanresorts.com; r US$650-2600 plus 21% tax;) Amanjiwo rivals Borobudur temple in architectural extravagance. Perched among the Menoreh Hills 3km south of Borobudur, with panoramic views over the pyramid, this hotel is practically a tourist attraction in its own right. Exclusive suites, many with their own pool, are among the finest in Java.

As well as the Pondok Tinggal Restaurant, which serves up a broad spread of Western and Indonesian fare, dining options include the pleasant **Borobudur Restaurant** (mains around 30,000Rp; lunch) and the countless warungs outside the monument enclosure and around the bus terminal.

Getting There & Away

Direct buses make the 42km trip from Yogyakarta's Umbulharjo bus terminal to Borobudur (10,000Rp, 1½ hours) via Muntilan. These buses skirt the central city but can also be caught at Jombor, about 4km north of Yogyakarta on Jl Magelang, near the northern ring road. Bus 5 runs from Jombor to the city centre.

From Borobudur terminal, buses also go to Muntilan (5000Rp) and Magelang (5000Rp).

In Borobudur the hotels are within walking distance of the bus terminal; a becak should cost no more than 5000Rp to anywhere in the village. It's a fine walk to Mendut and Pawon; otherwise a bus or bemo is 2000Rp to hop from one temple to the next, or hire a becak or bicycle (from hotels).

Tours of Borobudur (p177) are easily arranged in Yogyakarta at the Prawirotaman or Sosrowijayan agents.

YOGYAKARTA

☎ 0274 / pop 450,000

If Jakarta is Java's financial and industrial powerhouse, Yogyakarta is its soul. Central to the island's artistic and intellectual heritage, Yogyakarta (pronounced 'Jogjakarta'), called Yogya for short, is where the Javanese language is at its purest, Java's arts at their brightest and its traditions at their most visible.

Fiercely independent and protective of its customs, Yogya is now the site of an uneasy truce between the old ways of life and the trappings of modernity that have swept across the island in recent decades. Still headed by its sultan, whose *kraton* remains the hub of traditional life, contemporary Yogya is nevertheless as much a city of burger bars, traffic jams and advertising hoardings as batik, gamelan and ritual. But while the process of modernisation homogenises many of Java's cities, Yogya continues to juggle past and present with relative ease, sustaining a slower, more conservative way of life in the quiet *kampung* that thrive only a stone's throw from the throbbing main streets.

Yogya's potency has long outweighed its size, and it remains Java's premier tourist city, with countless hotels, restaurants and attractions of its own. It is also an ideal base for exploring nearby attractions, including

THE BANTUL EARTHQUAKE *Atik Wildan*

Early in the morning of 27 May 2006, Central Java was hit by an earthquake measuring 6.3 on the Richter scale. Its epicentre was the small village of Bantul – a town of farmers and artists, located 25km south of the ancient capital of Yogyakarta – but the quake was felt as far away as Borobudur.

Bantul was all but flattened – only 20% of the village's homes and community centres remained standing after the earthquake subsided. The rest of the affected area came through the quake in better condition, but a total of 200,000 people were left homeless, and around 6000 died. Aftershocks forced many to find shelter in the open, and nearby Mt Merapi sent debris some 3½km down its western flank.

Transport links (including the airport), shops, and the general infrastructure of Yogyakarta and its surrounds were back in operation soon after the quake, but the overall damage to some areas will take longer to rectify. Bantul and its neighbouring villages could possibly take years to fully recover, and while the southern half of Yogyakarta – an area that includes the *kraton* (p174) and Prawirotaman – is recuperating at a fast pace, it was hit hard by the quake, which could result in buildings lying indefinitely derelict.

Around 30% of the region's sights and hotels and 20% of the restaurants mentioned in this book sustained damage; however, most will be up and running by the time you read this. Worst hit are Candi Brahma and Vishnu (p192) at Prambanan, Museum Kareta Kraton (p176), and Taman Sari (p175); check with the tourist office (p172) for more information. The *kraton* itself only incurred cracks to its walls, but the caves of Gua Cerma and Langse near Parangtritis (p187) will probably be out of action for some time.

If you'd like to help out, donations are always welcomed by the Indonesian arm of the **Red Cross** (☎ 021-7992325; www.palangmerah.org in Indonesian; Jl Jenderal Datot Subroto Kav 96, 12790 Jakarta) and the **Indonesian Forum for the Environment** (WALHI/Friends of the Earth Indonesia; www.eng.walhi.or.id).

Indonesia's most important archaeological sites, Borobudur and Prambanan.

History

Yogyakarta owes its establishment to Prince Mangkubumi, who in 1755 returned to the former seat of Mataram and built the *kraton* of Yogyakarta. He took the title of sultan, adopted the name of Hamengkubuwono (The Universe on the Lap of the King) and created the most powerful Javanese state since the 17th century.

Yogya has always been a symbol of resistance to colonial rule; it was the heart of Prince Diponegoro's Java War (1825–30) and became the capital of the republic from 1946 until independence in 1949.

When the Dutch occupied Yogya in 1948, the patriotic sultan locked himself in the *kraton* and let rebels use the palace as their headquarters. The Dutch did not dare move against the sultan for fear of arousing the anger of millions of Javanese who looked upon him almost as a god. As a result of the sultan's support of the rebels, Yogya was granted the status of a special region when independence finally came.

Orientation

It is easy to find your way around Yogya. Jl Malioboro, named after the Duke of Marlborough, is the main road and runs straight down from the train station to the *kraton* at the far end. The road becomes Jl A Yani further south but is generally referred to as Jl Malioboro. The tourist office and many souvenir shops and stalls are along this street and most of the budget places to stay are west of it, in the Jl Sosrowijayan area near the railway line.

The old, walled *kraton* is the centre of old Yogya, where you will also find the Taman Sari (Water Castle), Pasar Ngasem (Bird Market) and numerous batik galleries. A second midrange hotel enclave is south of the *kraton* area around Jl Prawirotaman.

MAPS

The city's **tourist information office** (Map p173; ☎ 562000; Jl Malioboro 16; 8am-7pm Mon-Thu, 8-11.30am & 1-3pm Fri, 8am-6pm Sat) hands out free maps that will satisfy most tourist needs.

Information

INTERNET ACCESS

Internet cafés can be found all over town, although many of the cheaper cafés (3000Rp per hour) are located north of Jl Diponegoro.

Caferina (Map p178; Jl Sosrowijayan; per hr 8000Rp; 8am-11pm) Also food on offer.

Internet Queen (Map p178; Jl Pasar Kembang 17; per hr 7000Rp; 24hr)

Kresna Tourist Service (Map p179; ☎ 375502; Jl Prawirotaman I; per hr 7000Rp; 8am-11pm)

Metro Internet (Map p179; Jl Prawirotaman II; 8am-11pm) In the Metro Guest House.

MEDICAL SERVICES

Ludira Husada Tama Hospital (Map p173; ☎ 620333; Jl Wiratama 4; 24hr)

MONEY

Yogya has plenty of banks and numerous moneychangers in the tourist areas, and many banks have ATMs that accept Visa and MasterCard.

BNI bank (Bank Negara Indonesia; Map p173; Jl Trikora 1) Opposite the main post office.

Mulia (Map p178; Inna Garuda Hotel, Jl Malioboro 60) Along with Pt Barumun Abadi, this has the best exchange rates in Yogya.

Pt Barumun Abadi (Map p178; Inna Garuda Hotel, Jl Malioboro 60) Offers excellent exchange rates, often better than the banks.

POST

Main post office (Map p173; Jl Senopati; 7am-8pm Mon-Sat, 9am-8pm Sun)

TELEPHONE

You'll find wartels all over town.

Telkom office (Map p173; Jl Yos Sudarso; 24hr) One kilometre east of Jl Malioboro, this has Home Country Direct phones.

TOURIST INFORMATION

Tourist information office (Map p173; ☎ 562000; Jl Malioboro 16; 8am-7pm Mon-Thu, 8-11.30am & 1-3pm Fri, 8am-6pm Sat) Produces a number of publications (including a calendar of events) and can answer most queries. Also has counters at the airport and on the eastern side of the Tugu train station.

TRAVEL AGENCIES

Great Tours (Map p178; ☎ 583221; Jl Sosrowijayan 29; 8am-11pm) Recommended by the tourist information office.

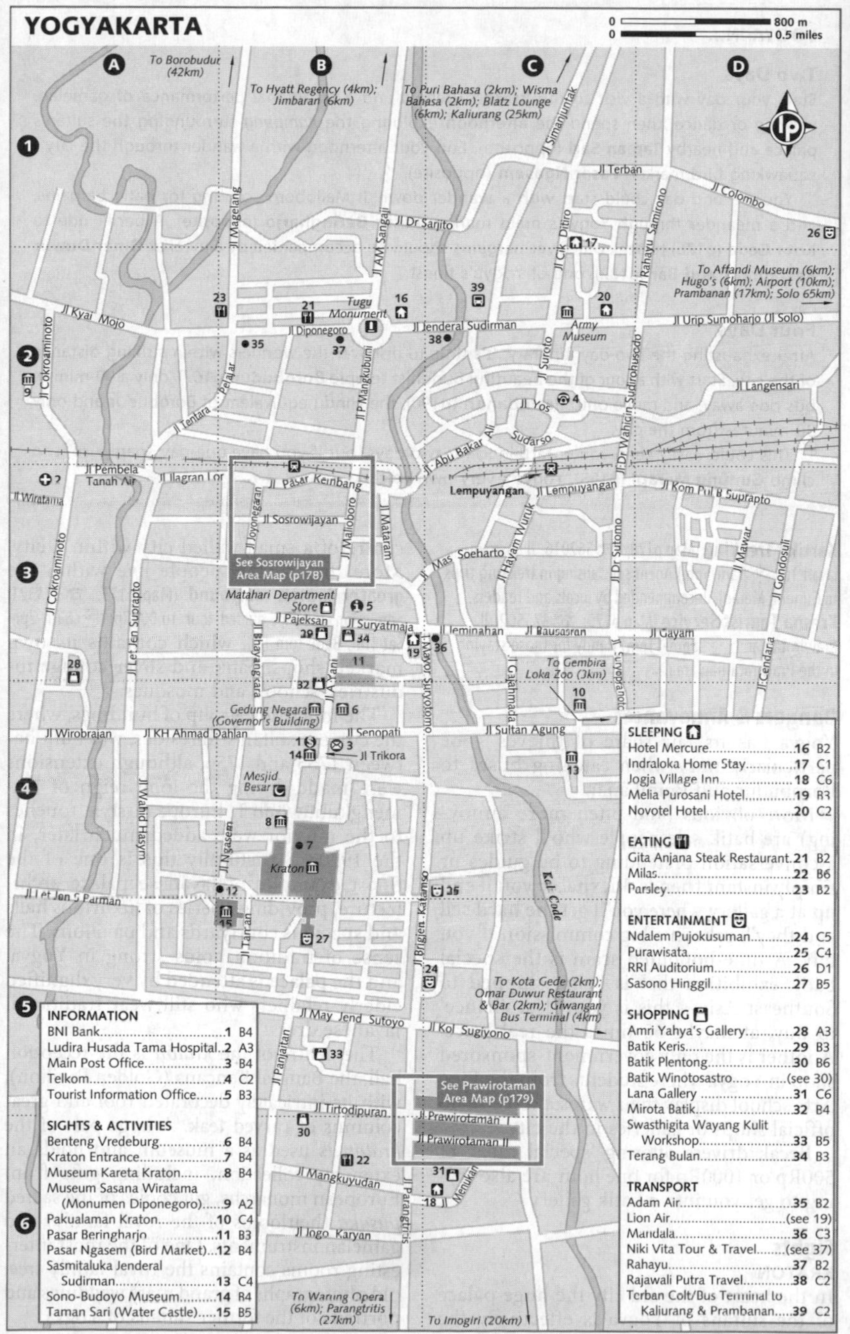
YOGYAKARTA
0 800 m
0 0.5 miles
A
B
C
D
1
2
3
4
5
6
To Borobudur (42km)
To Hyatt Regency (4km); Jimbaran (6km)
To Puri Bahasa (2km); Wisma Bahasa (2km); Blatz Lounge (6km); Kaliurang (25km)
To Affandi Museum (6km); Hugo's (6km); Airport (10km); Prambanan (17km); Solo 65km)
To Gembira Loka Zoo (3km)
To Kota Gede (2km); Omar Duwur Restaurant & Bar (2km); Giwangan Bus Terminal (4km)
To Warung Opera (6km); Parangtritis (27km)
To Imogiri (20km)
See Sosrowijayan Area Map (p178)
See Prawirotaman Area Map (p179)
Jl Terban
Jl Colombo
Jl Simanjuntak
Jl Dr Sarjito
Jl AM Sangaji
Jl Magelang
Jl Cik Ditiro
Jl Rahayu Samirono
Jl Kyai Mojo
Jl Diponegoro
Tugu Monument
Jl Jenderal Sudirman
Jl Urip Sumoharjo (Jl Solo)
Army Museum
Jl Cokroaminoto
Jl P Mangkubumi
Jl Suroto
Jl Dr Wahidin Sudirohusodo
Jl Langensari
Jl Tentara Pelajar
Jl Yos Sudarso
Jl Abu Bakar Ali
Jl Pembela Tanah Air
Jl Ilagran Lor
Jl Pasar Kembang
Jl Wiratama
Lempuyangan
Jl Lempuyangan
Jl Kom Pol B Suprapto
Jl Sosrowijayan
Jl Joyonegaran
Jl Malioboro
Jl Mataram
Jl Mas Soeharto
Jl Hayam Wuruk
Jl Dr Sutomo
Jl Mawar
Jl Gondosuli
Jl Let Jen Suprapto
Matahari Department Store
Jl Pajeksan
Jl Suryatmaja
Jl Jeminahan
Jl Bausasran
Jl Gayam
Jl Bhayangkara
Jl A Yani
Jl Mayor Suryotomo
Jl Gajahmada
Jl Suryopranoto
Jl Cendana
Gedung Negara (Governor's Building)
Jl Wirobrajan
Jl KH Ahmad Dahlan
Jl Senopati
Jl Sultan Agung
Jl Trikora
Mesjid Besar
Jl Wahid Hasym
Jl Ngasem
Kraton
Jl Let Jen S Parman
Jl Taman
Kali Code
Jl Brigjen Katamso
Jl May Jend Sutoyo
Jl Kol Sugiyono
Jl Panjaitan
Jl Tirtodipuran
Jl Prawirotaman I
Jl Prawirotaman II
Jl Mangkuyudan
Jl Menukan
Jl Parangtritis
Jl Jogo Karyan
SLEEPING
Hotel Mercure 16 B2
Indraloka Home Stay 17 C1
Jogja Village Inn 18 C6
Melia Purosani Hotel 19 B3
Novotel Hotel 20 C2
EATING
Gita Anjana Steak Restaurant 21 B2
Milas 22 B6
Parsley 23 B2
ENTERTAINMENT
Ndalem Pujokusuman 24 C5
Purawisata 25 C4
RRI Auditorium 26 D1
Sasono Hinggil 27 B5
SHOPPING
Amri Yahya's Gallery 28 A3
Batik Keris 29 B3
Batik Plentong 30 B6
Batik Winotosastro (see 30)
Lana Gallery 31 C6
Mirota Batik 32 B4
Swasthigita Wayang Kulit Workshop 33 B5
Terang Bulan 34 B3
TRANSPORT
Adam Air 35 B2
Lion Air (see 19)
Mandala 36 C3
Niki Vita Tour & Travel (see 37)
Rahayu 37 B2
Rajawali Putra Travel 38 C2
Terban Colt/Bus Terminal to Kaliurang & Prambanan 39 C2
INFORMATION
BNI Bank 1 B4
Ludira Husada Tama Hospital 2 A3
Main Post Office 3 B4
Telkom 4 C2
Tourist Information Office 5 B3
SIGHTS & ACTIVITIES
Benteng Vredeburg 6 B4
Kraton Entrance 7 B4
Museum Kareta Kraton 8 B4
Museum Sasana Wiratama (Monumen Diponegoro) 9 A2
Pakualaman Kraton 10 C4
Pasar Beringharjo 11 B3
Pasar Ngasem (Bird Market) 12 B4
Sasmitaluka Jenderal Sudirman 13 C4
Sono-Budoyo Museum 14 B4
Taman Sari (Water Castle) 15 B5

YOGYA IN...

Two Days

Start your day with a visit to the **kraton** (below) and a traditional performance of gamelan, *wayang* or dance, then spend the afternoon exploring the *kampung* surrounding the sultan's palace and nearby **Taman Sari** (opposite). End your afternoon with a wander through the city's squawking bird market, **Pasar Ngasem** (opposite).

Your second day could start with a wander down Jl Malioboro scouting for batik bargains, and a meander through Yogya's main market, **Pasar Beringharjo** (opposite). A becak ride to **Kota Gede** (p176) to seek out silver bargains should be accompanied by a meal at **Omar Duwur Restaurant and Bar** (p182), one of Yogya's finest.

Four Days

After exhausting the two-day itinerary, it's time to discover the wonders within striking distance of the city. Start with a tour of the beautiful Buddhist temple **Borobudur** (p167), only a 90-minute bus ride away, and move onto **Prambanan** (p190), the Hindu equivalent of Borobudur and only 30 minutes from the city.

This could easily keep you entertained for two days, but if you have one day spare, use it to climb **Gunung Merapi** (p188), Yogya's very own volcano.

Kartika Trekking (Map p178; ☎ 562016; Jl Sosrowijayan 10; 9am-5pm) Agent specialising in trekking trips to Gunung Merapi. Recommended by locals and readers.

Kresna Tourist Service (Map p179; ☎ 375502; Jl Prawirotaman I; 8am-11pm) Handy for those staying in the Prawirotaman area.

Dangers & Annoyances

Yogya has its fair share of thieves – be particularly wary when catching buses to Borobudur and Prambanan.

More obvious (and often more annoying) are batik salespeople who'll strike up a conversation pretending to be guides or simply instant friends. Inevitably you'll end up at a gallery where you'll get the hard sell and they'll rake in a big commission if you buy. A time-honoured scam is the special batik exhibition that is being shipped to Southeast Asia – this is your 'last chance' to buy, at maybe 50 times the real price. Another is the only government-sponsored shop in Yogya where students from the Fine Arts school display their wares: there are no official shops or galleries in the city.

Becak drivers offering 'special rates' of 500Rp or 1000Rp for one hour are also trying to get you into a batik gallery.

Sights

KRATON

In the heart of the old city the huge palace of the sultans of Yogya is effectively the centre of a small walled city within a city. More than 25,000 people live within the **greater kraton compound** (Map p173; ☎ 373321; admission 7500Rp, guided tour 10,000Rp; 8am-2pm Sat-Thu, 8am-1pm Fri), which contains its own market, shops, batik and silver cottage industries, schools and mosques.

The innermost group of buildings, where the current sultan still resides, was built between 1755 and 1756, although extensions were made during the long reign of Hamengkubuwono I. European-style touches to the interior were added much later, in the 1920s. Structurally this is one of the finest examples of Javanese palace architecture, providing a series of luxurious halls and spacious courtyards and pavilions. The sense of tradition holds strong in Yogya, and the palace is attended by very dignified elderly retainers who still wear traditional Javanese dress.

The centre of the *kraton* is the reception hall, the Bangsal Kencana (Golden Pavilion), with its intricately decorated roof and great columns of carved teak. A large part of the *kraton* is used as a museum and holds an extensive collection, including gifts from European monarchs, gilt copies of the sacred *pusaka* (heirlooms of the royal family) and gamelan instruments. One of the most interesting rooms contains the royal family tree, old photographs of grand mass weddings and portraits of the former sultans of Yogya.

An entire museum within the *kraton* is dedicated to the beloved Sultan Hamengkubuwono IX, with photographs and personal effects of the great man.

Other points of interest within the *kraton* include the 'male' and 'female' entrances indicated by giant-sized 'he' and 'she' dragons (although the dragons look very similar). Outside the *kraton*, in the centre of the northern square, there are two sacred *waringin* (banyan trees), where, in the days of feudal Java, white-robed petitioners would patiently sit hoping to catch the eye of the king. In the *alun-alun kidul* (southern square), two similar banyan trees are said to bring great fortune if you can walk between them without mishap while blindfolded; on Friday and Saturday nights you can see the youth of Yogya attempting the feat to a chorus of laughter from friends.

There are gamelan performances in the inner pavilion at 10am on Monday, Tuesday and Thursday. *Wayang golek* (9am Wednesday), Javanese singing performances (10am Friday), *wayang kulit* (9am Saturday) and classical dance (11am Sunday) are also held.

The *kraton*'s entrance is on the northwest side and it is closed on national holidays and for special *kraton* ceremonies, but batik touts will tell you it's closed to lure you to Taman Sari and a batik gallery.

TAMAN SARI

Just to the west of the *kraton* is the **Water Castle** (Map p173; admission 7000Rp; 8am-2pm), which once served as a splendid pleasure park of palaces, pools and waterways for the sultan and his entourage. The Portuguese architect of this elaborate retreat, built between 1758 and 1765, was from Batavia – the story goes that the sultan had him executed in order to keep his hidden pleasure rooms secret.

The complex was damaged first by Diponegoro's Java War, and an earthquake in 1865 helped finish the job. While much of what you see today lies in ruins, the bathing pools have been restored. From the tower overlooking the pools, the sultan was able to dally with his wives and witness the goings-on below.

The entrance to the restored bathing pools is on Jl Taman. Batik touts will try to lure you to a batik gallery or pretend to be official guides – shake them off.

PASAR NGASEM

At the edge of Taman Sari, Yogya's **bird market** (Map p173; Jl Polowijan; 8am-6pm) is a colourful menagerie crowded with hundreds of budgerigars, orioles, roosters and singing turtledoves in ornamental cages, but pigeons are the big business here (for training, not eating). Lizards and other small animals are also on sale, as are big trays of bird feed (swarming maggots and ants). From the back of Pasar Ngasem, an alleyway leads up to the broken walls of Taman Sari for fine views across Yogya.

PASAR BERINGHARJO

Yogya's **main market** (Map p173; Jl A Yani; 8am-6pm), on the southern continuation of Jl Malioboro, is a lively and fascinating place. The renovated front section has a wide range of batik – mostly cheap *batik cap* (stamped batik) – while the 2nd floor is dedicated to cheap clothes and shoes. Most interesting of all, though, is the old section towards the back. Crammed with warungs and stalls selling a huge variety of fruit and vegetables, this is still very much a traditional market. The range of *rempah rempah* (spices) on the 1st floor are quite something.

MUSEUMS

On the northern side of the main square in front of the *kraton*, **Sono-Budoyo Museum** (Map p173; ☎ 376775; admission 750Rp; 8am-1.30pm Tue-Thu, 8-11.15am Fri, 8am-noon Sat & Sun) is the pick of Yogya's museums, even if it is dusty and dimly lit. It has a first-class collection of Javanese art, including *wayang kulit* puppets, *topeng* (masks), kris and batik. It also has a courtyard packed with Hindu statuary and artefacts from further afield, including superb Balinese carvings. *Wayang kulit* performances are held here (p182).

Up until his death in 1990, Affandi, Indonesia's best-known artist internationally, lived and worked in an unusual tree-house studio overlooking the river, about 6km east of the town centre. The **Affandi Museum** (Jl Solo; admission 5000Rp; 9am-4pm Tue-Fri, 9am-1pm Sat) in the grounds exhibits his impressionist works, as well as paintings by his daughter Kartika and other artists. Affandi is buried in the back garden.

Dating from 1765, **Benteng Vredeburg** (Map p173; Jl A Yani 6; admission 750Rp; 8.30am-1.30pm

Tue-Thu, 8.30-11am Fri, 8.30am-noon Sat & Sun) is a Dutch-era fort opposite the main post office. The restored fort is now a museum that houses dioramas showing the history of the independence movement in Yogyakarta. The architecture is worth a look, but the dioramas are designed for Indonesian patriots.

Near the *kraton* entrance, **Museum Kareta Kraton** (Map p173; admission 2000Rp; 8am-2pm Sat-Thu, 8am-noon Fri) has exhibits of the opulent chariots of the sultans, although the bug-eyed horse statues are almost more interesting than the main event.

Sasmitaluka Jenderal Sudirman (Map p173; Jl B Harun; admission by donation; 8am-noon Tue-Sun) is the memorial home of General Sudirman, who commanded revolutionary forces and died shortly after the siege of Yogya in 1948.

Museum Sasana Wiratama (Monumen Diponegoro; Map p173; admission by donation; 8am-noon Tue-Sun) honours the Indonesian hero, Prince Diponegoro, who was leader of the bloody but futile rebellion of 1825–30 against the Dutch. A motley collection of the prince's belongings and other exhibits are kept in the small museum at his former Yogya residence.

KOTA GEDE

Kota Gede has been famed as the hub of Yogya's silver industry since the 1930s. But this quiet old town, which is now a suburb of Yogyakarta, was the first capital of the Mataram kingdom, founded by Panembahan Senopati in 1582. Senopati is buried in the small mossy graveyard of an old mosque to the south of the town's central market. You can visit the **sacred tomb** (admission 1000Rp; around 9am-noon Sun, Mon & Thu, around 1-3pm Fri), but be sure to wear conservative dress when visiting; on days when the tomb is closed there is little to see here.

Jl Kemasan, the main street leading into town from the north, is lined with busy silver workshops. Most of the shops have similar stock, including hand-beaten bowls, boxes, fine filigree and modern jewellery (see p183).

Kota Gede is about 5km southeast of Jl Malioboro. Catch bus 4, a becak (about 15,000Rp) or cycle there; it is flat most of the way.

OTHER SIGHTS

The small **Pakualaman Kraton** (Map p173; Jl Sultan Agung; 9.30am-1.30pm Tue, Thu & Sun), northeast of the main *kraton*, houses a small museum, a *pendopo* that can hold a full gamelan orchestra, and a curious colonial house. Outside opening times you can explore the grounds.

In the evening you can head along to the **Purawisata** (Map p173; Jl Brigjen Katamso), an amusement park noted more for its dance performances, but there are also rides, funfair games and a *pasar seni* (art market) with a basic collection of souvenirs.

Yogya's **Gembira Loka Zoo** (admission 4000Rp; 8am-6pm), about 5km east of Jl A Yani, has its fair share of cramped cages, but on the whole it is spacious and has some interesting exotica such as some Komodo dragons, which are successfully breeding.

Walking Tour

Yogya is a very manageable city and many of its blockbuster sights can be seen on foot. A good place to start a walking tour of the city is **Tugu train station** (**1**), from where **Jl Malioboro** (**2**), Yogya's premier shopping street, is laid out in front of you. Head south along Jl Malioboro until Jl Suryatmajan, from which point Malioboro becomes Jl A Yani. Only one block south of Jl Suryatmajan is the market **Pasar Beringharjo** (**3**; p175), and only another block south again is the city's old Dutch fort, **Benteng Vredeburg** (**4**; p175).

Continuing south once more, cross Jl Senopati onto Jl Trikora and the **alun-alun** (**5**) will appear. Swing right and past the **Sono-Budoyo Museum** (**6**; p175) before heading south again, walking by the **Mesjid Besar** (**7**) and **Museum Kareta Kraton** (**8**; left). The entrance to the **Kraton** (**9**; p174) is only a few metres to the left.

From the *kraton*, head west until you hit Jl Ngasem, then turn left. Walk south and the city's **bird market** (**10**; p175) will be impossible to miss. Take Jl Taman east from outside the bird market; it quickly turns south and passes the **Taman Sari** (**11**; p175). At the end of Jl Taman turn left and make a beeline for the city's southern **alun-alun** (**12**). If you're with friends (or are simply feeling adventurous), have yourself blindfolded and try your luck walking between the square's two banyan trees; local folk-

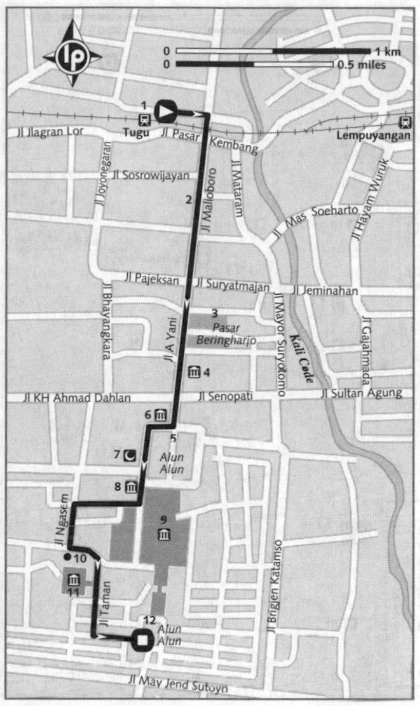

WALK FACTS

Start Tugu train station
Finish alun-alun
Distance 3km
Duration two hours, excluding stops at attractions along the way

lore predicts good fortune for those who succeed.

Courses

Plenty of places in the Sosrowijayan (such as Losmen Lucy, p178) and Prawirotaman areas (such as Via Via, p181) offer short batik T-shirt courses of one or two days' duration. High art they aren't, but they provide a good introduction. The **tourist information office** (Map p173; ☎ 562000; Jl Malioboro 16; 🕑 8am-7pm Mon-Thu, 8-11.30am & 1-3pm Fri, 8am-6pm Sat) also has a list of those offering courses.

Bahasa Indonesia courses are offered in Yogya. **Puri Bahasa** (☎ 583789; Komplex Colombo, Jl Rajawali) and **Wisma Bahasa** (☎ 588409; Komplex Colombo, Jl Rajawali) are well-established schools; the tourist information office can supply you with more options.

Tours

The tour agents on Jl Prawirotaman (Map p179) and Jl Sosrowijayan, Jl Dagen and Jl Pasar Kembang (Map p178) offer a host of similar tours at competitive prices that often include a snack and drink, but entrance fees are usually extra. Typical day tours and per-person rates (excluding entrance fees) are: Borobudur (60,000Rp); Dieng (150,000Rp); Prambanan (70,000Rp); Prambanan and Parangtritis (130,000Rp); Gunung Merapi climb from Selo (150,000Rp); and Gedung Songo and Ambarawa (150,000Rp).

Longer tours, such as to Gunung Bromo and on to Bali (300,000Rp, two days/one night) are also offered. Tours are often dependent on getting enough people to fill a minibus (usually a minimum of four), and prices vary depending on whether air-con is provided. Note that tours may also stop at batik or silver galleries to earn extra commission for tour operators.

Operators also arrange cars with driver (at some of the best rates in Java if you bargain).

Festivals & Events

Gerebeg The three Gerebeg festivals – held each year at the end of January and April and the beginning of November – are Java's most colourful and grand processions. In traditional court dress, palace guards and retainers, not to mention large floats of decorated mountains of rice, all make their way to the mosque, west of the *kraton*, to the sound of prayer and gamelan music.

Arts festival Yogya hosts this annual festival from 7 June to 7 July. Offers a wide range of shows and exhibitions. Most events are held at the Benteng Vredeburg.

Sleeping

Yogya has more than enough losmen, guesthouses and upmarket hotels to go round, although in the high season – July, August and December – things can get crowded. Outside these times, you should have no problem finding a bed and discounts should be easy to come by.

BUDGET

Sosrowijayan Area

Most of Yogya's cheap hotels are in the Sosrowijayan area, immediately south of the train line, near Jl Malioboro. Running

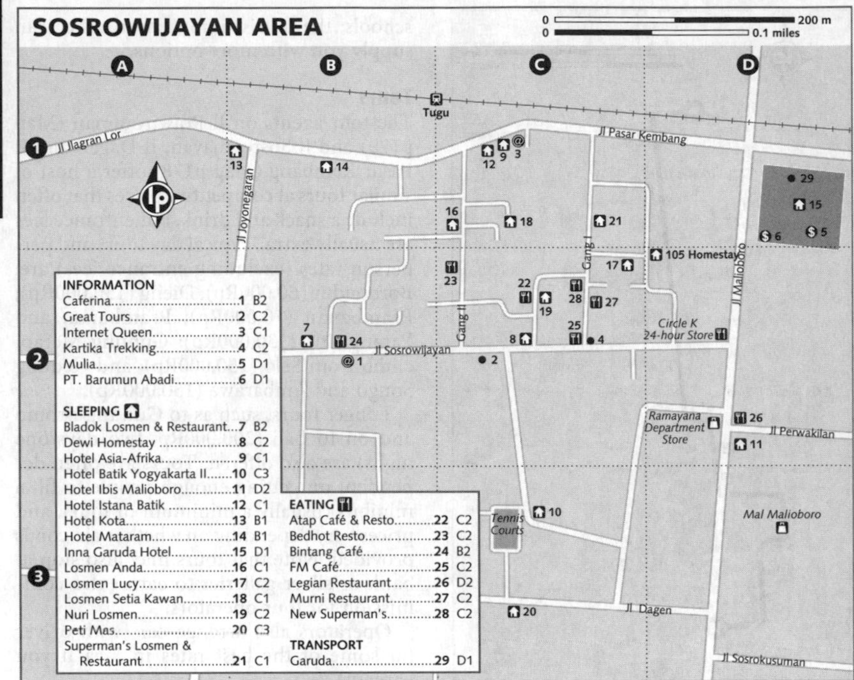

between Jl Pasar Kembang and Jl Sosrowijayan, the narrow alleys of Gang Sosrowijayan I and II are lined with cheap (but often bland) accommodation and popular eating places. Despite mass tourism, the *gang* (alleys) are quiet and still have a *kampung* atmosphere.

Losmen Anda (Map p178; ☎ 512452; r 25,000-30,000Rp) Friendly smiles come free of charge at Anda, a very basic losmen on Gang II. Rooms are a little scrungy (the better ones are upstairs), but they're cheap, and you can pass the time helping grandma with the family's evening meal.

Dewi Homestay (Map p178; ☎ 516014; dewi homestay@hotmail.com; r from 30,000Rp) With a true rustic look and feel, art covering the walls, four-poster beds and massive mosquito nets, Dewi is one of the better budget options in Sosrowijayan. It's just off Jl Sosrowijayan.

Losmen Lucy (Map p178; ☎ 513429; r 35,000Rp) Just off Gang I, Lucy's is one of the better, bargain-basement options and gets good marks for cleanliness and all-round homely feel. Rooms have teeny-tiny fans, but there's space to sit out the front to catch some air.

Losmen Setia Kawan (Map p178; ☎ 512452; www.bedhots.com; s/d 40,000/50,000Rp, with a/c from 60,000/70,000Rp;) Down an alley off Gang II, this losmen is in a well-kept, old-style building with plenty of charm. Rooms are simple but very attractive, with each sporting its own esoteric-style wall mural to liven things up. Communal areas (including a rooftop patio) are also lovingly designed and inviting.

Bladok Losmen & Restaurant (Map p178; ☎ 560452; Jl Sosrowijayan 76; r 60,000Rp, with European bathroom & balcony 100,000Rp, with air-con & TV 190,000Rp;) With oodles of charm, good facilities and a range of snug rooms, Bladok caters to both budget and midrange travellers, and remains a perennial favourite. It also has an excellent restaurant (p181).

Hotel Kota (Map p178; ☎ 515844; hotelkota@eudoramail.com; Jl Jlagran Lor 1; r from 120,000Rp;) Once a beautiful, colonial-style hotel with plenty of charm, Kota is now looking a bit washed up these days, with smudged walls and dim light bulbs, but some of its old charisma still shines through the murk. Rooms range from small, cheapish economies to glitzier top-enders featuring all the trimmings.

Hotel Asia-Afrika (Map p178; ☎ 566219; Jl Pasar Kembang 21; r with fan 150,000Rp, with air-con from 200,000Rp;) Asia-Afrika is a sensible place to start looking for hotels bordering on midrange. It has a nice garden café and rooms in good condition.

Also recommended:

Nuri Losmen (Map p178; ☎ 543654; s/d from 25,000/30,000Rp) In a quiet alley between Gang I and Gang II, with basic rooms and an upstairs terrace for tea-sipping and people-watching.

Superman's Losmen & Restaurant (Map p178; ☎ 515007; r 40,000Rp) Simple losmen midway along Gang I, with very friendly staff and very basic and clean rooms. See also p181.

Prawirotaman Area

This area used to be the centre for the midrange hotels in Yogya, but many have slashed prices – and sometimes standards – in recent years.

Delta Homestay (Map p179; ☎ 081 7271047; www.dutagardenhotel.com; Jl Prawirotaman II 597A; s/d 42,500/50,000Rp, with mandi 70,000/80,000Rp, with air-con 90,000/100,000Rp;) This excellent place has comfy rooms in very good condition, a peaceful ambience and a central pool. It's one of the few places in town you may have problems getting into if you haven't booked ahead.

Metro Guest House (Map p179; ☎ 372364; caféyg2@idola.net.id; Jl Prawirotaman II 71; r 50,000-75,000Rp, with air-con & hot shower 150,000Rp;) Metro is a popular travellers' hang-out, with branches on both sides of the road, a range of rooms, a restaurant and an internet café. The rooms are a bit dingy, though.

Mercury Guest House (Map p179; ☎ 370846; Jl Prawirotaman II 595; s/d with fan & hot shower 55,000/75,000Rp;) Mercury attracts guests with its *kraton*-style architecture and a wonderful dining area, furnished with antique pieces and some floor cushions. Rooms don't share the restaurant's charm and are surprisingly simple, but are super-clean and peaceful.

Rose Guest House (Map p179; ☎ 377991; Jl Prawirotaman I 22; s/d with fan from 60,000/75,000Rp, with air-con 110,000/120,000Rp;) Rose Guest House is a large establishment with clean but dark rooms centred around a swimming pool. The more expensive rooms come with a small terrace, and the staff here are friendly and accommodating. The only drawback is the rowdy birds in cages.

Prambanan Guest House (Map p179; ☎ 376167; Jl Prawirotaman I No 14; r with cold shower/air-con 70,000/130,000Rp;) An attractive hotel with an airy garden and attentive staff, Prambanan is a very good option in the midrange category. Cheaper rooms are bland but the better doubles are comfortable and have bamboo trimmings and art on the walls.

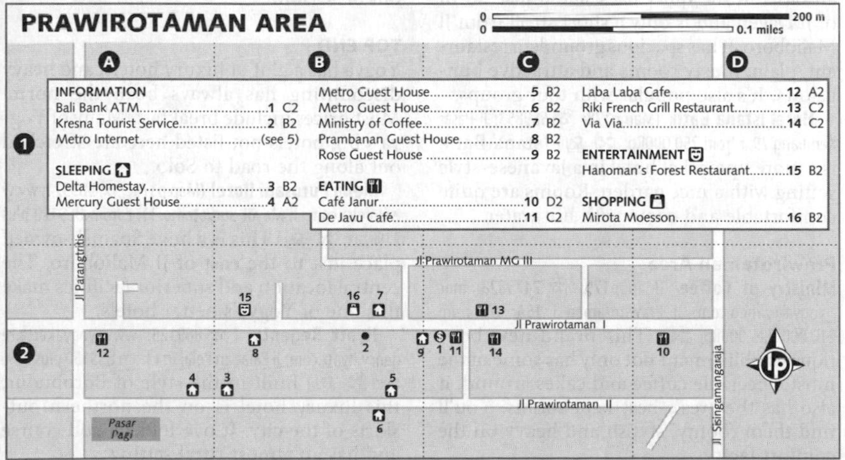

Other Areas

Jl Tirtodipuran is an extension of Prawirotaman I, on the other side of Jl Parangtritis. As well as a few restaurants and some large batik shops, it has a couple of decent hotels.

Indraloka Home Stay (Map p173; ☎ 564341; manunggal@yogya.wasantara.net.id; Jl Cik Ditiro 18; r with breakfast, air-con & hot water from 175,000Rp;) North of Jl Jenderal Sudirman, this true homestay has bags of charm, with antique furniture, faded, but classy, old-world décor and a small garden out back. The cheaper rooms are quite pokey, so shell out for the more expensive ones.

MIDRANGE

Sosrowijayan Area

Peti Mas (Map p178; ☎ 561938; petimas@yahoo.com; Jl Dagen 27; s/d from 99,000/115,000Rp, with air-con, TV & hot water from 226,000/246,000Rp;) Peti Mas is a peaceful hotel popular with families. Its rooms are clean and attractive with partially open-air bathrooms, and there's coiffed gardens and a pleasant restaurant.

Hotel Mataram (Map p178; ☎ 581721; Jl Pasar Kembang 61; r 175,000-350,000Rp;) A glossy, business-style hotel within stumbling distance of the train station, Mataram will serve those looking for a hotel with medium facilities and prompt service. Rooms are a bit charmless but offer predictable, motel-style comfort.

Hotel Batik Yogyakarta II (Map p178; ☎ 561828; batikcottage@yahoo.com; r/bungalows from 225,000/275,000Rp;) Batik Yogyakarta is an oasis in the quiet back alleys just north of Jl Dagen and is only a short stroll from Jl Malioboro. It has spacious grounds, a restaurant, plain, musty rooms and attractive bungalows. It's also popular with tour groups.

Hotel Istana Batik (Map p178; ☎ 589853; Jl Pasar Kembang 29; r from 250,000Rp;) Istana Batik is a more upmarket hotel in a Javanese-style setting with a nice garden. Rooms are quite comfortable and come with hot water.

Prawirotaman Area

Ministry of Coffee (Map p179; ☎ 7473828; moc_yogya@yahoo.com; Jl Prawirotaman I 15A; s/d from 210,000/226,000Rp;) This brand-new boutique establishment not only has some of the most delectable coffee and cakes around, it also has the area's best-kept rooms. You'll find them roomy, stylish and heavy on the comfort factor.

Other Areas

Jogja Village Inn (Map p173; ☎ 373031; www.jvidusun.co.id; Jl Menukan 5; r 346,000-579,000Rp plus 21% tax;) Jogja Village Inn is something of an institution in the city, and rightly so. This chic, boutique hotel has a traditional Javan feel, with top-notch rooms and a decent pool set in exotic gardens. It's quite the place for a few sundowners.

Novotel Hotel (Map p173; ☎ 580930; admin@novotelyogya.com; Jl Jenderal Sudirman 89; r from 370,000Rp;) While style and individuality don't go hand and hand with this chain hotel, it has well-kept rooms and all the facilities you'd expect from a business hotel. A gallery and a pastry shop are also on site.

Hotel Mercure (Map p173; ☎ 566617; info@mercureyogya.com; Jl Jenderal Sudirman 9-11; r from 385,000Rp plus 21% tax;) Close to Jl P Mangkubumi and the centre of town, this is a smaller hotel with some class. There's an army of attentive staff on hand, and discounts are readily handed out.

Inna Garuda Hotel (Map p178; ☎ 566353; www.innagaruda.com; Jl Malioboro 60; s/d from 500,000/600,000Rp;) Right in the thick of things on Jl Malioboro is Inna Garuda, once the grand old man of Yogya's top-class hotels. It is now looking a bit past its use-by date, but rooms are still quite comfy.

Hotel Ibis Malioboro (Map p178; ☎ 516974; admin@ibisyogya.com; Jl Malioboro 52-58; r from 675,000Rp;) This very central hotel offers homogenous, but fully functional, business-class comfort. Expect large discounts out of season.

TOP END

Yogya has a glut of luxury hotels, and heavy discounting has always been the norm. Most prices include breakfast. Many of Yogya's big hotels not listed here are stretched out along the road to Solo.

Melia Purosani Hotel (Map p173; ☎ 589521; www.solmelia.com; Jl Mayor Suryotomo 31; r from US$120 plus 21% tax;) This is a huge Spanish-owned place just to the east of Jl Malioboro. The central location and superior facilities make this one of Yogya's better hotels.

Hyatt Regency (☎ 869123; www.yogyakarta.regency.hyatt.com; Jl Palagan Pelajar; r from US$150 plus 20% tax;) Built in the style of Borobudur, this luxury hotel is on the northern outskirts of the city. It overlooks a golf course and has an almost rural setting.

Eating

SOSROWIJAYAN AREA

This area is inundated with cheap and cheerful eateries featuring Indonesian and Western dishes. It's also the place to join locals for a bite to eat; after 10pm, the souvenir vendors along the northern end of Jl Malioboro pack up and a *lesahan* area (where diners sit on straw mats) comes alive. Here you can try Yogya's famous *ayam goreng* (chicken deep-fried after soaking in coconut milk) and listen to young Indonesians strumming their guitars into the wee small hours.

A whole host of good warungs also line Jl Pasar Kembang, beside the train line.

Bedhot Resto (Map p178; Gang II; mains 10,000-20,000Rp; ⏰ breakfast, lunch & dinner) Bedhot means 'creative' in old Javanese and is perhaps the most stylish eatery in Sosrowijayan, with art on the walls and ebullient staff. The big menu stretches from pizza and cereals to salads and sate.

Atap Café & Resto (Map p178; Jl Sosrowijayan GT 1/113; mains 15,000Rp; ⏰ dinner) Just down a small alleyway opposite Nuri Losmen, this ecofriendly café has good Indonesian food, great puddings and a crowd of trendy, earth-loving locals. Slightly less politically correct is its *Osama bin Coffee*, which comes served with a hefty slug of brandy and rum.

FM Café (Map p178; Jl Sosrowijayan 14; mains around 15,000Rp; ⏰ breakfast, lunch & dinner) FM Café has seen its popularity wane, but it still has stacks of atmosphere and an eclectic, well-priced menu, ranging from nasi goreng to greasy-spoon fry-ups. Friday and Saturday nights see live bands performing.

New Superman's (Map p178; mains around 15,000Rp; ⏰ breakfast, lunch & dinner) A bit further down Gang I is Superman's offshoot; it's more popular, and has pizzas, steak, and Indonesian and Chinese food.

Bintang Café (Map p178; Jl Sosrowijayan 54; mains 15,000Rp; ⏰ breakfast, lunch & dinner) This imaginatively named café is easily the busiest place after sundown. The food is quite standard (Western, Chinese and Indonesian food), but the atmosphere makes up for it; expect live bands as the evening wears on.

Bladok Losmen & Restaurant (Map p178; Jl Sosrowijayan 76; mains 20,000-40,000Rp; ⏰ breakfast, lunch & dinner) Bladok ranks among Sosrowijayan's best; it has plenty of Alpine-style woodwork, a wholesome and inviting air, and a mainly European menu. See also p178.

Superman's Losmen & Restaurant (Map p178; Gang I; mains around 20,000Rp; ⏰ breakfast, lunch & dinner) One of the original purveyors of banana pancakes, Superman's has been around for decades. The owner, Pak Suparman, adapted his name, and likewise his food, to suit Western sensibilities. See also p179.

Also worth a mention:

Murni Restaurant (Map p178; Gang I; mains around 20,000Rp; ⏰ lunch & dinner) Alcohol-free and serves tasty curries with flaky *paratha* (Indian-style fried bread) and good ice juices.

Legian Restaurant (Map p178; cnr Jl Malioboro & Jl Perwakilan; mains 20,000-40,000Rp; ⏰ lunch & dinner) Serves Indonesian, Chinese, French and Italian food in a leafy roof-terrace setting overlooking Jl Malioboro.

PRAWIROTAMAN AREA

Ministry of Coffee (Map p179; ☎ 7473828; moc_yogya@yahoo.com; Jl Prawirotaman I 15A; coffee 5000Rp; ⏰ breakfast, lunch & dinner) For quality coffee and sweets the sultan wouldn't turn his nose up at, take a pew at the Ministry of Coffee's downstairs café or upstairs terrace. See also opposite.

Via Via (Map p179; ☎ 386557; www.viaviacafé.com; Jl Prawirotaman I 30; mains 12,000-35,000Rp; ⏰ breakfast, lunch & dinner) Stripped back and stylish, Belgian-run Via Via has a mixed menu and imaginative daily specials, along with loads of information for travellers to digest. There's also terrace seating upstairs. Tours are offered downstairs.

Café Janur (Map p179; Jl Prawirotaman I 44; mains 15-30,000Rp; ⏰ breakfast, lunch & dinner) With a well-endowed totem figure guarding the entrance, it's hard to miss Janur. Inside, the décor is an emporium of tribal guff. The mixed menu and cheap drinks attract a crowd of expats and tipsy locals.

Laba Laba Cafe (Map p179; Jl Prawirotaman I 2; mains 20,000Rp; ⏰ lunch & dinner) Laba Laba (which means 'spider') has been attracting expats and locals for years with its lively bar and grungy atmosphere. The menu ranges from steak and fries to some decent Indonesian fare, and there's a pleasant garden out the back.

Riki French Grill Restaurant (Map p179; Jl Prawirotaman I 31; mains 20,000Rp; ⏰ lunch & dinner) Riki is another restaurant-bar that fills up when the tourists are in town; the atmosphere is convivial and the steaks and waffles are rather good. Its happy hour between 4pm and 7pm gets the punters in early.

De Javu Café (Map p179; Jl Prawirotaman I 28; mains 20,000-40,000Rp; breakfast, lunch & dinner) This sweet little café sports local art, a mixture of Western and Indonesian cuisine and a relaxed, refined air.

OTHER AREAS

our pick **Jimbaran** (7452882; Jl Damai; fish 8000Rp per ounce, lobster & prawns from 12,000Rp per ounce; lunch & dinner) Combine a lazy location overlooking rice fields (or kids' football pitch, depending on the season), a speciality in seafood, and an open pagoda styled after traditional restaurants in Bali, and you have Jimbaran. Everything is priced by the ounce, but it's a hard choice between live crabs, lobsters, prawns and fresh fish on ice. Jimbaran is about 6km north of Yogya, and about 2km north of the Hyatt.

Milas (Map p173; Jl Mantrijeron MJ III 897A; mains 10-15,000Rp; lunch & dinner Tue-Sun) A vegetarian restaurant with an Indonesian and European menu, Milas is popular with both locals and visitors for its organic produce, relaxed air and peaceful surroundings.

Warung Opera (7181977; Jl Parangtritis, Km 6.3; mains 10,000-30,000Rp; dinner) Warung Opera serves up excellent Indonesian dishes, but that's not what sets it apart from the competition. Here you can not only dine well, but also have your fortune told by Donny, the owner. We're not sure of his success rate, but it's fun all the same.

Omar Duwur Restaurant and Bar (374952; Jl Mondorakan 252; mains 30,000-70,000Rp; lunch & dinner) Omar Duwur is quite a hike from the centre of town, but if you're a lover of fine food, it's well worth the effort of getting out to Kota Gede. This remains one of Yogya's best restaurants, offering a wide selection of Western and Eastern dishes in contemporary, colonial-style surrounds.

Other places worth a look-in:

Parsley (Map p173; Jl Magelang; cakes 2000Rp; 7am-7pm) Attempts to serve cakes, pies and pastries with a healthier twist.

Gita Anjana Steak Restaurant (Map p173; Jl Diponegoro 48; mains 20,000-50,000Rp; lunch & dinner) Not the place for vegetarians; meat feasts are the order of the day here.

Entertainment

Yogya is by far the easiest place to see traditional Javanese performing arts, with performances of one sort or another held daily. Dance, *wayang* or gamelan is performed every morning at the *kraton* (p174), and provides a useful introduction to Javanese arts. Check with the tourist office for current listings and any special events.

Most famous of all performances is the spectacular Ramayana ballet (p193) held in the open air at Prambanan in the dry season.

WAYANG KULIT

Leather puppet performances can be seen at several places around Yogya every night of the week.

Sasono Hinggil (Map p173; South Main Square) Most of the centres offer shortened versions for tourists, but here in the *alun-alun selatan* of the *kraton*, marathon all-night performances are held every second Saturday from 9pm to 5am (15,000Rp). Bring a pillow.

Sono-Budoyo Museum (Map p173; 376775; admission 750Rp; 8am-1.30pm Tue-Thu, 8-11.15am Fri, 8am-noon Sat & Sun) This museum also holds popular two-hour performances nightly from 8pm to 10pm (15,000Rp). The first half-hour involves the reading of the story in Javanese, so most travellers skip this and arrive later.

DANCE

Most performances are based on the Ramayana or at least billed as 'Ramayana ballet' because of the famed performances at Prambanan.

Purawisata (Map p173; 375705; Jl Brigjen Katamso) This amusement park stages Ramayana performances daily at 8pm (tickets 100,000Rp).

Ndalem Pujokusuman (Map p173; Jl Brigjen Katamso 45) Performances are here on Monday and Friday between 8pm and 10pm, but they're not as popular as Purawisata. Tickets cost 50,000Rp.

OTHER PERFORMANCES

RRI auditorium (Map p173; cnr Jl Gejayan & Jl Colombo) Here you can see *ketoprak* performances from 8pm to midnight on the first Saturday of every month for 20,000Rp.

Hanoman's Forest Restaurant (Map p179; Jl Prawirotaman I) Hanoman's has been hosting various *wayang* performances for years, but at the time of research it had closed its doors due to a lack of interest. This may change if tourist numbers pick up again.

LIVE MUSIC

Blatz Lounge (☎ 7488898; Jl Kaliurang, Km 6.3) The deep reds and delicious cocktails at this groovy bar are perfectly complemented by sublime live jazz every Tuesday night. If that's not enough to entice you, there are also pool tables and free internet.

Also worth a peek:

FM Café (Map p178; Jl Sosrowijayan 14) Regular bands on weekends; see also (p181).

Bintang Café (Map p178; Jl Sosrowijayan 54) Bands most nights; see also (p181).

NIGHTCLUBS

Hugo's (☎ 484208; Sheraton Mustika Resort & Spa, Jl Adisucipto) Hugo's is *the* place to be seen on weekends in Yogya, when the music pumps and the enormous dance floor fills to bursting point.

Shopping

Yogya is a shopper's paradise for crafts and antiques, primarily from Java, though bits and pieces from all over the archipelago can be found here.

Jl Malioboro is one great long throbbing bazaar of souvenir shops and stalls selling cheap clothes, leatherwork, batik bags, *topeng* masks and *wayang golek* puppets. Look in some of the fixed-price shops on Jl Malioboro or nearby streets to get an idea of prices; **Mirota Batik** (Map p173; ☎ 588524; Jl A Yani 9) is good place to start looking.

The other major area to shop is Jl Tirtodipuran, the continuation of Jl Prawirotaman. This is an interesting, more upmarket shopping stretch, with galleries, art shops and expensive batik factories. You'll find furniture, antiques, and a variety of crafts and curios from Java and further afield.

BATIK

Most of the batik workshops and several large showrooms are along Jl Tirtodipuran, south of the *kraton*. Many, such as **Batik Plentong** (Map p173; Jl Tirtodipuran 48) and **Batik Winotosastro** (Map p173; Jl Tirtodipuran 54), give free guided tours of the batik process. These places cater to tour groups, so prices are very high – view the process here and shop elsewhere.

In the markets, especially Pasar Beringharjo, you'll find batik is cheaper than in the shops, but you need to be careful about quality and should be prepared to bargain. Many other reasonably priced shops are on Jl Malioboro and Jl A Yani, but particularly good fixed-price places to try include the following:

Terang Bulan (Map p173; Jl A Yani 108)

Batik Keris (Map p173; ☎ 557893; Jl A Yani 71) A branch of the big Solo batik house; more expensive.

BATIK PAINTING

Given that the batik painting industry is Yogya's biggest blight (due to the excessive hard sell directed at tourists), perhaps the best advice is to avoid it altogether. However, batik paintings can be attractive souvenirs, and small paintings (around 300mm x 300mm) can be as cheap as 40,000Rp (although the asking price may be 400,000Rp). Most of the mass-production galleries are found around Taman Sari. It pays to shop around for something different and to bargain hard.

A few artists who pioneered and grew famous from batik painting still produce some batik.

Amri Yahya's Gallery (Map p173; Jl Gampingan 67; ⏲ Tue-Sun) Amri Yahya's gallery has a few early batik works on display, although he mostly produces abstract oil paintings these days.

ANTIQUES, CURIOS & FURNITURE

Although a few antiques can be found in the shops and markets, they are best left to collectors who know their stuff. Yogya art shops spend an inordinate amount of time defacing *wayang golek* puppets and *topeng* masks in the name of antiquity, and many other items get similar treatment.

Jl Tirtodipuran has the best selection of artefacts from all over Java and Indonesia. Prices are generally high here – bargain furiously, or get an idea of quality and look around for somewhere else to shop.

Furniture, mostly antique copies, can be found on Jl Tirtodipuran and in the back lanes nearby.

Mirota Moesson (Map p179; Jl Prawirotaman I 15) In the heart of the Prawirotaman area, this store has a large and interesting collection of furniture.

SILVER

The best area to shop for silverwork is in the silver village of Kota Gede (p176), although it can be found all over town. Fine filigree work is a Yogya speciality, but many styles and designs are available. Kota Gede has some very attractive jewellery, boxes, bowls, cutlery and miniatures, and there are dozens of smaller silver shops on Jl Kemesan and Jl Mondorakan, where you can get some good buys if you bargain.

You can get a guided tour of the process, with no obligation to buy, at the large factories:

Tom's Silver (☎ 525416; Jl Ngeski Gondo 60) Tom's has an extensive selection and some superb large pieces, but prices are very high.

HS (Jl Mandarokan I) Marginally cheaper; always ask for a substantial discount off the marked prices.

MD (☎ 375063; Jl Pesegah KG 8/44) Down a small alley off the street; as at HS, try for discounts.

OTHER CRAFTS

Yogya's leatherwork can be excellent value for money and the quality is usually high, but you should always check the quality and stitching. Shops and street stalls on Jl Malioboro are the best places to shop for leatherwork.

Lana Gallery (Map p173; ☎ 7150465; Jl Menukan 276A; 🕑 9am-6pm Tue-Sun) Lana Gallery displays contemporary art from artists of Yogya's Fine Arts school, and is run by two of the friendliest Indonesians you'll ever meet. You're welcome to browse or buy up the whole gallery.

Swasthigita (Map p173; ☎ 378346; Ngadinegaran MJ 7/50; 🕑 9am-4pm) Just north of Jl Tirtodipuran, this is a top-rate *wayang kulit* puppet manufacturer; it also holds the occasional *wayang* show.

Getting There & Away

AIR

Yogyakarta is well served by a number of airlines, including **Garuda** (Map p178; ☎ 551515; Inna Garuda Hotel, Jl Malioboro 60), **Mandala** (Map p173; ☎ 520603; Jl Mayor Suryotomo 537A), **Adam Air** (Map p173; ☎ 580999; Jl Diponegoro 121) and **Lion Air** (Map p173; ☎ 555028; Melia Purosani Hotel, Jl Mayor Suryotomo 31). The latter also flies to Denpasar and Surabaya. Consult the Java Airfares map (p98) for prices.

BUS

Yogya's **Giwangan bus terminal** (Jl Imogiri) is 5km southeast of the city centre; city bus 4 connects the terminal with Jl Malioboro; 15 with the *kraton*.

Buses run from Giwangan all over Java and also to Bali. Normal/air-con buses go to Solo (8000/15,000Rp, two hours), Semarang (15,000/30,000Rp, 3½ hours), Bandung (65,000/95,000Rp, 10 hours), Jakarta (85,000/115,000Rp, 12 hours) and Surabaya (50,000/60,000Rp, eight hours).

For long trips it's best to take luxury buses. It's cheaper to buy tickets at the bus terminal, but it's less hassle to simply check fares and departures with the ticket agents along Jl Mangkubumi, along Jl Sosrowijayan near Kartika Trekking, or along Jl Prawirotaman. These agents can also arrange pick-up from your hotel. Check more than one agent – some charge excessive commission. Typical fares include Denpasar (185,000Rp; 220,000Rp with toilet), Surabaya and Malang (75,000Rp), Bandung (85,000Rp) and Jakarta (90,000Rp).

Local buses also operate regularly from the main bus terminal to all the towns in the immediate area, including Borobudur (10,000Rp, 1½ hours), Parangtritis (7000Rp, one hour) and Kaliurang (37000Rp, one hour). To go to Prambanan (7000Rp), take the yellow Pemuda bus. To go to Imogiri (3000Rp, 40 minutes), take a Colt or the Abadi bus 5 to Panggang and ask the conductor to let you off at the *makam* (graves).

As well as the main bus terminal, Colts operate to the outlying towns from various subterminals. The most useful is the Terban Colt terminal (Map p173) to the north of the city centre on Jl Simanjuntak. From here Colts go to Kaliurang and Prambanan.

Buses, and particularly Colts, to the tourist attractions around Yogya are renowned for overcharging. Know the correct fare before boarding, and tender the right money, but expect to pay extra if you have luggage taking up passenger space.

MINIBUS

Door-to-door minibuses run to all major cities from Yogya. Sosrowijayan and Prawirotaman agents sell tickets. You can also buy direct from the minibus companies, which include **Rajawali Putra** (Map p173; ☎ 583535; Jl Jenderal Sudirman 42), **Rahayu** (Map p173; ☎ 561322; Jl Diponegoro 9A) and **Niki Vita Tour & Travel** (Map p173; ☎ 561884; Jl Diponegoro 25).

Destinations served by minibuses from Yogya include Solo (air-con 20,000Rp, two hours), Cilacap (60,000Rp, five hours), Pangandaran (100,000Rp, eight hours), Semarang (36,000Rp, three hours), Surabaya (75,000Rp), Malang (75,000Rp), Jakarta (170,000Rp, 14 hours) and Bali (200,000Rp).

The Gunung Bromo connection (100,000Rp to 150,000Rp, 10 hours) has a reputation for terminating short of Cemoro Lawang, so don't be surprised if it does (see p248). There are also two-day tours available – Yogyakarta/Solo to Bromo and Bali – which cost around 200,000Rp from travel agencies. Some travellers have experienced problems with onward connections upon reaching Bali, so purchase your ticket from a reliable agent and check up-to-date information with other travellers.

TRAIN

Centrally located, Yogya's **Tugu train station** (Map p178; ☎ 514270) handles all business- and executive-class trains. Economy-class trains also depart from and arrive at Lempuyangan station (Map p173), 1km to the east.

The *Senja Utama Yogya* (business 100,000Rp, nine hours) departs for Jakarta at 6.30pm. The executive *Argo Lawu* (from 200,000Rp, seven hours) leaves at 9.01am.

To go to Solo, the best option is the *Prameks*, departing from Tugu at 6.50am, 9.45am, 1pm, 4.10pm and 6.52pm. It costs 6500Rp and takes just over an hour.

The overnight *Mutiara Selatan* (business 110,000Rp, six hours) leaves for Surabaya at 1.08am. Numerous other night trains from Jakarta, such as the *Bima* (executive 170,000Rp), stop in Yogya (9.40pm) on the way to Surabaya.

Heading for Bandung, the *Lodaya* (business/executive 90,000/150,000Rp, eight hours) passes through Yogya at 9.17pm. Alternatively, the *Mutiara Selatan* (business 110,000Rp, 7½ hours) leaves at 10.27pm.

From Lempuyangan train station, most of the economy-class services are overnight trains that run between Surabaya and Jakarta (40,000Rp, 11 hours) and Bandung (35,000Rp, 10 hours).

Getting Around

TO/FROM THE AIRPORT

Taxis from Yogya's Adisucipto airport, 10km to the east, cost 45,000Rp to the city centre, and are slightly cheaper going to the airport on the meter.

If you stroll out to the main road, Jl Solo, only 200m from the airport, you can catch a Colt that goes to Yogya's Terban Colt station (about 1.5km from Jl Sosrowijayan) for only 3500Rp.

BECAK & ANDONG

Yogyakarta has an oversupply of becak; it is impossible to go anywhere in the main tourist areas without being greeted by choruses of 'becak'. Fares cost around 2000Rp per kilometre, but the minimum fare for tourists is usually 3000Rp and the asking rate is a lot more. The trip from Jl Prawirotaman to Jl Malioboro costs at least 7000Rp. Avoid becak drivers who offer cheap hourly rates unless you want to do the rounds of all the batik galleries that offer commission. There are also horse-drawn *andong* around town, which cost about the same or less than becak.

BICYCLE

For as little as 15,000Rp a day from hotels you can cycle around the city; or try the shops at the southern end of Gang I in Sosrowijayan. Always lock your bike and look for bicycle *parkir*, who will look after your bike for a couple of hundred rupiah.

BUS

Yogya's city buses *(bis kota)* operate on dozens of set routes around the city for a flat 2000Rp fare. They work mostly straight routes – going out and then coming back the same way.

Bus 2 is one of the more useful services. It runs from the bus terminal and turns down Jl Sisingamangaraja, past Jl Prawirotaman, then loops around, coming back up Jl Parangtritis and on to Jl Mataram, a block from Jl Malioboro, before continuing to the university and returning to the terminal.

Bus 15 runs from the *kraton* to the Giwangan terminal and bus 4 runs from Jl Malioboro.

CAR & MOTORCYCLE

Travel agencies on Jl Sosrowijayan and Jl Prawirotaman rent out cars with drivers for trips in and around town for 50,000Rp per hour, with or without petrol, depending on the travel agent. They have inflated price

A CUP OF JAVA

Java is so synonymous with coffee, one of the world's favourite drugs, sorry, *drinks*, that in some countries the term 'Java' has become a catch phrase for a cup of the hot brown stuff.

Coffee was introduced to Indonesia by the Dutch, who initially founded plantations around Jakarta, Sukabumi and Bogor. Due to the country's excellent coffee-growing conditions, plantations began springing up across Java, and even in parts of Sulawesi and Sumatra. Early on, the prominent coffee was Arabica; Arabica coffees were traditionally named after the port they were exported from, hence the common worldwide terms of Java and Mocha (from Yemen) for coffee.

Commonly thought of as a bean, coffee is actually a fruit pit or berry. Around 2000 berries are needed to make one pound of coffee. The most expensive coffee in the world, fetching US$300 a pound, is *kopi luwak*, a fully flavoured coffee produced in Java (it is also exported from the Philippines, Vietnam and southern India). What makes *kopi luwak* – also known as civet coffee – so expensive is the process by which it gains its unusually rich flavour. The local palm civet, a cat-like animal, gorges itself on coffee berries and passes the inner pit through its digestive tract unharmed. Along the way the pits are affected by the animal's stomach enzymes and come out the other end smelling of roses (or rich coffee in this case). The coffee has been appetisingly nicknamed 'cat poop' or 'monkey poo' coffee.

Today, Indonesia is the fourth-largest producer of coffee in the world after Brazil, Colombia and Vietnam. Robusta has replaced Arabica as the leading coffee of choice, currently making up some 88% of the country's exports. For further reading on Indonesia's love affair with coffee pick up a copy of *A Cup of Java* by Gabriella Teggia and Mark Hanusz.

lists for more distant destinations, but you can usually get a car or small minibus with driver for around 400,000Rp per day.

Motorcycles can be hired for approximately 40,000Rp a day, sometimes less. An International Driving Permit is required by law, but they are not often checked.

TAXI

In Yogyakarta the taxis are metered and efficient. They cost 5000Rp for the first kilometre, then 2500Rp for each subsequent kilometre.

AROUND YOGYAKARTA

Imogiri

Perched on a hilltop 20km south of Yogyakarta, Imogiri was built by Sultan Agung in 1645 to serve as his own mausoleum. Imogiri has since been the burial ground for almost all his successors and for prominent members of the royal family, and it is still a holy place. The cemetery contains three major courtyards – in the central courtyard are the tombs of Sultan Agung and succeeding Mataram kings, to the left are the tombs of the *susuhunan* (sultan or king) of Solo and to the right those of the sultans of Yogyakarta. The tomb of Hamengkubuwono IX, the father of the present sultan, is one of the most visited graves.

Of major interest to pilgrims is the **tomb of Sultan Agung** (admission 1000Rp; 10am-1pm Sun & Mon, 1.30-4pm Fri). There is no objection to visitors joining the pilgrims at these specified times, although to enter the tombs you must don full Javanese court dress, which can be hired for 2500Rp.

It's an impressive complex, reached by a daunting flight of 345 steps. From the top of the stairway, a walkway circles the whole complex and leads to the actual hill summit, with a superb view over Yogyakarta to Gunung Merapi.

Colts and buses from Yogyakarta (3000Rp) stop at the car park, from where it is about 500m to the base of the hill and the start of the steps. Like most pilgrimage sites, there will be various demands for 'donations'. The only compulsory entry charge is payable when you sign the visitors book, inside the main compound on the hilltop.

Kasongan

This is Yogyakarta's pottery centre. Dozens of workshops produce pots and some superb figurines, including 2m-high dragons and pony-sized horses. Kasongan pottery is sold painted or unpainted – very little glazing work is done.

Catch a Bantul-bound bus and get off on the main road at the entrance to the village,

6.5km south of Yogyakarta. It is then about a 1km walk to the centre of the village and most of the pottery workshops.

Parangtritis

☎ 0274

Windswept and sandblasted, with crashing waves on one side and craggy, looming cliffs on the other, Parangtritis has all the makings of a dusty frontier town. Or at least it would do if it weren't for the thousands of local tourists who flock here every weekend. Weekends in Yogyakarta's favourite seaside escape are a whirlwind of overpriced hotels, jostling crowds and souvenir salespeople.

During the week, however, Parangtritis becomes that dusty frontier town. Prices fall, an eerie quiet descends and it becomes a half-decent place to spend the day ambling through the dunes.

SIGHTS

The seas off Parangtritis are extremely dangerous, but you can swim safely in *pemandian* (freshwater pools) at the base of the hill near the village, where spring water spills out from the hilltop through high bamboo pipes. If you'd prefer hot springs, head for **Parang Wedang** just beyond the nearby village of Parangkusumo.

Trails along the hills above the sea to the east of Parangtritis lead to a meditation cave, **Gua Cerme**. A couple of kilometres from the town and past the Queen of the South resort is **Gua Langse**, used by mystics as a meditation cave.

FESTIVALS & EVENTS

Like so many places along the south coast, Parangtritis is a centre for the worship of Nyai Loro Kidul; during the annual festival of **Labuhan** staged to appease her, the sultans of Yogyakarta still send offerings to the sacred point at Parangkusumo.

SLEEPING & EATING

The centre of the village is the plaza, marked by the Sudirman monument. Leading down to the beach, the main promenade has plenty of basic hotels and *rumah makan*. Alternatively, some of the better options are on the main road, to the east of the bus

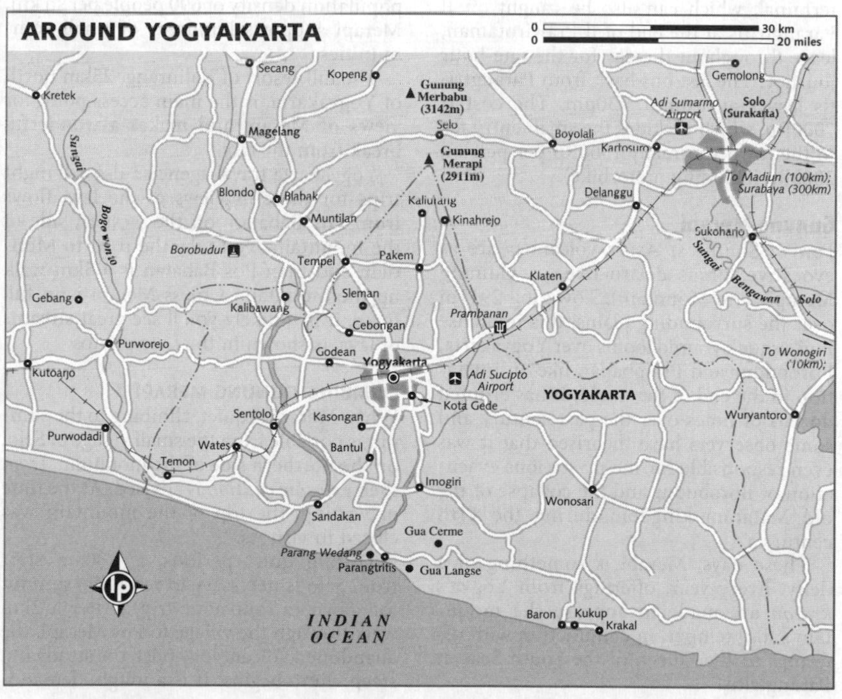

terminal. Hard bargaining is required; during the week, some places have rooms with *mandis* for as little as 20,000Rp.

Losmen Mutiara Samodra (☎ 368497; r from 30,000Rp) On the main road 200m east of the bus stop, this losmen is housed in a crumbling villa with at least a touch of Mediterranean charm. Opt for the upstairs rooms with cooler breezes.

Losmen Dinasti (☎ 368536; r 40,000Rp) With simple yet clean rooms and a homely feel, Dinasti is a top bet for a cheap bed; there is also a small restaurant.

Queen of the South (Puri Ratu Kidul; ☎ 367196; www.queen-of-the-south.com; bungalows from 450,000Rp plus 21% tax;) The best hotel by far is this small oasis (on weekdays at least) perched on the cliff tops high above town. It has excellent views from its fine *pendopo*-style restaurant and beach-front rooms. Its bungalows could do with a new paint job, but they're comfortable all the same; a 50% discount is sometimes available.

GETTING THERE & AWAY

Buses from Yogyakarta's Giwangan bus terminal, which can also be caught on Jl Parangtritis at the end of Jl Prawirotaman, leave throughout the day for the one-hour journey. The last bus back from Parangtritis leaves at around 5.30pm. The cost is 7000Rp, which includes the small entry fee to the town (normally 1500Rp per person, 2000Rp including motorbike).

Gunung Merapi

Few of Southeast Asia's volcanoes are as evocative, or as destructive, as Gunung Merapi (Fire Mountain). Towering 2911m over the surrounding plains, this immense Fuji-esque pyramid looms over Yogyakarta, Borobudur and Prambanan like an invitation to the end of the world. It has erupted dozens of times over the past century and some observers have theorised that it was even responsible for the mysterious evacuation of Borobudur and the collapse of the old Mataram kingdom during the 11th century.

These days, Merapi is something of a deity. Every year, offerings from Yogya's *kraton* are made to appease the mountain's foul temper, in conjunction with offerings to the Queen of the South Seas at Parangtritis.

> **VOLCANO WARNING**
>
> As this book went to print, Gunung Merapi was once again rumbling, sending out more than 180 tremors in one week alone. Its eruption status was upgraded and 10,000 villagers were put on alert for possible evacuation. It is essential to seek local knowledge on climbing the mountain and to not attempt a climb or hike into the 'danger zone'.

But Merapi isn't so easy to appease. On 22 November 1994 it erupted, killing more than 60 people, and it has been on the boil ever since. In June 1998, pyroclastic flows raced down its western flank, damaging farmland; and in January 2001, more flows and thousands of earthquakes prompted the Volcanological Survey of Indonesia to raise the status of its warning still further. The last major eruption, in July 2004, resulted in even more flows.

Eruptions, however, have not put a stop to people living on the mountain. With a population density of 690 people per sq km, Merapi supports hundreds of small communities.

The hill resort of Kaliurang, 25km north of Yogyakarta, is the main access point for views of Merapi and makes a wonderful break from the city.

Yogyakarta travel agencies also sell night trips for drive-in views of the lava flows from Pos Babatan, on the western side of the mountain. You take the road to Muntilan and then Pos Babatan is a 5km walk up the mountain. Unless Merapi is in full force, it is unlikely you'll see great streams of lava as shown in the tour photos.

CLIMBING GUNUNG MERAPI

When Merapi is quiet, climbing to the summit is possible from the small village of Selo, on the northern side of the mountain. Even then *extreme caution* is advised. At the time of writing, the top of the mountain was closed to visitors.

During quiet periods, a 1.30am start from Selo is necessary to reach the summit for dawn (a four-hour trip). After a 2km walk through the village to Pos Merapi, the abandoned volcanology post, the steady but steep climb begins. It is a tough, demanding walk but manageable by anyone with a reasonable level of fitness.

The last stages are through loose volcanic scree, but guides may stop short of the summit. Check with your guide whether it is possible to go to the top before setting off. Treks from Selo are not always well organised. Guides should warn against climbing if it looks dangerous. While they don't want to endanger lives, they may be prepared to take risks in order to be paid. Even during quieter periods, Merapi can suddenly throw out a stream of lava; in September 2002 an Indonesian student was killed when he got lost and fell into a ravine. There are two vents where lava can be seen, but it is not advisable to approach them.

Check the latest situation in Kaliurang, but at the time of writing the climb to the peak from Kaliurang had been strictly off limits since 1994 because of volcanic activity. **Christian Awuy** (☎ 081 75412572), owner of Vogels Hostel, has organised climbs for years and is an essential first reference point.

Alternatively, you can contact the **Merapi Volcano Observatory** (☎ 0274 514180, 514192; Jl Cendana 15) or **Kartika Trekking** (p174) in Yogyakarta.

Kaliurang

☎ 0274

Kaliurang, 25km north of Yogyakarta, is the nearest hill resort to the city. At 900m it has a cool, refreshing climate. During the monsoon, Kaliurang often sits in a thick blanket of cloud, but on clear days the views of Merapi are magical.

All visitors to Kaliurang must pay a 1000Rp entrance fee.

SIGHTS & ACTIVITIES

The **Ullen Sentalu Museum** (☎ 895161; admission 15,000Rp; ⌚ 9am-4pm Tue-Sun) is a surprise find on the slopes of Merapi. It devotes itself entirely to the richness of Javanese culture, and is one of the best museums on the island. Unusually, it focuses heavily on notable women of Java, particularly the wives of sultans, through pictures and stories. Batik also takes pride of place; here you can gauge the subtle differences between Yogya and Solo designs, alongside those from coastal towns to the north. Once you've had your fill of culture, the museum's peaceful restaurant is a fine place to while away an hour or two. Admission includes a two-hour tour of the private collection.

Day-trippers can explore the excellent **forest park** (Hutan Wisata Kaliurang; admission 1000Rp; ⌚ 8am-4pm) on the slopes of the mountain. Maps at the park entrance show areas you are allowed to explore. Heed them and don't venture further; in a sudden eruption lava can flow down the mountain at 300km/h. At the time of writing you could take the 15-minute walk to the Promojiwo viewpoint for views of Merapi and then on to the Tlogo Muncar waterfall, which is just a trickle in the dry season, and then back to the entrance.

Vogels Hostel arranges **mountain walks** to see the lava flows. The five-hour return trek starts at 4am and climbs 1400m up the mountain to see the glowing lava at its best (50,000Rp per person). Overnight camping trips (150,000Rp), village tours (100,000Rp) and bird-watching walks (50,000Rp) can also be arranged. A minimum of four people is required for all trips.

SLEEPING & EATING

Kaliurang is a downmarket resort, but it has more than 100 places to sleep.

Vogels Hostel (☎ 895208; Jl Astamulya 76; dm 10,000Rp, d with shared facilities 20,000-25,00Rp, bungalows with bath 75,000-100,000Rp) Vogels is a travellers institution and has been serving up the same mixture of cheap accommodation, hearty food and excellent information for years. The owner, Christian Awuy, is a particular authority on Merapi and its many moods.

Christian Hostel (r 40,000Rp) This offshoot of Vogels is just down the hill from its owner. Rooms are simple and clean but lack character. There are good views from the upstairs terrace.

Hotel Satriafi (☎ 895128; Jl Kesehatan 193; r with/without hot water & TV from 95,000/75,000Rp) Rooms at Satriafi are clean but generally quite basic, but they're more upmarket than those at Vogels. It gets cold at night in Kaliurang, so taking a room with hot water wouldn't be a bad idea.

Villa Taman Eden (☎ 895443; r with TV & hot water 150,000-200,000Rp; 🏊) One kilometre south of Vogels, Taman Eden is the closest thing Kaliurang has to a resort. The rooms teeter on the edge of smart, but standards have been falling in the last few years.

Restaurant Joyo (Jl Astamulya 63; mains around 10,000Rp; lunch & dinner) Across the road from Vogels, Joyo is half shop, half restaurant, with good Chinese and Indonesian food and a hodgepodge collection of traditional art.

GETTING THERE & AWAY

Colts from Yogyakarta's Terban Colt station to Kaliurang cost 7000Rp; the last leaves at 4pm. If you have your own transport, you can follow the quieter, *Solo Alternatif* route from here to Prambanan. From Pakem, buses go to Prambanan as well as to Tempel, from where another bus does the run to Borobudur.

A taxi from Malioboro will cost around 65,000Rp.

Selo

On the northern slopes of Gunung Merapi, 50km west of Solo, Selo has a few basic homestays where guides can be arranged for the Merapi climb. The views of the mountain from the village are superb.

From Selo it is a four-hour trek to the volcano's summit (see p188).

The host at popular **Pak Auto** (r per person 20,000Rp) has been guiding trips to the top for years. Accommodation is very basic but clean. Elderly Pak Darto rarely ventures far these days, but he can offer good advice and arrange other guides. Prices are variable, depending on the guide, your fitness, how many people are in the group and the risk factor. Count on around 50,000Rp to 100,000Rp for two to three people.

Hotel Agung Merapi (r 60,000Rp) is a crumbling place that is a slight step up from Pak Auto even though standards are poor; it also has a restaurant.

Selo is most easily reached from Solo: take a bus to Magelang, stopping at Selo (7000Rp, two hours) on the way. However, the route from Yogyakarta is far more beautiful. Take a Magelang bus to Blabak (5000Rp) and then a Colt or bus to Selo (5000Rp). Travel agents in Solo and Yogyakarta arrange Merapi climbing trips via Selo.

PRAMBANAN

☎ 0274

On the road to Solo 17km northeast of Yogyakarta, the temples at Prambanan village are the best remaining examples of Java's period of Hindu cultural development. Not only do these temples form the largest Hindu temple complex in Java, but the wealth of sculptural detail on the great Shiva temple makes it easily the most outstanding example of Hindu art.

All the temples in the Prambanan area were built between the 8th and 10th centuries AD, when Java was ruled by the Buddhist Sailendras in the south and the Hindu Sanjayas of Old Mataram in the north. Possibly by the second half of the 9th century, these two dynasties were united by the marriage of Rakai Pikatan of Hindu Mataram and the Buddhist Sailendra princess Pramodhavardhani. This may explain why a number of temples, including those of the Prambanan temple complex and the smaller Plaosan group, reveal Shivaite and Buddhist elements in architecture and sculpture. These two elements are also found to some degree in India and Nepal.

Following this creative burst over a period of two centuries, the Prambanan Plain was abandoned when the Hindu-Javanese kings moved to East Java. In the middle of the 16th century there is said to have been a great earthquake which toppled many of the temples. In the centuries that followed, their destruction was accelerated by treasure hunters and locals searching for building materials. Most temples have now been restored to some extent, and like Borobudur, Prambanan made the Unesco World Heritage list in 1991.

Orientation & Information

The **Prambanan temples** (☎ 496401; adult/student US$10/6; temple complex 6am-6pm, last admission at 5.15pm) are usually visited as a day trip from Yogyakarta (17km away), but they can also be visited from Solo (50km away). The main temple complex lies on the Yogyakarta–Solo highway, opposite Prambanan village. From the main entrance on the southeastern side, it is a short walk to Candi Shiva Mahadeva, the largest of the temples, locally called Candi Loro Jonggrang (Slender Virgin Temple). Behind it, on the western side near the highway, is the outdoor theatre where the Ramayana ballet is performed.

To the north of the Shiva Mahadeva temple, which is flanked by the smaller Brahma and Vishnu temples, is the archaeological museum. Further north are smaller, partly renovated temples leading to Candi Sewu. A 'minitrain' (5000Rp) from the museum loops to Candi Sewu. All of these temples form the main Prambanan complex.

On the left after passing through the main gate there is a small **information desk** with info on the site and Ramayana performances. As at Borobudur, the admission price includes camera fees and admission to the museum. Hiring a guide can be a good investment at 40,000Rp for a one-hour tour for one to 20 people. There is also an audiovisual show every 30 minutes (2000Rp).

Most of the outlying temples are within a 5km radius of Prambanan village. You'll need at least half a day to see them on foot, or they can be explored by bicycle or motorcycle if you ride to Prambanan. A standard entry fee of 5000Rp applies in most of the outlying temples.

As with any of Java's major tourist attractions, the best time to visit Prambanan is early morning or late in the day when it's quiet, though you can never expect to get Prambanan to yourself. Very few people visit the other sites away from the main grouping of temples, and the walk to the outlying temples can be as much a pleasure as the temples themselves.

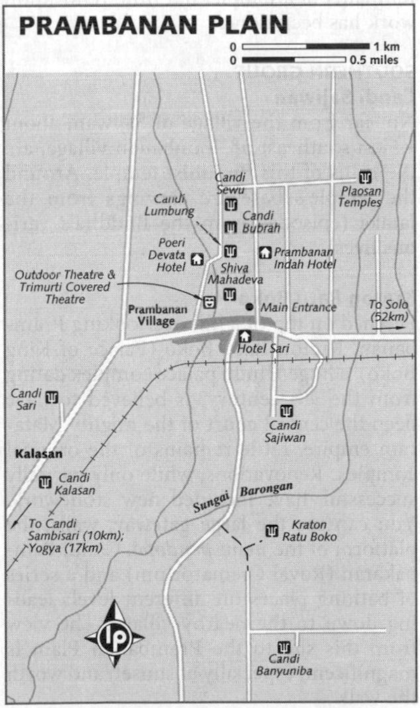

PRAMBANAN PLAIN

Sights

PRAMBANAN TEMPLES

The huge Prambanan complex was erected in the middle of the 9th century – around 50 years later than Borobudur – but little is known about its early history. It's thought that it was built by Rakai Pikatan to commemorate the return of a Hindu dynasty to sole power in Java.

Prambanan was in ruins for years, and while efforts were made in 1885 to clear the site, it was not until 1937 that reconstruction was first attempted. Of the original group, the outer compound contains the remains of 244 temples. Eight minor and eight main temples stand in the highest central courtyard.

Candi Shiva Mahadeva

This temple, dedicated to Shiva, is not only the largest of the temples, it is also the finest. The main spire soars 47m and the temple is lavishly carved. The 'medallions' that decorate its base have a characteristic Prambanan motif – small lions in niches flanked by *kalpatura* (trees of heaven) and a menagerie of stylised half-human and half-bird *kinnara* (heavenly beings). The vibrant scenes carved onto the inner wall of the gallery encircling the temple are from the Ramayana – they tell how Lord Rama's wife, Sita, is abducted and how Hanuman the monkey god and Sugriwa the white monkey general eventually find and release her. To follow the story, ascend the main eastern stairway and go around the temple clockwise.

In the main chamber at the top of the eastern stairway, the four-armed statue of Shiva the Destroyer is notable for the fact that this mightiest of Hindu gods stands on a huge lotus pedestal, a symbol of Buddhism. In the southern cell is the pot-bellied and bearded Agastya, an incarnation of Shiva as divine teacher; in the western cell is a superb image of the elephant-headed Ganesha, Shiva's son. In the northern cell, Durga, Shiva's consort, can be seen killing the demon buffalo. Some people believe that the Durga image is actually an image of the Slender Virgin, who, legend has it, was turned to stone by a man she refused to marry. She is still the object of pilgrimage and her name is often used for the temple group.

Candi Brahma & Candi Vishnu

These two smaller temples flank the large Candi Shiva Mahadeva. Candi Brahma to the south, carved with the final scenes of the Ramayana, has a four-headed statue of Brahma, the god of creation. Reliefs on Candi Vishnu to the north tell the story of Lord Krishna, a hero of the Mahabharata epic. Inside is a four-armed image of Vishnu the Preserver.

Candi Nandi

This small shrine, facing Candi Shiva Mahadeva, houses one of Prambanan's finest sculptures – a huge, powerful figure of the bull Nandi, the vehicle of Shiva.

Candi Sewu

The 'Thousand Temples', dating from around AD 850, originally consisted of a large central Buddhist temple surrounded by four rings of 240 smaller 'guard' temples. Outside the compound stood four sanctuaries at the points of the compass, of which Candi Bubrah is the most southern one.

The renovated main temple is interesting for the unusual finely carved niches around the inner gallery, with shapes resembling those found in the Middle East. These niches would once have held bronze statues, but plundering of the temple went on for many years and many statues have been whisked away.

Candi Sewu lies about 1km north of the Shiva Mahadeva temple, past the small, partly renovated Candi Lumbung and Candi Bubrah.

PLAOSAN TEMPLES

This northeastern group of temples is 3km from the Prambanan complex. It can be reached on foot by taking the road north from the main gate, going past Candi Sewu at the end of the main complex, and then taking a right turn. Stay on this road for about 1km.

Built around the same time as the Prambanan temple group by Rakai Pikatan, the Plaosan temples combine both Hindu and Buddhist religious symbols and carvings. The temples are comprised of the main Plaosan Lor (Plaosan North) compound and the smaller Plaosan Kidul (Plaosan South), just a couple of hundred metres away.

Plaosan Lor comprises two restored, identical main temples, surrounded by some 126 small shrines and solid stupas, most of which are now just a jumble of stone.

Two giant *dwarapala* (temple guardian statues) stand at the front of each main temple. The main temples, notable for their unusual three-part design, are two-storey, three-room structures, with an imitation storey above and a tiered roof of stupas rising to a single, larger one in the centre. Inside each room are impressive stone Bodhisattvas on either side of an empty lotus pedestal, and intricately carved *kala* (dragon) heads above the many windows. The bronze Buddhas that once sat on the lotus pedestals have been removed.

Plaosan Kidul has more stupas and the remnants of a temple, but little renovation work has been done.

SOUTHERN GROUP

Candi Sajiwan

Not far from the village of Sajiwan, about 1.5km southeast of Prambanan village, are the ruins of this Buddhist temple. Around the temple's base are carvings from the Jataka (episodes from the Buddha's various lives).

Kraton Ratu Boko

Perched on top of a hill overlooking Prambanan, Kraton Ratu Boko (Palace of King Boko), a huge Hindu palace complex dating from the 9th century, is believed to have been the central court of the mighty Mataram empire. Little remains of the original complex. Renovations, while only partially successful, have included new stonework. You can see the large gateway, walls, the platform of the main *pendopo*, Candi Pembakaran (Royal Crematorium) and a series of bathing places on different levels leading down to the nearby village. The view from this site to the Prambanan Plain is magnificent, especially at sunset, and worth the walk.

To reach Ratu Boko, travel 1.5km south on the road from Prambanan village to just southwest of where the river crosses the road. Near the 'Yogya 18km' signpost a steep rocky path leads up to the main site. Altogether it is about a one-hour walk. The site can be reached by car or motorcycle via a much longer route that goes around the back of the mountain.

WESTERN GROUP

There are three temples in this group between Yogyakarta and Prambanan, two of them close to Kalasan village on the main Yogyakarta road. Kalasan and Prambanan villages are 3km apart, so it is probably easiest to take a Colt or bus to cover this stretch.

Candi Kalasan

Standing 50m off the main road near Kalasan village, this temple is one of the oldest Buddhist temples on the Prambanan Plain. A Sanskrit inscription of AD 778 refers to a temple dedicated to the female Bodhisattva, Tara, though the existing structure appears to have been built around the original one some years later. It has been partially restored during this century and has some fine detailed carvings on its southern side, where a huge, ornate *kala* head glowers over the doorway. At one time it was completely covered in coloured shining stucco, and traces of the hard, stonelike 'diamond plaster' that provided a base for paintwork can still be seen. The inner chamber of Kalasan once sheltered a huge bronze image of Buddha or Tara.

Candi Sari

About 200m north from Candi Kalasan, in the middle of coconut and banana groves, the Sari Temple has the three-part design of the larger Plaosan temple but is probably slightly older. Some students believe that its 2nd floor may have served as a dormitory for the Buddhist priests who took care of Candi Kalasan. The sculptured reliefs around the exterior are similar to those of Kalasan but are in much better condition.

Candi Sambisari

A country lane runs to this isolated temple, about 2.5km north of the main road. Sambisari is a Shiva temple and possibly the latest temple at Prambanan to be erected by the Mataram empire. It was discovered by a farmer in 1966. Excavated from under ancient layers of protective volcanic ash and dust, it lies almost 6m below the surface of the surrounding fields and is remarkable for its perfectly preserved state. The inner sanctum of the temple is dominated by a large lingam and yoni (stylised penis and vagina), typical of Shiva temples.

Sleeping

Very few visitors stay at Prambanan given its proximity to Yogyakarta. There are plenty of hotels but most are pretty seedy.

Hotel Sari (☎ 496595; s/d with mandi 30,000/35,000Rp) Sari is about as basic as you can get near the temples, but the traffic outside can be very noisy.

Prambanan Indah (☎ 497353; Jl Candi Sewu 8; r with fan/air-con 70,000/156,000Rp, ste 291,000Rp; ❄) Prambanan is close to the main temple (you can see the top of it from the front rooms) and is one of the bigger places here. It has a handful of economy rooms; most come with air-con.

Poeri Devata Hotel (☎ 496435; cottages from 350,000Rp plus 21% tax; ❄ 🏊) Down a quiet country lane at the northwest corner of the temple complex, this is the most exclusive choice, with gardens, a restaurant, and views of the temples.

Entertainment

Ramayana Ballet (☎ 496408; www.borobudurpark.com) Held at the outdoor theatre just west of the main temple complex, the famous *Ramayana Ballet* is Java's most spectacular dance-drama. The story of Rama and Shinta unfolds over four successive nights, twice or three times each month from May to October (the dry season), leading up to the full moon. With the magnificent floodlit Candi Shiva Mahadeva as a backdrop, nearly 200 dancers and gamelan musicians take part in a spectacle of monkey armies, giants on stilts, clashing battles and acrobatics.

Performances last from 7.30pm to 9.30pm. Tickets are sold in Yogyakarta through the tourist information office (p172) and travel agencies (p172) at the same price you'll pay at the theatre box office, but they usually offer packages that include transport direct from your hotel for 20,000Rp to 30,000Rp extra. Tickets cost 30,000Rp for economy seats, 75,000Rp for 1st-class seats and 100,000Rp for VIP seats (padded chairs up the front). There are no bad seats in the amphitheatre – all have a good view and are not too far from the stage, but the cheapest seats are stone benches side on to the stage.

Alternatively, the *Ramayana Ballet Full Story* is a good two-hour performance (condensing the epic into one night), and alternates with the four-part episodic performances. It features only 50 performers but is still a fine spectacle, held at the Trimurti Covered Theatre from November to April. Performances start at 7.30pm every Tuesday and Thursday.

Getting There & Away

BICYCLE & MOTORCYCLE

You can visit all the temples by bicycle from Yogya. The most pleasant route, though it's a longer ride, is to take Jl Senopati out past the zoo to the eastern ring road, where you turn left. Follow this right up to Jl Solo, turn right and then left at Jl Babarsari. Go past the Sahid Garden Hotel and follow the road anticlockwise around the school to the Selokan Mataram. This canal runs parallel to the Solo road, about 1.5km to the north, for around 6km to Kalasan, about 2km before Prambanan.

To view the western temples you really need to come back via the Solo road. The turn-off north to Candi Sambisari from the Solo road crosses the canal before leading another 1km to the temple. You can visit the temple, backtrack to the canal path and continue back to Yogyakarta.

If you are coming by motorcycle, you can combine the visit with a trip to Kaliurang. From Kaliurang, instead of going back to the main Yogyakarta–Solo road, take the *Solo Alternatif* route signposted in the village of Pakem, about halfway between Yogyakarta and Kaliurang. From there the road passes through some beautiful countryside, before tipping you onto the main highway just before Prambanan's main entrance.

BUS

From Yogyakarta, take the bus (7000Rp, 30 minutes) from the main bus terminal, or from the Sosrowijayan area take bus 4 along Jl Mataram and get off at the Jl Cik Ditiro/Jl Terbau corner and then take a bemo to Prambanan bus terminal. From Solo, buses take 1½ hours and cost 5600Rp.

SOLO (SURAKARTA)

☎ 0271 / pop 525,000

Solo, a traditional and unhurried city 65km northeast of Yogyakarta, often plays second fiddle to its more conspicuous neighbour. But this is just plain unfair. With its backstreet *kampung*, wide thoroughfares, laid-back locals and rich cultural heritage, Solo has more than enough to warrant at least an overnight visit. Plus the usual cries of 'Hello mister', 'Becak, becak' and 'Come to my gallery' – so ingrained in many of Java's cities – are less frequent here, as are the tourists; more often than not you won't bump into another traveller as you wander the alleyways and markets of this attractive city.

In many ways, Solo is also Java writ small, incorporating its vices and virtues and embodying much of its heritage. On the downside, the island's notoriously fickle temper tends to flare in Solo first – the city has been the backdrop for some of the worst riots in Java's recent history. This fact will come as quite a surprise to most visitors, who will find the locals some of the friendliest on this crowded island. On the upside, the city's long and distinguished past as a seat of the great Mataram empire means that it competes with Yogyakarta as the hub of Javanese culture.

As well as visitors to its two beautiful palaces, Solo attracts many students and scholars to its academies of music and dance. The city is an excellent place to see traditional performing arts, and traditional crafts, especially batik, are also well represented, as Solo is a major textile centre.

History

Surakarta's founding in 1745 has a mystical history. Following the sacking of the Mataram court at Kartosuro in 1742, the *susuhunan*, Pakubuwono II, decided to look for a more auspicious site. According to legend, 'voices' told the king to go to the village because 'it is the place decreed by Allah and it will become a great and prosperous city'.

Pakubuwono II died after only fours years in the city, and his heir, Pakubuwono III, managed to lose half of his kingdom to the court of Yogyakarta. Pakubuwono X (1893–1938), however, had more luck. He revived the prestige of the court through the promotion of culture and gave no time to fighting rival royals.

Following WWII, the royal court fumbled opportunities to play a positive role in the revolution, and lost out badly to Yogyakarta, which became the seat of the independence government. The palaces of the city soon became mere symbols of ancient Javanese feudalism and aristocracy.

With the overthrow of Soeharto, Solo erupted following the riots in Jakarta in May 1998. For two days rioters went on a rampage, systematically looting and burning every shopping centre and department store.

Brows still furrow whenever you mention Surakarta (Solo) elsewhere in Java, but the golden arches and Colonel Sanders are back on the billboards and fancy new shopping malls are gradually rising from the ashes of the old. Solo, with its links to extremist groups such as Jemaah Islamiah, remains a politically volcanic city, however, and no-one can predict when the next eruption might take place.

Orientation

Jl Slamet Riyadi, the broad and busy avenue running east–west through the centre of Solo, is the main thoroughfare; most hotels and restaurants are on or just off it.

Solo's Balapan train station is in the northern part of the city, about 2km from the city centre; the main bus terminal, Tirtonadi, is 1.5km north again. The Gilingan minibus terminal is near the bus terminal.

The oldest part of the city is centred around the Kraton Surakarta to the southeast.

Information

Banks with ATMs line Jl Slamet Riyadi and offer far better rates than most hotels.

BumiNet (Jl Ahmad Dahlan 39; per hr 6000Rp) Internet access handy to most travellers accommodation.

Main post office (Jl Jenderal Sudirman; ⌚ 8am-7pm) Efficient and open daily for most postal services.

Solonet (Jl Slamet Riyadi 388; per hr 4500Rp) For internet access.

Telkom wartel (Jl Mayor Kusmanto) Near the post office, and has a Home Country Direct phone. Other wartel can be found around town.

Tourist office (☎ 711435; Jl Slamet Riyadi 275; ⌚ 8am-4pm Mon-Sat) Extremely helpful office with some useful pamphlets, a map of Solo, and information on cultural events and places to visit. It also has desks at the bus and train stations which can help with ticket bookings.

Sights

KRATON SURAKARTA

In 1745 Pakubuwono II moved from Kartosuro to **Kraton Surakarta** (Kraton Kasunanan; ☎ 656432; admission 8000Rp; ⌚ 9am-2pm Tue-Fri, 9am-3pm Sat & Sun) in a day-long procession that transplanted everything belonging to the king, including the royal banyan trees and the sacred **Nyai Setomo cannon** (the twin of Si Jagur, p104, in old Jakarta), which now sits in the northern palace pavilion. Ornate European-style decorations were later added by Pakubuwono X, the wealthiest of Surakarta's rulers, between 1893 and 1939.

The main entrance to the kraton fronts the *alun-alun*. Here, at the main entrance, the Pagelaran is the largest audience hall, where the *susuhunan* held court in front of his people. Over the street behind the Pagelaran is the *kraton* proper, though the main gateway is not open to the public and entry is from around the eastern side at the museum. Much of the *kraton* was destroyed by fire in 1985, attributed by the Solonese to the *susuhunan*'s lack of observance of tradition. Many of the inner buildings, including the *pendopo,* were destroyed and have been rebuilt. One that has survived is the distinctive tower known as **Panggung Songgo Buwono** (recently enjoying some much-needed restoration), which was built in 1782 and looks like a cross between a Dutch clock tower and a lighthouse. Its upper storey is a meditation sanctum where the *susuhunan* is said to commune with Nyai Loro Kidul (Queen of the South Seas).

A heavy carved doorway leads through from the museum across the inner courtyard of shady trees to the *pendopo*, but most of the *kraton* is off limits and is in fact the *dalem* (residence) of the *susuhunan*. The main sight for visitors is the **Sasono Sewoko museum**. Its exhibits include fine silver and bronze Hindu-Javanese figures, Javanese weapons, antiques, carriages and other royal heirlooms.

Admission includes entry to the *kraton* complex and museum, and guides can be hired for an extra 20,000Rp. Children's

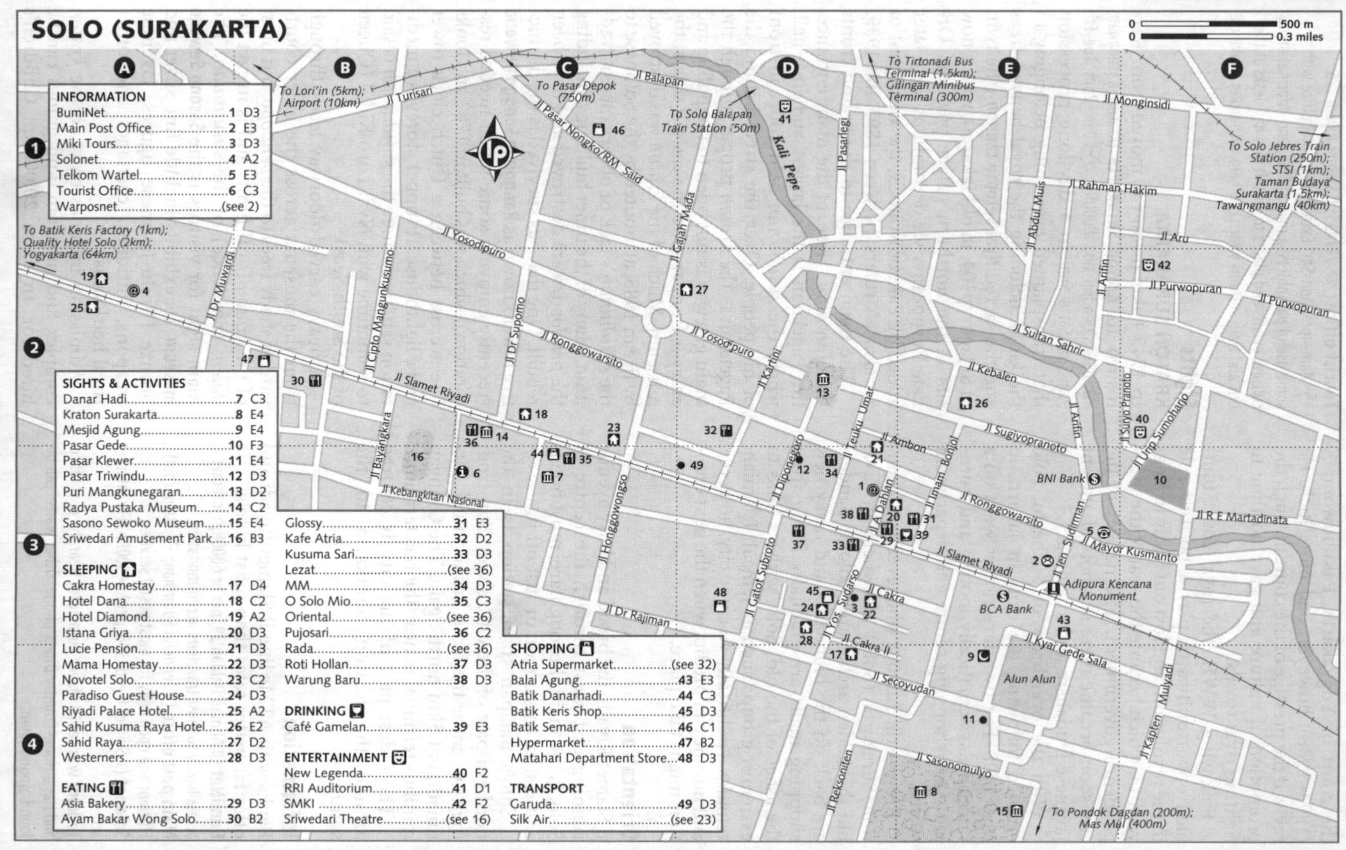
SOLO (SURAKARTA)
0 500 m
0 0.3 miles
INFORMATION
BumiNet 1 D3
Main Post Office 2 E3
Miki Tours 3 D3
Solonet 4 A2
Telkom Wartel 5 E3
Tourist Office 6 C3
Warposnet (see 2)
SIGHTS & ACTIVITIES
Danar Hadi 7 C3
Kraton Surakarta 8 E4
Mesjid Agung 9 E4
Pasar Gede 10 F3
Pasar Klewer 11 E4
Pasar Triwindu 12 D3
Puri Mangkunegaran 13 D2
Radya Pustaka Museum 14 C2
Sasono Sewoko Museum 15 E4
Sriwedari Amusement Park 16 B3
SLEEPING
Cakra Homestay 17 D4
Hotel Dana 18 C2
Hotel Diamond 19 A2
Istana Griya 20 D3
Lucie Pension 21 D3
Mama Homestay 22 D3
Novotel Solo 23 C2
Paradiso Guest House 24 D3
Riyadi Palace Hotel 25 A2
Sahid Kusuma Raya Hotel 26 E2
Sahid Raya 27 D2
Westerners 28 D3
EATING
Asia Bakery 29 D3
Ayam Bakar Wong Solo 30 B2
Glossy 31 E3
Kafe Atria 32 D2
Kusuma Sari 33 D3
Lezat (see 36)
MM 34 D3
O Solo Mio 35 C3
Oriental (see 36)
Pujosari 36 C2
Rada (see 36)
Roti Hollan 37 D3
Warung Baru 38 D3
DRINKING
Café Gamelan 39 E3
ENTERTAINMENT
New Legenda 40 F2
RRI Auditorium 41 D1
SMKI 42 F2
Sriwedari Theatre (see 16)
SHOPPING
Atria Supermarket (see 32)
Balai Agung 43 E3
Batik Danarhadi 44 C3
Batik Keris Shop 45 D3
Batik Semar 46 C1
Hypermarket 47 B2
Matahari Department Store 48 D3
TRANSPORT
Garuda 49 D3
Silk Air (see 23)
To Lori'in (5km); Airport (10km)
To Pasar Depok (750m)
To Solo Balapan Train Station (50m)
To Tirtonadi Bus Terminal (1.5km); Gilingan Minibus Terminal (300m)
To Solo Jebres Train Station (250m); STSI (1km); Taman Budaya Surakarta (1.5km); Tawangmangu (40km)
To Batik Keris Factory (1km); Quality Hotel Solo (2km); Yogyakarta (64km)
To Pondok Dagdan (200m); Mas Mul (400m)
Kali Pepe
BNI Bank
BCA Bank
Adipura Kencana Monument
Alun Alun
Jl Turisari
Jl Balapan
Jl Pasar Nongko/RM Said
Jl Monginsidi
Jl Rahman Hakim
Jl Pasarlegi
Jl Abdul Muis
Jl Aru
Jl Purwopuran
Jl Arifin
Jl Yosodipuro
Jl Gajah Mada
Jl Dr Muwardi
Jl Cipto Mangunkusumo
Jl Dr Supomo
Jl Ronggowarsito
Jl Slamet Riyadi
Jl Kartini
Jl Sultan Sahrir
Jl Kebalen
Jl Teuku Umar
Jl Ambon
Jl Sugiyopranoto
Jl Suryo Pranoto
Jl Urip Sumoharjo
Jl Bayangkara
Jl Kebangkitan Nasional
Jl Honggowongso
Jl Diponegoro
Jl Imam Bonjol
Jl A Dahlan
Jl R E Martadinata
Jl Mayor Kusmanto
Jl Jen Sudirman
Jl Gatot Subroto
Jl Yos Sudarso
Jl Cakra
Jl Cakra II
Jl Dr Rajiman
Jl Secoyudan
Jl Kyai Gede Sala
Jl Mulyadi
Jl Kapten
Jl Reksoniten
Jl Sasonomulyo

dance practice can be seen on Sunday from 10am to noon, while adult practice is from 1pm to 3pm.

PURI MANGKUNEGARAN

In the centre of the city and dating back to 1757, **Puri Mangkunegaran** (☎ 644946; admission 10,000Rp; ⏰ 8.30am-2pm Mon-Sat, 8.30am-1pm Sun) is the home of the second house of Solo. Technically a *puri* (palace) rather than a *kraton* (a *kraton* is occupied by the first ruling house), it was founded after a bitter struggle against Pakubuwono II, launched by his nephew Raden Mas Said (an ancestor of Madam Tien Soeharto, the late wife of the former president). Though much smaller in scale and design, this palace is better maintained and obviously wealthier than the more important Kraton Surakarta. It also tends to have better organised tours. Members of the royal family still live at the back of the palace.

The centre of the palace compound is the *pendopo*, bordered on its northern side by the *dalem*, which now forms the **palace museum**. The pavilion has been added to over the centuries and is one of the largest in the country. Its high rounded ceiling was painted in 1937 and is intricately decorated with a central flame surrounded by figures of the Javanese zodiac, each painted in its own mystical colour. In Javanese philosophy yellow guards against sleepiness, blue against disease, black against hunger, green against desire, white against lust, rose against fear, red against evil and purple against wicked thoughts. The pavilion contains one of the *puri*'s oldest sets of gamelan instruments, known as Kyai Kanyut Mesem (Drifting in Smiles).

The museum here is a real delight but can only be visited on a guided tour (around 20,000Rp). Most of the exhibits are from the personal collection of Mangkunegara VII. Among the items on display are gold-plated dresses for the royal Srimpi and Bedoyo dances, jewellery and a few oddities, which include huge Buddhist rings and gold genital covers – one for a queen, and a decidedly small penis cover for a king.

At the pavilion, you can see excellent music and dance practice sessions on Wednesday from 10am until noon.

Dinner with the royal family can also be arranged through *puri* staff or via **Herwasto Kusomo** (☎ 642637). Tickets cost US$30 per head for a minimum of 25 guests.

RADYA PUSTAKA MUSEUM

This small **museum** (Jl Slamet Riyadi; admission 1000Rp; ⏰ 9am-1pm Tue-Sun), next to the tourist office, has good displays of gamelan instruments, jewelled kris, *wayang* puppets from Thailand and Indonesia, a small collection of *wayang beber* (scrolls that depict *wayang* stories) and Raja Mala, a hairy puppet figurehead from a royal barge. Offerings must be made regularly to Raja Mala; otherwise, it is said, it will exude a pungent odour. The museum often closes earlier than the official closing time listed here.

MARKETS

Pasar Klewer (Jl Secoyudan; ⏰ 8am-6pm), supposedly the largest batik and textile market in Indonesia, is the ever-crowded three-storey textile market near Kraton Surakarta. This is the place to buy batik (mainly *batik cap*) – and it helps if you know your stuff and are prepared to bargain.

Pasar Triwindu (Jl Diponegoro; ⏰ 9am-4 or 5pm Mon-Sat), Solo's flea market, is always worth a browse. It sells antiques and all sorts of bric-a-brac, and is the place to pick up that fancy light fitting you've always wanted. An ever-increasing amount of the market is also devoted to car and motorcycle parts.

Pasar Gede (Jl Urip Sumoharjo; ⏰ 8am-6pm) is the city's largest general market, selling all manner of produce, particularly fruit and vegetables.

At the northwestern end of Jl Raden Mas Said, **Pasar Depok** (⏰ 8am-5pm Mon-Sat) is Solo's squawking bird market.

OTHER SIGHTS

Directly behind Batik Danarhadi, **Danar Hadi** (☎ 714253; Jl Slamet Riyadi 216; admission 15,000Rp; ⏰ 9.30am-2.30pm Mon-Sat) is a small museum big on batik, with row after row of traditional textile. Entry includes a guided tour in English, which endeavours to explain the history of many pieces. Old photos also help to paint a picture of the history of batik, but the real gem is watching women create the textile on site.

On the western side of the *alun-alun*, **Mesjid Agung**, featuring classical Javanese architecture, is the largest and most sacred mosque in Solo.

Solo's **Sriwedari Amusement Park** (admission 3000Rp; 5-10pm Mon-Fri, 5-11pm Sat, 9am-10pm Sat) has fair rides, sideshow stalls and other dated diversions. The main reason to come is for the nightly *wayang orang* performances and other cultural shows that are held regularly.

Courses

Traditionally, Solo is well known as a meditation centre, but the number of courses offered have been dwindling of late. The tourist office (p195) still lists a couple of places on its books for interested parties, though.

Mama Homestay (right) The eponymous Mama offers a one-day introductory batik course for 60,000Rp (you supply the T-shirt), although she is getting old these days and her English is limited.

Warung Baru (opposite) Never to be outdone, Baru also offers batik courses (70,000Rp, including T-shirt).

Tours

Various travel agents around town run tours, including **Miki Tours** (☎ 653278; Jl Yos Sudarso 17), and many guesthouses and hotels can book a variety of tours. They include tours to Candi Sukuh and the hill resort Tawangmangu (100,000Rp), and one-day trekking tours to Gunung Merapi (350,000Rp) and Gunung Lawu (250,000Rp). Most require a minimum of two people.

Bicycle tours to sites outside the city limits are a perennial favourite in Solo. For 60,000Rp to 75,000Rp a full-day tour takes you through beautiful countryside to 15 destinations, including stops to watch batik production, gamelan making, and tofu, *arak* (colourless, distilled palm wine) and rice-cracker processing. Warung Baru (opposite), Istana Griya, Mama, Westerners (right) and Miki tours all offer such tours.

Festivals & Events

As a historic centre, Solo plays host to a number of annual events. The following two are of the most interest:

Kirab Pusaka (Heirloom Procession) Held on the first day of the Javanese month of Suro (which can fall any time from March to May) since 1633, these colourful processions start at Puri Mangkunegaran in the early evening and continue late into the night.

Sekaten This festival marks the birth of the Prophet Muhammed and is held in the Islamic month of Maurud (from May to July). First staged in 1478, the event comprises two ceremonies with a week in between. The closing ceremony sees a fair erected in the *alun-alun* and culminates in the cutting up and sharing out of a huge rice mountain.

Sleeping

BUDGET

Solo has an excellent, though ever-decreasing, selection of friendly homestays. Almost all offer good travel information, tours, bus bookings, bicycles, breakfast, and free tea and coffee.

Pondok Dagdan (☎ 669324; Jl Carangan Baluarti 42; r without mandi 25,000RP) In the shadow of Kraton Surakarta, this quintessential homestay benefits from a welcoming owner and a peaceful setting. Rooms, which are built around a leafy courtyard, are very basic and popular with foreign students and English teachers.

Lucie Pension (☎ 653375; Jl Ambon 12; s/d 30,000/40,000Rp) Near Puri Mangkunegaran, this proper homestay has friendly owners (no English) and a handful of spotless rooms with tatami-style mats and mattresses on the floor. The terrace out front is perfect for watching the comings and goings of the *kampung*.

Westerners (☎ 633106; Kemlayan Kidul 11; r 40,000Rp) On the first alley north of Jl Secoyudan off Jl Yos Sudarso, this friendly, well-run and very secure losmen is Solo's original homestay. It's a little dog-eared these days but highly adequate.

Mama Homestay (☎ 652248; Kauman Gang III; s/d with breakfast 35,000/45,000Rp) Basic rooms that share *mandis* in tumbling surrounds; standards aren't high, but there's a supremely homey atmosphere.

Paradiso Guest House (☎ 652960; Kemlayan Kidul 1; r without mandi 30,000Rp, with mandi 50,000-60,000Rp) Not to be confused with Westerners (a misleading 'Westerners' sign hangs over the gate), which is further down the same alley, Paradiso is a homely place, with a *pendopo*-style sitting area and slightly smudged, all-white rooms. It's deathly quiet in the off season.

Istana Griya (☎ 632667; istanagriya@yahoo.com; Jl Ahmad Dahlan 22; r with fan/air-con from 70,000/100,000Rp;) Istana Griya is high on the list of top places to stay in Solo due to its quiet location, knowledgeable and friendly staff, and colourful, spotless and comfy rooms. A wide range of tours and activities can be arranged here.

Cakra Homestay (☎ 634743; Jl Cakra II/15; r with/without mandi 75,000/65,000Rp, with air-con 100,000Rp;) Occupying a charming, traditional property down an alley on the opposite side of Jl Yos Sudarso, Cakra wins the prize for one of the best-looking hostels in Central Java. It loses marks on the rooms, which are basic, but gains them back with free gamelan performances on random evenings, and staff with extensive knowledge of Javanese culture.

MIDRANGE

Many of the hotels in this bracket are strung along or just off Jl Slamet Riyadi, west of the city centre. Standards generally don't match the price, however.

Hotel Dana (☎ 711976; danasolo@indo.net.id; Jl Slamet Riyadi 286; r/ste with breakfast 225,000/450,000Rp) This fine colonial hotel has undergone extensive renovation, not all of it sympathetic, but it still has a modicum of grace and decent rooms, most with private sitting areas.

Riyadi Palace Hotel (☎ 717181; riyadi@indo.net.id; Jl Slamet Riyadi 335; r 225,000-555,000Rp) Riyadi is certainly no palace, but it has well-appointed rooms and a business feel; rooms at the back of the hotel are in better shape.

Hotel Diamond (☎ 733888; Jl Slamet Riyadi 392; r with air-con 230,000Rp, ste 1,000,000Rp;) This newly renovated motel-style hotel across the street from the Riyadi Palace has rooms that are a touch better than most, a glossy lobby and shiny fittings. Discounts are readily offered.

Sahid Raya (☎ 0800 271002, 644144; sahidslo@indosat.net.id; Jl Gajah Mada 82; r from 350,000Rp;) This upmarket hotel generally caters to business clients, and has well-kept rooms and staff who can help you with most queries regarding Solo.

Novotel Solo (☎ 724555; reservation@novotelsolo.com; Jl Slamet Riyadi 272; r from 385,000Rp;) Novotel is one of the most popular midrange/top-end hotels because of its excellent central position and quality facilities. Its bar, which has nightly cover-band performances, is a busy late-evening haunt.

Sahid Kusuma Raya Hotel (☎ 646356; www.sahidkusuma.com; Jl Sugiyopranoto 20; r from 370,000Rp;) An opulent old-style resort designed around a former Solonese palace, Kusuma Raya is a grand choice for those looking for comfort. While the main building is getting on a bit, most rooms are renovated; it has lashings of stylish charm. Published room rates may be discounted up to 25%.

Quality Hotel Solo (☎ 731312; Jl Ahmad Yani 40; r from 385,000Rp;) This hotel is popular with business types due to its top facilities and professional staff. It's 3km west of the city centre.

TOP END

Solo isn't loaded with top-end hotels, but there are a couple of luxury options around.

Lor'in (☎ 724500; Jl Adisucipto 47; r from US$75;) Lor'in is a stylish, resort-style hotel that is the most luxurious of all on offer. It is 5km from town, on the airport road. Rooms are rarely discounted, but posted prices are already good value.

Eating

Indulging in Solo's street food should on be everyone's list of things to do. Roaming hawkers pack the streets at night advertising their wares by screeching, striking buffalo bells or clattering cutlery. Of the plethora of dishes on offer, try *nasi gudeg* (unripe jackfruit served with rice, chicken and spices), *nasi liwet* (a local speciality incorporating rice cooked in coconut milk and eaten with a host of side dishes) or *srabi* (mini rice puddings served on a crispy pancake with banana, jackfruit or chocolate topping).

If you're looking for a quick fix head to Pujosari, a collection of warungs next to the tourist office. The best of the bunch include Lezat, which stays open 24 hours and does a mean *ayam kampung* (village chicken), Rada, which specialises in dim sum, and Oriental, which dishes up some fine Chinese.

Asia Bakery (Jl Slamet Riyadi; cakes around 2000Rp; 7am-7pm) This small, sparkling bakery will satisfy anyone's sweet tooth, with sticky buns and stacks of sugary delights.

Warung Baru (☎ 656369; Jl Ahmad Dahlan 23; mains from 8500Rp; breakfast, lunch & dinner) This backpacker institution has some of the best bread in the city, but the rest of the enormous menu is often a letdown. Still, the atmosphere is convivial, the owners are more than friendly and tours can be organised over a bite to eat.

Kusuma Sari (☎ 656406; Jl Yos Sudarso 81; mains around 10,000Rp; ⏰ lunch & dinner) Kusuma Sari is a stripped-back and spotless diner. It attracts Solonese by the dozen with pseudo-Western cuisine and mountains of ice cream.

Glossy (Jl Imam Bonjol 1; mains around 15,000Rp; ⏰ lunch & dinner) This small and easy-going eatery close to Solo's backpacker quarter is big on hot-plate steaks, coffee and freshly squeezed juices; the menu has extensive lists of all three. Glossy also supports local artists by moonlighting as a gallery.

MM (Jl Ronggowarsito; mains around 15,000Rp; ⏰ lunch & dinner) MM is popular with students for its cheap, good hot-plate steaks, relaxed air, live music on weekends, and open setting. If you've got the runs, it's not the place to head, though – the toilet is just a bare floor with accompanying water tap.

Mas Mul (Jl Veteran; ⏰ 3-11pm) At the southern entrance to the *kraton* is this, one of Solo's snake restaurants. For 25,000Rp, you can select a live cobra for sateing or frying, and can take the skin home as a gruesome souvenir. Those wishing to booster their virility can then opt to drink the snake's blood with wine or Red Bull.

O Solo Mio (☎ 727264; Jl Slamet Riyadi 253; pizzas around 30,000Rp; ⏰ lunch & dinner) This place is as close as you'll get to a slice of little Italy in the heart of Solo. With a wood-fired pizza oven, fashioned from bona fide Gunung Merapi stone, O Solo Mio produces excellent pizzas, but you'll also find ciabatta, pasta and cappuccino on the menu.

Also-rans include the following:

Roti Hollan (Jl Slamet Riyadi 135; mains around 10,000Rp; ⏰ lunch & dinner) With a restaurant upstairs and a bakery downstairs (plus beer at both), this dowdy place caters to most eating wishes.

Ayam Bakar Wong Solo (Jl Slamet Riyadi 299; mains 15,000Rp; ⏰ lunch & dinner) Fans of barbecued chicken pack this place.

Kafe Atria (cnr Jl Ronggowarsito & Jl Kartini; mains around 30,000Rp; ⏰ lunch & dinner) Decent grills and meat feasts can be had in this café above the Atria supermarket.

Drinking

Solo isn't the town to drink up large and party into the wee small hours, but there are a couple of places to down a few brewskies.

Café Gamelan (Jl Slamet Riyadi 58) With outdoor seating, constant entertainment from busy Jl Slamet Riyadi, and staff willing to sit and chat a while, Gamelan is a good bet for a beer in the evenings. Just avoid the food.

MM (Jl Ronggowarsito; ⏰ lunch & dinner) MM is the place to mingle with Solo's student crowd on the weekends; many flock here for the live music and buzzing atmosphere.

Entertainment

CULTURAL PERFORMANCES

Solo is an excellent place to see traditional Javanese performing arts.

At the back of Sriwedari Amusement Park, **Sriwedari Theatre** (⏰ performances 8pm) has a long-running *wayang orang* troupe. Though it's no longer a premier troupe, it only costs 3000Rp to sample this unique vaudeville-style of telling the classics, complete with singing, comedy and action drama. You can come and go as you please, and performances are staged from 8pm to 10pm nightly except Sunday.

RRI auditorium (☎ 641178; Jl Abdul Rahman Saleh 51) RRI holds various cultural performances, which are popular and often excellent. The station has *wayang orang* on the second Tuesday of the month from 8pm to midnight and *ketoprak* performances on the fourth Tuesday of the month from 8pm to midnight.

Sekolah Tinggi Seni Indonesia (STSI; ☎ 647658) This arts academy located at the Kentingan campus in Jebres, in the northeast of the city, has dance practice from 7.30am to 2pm Monday to Thursday, from 7.30am to 11am on Friday and from 7.30am to noon on Saturday.

SMKI (☎ 632225; Jl Kepatihan Wetan) The high school for the performing arts also has dance practice from around 8am to noon Monday to Thursday and Saturday, and 8am to 11am Friday.

Taman Budaya Surakarta (TBS; ☎ 635414; Jl Ir Sutami 57) This, the cultural centre to the east of the city, holds all-night *wayang kulit* performances. Ki Mantep Sudarsono is one of Indonesia's most famous *dalang* and often performs in Solo. Private dance lessons are also available here.

Puri Mangkunegaran (☎ 644946; ⏰ 8.30am-2pm Mon-Sat, 8.30am-1pm Sun) and **Kraton Surakarta** (Kraton Kasunanan; ☎ 656432; ⏰ 9am-2pm Tue-Fri, 9am-3pm Sat & Sun) each have traditional Javanese dance practice, **Balai Agung** (Jl Kyai Gede Sala; ⏰ 9am-5pm Mon-Sat) offers *wayang kulit* performances every Tuesday night from 8pm, and **Cakra Homestay** (☎ 634743; Jl Cakra II/15) hosts the occasional gamelan performance at 8pm.

Solo also plays host to regular art exhibitions (ask the tourist office for the current listings).

NIGHTCLUBS

Hedonists can also find a few lively nightspots for an evening of deafening bump-and-grind.

New Legenda (Jl Suryo Pranoto; admission 15,000Rp; 🕑 8pm-2am) Like most Javanese clubs New Legenda is incredibly dark and incredibly loud, but it's a riot of a night out. Just look for the lascivious-looking Statue of Liberty.

Shopping

Solo is one of Indonesia's main textile centres, producing not only its own unique, traditional batik but every kind of fabric for domestic use and export.

For everyday shopping, check out the markets or the shops on Jl Secoyudan or head to **Matahari department store** (cnr Jl Gatot Subroto & Jl Dr Rajiman), which offers everything you would expect.

The best of the modern supermarkets include the rebuilt **Hypermarket** (Jl Slamet Riyadi) and the newer **Atria** (Jl Ronggowarsito). For everyday shopping, check out the markets or the shops on Jl Secoyudan.

BATIK

The following are all large, well-established manufacturers with showrooms for their range of sophisticated work.

Batik Keris factory (☎ 714400; 🕑 8am-5pm Mon-Sat) In Lawiyan, west of the city, this is one place to see the batik process up close. Its shop (Jl Yos Sudarso 62) has icy air-con, a café and two full floors of fixed-price batik bags, skirts and shirts.

Batik Danarhadi (Jl Slamet Riyadi 261) Danarhadi is another big Solonese manufacturer. It has a good range of batik fabrics and ready-made clothes.

Batik Semar (Jl Adisucipto 101) Semar is good for modern cotton and beautiful silk batiks.

Pasar Klewer (Jl Secoyudan; 🕑 8am-6pm) Near Kraton Surakarta, Pasar Klewer has hundreds of stalls selling fabrics.

CURIOS

Kris and other souvenirs can be purchased from street vendors at the eastern side of the *alun-alun* near Kraton Surakarta. The gem sellers have a mind-boggling array of semiprecious stones.

Jl Dr Rajiman (Secoyudan), which runs along the southern edge of the *alun-alun*, is the goldsmiths street. Buy gold in the Chinese shops and have its weight and purity verified by the streetside gold testers along Jl Dr Rajiman and the side street of Jl Reksoniten near the *kraton*.

Pasar Triwindu (Jl Diponegoro; 🕑 9am-4 or 5pm Mon-Sat) All kinds of bric-a-brac plus a few genuine antiques are sold at Solo's fun flea market – fine porcelain, puppets, *batik tulis* (hand-painted or literally 'written' batik), pens, lamps and furniture. Many of the antiques are newly aged, so be prepared to bargain hard.

Balai Agung (Jl Kyai Gede Sala; 🕑 9am-5pm Mon-Sat) Here, on the north side of the *alun-alun* in front of the Kraton Surakarta, you can see high-quality *wayang kulit* puppets being made (and put through their paces). Gamelan sets are also on sale, but these are produced in Bekonang village, 5km east of Solo.

Vendors at Sriwedari Amusement Park also sell souvenirs.

Getting There & Away

AIR

On Tuesday, Thursday, Saturday and Sunday, **Silk Air** (☎ 724604/5; www.silkair.com; Novotel Hotel, Jl Slamet Riyadi 272) flies to Singapore for US$214 return (one way is US$50 more expensive). At the time of writing, domestic services were limited to two daily flights to Jakarta with **Garuda** (☎ 630082; Hotel Cakra; Jl Slamet Riyadi 201).

BUS

The Tirtonadi bus terminal is 3km from the centre of the city. Only economy buses leave from here to destinations such as Prambanan (5600Rp, 1½ hours), Yogyakarta (8500Rp, two hours) and Semarang (11,700Rp, 2½ hours). Buses also travel to a number of destinations in East Java, including Pacitan (15,000Rp, four hours), Surabaya (31,600Rp, six hours) and Malang (42,600Rp, seven hours).

Near the bus terminal, the Gilingan minibus terminal has express air-con minibuses to almost as many destinations as the larger buses. Door-to-door minibuses go to Yogyakarta (25,000Rp), Semarang (35,000Rp), Surabaya or Malang (85,000Rp), Denpasar (210,000Rp) and Jakarta (160,000Rp). Homestays, cafés and travel agents also sell these tickets.

TRAIN

Solo is located on the main Jakarta–Yogyakarta–Surabaya train line and most trains stop at **Balapan** (☎ 714039), the main train station.

The quickest and most convenient way to get to Yogyakarta is on the *Prameks* (business 6500Rp, one hour), which departs from Balapan five times a day at 5.45am, 8.25am, 11.35am, 2.41pm and 5.43pm.

Express trains to Jakarta include the *Argo Lawu* (executive 210,000Rp, 7½ hours, once daily at 8.10am), which is the most luxurious day train; the *Senja Utama* (business 100,000Rp, 10 hours, once a day at 6pm); and the executive *Bima* (from 200,000Rp, nine hours, once daily at 9pm).

The *Lodaya* (business/executive 100,000/150,000Rp, nine hours) departs for Bandung at 8pm and the *Sancaka* (business/executive 60,000/85,000Rp, five hours) swings through Balapan at 8.14am and 4.58pm on its way from Yogyakarta to Surabaya.

For Semarang, catch the *Pandan Wangi* (business 13,000Rp, two hours) at 5.15am and 1.30pm.

Jebres train station in the northeast of Solo has a few economy-class services to Surabaya and Jakarta, but if you're saving pennies, the bus is a more comfortable option.

Getting Around

A taxi to/from Adi Sumarmo airport, 10km northwest of the city centre, costs 50,000Rp, or you can take a bus to Kartosuro and then another to the airport. Around town, reliable, metered **Kosti Solo taxis** (☎ 856300) can be called or hailed on the street and cost 5000Rp for the first kilometre and 2500Rp per kilometre thereafter. Becak can be hired for 30,000Rp to 35,000Rp per hour, or will cost around 7000Rp from the train station or bus terminal into the centre; otherwise take the orange minibus 06 (2000Rp) to Jl Slamet Riyadi. Public buses run up and down Riyadi and cost 2000Rp.

Many homestays and travellers cafés can arrange bike hire for around 10,000Rp to 15,000Rp; a motorcycle – Solo is one of Java's quietest cities traffic-wise – will cost around 60,000Rp. Cars with drivers can be arranged for around 350,000Rp per day, not including petrol.

AROUND SOLO

Sangiran

Fifteen kilometres north of Solo, Sangiran is an important archaeological excavation site (so important it gained World Heritage status in 1996), where some of the best examples of fossil skulls of prehistoric 'Java Man' *(Pithecanthropus erectus)* were unearthed by a Dutch professor in 1936.

The town's main (if not only) attraction is its small **museum** (admission 10,000Rp; 🕘 9am-4pm Tue-Sun), with a few skulls (one of *Homo erectus*), various pig and hippopotamus teeth, and fossil exhibits, including huge mammoth bones and tusks. Souvenir stalls outside sell bones, 'mammoth tusks' carved from stone and other dubious fossil junk. Guides will also offer to take you to the area where shells and other fossils have been found in the crumbling slopes of the hill.

Take a Purwodadi bus from Solo's main bus terminal to Kalijambe (3000Rp). Ask for Sangiran and you will be dropped at the turn-off, 15km from Solo. It is then 4km to the museum (10,000Rp by *ojek*).

Gunung Lawu

Towering Gunung Lawu (3265m), lying on the border of Central and East Java, is one of the holiest mountains in Java. Mysterious Hindu temples dot its slopes and each year thousands of pilgrims seeking spiritual enlightenment climb its peak.

Although popular history has it that when Majapahit fell to Islam, the Hindu elite all fled east to Bali, Javanese lore relates that Brawijaya V, the last king of Majapahit, went west. Brawijaya's son, Raden Patah, was the leader of Demak and led the conquering forces of Islam against Majapahit, but rather than fight his own son, Brawijaya retreated to Gunung Lawu to seek spiritual enlightenment. There he achieved nirvana as Sunan Lawu, and today pilgrims come to

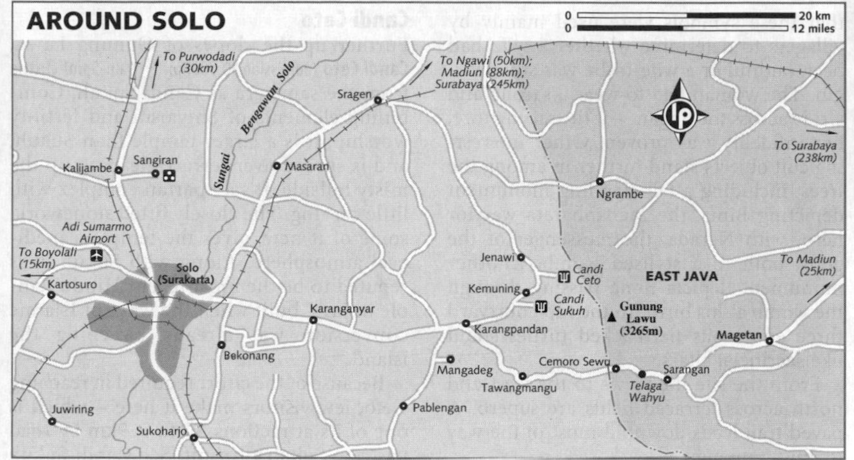

the mountain to seek his spiritual guidance or to achieve magic powers.

The unique temples on the mountain – the last Hindu temples built in Java before the region converted to Islam – show the influence of the later *wayang* style of East Java, though they incorporate elements of fertility worship. The most famous temple is Candi Sukuh; Candi Ceto is another large complex that still attracts Hindu worshippers.

CLIMBING GUNUNG LAWU

Colts between Tawangmangu and Sarangan pass Cemoro Sewu (5000Rp), 5km from Sarangan on the East and Central Java border. This small village is the starting point for the 6.7km hike to the summit of Gunung Lawu. Thousands of pilgrims flock to the summit on 1 Suro, the start of the Javanese new year, but pilgrims and holidaying students make the night climb throughout the year, especially on Saturday night. Most start around 8pm, reaching the peak at around 2am for meditation.

To reach the top for a sunrise free of clouds, start by midnight at the latest, though superfit hikers can do the climb in as little as four hours. It is a long, steady hike, but one of the easiest mountains in Java. The stone path is easy to follow – bring a strong torch (flashlight). Alternatively, guides can make a night climb easier and can lead you to the various pilgrimage sites along the way. Guides in Cemoro Sewu cost around 80,000Rp; in Sarangan try at the Hotel Nusa Indah. Sign in at the PHKA post before starting the climb (admission to walk 2000Rp).

Candi Sukuh

One of Java's most mysterious and striking temples, **Candi Sukuh** (admission 10,000Rp; 9am-5pm) stands 900m above sea level on the slopes of Gunung Lawu, 36km east of Solo. It is a large truncated pyramid of rough-hewn stone, which is curiously Inca-like, and while the sculpture is carved in the *wayang* style found particularly in East Java, the figures are crude, squat and distorted. The temple isn't wildly erotic as is sometimes suggested, but there are fairly explicit and humorous representations of a stone penis or two and the elements of a fertility cult are quite clear.

Built in the 15th century during the declining years of the Majapahit empire, Candi Sukuh seems to have nothing whatsoever to do with other Javanese Hindu and Buddhist temples, and the origins of its builders and strange sculptural style remain a mystery. It is the most recent Hindu-Buddhist temple in the region, yet it seems to mark a reappearance of the pre-Hindu animism that existed 1500 years before. It's a quiet, isolated place with a strange, potent atmosphere.

At the gateway before the temple are a large stone lingam and yoni. Flowers are still often scattered here, and there's a story that these symbols were used mainly by villagers to determine whether a wife had been faithful or a wife-to-be was still a virgin. The woman had to wear a sarong and stride across the lingam – if the sarong tore, her infidelity was proven. Other interesting cult objects stand further in among the trees, including a tall-standing monument depicting Bima, the Mahabharata warrior hero, with Narada, the messenger of the gods, both in a stylised womb. Another monument depicts Bima passing through the womb at his birth. In the top courtyard three enormous flat-backed turtles stand like sacrificial altars.

From the site the views to the west and north across terraced fields are superb. A paved trail leads downhill most of the way to Tawangmangu.

To get there, take a bus bound for Tawangmangu from Solo to Karangpandan (5000Rp), then a Kemuning minibus (3000Rp) to the turn-off to Candi Sukuh; from here it's a steep 2km walk uphill to the site or a 10,000Rp *ojek* ride. For 25,000Rp, *ojeks* will take you to both Sukuh and Ceto.

Candi Ceto

Further up the slopes of Gunung Lawu, **Candi Ceto** (admission 10,000Rp; 9am-5pm) dates from the same era as Candi Sukuh. Combining elements of Shivaism and fertility worship, it is a larger temple than Sukuh, and is spread over terraces leading up the misty hillside. It's a Spartan complex with little carving. The closely fitted stonework, some of it new, gives the temple a medieval atmosphere. Along with Sukuh, it is reputed to be the most recent Hindu temple in Java, built when the wave of Islamic conversion was already sweeping the island.

Because of the effort required in reaching Ceto, few visitors make it here – which is one of its attractions. Ceto is 9km by road past the Sukuh turn-off. See Candi Sukuh for transport details.

Tawangmangu

☎ 0271

Tawangmangu, a hill resort on the western side of Gunung Lawu, is a popular weekend retreat for Solonese. There isn't much here to attract tourists, but it's a pleasant enough

JAVA MAN

Charles Darwin's *On the Origin of Species* (1859) spawned a new generation of naturalists in the 19th century, and his theories sparked acrimonious debate across the world. Ernst Haeckel's *The History of Natural Creation* (1874) expounded on Darwin's theory of evolution and surmised the evolution of primitive humans from a common ape-man ancestor, the famous 'missing link'.

One student of the new theories, Dutch physician Eugene Dubois, went to Java in 1889 after hearing of the uncovering of a skull at Wajak, near Tulung Agung in East Java. Dubois worked at the dig, uncovering other human fossils closely related to modern man. In 1891 at Trinil in East Java's Ngawi district, Dubois unearthed an older skullcap, along with a femur and three teeth he later classified as originating from *Pithecanthropus erectus,* a low-browed, prominent-jawed early human ancestor, dating from the Middle Pleistocene epoch. His published findings of 'Java Man' caused such a storm in Europe that Dubois even reburied his discovery for 30 years.

Since Dubois' findings, many older examples of *Homo erectus* (the name subsequently given to *Pithecanthropus erectus*) have been uncovered in Java. The most important and most numerous findings have been at Sangiran, where in the 1930s Ralph von Koenigswald found fossils dating back to around 1 million BC; in 1936, at Perning near Mojokerto, the skull of a child was discovered and was purported to be even older. Most findings have been along Sungai Bengawan Solo in Central and East Java.

Geochronologists have now dated the bones of Java's oldest *Homo erectus* specimens at 1.7 million years, but also postulate that the youngest fossils may be less than 40,000 years old. This means that *Homo erectus* existed in Java at the same time as *Homo sapiens,* who arrived on the island some 60,000 years ago, and reignites the debate about whether humankind evolved in Africa and migrated from there, or whether humans evolved on several continents concurrently. Those interested in learning more should pick up a copy of Carl Swisher, Garniss Curtis and Roger Lewin's extremely readable book, *Java Man*.

place to escape the city heat and partake in hiking on the slopes of the mountains.

SIGHTS & ACTIVITIES

On the back road in Tawangmangu, about 2km from the bus terminal, **Grojogan Sewu** (admission 3500Rp; 6am-6pm), a 100m-high waterfall, is a favourite playground for monkeys. This is perhaps the most famous waterfall in Java, though apart from its height it isn't very spectacular. It's reached by a long flight of steps down a hillside, and you can **swim** in the very chilly and dirty swimming pool at the bottom. From the bottom of the waterfall a walking trail leads to the path to Candi Sukuh; *ojek* also hang out here on weekends.

Trekkers can take an interesting 2½-hour **walk** to Candi Sukuh, 6km along a paved path from Tawangmangu. This path is steep in parts but is also negotiable by motorbike.

SLEEPING & EATING

Prices and quality rise as you head up the hill, a long grunt from the bus terminal. There are plenty of losmen on Jl Grojogan Sewu, a quieter street running between the waterfall and Jl Raya Lawu.

Wisma Yanti (☎ 697056; Jl Raya Lawu 65; r without mandi 30,000Rp, main house r 75,000Rp, whole house 250,000Rp) Its rooms may not exude the most charm, but this homestay has a peaceful ambience and a nice garden to relax in, and you may be invited for sate with the owners in the evening.

Pondok Garuda (☎ 697239; r with hot water 50,000-200,000Rp) About 500m uphill from the bus terminal, Garuda is a large hotel with a variety of rooms, all of which are a good size and come with the all-important hot water. If you're sensitive to noise, it may not be the best bet (a mosque is next door) and prices increase by 20% at weekends.

Hotel Wahayu Sari (☎ 697470; Jl Grojogan Sewu 6; r 70,000Rp) Of the small hotels near the waterfall, this is one of the best. Rooms are fairly basic, but they're clean and comfortable.

Komajaya Komaratih Hotel (☎ 697125; Jl Raya Lawu 150-151; r 102,000-282,000Rp) Like Pondok Indah, the owners of this hotel just love their kitsch statues of everything from Snow White to Mickey Mouse. The English-speaking staff are very friendly and rooms are of a better standard than most in these parts.

Pondok Indah (☎ 697024; Jl Raya Lawu 22; r/villas 120,000/240,000Rp) Pondok Indah is a good option for families; it has a children's playground and a plethora of Disney-character statues decorating the front lawn. Rooms are well kept and come with hot water.

Sapto Argo (Jl Raya Lawu; mains from 7000Rp; lunch & dinner) Argo has good, cheap Indonesian dishes and serves the local speciality, *sate kelinci* (rabbit sate).

Lesahan Pondok Indah (Jl Raya Lawu; mains 10,000-30,000Rp; lunch & dinner) This is a more tranquil spot, with excellent food to enjoy while seated cross-legged on bamboo mats or on bamboo seats.

For cheaper eats, the road near the waterfall is inundated with warungs.

GETTING THERE & AWAY

Buses travel to Solo (7500Rp) and less-frequent Colts go to Sarangan (9000Rp). Minibuses (2000Rp) loop through town from the bus terminal up the main road, across to the waterfall and back around to the bus terminal. They are frequent on Sunday, but on other days expect to wait forever until they are jam-packed.

Sarangan

☎ 0351

An interesting alternative to backtracking to Solo is to take a Colt to Sarangan, 18km from Tawangmangu on the mountain road to Madiun. It is just over the provincial border in East Java, though most foreign visitors come via Solo. On weekends, local crowds pack the place, as happy as clams with a short speedboat ride around the town's 'lake', which in most countries equates to a 'pond'. A 2500Rp fee is payable at the entrance to the town.

The vistas en route are far more spectacular than the town of Sarangan itself, which is just another crowded holiday resort, albeit one with the aforementioned muddy lake.

At 1287m, however, the climate is fresh and the views far more impressive than in Tawangmangu. Sarangan is also a good base for tackling the ascent of Gunung Lawu, which rises almost vertically from the outskirts of town. In fact, the roads are so steep here that the roadsides between Sarangan and Tawangmangu are often littered with overheating cars billowing steam. If you are driving, take care.

SLEEPING

Many hotels are on the main road as you enter town.

Hotel Merah (☎ 888182; Jl Raya Telaga; r from 125,000Rp) Rooms at the Merah are rather bland and clinical, but they have direct views onto the town's small lake, and the top floor, which has been converted into a huge terrace, is just made for sundowners.

Hotel Nusa Indah (☎ 888021; Jl Raya Telaga 171; r with hot water from 150,000Rp; ❄) This friendly hotel is well kept and can arrange English-speaking guides (200,000Rp) for climbing Gunung Lawu. Ask for a room at the back with bird's-eye views of East Java.

Hotel Sarangan (☎ 888022; saranga_hotel@plasa.com; r from 230,000Rp; 💻) At the top of the village, Hotel Sarangan has excellent views of the lake and East Java, as well as cheery English-speaking staff. Most rooms sleep four or more people, and have their own sitting rooms with open fireplaces.

Telaga Mas International (☎ 888762; Jl Raya Telaga; r 350,000-700,000Rp) Sarangan's biggest hotel is located right on the lake and is staffed by a friendly bunch. Rooms, however, are incredibly drab for the price.

GETTING THERE & AWAY

Colts make the run to Tawangmangu (9000Rp), passing Cemoro Sewu for the climb to Gunung Lawu, but they only leave when full and waits can be eternal on slow days.

Mangadeg

Near Karangpandan, a road branches south from the main Solo–Tawangmangu road about 5km to Mangadeg, the burial hill of Solo's royal Mangkunegoro family. Make a small donation and visit the graves or simply take in the superb views.

A couple of kilometres away in the same sacred hills, the lavish **Astana Giribangun** is the Soeharto family burial palace, where the former president's wife, Madame Tien Soeharto, is buried.

Just past Mangadeg is **Pablengan**, the former bathing pools of the Mangkunegoro, which has dilapidated, ancient bathing pavilions fed by seven types of spring water.

NORTH COAST

Central Java's north coast features little on the itineraries of most tourists, who tend to opt for the more prominent attractions in and around Yogyakarta and Solo. And while there isn't a huge amount to see and do in this steamy corner of the island, it is not without its charm.

For starters, the towns dotting the north coast are steeped in history. For many centuries the north coast was the centre for trade with merchants from Arabia, India and China, who brought with them not only goods but also ideas and cultures. In the 15th and 16th centuries the area was a springboard for Islam into Java, and the tombs of the country's great saints all lie between Semarang and Surabaya (with the exception of Sunan Gunungjati in Cirebon).

For those looking for authentic arts and crafts, the north coast will also please. Pekalongan is celebrated for its batik, while Jepara is a major centre for wooden furniture. If the sweet smell of *kretek* (clove cigarettes) is to your liking, then a trip to Kudus, the birthplace of the *kretek*, may appeal.

Central Java's capital, Semarang, is located here, and while it won't hold your interest for too long, it is a gateway to the splendid (and often forgotten) Karimunjawa islands and peaceful mountains between it and Yogyakarta.

PEKALONGAN

☎ 0285 / pop 325,000

On the north coast between Semarang and Cirebon, Pekalongan (its name is said to be derived from the Chinese *a-pek-along-an*, meaning 'a place for catching fish') is known as Kota Batik (Batik City), and its batiks are some of the most sought-after in Indonesia. It is less formal, more colourful and more innovative in design than the traditional styles of Yogyakarta and Solo.

Pekalongan is a steamy city that sees few tourists, but it does have a neglected, old-fashioned atmosphere and an ethnically diverse population, which may appeal to some. While the main street, Jl Gajah Mada/Hayam Wuruk, can bustle, Pekalongan is relatively quiet for its size (and a dry city at that).

Information

BII bank (Bank Internasional Indonesia; Jl Diponegoro 4) For changing money.

Main post office (Kantor Pos dan Giro) Opposite the Balai Kota on the *alun-alun*.

Telkom office (Jl Merak 2) Next door to the main post office. You can make international telephone calls here.

Tourist office (☎ 423221; Jl Angkatan 45; 7am-2pm Mon-Thu, 7-11am Fri) Just north of Jl Gajah Mada; unfortunately it isn't much help.

Sights

Pekalongan's microscopic **Batik Museum** (Jl Majapahit 7A; admission free; 9am-1pm Mon-Sat), 2km south of the train station, has a few examples of batik, with explanations in Bahasa Indonesia. Of more interest is the **bird market** (Jl Kurinci) nearby.

The most interesting area of town is to the north, along Jl Blimbing with its old **Chinese quarter**; here you'll find a Chinese temple and old terraced houses. To the east, Jl Patiunus and the streets leading off it, make up the **Arab quarter**, another good area for batik (see right). Not far to the south is the town's main batik market, **Pasar Banjarsari**.

Facing the surprisingly quiet and pretty *alun-alun*, the **Mesjid Jami Yasmaja** has impressive Arabic architecture enclosing an older Javanese-style mosque.

Sleeping & Eating

Budget hotels are directly opposite the train station on Jl Gajah Mada.

Hotel Damai (☎ 422768; Jl Gajah Mada 7; r with fan from 37,000Rp, with air-con 110,000Rp) The best of a bunch of budget options with prison-like rooms on Jl Gajah Mada, Damai has the added bonus of being directly opposite the train station.

Nirwana Hotel (☎ 422446; Jl Dr Wahidin 11; r with fan/air-con from 105,000/210,000Rp) Nirwana is top dog in town when it comes to hotels, with pleasant rooms, an outdoor coffee shop and one of Pekalongan's better restaurants.

Hotel Istana (☎ 428029; Jl Gajah Mada 23; r with fan 110,000Rp, with air-con from 156,000Rp) This is an excellent midrange hotel, with clean rooms and a quiet ambience despite having a disco on the premises (which is about the only nightlife in town).

Purimas Bakery (Jl Hayam Wuruk; cakes from 2000Rp; breakfast, lunch & dinner) Purimas is Pekalongan's favourite bakery, with good cakes, pastries, cold drinks and a sit-down area. There are branches on Jl Gajah Mada and Jl Cempaka.

Es Teler 77 (Jl Raya Dr Cipto 66; mains from 6000Rp; lunch & dinner) This spotless franchise affair with garish green and yellow seats serves fine local dishes in a relaxed alfresco setting.

Shopping

Pekalongan batik is constantly evolving and new designs are more suited to Western and modern Indonesian tastes. Traditional batik is still popular, however, and Indonesians are often required to don it for formal occasions.

Street peddlers casually wave batik from the doorways of hotels and restaurants – mostly cheap clothes and poor-quality sarongs, but you might get lucky. Shops around town, many on Jl Hayam Wuruk, sell clothes, lengths of cloth, and sarongs in cotton and silk.

Pasar Banjarsari (Jl Sultan Agung; 8am-5pm) On the ground floor of new Plaza Pekalongan, this market has lost some of its character with its recent move, but it's still a fun place to pick up cheap (albeit often poor-quality) batik.

Huza (Jl Kenanga 7; 9am-4pm Mon-Fri) Locally recommended as one of the best places in town for quality and price, Huza has an extensive range of batik on offer.

Tobal (Jl Teratai 24; 9am-4pm Mon-Fri) Tobal is a large rag-trade business that produces clothes for the export market; you can view the process.

Most of the traditional batik is produced in the villages around Pekalongan. In the batik village of Kedungwuni, 17km south of town, Oey Soe Tjoen's workshop is famous for its intricate *batik tulis*. You can see it being made every day of the week except Friday.

Getting There & Away

Pekalongan is located on the main Jakarta–Semarang–Surabaya road and train route. There is also a road linking Pekalongan and the Dieng Plateau.

Pekalongan's bus terminal is about 4km southeast of town, 2000Rp by Colt or 7000Rp by becak. Buses from Cirebon can drop you off in town on their way through. Frequent buses go to Semarang (normal/air-con 15,000/25,000Rp, three hours); buses also go to Cirebon (18,000/25,000Rp, four hours), but often you will first have to take a bus to Tegal and then another to Cirebon.

As Pekalongan is midway for most trains running between Semarang and Jakarta, it's not the best place to pick up tickets, but it is possible.

The *Senja Bisnis* (9.28pm) and *Fajar Bisnis* (9.35pm) expresses run from Semarang to Jakarta (business 75,000Rp) and stop in the town, as does the luxury *Argo Muria* (5.24pm, 200,000Rp).

Getting Around

Pekalongan has plenty of becak, and anything between 500Rp and 7000Rp will get you most places in town. Orange bemos run all over Pekalongan for a standard 2000Rp. For Kedungwuni, take a bemo down Jl Mansyur.

SEMARANG

☎ 024 / pop 1.4 million

The bustling, north-coast port of Semarang is a schizophrenic city, embodying the polarity of modern Java. On one side, this old, Dutch administrative centre is still deeply traditional, with rambling colonial architecture and vibrant Chinese and Arab quarters. On the other side, the commercial area around Simpang Lima (Five Ways), with its shopping malls, clogged freeways and business hotels, is emblematic of Java's sudden and dramatic shift into the 21st century.

It may well be the provincial capital of Central Java, but Semarang lacks the pull of Solo and Yogyakarta. It does, however, have some appealing corners and is a good starting point for trips along the north coast or south to the central mountains.

Orientation

Semarang has two parts: 'old' Semarang is on the coastal plain, sandwiched between the two Banjir canals, while the new town sprawls southwards. An important hub in the old town is the Pasar Johar on the roundabout at the top of Jl Pemuda.

Jl Pemuda, Semarang's premier boulevard in Dutch times, is still a major artery and shopping street, though nowadays the busy, commercial hub of Simpang Lima square is the real centre of Semarang.

Information

INTERNET ACCESS

GAMA Warnet (Jl Gajah Mada 58; 6500Rp per hr; ⏲ 24hr)

MEDICAL SERVICES

RS Saint Elizabeth (☎ 8310076; Jl Kawi) The best hospital and first choice of the sizable Semarang expat community is in the Candi Baru district.

MONEY

All the banks listed here have ATMs.

ABN Amro (Jl Jenderal A Yani) Just off Simpang Lima.

BCA bank (Bank Central Asia; Jl Pemuda 90-92) You can change most currencies here.

POST & TELEPHONE

Main post office (Jl Pemuda; ⏲ 8am-8pm Mon-Sat) On a busy intersection near the Chinese market.

Telkom office (Jl Jenderal Suprapto 7) Like the post office, close to the Chinese market.

TOURIST INFORMATION

Central Java tourist office (☎ 3515451; Jl Pemuda 147; ⏲ 7.30am-4pm Mon-Fri) Has information on Semarang and the entire Central Java Region; may also provide internet access in the future.

Sights

OLD CITY

Semarang's old city, also known as **Outstadt**, is the highlight of any visit. The broad, colonial sweep of Jl Jenderal Suprapto plays host to many of the city's most impressive historic buildings, including the spires and solid walls of the Dutch church **Gereja Blenduk** (Jl Jenderal Suprapto); built in 1753, it still holds services. This area was the main port during colonial times, and towards the river from the church there are old Dutch warehouses with shuttered windows, flaking plaster and peeling paint. Just south of here along the canal behind the post office is a fading equatorial Amsterdam – albeit without the coffee shops.

Further south you plunge into the narrow streets of Semarang's old **Chinatown**. Though Chinese characters are rarely on show (the Chinese language was long discriminated

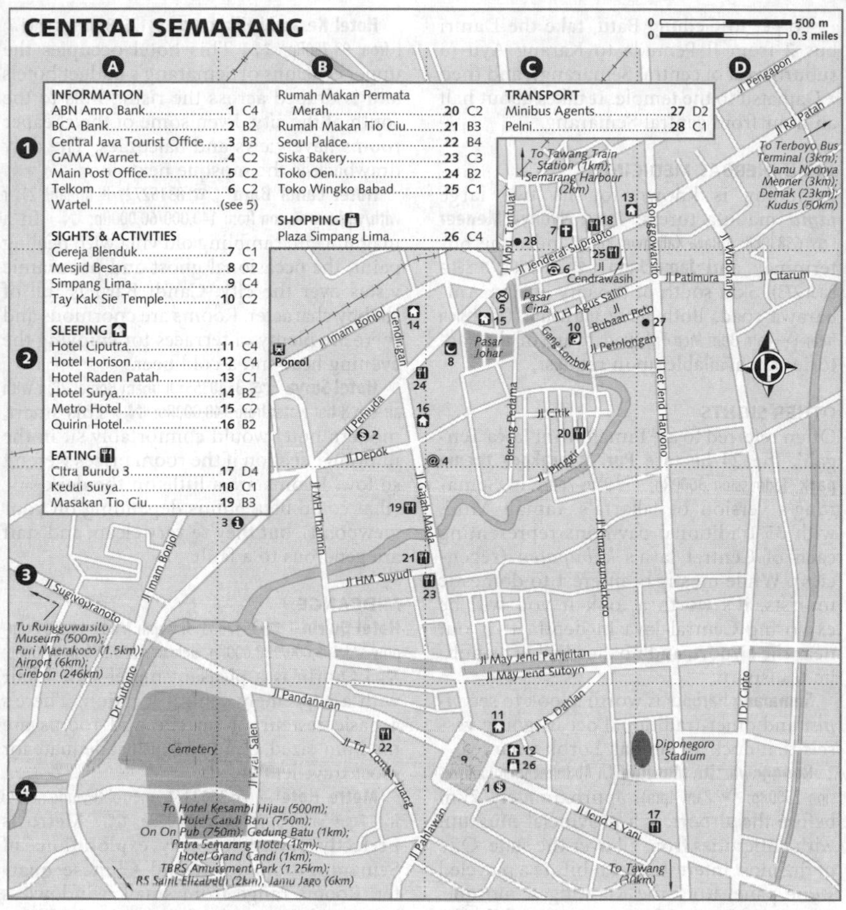

against by law), Semarang is Indonesia's most Chinese city.

Chinatown's highlight is the brightly painted **Tay Kak Sie Temple** (Gang Lombok), which dates from 1772. The temple is on the small alley running along the river off Jl Pekojan. **Pasar Cina** (Chinese Market; 7am-4pm), also called Pasar Gang Baru, is a fascinating mix of Chinese and Indonesian market flair.

Back towards the centre of the city, **Pasar Johar** (Jl H Agus Salim; 7am-5pm) is Semarang's most intriguing market. Facing the market is Semarang's **Mesjid Besar** (Grand Mosque).

GEDUNG BATU (SAM PO KONG TEMPLE)

This well-known Chinese temple (admission free; 24hr) stands 5km southwest of the centre of the city. It was built in honour of Admiral Cheng Ho, the famous Muslim eunuch of the Ming dynasty, who led a Chinese fleet on seven expeditions to Java and other parts of Southeast and West Asia in the early 15th century. Cheng Ho has since become a saint known as Sam Po Kong and is particularly revered in Melaka, Malaysia. He first arrived in Java in 1405 and is attributed with helping to spread Islam. This temple is also revered by Muslims.

The main hall of the temple complex is built around an inner chamber in the form of a huge cave flanked by two great dragons, hence the temple's popular name, *gedung batu* (stone building). Inside the cave is an idol of Sam Po Kong.

To get to Gedung Batu, take the Damri bus 2 from Jl Pemuda to Karang Ayu (a suburb west of central Semarang), and then a Daihatsu to the temple. It takes about half an hour from central Semarang.

JAMU (HERBAL MEDICINES)

Semarang is known for its two large *jamu* manufacturers: **Jamu Nyonya Meneer** (☎ 6583088; Jl Raya Kaligawe, Km 4), near the bus terminal; and **Jamu Jago** (☎ 7472762; Jl Setia Budi 273), 6km south of the city on the Ambarawa road. Both have **museums** (admission free; 8am-3pm Mon-Fri) and tours of the factories are available upon request.

OTHER SIGHTS

Often referred to as 'Taman Mini Jawa Tengah', the 24-hectare **Puri Maerakoco theme park** (admission 3000Rp; 9am-7pm) is Semarang's version of Jakarta's Taman Mini, with 35 traditional pavilions representing each of Central Java's *kabupaten* (regencies). While mostly of interest to domestic tourists, it's worth a look if you will be exploring Central Java in depth. It is out near the airport, and not accessible by public transport.

Semarang harbour is worth a look to see *pinisi* and other traditional ocean-going vessels that dock at Tambak Lorok wharves.

Ronggowarsito Museum (Jl Abdulrachman; admission 2500Rp; 8am-4pm), approximately 2km before the airport, is a provincial museum with antiquities from all over the state. One of the most interesting exhibits is a recycled stone panel from the Mantingan mosque. One side shows Islamic motifs, while the reverse shows the original Hindu-Buddhist scene.

Simpang Lima is a square that houses Semarang's cinema complexes and big malls. Crowds congregate in the evenings and browse aimlessly through shops that display countless consumer items that few can afford.

Sleeping

BUDGET

Hotel Raden Patah (☎ 3511328; Jl Jenderal Suprapto 48; r with/without mandi 40,000/30,000Rp) This basic hotel in the heart of the colonial district is perfect for those looking for a bed and nothing else. Rooms at the rear of the quiet inner courtyard are the most attractive.

Hotel Kesambi Hijau (☎ 8312528; Jl Kesambi 7; r from 93,750Rp;) This hotel occupies the upper echelons of Semarang's budget hotels and is draped across the rising hills to the south of the city. Even some of the cheaper rooms have views and balconies. The only drawback is the mosque next door.

Hotel Candi Baru (☎ 8315272; Jl Rinjani 21; r with/without air-con from 140,000/60,000Rp;) In a magnificent, rambling old villa with peeling paint, the occasional ghost and panoramic vistas over the city, Candi Baru is full of shabby character. Rooms are enormous and there are plenty of terraces for enjoying the evening heat and a cold beer.

Hotel Surya (☎ 3540355; Jl Imam Bonjol 28; r with air-con & hot water from 140,000Rp;) This smart, modern hotel would comfortably sit in the midrange section if the room prices weren't so low. Rooms are a little on the dark side (that could be a bonus depending on your viewpoint), but they're very clean, and staff are generous to a fault.

MIDRANGE

Hotel Quirin (☎ 3547063; Jl Gajah Mada 44-52; economy s/d 165,000/198,000Rp, deluxe r 250,000-340,000Rp;) Quirin is a pleasant motel-style affair with a supremely central location. There's a basic restaurant on site and rooms are medium-sized, clean and quite adequate for most travellers' needs.

Metro Hotel (☎ 3547371; metrohtl@indo.net.id; Jl H Agus Salim 3; r from 250,000Rp;) Metro is perfectly placed for easy explorations of Semarang's old town and Chinese quarter. Rooms range from small, windowless boxes with air-con to plush top-end jobbies; they're all spotless.

Hotel Ciputra (☎ 8449888; www.hotelciputra.com; Simpang Lima; r from 500,000Rp;) Ciputra may be looking a little dated these days, but it still has well-presented rooms and facilities that border on top end. It's located in the heart of Semarang's modern, glitzy district.

Patra Semarang Hotel (☎ 8414141; www.patra-jasa.com/semarang; Jl Sisingamangaraja; r from 600,000Rp plus 21% tax;) Patra Semarang was undergoing substantial renovations when we visited, so expect to find brand-new rooms when you do. The fine view of Semarang will still be the same, as will the range of sporting facilities. Discounts are readily available.

TOP END

Semarang has more than enough top-end hotels, most of which cater to business types.

Hotel Horison (☎ 8450045; www.horisonhotel.com; Jl Ahmad Dahlan; r from 650,000-750,000Rp, ste 950,000-2,000,000Rp plus 21% tax;) Horison is a multistorey hotel supremely handy for shopaholics; it's attached to Plaza Simpang Lima. Rooms are of the highest standard. With the hotel's spa, massage centre, three restaurants and two bars, you may never venture out onto the steamy city streets.

Hotel Grand Candi (☎ 8416222; gchotel@indosat.net.id; Jl Sisingamangaraja 16; r from US$120 plus 21% tax;) Grand Candi is indeed grand – it's Semarang's most luxurious hotel. Its highlights include an elevated location, a plethora of facilities, first-class rooms and professional staff. Ask for a discount, or pay in rupiah and instantly receive one.

Eating

Unlike many of Java's large cities, Semarang doesn't have a major concentration of good restaurants. If anything, most are quite average, and spread throughout the city. With such a large Chinese population, this is, however, the place to sample Chinese food.

For cheap eats at night, it's a toss-up between Simpang Lima and Pasar Johar. The former often pips the later for atmosphere, though; dozens of *kaki lima* (food carts) set up around the huge square, serving a bit of everything and offering traditional *lesahan* dining (on straw mats). Plaza Simpang Lima also has an extensive food court on the 4th floor.

Toko Wingko Babad (Jl Cendrawasih 14; cakes 2000Rp; breakfast & lunch) Any self-respecting Javan city would be nothing without a quality bakery, and Semarang is no exception. This place bakes local specialities such as *wingko babad*, delicious coconut cakes – buy them hot here.

Kedai Surya (Jl Let Jenderal Suprapto 34; mains 15,000Rp; lunch & dinner) In the heart of the old town is this basic Indonesian eatery housed in a towering, colonial warehouse. Try the frog cooked in spicy flour.

Masakan Tio Ciu (Gajah Mada 71; mains 15,000-30,000Rp; lunch & dinner) The smaller and simpler cousin of its namesake, Rumah Makan Tio Ciu, this is yet another Semarang restaurant specialising in seafood and Chinese, but why stop when you're onto a good thing? Service is friendly and quick, and the food piping hot.

Toko Oen (Jl Pemuda 52; mains from 20,000Rp; lunch & dinner) Toko Oen is a quintessential colonial teahouse showing its age, but it's allowed to; it's been around since 1936. It's still a calm spot to sample local Chinese and Indonesian food while watching Chinese businessmen discuss future dealings and old gentlemen sip hot tea. Plus, the jars of cookies are just too good to pass over.

Rumah Makan Tio Ciu (Jl Gajah Mada; mains around 25,000Rp; lunch & dinner) Tio Ciu is an open-air restaurant with some of the finest seafood and Chinese in the city, and is all steam and sizzling woks in the evenings.

Seoul Palace (Jl Pandanaran 109; mains 30,000Rp; dinner) This is the city's choicest Korean eatery and has excellent meat- and fish-feast barbecues served in colourful surroundings.

Also recommended:

Siska Bakery (Jl Gajah Mada 99; cakes 2000Rp; breakfast & lunch) The place to go for all things sticky and sweet.

Citra Bundo 3 (Jl Jenderal A Yani 184; mains 10,000-20,000Rp; lunch & dinner) Cheap and cheerful local fare can be had at this garish eatery.

Rumah Makan Permata Merah (Jl Pinggir 86-92; mains 10,000-30,000Rp; lunch & dinner) For authentic Chinese (it has one of the few Chinese signs in Semarang).

Drinking

On On Pub (Jl Rinjani 21) At the Hotel Candi Baru, this is one of Semarang's liveliest bars. It has pool, darts and pub grub in an old-world, colonial setting.

Entertainment

TBRS amusement park (☎ 8311220; Jl Sriwijaya 29, Tegalwareng) This amusement park holds *wayang orang* performances every Saturday from 7pm to midnight, and *wayang kulit* every Thursday Wage and *ketoprak* every Monday Wage of the Javanese calendar (5000Rp).

Getting There & Away

AIR

There are limited flights out of Semarang, but schedules and destinations change regularly. At the time of writing, **Garuda** (☎ 8454737), in the Hotel Horison (left), had six flights a day to Jakarta; **Adam Air** (☎ 3584000) and **Sriwijaya** also operate one flight per day. See the Java Airfares map (p98) for prices.

BOAT

For ferry information, the **Pelni office** (☎ 3540381/6722; Jl Mpu Tantular 25; 🕑 8am-noon & 1-2pm Mon-Thu, 8am-noon Fri & Sat) is near Tawang train station. Pelni's *Lawit*, *Leuser* and *Binaiya* ferries run between Semarang and the Kalimantan ports of Sampit (economy/1st class 123,500/384,000Rp), Kumai (108,500/335,000Rp), Pontianak (162,000/513,000Rp) and Banjarmasin (3rd/2nd class 230,500/274,500Rp). Other Pelni-operated boats include the *Wilis* to Ketapang (Banyuwangi) (economy/2nd class 126,000/303,500Rp) and the *Ciremai* to Makassar (economy/1st class 233,000/740,000Rp).

BUS

Semarang's Terboyo bus terminal is 4km east of town, just off the road to Kudus. Destinations for normal/air-con buses are Yogyakarta (20,000/30,000Rp, three hours), Pekalongan (15,000/25,000Rp, three hours), Cirebon (35,000/45,000Rp, six hours) and Surabaya (35,000/50,000Rp, nine hours). There are also economy-only buses to Kudus (6000Rp, one hour), Jepara (9000Rp) and Wonosobo (20,000Rp, four hours).

Agents for luxury buses and express minibuses are located near Losmen Jaya and include **Rahayu agent** (☎ 3543935; Jl Let Jenderal Haryono 9) and **Nusantara Indah agent** (☎ 3553984; Jl Let Jenderal Haryono 9B).

Air-con minibuses travel to destinations across the island, including Pekalongan (35,000Rp), Wonosobo (35,000Rp), Solo (35,000Rp), Yogyakarta (40,000Rp), Surabaya (100,000Rp) and Jakarta (150,000Rp). Air-con minibuses to Denpasar cost 160,000Rp.

TRAIN

Semarang lies on the main Jakarta–Cirebon–Surabaya train route. **Tawang** (☎ 3544544) is Semarang's main station.

Good trains heading for Jakarta (8pm) and Semarang (8am) are the *Senja Bisnis* and *Fajar Bisnis* (business 75,000Rp, seven hours). The luxury *Argo Muria* does the run in six hours and costs 200,000Rp. It leaves Tawang at 5am and 4pm respectively. The *Sembrani* (executive 180,000Rp, six hours) passes through Semarang at 11.05pm en route to Jakarta from Surabaya and at 11.39pm going the other way (110,000Rp, four hours).

Most of the economy-class services depart from Semarang's Poncol train station. The *Tawangjaya* (36,000Rp, nine hours) for Jakarta leaves at 6.40pm. All economy-class trains to Surabaya are overnight trains, such as the *Kertajaya* (28,000Rp, 4½ hours), which leaves at 1am.

Getting Around

TO/FROM THE AIRPORT

Ahmad Yani airport is 6km to the west of town. A taxi into town costs 30,000Rp and around 20,000Rp when returning to the airport using the taxi meter.

PUBLIC TRANSPORT

City buses charge a fixed 2000Rp fare and terminate at the Terboyo bus terminal. Buses 1, 2 and 3 run south along Jl Pemuda to Candi Baru. Minibuses cost the same and operate all around town.

A becak from Tawang train station or the bus terminal to Hotel Metro will cost about 7000Rp, as will most rides from around town.

Semarang has metered taxis, which congregate around the big hotels, Simpang Lima and the post office. You can call **Kosti taxis** (☎ 7613333) in advance; a minimum of 10,000Rp is charged.

AMBARAWA

☎ **0298**

The market town of Ambarawa, 28km south of Semarang, will be of interest to train spotters; it's the site of the **Ambarawa Train Station Museum** (Museum Kereta Api Ambarawa; admission 3000Rp; 🕑 8am-4pm). Originally the Koening Willem I station, opened in 1873, the museum has exhibits of rail memorabilia and steam locomotives built between 1891 and 1928.

Though the line has closed, groups of up to 100 passengers can charter a train for the 18km round trip from Ambarawa to Bedono for 2,200,000Rp. Book through the **Ambarawa train station** (☎ 591035) a few days in advance.

The museum is a couple of kilometres outside town, just off the road to Magelang. Ambarawa has hotels, but nearby Bandungan is a nicer place to stay.

our pick Nestled in the heart of 22 hectares of coffee plantation, at an altitude of 900m, and surrounded by eight volcanoes, **Losari Coffee Plantation** (☎ 596333; www.losaricoffeeplantation.com; Desa Losari, Grabag; villa from US$275 plus 21% tax;) has arguably the most glorious location of any resort in Java. But it's not only the scenery that will impress. Each of the resort's 18 villas are individually decorated with lavish touches of Mediterranean and Javanese flair, and feature stunning views of the countryside. And there's plenty to do if lazing by the pool doesn't appeal: take a tour of the plantation; soak up some steam in the Hamam, the resort's Turkish bath; or sample the plantation's organic tea and coffee in the historic Club House. Losari is located near Grabag, some 12km southwest of Ambarawa. From Ambarawa, it's best to take a taxi (30,000Rp) to the resort.

Ambarawa can be reached by public bus from Semarang (6000Rp, one hour), and Yogyakarta (20,000Rp, 2½ hours) via Magelang.

BANDUNGAN

☎ 0298

Bandungan is a pleasant hill resort at 980m, but the main attraction is the nearby Gedung Songo temples. It is one of the best places in the area to base yourself for exploration of the temples and to escape the heat of the north coast.

In town, **Hotel Parahita** (☎ 711017; r 50,000Rp), just down the back road to Semarang from the market, has basic rooms and a friendly owner who speaks no English.

Hotel Rawa Pening Eltricia (☎ 711445; r from 120,000Rp, cottages from 200,000Rp;), 1km west of town, is perched on a hill with fine views and a terraced garden. Rooms are in good nick, and it has a lovely old colonial-style restaurant and a tennis court.

Buses make the run directly from Semarang to Bandungan (10,000Rp). If you are coming from the south, get off at Ambarawa and take a Colt to Bandungan (2000Rp).

GEDUNG SONGO TEMPLES

These nine (Gedung Songo means 'nine buildings' in Javanese) small **Hindu temples** (admission 2500Rp; 7am-5pm) are scattered along the tops of the foothills around Gunung Ungaran. The architecture may not be overwhelming, but the setting is superb. The 1000m perch gives one of the most spectacular views in Java – south across shimmering Danau Rawa Pening to Gunung Merbabu and, behind it, smouldering Gunung Merapi; and west to Gunung Sumbing and Gunung Sundoro.

Built in the 8th and 9th centuries AD and devoted to Shiva and Vishnu, five of the temples are in good condition after major restoration in the 1980s; however, most of the carvings were lost. A hill path goes past three temple groupings – the temples at the third grouping are the most impressive. Halfway up, the trail leads down to a ravine and hot sulphur springs, and then up again to the final temple and its expansive views. The 3km loop can be walked in an hour, but allow longer to savour the atmosphere. Horses can also be hired.

Arrive early in the morning for the best views. A couple of small hotels with rooms for around 35,000Rp are just outside the gate. Camping inside the temple complex is also possible, for a small fee.

The temples are about 6km from Bandungan. Take a Sumawono bus (2000Rp) 3km to the turn-off to the temples. Buses also run from Semarang and Ambarawa (4000Rp). The final 3km uphill to Gedung Songo (4000Rp) can be tackled either by foot or *ojek* (10,000Rp).

DEMAK

Demak was the springboard from which Islam made its leap into Java. As the capital of the island's first Islamic state, it was from here that the Hindu Majapahit kingdom was conquered and much of Java's interior was converted.

The town's economic heyday has now passed and even the sea has retreated several kilometres, leaving this former port curiously landlocked. But the role this small town, 25km east of Semarang, once played has not been forgotten, and Demak's **Mesjid Agung** remains one of the archipelago's foremost Muslim pilgrimage sites.

Constructed in 1466, this is Java's oldest mosque. Legend tells how it was built from wood by the *wali songo* in a single night. Four main pillars in the central hall were originally made by four of the Muslim saints, and one pillar, erected by Sunan Kalijaga, is said to be made from scraps of timber magically fused together.

The history of the mosque is outlined in the small **museum** (admission by donation; 8am-5pm) to the side. Some of the original woodwork, including magnificent carved doors, is on display.

The tombs of Demak's rulers are next to the mosque; the tomb of Raden Trenggono (leader of Demak's greatest military campaigns), however, attracts the most pilgrims. During Grebeg Besar, when various heirlooms are ritually cleansed, thousands of pilgrims visit Demak (the date is different each year; check with the Semarang's Central Java tourist information office, p208).

The mosque is on the main road in the centre of town and through-buses from either Semarang or Kudus (5000Rp) can drop you on the doorstep.

KUDUS

☎ 0291

Kudus takes its name from the Arabic word *al-Quds* (holy) – it's the only town in Java to have an Arabic name – and was founded by the Muslim saint Sunan Kudus. It is therefore an important pilgrimage site but, like much of Java, retains links with its Hindu past and the slaughter of cows is still forbidden within the town.

The town itself, however, holds little charm for passing tourists, unless they're huge fans of Indonesia's famous *kretek*. This is where the first cigarettes were produced, and today Kudus is still a stronghold of *kretek* production.

Information

For money, try either the **BII bank** (Bank Internasional Indonesia; Jl Dr Lukmonohadi), which has an ATM, or the **BCA bank** (Bank Central Asia; Jl Dr Ramelan). The **tourist office** (☎ 435958; Komplek Kriday Wisata, Jl Gor Werga Wetan; 7am-2pm Mon-Thu, 7-11am Fri, 7am-12.30pm Sat) is in the east of town (look out for the concrete animals), but can't help with much.

Sights

OLD TOWN

West of the river, **Kauman**, the oldest part of town, has narrow streets and a Middle Eastern atmosphere. Here you'll find the **Mesjid Al-Manar** (also known as Al-Aqsa); constructed in 1549 by Sunan Kudus, it is famous for its tall red-brick *menara* (minaret), which may have originally been the watchtower of the Hindu temple the mosque is said to be built on.

In the courtyards behind the mosque, the imposing **Tomb of Sunan Kudus** is shrouded with a curtain of lace. The narrow doorway, draped with heavy gold-embroidered curtains, leads through to an inner chamber and the grave. During Buka Luwur, held once a year on 10 Muharram of the Islamic calendar, the curtains around the tomb are changed and thousands of pilgrims flock to Kudus for the ceremony.

KRETEK PRODUCTION

Djarum, which started in 1952, is the third-biggest *kretek* producer in Indonesia. It's possible to tour its modern **factory** (☎ 431901; Jl A Yani 28); tours leave at 9am Monday to Friday and are free of charge. **Sukun**, outside the town, still produces *rokok klobot*, the original *kretek* rolled in corn leaves.

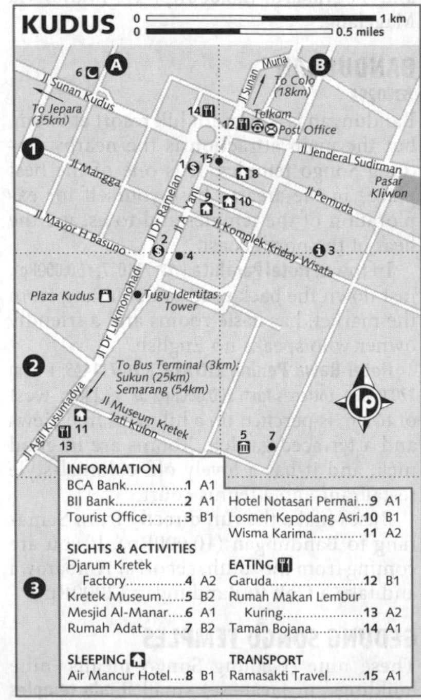

KRETEK CIGARETTES

If Java has a smell, it is the sweet, spicy scent of the clove-flavoured *kretek*. The *kretek* has only been around since the early 20th century, but today the addiction is nationwide and accounts for 90% of the cigarette market, while sales of *rokok putih* (cigarettes without cloves) are languishing. So high is the consumption of cloves used in the *kretek* industry that Indonesia, traditionally a supplier of cloves in world markets, has become a substantial net importer from other world centres.

The invention of the *kretek* is attributed to a Kudus man, Nitisemito, who claimed the cigarettes relieved his asthma. He mixed tobacco with crushed cloves rolled in *rokok klobot* (corn leaves) – this was the prototype for his Bal Tiga brand, which he began selling in 1906.

Kudus became the centre for the *kretek* industry and at one stage the town had more than 200 factories, though today less than 50 cottage industries and a few large factories remain. Rationalisation in the industry has seen *kretek* production dominated by big producers, such as Sampoerna in Surabaya, Gudang Garam in Kediri, and Djarum in Kudus. Nitisemito became a victim of the industry he started and died bankrupt in 1953.

Although filtered *kretek* are produced by modern machinery – Djarum churns out up to 140 million a day – nonfiltered *kretek* are still rolled by hand on simple wooden rolling machines. The best rollers can turn out about 7000 cigarettes in a day.

As to the claim that *kretek* are good for smoker's cough, cloves are a natural anaesthetic and so do have a numbing effect on the throat. Any other claims to aiding health stop there – the tar and nicotine levels in the raw, slowly cured tobaccos are so high that some countries have banned or restricted their import.

Filtered *kretek* now dominate the market. There are now 'mild' versions on offer, but for the *kretek* purist, the conical, crackling, nonfiltered *kretek* has no substitute – the Dji Sam Soe ('234') brand is regarded as the Rolls Royce of *kretek*.

The **Kretek Museum** (donations accepted; Jl Museum Kretek Jati Kulon; 8am-2pm Sat-Thu) has exhibits of a number of interesting photographs and implements used in *kretek* production, (almost all of the explanations are in Bahasa Indonesia). Next door, **Rumah Adat** is a traditional wooden Kudus house exhibiting the fabulous carving work the town is noted for.

Sleeping

Wisma Karima (431712; Jl Museum Kretek Jati Kulon 3; r with/without mandi 40,000/32,500Rp, with air-con 85,000Rp;) Karima is one of the town's better budget options, with well-presented rooms and welcoming owners, although it is near a busy road.

Hotel Notasari Permai (437245; Jl Kepodang 12; r 100,000Rp, with air-con, TV & minibar from 175,000Rp;) Notasari is one step up from most hotels in Kudus; rooms are bright and clean and the entire place exudes a friendly, wholesome feel. It also has a restaurant.

Also recommended:

Air Mancur (432514; Jl Pemuda 70; r from 50,000Rp) Worn rooms but surprisingly peaceful location given busy Jl Pemuda.

Losmen Kepodang Asri (433795; Jl Kepodang 17; r 50,000Rp) Central, with newly spruced rooms.

Eating

Local specialities include *soto Kudus* (chicken soup) and *jenang Kudus*, a sweet that's made of glutinous rice, brown sugar and coconut.

Garuda (Jl Jenderal Sudirman 1; mains 20,000-40,000Rp; lunch & dinner Mon-Sat) Near the *alun-alun*, this is the town's swishest Chinese restaurant, with an extensive menu of Asian delights.

Rumah Makan Lembur Kuring (Jl Agil Kusumadya 35; mains 15,000-30,000Rp; lunch & dinner) Makan Lembur Kuring has all Kudus' restaurants beat for ambience even though it's big and popular. Good Sundanese and Javanese food is served here under a shady pagoda.

The best place for cheap eats and a range of local specialities is Taman Bojana, a food-stall complex with more than a dozen stalls downstairs (and every ATM under the sun).

Getting There & Away

Kudus is on the main Semarang to Surabaya road. The bus terminal is about 4km south of town. City minibuses run from behind the bus terminal to the town centre (2000Rp), or you can take an *ojek* or becak.

Buses go from Kudus to Demak (3000Rp, 30 minutes) and Semarang (6000Rp, one hour), while brown-and-yellow minibuses go to Colo for 8000Rp. Buses to Jepara (10,000Rp, 45 minutes) leave from the Jetak subterminal, 4km west of town (2000Rp by purple minibus).

For minibuses, try **Ramasakti Travel** (☎ 432153; Jl A Yani 110).

AROUND KUDUS

The small hill resort of **Colo**, 700m up the slopes of Gunung Muria, is 18km north of Kudus. Colo is famed for its **Tomb of Sunan Muria** (Raden Umar Said), one of the nine *wali songo* buried here in 1469. (The *wali songo* are the nine holy men who propagated the Islam religion in Java.) Built in the 19th century, the mosque surrounding the tomb is high on a ridge overlooking the plains to the south. Pilgrims pray at the tomb, and during Buka Luwur, held in Colo on 16 Muharram of the Islamic calendar, up to 10,000 pilgrims line the road to the top.

A waterfall, **Air Terjun Monthel**, is 1.5km away or about a half-hour stroll from the village.

Local artist Mustaqim paints and sculpts out of his **Taqim Arts Studio** in the village of Kajar, 1km from Colo. Visits can be arranged through the tourist office (p214) in Kudus.

JEPARA

☎ 0291

Famed as the best woodcarving centre in Java, Jepara's expansive furniture business has brought it all the trappings of booming prosperity. It's also as sleepy as an afternoon becak driver and more affluent than many of Java's small towns, making it a tranquil spot to take a break from the road.

If you are just here for the furniture, the road into town passes more woodcarving workshops than you can shake a table-leg at. The best tactic is to keep an eye out for potential bargains on the bus in and go back armed with your wallet, and a mind to haggle, later.

Information

The town's **tourist office** (☎ 591493; Jl AR Hakim 51; 7am-2pm Mon-Thu, 7-11am Fri) is in the western part of town and is not particularly helpful.

Sights

Raden Ajeng Kartini, a 19th-century writer and progressive thinker, was the daughter of the *bupati* (regent) of Jepara. She grew up in the *bupati*'s residence, on the east side of the *alun-alun*, and it is sometimes possible to visit Kartini's rooms – if you contact the tourist office first. It was in this residence that Kartini spent her *pingit* ('confinement' in Javanese), when girls from 12 to 16 were kept in virtual imprisonment and forbidden to venture outside the family home. The small **Museum RA Kartini** (admission 1500Rp; 7am-4pm Mon-Sat, 9am-4pm Sun), on the north side of the *alun-alun*, has memorabilia from the family home, and a smattering of folk art.

Heading north from the museum, cross the river and veer left up the hill to the old Dutch **Benteng VOC**. Over the last 50 years the fort's stonework has been pillaged, but the site has good views across town to the Java Sea. The cemetery nearby has some Dutch graves.

The most popular seaside recreation park is **Pantai Kartini**, 3km west of town. From there you can rent a boat (60,000Rp return) to nearby **Pulau Panjang**, which has excellent white-sand beaches. Café SA (opposite) offers fishing trips to the island as well.

Sleeping

Pondok Wisma Kota Baru (☎ 593356; Pantai Kartini; r with/without air-con 60,000/40,000Rp;) This small homestay is within eyesight of the ocean at Kartini Beach and offers comfy, spotless rooms with shared *mandis* away from the city.

Hotel Elim (☎ 591406; Jl Dr Soetomo 13-15; r 50,000Rp, with hot water, air-con & TV from 110,000Rp;) Elim is an attractive option with a good spread of rooms (with shared *mandis*) in better-than-average condition and a pleasant outdoor restaurant.

Kalingga Star (☎ 591054; Jl Dr Soetomo 16; r with air-con 90,000Rp, ste from 135,000Rp;) A couple of doors down from Hotel Elim, Kalingga Star is a notch up in size, but not looks. Inside, it's all white tiles and plastic flowers; nonetheless the spacious rooms are quite good.

Hotel Jepara Indah (☎ 593548; jeparaindah@hotmail.com; Jl HOS Cokroaminoto 12; r 250,000-360,000Rp;) Jepara Indah is the town's most plush residence for visitors; its service and facilities are aimed at the business crowd and rooms are above average.

Eating

All of the hotels in Jepara have decent restaurants.

Café SA (☎ 081 79552266; Pantai Kartini; fish per 100g 4000Rp; lunch & dinner) With the sea splashing at the edge of its individual huts and its seafood as fresh as you can get, SA is ideal for dinner and a few sundowners.

Pondok Rasa (Jl Pahlawan 2; mains 8000-20,000Rp; lunch & dinner) Just across the river from the *alun-alun*, Rasa has a pleasant garden and good Indonesian food served *lesahan* style.

Rumah Makan Citra (cnr Jl Ringn Jaya & Soeprapto; mains around 15,000Rp; lunch & dinner) Close to the tourist office, this is another of Jepara's flashier restaurants and dishes up delicious seafood.

Shopping

Intricately carved *jati* (teak) and mahogany furniture and relief panels are on display at shops and factories all around Jepara. However, the main furniture centre is the village of **Tahunan**, 4km south of Jepara on the road to Kudus, where it's wall-to-wall furniture.

Brightly coloured ikat weavings using motifs from Sumba are sold in Bali, but they are actually crafted in the village of **Torso**, 14km south of Jepara and 2km off the main road. Other original designs are also produced and men instead of women perform the weaving, allowing broader looms to be used. Srikandi Ratu and Lestari Indah are two workshops with fixed-price showrooms.

Pecangaan, 18km south of Jepara, produces rings, bracelets and other jewellery from *monel* (stainless-steel alloy).

Getting There & Around

Frequent buses make the trip from Jepara to Kudus (10,000Rp, 45 minutes) and Semarang (10,000Rp, 1½ hours). A few buses also go to Surabaya, but Kudus has more connections. Air-con buses to Jakarta cost 80,000Rp.

Becak are cheap and the best way to get around town. From the terminal, about 1km west of the town centre, 5000Rp will get you to anywhere in town.

AROUND JEPARA

Mantingan

The mosque and tomb of Ratu Kali Nyamat, the great warrior-queen, are in Mantingan village, 4km south of Jepara. Kali Nyamat twice laid siege to Portugal's Melaka stronghold in the latter part of the 16th century.

The mosque, dating to 1549, was restored some years ago and the tomb lies to the side of it. The mosque is noted for its Hindu-style embellishments and medallions.

Mantingan is easily reached from Jepara. *Angkudes* (minibuses) from the bus terminal can drop you outside the mosque for 2000Rp.

Beaches

Jepara has some pleasant, white-sand beaches. **Pantai Bandengan** (aka Tirta Samudra), 8km northeast of town, is one of the best beaches on the north coast. The main public section can be littered, but a short walk away the sand is clean, the water clear and the swimming safe. To get there from Jepara, take a brown-and-yellow bemo (2000Rp) from Jl Pattimura. On weekdays you may have to charter a whole bemo for around 20,000Rp.

KARIMUNJAWA

☎ 0297

Distant and undeveloped, Karimunjawa consists of 27 islands, scattered 80km north of Semarang. This is one of Java's last forgotten corners and also one of its least-visited treasures.

Relatively difficult to reach and with only limited facilities, the archipelago is still little more than a pinprick on the tourist trail. And yet that is its charm. With brilliant white beaches, iridescent seas and only a trickle of visitors each year, these tiny islands are everything that hectic, crowded Java isn't.

Orientation

The main island, **Pulau Karimunjawa**, is home to most of the islanders and the majority of the archipelago's facilities, It is also the site of the islands' only real town, **Karimunjawa**, and, despite widespread mangroves, some reasonable beaches. A small airport is located on adjacent **Pulau Kemujan**.

Information

The islands don't have a tourist office per se, but a small information booth at the harbour is usually open to greet boats. Pulau Karimunjawa is home to both a telecom and a post office.

Sights & Activities

If you can find one of the rangers, they may be able to organise a hike up Pulau Karimunjawa's 600m peak, **Gunung Gendero**, but the real attractions lie offshore. The uninhabited islands of **Menjangan Besar** and **Menjangan Kecil** both have sweeping white sands, good snorkelling and are within easy reach of Karimunjawa town.

Further out, **Pulau Menyawakan** is the site of Karimunjawa's only major resort. **Pulau Nyamuk**, **Pulau Parang**, **Pulau Bengkoang** and **Pulau Genting** are all home to small, traditional communities. The reefs around many of these islands offer good diving and snorkelling, which can be arranged through the **Kura Kura Resort** on Pulau Menyawakan.

As a marine park, many parts of Karimunjawa are off limits. **Pulau Burung** and **Pulau Geleang** are home to nests of sea eagles and are strictly protected.

The islands can experience violent weather in January and February; during this time, flights and boat trips can be badly disrupted.

Sleeping & Eating

The main village of Karimunjawa has a handful of homestays and one *wisma* (guesthouse); the tourist office (p208) in Semarang can supply you with names and contact numbers.

Wisma Wisata (☎ 312118; r 50,000Rp) On the *alun-alun*, Wisata is the pick of the crop of the cheaper accommodation, with beer, clean rooms and a good spot near the harbour.

Prapatan (☎ 312227; Jl Dermaga Baru; r 50,000Rp) Prapatan is a cheerful homestay in Karimunjawa's main village; for an extra 40,000Rp, the host will also provide three meals a day.

Pak Cuming (r 50,000Rp) For something unusual, rent out a room on a fishing platform 1km offshore. You'll have to ask around the village for information, as the owner has no telephone.

Melati Karimunjawa Hotel (☎ 312253; info_wisata@yahoo.com; r with fan/air-con 96,000/272,000Rp; ❄) Melati is a quite decent hotel near the main town on Pulau Karimunjawa. It is spotless, friendly, surrounded by plenty of greenery and has a good open-air eatery with sea views. It's advisable to book ahead for weekend stays.

Kura Kura Resort (Jepara ☎ 0291-595932; www.kurakuraresort.com; minimum 2 nights from US$175; ❄ 🏊) Kura Kura is Karimunjawa's only luxury hotel. It's situated on its own private island, with a bar, restaurant, PADI-certified dive and water sports facilities, and about 800m of fine, white sand. Prices are per person per night and include good-quality bungalow accommodation, flights (or speedboat connections) and meals. Hefty supplements are charged if boats or planes from the mainland aren't full (a minimum of three people is needed for planes to take off).

Ibu Joyce (Jl Pattimura) This friendly shop owner speaks English and runs a shop selling food and beer; she will cook meals if asked in advance and is savvy about all things Karimunjawa.

Melati hotel has the best restaurant in town, and **Ester's** (mains around 20,000Rp; 🕑 lunch & dinner) on the *alun-alun* has a basic, seafood-oriented menu.

Getting There & Away

At the time of writing, **Kura Kura Resort** operated the only planes flying into Karimunjawa. Most flights shuttle guests between the resort and Semarang or Yogyakarta, and last-minute deals can be as low as 350,000Rp and 500,000Rp respectively. Four-seater Cessnas can also be chartered.

The *Muria* sails to Karimunjawa (economy/VIP 25,000/40,000Rp, six hours) from Pantai Kartini in Jepara on Wednesday and Saturday at 9am, returning from Karimunjawa on Monday and Thursday at the same time.

The faster *Kartini I* (economy/executive 100,000/130,000Rp, 3½ hours) leaves from Semarang at 9am on Saturday and returns at 2pm Sunday from Karimunjawa. Tickets can be reserved on ☎ 024-7602952.

From Pulau Karimunjawa, it costs around 300,000Rp to charter a wooden boat for a day trip to the outer islands or 50,000Rp for the short hop to Pulau Menjangan Besar and Kecil.

There are no buses or *angkot* operating on the islands, but *ojek* or mopeds (50,000-70,000Rp per day) can be hired to get around the main island's 22km of roads.

EAST JAVA

The least densely populated of Java's provinces, East Java (Jawa Timur) is a wild, rolling region with dizzying peaks, smoking volcanoes and unspoiled panoramas. While the regional capital, Surabaya, has all the accoutrements of a booming Indonesian city, including six-lane freeways, multiplexes and a trademark traffic problem, this is Java at its natural, naked best.

For most visitors, this rugged face of East Java is synonymous with the sublime Bromo-Tengger Massif, incorporating the volcanic peaks of Gunung Bromo (2392m) and Gunung Semeru (3676m) – Java's highest mountain. But while these puffing giants are the region's undisputed highlights, this is also the place to leave both the road and the madding crowds far behind and throw yourself right into Java's untamed parts.

Baluran National Park is the most accessible of Java's wildlife reserves, but the southern route through East Java is the most scenic. It is worth making the effort to get to the more remote areas, such as the stunning crater lake of Kawah Ijen and the national parks – Meru Betiri, where there is a protected turtle beach, and Alas Purwo, which is hallowed among surfers for its gigantic reef breaks. Just off the coast near Surabaya in the northeast is the rugged island of Madura, a place where traditions are particularly strong and famous bull races, known as *kerapan sapi*, are staged during August and September.

SURABAYA

☎ 031 / pop 2.6 million

There's no denying that Surabaya is big, noisy, polluted and intimidating. As Indonesia's second-largest city and the home of the country's navy, Surabaya is a colossal port peppered with cranes, corporate buildings and crowded spaces. Against the calm of rural East Java, it is pandemonium writ large.

But while Surabaya has all the trappings of a modern city, it too has its contrasts. Brightly daubed becak still cut blindly through the waves of Japanese saloon cars, and the claustrophobic streets of the city's old town hum with the sights, sounds and smells of earlier times.

For most foreign visitors, the city is merely a place to change buses or trains for Bali. For locals, however, Surabaya is closely linked to the birth of the Indonesian nation, as it was here that the battle for independence began. To them, Surabaya is Kota Pahlawan (City of Heroes), and statues commemorating independence are scattered all over the city.

Orientation

The centre of the sprawl is the area around Jl Pemuda, which runs west from Gubeng train station, Plaza Surabaya and a number of big hotels and banks. Jl Pemuda runs into Jl Tunjungan/Jl Basuki Rahmat, another main commercial street, where you'll find Tunjungan Plaza.

The old city is centred around Jembatan Merah (Red Bridge) and Kota train station to the north. Further north is Tanjung Perak harbour. Surabaya's zoo is 5km south of the city centre, and the main bus terminal, Purabaya, is just outside the city limits, 10km south.

Information

BOOKSHOPS

Gramedia (🕑 9am-5pm Mon-Sat) On the 1st floor of Tunjungan Plaza.

CULTURAL CENTRES

French Cultural Centre (☎ 5678639; Jl Darmokali 10-12; 🕑 8am-8pm Mon-Fri) At the French consulate.

Goethe Institut (☎ 5343735; Jl Taman Ade Irma Suryani Nasution 15; 🕑 7.30am-3.30pm Mon-Thu, 7.30-11.30am Fri)

INTERNET ACCESS & TELEPHONE

All the following have internet access and telephone booths.

Transnet (cnr Jl Pemuda & Jl Basuki Rahmat; per hr 6000Rp; 🕑 24hr)

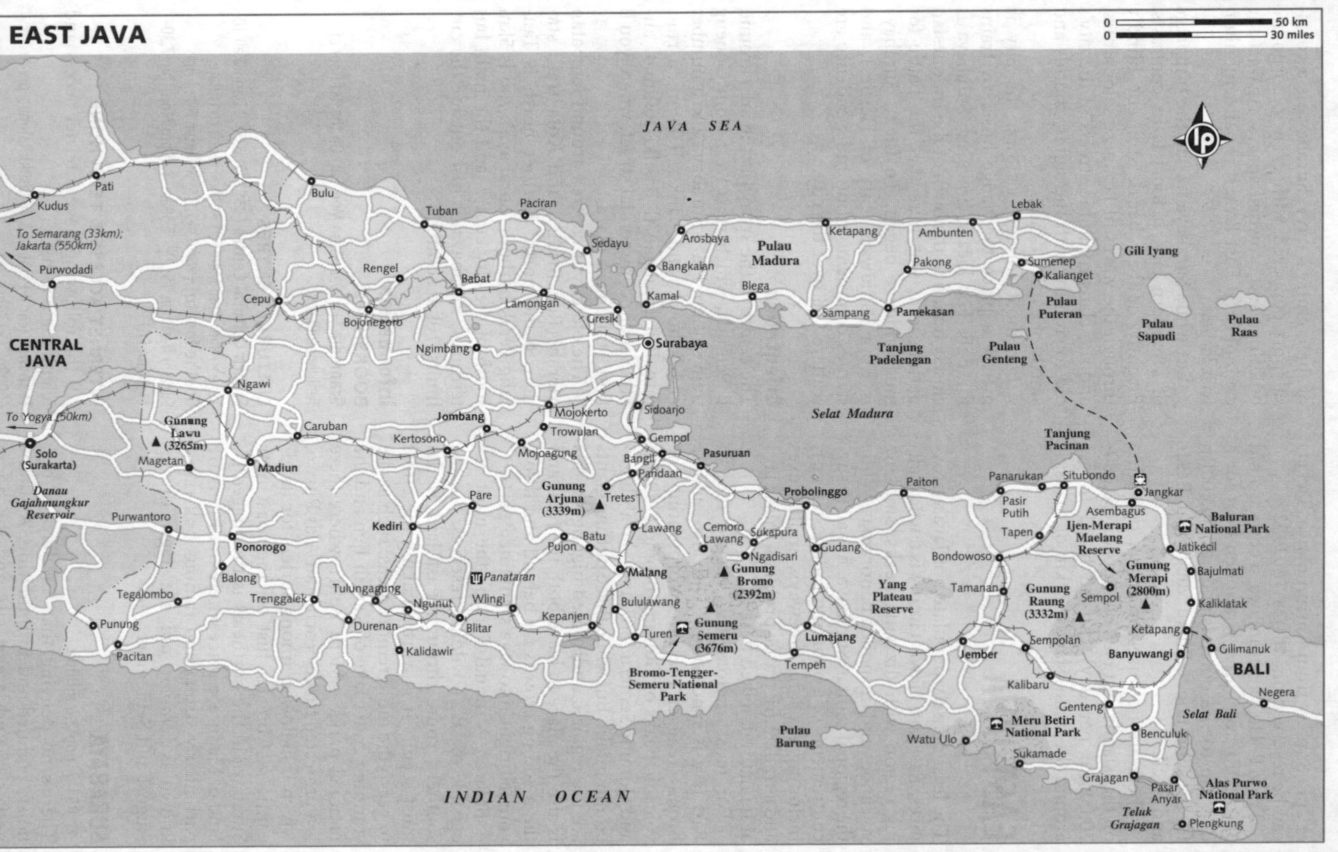
EAST JAVA
0 50 km
0 30 miles
JAVA SEA
Selat Madura
INDIAN OCEAN
CENTRAL JAVA
BALI
Selat Bali
Pulau Madura
Pulau Raas
Pulau Sapudi
Gili Iyang
Pulau Puteran
Pulau Genteng
Pulau Barung
Tanjung Pacinan
Tanjung Padelengan
Teluk Grajagan
To Semarang (33km); Jakarta (550km)
To Yogya (50km)
Kudus
Pati
Purwodadi
Solo (Surakarta)
Danau Gajahmungkur Reservoir
Bulu
Cepu
Tuban
Rengel
Bojonegoro
Babat
Paciran
Lamongan
Sedayu
Gresik
Ngimbang
Ngawi
Madiun
Caruban
Magetan
Gunung Lawu (3265m)
Purwantoro
Ponorogo
Balong
Tegalombo
Punung
Pacitan
Trenggalek
Tulungagung
Durenan
Ngunut
Kalidawir
Kediri
Kertosono
Jombang
Pare
Panataran
Wlingi
Blitar
Kepanjen
Mojokerto
Trowulan
Mojoagung
Gunung Arjuna (3339m)
Pujon
Batu
Tretes
Malang
Bululawang
Turen
Lawang
Pandaan
Bangil
Gempol
Sidoarjo
Surabaya
Kamal
Bangkalan
Arosbaya
Blega
Sampang
Ketapang
Pamekasan
Pakong
Ambunten
Lebak
Sumenep
Kalianget
Pasuruan
Cemoro Lawang
Gunung Bromo (2392m)
Gunung Semeru (3676m)
Bromo-Tengger-Semeru National Park
Sukapura
Ngadisari
Probolinggo
Gudang
Lumajang
Tempeh
Yang Plateau Reserve
Paiton
Panarukan
Pasir Putih
Situbondo
Tapen
Bondowoso
Tamanan
Jember
Gunung Raung (3332m)
Sempolan
Kalibaru
Meru Betiri National Park
Sukamade
Watu Ulo
Genteng
Grajagan
Benculuk
Pasar Anyar
Alas Purwo National Park
Plengkung
Banyuwangi
Ketapang
Sempol
Ijen-Merapi Maelang Reserve
Gunung Merapi (2800m)
Asembagus
Jangkar
Jatikecil
Baluran National Park
Bajulmati
Kaliklatak
Gilimanuk
Negera

Wartel (per hr 10,000Rp; 24hr) On the 5th floor next to the Tunjungan 21 Cinema in Tunjungan Plaza.

Wasantara-net office (per hr 4000Rp; 8am-9pm Mon-Sat, 9am-7pm Sun) Next door to the main post office; can be loud and chaotic.

MEDICAL SERVICES

Rumah Sakit Darmo (☎ 5676253; Jl Raya Darmo 90) Hospital with English- and Dutch-speaking doctors.

MONEY

Jl Pemuda has plenty of banks with ATMs, as does Jl Tunjungan.

BNI Bank (Bank Negara Indonesia; Jl Pemuda) Usually offers good rates.

POST

Main post office (Jl Kebon Rojo; 7.30am-7.30pm Mon-Sat) Inconveniently located 4km north of the city centre.

TOURIST INFORMATION

East Java Regional Tourist Office (☎ 8531822; Jl Wisata Menanggal; 7am-2pm Mon-Fri) About 3km south of the centre; has a few brochures on the province.

Surabaya City Tourist Office (☎ 5617907; Jl Adityawarman 110; 7am-2pm Mon-Fri) About 2km south of the centre behind the zoo.

Sights

OLD CITY

Even though much of Surabaya's historical centre is literally falling to pieces, the old city easily wins the 'Most Attractive Neighbourhood' prize. With crumbling Dutch architecture, strong Chinese influences and an Arab quarter, it's also the most interesting and idiosyncratic.

A good place to start exploring the old city is **Jembatan Merah**, the so-called 'Red Bridge' that saw fierce fighting during Indonesia's battle for independence. Jl Jembatan Merah, running south of the bus terminal along the canal, is a grungy replica of Amsterdam, but worthy (although rundown) examples of **Dutch architecture** can be seen here. The area further south around the post office and Pelni office also has some fine buildings, though the most impressive is the Indo-European-style **Gedung PTP XXII** government office building, just west of Jl Jembatan Merah, along Jl Merak Cendrawasih.

To the east of Jembatan Merah is Surabaya's **Chinatown**, with hundreds of small businesses and warehouses. Becak and hand-pulled carts are still the best way to transport goods in the crowded, narrow streets. **Pasar Pabean** (Jl Pabean) is a sprawling, darkly lit market, where you can buy everything from Madurese chickens to Chinese crockery.

Further east, near the canal, the stunningly atmospheric **Kong Co Kong Tik Cun Ong temple** (Jl Dukuh) is primarily Buddhist, but has a variety of Confucian and Taoist altars if you can see them through the plumes of incense smoke.

The highlight of a visit to the old city is **Mesjid Ampel** (Jl Ampel Suci), in the heart of the Arab quarter. From the Kong Co Kong Tik Cun Ong temple, proceed north along Jl Nyamplungan and then take the second left down Jl Sasak. A crowd of becak marks the way to the mosque. Through the arched stone entrance is Jl Ampel Suci, a narrow, covered bazaar with perfumes, sarongs, *peci* (black Muslim felt hats) and other religious paraphernalia for sale. Follow the pilgrims past the beggars to the mosque. This is the most sacred mosque in Surabaya; it was here that Sunan Ampel, one of the *wali songo* who brought Islam to Java, was buried in 1481. Pilgrims chant and present rose-petal offerings at the grave behind the mosque.

From the old city you can then head north to the **Kalimas harbour**, where brightly painted *pinisi* from Sulawesi and Kalimantan unload their wares.

SURABAYA ZOO

South of the city centre, **Surabaya Zoo** (Kebun Binatang; Jl Diponegoro; admission 7500Rp; 7am-5pm) has the usual collection of lions, tigers and reptiles, as well as an eccentric concrete statue of a shark tussling with a crocodile, the city's unofficial symbol (*sura* means 'shark' and *baya* means 'crocodile'). The animals look typically nonchalant, but the park is well laid out, with large open enclosures. If you're not planning to visit Komodo, the dragons are worth a visit.

Sunday is crowded and entertainment is often featured in the afternoon. Any bus that is heading down Jl Panglima Sudirman, such as P1 (2000Rp), will take you to the zoo; alternatively you can take an M bemo (2000Rp).

MONUMEN KAPAL SELAM

In keeping with Indonesia's fascination with all things military, Surabaya's foremost

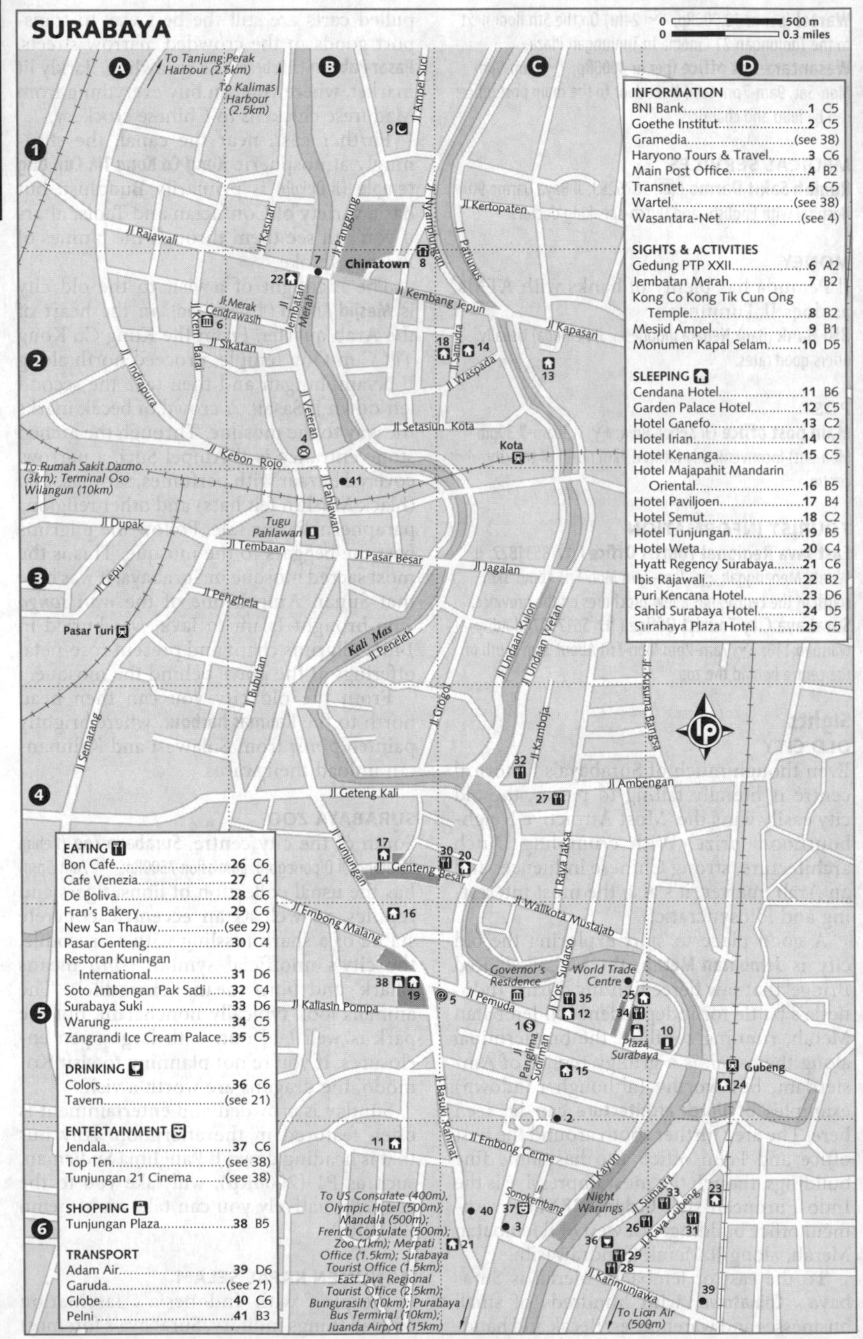
SURABAYA
0 500 m
0 0.3 miles
A
B
C
D
1
2
3
4
5
6
INFORMATION
BNI Bank....................1 C5
Goethe Institut....................2 C5
Gramedia....................(see 38)
Haryono Tours & Travel....................3 C6
Main Post Office....................4 B2
Transnet....................5 C5
Wartel....................(see 38)
Wasantara-Net....................(see 4)
SIGHTS & ACTIVITIES
Gedung PTP XXII....................6 A2
Jembatan Merah....................7 B2
Kong Co Kong Tik Cun Ong Temple....................8 B2
Mesjid Ampel....................9 B1
Monumen Kapal Selam....................10 D5
SLEEPING
Cendana Hotel....................11 B6
Garden Palace Hotel....................12 C5
Hotel Ganefo....................13 C2
Hotel Irian....................14 C2
Hotel Kenanga....................15 C5
Hotel Majapahit Mandarin Oriental....................16 B5
Hotel Paviljoen....................17 B4
Hotel Semut....................18 C2
Hotel Tunjungan....................19 B5
Hotel Weta....................20 C4
Hyatt Regency Surabaya....................21 C6
Ibis Rajawali....................22 B2
Puri Kencana Hotel....................23 D6
Sahid Surabaya Hotel....................24 D5
Surabaya Plaza Hotel....................25 C5
EATING
Bon Café....................26 C6
Cafe Venezia....................27 C4
De Boliva....................28 C6
Fran's Bakery....................29 C6
New San Thauw....................(see 29)
Pasar Genteng....................30 C4
Restoran Kuningan International....................31 D6
Soto Ambengan Pak Sadi....................32 C4
Surabaya Suki....................33 D6
Warung....................34 C5
Zangrandi Ice Cream Palace....................35 C5
DRINKING
Colors....................36 C6
Tavern....................(see 21)
ENTERTAINMENT
Jendala....................37 C6
Top Ten....................(see 38)
Tunjungan 21 Cinema....................(see 38)
SHOPPING
Tunjungan Plaza....................38 B5
TRANSPORT
Adam Air....................39 D6
Garuda....................(see 21)
Globe....................40 C6
Pelni....................41 B3
To Tanjung Perak Harbour (2.5km)
To Kalimas Harbour (2.5km)
Jl Ampel Suci
Jl Nyamplungan
Jl Kertopaten
Jl Pattunus
Jl Kasuari
Jl Panggung
Jl Rajawali
Chinatown
Jl Kembang Jepun
Jl Jembatan Merah
Jl Merak Cendrawasih
Jl Krem Barat
Jl Sikatan
Jl Samudra
Jl Waspada
Jl Kapasan
Indrapura
Jl Veteran
Jl Setasiun Kota
Kota
Jl Kebon Rojo
To Rumah Sakit Darmo (3km); Terminal Oso Wilangun (10km)
Jl Pahlawan
Jl Dupak
Tugu Pahlawan
Jl Tembaan
Jl Pasar Besar
Jl Jagalan
Jl Cepu
Jl Penghela
Pasar Turi
Kali Mas
Jl Peneleh
Jl Undaan Kulon
Jl Undaan Wetan
Jl Kusuma Bangsa
Jl Bubutan
Jl Grogol
Jl Kamboja
Jl Semarang
Jl Ambengan
Jl Geteng Kali
Jl Tunjungan
Jl Genteng Besar
Jl Raya Jaksa
Jl Walikota Mustajab
Jl Embong Malang
Governor's Residence
World Trade Centre
Jl Kaliasin Pompa
Jl Pemuda
Jl Yos Sudarso
Jl Panglima Sudirman
Plaza Surabaya
Gubeng
Jl Basuki Rahmat
Jl Embong Cerme
Jl Kayun
Jl Sonokembang
Night Warungs
Jl Sumatra
Jl Raya Gubeng
Jl Karimunjawa
To US Consulate (400m), Olympic Hotel (500m); Mandala (500m); French Consulate (500m); Zoo (1km); Merpati Office (1.5km); Surabaya Tourist Office (1.5km); East Java Regional Tourist Office (2.5km); Bungurasih (10km); Purabaya Bus Terminal (10km); Juanda Airport (15km)
To Lion Air (500m)

stretch of renovated, waterside real estate centres around the hulk of the *Pasopati*, a Russian submarine (Jl Pemuda; admission 5000Rp; 9am-9pm) commissioned into the Indonesian navy in 1962. The *Pasopati* itself is well maintained and there is a small landscaped **park** with a couple of cafés popular with young smoochers.

Sleeping

BUDGET

Plenty of cheap hotels can be found near Kota train station. It's an interesting area, but it's a long way from the city centre, so few travellers stay this far north.

Hotel Ganefo (3711169; Jl Kapasan 169-171; r with shared/private mandi 65,000/75,000Rp, with air-con 90,000Rp;) If you love sipping tea and whiling away the day in old-worldly surroundings, then Ganefo may be for you. Its fantastic colonial lobby and terrace are perfect for late-afternoon tea drinking, but the rooms are quite cell-like, with iron beds.

Hotel Paviljoen (5343449; Jl Genteng Besar 94; r 66,000Rp, with air-con from 104,000Rp;) This airy colonial villa has fallen on hard times, but it's still one of the most pleasant budget hotels in town. The helpful managers speak English and Dutch and the elderly owner has read just about any book you can put in front of him. On the downside, the basic rooms are inundated with mosquitoes.

Olympic Hotel (5343216; Jl Urip Sumoharjo 65-67; r 70,000Rp, with air-con 85,000Rp, bigger VIP r 98,000Rp;) South of the city centre, Olympic is reminiscent of a derelict hospital. Inside, however, some of the rooms are surprisingly good. Ask the friendly receptionist for a good look around and ask for a discount.

Puri Kencana Hotel (5033161; Jl Kalimantan 9; r from 100,000Rp;) Puri Kencana is a small, semi-stylish hotel handy to the Gubeng train station, with a range of decent rooms (no hot water though) and friendly staff.

Hotel Semut (3524578; Jl Samudra 9-15; d from 145,000Rp;) With a hint of style and a swathe of Chinese furniture, Semut will appeal to travellers looking for a room with more class than most budget options. Rooms are sizable and face a large veranda around a central quadrangle.

Hotel Kenanga (5341359; Jl Embong Kenongo 12; s/d from 150,000/160,000Rp;) Kenanga may have changed its name, but the hotel itself has yet to reinvent itself; it occupies a quiet spot just off Jl Pemuda and has highly adequate but bland rooms. Breakfast is not included in the price.

MIDRANGE

Surabaya has a wide selection of midrange accommodation. Competition is fierce, particularly at the higher end.

Cendana Hotel (5455101; www.cendanahotel.com; Jl Kombes Pol M Doeryat 6; r from 275,000Rp;) Cendana is one of the newer hotels in Surabaya and is a good bet. It has well-appointed rooms and is located just far enough away from the city's main streets to offer some respite from the noise.

Hotel Weta (5319494; hotelweta@hotmail.com; Jl Genteng Kali 3-11; r from 315,000Rp;) Weta is arguably the best of Surabaya's midrange options. Its high-rise views overlook the murky Kali Mas River across the city landscape, and rooms are well polished and come with a bathtub for soaking those weary bones.

Garden Palace Hotel (5344056; Jl Yos Sudarso 11; s/d from 348,000/363,300Rp plus 21% tax;) This older four-star hotel sure isn't a palace and there isn't much evidence of a garden, but generous discounts can make this a good buy. It also has a cheaper three-star wing.

Surabaya Plaza Hotel (5316833; www.primeplazahotels.com; Jl Pemuda 31-37; r from 375,000Rp;) This is one of Surabaya's ritzier establishments and is well located in the thick of things. Rooms range from standard to plush suites.

Ibis Rajawali (3539994; cnr Jl Rajawali & Jl Jembatan Merah; r from 380,000Rp;) Rajawali is a fine choice if you're looking to stay in the north of town. The entire place, from the reception to the rooms, is stylish and businesslike, and discounts are often handed out.

Sahid Surabaya Hotel (5031106; sahidsub@telkom.net; Jl Sumatra 1-15; r from 400,000Rp;) Only a stone's throw from Gubeng train station, Sahid Surabaya is perfect for travellers arriving late into town and looking for a hotel with its fair share of creature comforts. It has also received a number of readers' recommendations.

Hotel Tunjungan (5466666; www.tunjungan-hotel.com; Jl Tunjungan 102-104; r from 550,000Rp;) From the outside this high-rise three-star hotel doesn't look like it could make the cut, but inside things are quite different. Rooms are in very good condition and come with all the trimmings, and who can deny the attraction of a rooftop pool and restaurant?

TOP END

Surabaya has a glut of luxury hotels and competition is cut-throat. Most cater to Indonesian business types.

Hyatt Regency Surabaya (☎ 5311234; Jl Basuki Rahmat 124-128; r from US$70 plus 21% tax; ❄ 💻) The five-star Hyatt has long been one of Surabaya's plushest hotels. Discounts are often offered, but prices rise substantially during peak times.

Hotel Majapahit Mandarin Oriental (☎ 545 4333; www.mandarinoriental.com; Jl Tunjungan 65; r from US$72 plus 21% tax; ❄) This superb colonial hotel built in 1910 has all the trimmings of a top-class establishment, and more charm than most. It's easily Surabaya's finest, and is a tranquil spot in such a busy city. Ask for a discount.

Eating

Surabaya has a huge array of eating options which cover all price ranges. For cheap eats, **Pasar Genteng** (Jl Genteng Besar; mains 8000Rp; 🕑 9am-9pm) has good night warungs. Late-night munchies can be had at the offshoot of Jl Pemuda, opposite the Plaza Surabaya, which buzzes with food-stall activity around the clock, or the strip of warungs with their backs to the river along Jl Kayun. Try *rawon*, a thick black beef soup Surabaya is famous for. For something more Western, Tunjungan Plaza has a colossal selection of squeaky-clean restaurants and fast-food outlets.

Zangrandi Ice Cream Palace (Jl Yos Sudarso 15; ice cream 2000Rp; 🕑 lunch & dinner) Zangrandi is a well-established parlour favoured by Surabayan 20-somethings. Relax in planters chairs at low tables and try to ignore the traffic noise.

Soto Ambengan Pak Sadi (Jl Ambengan 3A; mains 20,000Rp; 🕑 lunch & dinner) If you're looking for chicken dishes, then look no further than Pak Sadi's. But don't overlook the famed lemon grass and coriander Madurese chicken soup, which is sublime.

Cafe Venezia (☎ 5343335; Jl Ambengan 16; mains 30,000-60,000Rp; 🕑 lunch & dinner) Venezia is an old-school establishment in a venerable Dutch villa. The menu is a smorgasbord of tastes, ranging from steaks to Korean barbecue and Japanese dishes. The ice cream is particularly good too.

The area south of Gubeng station, particularly along Jl Raya Gubeng, has some of the city's better restaurants.

New San Thauw (☎ 5035776; Jl Raya Gubeng 64; fish & crab from 9000Rp per 100g; 🕑 lunch & dinner) San Thauw offers seafood that only comes fresher directly from the sea; walk in the door, choose your meal from the tank and wait patiently for the food to arrive.

De Boliva (☎ 5963202; Jl Raya Gubeng 36; mains 30,000Rp; 🕑 lunch & dinner) Housed in a beautifully converted Dutch villa, De Boliva is a stylish restaurant with a menu touching on the four corners of the globe. Don't pass over the excellent sorbet and vitamin-rich smoothies.

Surabaya Suki (☎ 5015979; Jl Raya Gubeng; mains 30,000-100,000Rp; 🕑 lunch & dinner) This very popular Chinese restaurant has a vast menu that features excellent but expensive shark soup and abalone. An extensive vegetarian selection is also featured.

Restoran Kuningan International (☎ 5035103; Jl Kalimantan 14; mains 40,000-200,000Rp; 🕑 dinner) Kuningan is another of Surabaya's top-class restaurants, housed in a converted Dutch villa. The large, mixed menu specialises in seafood, indicated by the huge stained-glass window over the front entrance sporting a gigantic lobster.

Also recommended:

Fran's Bakery (Jl Raya Gubeng 64; cakes 2000-5000Rp; 🕑 breakfast & lunch) Caketastic for those with a sweet tooth.

Bon Café (Jl Raya Gubeng 46; mains 20,000-40,000Rp; 🕑 lunch & dinner) Has a big menu of mostly Western dishes and grills.

Drinking

Most of the big hotels have bars that double as nightclubs; Tavern in the Hyatt Regency (left) rates as one of the best with locals. If you're looking for cheap drinks, a chat with Surabayans and some quality live music, don't pass over Colors (opposite).

Entertainment

CULTURAL PERFORMANCES

Jendala (☎ 5314073; Jl Sonokembang 4-6) This restaurant, in a beautiful colonial lodge, has a varied programme of so-called 'culturetainment', ranging from theatre to dance to disco.

NIGHTCLUBS

Surabayans love their nightclubs, and pack them out on weekends. **Top Ten** (Tunjungan Plaza; Jl Tunjungan; 8pm-3am) is one of the better ones, and can be found in Surabaya's largest shopping centre.

LIVE MUSIC

Colors (☎ 5030562; www.colorspub.com; Jl Sumatra 81; 5pm-3am) Colors is a small venue that's big on live music. The bartenders and some locals will treat you like a long-lost cousin, and if you turn up early enough, you may get the chance to perform some karaoke with live backing. Bands play nightly until 2am.

CINEMA

Cinema complexes are found all around the city.

Tunjungan 21 (Tunjungan Plaza, Jl Tunjungan; tickets 17,000-25,000Rp) This large cinema complex shows recent Hollywood releases in English.

Getting There & Away

AIR

Surabaya has a number of international connections, though services are rapidly diminishing. The most-popular flights head to Singapore (US$220).

Surabaya is an important hub for domestic flights, including those coming from Bandung and Jakarta. Airlines operating out of Surabaya include the following:

Adam Air (☎ 5055111; Jl Biliton 44-46) Has desk at airport as well.

Garuda (☎ 08071-427832 24hr booking line; 546 8505; Hyatt Regency, Jl Basuki Rahmat 124-128) Also offers flights to Singapore.

Lion Air (☎ 503611; Jl Sulawesi 75)

Mandala (☎ 5610777; Jl Raya Diponegoro 91D)

Travel agencies sell domestic tickets at a small discount and international tickets with a bigger cut. See the Java Airfares map (p98) for prices.

Agencies include **Haryono Tours & Travel** (☎ 5325800; Jl Panglima Sudirman 93; 8am-4pm Mon-Fri, 8am-1pm Sat).

BOAT

Surabaya is an important port and a major transport hub for ships to the other islands. Boats depart from Tanjung Perak harbour; bus P1 from outside Tunjungan Plaza heads here.

Popular Pelni connections run to Sulawesi, with several ships running direct to Makassar (economy/1st class 161,500/507,000Rp), and Pontianak (195,000Rp to 617,000Rp) in Kalimantan. See the Transport chapter (p872) or head to the **Pelni ticket office** (☎ 3521044; www.pelni.co.id; Jl Pahlawan 112; 8am-6pm Mon-Fri, 9am-3pm Sat & Sun) for more information.

Ferries to Kamal on Madura (4000Rp, 30 minutes) leave every half-hour from Tanjung Perak, at the end of Jl Kalimas Baru.

BUS

Most of Surabaya's buses operate from the main Purabaya bus terminal, 10km south of the city centre at Bungurasih. Crowded Damri buses run between the bus terminal and the city centre – the P1 service (2000Rp) from the bus terminal is best and can drop you at the Jl Tunjungan/Jl Pemuda intersection. A metered taxi costs around 30,000Rp. Buses along the north coast to Kudus (normal/*patas* 25,000/45,000Rp, eight hours) and Semarang (35,000/50,000Rp, nine hours) depart from Terminal Oso Wilangun, 10km west of the city.

Buses from Purabaya head to Malang (9500/15,000Rp, two hours), Probolinggo (12,000/20,000Rp, three hours), Banyuwangi (33,000/50,000Rp, six hours), Solo (28,000/50,000Rp, 6½ hours) and to Yogyakarta (35,000/60,000Rp, eight hours). Buses also operate from Purabaya bus terminal to Madura.

Luxury buses from Purabaya also do the long hauls to Solo, Yogyakarta, Bandung and Denpasar. Most are night buses leaving in the late afternoon/evening. Bookings can be made at Purabaya bus terminal, or travel agencies in the city centre sell tickets with a mark-up. The most convenient bus agents are those on Jl Basuki Rahmat. Intercity buses are not allowed to enter the city, so you will have to go to Purabaya to catch your bus.

MINIBUS

Door-to-door minibuses will collect passengers from their hotels, which saves a slog to the terminal, but they aren't always quicker because of the time spent driving between pick-ups.

Destinations and sample fares include Malang (40,000Rp), Denpasar (150,000Rp), Solo (65,000Rp), Yogyakarta (75,000Rp) and Semarang (80,000Rp). Hotels can make bookings and arrange pick-up or you can try the agencies along Basuki Rahmat.

TRAIN

From Jakarta, trains taking the fast northern route via Semarang arrive at the Pasar Turi train station southwest of Kota train station. Trains taking the southern route via Yogyakarta, and trains from Banyuwangi and Malang, arrive at Gubeng and most carry on through to Kota. **Gubeng train station** (☎ 5033115) is much more central and sells tickets for all trains.

Most Jakarta-bound trains leave from **Pasar Turi** (☎ 5345014), including the luxury *Argo Anggrek* (from 200,000Rp, nine hours), which leaves at 8.15am and 8.15pm, and the *Gumarang* (business/executive 130,000/180,000Rp, 11 hours), departing at 5.05pm.

From Gubeng, the slower *Bima* (executive 220,000Rp, 13 hours) departs at 4pm for Jakarta via Yogyakarta, and the business *Mutiara Selatan* (120,000Rp, 13 hours) at 4.35pm for Bandung.

The *Sancaka* is the best day train for Yogyakarta, leaving Gubeng at 7.30am and 3pm for Solo (four hours) and Yogyakarta (five hours). It costs 60,000/85,000Rp in business/executive class to either destination. The faster 1.15pm *Sri Tanjung* (21,000Rp, six hours) is a reasonable economy-class service to Yogyakarta's Lempungan train station via Solo, but schedules change regularly.

Apart from services to the main cities, trains leave Gubeng for Malang (6000Rp, two hours) at 4.40am, 8am, 10.45am and 4.20pm and most continue on to Blitar. The *Mutiara Timur* goes to Banyuwangi (business/executive 40,000/55,000Rp, six hours) via Probolinggo at 9.10am and 10.45pm.

Getting Around

TO/FROM THE AIRPORT

Taxis from Juanda airport (15km) operate on a coupon system and cost 40,000Rp to the city centre; from the city centre expect to pay around 80,000Rp. The Damri airport bus (7000Rp) runs infrequently between 8am and 3pm and goes to Purabaya bus terminal and then on to the city centre.

BUS

Surabaya has an extensive Damri city bus network, with normal buses (2000Rp flat rate) and *patas* buses (3000Rp per journey). They can be very crowded, especially the normal buses, and are a hassle if you have luggage.

One of the most useful services is the *patas* P1 bus, which runs from Purabaya bus terminal past the zoo and into the city along Jl Basuki Rahmat. It then turns down Jl Bubutan and continues on to the Tanjung Perak harbour. In the reverse direction, catch it on Jl Tunjungan. The normal buses also cover the same route.

Surabaya also has plenty of bemo labelled A, B and so on, and all charge 2000Rp, depending on the length of the journey. Bemo M runs to the zoo.

TAXI

Surabaya has air-con metered taxis charging 4000Rp for the first kilometre and 2500Rp for subsequent kilometres. Reliable **Bluebird taxis** (☎ 3721234) can be called in advance.

Cars with drivers can be hired from **Globe** (☎ 5481111; Jl Basuki Rahmat 147), or ask in your hotel. Rates start at 400,000Rp per day plus petrol.

TROWULAN

Trowulan was once the capital of the largest Hindu empire in Indonesian history. Founded by Singosari prince Wijaya in 1294, it reached the height of its power under Hayam Wuruk (1350–89), who was guided by his powerful prime minister, Gajah Mada. During this time Majapahit received tribute from most of the regions encompassing present-day Indonesia and even parts of the Malay Peninsula.

Its wealth was based on its control of the spice trade and the fertile rice-growing plains of Java. The religion was a hybrid of Hinduism – with worship of the deities Shiva, Vishnu and Brahma – and Buddhism, but Islam was tolerated, and Koranic burial inscriptions found on the site suggest that Javanese Muslims resided within the royal court. The empire came to a catastrophic end in 1478 when the city fell to the north-coast power of Demak, forcing the Majapahit elite to flee to Bali and opening Java up to the Muslim conquest.

The remains of the court are scattered over a large area around the village of Trowulan, 12km from Mojokerto. The Majapahit temples were mainly built from red clay bricks that quickly crumbled. Many have been rebuilt and are relatively simple compared to the glories of structures such as Borobudur, but they do give a good idea of what was once a great city. It's possible to walk around the sites in one day, or you can hire a becak. Given the heat and the fact that the temples are spread over a large area, a car is ideal.

One kilometre from the main Surabaya–Solo road, the **Trowulan Museum** (admission 2000Rp; 7am-3.30pm Tue-Sun) houses superb examples of Majapahit sculpture and pottery from East Java. Pride of place is held by the splendid statue of Kediri's King Airlangga-as-Vishnu astride a huge Garuda, taken from Belahan. It should be your first port of call for an understanding of Trowulan and Majapahit history, and it includes descriptions of the other ancient ruins in East Java.

Some of the most interesting ruins include the **Kolam Segaran** (a vast Majapahit swimming pool); the gateway of **Bajang Ratu**, with its strikingly sculptured *kala* heads; the **Tikus Temple** (Queen's Bath); and the 13.7m-high **Wringinlawang Gate**. The **Pendopo Agung** is an open-air pavilion built by the Indonesian army. Two kilometres south of the pavilion, the **Troloyo cemetery** is the site of the oldest Muslim graves found in Java, the earliest dating from AD 1376.

Getting There & Away

Trowulan can be visited as a day trip from Surabaya, 60km to the northeast.

From Surabaya's Purabaya bus terminal take a Jombang bus (6000Rp, one hour), which can drop you at the turn-off to the museum; a becak tour of the sites will cost around 50,000Rp with bargaining.

PULAU MADURA

pop 3 million

Separated from Surabaya by a narrow channel, the island of Madura is a flat, rugged expanse of land with few hills and fewer visitors. It is famous for its colourful bull races, *kerapan sapi*, and its virility drink, *jamu madura*, a spicy concoction meant to put fire in men's veins. It also has several historical sites, some passable beaches and an unwavering traditional culture.

Madurese men claim that the name Madura is derived from *madu* (honey) and *dara* (girl), and Madurese women are, so the story goes, known throughout Java for their sexual prowess. Madura is, however, a very traditional and devoutly Islamic society. The sarong and *peci* are still the norm – mall fever has not found its way to Madura. In general, the Madurese are rugged *kasar* people according to the Javanese, and are said to be adept at wielding knives when disputes arise. While the Madurese can be disconcertingly blunt at times, and in remote areas you may attract a crowd of curious onlookers, they can also be extremely hospitable.

The island is about 160km long by 35km wide. Its southern side is lined with shallow beaches and cultivated lowland, while the northern coast alternates between rocky cliffs and great rolling sand-dune beaches, the best of which is at Lombang. At the extreme east is a tidal marsh and vast tracts of salt around Kalianget. The interior is riddled with limestone slopes, and is either rocky or sandy, so agriculture is limited.

HISTORY

In 1624 the island was conquered by Sultan Agung of Mataram and its government united under one Madurese princely line, the Cakraningrats. Until the middle of the 18th century the Cakraningrat family fiercely opposed Central Javanese rule and harassed Mataram, often conquering large parts of the kingdom. The famous Prince Raden Trunojoyo even managed to carry off the royal treasury of Mataram in 1677, which was restored only after the Dutch intervened and stormed Trunojoyo's stronghold at Kediri.

By the beginning of the 1700s, however, the Dutch had secured control of the eastern half of Madura. The Cakraningrats then agreed to help the Dutch put down the rebellion in Central Java that broke out after the Chinese massacre in 1740, but in the end fared little better than their Javanese counterparts. Although Cakraningrat IV attempted to contest the issue, a treaty was eventually signed in 1743 in which Pakubuwono II ceded full sovereignty of Madura to the Dutch. Cakraningrat fled to Banjarmasin and took refuge on an English ship, but was robbed, betrayed by the sultan and finally captured by the Dutch and exiled to the Cape of Good Hope (South Africa).

Under the Dutch, Madura continued as four states, each with its own regent. Madura was initially important as a major source of colonial troops, but in the second half of the 19th century it acquired greater economic value as the main supplier of salt to Dutch-governed areas of the archipelago.

South Coast

The first port of call for most visitors is **Kamal**, a scruffy town of little importance to sightseers. Many head directly to **Bangkalan**, the next town north of Kamal, to watch the bull races. If you've time to kill before a race, **Museum Cakraningrat** (8am-2pm Mon-Sat) will entertain you for an hour or so with displays on Madurese history and culture.

Sampang, 61km from Bangkalan, also stages bull races and is the centre of the regency of the same name. **Camplong**, 9km further east, is a safe and popular, if grungy, swimming beach on the south coast. The Pertamina storage tanks nearby do nothing for its visual appeal, but it is a breezy oasis from the hot interior of Madura.

About another 15km further east is the pleasant (for Madura) town of **Pamekasan**, the island's capital. Bull races are held in and around Pamekasan every Sunday from the end of July until early October; during October each year it throbs with the festivities of the **Kerapan Sapi Grand Final**. The **BCA bank** (Bank Central Asia; Jl Jokotole; 9am-2pm Mon-Fri), just east of the *alun-alun*, changes money and allows cash advances on credit cards.

About 35km east of Pamekasan, before Bluto, is **Karduluk**, a woodcarving centre.

SLEEPING

Bangkalan has a couple of hotels. **Hotel Ningrat** (031-3095388; Jl Kahaji Muhammed Kholil 113; s/d 50,000/60,000Rp, r 100,000Rp, with air-con 180,000Rp;), on the main road south of town, is one of the island's best hotels – though that's not saying much. All in all, its rooms are comfortable but small, with the bigger air-con variety decorated in traditional Madurese style. Closer to the town centre is the very basic **Hotel Melati** (031-3096457; Jl

A BULL RACE AT PACE

In Madurese folklore, the tradition of *kerapan sapi* (bull racing) began long ago when plough teams raced each other across the arid fields. This pastime was encouraged by Panembahan Sumolo, an early king of Sumenep. Today, with stud-bull breeding big business on Madura, *kerapan sapi* are an incentive for the Madurese to breed good stock. Only bulls of a high standard can be entered for important races – the Madurese keep their young bulls in superb condition, dosing them with an assortment of medicinal herbs, honey, beer and raw eggs.

Traditional races are run in bull-racing stadiums all over Madura. Practice trials are held throughout the year, but the main season starts in late August and September, when contests are held at district and regency levels. The finest bulls fight it out for the big prize in October at the grand final in Pamekasan, the island's capital.

This is the biggest and most colourful festival and as many as 100 bulls, wearing richly decorated halters, ribbons and flowers, are paraded through town to a loud fanfare. For each race, two pairs of bulls, stripped of their finery, are matched, with their 'jockeys' perched behind on wooden sleds. Gamelan music is played to excite the bulls and then, after being fed a generous tot of *arak*, they're released and charge flat out down the track – just as often plunging straight into the crowd. The race is over in a flash – the best time recorded so far is nine seconds over 100m. After the elimination heats the victors get to spend the rest of the year as studs.

Pamekasan is the main centre for bull racing but Bangkalan, Sampang, Sumenep and some of the surrounding villages also host races. The East Java Calendar of Events, available from tourist offices in Surabaya (p221), has a general schedule for the main races, but if you are on Madura over a weekend during the main season, you can be guaranteed that races or practices will be held somewhere on the island.

Majen Sungkono 48; r from 20,000Rp); it's back from the street down an alleyway.

In Camplong, the imaginatively named **Hotel Camplong** (☎ 0323-321568; r 110,000Rp) is a reasonable place to bed down for the night.

In the island's capital, try either **Hotel Trunojoyo** (☎ 0324-322181; Jl Trunojoyo 48; r with/without mandi 55,000/25,000Rp, with air-con 65,000Rp; ❄), near Hotel Garuda on the road to Bangkalan, which is equipped with clean and quiet rooms, or **Hotel Ramayana** (☎ 0324-324575; Jl Niaga 55; r with fan from 40,000Rp, with air-con from 80,000Rp; ❄), which is slightly better, with reasonably bright, comfortable rooms.

Sumenep

☎ 0328

Compared with the rest of rugged Madura, Sumenep, in the far east of the island, is a sleepy, refined town, with a Mediterranean air and quiet lazy streets. The goats and belching pick-ups that clog the streets of the island's other main communities are a rarity here and by mid-afternoon the whole town seems to settle into a slow, collective siesta. With dozens of crumbling villas and a fine *kraton* and mosque, it is easily Madura's most interesting town.

INFORMATION

It's taken a while, but finally Madura has a **tourist office** (☎ 667148; Jl Sutomo 5; 🕑 7am-3pm Tue-Sat), which has information on both Sumenep and the island.

Sumenep's post office is on the road to Kalianget, and the Telkom office is further out past the Chinese temple. Both the **BCA bank** (Bank Central Asia; Jl Trunojoyo; 🕑 9am-2pm Mon-Fri) and **BNI bank** (Bank Negara Indonesia; Jl Trunojoyo; 🕑 9am-2pm Mon-Fri) change cash at poor rates.

Wahana Computers (Jl Dr Cipto 3; 🕑 8am-midnight) has internet access costing 6000Rp per hour.

SIGHTS

Occupied by the present *bupati* of Sumenep, the **kraton** and its **taman sari** (pleasure garden; admission included in carriage-house museum entry; 🕑 7am-5pm) were built in 1750 by Panembahan Sumolo, son of Queen Raden Ayu Tirtonegoro and her spouse, Bendoro Saud. The architect is said to have been the grandson of one of the first Chinese to settle in Sumenep after the Chinese massacre in Batavia. Part of the *kraton* building is a small museum with an interesting collection of royal possessions, including Madurese furniture, stone sculptures and *binggel* (heavy silver anklets worn by Madurese women). The complex can only be visited on a guided tour arranged at the royal carriage-house museum.

Opposite the *kraton*, the **royal carriage-house museum** (admission 1000Rp; 🕑 7am-5pm) contains the throne of Queen Tirtonegoro and a Chinese-style bed reputedly 300 years old. On the first Sunday of the month, traditional dance or gamelan practice (admission free; 🕑 10am-1pm) is held at the *kraton*.

Sumenep's 18th-century **Mesjid Jamik** is notable for its three-tiered Meru-style roof, Chinese porcelain tiles and ceramics. Sumenep also has a **Chinese temple**.

The tombs of the royal family are at the **Asta Tinggi cemetery**, which looks out over the town from a peaceful hilltop 2km away. The main royal tombs are decorated with carved and painted panels; two depict dragons said to represent the colonial invasion of Sumenep. The biggest mausoleum is that of Panembahan Notokusomo (1762–1811), but it is the grave of Tirtonegoro that attracts pilgrims from all over Madura and Java. One of the small pavilions in the outer courtyard still bears the mark of an assassin's sword from an unsuccessful attempt to murder Bendoro Saud.

Sumenep is a centre for champion bull-breeding, and on most Saturday mornings practice **bull races** can be seen at the Giling stadium.

FESTIVALS & EVENTS

The **Festival of Sumenep** is usually celebrated biannually on 31 October and marks the founding of the town, with a programme of cultural performances.

SLEEPING & EATING

Hotel Wijaya II (☎ 662532; Jl KH Wahid Hasyim 3; r with fan/air-con from 20,000/70,000Rp; ❄) This is the sister of Wijaya I; rooms are darker and scruffier, but it is a quieter spot to bed down for the night.

Hotel Wijaya I (☎ 662433; Jl Trunojoyo 45-47; r with/without air-con from 65,000/25,000Rp; ❄) Hotel Wijaya I is probably the best of a bunch of bad budget places, with a range of reasonably

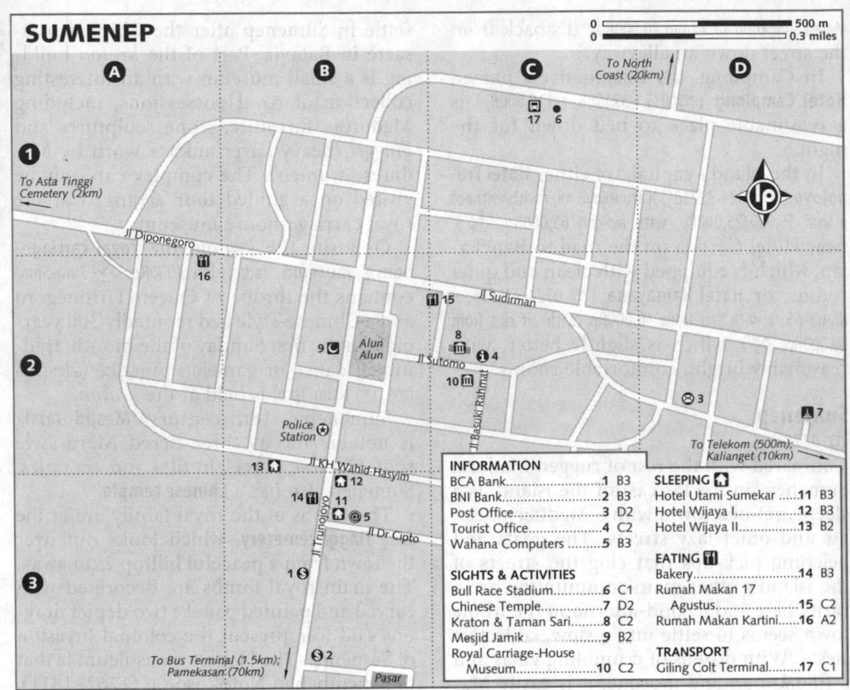

clean but bland rooms. There is a restaurant on site, which is open for dinner, as well as a wartel.

Hotel Utami Sumekar (☎ 672221; Jl Trunojoyo 53; s/d 100,000/120,000Rp, ste from 145,000Rp;) This huge, rambling place is a bit down at heel and has characterless rooms, but at least the beds are good and firm, and you won't be disturbed by neighbours.

Decent but simple restaurants around town include **Rumah Makan Kartini** (Jl Diponegoro 83; mains around 8000Rp; lunch & dinner) and **Rumah Makan 17 Agustus** (Jl Sudirman 34; mains 8000Rp; lunch & dinner); don't expect much and you'll be satisfied.

There are good day and night markets down a lane next to the BNI bank, and a **bakery** (Jl Trunojyo; pastries 2000Rp; lunch & dinner) opposite Hotel Wijaya I.

SHOPPING

The main business in town is antiques, but the best antiques are carted off by the truckload to Bali and Jakarta. Every second house seems to have something for sale. Sumenep is a centre for batik on Madura, though Madurese batik isn't as fine as that in Java.

Rachma Batik (Pasar; 9am-5pm Mon-Fri) For batik, try this place in the market.

GETTING THERE & AWAY

The main Sumenep bus terminal is on the southern outskirts of the town, a 5000Rp becak ride from the centre. Buses leave from here roughly every 1½ hours until evening for Surabaya's Purabaya bus terminal (35,000Rp, four hours), and there are also direct buses to Banyuwangi, Malang, Semarang, Jakarta and Denpasar. Bus agents along Jl Trunojoyo sell tickets.

The Giling bus terminal for Colts to the north is right near the stadium, 1.5km from the market, or around 5000Rp by becak. From Giling, Colts go to Lombang, Slopeng, Ambunten and other north-coast destinations.

Around Sumenep

From Sumenep, the road to **Kalianget**, 10km southeast, passes many fine villas with façades of heavy, white columns under overhanging red-tiled roofs. Kalianget is a centre for **salt production**, and from here you can take boats to the other islands of the Sumenep district.

You can go **snorkelling** at Pulau Talango, just offshore. The larger islands include Sapudi, Rass and Kangean, well to the east.

North Coast

Fishing villages and their brightly painted *perahu* (boats) dot the north coast. The coast is lined with sandy beaches, but few are particularly wonderful.

Near Arosbaya, 27km north of Kamal, the tombs of the Cakraningrat royalty are at **Air Mata** (Tears) cemetery, superbly situated on the edge of a small ravine. The ornately carved *gunungan* (*wayang* mountain motif) headstone on the grave of Ratu Ibu, consort of Cakraningrat I, is the most impressive and is on the highest terrace. The turn-off to Air Mata is just before Arosbaya. From the coast road it's a 4km walk inland.

The village of **Tanjungbumi** is situated on the northwest coast of Madura, about 60km from Kamal. Although primarily a fishing village, it is also a manufacturing centre for traditional Madurese batik and *perahu*.

Pasongsongan is a fishing village on the beach, where it may be possible to stay with villagers. Further east, **Ambunten** is the largest village on the north coast and has a bustling market. Just over the bridge, you can walk along the picturesque river, which is lined with *perahu*, and through the fishing village to the beach.

Just outside Ambunten to the east, **Slopeng** has a wide beach with sand dunes, coconut palms and usually calm water for swimming, but it is not always clean. Men fish the shallower water with large cantilevered hand nets, which are rarely seen elsewhere in Java.

Slopeng is also known for its *topeng* making and its beach is best visited on a day trip from Sumenep, only 20km away.

Pantai Lombang, 30km northeast of Sumenep, is touted as the best beach on Madura. It has a wide stretch of sand but little else.

Getting There & Away

Ferries sail to Kamal (4000Rp, 30 minutes), the port town on the western tip of Madura, roughly every half-hour around the clock from Surabaya's Tanjung Perak harbour. Buses go directly from Surabaya's Purabaya bus terminal via the ferry right to Sumenep (normal/*patas* 25,000/35,000Rp, four hours) almost every 1½ hours; alternatively, catch them at the harbour. Buses run right across to Sumenep (passing through Surabaya on their way) from Banyuwangi (via Probolinggo), Denpasar (also via Probolinggo), Malang, Semarang and Jakarta.

Another possibility, if you are coming from the east, is to take the **passenger and car ferry** (☎ 0328-663054) from Jangkar harbour (near Asembagus) to Kalianget (31,800Rp, five hours) on the eastern tip of Madura. The ferry departs Jangkar at 8am and 2pm daily but schedules change regularly, so it's a good idea to phone ahead. Buses run from Situbondo to Jangkar, or you can take a bus to Asembagus, then a becak or *andong* for the 4.5km trip to Jangkar. From Kalianget, the ferry departs Kalianget at 8am and 2pm daily. Colt 'O' (2000Rp, 20 to 30 minutes) travels between Kalianget and Sumenep.

Getting Around

On arrival by ferry from Surabaya in Kamal, it's possible to pick up a Colt to Terminal Baru on the southern outskirts of Bangkalan. From here, Colts run along the main highway to Bangkalan (2000Rp, 30 minutes), Pamekasan (10,000Rp, 2½ hours) and Sumenep (20,000Rp, four hours). If heading straight to Sumenep, try to get on a bus at Tanjung Perak in Surabaya. Colts are much more frequent than buses and run all over the island, but can spend a lot of time picking up passengers. Colts travel along the northern route to Arosbaya, Tanjungbumi, Pasongsongan and Ambunten.

To see something of the island, it's interesting to take a Colt from Pamekasan inland through tobacco country to Waru, and then another on to Pasongsongan, from where you can head back to Sumenep via Ambunten and Slopeng.

Madura's roads are almost all paved and in excellent condition, with relatively little traffic. As the island is mostly flat, Madura is a good cycling destination, although it does get very hot.

MALANG

☎ 0341 / pop 710,000

With leafy, colonial-era boulevards and a breezy climate, Malang moves at a far more leisurely pace than the regional capital, Surabaya, sprawling over the hilltops with the airs and graces of an overgrown market town.

Established by the Dutch in the closing decades of the 18th century, Malang earned its first fortunes from coffee, which flourished on the surrounding hillsides. Today, the city's colonial grandeur is quickly disappearing behind the homogenous façades of more modern developments, but the streets of the Tugu area still have a rare and intriguing serenity.

The main attractions lie outside the city, but much of Malang's charm can be discovered by leaving your map in the hotel and simply setting off into the suburbs.

Orientation

City life – both during the day and at night – revolves around the *alun-alun* and the busy streets flowing into Jl Agus Salim and Pasar Besar near the central market. This is where you'll find the main shopping plazas, restaurants, cinemas and many of Malang's hotels. Banks and the Telkom office are northwest of the *alun-alun* along Jl Basuki Rahmat. Malang's best restaurants are in the west of the city, a becak ride from the centre, and for more historical wanderings, start with the circular Jl Tugu.

Information

INTERNET ACCESS

Prima Warung Internet (Jl Basuki Rahmat 33; per hr 4500Rp; 24hr) Fastest internet connection in town, which is why there are often queues.

Warposnet (Jl Kauman Merdeka; per hr 3500Rp; 7am-11pm) Next to the post office.

MONEY

Malang has plenty of banks, with ATMs and moneychangers. Compare the BNI and BII banks on Jl Basuki Rahmat for the best rates, or try **Lippo Bank** opposite the *alun-alun*.

POST & TELEPHONE

Main post office (Jl Kauman Merdeka; 8am-7.30pm Mon-Sat) Opposite the *alun-alun*.

Telkom office (Jl Basuki Rahmat; 24hr) Has a Home Country Direct phone.

TOURIST INFORMATION

Gunung Bromo National Park head office (☎ 490885; tn-bromoru@malang.wasantaranet.id; Jl Raden Intan 6; 7.30am-3pm Mon-Thu, 7.30-11am Fri) Brochures and information on Bromo.

Tourist Information box (☎ 323966; Jl Majapahit; 8am-5pm) Has a tiny amount of information on the town and its surrounds; long opening hours but rarely occupied.

Tourist Information Office (☎ 562680; Jl Gede 6) More helpful, but 3km northwest of the *alun-alun*. Closed for renovation at the time of writing.

TRAVEL AGENCIES

Sunrise Holiday (☎ 359070; www.sunriseholiday.com; Jl Majapahit 1K; 8am-8pm) Knowledgeable agent offering tourist information and tours. Dutch- and English-speaking guides; has a branch at the Toko Oen restaurant (p234).

Wijaya Travel (☎ 327072; Jl Pajajaran 7; 8am-5pm) Can arrange minibus pick-ups from hotels.

Sights & Activities

The city is noted for its colonial architecture. The **Balai Kota** (Town Hall; Jl Tugu Circle) is a sprawling Dutch administrative building, and nearby are some former old mansions, such as the **Splendid Inn** and the **Wisma IKIP** next door on Jl Majapahit. Near the *alun-alun*, the **Gereja Kathedral Kuno** is the old Dutch Reform Church. To the north of town, Jl Besar Ijen is Malang's millionaire's row. Most of the large houses date from the colonial era, but many have been substantially renovated, losing architectural detail in the process.

On the northwestern outskirts of town, **Candi Badut** is a small Shivaite temple dating from the 8th century. West of town, the modern **Army Museum** (Jl Besar Ijen; admission 1500Rp; 8am-3pm Mon-Thu, 8-11am Fri, 8am-1pm Sat & Sun) is devoted to Malang's Brawijaya Division.

Malang has some good markets. The huge central market, the **Pasar Besar** (Jl Pasar Besar; 9am-5pm), is always worth browsing in. The flower market, **Pasar Bunga** (7am-5pm), has a pleasant aspect down by the river, and it is the place to stroll in the morning. The most intriguing market, though, is **Pasar Senggol** (7am-5pm), Malang's bird market, which also sells snakes and fish. **Pasar Kebalen**, near the **Eng An Kiong Chinese temple**, is the most active market in

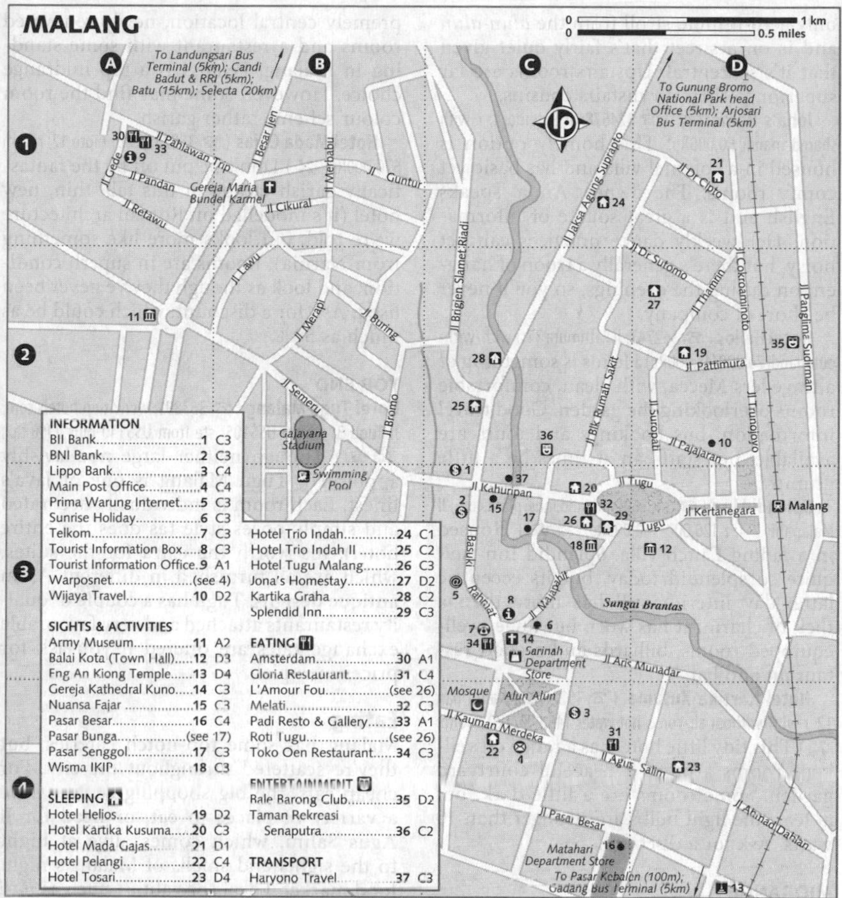

the evenings, open until around 9pm most nights.

A great way to combine relaxation for yourself and support for the local community is a visit to **Nuansa Fajar** (☎ 324482; Jl Kahuripan 114; massage per hr 17,000Rp, house calls per hr 24,000Rp), an outfit training and employing blind masseurs from all over the country. The beds are set up at the back of a small restaurant and while the surroundings aren't the most tranquil, the masseurs are skilled and it's for a good cause.

Tours

A number of operators offer tours to southern beaches (from 300,000Rp per person, minimum of two), Batu (200,000Rp) and Bromo (via Tosari for about 375,000Rp). The following can all also arrange car hire with driver from about 350,000Rp to 400,000Rp per day, or scooter and driver from 85,000Rp.

Hotel Helios (☎ 362741; Jl Pattimura 37) Well-known operator (the staff speak Dutch as well as English); works in tandem with Sunrise Holiday.

Jona's Homestay (☎ 324678; Jl Sutomo 4) Anna is the helpful English-speaking owner of this place; will only rent scooters to people overnighting at the homestay.

Sunrise Holiday (☎ 359070; www.sunriseholiday.com; Jl Majapahit 1K; 🕓 8am-8pm) Also rents scooters.

Sleeping

BUDGET

Hotel Tosari (☎ 326945; Jl Ahmad Dahlan 31; r 30,000Rp, with mandi/air-con 45,000/155,000Rp; ❄) Tosari is only a 10-minute stroll from the *alun-alun* and is on a street that's fairly quiet given that it's so central. Upstairs rooms are far superior to their downstairs cousins.

Jona's Homestay (☎ 324678; Jl Sutomo 4; r with shared mandi 60,000Rp) This homely option is housed in a colonial villa and has basic yet comfy rooms. The owner, Anna, speaks English and is a great source of information. Her weekly dance practices can get noisy, but there's generally a troop of hangers-on during the evenings, so you'll never be short of company.

Hotel Helios (☎ 362741; Jl Pattimura 37; r with/without mandi 70,000/45,000Rp) Helios is something of a travellers Mecca, with clean, comfortable rooms overlooking the garden. Good travel information, bus bookings and tours are available, but staff can at times be a little grumpy.

Splendid Inn (☎ 366860; splendid.inn@plasa.com; Jl Majapahit 2-4; r 120,000-160,000Rp; ❄ 🏊) Housed in a fading Dutch villa, Splendid Inn isn't quite so splendid today, but its eccentric latter-day interior still has more than a flick of charm. It has worn but huge, well-equipped rooms, billiards and a good restaurant and bar.

Hotel Kartika Kusuma (☎ 352266; Jl Kahuripan 12; r with/without air-con & hot water 145,000/120,000Rp; ❄) This tidy little hotel has a range of well-kept rooms around a peaceful courtyard garden. Some rooms are a little dark, but at least the light bulbs are stronger than 10 watts. Ask for a discount.

MIDRANGE

Hotel Trio Indah II (☎ 359083; Jl Brigjen Slamet Riadi 1-3; r 215,000-380,000Rp; ❄ 💻) This newly built hotel has small but comfy rooms and eager-to-please staff. It shares a busy corner with McDonald's, so ask for a room at the back.

Trio Indah (☎ 341661; Jl Jaksa Agung Suprapto 18-20; r from 250,000Rp) Not as good as its number II, Trio Indah is still a fine bet, with large, if bland, rooms and discounts available.

Kartika Graha (☎ 361900; Jl Jaksa Agung Suprapto 17; r from 285,000Rp; ❄ 🏊) Kartika Graha is a modern hotel with pleasant rooms and bars, restaurants and karaoke lounges aplenty. Sadly, there doesn't seem to be anyone about to fill them.

Hotel Pelangi (☎ 365156; www.hotelpelangi.com; Jl Kauman Merdeka 3; r from 286,000Rp) With a supremely central location, newly renovated rooms and a restaurant with some standing in Malang, Pelangi is a top midrange choice. However, some may find the room colour scheme rather garish.

Hotel Mada Gajas (☎ 358785; Jl Dr Cipto 17; r from 670,000Rp; ❄) Don't be put off by the fantastically garish façade of this tall, thin, new hotel (it's modelled on Roman architecture we're told, but looks more like something from Narnia). Rooms are in superb condition, and look as though they've never been used. Ask for a discount, which could be as much as 50%.

TOP END

Hotel Tugu Malang (☎ 363891; www.tuguhotels.com; Jl Tugu 3; r from US$105, ste from US$140 plus 21% tax; ❄ 🏊) Though neither large nor lavishly appointed, Tugu Malang is one of Java's finest. Each room is individually decorated and simply oozes style (as does the entire hotel); it's worth the extra for the suites, which are all furnished in different Asian antique designs. Tugu has a couple of quality restaurants attached and very favourable exchange rates are offered if you ask for prices in rupiah.

Eating

Malang has some top-notch eateries, but they're scattered throughout the city. For cheap eats, the big shopping centres have a variety of places to eat, or head for Jl Agus Salim, which comes alive at night to the sights and smells of Malang's night food market. Local specialities, such as *nasi rawon* (beef soup served with rice), are always worth a try.

Roti Tugu (Jl Tugu 3; cakes around 2000Rp; 🕑 breakfast, lunch & dinner) Sublime pastries, along with an assortment of cookies, drinks and fruits, can be picked up from the bakery of the Tugu Hotel.

Gloria Restaurant (Jl Agus Salim 23; mains 10,000-30,000Rp; 🕑 lunch & dinner) Gloria is your quintessential Chinese restaurant, with a huge array of Chinese cuisine served in stripped-back yet clean surrounds. The staff are friendly and keen to practise their English.

Toko Oen (Jl Basuki Rahmat; mains 20,000-40,000Rp; 🕑 breakfast, lunch & dinner) Opposite the Sarinah department store is this anachronism from colonial days, with tea tables and cane chairs. These days, the ambience is more English seaside than imperial grandeur, but the Western and Indonesian food is reasonably good and it is an inviting place to kick back with a beer or an ice cream. There's also tourist information available and a small selection of English books and maps for sale.

Melati (☎ 363891; Jl Tugu 3; mains 30,000-160,000Rp; 24hr) Melati is Hotel Tugu Malang's smaller restaurant, but it by no means takes second place in the restaurant race. Set beside the hotel's pool and lit by an army of candles, it exudes plenty of romantic charm and has an inviting mix of Western, Indonesian and Malang cuisine. The service, which is close to impeccable, is an added bonus.

L'Amour Fou (☎ 363891; Jl Tugu 3; mains 40,000-120,000Rp; dinner) This eccentric, eclectic and extravagant restaurant is not only a dining option but an attraction in its own right. Almost everything inside L'Amour Fou touches on *love*, from the heart-shaped pizzas to the labyrinth of lovers' nooks and secret balconies. The menu is a heady mix of Indonesian and Western delights and the wine selection is extensive; the only drawback is the loud cover band, which you'll have to shout over to be heard.

Padi Resto & Gallery (Jl Pahlawan Trip 19; mains 50,000Rp; lunch & dinner) Padi is at the cutting edge of Malang's cuisine scene, with live music, a chic garden setting and plenty of starched linen and gleaming glassware. Pick from a menu of tip-top steaks and fish specials before tucking into the stunning puds. Even the toilets are chic.

Amsterdam (☎ 326536; Jl Pahlawan Trip 25; mains 50,000Rp; lunch & dinner) A couple of doors down from Padi Resto, Amsterdam is a more gregarious steakhouse, with louder punters and less formality. This is a good place to mingle over a mixer with the city's upwardly mobiles.

Entertainment

CULTURAL PERFORMANCES

Taman Rekreasi Senaputra (Jl Basuki Rahmat) This is Malang's cultural and recreational park. Every Sunday morning at 10am, *kuda lumping* (horse trance) dances are held here (2500Rp). The dancers ride plaited-cane horses until they fall into a trance, allowing them to eat glass and perform other masochistic acts without harm. The park also features *wayang kulit* performances on special occasions; check with the tourist information offices for the next performance.

RRI (☎ 387500; Jl Candi Panggung) About 5km northwest of the city, this place has *wayang kulit* from 9pm on the first Saturday of the month.

NIGHTCLUBS

For a city with such a large student population, things are decidedly quiet during the evening. One place to mix and mingle with the local populace at night though is **Bale Barong Club** (Hotel Mandala Puri; Jl Panglima Sudirman 81; cover charge 25,000Rp). The club kicks off after 10pm on weekends when cover bands take the stage.

Getting There & Away

BUS & MIKROLET

Malang has three bus terminals. Arjosari, 5km north of town, is the main one, with regular buses mostly along the northern route to destinations such as Surabaya (normal/air-con 9500/14,000Rp, two hours), Probolinggo (11,000/15,000Rp, 2½ hours), Jember (21,600Rp, 4½ hours), Banyuwangi (34,200Rp, six hours) and Denpasar (60,000/95,000Rp, 10 hours). *Mikrolet* run from Arjosari to nearby villages such as Singosari (2000Rp) and Tumpang (2000Rp).

The Gadang bus terminal is 5km south of the city centre, and has buses along the southern routes to destinations such as Blitar (9000Rp, two hours).

The Landungsari bus terminal, 5km northwest of the city, has buses to destinations west of the city, such as Batu (2500Rp, 30 minutes).

Numerous bus companies offer deluxe services from Arjosari for the long hauls. The buses to Bandung (around 185,000Rp) and Jakarta (205,000Rp) leave around 2.30pm. Numerous buses to Solo and Yogyakarta cost around 120,000Rp, and leave around 7pm. Night buses also do the run to Bali for 135,000Rp.

The travel agent (p232) at the Toko Oen restaurant books a wide range of bus tickets; otherwise, try **Haryono Travel** (☎ 367500; Jl Kahuripan 22) for other transport needs, including flights.

MINIBUS

Plenty of door-to-door minibus companies operate from Malang, and hotels and travel agencies can book them. **Wijaya Travel** (☎ 327072; Jl Pajajaran 7; 🕒 8am-5pm) is one reliable agency, as is **Sunrise Holiday** (☎ 359070; www.sunriseholiday.com; Jl Majapahit 1K; 🕒 8am-8pm). Minibuses travel to Solo (75,000Rp), Yogyakarta (75,000Rp), Probolinggo (50,000Rp) and Denpasar (135,000Rp). Minibuses to Surabaya (50,000Rp) will drop you off at hotels in Surabaya, thus saving the long haul from Surabaya's bus terminal.

TRAIN

Some useful services, mostly economy class, operate out of **Malang train station** (☎ 362208). The economy-class *Penataran* (4500Rp, 2½ hours) is the most convenient train to Surabaya. It leaves Malang every day at 4.15am, 6.55am, 8.40am, 12.18pm and 6.32pm. The executive-class *Gajayana* (185,000Rp, 13 hours) leaves Malang at 3.40pm, bound for Jakarta's Gambir station. The economy/business *Matar Maja* goes west from Malang to Solo, Yogyakarta (55,000Rp, seven hours), Cirebon and Jakarta at 2.10pm.

Getting Around

Mikrolet run all over town from the main bus terminals and to other *mikrolet* stations. Most run between the bus terminals through the town centre. These are marked A-G (Arjosari to Gadung and return), A-L (Arjosari to Landungsari) or G-L (Gadang to Landungsari). A trip anywhere in town costs 2000Rp.

Becak and metered taxis (minimum charge 20,000Rp) are also available around the town.

AROUND MALANG

Singosari Temples

The Singosari temples lie in a ring around Malang and are mostly funerary temples dedicated to the kings of the Singosari dynasty (AD 1222 to 1292), the precursors of the Majapahit empire.

CANDI SINGOSARI

Right in the village of Singosari, 12km north of Malang, this **temple** (admission free; 🕒 7am-5pm) stands 500m off the main Malang to Surabaya road. One of the last monuments erected to the Singosari dynasty, it was built in 1304 in honour of King Kertanegara, the fifth and last Singosari king, who died in 1292 in a palace uprising. The main structure of the temple was completed, but for some reason, the sculptors never finished their task. Only the top part has any ornamentation and the *kala* heads have been left strangely stark. Of the statues that once inhabited the temple's chambers, only the statue of Agastya, the Shivaite teacher who walked across the water to Java, remains. Statues of Durga and Ganesha were originally carted off to the Netherlands and are now housed in the National Museum in Jakarta.

About 200m beyond the temple there are two enormous figures of *dwarapala* (guardians against evil spirits) wearing clusters of skulls and twisted serpents.

To reach Singosari, take a green *mikrolet* (2000Rp) from Malang's Arjosari bus terminal and get off at the Singosari market on the highway, then walk or take a becak.

CANDI SUMBERAWAN

This small, plain **Buddhist stupa** (admission free; 🕒 7am-5pm) lies in the foothills of Gunung Arjuna, about 5km northwest of Singosari. Originating from a later period than the Singosari temples, it was built to commemorate the visit of Hayam Wuruk, the great Majapahit king, who visited the area in 1359.

Take a Colt (2000Rp) from Singosari *pasar* on the highway to Desa Sumberawan, and from where the Colts terminate, walk 500m down the road to the canal, turn right and follow the canal through picturesque rice paddies for 1km to the temple. This delightful walk is the highlight of the visit.

CANDI JAGO

Along a small road near the market in Tumpang, 18km from Malang, **Candi Jago** (Jajaghu; admission 5000Rp; 🕒 7am-5pm) was built in 1268 and is thought to be a memorial to the fourth Singosari king, Vishnuvardhana. The temple is in fairly poor condition, but it still has some interesting decorative carving – in the three-dimensional, *wayang kulit* style typical of East Java – from the Jataka and the Mahabharata. This primarily Buddhist temple also has Javanese-Hindu statues, including a six-armed, death-dealing goddess

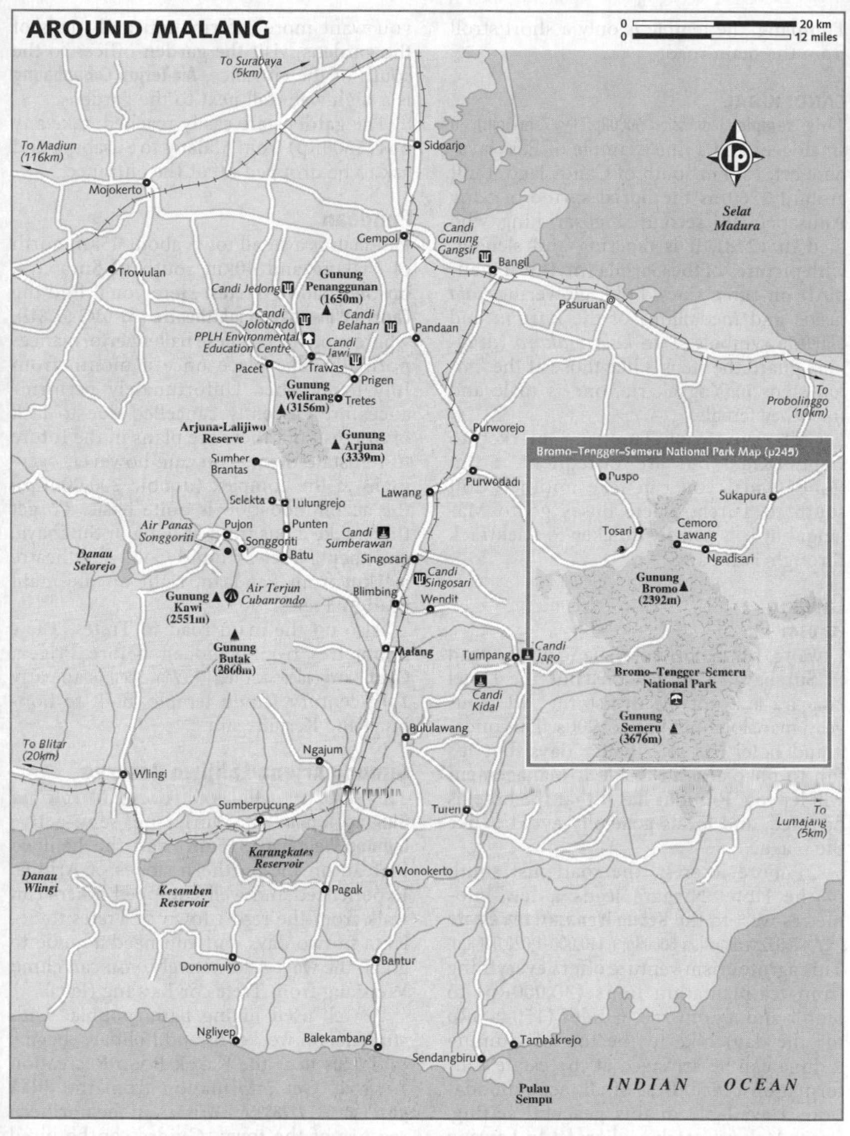

and a lingam, the symbol of Shiva's male potency.

To reach Candi Jago take a white *mikrolet* from Malang's Arjosari bus terminal to Tumpang (3000Rp). In Tumpang you can also visit the **Mangun Dhama Art Centre**, which is noted for its dance classes; it also has gamelan, *wayang* and woodcarving courses. *Wayang kulit* and dance shows will be staged if pre-arranged; check with the tourist office (p232) and travel agencies (p232) in Malang for information on schedules and prices.

If coming from Singosari, go to Blimbing where the road to Tumpang branches off the highway, and then catch a *mikrolet*. In

Tumpang, the temple is only a short stroll from the main road.

CANDI KIDAL

This **temple** (admission 5000Rp; 7am-5pm), a small gem and a fine example of East Javanese art, is 7km south of Candi Jago. Built around 1260 as the burial shrine of King Anusapati (the second Singosari king, who died in 1248), it is tapering and slender, with pictures of the Garuda (mythical man-bird) on three sides, bold, glowering *kala* heads and medallions of the *haruna* and Garuda symbols. Two *kala makara* (dragons) guard the steps – like those at the *kraton* steps in Yogyakarta, one is male and the other female.

Colts run from Tumpang market to Candi Kidal but are infrequent. From Candi Kidal you can take another Colt south to Turen, where buses go to Malang, but it is usually quicker to backtrack through Tumpang.

Lawang

☎ 0341

Lawang, 18km north of Malang on the road to Surabaya, is forgettable, but the Hotel Niagara is a notable five-storey Art Nouveau mansion built in the 1900s. This once-grand hotel has seen better days, but it's fun to poke around inside if management will let you. Rumour has it that the hotel is haunted, and locals generally avoid it like the plague.

Of more interest, the road just south of the Hotel Niagara leads a few kilometres west to the **Kebun Wonasari tea estate** (☎ 426032; admission 6000Rp; r 110,000-1,020,000Rp). This agrotourism venture offers everything from tea-plantation tours (30,000Rp) to tennis and a mini zoo. Guides (150,000Rp for the day) hike to the top of Gunung Arjuna can be arranged at the estate's information office. Best of all, accommodation is available in this peaceful setting. From Malang, catch a *mikrolet* to Lawang (4000Rp) and then an *ojek* to Wonosari from there (10,000Rp).

Purwodadi

A few kilometres north of Lawang on the road to Surabaya, the **Kebun Raya Purwodadi** (admission 3700Rp, tours 6000Rp; 7am-4pm) are expansive dry-climate botanical gardens. If you want more information and maps of the gardens, visit the garden offices to the south of the entrance. **Air Terjun Cobanbaung** is a high waterfall next to the gardens.

The gardens are easily reached; take any bus (5500Rp) from Malang to Surabaya and ask to be dropped off at the entrance.

Pandaan

Pandaan is a small town about 45km north of Malang and 40km south of Surabaya, on the road to Tretes. Here you'll find the **Candra Wilwatika Amphitheatre** (☎ 0343-631842), where modern Javanese ballet performances normally take place once a month from July to October. Unfortunately performances are currently cancelled due to lack of interest, but there are plans in the future to reinstate them. You can, however, overnight at the complex (double 200,000Rp); the accommodation is quite basic. To get there, take a bus from Malang or Surabaya, and then a Tretes-bound Colt. The theatre is 1km from Pandaan, right on the main road to Tretes.

Also on the main road to Tretes, a few kilometres from Pandaan before Prigen, **Candi Jawi** (admission free; 7am-5pm) is an early 14th-century Hindu temple, built to honour King Kertanegara.

Gunung Arjuna-Lalijiwo Reserve

This reserve includes the dormant volcano **Gunung Arjuna** (3339m), the semi-active **Gunung Welirang** (3156m) and the Lalijiwo Plateau on the northern slopes of Arjuna. Experienced and well-equipped hikers can walk from the resort town of Tretes to Selekta in two days, but you need a guide to go all the way. Alternatively, you can climb Welirang from Tretes or Lawang (left).

A well-used hiking path, popular with students on weekends and holidays, begins in Tretes near the Kakak Bodo Recreation Reserve. Get information from the **PHKA post** (☎ 081 21788956; Jl Wilis 523) in the northern reaches of the town. Guides can be hired here for 300,000Rp per day; allow two days to climb one mountain and three days for both.

It's a hard five-hour, 17km walk to the very basic huts used by the Gunung Welirang sulphur collectors. It is usual to stay overnight at the huts in order to reach the summit before the clouds and mist roll in around mid-morning. Bring your own camping gear, food and drinking water (or hire it all at the PHKA post for 100,000Rp per day), and be prepared for freezing conditions. From the huts it's a 4km climb to the summit. Allow at least six hours in total for the ascent, and 4½ hours for the descent.

The trail passes Lalijiwo Plateau, a superb alpine meadow, from where a trail leads to Gunung Arjuna, the more demanding peak. From Arjuna a trail leads down the southern side to Junggo, near Selekta and Batu. It's a five-hour descent from Arjuna this way; a guide is essential.

GETTING THERE & AWAY

To get to the start of the hike, take a bus to Pandaan (7500Rp) from Malang or Surabaya and then a minibus to Tretes (7000Rp).

Gunung Penanggungan

The remains of no less than 81 temples are scattered over the slopes of Gunung Penanggungan (1650m), a sacred Hindu mountain said to be the peak of Mt Mahameru, which broke off and landed at its present site when Mt Mahameru was transported from India to Indonesia.

This was an important pilgrimage site for Hindus. Pilgrims made their way to the top of the mountain and stopped to bathe in the holy springs adorned with Hindu statuary. The two main bathing places are **Candi Jolotundo** and **Candi Belahan**, the best examples of remaining Hindu art. Both are difficult to reach.

our pick In a stunning, unspoilt setting on the western slopes of Penanggungan, **PPLH Environmental Education Centre** (☎ 0321-7221045; www.pplh.org; dm 20,000Rp, bungalows 220,000Rp) is the perfect place to take a break from the intensity of travel in Java. It mainly caters to groups, but its hiking packages (guides 80,000Rp) and herbal medicine and ecology courses are also open to individuals. It has a good organic restaurant and fine accommodation in pretty bungalows or more-basic dorms. During the week you'll generally have the place to yourself, aside from the occasional school group passing through. To get there, take a Trawas-bound bemo (7000Rp) from Pandaan and an *ojek* (10,000Rp) from Trawas.

Batu

☎ 0341

Batu, 15km northwest of Malang, is a featureless sprawl on the lower reaches of Gunung Arjuna, but it has superb mountain scenery, a cool climate and a scattering of nearby attractions. It recently hit international headlines when Azahari Husin, a Malaysian bomb maker linked with Jemaah Islamiah and wanted in connection with the Bali bombings, was cornered in his home and killed.

SIGHTS

Without leaving the confines of the town, the only sight is the **apple and strawberry orchard** surrounding the Kusuma Agrowisata hotel (p240). **Tours** (15,000Rp per orchard; 🕒 7am-5pm) are offered and the price includes a generous two apples *or* three strawberries, and entry to the nearby mini zoo.

Songgoriti, 3km west of Batu, has well-known **hot springs** (admission 7500Rp; 🕒 7.30am-5pm) and a small ancient Hindu temple in the grounds of the Hotel Air Panas Songgoriti. Nearby, Pasar Wisata is a tourist market selling mostly apples, bonsai plants, and stone mortars and pestles. The waterfall **Air Terjun Cubanrondo** (admission 10,000Rp; 🕒 7.30am-5pm) is 5km southwest of Songgoriti.

Selekta, a small resort 5km further up the mountain from Batu and 1km off the main road, is home to the **Pemandian Selekta**, a large swimming pool with a superb setting in landscaped gardens (admission 12,500Rp; 🕒 7.30am-5pm).

Higher up the mountain, the small village of **Sumber Brantas**, far above Selekta, is at the source of Sungai Brantas. From here you can walk 2km to **Air Panas Cangar** (admission 5000Rp; 🕒 7.30am-5pm), a hot springs high in the mountains surrounded by forest and mist.

SLEEPING

Accommodation is available in Batu, Songgoriti and all along the road to Selekta at Punten and at Tulungrejo, where the road to Selekta turns off. Songgoriti and Selekta are small, quiet resorts, though Selekta is more elevated with better views. Batu has better facilities and makes a good base. You'll find most hotels scattered along Jl Panglima Sudirman, the main road to Kediri running west from the town centre.

Add around 25% to the prices listed here for weekend rates.

Hotel Baru (☎ 591775; Jl Agus Salim 27; d 50,000-80,000Rp) A pleasant guesthouse slap-bang in the middle of what little action Batu has, Baru has friendly owners and surprisingly spotless rooms; the bigger they are the more expensive they are.

Mutiara Baru (☎ 511259; Jl Panglima Sudirman 89; d from 60,000Rp;) The newly renovated Mutiara Baru has simple but very good rooms and a quiet garden with a children's playground out the back.

Hotel Selekta (☎ 591025; r from 265,000Rp;) Near the Pemandian Selekta, Hotel Selekta is a midrange option with a quiet setting and views of the valley below.

Royal Orchids Hotel (☎ 593083; www.royalorchidsgarden.com; Jl Indragiri 4; r from 299,000Rp, condominiums from 750,000Rp;) This plush hotel is newer than the nearby Kartika Wijaya and has a lovely resort feel. The collection of old-timer cars in the reception and parking lot only add to the ambience.

Kusuma Agrowisata (☎ 593333; www.hotelkusumaagro.com; Jl Abdul Gani Atas; weekday/weekend r from 375,000/510,000Rp;) This sprawling place 3km south of the town centre has well-presented rooms in a quiet location. Cottages are also available and tours of the attached apple orchard and strawberry farm are thrown in for free.

Hotel Kartika Wijaya (☎ 592600; Jl Panglima Sudirman 127; r from 405,000Rp;) Kartika Wijaya is an upmarket hotel with a delightful colonial lobby, fitness centre and landscaped gardens. The rooms are styled after different regions in Indonesia, and the reception features a huge stained-glass window of Java. Fork out a little more for the cottages at the back; the hotel is on a busy road.

EATING

Jl Panglima Sudirman in Batu also has plenty of restaurants.

Rumah Makan Cairo (Jl Panglima Sudirman 60; mains 10,000-30,000Rp; lunch & dinner) This simple eatery has *martabak* (meat, egg and vegetable pancake-like dish) and Middle-Eastern inspired fare.

Pantara Café (Jl Panglima Sudirman 123; mains around 15,000Rp; lunch & dinner) Pantara is an atmospheric, traditional-style eatery, serving local dishes in bamboo surroundings.

Both Hotel Kartika Wijaya and Mutiara Baru have decent restaurants.

GETTING THERE & AWAY

From Malang's Landungsari bus terminal take a Kediri bus or one of the frequent pink *mikrolet* to Batu (2500Rp, 30 minutes). Batu's bus terminal is 2km from the centre of town – take another *mikrolet* (1000Rp) from the bus terminal.

From the bus terminal, orange *mikrolet* run through town to Selekta (2000Rp, 30 minutes) and Sumber Brantas (3000Rp, one hour), but they often linger for a full complement of passengers. *Mikrolet* turn off to Sumber Brantas at Jurangkuwali village. For Air Panas Cangar, walk 2km straight ahead from Jurangkuwali.

An *ojek* to Selekta costs 10,000Rp.

Gunung Kawi

On Gunung Kawi (2551m), west of Malang and 18km northwest of Kepanjen, is the tomb of the Muslim sage Kanjeng Penembahan Djoego, who died in 1871. Descended from Pakubuwono I, king of the Mataram empire, the sage is better known as Mbah Jugo.

From the parking area, a long path leads up the slope past shops, souvenir stalls and beggars. Before the tombs at the top, there is a Chinese temple and the house of Mbah Jugo, which attracts non-Muslim Chinese worshippers from as far away as Jakarta. Legend has it that the saint will answer the prayers of fortune-seeking pilgrims. Apparently he did so for one Chinese couple, who went on to form one of Indonesia's biggest *kretek* companies.

This strange cross-religious mountain resort can be experienced on a day trip, or there are plenty of basic *penginapan* and restaurants if you want to stay the night. Gunung Kawi can be reached by taking a bus to Kepanjen (7000Rp), 3km east of the turn-off, and then a Colt (7000Rp) for the final 19km.

South-Coast Beaches

The coast south of Malang has some good beaches, but facilities are limited. **Sendangbiru** is a picturesque fishing village separated by a narrow channel from **Pulau Sempu**, a nature reserve with the **Telaga Lele** and **Telaga Sat** lakes in the centre, ringed by jungle. Boats can be hired (150,000Rp per person) for the 800m crossing. Take your own provisions.

A few kilometres before Sendangbiru, a rough track to the left leads 3km to **Tambakrejo**, a small fishing village with a sweeping sandy bay, which despite the surf is generally safe for swimming.

Balekambang is best known for its picturesque Hindu temple on the small island of Pulau Ismoyo, connected by a footbridge to the beach. This is Java's answer to Bali's Tanah Lot and was built by Balinese artisans in 1985 for the local Hindu communities. Balekambang is one of the most popular beaches and is crowded on weekends. Accommodation in the village is limited to the very basic Pesanggrahan Balekambang.

Ngliyep, further west, is a popular rocky beach. It has a *pasanggrahan* (guesthouse) offering basic accommodation.

GETTING THERE & AWAY

Minibuses from Malang's Gadang bus terminal travel the 69km to Sendangbiru (12,000Rp, two hours), past the turn-off to Tambakrejo; otherwise take a bus to Turen and then another to Sendangbiru. For Balekambang, buses run direct from Malang along the upgraded road for 7000Rp. The road to Ngliyep is also good, and occasional white minibuses run direct; otherwise first take a bus to Bantur.

BLITAR

☎ 0342 / pop 125,000

Blitar is the usual base from which to visit Panataran, and is also of interest as the site of former president Soekarno's grave.

Information

The post office is next to the train station. Both the **BNI bank** (Bank Negara Indonesia; Jl Kenanga 9) and **BCA bank** (Bank Central Asia; Jl Merdeka) are in the centre of town. **Telkom** (Jl A Yani 10) is the place to go for international telephone calls; it's on the continuation of Jl Merdeka, about 1km east of the Hotel Lestari. **Warnet** (Jl Mastrip 34; per hr 4500Rp; 🕑 9am-7pm Mon-Sat) has internet access and is behind the main street.

Sights

MAKAM BUNG KARNO

At Sentul, 2km north of the town centre on the road to Panataran, there is an elaborate **monument** (admission 1500Rp; 🕑 8am-5pm) that marks the spot where former president Soekarno was buried in 1970. Soekarno is looked on by many as the 'father of his country', although he was only reinstated as a national hero in 1978.

Soekarno, affectionately referred to as Bung Karno, was given a state funeral, but despite family requests that he be buried at his home in Bogor, he was buried as far as possible from Jakarta in an unmarked grave next to his mother in Blitar. His father's grave was also moved from Jakarta to Blitar. It was only in 1978 that the lavish million-dollar monument was built over the grave and opened to visitors. At the southern edge of the monument a new museum devoted to the man and his achievements has been built; entry is included in the admission price.

A becak from the town centre will cost anything between 5000Rp and 10,000Rp depending on your bargaining skills; otherwise take a Panataran *angkudes* (yellow minibus; 2000Rp) and ask for the *makam* (grave). Bemos turn off before the souvenir stalls, from where it is a walk of a few hundred metres.

OTHER SIGHTS

For a more personal look into the life of Soekarno, head for the **Museum Soekarno** (Jl Sultan Agung 59; admission 5000Rp; 🕑 8am-3pm), located in the house where he lived as a boy. Photos and memorabilia line the front sitting room, and you can see the great man's bedroom and check out the old Mercedes in the garage, a former state car. The museum is about 1.5km from the centre of town.

Blitar's large **Pasar Legi**, next to the bus terminal, is also worth a gander.

Sleeping & Eating

Hotel Sri Rejeki (☎ 801718; Jl TGP 13; r with/without mandi from 35,000/25,000Rp, with air-con from 65,000Rp; ❄) With a range of rooms and a central location, Sri Rejeki should have something to suit everyone's taste.

Hotel Tugu Blitar (☎ 801766; blitar@tuguhotels.com; Jl Merdeka 173; r 80,000-390,000Rp; ❄) Located right in the centre of town, this fine boutique hotel has quite bland economy rooms but superb superior doubles, decked out with antiques, in the old colonial-era building. It also has an excellent restaurant.

Blitar has some good restaurants on Jl Merdeka:

Ramayana (Jl Merdeka 65; mains around 15,000Rp; lunch & dinner) Large Chinese establishment east of the *alun-alun*.

Rumah Makan Sarinah (Jl Merdeka; mains 10,000Rp; lunch & dinner) Has varied fare and does good *sop buntut* (oxtail soup) and *ayam goreng*.

Getting There & Away

Regular buses run from Blitar to Malang (9000Rp, two hours) and Surabaya (20,000Rp, four hours), as well as Solo (30,000Rp, six hours). The bus terminal is 4km south of town along Jl Veteran (2000Rp by *angkot* from the centre). *Angkudes* run from the western end of Jl Merdeka, by the Rumah Makan Sarinah, to Panataran for 5000Rp – they stop right outside the temple. They also pass near Makam Bung Karno, but the road in front of the grave is closed and they skirt around the side streets to the east.

The easiest way to reach Malang is by train. The express economy-class *Penataran* departs for Malang (4500Rp, 1½ hours) and Surabaya (6000Rp, 3½ hours) at 4.40am, 6.35am, 10.10am, 1.10pm and 4.37pm. The *Matar Maja* runs east from Malang, through Blitar, to Solo, Semarang, Cirebon and Jakarta (45,000Rp).

PANATARAN

The **Hindu temples** (admission by donation; temple complex 7am-5pm) at Panataran are the largest intact Majapahit temples, and the finest examples of East Javanese architecture and sculpture. Construction began in around 1200, during the Singosari dynasty, but the temple complex took some 250 years to complete. Most of the important surviving structures date from the great years of the Majapahit empire during the 14th century and are similar to many Balinese temples.

Around the base of the first-level platform, which would once have been a meeting place, the comic-strip carvings tell the story of a test between the fat, meat-eating Bubukshah and the thin, vegetarian Gagang Aking.

Further on is the small Dated Temple, so called because of the date '1291' (AD 1369) carved over the entrance. On the next level are colossal serpents snaking endlessly around the Naga Temple, which once housed valuable sacred objects.

At the rear stands the Mother Temple – or at least part of it, for the top of the temple has been reconstructed alongside its three-tiered base. Followed anticlockwise, panels around the base depict stories from the Ramayana. The more realistic people of the Krishna stories on the second tier of the base show an interesting transition from almost flat to three-dimensional figures.

Behind is a small royal *mandi* with a frieze depicting lizards, bulls and dragons around its walls.

Three hundred metres beyond the turn-off to the temples is the **Museum Panataran**. It contains an impressive collection of statuary from the complex, but labelling is poor and opening hours are haphazard.

Getting There & Away

Panataran is 16km from Blitar (5000Rp by bus), and 3km north of the village of Nglegok. It is possible to see the Panataran temples comfortably in a day from Malang – and possibly from Surabaya also.

PACITAN

☎ 0357

On the south coast near the provincial border with Central Java, the small town of Pacitan is on a horseshoe bay ringed by rocky cliffs. Pacitan's **Pantai Ria Teleng** is 4km from town and makes a good beach break from Solo. The sand is a dark yellow and the surf is rough, but it is very peaceful, and the coastline is scenic. Swimming is possible when the seas are calm – the safest area is towards the fishing boats at the southwestern end of the bay, where there is also a swimming pool.

Information

BNI bank (Bank Negara Indonesia; Jl A Yani) On the main street; changes cash for a number of currencies, at poor rates.

BRI bank (Bank Rakyat Indonesia; Jl A Yani) Also on the main street.

Telkom office (Jl A Yani) Located at the western end of the main street.

Tourist Information Office (☎ 885326; Jl W R Suprapmanto; 7am-3pm Mon-Thu, 7-11am Fri) Helpful; 2km from the Hotel Pacitan.

Wartel Next to the Hotel Remaja.

Sleeping & Eating

The beach is the main reason to visit, so there is not a lot of reason to stay in town. If you're stuck, though, there are budget hotels in Pacitan are along Jl A Yani. The best place to stay is 4km out of town at Pantai Ria Teleng.

Happy Bay Beach Bungalows (☎ 881474; r 55,000Rp, private bungalows 65,000Rp) Happy Bay has comfortable accommodation and is directly opposite the beach. There are also bicycles (10,000Rp) and motorbikes (50,000Rp) available for rent and a restaurant that may or may not be open.

Srikandi (☎ 881252; Jl A Yani 67; r with TV & fan/air-con 85,000/120,000Rp; ❄) Overlooking rice paddies on the western edge of the town is Srikandi, the area's best place to stay. Staff are more than helpful and the hotel's restaurant serves cheap Indonesian dishes and fresh fish.

Depot Makan Bu Jabar (Jl H Samanhudi 3; mains around 15,000Rp; 🕐 lunch & dinner) This simple eatery is a block behind the police station on Jl A Yani; it's the next best dining option to Srikandi's restaurant.

Getting There & Away

Pacitan can be approached by bus from Solo (15,000Rp, four hours), or hourly buses run along the scenic road to Ponorogo (9000Rp, 2½ hours), just south of Madiun. From Ponorogo, direct buses go to Blitar (15,000Rp, four hours) throughout the day. From Blitar to Malang take a Colt or bus.

Pacitan's bus terminal is 500m from the centre of town on the road to Solo and the beach. Buses from Solo pass the turn-off to the beach and can drop you there. Happy Bay is a 500m walk away; a becak from the terminal costs 7000Rp.

AROUND PACITAN

At Punung village, on the Solo road 30km northwest of Pacitan, is the turn-off to the limestone caves of **Goa Putri**, 2km away, and the much more impressive **Gua Gong**, 8km from the highway. Only open to the public since 1995, Gua Gong is the largest and most spectacular cave in an area famed for its caves.

The more famous **Gua Tabuhan** (Musical Cave) is 4km north on the highway beyond Punung, and then another 4km to the cave. This huge limestone cavern is said to have been a refuge for the 19th-century guerrilla leader Prince Diponegoro. Guides will give an excellent 'orchestral' performance by striking rocks against stalactites, each in perfect pitch, and echoing pure gamelan melodies. The concert lasts about 10 minutes. You must hire a guide and lamp.

This is also agate country, and hawkers sell reasonably priced polished stones and rings.

PROBOLINGGO

☎ 0335 / pop 180,000

Among Indonesians and fruit lovers, Probolinggo is best known as the producer of Java's finest mangoes (it also receives kudos for its grapes). For most tourists, however, the town is little more than a transit point on the route to Gunung Bromo.

Information

The main post office and most of the banks, including the BCA and BNI, are on Jl Suroyo, which leads off the main street to the train station.

Sleeping & Eating

Hotel Bromo Permai (☎ 422256; Jl Panglima Sudirman 327; r 65,000Rp, with air-con from 95,000Rp; ❄) This is the town's most popular travellers hotel, and has comfortable rooms and a very helpful, English-speaking owner. It's on the busy main road close to the centre of town at the eastern end, but rooms at the back are quiet. It also has a wartel.

Hotel Paramita (☎ 421535; Jl Siaman 7; r with fan/air-con from 75,000/140,000Rp; ❄) Paramita is handy to the town's main street and is so new the finishing touches were being added when we visited. Rooms – which are spotless and sizable, but a little plain – are centred on a landscaped garden.

Hotel Ratna (☎ 421597; Jl Panglima Sudirman 16; economy r with/without fan 90,000/50,000Rp, VIP from 150,000Rp plus 10% tax; ❄) Two kilometres further west of the Bromo Permai you'll find Ratna, the best hotel in town. The building has plenty of (fake) colonial charm and the rooms are spacious and come with balcony.

Most of the hotels have restaurants and there are also some good Chinese eateries in Probolinggo.

Restaurant Malang (Jl Panglima Sudirman 104; mains around 15,000Rp; 🕐 lunch & dinner) Has a big menu, cold beer and stacks of mangoes.

PROBOLINGGO PROBLEMS

Of all the bus terminals in Java, Probolinggo's has the worst reputation. It's by no means dangerous, just not very honest. Travellers have reported problems with arranging onward tickets, particularly at night, when overcharging is the norm. Even what looks like a reputable ticket agent may charge double or even triple the standard price. The best thing to do is find the bus you need and pay the fare on board; at least you'll have a chance to compare prices with other passengers. Also, when travelling to Probolinggo, make it clear to the ticket collector you want to be dropped off at the Bayuangga bus terminal; we've received letters from travellers complaining of being left at random travel agents and charged exorbitant fares for bus tickets.

Thieves are common on the buses in East Java, especially on buses departing from Probolinggo.

Sumberhidup (Jl Panglima Sudirman; mains around 15,000Rp; lunch & dinner) Near Restaurant Malang; cooks up Chinese and Indonesian fare.

Getting There & Away

BUS

Probolinggo's Bayuangga bus terminal is about 5km from town on the road to Gunung Bromo. Yellow *angkot* run to/from the main street and the train station for 2000Rp. Buses to destinations in East Java (eg Banyuwangi and Surabaya) are frequent, so avoid the crowds of touts and just pay for your fare on the bus. Advance bookings for the long-distance executive buses will cost a little more – shop around.

From Probolinggo, buses travel to destinations such as Surabaya (15,000Rp, two hours); Malang (economy/air-con 15,000/30000Rp, 2½ hours); Banyuwangi (35,000/50,000Rp, five hours) via Situbondo; Bondowoso (15,000/30,000Rp); Yogyakarta (45,000/80,000Rp, eight hours); and Denpasar (55,000/120,000Rp).

MINIBUS

Gunung Bromo Colt minibuses from Probolinggo's Bayuangga bus terminal go to Cemoro Lawang (15,000Rp, two hours) via Ngadisari (12,000Rp, 1½ hours) until around 5pm, sometimes later during peak tourist periods if there is demand. The late-afternoon buses charge more to Cemoro Lawang, when fewer passengers travel beyond Ngadisari. Make sure it goes all the way to Cemoro Lawang when you board.

TRAIN

About 2km north of town, the train station is 7km from the bus terminal. Probolinggo is on the Surabaya–Banyuwangi train line. Most services are economy class. The *Mutiara Timur* costs 40,000/55,000Rp (business/executive) to Surabaya (departing at 1.25pm) or Banyuwangi (departing at 11am). The pick of the economy-class services is the *Tawang Alun* to Banyuwangi (19,000Rp) at 3.45pm and to Malang (18,000Rp) at 11am. The slow *Sri Tanjung* goes to Yogyakarta (32,000Rp) via Solo at 10.50am.

GUNUNG BROMO & BROMO-TENGGER-SEMERU NATIONAL PARK

☎ 0335

Gunung Bromo is nature's Borobudur; it's a landscape that's as evocative and resonant as any in Southeast Asia, and is the raw material for countless legends and as many picture postcards.

Compared with Java's other major peaks, Gunung Bromo (2392m) is a midget, but this volcano's beauty is in its setting, not its size. Rising from the guts of the ancient Tengger caldera, Bromo is one of three volcanoes to have emerged from a vast crater, stretching 10km across. Flanked by the peaks of Kursi (2581m) and Batok (2440m), the steaming cone of Bromo stands in a sea of ashen, volcanic sand, surrounded by the towering cliffs of the crater's edge. Nearby, Gunung Semeru (3676m), Java's highest peak and one of its most active volcanoes, throws its shadow – and occasionally its ash – over the whole scene.

Orientation & Information

Access is usually via Probolinggo from the northeast, but Bromo can be approached from a number of routes, including Wonokitri from the northwest and Ngadas from the southwest. The ideal time to visit is during the dry season from April to October. At any time of year it's cold on these mountains and night temperatures can drop to single figures.

Whichever approach you take, an entrance fee of 4000Rp is payable. Information is available from the **PHKA post** (☎ 541038; 🕑 8am-3pm Tue-Sun), opposite Hotel Bromo Permai in Cemoro Lawang, and at the **PHKA post** (☎ 0343-571048; 🕑 8am-3pm Tue-Sun) on the southern outskirts of Wonokitri. Both extend their opening hours during busy periods. The park's official office is located in Malang (p232).

Activities

PROBOLINGGO APPROACH

This is the easiest and most popular route. From Probolinggo, it's 28km to Sukapura, then another 7km to Ngadisari and then 3km to Cemoro Lawang. Minibuses ply the route all the way to Cemoro Lawang from Probolinggo.

As with mountain scaling anywhere in Asia, it is important to be at the top of Gunung Bromo for the impressive sunrise.

From Cemoro Lawang, it's 3km down the crater wall and across the Sand Sea (Laotian Pasir) to the slopes of Bromo, about a one-hour walk. Get up at 4.30am or even earlier for the flat stroll across the eerie sea. White stone markers are easy to follow during the day, but can be more elusive in the dark; alternatively, hire a jeep (300,000Rp) or horse (60,000Rp) from Cemoro Lawang. By the time you have crossed the lava plain from Cemoro Lawang and started to climb up the 253 steps to the top of Bromo, it should be fairly light and you'll get fantastic views of the smoking crater and of the sun clearing the higher peaks.

The colours are better at dawn, but visibility is usually good throughout the day in the dry season, even though the slopes below Cemoro Lawang may be covered in mist. Later in the day you'll also avoid the dawn crowds, especially during busy holiday periods. In the wet season the clouds and the dawn often arrive at the same time.

From Cemoro Lawang, it is also possible to visit **Gunung Penanjakan** (2770m), the

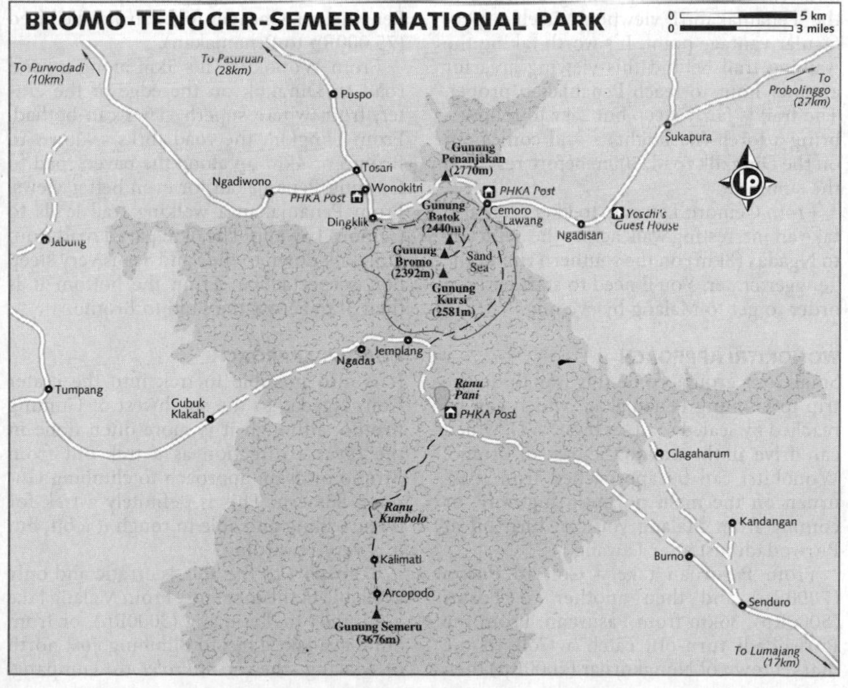

THE LEGENDS OF BROMO

Unsurprisingly, the eerie landscape of Bromo and its neighbouring volcanoes has spawned countless myths and legends. It is said that the Tengger crater was originally dug out with just half a coconut shell by an ogre smitten with love for a princess.

But Bromo is of particular religious significance to the Hindu Tengger people, who still populate the massif and first fled here to escape the wave of Islam that broke over the Majapahit empire in the 16th century. The Tengger believe that Bromo once fell within the realm of the childless King Joko Seger and Queen Roro Anteng, who asked the god of the volcano for assistance in producing an heir. The god obliged, giving them 25 children, but demanded that the youngest, a handsome boy named Dian Kusuma, be sacrificed to the flames in return. When the queen later refused to fulfil her promise, the young Dian bravely sacrificed himself to save the kingdom from retribution.

Today, the mountain is appeased during the annual Kasada festival (the park's PHKA offices can tell you when it occurs during the year), when local Tenggerese come to Bromo to throw offerings of vegetables, chickens and money into the crater of the volcano.

highest point on the outer crater. Hired jeeps (200,000Rp) go down to the Sand Sea and up to Penanjakan for the dawn, then return via Gunung Bromo. Penanjakan is where those picture-postcard shots are taken, with Bromo in the foreground and Semeru smoking in the distance. Alternatively, it is two hours on foot. Walk one hour (or charter a jeep) along the road to the 'Penanjakan II' viewpoint, itself a spectacular vantage point. It's worth taking the walking trail behind this viewing area for another hour to reach Penanjakan proper. The trail is fairly steep but easy to follow – bring a torch (flashlight) – and comes out on the Dingklik road, 500m before reaching the summit.

From Cemoro Lawang, trekkers can also take an interesting walk across the Sand Sea to Ngadas (8km) on the southern rim of the Tengger crater. You'll need to start early in order to get to Malang by evening.

WONOKITRI APPROACH

Small tour groups come this way to do the trip to Gunung Penanjakan, which can be reached by sealed road, or by a 4WD, which can drive all the way to the base of Bromo. Wonokitri can be approached from Pasuruan on the main northern highway, or coming from Malang you can turn off at Purwodadi just after Lawang.

From Pasuruan take a Colt to Puspo (7000Rp) and then another to Tosari (5000Rp), 36km from Pasuruan. From the Purwodadi turn-off, catch a Colt to the market town of Nongkojajar (7000Rp) then an *ojek* to Tosari (20,000Rp to 25,000Rp). Note that the latter route is not a common tourist trail, so you may have to hunt for an *ojek* to take you the last leg.

From Tosari market another *ojek* will take you to Wonokitri (10,000Rp), from where jeeps can be hired for the last stretch to Bromo (300,000Rp, less in the afternoon), including a side trip to Gunung Penanjakan. Cheaper *ojek* can also be hired (75,000Rp to Penanjakan).

From Wonokitri, it's 5km along a good road to Dingklik on the edge of the crater, from where superb views can be had. From Dingklik the road forks – down to Bromo or 4km up along the paved road to Gunung Penanjakan for even better views. From Penanjakan a walking trail leads to Cemoro Lawang. The 6km paved road from Dingklik down to the Sand Sea is very steep but is spectacular. From the bottom it is then 3km across the sand to Bromo.

NGADAS APPROACH

It is also possible to trek into the crater from Ngadas to the southwest of Gunung Bromo, although it is more often done in the reverse direction as a trek out from Bromo or as an approach to climbing Gunung Semeru. This is definitely a trek for those willing and able to rough it a bit, but it is very rewarding.

Transport to the area is erratic and only available in the morning. From Malang take a *mikrolet* to Tumpang (3000Rp), or from Surabaya take a bus to Blimbing, just north of Malang, then a *mikrolet* to Tumpang.

From here take another *mikrolet* to Gubug Klakah (3000Rp), from where you walk 12km to Ngadas. From Ngadas it is 2km to Jemplang at the crater rim, and then three hours on foot (12km) across the floor of the Tengger crater to Gunung Bromo and on to Cemoro Lawang. From Jemplang, you can also head south for the Gunung Semeru climb.

Jeeps can also be chartered in Tumpang or Ngadas for around 300,000Rp.

CLIMBING GUNUNG SEMERU

Part of the huge Tengger Massif, Gunung Semeru is the highest peak in Java, at 3676m. Also known as Mahameru (Great Mountain), it is looked on by Hindus as the most sacred mountain of all and the father of Gunung Agung on Bali.

Semeru is one of Java's most active peaks and has been volatile ever since its first recorded eruption in 1818. In 1981, 250 people were killed during one of its worst eruptions, and only recently, in March 2002, two huge pyroclastic flows travelled 2.5km down the mountainside to Besuk Kembar. At the time of writing the mountain was open to climbers, but this situation could change at any time; check with the local tourist office, other travellers or the nearest *pos pengamatan* (observation post) for Gunung Semeru's eruption status.

It's a rough three-day trek to the summit, and you must be well equipped and prepared for camping overnight. Nights on the mountain are freezing and inexperienced climbers have died of exposure. The best time to make the climb is May to October.

Hikers usually come through Tumpang in the west, from where you can charter jeeps to Ranu Pani (500,000Rp return), the start of the trek; otherwise take a Colt from Tumpang to Gubug Klakah and walk 12km to Ngadas, and then on to Jemplang. It is also possible to cross the Tengger Sand Sea from Gunung Bromo (12km) to Jemplang, 2km from Ngadas at the Tengger crater rim. From Jemplang, the road skirts around the crater rim before heading south to Ranu Pani (6km; 1½ hours on foot).

Ranu Pani is a lake with a small village nearby. Pak Tasrip runs a homestay costing 80,000Rp per person (meals are served). He can help organise a climb of Gunung Semeru, and he also rents out sleeping bags, which are essential. Ranu Pani is the usual overnight rest spot, and the Ranu Pani **PHKA post** (☎ 0341-787972 for office in Tumpang) is towards the lake. Register with the PHKA and obtain advice on the climb. It can also help arrange guides (from 200,000Rp for one day; 75,000Rp for porters), which are not essential but recommended unless there are a lot of other climbers.

The main trail begins behind the PHKA post. This new trail is lined with scrubby growth, but is an easier walk than the old trail, which is steeper. Both trails lead to Ranu Kumbolo crater lake (2400m), 13km or 3½ hours from Ranu Pani. From Ranu Kumbolo, which has a shelter, the trail climbs to Kalimati (three hours) at the foot of the mountain. From Kalimati it is a steep 1½-hour climb to Arcopodo, where there is a camp site for the second night on the mountain.

From Arcopodo, it is a short, steep climb to the start of the volcanic sands, and then a tough three-hour climb through loose scree to the peak. Semeru explodes every half-hour and these gases and belching lava make Semeru dangerous – stay away from the vent. On a clear day, there are breathtaking views of Java's north and south coasts, as well as views of Bali. To see the sunrise it is necessary to start at 2am for the summit. It is possible to make it back to Ranu Pani on the same day.

Sleeping & Eating

CEMORO LAWANG

Right on the lip of the Tengger crater and the start of the walk to Bromo, Cemoro Lawang is the most popular place to stay. Prices for everything, including accommodation, are inflated, but the views are stunning and the cool climate can come as quite a relief. You may be able to bargain a discount during quiet periods.

Cafe Lava Hostel (☎ 541020; r with shared bath 50,000Rp, with breakfast & hot shower 110,000Rp) This archetypal travellers hang-out has a laid-back air, gregarious English-speaking staff and a good backpacker buzz. Economy rooms are scuzzy and small, but the more expensive standard rooms are in quite good nick.

Cemara Indah Hotel (☎ 541019; old block r with/without mandi from 150,000/50,000Rp, with air-con, TV & hot water 250,000Rp;) This place teeters on the edge of the crater and has sublime views over Bromo. Rooms range from prison-block Spartan to comfortable. Discounts are available for YHA and ISIC cardholders.

Hotel Bromo Permai I (☎ 541021; bromopermai_hotel@yahoo.com; r 60,000Rp, with hot shower/TV 210,000/245,000Rp) Bromo Permai is the fanciest hotel in the village centre. Rooms are rather ho-hum, though, and luxury certainly doesn't come as standard.

Lava View Lodge (☎ 541009; globaladventure@indo.net.id; r from 150,000Rp, bungalows 250,000Rp) The upmarket cousin of the Cafe Lava Hostel is 500m along a side road through the parking/souvenir-stall area below Hotel Bromo Permai I. Views are superb and rooms are comfortable and the closest Cemoro Lawang has to plush. Add 75% to prices in peak season (mid-October to the beginning of January).

Guest House Rumah Tamu (☎ 541038; cottages 500,000Rp) This PHKA establishment located opposite Hotel Bromo Permai I has two cottages to rent that sleep four people. They're a bit rough around the edges, but each has two bedrooms, a sitting room and hot water.

All the hotels have restaurants, and there are a couple of warungs near the PHKA office.

Bromo Corner Cafe (mains around 20,000Rp; 🕒 lunch & dinner) Next to the information centre; serves nasi goreng and other favourites in pleasant surrounds.

Café Lava (mains around 20,000Rp; 🕒 breakfast, lunch & dinner) The cheeriest place around, with cold beer and friendly staff.

Cemara Indah (mains 20,000-40,000Rp; 🕒 breakfast, lunch & dinner) Has the best views.

NGADISARI

Yoschi's Guest House (☎ 0335-541018; yoschi_bromo@telkom.net; r with/wthout shower 150,000/75,000Rp, cottages with hot water from 300,000Rp plus 15% tax; 💻) With loads of character, Alpine kitsch décor, a fab restaurant and friendly staff, Yoschi's is a great option away from the crater. Rooms are a little small but very comfortable, and there's a peaceful garden to relax in. Tours and transport for the 3km to Bromo (50,000Rp person) are also offered.

SUKAPURA

Grand Bromo Hotel (☎ 031-7329945; r from 302,500Rp, cottages from 1,210,000Rp; 🏊) The resort-style Grand Bromo is a few kilometres up the mountain from Sukapura village and a full 9km from the crater. If you want luxury accommodation and have a car, this may be your best bet; otherwise it's too far from the crater to be convenient.

TOSARI & WONOKITRI

Bromo Cottages (☎ 0343-571222; r from 375,000Rp, cottages from 625,000Rp) Perched on the side of the hill in Tosari, Bromo Cottages has fine mountain views and a restaurant. Rooms and cottages are quite plush for the area, and transport and tours to Bromo are available.

It's also possible to stay with villagers in Wonokitri or at the **Surya Nata Homestay** (r from 100,000Rp). Ask around or arrange something through Wonokitri's PHKA office.

Getting There & Away

Most visitors come through Probolinggo. Hotels in Cemoro Lawang and Ngadisari can make bookings for expensive onward bus tickets from Probolinggo (15,000Rp by public bus) to Yogyakarta (125,000Rp to 140,000Rp) and Denpasar (125,000Rp to 140,000Rp).

Travel agencies in Solo and Yogyakarta book minibuses to Bromo for 100,000Rp to 150,000Rp. These are not luxury minibuses, and sometimes they run a bigger bus to Probolinggo and change there. Occasionally buses will stop short of Cemoro Lawang – specify this as your end destination when purchasing your ticket.

Tours to Bromo are easily organised in Malang, and you can also arrange jeep hire in hotels and travel agents there.

PASIR PUTIH

☎ 0338

On the north coast, roughly halfway between Probolinggo and Banyuwangi, Pasir Putih is one of East Java's most popular seaside resorts and is mobbed on the weekend by sun 'n' sand worshippers from Surabaya. While the beaches are OK, this strip of rickety warungs, souvenir stalls and *rumah makan* is run down, infested with sand flies and has few passable hotels.

The **Hotel Pasir Putih** (☎ 390022; r 55,000-175,000Rp) is in the heart of the 'action', but rooms are desperately dowdy; the more expensive variety come with hot water. If you are staying for a while, **San Sui Hotel** (☎ 675432; r from 155,000Rp; ❄ 🏊), 6km east of Pasir Putih's main drag, is a far more comfortable bet. It has some quiet stretches of sand nearby.

BONDOWOSO

☎ 0332

Bondowoso, 34km southwest of Situbondo, is one of the cleanest towns in Java – itself an attraction – and the home of some of the island's best *tape*, a tasty, sweet-and-sour snack made from boiled vegetable roots. Otherwise, it is merely a transit point for nearby attractions such as Ijen.

Hotel Anugerah (☎ 421870; Jl Sutoyo 12; r 75,000Rp, with TV/air-con 100,000/125,000Rp; ❄) Anugerah is a very friendly establishment with large, clean rooms in garish green. Staff can arrange transport to Ijen (300,000Rp return for up to two persons), but you're better off overnighting on the plateau.

Palm Hotel (☎ 421201; www.palm-hotel.net; Jl A Yani 32; r with mandi/air-con from 62,500/156,250Rp; ❄ 🏊) Near Hotel Anugerah, this is Bondowoso's best hotel, with spotless, newly renovated rooms and a lovely pool. It also has a good restaurant and can arrange transport to Ijen.

Both hotels have restaurants, but *tape* can be found on Jl PB Sudirman, where dozens of shops sell it by the basket (15,000Rp). The '321' brand is reportedly the best.

Buses from Bondowoso include Jember (5000Rp, 45 minutes), Probolinggo (9000Rp, two hours) and Surabaya (normal/air-con 25,000/40,0000Rp, five hours).

IJEN PLATEAU

Ijen Plateau, part of a reserve that stretches northeast to Baluran National Park, was at one time a huge active crater, 134 sq km in area. Today, it is a quiet but active volcano, and the landscape is dominated by the volcanic cones of Ijen (2368m) and Merapi (2800m) on the northeastern edge of the plateau, and Raung (3332m) on the southwestern corner. Coffee plantations cover much of the western area of the plateau (alongside lush forest), where there are a few settlements. The plateau has a number of difficult-to-reach natural attractions, but most visitors come for the hike to spectacular Kawah Ijen. There are few people in this unspoilt area, which is as much an attraction as the volcanoes themselves.

Sights & Activities

KAWAH IJEN HIKE

The magnificent turquoise sulphur lake of Kawah Ijen lies at 2148m above sea level and is surrounded by the volcano's sheer crater walls. Ijen's last major eruption was in 1936, though a minor ash eruption occurred in 1952. At the edge of the lake, smoke billows out from the volcano's vent and the lake bubbles when activity increases.

The vent is a source of sulphur, and collectors work here, making the trek up to the crater and down to the lake every day. The best time to make the Kawah Ijen hike is in the dry season between April and October. Sulphur collectors hike up in the morning and return around 1pm when the clouds roll in. Trekkers are advised to do the same, but the clouds often disappear in the late afternoon. Make it for sunrise if you can.

The starting point for the trek to the crater is the **PHKA post** (🕐 7am-5pm) at Pos Paltuding, which is usually reached from Bondowoso but can also be accessed from Banyuwangi. Sign in and pay your 20,000Rp entry fee here. The steep 3km path up to the observation post takes about 1½ hours; keep an eye out for gibbons. Just past the PHKA post, the road forks – to the left is the walk to the 'safety-valve' dam, built to regulate the flow of water into Banyu Pahit (Bitter River), but the main area of interest lies along the right fork, a 30-minute walk to the top of the crater and its stunning views.

From the crater, a steep gravely path leads down to the sulphur deposits and the steaming lake. The walk down takes about 20 minutes; the path is slippery in parts and the sulphur fumes towards the bottom can be overwhelming. Take great care – a French tourist fell and died some years ago.

Back at the lip of the crater, turn left for the climb to the crater's highest point (2368m) and magnificent views, or keep walking anticlockwise for even more expansive views of the lake. On the other side of the lake opposite the vent, the trail disappears into crumbling volcanic rock and deep ravines.

COFFEE PLANTATIONS

Java's finest coffee, both Arabica and Robusta varieties, is produced in the Ijen Plateau area, as well as cacao, cloves and rubber. It's possible to visit various coffee plantations, including **Kebun Kalisat** (admission 50,000Rp) and **Kebun Balawan** (admission free); visits will usually include a wander through coffee groves and an impromptu tour of the plantation's factory. The latter plantation has thermal pools and a gushing thermal waterfall (1000Rp) set among lush jungle and the incessant pulse of cicadas. Both plantations have accommodation (below).

Sleeping & Eating

Pos Paltuding (dm 50,000Rp, r 120,000Rp, Pesanggrahan cottage 350,000Rp) The PHKA post at the start of the Kawah Ijen hike has a bare but peaceful cottage with three comfortable rooms. There's no hot water and blankets are not provided, so bring a sleeping bag – it gets very cold at this altitude. The post also has an open-sided shelter for campers, and beds in its café.

Arabika Homestay (☎ 0868 12107424; r from 92,000Rp plus 10% tax) At Sempol, 13km before Pos Paltuding on the Bondowoso side, the Kebun Kalisat coffee plantation maintains this guesthouse, 1km from the main road. Service is friendly and the more expensive rooms are comfy and have attached bathrooms and hot water. Meals are served here.

Catimore Homestay (☎ 0868 12107942; r 100,000-200,000Rp) This quality homestay is on the Kebun Balawan coffee plantation some 6km from Sempol. Its basic rooms have a quiet atmosphere. Dinner is available and rooms come with attached bathroom and the all-important hot water. An *ojek* from Sempol costs 15,000Rp.

Jampit Villa (☎ 031-3524893, Jember 0331-486861; ptpn12@rad.net.id; 1,000,000Rp; 🅿) Kebun Kalisat coffee plantation is the proud owner of this luxurious villa, 14km south of Sempol at Jampit. The villa sleeps 20 and has a kitchen and a communal living room. Book through PT Perkubunan Nusantara XII (opposite).

Sempol village has a couple of warungs if you need a place to eat. Pos Paltuding has a small shop for provisions and a café serving little more than noodles.

Getting There & Away

It is possible to travel nearly all the way to Kawah Ijen by public transport, but most visitors charter transport.

FROM BONDOWOSO

From Wonosari, 8km from Bondowoso towards Situbondo, an upgraded road (with its fair share of potholes) runs via Sukosari and Sempol all the way to Pos Paltuding. Apart from a few rough stretches, it is a good paved road and takes about two hours by car. Sign in at the coffee plantation checkpoints (4000Rp) on the way. The Palm Hotel and Hotel Anugerah in Bondowoso (p249) can arrange day tours.

Minibuses run from Bondowoso to Sempol (20,000Rp, 2½ hours), but they only leave when full, and departure times are haphazard. You should be able to find someone in Sempol who will take you the 13km to Pos Paltuding on the back of their motorbike for around 50,000Rp one way. At Pos Paltuding, there are usually a few motorbikes to take you back.

FROM BANYUWANGI

Ijen is closer to Banyuwangi, but the road is very steep and has deteriorated badly. A 4WD is essential (500,000Rp per vehicle) and can be hired through the Banyuwangi Tourist Office (p263).

From Banyuwangi's Blambangan bemo station, take a Lin 3 bemo to Sasak Perot (2000Rp) on the eastern outskirts of town and then a Colt on to Jambu (7500Rp) at the turn-off to Kawah Ijen, a further 17km away. Start at 5.30am to reach the crater in time for good views. From Jambu, *ojek* can take you 9km along the paved road to Sodong through the clove and coffee plantations for 50,000Rp. Beyond Sodong it is a hair-raisingly steep ride and *ojek* are not always keen to do it.

Sodong used to be where the sulphur collectors would bring their loads to be taken by truck to Banyuwangi. It has now been abandoned and the washed-out road is a very steep, rock-strewn track for about 4km, though the last stretch is better.

The 8km from Sodong to Pos Paltuding winds its way through dense rainforest with towering ferns and palms. It's possible to attack this on foot, but expect a tough three-hour battle uphill; most people travel by jeep. Halfway up, the PHKA Pos Totogan, which is at the edge of the reserve, is not always staffed.

Only 4WD vehicles and motorcycles can make it up, but cars and minibuses can go down from Pos Paltuding to Banyuwangi. It's a slow, bumpy ride in first gear with brakes on all the way.

JEMBER

☎ 0331

Jember is the thriving service centre for the surrounding coffee, cacao, rubber, cotton and tobacco plantations. It has all the amenities of a large city, but is relatively free of traffic and competes with Bondowoso for the tidy town award.

From Jember groups can arrange a plantation tour, though Kalibaru is the usual centre for plantation visits. **PT Perkubunan Nusantara XII** (☎ 486861; Jl GaJah Mada 249) is the state-owned company that controls most of the plantations – it offers day or overnight tours with accommodation on the plantations (including Jampit Villa, opposite). It is also home to the **Meru Betiri National Park Office** (☎ 335535; www.merubetiri.or.id; Jl Sriwidjaya 53; 7.30am-3pm Mon-Fri), which has background and accommodation information on the park.

If you need a place to stay overnight, **Hotel Sulawesi** (☎ 333555; Jl Let Jenderal Suprapto 48; r from 175,000Rp;), about 1km from the town centre, is spotlessly clean, with well-equipped rooms.

Getting There & Away

The main terminal, Tawung Alun, 6km west of town, has buses to Bondowoso (7000Rp, 45 minutes), Banyuwangi (15,000Rp, three hours) and Kalibaru (7000Rp, one hour), but buses from Bondowoso usually terminate at the subterminal, 5km north of town; there are also subterminals to the east (for Banyuwangi) and south (for Watu Ulo). Yellow Lin bemo (2000Rp) run from the terminals to the centre of town.

Jember is also located on the Surabaya–Banyuwangi train line; the station is in the town centre.

WATU ULO & PAPUMA

☎ 0331

Watu Ulo is popular on weekends, but like most of the beaches on Java's south coast, it has grey sand, and crashing surf makes swimming dangerous. The real surprise lies just west around the headland from Watu Ulo at Papuma – a small beach with white sand, turquoise waters and sheltered swimming. **Hotel Vishnu** (☎ 481028; r from 45,000Rp) is a basic place in the heart of Watu Ulo.

To reach Watu Ulo, take a Jember city bemo (2000Rp) to the Ajung subterminal and then a taxi (the confusing name for a public minibus in these parts) to Ambulu

THE THREAT OF LANDSLIDES

Landslides are common occurrences that leave dozens dead and thousands homeless on an all-too-frequent basis.

It seems the steep slopes of Java are simply slip-sliding away every time the wet season – November to March – hits the island. In February 2006 alone, landslides swept through the village of Sijeruk in Central Java and Jember in East Java, claiming more than 150 lives. In recent years, Purworejo and Cilacap in Central Java and Cimahi in West Java all suffered at the hands of huge mud slides.

Unsurprisingly, environmentalists blame much of the problem on deforestation and illegal logging. But while stripping the land of its much-needed blanket of vegetation is just asking for trouble (and utterly short-sighted), it may not be the main cause of landslide disasters. Sijeruk's landslide occurred on a densely forested hill and most of the villagers affected in the Jember slide live on coffee plantations and along river banks, areas prone to flooding each year. The UN's Food and Agriculture Organization has even been so bold as to suggest that deforestation cannot be blamed for small-scale landslides and floods, but rather that the change in climatic patterns is the culprit.

Indonesia's government has made significant progress in halting the illegal trade in timber in recent years, but there is still plenty of work to do. In the near future, however, it seems likely that landslides will play a major role in far too many people's lives when the rains come.

(6000Rp, one hour). From Ambulu yellow bemos go to Watu Ulo (2000Rp, 30 minutes). Papuma is then a half-hour walk along the paved road over the steep headland, though bemos can drop you at the beach.

KALIBARU

☎ 0333

The picturesque road from Jember to Banyuwangi winds around the foothills of Gunung Raung (3322m) up to the small hill town of Kalibaru. It has a refreshing climate and makes a pleasant stop on this route.

The village itself is basically strung out along the main road and quite unremarkable, but it does have a remarkable array of excellent midrange accommodation for such a small town. This makes it a good base for visiting the nearby plantations around **Glenmore**, 10km east, or the smaller, easily visited plots of coffee and cloves to the north of Kalibaru's train station.

The area has many plantations but the main plantation of interest is **Kebun Kandeng Lembu** (admission 20,000Rp; 9am-noon Mon-Thu & Sat, 8.30am-noon Fri), 5km south of Glenmore. Guides can be hired (70,000Rp) for groups to see rubber tapping and processing, as well as cacao and coffee plantations.

Tours

Margo Utomo (right) This resort has plantation tours for 375,000Rp for two people. It also organises transport and group tours to Kawah Ijen (750,000Rp for one to four people), Alas Purwo (735,000Rp for one to five people) and Sukamade (1,100,000Rp for one or two people including accommodation and food).

Kalibaru train station (☎ 897322) Small diesel lorries can be taken from the train station through 35km of impressive mountain countryside (500,000Rp for eight people).

Sleeping & Eating

Kalibaru Cottages (☎ 897333; r with breakfast 165,000Rp;) Four kilometres west of town on the Jember road is yet another of Kalibaru's excellent midrange hotels. It's larger than its competition but still retains a peaceful resort atmosphere. The central pool, surrounded by palm trees, is inviting any time of the night or day and rooms are more than spacious, with comfy beds and pleasant, open-air bathrooms. There's also a restaurant attached.

our pick **Margo Utomo Resort** (☎ 897700; Jl Lapangan 10; r 200,000Rp;) This old Dutch inn, which now moonlights as a resort, is full of colonial style, and is one of the best places to stay in East Java. Its small bungalows are attractively arranged along a central walkway lined with tropical flowers leading to the resort's aqua-blue pool, all of which is backed by a coffee plantation (tours free for guests, 30,000Rp for nonguests). Its collection of tropical birds can be a little noisy at times and rooms are surprisingly mediocre, but the setting is hard to beat. Rates skyrocket from June to August, at which time it's advisable to book well ahead.

Margo Utomo Cottages (☎ 897420; margoutomo@hotmail.com; Jl Putri Gunung 3; r 200,000Rp;) Newer than Margo Utomo Homestay and without the same colonial atmosphere, Margo Utomo Cottages loses out in the charm stakes but makes up ground with a superb, restful setting down by the river, 3km east of town. It also has a restaurant.

Getting There & Away

Any bus between Jember (7000Rp, one hour) and Banyuwangi (10,000Rp, two hours) can drop you near the hotels. The train station is right near the Margo Utomo Homestay and Kalibaru is on the main Banyuwangi–Jember–Probolinggo–Surabaya train line.

MERU BETIRI NATIONAL PARK

The Meru Betiri National Park, covering 580 sq km between Jember and Banyuwangi districts, is an area of magnificent coastal rainforest and abundant wildlife, making it one of Java's finest parks. Its biggest drawback, however, is its difficult access, which keeps the number of visitors to a trickle.

Orientation & Information

Named after Gunung Betiri (1223m) in the north of the park, the coastal mountains trap the rain and the park is very wet for much of the year. Visit in the dry season from April to October – the road into the park fords a river, which easily floods. Even in the dry season you may have to wade across the river and walk into the park.

The park's office (p251) in Jember has plenty of information; entrance to the park costs 15,000Rp.

(Continued on page 261)

JEFF YATES

The shores of Danau Toba (p399), Sumatra

PETER PTSCHELINZEW

A ferry crosses Danau Toba (p399), Sumatra

Orang-utan in Bukit Lawang (p389), Sumatra

JEFF YATES

ALAIN E

Bustling Jakarta (p99) by night

JERRY ALEXANDER

Coffee store in Bandung (p136), Java

Three-wheeled *bajaj* (p118) in Jakarta

PAUL KE

DIMAS ADRIAN

Street art in Yogyakarta (p171), Java

Cycling around Gunung Bromo (p244), Java

CHRIS MELLOR

JERRY ALEXANDER

Houses near Gunung Bromo (p244), Java

Ijen Plateau (p249), Java

JANE SWEENEY

PAUL BEINSSEN

Beach sunset at Legian (p276), Bali

Seminyak nightlife (p291), Bali

PAUL BEINSSEN

Surfboards for hire on the beach at Kuta (p276), Bali

RICHARD I'A

BILL WASSMAN

Rice fields near Tampaksiring (p326), Bali

LEE FOSTER

Market in Ubud (p307), Bali

Waterfall near Lovina (p369)

JOHN BORTHWICK

Diving (p349), Bali

STEPHANE VICTOR

Rafting on Sungai Ayung (p314), Bali

Surfing at Pantai Nihiwatu (p601), Nusa Tenggara

PAUL KENNEDY

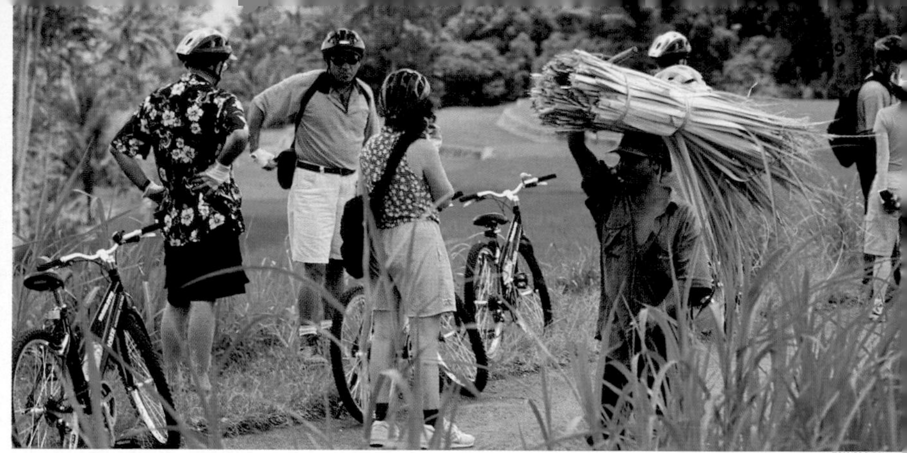

TOM COCKREM

Cycling past rice fields near Ubud (p307), Bali

Trekking on the Mentawai Islands (p437), Sumatra

JANE SWEENEY

LEE FOSTER

Batik workshop in Yogyakarta (p171), Java

Young craftsman painting ceramic pots in Banyumulek (p498), Lombok

RICHARD I'ANSON

Woman weaving on a traditional loom in Sukarara (p524), Lombok

RICHARD I

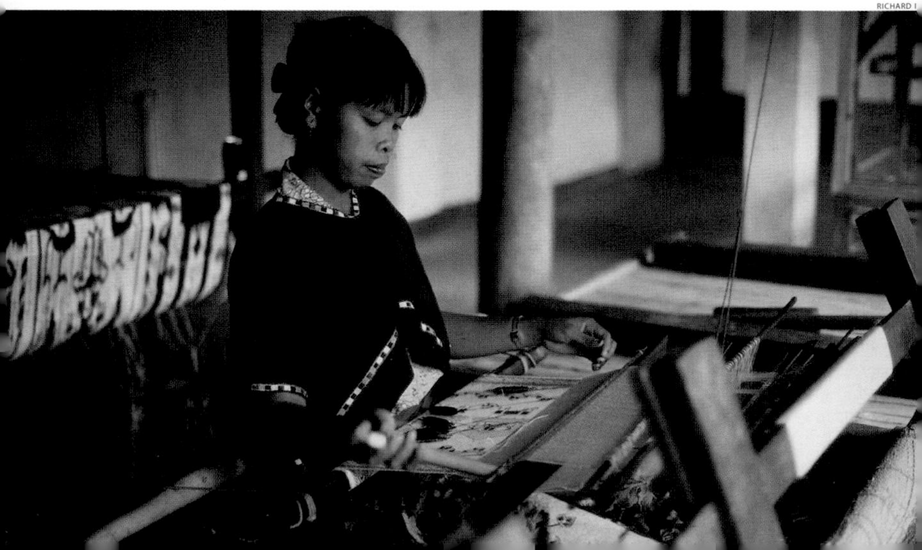

(Continued from page 252)

Sights & Activities

The park's major attraction is the protected turtle beach at **Sukamade**, one of Indonesia's most important turtle-spawning grounds, where five species of turtle come ashore to lay their eggs. Green turtles are most common, but giant leatherbacks also visit. Usually seen in the wet season from December to February, giant leatherbacks are affected by conditions in the Indian Ocean and sometimes arrive between February and July instead; Mess Pantai (below) arranges night trips.

Wildlife, found mostly in the mountain forests, includes leopard, wild pigs, deer, banteng, black giant squirrels, civets and pangolin. Bird life is prolific and hornbills, including the rhinoceros hornbill, whoosh and honk overhead. Meru Betiri is most famous as the last known home of the Javan tiger, and though they are now widely believed to be extinct, tracks have been recorded as recently as 1997.

Trails are limited in the park and a guide (50,000Rp), arranged through the park office or accommodation, is usually necessary. Apart from some coastal walks, a trail leads about 7km northwest of Sukamade to the **Sumbersari** grazing ground part of the way through rainforest and bamboo thicket.

Rajegwesi, at the entrance to the park, is on a large bay with a sweeping beach and a fishing village. Past the park entrance the road climbs, giving expansive views over spectacular **Teluk Hijau** (Green Bay), with its cliffs and white-sand beach. A trail leads 1km from the road down to Teluk Hijau, or it is about a one-hour walk east from Mess Pantai.

Sleeping

Mess Pantai (☎ 0331-335535; cottages with shared mandi per r 75,000Rp, entire cottage 300,000Rp, VIP r with fan 250,000Rp) Nestled in the forest back from Sukamade beach, Mess Pantai is the best place to stay when exploring the park. It has simple, four-bedroom cottages and a bigger, more comfy two-bedroom cottage. There's cooking facilities and the staff can provide meals (10,000Rp), but as a safe bet bring your own food – you can stock up in Sarongan, or the Sukamade estate in the nearby plantation has a shop selling basic supplies. If you have your own equipment, you can also camp on the beach (15,000Rp per tent).

Wisma Sukamade (☎ 0331-484711; r from 120,000Rp) Approximately 5km north of the beach, Sukamade plantation has much more comfortable accommodation with electricity and all the creature comforts. It has a variety of rooms and meals are provided. Though the accommodation is good, it's not as convenient unless you have your own transport or are on a tour.

Getting There & Away

This is one of the most isolated parts of Java, and it is a long bumpy trip, even by 4WD vehicle.

The most direct way to Sukamade from Banyuwangi or Jember is to first take a bus to Jajag (15,000Rp, 1½ hours), then a minibus to Pesanggaran (9000Rp, one hour). From Pesanggaran take a taxi (the local name for a public truck) to Sukamade (25,000Rp, two hours). The taxi leaves Pesanggaran at noon on the dot (a rarity in Java); to make it on time, you'll need to leave Jember around 6.30am.

The taxi passes through Sarongan, a small town where you can stock up on supplies. *Ojeks* to Sukamade (around 50,000Rp) can be arranged here, but generally only in the dry season; during the wet season the rivers are too high to cross. There are two river crossings: the deeper one further south and the shallower crossing further upstream. If the river is up but not flooded, you can wade across and get another *ojek* or walk the 4km to Mess Pantai. The taxi has no problem with swollen rivers unless there is severe flooding.

About 4km on from Sarongan you reach the Rajegwesi PHKA post at the entrance to the park; this is a good place to check on the condition of the river.

ALAS PURWO NATIONAL PARK

This 434.2-sq-km national park occupies the whole of the remote Blambangan Peninsula on the southeastern tip of Java. Facilities are limited and it is not easy to reach, but Alas Purwo has fine beaches, good opportunities for wildlife spotting, and savannah, mangrove and lowland monsoon forests. Apart from day-trippers and local beach parties on weekends, the park gets few visitors.

Alas Purwo means First Forest in Javanese – according to legend this is where the earth first emerged from the ocean. It is an important Hindu spiritual centre and **Pura Giri Selokah**, a temple in the park, attracts many pilgrims, especially during Pagerwesi, the Hindu new year.

More recently, the huge breaks – which stretch for 2km – at Plengkung, on the isolated southeastern tip of the peninsula, have made it famous among surfers who have dubbed it 'G-Land' (for Grajagan, another name for the area).

Orientation & Information

Surfers come by charter boat from Grajagan at the western end of the bay, but the usual park entry is by road via the village of Pasar Anyar, which has a large national park office and interpretive centre. Call in here to check on accommodation; alternatively check with the head office (opposite) in Banyuwangi.

The actual gateway to the park is at Rowobendo, 10km south along a bad road, where you need to pay your admission fee (20,000Rp). From Rowobendo the road runs past the temple before hitting the beach at Trianggulasi, 2km away. Trianggulasi has hut accommodation but nothing else.

Sights & Activities

This limestone peninsula is relatively flat and the rolling hills reach a peak of only 322m. Alas Purwo has plenty of lowland coastal forest but few trails to explore it – vast expanses of the eastern park are untrammelled, even by park staff.

Using Trianggulasi as a base, there are some interesting short walks. The white-sand beach here is beautiful, but swimming is usually dangerous.

It's common to see herds of wild banteng, *kijang* and peacocks in the early morning and late afternoon at the **Sadengan** grazing ground, which has a viewing tower. This beautiful meadow backed by forest is a 2km walk from Trianggulasi along a road and then a swampy trail.

Alas Purwo also has a small population of *ajag* (Asiatic wild dogs), jungle fowl, leaf monkeys, *muntjac* deer, sambar deer and leopards (mostly black panthers). The park guards can arrange interesting, although often fruitless, night leopard-spotting expeditions for around 100,000Rp.

Guards can also arrange a motorbike trip to the turtle hatchery at **Ngagelan**, or you can walk. It's 6km from Rowobendo along a rough road, or a 7km walk along the beach at low tide from Trianggulasi.

It is also possible to walk along the beach all the way to Plengkung via **Pancur**, 3km southeast of Trianggulasi, where there is a small waterfall that flows onto the beach, another PHKA post and a camping ground.

From Pancur a trail heads 2km inland through some good forest to **Gua Istana**, a small cave, and another 2km further on to **Gua Padepokan**.

From Pancur it is a further 11km walk (two hours) around Grajagan Bay to the fine beach at **Plengkung**, one of Asia's premier surfing spots. Between 1995 and 1998 the Quiksilver Pro surfing championship was held here every year around June as part of the Association of Surf Professionals World Championships. The surf camps at Plengkung are by no means five-star but do provide unexpected luxury in the wilderness.

Tours

The bigger and better surf camps, away from the beach at Plengkung, are for tours only. Accommodation costs around US$50 a day at all the camps, but everyone comes on a surfing package that includes all transfers, usually from Bali. Established tour operators include the following:

Bobby's Camp (bookings in Bali ☎ 0361-755588; www.grajagan.com) The biggest of them, this is run out of Bali and offers three-night packages from US$300.

G-Land Jungle Surf Camp (bookings in Bali ☎ 0361-777649; www.g-land.com) The other main operator. The elevated bungalows are comfortable and have most of the facilities a surfer could want; packages start at US$350 for three nights.

Sleeping & Eating

Pesanggrahan (☎ 0333-428675; s/d 50,000/75,000Rp) Close to the beach at Trianggulasi, this PHKA establishment has elevated bungalows. The rooms are Spartan, with only a bed. Water is from a well, and electricity is provided by a generator. Though primitive, this is a lovely, relaxing spot and many who come for a day or two end up staying longer.

Even though staff at Pesanggrahan *may* sell supplies and cook meals in the high season, it's best to bring all food and drink with you. Trianggulasi has no warungs and is deserted if no guests stay, but the Pesanggrahan has a kitchen with a kerosene stove and hurricane lamps.

The PHKA office at Pasar Anyar has a shop selling basic provisions for visitors, such as packet noodles, but it is better to stock up on food at the general stores in Dambuntung, where the bus drops you. There is also a camping ground and a PHKA post at Pancur.

Getting There & Away

From Banyuwangi's southern Brawijaya bus terminal, the Putra Jaya company has buses to Kalipahit (10,000Rp, 1½ hours) via Benculuk and Tegaldelimo until 4pm. Buses can drop you at the small village of Dambuntung, where you can stock up on food. Then take an *ojek* for around 35,000Rp to 50,000Rp first to the park office in Pasar Anyar, 3km from Dambuntung, to check on accommodation, and then on to the park. The 12km road from Pasar Anyar to Trianggulasi is badly potholed but is flat and negotiable by car.

Jeeps can be hired in Banyuwangi (700,000Rp) for one-day trips to Plengkung.

BANYUWANGI

☎ 0333

This pleasant, clean town has no major sites to drag you here, but schedules, inquisitiveness or the need for a break might take you to Banyuwangi, the ferry departure point for Bali.

Orientation

The ferry terminus, bus terminal and train station are all at Ketapang, 8km north of town, so most people go straight through to Gunung Bromo or Yogyakarta.

Information

Alas Purwo National Park head office (☎ 428675; Jl A Yani 108; ⏲ 7.30am-3pm Mon-Thu, 7.30-11am Fri) Two kilometres south of the town centre.

Baluran National Park head office (☎ 424119; www.balurannationalpark.go.id; Jl Agus Salim 132; ⏲ 7am-3pm Mon-Thu, 7-11am Fri) Four kilometres southwest of the centre.

Banyuwangi Tourist Office (☎ 424172; Jl Ahmad Yani 78; ⏲ 7am-3.30pm Mon-Thu, 7-10.30am Fri) Extremely helpful office; Mr Aekanu (☎ 081 55905197; aekanu@plasa.com), who works at the office, can organise tours.

Sights

One of the few sights in town is the **Kongco Tan Hu Cin Jin Chinese temple** (Jl Ikam Gurani 54); built in 1784, it's well worth a peek.

At the Banyuwangi Tourist Office is a small **museum** (admission free; ⏲ 7am-3.30pm Mon-Fri) devoted to culture from the area.

Sleeping & Eating

Hotel Baru (☎ 421369; Jl MT Haryono 82-84; r with fan/air-con 30,000/70,000Rp; ❄) Baru is a solid option with friendly staff and a variety of rooms. There's also a small restaurant on site.

Hotel Ketapang Indah (☎ 422280; Jl Gatot Subroto; r from 200,000Rp, sea-view r 400,000Rp; ❄ 🏊) About 2km south of the ferry terminal in Ketapang is this, Banyuwangi's most stylish hotel. Rooms and cottages are scattered around a landscaped garden, and there are uninterrupted views of Bali.

our pick **Ijen Resort and Villas** (☎ 429000; www.ijenhotel.com; Dusun Randuagung, Licin; r from US$115, ste US$195 plus 21% tax; 🏊) Nestled among rice fields at the foot of Ijen Plateau, miles from the hustle and bustle of city living, is this East Java oasis. Privacy is paramount here, which is probably why the resort attracts so many honeymooners. Rooms are more than inviting, with stone floors, open-air bathrooms, supremely thick mattresses and balconies with either views of the Ijen mountains or Bali. The pool itself has possibly the best view of all – across terraced rice fields to the rising peak of Gunung Raung. Meals are available, so you never have to venture away from the peaceful setting. The resort is about 25 minutes from Banyuwangi; take a bus to Licin then hire an *ojek* for the rest of the journey.

Wina Ayam Goreng Blambangan (mains 20,000Rp; ⏲ lunch & dinner) This large eatery in Blambangan bemo station has some of the best chicken in town.

For cheap eats, there are plenty of warungs on the corner of Jl MT Haryono and Jl Wahid Haysim. There are also several budget eateries on Jl Kapt Piere Tendean. In the evening, Pondok Ikan Bakar at No 17 does a cracking fish barbecue.

Getting There & Away

BOAT

Ferries from Ketapang depart roughly every 30 minutes around the clock for Gilimanuk in Bali. The ferry costs 4300Rp for passengers, 16,000Rp for a rider and motorcycle and 85,000Rp for a car, including driver. Through-buses between Bali and Java include the fare in the bus ticket and are the easiest option.

Pelni's *Tatamailau* stops in Banyuwangi once a month on its route to Sulawesi, Maluku and Papua. It docks at Tanjungwangi, along from the Bali ferry dock. Tickets can be bought at the **Pelni agent** (☎ 510291; Jl Raya Dodol 16) nearby.

BUS

Banyuwangi has two bus terminals. The Sri Tanjung bus terminal is 3km north of the Bali ferry terminal at Ketapang, and 11km north of town. Buses from this terminal travel to northern destinations, such as Baluran (6000Rp, one hour), Probolinggo (normal/*patas* 26,000/34,000Rp, four hours) and Surabaya (36,000/51,000Rp, six hours). Buses also go right through to Yogyakarta (*patas* 105,000Rp, 14 hours) and Denpasar (51,000Rp, four hours including the ferry trip).

Brawijaya terminal (also known as Karang Ente), 4km south of town, has most of the buses to the south. These include Kalipahit (10,000Rp, 1½ hours), Kalibaru (10,000Rp, two hours) and Jember (15,000Rp, three hours).

TRAIN

The main Banyuwangi train station is just a few hundred metres north of the ferry terminal.

The express *Mutiara Timur* leaves at 9am and 10.45pm for Probolinggo (four hours) and Surabaya (business/executive 40,000/55,000Rp, six hours). Economy-class trains include the *Sri Tanjung*, which leaves at 6am for Yogyakarta (38,000Rp, 13 hours); and the *Blambangan*, which leaves at 1.10pm for Probolinggo (19,000Rp, six hours).

BALURAN NATIONAL PARK

Baluran National Park is quite unlike any other park on the island. Nicknamed 'Indonesia's little bit of Africa', this park was once extensive grasslands covering some 250 sq km on the northeastern corner of Java. Unfortunately much of the grasslands have disappeared due to encroachment by acacia thorn scrub, but you can find pockets of the park that still live up to its nickname.

Orientation & Information

The main service town for Baluran is Wonorejo, on the main coast road between Surabaya and Banyuwangi, where food supplies can be bought. The **PHKA office** (☎ 0333-461650; 🕑 7am-5pm) is on the highway, where guides can be arranged for 60,000Rp per hour. The park's head office (p263) is in Banyuwangi. The park entry fee is 20,000Rp and an extra 6000Rp is charged for a car.

Baluran can be visited at any time of the year, but the dry season (June to November) is usually the best time because the animals congregate near the waterholes at Bekol and Bama.

Sights & Activities

Baluran is rich in wildlife and supports important populations of banteng and *ajag* plus sambar deer, *muntjac* deer, two species of monkey, and wild pigs. The park is also home to between 10 and 12 leopards, but there have only been two sightings in the last 17 years. The bird life is depleted, due to extensive illegal trapping for the caged-bird trade. However, green peafowl, red and green jungle fowl, hornbills and bee-eaters are still easy to see.

On the hill above the guesthouses at Bekol there is a viewing tower that provides a panoramic view over a 300-hectare clearing. Banteng and sambar herds can be seen here, and wild dogs can sometimes be seen hunting sambar, usually in the early morning. There are walking trails around Bekol.

Bama, on the coast, is a 3km walk or drive from Bekol. It has accommodation and a half-decent beach where you can snorkel. The nearby coastal forest has numerous waterholes and is a good place to see water monitor lizards and monkeys.

Sleeping

Bookings can be made in advance through the **Baluran National Park head office** (☎ 424119; www.balurannationalpark.go.id; Jl Agus Salim 132; 🕑 7am-3pm Mon-Thu, 7-11am Fri) in Banyuwangi. Most visitors tend to day-trip, so accommodation is not usually full, but it pays to book, especially in the peak June to July holiday period when school groups visit the park.

PANGANDARAN'S TSUNAMI *Atik Wildan*

On the afternoon of 17 July 2006, an undersea earthquake measuring 7.7 on the Richter scale triggered a tsunami that struck a 200km stretch of Java's central coast. The earthquake caused a wave 3m high to race 400m inland, and, while far less severe than the devastating tsunami of December 2004, it still wreaked havoc as far west as the Bandung province and as far east as Yogyakarta's coastal settlements. Approximately 550 people died and close to 50,000 were displaced.

Worst hit was the beach resort of Pangandaran and its neighbouring villages. Little warning of the wave reached locals and tourists (the promised tsunami-warning system of alarms and sirens had yet to be installed), but fortunately many managed to flee to the inland hills. Beachfront restaurants and hotels were badly damaged by the wave and all the shops and stalls on the beach itself were completely washed away; those further inland suffered little damage.

As little as two months after the tsunami, much of Pangandaran was back to normal. Transport facilities along the coastline were up and running, some hotels had opened their doors, and the fish market was once again crowded. The most severely damaged hotels were planning to open six months after the tsunami, but it's advisable to call ahead to check whether your hotel of choice is currently operating. The government has banned further development on the beach so the warungs at the southern end of the west beach are no longer.

Support and donations for victims of the tsunami are welcomed by the Indonesian arm of the **Red Cross** (☎ 021-7992325; www.palangmerah.org in Indonesian; Jl Jenderal Datot Subroto Kav 96, 12790 Jakarta).

Atik Wildan lives in Yogyakarta and with her husband runs the Lana Gallery (p184), one of the few contemporary art galleries in the country to directly support up-and-coming artists.

our pick **Rosa's Ecolodge** (☎ 0338-453005; www.rosasecolodge.com; Ds Sidomulyo RT 03/03, Sumberwaru; r 250,000Rp;) On the northern edge of the park in tiny Sumberwaru is this peaceful lodge run by the affable Rene and Rosa. This is a place to kick back for a few days and soak up village life, and let yourself be entertained by the hosts' captivating stories. Rooms are spacious and of the highest standard, with tiled floors you could eat off, bamboo lining the walls, and traditional wood furniture. Home-cooked meals – veritable banquets of local specialities using local produce – are available for 40,000Rp, and tours of Baluran can be arranged. You can sleep easy, knowing part of the room rate is being channelled into educating local children on the importance of nature and natural resources.

At Bekol, 12km into the park, **Pesanggrahan** (per person 25,000Rp) has six rooms; there's a *mandi* and kitchen, but you must bring your own provisions.

Bekol also has two wisma; **Wisma Tamu** (beds per person 35,000Rp) has three comfortable rooms with attached *mandis*, while **Wisma Peneliti** (beds per person 55,000Rp) is a little more expensive but also a little more plush.

Bama, 3km east of Bekol on the beach, also has its fair share of accommodation. **Bama Guesthouse** (beds 25,000Rp per person) is a very basic option but has cooking facilities, although you must bring your own food. **Rumah Panggung** (cottage 150,000Rp) is bigger, newer and cosier, but is closer to the waterhole than the beach.

The canteen at Bekol sells drinks and some provisions, but meals are cooked only for groups of 10 or more. You might be able to arrange something with the PHKA staff, but you have to bring your own food.

Getting There & Away

Surabaya to Banyuwangi buses, taking the coast road via Probolinggo, can drop you right at the park entrance; and when leaving the park, buses are easily flagged down. From Banyuwangi (or Ketapang ferry, if you are coming from Bali) it's only a half-hour journey on the Wonorejo bus (6000Rp). Ask the driver to let you off at the park entrance, and ask a PHKA ranger to arrange an *ojek* (30,000Rp) to take you the next 12km to Bekol along the badly rutted road. If you are coming from the west, Baluran is 3½ hours from Probolinggo.

Bali

Bali may be small in size – you can drive around the entire coast in one long day – but its prominence as a destination is huge, and rightfully so. Ask travellers what Bali means to them and you'll get as many answers as there are flowers on a frangipani tree. Virescent rice terraces, pulse-pounding surf, enchanting temple ceremonies, mesmerising dance performances and ribbons of beaches are just some of the images people cherish.

And those are just some of the more obvious qualities. A visit to Bali means that you are in the most visitor-friendly island of Indonesia. There are pleasures of the body, whether a massage on the beach or a hedonistic interlude in a sybaritic spa. Shopping that will put 'extra bag' at the top of your list. Food and drink ranging from the freshest local cuisine bursting with the flavours of the markets to food from around the globe, often prepared by chefs and served in restaurants that are world class. From a cold Bintang at sunset to an epic night clubbing, your social whirl is limited only by your own fortitude.

Small obviously doesn't mean limited. The manic whirl of Kuta segues into the luxury of Seminyak. The artistic swirl of Ubud is a counterpoint to misty treks amid the volcanoes. Mellow beach towns like Amed, Lovina and Pemuteran can be found right round the coast and just offshore is the laid-back idyll of Nusa Lembongan.

As you stumble upon the exquisite little offerings left all over the island that materialise as if by magic, you'll see that the tiny tapestry of colours and textures is a metaphor for Bali itself.

HIGHLIGHTS

- Sunbathing and partying at **Kuta Beach** (p281)
- Hitting the latest bars, restaurants and clubs at **Seminyak** (p287)
- Experiencing Bali's elaborate cultural life in **Ubud** (p307) and surrounding villages
- Chilling out – or maybe catching a wave – on **Nusa Lembongan** (p346)
- Hiking through and enjoying the superb views of lush valleys from the region around **Munduk** (p364)

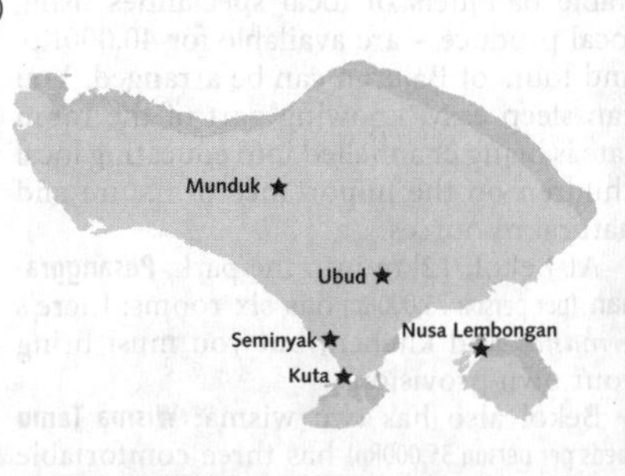

- POPULATION: 3.2 MILLION
- LAND AREA: 5632 SQ KM
- HIGHEST PEAK: GUNUNG AGUNG (3142M)

HISTORY

It's certain that Bali has been populated since early prehistoric times, but the oldest human artefacts found are 3000-year-old stone tools and earthenware vessels from Cekik. Not much is known of Bali during the period when Indian traders brought Hinduism to the Indonesian archipelago, but the earliest written records are stone inscriptions dating from around the 9th century. By that time, rice was being grown under the complex irrigation system known as *subak,* and there were precursors of the religious and cultural traditions that can be traced to the present day.

Hindu Influence

Hindu Java began to spread its influence into Bali during the reign of King Airlangga, from 1019 to 1042. At the age of 16, Airlangga had fled into the forests of western Java when his uncle lost the throne. He gradually gained support, won back the kingdom once ruled by his uncle and went on to become one of Java's greatest kings. Airlangga's mother had moved to Bali and remarried shortly after his birth, so when he gained the throne there was an immediate link between Java and Bali. At this time, the courtly Javanese language known as Kawi came into use among the royalty of Bali, and the rock-cut memorials seen at Gunung Kawi (Mt Kawi) near Tampaksiring are a clear architectural link between Bali and 11th-century Java.

After Airlangga's death, Bali retained its semi-independent status until Kertanagara became king of the Singasari dynasty in Java two centuries later. Kertanagara conquered Bali in 1284, but his power lasted only eight years until he was murdered and his kingdom collapsed. With Java in turmoil, Bali regained its autonomy and the Pejeng dynasty, centred near modern-day Ubud, rose to great power. In 1343 Gajah Mada, the legendary chief minister of the Majapahit dynasty, defeated the Pejeng king Dalem Bedaulu and brought Bali back under Javanese influence.

Although Gajah Mada brought much of the Indonesian archipelago under Majapahit control, Bali was the furthest extent of its power. Here the 'capital' moved to Gelgel, near modern-day Semarapura (once known as Klungkung), around the late 14th century, and for the next two centuries this was the base for the 'king of Bali', the Dewa Agung. The Majapahit kingdom collapsed into disputing sultanates. However, the Gelgel dynasty in Bali, under Dalem Batur Enggong, extended its power eastwards to the neighbouring island of Lombok and even crossed the strait to Java.

As the Majapahit kingdom fell apart, many of its intelligentsia moved to Bali, including the priest Nirartha, who is credited with introducing many of the complexities of Balinese religion to the island. Artists, dancers, musicians and actors also fled to Bali at this time, and the island experienced an explosion of cultural activities. The final great exodus to Bali took place in 1478.

European Contact

The first Europeans to set foot in Bali were Dutch seafarers in 1597. Setting a tradition that prevails to the present, they fell in love with the island, and when Cornelius Houtman – the ship's captain – prepared to set sail from Bali, some of his crew refused to leave with him. At that time, Balinese prosperity and artistic activity, at least among the royalty, were at a peak, and the king who befriended Houtman had 200 wives and a chariot pulled by two white buffaloes, not to mention a retinue of 50 dwarfs. When the Dutch returned to Indonesia in later years, they were interested in profit, not culture, and barely gave Bali a second glance.

Dutch Conquest

In 1710 the capital of the Gelgel kingdom was shifted to nearby Klungkung (now called Semarapura), but local discontent was growing, lesser rulers were breaking away from Gelgel domination and the Dutch began to move in, using the old policy of divide and conquer. In 1846 the Dutch used Balinese salvage claims over shipwrecks as the pretext to land military forces in northern Bali. In 1894 the Dutch chose to support the Sasaks of Lombok in a rebellion against their Balinese rajah. After some bloody battles, the Balinese were defeated in Lombok, and with northern Bali firmly under Dutch control, southern Bali was not likely to retain its independence for long. Once again, salvaging disputes gave

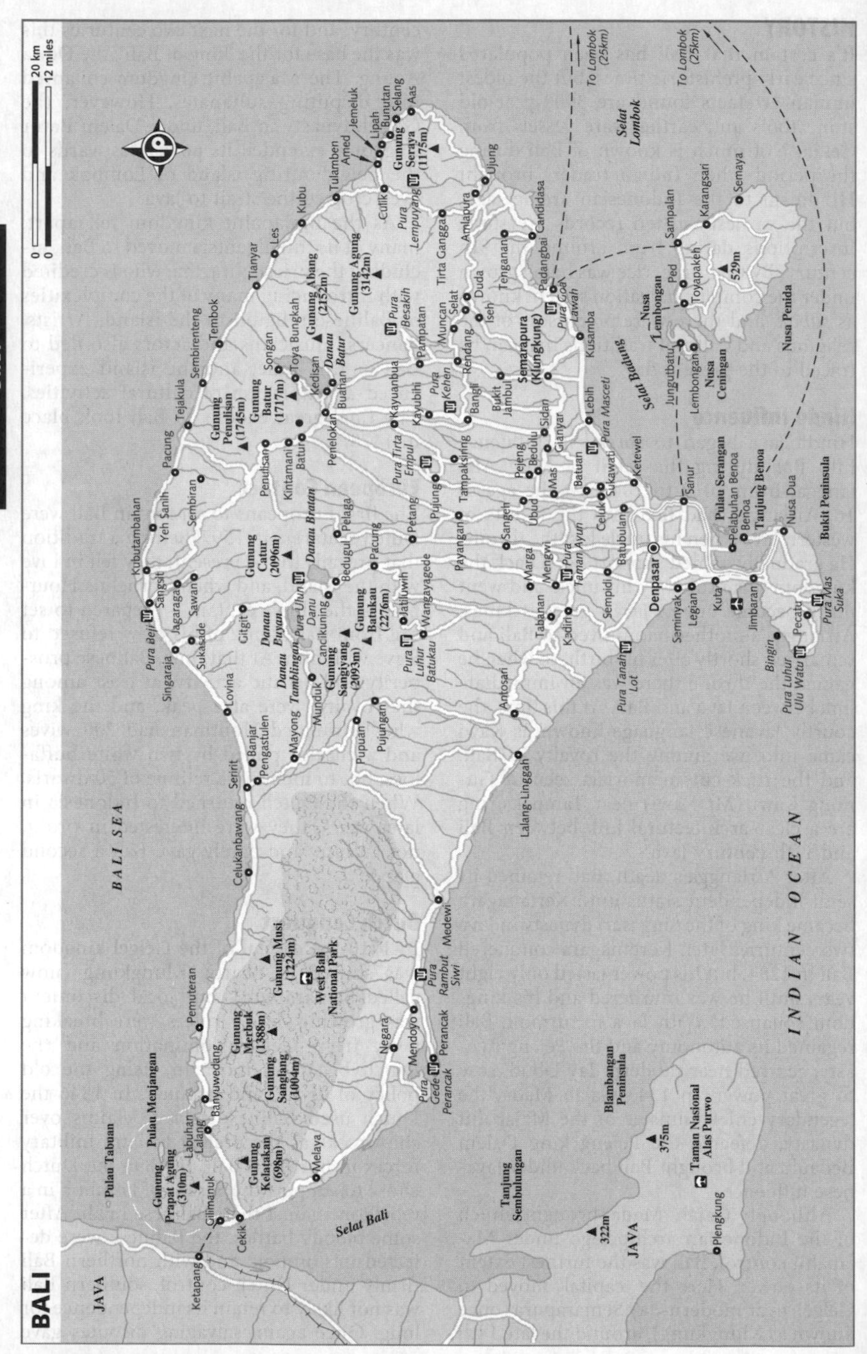
BALI
0 20 km
0 12 miles
JAVA
BALI SEA
INDIAN OCEAN
Selat Bali
Selat Badung
Selat Lombok
To Lombok (25km)
To Lombok (25km)
Pulau Tabuan
Pulau Menjangan
Ketapang
Gilimanuk
Cekik
Gunung Prapat Agung (310m)
Labuhan Lalang
Gunung Kelatakan (698m)
Melaya
Banyuwedang
Gunung Sanglang (1004m)
Gunung Merbuk (1388m)
Pemuteran
Gunung Musi (1224m)
West Bali National Park
Negara
Mendoyo
Perancak
Pura Gede Perancak
Pura Rambut Siwi
Medewi
Celukanbawang
Seririt
Banjar
Pengastulen
Lovina
Singaraja
Pura Beji
Sangsit
Jagaraga
Sawan
Sukasade
Gitgit
Kubutambahan
Yeh Sanih
Sembiran
Pacung
Tejakula
Sembirenteng
Tembok
Tianyar
Les
Kubu
Tulamben
Culik
Amed
Jemeluk
Lipah
Bunutan
Selang
Aas
Gunung Seraya (1175m)
Pura Lempuyang
Ujung
Amlapura
Tirta Gangga
Candidasa
Padangbai
Pura Goa Lawah
Tenganan
Duda
Iseh
Selat
Muncan
Sidemen
Rendang
Pura Besakih
Gunung Agung (3142m)
Gunung Abang (2152m)
Toya Bungkah
Songan
Kedisan
Danau Batur
Buahan
Gunung Batur (1717m)
Batur
Kintamani
Penulisan
Gunung Penulisan (1745m)
Penelokan
Kayuambua
Kayubihi
Pura Kehen
Bangli
Bukit Jambul
Semarapura (Klungkung)
Kusamba
Pampatan
Pura Tirta Empul
Tampaksiring
Pujung
Petang
Pelaga
Danau Bratan
Bedugul
Pacung
Gunung Catur (2096m)
Pura Ulun Danu
Candikuning
Danau Buyan
Danau Tamblingan
Munduk
Mayong
Gunung Sangiyang (2093m)
Gunung Batukau (2276m)
Jatiluwih
Wangayagede
Pura Luhur Batukau
Pupuan
Pujungan
Antosari
Lalang-Linggah
Tabanan
Kediri
Pura Tanah Lot
Marga
Mengwi
Pura Taman Ayun
Sangeh
Payangan
Ubud
Pejeng
Bedulu
Mas
Gianyar
Sidan
Lebih
Pura Masceti
Batuan
Celuk
Sukawati
Ketewel
Batubulan
Sempidi
Denpasar
Seminyak
Legian
Kuta
Jimbaran
Bingin
Pura Luhur Ulu Watu
Pecatu
Pura Mas Suka
Bukit Peninsula
Nusa Dua
Tanjung Benoa
Benoa
Pelabuhan Benoa
Pulau Serangan
Sanur
Jungutbatu
Nusa Lembongan
Lembongan
Nusa Ceningan
Toyapakeh
Ped
Sampalan
Karangsari
Semaya
529m
Nusa Penida
Blambangan Peninsula
Taman Nasional Alas Purwo
375m
Tanjung Sembulungan
322m
Plengkung

the Dutch the excuse they needed to move in. A Chinese ship was wrecked off Sanur in 1904 and ransacked by the Balinese. The Dutch demanded that the rajah of Badung pay 3000 silver dollars in damages – this was refused. In 1906 Dutch warships appeared at Sanur; Dutch forces landed and, despite Balinese opposition, marched the 5km to the outskirts of Denpasar.

On 20 September 1906, the Dutch mounted a naval bombardment of Denpasar and then commenced their final assault. The three rajahs of Badung (southern Bali) realised that they were outnumbered and outgunned, and that defeat was inevitable. Surrender and exile, however, was the worst imaginable outcome, so they decided to take the honourable path of a suicidal *puputan* – a fight to the death.

The Dutch begged the Balinese to surrender rather than make their hopeless stand, but their pleas went unheard and wave after wave of the Balinese nobility marched forward to their deaths. In all, nearly 4000 Balinese died in the *puputan*. Later, the Dutch marched east towards Tabanan, taking the rajah of Tabanan prisoner, but he committed suicide rather than face the disgrace of exile.

The kingdoms of Karangasem and Gianyar had already capitulated to the Dutch and were allowed to retain some powers, but other kingdoms were defeated and the rulers exiled. Finally, the rajah of Klungkung followed the lead of Badung and once more the Dutch faced a *puputan*. With this last obstacle disposed of, all of Bali was now under Dutch control and became part of the Dutch East Indies. Dutch rule over Bali was short-lived, however, as Indonesia fell to the Japanese in WWII.

Independence

On 17 August 1945, just after WWII ended, the Indonesian leader Soekarno proclaimed the nation's independence, but it took four years to convince the Dutch that they were not going to get their great colony back. In a virtual repeat of the *puputan* nearly half a century earlier, a Balinese resistance group was wiped out in the Battle of Marga on 20 November 1946; Bali's airport, Ngurah Rai, is named after its leader. It was not until 1949 that the Dutch finally recognised Indonesia's independence.

The huge eruption of Gunung Agung in 1963 killed thousands, devastated vast areas of the island and forced many Balinese to accept transmigration to other parts of Indonesia. Two years later, in the wake of the attempted communist coup, Bali became the scene of some of the bloodiest anticommunist killings in Indonesia. These were perhaps inflamed by some mystical desire to purge the land of evil, but also came about because the radical agenda of land reform and abolition of the caste system was a threat to traditional Balinese values. The brutality of the killings was in shocking contrast to the stereotype of the 'gentle' Balinese.

Modern Bali

The tourism boom, which started in the early 1970s, has brought many changes, and has helped pay for improvements in roads, telecommunications, education and health. Though tourism has had some marked adverse environmental and social effects, Bali's unique culture has proved to be remarkably resilient. Beginning in the 1990s there has been vocal public opposition to some controversial tourist developments, which indicates that Balinese people will play a more active role in the development of their island.

Bali, like most places, has also been affected by global politics. In October 2002, two simultaneous bomb explosions in Kuta – targeting an area frequented by tourists – injured or killed more than 500 people; see p281. The island's vital tourist industry was dealt a severe blow. It had mostly recovered by 2005 when in October of that year more bombs went off, albeit with less loss of life. Still, the bombs caused an immediate sharp drop in tourists and have forced the Balinese to yet again ponder their role in the world's greater geopolitics.

CULTURE

The population in Bali is almost all Indonesian; 95% are of Balinese Hindu descent and could be described as ethnic Balinese. The remaining residents are mostly from other parts of the country, particularly Java.

Balinese have traditional caste divisions that resemble the Indian Hindu system, although there are no 'untouchables'. Nor is there separation of labour based on caste, except for the Brahmana priesthood. Over

90% of the population belong to the common Sudra caste, which now includes many wealthy Balinese. The main significance of caste is in religious roles and rituals, and its influence on Balinese language.

The traditional Balinese society is intensely communal; the organisation of villages, the cultivation of farmlands and even the creative arts are communal efforts. A person belongs to their family, clan, caste and to the village as a whole. The roles of the sexes are fairly well delineated, with certain tasks handled by women and others reserved for men. For instance, the running of the household is very much the woman's task, while caring for animals is mostly a male preserve.

Balinese society is held together by collective responsibility. If a woman enters a temple while menstruating, for instance, it is a kind of irreverence, an insult to the gods, and their displeasure falls not just on the transgressor but on the whole community. This collective responsibility produces considerable pressure on the individual to conform to *adat* – the traditional values and customs that form the core of society.

Religion

The Balinese are nominally Hindus, but Balinese Hinduism is half a world away from that of India. When the Majapahits evacuated to Bali they took with them their religion and its rituals, as well as their art, literature, music and culture. The Balinese already had strong religious beliefs and an active cultural life, and the new influences were simply overlaid on existing practices – hence the peculiar Balinese interpretation of Hinduism.

The Balinese worship the same gods as the Hindus of India – the trinity of Brahma, Shiva and Vishnu – but they also have a supreme god, Sanghyang Widi. Unlike in India, the trinity is never seen – a vacant shrine or empty throne tells all. Nor is Sanghyang Widi often worshipped, though villagers may pray to him when they have settled new land and are about to build a new village. Other Hindu gods such as Ganesh, Shiva's elephant-headed son, may occasionally appear, but a great many purely Balinese gods, spirits and entities have far more relevance in everyday life.

The Balinese believe that spirits are everywhere, an indication that animism is the basis of much of their religion. Good spirits dwell in the mountains and bring prosperity to the people, while giants and demons lurk beneath the sea, and bad spirits haunt the woods and desolate beaches. The people live between these two opposites and their rituals strive to maintain this middle ground. Offerings are carefully put out every morning to pay homage to the good spirits and nonchalantly placed on the ground to placate the bad ones. You can't get away from religion in Bali – there are temples in every village, shrines in every field and offerings made at every corner.

TEMPLES

The word for temple is *pura*, which is a Sanskrit word meaning 'a space surrounded by a wall'. As in so much of Balinese religion, the temples, though nominally Hindu, owe much to the pre-Majapahit era. Their *kaja, kelod* or *kangin* (alignment towards the mountains, the sea or the sunrise) is in deference to spirits that are more animist than Hindu.

Almost every village has at least three temples. The most important is the *pura puseh* (temple of origin), which is dedicated to the village founders and is at the *kaja* end of the village. In the middle of the village is the *pura desa* for the spirits that protect the village community in its day-to-day life. At the *kelod* end of the village is the *pura dalem* (temple of the dead). The graveyard is also here and the temple will often include representations of Durga, the terrible incarnation of Shiva's wife.

Families worship their ancestors in family temples, clans in clan temples and the whole village in the *pura puseh*. Certain temples in Bali are of such importance that they are deemed to be owned by the whole island rather than by individual villages. These include Pura Besakih (p332) on the slopes of Gunung Agung, the most revered place in Bali, often called 'The Mother Temple'.

The simple shrines or thrones you see – for example, in rice fields or next to sacred old trees – are not real temples, as they are not walled. You'll find these shrines in all sorts of places, often overlooking intersections or dangerous curves in the road to protect road users.

For much of the year Balinese temples are deserted, but on holy days the deities and ancestral spirits descend from heaven to visit their devotees, and the temples come alive with days of frenetic activity and nights of drama and dance. Temple festivals come at least once every Balinese year (210 days). Because most villages have at least three temples, you're assured of at least five or six annual festivals in every village. The full-moon periods, around the end of September to the beginning of October, or early to mid-April, are often times of important festivals. **Galungan-Kuningan** is a 10-day festival when *lots* of activity takes place at family and community temples all over the island.

Arts

The Balinese had no words for 'art' and 'artist' because, traditionally, art has never been regarded as something to be treasured for its own sake. Prior to the tourism boom, art was just part of everyday life, and what was produced went into temples, palaces or festivals. Although respected, the painter or carver was not considered a member of some special elite, the artist's work was not signed and there were no galleries or craft shops.

It's a different story today, with thousands of art outlets tucked into every possible crevice. Although much Balinese art is churned out quickly as cheap souvenirs, buried beneath the reproductions of reproductions there's still much beautiful work to be found.

Even the simplest activities are carried out with care, precision and artistic flair. Just glance at those little offering trays thrown down on the ground for the demons every morning – each one a throwaway work of art. Look at the temple offerings, the artistically stacked pyramids of fruit or other beautifully decorated foods. Look for *penjor*, long decorated bamboo poles at doorways during festivals, the woven decorative palm-leaf strips called *lamak*, stylised female figures known as *cili* and the intricately carved coconut-shell wall-hangings.

Traditionally most visitors to the island have found the greatest concentration of the arts in and around Ubud (p307).

BALINESE PAINTING

The art form most influenced both by Western ideas and tourist demand is painting. Traditional painting was very limited in style and subject matter, and was used primarily for temple decoration. The arrival of Western artists following WWI introduced new subject matters and materials with which artists could work.

Traditional Balinese painting was strictly limited to three basic kinds: *langse, iders-iders* and calendars. *Langse* are the large, rectangular hangings used as decoration or curtains in palaces or temples. *Iders-iders* are scroll paintings that are hung along the eaves of temples. The calendars are usually astrological, showing the auspicious days of each month.

Most of the paintings were narratives with mythological themes, illustrating stories from Hindu epics and literature. Paintings were executed in the *wayang* style – the flat two-dimensional style that imitates the *wayang kulit* (shadow puppets), with the figures invariably shown in three-quarter view. The colours that artists could use were strictly limited to a set list of shades (red, blue, brown, yellow and light ochre for flesh).

In these narratives the same characters appeared in several different scenes, each depicting an episode from the story. The individual scenes were usually bordered by mountains, flames or ornamental walls. The deities, princes and heroes were

BALI MEDIA

To find out what's happening locally pick up any of a number of local publications, including the following.

Bali Advertiser Free newspaper with voluminous ads, comprehensive information, and idiosyncratic columnists.

Bali Style Glossy features for the posh set.

Hello Bali Good features and restaurant and entertainment reviews.

What's Up Bali Useful map-based weekly brochure with complete entertainment listings.

The website **Bali Discovery** (www.balidiscovery.com) has a first-rate section on Bali news. For news from further afield, the *International Herald Tribune* is sold at convenience stores in South Bali and Ubud. Same-day copies of Australian newspapers are sold by vendors for ridiculous sums.

identified by opulent clothing, jewellery, elaborate headdresses and by their graceful postures and gestures; and the devils and giants by their bulging eyes, canine teeth, bulbous noses and bulky bodies. Semarapura (p330) is still a centre for traditional painting – the painted ceiling of the Kertha Gosa (p331) there is a fine example of the style.

ARCHITECTURE

The basic feature of Balinese architecture is the *bale* (pronounced 'bal-ay'), a rectangular, open-sided pavilion with a steeply pitched roof of palm thatch. A family compound will have a number of *bale* for eating, sleeping and working. The focus of a community is the *bale banjar*, a large pavilion for meeting, debate, gamelan practise and so on. Buildings such as restaurants and the lobby areas of hotels are often modelled on the *bale* – they are airy, spacious and handsomely proportioned.

Like the other arts, architecture has traditionally served the religious life of Bali. Balinese houses, although attractive, have never been lavished with the architectural attention that is given to temples. Even Balinese palaces are modest compared with the more important temples. Temples are designed to fixed rules and formulas, with sculpture serving as an adjunct, a finishing touch to these design guidelines.

SCULPTURE

In small or less-important temples, sculpture may be limited or even nonexistent, while in other temples – particularly some of the exuberantly detailed temples of northern Bali – it may be almost overwhelming in its detail and intricacy. Throughout the island you will see elaborate carved stone decorations and accents. These are relatively easy to produce in the soft local stones.

WOODCARVING

Like painting, woodcarving is no longer done simply for decoration or other symbolic purposes in temples and palaces but is now created for its own sake. Influences from outside inspired new subjects and styles, and some of the same Western artists provided the stimulus.

Especially around Ubud, carvers started producing highly stylised and elongated figures, leaving the wood in its natural state rather than painting it, as was the traditional practice. Others carved delightful animal figures, some totally realistic and others wonderful caricatures, while other artists carved whole tree trunks into ghostly, intertwined 'totem poles' or curiously exaggerated and distorted figures.

DANCE

Music, dance and drama are closely related in Bali. In fact, dance and drama are synonymous, though some 'dances' are more drama and less dance, and others more dance and less drama.

Balinese dance tends to be precise, shifting and jerky, like the accompanying gamelan music, which has abrupt shifts of tempo and dramatic changes between silence and crashing noise. There's virtually no physical contact in Balinese dancing – each dancer moves independently, but every movement of wrist, hand and finger is important. Even facial expressions are carefully choreographed to convey the character of the dance.

The dances are a blend of seriousness and slapstick. Basically, they are straightforward ripping yarns, where you cheer the goodies and boo the baddies. Some dances have a comic element, with clowns who counterbalance the staid, noble characters. The clowns often have to convey the story to the audience, since the noble characters may use the classical Javanese Kawi language, while the clowns (usually servants of the noble characters) converse in Balinese.

Dances are a regular part of almost every temple festival, and Bali has no shortage of these. There are also dances virtually every night at tourist centres, although the most authentic are found in and around Ubud; admission to a first-class performance here, for example, costs around 50,000Rp.

Kecak

One of the best-known dances of Bali is the Kecak. It is unusual because it does not have a gamelan accompaniment. Instead, the background is provided by a chanting 'choir' of men who provide the 'chak-a-chak-a-chak' noise that distinguishes the dance.

The Kecak tells the tale of the Ramayana, the quest of Prince Rama to rescue his wife Sita after she had been kidnapped by

Rawana, the King of Lanka. Rama is accompanied to Lanka by Sugriwa, the king of the monkeys, with his monkey army. Throughout the Kecak dance, the circle of men, all bare-chested and wearing checked cloth around their waists, provide a non-stop accompaniment, rising to a crescendo as they play the monkey army and fight it out with Rawana and his cronies. The chanting is accompanied by the movements of the monkey army whose members sway back and forth, raise their hands in unison, flutter their fingers and lean left and right, all with an eerily exciting coordination.

Barong & Rangda

The Barong Keket is half shaggy dog, half lion – and is played by two men in much the same way as a circus clown-horse. Its opponent is the *rangda* (witch).

The Barong represents good and protects the village from the *rangda*, but is also a mischievous creature. It flounces into the temple courtyard, snaps its jaws at the gamelan, dances around and enjoys the acclaim of its supporters – a group of men with kris. Then the *rangda* makes her appearance, with long tongue lolling, pendulous breasts wobbling, human entrails draped around her neck, fangs protruding from her mouth and sabre-like fingernails clawing the air.

The two duel with their magical powers, and the Barong's supporters draw their kris and rush in to attack the witch. The *rangda* puts them in a trance and the men try to stab themselves, but the Barong also has great magical powers and casts a spell that stops the kris from harming the men. This is the most dramatic part of the dance – as the gamelan rings crazily the men rush back and forth, waving their kris around, all but foaming at the mouth, sometimes even rolling on the ground in a desperate attempt to stab themselves. Finally, the *rangda* retires defeated – good has won again. Good must always triumph over evil in Bali, and no matter how many times the spectators have seen the performance or how well they know the outcome, the battle itself remains all-important.

Legong

This is the most graceful of Balinese dances and, to connoisseurs of Balinese dancing, the one of most interest.

There are various forms of the Legong but the Legong Kraton (Legong of the Palace) is the one most often performed. A performance involves just three dancers – the two Legongs and their 'attendant' known as the Condong. The Legongs are identically dressed in tightly bound gold brocade. So tightly are they encased that it's something of a mystery how they manage to move with such agility and speed. Their faces are elaborately made up, their eyebrows plucked and repainted, and their hair decorated with frangipanis.

The dance relates how a king takes a maiden, Rangkesari, captive. When Rangkesari's brother comes to release her, he begs the king to let her free rather than go

TOP FIVE BALI READS

The stacks of books about Bali are like coconuts on trees, there are so many they could easily topple over and hit you on the head. However, here's five you'll enjoy before or during your stay.

Eat, Pray, Love by Elizabeth Gilbert is, as the subtitle says, 'One Woman's Search for Everything Across Italy, India and Indonesia'. The climax occurs in Bali and answers questions posed throughout the book.

Fragrant Rice by Janet De Neefe follows her from her time as a naive backpacker from Melbourne to her life today as a mother of a Balinese family. She brings her experience running the wonderful Casa Luna empire in Ubud to her chapters, which cherish local food.

A House in Bali by Colin McPhee is the timeless classic about a Canadian who experienced Bali's cultural and village life to the core in the 1930s.

Our Hotel in Bali by Louise Koke is another classic about Westerners in Bali in the 1930s. She and her husband Bob created the first-ever Kuta Beach hotel and had numerous delightful encounters along the way. It's a quick and fun read with lots of photos.

Bali Blues by Jeremy Allan is a highly readable tale of love set in the tumultuous year after the 2002 bombings. It contains many an insight into life on the island.

to war. The king refuses and on his way to the battle meets a bird bringing ill omens. He ignores the bird and continues on to meet Rangkesari's brother, who kills him. The dance, however, relates only the lead up to the battle and ends with the bird's appearance. When the king leaves the stage he is going to the battle that will end in his death.

The dance starts with an introduction by the Condong. She departs as the Legongs enter. The Legongs dance solo, in close identical formation, and even in a mirror-image formation when they dance a nose-to-nose love scene. They relate the king's sad departure from his queen, Rangkesari's request that he release her and the king's departure for battle. Finally, the Condong reappears with tiny golden wings as the bird of ill fortune and the dance ends.

GAMELAN

As in Sumatra and Java, Balinese music is based around the gamelan orchestra. The whole gamelan orchestra is known as a *gong* an old fashioned *gong gede* or a more modern *gong kebyar*. There are even more ancient forms of the gamelan, such as the *gong selunding*, still occasionally played in Bali Aga villages like Tenganan.

Although the instruments used are much the same, Balinese gamelan is very different from the more gentle, reserved and formal form you'll hear in Java. Balinese gamelan often sounds like everyone is going for it full pelt. In Java gamelan music is rarely heard except at special performances, whereas in Bali you'll hear gamelan playing everywhere you go.

GETTING THERE & AWAY

Air

Bali's Ngurah Rai Airport (DPS) is just south of Kuta. It is named after a hero of the struggle for independence from the Dutch.

The airport is spacious and modern and is well-served with international flights. It has a hotel-booking counter, a left-luggage room, several moneychangers, an expensive duty-free shop and many souvenir shops, ATMs and lots of familiar fast-food places.

The **domestic terminal** (☎ 0361-751011) and **international terminal** (☎ 0361-751011) are a few hundred metres apart.

International airlines flying to and from Bali include the following:

Air Asia (airline code AK; ☎ 0361-760116; www.airasia.com) Hub Kuala Lumpur.

Cathay Pacific Airways (airline code CX; ☎ 0361-766931; www.cathaypacific.com) Hub Hong Kong.

Continental Airlines (airline code CO; ☎ 0361-768358; www.continental.com) Hubs Newark and Houston.

Eva Air (airline code BR; ☎ 0361-751011; www.evaair.com) Hub Taipei.

Japan Airlines (airline code JL; ☎ 0361-757077; www.jal.co.jp) Hub Tokyo.

Korean Air (airline code KE; ☎ 0361-768377; www.koreanair.com) Hub Seoul.

Malaysia Airlines (airline code MH; ☎ 0361-764995; www.mas.com.my) Hub Kuala Lumpur.

Qantas Airways (airline code QF; ☎ 0361-288331; www.qantas.com.au) Hubs Sydney and Melbourne. Plans to rebrand its service as Jetstar.

Singapore Airlines (airline code SQ; ☎ 0361-768388; www.singaporeair.com) Hub Singapore.

Thai Airways International (airline code TG; ☎ 0361-288141; www.thaiair.com) Hub Bangkok.

Domestic services in Bali seem to be in a constant state of flux. However competition is fierce and you can usually find flights to a range of destinations for under US$100. The best thing to do is to go to the airport and shop at the airline ticket offices. Often you'll come close to long-distance bus and ferry fares. Places served often from Bali include Jakarta, Surabaya, Lombok, Yogyakarta, Bima, Maumere, Bandung, Kupang and more.

Garuda Indonesia (airline code GA; ☎ 0361-227824; www.garuda-indonesia.com) Hubs Bali and Jakarta.

Lion Air (airline code JT; ☎ 0361-763872; www.lionairlines.com)

Merpati Nusantara Airlines (airline code MZ; ☎ 0361-235358; www.merpati.co.id)

Mandala Airlines (airline code RI; ☎ 0361-751011; www.mandalaair.com)

Pelita (airline code 6D; ☎ 0361-762248; www.pelita-air.com)

Public Bus

JAVA

Many buses from numerous bus companies travel daily between the Ubung terminal in Denpasar and major cities in Java (via ferry); most travel overnight. Fares vary between operators, and depend on what sort of comfort you want – it's worth paying extra for a decent seat and air-con. For details, see p306.

Sea

JAVA

Ferries operate between Gilimanuk in western Bali and Ketapang (Java), see p358.

LOMBOK

This island is accessible by regular public boat from Padangbai, see p334.

OTHER INDONESIAN ISLANDS

Three ships from Pelni stop at Benoa Harbour (p297) as part of their regular loops throughout Indonesia. *Dobonsolo* travels to Java, Nusa Tenggara, Maluku and northern Papua; and *Awu* and *Tilongkabila* to Nusa Tenggara and southern Sulawesi. Prices are dependent on the route and the class of travel. Check for details locally.

You can inquire and book at the **Pelni office** (☎ 0361-763963; www.pelni.co.id; Jl Raya Kuta 299; 🕒 8am-noon & 1-4pm Mon-Thu, 8-11.30am & 1-4pm Fri, 8am-1pm Sat) in Tuban and the **Pelni office** (☎ 0361-721377; 🕒 8am-4pm Mon-Fri, 8am-12.30pm Sat) at Benoa Harbour.

GETTING AROUND

Bali is a small island with good roads and regular, inexpensive public transport. Traffic is heavy on the main roads from Denpasar south to the Kuta region and Sanur, east about as far as Semarapura and west across to the port of Gilimanuk. Roads are uncrowded on the rest of the island. If you rent your own vehicle, it's generally easy to find your way around – main roads are signposted and maps are readily available. Off the main routes, most roads are surfaced but often potholed and signage is not good.

It's worth noting that many pricier restaurants in places such as South Bali and Ubud will arrange free transport to/from the establishment. Just ask.

To/From the Airport

Ngurah Rai airport is just south of Kuta Beach, a 25-minute walk max. You can arrange usually hassle-free prepaid taxis from the official counters, just outside the terminals. See the boxed text (above) for approximate costs to various destinations.

If you have a surfboard, you will be charged at least 35,000Rp extra, depending on its size.

The thrifty can walk across the airport car park to the right from the terminals and continue a couple of hundred metres to the airport road, where you can hail a regular cab for about half the above amounts. You can also get a bemo (minibus) into Denpasar here as well.

PREPAID TAXIS FROM NGURAH RAI AIRPORT

Destination	Fare (Rp)
Denpasar	70,000
Jimbaran	50,000
Kuta Beach	40,000
Legian	45,000
Nusa Dua	85,000
Sanur	85,000
Seminyak	55,000
Ubud	175,000

Bemo

Most of Bali's public transport is provided by cramped minibuses, usually called bemo, but on some longer routes the vehicle may be a full-sized bus. Denpasar is the transport hub of Bali and has bus/bemo terminals for all the various destinations. Travel in southern Bali often requires travelling via one or more of the Denpasar terminals, which can make for an inconvenient and time-consuming trip.

The fare between main towns may be posted at the terminals, or you can ask around. You can also flag down a bemo pretty much anywhere along its route, but you may be charged the *harga turis* (tourist price) – Bali bemos are notorious for overcharging tourists. Ask a local the correct fare before starting a journey, or watch what people pay and give the same when you get off. Local rides cost a minimum of 2000Rp.

Beware of pickpockets on bemos – they often have an accomplice to distract you, or use a package to hide the activity.

Boat

Small boats go to a number of islands around Bali, notably those in the Nusa Lembongan group. They will usually pull up to a beach, and you have to wade to and from the boat with your luggage and clamber aboard over the stern. Details of boat services are given in the relevant sections. There are also larger tourist boats to Nusa Lembongan (p349).

Car & Motorcycle

A small Suzuki or Toyota jeep is the typical rental vehicle in Bali. Typical costs are 80,000Rp to 120,000Rp per day, including insurance and unlimited kilometres but not including fuel. Hiring a car with driver will cost, all-inclusive, around 350,000Rp for an eight- to 10-hour day.

Motorcycles are a popular way to get around Bali, but can be dangerous. Most rental motorcycles are between 90cc and 125cc, with 100cc being the usual size. Rental charges vary with the bike, period of hire and demand. The longer the hire period the lower the rate; the bigger or newer the bike the higher the rate. Typically you can expect to pay from around 30,000Rp a day. This includes a flimsy helmet, which is compulsory and provides protection against sunburn but not much else.

You can arrange rentals from any place you are staying, or in tourist areas just by walking down the street. Offers will pour forth.

Taxi

Metered taxis are common in South Bali, Denpasar and Ubud. They are essential for getting around Kuta and Seminyak, where you can easily flag one down. Elsewhere, they're often a lot less hassle than haggling with bemo jockeys and charter drivers.

The usual rate for a taxi is 5000Rp flag fall and 2000Rp per kilometre, but the rate is higher in the evening. If you phone for a taxi, the minimum charge is 10,000Rp. Any driver who claims meter problems or who won't use it should be avoided.

The most reputable taxi agency is **Bali Taxi** (☎ 0361-701111), which uses distinctive blue vehicles with the words 'Bluebird Group' over the windshield. Drivers speak reasonable English and use the meter at all times. There's even a number to call with complaints (☎ 0361-701621).

After Bali Taxi, standards decline rapidly. Some are acceptable, although you may have a hassle getting the driver to use the meter and fending off offers for shopping, massage etc.

Tourist Shuttle Bus

Tourist shuttle buses travel between the main tourist centres in Bali and connect to destinations on Lombok. Shuttle buses are quicker, more comfortable and more convenient than public transport, and though more expensive, they are very popular with budget and midrange travellers. If you're with a group of three or more people (or sometimes even two), it will probably be cheaper to charter a vehicle, however.

Perama (www.peramatour.com) is the main operator. It also has offices or agents in Kuta (p287), Sanur (p297), Ubud (p324), Lovina (p373), Padangbai (p337) and Candidasa (p340). At least one bus a day links these tourist centres with more frequent services to the airport. There are also services to Kitimani and along the east coast between Lovina and Candidasa via Amed by demand.

Fares are reasonable (for example Kuta to Lovina is 70,000Rp). Be sure to book your trip at least a day ahead in order to confirm schedules. It is also important to understand where Perama buses will pick you up and drop you off, as you may need to pay an extra 5000Rp to get to/from your hotel.

SOUTH BALI

For many people South Bali *is* Bali; for many others it is anything but. Chaotic Kuta and upscale Seminyak throb around the clock. In the south, the Bukit Peninsula is home to some of the island's largest resorts, while in the east Sanur follows the subdued beat of its reef-protected surf. The coast features a fine range of beaches.

KUTA & LEGIAN

☎ 0361

The Kuta region is overwhelmingly Bali's largest and tackiest tourist beach resort. Most visitors come here sooner or later because it's close to the airport and has the greatest range of budget hotels, restaurants and tourist facilities. Some find the area overdeveloped and seedy, but if you have a taste for a busy beach scene, shopping and nightlife, you will probably have a great time. Go elsewhere on the island if you want a quiet, unspoilt tropical hideaway.

It is fashionable to disparage Kuta and its immediate neighbour to the north, Legian, for their rampant development, low-brow nightlife and crass commercialism, but the cosmopolitan mixture of beach-party he-

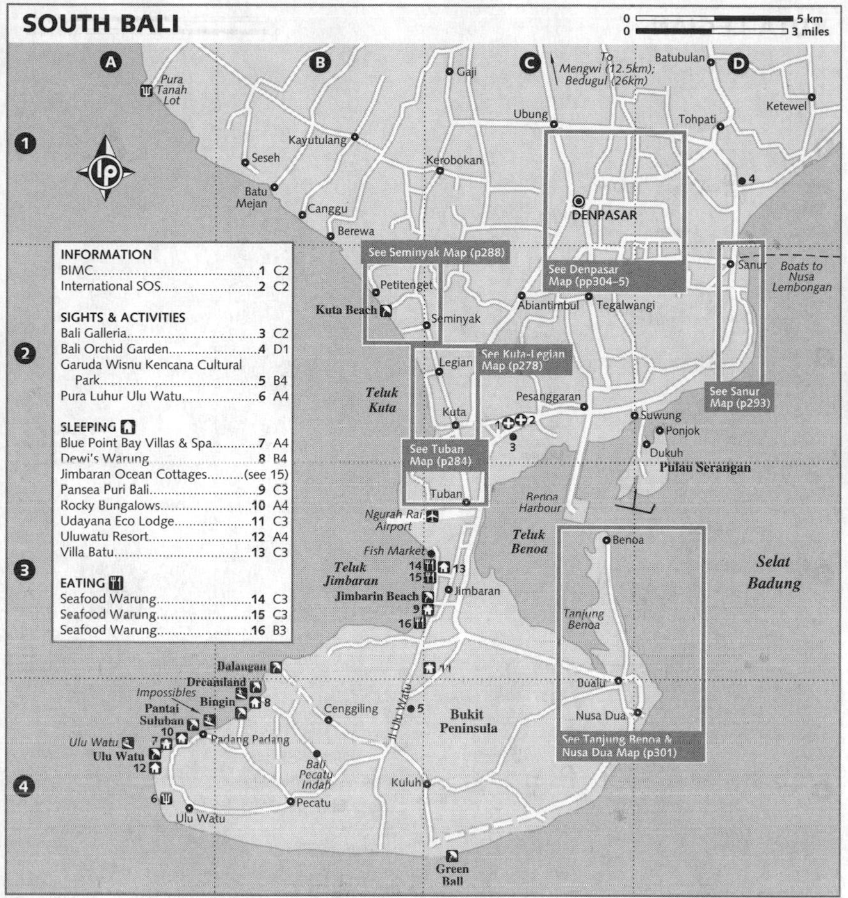

donism and entrepreneurial energy can be exciting. It's not pretty, but it's not dull either, and the amazing growth is evidence that a lot of people find something to like in Kuta.

Kuta has the most diversions and the best beach – but the worst traffic and most persistent hawkers.

Legian is a slightly quieter version of Kuta and seems to appeal mostly to sunseekers who have outgrown Kuta. The hotels are slightly more genteel, as is everything else.

Tuban, a small area between Kuta and the airport to the south, is short on character but does boast several large hotels and a vast new shopping centre.

History

Mads Lange, a Danish copra trader and an adventurer of the 19th century, established a successful trading enterprise near modern Kuta, and had some success in mediating between local rajahs and the Dutch, who were encroaching from the north. His business soured in the 1850s, and he died suddenly, perhaps murdered. His grave, and a monument erected later, are near Kuta's night market.

The original Kuta Beach Hotel was started by a Californian couple in the 1930s, but closed with the Japanese occupation of Bali in 1942. In the late 1960s, Kuta became a stop on the hippie trail between Australia and Europe, and an untouched

KUTA-LEGIAN

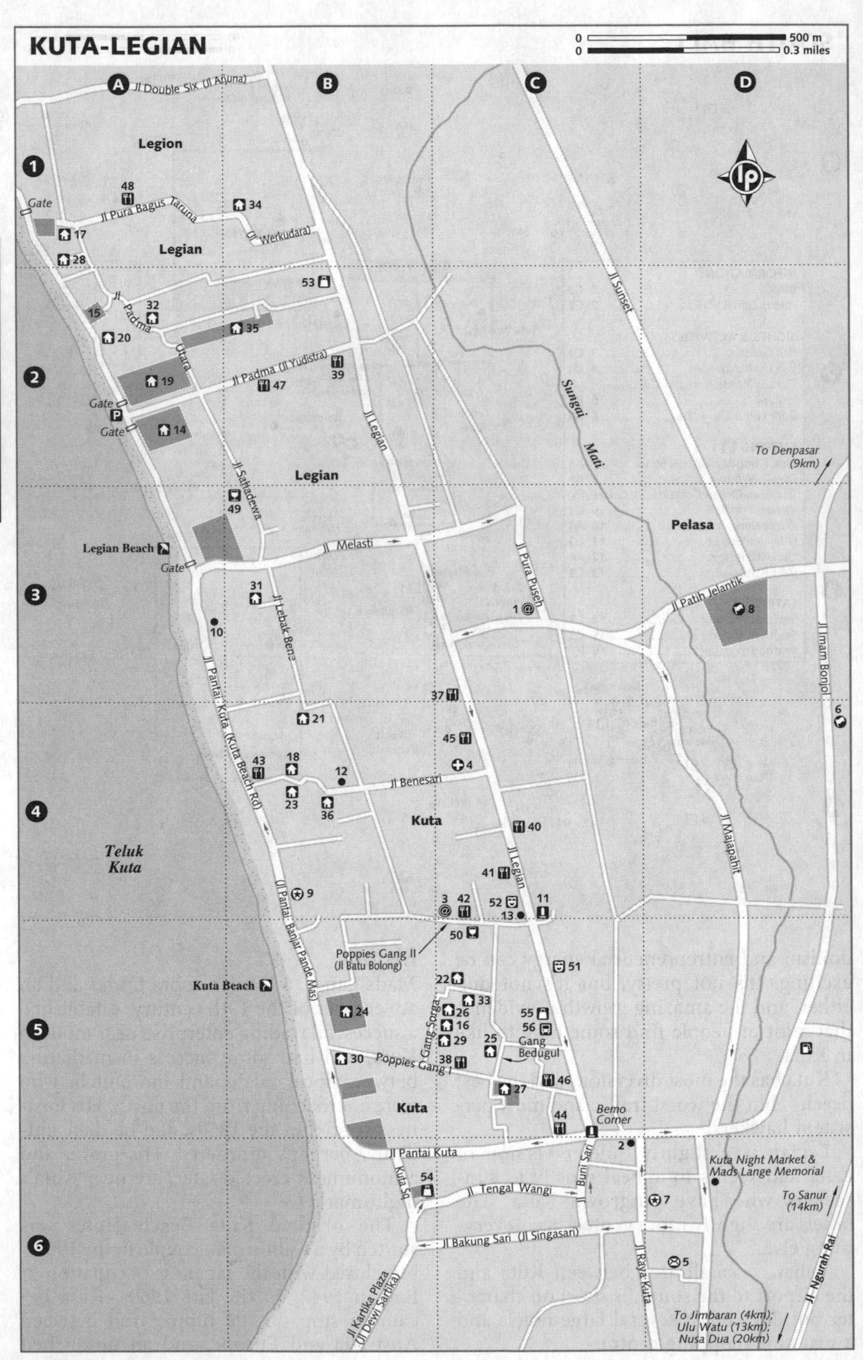

0 500 m
0 0.3 miles
Jl Double Six (Jl Arjuna)
Legion
Legian
Jl Pura Bagus Taruna
Jl Werkudara
Jl Padma Utara
Jl Padma (Jl Yudistra)
Jl Sahadewa
Jl Legian
Jl Melasti
Legian Beach
Gate
Jl Lebak Bene
Jl Pura Puseh
Jl Patih Jelantik
Jl Sunset
Sungai Mati
Pelasa
To Denpasar (9km)
Jl Imam Bonjol
Jl Pantai Kuta (Kuta Beach Rd)
Jl Benesari
Kuta
Teluk Kuta
Jl Majapahit
(Jl Pantai Banjar Pande Mas)
Poppies Gang II (Jl Batu Bolong)
Kuta Beach
Gang Sorga
Poppies Gang I
Gang Bedugul
Bemo Corner
Jl Pantai Kuta
Kuta Sq
Jl Tengal Wangi
Jl Buni Sari
Kuta Night Market & Mads Lange Memorial
To Sanur (14km)
Jl Bakung Sari (Jl Singasari)
Jl Raya Kuta
Jl Kartika Plaza (Jl Dewi Sartika)
Jl Ngurah Rai
To Jimbaran (4km); Ulu Watu (13km); Nusa Dua (20km)

'secret' surf spot. Accommodation opened and by the early 1970s Kuta had a delightfully laid-back atmosphere. Enterprising Indonesians seized opportunities to profit from the tourist trade, often in partnership with foreigners who wanted a pretext for staying longer.

As Kuta expanded, Legian further north became the quiet alternative, but now you can't tell where one ends and the other begins. Immediately north again, Seminyak continues north from Legian. All this has taken its toll, and the area is a chaotic mixture of shops, bars, restaurants and hotels on a confusing maze of streets and alleys, often congested with heavy traffic, thick with fumes and painfully noisy.

Orientation

The Kuta region is a disorienting place – it's flat, with few landmarks or signs, and the streets and alleys are crooked and often walled on one or both sides so it feels like a maze. The busy Jl Legian runs roughly parallel to the beach through Legian to Kuta. It's a two-way street in Legian, but in most of Kuta it's one way going south, except for an infuriating block near Jl Melasti where it's one way going north.

Between Jl Legian and the beach is a tangle of narrow side streets, with an amazing hodgepodge of tiny hotels, souvenir stalls, warung, bars, construction sites and even a few remaining stands of coconut palms. A small lane or alley is known as a *gang*; most are unsigned and too small for cars, although this doesn't stop some drivers trying. The best known are called Poppies Gang I and II – use these as landmarks. Most of the bigger shops, restaurants and nightspots are along Jl Legian and a few of the main streets that head towards the beach.

Note, too, that many of the English street names such as Jl Double Six (named after the beachside nightclub) are being renamed with local names (in this case Jl Arjuna). Maps in this book show both street names, and you'll find that old or new work equally well.

Information

You'll find tourist-information offices and tour-booking agencies every few metres along the main tourist streets of Kuta.

BOOKSHOPS

Little used bookstores and exchanges can be found scattered along the *gang* and roads, especially the Poppies.

Periplus Bookshop (Map p278; ☎ 763988; Matahari department store, Kuta Sq) On the 4th floor of this department store there is a good selection of books, magazines and newspapers. There is also a newsstand near the grocery section on the ground floor.

EMERGENCY

Police station (Map p278; ☎ 751598; Jl Raya Kuta; 24hr) Next to the Badung Tourist Office.

Tourist police post (Map p278; ☎ 224111; Jl Pantai Kuta; 24hr) Is a branch of the main police station in Denpasar. Right across from the beach, the officers – who have a gig that is sort of like a Balinese Baywatch – are friendly and anxious to help.

INTERNET ACCESS

Slow internet shops abound. The following have broadband connections and many services. Expect to pay 3000Rp to 5000Rp for 10 minutes.

Bali@Cyber Café & Restaurant (Map p278; ☎ 761326; Jl Pura Puseh; 8am-11pm) Has a full range of computer options as well as a good menu of snacks, meals and tasty smoothies.

Internet Outpost (Map p278; ☎ 763392; Poppies Gang II; 8am-2am) Has desks, couches and cold drinks.

MEDICAL SERVICES

BIMC and International SOS are major clinics aimed at foreigners.

BIMC (Map p277; ☎ 761263; www.bimcbali.com; Jl Ngurah Rai 100X; 24hr) On the bypass road just east of Kuta, near the Bali Galleria, and easily accessible from most of southern Bali. It's a modern Australian-run clinic that can do tests, hotel visits and arrange medical evacuation.

A basic consultation costs 600,000Rp.

International SOS (Map p277; ☎ 710505; www.sos-bali.com; Jl Ngurah Rai 505X; 24hr) Near BIMC; offers similar services at similar prices.

Legian Medical Clinic (Map p278; ☎ 758503; Jl Benesari; on call 24hr) Has an ambulance and dental service. It's 300,000Rp for a consultation with an English-speaking Balinese doctor, or 700,000Rp for an emergency visit to your hotel room. It has a well-stocked pharmacy attached to the clinic.

MONEY

There are several banks along Jl Legian, at Kuta Sq and Jl Pantai Kuta. In addition, ATMs abound, including at the ubiquitous Circle K and Mini Mart convenience stores.

The numerous 'authorised' moneychangers are efficient, faster, open long hours and offer better exchange rates. Rates can vary considerably, but be cautious, especially where the rates are markedly better than average – they may not have mentioned that they charge a commission or, judging by the number of readers' letters we've received, there may be a few that make their profit by adeptly shortchanging their customers.

POST

There are plenty of postal agencies along the streets for uncomplicated transactions of the stamp-and-postcard type.

Main post office (Map p278; Jl Selamet; 7am-2pm Mon-Thu, 7-11am Fri, 7am-1pm Sat) Is on a small road east of Jl Raya Kuta. It's small, efficient and has an easy, sort-it-yourself poste restante service. This post office is well-practised in shipping large packages.

TELEPHONE

Wartels (private telephone offices) are concentrated in the main tourist areas, particularly along Jl Legian and along the main *gang* between Jl Legian and the beach.

Dangers & Annoyances

Although the streets and *gang* are usually quite safe, beware of a dubious *gang* linking Poppies Gang I with Jl Pantai Kuta. Scooter-borne prostitutes (who may hassle single men late at night) consummate their business here.

HAWKERS

Occasional crackdowns mean that it's rare to find any food or souvenir carts in the Kuta tourist area, but street selling is common, especially on hassle street, Jl Legian. The beach is not unbearable, although the upper part features souvenir sellers and licensed massage ladies. Closer to the water, you can sunbake on the sand in peace – you'll soon find where the invisible line is. Most annoying are the touts pelting you with cries of 'Transport?'.

SURF

The surf can be very dangerous, with a strong current on some tides, especially up north in Legian. Lifeguards patrol swimming areas of the beaches at Kuta and Legian, indicated by red-and-yellow flags. If they say the water is too rough or unsafe to swim in, they mean it.

THEFT

This is not a big problem, but visitors do lose things from unlocked hotel rooms or from the beach. Going into the water and leaving valuables on the beach is simply asking for trouble (in any country). Snatch thefts are rare. Valuable items can be left at your hotel reception.

THE BALI BOMBINGS

On Saturday 12 October 2002, two bombs exploded on Kuta's bustling Jl Legian. The first blew out the front of Paddy's Bar. A few seconds later a far more powerful bomb obliterated the Sari Club. The blast and fireballs that followed destroyed or damaged neighbouring clubs, pubs, shops and houses. More than 300 people from at least 23 countries were injured. The number dead, including those unaccounted for, reached over 200, although the exact number will probably never be known.

Beyond the human toll, the bombings were disastrous to Bali economically. But almost three years later the economy had largely recovered. Devastatingly, in 2005 more bombs went off at a Kuta restaurant and seaside restaurants in Jimbaran. Over 20 were killed and tourism took another hit.

Laying blame for the acts has been mired in controversy. Jemaah Islamiyah, an Islamic terror group, was blamed for the 2002 blasts. Dozens were convicted but many sentences were short. Much speculation centres on the role of terror groups such as al-Qaeda in all the blasts. What is certain is that Bali's innocence is truly over.

Meanwhile many people visit the site of the 2002 blasts. A **memorial** (Map p278) is across from the site of the Sari Club and has an emotional effect on many who view it.

WATER POLLUTION

The sea water around Kuta is quite commonly contaminated by run off from both built-up areas and surrounding farmland, especially after heavy rain.

Activities

From the Kuta region you can easily go surfing, sailing, diving, fishing or rafting anywhere in southern Bali, and be back for the start of the evening happy hour. Many of your activities in Kuta will centre on the superb **beach**. Hawkers will sell you sodas and beer, snacks and other treats. You can rent lounge chairs and umbrellas (negotiable at 10,000Rp to 20,000Rp) or just crash on the sand.

MASSAGES & SPAS

The sybaritic pleasures of a massage or an interlude at a spa are an important part of many people's visit, and the choices are many. Professional masseurs, with licence numbers on their conical hats, offer massages on the beach. A realistic price is about 20,000Rp for a half-hour massage, or 40,000Rp for one hour, but you might have to bargain hard to get near this price if things are busy. Most spas offer facials, waxing and numerous indulgent services.

In the typically calm setting at **Jamu Spa** (Map p278; ☎ 752520; www.jamutraditionalspa.com; Alam Kul Kul, Jl Pantai Kuta; traditional massage US$35; 🕑 9am-9pm) you can enjoy indoor massage rooms that open onto a pretty garden courtyard. If you've ever wanted to be a fruit salad, here's your chance, as you can have various treatments that involve tropical nuts, coconut, papaya and more.

There are many **Mandara Spas** (www.mandaraspa-asia.com) in top-end hotels including **Hotel Padma Bali** (Map p278; ☎ 752111; Jl Padma 1; massages from US$35; 🕑 10am-8pm), where the divine spa is decorated with water features and impressive stone sculptural reliefs.

Kuta for Children

Minigolf is available at many resort hotels and, if it's too hot to be outside, Timezone video arcades are located in the two Matahari department stores.

Le Speed Karts (Map p284; ☎ 757850; Jl Kartika Plaza, Tuban; 5-min ride 40,000Rp; 🕑 10am-10pm) Fun, small go-kart track.

Waterbom Park (Map p284; ☎ 755676; www.waterbom.com; Jl Kartika Plaza, Tuban; adult/child/family US$18.50/9.50/50; 🕑 9am-6pm) Popular activities for kids include waterslides and pools at this park.

Tours

A vast range of tours all around Bali, from half-day to three-day tours, can be booked through travel agents or hotels in Kuta. These tours are a quick and easy way to see a few sights if your time is limited and you don't want to rent or charter a vehicle.

Sleeping

Kuta, Legian and Tuban have hundreds of places for you to stay. The top-end hotels

SURFING IN BALI

It really is a surfer's paradise in Bali. Breaks are found right around the south side of the island and there's a large infrastructure of schools, board rental places, cheap surfer dives and more that cater to the crowds.

Five famous spots you won't want to miss:

Kuta Beach (Map p277) Where surfing came to Asia. This is a good place for beginners, with long, steady breaks.

Dreamland (Map p277) Up-and-coming spot that of late has been all the rage. See p298.

Ulu Watu (Map p277) Some of the largest sets in Bali. See p299.

Medewi (Map p268) Famous point break with a ride right into a river mouth. See p355.

Nusa Lembongan (Map p347) The island is a mellow scene for surfers and non-surfers. The breaks are right in front of the places to stay. See p347.

Surfboard rentals start at 30,000Rp per day. One good place is **Redz** (Map p278; ☎ 763980; redzsurf@iol.it; Jl Benesari).

Tubes Surf Bar & Restaurant (Map p278; Poppies Gang II; 🕑 10-2am) is *the* surfers' hang-out. It shows surfing videos and publishes a tide chart, which is widely circulated. Also keep an eye out for free surfing magazines such as *Magic Wave*.

Quicksilver Boardriding School (Map p288; ☎ 751214; qbs@quicksilver.co.id; Jl Double Six; half-day lesson US$40) is one of the major surf schools, with classes every day.

are along the beachfront, midrange places are mostly on the bigger roads between Jl Legian and the beach, and the cheapest losmen (basic, often family-run, accommodation) are generally along the smaller lanes in between.

BUDGET

The best budget accommodation is in a losmen with rooms facing a central garden. Look for a place that is far enough off the main roads to be quiet, but close enough so that getting to the beach, shops and restaurants is no problem. Many losmen offer a simple breakfast.

Kuta

Many of the cheap places are along the tiny alleys and lanes between Jl Legian and the beach in central Kuta. This is a good place to base yourself: it's quiet, but only a short walk from the beach, shops and nightlife.

Komala Indah I (Map p278; ☎ 753185; Jl Benesari; r 40,000-150,000Rp; ❄) The range of rooms here is set around a pleasant garden. The cheapest of the 33 rooms have squat toilets, fans and twin beds only. Breakfast is included.

Rita's House (Map p278; ☎ 751760; s/d 50,000/60,000Rp) Since 1971 this cheap, clean, cramped and cheerful 23-room inn just north of Poppies Gang I has been renting rooms to weary surfers and budget travellers. The showers are cold and the air is fan-driven.

Berlian Inn (Map p278; ☎ 751501; s/d 60,000/80,000Rp, with hot water 90,000/120,000Rp) Located off Poppies Gang I, this is a cut above other budget accommodation. The 24 rooms at Berlian Inn are quiet and have ikat (cloth where a pattern is produced by dyeing the individual threads before weaving) bedspreads and an unusual open-air bathroom design.

Mimpi Bungalows (Map p278; ☎ 751848; kumimpi@yahoo.com.sg; r 80,000R-150,000Rp; ❄ 🏊) The cheapest of the 10 rooms here, off Gang Sorga, are actually the best value. The gardens boast plenty of shade and privacy and the pool is a good-size.

Kedin's II (Map p278; ☎ 763554; Gang Sorga; s/d 70,000/90,000Rp; 🏊) One of the best budget choices, the 16 cold-water rooms here have hints of style and are set in some fine gardens that feature a good-sized pool.

Hotel Lusa (Map p278; ☎ 753714; www.hotellusa.net; Jl Benesari; r US$11-37; ❄ 🏊) Older rooms here lack the flash of the rooms in a new block but they are the better value. All guests of the 57 rooms can enjoy the pool, café and leafy grounds.

Lima Satu Cottages (Map p278; ☎ 754944; Gang Bedugul; s/d 120,000/170,000Rp; ❄ 🏊) On a *gang* of cheapies off Poppies Gang I, the 11 rooms here are the best of the lot and quite comfortable.

Legian

The streets are wider and the pace is less frenetic than just south in Kuta. Budget places tend to be larger as well.

Senen Beach Inn (Map p278; ☎ 755470; Gang Camplung Mas 25; s/d 50,000/60,000Rp) In a little *gang* near Jl Melasti, this low-key place is run by friendly young guys. Rooms have outdoor bathrooms and are set around a small garden. It's an atmospheric, quiet place to stay. It has a small café.

Sinar Indah (Map p278; ☎ 755905; Jl Padma Utara; r 150,000-200,000Rp;) This standard, fairly basic losmen is handy to the beach. It offers 18 plain, clean rooms, which have hot water.

MIDRANGE

The bulk of accommodation in the Kuta area falls into the midrange category. Quality varies widely, with some places offering quite a bit in terms of location, amenities and service.

Kuta

Most of these places are handy to the beach.

Suji Bungalow (Map p278; ☎ 765804; www.sujibglw.com; r US$19 29;) Off Poppies Gang I, this fine, friendly place has a choice of bungalows and 47 rooms set in a spacious, quiet garden around a pool. It's not flash, but it's better than many similarly priced options. There's also a shady poolside café.

Sari Yasa Samudra Bungalows (Map p278; ☎ 751562; fax 752948; Jl Pantai Kuta; s/d US$20/23, with air-con US$35/40;) An excellent location directly opposite the beach makes this place fine value. It has pleasant bungalows set in lush gardens and the large pool has been renovated. Breakfast is included.

Un's Hotel (Map p278; ☎ 757409; www.unshotel.com; Jl Benesari; s/d US$25/28, with air-con US$33/48;) Un's is one of those Kuta places that somehow feels like a remote resort even though it is the heart of the action. It's a two-storey place, with bougainvillea spilling over the balconies which face a pool. The 30 spacious rooms have solar hot water, antiques and open-air bathrooms.

Kuta Seaview Cottages (Map p278; ☎ 751961; www.kutaseaviewhotel.com; Jl Pantai Kuta; r US$60-85;) The 27 stylishly decorated cottages and 45 large rooms come complete with fresh flowers on the beds, and a lovely garden setting. It's popular with a younger crowd and its azure pool is well-placed facing the ocean.

Poppies Cottages (Map p278; ☎ 751059; www.poppies.net; Poppies Gang I; r US$70-85;) This Kuta institution has a lush, green garden setting for its 20 thatch-roofed cottages, which have outdoor sunken baths. The peaceful pool is surrounded by stone sculptures and water fountains, and almost makes you forget you are in the heart of Kuta.

Legian

Hotel Sayang Maha Mertha (Hotel Sayang Beach Lodging; Map p278; ☎ 751249; www.sayanghotel.com; r US$8-45;) The 56 rooms here, off Jl Lebak Bene, range from basic with cold water to quite comfortable with a range of amenities like satellite TV. It has a bar and billiards, and is popular with surfers.

Three Brothers Inn (Map p278; ☎ 751566; www.threebrothersbungalows.com; Jl Padma Utara; r US$20-35, with air-con US$30-32;) Twisting banyan trees shade scores of brick bungalows holding 90 rooms in the Brothers' sprawling and garden-like grounds. The fan rooms are the best option, but all rooms are spacious, some have lovely outdoor bathrooms, and most have solar hot water.

Hotel Kumala Pantai (Map p278; ☎ 755500; www.kumalapantai.com; Jl Werkudara; r US$30-50;) One of the great deals in Legian. The 88 rooms are large, with marble baths that have separate shower and tub. The three-storey blocks are set in nicely landscaped grounds across from the beach. The breakfast buffet is bountiful.

Puri Tantra Beach Bungalows (Map p278; ☎ 753195; puritantra@telkom.net; Jl Padma Utara 50X; s/d/f US$35/40/55) These six charming, traditional, fan-only cottages are a step back in time and make for a mellow retreat. All have outdoor bathrooms and are right by the beach, which is reached through a small red door.

Hotel Puri Raja (Map p278; ☎ 755902; www.puriraja.com; Jl Padma Utara; r US$45-65;) Right on a great stretch of beach, the Puri Raja offers good value with its two large, circular pools and uncrowded grounds. The 72 rooms have balconies or patios and include satellite TV. More money gets you up by the pools or beach.

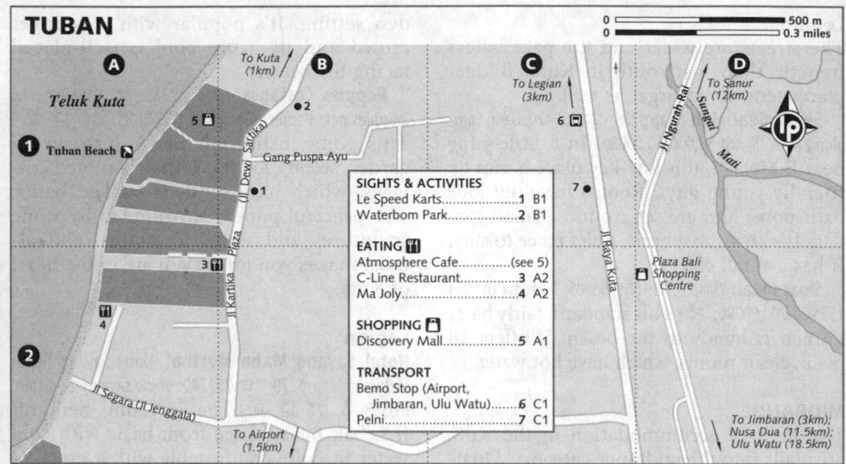

TOP END

Getting a room on Kuta Beach is one of Bali's great pleasures. Note that those in Kuta proper are separated from the beach by a busy main road.

Kuta

Alam Kul Kul (Map p278; ☎ 752520; www.alamkulkul.com; Jl Pantai Kuta; r/villas US$125/250;) The Alam has a gorgeous setting among majestic, gnarled banyan trees. Rooms and villas have contemporary styling with lots of attention to detail and elaborate and romantic furnishings. There's a kids' daycare centre. The Jamu Spa (p281) is on-site.

Legian

Most of the top-end places in Legian are directly opposite the beach on stretches of road closed to traffic. These tend to be relaxed places favoured by families.

Bali Niksoma Beach Resort (Map p278; ☎ 751946; www.baliniksoma.com; Jl Padma Utara; r US$88-125, villas US$438;) The mannered and minimalist style here comes right from the pages of a design magazine. There are two multilevel pools, one of which seems to disappear into the ocean and horizon. The 58 rooms are exquisite and the villas sublime. There is a health club and a noteworthy spa.

Bali Mandira Hotel (Map p278; ☎ 751381; www.balimandira.com; Jl Pantai Kuta; r US$120, cottages from US$150;) Gardens filled with bird of paradise flowers set the tone at the Bali Mandira. Cottages have modern interiors, and the bathrooms are partly open-air. A dramatic pool at the peak of a stone ziggurat housing the spa offers uninterrupted ocean views. It also has a pleasant open-air beachfront café.

Eating

There's a profusion of places to eat around Kuta and Legian. Travellers' and surfers' cafés with their cheap menus of Indonesian standards, sandwiches and pizza are ubiquitous. Other forms of Asian fare can be found as well and numerous places serve fresh seafood, steaks and pasta.

If you're looking for the laid-back scene of a classic travellers' café, wander the various *gang* and look for the crowds. Often what's busy one night will be quiet the next. For quick snacks and other victuals, Circle K and Mini Mart convenience stores are everywhere and open 24 hours.

TUBAN

The beachfront hotels all have numerous restaurants. In most cases the best feature for nonguests are the beachside cafés, which are good for a tropical snack or a sunset drink.

C-Line Restaurant (Map p284; ☎ 751285; Jl Kartika Plaza 33; dishes 20,000-50,000Rp) Local art lines the walls and bougainvillea shades the tables. Breakfasts, pasta, Indo standards, seafood and more are on the menu. The banana smoothies are tops.

Atmosphere Cafe (Map p284; ☎ 769501; Discovery Mall, Jl Kartika Plaza; dishes 20,000-60,000Rp; 11am-1am;) This posh, stylish café overlooks the surf. There's a large, umbrella-shaded patio and sleek lounge inside.

Ma Joly (Map p284; ☎ 753708; Jl Segara; dishes 25,000-80,000Rp; noon-11pm) An upscale restaurant right on the beach, Ma Joly has a creative menu of seafood and pasta, and a good wine list.

KUTA

On the Beach

Busy Jl Pantai Kuta keeps beachside businesses to a minimum in Kuta. Beach vendors are pretty much limited to drinks.

La Cabana (Map p278; ☎ 766156; Jl Benesari at Jl Pantai Kuta; dishes 15,000-25,000Rp) A nice place on an otherwise barren strip, there are little fountains to cover the traffic noise and you have a clear view of sunsets. The menu has all the Kuta standards.

Central Kuta

Bamboo Corner (Map p278; Poppies Gang I; dishes 6000-9,000Rp) This surfer classic has vegetarian plus local dishes. It's very popular and the fast turnover keeps things ultra fresh. The atmosphere can be described as veteran.

Made's Warung (Map p278; ☎ 755297; Jl Pantai Kuta; dishes 18,000-90,000Rp) Longtime visitors debate whether longtime favourite Made's still 'has it', but service has definitely improved over recent years. What's certain is that the menu of Indonesian classics is prepared and served with more flair and care than the usual warung.

Poppies Restaurant (Map p278; ☎ 751059; Poppies Gang I; dishes 30,000-80,000Rp) Poppies was one of the first restaurants in Kuta (Poppies Gang I is named after it), and is popular for its lush garden setting and romantic atmosphere. Refined Balinese fare joins steaks and seafood on a menu that features many items made with local organic ingredients. You may need to book.

Along Jalan Legian

The eating choices along Jl Legian seem endless, but avoid tables close to the busy street.

Aroma's Café (Map p278; ☎ 751003; Jl Legian; dishes 20,000-45,000Rp) A gentle garden setting encircled by water fountains is a perfect place to start the day over great juices, breakfasts and coffee. Other times the menu has good versions of Western and Indonesian classics.

Kopi Pot (Map p278; ☎ 752614; Jl Legian; dishes 22,000-40,000Rp) Shaded by trees, Kopi Pot is popular for its coffees, milk shakes and yummy desserts, as well as seafood and European and Indonesian main dishes. The upstairs dining area offers shelter if rain threatens the street-level outdoor tables.

Ketupat (Map p278; ☎ 754209; Jl Legian; dishes 25,000-120,000Rp) Hidden behind the Jonathan Gallery, Ketupat is a calm, serene oasis. The dining pavilions all centre on a strikingly blue pool. Dishes originate from across Indonesia, including Javanese curries, such as *nasi hijau harum* (fried rice with greens, shrimp and herbs). Gelato is sold out front.

Mama's (Map p278; ☎ 761151; Jl Legian; dishes 30,000-70,000Rp; 24hr) This German classic serves up schnitzel and other meaty dishes around the clock. The beer comes by the litre and the open-air bar is a fine place for enjoying satellite sports.

Poppies Gang II

Kori Restaurant & Bar (Map p278; ☎ 758605; Poppies Gang II; meals 15,000-80,000Rp) Kori wanders through a gorgeous assemblage of gardens and ponds. Popular with expats, it has a good selection of steaks, pasta, upscale Indonesian, burgers and more. You can have a secluded rendezvous in the flower-bedecked nooks out back. The drink list is long and includes many non-clichéd tropical drinks. There's live jazz some nights.

LEGIAN

Legian has some good restaurants with good views of the surf in its seaside hotels. Many places on Jl Melasti don't aspire to anything more than luring in jet-lagged tourists.

Wayan & Friends (Map p278; ☎ 761024; Jl Padma; dishes 9000-40,000Rp) Wayan and his pals have a relaxed place with vivid tablecloths and low lighting. It has delicious vegetable juices, and gourmet sandwiches, which you can customise, made with freshly baked baguettes. There's a small kids' menu.

Indo-National (Map p278; ☎ 759883; Jl Padma; dishes 20,000-90,000Rp) Thanks to its popularity, the Indo-National has moved to larger quarters. Many of the dishes – there are nightly specials – are seafood, and the mixed platter (45,000Rp) is a feast. The welcome is effusive and genuine. The hosts and staff remember you after one visit, and after a week you can feel like a longtime regular.

Yut'z (Map p278; ☎ 765047; Jl Pura Bagus Taruna 52; 30,000-70,000Rp) An upscale and modern version of a Swiss and European restaurant, Yut'z overlooks the street and a small garden. Fruhstuck fanatics can get their fix here. Later in the day, the menu has a changing selection of specials from the creative kitchen.

Entertainment

Around 6pm, the sunset at the beach is the big attraction, perhaps while enjoying a drink at a café with a sea view. After a good dinner, many visitors are happy with another drink (or two) and a stroll in the cooler evening air. But a lot of people are on holiday and here to party, and in Kuta that means lots of drinking, dancing and late nights. The more sophisticated nightspots are mainly in Seminyak, where the ambience is decidedly hipper, and where many clubs don't get going until after 11pm.

BALINESE DANCE & MUSIC

The Ubud area is really the place to go for authentic dance and you'll see offers in many hotels from tour operators. But note that you'll not get back to Kuta until after 10pm with most of these. Expect to pay around US$20 each. Otherwise brochures touting Kuta-area performances can be found at every hotel reception.

BARS & CLUBS

Most bars are free to enter, and often have special drink promotions and 'happy hours' between about 5pm and 8pm. During the low season, when tourist numbers are down, you might have to visit quite a few venues to find one with any life. A cover charge is a rarity. Ambience ranges from the laid-back vibe of the surfer dives to the high-concept nightclubs with their long drink menus and hordes of prowling servers.

You'll find many low-key boozers, amid their flashier brethren, along Jl Legian.

Apache Reggae Bar (Map p278; ☎ 761212; Jl Legian 146; 🕑 11pm-3am) One of the rowdier spots in Kuta, Apache jams in locals and visitors, many of whom are on the make. The music is highly variable but the *arak* (colourless, distilled palm wine) flows very freely (often in huge plastic jugs) and, the next day, there's a good chance you won't remember what you heard anyway.

Bounty (Map p278; ☎ 752529; Jl Legian; 🕑 10pm-6am) Set on a faux sailing boat, the Bounty is a vast open-air disco that humps, thumps and pumps all night. Climb the blue-lit staircase and get down on the poop deck to hip hop, techno, house and anything else the DJs come up with. Frequent foam parties.

Dolphin (Map p278; ☎ 755376; Jl Sahadewa; 🕑 3-11pm) A popular spot in the heart of Legian, the Dolphin draws crowds nightly for shows that include bands playing everything from pop to country.

Fuel (Map p278; ☎ 765777; Jl Legian 62; 🕑 11am-5am) This high-concept café has a stark red-and-black design and such popular additions as 'sexy dancers'. There are lots of shot specials and the motto is 'eat, drink, groove'.

Shopping

Parts of the Kuta region are door-to-door shops and over the years these have steadily become more sophisticated. But there are still many simple stalls, where T-shirts, souvenirs and beachwear are the main lines, and where the price depends on your bargaining ability. Many of these stalls are crowded together in 'art markets' like the one near the beach end of Jl Bakung Sari or the one on Jl Melasti.

The bigger, Western-style stores generally have higher quality goods at higher fixed prices. Jl Legian is lined with shops, and although there are exceptions, the quality generally gets better as you head north to Seminyak.

ARTS & CRAFTS

Kuta shops sell arts and crafts from almost every part of the island, from Mas woodcarvings to Kamasan paintings to Gianyar textiles, and just about everything else in between. There are also many interesting pieces from other parts of Indonesia, some of questionable authenticity and value. There's a good selection of quality craft shops on Jl Legian, between Poppies Gang II and Jl Padma.

BEACHWEAR & SURF SHOPS

A huge range of surf shops sell big-name surf gear – including brands such as Mambo, Rip Curl, Quicksilver and Billabong – although the quality may not be as good as you'll find overseas, and is only marginally cheaper. Local names include Surfer Girl and Dreamland.

CLOTHING

The local fashion industry has diversified from beach gear to sportswear to fashion clothing. Most of the fashion shops are on or near Jl Legian.

From the intersection of Jl Padma and Jl Legian, north to Seminyak, you'll find some of the more interesting women's (and men's) clothing shops as well as interesting homeware shops (often the two are combined).

Uluwatu (Map p278; ☎ 751933; Jl Legian) There are numerous branches across South Bali. This is one of the largest and is an elegant shop for browsing through the collections of lace-accented linen and cotton clothing. The items are made in villages around Tabanan in West Bali.

Komodo (Map p278; ☎ 761147; Jl Legian 427, Legian) A licensed store for the well known fun and funky UK label. It carries other lines as well.

DEPARTMENT STORES & MALLS

Discovery Mall (Map p284; ☎ 755522; www.discoveryshoppingmall.com; Jl Kartika Plaza; 9am-9pm) Your eyes follow the beautiful sweep of sand south along the Kuta shore until you see…this! Huge and hulking, this enormous new mall is built on the water and is filled with stores of every kind – most somewhat upscale.

Matahari department store (Map p278; ☎ 757588; Kuta Sq; 9.30am-10pm) This store has fairly staid clothing, a floor full of souvenirs, jewellery, a supermarket and the recommended Periplus bookshop.

Bali Galleria (Map p277; ☎ 758875; Jl Ngurah Rai) A large open-air Western-style mall that is busy with locals and tourists alike. There's numerous large stores and plenty of shops with well-known names (Body Shop, Marks & Spencer etc).

Getting There & Away

BEMO

Public bemos regularly travel between Kuta and the Tegal terminal in Denpasar – the fare should be 8000Rp. Most bemos go only to the terminal area in Kuta (on Jl Raya Kuta just east of Bemo Corner).

PERAMA TOURIST SHUTTLE BUSES FROM KUTA

Destination	Fare (Rp)
Candidasa	40,000
Lovina	70,000
Padangbai	40,000
Sanur	15,000
Ubud	30,000

BUS

Public Bus

Travel agents in Kuta sell tickets to Java and Lombok for buses that depart from Ubung terminal in Denpasar; you'll have to get yourself to Ubung. The tickets will be slightly more expensive than if you buy them at Ubung, but it's worth it to avoid a trip into Ubung and to be sure of a seat when you want to go. For public buses to anywhere else in Bali you'll have to go first to the appropriate terminal in Denpasar, and pay your money there.

Tourist Shuttle Bus

Shuttle bus tickets are sold at most travel agents – buy them a day ahead, or call the company and pay when you check in.

Perama (Map p278; ☎ 751551; www.peramatour.com; Jl Legian 39; 7am-10pm) is the main shuttle bus operation, and will sometimes pick you up from your hotel for free (confirm this when making arrangements). Perama usually has at least one bus a day to its destinations (see boxed text, above). In busy seasons, there will be three or more to popular spots like Ubud.

Getting Around

See p275 for details on getting around. Besides the frequent taxis, you can rent a scooter – often with a surfboard rack – or a bike. Just ask where you are staying. One of the nicest ways to get around the Kuta and Legian area is by foot, along the beach.

SEMINYAK

Seminyak is the most exciting part of South Bali. It's the home of the best restaurants, bars and clubs. In fact, new ones literally open every week.

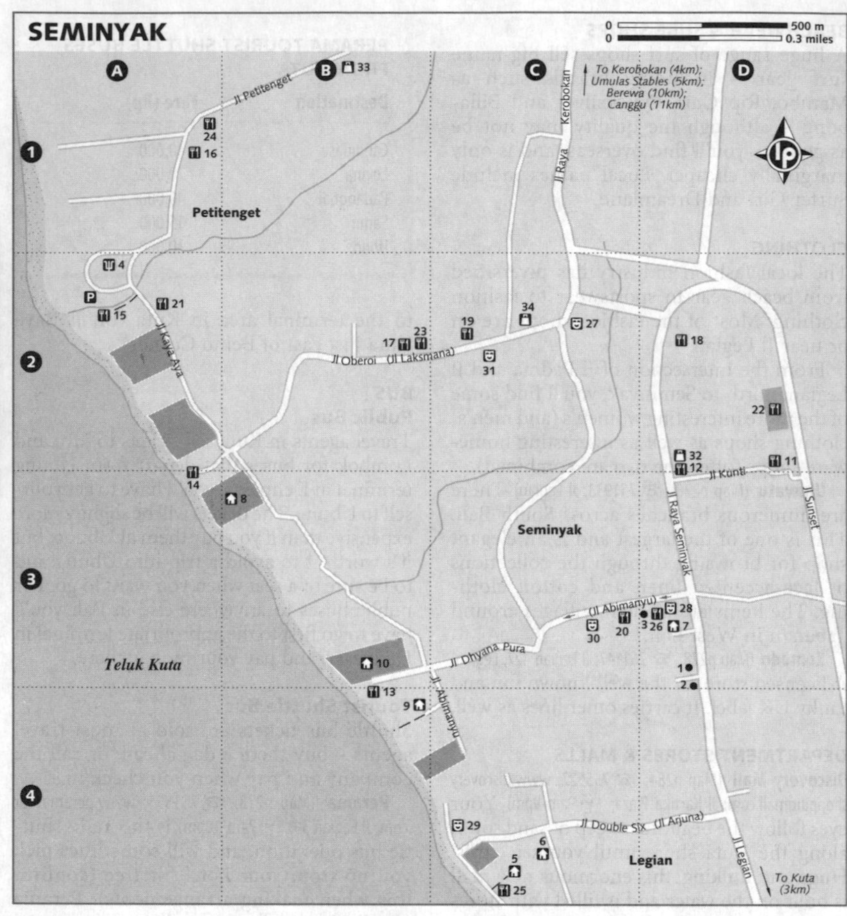

All this creative energy is yours to enjoy, possibly from the luxury of one of the world-class hotels found along the water. Although all this fun comes at a price, Seminyak is an exciting place where half the fun is just finding out what's new.

Orientation

The southern border of Seminyak runs along Jl Double Six. The only road along the beach is down here, it passes several notable clubs and restaurants. Jl Raya Seminyak is the continuation of Jl Legian from Kuta. Jl Oberoi heads west to the resort of same name and meets Jl Kaya Aya, which passes most of the resorts on the land side.

Seminyak shares many services with Kuta and Legian immediately to the south.

Information

Most of the hotels have broadband connections for guests. Cheap and slow internet shops can be found along the main streets including Jl Dhyana Pura and Jl Oberoi. ATMs can be found along all the main roads.

For medical services, see the Kuta & Legian section (p280).

Bintang Supermarket (☎ 730552; Jl Raya Seminyak 17) Newspapers, magazines, best-sellers and art books.

Tiger Pharmacy (☎ 732621; Jl Raya Seminyak 19; 🕑 24hr) Has a full range of prescription medications.

Sights

North of the string of hotels on Jl Kaya Aya, **Pura Petitenget** is an important temple and a scene of many ceremonies. It is one of a string of sea temples that stretches from Pura Luhur Ulu Watu on the Bukit Peninsula north to Tanah Lot in western Bali. It honours the visit of a 16th-century priest.

Activities

Because of the limited road access, the beach in Seminyak tends to be less crowded than further south in Kuta. This also means that it is less patrolled and the water conditions are less monitored. The odds of encountering dangerous riptides and other hazards are ever present especially as you head north.

The beach at the end of Jl Double Six is popular with locals and visitors alike for sports and general lounging.

SPAS

Look for lavish spas in all of the top hotels in Seminyak.

NT Health & Beauty Spa (☎ 732226; Jl Dhyana Pura 6B; 9am-10pm) offers a variety of services from simple haircuts (90,000Rp) to two-hour long treatments featuring exfoliations and other pleasures (200,000Rp).

BUNGY JUMPING

AJ Hackett Bungy (☎ 731144; Jl Arjuna; US$50; 10am-7pm Sun-Thu, 10am-7pm & 2-4am Fri & Sat), beside the beach at the Double Six Club (p291), has a great view of the coast that means you can't see the hideous tower you're standing on (or bouncing from).

Sleeping

Seminyak isn't just about top-end hotels. There's a good bunch of cheaper places to the south and they're close to the beach. But if you're looking for the best places to stay in Bali, you'll find several here.

BUDGET

Ned's Hide-Away (☎ 731270; nedshide@dps.centrin.net.id; Gang Bima 3; r from 80,000Rp) Named after Aussie icon Ned Kelly, this simple 15-room place is popular with those hoping to lie low between bouts of fun. Rooms have hot water and there's a character-filled bar. Look for the sign on Jl Legian, near Bintang Supermarket.

Blue Ocean (☎ 730289; r 120,000-130,000Rp, with air-con 150,000Rp;) Right near the beach, the Blue Ocean is a clean and basic place with hot water and pleasant outdoor bathrooms. Many of the 24 rooms have kitchens and there's action nearby day and night.

MIDRANGE

Hotel Kumala (☎ 732186; Jl Pura Bagus Taruna; r US$15-25;) Great value and convenient to both Legian and Seminyak, the Kumala has large older-style rooms with teak furniture, modern bathrooms, and two pools in a garden filled with bamboo stands, frangipani and bougainvillea.

Raja Gardens (☎ 730494; jdw@eksadata.com; Jl Abimanyu; r 200,000-300,000Rp;) Look for spacious, lush grounds in this quiet and secluded spot near the beach. The seven rooms are spotless and have touches of tropical style. The open-air bathrooms are filled with plants.

TOP END

Sofitel Seminyak Bali (☎ 730730; www.theroyal-seminyak.com; Jl Dhyana Pura; r from US$150, villas from US$500;) This hotel's beachside location is ideal and you can walk to the clubs

A WALK ON THE BEACH

That fabulous stretch of sand that starts in Kuta and runs north right to the west coast can be the focus for a great day out exploring. Start where Jl Pantai Kuta meets the shore and head north. As your mood demands, frolic in and out of the surf while taking breaks on the sand. Time yourself so that at about noon you'll be at the patch of beach where Jl Double Six meets the sand. Here you'll find a strip of shady outdoor cafés that have ocean views. After lunch you can join the many locals and visitors in a variety of beach games that give this fine patch of beach relentless energy. Continue north along the sand and ponder your massage options: choose from one of the ladies on the beach or something more elaborate at one of the spas in the beachside hotels. With the afternoon starting to wind down, take a break on a rental lounger on the sand and enjoy a beverage from the vendor. Finally as the sun heads down in the west, finish up at Ku De Ta (opposite), the popular beachside club that's not just a café but a scene. Eventually you can have dinner at one of the many dining options in Seminyak and then grab a cab home.

and restaurants on Jl Dhyana Pura. The rooms are done in a smart contemporary style. What really sets the property apart are the private walled units where the feel is like an old Balinese village.

our pick **Oberoi** (☎ 730361; www.oberoihotels.com; Jl Oberoi; r US$255-300, villas US$400-850;) One of the world's top hotels, the Oberoi has been a refined beachside retreat since 1971. The low-rise architecture is understated, as is the service. But every detail is spot on, right down to the selection of fruit that graces your room. All accommodation here have a private lanai (veranda) each, and as you move up through the food chain additional features include private villas, ocean views and private, walled pools. From the café overlooking the almost private sweep of beach to the numerous luxuries found in each unit, this is a place to spoil yourself. Many find it hard to leave even though the best of Seminyak nightlife is nearby.

In addition to luxurious hotels, Seminyak and the coast north is home to many rental villas. At the minimum they have a kitchen, living room and private garden, and often two or more bedrooms, so they are suitable for a family or a group of friends. Rates can range anywhere from US$500 for a modest villa to US$4000 per week and beyond for your own tropical estate. The following agencies are two among many: **Bali Villas** (☎ 0361-703060; www.balivillas.com) and **Elite Havens** (☎ 0361-731074; www.elitehavens.com).

Eating

Seminyak is spread out, so you won't be walking among the many dining choices, rather you'll be choosing a neighbourhood first. Note that, where indicated, some restaurants morph into clubs as the night wears on. Conversely some of the places listed under Bars & Clubs also do decent food.

JALAN DOUBLE SIX

Numerous places here near the beach have a funky atmosphere and are more hip than similar joints in Kuta.

Zanzibar (☎ 733529; Jl Double Six; dishes 20,000-45,000Rp) Sunset is prime time, but during the day you can enjoy the shade of the large trees overhead. The menu features vegetarian and pasta dishes with a dash of style. Breakfasts are good too.

JALAN DHYANA PURA

Zula Vegetarian Paradise (☎ 732723; Jl Dhyana Pura 5; dishes 15,000-40,000Rp; 8am-4am) It's all vegetarian at this fun little place where you can get tofu cheese, a tofu spring roll, tofu cheesecake, not to mention a tofu-chickpea burger. The long list of juices includes the highly appropriate (for Jl Dhyana Pura) 'Liver Cleanser' special.

Santa Fe Bar & Grill (☎ 731147; Jl Dhyana Pura 11A; dishes 15,000-45,000Rp; 7am-4am) The pizza and Southwest food here is popular and deservedly so. People can be found dining here at all hours, especially late when there's live music (mostly rock). Not surprisingly, tequila is popular.

Gado Gado (☎ 736966; Jl Dhyana Pura; mains 90,000-190,000Rp; lunch & dinner) This stylish place has a magical location on the beach. To the sound of the surf, enjoy the excellent service and the fine menu of Asian and Mediterranean fusion dishes. The bar is popular and refined.

JALAN RAYA SEMINYAK

Bali Deli (☎ 738686; Jl Kunti 117X) The deli counter at this upscale market is loaded with imported cheeses, meats and baked goods. This is the place to get food from home. A small café has wi-fi.

Pondok Duo (☎ 738834; Jl Raya Seminyak; dishes 6000-9000Rp) Choose from an array of traditional dishes at this modest Padang-style spot. Its popularity ensures fast turnover of the prepared dishes.

Café Moka (☎ 731424; Jl Raya Seminyak; dishes 15,000-40,000Rp;) Enjoy French-style baked goods at this fine bakery, which is popular for breakfast. Fresh deli cuisine like superb salads and tapas is served for lunch and dinner. The bulletin board is a window into the local expat community.

JALAN OBEROI

Otherwise known as 'Eat St', the new name Jl Laksmana is slowly catching on.

Mykonos (☎ 733253; Jl Oberoi 52; dishes 15,000-45,000Rp; 5pm-midnight) The island food of Greece comes to the island of Bali at this wildly popular spot. All the classics are here from meze like tzatziki to various grilled souvlakis. Cheap wine fuels the fun.

Rumours (☎ 738720; Jl Oberoi 100; mains 20,000-50,000Rp; 6pm-midnight) The menu spans steaks and Italian favourites. Portions are large and the quality is good which ensures its popularity. Be ready to wait.

Tuesday Night Pizza Club (☎ 730614; Jl Oberoi; pizza 25,000-118,000Rp; 6pm-midnight) Pizzas come in four sizes at this simple joint and have a range of goofy names like Hawaii Five-O (ham and pineapple) and The Italian Job (mozzarella and tomato). And guess what? They deliver.

La Lucciola (☎ 730838; Jl Oberoi; dishes 80,000-140,000Rp) A sleek beachside restaurant offers good views across a lovely lawn and sand to the surf from the 2nd-floor tables. The bar downstairs is big with sunset watchers. The menu is modern Australian (a tasty melange of Mediterranean, Asian, seafood and more) and Italian (try the risotto).

Ku De Ta (☎ 736969; Jl Oberoi; dishes 140,000-200,000Rp; 7am-1pm) Restaurant? Bar? Way of life? Ku De Ta swarms with Bali's beautiful. Kids play in the stylish pool while adults ponder drinks in the cigar bar and everyone ponders the gorgeous sunsets over the beach. The menu is a creative fusion mix and the service is professional.

Sate Bali (☎ 736734; Jl Oberoi 22; meals 195,000Rp; lunch & dinner) Some very fine traditional Balinese meals are served at this small but artful café. Prepare for dozens of small plates of fresh food. Service is sublime.

NORTHERN SEMINYAK

Seminyak Night Market (Jl Sunset) Gets going around 6pm and plenty of warung sell delicious *bakso* (meatball soup) and *soto ayam* (chicken soup). Loud music plays and there's a convivial atmosphere.

Waroeng Bonita (☎ 731918; Jl Petitenget; dishes 17,000-49,000Rp) Balinese dishes such as *ikan rica-rica* (fresh fish in a spicy green chilli sauce) are the specialitics at this cute little place with tables under the trees.

Living Room (☎ 735735; Jl Petitenget; mains 80,000-100,000Rp; 11am-11pm) At night hundreds of candles twinkle on and about the scores of outdoor tables at the new location of this lacy fantasy of a restaurant. The menu is Asian with good Thai, Vietnamese and Balinese dishes.

Entertainment

Jl Double Six is named for the legendary club on the beach and this area remains a centre of 3am Kuta-area club culture. Jl Dhyana Pura is popular for its ever-changing line-up of high-concept clubs and bars. Note that, where indicated, some of the places do good food in the evening while some of the places listed under Eating also do music.

JALAN DOUBLE SIX

The club of the same name is the big destination here. There are several other trendy clubs nearby.

Double Six Club (☎ 0812 462 7733; Jl Double Six; 11pm-6am) This veteran club got a massive remake, which has made it into a playground for the beautiful. The swimming pool is mostly for show and there are top international DJs playing hot mixes. An adjoining café seeks to nab sunset watchers.

JALAN DHYANA PURA

One of the joys of Jl Dhyana Pura is bouncing from place to place all night long. Many pure clubs snooze until after midnight.

Q-Bar (☎ 762361; Jl Dhyana Pura; 🕑 8pm-3am) This bright bar caters to gay clubbers but by no means exclusively. Rainbow lovers will rejoice; the music of choice is house. There are good views of the action – inside and out – from the upper floor.

Bali Pub (Jl Dhyana Pura; 🕑 6pm-1am) A laid-back place for cool jazz on a street of driving techno.

JALAN OBEROI

Aina Bar (☎ 730182; Jl Oberoi; 🕑 6pm-2am) Mellow rock is the music of choice at this intimate little open-fronted bar. Pull up a stool and chat up the bartender.

Woodstock (☎ 730629; Jl Oberoi; 🕑 6pm-3am) Love, peace and music. Hammocks hang from the rafters and there's a large garden out back. Music reflects the name.

Shopping

In Seminyak, fashion shops are much funkier than in Kuta. There are many interesting clothing stores and boutiques on this stretch of Jl Raya Seminyak. North of Jl Dhyana Pura there are numerous shops selling artworks, housewares, furniture and other designer goods aimed at helping you create your own 'Bali Style'.

Blue Glue (☎ 844 5956; Jl Raya Seminyak) Has a collection of Bali-made bathing suits from teensie to trendy.

Richard Meyer Culture (☎ 744 5179; Jl Petitenget 200X) This gallery sells works – mostly photos – by renowned contemporary Bali artists and is known for its shows and historical collection.

Salim Gallery (Jl Oberoi) A good-sized space that frequently has shows by noted local artists, such as the luminous work of Martin Agam Sitepu.

Getting There & Around

Most transport information is the same as for Kuta. Metered taxis are easily hailed. A taxi to the heart of Kuta will be about 10,000Rp. You can beat the traffic and have a good stroll by walking the beach south – Legian is about 20 minutes.

NORTH OF SEMINYAK

☎ 0361

As Seminyak grows, the small towns to its north grow as well. Kerobokan is where Seminyak was 10 years ago – on the cusp of major growth. Expats and land speculators are snatching up property here and in Canggu along the coast. Getting to most of the places listed is really only convenient with your own transport or by taxi. Think 20,000Rp or more from Kuta.

Kerobokan

Lots of interesting little places can be found here, a trend sure to continue. To get here from Kuta and other points in the south, follow Jl Legian north, through its Jl Raya Seminyak phase, until it becomes Jl Raya Kerobokan just north of Seminyak. Look for an ever-growing range of upscale shops and galleries along here.

Just past the jail off Jl Raya Kerobokan, **Warung Gossip** (☎ 0817 970 3209; Jl Pengubengan Kauh; meals 15,000-20,000Rp; 🕑 lunch) serves top-notch versions of Balinese warung staples. The line-up of food changes daily. There's also a café area for more formal dining.

Canggu

A popular surf spot with right- and left-hand breaks, Canggu is literally getting on the map. You'll spot quite a few satellite dishes poking above the rice paddies, denoting the locations of lavish expat homes. Surfers congregate at beaches where various local roads hit the sand. There's usually a few unnamed warung a few metres from the beach.

To get to Canggu, go west at Kerobokan and south at Kayutulang. Bemos leave from Gunung Agung terminal in Denpasar (5000Rp). Taxis from Kuta will run to 30,000Rp or more.

Batu Mejan

The next popular bit of beach northwest of Canggu Beach is Batu Mejan or Echo Beach. Besides the surfers' warung, there's the **Beach House** (☎ 738471; Jl Pura Batu Mejan; dishes 5000-40,000Rp), which faces the waves. It has a variety of couches and tables where you can hang out, watch the waves and enjoy the breakfasts, sandwiches and salads.

SANUR

☎ 0361

Sanur is a slightly upmarket sea, sun and sand alternative to Kuta. The white-sand beach is sheltered by a reef. The resulting low-key surf contributes to Sanur's nickname 'Snore', although this is also attributable to the area's status as a haven for expat retirees. Some parents prefer the beach at Sanur because its calmness makes it a good place for small children to play.

Sanur was one of the places favoured by Westerners during their prewar discovery of Bali. Artists Miguel Covarrubias, Adrien Jean Le Mayeur and Walter Spies, anthropologist Jane Belo and choreographer Katharane Mershon all spent time here.

Orientation

Sanur stretches for about 5km along an east-facing coastline, with the lush and green landscaped grounds of resorts fronting right onto the sandy beach. The appalling Grand Bali Beach Hotel, located at the northern end of the strip, fronts the best stretch of beach. West of the beachfront hotels is the noisy main drag, Jl Danau Tamblingan, with hotel entrances, oodles of tourist shops, restaurants and cafés.

Jl Ngurah Rai, commonly called Bypass Rd, skirts the western side of the resort area, and is the main link to Kuta and the airport.

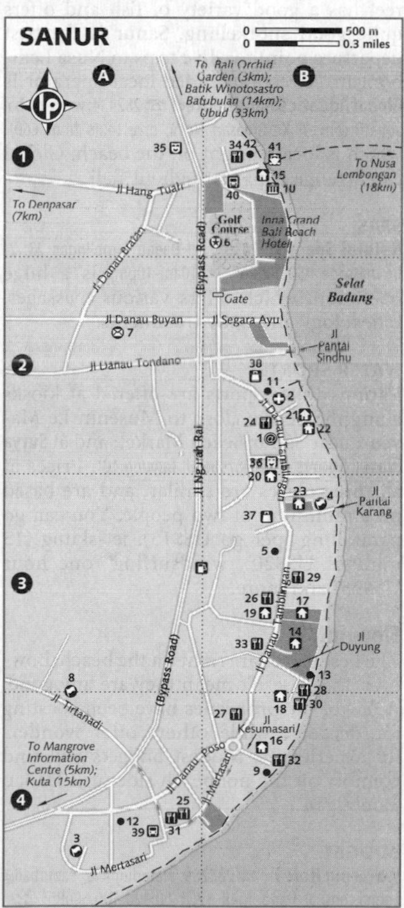

INFORMATION
Cybergate 1 B2
Dokter Paktek Umum 2 B2
French Consulate 3 A4
German Consulate 4 B3
Hardy's Supermarket 5 B3
Police Station 6 B1
Post Office 7 A2
UK Consulate 8 A3

SIGHTS & ACTIVITIES
Global Aquatic Diving Center 9 B4
Museum Le Mayeur 10 B1
Natural Spa 11 B2
Stone Pillar 12 A4
Surya Water Sports 13 B3

SLEEPING
Bali Hyatt 14 B3
Diwangkara Beach Hotel 15 B1
Hotel Palm Gardens 16 B4
Hotel Paneeda View 17 B3
Hotel Segara Agung 18 B4
Jati Homestay 19 B3
Keke Homestay 20 B3
Respati Bali 21 B2
Tandjung Sari 22 B2
Yulia 2 Homestay 23 B3

EATING
Alise's Restaurant 24 B2
Cat & Fiddle 25 A4
Lumut 26 B3
Massimo 27 B4
New Banjar Club 28 B3
Palay Restaurant 29 B3
Retro Café & Gallery (see 37)
Sanur Bay 30 B4
Sari Laut 31 A4
Stiff Chili 32 B4
Telaga Naga 33 B3
Watering Hole I Restaurant 34 B1

ENTERTAINMENT
Jazz Bar & Grille 35 A1
Speakezy's 36 B2

SHOPPING
Mama & Leon 37 B3
Rare Angon 38 B2

TRANSPORT
Bemo Stop 39 A4
Bemo Stop 40 B1
Boats to Nusa Lembongan 41 B1
Perama Office 42 B1

BALI

Information

Moneychangers here have a dubious reputation. There are numerous ATMs and banks along Jl Danau Tamblingan.

Other than a few used-book exchanges in hotels that will allow you to complete your Danielle Steele collection, Sanur lacks a good bookshop.

Some other services in town:

Cybergate (☎ 287274; Jl Danau Tamblingan; per hr 15,000Rp; 🕑 8am-10pm) Broadband, burns CDs.

Dokter Paktek Umum (☎ 282678; Jl Danau Tamblingan 27; 🕑 on call 24hr) Charges 100,000Rp per consultation.

Hardy's Supermarket (☎ 281914; Jl Danau Tamblingan 136; 🕑 8am-10pm) Sells newspapers and magazines.

Police station (☎ 288597; Jl Ngurah Rai)

Post office (☎ 754012; Jl Danau Buyan; 🕑 8am-7pm Mon-Sat) Located west of Jl Ngurah Rai.

Sights

MUSEUM LE MAYEUR

The Belgian artist Adrien Jean Le Mayeur de Merpes (1880–1958) arrived in Bali in 1932. Three years later he met and married the beautiful Legong dancer Ni Polok when she was 15. They lived in this compound when Sanur was still a quiet fishing village. The main house must have been a delightful place then – a peaceful and elegant home filled with art and antiques right by the tranquil beach. After his death, Ni Polok lived in the house until she died in 1985. The house is an interesting example of Balinese architecture – notice the beautifully carved shutters that recount the story of Rama and Sita from the Ramayana.

Some Le Mayeur paintings are displayed inside the **museum** (☎ 286201; adult/child 2000/1000Rp; 🕑 7.30am-3.30pm Sun-Thu, 7.30am-1pm Fri), with information in Indonesian and English. Some of Le Mayer's early works are interesting, Impressionist-style paintings from his travels in Africa, India, Italy, France and the South Pacific. Paintings from his early period on Bali are romantic depictions of Balinese daily life and beautiful Balinese women – often Ni Polok.

BALI ORCHID GARDEN

Given Bali's weather and volcanic soil, no one should be surprised that orchids grow very well. At this **garden** (Map p277; ☎ 466010; Jl Bypass Tohpati; adult/child 50,000/25,000Rp; 🕑 8am-6pm) you can see thousands of orchids in a variety of settings. It's 3km north of Sanur along Jl Ngurah Rai just past the major intersection with the coast road, Jl Bypass Tohpati.

STONE PILLAR

The pillar, behind Pura Belangjong, is Bali's oldest dated artefact and has ancient inscriptions recounting military victories of more than 1000 years ago. These inscriptions are in Sanskrit and are evidence of Hindu influence 300 years before the arrival of the Majapahit court.

Activities

DIVING & SNORKELLING

The diving near Sanur is not great, but the reef has a good variety of fish and offers quite good snorkelling. Sanur is the best departure point for dive trips to Nusa Lembongan. A recommended local operator is **Global Aquatic Diving Center** (☎ 282434; www.globalaquatic.com; Jl Kesumasari No 9; dive tours from €60), which is located right on the beach. Global can arrange trips throughout Bali.

SPAS

Natural Spa (☎ 283677; Jl Danau Tamblingan 23; 2-hr massage 450,000Rp; 🕑 10am-10pm) is a huge operation, which offers various massages, reflexology and body treatments.

WATER SPORTS

Various water sports are offered at kiosks along the beach: close to Museum Le Mayeur; near Sanur Beach Market; and at **Surya Water Sports** (☎ 287956; Jl Duyung 10). Prices at all three places are similar, and are based on a minimum of two people. You can go parasailing (per go US$15), jet-skiing (15 minutes US$20), windsurfing (one hour US$25) and more.

Sleeping

The best places are right on the beach; however, that doesn't mean they are any good. A few of the properties have been coasting for decades, while others offer wonderful experiences. Modest budgets will find comfort on the nonbeach side of Jl Danau Tambligan.

BUDGET

Watering Hole I (☎ 288289; wateringhole_sanurbali@yahoo.com; Jl Hang Tuah 37; r 60,000-100,000Rp; ❄)

In the northern part of Sanur, the Hole is a busy, friendly place, with 25 pleasant, clean rooms over a few storeys. The cheapest rooms have fan cooling and cold water. It also has the Watering Hole Restaurant, right.

Keke Homestay (☎ 287282; Jl Danau Tamblingan 96; s/d 60,000/75,000Rp; with air-con 100,000/150,000Rp;) Set back a little from the noisy main road, Keke welcomes travellers with seven quiet, clean rooms. They all have cold water and fans.

Yulia 2 Homestay (☎ 287495; kf_billy@indo.net.id; Jl Danau Tamblingan; s/d 80,000/90,000Rp) Yulia 2 has seven clean, pleasant rooms in a somewhat cramped compound. All have hot water and fans and there's a fun little café.

Jati Homestay (☎ 281730; www.balivision.com/hotels/jatihomestay; Jl Danau Tamblingan; r 150,000-200,000Rp) Situated in pretty grounds, Jati has 15 pleasant and clean bungalows, with small but well-organised kitchen facilities and hot water.

MIDRANGE

Hotel Segara Agung (☎ 288446; www.segaraagung.com; Jl Duyung 43; r US$20-35, f US$50;) Down a quiet, unpaved residential street, this hotel is only a two-minute walk to the beach. The 16 rooms are clean and pleasant, staff are friendly and there's a big swimming pool.

Hotel Palm Gardens (☎ 287041; plmgrd@indosat.net.id; Jl Kesumasari 3; r from 250,000Rp;) Everything is peaceful here, from the 17 low-key rooms to the relaxed service. It's close to the beach and there is a nice medium-sized pool with a small waterfall.

Diwangkara Beach Hotel (☎ 288577; dhvbali@indosat.net.id; Jl Hang Tuah 54; r from US$40;) Facing the beach near the end of Jl Hang Tuah, this 38-room hotel is a tad old-fashioned (especially the pool), but the smaller bungalows are right by the beach.

Respati Bali (☎ 288427; brespati@indo.net.id; Jl Danau Tamblingan 33; r US$40-60;) Despite its narrow site, the Respati's 32 contemporary bungalow-style rooms don't feel cramped. The beach frontage is a plus and the pool is a decent-size.

Hotel Paneeda View (☎ 288425; www.paneedaview.com; Jl Danau Tamblingan 89; r from US$55;) Right on the beach, this hotel has three small pools and 55 rooms. Much attention to detail is devoted to the attractively redecorated rooms; each has a patio.

TOP END

Bali Hyatt (☎ 281234; www.bali.resort.hyatt.com; Jl Danau Tamblingan; r US$90-350;) The gardens are an attraction themselves at this 390-room beachfront resort. Hibiscus, wild ginger, lotus and many more species can be found in profusion. Rooms are comfortable and the resort is regularly updated. The two pools are vast; one has a waterfall-shrouded cave.

Tandjung Sari (☎ 288441; www.tandjungsarihotel.com; Jl Danau Tamblingan 29; bungalows US$130-260;) The mature trees along the shaded driveway set the gracious tone at this Sanur veteran, which was one of the first Balinese bungalow hotels. Like a good tree it has flourished since its start in 1967; the 26 gorgeous traditional-style bungalows are superbly decorated with crafts and antiques. The staff is a delight. Highly recommended.

Eating

There's great eating in Sanur at every budget level. Cheap warung and street food carts can be found around the Pasar Sindhu night market, at the beach end of Jl Segara Ayu, and along Jl Danau Poso, at the southern end of Sanur, beyond the resort area.

NORTHERN SANUR

There are numerous little cafés and warungs down by the beach.

Watering Hole Restaurant (☎ 288289; Jl Hang Tuah; dishes 10,000-40,000Rp) Popular for Chinese, Indonesian and Western meals that are served at decent prices. This is a good travellers' hang-out at this end of town.

BEACH

The beach path offers restaurants, warung and bars where you can catch a meal, a drink or a sea breeze. There are several places near the end of each road that ends at the beach.

Stiff Chili (Jl Kesumasari; dishes 8000-20,000Rp) Besides the evocative name, this beachside hut features good sandwiches, pizza and gelato.

New Banjar Club (☎ 287359; dishes 20,000-40,000Rp) Near Jl Duyung, this is a nice beachfront restaurant. Look for a typical menu of pizza, pasta and Indo classics.

Sanur Bay (☎ 288153; Jl Duyung; 25,000-40,000Rp) Tables right on the sand allow for great views at this classic beachside seafood grill.

BALI

JALAN DANAU TAMBLINGAN

Lumut (☎ 270009; Jl Danau Tamblingan; dishes 15,000-55,000Rp; ⏰ 10am-10pm) This gracious 2nd-floor café is set back from the road. The menu has the usuals but the emphasis is on fusion Asian cuisine and seafood. It's also good for a coffee or juice during the day.

Alise's Restaurant (☎ 282510; Tamu Kami Hotel, Jl Danau Tamblingan 64X; dishes 20,000-60,000Rp; ⏰ 7.30-10pm Sun, Tue, Thu & Fri) Alise's has a romantic, lantern-lit outdoor dining area by the pool and serves a good range of European dishes. Local musicians perform Balinese and Western music while the solicitous owners chat you up.

Palay Restaurant (☎ 288335; Jl Danau Tamblingan 81; dishes 20,000-80,000Rp; ⏰ lunch & dinner) Like an upscale surfers joint, look for fine versions of pasta, burgers, pizza and local faves here. It's all served under a soaring thatched roof.

Retro Café & Gallery (☎ 282472; Jl Danau Tamblingan 126; dishes 25,000-45,000Rp) There's a relaxed back section here, well away from the traffic noise, with walls filled with paintings. The menu has all the classics.

Telaga Naga (☎ 281234; Jl Danau Tamblingan 180; dishes 25,000-100,000Rp; ⏰ dinner) Torches light the pathway to this jewel-like restaurant where red lanterns glow over tables. Offerings on the Chinese Szechwan menu are gourmand, such as *abalone masak jamur hitam* (abalone with black mushrooms). Fine gardens.

Massimo (☎ 288942; Jl Danau Tamblingan 206; dishes 30,000-125,000Rp) The interior here is like an open-air Milan café, the outside is like a Balinese garden – a perfect combo. The menu boasts highly authentic pastas, pizzas and more.

SOUTH SANUR

Sari Laut (☎ 289151; dishes 12,500-25,000Rp) Among a cluster of warungs offering cheap dining by the bemo stop, Sari Laut is always full of locals.

Cat & Fiddle (☎ 282218; Jl Cemara 36; dishes 25,000-50,000Rp) Look for Brit standards like fish and chips on the menu at this open-air place, which is, not surprisingly, popular with expats. Trad breakfasts in the morning balance live music many nights.

Entertainment

Many of Sanur's drinking establishments cater to retired expats and are thankfully air-conditioned. Several serve food. For a real Sanur experience, have a drink at one of the many little beachside bars that can be found along the promenade.

Jazz Bar & Grille (☎ 285892; Komplek Sanur 15, Jl Ngurah Rai; dishes 35,000-75,000Rp; ⏰ 10am-2am; ❄) There's live jazz from Sunday to Thursday and pop on Friday and Saturday.

Speakezy's (☎ 288825; Jl Danau Tamblingan 94; ⏰ 4pm-1am) One of the few true bars on the strip, this place has a cheesy theme, lots of drink specials and cheap beer. There's live acoustic music many nights.

Shopping

Sanur is within easy reach of much of the good arts-and-crafts shopping around Ubud. Locally, there are several painting studio shops, with a wide selection of paintings on offer on Jl Danau Tamblingan and also around Jl Pantai Sindhu.

Rare Angon (☎ 288962; Jl Danau Tamblingan 17) A gallery with works from over a dozen local artists. Many are often working right in the shop.

Mama + Leon (☎ 288044; Jl Danau Tamblingan 99A) An upmarket women's fashion shop specialising in cool, classic cuts and colours, where many of the locally made works feature embroidery.

Getting There & Away

BEMO

The public bemo stops are at the southern end of Sanur on Jl Mertasari, and just outside the main entrance to the Inna Grand Bali Beach Hotel on Jl Hang Tuah. You can hail a bemo anywhere along Jl Danau Tamblingan and Jl Danau Poso.

Green bemos go along Jl Hang Tuah and up Jl Hayam Wuruk to the Kereneng terminal in Denpasar (5000Rp).

BOAT

Public boats to Nusa Lembongan leave from the northern end of Sanur beach at 7.45am (40,000Rp, 1½ to two hours). This is the boat used by locals and you may have to share space with a chicken. The Perama tourist boat (more reliable) leaves at 10.30am (70,000Rp).

From Nusa Lembongan to Sanur, public boats leave Jungutbatu Beach at 7.45am. The Perama boat to Sanur leaves at 8.30am and connects with a through service to Kuta (85,000Rp) and Ubud (90,000Rp).

PERAMA TOURIST SHUTTLE BUSES FROM SANUR

Destination	Fare (Rp)
Candidasa	40,000
Kuta	15,000
Lovina	70,000
Padangbai	40,000
Ubud	30,000

For details about various other boats to Nusa Lembongan, see p349.

TOURIST SHUTTLE BUS

The **Perama office** (☎ 285592; Jl Hang Tuah 39; 🕑 7am-10pm) is at Warung Pojok at the northern end of town. It runs shuttles to various destinations (see boxed text, above), most only once daily.

Getting Around

Bemos go up and down Jl Danau Tamblingan and Jl Danau Poso for 3000Rp. Metered taxis can be flagged down in the street, or call **Bali Taxi** (☎ 701111).

BENOA HARBOUR

Bali's main port is at the entrance of Teluk Benoa (Benoa Bay), the wide but shallow bay east of the airport runway. Benoa Harbour is on the northern side of the bay – a square of docks and port buildings on reclaimed land, linked to mainland Bali by a 2km causeway.

Benoa Harbour is the port for tourist day-trip boats to Nusa Lembongan (see p349) and for Pelni ships to other parts of Indonesia.

Visitors must pay a toll to go on the causeway (1000Rp per vehicle). Public bemos (5000Rp) leave from Sanglah terminal in Denpasar. A taxi from Kuta or Sanur should cost around 18,000Rp one way, plus the toll.

BUKIT PENINSULA

☎ 0361

The southern peninsula is known as Bukit (*bukit* means 'hill' in Indonesian). It's arid by Bali standards. Hotel developments can be found at Jimbaran, Tanjung Benoa and the tourist enclave of Nusa Dua. The western and southern coasts are magnificent, and have some lovely, isolated beaches and great surf.

Jimbaran

South of Kuta and the airport, Teluk Jimbaran (Jimbaran Bay) is a superb crescent of white sand and blue sea, fronted by a long string of seafood warung, and ending at the southern end in a bushy headland, home to the Four Seasons Resort. The sunset towering over the horizon is what brings travellers to Jimbaran to feast on seafood grilled over coconut husks, fresh from the local fishing fleet.

It's pretty sleepy here and facilities are very limited. Jl Raya Uluwatu has a couple of small markets for supplies like water but for most things you will need to head to Kuta or Nusa Dua.

SLEEPING

The Jimbaran area is home to luxurious resorts, as well as more modest accommodation options.

Villa Batu (Map p277; ☎ 703186; Jl Pemelisan Agung 21A; r 150,000-250,000Rp; ❄) Behind Café Layar, this simple place has small rooms with open-air cold-water bathrooms.

Jimbaran Ocean Cottages (Map p277; ☎ 702253; info@kirakira-stay.com; Jl Pantai Jimbaran 3; r 150,000Rp, with air-con 200,000-250,000Rp; ❄) Things are pretty tight here but you cannot beat the site across from the beach. All 15 rooms have hot water and there is a nice café, with good views, on the 2nd floor.

Udayana Eco Lodge (Map p277; ☎ 261204; www.ecolodgesindonesia.com; s/d US$55/60; ❄ 🏊) Inland near Udayana University, this lodge has grand views over South Bali from its perch on a knoll in 70 hectares of bushland. The 15 rooms are comfortable and there is an inviting common area with a fine library.

Pansea Puri Bali (Map p277; ☎ 701605; www.pansea.com; Jl Yoga Perkanti; cottages US$150-250; ❄ 💻 🏊) Set on nice grounds complete with a figure-eight pool that looks out on open ocean, the 48 cottages here have private gardens, deeply shaded patios and stylish room design.

EATING

The destination of many Kuta-area tourists, Jimbaran's three groups of seafood warung (Map p277) do fresh barbecued seafood every evening (and many are also open for lunch). The simple open-sided shacks are right by the beach and perfect for enjoying sea breezes and sunsets. The usual deal is to select your seafood fresh from an ice bucket and pay according to weight. Per 100g, expect to pay around 25,000Rp for live lobster, 13,000Rp to 20,000Rp for prawns, and 5000Rp for fish, squid and clams. Prices are open to negotiation and the accuracy of the scales is a joke among locals. However, the best places can combine garlic and lime marinade with a chilli and oil dousing during grilling for fabulous results.

The longest row of restaurants is at the northern end of the beach, south of the fish market (Map p277). This is the area where you will be taken by taxi if you don't specify otherwise. The middle area, however, is a better choice and is just south of Jl Penelisan Agung. The atmosphere is more relaxed and the operators less avaricious.

GETTING THERE & AWAY

Public bemos from Tegal terminal in Denpasar go via Kuta to Jimbaran (10,000Rp), and continue to Nusa Dua. They don't run after about 4pm, but plenty of taxis wait around the beachfront warung in the evening to take replete diners back to Kuta (about 25,000Rp), Seminyak or wherever.

Central Bukit

The centrepiece of **Garuda Wisnu Kencana Cultural Park** (GWK; ☎ 703603; admission 15,000Rp, parking 5000Rp; 8am-10pm) is the yet to be completed 66m-high *garuda* (mythical man-bird) statue, to be erected on top of a shopping and gallery complex, for a total height of 146m. Well, that's the plan. So far the only completed part of the statue is the large bronze head. A shopping mall is completed as are two restaurants, but they are mostly empty. As it stands – or doesn't – the deserted site is not worth going out of your way for except for the views. Optimistic predictions for eventual completion of the site are regularly issued.

Dreamland

Once a remote surf break, Dreamland, as it's commonly known, is now a trendy scene. Reached by passing through the vast and mostly moribund development of Bali Pecatu Indah, this perfect cove of a beach is surrounded by cliffs. On most days, those in the know line the sands watching surfers and taking comfort at the growing number of simple cafés. It's all a little wild: planning is nonexistent as are pavements (after the grand boulevard ends) and it's not uncommon to see a cow wandering past lithe Versace-clad beauties.

Dewi's Warung (☎ 081 5555 1722; r 150,000-250,000) is right on the sand. The simple rooms have fans and stunning views.

Dreamland (locals call it Lemongkak) is 4km off the Ulu Watu road. There's an entrance fee of 5000Rp to park on the deeply rutted terrain. Taxis from the Kuta area cost 30,000Rp to 40,000Rp per hour for the round trip and waiting time.

Ulu Watu Area

The west coast around Ulu Watu has legendary surf breaks as well as the important Pura Luhur Ulu Watu.

The surf break at Padang Padang is the centre of development of late and boasts numerous small inns and warung that sell and rent surfboards, and provide food, drink, ding repairs or a massage – whatever you need most. It is the only good place to swim in the area. From its bluff, you get a good view of all the area surf breaks.

Coming from the east you will first encounter a gated parking area (car/motorcycle 2000/1000Rp), which is about a 400m walk from the water. Continuing on over a bridge, there is an older parking area (car/motorcycle 1000/500Rp) that is a hilly 200m from the water. Watch out for 'gatekeepers' looking for bonuses.

SIGHTS & ACTIVITIES

Pura Luhur Ulu Watu (admission incl sarong & sash rental 3000Rp; parking 1000Rp; 8am-7pm) is one of several important temples to the spirits of the sea along the south coast of Bali.

The temple is perched precipitously on the southwestern tip of the peninsula, atop sheer cliffs that drop straight into the pounding surf. You enter through an unusual arched gateway flanked by statues of Ganesha. At sunset, walk around the cliff top to the left (south) of the temple. Watch out for monkeys, who – when not reproducing – like to snatch sunglasses and anything else within reach.

An enchanting **Kecak dance** (tickets 35,000Rp; 6-7pm) is held in the temple grounds at sunset. Although obviously set up for tourists, the gorgeous setting makes it one of the more delightful performances on the island.

For the best surfing spots, a paved road goes northwest towards **Padang Padang** from Pecatu village (turn right at the small temple), passing a small side road branching off to **Bingin**, a popular beach with savage surf and a renowned left break. **Impossibles** is nearby.

Ulu Watu, or Ulu's, is a legendary surf spot – the stuff of dreams and nightmares. It's about 1km south of Padang Padang and its legend is nearly matched by nearby **Pantai Suluban**.

SLEEPING

There's a whole string of cheap and very basic surfing dives on the road from Padang Padang through Ulu Watu. Expect to pay about 50,000Rp for a room with cold water, a fan and a shared bath. Many surfers choose to stay in Kuta and make the drive, which is less than an hour.

Rocky Bungalows (☎ 0817 346 209; r 250,000-450,000Rp;) This low-key place off Jl Ulu Watu near Padang Padang has 10 rooms with great water views from the balconies. It's a three-minute walk to the water.

Uluwatu Resort (☎ 7420610; www.uluwaturesort.com; Jl Pantai Suluban; villas US$83-93;) On the cliff top across the river from Padang Padang, this stylish place has impressive ocean views. It's laid-back and a good place to chill out.

Blue Point Bay Villas & Spa (☎ 7441077; www.bluepointbayvillas.com; Jl Labuansait; villas from US$230;) A swanky 31-villa resort right above the Padang Padang break, it has stunning views. There's a high level of service and a good restaurant.

EATING

Most of the hotels and inns have restaurants and any beach where there are surfers will have a few warung selling necessities like beer, sandwiches and Indonesian staples. There are several cafés on the road from Pecatu.

GETTING THERE & AWAY

The best way to see the west coast is with your own vehicle or by chartering a taxi.

Public bemos to Ulu Watu are infrequent, and stop running by mid-afternoon. Some of the dark blue bemos from Kuta serve Jimbaran and Ulu Watu (8000Rp) – it's best to catch one west of Tuban (on Jl Raya Kuta, outside the Supernova shopping centre) or Jimbaran (on Jl Ulu Watu).

You may encounter offers to see the sunset or the Kecak dance at the temple, these cost from about 80,000Rp and sometimes include a side trip to a beach or to Jimbaran.

Nusa Dua

Nusa Dua translates literally as 'Two Islands' – the islands are actually small raised headlands, each with a little temple. Nusa Dua is better known as Bali's gated beach-resort enclave – a gilded ghetto of enormous hotels. There are no independent developments, no hawkers, no warung, no traffic, no pollution and no noise. The drawback is the isolation from any sense of Balinese community life; in many ways, you could be at any international tropical beach resort the world over.

As a planned resort, Nusa Dua is very spread out. You enter the enclave through one of the big gateways, and inside there are expansive lawns, manicured gardens and sweeping driveways leading to the lobbies of large hotels.

ACTIVITIES

One of the nicest features of Nusa Dua is the 5km beach promenade that stretches the length of the resort and continues north along much of the beach in Tanjung Benoa as well. Not only is it a good stroll at any time but it also makes it easy to sample the pleasures of the other beachside resorts.

The reef-protected beach at Nusa Dua is shallow at low tide, and the wave action is pretty flaccid.

The **Bali Golf & Country Club** (☎ 771791; green fees US$142) is a top-flight 18-hole course lined with timeshare condos. Designed by Nelson & Wright, it features the best links in Bali (and almost the *only* links in Bali).

SLEEPING

The eight Nusa Dua hotels are similar in several ways: they are all big (although some are just plain huge) and they have long beachfronts. Each has several restaurants and bars, as well as various pools and other resort amenities. Many of the properties cater primarily to groups and aren't terribly special, despite their size. But a couple of choices are very good if you're ready for a full-on resort experience.

Westin Resort (☎ 771906; www.westin.com/bali; r from US$220;) There are 355 rooms on offer. Attached to a large convention centre, the Westin has an air-con lobby (one of three in Bali) and vast public spaces. Formerly a Sheraton, it has been comprehensively renovated. Its acres of pools are Nusa's best and feature waterfalls. The Kids Club has extensive activities and facilities.

Grand Hyatt Bali (☎ 771234; www.bali.grand.hyatt.com; r from US$220;) Sort of a little city, the 648-room Hyatt has directional signs scattered across the grounds, which have up to 21 arrows. Like any city, some neighbourhoods are better than others. Some in the West Village (there are four, the East and South Villages are best located) face the taxi parking lot. The riverlike pool is huge and has a fun slide. The children's club will keep the little buggers busy for days.

EATING

Restaurants in the hotels are abundant. South of the enclave, the various warung at the beach serve some typically fresh local standards.

Along Jl Pantai Mengiat, just outside the gate, there are a string of open-air eateries offering an unpretentious alternative to Nusa Dua dining. None will win any culinary awards but they are fun, and if you pause long enough in front of any, the staff will offer you escalating inducements to step inside.

SHOPPING

Bali Collection (☎ 771664; www.bali-collection.com) Built on the bones of the failed Galleria Nusa Dua, this upscale shopping mall is designed to milk the wallets of those staying at the huge local resorts. However the fate of its over 100 shops will rest upon whether it can attract a local following, much like the wildly popular malls in Kuta and Denpasar.

GETTING THERE & AROUND

Public bemos travel between Denpasar's Tegal terminal and the terminal at Bualu (8000Rp). From Bualu, it's at least 1km to the hotels. But who takes a bemo to a four-star resort? Call a taxi.

Find out what shuttle-bus services your hotel provides. A free **shuttle bus** (☎ 771662; 9am-10pm) connects Nusa Dua and Tanjung Benoa resort hotels with the Bali Collection shopping mall.

Tanjung Benoa

The peninsula of Tanjung Benoa extends about 4km north from Nusa Dua to the fishing village of Benoa. It is not a gated community by any means and resorts bump up against modest local homes.

Like beaches at Sanur and Nusa Dua, those here are protected from waves by an off-shore reef.

Restaurants and hotels are spread out along Jl Pratama, which runs the length of the peninsula. It may be one of the most perilous streets in South Bali for a stroll. There are few sidewalks and in many places nowhere to walk but on the narrow road. Fortunately, the delightful beach promenade is just steps away.

SIGHTS

Benoa is one of Bali's multi-denominational corners, with an interesting **Chinese Buddhist temple**, a **mosque** and a **Hindu temple** within 100m of each other. It's an interesting little fishing town that makes for a good stroll.

ACTIVITIES

Quite a few water-sports centres along Jl Pratama offer daytime diving, cruises, windsurfing, water-skiing etc. Check equipment and credentials before you sign up. Most have a thatched-roof bar and restaurant attached to their premises. Each morning convoys of buses arrive from all over South Bali bringing day-trippers to enjoy the calm waters and various activities.

Among the established water-sports operators is **Pandawa Marine Adventures** (☎ 778585). As if by magic, all operators have similar prices.

Water sports include the very popular parasailing (per round US$25) and jet-skiing (per 15 minutes US$25). You'll need at least two people for banana-boat rides (per 15 minutes US$25), or glass-bottomed boat trips (90-minute tour with snack US$35).

SLEEPING

Accommodation here is a mixed bag. Several lesser resorts along the beach charge

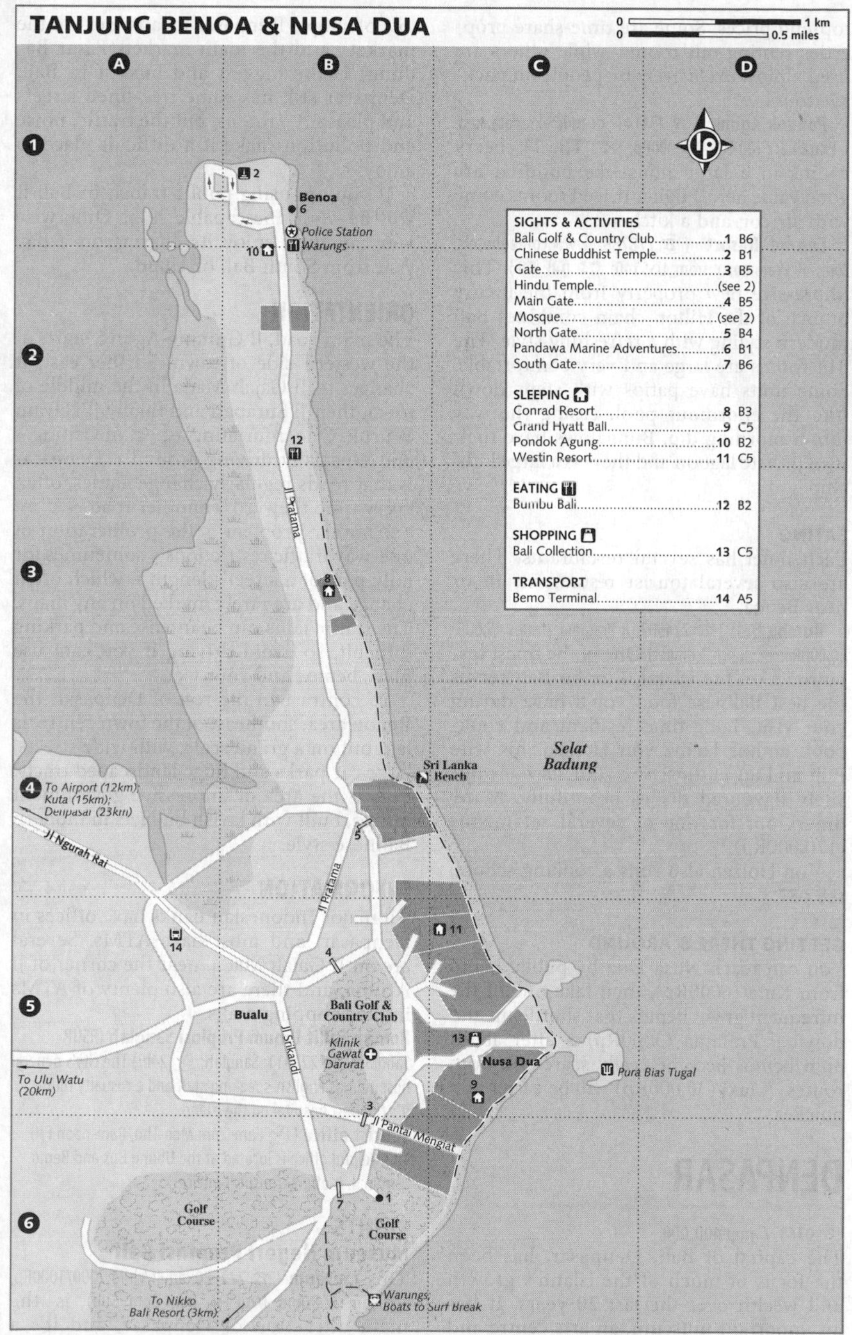
TANJUNG BENOA & NUSA DUA
0 1 km
0 0.5 miles
SIGHTS & ACTIVITIES
Bali Golf & Country Club....1 B6
Chinese Buddhist Temple....2 B1
Gate....3 B5
Hindu Temple....(see 2)
Main Gate....4 B5
Mosque....(see 2)
North Gate....5 B4
Pandawa Marine Adventures....6 B1
South Gate....7 B6
SLEEPING
Conrad Resort....8 B3
Grand Hyatt Bali....9 C5
Pondok Agung....10 B2
Westin Resort....11 C5
EATING
Bumbu Bali....12 B2
SHOPPING
Bali Collection....13 C5
TRANSPORT
Bemo Terminal....14 A5
Benoa
Police Station
Warungs
Jl Pratama
Selat Badung
Sri Lanka Beach
To Airport (12km); Kuta (15km); Denpasar (23km)
Jl Ngurah Rai
Bualu
Bali Golf & Country Club
Jl Srikandi
Klinik Gawat Darurat
Nusa Dua
Pura Bias Tugal
To Ulu Watu (20km)
Jl Pantai Mengiat
Golf Course
Golf Course
To Nikko Bali Resort (3km)
Warungs; Boats to Surf Break

top-end prices. Some are time-share properties renting out rooms, while others are used almost exclusively by people on package tours.

Pondok Agung (☎ 771143; roland@eksadata.com; Jl Pratama; r 100,000-260,000Rp;) The 11 cheery rooms in a large houselike building are good value here. Higher priced rooms come with air-con and a kitchen.

Conrad Resort (☎ 778788; www.conradhotels.com; Jl Pratama; r from US$140;) This impressive new property from the luxury branch of the Hilton chain combines Bali modern styling with a refreshing style. The 314 rooms are large and very comfortable. Some units have patios with steps down into the enormous pool, easing the way into a morning dip. Bungalows have their own private lagoon and there is a large kids' club.

EATING

Each hotel has several restaurants. There are also several tourist restaurants in or near Benoa.

Bumbu Bali (☎ 774502; Jl Pratama; dishes 45,000-60,000Rp; lunch & dinner) One of the finest restaurants on the island, Bumbu Bali serves the best Balinese food you'll have during your visit. Long-time resident and cookbook author Heinz von Holzen, his wife Puji and an enthusiastic staff serve exquisitely flavoured dishes beautifully. Many diners opt for one of several set menus (170,000Rp).

Von Holzen also runs a cooking school; see p87.

GETTING THERE & AROUND

You can reach Nusa Dua by public bemo from Kuta (6000Rp), then take one of the infrequent green bemos that shuttle up and down Jl Pratama (3000Rp) – after about 3pm bemos become really scarce on both routes. A taxi (30,000Rp) will be easier and quicker.

DENPASAR

☎ 0361 / pop 400,000

The capital of Bali, Denpasar, has been the focus of much of the island's growth and wealth over the last 20 years. It has an important museum, an arts centre and lots of shops. Denpasar means 'next to the market', and the main market (Pasar Badung) is the biggest and busiest in Bali. Denpasar still has some tree-lined streets and pleasant gardens, but the traffic, noise and pollution make it a difficult place to enjoy.

If you are using public transit in Bali it will be your inescapable hub. Otherwise you can fully enjoy its charms on a day visit from South Bali or Ubud.

ORIENTATION

The main road, Jl Gunung Agung, starts at the western side of town. Further east, it changes to Jl Gajah Mada in the middle of town, then Jl Surapati and finally Jl Hayam Wuruk. One infuriating aspect of visiting – and especially driving around – Denpasar is that roads regularly change names, often every time they cross another road.

Another problem is the proliferation of one-way traffic restrictions – sometimes for only part of a street's length – which often change and are rarely marked on any maps. The traffic jams can be intense and parking difficult, so avoid driving if you can; use taxis, bemos and your feet.

In contrast to the rest of Denpasar, the Renon area, southeast of the town centre, is laid out on a grand scale, with wide streets, large car parks and huge landscaped tracts. This is the area of impressive government offices, built with lavish budgets in modern Balinese style.

INFORMATION

All major Indonesian banks have offices in Denpasar, and most have ATMs. Several are on Jl Gajah Mada, near the corner of Jl Arjuna, and there are also plenty of ATMs in the shopping malls.

Rumah Sakit Umum Propinsi Sanglah (RSUP Sanglah; ☎ 227911; Sanglah; 24hr) The city's general hospital has English-speaking staff and a casualty room. It's the best hospital on the island.

Tourist office (8am-2pm Mon-Thu, 8am-noon Fri) This helpful office is located at the Ubung Bus and Bemo Terminal. It offers transport advice.

SIGHTS

Museum Negeri Propinsi Bali

This **museum** (☎ 222680; adult/child 2000/1000Rp; 8am-12.30pm Mon-Fri, 8am-3pm Sun) is the main attraction of Denpasar, and it's a good one. It gained prominence in 1932 when German artist Walter Spies and some Dutch officials revived the idea of collecting and preserving Balinese antiquities and cultural objects, and creating an ethnographic museum. Now it's quite well set up, and most displays are labelled in English. You can climb one of the towers inside the grounds for a better view of the whole complex.

The **main building** (Gedung Timur) has a collection of prehistoric pieces downstairs, including stone sarcophagi, and stone and bronze implements. Upstairs are examples of traditional tools and artefacts, including types still in everyday use.

The **northern pavilion** (Gedung Tabanan) houses shadow puppets, dance costumes and masks, including a sinister *rangda,* a healthy-looking Barong and a towering *barong landung* (giant puppet dance) figure. The **central pavilion** (Gedung Karangasem) is like the palace pavilions of Amlapura where rajahs held audiences. The **southern pavilion** (Gedung Buleleng) has a varied collection of textiles, including *endek* (a Balinese method of weaving with pre-dyed threads), double ikat (cloth in which the pattern is produced by dyeing individual threads before weaving), *songket* (silver- and gold-threaded cloth, hand-woven using a floating weft technique) and *prada* (the application of gold leaf or gold or silver thread in traditional Balinese clothes).

Museum staff often play music on a bamboo gamelan to magical effect.

Pura Jagatnatha

Next to the museum, the state Jagatnatha Temple was built in 1953, and is dedicated to the supreme god, Sanghyang Widi. Part of its significance is its statement of monotheism. The *padmasana* (shrine) is made of white coral, and consists of an empty throne (symbolic of heaven) on top of the cosmic turtle and two *naga* (mythological serpents) that symbolise the foundation of the world. The walls are decorated with carvings of scenes from the Ramayana and Mahabharata. Pura Jagatnatha is more frequently used than many Balinese temples, with local people coming every afternoon to pray and make offerings, so it can often be closed to tourists.

Taman Wedhi Budaya

This **arts centre** (☎ 222776; admission free; 🕑 8am-5pm Tue-Sun) is a sprawling complex in the eastern part of Denpasar. It was established in 1973 as an academy and showplace for Balinese culture, and has lavish architecture and not much else for most of the year (there are no regular dance performances here). The impressive-looking art gallery has a fair collection.

From mid-June to mid-July, the centre hosts the Bali Arts Festival (below), with dances, music and craft displays from all over Bali. You may need to book tickets at the centre for more popular events.

FESTIVALS & EVENTS

The annual **Bali Arts Festival** (www.baliartsfestival.com) is based at the Taman Wedhi Budaya arts centre (above) in Denpasar, and lasts for about one month from mid-June to mid-July. It's a great time to be visiting Bali, and the festival is an easy way to see an enormous variety of traditional dance, music and crafts from all over the island. The productions of the Ramayana and Mahabharata ballets are grand, and the opening ceremony and parade in Denpasar are particularly colourful.

The festival is the main event of the year for the scores of village dance and musical groups. Competition is fierce, with local pride on the line at each performance. To do well here sets a village on a good course for the year. Some events are held in a 6000-seat amphitheatre, a venue that allows you to realise the mass appeal of traditional Balinese culture. Tickets are usually available right before performances and schedules are widely available throughout South Bali and Ubud.

SLEEPING

Denpasar has several hotels, but it's hard to think of a compelling reason to stay here unless you want to be close to the bus terminals or have some other business here. At times when many Indonesians travel (July, August, around Christmas and Idul Fitri – November/December), it may be wise to book a room.

Adi Yasa (☎ 222679; Jl Nakula 23B; s/d 25,000/40,000Rp) Budget travellers have crashed here since the 1970s. It's centrally located and friendly, but the nine rooms are very basic.

DENPASAR

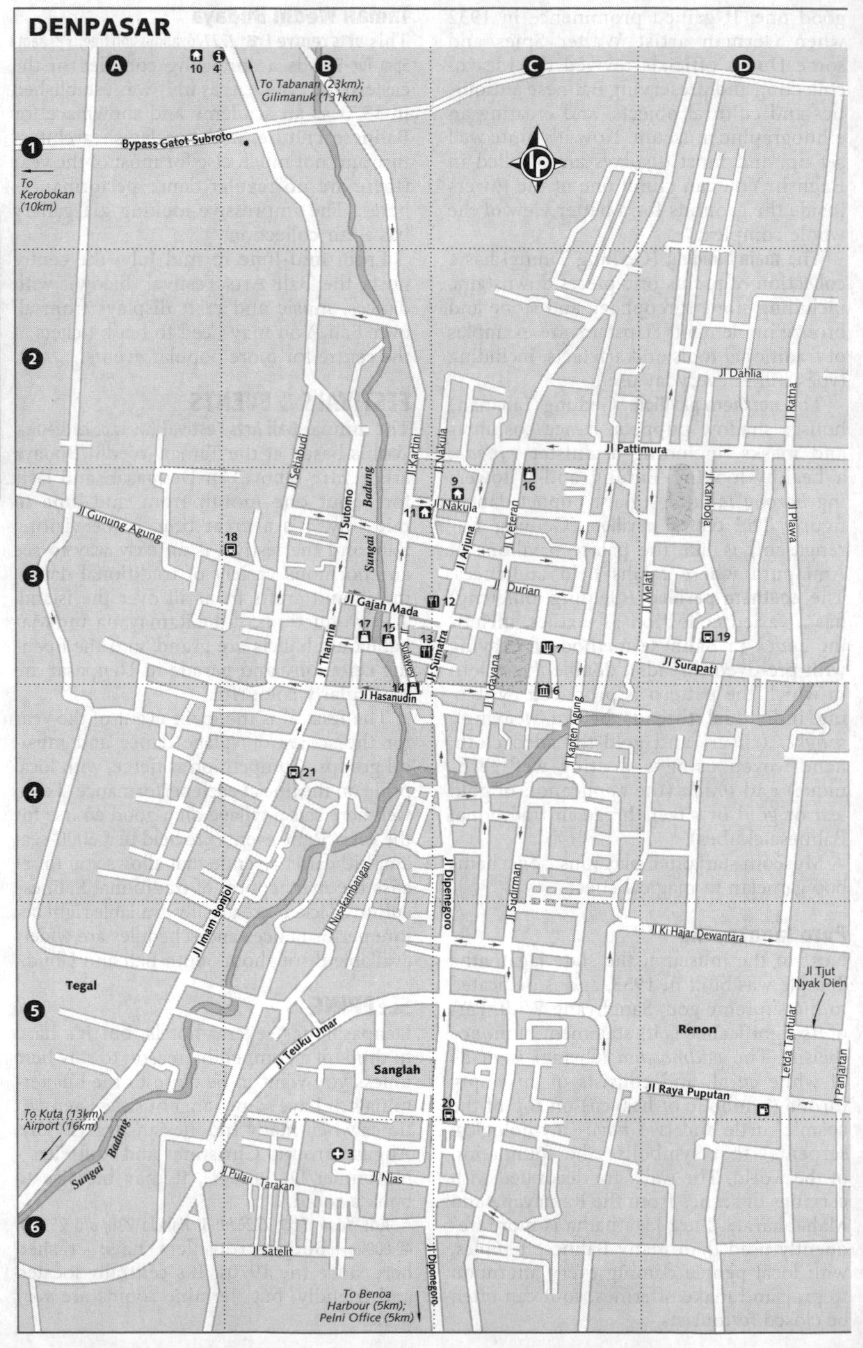
A
B
C
D
1
2
3
4
5
6
To Tabanan (23km); Gilimanuk (131km)
Bypass Gatot Subroto
To Kerobokan (10km)
Jl Dahlia
Jl Ratna
Jl Pattimura
Jl Setiabudi
Jl Kartini
Jl Nakula
Jl Kamboja
Jl Plawa
Jl Gunung Agung
Jl Sutomo
Sungai Badung
Jl Arjuna
Jl Veteran
Jl Melati
Jl Durian
Jl Gajah Mada
Jl Thamrin
Jl Sulawesi
Jl Sumatra
Jl Surapati
Jl Udayana
Jl Hasanudin
Jl Kapten Agung
Jl Nusakambangan
Jl Dipenegoro
Jl Sudirman
Jl Imam Bonjol
Jl Ki Hajar Dewantara
Jl Tjut Nyak Dien
Tegal
Renon
Letda Tantular
Jl Teuku Umar
Sanglah
Jl Panjaitan
Jl Raya Puputan
To Kuta (13km); Airport (16km)
Sungai Badung
Jl Pulau Tarakan
Jl Nias
Jl Satelit
To Benoa Harbour (5km); Pelni Office (5km)
Jl Dipenegoro
1
2
3
4
6
7
9
10
11
12
13
14
15
16
17
18
19
20
21

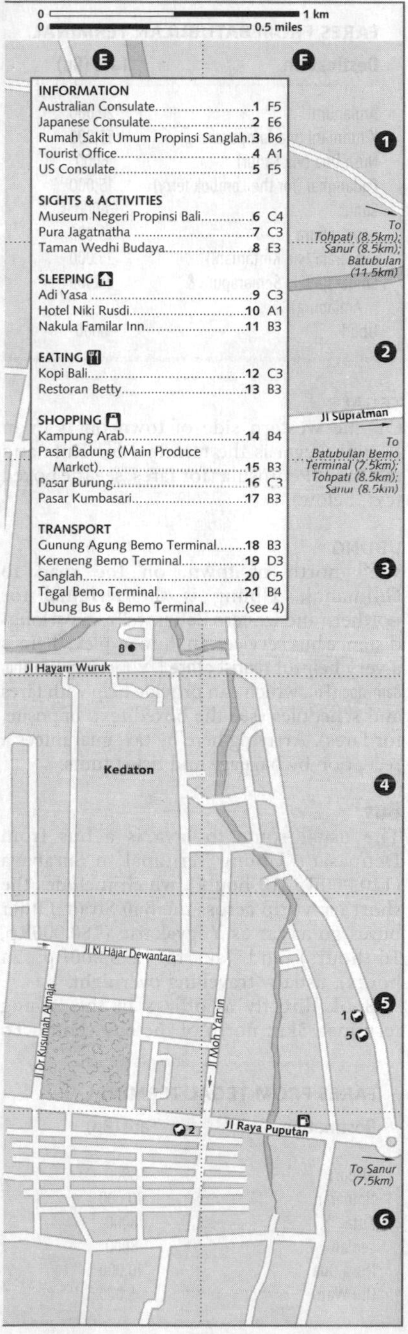

Nakula Familar Inn (☎ 226446; Jl Nakula 4; s/d 50,000/75,000Rp) Across the road and 100m west from the Adi Yasa, the eight rooms are decent (cold-water showers only) and clean, and all have a small balcony area. The traffic noise isn't too bad and there is a nice little enclave in the middle. Tegal–Kereneng bemos go along Jl Nakula.

Hotel Niki Rusdi (☎ 416397; Jl Pidada XIV; r 80,000-200,000Rp;) This simple place is located right behind the Ubung Bus Terminal and is a good choice if you have an early or late bus. Rooms are very clean. There are other options nearby if this one is full.

EATING

Most places cater to local people and Indonesian visitors, so they offer a good selection of authentic food at reasonable prices. The cheapest places are warungs at the bemo/bus terminals and the markets. At the Pasar Malam Kereneng (Kereneng Night Market) dozens of vendors dish up food till dawn. A number of places along Jl Teuku Umar cater to more affluent ocals.

Restoran Betty (Jl Sumatra 56; mains 7000-12,000Rp) This calm place (compared to the madness of the street outside) has a good range of juices and Indonesian dishes. Don't be put off by the antique plastic food models.

Kopi Bali (☎ 224016; Jl Gajah Mada 80; coffee 3000Rp; 9am-4pm Mon-Sat) Home to Bali's Coffee Co, this storefront sells locally grown beans and makes a mean cup of coffee or espresso, which you can enjoy at the two tiny tables while watching the bustle of Denpasar's old main drag.

SHOPPING

Denpasar's markets are vast and a good reason to visit.

Pasar Badung is a pungent market, and is the largest and oldest in Bali. It's very busy in the morning and evening, and a great place to browse and bargain, except for the unsolicited guides/commission-takers who sometimes attach themselves to you. Most visitors head to the clothing and handicrafts section on the top floor; the 'wet market' – the fruit and veg – is downstairs. Pasar Kumbasari, along the opposite side of the river from Pasar Badung, has handicrafts, fabrics and gold work. Pasar Burung is a bird market with hundreds of caged birds and small animals for sale. It's lovely to listen to and very colourful to see, but the animals' conditions are hardly ideal. Kampung Arab, located near Pasar Badung, has plenty of gold shops *(toko mas)*.

Jl Sulawesi, east of Pasar Badung, has many shops with batik, ikat and other fabrics.

GETTING THERE & AWAY

Denpasar is *the* hub of road transport in Bali – you'll find buses and minibuses bound for all corners of the island. See p274 for details of air transport.

Bemo

The city has several bemo terminals, so if you're travelling independently from one part of Bali to another, you'll often have to go via Denpasar, and transfer from one terminal to another. The terminals for transport around Bali are Ubung, Batubulan and Tegal, while the Gunung Agung, Kereneng and Sanglah terminals serve destinations in and around Denpasar. Each terminal has regular bemo connections to the other terminals in Denpasar for 5000Rp. These can be cumbersome.

Bemos and minibuses cover shorter routes between towns and villages, while full-sized buses are often used on longer, more heavily travelled routes. Buses are quicker and more comfortable, but they're less frequent.

BATUBULAN

This terminal, a very inconvenient 6km northeast of Denpasar on a road to Ubud, is for destinations in eastern and central Bali (for fares, see the boxed text, above).

FARES FROM BATUBULAN TERMINAL

Destination	Fare (Rp)
Amlapura	20,000
Kintamani (via Tampaksiring)	15,000
Nusa Dua (via Sanur)	6000
Padangbai (for the Lombok ferry)	15,000
Sanur	6000
Semarapura	15,000
Singaraja (via Kintamani)	25,000
Singaraja (via Semarapura & Amlapura)	25,000
Ubud	6000

GUNUNG AGUNG

This terminal, at the northwestern corner of town (look for orange bemos), is on Jl Gunung Agung, and has bemos to Kerobokan and Canggu (6000Rp).

KERENENG

East of the town centre, Kereneng has bemos to Sanur (5000Rp).

SANGLAH

On Jl Diponegoro, near the general hospital in the south of the city, Sanglah has bemos to Suwung and Benoa Harbour (5000Rp).

TEGAL

On the western side of town on Jl Iman Bonjol, Tegal is the terminal for Kuta and the Bukit Peninsula (for fares, see the boxed text, below).

UBUNG

Well north of town, on the road to Gilimanuk, Ubung is the terminal for northern and western Bali as well as most long-distance bus services. In the complex, there is a very helpful **tourist office** (8am-2pm Mon-Thu, 8am-noon Fri), which can provide help with fares and schedules (see the boxed text, opposite, for fares). Arriving here by taxi guarantees a reception by baggage and ticket touts.

Bus

The usual route to Java is a bus from Denpasar's Ubung Terminal to Surabaya (120,000Rp, 10 hours), which includes the short ferry trip across the Bali Strait. Other buses go as far as Yogyakarta (180,000Rp, 16 hours) and Jakarta (275,000Rp, 24 hours), usually travelling overnight.

Book directly at offices in the Ubung terminal, 3km north of the city centre. To

FARES FROM TEGAL TERMINAL

Destination	Fare (Rp)
Airport	8000
Jimbaran	10,000
Kuta	8000
Legian	8000
Nusa Dua	10,000
Ulu Watu	15,000

FARES FROM UBUNG TERMINAL

Destination	Fare (Rp)
Gilimanuk (for the ferry to Java)	25,000
Kediri (for Tanah Lot)	6000
Mengwi	6000
Negara	20,000
Pancasari (for Danau Bratan)	15,000
Singaraja (via Pupuan or Bedugul)	28,000
Tabanan	6000

Surabaya or even Jakarta, you may get on a bus within an hour of arriving at Ubung, but at busy times you should buy your ticket at least one day ahead.

There are no tourist shuttle buses to/from Denpasar.

GETTING AROUND

Bemo

Bemos take various circuitous routes from and between the bus/bemo terminals. They line up for various destinations at each terminal, or you can hail them from anywhere along the main roads – look for the destination sign above the driver's window. The Tegal–Nusa Dua bemo (dark blue) is handy for Renon; and the Kereneng–Ubung bemo (turquoise) travels along Jl Gajah Mada, past the museum.

Taxi

As in South Bali, taxis prowl the streets of Denpasar looking for fares. As always, the blue cabs of **Bali Taxi** (☎ 701111) are the most reliable choice.

UBUD

☎ **0361**

Perched on the gentle slopes leading up towards the central mountains, Ubud is the other half of Bali's tourism duopoly. Unlike South Bali, however, Ubud's focus remains on the remarkable Balinese culture in its myriad forms.

It's not surprising that many people come to Ubud for a day or two and end up staying longer, drawn in by the rich culture and many activities. Besides the very popular dance-and music shows, there are numerous courses on offer that allow you to become fully immersed in Balinese culture.

Sensory pursuits are amply catered to with some of the best food on the island. From fabled world-class resorts to surprisingly comfortable little family-run inns, there is a fine choice of hotels. Many places come complete with their own spas, for hours or days of pampering packages.

Around Ubud are temples, ancient sites and whole villages producing handicrafts (albeit mostly for visitors). Although the growth of Ubud has engulfed several neighbouring villages, leading to an urban sprawl, parts of the surrounding countryside remain unspoiled, with lush rice paddies and towering coconut trees. You'd be remiss if you didn't walk one or more of the dozens of paths during your stay.

ORIENTATION

The once small village of Ubud has now expanded to encompass its neighbours – Campuan, Penestanan, Padangtegal, Peliatan and Pengosekan are all part of what we see as Ubud today. The centre of town is the junction of Monkey Forest Rd and Jl Raya Ubud, where the bustling market and crowded bemo stops are found, as well as Ubud Palace and the main temple, Pura Desa Ubud. Monkey Forest Rd (officially Jl Wanara Wana, but always known by its unofficial name) runs south to Sacred Monkey Forest Sanctuary and is lined with shops, hotels and restaurants. The roughly parallel Jl Hanoman is also lined with shops, cafés and more.

Jl Raya Ubud ('Ubud Main Rd' – often Jl Raya for short) is the main east–west road. West of Ubud, the road drops steeply down to the ravine at Campuan, where an old suspension bridge, next to the new one, hangs over Sungai Wos. West of Campuan, the pretty village of Penestanan is famous for its painters and beadwork. East and south of Ubud proper, the 'villages' of Peliatan, Nyuhkuning and Pengosekan are known variously for painting, woodcarving and traditional dance. The latter has been the focus of recent development, with rice paddies giving way to new hotels. The area north of Ubud is less densely settled, with picturesque rice paddies interspersed with small villages, many of which specialise in a local craft.

INFORMATION

Along the main roads, you'll find most services you need. There are numerous travel agents and several wartels.

Bookshops

Ubud is the best place for book shopping. Selections are wide and varied and you can get numerous books about Balinese art and culture. Many carry books by small and obscure publishers. Shops typically carry newspapers such as the *International Herald Tribune*.

Ary's Bookshop (Map p312; ☎ 978203; Jl Raya Ubud) Good for art books, periodicals and maps.

Cinta Bookshop (Map p312; ☎ 973295; Jl Dewi Sita) A nice assortment of used novels and vintage books about Bali.

Ganesha Bookshop (Map pp310-11; ☎ 970320; www.ganeshabooksbali.com; Jl Raya Ubud) Ubud's best bookshop has an amazing amount of books jammed into a small space. Excellent selection of titles on Indonesian studies, travel, arts and music, fiction (including some used titles) and maps.

Periplus (Map p312; ☎ 975178; Monkey Forest Rd) A typically glossy branch of the Bali chain.

Emergency

Police station (Map pp310-11; ☎ 975316; Jl Raya Andong; 24hr) Located on the eastern side of town at Andong.

Internet Access

Internet centres are common on the main streets; most have slow connections and charge 200Rp to 300Rp per minute. The following places are a cut above average, with fast broadband connections.

Bali 3000 (Map pp310-11; ☎ 978538; Jl Raya Ubud; per hr 16,000Rp; 8am-11pm;) Like a fashionable internet café in Milan with a full range of computing services. Serves good sandwiches, coffees and juices.

Ubud Music (Map p312; ☎ 971837; Jl Raya Ubud; per 10min 5000Rp; 8am-8pm) Sells music and has a photocopier.

Libraries

Pondok Pecak Library & Learning Centre (Map p312; ☎ 976194; Monkey Forest Rd; 9am-5pm Mon-Sat, 1-5pm Sun) A relaxed place, which also has a children's book section. It charges a membership fee starting at 40,000Rp. It has a small café and a pleasant reading area on the roof. Located on the far side of the football field. See p314 for information on cultural courses.

Medical Services

See p280 for details on international clinics in Bali.

Mua Pharmacy (Map p312; ☎ 974674; Monkey Forest Rd; 8am-9pm)

Ubud Clinic (Map pp310-11; ☎ 974911; Jl Raya Campuan 36; 24hr) Best medical centre in Ubud. Charges from 200,000Rp for a clinical consultation.

Money

Ubud has numerous banks, ATMs and moneychangers along Jl Raya Ubud and Monkey Forest Rd.

Post

Main post office (Map pp310-11; Jl Jembawan; 8am-6pm) Has a sort-it-yourself poste restante system –

UBUD IN...

One Day

Stroll the streets of Ubud, enjoying the galleries and sampling the fine cuisine. Try to get out on one of the short nearby walks through the verdant rice fields. Go to an evening dance performance in the centre.

Three Days

Take longer walks in the countryside, especially the Campuan Ridge and Satan Valley. Visit the art museums and attend dance performances not just in Ubud, but in the nearby villages. Indulge at a local spa. Drop by the market in the morning.

One Week or More

Do everything above but take time to simply chill out. Get in tune with Ubud's rhythm. Take naps, read books, wander about. Think about a course in Balinese culture. Compare and choose your favourite café.

address poste restante mail to Kantor Pos, Ubud 80571, Bali, Indonesia.

Tourist Information

Ubud Tourist Information (Yayasan Bina Wisata; Map p312; ☎ 973285; Jl Raya Ubud; 🕑 8am-8pm) The one really useful tourist office in Bali. It has a good range of information and a notice board listing current happenings and activities. The staff can answer most regional questions and have up-to-date information on ceremonies and traditional dances held in the area; dance tickets are sold here.

SIGHTS

Palaces & Temples

Ubud Palace and **Puri Saren Agung** (Map p312; cnr Jl Raya Ubud & Jl Suweta) share space in the heart of Ubud. The compound has many ornate corners and was mostly built after the 1917 earthquake. The local royal family still lives here and you can wander around most of the large compound exploring the many traditional and not excessively ornate buildings. If you really like it, you can stay the night (p318).

Just north, **Pura Marajan Agung** (Map p312; Jl Suweta), has one of the finest gates you'll find and is the private temple for Ubud's royal family. **Pura Desa Ubud** (Map p312; Jl Raya Ubud) is the main temple for the Ubud community. Just a bit west is the very picturesque **Pura Taman Saraswati** (Ubud Water Palace; Map p312; Jl Raya Ubud). Waters from the temple at the rear of the site feed the pond at the front, which is a riotous tangle of pink lotus blossoms. There are carvings that honour Dewi Saraswati, the goddess of wisdom and the arts, who has clearly given her blessing to Ubud. There are weekly dance performances.

Art Museums

MUSEUM PURI LUKISAN

This **Palace of Fine Arts** (Map p312; ☎ 975136; www.museumpurilukisan.com; admission 20,000Rp; 🕑 9am-5pm), off Jl Raya Ubud, displays excellent examples of all schools of Balinese art. The modern Balinese art movement started in Ubud, where artists first used modern materials, were influenced by foreign styles and began to depict scenes of everyday Balinese life.

The pavilion straight ahead as you enter has a collection of early works from Ubud and the surrounding villages. The pavilion on the left has some colourful examples of the 'Young Artist' style of painting and a good selection of 'modern traditional' works. The pavilion on the right is used for temporary exhibitions, which change every month or so. Paintings are well displayed and labelled in English, and some of the artwork is often for sale.

You enter the museum by crossing a river gully beside the road and wander from building to building through a beautiful garden with pools, statues and fountains.

NEKA ART MUSEUM

Quite distinct from Neka Gallery, the **Neka Art Museum** (Map pp310-11; ☎ 975074; Jl Raya Sanggingan; adult/child 20,000Rp/free; 🕑 9am-5pm) is the creation of Suteja Neka, a private collector and dealer in Balinese art. It has an excellent and diverse collection and is the best place to learn about the development of painting in Bali.

The **Balinese Painting Hall** provides an overview of local painting, showing influences from classic *wayang kulit* puppetry through to abstract expressionism. The **Arie Smit Pavilion** features Smit's works and examples of the 'Young Artist' school, which he inspired. The **Lempad Pavilion** houses Bali's largest collection of works by I Gusti Nyoman Lempad.

The **Contemporary Indonesian Art Hall** has paintings by artists from other parts of Indonesia, many of whom have worked in Bali. Abdul Aziz, Affandi, Dullah and Anton Kustia Wijaya, among others, are represented. The upper floor is devoted to the work of foreign artists, such as Louise Koke, Miguel Covarrubias, Rudolph Bonnet, Donald Friend, Han Snel and Antonio Blanco. It often hosts temporary exhibitions.

There is a good **bookshop** in the lobby. Bemos travelling between Ubud and Kintamani stop outside the museum.

AGUNG RAI MUSEUM OF ART (ARMA)

Founded by Agung Rai as a museum, gallery and cultural centre, the impressive **ARMA** (Map pp310-11; ☎ 976659; Jl Raya Pengosekan; admission 20,000Rp; 🕑 9am-6pm) is the only place in Bali to see works by the influential German artist Walter Spies. It also has work by 19th-century Javanese artist Raden Saleh. It exhibits classical Kamasan paintings, Batuan-style work from the 1930s and 1940s,

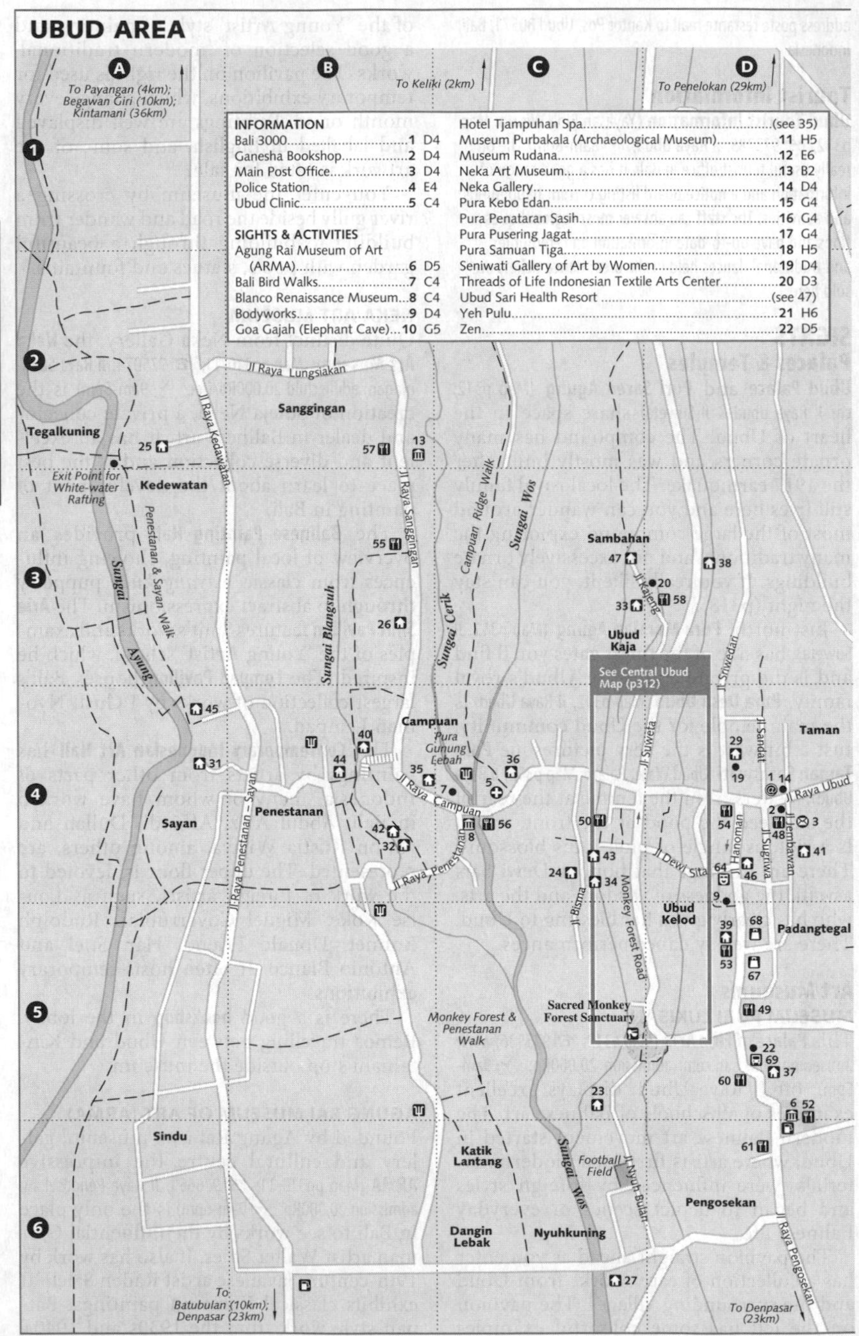
UBUD AREA
INFORMATION
Bali 3000.......................................1 D4
Ganesha Bookshop..........................2 D4
Main Post Office..............................3 D4
Police Station..................................4 E4
Ubud Clinic......................................5 C4
SIGHTS & ACTIVITIES
Agung Rai Museum of Art (ARMA)......................6 D5
Bali Bird Walks...................................7 C4
Blanco Renaissance Museum...8 C4
Bodyworks...9 D4
Goa Gajah (Elephant Cave).....10 G5
Hotel Tjampuhan Spa..........................(see 35)
Museum Purbakala (Archaeological Museum).........11 H5
Museum Rudana...............................12 E6
Neka Art Museum...............................13 B2
Neka Gallery......................................14 D4
Pura Kebo Edan..................................15 G4
Pura Penataran Sasih..........................16 G4
Pura Pusering Jagat...........................17 G4
Pura Samuan Tiga...............................18 H5
Seniwati Gallery of Art by Women...........19 D4
Threads of Life Indonesian Textile Arts Center..........20 D3
Ubud Sari Health Resort.........................(see 47)
Yeh Pulu..21 H6
Zen...22 D5
To Payangan (4km); Begawan Giri (10km); Kintamani (36km)
To Keliki (2km)
To Penelokan (29km)
Jl Raya Lungsiakan
Sanggingan
Tegalkuning
Exit Point for White-water Rafting
Kedewatan
Jl Raya Kedewatan
Penestanan & Sayan Walk
Jl Raya Sanggingan
Campuan Ridge Walk
Sungai Wos
Sungai Cerik
Sungai Blangsuh
Sungai Ayung
Sambahan
Jl Kajeng
Ubud Kaja
See Central Ubud Map (p312)
Jl Sriwedari
Jl Sandat
Taman
Campuan
Pura Gunung Lebah
Jl Raya Campuan
Jl Raya Ubud
Sayan
Penestanan
Jl Raya Penestanan – Sayan
Jl Raya Penestanan
Jl Suweta
Jl Dewi Sita
Jl Hanoman
Jl Sugriwa
Jl Jembawan
Jl Bisma
Monkey Forest Road
Ubud Kelod
Padangtegal
Sacred Monkey Forest Sanctuary
Monkey Forest & Penestanan Walk
Sindu
Katik Lantang
Football Field
Jl Nyuh Bulan
Pengosekan
Dangin Lebak
Nyuhkuning
Jl Raya Pengosekan
To Batubulan (10km); Denpasar (23km)
To Denpasar (23km)

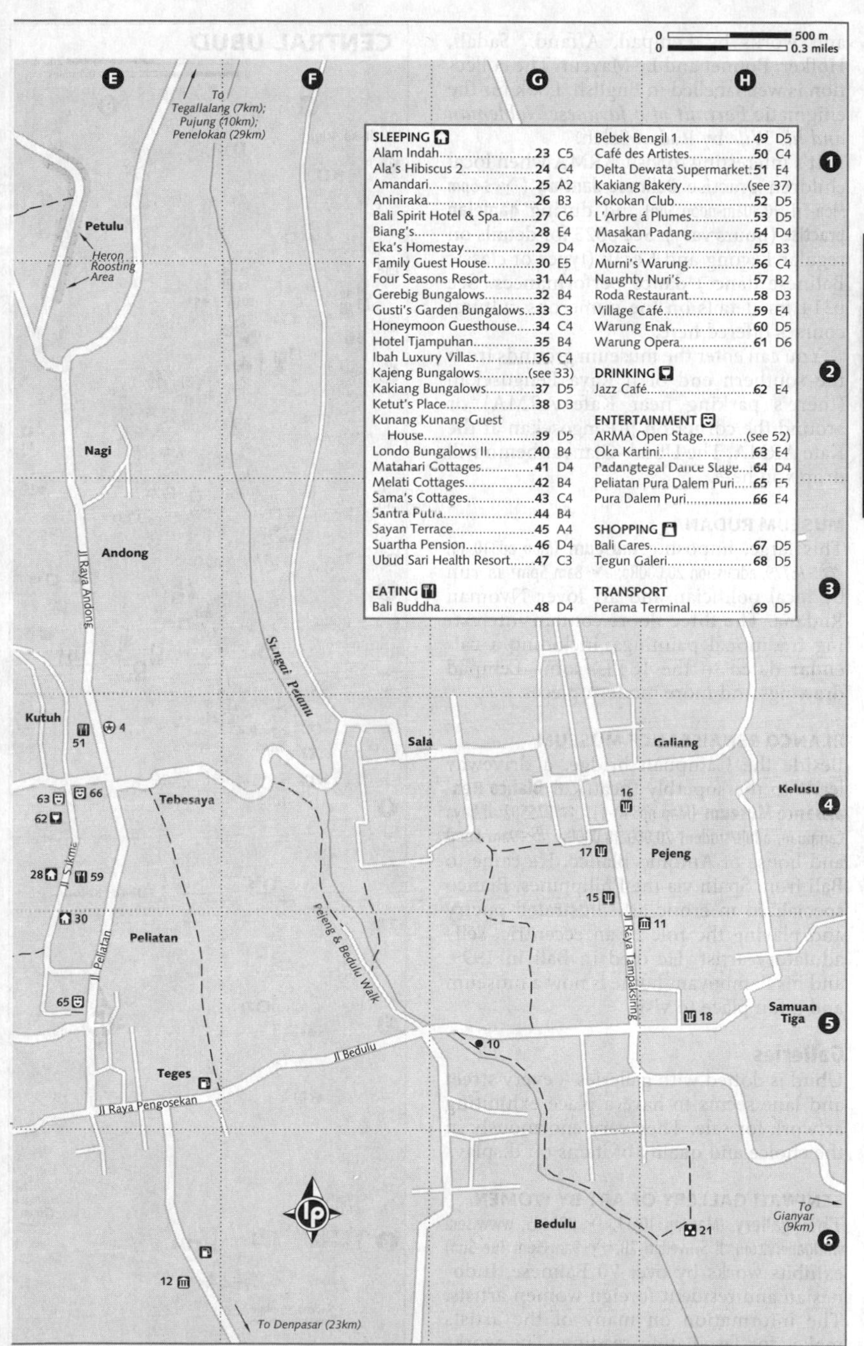
0 500 m
0 0.3 miles
E
F
G
H
To Tegallalang (7km); Pujung (10km); Penelokan (29km)
SLEEPING
Alam Indah....23 C5
Ala's Hibiscus 2....24 C4
Amandari....25 A2
Aniniraka....26 B3
Bali Spirit Hotel & Spa....27 C6
Biang's....28 E4
Eka's Homestay....29 D4
Family Guest House....30 E5
Four Seasons Resort....31 A4
Gerebig Bungalows....32 B4
Gusti's Garden Bungalows....33 C3
Honeymoon Guesthouse....34 C4
Hotel Tjampuhan....35 B4
Ibah Luxury Villas....36 C4
Kajeng Bungalows....(see 33)
Kakiang Bungalows....37 D5
Ketut's Place....38 D3
Kunang Kunang Guest House....39 D5
Londo Bungalows II....40 B4
Matahari Cottages....41 D4
Melati Cottages....42 B4
Sama's Cottages....43 C4
Santra Putra....44 B4
Sayan Terrace....45 A4
Suartha Pension....46 D4
Ubud Sari Health Resort....47 C3
EATING
Bali Buddha....48 D4
Bebek Bengil 1....49 D5
Café des Artistes....50 C4
Delta Dewata Supermarket....51 E4
Kakiang Bakery....(see 37)
Kokokan Club....52 D5
L'Arbre á Plumes....53 D5
Masakan Padang....54 D4
Mozaic....55 B3
Murni's Warung....56 C4
Naughty Nuri's....57 B2
Roda Restaurant....58 D3
Village Café....59 E4
Warung Enak....60 D5
Warung Opera....61 D6
DRINKING
Jazz Café....62 E4
ENTERTAINMENT
ARMA Open Stage....(see 52)
Oka Kartini....63 E4
Padangtegal Dance Stage....64 D4
Peliatan Pura Dalem Puri....65 F5
Pura Dalem Puri....66 E4
SHOPPING
Bali Cares....67 D5
Tegun Galeri....68 D5
TRANSPORT
Perama Terminal....69 D5
1
2
3
4
5
6
Petulu
Heron Roosting Area
Nagi
Andong
Jl Raya Andong
Sungai Petanu
Kutuh
Sala
Galiang
Kelusu
Tebesaya
Pejeng
Jl Sukma
Peliatan
Jl Peliatan
Pejeng & Bedulu Walk
Jl Raya Tampaksiring
Samuan Tiga
Jl Bedulu
Teges
Jl Raya Pengosekan
Bedulu
To Gianyar (9km)
To Denpasar (23km)

BALI

and works by Lempad, Affandi, Sadali, Hofker, Bonnet and Le Mayeur. The collection is well labelled in English. Look for the enigmatic *Portrait of a Javanese Nobleman and his Wife* by Raden Saleh.

It's interesting to visit ARMA when local children practise **Balinese dancing** (3-5pm Mon-Fri, 10.30am-noon Sun) and during **gamelan practise** (hours vary). See p323 for details on regular Legong and Kecak (types of classic Balinese dance) dance performances. See p314 for details on the numerous cultural courses offered here.

You can enter the museum grounds from the southern end of Jl Raya Pengosekan (there's parking near Kafe ARMA) or around the corner on Jl Pengosekan at the Kafe ARMA. The Ubud–Gianyar bemo will drop you here.

MUSEUM RUDANA

This large, imposing **museum** (Map pp310-11; ☎ 975779; admission 20,000Rp; 8am-5pm) is run by local politician and art lover Nyoman Rudana. The three floors contain interesting traditional paintings, including a calendar dated to the 1840s, some Lempad drawings and more modern pieces.

BLANCO RENAISSANCE MUSEUM

Beside the Campuan bridge, a driveway leads to the superbly theatrical **Blanco Renaissance Museum** (Map pp310-11; ☎ 975502; Jl Raya Campuan; adult/student 20,000/10,000Rp; 9am-5pm) and house of Antonio Blanco. He came to Bali from Spain via the Philippines. Blanco specialised in erotic art, illustrated poetry and playing the role of an eccentric, self-adulatory artist. He died in Bali in 1999, and his flamboyant home is now a museum and a fun place to visit.

Galleries

Ubud is dotted with galleries – every street and lane seems to have a place exhibiting artwork for sale. They vary enormously in the choice and quality of items on display.

SENIWATI GALLERY OF ART BY WOMEN

This **gallery** (Map pp310-11; 975485; www.seniwatigallery.com; Jl Sriwedari 2B; 9am-5pm Tue-Sun) exhibits works by over 70 Balinese, Indonesian and resident foreign women artists. The information on many of the artists makes for fascinating reading. The works

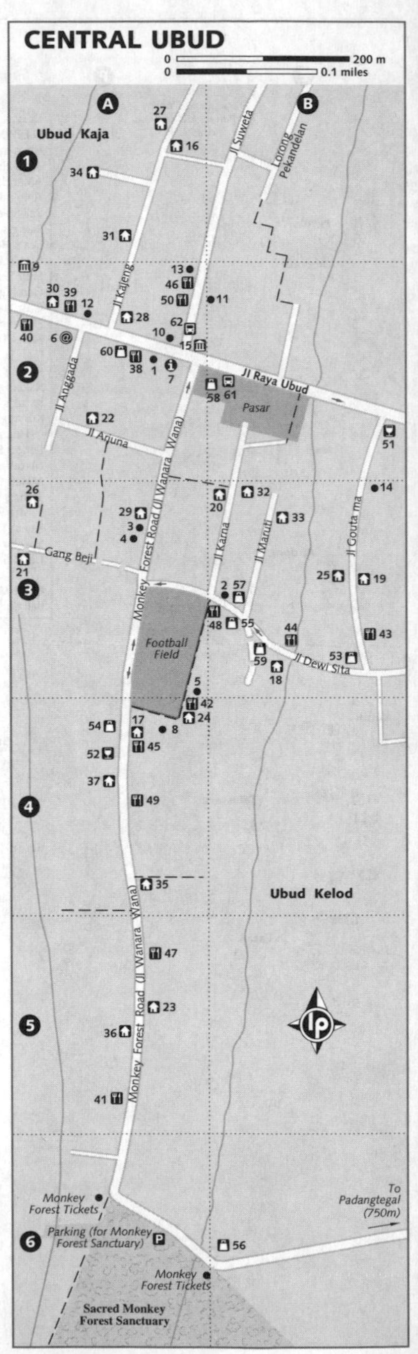

INFORMATION
Ary's Bookshop......1 A2
Cinta Bookshop......2 B3
MUA Pharmacy......3 A3
Periplus......4 A3
Pondok Pecak Library & Learning Centre......5 A3
Ubud Music......6 A2
Ubud Tourist Information......7 A2

SIGHTS & ACTIVITIES
Milano Salon......8 A4
Museum Puri Lukisan......9 A2
Pura Desa Ubud......10 A2
Pura Marajan Agung......11 B2
Pura Taman Saraswati......12 A2
Puri Saren Agung......(see 15)
Rio Helmi Gallery......13 A2
Studio Perak......14 B3
Ubud Palace......15 A2

SLEEPING
Arjana Accommodation......16 A1
Cendana Resort & Spa......17 A4
Dewangga Bungalows......18 B3
Donald Homestay......19 B3
Gandra House......20 B3
Gayatari Bungalows 2......21 A3
Jungut Inn......22 A2
Kubu Saren......23 A5
Loka House......24 A4
Nirvana Pension & Gallery......25 B3
Oka Wati Hotel......26 A3
Padma Accommodation......27 A1
Pradha Guesthouse & Restaurant......28 A2
Puri Muwa Bungalows......29 A3
Puri Saraswati Bungalows......30 A2
Roja's Bungalows......31 A1
Sania's House......32 B3
Sayong House......33 B3
Siti Bungalows......34 A1
Sri Bungalows......35 A4
Ubud Terrace Bungalows......36 A5
Ubud Village Hotel......37 A4

EATING
Ary's Warung......38 A2
Bumbu Bali Restaurant......(see 50)
Café Lotus......39 A2
Casa Luna......40 A2
Coffee & Silver......41 A5
Deli Cat......42 A4
Dewa Warung......43 B3
Kafé Batan Waru......44 B3
Lamak......45 A4
Terazo......46 A2
Three Monkeys......47 A5
Tutmuk Cafe......48 B3
Waroeng......49 A4
Warung Ibu Oka......50 A2

DRINKING
Nomad......51 B2
Putra Bar......52 A4

SHOPPING
Alamkara......53 B3
Alamkara......54 A4
Kertas Gingsir......55 B3
Kites Centre......56 B6
Kou......57 B3
Pasar Seni (Art Market)......58 B2
Thebb......59 B3
Treasures - a Gallery of Gold Creations......60 A2

TRANSPORT
Bemo Stop......61 B2
Bemo Stop......62 A2

span all mediums and many are for sale to aid charitable causes.

THREADS OF LIFE INDONESIAN TEXTILE ARTS CENTER

This small, professional **textile gallery and educational studio** (Map pp310-11; ☎ 972187; Jl Kajeng 24; 10am-6pm Mon-Sat) sponsors the production of naturally dyed, handmade ritual textiles, helping to recover skills in danger of being lost to modern dyeing and weaving methods. Commissioned pieces are displayed in the gallery, which has good explanatory material. It also runs regular textile appreciation courses (p314) and has a good shop.

NEKA GALLERY

Operated by Suteja Neka, the **Neka Gallery** (Map pp310-11; ☎ 975034; Jl Raya Ubud; 9am-5pm) is separate from the Neka Art Museum. It has an extensive selection from all the schools of Balinese art, as well as works by European residents such as the renowned Arie Smit.

RIO HELMI GALLERY

The man who has taken photographs for many of those coffee-table books about Bali lives in Ubud and has a small **gallery** (Map p312; ☎ 972304; Jl Suweta 5; 10am-6pm) where you can see examples of some of his works.

Artists' Homes

The home of Walter Spies is now part of **Hotel Tjampuhan** (p319). Dutch-born artist Han Snel lived in Ubud from the 1950s until his death in early 1999, and his family runs **Siti Bungalows** on Jl Kajeng (p318), where his work is exhibited in a gallery.

Music scholar Colin McPhee is well known thanks to his perennial favourite *A House in Bali*. Although the actual 1930s house is long gone, you can visit the riverside site (which shows up in photographs in the book) at **Sayan Terrace** (p319).

Sacred Monkey Forest Sanctuary

This cool and dense swathe of jungle, officially called **Mandala Wisata Wanara Wana** (Map p312; ☎ 971304; Monkey Forest Rd; adult/child 10,000/5000Rp; 8.30am-6pm), houses three holy temples. The sanctuary is inhabited by a band of grey-haired and greedy long-tailed Balinese macaques who are nothing like the innocent-looking doe-eyed monkeys on the brochures. They are ever vigilant for passing tourists who just might have peanuts and ripe bananas available for a quick hand-out. Don't hand food directly to these creatures.

The interesting **Pura Dalem Agung** (Temple of the Dead) is in the forest and has a real Indiana Jones feel to it. Look for the Rangda figures devouring children at the entrance to the inner temple.

You can enter through one of the three gates: at the southern end of Monkey Forest Rd; 100m further east, near the car park; or from the southern side, on the lane from Nyuhkuning.

ACTIVITIES

Massage, Spas & Salons

Ubud has numerous salons and spas where you can seriously pamper yourself.

Bodyworks (Map pp310-11; ☎ 975720; Jl Hanoman; 1-hr massage 90,000Rp; 9am-9pm) is set in a traditional Balinese compound. Treatment rooms are light-filled, although traffic noise competes with the gurgling fountains. A facial is 75,000Rp while a spice, salt, milk or seaweed bath costs from 125,000Rp to 150,000Rp.

Milano Salon (Map p312; ☎ 973448; Monkey Forest Rd; 1-hr massage 60,000Rp; 9am-8pm) offers facials and massages in a simple setting.

Ubud Sari Health Resort (Map pp310-11; ☎ 974393; Jl Kajeng; 1-hr massage US$15; 8am-8pm) is a spa and hotel in one. Besides a long list of one-day spa and salon services, there are a vast range of packages that include stays at the hotel (p318).

Zen (Map pp310-11; ☎ 970976; Jl Hanoman; 1-hr massage 75,000Rp; 9am-8pm) has a good reputation. It offers body scrubs, 90-minute *mandi lulur* and massage treatments (90,000Rp).

Rafting

The nearby Sungai Ayung is the most popular river in Bali for white-water rafting. **Bali Adventure Tours** (☎ 721480; www.baliadventuretours.com) offers trips down Sungai Ayung from US$42 to US$66, and can combine rafting with a big choice of other outdoor activities.

Another operator offering rafting and other adventurous outings is **Sobek** (☎ 287059; www.balisobek.com).

COURSES

Ubud is a very pleasant place to spend a few weeks developing your artistic skills, or learning about Balinese culture. Most places ask that you register in advance. Cooking courses are also offered, see p87.

ARMA (Map pp310-11; ☎ 976659; www.armamuseum.com; Jl Raya Pengosekan; 9am-6pm) A cultural powerhouse offering classes in painting, woodcarving and batik. Other courses include Balinese history, Hinduism and architecture. Classes cost US$22 to US$50 depending on duration and materials used.

Nirvana Batik Course (☎ 975415; Nirvana Pension & Gallery, Jl Goutama 10; classes 10am-3pm Mon, Wed & Sat) Nyoman Suradnya teaches the highly regarded batik courses here. One-day courses are $35, two- to three-day courses are $30 per day, and four- to five-day courses are $25 per day. Courses are conducted at Nirvana Pension & Gallery (Map p312).

Pondok Pecak Library & Learning Centre (Map p312; ☎ 976194; Monkey Forest Rd; 9am-5pm Mon-Sat, 1-5pm Sun) Painting and mask-carving classes are run here for tourists. Sessions cost from 50,000Rp for one hour. This is also a good place to find out about other courses being offered in the Ubud area, including language classes.

Santra Putra (Map pp310-11; ☎ 977810; Penestan; classes per hr 100,000Rp) Intensive painting and drawing classes are run by abstract artist I Wayan Karja, whose studio is also on-site. Accommodation is also available, see p317.

Studio Perak (Map p312; ☎ 0812 365 1809; Jl Goutama) This studio has a friendly atmosphere and it specialises in Balinese-style silversmithing courses. A three-hour lesson, where you'll make a finished piece, costs 150,000Rp.

Threads of Life Indonesian Textile Arts Center (Map pp310-11; ☎ 972187; www.threadsoflife.com; Jl Kajeng 24) Textile appreciation courses are run in the gallery and educational studio. There is a range of classes, including ones lasting eight days that involves extensive travel around Bali.

TOURS

Day tours around Ubud are popular. Many nearby attractions are quite difficult to reach by public transport, and finding your way around the back roads isn't always easy.

All travel agencies in Ubud can arrange tours, but it's worth shopping around as some will include entrance fees and some don't.

Bali Bird Walks (Map pp310-11; ☎ 975009; US$33; Tue, Fri, Sat & Sun 9am-12.30pm) For the keen birdwatcher, this tour is still going strong. A gentle morning's walk will give you the opportunity to see maybe 30 of the 100 or so local species.

Bali Eco and Educational Cycling Tour (Bali Budaya Tours; ☎ 975557, 081 833 6580; per person 360,000Rp) For the active. Offers a combination of mountain biking (downhill!) and cultural and culinary activities.

Ubud Tourist Information (Yayasan Bina Wisata; Map p312; ☎ 973285; Jl Raya Ubud; 8am-8pm) Runs interesting and affordable half- and full-day trips (125,000Rp to 200,000Rp) to a huge range of places, including Uluwatu, Mengwi, Alas Kedaton and Tanah Lot, or Goa Gajah, Pejeng, Gunung Kawi and Kintamani.

WALKS AROUND UBUD

There are lots of awe-inspiring walks to surrounding villages or through the rice paddies.

It's good to start walks at daybreak, before it gets too hot. In the walks below, distances are approximate and are measured with the Ubud Palace as the start and end point.

Monkey Forest & Penestanan

This 8km walk features a good range of rice paddies and rural Ubud scenery.

Take your time strolling through the **Sacred Monkey Forest Sanctuary** (p313). Continue south on the lane to the village of **Nyuhkuning**, and turn west along the south end of the football field, then turn south down the narrow road. At the southern end of the village, turn right and follow the paved road across the bridge over Sungai Wos to Dangin Lebak. Take the track to the right just after the large Bale Banjar Dangin Lebak (Dangin Lebak Community Hall). From here follow paths due north through the rice paddies, and veer left, westwards through the rice paddies to a paved road to reach **Katik Lantang**, where you join a paved road that continues north to Penestanan, where many artists live. Follow the paved road through the village, veering east, and go down through a deep cutting and back to Ubud.

Campuan Ridge

This 7km walk passes over the lush river valley of Sungai Wos, offering views of Gunung Agung and glimpses of small village communities and rice fields.

The walk leaves Jl Raya Campuan at the Ibah Luxury Villas (p319). Enter the hotel driveway and take the path to the left, where a walkway crosses the river to Pura Gunung Lebah. From there follow the concrete path north, climbing up onto the ridge between the two rivers.

Continuing north along the Campuan ridge, the road improves as it passes through rice paddies and the small village of **Bangkiang Sidem**. On the outskirts of the village, an unsigned road heads west, which winds down to Sungai Cerik (the west branch of Sungai Wos), then climbs steeply up to **Payogan**. From here you can walk south to the main road and on to the centre of Ubud.

Penestanan & Sayan

The wonders of Sungai Ayung are the focus of this 6.5km walk, where you will walk below the luxury hotels built to take advantage of this lush, tropical river valley.

Just west of the Campuan bridge, a steep uphill road, Jl Raya Penestanan, bends away to the left and winds across the forested gully of Sungai Blangsuh to the artists' village of Penestanan. West of Penestanan, take a small road north that curves around to **Sayan** and the Sayan Terrace hotel (p313). The best place to get down to the riverside is just north of Sayan Terrace – follow the narrow tracks down.

Head north along the eastern side of the Ayung, traversing steep slopes and rice paddies. After about 1.5km you'll reach the finishing point for many of the white-water rafting trips – a good but steep trail goes from there up to the main road at **Kedewatan**, where you can walk back to Ubud.

FESTIVALS & EVENTS

The Ubud area is one of the best places in Bali to see the many religious and cultural events that are celebrated on the island each year.

The **Ubud Writers & Readers Festival** (www.ubudwritersfestival.com) brings together scores of writers and authors from around the world in a celebration of writing – especially that which touches on Bali. It is usually held in October.

SLEEPING

Ubud has hundreds of places to stay. Choices range from simple little losmen to luxurious retreats that are among the best in the world. Generally, Ubud accommodation offers good value for money at any price level. A simple, clean room within a family home compound is the least expensive option. The midrange hotels generally offer swimming pools and other amenities, while the top-end hotels are often perched on the edges of the deep river valleys, with superb views and service. (Although some very cheap places also boast amazing views that urge you to curl up with a book and contemplate.)

Addresses in Ubud can be imprecise – but signage at the end of a road will often list the names of all the places to stay. Away from the main roads there are no streetlights and it can be very difficult to find your way after dark. If walking, you will definitely want a torch (flashlight).

Budget

Many inexpensive family lodgings are very small, often with just two, three or four rooms. They tend to operate in clusters, so you can easily look at a few before making your choice.

CENTRAL UBUD

Monkey Forest Rd

This was the first place developed for tourists in Ubud and there are many good-value places here.

Jungut Inn (Map p312; ☎ 978237; Jl Arjuna; s/d 30,000/40,000Rp) The torch-bearer for value on budget-friendly Jl Arjuna just off Monkey Forest Rd, Jungut's three rooms are barebones but very cheap. The family is usually sitting in the compound making offerings.

Kubu Saren (Map p312; ☎ 975704; Monkey Forest Rd; s/d 60,000/75,000Rp) This old-style simple place has eight bungalow rooms in a dark and shady compound.

Puri Muwa Bungalows (Map p312; ☎ 976441; Monkey Forest Rd; r 75,000-125,000Rp) Near the top of Monkey Forest Rd in a thicket places is this basic family-run establishment. It's reasonably quiet considering its location, and everything is very mellow. Cheaper rooms are cold-water only.

Loka House (Map p312; ☎ 973326; s/d 90,000/100,000Rp) Once through the lush entrance, Loka is a peaceful place, where the two-storey main building overlooks a small carp pond in the garden. The three rooms have hot water and fans. Located off Monkey Forest Rd.

Ubud Terrace Bungalows (Map p312; ☎ 975690; Monkey Forest Rd; r 100,000Rp;) Good value, as the basic rooms come with a pool and hot water.

Gayatri Bungalows 2 (Map p312; ☎ 979129; meggy292003@yahoo.com; r 150,000-200,000Rp;) The 12 large rooms have hot water and fans. It's a nice jaunt past rice paddies off Monkey Forest Rd.

East of Monkey Forest Rd

Small streets east of Monkey Forest Rd, including Jl Karna, have numerous, family-style homestays, which are secluded but still handy to the centre.

Gandra House (Map p312; ☎ 976529; Jl Karna; r 40,000-70,000Rp) Modern bathrooms and spacious gardens are the highlights of this cold-water 10-room place. One of several on this street.

Sayong House (Map p312; ☎ 973305; Jl Maruti; s/d 80,000/100,000Rp;) At the northern end of this deliciously quiet lane, Sayong has seven basic hot-water rooms, and there's a gorgeous pool in a private location across the lane from the rooms.

Sania's House (Map p312; ☎ 975535; sania_house@yahoo.com; Jl Karna 7; r 150,000-250,000Rp;) Pets wander about this family-run place, where the pool with fountains, huge terrace and large rooms will have you wagging your tail.

Jalan Goutama

This charming street has several cheap, quiet and accessible places to stay.

Donald Homestay (Map p312; ☎ 977156; Jl Goutama; r 40,000-70,000Rp) The four rooms – some with hot water – are in a nice back corner of the family compound. Chickens run about, some shortly to be turned into satay.

North of Jalan Raya Ubud

Both Jl Kajeng and Jl Suweta, leading north from Jl Raya, offer an excellent choice of budget lodgings, some quite close to the centre of town.

Arjana Accommodation (Map p312; ☎ 975583; Jl Kajeng 6; s/d 40,000/50,000Rp) The good-value leader. Bathrooms are outdoors in a mini-jungle, and the simple rooms are clean.

Roja's Bungalows (Map p312; ☎ 975107; Jl Kajeng 1; r 70,000-90,000Rp) One of the first of several places on Jl Kajeng, Roja's maintains a friendly atmosphere. Rooms are clean and well kept; some have hot water.

Padma Accommodation (Map p312; ☎ 977247; aswatama@hotmail.com; Jl Kajeng 13; r 120,000Rp) A very friendly place, Padma has only two adjoining, very private bungalows in a tropical garden. Rooms are decorated with local crafts and the modern outdoor bathroom has hot water. Nyoman Sudiarsa, a painter and family member, has a studio on the grounds and offers bike tours.

NORTH OF THE CENTRE

Things get quiet as you head north from Jl Raya Ubud, but note that some places are almost a kilometre to the north.

Kajeng Bungalows (Map pp310-11; ☎ 975018; Jl Kajeng; r 60,000-150,000Rp;) There are two big features here: a pool and a stunning setting overlooking a lush valley. The most expensive rooms have hot water, tubs and the best views.

Gusti's Garden Bungalows (Map pp310-11; ☎ 973311; gustigarden@yahoo.com; Jl Kajeng 27; s/d 140,000/170,000Rp;) Gusti opens onto a lavish garden, where the comfortable rooms are perched overlooking a swimming pool with a café. Excellent valley panorama.

EAST OF THE CENTRE

Eka's Homestay (Map pp310-11; ☎ 970550; Jl Sriwedari 8; r 50,000Rp) In a nice little family compound Eka's has six peaceful cold-water rooms. It is the home of Wayan Pasek Sucipta, a teacher of Balinese music.

Biangs (Map pp310-11; ☎ 976520; Jl Sukma 28; r 50,000-100,000Rp) In a little garden, Biangs – which means 'mama' – has six well-maintained rooms, with hot water. The views expand as you rise up the price chart.

Suartha Pension (Map pp310-11; ☎ 974244; Jl Hanoman 17; r 50,000-150,000Rp) There's a charming, traditional family setting here. Ikat and decorative features like fresh flowers strewn about make for a welcoming setting. More expensive rooms have hot water.

Family Guest House (Map pp310-11; ☎ 974054; familyhouse@telkom.net; Jl Sukma; r 80,000-350,000Rp) A gem, this popular place is set in a pleasant garden. Healthy breakfasts featuring brown bread are served. Some of the 12 rooms have hot water.

Kunang Kunang Guest House (Map pp310-11; ☎ 976052; Jl Hanoman; r 90,000-160,000Rp) All nine rooms in this quiet retreat have hot water. More money buys you sublime rice-paddy views from 2nd-floor rooms.

WEST OF THE CENTRE

Ala's Hibiscus 2 (Map pp310-11; ☎ /fax 970476; r 80,000-100,000Rp) Smack bang in the middle of rice paddies, this good place is about 150m down a path off Jl Bisma. The clean rooms have exceptional views, hot water and mosquito nets and are decorated with local handicrafts.

Sama's Cottages (Map pp310-11; ☎ 973481; Jl Bisma; s/d 100,000/150,000Rp;) This lovely little hideaway is terraced down a hill. It also has a well-maintained pool, and for companionship, you can befriend the cocks pecking about.

Campuan & Penestanan

West of Ubud but still within walking distance, places in the rice paddies are pitched at those seeking low-priced, longer-term lodgings. These places are a steep climb up a set of concrete stairs off Jl Raya Campuan.

Londo Bungalows II (Map pp310-11; ☎ 976764; londobungalows@hotmail.com; bungalows 60,000Rp) Off Jl Raya Campuan, this is ridiculously cheap. The three simple hot-water bungalows have gorgeous rice paddy– and morning-views of Gunung Batukau.

Santra Putra (Map pp310-11; ☎ 977810; karja bali@yahoo.com; Penestan; r US$12-15) Run by internationally exhibited abstract artist I Wayan Karja whose studio/gallery is also on-site, this place has five big, open airy rooms with hot water. Enjoy paddy-field views from all vantage points. Painting and drawing classes are offered by the artist, see p314. Located off Jl Raya Campuan.

Gerebig Bungalows (Map pp310-11; ☎ /fax 974582; s/d 125,000/150,000Rp) Walking through rice paddies 150m south of Londo Bungalows II rewards with wonderful views and good-value two-storey hot-water bungalows. South of Jl Raya Campuan.

Midrange

There is no end to the options at this price range.

CENTRAL UBUD

Nirvana Pension & Gallery (Map p312; ☎ 975415; rodanet@denpasar.wasantara.net.id; Jl Goutama 10; r 150,000-300,000Rp) There are *alang alang* (grass) roofs, a plethora of paintings, ornate doorways and modern bathrooms with hot water here. Batik courses also take place here (see p314).

Dewangga Bungalows (Map p312; ☎ 973302; www.dewangga-ubud.com; Jl Dewi Sita; r 150,000-

BALI

400,000Rp) Close to Jl Goutama, the 10 rooms here – some very large – have a variety of wood and stone carvings, some playfully lurid. The grounds are large and decorated with colourful mosaic tiles.

Siti Bungalows (Map p312; ☎ 975699; fax 975643; Jl Kajeng 3; bungalows US$30-60;) Owned by the family of the late Han Snel, a well-known Ubud painter for many years, this quiet compound has eight bungalows and a small pool. Some rooms are perched right on the edge of the river gorge and have sweeping views.

Sri Bungalows (Map p312; ☎ 975394; sribungalows@hotmail.com; Monkey Forest Rd; r US$35;) Some 50m off the busy road, this place has 16 bright bungalow-style rooms with hot water. The pool is large and there's an internet café.

Oka Wati Hotel (Map p312; ☎ 973386; www.okawatihotel.com; r US$25-60;) Opened in 1977, the Oki Wati is an unassuming veteran in old-Ubud style. The 19 rooms have large verandas where the delightful staff will deliver your choice of breakfast. The décor features vintage details like four-poster beds. The pool is very large and the site, off Monkey Forest Rd, is surrounded by rice paddies and lush tropical foliage.

Cendana Resort & Spa (Map p312; ☎ 973243; www.cendanaresort-spa.com; Monkey Forest Rd; r US$45-95;) Rooms have TV and face a lone paddy field. Both higher priced rooms have modern bathrooms and face pools. The landscaping is superb, with the two pools appearing to cascade over the rice paddies.

Pradha Guesthouse & Restaurant (Map p312; ☎ 975122; www.pradhaubud.com; Jl Kajeng 1; r from US$50;) Overlooking a deep, lush pool and nice café, the Pradha has six stylish and comfortable rooms; traffic noise from Jl Raya Ubud is minimal.

Puri Saren Agung (Map p312; ☎ 975057; fax 975137; Jl Raya Ubud; r US$50-65;) Part of the Ubud royal family's palace, this place is behind the courtyard where the regular dance performances are held. Accommodation is in traditional Balinese pavilions, with big verandas, four-poster beds, antique furnishings and hot water. There are lots of over-stuffed chairs about.

Puri Saraswati Bungalows (Map p312; ☎ 975164; www.purisaraswati.com; Jl Raya Ubud; r US$50-90;) This 18-room place is very central and pleasant, with lovely gardens that open onto the Ubud Water Palace. Rooms are well back from Jl Raya Ubud, so it's quiet. Cheaper rooms have fans.

NORTH OF THE CENTRE

Ketut's Place (Map pp310-11; ☎ 975304; www.indo.com/hotels/ketut-place; Jl Suweta 40; r US$20-48;) The elegant rooms here range from simple with fans to deluxe with air-con and bathtub. All have stunning views of the pool glittering down the hillside and the river valley. See p321 for details on its popular Balinese feasts.

Ubud Sari Health Resort (Map pp310-11; ☎ 974393; www.ubudsari.com; Jl Kajeng; r US$25-45, villas US$45-75;) There's charming accommodation and colonic irrigation for all guests here. See p314 for details on the spa. Daily health classes are held and even the plants in the gardens are labelled for their medicinal qualities. The 10 rooms feature lots of glass and white linen.

EAST OF THE CENTRE

Matahari Cottages (Map pp310-11; ☎ 975459; www.matahariubud.com; Jl Jembawan; r US$25-60;) This wild place has flamboyant themed rooms, including the 'Batavia Princess' and the 'Indian Pasha'. The Library is a vision out of a 1920s fantasy. You can wash those men right outa your hair in the South Pacific suite.

our pick **Alam Indah** (Map pp310-11; ☎ 974629; www.alamindahbali.com; Jl Nyuh Bulan; r US$50-95;) Just south of the Monkey Forest in Nyuhkuning, this isolated and spacious 10-room resort has a good riverside location and rooms that are beautifully finished in natural materials to traditional designs. The Wos river-valley views are tranquil, especially from the serene pool area where you can take your lunch while soaking up the sun. In the background a small waterfall burbles away peacefully. At night a trail of candles leads you down the winding drive through the trees to the hotel. The 'commute' to Ubud through the Monkey Forest is a bonus.

SOUTH OF THE CENTRE

Kakiang Bungalows (Map pp310-11; ☎ 978984; www.kakiang.com; Jl Raya Pengosekan; r US$50-80;) This elegant place has 10 bungalows with a rural design but modern conveniences. All have nice verandas. The pool area

BALI

is attractive and a study in cut stone. There's also the good Kakiang Bakery (p322).

WEST OF THE CENTRE

Honeymoon Guesthouse (Map pp310-11; ☎ 973282; www.casalunabali.com; Jl Bisma; r 325,000-550,000Rp;) Run by the Casa Luna (p320) clan and set in a family compound, there's a high rate of return visitors, so it's recommended to book ahead here. The 16 rooms have terraces, fans and tubs. More money gets you fridges and better views. The café is suitably tasty. See p87 for details about the cooking classes held here.

Campuan & Penestanan

Just west of the Campuan bridge, steep Jl Raya Penestanan branches off to the left, and climbs up and around to Penestanan.

Melati Cottages (Map pp310-11; ☎ 974650; melaticottages@hotmail.com; r US$30-50;) You can quack like a classic Ubud rice-paddy duck as you stroll out to these traditional-style rooms set around a café by the pool. Located off Jl Raya Penestanan; walk in from the north or south.

Aniniraka (Map pp310-11; ☎ 975213; www.aniniraka.com; Jl Raya Sanggingan; r US$75-125;) On the western side of the road in a paddy field, the inn has a soaring public area and a wonderfully situated swimming pool with Jacuzzi. The 11 rooms are attractive, with the current trend for dark woods and light fabrics well-represented.

Sayan & Ayung Valley

Sayan Terrace (Map pp310-11; ☎ 974384; www.sayanterraceresort.com; Jl Raya Sayan; r US$60-150;) With a million-dollar view of Sungai Ayung Valley below and the tops of palm trees stretching west, the Sayan Terrace is a good place to relax. The nine rooms are large and open onto terraces and are best value at the lower end of the price range. This is the site of Colin McPhee's *A House in Bali;* see p313 for details.

Top End

At this price range you have your choice of prime properties in the area. The big decision: close to town or not. Look for views, expansive pools, rooms with architectural features such as marble and/or outdoor bathrooms and a full range of amenities. Excellent service is a given.

CENTRAL UBUD

Ubud Village Hotel (Map p312; ☎ 975571; www.theubudvillage.com; Monkey Forest Rd; r US$70-150;) Close to Ubud's urban action – such as it is – the Village features a big pool, lush garden and 28 tasteful, fully equipped rooms. The hotel also has an impressive two-level restaurant and an open-air spa. Open-air bathrooms let you know you're in the tropics.

SOUTH OF THE CENTRE

Bali Spirit Hotel & Spa (Map pp310-11; ☎ 974013; www.balispirithotel.com; Nyuhkuning Village; r US$100-160;) Overlooking the Wos Valley, the Bali Spirit has stylish rooms and stunning views. The 19 rooms tumble down the hillside and feature Balinese art works and antiques. The spring-fed pool sits in a tropical bowl down by the rapids. The hotel also boasts a winsome spa and complimentary car service to area locations.

WEST OF THE CENTRE

Properties generally go from posh to posher as you near the fabled Ayung Valley.

Hotel Tjampuhan (Map pp310-11; ☎ 975368; www.indo.com/hotels/tjampuhan; Jl Raya Campuan; r US$70, with air-con US$115;) This venerable place overlooks the confluence of Sungai Wos and Sungai Cerik. The influential German artist Walter Spies lived here in the 1930s, and his former home, which sleeps four people (US$175), is now part of the hotel. There are shared modern bungalows in the wonderful garden. The hillside swimming pool is especially delightful with a verdant view in all directions.

Ibah Luxury Villas (Map pp310-11; ☎ 974466; www.ibahbali.com; ste from US$250, villas from US$450;) Off Jl Raya Campuan, and overlooking the lush Wos Valley, the Ibah offers an elegant environment and 18 spacious, stylish individual suites scattered across the hillside. The garden is decorated with stone carvings, handcrafted pots and antique doors, and the saltwater swimming pool is set into the hillside beneath an ancient-looking stone wall.

Sayan & Ayung Valley

Two kilometres west of Ubud, the fast flowing Sungai Ayung has carved out a deep valley, its sides sculpted into terraced rice paddies or draped in thick rainforest. Overlooking this verdant valley are some of the most stylish, luxurious and expensive hotels in Bali.

Four Seasons Resort (Map pp310-11; ☎ 977577; www.fourseasons.com; ste US$450, villas from US$575;) Set slightly into the valley, the curved open-air reception area is looks like a Cinerama screen of virescent Ubud landscape. Many of the villas have private pools and all units share the same amazing views. If you don't like green, consider a desert holiday. The many services include a spa.

Amandari (Map p312; ☎ 975333; www.amanresorts.com; ste from US$600;) In Kedewatan village, the Amandari is unquestionably classy with superb views over the paddies and down to the river – the main swimming pool seems to drop right over the edge. The 30 private pavilions have stone gateways and private gardens. They are spacious and exquisitely decorated. The best units have their own private pool.

NORTHWEST OF UBUD

Begawan Giri (☎ 978888; www.begawan.com; ste US$500-3000;) Secluded in a remote location 10km northwest of Ubud is the most fabled hotel in Bali. Set amid 20 acres of riverside forest and rice paddies, the 22 unique suites are grouped into five 'residences', each with its own swimming pool, library, kitchen and butler. The design by Cheong Yew Kuan emphasises the natural surroundings and combines new and old materials from the archipelago.

EATING

Ubud's restaurants offer the most diverse and interesting food on the island. It's a good place to try authentic Balinese dishes, as well as a range of other Asian and international cuisine. The quintessential Ubud restaurant has fresh ingredients, a delightful ambience and an eclectic menu, with dishes fusing inspiration from around the world.

Central Ubud

JALAN RAYA UBUD

There's plenty to chose from on Ubud's main street.

Casa Luna (Map p312; ☎ 977409; Jl Raya Ubud; dishes 9000-35,000Rp) This well-known bakery has a creative international menu and a delicious range of bread, pastries, cakes and more. Crisp salads, homemade pasta and simple main courses are not to be missed. The owner, Janet de Neefe, runs regular Balinese cooking courses (p87).

Café Lotus (Map p312; ☎ 975357; Jl Raya Ubud; dishes 26,000-55,000Rp) A leisurely meal at this shady Ubud classic overlooking the lotus pond is a relaxing option. The menu features Western and Indonesian fare that's well-prepared. For 50,000Rp you can book front-row seats for dance performances at Pura Taman Saraswati.

Ary's Warung (Map p312; ☎ 978359; Jl Raya Ubud; mains 30,000-85,000Rp) 'Warung' is something of a misnomer, as crisp table linen, architectural food presentation, well-trained waiters and high prices won't be found in any other warung. Organic ingredients are favoured on the seasonally changing menu.

MONKEY FOREST RD

our pick **Deli Cat** (Map p312; ☎ 971284; dishes 12,000-30,000Rp) A character-filled place filled with characters, Deli Cat (off Monkey Forest Rd behind the football field) is like a little tropical bodega. Wine – some delightfully cheap – is sold along with snacks and cheese and larger dishes like sandwiches, meatballs and soups, including an excellent mushroom. Try the little grilled sausages outside at the tables right on the football field. Or you can get carried away and have a bottle of French champagne for 225,000Rp – not a bad deal, actually. There are shared tables inside and out and a bed if it all becomes too much. Many people end their Ubud evenings with a nightcap here.

Waroeng (Map p312; ☎ 970928; Monkey Forest Rd; dishes from 15,000Rp) A small and artful upmarket warung with music befitting its owners (it's behind the Jazz Café– see p322). Create your own *nasi campur* from an array of fresh items.

Coffee & Silver (Map p312; ☎ 975354; Monkey Forest Rd; dishes 20,000-70,000Rp; 10am-midnight) Tapas and more substantial items make up the menu at this comfortable place with seating inside and out. Vintage photos of Ubud line the walls. Good coffee drinks.

Three Monkeys (Map p312; ☎ 974830; Monkey Forest Rd; mains 20,000-70,000Rp) A top choice, the dining room opens onto rice fields out back. Add in the glow of tiki torches for a magical effect. By day there are sandwiches, salads and gelato. At night there's a fusion menu of Asian classics, pasta and steaks. Local art decorates the walls.

Lamak (Map p312; ☎ 974668; Monkey Forest Rd; dishes 40,000-155,000Rp; 11am-midnight) Artful presentations from the eclectic menu set the mood at this excellent place. The large kitchen is open and each day there are specials of Indonesian food that are not found on your average menu. Long wine list.

EAST OF MONKEY FOREST RD

Dewa Warung (Map p312; Jl Goutama; dishes 4000-10,000Rp) You feel like you're in the country at this place with its tin roof and its shady position above the street. Inexpensive offerings include local curries. Beers are cheap.

Tutmak Café (Map p312; ☎ 975754; Jl Dewi Sita; dishes 15,000-30,000Rp) The location here facing both Jl Dewi Sita and the football field makes this a breezy stop on a hot day. It's also a stylish one with several levels of seating. Break the banana shackles and have a blueberry shake or try one of the sandwiches, burgers, juices or coffees.

Kafé Batan Waru (Map p312; ☎ 977528; Jl Dewi Sita; dishes 20,000-70,000Rp; 10am-midnight) One of Bali's best restaurants, Batan Waru serves consistently excellent Indonesian food. Western dishes include sandwiches and salads. The care and talent in the kitchen is apparent in the presentations. Most of the ingredients are organic. Smoked duck (*bebek betutu*) and suckling pig (*babi guling*) can be ordered in advance.

NORTH OF JALAN RAYA UBUD

Warung Ibu Oka (Map p312; Jl Suweta; dishes 15,000Rp) Noontime crowds of locals opposite Ubud Palace are here for one thing: the Balinese-style roast piglet. Line up and find a place at the communal tables under the shelter for one of the best meals you'll have in Ubud. Order a *spesial* to get the best cut.

Bumbu Bali Restaurant (Map p312; ☎ 974217; Jl Suweta 1; dishes 18,000-50,000Rp) Indian, Balinese and vegetarian influences combine at this excellent restaurant where many of its candlelit tables face Ubud Palace. Dishes are inventive and the flavours complex.

Terazo (Map p312; ☎ 978941; Jl Suweta; dishes 30,000-80,000Rp lunch & dinner) This stylish place serves brilliantly presented, eclectic Balinese fusion cuisine. The wine list is long and features numerous French, Italian and Australian choices. The austere interior is accented by vintage travel posters.

North of the Centre

Roda Restaurant (Map pp310-11; Jl Kajeng 24; dishes 6000-15,000Rp) Above Threads of Life Indonesian Textile Art Center, Roda is a pleasant little restaurant. It has good Indonesian dishes, including hard-to-find Balinese desserts, such as the Moorish *jaja Bali* (sticky rice, coconut, palm sugar and fruit steamed in banana leaves). Roda also holds traditional meals (30,000Rp per person; minimum five people); book in advance.

Ketut's Place (Map pp310-11; ☎ 975304; Jl Suweta 40; feast 100,000Rp; dinner Sun, Wed & Fri) Ketut's famous traditional Balinese feast is an excellent introduction to Balinese life and customs. The range of dishes is amazing and the quality is tops. There's usually an interesting group, so it's very sociable. See p318 for details on accommodation.

East of the Centre

Delta Dewata Supermarket (Map pp310-11; ☎ 973049; Jl Raya Andong) Located on the eastern side of town, this place gives you a Wal-Mart–like shopping experience (vast array of goods) without the social guilt.

Masakan Padang (Map pp310-11; Jl Hanoman; dishes 6000-12,000Rp; noon-1am) This Padang-style eatery – where you choose from the plates on display – has some of the cheapest, tastiest eats in town. Food is fresh and much of it is spicy.

Village Café (Map pp310-11; ☎ 973229; Rona Inn, Jl Sukma; dishes 7500-20,000Rp) Friendly staff serve up the usual suspects as well as extra-tasty juice concoctions featuring watermelon, carrot and apple juice. There's also internet access.

L' Arbre á Plumes (Map pp310-11; Jl Hanoman; dishes 8000-20,000Rp) There's good northern light for letter writing at this tiny French café. Baguette sandwiches and crepes lead the small menu. French publications line the walls.

Bali Buddha (Map pp310-11; ☎ 976324; Jl Jembawan 1; dishes 12,000-35,000Rp) This second-storey place offers a full range of vegetarian *jamu* (health tonics), salads, tofu curries, savoury crepes, pizza and bagels, as well as gelato. It has a comfy lounging area and is candlelit in the evening. The café also doubles as an exhibition space for local artists. On the ground floor, a market sells fresh organic fruit and vegetables, other healthy foods such as muesli and olive oil, and home-baked date bars, breads and cookies. Other items include cosmetics.

Bebek Bengil 1 (Dirty Duck Diner; Map pp310-11; ☎ 975489; Jl Hanoman; dishes 18,000-50,000Rp; 🕑 10am-10pm) This sprawling place does a special line in crispy deep-fried duck dishes. Water courses through the delightful dining area with its low tables and cushions on the floor.

South of the Centre

Kakiang Bakery (Map pp310-11; ☎ 978984; Jl Raya Pengosekan; dishes 8000-20,000Rp; ❄) This modern little café is a good place for a coffee, a snack or sandwich. You could even share a tart.

Warung Opera (Map pp310-11; ☎ 977564; Jl Raya Pengosekan; dishes 15,000-45,000Rp) This big, open place is popular for its diverse menu of snacks, steaks, sandwiches and local fare. The chicken salad and crispy duck are two favourites. Many come for the sophisticated entertainment that includes live jazz and blues many nights.

Warung Enak (Map pp310-11; ☎ 972911; Jl Raya Pengosekan; dishes 15,000-150,000Rp) There are peaceful rice-paddy views from the breezy upper level of this brightly coloured place that specialises in Indonesian food. The *rijstaffel* (selection of Indonesian dishes served with rice) is always a good choice and you can wash it down with a long list of imported wines.

Kokokan Club (Map pp310-11; ☎ 973495; Jl Raya Pengosekan; mains 35,000-55,000Rp; 🕑 lunch & dinner) On the grounds of the ARMA Resort, this elegant restaurant serves superb southern Thai and seafood dishes. *Hor mok goong* (prawns steamed in banana leaf) is as good as you'll find anywhere. The open-sided upstairs dining area has an air of understated elegance. Phone for transport.

West of the Centre

The restaurants and cafés in this section are all pretty spread out.

Murni's Warung (Map pp310-11; ☎ 975233; Jl Raya Campuan; dishes 16,000-50,000Rp) Since 1977 Murni's has been an Ubud favourite. The setting is beautiful and a four-level dining room overlooks the lush river valley. The diverse menu includes many desserts. There's a nice bar on the 2nd level down. One quibble: the gift shop gets bigger every year.

Café des Artistes (Map pp310-11; ☎ 972706; Jl Bisma 9X; dishes 22,000-86,000Rp; 🕑 10am-midnight) In a quiet and cultured perch off Jl Raya Ubud, the popular Café des Artistes brings Belgian food to Ubud. But the menu strays into France and Indonesia as well, with a foray to other places for sandwiches and salads at lunch. Dinner mains show the care in the kitchen from the talented staff. Art by locals such as Theo Zantman is on display. The wicker chairs are most comfortable.

SANGGINGAN

Naughty Nuri's (Map pp310-11; ☎ 977547; Jl Raya Sanggingan; dishes 15,000-50,000Rp) Huge burgers are the speciality here – you can get them to go. Or choose from local items or steaks, ribs and seafood. Thursday night grilled tuna specials are very popular at this rustic place, as are the martinis.

Mozaic (Map pp310-11; ☎ 975768; Jl Raya Sanggingan; menus 295,000-395,000Rp; 🕑 lunch & dinner Tue-Sun) Chef Chris Salans has created a fine restaurant that brings excellent French fusion cuisine into a lush garden setting. One of Bali's finest, Mozaic is consistently popular for its high standards, putting it on par with top international restaurants. There are many vegetarian choices.

DRINKING

No one comes to Ubud for wild nightlife. A few bars do get quite lively around sunset and later into the night, but the venues certainly don't aspire to the extremes of beer-swilling debauchery and first-world hip clubs found in Kuta and Seminyak.

Bars close early in Ubud – around 1am – by local ordinance. Many places listed under Eating, such as Deli Cat (p320) or Warung Opera (left), are also good just for a drink.

Nomad (Map p312; ☎ 977169; Jl Raya Ubud; dishes 15,000-45,000Rp) There's a barbecue here daily and often a gamelan player as well. It's a good central spot for a drink, especially back in the dark corners.

Jazz Café (Map pp310-11; ☎ 976594; Jl Sukma 2; dishes 35,000-60,000Rp; 🕑 5pm-midnight) An expat meeting place, Jazz Café has a relaxed atmosphere in a garden of coconut palms and ferns, good Asian fusion food and live music Tuesday to Saturday from 7.30pm.

The cocktail list is long. It provides free pick-up and drop-off around Ubud.

Putra Bar (Map p312; Monkey Forest Rd; draught beer 12,000Rp) Ubud's rasta wannabes hang out at this dark place, which features live reggae music from 9pm on Sunday, Tuesday, Wednesday and Friday, and movies or sports telecasts on Marley-free evenings.

ENTERTAINMENT

The joy of Ubud – and what makes people stay weeks instead of days – is the cultural entertainment. This is where you can base yourself not only for the nightly array of performances, but also to keep up with news of scheduled events in surrounding villages.

In a week in Ubud, you can see Kecak, Legong and Barong dances, Mahabharata and Ramayana ballets, *wayang kulit* puppets and gamelan orchestras. The main venues are the **Ubud Palace** (Map p312; Jl Raya Ubud), **Padangtegal Dance Stage** (Map pp310-11; Jl Hanoman), **Pura Dalem Puri** (Map pp310-11; Jl Raya Ubud), the **ARMA Open Stage** (Map pp310-11; ☎ 976659; Jl Raya Pengosekan), and **Peliatan Pura Dalem Puri** (Map pp310-11; Jl Peliatan). Other performances are in nearby towns like Batuan, Mawang and Kutuh.

You can also find shadow-puppet shows – although these are greatly attenuated from traditional village performances that often last the entire night. Regular performances are held at **Oka Kartini** (Map pp310-11; ☎ 975193; Jl Raya Ubud; tickets 50,000Rp).

Ubud's **Tourist Information office** (Yayasan Bina Wisata; Map p312; ☎ 973285; Jl Raya Ubud; 🕙 8am-8pm) has performance information, and sells tickets (from 50,000Rp). For performances outside Ubud, transport is usually included in the price. Tickets are also sold at the venues. Vendors sell drinks at the performances, which typically last about 90 minutes.

SHOPPING

Ubud has a huge variety of quality art shops, boutiques and galleries. Many places have clever and unique items made in and around the area.

The euphemistically named **Pasar Seni** (Art Market; Map p312; Jl Raya Ubud) is a busy two-storey place that sells a wide range of clothing, sarongs, footwear and souvenirs of variable quality at negotiable prices. Decent souvenirs include leather goods, batiks, baskets and silverware. More interesting is Ubud's colourful produce market, which operates to a greater or lesser extent every day and is buried within Pasar Seni. It starts early in the morning and winds up by lunch time.

You can spend days in and around Ubud shopping. Jl Raya Ubud, Monkey Forest Rd, Jl Hanoman and Jl Dewi Sita should be the focus of your expeditions. The following is just a taste of what's available.

Tegun Galeri (Map pp310-11; ☎ 973361; Jl Hanoman 44) Everything the souvenir stores are not; beautiful handmade items from around the island.

Thebb (Map p312; ☎ 975880; Jl Dewi Sita) Smart and hip houseware in distinctive designs made in Bali.

Alamkara Monkey Forest Rd (Map p312; ☎ 972213); Jl Dewi Sita (Map p312; ☎ 971004) One of the best jewellery galleries in Ubud, if not Bali, where the craftsmanship is of a high standard. On display are unusual, but very wearable designs in gold and silver, featuring black pearls and gems. The work of foreign and local jewellers is on display.

Treasures – a Gallery of Gold Creations (Map p312; ☎ 976697; Jl Raya Ubud) A posh place with ornate and expensive gold jewellery encrusted with gems.

Kou (Map p312; ☎ 971905; Jl Dewi Sita) Luscious handmade organic soaps made locally. Breathe deep on the way in.

Bali Cares (Map pp310-11; ☎ 981504; www.idepfoundation.org; Jl Hanoman 44B) This lovely shop sells goods to benefit several local charities. Items range from woodcarvings made from sustainable woods to paintings, handicrafts and other items produced by local people. There's an adjoining small café.

Kertas Gingsir (Map p312; ☎ 973030; Jl Dewi Sita) Specialises in interesting paper handmade from banana, pineapple and taro plants. If you're a real fan, ask about factory visits.

Kites Centre (Map pp310-11; ☎ 970924; Monkey Forest Rd) There are colourful wind-born creations such as dragons and sailing ships. A small frog goes for 25,000Rp.

GETTING THERE & AWAY

Bemo

Ubud is on two bemo routes. Orange bemos travel from Gianyar to Ubud (7000Rp) and larger brown bemos from Batubulan terminal in Denpasar to Ubud (6000Rp), and then head to Kintamani via Payangan. Ubud doesn't have a bemo terminal; bemos stop near the market in the centre of town.

Taxi

There are very few taxis in Ubud – those that honk their horns at you have usually dropped off passengers from southern Bali in Ubud and are hoping for a fare back. Instead, use one of the drivers with private vehicles hanging around on the street corners.

Tourist Shuttle Bus

Perama (Map pp310-11; ☎ 973316; Jl Hanoman; 9am-9pm) is the major tourist shuttle operator, but its terminal is inconveniently located in Padangtegal; to get to your final destination in Ubud will cost another 5000Rp. See the boxed text (below) for information on fares.

GETTING AROUND

To/From the Airport

Prepaid taxis from the airport to Ubud cost 175,000Rp. A taxi or car with driver to the airport will cost about half.

Bemo

Bemos don't directly link Ubud with nearby villages; you'll have to catch one going to Denpasar, Gianyar, Pujung or Kintamani and get off where you need to. Small bemos to Gianyar travel along eastern Jl Raya, down Jl Peliatan and east to Bedulu. To Pujung, bemos head east along Jl Raya and then north through Andong and past the turn-off to Petulu. Larger brown bemos to Batubulan terminal go east along Jl Raya and down Jl Hanoman.

Bicycle

Many shops, agencies and hotels in central Ubud rent mountain bikes. The standard charge is around 20,000Rp per day. Ask at your accommodation.

PERAMA TOURIST SHUTTLE BUSES FROM UBUD

Destination	Fare (Rp)
Candidasa	40,000
Kuta	30,000
Lovina	70,000
Padangbai	40,000
Sanur	20,000

Car & Motorcycle

With numerous nearby attractions, many of which are difficult to reach by bemo, renting a vehicle is sensible. Ask at your accommodation.

AROUND UBUD

☎ 0361

The region east and north of Ubud has many of the most ancient monuments and relics in Bali. Many of them predate the Majapahit era and raise as yet unanswered questions about Bali's history. Some are more recent, and newer structures have also been built on and around the ancient remains. They're interesting to history and archaeology buffs but, with the exception of Gunung Kawi and Yeh Pulu, which are both very impressive and beautiful, may not be so interesting to others. Perhaps the best approach is to plan a whole day walking or cycling around the area, stopping at the places that interest you, but not treating any as a destination in itself.

If you're travelling by public transport, start early and take a bemo to the Bedulu intersection, and another to Tirta Empul (about 15km from Ubud). See the temple of Tirta Empul, then follow the path beside the river down to Gunung Kawi – you may need to ask directions. From there you can return to the main road and walk downhill about 8km to Pejeng, or flag down a bemo going towards Gianyar. The temples and museum at Pejeng and the archaeological sites at Bedulu are all within about 3km of each other.

South of Ubud, the main road connecting the region to South Bali is lined with literally hundreds of craft and artisan shops. Stone and wood are carved into a myriad shapes – including custom orders – and you won't want for jewellery.

BEDULU

Bedulu was once the capital of a great kingdom. The legendary Dalem Bedaulu ruled the Pejeng dynasty from here, and was the last Balinese king to withstand the onslaught of the powerful Majapahits from

Java. He was eventually defeated by Gajah Mada in 1343. The capital shifted several times after this, to Gelgel and then later to Semarapura.

Sights

GOA GAJAH

About 1km east of Teges is **Goa Gajah** (Elephant Cave; Map pp310-11; adult/child 4100/2100Rp, car parking 1000Rp, motorbike parking 300Rp; 8am-6pm). The origins of the cave are uncertain – one tale relates that it was created by the fingernail of the legendary giant Kebo Iwa. It probably dates at least to the 11th century, and it was certainly in existence at the time of the Majapahit takeover of Bali. In modern times the cave was rediscovered by Dutch archaeologists in 1923; the fountains and bathing pool were not unearthed until 1954.

The small cave is carved into a rock face and you enter through the cavernous mouth of a demon. The gigantic fingertips pressed beside the face of the demon push back a riotous jungle of surrounding stone carvings. Inside the T-shaped cave you can see fragmentary remains of lingam, the phallic symbols of the Hindu god Shiva, and their female counterpart the yoni, plus a statue of the elephant-headed god Ganesh. In the courtyard in front of the cave are two square bathing pools with water gushing into them from waterspouts held by six female figures. To the left of the cave entrance, in a small pavilion, is a statue of Hariti, surrounded by children. In Buddhist lore, Hariti was an evil woman who devoured children, but under the influence of Buddhism she reformed completely to become a protector of children and a symbol of fertility.

If you're travelling independently, arrive before 10am, when the tour groups start to arrive.

YEH PULU

This 25m-long carved **cliff face** (Map pp310-11; adult/child 4100/2100Rp; 8am-6pm) is believed to be a hermitage dating from the late 14th century. It was rediscovered by a local official in 1925, and excavated by the Dutch in 1929. Apart from the figure of elephant-headed Ganesh, the son of Shiva, there are no obviously religious scenes here. The energetic frieze includes various scenes of everyday life (check out the horse and owner struggling uphill and the woman peering from behind her doorway), and the position and movement of the figures suggests that it could be read from left to right as a story. One theory is that they are events from the life of Krishna, the Hindu god.

The Ganesh figures of Yeh Pulu and Goa Gajah are similar, indicating a close relationship between the two sites. You can walk between the sites, following small paths through the rice fields, but you might need to pay a local to guide you. If travelling by car or bicycle, look for the signs to 'Relief Yeh Pulu' or 'Villa Yeh Pulu' east of Goa Gajah. The entry fee includes a small brochure with an explanation in creative English.

PURA SAMUAN TIGA

The majestic **Pura Samuan Tiga** (Temple of the Meeting of the Three; Map pp310-11) is about 200m east of the Bedulu junction. The name is possibly a reference to the Hindu trinity, or it may refer to meetings held here in the early 11th century. Despite these early associations, all the temple buildings have been rebuilt since the 1917 earthquake. The imposing main gate was designed and built by I Gusti Nyoman Lempad, one of Bali's renowned artists and a native of Bedulu.

MUSEUM PURBAKALA

This archaeological **museum** (Map pp310-11; ☎ 942354; Jl Raya Tampaksiring; admission by donation; 8am-3pm Mon-Thu, 8am-12.30pm Fri) has a reasonable collection of artefacts from all over Bali, and most displays are in English. The exhibits in several small buildings include some of Bali's first pottery from near Gilimanuk, and sarcophagi dating from as early as 300 BC – some originating from Bangli are carved in the shape of a turtle, which has important cosmic associations in Balinese mythology. The museum is about 500m north of the Bedulu junction, and easy to reach by bemo or by bicycle.

Getting There & Away

About 3km east of Teges, the road from Ubud reaches a junction where you can turn south to Gianyar or north to Pejeng, Tampaksiring and Penelokan. Any Ubud to Gianyar bemo will drop you off at the Bedulu junction, from where you can walk. The road from Ubud is reasonably flat, so coming by bicycle is a good option.

PEJENG

Further up the road to Tampaksiring is Pejeng and its famous temples. Like Bedulu, Pejeng was once an important seat of power, the capital of the Pejeng kingdom, which fell to the Majapahit invaders in 1343.

Pura Kebo Edan

Also called the **Crazy Buffalo Temple** (Map pp310-11; 7am-6pm), this is not an imposing structure but is famous for its 3m-high statue, known as the Giant of Pejeng and thought to be about 700 years old. The temple is a place where prayer and offerings are thought to cure sick animals. It's on the western side of the road.

Pura Pusering Jagat

This large **temple** (Navel of the World Temple; Map pp310-11) is said to be the centre of the old Pejeng kingdom. Dating from 1329, it is visited by young couples who pray at the stone lingam and yoni. Further back is a large stone urn with elaborate but worn carvings of gods and demons searching for the elixir of life in a depiction of the Mahabharata tale 'Churning the Sea of Milk'. The temple is on a small track running west of the main road.

Pura Penataran Sasih

This **temple** (Map pp310-11; Jl Raya Tampaksiring) was once the state temple of the Pejeng kingdom. In the inner courtyard, high up in a pavilion and difficult to see in any detail, is the huge bronze drum known as the **Moon of Pejeng**. The hourglass-shaped drum is more than 2m long, the largest single-piece cast drum in the world. Estimates of its age vary from 1000 to 2000 years, and it is not certain whether it was made locally.

TAMPAKSIRING

Tampaksiring is a small town where Gunung Kawi, the most impressive ancient monument in Bali, is located. There's also a large and important temple, with bathing pools, nearby at Tirta Empul. There is nowhere to stay in Tampaksiring.

Sights

GUNUNG KAWI

On the southern outskirts of town a sign points east off the main road to the wondrous **Gunung Kawi** (adult/child 4100/2100Rp; 7am-5pm). From the end of the access road a steep stone stairway leads down to the river, at one point making a cutting through an embankment of solid rock. There, in the bottom of this lush green valley, is one of Bali's oldest, most charming and certainly largest ancient monuments.

Gunung Kawi consists of 10 rock-cut *candi* (shrines), memorials cut out of the rock face in imitation of actual statues. They stand in 7m-high sheltered niches cut into the sheer cliff face. A solitary *candi* stands about 1km further down the valley to the south; this is reached by a trek through the rice paddies on the western side of the river. Each is believed to be a memorial to a member of 11th-century Balinese royalty, but little is known for certain. Legends relate that the whole group of memorials was carved out of the rock face in one hard-working night by the mighty fingernails of Kebo Iwa.

The five monuments on the eastern bank are probably dedicated to King Udayana, Queen Mahendradatta, their son Airlangga and his brothers Anak Wungsu and Marakata. While Airlangga ruled eastern Java, Anak Wungsu ruled Bali. The four monuments on the western side are, according to this theory, dedicated to Anak Wungsu's chief concubines. Another theory is that the whole complex is dedicated to Anak Wungsu, his wives, concubines and, in the case of the remote 10th *candi*, a royal minister.

The steps require a steep 10-minute hike up on the way back. The valley is hot and doesn't get much breeze, so wear a hat and take water. The hawkers are persistent, but there are, thankfully, few within the temple compound itself. You'll need a temple sarong and sash, and if you're travelling independently go early or late to avoid the tour groups; it's simply a wonderful place when it's quiet.

TIRTA EMPUL

A well-signposted fork in the road north of Tampaksiring leads to the holy springs at **Tirta Empul** (adult/child 4100/2100Rp; 8am-6pm). Founded in 962, the springs are believed to have magical powers, so the temple is important. The springs are a source of Sungai Pakerisan, which rushes by Gunung Kawi only 1km or so away. The actual springs bubble up into a large, crystal-clear tank within the temple and gush out through waterspouts into a bathing pool. Despite its antiquity, the temple looks glossy and new – it was totally restored in the late 1960s – but you still need to wear long pants or a temple sarong. The bathing pools can be visited, but you probably won't be able to bathe in them.

Overlooking Tirta Empul springs is Soekarno's palace, **Istana Negara**. It's a simple single-storey structure built on a ridge, and was designed by Soekarno himself. It was erected in 1954 on the site of a Dutch rest house. It's sometimes open to the public.

The exit route from the temple is through a lengthy warren of souvenir stalls – grit your teeth and follow the painted arrows on the ground to find your way out.

Getting There & Away

Tampaksiring is an easy day trip from Ubud, or a stopover between Ubud and Danau Batur. If travelling by bemo, get a connection in Bedulu. Tirta Empul and Gunung Kawi are easy to find along the Penelokan to Ubud road, and are only about 1.5km apart.

NORTH OF UBUD

The usual road from Ubud to Batur is through Tampaksiring, but there are other lesser roads up the gentle mountain slope. One of the most attractive goes north from Peliatan, past Petulu, and through Tegallalang and Pujung, to bring you out on the crater rim between Penelokan and Batur. It's a sealed road all the way. **Tegallalang**, **Jati** and **Pujung** are all noted woodcarving centres.

A good lunch stop about 12km from Ubud, with picturesque paddy-field views, is **Blue Yogi Cafe** (☎ 901368; dishes 15,000-40,000Rp; ⌚ 8am-5pm). After lunch, walk things off with a stroll among the rice.

SOUTH OF UBUD

The road from Ubud to Denpasar, Sanur and South Bali, via Mas, Batuan, Sukawati, Celuk and Batubulan is lined with places making and selling handicrafts. (You may not have realised there could be so many stone-carvers on one island.) Many tourists stop and shop along this route, but there are some quieter back roads where much of the craft work is done in small workshops and family compounds; this means the selection is better, and cutting out the retailer means that prices are cheaper and more money stays with the craftsperson.

There are regular bemos along this route, but if you want to stop at craft workshops it's more convenient to have your own transport so you can explore the back roads and carry your purchases without any hassles. If you decide to charter a vehicle, the driver may receive a commission from any place you spend your money – this can add 10% or more to the cost of purchases. Also, a driver may steer you to workshops or artisans that he favours, rather than those of most interest to you.

Mas

Mas means 'gold', but **woodcarving**, particularly mask carving, is the craft practised here. The road through Mas is lined with craft shops for the tour-bus loads, but there are plenty of smaller carving operations in the back lanes.

Along the main road in Mas is the **Taman Harum Cottages** (☎ 975567; www.tamanharumcottages.com; r from US$35, villas US$50-75; ❄ 🏊). There are 17 rooms and villas – some are quite large and excellent value. By all means get one overlooking the paddy fields. It has a gallery, which is a venue for a range of art and cultural courses.

Batuan

Batuan is a noted **painting centre** with a number of art galleries. It came under the influence of Bonnet, Spies and the Pita Maha artists' cooperative at an early stage. Traditionally, Batuan painters produced dynamic black-ink drawings, but the newer 'Batuan style' of painting is noted for including a large number of different subjects in a single canvas, even the odd windsurfer or a tourist with a video camera. Batuan is also noted for the ancient Gambuh dance performed in the *pura puseh* every full moon.

Taman Burung Bali Bird Park & Rimba Reptil Park

Just north of Tegaltama, the **bird park** (☎ 299352; www.bali-bird-park.com; adult/child US$8/4; ⌚ 8am-6pm) boasts more than 1000 birds from over 250 species, including rare *cendrawasih* (birds of paradise) from Papua and highly endangered Bali starlings – many of which are housed in special walk-through aviaries. The 2 hectares of landscaped gardens feature a fine collection of tropical plants and a couple of non-native Komodo dragons.

Next door, **Rimba Reptil Park** (☎ 299344; adult/child US$8/4; ⏰ 8am-6pm) has about 20 species of creatures from Indonesia and Africa, including turtles, crocodiles, a python and more Komodo dragons.

Both places are popular with kids. You can buy a combination ticket to both parks (adult/child US$15/7.50). Allow at least two hours for the bird park alone, which also has a good restaurant.

Many tours stop at the parks, or you can take a Batubulan–Ubud bemo, get off at the junction at Tegaltamu and follow the signs north for about 600m. There is a large parking lot.

Sukawati

Sukawati is a centre for the manufacture of wind chimes, temple umbrellas and *lontar* (palm leaf) baskets dyed with intricate patterns. It has a busy **craft market** in an obvious, two-storey building on the main road – bemos stop right outside. Every type of quality craftwork and touristy trinket is on sale, at cheap prices for those who bargain hard. Across the road is the colourful morning produce-market, with the old royal palace behind; it's worth a stop.

Wayang kulit (shadow puppets) and *topeng* (masks) are also made in the backstreets of Sukawati and in **Puaya**, about 1km northwest of the main road.

Celuk

Celuk is a **silver- and gold-smithing centre** with numerous jewellery specialists and a wide variety of pieces on sale. Most of the work is done in workshops in the back streets; after the main line of showrooms turn left (if you're coming from Denpasar) into Jl Jagaraga and check out the artisans at work.

Batubulan

Stonecarving is the main craft of Batubulan, which means 'moon stone', and the temples around Batubulan are noted for their fine **sculptures**. You'll see hundreds of statues beside the road, and you're welcome to watch the workers, many of them young boys, chipping away at big blocks of soft volcanic stone.

Batubulan also has some well-regarded **dance troupes**. Dances are performed daily at several venues along the road, with Barong usually at 9.30am and Fire and/or Kecak dances at 6.30pm. The shows last for an hour or so, and cost 50,000Rp. The *pura puseh,* about 200m to the east of the busy main road, is worth a visit; there may be a morning Barong dance performed there.

Batubulan is the major bemo terminal for eastern and central Bali – see p306 for details.

EAST BALI

The eastern end of Bali is dominated by the mighty Gunung Agung, the 'navel of the world' and Bali's 'mother mountain'. The slopes of this and the other peaks at this end of the island hold some of the most verdant rice fields and tropical vistas you can imagine. It's a good place to have your own transport, as you can simply 'get lost' wandering side roads and revel in the exquisite scenery.

At the coast, there are attractive beaches galore, especially those south of Semarapura, that are now easily accessible thanks to the ever-lengthening coastal road. Add in some ancient cultural sites and the popular areas of Candidasa and Amed and you have an area that will figure in the itinerary of anyone who breaks free from the South Bali–Ubud juggernaut.

GIANYAR

☎ 0361

Gianyar is the capital of Gianyar district (which includes Ubud). It has some small **textile factories** on the west side of town, where you can see ikat being woven and buy fabric and clothes. It's a place that most tourists will pass through, rather than spend time in.

The Gianyar royal family saved its palace, and its position, by capitulating to the Dutch. The original 18th-century **Puri Gianyar** was destroyed in a conflict with the Klungkung kingdom in the mid-1880s, was rebuilt and then severely damaged again in the 1917 earthquake. It's a fine example of traditional

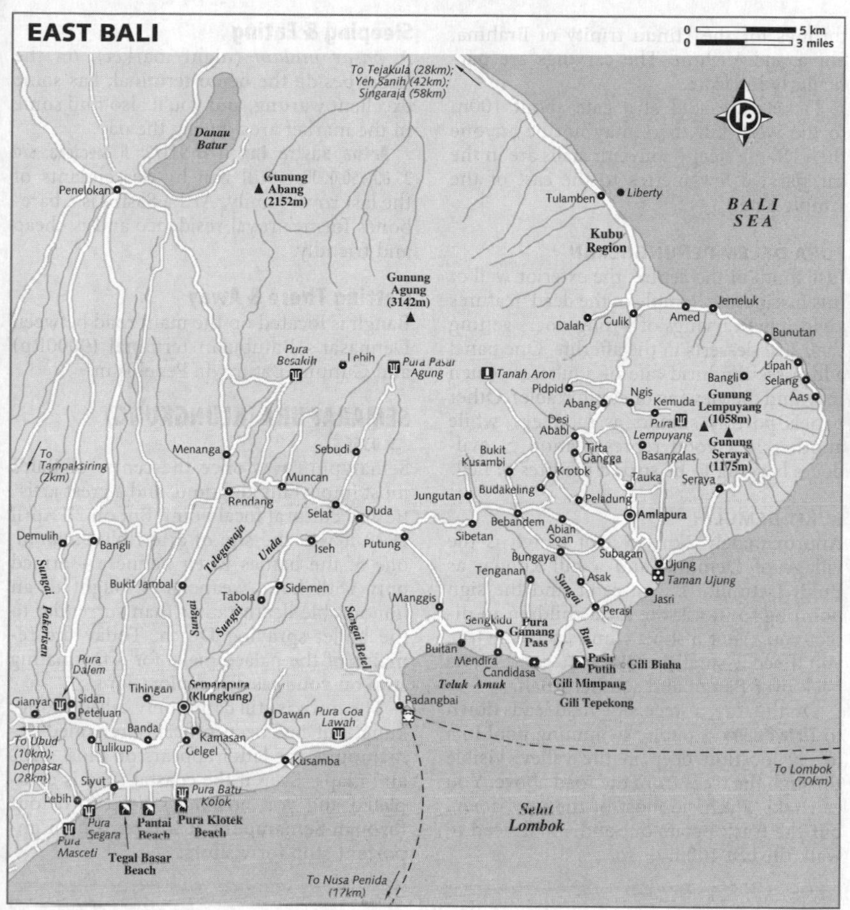

palace architecture, and though foreigners are not normally allowed inside, you can get a good sense of it from the outside.

Gianyar's **warung** on the main street and market are noted for their fine *babi guling* (roast pig), a local speciality.

Regular bemo travel is between the main terminal in Gianyar and Batubulan terminal (8000Rp). Gianyar is the junction for Ubud and Tampaksiring. The bemo terminal is on the west side of town, about 500 metres from the centre.

BANGLI

☎ 0366

Halfway up the slope to Penelokan, Bangli – once the capital of a kingdom – has an interesting temple and cultural centre, though if there's no ceremony or festival happening, it's pretty quiet.

Sights

PURA KEHEN

Pura Kehen (admission 4100Rp; 9am-5pm), the state temple of the Bangli kingdom, is one of the finest temples in east Bali; it's a little like a miniature version of Pura Besakih.

The temple is terraced up the hillside, with a great flight of steps leading to the beautifully decorated entrance. The first courtyard has a huge banyan tree with a *kulkul* (alarm drum) entwined in its branches. The inner courtyard has a *meru* (multiroofed shrine) with 11 roofs, and thrones for the Hindu trinity of Brahma, Shiva and Vishnu. The carvings are particularly intricate.

Tickets are sold at a gate about 100m to the west, but there may not be anyone there. Some sleepy souvenir stalls are in the car park, a few metres to the east of the temple gate.

PURA DALEM PENUNGGEKAN

Just south of the centre, the exterior wall of this fascinating 'temple of the dead' features vivid relief carvings of wrong-doers getting their just desserts in the afterlife. One panel addresses the lurid fate of adulterers (men may find the viewing uncomfortable). Other panels portray sinners as monkeys, while another is a good representation of evil-doers begging to be spared the fires of hell.

BUKIT DEMULIH

Approximately 3km west of Bangli is the village of Demulih and a hill known as Bukit Demulih. If you can't find the sign pointing to it, ask the local children to direct you. After a short climb up to the top, you'll see a small **temple** with good views back over Bangli and southern Bali.

On the way, a steep side road leads down to **Tirta Buana**, a public swimming pool in a lovely location deep in the valley, visible through the trees from the road above. You can take a vehicle most of the way down, but the track peters out and you'll need to walk the last 100m or so.

Sleeping & Eating

A *pasar malam* (night market), on the street beside the bemo terminal, has some excellent warung, and you'll also find some in the market area during the day.

Artha Sastra Inn (☎ 91179; Jl Merdeka; s/d 35,000/50,000Rp) Still run by descendants of the last royal family, Artha Sastra is a bare-bones former royal residence and is cheap and friendly.

Getting There & Away

Bangli is located on the main road between Denpasar's Batubulan terminal (9000Rp) and Gunung Batur, via Penelokan.

SEMARAPURA (KLUNGKUNG)

☎ 0366

Semarapura was once the centre of Bali's most important kingdom, and a great artistic and cultural focal point. But on 28 April 1908 it was the site of a terrible *puputan*, one of the battles when Balinese – armed only with hand-weapons – fought to an honourable death rather than surrender to the bullet-spraying Dutch. Today the remains of the palace make for a fascinating stop on your eastern explorations.

The town is still commonly called Klungkung, but has been officially renamed Semarapura; the latter appears on most signs and maps. Even if the coastal road is completed and you no longer need to detour through Semarapura, it will remain an important stop for visitors.

BALI'S 'NEW' BEACHES

The new road running from Sanur east along the coast has made it easy to get to large stretches of shore that were until recently pretty inaccessible.

The coast is striking, with seaside temples, black-sand beaches and pounding waves. Here are some places worth exploring, starting in the west and heading east.

Pura Masceti One of Bali's most important temples, is on the beach. Gaudy statuary and a few drink vendors complete the scene.

Pura Segara Looks across the strait to Nusa Penida, home of Jero Gede Macaling – the temple helps protect Bali from his evil influence. The site is very quiet.

Lebih Has a beach made of mica that sparkles with a billion points of light. There are a couple of cafés.

Tegal Basar Beach A turtle sanctuary with a good view of Nusa Lembongan.

Pantai Beach A must for fans of the tautological (*pantai* means beach). There's a tiny café and long row of dunes at this picture-perfect spot.

Pura Klotek Beach Has a small temple and some very fine black sand.

Note that swimming in the often pounding surf is dangerous. You'll need your own transport to visit these places and you'll find services are few, so bring your own water and towels.

Sights

SEMARA PURA COMPLEX

When the Dewa Agung dynasty moved here in 1710, a new palace, the **Semara Pura** (adult/child 5000/2000Rp, parking 1000Rp; 7am-6pm), was established. Most of the original palace and grounds were destroyed during Dutch attacks in 1908, and the **Pemedal Agung**, the gateway on the southern side of the square, is all that remains of the palace itself – the carved wooden doors are beautiful.

Kertha Gosa

The 'Hall of Justice' was effectively the supreme court of the Klungkung kingdom, where disputes and cases that could not be settled at the village level were brought. This open-sided pavilion is a superb example of Klungkung architecture, and its ceiling is covered with fine paintings in the Klungkung style. The paintings, done on asbestos sheeting, were installed in the 1940s, replacing cloth paintings that had deteriorated.

Bale Kambang

The ceiling of the beautiful 'Floating Pavilion' is painted in Klungkung style. As in the Kertha Gosa, the different rows of paintings deal with different subjects. The first row is based on the astrological calendar; the second on the folk tale of Pan and Men Brayut and their 18 children; and the upper rows on the adventures of the hero Sutasona.

Museum Semarajaya

This recently renovated museum has an interesting collection of archaeological and other pieces. There are exhibits of *songket* weaving, salt-making, palm toddy and palm-sugar extraction, and a moving display about the 1908 *puputan*, along with some interesting old photos.

Getting There & Away

Frequent bemos from Denpasar (Batubulan terminal) pass through Semarapura (9000Rp) on the way to Padangbai, Amlapura, Selat and Singaraja. They can be hailed from near the Puputan Monument.

Bemos heading north to Besakih (9000Rp) leave from the centre of Semarapura, a block northeast of Kertha Gosa. Most other bemos leave from the inconvenient Terminal Kelod, about 2km south of the city centre.

Perama shuttle buses between South Bali or Ubud and the east will stop in Semarapura on request, although this may change when the coastal road is completed.

AROUND SEMARAPURA

Nyoman Gunarsa, one of the most respected and successful modern artists in Indonesia, established the **Museum Seni Lukis Klasik** (☎ 0366-22255; adult/child 20,000Rp/free; 9am-4pm), a museum and arts centre, near his home village. The huge three-storey building exhibits an impressive variety of older pieces, including carvings in stone and wood, architectural antiques, masks, ceramics and textiles. Many of the classical paintings are on bark paper and are some of the oldest surviving examples of this style. The top floor is devoted to Gunarsa's own work of colourful, semi-abstract depictions of traditional dancers and musicians.

The museum is about 6km west from Semarapura, near a bend on the road to Denpasar – look for the dummy policemen at the base of a large statue nearby.

SIDEMEN ROAD

☎ 0366

A less-travelled road to Pura Besakih goes northeast from Semarapura, via Sidemen and Iseh, to the Rendang–Amlapura road. The area offers marvellous paddy-field scenery, a delightful rural character and exciting views of Gunung Agung (when the clouds permit). The road is in good shape and regular bemos shuttle up and down from Semarapura.

Sidemen has a spectacular location and is a centre for culture and arts, particularly *endek* (ikat) cloth and *songket*, which is woven with threads of silver and gold. German artist Walter Spies lived in Iseh for some time from 1932 in order to escape the perpetual party of his own making in Ubud. Later, the Swiss painter, Theo Meier, nearly as famous as Spies for his influence on Balinese art, lived in the same house.

There are many walks throughout the verdant valley.

Sleeping & Eating

Near the centre of Sidemen, a small road heads west, signposted with the names of several places to stay. Views throughout the

BALI

area are often spectacular, from terraced green hills to Gunung Agung. Places to stay always have restaurants.

Lihat Sawah (☎/fax 24183; r 150,000-250,000Rp) Take the right fork in the road to this very friendly place with great gardens. All nine rooms (the cheapest have cold water) have views of the valley and mountain. The surrounding rice fields course with water. Lihat Sawah also has food on offer – dishes cost 12,500Rp to 25,000Rp.

Patal Kikian (☎/fax 23005; villas US$50-70;) Two kilometres north of Sideman, look for a steep driveway on the eastern side of the road. This retreat has four spacious, stylishly furnished villas with vast verandas overlooking terraced hillsides for one of the best views in East Bali. Rates include all meals, which are served as private banquets on your own veranda. Rooms have hot water and there is a soaking pool.

Sacred Mountain Sanctuary (☎ 24330; www.sacredmountainresortresort.com; villas US$90-140;) Close to the river, this remote and rusticated resort has a New Age vibe and a huge spring-fed swimming pool. The 19 bamboo villas have open-air bathrooms and many artistic touches. The resort can arrange treks of Gunung Agung (from US$55), as well as a range of courses. Massage is available, as is food (dishes 20,000Rp to 35,000Rp).

PURA BESAKIH

Perched nearly 1000m up the side of Gunung Agung is Bali's most important temple, Pura Besakih. In fact, it is an extensive complex of 23 separate-but-related temples, with the largest and most important being Pura Penataran Agung. Unfortunately, many people find it a deeply disappointing experience due to the avarice of numerous local characters. See the boxed text, below, for the details, which may well help you decide whether to skip it.

Orientation

The main entrance is 2km south of the complex on the road from Menanga and the south. The fees are as follows: adult/child 7500/6000Rp, still camera 1000Rp, video camera 2500Rp and car park 1000Rp. The fact that you may well be charged for a video camera whether you have one or not gives you a taste of things to come.

About 200m past the ticket office, there is a fork in the road with a sign indicating Besakih to the right and Kintamani to the left. Go left because going to the right puts you in a large parking lot at the bottom of a hill some 300m from the complex. Going past the road to Kintamani, where there is another ticket office, puts you in a parking lot only 20m from the complex. Snack stands and warung are found along the trash-strewn approaches and at both parking lots.

Sights

The largest and most important temple is **Pura Penataran Agung**. It is built on six levels, terraced up the slope, with the entrance approached from below, up a flight of steps. This entrance is an imposing *candi bentar* (split gateway) and, beyond it, the even more impressive *kori agung* is the gateway to the second courtyard. It's most enjoyable during one of the frequent festivals, when hundreds, perhaps thousands, of gorgeously dressed devotees turn up with beautifully arranged offerings. Note that

AN UNHOLY EXPERIENCE

So intrusive are the scams and irritations faced by visitors to Besakih that many wish they had skipped the complex altogether. What follows are some of the ploys you should be aware of before a visit.

- Near the main parking area is a building labelled Tourist Information Office. Guides here may emphatically tell you that you need their services. You don't. You may always walk among the temples. No 'guide' can get you into a closed temple.
- Other 'guides' may foist their services on you throughout your visit. There have been reports of people agreeing to a guide's services only to be hit with a huge fee at the end.
- Once inside the complex, you may receive offers to 'come pray with me'. Visitors who seize on this chance to get into a forbidden temple can face demands of 50,000Rp or more.

tourists are not allowed inside this temple. The other temples – all with individual significance and often closed to visitors – are markedly less scenic.

When it's mist-free, the view down to the coast is superb.

Getting There & Away

The best way to visit is with your own transportation, which allows you to explore the many gorgeous drives in the area.

You can visit by bemo from Semarapura (9000Rp), but from other parts of Bali this can make the outing an all-day affair. Be sure to ask the driver to take you to the temple entrance, not to the village about 1km from the temple complex. Make certain you leave the temple by 3pm if you want to return to either Semarapura or Denpasar by bemo.

RENDANG TO AMLAPURA ROAD

☎ 0366

A scenic road goes around the southern slopes of Gunung Agung from Rendang to near Amlapura. It runs through some superb countryside, descending more or less gradually as it goes further east.

Starting in the west, Rendang is an attractive town, easily reached by bemo from Semarapura or via a particularly pretty minor road from Bangli. About 4km along a winding road is the old-fashioned village of **Muncan** with its quaint shingle roofs.

The road then passes through some of the most attractive rice country in Bali before reaching **Selat**, where you turn north to get to Pura Pasar Agung, a starting point for climbing Gunung Agung. **Puri Agung Inn** (☎ 23037; r 125,000-175,000Rp) has 10 clean and comfortable rooms with rice-field views. Here you can arrange rice-field walks or climbs up Gunung Agung (right).

Further on is **Duda**, where the scenic Sidemen Road (p331) branches southwest to Semarapura.

Continuing east, **Sibetan** is famous for growing *salak*, the delicious fruit with a curious 'snakeskin' covering that you can buy between December and April. *Salak* are the spiky low palm trees you'll see, and the fruit grows in clusters at the base of the trunks. Nearby, a poorly signposted road leads north to Jungutan, with its **Tirta Telaga Tista**, a pleasant fish pool and garden complex built for the water-loving rajah of Karangasem. It's a good spot for a picnic if you've got time and your own transport, but it's not a place for swimming.

The scenic road finishes at **Bebandem**, where there's a cattle market every three days, with plenty of other stuff for sale as well. Bebandem and several nearby villages are home to members of the traditional metalworkers caste, which includes silversmiths and blacksmiths.

GUNUNG AGUNG

Bali's highest and most revered mountain, Gunung Agung is an imposing peak seen from most of South and East Bali, although it's often obscured by cloud and mist. Many references give its height as 3142m, but some say it lost its top in the 1963 eruption and opinion varies as to the real height. The summit is an oval crater, about 700m across, with its highest point on the western edge above Besakih.

Climbing Gunung Agung

It's possible to climb Agung from various directions. The two shortest and most popular routes are from Pura Besakih, on the southwest side of the mountain, and from Pura Pasar Agung, on the southern slopes. The latter route goes to the lower edge of the crater rim (2900m), but you can't make your way from there around to the very highest point. You'll have great views south and east, but you won't be able to see central Bali.

To have the best chance of seeing the view before the clouds form, get to the top before 8am. You'll have to start at night, so plan your climb when there will be some moonlight. Take a strong flashlight, extra batteries, plenty of water (2L per person), snack food, waterproof clothing and a warm jumper (sweater). The descent is especially hard on the feet, so you'll appreciate strong shoes or boots and pedicured toes.

You should take a guide for either route. Early in the climb the guide will stop at a shrine to make an offering and say some prayers. This is a holy mountain and you should show respect.

It's best to climb during the dry season (April to September); July to September are the most reliable months. At other times, the paths can be slippery and dangerous and the views are clouded over. Climbing Gunung Agung is not allowed when major religious events are being held at Pura Besakih, which generally includes most of April. No guide will take you up at these times.

GUIDES

Trips with guides on either of the following routes up Gunung Agung generally include breakfast and other meals and a place to stay, but be sure to confirm all details in advance. They can also arrange transportation.

Most of the places to stay in the region, including those around Sidemen and Tirta Gangga, will recommend guides for Gunung Agung climbs, but it's more convenient to start from a base nearer the mountain, and the local guides from places like Selat (p333) and Muncan (p333) are more experienced. Expect to pay a negotiable 300,000Rp to 600,000Rp per person for your climb.

Recommended guides:

Gung Bawa Trekking (☎ 0366-24379; gbtrekk@yahoo.com; Selat) A reliable operation near the market.

Ketut Uriada (☎ 0812 3646 426; Muncan) It's easiest if you have your own car, but this experienced guide can arrange transport for an extra fee (look for his small sign on the road east of the village).

FROM PURA BESAKIH

This climb is much tougher than from the south and is only for the very physically fit. For the best chance of a clear view before the clouds close in, you should start at midnight. Allow at least six hours for the climb, and four to five hours for the descent. The starting point is Pura Pengubengan, northeast of the main temple complex, but it's easy to get lost on the lower trails, so definitely hire a guide.

FROM PURA PASAR AGUNG

This route involves the least walking, because Pura Pasar Agung (Agung Market Temple) is high on the southern slopes of the mountain (around 1500m) and can be reached by a good road north from Selat. From the temple you can climb to the top in three or four hours, but it's a pretty demanding trek. With or without a guide, you must report to the police station at Selat before you start; if you don't have a guide, the police will strongly encourage you to take one.

It is much better to stay the night near Muncan or Selat so that you can drive up early in the morning to Pura Pasar Agung. This temple has been greatly enlarged and improved, in part as a monument to the 1963 eruption that devastated this area.

Start climbing from the temple at around 3am. There are numerous trails through the pine forest but after an hour or so you'll climb above the tree line. Then you're climbing on solidified lava, which can be loose and broken in places, but a good guide will keep you on solid ground. At the top, you can gawk into the crater, watch the sun rise over Lombok and see the shadow of Agung in the morning haze over southern Bali.

Allow at least two hours to get back down to the temple. If you don't have a car waiting for you, walk down to Sebudi, from where there are public bemos down to Selat.

PADANGBAI

☎ 0363

Located on a perfect little bay, tiny Padangbai is the port for ferries between Bali and Lombok, and passenger boats to Nusa Penida. It is also a popular place to break a journey and relax while you plan your assault on Bali or Lombok (depending on which way you're heading), and it's a smaller, quieter, more beachy option than Candidasa. It takes about 10 minutes to walk from one end of town to the other. Take time to choose one of the many places to stay and eat; they're all very close together.

Information

Moneychangers along Jl Pelabuhan offer rates lower than in the South Bali tourist resorts – check the rates at **Bank BRI** (Bank Raykat Indonesia; Jl Pelabuhan) first. There are ATMs here.

You can find internet access at numerous places along the main streets such as Gang Segara and Jl Pelabuhan.

Dangers & Annoyances

Female travellers will notice a change in attitude towards women around the ferry terminal area. Expect a few snide remarks and unwanted stares. Ferry ticket touts and freelance porters can also cause irritation. Don't let anyone touch your luggage without agreeing to a price first, or better yet just don't let anyone touch it.

Sights

With its protected bay, Padangbai has a good beach. Others are nearby; walk southwest from the ferry terminal and follow the trail up the hill to idyllic **Bias Tugal**, also called Pantai Kecil (Little Beach), on the exposed coast outside the bay. Be careful in the water; it is subject to strong currents. There are a couple of daytime warung here.

On a headland at the northeast corner of the bay, a path uphill leads to three temples. On the other side is the small, light-sand **Blue Lagoon Beach**.

Activities

DIVING

There's some pretty good diving on the coral reefs around Padangbai, but the water can be a little cold and visibility is not always ideal. The most popular local dives are Blue Lagoon and Teluk Jepun (Jepun Bay), both in Teluk Amuk, the bay just east of Padangbai. There are a good variety of soft and hard corals and varied marine life, including sharks, turtles and wrasse, and a 40m wall at the Blue Lagoon.

Several good local outfits offer diving trips in the area, including to Gili Tepekong and Gili Biaha, and on to Tulamben and Nusa Penida. All dive prices are competitive, costing US$40 to US$90 for two boat dives, depending on the site. Dive courses are available.

Recommended operators:

Geko Dive (☎ 41516; www.gekodive.com; Jl Silayukti) The longest-established operator; nice café across from the beach.

Water Worx (☎ 41220; www.waterworxbali.com; Jl Silayukti) Another good dive operator.

SNORKELLING

One of the best and most accessible walk-in snorkel sites is off Blue Lagoon Beach. Note that it is subject to strong currents when the tide is out. Other sites such as Teluk Jepun can be reached by local boat (or check with the dive operators to see if they have any

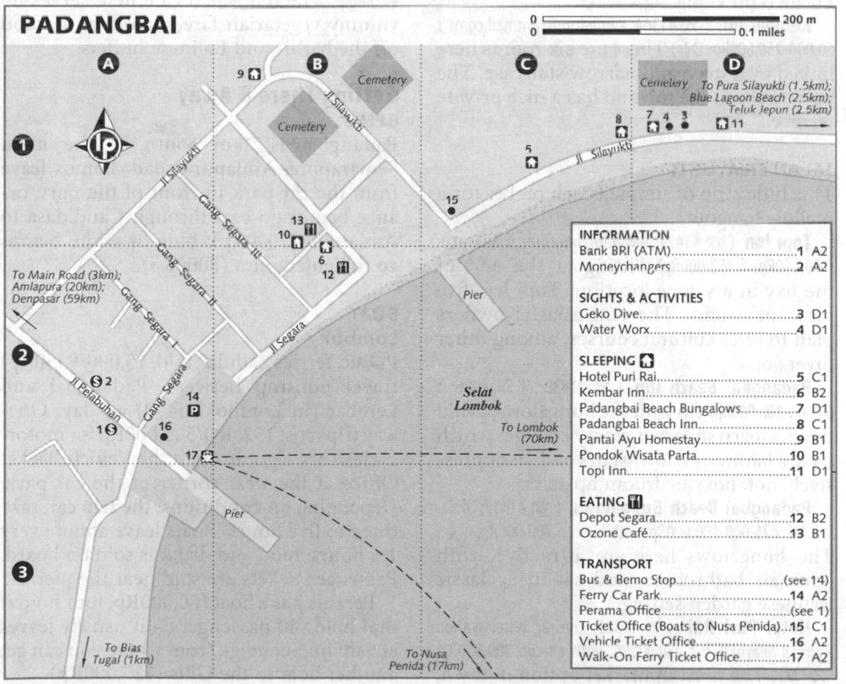

room on their dive boats). Snorkel sets cost about 20,000Rp per day.

Local *jukung* (boats) offer snorkelling trips for two passengers (bring your own snorkelling gear) around Padangbai (140,000Rp), and as far away as Nusa Lembongan (250,000Rp).

Sleeping

Accommodation in Padangbai – like the town – is pretty laid-back. Prices are fairly cheap and it's pleasant enough here that there's no need to hurry to or from Lombok if you want to hang out in the beach and cafés with other travellers.

VILLAGE

In the village, there are several tiny places in the alleys, some with a choice of small, cheap downstairs rooms or bigger, brighter upstairs rooms.

Pondok Wisata Parta (☎ 41475; r 40,000-150,000Rp; ❄) The pick of the 10 rooms in this nice place is the 'honeymoon room', which has a harbour view and good breezes. The most expensive rooms have air-con. Located off Gang Segara III.

Kembar Inn (☎ 41364; kembarinn@hotmail.com; r 50,000-150,000Rp; ❄) There are six rooms here linked by a steep and narrow staircase. The best awaits at the top and has a nice private terrace.

JALAN SILAYUKTI

This little strip of simple beach makes for a mellow hangout.

Topi Inn (☎ 41424; www.topiinn.com; Jl Silayukti; r 40,000Rp, f 150,000Rp) Sitting at the end of the bay in a serene location, Topi has five pleasant rooms. The enthusiastic owners plan to offer cultural courses, among other diversions.

Padangbai Beach Inn (☎ 41439; Jl Silayukti; r 60,000-100,000Rp) Go with the bungalows; avoid the rice-barn style two-storey cottages which have a bathroom downstairs and an oppressively hot, boxy bedroom upstairs.

Padangbai Beach Bungalows (☎ 41417; Jl Silayukti; r 75,000-100,000Rp, with air-con 200,000Rp; ❄) The bungalows here are attractive, with open-air bathrooms, and set in a classic Balinese garden setting.

Hotel Puri Rai (☎ 41385; purirai_hotel@yahoo.com; Jl Silayukti 3; r 250,000Rp, with air-con 300,000Rp; ❄ 🏊) The most upmarket option in town, the Puri Rai has 30 rooms, some with fans in a double-storey stone building, pleasantly facing the pool. Others with air-con enjoy harbour views or overlook a parking area.

Eating & Drinking

Beach fare and backpackers' staples are on offer in Padangbai – lots of fresh seafood, Indonesian classics, pizza and, yes, banana pancakes. Most of the places to stay have a café. The beachfront restaurants on Jl Segara and Jl Silayukti have similar menus and prices, harbour views during the day and cool breezes in the evening.

Depot Segara (☎ 41443; Jl Segara; dishes 10,000-20,000Rp) Fresh seafood is prepared in a variety of ways at this popular café with a touch of style. Ponder the murals while you gobble down one of the good breakfasts.

Ozone Café (☎ 41501; dishes 15,000-35,000Rp) This popular travellers' gathering-spot has been spruced up with a full bar and incomprehensible slogans on the wall (example: Acting like a monkey when you see a nice girl is so important for you).

Topi Inn (☎ 41424; Jl Silayukti; mains 18,000-40,000Rp) The renovated café here serves up yummy vegetarian fare, as well as seafood off the barbie and Balinese buffets.

Getting There & Away

BEMO

Padangbai is 2km south of the main Semarapura–Amlapura road. Bemos leave from the car park in front of the port; orange bemos go east through Candidasa to Amlapura (7000Rp); blue or white bemos go to Semarapura (8000Rp).

BOAT

Lombok

Public ferries (adult/child 15,000/9350Rp) travel nonstop between Padangbai and Lembar (in Lombok, p499) all day. One-way trips cost 152,000/322,000Rp for motorcycles/cars – go through the Vehicle Ticket Office at the west corner of the car park. Depending on conditions, the trip can take three to five hours. Boats leave about every 1½ hours; food and drink is sold on board. Passenger tickets are sold near the pier.

Perama has a boat (60,000Rp, four hours) that holds 40 passengers – it usually leaves at 9am for Senggigi, from where you can get another boat to the Gilis (125,000Rp).

PERAMA TOURIST SHUTTLE BUSES FROM PADANGBAI

Destination	Fare (Rp)
Candidasa	15,000
Kuta	40,000
Lovina	100,000
Sanur	40,000
Ubud	40,000

Nusa Penida

On the beach just east of the car park you'll find the twin-engine fibreglass boats that run across the strait to Buyuk on Nusa Penida (50,000Rp, one hour). The inconspicuous ticket office is nearby. Boats leave at infrequent intervals.

BUS

To connect with Denpasar, catch a bemo out to the main road and hail a bus to the Batubulan terminal (15,000Rp).

TOURIST SHUTTLE BUS

Perama (☎ 41419; Café Dona, Jl Pelabuhan; 🕑 7am-8pm) has a stop here for its services around the east coast. See the boxed text (above) for information on fares.

AROUND PADANGBAI

Pura Goa Lawah

About 3km west of Padangbai is **Pura Goa Lawah** (Bat Cave Temple; admission 3000Rp, car park 1000Rp, sash rental 1000Rp; 🕑 8am-6pm). The cave in the cliff face is jam-packed full of bats that fly out after dusk, and the complex is equally overcrowded with tour groups later in the day; the hawkers are a hassle. The temple itself is small, although it's very old and of great significance to the Balinese.

The cave is said to lead all the way to Besakih, but it seems nobody has volunteered to confirm this. The bats provide sustenance for the legendary giant snake Naga Basuki, which is also believed to live in the cave. There has been no evidence found of stately Wayne Manor above the bat cave, either.

Kusamba

A side road southwest of Padangbai goes to this fishing and salt-making village, where you'll see lines of colourful fishing *perahu* (outriggers) lined up on the beach. Fishing is normally done at night and the 'eyes' on the front of the boats help navigation through the darkness. East and west of Kusamba, the thatched roofs of salt-making huts can be seen along the beach.

PADANGBAI TO CANDIDASA

Buitan

☎ 0363

Balina Beach is the name bestowed on the tourist development in the village of Buitan. It is pretty and quiet, but beach-lovers may be disappointed with the black sand and rocks along the high-tide line.

One of Bali's best resorts, the **Amankila** (☎ 41333; www.amankila.com; villas from US$650; ❄ 💻 🏊), is hidden by jutting cliffs. About 5.6km beyond the Padangbai turn-off and 500m past the road to Manggis, a discreetly marked side road leads to the hotel. It features an isolated seaside location with views to Lombok and understated architecture – classically simple rectangular structures with thatched roofs and lots of natural wood and stone. The three main swimming pools step down into the sea, in matching shades of blue. The Beachclub pool (150,000Rp) is on a stretch of sand and is open to nonguests. It has a café and water sports. The restaurants at the Amankila are open to nonguests. The superb Terrace (lunch 80,000Rp to 200,000Rp) has creative and varied cuisine.

Mendira

☎ 0366

Mendira has a few scattered places to stay. It's a pretty area and a quieter alternative to Padangbai or Candidasa.

Amarta Beach Inn Bungalows (☎ 41230; r 100,000-150,000Rp) has 10 units right on the sea. They're in a gorgeous location and are great value. The more expensive ones have hot water and spiffy open-air bathrooms. At low tide there is a tiny beach; at other times you can sit and watch the bananas grow.

Lotus Bungalows (☎ 41104; www.lotusbungalows.com; r US$20-45; ❄ 💻 🏊) has 24 rooms (some with air-con, all with hot water) in bungalow-style units. Four (numbers one, two, 13 and 14) are right on the ocean, with the last being the top pick. The décor is bright and airy and there is a large pool.

Candi Beach Cottage (☎ 41234; www.candibeachbali.com; r US$60-80, bungalows US$110-130;) is a delightfully low-key resort. It has two pools and lovely grounds right at the crashing waves. There are 32 rooms and 32 bungalows, all with satellite TV.

TENGANAN

Tenganan is occupied by the Bali Aga people, descendants of the original Balinese who inhabited Bali prior to the Majapahit arrival. The village is surrounded by a wall, and basically consists of two rows of identical houses stretching up the gentle slope of the hill.

Tenganan retains strong and distinct **craft traditions** that include basket weaving, *lontar* strips (specially prepared palm leaves with hand-drawn stories) and the weaving of double and single ikat. A peculiar, old-fashioned version of the gamelan known as the *gamelan selunding* is still played here, and girls dance an equally ancient dance known as the Rejang.

As you enter the village you may be greeted by a guide who will take you on a tour of the village – and generally lead you back to his or her family compound to look at various craft items. Delightfully, its all very low-key, but you should offer to pay 20,000Rp or so for your guide's time.

Getting There & Away

Tenganan is at the end of a road 4km uphill from a coast road junction just west of Candidasa. At the turn-off, a posse of *ojeks* (motorcycles that take passengers) offer rides to the village for about 6000Rp. If you're using public transport, take an *ojek* up, and enjoy the gentle walk back downhill to the main road.

CANDIDASA

☎ 0363

Tourist development ran amok in Candidasa and now there's shoulder-to-shoulder development, an unattractive proposition for many. The main drawback is the lack of a beach, which, except for the far eastern stretch, has eroded away as fast as hotels were built. Most of the coastline has breakwaters, so you can't even walk along it. The main drag is noisy and doesn't get sea breezes.

Despite all this, Candidasa is much less hectic than South Bali and is often as sleepy as the lotus blossom–filled lagoon. Many find it a fine base to explore eastern Bali and there are some good restaurants. It's popular with divers and snorkellers, although beach-lovers will prefer Padangbai.

Information

There are several moneychangers near Foto Asri, as is a Bank BPD ATM. There are plenty of not-very-fast internet options along Jl Raya Candidasa.

Foto Asri (☎ 41098; Jl Raya Candidasa) Sells groceries and sundries and has a postal agency.

Happy's Internet (☎ 41052; Jl Raya Candidasa; per 20min 8000Rp) This suitably amiable spot is a good choice.

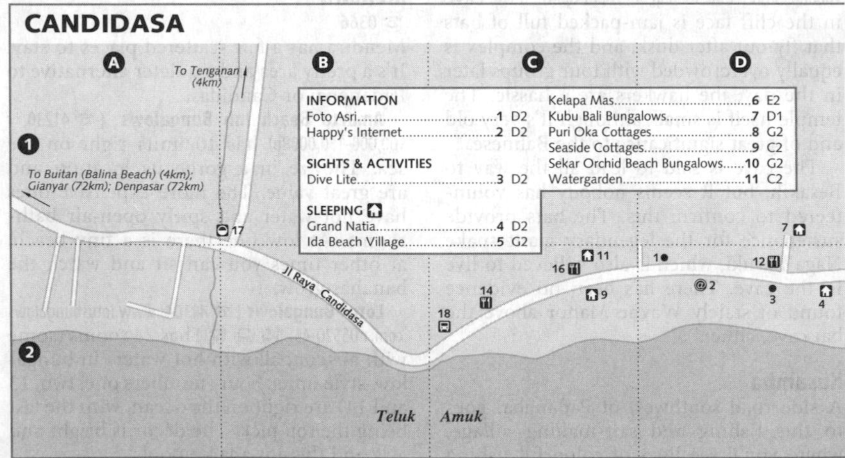

Activities

Diving and snorkelling are popular activities in Candidasa. Gili Tepekong, which has a series of coral heads at the top of a sheer drop-off, is perhaps the best dive site. It offers the chance to see lots of fish, including some larger marine life.

A recommended dive operator is **Dive Lite** (41660; www.divelite.com; Jl Raya Candidasa; 2 dives US$60-95), which offers dives at Tulamben, Amed, Nusa Penida/Lembongan and Menjangan. A four-day PADI open-water course is US$360. Snorkelling tours are US$25.

Hotels and shops along the main road rent snorkel sets for about 20,000Rp per day. For the best snorkelling, take a boat to offshore sites or to Gili Mimpang (a one-hour boat trip for up to three people should cost about 70,000Rp to 100,000Rp).

Sleeping

Candidasa's main drag is well supplied with seaside accommodation, as well as restaurants and other tourist facilities. More relaxed, and only slightly less convenient, are the places east of the lagoon, hidden among the palm trees near the original fishing village.

BUDGET

Seaside Cottages (41629; www.bali-seafront-bungalows.com; Jl Raya Candidasa; cottages 30,000-230,000Rp;) There are lodging options galore at this clean and well-run place. Basic rooms have cold water and fan. As you move up the rate card you add hot water, air-con, open-air garden bathrooms, kitchens and delightful views. The Temple Café (p340) here is a fun place.

Puri Oka Cottages (41092; puri_oka@hotmail.com; Jl Pantai Indah; r 100,000-250,000Rp;) Hidden by a banana grove east of town, the cheapest of the 24 rooms here are small, while the better ones have tasteful décor and water views. The pool is medium-sized, and at low tide there's a small beach out the front.

Sekar Orchid Beach Bungalows (41086; www.sekar-orchid.com; Jl Pantai Indah 26; bungalows 120,000-150,000Rp) The grounds here live up to the name with orchids growing in profusion. There's a small beach and the seven large rooms are very good value with nice views from the 2nd floor. The site is nicely isolated.

Kelapa Mas (41369; www.kelapamas.com; Jl Raya Candidasa; r 150,000-250,000Rp;) This relaxing hideaway deserves its name – the grounds are filled with tall coconut palms. Bamboo rooms with lounging verandas are set in lush gardens, with even a little sand lining the seashore. Some have views; others have hot water and air-con.

MIDRANGE

Ida Beach Village (41118; fax 41041; Jl Pantai Indah; bungalows US$45-60;) Accommodation ranges from Balinese rice-barn-style bungalows with private gardens to more

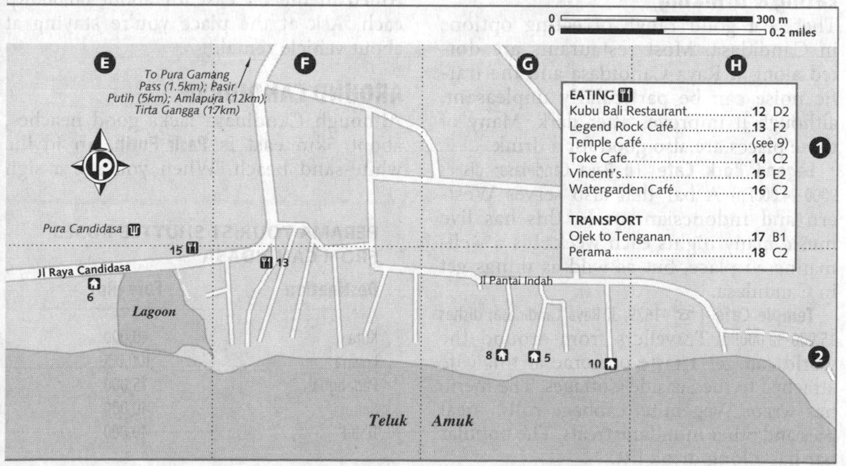

modest cottages for 17 units in all. The seaside swimming pool is a highlight; the location is very quiet.

Kubu Bali Bungalows (☎ 41532; www.kububali.com; s/d US$50/55, ste US$60-65; ❄ 🏊) Behind Kubu Bali restaurant and up a lane, there are 20 beautifully finished individual bungalows. Streams, ponds and a swimming pool are landscaped into the steep hillside, with views over palm trees, the coast and the sea. You'll have to climb a bit to get to your room. There's also a café by the pool with wonderful views.

Grand Natia (☎ 42007; hotelnatia@yahoo.com; Jl Raya Candidasa; r US$50-85; ❄ 🏊) This hotel resembles a modern water palace – elegant pathways are lined with waterways teeming with carp. Each of the 12 rooms has an open-air bathroom. The small pool drops away to a gorgeous ocean view, although the two 'ocean-view' rooms are not worth the extra swag.

TOP END

Watergarden (☎ 41540; www.watergardenhotel.com; Jl Raya Candidasa; r US$70-85, 2-bedroom ste US$160; ❄ 🏊) The best choice in town, the Watergarden lives up to its name with a swimming pool and fish-filled ponds that wind around the buildings and through the lovely garden. The design has a Japanese influence, and each of the 14 rooms has a veranda projecting over the lily ponds. See right for details on its Watergarden Café.

Eating & Drinking

There's a good range of eating options in Candidasa. Most restaurants are dotted along Jl Raya Candidasa and the traffic noise can be particularly unpleasant, although it improves after dark. Many of these places are also good for a drink.

Legend Rock Café (Jl Raya Candidasa; dishes 9000-24,000Rp) A bar that also serves Western and Indonesian meals, this has live music many nights each week. It's a well-mannered place, but as wild as things get in Candidasa.

Temple Café (☎ 41629; Jl Raya Candidasa; dishes 15,000-30,000Rp) Travellers from around the world can get a taste of home at this café attached to the Seaside Cottages. The menu has wraps, Vegemite, cabbage rolls, meat pies and other mundane treats. The popular bar has a long drink list.

Watergarden Café (☎ 41540; Jl Raya Candidasa; dishes 15,000-40,000Rp) Overlooking a carp pond, this stylish café somehow manages to maintain a peaceful atmosphere amid the zooming trucks. The food is excellent, including Asian specialities. Breakfast here comes with oodles of fresh fruit.

Kubu Bali Restaurant (☎ 41532; Jl Raya Candidasa; dishes 18,000-50,000Rp) This big stylish place has an open kitchen out the front, where Indonesian and Chinese dishes are turned out with great energy and panache. The seafood is excellent.

Toke Café (☎ 41991; Jl Raya Candidasa; dishes 20,000-35,000Rp) The open kitchen on the street serves up some top seafood. It's got a nice old bar and is a good place for a drink or something for the munchies.

Vincent's (☎ 41368; Jl Raya Candidasa; dishes 25,000-80,000Rp) A long and open place with several distinct rooms and a lovely rear garden with rattan lounge furniture. There's a plethora of artfully prepared Thai and veggie options but the real stars are the local dishes.

Getting There & Away

Candidasa is on the main road between Amlapura and South Bali, but there's no terminal, so hail down bemos (buses probably won't stop). You'll need to change in either Padangbai or Semarapura.

Perama (☎ 41114; Jl Raya Candidasa; 🕑 7am-7pm) is at the western end of the strip. See the boxed text (below) for information on bus fares. Two or more people can charter a ride to Amed in the far east for about 60,000Rp each. Ask at the place you're staying at about vehicle rental.

AROUND CANDIDASA

Although Candidasa lacks good beaches, about 5km east is **Pasir Putih**, an idyllic white-sand beach. When you see a sign

PERAMA TOURIST SHUTTLE BUSES FROM CANDIDASA

Destination	Fare (Rp)
Kuta	40,000
Lovina	100,000
Padangbai	15,000
Sanur	40,000
Ubud	40,000

with 'Virgin Beach Club', turn off the main road and follow a paved track for about 1km to a bridge where locals will collect a fee (5000Rp). Another 1km brings you to a small temple that has good parking. You can drive a further 600m directly to the beach but the road is a disaster and the walk is quite pretty.

The beach is almost a cliché: a long crescent of white sand backed by coconut trees. At one end cliffs provide shade; at the other is a little line of fishing boats. At times a stand sells drinks.

AMLAPURA

☎ 0363

Amlapura is the main town and transport junction in eastern Bali, and the capital of the Karangasem district. It's known for the frayed grandeur of its palaces (although that's changing), and is on the way to or from Tirta Gangga. It has a confusing array of one-way streets; persevere, and keep asking your way to a palace. Like many regional towns it's short on places to stay or eat.

Banks and ATMs can be found on Jl Gajah Mada. They are the last going around the island until Singaraja.

Sights

Amlapura's three palaces, on Jl Teuk Umar, are stolid reminders of Karangasem's period as a kingdom at its most important when supported by Dutch colonial power in the late 19th and early 20th centuries.

Outside the **Puri Agung Karangasem** (Jl Teuku Umar; admission 5000Rp; 8am-6pm), there is an impressive three-tiered entry gate and beautiful sculpted panels. After you pass through the entry courtyard, a left turn takes you to the main building, known as the Maskerdam (Amsterdam), because it was the Karangasem kingdom's acquiescence to Dutch rule that allowed it to hang on long after the demise of the other Balinese kingdoms. Inside you can see several rooms, including the royal bedroom and a living room with furniture that was a gift from the Dutch royal family.

Across the street, **Puri Gede** (Jl Teuku Umar; admission free; 8am-6pm) is being extensively renovated. The rambling palace grounds feature many brick buildings dating from the Dutch colonial period. Look for stone and wood carvings from the 19th century. The Rangki (a sort of pavilion) has been returned to its glory and is surrounded by fish ponds. Look for the stern portrait of the late king AA Gede Putu; his wife still lives in one of the buildings.

The other royal palace building, **Puri Kertasura**, is not open to visitors.

Getting There & Away

Amlapura is a major transport hub. Buses and bemo regularly ply the main road to Denpasar's Batubulan terminal (20,000Rp), via Candidasa and Padangbai. Plenty of buses also go around the north coast to Singaraja (about 15,000Rp), via Tirta Gangga, Amed and Tulamben.

If you are driving to Amed and beyond, fill up at the petrol station on the road to Tirta Gangga. It's the last one until Yeh Sanih in the north.

AROUND AMLAPURA

Five kilometres south of Amlapura, **Taman Ujung** is a major complex that may leave you slack-jawed – and not with wonder. The last king of Karangasem completed the construction of a grand water palace here in 1921, which was extensively damaged by an earthquake in 1979. A tiny vestige of the old palace is surrounded by vast new ponds and terraces built for untold billions of rupiah. Today it is backed by a failed hotel and the wind-swept grounds are seldom trod by visitors. A better bet is the neighbouring fishing village of **Ujung**. It has authentic colour and the surf in these parts can be dramatic.

TIRTA GANGGA

☎ 0363

The tiny village of Tirta Gangga (Water of the Ganges), high on a ridge with sublime views of rice paddies sprawling over the hills down to the sea, is a relaxing place to stop. The main attraction is the old water palace and guided treks through the gorgeous landscape. Facilities are limited.

Sights

Amlapura's water-loving rajah, after completing his lost masterpiece at Ujung, had another go at **Taman Tirta Gangga** (adult/child 5100/3100Rp, parking 1000Rp; site 24hr, ticket office 6am-6pm). Originally built in 1948, the water palace was damaged in the 1963 eruption of Gunung Agung. The palace has several

BALI

swimming pools and ornamental ponds, which serve as a fascinating reminder of the old days of the Balinese rajahs. 'Pool A' (adult/child 6000/4000Rp) is the cleanest and is in the top part of the complex. It's a good place for a break and a stroll.

Activities

HIKING AROUND TIRTA GANGGA

The rice terraces around Tirta Gangga are some of the most beautiful in Bali. They sweep out from Tirta Gangga, almost like a sea surrounding an island. Back roads and walking paths take you through a world of green to many picturesque traditional villages. Going to smaller, more remote villages, it's sensible and inexpensive to engage a guide – ask at your accommodation or at the Good Karma café (right). Guide prices are negotiable at around 15,000Rp per person per hour for local treks, plus transport and food.

Some of the more interesting hikes include Pura Lempuyang (768m), one of Bali's nine directional temples (five hours return from Ngis); Bukit Kusambi, a small hill with a big view (five hours return); and Budakeling village, home to several Buddhist communities (about six hours return from Tirta Gangga).

Sleeping & Eating

Most places to stay have cafés and there's another cluster by the sedate shops around the parking area.

Dhangin Taman (☎ 22059; r 40,000-80,000Rp) Adjacent to the water palace, this fascinating place features elaborate tiled artworks in a garden. It has a range of 14 simple rooms – the cheapest ones facing the rice paddies are the best – and a restaurant (dishes 5000Rp to 8000Rp) with tables overlooking the palace. You leave your breakfast order hanging on the door, just like the Hilton.

Pondok Lembah Dukah (r 50,000-100,000Rp) Down the path to the right of Good Karma and past Dua Homestay, this basic place is a 300m walk, but worth it. It has three bungalows; rooms are clean, have fans and cold water and incredible views.

Puri Prima (☎/fax 21316; r 50,000-100,000Rp) About 1km north of Tirta Gangga, this offers outstanding views and nine pleasant rooms. It has a small restaurant (dishes 10,000Rp to 16,000Rp). Staff can also organise trekking to Gunung Agung (two people 600,000Rp).

Good Karma (☎ 22445; s/d 70,000/90,000Rp) In the middle of a picturesque rice paddy, Good Karma has good vibes thanks to four very clean and simple bungalows. The restaurant serves excellent food (dishes 10,000Rp to 16,000Rp) in a comfortable setting; there are many vegetarian options. It's right off the main parking lot.

Puri Sawah Bungalows (☎ 21847; fax 21939; bungalows 100,000-200,000Rp) Just up the road from the palace, Puri Sawah has four comfortable and spacious rooms with great views. It also has larger, two-bedroom bungalows, which sleep six (with hot water). The restaurant (dishes 16,000Rp to 22,000Rp) has rice-paddy views and serves sandwiches and local food.

Tirta Ayu Homestay (☎ 22697; fax 21383; r 150,000-250,000Rp, villas US$50-150; 🏊) Right in the palace compound, this has four pleasant bungalows (cold water only) and three spacious villas with nice outdoor bathrooms. Free use of the palace swimming pool is included. A café (dishes 10,000Rp to 25,000Rp) overlooks the palace grounds. One of the villas is huge and has its own plunge pool.

Ryoshi (☎ 081 2368 2791; dishes 10,000-35,000Rp; 🕑 10am-10pm) This last outpost heading east of the Bali Japanese restaurant chain, is about 500m past central Tirta Gangga and enjoys fabulous views of the region. The grilled seafood is good and you can dine under a canopy of frangipani.

Getting There & Away

Bemo and minibuses making the haul between Amlapura and Singaraja stop at Tirta Gangga right outside the water palace or any hotel further north. The fare to Amlapura should be 3000Rp.

AMED & THE FAR EAST COAST

☎ 0363

This once-remote stretch of coast, from Amed to Bali's far eastern tip, has reached that nefarious critical mass where it becomes a destination just because of its size. Yet unlike some other places on the Bali coast, it is holding onto the charms that drove the development in the first place.

The mostly arid coastline has superb views across to Lombok and behind to

Gunung Agung. Hotels, restaurants, dive operators and other facilities serve visitors who come to enjoy the fine scenery, the relaxed atmosphere and the excellent diving and snorkelling.

Amed itself has no standard tourist centre but is instead a series of small villages in scalloped inlets. It's the perfect hideaway if you want to simply stay put and never leave your village.

Orientation & Information

In the rest of Bali, and to identify itself as a destination, this whole strip of coast is commonly called 'Amed' but, strictly speaking, Amed is just the first of several *dusun* (small villages) set in a dramatic landscape of black-sand beaches spread over 10km.

Visitors may be charged a tourist tax. Enforcement of a 5000Rp per person fee at a tollbooth on the outskirts of Amed is sporadic. Phone lines only extend as far as Lipah; after that it's cell phones only. Internet service is limited to a couple of places between Amed and Lipah. There are no ATMs or banks.

Activities

DIVING & SNORKELLING

Snorkelling is excellent at several places along the coast. **Jemeluk** is a protected area where you can admire live coral and plentiful fish within 100m of the beach. There's a wreck of a Japanese fishing boat near **Aas**, offshore from Eka Purnama bungalows, and coral gardens and colourful marine life at **Selang**. Almost every hotel rents snorkelling equipment for about 20,000Rp per day.

Scuba diving is good and the *Liberty* wreck at Tulamben (p344) is only a 20-minute drive away. Two good operators with similar prices (local dives from about US$45, open-water dive course about US$300):

Eco-dive (☎ 081 658 1935; www.ecodivebali.com; Jemeluk; dives from US$45) Full-service shop with simple accommodation for clients.

Euro Dive (☎ 23469; www.eurodivebali.com; dives from US$45) Located east of Amed. Has a long list of services.

TREKKING

Quite a few trails go inland from the coast, up the slopes of Gunung Seraya (1175m) and to some little-visited villages. The countryside is sparsely vegetated and most trails are well defined, so you won't need a guide for shorter walks. Allow a good three hours to get to the top of Seraya, starting from the rocky ridge just east of Jemeluk Bay.

Sleeping

For accommodation, you'll have to make the choice between places in the little beachside villages or places on the sunny and dry headlands connecting the inlets. The former put you right on the sand and offer a small amount of life while the latter give you broad, sweeping vistas and isolation.

Accommodation can be found in every price category, and rates are often negotiable. Almost every place has a modestly priced restaurant or café.

EAST OF AMED VILLAGE

Three Brothers Bungalows (☎ 23472; r 80,000-120,000Rp) The boys have popular and basic beachfront accommodation, plus an adjoining café with a few tables right on the sand. You can't get closer to the water.

JEMELUK

Galang Kangin Bungalows (s/d from 50,000/80,000Rp) One of several budget places, it has clean, basic cold-water rooms.

Waeni's Sunset View Bungalows & Restaurant (☎ 23515; madesani@hotmail.com; r 80,000-100,000Rp) Waeni's has unusual rustic stone cottages with gorgeous views of the mountains behind and the bay below. The café with its views is a good place for a sunset drink.

Hotel Prema Liong (☎ 23486; www.bali-amed.com; r 150,000-400,000Rp) Javanese-style two-storey bungalows are terraced up the hillside and have a New Age ethos. The cold-water, open-air bathrooms are lush and almost double as a garden, while the balconies have comfy cushions and day beds.

Santai (☎ 23487; www.santaibali.com; r US$50-95; ❄ 🏊) This stylish top-end option is a great little retreat. The six rooms have four-poster beds, timber floors, open-air bathrooms and big comfy balcony sofas. A snaking swimming pool, fringed by purple bougainvillea, adds to the atmosphere.

Apa Kabar (☎ 23492; www.apakabarvillas.com; bungalows US$75-95, villas US$110-150; ❄ 🏊) Right in front of fishing boats on the beach, Apa Kabar has stylish and spacious villas overlooking a swimming pool that gurgles with a small waterfall. Some units have ocean views.

LIPAH

Bayu Cottages (☎ 23495; www.bayucottages.com; r US$22-28;) The good-value Bayu has rooms with balconies overlooking the coast from the knoll. There's a pool and amenities including open-air marble bathrooms.

SELANG

Eka Purnama (☎ 0868 1212 1685; www.eka-purnama.com; r 100,000-180,000Rp) This gorgeous, cold water–only place is set high on a hill. The balconies, complete with hammocks, have pure ocean views.

Blue Moon Villas (☎ 0817 4738 100; www.bluemoonvilla.com; r from US$55, villas US$120-185;) On a knoll across the road from the cliffs, Blue Moon is a small and upmarket place, complete with a little pool. The five rooms set in three villas have open-air stone bathrooms. The café takes usual fare and gives it a dash of panache.

AAS

Meditasi (fax 22166; r 150,000-200,000Rp) Rooms are close to good swimming and snorkelling at this chilled out yet tidy place where the bamboo bungalows have balconies overlooking the beach.

Eating

Most of the hotels listed have places for a meal or a sunset drink.

Cafe Senang (dishes 6000-15,000Rp) Located east of Amed at Euro Dive, this small bar/café is popular with travellers.

Sama Sama Cafe (Jemeluk; dishes 15,000-30,000Rp) Prawns, barracuda, and other seafood almost jump from the boats onto the grill at this four-table beachside joint.

Café Garam (☎ 23462; dishes 15,000-40,000Rp) East of Amed, this place has ambience and a good Asian menu that goes beyond the norm. The café has a small exhibition on local salt-making, and local salt is on sale.

Getting There & Around

Most people drive here via the main highway from Amlapura and Culik. The spectacular road going all the way around the headlands has been improved; it's possible to do the journey as a circle, with the foreknowledge that conditions between Ujung and Aas are twisting and narrow.

All the places east of Culik are difficult to reach by public transport. Minibuses and bemos from Singaraja and Amlapura pass through Culik, the turn-off for Amed. Infrequent public bemos go from Culik to Amed (3.5km), and some continue to Seraya until 1pm. A public bemo should cost around 7000Rp from Culik to Lipah.

You can also charter transport from Culik for a negotiable 40,000Rp (by *ojek* it costs less than half this price). Be careful to specify which hotel you wish to go to – if you agree on a price to 'Amed', you may be taken only to Amed village, far short of your destination.

Perama offers charter tourist-bus services from Candidasa (p340) and Lovina (p373), but you can do usually do better by hiring a car and driver.

KUBU REGION

Driving along the main road you will pass through vast old lava flows from Gunung Agung down to the sea. The landscape is strewn with lava, boulders and is nothing like the lush rice paddies elsewhere.

TULAMBEN

☎ 0363

The big attraction here is the wreck of the US cargo ship *Liberty* – among the best and most popular dive sites in Bali. Other great dive sites are nearby, and even snorkellers can easily swim out and enjoy the wreck and the coral. Tulamben's beachfront is quite different from other beach resorts – heavy, black, round boulders and pebbles make it unappealing for sunbathers or casual swimmers. Services beyond the hotels are few.

Activities

DIVING & SNORKELLING

The wreck of the *Liberty* is about 50m directly offshore from Puri Madha Bungalows (there's also a shady car park here; 1000Rp). Swim straight out and you'll see the stern rearing up from the depths, heavily encrusted with coral, and swarming with dozens of species of colourful fish – and with scuba divers most of the day. Many divers commute to Tulamben from Candidasa or Lovina, and in busy times it can get quite crowded between 11am and 4pm, with up to 50 divers around the wreck at a time. Stay the night in Tulamben or – better – in nearby Amed and get an early start.

> **THE WRECK OF THE LIBERTY**
>
> In January 1942 the US Navy cargo ship USAT *Liberty* was torpedoed by a Japanese submarine near Lombok. Taken in tow, it was beached at Tulamben so that its cargo of rubber and railway parts could be saved. The Japanese invasion prevented this and the ship sat on the beach until the 1963 eruption of Gunung Agung broke it in two and left it just off the shoreline, much to the delight of divers.

Most hotels have their own diving centre, and some will give a discount on accommodation if you dive with their centre, but not all of them can be recommended to inexperienced divers.

Expect to pay as little as US$25/40 for one/two dives at Tulamben, and a little more for a night dive or dives around Amed.

Most hotels and dive centres rent out snorkelling gear for a negotiable 20,000Rp.

Among the many dive operators, **Tauch Terminal** (☎ 0361-730200; www.tauch-terminal.com) is one of the longest-established, and runs the Tauch Terminal Hotel (below). A four-day PADI open-water certificate course costs about US$400.

Sleeping & Eating

At high tide, none of the places situated on the water have much rocky beach at all, but the waves are dramatic. Look for signs along the main road for the following places; most have their own dive operations. Every place to stay has at least a café.

Puri Madha Bungalows (☎ 22921; r 60,000Rp) This is the first hotel you approach from the northwest; it faces the wreck and the day-use parking area. There are nine small, clean cold-water rooms on the water.

Bali Coral Bungalows (☎/fax 22909; r 100,000Rp, with air-con 200,000Rp;) Ten pleasant, clean bungalows with modern bathrooms huddle here, some with sea views. Food is also available (dishes 10,000Rp to 25,000Rp).

Tauch Terminal Resort (☎ 0361-730200, 22911; www.tauch-terminal.com; r US$40-80;) Down a side road, this is the pick of Tulamben accommodation. Rooms have large terraces; the cheaper ones in bungalows are actually more atmospheric. There is an idyllic waterfront pool, beach bar and restaurant with a menu spanning Europe and Asia.

Mimpi Resort (☎ 21642; www.mimpi.com; r US$80-150;) Overlooking a picturesque stretch of waterfront, Mimpi has a range of 30 stylish bungalows with outdoor bathrooms, and an ocean-front pool, dive centre and spa.

Getting There & Away

Plenty of buses and bemos travel between Amlapura and Singaraja and will stop anywhere along the Tulamben road, but they're infrequent after 2pm. Expect to pay 6000Rp to 8000Rp to either town.

Perama offers charter tourist-bus services from Candidasa (p340) and Lovina (p373), but you can probably match their rates by hiring a car and driver.

TULAMBEN TO YEH SANIH

North of Tulamben, the road continues to skirt the slopes of Gunung Agung, with frequent evidence of lava flows from the 1963 eruption. Further around, the outer crater of Gunung Batur slopes steeply down to the sea. The rainfall is low and you can generally count on sunny weather. The scenery is very stark in the dry season and it's thinly populated. The route has regular public transport, but it's easier to make stops and detours with your own vehicle.

At Les, a road goes inland to lovely **Air Terjun Yeh Mampeh** (Yeh Mampeh Waterfall), said to be one of Bali's highest. Look for a large sign on the main road and then turn inland for 2km. Walk the last 2.5km or so on an obvious path by the stream. A 2000Rp donation is requested; there's no need for a guide.

The next main town is **Tejakula**, famous for its stream-fed public bathing area, said to have been built for washing horses, and often called the horse bath. The renovated bathing areas (separate for men and women) are behind walls topped by rows of elaborately decorated arches, and are regarded as a sacred area. The baths are 100m inland on a narrow road with lots of small shops – it's a quaint village, with some finely carved *kulkul* towers. Take a stroll above the baths, past irrigation channels flowing in all directions.

At Pacung, about 10km before Yeh Sanih, you can turn inland to **Sembiran**, which is believed to be a Bali Aga village, although it doesn't promote itself as such. The most striking thing about the place is its hillside location and brilliant coastal views.

NUSA LEMBONGAN & ISLANDS

One of three islands just off the southern coast of East Bali, Nusa Lembongan is overshadowed by its much larger sibling Nusa Penida, but it is first and foremost in terms of traveller popularity thanks to its enjoyable beach scene, great diving and surfing and an ever-expanding visitor-based economy.

Nusa Lembongan is easily reached from Bali. The island of Nusa Penida has several villages, but is right off the tourist track and has few facilities for visitors, while Nusa Ceningan is sparsely populated. The waters around the three islands have some of the best dive spots in Indonesia.

Lembongan is a delightful place, where surfers and nonsurfers alike can get away from the relative chaos of southern Bali. For a short visit, take a comfortable cruise boat, stopping to snorkel or bask on a beach, or do a more specialised diving or surfing trip.

It's been a poor region for many years. Income from tourists is padded with seaweed cultivation. You'll see plots of cultivation in the waters off Jungutbatu and smell the stuff drying on land. Extracts are used as food additives in products like ice cream. Yum.

NUSA LEMBONGAN

☎ 0366

The most developed island for tourism is the delightfully laid-back Nusa Lembongan, which is free of cars, motorcycle noise and hassles. It has a local population of about 7000 people, mostly living in two small villages, Jungutbatu and Lembongan. Tourism money means that the power now stays on around the clock.

Orientation

Most surfers, divers and budget travellers stay at Jungutbatu beach or one of the ever-growing number of places along the crescent of coast to Mushroom Bay, where many of the day-trip cruise boats stop.

About 4km southwest along the sealed road from Jungutbatu is Lembongan village, the island's other town. You can go right around the island, following the rough track that eventually comes back to Jungutbatu, but the roads are steep for cyclists and walkers.

There's no jetty at Jungutbatu – the boats usually beach in the shallows by the village. Local businesses do a good job of keeping the beach clean.

Information

It's advisable to bring sufficient cash with you, as rates are poor; there is no ATM or post office. Small markets can be found on the main street with the bank. Pondok Baruna has internet access, and any of the hotels can refer you to a small medical clinic in Jungutbatu village.

Bank BPD (🕒 8am-3pm Mon-Thu, 8am-1pm Fri) Can exchange traveller's cheques and cash.

Mainsky Inn (☎ 0361-283065) Operates a wartel (private telephone office).

Sights

JUNGUTBATU

The **beach** here, a lovely arc of white sand with clear blue water, has superb views across to Gunung Agung in Bali. The village itself is pleasant, with quiet lanes, no cars and a couple of temples, including **Pura Segara** and its enormous banyan tree.

MUSHROOM BAY

This gorgeous little bay, unofficially named for the mushroom corals offshore, has a perfect crescent of white-sand beach. During the day, the tranquillity may be disturbed by banana-boat rides or parasailing. In the morning and the evening, it's delightful.

The most pleasant way to get here from Jungutbatu is to walk along the trail that starts from the southern end of the main beach and follows the coastline for a kilometre or so past a couple of little beaches.

Activities

Most places will rent bicycles for 25,000Rp per day, surfboards for 50,000Rp, snorkelling gear for 20,000Rp to 30,000Rp per day, and motorbikes for 30,000Rp per hour.

SURFING

Surfing here is best in the dry season (April to September), when the winds come from the southeast. It's definitely not for beginners, and can be dangerous even for experts. There are three main breaks on the reef, all aptly named. From north to south are Shipwreck, Lacerations and Playground. Depending on where you're staying, you can paddle directly out to whichever of the three is closest; for others it's better to hire a boat. Prices are negotiable – from 20,000Rp for a one-way trip, and around 100,000Rp waiting time.

DIVING

The excellent **World Diving** (☎ 081 2390 0686; www.world-diving.com), based at Pondok Baruna on Jungutbatu Beach, has full PADI Resort status. It offers a range of courses, including five-day PADI open-water courses for US$345, and dive trips from US$60 to sites around all three islands. Other operators can be found in various hotels. See Diving the Islands, p349 for details on the area's dive sites.

SNORKELLING

There's good snorkelling just off the day-cruise pontoons off Jungutbatu Beach, as well as in areas off the north coast of the island. You can charter a boat from 40,000Rp to 50,000Rp per hour, depending on demand, distance and the number of passengers; for more information ask at

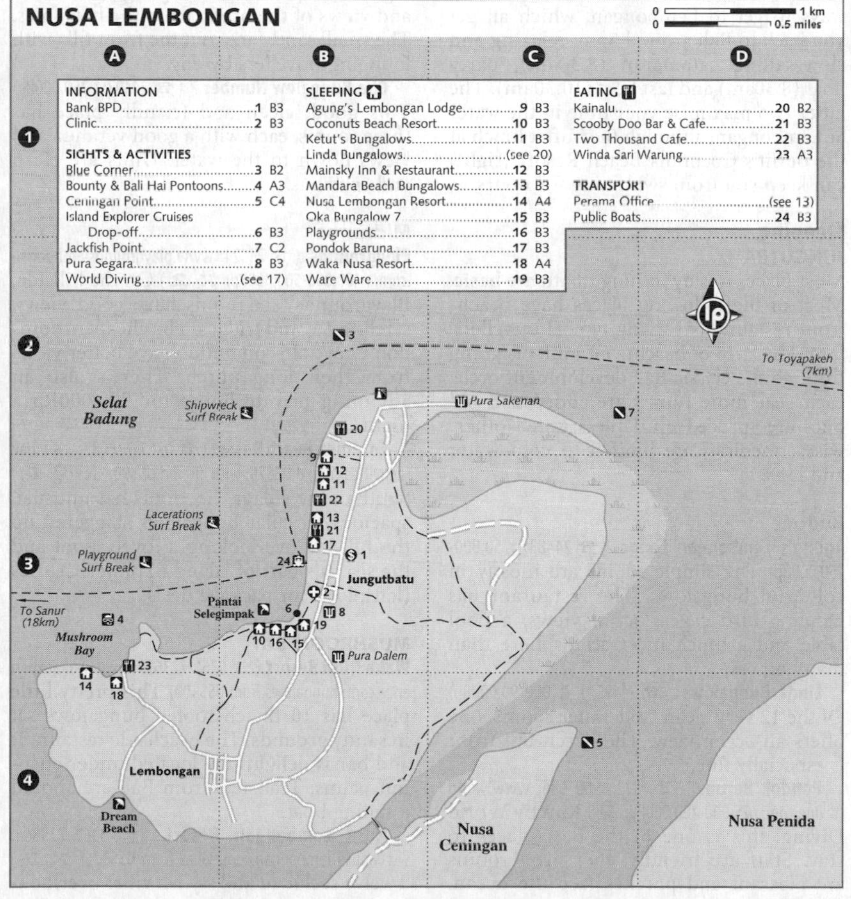

your hotel. **World Diving** (☎ 081 2390 0686; www.world-diving.com; Pondok Baruna, Jungutbatu Beach) allows snorkellers to join dive trips.

CRUISES

A number of cruise boats offer day trips to Nusa Lembongan from Benoa Harbour in South Bali. Trips include hotel transfer from South Bali, basic water sports, snorkelling, banana-boat rides and a buffet lunch. Note that with hotel transfers, the following day trips can make for a very long day.

Bounty Cruises (☎ 0361-726666; www.balibountycruises.com; adult/child US$85/42.50) has a huge offshore pontoon with slides and other tools of frolic; and does day trips.

Island Explorer Cruises (☎ 0361-728088; www.bali-activities.com; adult/child US$55/27.50) has three ways to get to Lembongan, which all get you back to Bali around 5pm: relaxing and slow-sailing catamaran (8.30am), party boat (8.30am) and fast boat (10.30am). The latter two maximise your time in the water at Lembongan, although the buffet lunch at the outfit's Coconuts Beach Resort (right) can keep you from swimming for hours.

Sleeping

JUNGUTBATU

Most places to stay in Jungutbatu are basic. Most of the following places have beachfront restaurants serving typical travellers' fare. The strip of beachfront joints is going through the classic Bali development cycle: each year more rooms are added and old ones are spruced up. Unless noted otherwise, amenities are limited to cold water and fans.

Budget

Agung's Lembongan Lodge (☎ 24483; r 50,000-150,000Rp) The simple rooms are mostly in colourful bungalows. The restaurant has hanging bird cages, ocean views, a pool table and a much nicer atmosphere than many others.

Linda Bungalows (☎ 24495; r 70,000-90,000Rp) Of the 12 very clean cold-water rooms, one offers an ocean view. The beach out front is especially fine.

Pondok Baruna (☎ 0812 3900 686; www.world-diving.com; r 75,000-100,000Rp; 💻) Run by World Diving, this is one of the best places to stay. Staff are friendly, the seven rooms are pleasant and porches face the ocean. The restaurant serves good meals (dishes 10,000Rp to 18,000Rp).

Mandara Beach Bungalows (☎ 24470; www.mandara-lembongan.com; r 100,000-160,000Rp, with air-con 250,000Rp; ❄) Eight large rooms are set around a popular café. There's a nascent garden away from the water.

Ware-Ware (☎ 0812 3970 572; r 120,000-200,000Rp) The eight units at this hillside place are a mix of traditional square and groovy circular numbers with thatched roofs. Rooms are large, with rattan couches and big bathrooms. The café has good, breezy views.

Ketut's Bungalows (☎ 24487; r 150,000-350,000Rp; ❄) The 12 rooms run the gamut from humble to modest. More expensive ones come with hot water, fridges, air-con and big beds. Upstairs rooms get good breezes and views of the ocean from the balconies. The small sandy area out the front fills with lounging travellers by day.

Oka Bungalow Number 7 (☎ 24497; r 250,000Rp) This good, clean and friendly place has three rooms, each with a good veranda and views down to the water. Units are clean and spacious.

Midrange

Playgrounds (☎ 24524; www.playgroundslembongan.com; r 400,000-500,000Rp; ❄ 🏊) On the hillside, Playgrounds' six rooms have good views, satellite TV and fridges. The cheaper rooms don't have air-con but do have better views from their long porch. There's also an adjoining private house for 700,000Rp a night.

Coconuts Beach Resort (☎ 0361-728088; www.bali-activities.com; d US$70, with air-con US$90; ❄ 💻 🏊) South of the village, Coconuts has unusual, spacious, circular bungalows staggered up the hillside overlooking a lovely pool and the sea. It's part of Island Explorer Cruises (left); look for package deals.

MUSHROOM BAY

Waka Nusa Resort (☎ 0361-723629; www.wakaexperience.com; bungalows from US$100) This pretty little place has 10 thatch-roofed bungalows set in sandy grounds. The beachside restaurant and bar is delightfully located under coconut palms. Transfers from Bali are aboard a sailing boat.

Nusa Lembongan Resort (☎ 0361-725864; www.nusa-lembongan.com; villas from US$175; ❄ 🏊) Twelve secluded and stylish villas overlooking a gorgeous sweep of ocean are the draw here. The resort has a creative restaurant with patio views over the bay.

Eating

JUNGUTBATU

Many of the places listed under Sleeping also have cafés and restaurants. The usual menu of Indonesian and Western dishes is omnipresent. There are some delightful warung on the path to Pura Sakenan.

Scooby Doo Bar & Cafe (dishes 7500-15,000Rp) Although probably not licensed to use the name of the popular pooch, Scooby's serves up a long list of snacks and drinks right on the sand to a big crowd every night. There are sofas for lounging.

Kainalu (dishes 12,000-30,000) Spread over two levels right on the sand, it has a pool table, serves up surfer classics and has chairs for sunbathing.

Two Thousand Cafe (☎ 0812 394 1273; dishes 15,000-30,000Rp) This pleasant café-bar is right on the sand and is a good sunset spot.

MUSHROOM BAY

Winda Sari Warung (dishes 10,000-30,000Rp) Near the Bali Hai Beach Club, this fun warung has a good spot overlooking the fishing boats at Mushroom Bay.

Getting There & Away

Getting to or from Nusa Lembongan offers numerous choices. In descending order of comfort are the Island Explorer boats used by day-trippers, the Perama boat and the public boats. Getting between the boats and shore and getting around once on land is not especially easy, so this is the time to travel very light.

BENOA HARBOUR

Island Explorer Cruises (☎ 0361-728088; www.bali-activities.com; return US$35) offers passage on its boats to the island. Drop-off is at either Coconuts Beach Resort or on the beach. This is the best way to make a day trip. See opposite for more info.

SANUR & SOUTH BALI

Public boats to Nusa Lembongan leave from the northern end of Sanur beach at roughly 7.45am (50,000Rp, 1½ to two hours). This is the boat used by locals and you may have to share space with a chicken. The Perama tourist boat (which is more reliable) leaves at 8.30am (70,000Rp, 1½ hours); the Lembongan office is in the Mandara Beach Bungalows (opposite). The ride is often rough and you're likely to get wet. You can charter a boat for 600,000Rp.

Getting Around

The island is fairly small and you can easily walk around it in a few hours; however, the roads across the middle of the island are quite steep. Bicycles and scooters are widely available for rent.

DIVING THE ISLANDS

There are great diving possibilities around the islands, from shallow and sheltered reefs, mainly on the northern side of Lembongan and Penida, to very demanding drift dives in the channel between Penida and the other two islands. Vigilant locals have protected their waters from dynamite bombing by renegade fishing boats, so the reefs are mostly still intact.

If you arrange a dive trip from Candidasa or South Bali, stick with the most reputable operators, as conditions here can be tricky and local knowledge is essential. A particular attraction are the large marine animals, including turtles, sharks and manta rays. The large (3m fin-to-fin) and unusual *mola mola* (sunfish) is sometimes seen around the islands between July and September, while manta rays are often seen south of Nusa Penida.

The best dive sites include **Blue Corner** and **Jackfish Point** off Nusa Lembongan and **Ceningan Point** at the tip of Nusa Ceningan. The channel between Ceningan and Penida is renowned for drift diving but it is essential that you have a good operator who can judge fast-changing currents and other conditions. Upswells can bring cold water from the open ocean to sites such as **Ceningan Wall**. This is one of the world's deepest natural channels and attracts all manner and sizes of fish.

Sites close to Nusa Penida include **Big Rock, Crystal Bay, SD, Pura Ped** and **Manta Point**. Of these, Crystal Bay, SD and Pura Ped are suitable for novice divers and are good for snorkelling.

BALI

NUSA CENINGAN

There is a narrow suspension bridge crossing the lagoon between Nusa Lembongan and Nusa Ceningan, which makes it quite easy to explore the network of tracks on foot or by bicycle – not that there is much to see. The lagoon is filled with frames for seaweed farming and there's also a fishing village and several small agricultural plots. The island is quite hilly, and if you're up for it, you'll get glimpses of great scenery as you wander or cycle around the rough tracks.

NUSA PENIDA

☎ 0366

The arid island of Nusa Penida is a limestone plateau with white-sand beaches on its north coast, and views over the water to the volcanoes in Bali. The beaches are not good for swimming as most of the shallows are filled with bamboo frames used for seaweed farming. The south coast has limestone cliffs dropping straight down to the sea and a row of offshore islets – it's rugged and spectacular scenery. The interior is hilly, with sparse-looking crops and old-fashioned villages. Nusa Penida can make for an adventurous daytrip from Nusa Lembongan.

Sampalan

Sampalan, the main town on thinly populated Penida, is quiet and pleasant, with a market, schools and shops strung out along the curving coast road. The market area, where the bemos congregate, is in the middle of town.

SLEEPING & EATING

Bungalow Pemda (☎ 21448, 23580; r 25,000-100,000Rp) Opposite the police station, a few hundred metres east of the market, is the government rest-house, which has four good-value renovated rooms with hot water. The older rooms are basic.

There are a few warungs along the main road and around the market.

Toyapakeh

If you come by boat from Lembongan, you'll probably be dropped at the beach at Toyapakeh, a pretty town with lots of shady trees. The beach has clean white sand, clear blue water, a neat line of boats, and Gunung Agung as a backdrop. Step up from the beach and you're at the road head, where bemos can take you to Ped or Sampalan (2000Rp).

Around the Island

A trip around the island, following the north and east coasts, and crossing the hilly interior, can be completed in a few hours by motorcycle. The following description goes clockwise from Sampalan.

The coastal road from Sampalan curves and dips past bays with rows of fishing boats and offshore seaweed gardens. After about 6km, just before the village of Karangsari, steps go up on the right side of the road to the narrow entrance of **Goa Karangsari** caves. There are usually people who can provide a lantern and guide you through the cave for a small negotiable fee of around 20,000Rp each. The limestone cave is over 15m tall in some sections. It extends more than 200m through the hill and emerges on the other side to overlook a verdant valley.

Continue south past a naval station and several **temples** to Suana. Here the main road swings inland and climbs up into the hills, while a very rough side track goes southeast, past more interesting temples to **Semaya**, a fishing village with a sheltered beach and one of Bali's best dive sites offshore.

About 9km southwest of Suana, **Tanglad** is an old-fashioned village and a centre for traditional weaving. Rough roads south and east lead to isolated parts of the coast.

A scenic ridge-top road goes northwest from Tanglad. At Batukandik, a rough road leads to a spectacular **air terjun** (waterfall). Limestone cliffs drop hundreds of feet into the sea, with offshore rock pinnacles surrounded by crashing surf.

Back on the main road, continue to Batumadeg, past **Bukit Mundi** (the highest point on the island at 529m), through Klumpu to Sakti, which has traditional stone buildings. Return to the north coast at Toyapakeh.

The important temple of **Pura Dalem Penetaran Ped** is near the beach at Ped, a few kilometres east of Toyapakeh. It houses a shrine for the demon Jero Gede Macaling. The temple structure is crude, which gives it an appropriately sinister ambience. From there, the road is straight and flat back to Sampalan.

Getting There & Away

The strait between Nusa Penida and southern Bali is very deep and subject to heavy swells – if there is a strong tide, boats often have to wait. You may also have to wait a while for the public boat to fill up with passengers. Boats to and from Kusamba are not recommended.

NUSA LEMBONGAN

There is a public boat connection (5000Rp, 20 minutes) between Toyapakeh and Jungutbatu (Nusa Lembongan) between 5am and 6am. Ask at your hotel or on the beach. Alternatively, charter a whole boat between the two islands for a negotiable 200,000Rp.

PADANGBAI

On the beach just east of the car park you'll find the twin-engine fibreglass boats that run across the strait to Buyuk, just west of Sampalan on Nusa Penida (50,000Rp, one hour). The inconspicuous ticket office is nearby. Boats leave at infrequent intervals.

Getting Around

To see the island you should charter your own bemo or private vehicle with driver for about 60,000Rp to 100,000Rp.

WEST BALI

Most places regularly visited in West Bali, like Sangeh or Tanah Lot, are easy day trips from Ubud or the Kuta region. The rest of the west tends to be a region travellers zip through on their way to or from Java, but it does offer a few secluded places to stay, the West Bali National Park (Taman Nasional Bali Barat) and long stretches of black-sand beach and rolling surf. Countless tracks run south of the main road, usually to fishing villages, which rarely see a tourist despite being so close to a main transport route.

TANAH LOT

☎ 0361

The brilliantly located **Pura Tanah Lot** (adult/child 3300/1800Rp, car park 1500Rp) is possibly the best-known and most photographed temple in Bali. It's an obligatory stop on many tours from South Bali, very commercialised, and especially crowded at sunset. It has all the authenticity of a stage set – even the tower of rock the temple sits upon was artfully reconstructed with Japanese money, as the entire structure was crumbling. Over one-third of the rock you see is artificial.

For the Balinese, Pura Tanah Lot is one of the most important and venerated sea temples. Like Pura Luhur Ulu Watu (p298), at the tip of the southern Bukit Peninsula, it is closely associated with the Majapahit priest, Nirartha.

Tanah Lot, however, is a well-organised tourist trap. To reach the temple, a walkway runs through a sort of sideshow alley with dozens of souvenir shops down to the sea. To ease the task of making purchases, there is an ATM.

To visit the temple you should pick the correct time – everybody shows up for sunset and the mobs obliterate any spiritual feel the place has. If you visit before noon, crowds are few and the vendors are all but asleep.

You can walk over to the temple itself at low tide (but non-Balinese are not allowed to enter), or if you need a pricey drink, walk up the slope to the left and sit at one of the many tables along the cliff top.

Sleeping & Eating

If you want to enjoy the sunset spectacle and also avoid traffic afterwards, there are lodging options near Tanah Lot. There are cheap warungs around the car park, and more expensive restaurants inside the grounds and on the cliff tops facing the temple.

Dewi Sinta Restaurant & Villa (☎ 812933; dewisinta@denpasar.wasantara.net.id; dishes 20,000-60,000Rp, buffet lunches 50,000Rp; ⚅ ⛱) Off a souvenir-shop gang, not far from the ticket office, lies this midrange hotel. There's a range of rooms (US$16 to US$55), and some look across the pool and beyond to rural views. The restaurant offers standard buffet lunches and Balinese dance performances some nights.

Getting There & Away

Coming from South Bali with your own transport, take the coastal road west from Kerobokan, which is north of the Kuta region, and follow the signs or the traffic. From other parts of Bali, turn off the

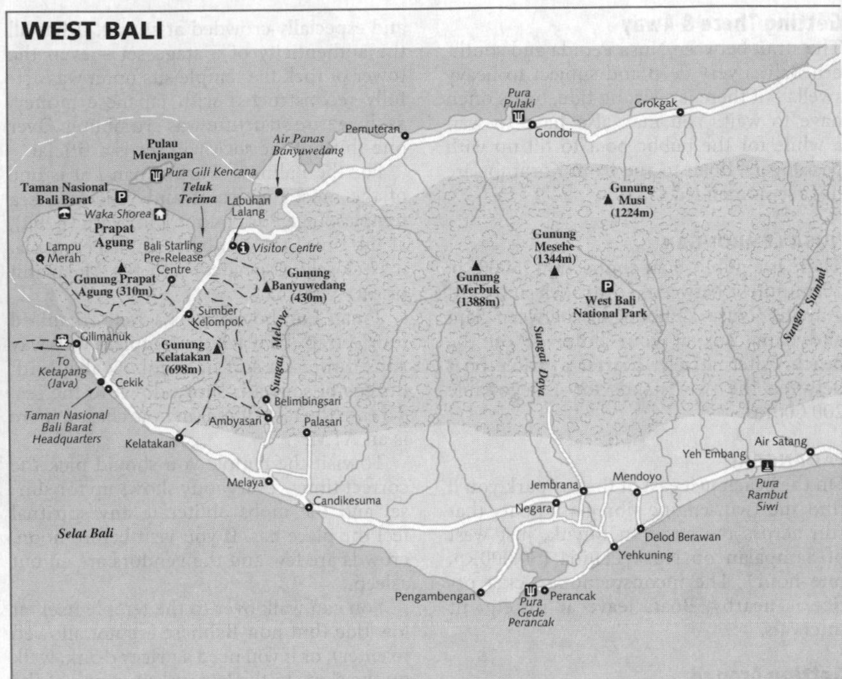

Denpasar–Gilimanuk road near Kediri and follow the signs.

By bemo, go from Denpasar's Ubung terminal to Tanah Lot (7000Rp) via Kediri. Alternatively, take an organised tour from Ubud or South Bali, which may include other sites such as Bedugul, Mengwi and Sangeh.

PURA TAMAN AYUN

The huge state temple of **Pura Taman Ayun** (adult/child 3300/1800Rp; 8am-6pm), surrounded by a wide, elegant moat, was the main temple of the Mengwi kingdom, which survived until 1891, when it was conquered by the neighbouring kingdoms of Tabanan and Badung. The large, spacious temple was built in 1634 and extensively renovated in 1937. It's a lovely place to wander around, especially before the tour buses arrive. The first courtyard is a large, open, grassy expanse and the inner courtyard has a multitude of *meru*.

Getting There & Away

Any bemo running between Denpasar (Ubung terminal) and Bedugul or Singaraja can drop you off at the roundabout in Mengwi, where signs indicate the road (250m) to the temple. Pura Taman Ayun is a stop-off on many organised tours from Ubud or southern Bali.

MARGA

Northwest of the village, **Margarana memorial** (admission by donation of around 5000Rp; 8am-4pm) commemorates the battle of Marga. On 20 November 1946, a force of 96 independence fighters was surrounded by a much larger and better-armed Dutch force fighting to regain Bali as a colony after the departure of the Japanese. The outcome was similar to the *puputan* of 40 years before. There was, however, one important difference: this time the Dutch suffered heavy casualties too, and this may have helped weaken their resolve to hang on to this rebellious colony.

On the site is a small **museum**, with a few photos, homemade weapons and other artefacts from the conflict. Get off any bemo between Denpasar and Bedugul or Singaraja, about 6km north of Mengwi, and walk

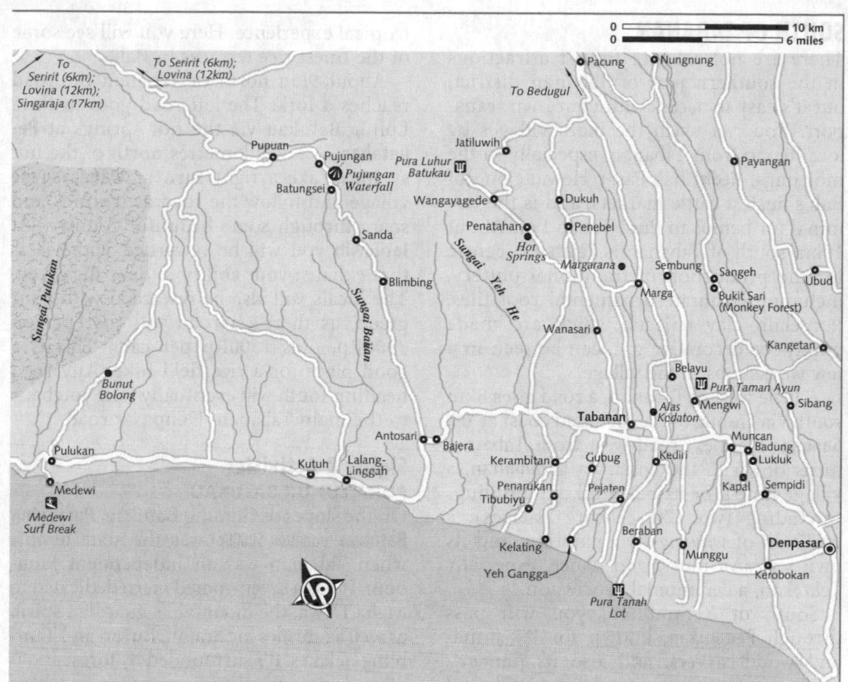

westward about 2km through Marga. It's easy to get lost, so ask for directions.

SANGEH

About 20km north of Denpasar, near the village of Sangeh, stands the monkey forest of **Bukit Sari**. There's a rare grove of nutmeg trees in the monkey forest and a temple, **Pura Bukit Sari**, with an interesting old *garuda* statue. Take note: the monkeys are all about business and will jump on you if you have a pocketful of peanuts and don't dispense them fast enough. The cheeky monkeys have also been known to steal hats, sunglasses and even sandals, from fleeing tourists. This place is definitely touristy, but the forest is cool, green and shady. The souvenir sellers are restricted to certain areas and are easy to avoid.

Getting There & Away

You can reach Sangeh and Bukit Sari on any bemo heading to Pelaga from Wangaya terminal in Denpasar (6000Rp). There is also road access from Mengwi and Ubud, but no public transport. Most people visit on an organised tour or drive themselves.

TABANAN

☎ 0361

Tabanan is the capital of the district of the same name. Like many such towns in Bali, it's a large, well-organised place. It is also a renowned centre for dancing and gamelan playing, although public performances are essentially nil. Mario, the renowned dancer of the prewar period, hailed from Tabanan. His greatest achievement was to perfect the Kebyar dance, and he is also featured in Miguel Covarrubias' classic book, *Island of Bali*.

A *subak* is the village association that deals with water, water rights and irrigation. The **Mandala Mathika Subak** (☎ 810315; Jl Raya Kediri) is quite a large complex devoted to Tabanan's *subak* organisations and incorporates the rather forlorn Subak Museum, which has displays about the irrigation and cultivation of rice, and the intricate social systems that govern it. The exhibits are poorly labelled and it's really only for rice-growing enthusiasts; this is a shame as there's a good story to tell here and the local waterways are some the most impressive in Bali.

SOUTH OF TABANAN

There are not a lot of tourist attractions in the southern part of Tabanan district, but it's easy to access with your own transport. You can reach the main villages by local bemo from Tabanan, especially in the mornings. **Kediri** has Pasar Hewan, one of Bali's busiest cattle markets, and is the terminal for bemos to Pura Tanah Lot. About 10km south of Tabanan is **Pejaten**, a centre for the production of traditional pottery, including elaborate ornamental roof tiles. Porcelain clay objects, which are made purely for decorative use, can be seen in a few workshops in the village.

A little west of Tabanan, a road goes 8km south via Gubug to the secluded coast at **Yeh Gangga**. The next road west from Tabanan turns down to the coast via **Kerambitan**, a village noted for its beautiful old buildings (including two 17th-century palaces); a tradition of *wayang*-style painting; and its own styles of music and dance, especially Tektekan, a ceremonial procession.

South of Kerambitan, you will pass through **Penarukan**, known for its stone- and wood-carvers, and also its dancers. Continue to the coast, where you'll find the beach at **Kelating** wide, black and usually deserted.

About 4km from southern Kerambitan is **Tibubiyu**. For a gorgeous drive through huge bamboo, fruit trees, rice paddies and more, take the scenic road northwest from Kerambitan to the main road.

To stay the night, consider **Puri Dewa** (☎ 081 2360 4517; Tibubiyu; bungalows 150,000-200,000Rp, dishes 12,000-25,000Rp). To find Puri Dewa, head straight south from Puri Anyar and turn right at the T-intersection. At the huge banyan tree, turn right and follow the road through to Tibubiyu. Bibi's is signposted on the left. It's wonderfully isolated, perfectly tranquil and has five rather nice bungalows. There are amazing rice-paddy views with the ocean beyond. There's a small, breezy restaurant for guests only.

NORTH OF TABANAN

The area north of Tabanan is good to travel around with your own transport. There are some strictly B-level attractions; the real appeal here is just driving the back roads with trees canopying the road for a full-on tropical experience. Here you will see some of the finest rice terraces in Bali.

About 9km north of Tabanan the road reaches a fork. The left road goes to Pura Luhur Batukau via the hot springs at **Penatahan**. A few kilometres north of the hot springs, take a right turn at **Wangayagede** village and follow the road as it winds and soars through some beautiful country. At **Jatiluwih** you will be rewarded with vistas that exhaust your ability to describe green. The locals will also be rewarded with your green, as there's a road toll (per person 3300Rp, plus 1500Rp per car). This is a good place for a rice-field hike. Any road heading south will eventually take you back to the main Tabanan–Denpasar road.

Sights & Activities

PURA LUHUR BATUKAU

On the slopes of Gunung Batukau, **Pura Luhur Batukau** (donation 5000Rp) was the state temple when Tabanan was an independent kingdom. It has a seven-roofed *meru* dedicated to Maha Dewa, the mountain's guardian spirit, as well as shrines for Bratan, Buyan and Tamblingan lakes. It's surrounded by forest and is often damp and misty. Sarongs can be rented and a donation to the temple is requested.

The main pagoda-like structures have little doors shielding small ceremonial items. This is certainly the most spiritual temple you can easily visit in Bali. There's a general lack of touts and other characters – including hordes of tourists. Facing the temple take a short walk around to the left to see a small white-water stream. The air vibrates with the coursing of water.

GUNUNG BATUKAU

At Pura Luhur Batukau you are fairly well up the side of **Gunung Batukau**, and you may wish to go for a climb. To reach the top of the 2276m peak, you'll need a guide. This can be arranged at the temple ticket booth. Expect to pay at least 800,000Rp for a muddy trek that will take at least seven hours in one direction. The rewards are amazing views, verdant scenery and the knowledge that you've taken the trail that is much less travelled compared to the peaks in the east.

Sleeping & Eating

Past the village of Wangayagede and signposted to the left off the main Pura Luhur

Batukau road, **Prana Dewi Mountain Resort** (☎ 732032; www.balipranaresort.com; bungalows from US$40) is set among rice paddies and coursing waterways. The eight rustic, beautifully furnished bungalows have thick slab timber floors and hot water. The restaurant, surrounded by low, terraced red-rice fields and a bamboo forest, has a lush vista. Most of the vegetables used in the creative dishes (15,000Rp to 35,000Rp) are grown organically in the surrounding fields.

LALANG-LINGGAH

☎ 0361

A little to the west of Lalang-Linggah, a road leads to the surf breaks near the mouth of Sungai Balian (Balian River). The main break, at the river mouth, is sometimes called Soka.

Among the smattering of places to stay hidden away on this quiet coast, **Gajah Mina** (☎ 0812 3811 630; www.gajahminaresort.com; villas from US$80;) is one of the nicer ones. There are eight private, exquisitely furnished bungalow-style villas. All have an outdoor and indoor bathroom, and inviting day lounges on the balcony. From the pool, there are views of the ocean in the near distance. The restaurant features an international Asian menu. The turn-off from the main road is near the village market and there is a gate where 1000Rp is collected before you make the very pretty 1km drive.

JEMBRANA COAST

About 34km west of Tabanan you cross into Bali's most sparsely populated district, Jembrana. The main road follows the south coast most of the way to Negara. There's some beautiful scenery but little tourist development along the way, with the exception of the surf action at Medewi.

Medewi

☎ 0365

Along the main road, a large sign points down the paved road (200m) to the surfing mecca of Pantai Medewi. The beach is a stretch of huge, smooth grey rocks interspersed among round black pebbles. It's a placid place where cattle graze by the beach. Medewi is noted not for its beach but for its *long* left-hand wave – there is little else here.

SLEEPING & EATING

For a casual meal, some of the finest fare is served up freshly stir-fried at a cart right by the beach.

Mai Malu Restaurant & Guesthouse (☎ 43897; s/d 60,000/80,000Rp) Near the highway on the Medewi side road, Mai Malu is popular with surfers, serving crowd-pleasing pizza, burgers and Indonesian meals (10,000Rp to 35,000Rp) in its modern, breezy upstairs eating area. The three rooms have cold water and fans. Other cheapies huddle nearby.

Medewi Beach Cottages (☎ 40029; r US$15-60;) These cottages have an ordinary two-storey building on the western side of the road with seven second-rate standard cold-water rooms aimed at surfers, and a more stylish wing on the other side with 22 well-furnished rooms around a pool. The posh side features satellite TV and lush grounds, but security measures have obstructed what should be a good view.

Puri Dajuma Cottages (☎ 43955; www.dajuma.com; r US$70-90;) Coming from the east, you won't be able to miss this seaside resort, thanks to its prolific signage. Happily, the 18 large rooms actually live up to the billing. Bathrooms are both inside and out, and its location on a pounding body-surfing break is dramatic. Medewi Beach is a 2km walk west. Ask for a deal on the listed rates.

NEGARA

☎ 0365

Negara, the district capital, is a prosperous little town and is useful for a pit stop, though there's not much to see. The town springs to life when the famous bull races (p356) are held nearby in July, August, September and/or October. Most banks change money and have ATMs.

Sleeping & Eating

The main road bypasses the town to the north – you'll need to turn in to the main drag, Jl Ngurah Rai. There are assorted warung in the market area.

Hotel Wira Pada (☎ 41161; Jl Ngurah Rai 107; r with fan/air-con 90,000/130,000Rp;) The cheap rooms are dark and dreary, while the more expensive ones have air-con. The setting is reasonably pleasant, however, and you can make friends with the talking mynah bird.

Rumah Makan Puas (Jl Ngurah Rai; dishes 6000-12,000Rp) A nice shady spot with good Padang-style food.

Hardy's Supermarket (☎ 40709; Jl Ngurah Rai) Hardy's has the best selection of goods in western Bali.

Getting There & Away

Most bemos and minibuses from Denpasar (Ubung terminal) to Gilimanuk drop you in Negara (12,000Rp).

AROUND NEGARA

At the southern fringe of Negara, **Loloan Timur** is largely a Bugis community (originally from Sulawesi) that retains 300-year-old traditions. Look for the distinctive houses on stilts, some decorated with wooden fretwork.

To reach **Delod Berawan**, turn off the main Gilimanuk–Denpasar road at Mendoyo and go south to the coast, which has a black-sand beach and irregular surf. You can see bull-race practices Sunday mornings at the nearby football field.

Perancak is the site of Nirartha's arrival in Bali in 1546, commemorated by a small temple, **Pura Gede Perancak**. Bull races are run at **Taman Wisata Perancak** (☎ 0365-42173), and Balinese buffets are sometimes staged for organised tours from South Bali. If you're travelling independently, give the park a ring before you go out there. In Perancak go for a walk along the picturesque fishing harbour.

Once capital of the region, **Jembrana** is the centre of the *gamelan jegog*, a gamelan using huge bamboo instruments that produce a very low-pitched, resonant sound. Performances often feature a number of gamelan groups engaging in musical contest. To see and hear them in action, time your arrival with a local festival, or ask in Negara where you might find a group practising.

TAMAN NASIONAL BALI BARAT

☎ 0365

The Taman Nasional Bali Barat (West Bali National Park) covers 19,003 hectares of the western tip of Bali. An additional 50,000 hectares are protected in the national park extension, as well as almost 7000 hectares of coral reef and coastal waters. On an island as small and densely populated as Bali, this represents a major commitment to nature conservation. Unfortunately, you'll soon see a lot of firewood vendors along the road, who cut down trees and replace them with coffee plants.

The **park headquarters** (☎ 61060; 🕑 7am-5pm) at Cekik displays a topographic model of the park area, and has a little information about plants and wildlife. You can arrange trekking guides and permits here. There is also a small visitors centre at Labuhan Lalang (p358) on the northern coast, where boats leave for Pulau Menjangan.

The main roads to Gilimanuk go through the national park, but you don't have to pay an entrance fee just to drive through. If you want to stop and visit any of the sites within the park, you must buy a ticket (2500Rp).

What most strikes many visitors who venture into the park is the symphony from the birds and the rustling trees. Just getting off the road a bit on one of the many trails (see opposite) transports you into the heart of nature.

BULL RACES

This part of Bali is famous for the bull races, known as *mekepung*, which culminate in the Bupati Cup in Negara in early August. The racing animals are actually the normally docile water buffalo, which charge down a 2km-long stretch of road or beach pulling tiny chariots. Gaily clad riders stand or kneel on top of the chariots forcing the bullocks on, sometimes by twisting their tails to make them follow the curve of the makeshift racetrack. The winner, however, is not necessarily first past the post. Style also plays a part and points are awarded to the most elegant runner. Gambling is not legal in Bali, but…

Important races are held during the dry season, from July to October. Occasional races are set up for tourist groups at a park in Perancak on the coast, and minor races and practices are held at several Perancak and other sites on Sunday mornings, including Delod Berawan (see above) and Yeh Embang. Check with your hotel or the **Jembrana Government Tourist Office** (☎ 41210, ext 224) for details.

Sights & Activities

WILDLIFE

Most of the natural vegetation in the park is not tropical rainforest, which requires rain year-round, but coastal savannah, with deciduous trees that become bare in the dry season. The southern slopes receive more regular rainfall, and hence have more tropical vegetation, while the coastal lowlands have extensive mangroves.

There are more than 200 species of plants in the park. Local fauna includes black monkeys, leaf monkeys and macaques (seen in the afternoon along the main road near Sumber Kelompok); rusa, barking, sambar, Java and mouse deer (*muncak*); and some wild pigs, squirrels, buffalo, iguanas, pythons and green snakes. There were once tigers, but the last confirmed sighting was in 1937 – and that one was shot. The bird life is prolific, with many of Bali's 300 species found here, including the extremely rare Bali starling.

TREKKING

All trekkers must be accompanied by an authorised guide. It's best to arrive the day before you want to trek, and make inquiries at the park headquarters at Cekik, the visitors' centre at Labuhan Lalang or any hotel in Gilimanuk. Guides may miraculously appear at your hotel within minutes of your arrival, but first make sure they are authorised.

The set rates for guides in the park depend on the size of the group and the length of the trek – with one or two people it's 150,000Rp for one or two hours, 200,000Rp for three or four hours, and 400,000Rp for five to seven hours; with three to five people it's 250,000Rp, 300,000Rp or 500,000Rp. Transport and food are extra and all the prices are very negotiable. Early morning, say 6am, is the best time to start – it's cooler and you're more likely to see some wildlife. The following are two of the more popular treks.

From a trail west of Labuhan Lalang, hike around the mangroves at **Teluk Terima**. Then partially follow Sungai Terima into the hills and walk back down to the road along the steps at Makam Jayaprana. You might see grey macaques, deer and black monkeys (allow two to three hours).

From Sumber Kelompok, go up **Gunung Kelatakan** (698m), then down to the main road near Kelatakan village (six to seven hours). You may be able to get permission from park headquarters to stay overnight in the forest – if you don't have a tent, your guide can make a shelter from branches and leaves, which will be an adventure in itself. Clear streams abound in the dense woods.

BOAT TRIPS

The best way to explore the mangroves of Teluk Gilimanuk or the west side of Prapat Agung is by chartering a boat (maximum of two people) for about 120,000Rp per boat per hour. You can arrange this at either of the park offices. A guide will cost another 100,000Rp. This is the ideal way to see bird life, including the kingfisher and the Javanese heron.

DIVING

Teluk Gilimanuk is a shallow bay with marine life quite different from that in other parts of Bali – it's especially interesting for divers with a strong interest in marine biology. The closest and most convenient dive operators are found at Pemuteran (p373) and Lovina (p370).

Pulau Menjangan is one of Bali's best-known dive areas, with a dozen distinct dive sites. The diving is excellent – lots of tropical fish (including clown fish, parrot fish, sharks and barracuda), soft corals, great visibility (usually), caves and a spectacular drop-off.

Sleeping

There's rough – and free – camping at the park headquarters in Cekik, although one of the guides hanging around may ask for a 10,000Rp donation. Besides the somewhat dire choices in Gilimanuk, there are nice options in the northwest, east of Labuhan Lalang. Your best bet is to go for Pemuteran (p373).

Waka Shorea (☎ 0362-94666; www.wakaexperience.com; units from US$165; ✈ 🏊) Located in splendid isolation in the park, Waka Shorea is a 10-minute boat ride from the hotel's reception area just east of Labuhan Lalang. It's a luxurious boutique resort and the emphasis is on nature, whether through diving, trekking or bird-watching.

Getting There & Away

The national park is too far away for a comfortable day trip from Ubud or South

Bali, though many dive operators do it. It is much more accessible from Lovina or Pemuteran – just get any Gilimanuk-bound bus or bemo to drop you at either the Labuhan Lalang visitors centre or the park headquarters at Cekik. Alternatively, you can take an organised tour or rent a vehicle.

LABUHAN LALANG

The jetty at this small harbour is the place to catch a boat to Pulau Menjangan (p357) in the national park. There's a **visitors centre** (7.30am-3pm) here, where you can pay the park entrance fee (2500Rp), as well as several warungs and a pleasant beach 200m to the east. Some of the warung rent snorkelling gear (50,000Rp for four hours) and can point out where the best sites are.

Local boat owners have a strict cartel and fixed prices: it costs 250,000Rp for a four-hour trip to Menjangan, and 20,000Rp for every subsequent hour in a boat holding 10 people (or five scuba divers with equipment). A guide costs an additional 60,000Rp.

GILIMANUK

☎ 0365

Gilimanuk is the terminus for ferries that shuttle back and forth across the narrow strait to Java.

Most travellers to or from Java can get an onward ferry or bus straight away, and won't need to stop in Gilimanuk. The museum is the only attraction – the town is really a place one passes through quickly. Services are few; there are no ATMs.

This part of Bali has been occupied for thousands of years. The **Museum Situs Purbakala Gilimanuk** (☎ 61328; donation 5000Rp; 8am-4pm Mon-Fri) is centred on a family of skeletons thought to be 4000 years old, which were found locally in 2004. It's 500m east from the ferry port.

Hotel Sari (☎ 61264; r 100,000Rp, with air-con 175,000Rp;) is the best of a dubious lot of hotels. On the ocean side of Jl Raya, it has basic rooms and a karaoke bar next door.

Getting There & Away

Frequent buses hurtle along the main road between Gilimanuk's huge bus depot and Denpasar's Ubung terminal (25,000Rp), or along the north coast road to Singaraja (20,000Rp).

FERRY

Boats to and from Ketapang on Java (adult/child 4300/2900Rp, car and driver 81,500Rp) run every 30 minutes round the clock, and are the main reason for coming here.

CENTRAL MOUNTAINS

Most of Bali's mountains are volcanoes; some are dormant, but some are definitely active. The mountains divide the gentle sweep of fertile land to the south from the narrow, more arid strip to the north. Northwest of Gunung Agung is the stark and spectacular caldera that contains the volcanic cone of Gunung Batur (1717m), the waters of Danau Batur and numerous smaller craters. In central Bali, around Bedugul, is another complex of volcanic craters and lakes, with much lusher vegetation. A string of smaller mountains stretches off into the sparsely inhabited western region.

It's all a big change from the coastal areas. Temperatures fall and you may need something more than shorts! There are two main routes through the mountains to the north coast (via Gunung Batur and via Bedugul), which allow you to make a circuit. There are treks to be had, clear lake waters to enjoy, plus a few other natural and sacred sites of note.

GUNUNG BATUR

☎ 0366

Most day-visitors come on organised tours and stop at the crater rim at Penelokan for views and lunch; most overnight visitors stay in the villages around the lake. The views both from above and from lake level are truly wonderful – if you hit the area on a clear day.

Orientation & Information

There are two main roads in the Gunung Batur area. The outer caldera-rim road links Penulisan and Penelokan, and from Penelokan you drop down onto the inner-rim road. The latter is rough in parts, especially the western side of the circuit, but drivable for all vehicles.

If you arrive by private vehicle, you will be stopped at ticket offices at Penelokan or Kubupenelokan; to save any hassle, you should stop and buy a ticket. Entry is 4000/2000Rp per adult/child. Bicycles are free (and should be, given the climb needed to get here). This ticket is for the whole Gunung Batur area; you shouldn't be charged any more down at the lakeside.

Dangers & Annoyances

Gunung Batur has developed a well-deserved reputation as a money-grubbing place where visitors (mainly around Penelokan) are hassled by touts and wannabe mountain guides (mainly around the lake area). Of course the guides themselves can be a problem, see p360). Don't leave valuables in your car, especially at any car park at the start of a volcano trail. Don't even leave a helmet with a motorcycle.

Trekking

The setting for Gunung Batur is otherworldly: it's like a giant dish, with the bottom half covered with water and a set of volcanic cones growing in the middle. Visit the area on a clear day and you'll understand what all the fuss is about. Soaring up in the centre of the huge outer crater is the cone of Gunung Batur (1717m), formed by a 1917 eruption. A cluster of smaller cones lies beside, created variously by eruptions in 1926, 1963, 1974 and 1994.

But is it worthwhile to go through the hassle and the expense of making the

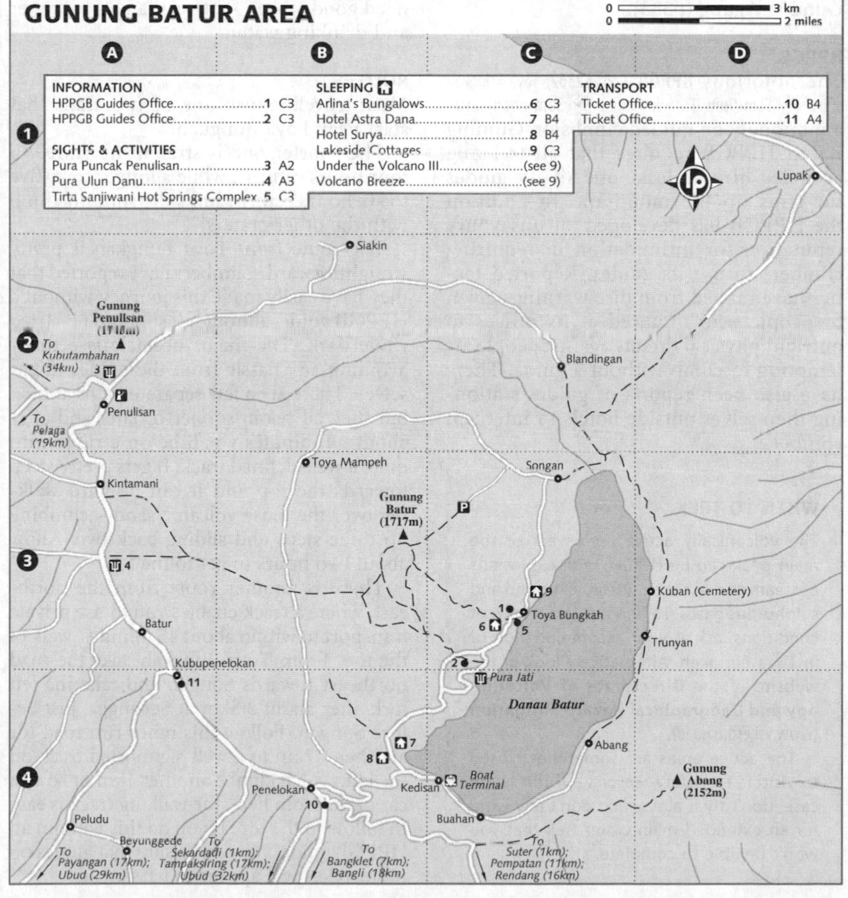

climb? You'll get some amazing pictures and come close to volcanic action not easily seen anywhere. But the flip side is that it's costly, you have to deal with various characters and at some point you may just say, 'I could have enjoyed all this from the parking lot viewpoint in Penelokan.'

Even reputable and highly competent adventure tour operators from elsewhere in Bali cannot take their customers up Gunung Batur without paying the HPPGB (see below) and using one of their guides, so these tours are relatively expensive.

Pretty much all the accommodation in the area can help you put a trek together. They can recommend alternatives to the classic Batur climb such as the outer rim of the crater, or to other mountains such as Gunung Agung (p333).

HPPGB

The notorious **HPPGB** (☎ 52362; Toya Bungkah office ⏰ 5am-9pm; Pura Jati office ⏰ 3am-noon) has a monopoly on guided climbs up Gunung Batur. HPPGB requires that all trekking agencies hire at least one of its guides for trips up the mountain. In addition the HPPGB has developed an unsavoury reputation for intimidation in requiring climbers to use its guides. Reported tactics have ranged from dire warnings given to people who inquired at its offices to outright physical threats against people attempting to climb without a guide. There have also been reports of guides stationing themselves outside hotels to intercept climbers.

WHEN TO TREK

The volcanically active area west of the main peak can be deadly, with explosions of steam and hot lava, unstable ground and sulphurous gases. To find out about current conditions, ask at your accommodation or in Toya Bungkah. Alternatively look at the website of the **Directorate of Volcanology and Geographical Hazard Mitigation** (www.vsi.esdm.go.id).

The active areas are sometimes closed to visitors for safety reasons – if this is the case, don't try it alone, and don't pay extra for an extended main crater trek that you won't be able to complete.

HPPGB GUIDED CLIMBS

Trek	Duration	Cost (Rp)
Batur Sunrise	4am-8am	200,000-300,000
Gunung Batur main crater	4am-10am	200,000-300,000

Pinning these guys down on rates can be enough to send you back to South Bali, but see the boxed text (above) for what you can expect to pay.

EQUIPMENT

If you're climbing before sunrise, take a torch (flashlight) or be absolutely sure that your guide provides you with one. You'll need good strong footwear, a hat, a jumper and drinking water.

ROUTES

Most travellers use one of two trails that start near Toya Bungkah.

The shorter one is straight up (three to four hours return), while a longer trek (five to six hours return) links the summit climb with the other craters.

The route from Toya Bungkah is pretty straightforward. Climbers have reported that they have easily made this journey without a HPPGB guide, although it shouldn't be tried while dark. The major obstacle is actually avoiding any hassle from the guides themselves. There are a few separate paths at first, but they all rejoin sooner or later and after about 30 minutes you'll be on a ridge with quite a well-defined track. It gets pretty steep towards the top and it can be hard walking over the loose volcanic sand – climbing up three steps and sliding back two. Allow about two hours to get to the top.

There is another route from the northeast, where a track enables you to use private transport to within about 45 minutes' walk of the top. From Toya Bungkah, take the road northeast towards Songan and take the left fork after about 3.5km at Serongga, just before Songan. Follow this inner-rim road for another 1.7km to a well-signposted track on the left, which climbs another 1km or so to a car park. From here, the walking track is easy to follow to the top. If you do this without an HPPGB guide, you can be sure that guides on motorbikes will appear to hassle you.

The Outer-Rim Road

PENELOKAN

On a clear day, Penelokan has superb views across to Gunung Batur and down to the lake at the bottom of the crater. It has numerous huge places catering to busloads of tourists. Enjoy the view and leave.

KINTAMANI

The village of Batur used to be down in the crater. A violent eruption in 1917 killed thousands of people and destroyed more than 60,000 homes and 2000 temples. The village was rebuilt, but Gunung Batur erupted again in 1926. This time the lava flow covered all but the loftiest temple shrine. The village was relocated up on the crater rim, and the surviving shrine was also moved up and placed in the temple, **Pura Ulun Danu**.

PENULISAN

At a bend in the road, at the junction to Singaraja, several steep flights of steps lead to Bali's highest temple, **Pura Puncak Penulisan** (admission 4100Rp) at 1745m. The views from the temple are superb: facing north you can see over the rice terraces clear to the Singaraja coast.

The Inner-Rim Road

The farming villages down on the lakeside grow onions and other aromatic crops. It's a crisp setting with often superb lake and mountain views.

KEDISAN

A hairpin-bend road winds its way down from Penelokan to Kedisan on the shore of the lake. There are a few good places to stay here if you are trekking.

Sleeping & Eating

Hotel Surya (☎ 51139; www.indo.com/hotels/surya; r 40,000-100,000Rp) Right at the bottom of the road from Penelokan, the Surya has a range of 22 decent rooms – the more expensive have views, hot water and bathtubs. Its restaurant has a fine view. Pick-up is offered from Ubud.

Hotel Astra Dana (☎ 52091; r 50,000-80,000Rp) The more expensive of the 12 rooms have hot water and views to the lake across onion and cabbage fields. This is the home of the always delightful Dizzy, local guide extraordinaire.

TOYA BUNGKAH

The main tourist centre is Toya Bungkah, which is scruffy but has a cute charm and a serene lakeside setting.

Hot springs bubble out in a couple of spots, and have long been used for bathing pools. Beside the lake, with a wonderful mountain backdrop, **Tirta Sanjiwani Hot Springs Complex** (☎ 51204; adult/child US$5/2.50; 🕑 8am-8pm) has lovely gardens near the lake. Entry includes use of the big cold-water pool (20°C) and hot spa (40°C).

Sleeping & Eating

Unless noted, hotels only have cold water, which can be a boon for waking up for a sunset climb. Most have restaurants, some of which serve *ikan mujair*, a delicious small lake fish, which is barbecued to a crisp with onion, garlic and bamboo shoots.

Under the Volcano III (☎ 0813 3860 081; r 60,000Rp) With a lovely, quiet lakeside location opposite vegetable plots, this inn has six clean and pretty rooms; go for room one right on the water. There are two other nearby inns in the Volcano empire, all run by the same cheery family.

Arlina's Bungalows (☎ 51165; s/d 50,000/80,000Rp, with hot water 70,000/100,000Rp) Clean, comfortable, friendly and above the average standard. Breakfast is included.

Lakeside Cottages (☎ 51249; jero_wijaya@hotmail.com; r US$10-35; 🖳) At the end of the track on the water's edge, this is definitely one of the better places. The top-end rooms feature hot water and satellite TV.

Volcano Breeze (☎ 51824; dishes 10,000 21,000Rp) A delightful and sociable travellers' café. Fresh lake fish in many forms is the speciality here.

Getting There & Away

From Batubulan terminal in Denpasar, bemos travel regularly to Kintamani (15,000Rp). You can also get a bus on the busy Denpasar (Batabulan) to Singaraja route, which will stop in Penelokan and Kintamani (about 15,000Rp).

Alternatively, you can just hire a car or use a driver. From South Bali expect to pay at least 400,000Rp.

Getting Around

Orange bemos regularly shuttle back and forth around the crater rim, between

Penelokan and Kintamani (7000Rp for tourists). Public bemos from Penelokan down to the lakeside villages go mostly in the morning (tourist price is about 5000Rp to Toya Bungkah). Later in the day, you may have to charter transport (40,000Rp or more).

DANAU BRATAN

☎ 0368

Driving inland from the humidity of southern Bali, you gradually leave the rice terraces behind and ascend into the cool, damp mountain country around Danau Bratan. This lovely area is an excellent place to relax and use as a base for hiking around the lakes and surrounding hills mentioned later in this section.

The neighbouring towns of Candikuning and Bedugul have a picturesque temple, botanical gardens and a colourful market where you can buy the local fruit that grows in profusion. Thankfully, the area lacks the tourists and touts found around Gunung Batur, though Sunday and public holidays are usually very busy with local visitors.

In the west, the area around Munduk is great for trekking and you can enjoy views all the way down to the north coast.

Bedugul & Candikuning

The name Bedugul is sometimes used to refer to the whole lakeside area, but strictly speaking, Bedugul is just the first place you

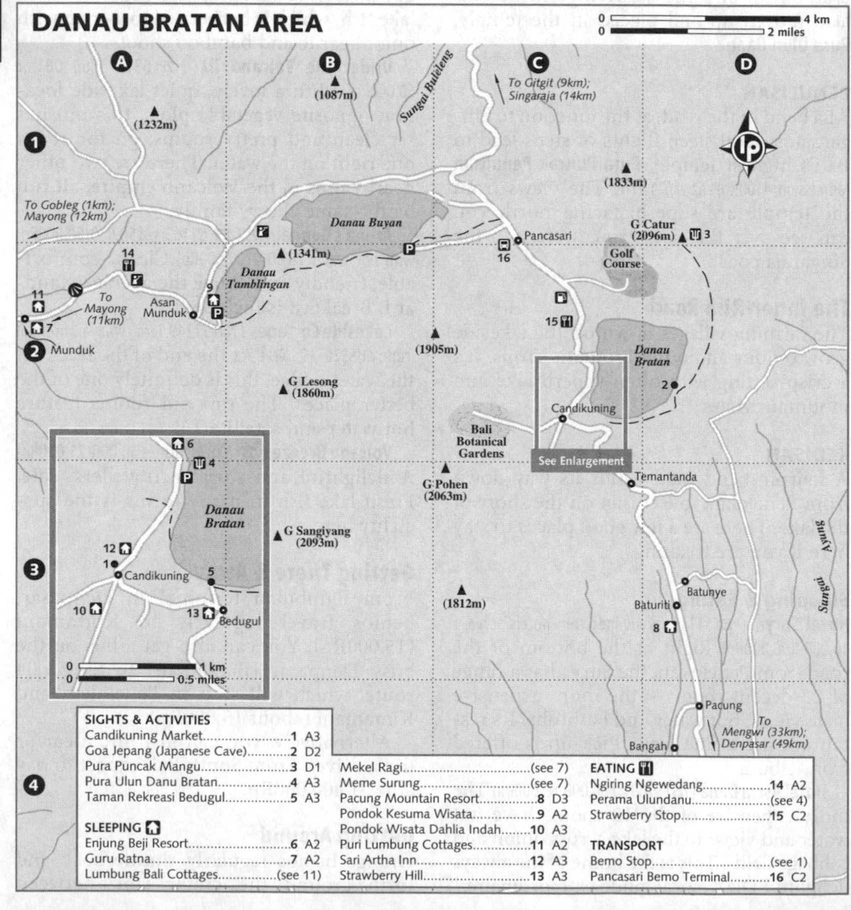

reach at the top of the hill when coming up from South Bali.

Spread out along the western side of the lake, Candikuning is the horticultural focus of central Bali. Its daily **market** was once the main supplier of vegetables, fruit and flowers for the southern hotels, but now its patrons are mostly tourists with a smattering of locals shopping for herbs, spices and potted plants. There's a wartel beside the market, and several moneychangers.

SIGHTS

There's a number of good sights up here. Note that **Taman Rekreasi Bedugal**, which is on the lake at Bedugal, is a pretty charmless amusement park aimed at day-tripping Balinese.

Bali Botanical Gardens

Established in 1959 as a branch of the national botanical gardens at Bogor, near Jakarta, the **Bali Botanical Gardens** (Kebun Raya Eka Karya Bali; ☎ 21273; admission 3500Rp, car parking 1500Rp; 🕑 7am-6pm) are a showplace. They cover over 154 hectares on the lower slopes of Gunung Pohen. The gardens boast an extensive collection of trees and flowers, including wild orchids. Some plants are labelled with their botanical names, and the booklet *Six Self Guided Walks in the Bali Botanical Gardens*, sold at the ticket office for 20,000Rp, is helpful. The gorgeous orchid area is often locked to foil flower filchers; ask that it be unlocked.

Coming north from Bedugul, at a junction conspicuously marked with a large, phallic corncob sculpture, a small side road goes 600m west to the gardens. Although normally cool, shady, scenic and uncrowded, on Sunday and public holidays they're very popular with Balinese families.

Pura Ulun Danu Bratan

About a kilometre north of the market, this very important Hindu-Buddhist **temple** (adult/child 3300/1800Rp, parking 2000Rp; 🕑 tickets 7am-5pm, site 24hr) was founded in the 17th century. It is dedicated to Dewi Danu, the goddess of the waters, and is actually built on small islands, which means it is completely surrounded by the lake. Both pilgrimages and ceremonies are held here to ensure that there is a supply of water for farmers all over Bali.

It is truly beautiful, with classical Hindu thatch-roofed *meru* reflected in the water and silhouetted against the often cloudy mountain backdrop – one of the most common photographic images of Bali. A large banyan tree shades the entrance, and you walk through manicured gardens and past an impressive Buddhist stupa to reach the lakeside.

An unfortunate aspect is the small animal zoo, left of the main entrance, where tourists are encouraged to be photographed alongside snakes, bats and iguanas, all of which appear to be kept in less than humane conditions.

If you are feeling hungry, **Perama Ulundanu** (☎ 21191; dishes 15,000-30,000Rp; 🕑 9am-5pm) in the grounds has a pleasant outdoor terrace and the usual Indonesian and Western standards.

ACTIVITIES

Trekking

From the water sports area, a trail around the south side of the lake goes to the mundane **Goa Jepang** (Japanese Cave), which was dug during WWII. From there, a difficult path ascends to the top of **Gunung Catur** (2096m), where the old **Pura Puncak Mangu** temple is popular with monkeys. Allow about four hours to go up and back from Taman Rekreasi Bedugul.

Water Sports

At the temple gardens, you can hire a four-passenger speedboat with a driver (per 30 minutes 125,000Rp), a five-person boat with boatman (per 30 minutes 80,000Rp), or a two-person pedal boat (per 30 minutes 35,000Rp).

For an almost surreal experience, take a quiet paddle across the lake and see Pura Ulun Danu Bratan at sunrise – arrange it with a boatman the night before.

SLEEPING

The Bedugul and Candikuning area can make a good place for a break in exploring the highlands. Upmarket hotels on the slope south of Bedugul offer outstanding views to the east and west.

Pondok Wisata Dahlia Indah (☎ 21233; r 50,000Rp, with hot water 80,000-125,000Rp) In Candikuning, along a lane near the road to the botanical gardens, this is a decent budget option with 17 comfortable, clean rooms.

Sari Artha Inn (☎ 21011; r 50,000Rp) Close to the market and lacking views, this place has five basic hot-water rooms.

Strawberry Hill (Bukit Stroberi; ☎ 21265; r from 60,000Rp) Opposite the Taman Rekreasi turn-off, this cosy place has 10 basic rooms with hot water – a fine budget choice. The excellent restaurant (dishes 10,000Rp to 18,000Rp) has polished floorboards and on a clear day you can see Kuta. It has a good bar and tasty burgers.

Enjung Beji Resort (☎ 21490; fax 21022; cottages 250,000-500,000Rp) Just north of Pura Ulun Danu Bratan and overlooking the lake, this 23-room place is a peaceful, pleasant option. The superior cottages are excellent quality and have outdoor showers and sunken baths. All have hot water, good on cool misty days.

Pacung Mountain Resort (☎ 21038; r US$90-200; 🏊) Well down the road to the south from the ridge, this resort is built on a steep terraced slope overlooking an exquisite valley carved with rice fields and early morning views of Gunung Batukau.

EATING

Food stalls at Candikuning market offer cheap eats, and there are food carts further north at the car park overlooking the lake. At the entrance to Pura Ulun Danu Bratan are several Padang warungs, and there's a restaurant on the grounds.

Strawberry Stop (☎ 21060; dishes 6000-15,000Rp, strawberry wine 65,000Rp; 🕑 8am-6pm) North of Candikuning, Strawberry Stop makes good use of locally grown strawberries in milk shakes, juices and pancakes. Jaffles and other simple snacks and dishes are also available. The wine will remind you of your misspent teenage years drinking plonk behind a fence.

GETTING THERE & AWAY

Danau Bratan is beside a main north–south road, so it's easy to reach from South Bali or Singaraja.

Most minibuses and bemos will stop along the main road in Bedugul and Candikuning. There are frequent connections from Denpasar's Ubung terminal (15,000Rp) and Singaraja's Sukasada terminal (15,000Rp). For Gunung Batur, you have to connect through Singaraja or hire transport.

Pancasari

The broad, green valley northwest of Danau Bratan is actually the crater of an extinct volcano. In the middle of the valley, on the main road, Pancasari is a nontourist town with a bustling market and the main terminal for public bemos.

Danau Buyan & Danau Tamblingan

Also northwest of Danau Bratan are two more lakes, Danau Buyan and Danau Tamblingan – neither has been heavily developed for tourism, which is an advantage. There are several tiny villages and abandoned temples along the shores of both lakes, and although the frequently swampy ground makes it unpleasant in parts to explore, this is still a good place for taking a walk.

SIGHTS & ACTIVITIES

Danau Buyan (admission 2000Rp, parking 1000Rp) has parking right on the lake, a delightful 1.5km drive off the main road. The entire area is home to market gardens growing produce such as strawberries.

A 4km **hiking trail** goes around the southern side of Danau Buyan from the parking lot, then over the saddle to Danau Tamblingan and on to Asan Munduk. It combines forest and lake views.

Danau Tamblingan (adult/child 3000/1500Rp, parking 1000Rp) also has a parking lot at the end of the road from the village of Asan Munduk. The lake is a 400m walk and this is where you can catch the trail to Danau Buyan. If you have a driver, you could walk this path in one direction and be met at the other end. There's usually a couple of guides hanging around the parking lot (you don't need them for the lake path) who will take you up and around **Gunung Lesong** (six hours, 300,000Rp).

SLEEPING & EATING

Pondok Kesuma Wisata (☎ 0817 472 8826; r 200,000Rp) This cute little guesthouse with hot-water rooms and a nice café (dishes 8000Rp to 20,000Rp) just up from the Danau Tamblingan parking lot has a surprise or two: you may be greeted by a monkey.

Munduk & Around

☎ 0362

Heading north from Pancasari, the main road climbs steeply up the rim of the old volcanic crater. It's worth stopping to enjoy the views back over the valley and lakes – watch out for the typically ill-behaved monkeys on the road. Turning right at the top will take you on a scenic descent to the coastal town of Singaraja, via the Gitgit waterfalls (p369). Taking a sharp left turn, you follow a ridge-top road with Danau Buyan on one side and a slope to the sea on the other; coffee is a big crop in the area.

The road winds beautifully through the lush scenery to the main village of Munduk. Watch for superb panoramas of North Bali and the ocean. About 2km west of Munduk look for signs indicating parking for a 15m waterfall near the road.

There's archaeological evidence of a developed community in the Munduk region between the 10th and 14th centuries, and accounts of the first Majapahit emissaries visiting the area. When the Dutch took control of North Bali in the 1890s, they experimented with commercial crops, establishing plantations for coffee, vanilla, cloves and cocoa. Quite a few Dutch buildings are still intact along the road in Munduk and further west, and the mountain scenery is sublime.

Almost everything is at an elevation of at least 1000m. Numerous trails are suitable for two-hour or much longer **treks** to coffee plantations, rice fields, four waterfalls, villages, and around both Danau Tamblingan and Danau Buyan. You will be able to arrange a guide through your lodgings. Many people come here to trek for a day and stay a week.

SLEEPING & EATING

Guru Ratna (☎ 92182; r 100,000-200,000Rp) The cheapest place right in town has five comfortable cold-water rooms in an old Dutch house. The best rooms have some style and nice porches. The restaurant does good meals (dishes 12,500Rp).

Meme Surung and **Mekel Ragi** (☎ 92811; r 200,000Rp) are atmospheric old Dutch houses right next to each other right in town and run by the same owner. The former has excellent views down the valleys.

Lumbung Bali Cottages (☎ 92818; r from US$40) About 800m west of Munduk, this place has nine two-level villas overlooking the lush local terrain. The open-air bathrooms are refreshing just as the porches are relaxing. Like all local places, there are a wide range of hikes on offer here.

Puri Lumbung Cottages (☎ 92810; www.purilumbung.com; s/d cottages US$67/75, f cottages US$95-149; 💻) This great hotel has bright two-storey cottages that have stunning views (units three, eight, 10 and 11 have the best views) all the way down to the coast from their upstairs balconies. Rice grows right outside each unit. Fifteen trekking options and a range of courses, including dance and cooking, are offered. The hotel's restaurant, Warung Kopi Bali, has a great outlook onto the lush valleys and also serves great food (dishes 15,000Rp to 24,000Rp), including the local dish *timbungan bi siap* (clear chicken soup with sliced cassava and fried shallots). The hotel is on the right-hand side of the road 700m before Munduk from Bedugul.

Ngiring Ngewedang (☎ 082 836 5146; dishes 15,000-40,000Rp; 🕑 10am-4pm) This coffee house 5km east of Munduk has views of the ocean when it's not clouded over. The café sells its own brand of coffee and staff will also take you through the coffee-production process.

GETTING THERE & AWAY

Bemos leave Ubung terminal in Denpasar for Munduk frequently (20,000Rp). Morning bemos from Candikuning also stop in Munduk (12,000Rp). If you're driving to or from the north coast, a decent road west of Munduk goes through a number of picturesque villages to Mayong, then down to the sea at Seririt.

ROUTES THROUGH PUPUAN

The two most popular routes between the southern and northern coasts are the roads via Kintamani and Bedugul, but there are two other routes over the mountains. Both branch north from the Denpasar to Gilimanuk road, one from Pulukan and the other from Antasari, and meet at Pupuan before dropping down to Seririt, west of Lovina.

The Pulukan to Pupuan road climbs steeply up from the coast, providing fine views back down to the sea. The route runs through spice-growing country. At one point, the narrow and winding road runs right through an enormous *bunut* tree, which bridges the road. This road was built by the Dutch using forced local labour – many Balinese died during its construction and this, together with the sacrilege of chopping into the living tree, makes the **Bunut Bolong** a sacred place. The views beyond the tree into the rainforest are gorgeous and the birdsong can be deafening. Further on, the road spirals down to Pupuan through some of Bali's most beautiful rice terraces.

The road from Antasari initially travels through rice fields, then climbs into the spice-growing country and finally descends through the coffee plantations to Pupuan. If you continue another 12km or so towards the north coast you reach Mayong, where you can turn east to Munduk and on to Danau Tamblingan and Danau Buyan.

NORTH BALI

Before people arrived by plane in South Bali, most people arrived at the island by steamship at the old port in Singaraja. It was a time of great prominence for the Buleleng area, which comprises most of North Bali. Although in recent decades it has been eclipsed by the south, the region retains its fierce pride.

There is a strong and distinct artistic and cultural tradition here. Dance troupes are highly regarded and a number of dance styles originated here, including Joged and Janger. Work in gold and silver, weaving, pottery, musical-instrument making and temple design all feature distinctive local styles. Distinctive too is the terrain: it's much drier here than in the lush south.

And in recent years Buleleng has developed its own resort area, Lovina, to draw people away from the hectic south. Each year this strip adds just enough polish to increase its allure to visitors. Many come here for the relaxing part of their holiday, and, for active sorts, Pemuteran at the west end of the coast has excellent diving.

YEH SANIH

☎ 0362

About 15km east of Singaraja, Yeh Sanih (also called Air Sanih) is a hassle-free seaside spot with a few guesthouses on a

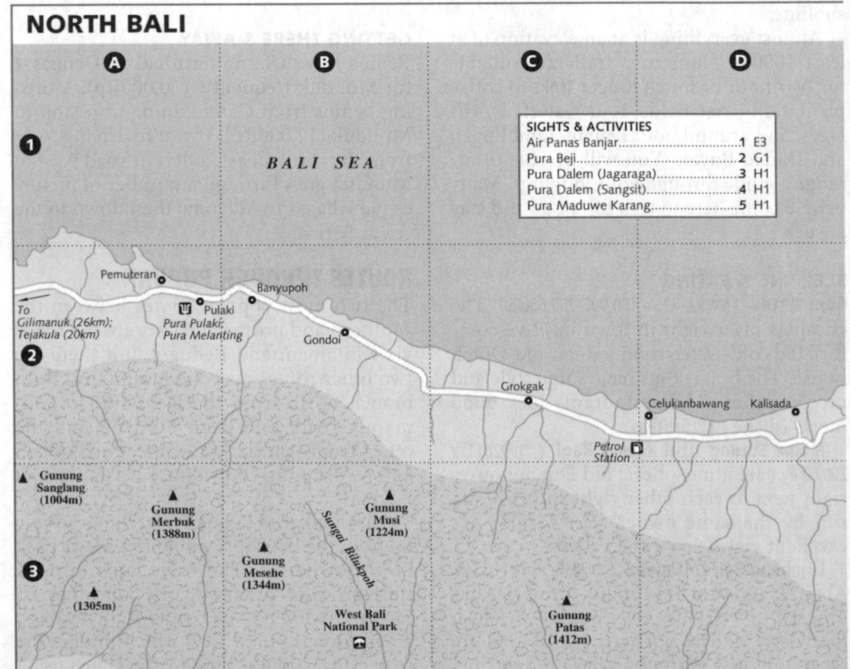

black-sand beachfront (albeit with a retaining wall). It's named for its fresh-water springs, **Air Sanih** (adult/child 2000/1000Rp; 8am-6pm), which are channelled into large swimming pools before flowing into the sea. The pools are particularly picturesque at sunset, when throngs of locals bathe under heavily blooming frangipani trees.

Pura Ponjok Batu has a commanding location between the sea and the road, some 7km east of Yeh Sanih. It has some very fine limestone carvings in the central temple area.

A surprise in the area is **Art Zoo** (8am-6pm), 5.7km east of Yeh Sanih on the Singaraja road. The American artist Symon has a gallery bursting with vibrant, exotic and often homoerotic paintings and sculpture. You can chat up his models.

Sleeping & Eating

Cilik's Beach Garden (26561; www.ciliksbeachgarden.com; s/d €40/60, villas €75-110;) Coming here is like visiting your rich friends. These villas, 1km east of Yeh Sanih, are large and have vast private gardens. Other accommodation is in stylish *lumbungs* (rice barns with round roofs) set in a delightful garden facing the ocean. Meals (dishes 20,000Rp to 40,000Rp) are served in a pavilion.

Getting There & Away

Yeh Sanih is on the main road along the north coast. Frequent bemos and buses from Singaraja stop outside the springs (7000Rp).

If you are driving the coast road to Amed and beyond, be sure to fill up at the petrol station just east of Yeh Sanih as there is not another until almost Amlapura.

SINGARAJA

0362

Singaraja (Lion King) is Bali's second largest city, and it's downright tidy compared to Denpasar. Singaraja was the centre of Dutch power in Bali and remained the administrative centre for the Lesser Sunda Islands (Bali through to Timor) until 1953. It is one of the few places in Bali where there are visible reminders of the Dutch period in the many colonial houses.

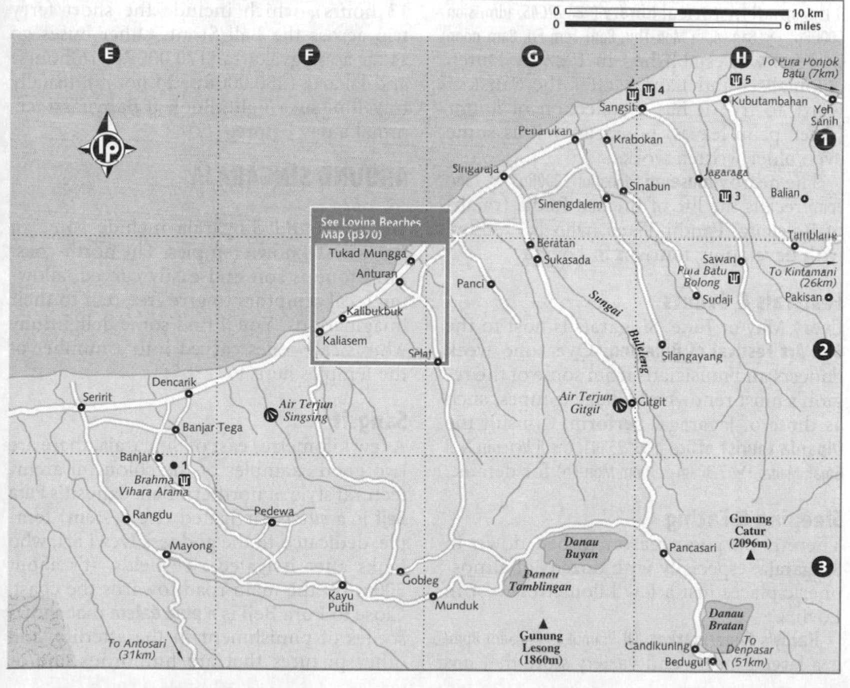

BALI

Sparkling gutters aside, it's not a place where travellers linger. It has few real attractions other than services and roads you're bound to travel whether by bus, bemo or car. However, a couple of royal museums are worth a pause.

Information

Facilities include the following:

Diparda (☎ 25141; cnr Jl Veteran & Jl Gajah Mada; 🕒 7.30am-3.30pm Mon-Fri) The regional tourist office loves visitors. Ask about dance and other cultural events.

RSUP Hospital (☎ 22046; Jl Ngurah Rai; 🕒 24hr) Singaraja's hospital is the largest in northern Bali.

Sights

OLD HARBOUR & WATERFRONT

The conspicuous **Yudha Mandala Tama monument** commemorates a freedom fighter killed by gunfire from a Dutch warship early in the struggle for independence. Close by, there's the colourful Chinese temple **Ling Gwan Kiong**. There are a few old canals here as well and you can still get a little feel of the old colonial port.

GEDONG KIRTYA LIBRARY & MUSEUM

This small historical **library** (☎ 22645; admission 5000Rp; 🕒 8am-4pm Mon-Thu, 8am-1pm Fri, 8am-noon Sat & Sun) was established in 1928 by Dutch colonialists and named after the Sanskrit word 'to try'. It has a collection of *lontar* (dried palm leaves) books as well as some even older written works.

The nearby **museum** (donation 5000Rp; 🕒 7am-3pm) recalls the life of the last Radja (rajah) of Buleleng, Pandji Tisna, who is credited with developing tourism in Lovina.

Festivals & Events

Every May or June, Singaraja is host to the **Bali Art Festival of Buleleng**. Over one week dancers and musicians from some of the region's most renowned village troupes, such as those of Jagaraga, perform. Consult the **Diparda tourist office** (☎ 25141; cnr Jl Veteran & Jl Gajah Mada; 🕒 7.30am-3.30pm Mon-Fri) for details.

Sleeping & Eating

There is no good reason to bed down in Singaraja, especially with dozens of atmospheric places just a few kilometres west in Lovina.

Hardy's Supermarket (Jl Pramuka; 🕒 8am-8pm) is a large grocery and variety store that has the best selection of goods this side of the volcanoes.

Getting There & Away

BEMO & BUS

Singaraja is the transport hub for the northern coast, with three main bemo/bus terminals. From the main Sukasada terminal, about 3km south of town, minibuses go to Denpasar (Ubung terminal, 28,000Rp) via Bedugul/Pancasari (13,000Rp) about every 30 minutes from 6am to 4pm.

The Banyuasri terminal, on the western side of town, has buses heading to Gilimanuk (15,000Rp, two hours) and Java, and plenty of blue bemos to Lovina (6000Rp).

The Penarukan terminal, 2km east of town, has bemos to Yeh Sanih (7000Rp) and Amlapura (15,000Rp, three hours) via the coastal road; and also minibuses to Denpasar (Batubulan terminal; 25,000Rp) via Kintamani.

To Java

From Singaraja, several bus companies have overnight services to Surabaya (110,000Rp, 13 hours), which include the short ferry trip across the Bali Strait. Other buses go as far as Yogyakarta (170,000Rp, 16 hours) and Jakarta (250,000Rp, 24 hours), usually travelling overnight. Book at Banyuasri terminal a day before.

AROUND SINGARAJA

☎ 0362

Sights around Singaraja include some of Bali's best-known temples. The north-coast sandstone is soft and easily carved, allowing local sculptors to give free rein to their imaginations. You'll find some delightfully whimsical scenes carved into a number of the temples here.

Sangsit

A few kilometres east of Singaraja, there are two good examples of the colourful architectural style of northern Bali. Sangsit's **Pura Beji** is a *subak* (irrigated rice system) temple, dedicated to the goddess Dewi Sri, who looks after irrigated rice fields. It's about 500m off the main road towards the coast. Close to Pura Beji is a **pura dalem** that shows scenes of punishment in the afterlife, and other pictures that are humorous and/or erotic. Turn left about 50m south of Pura Beji, and left again after about 100m. It's another 100m down the road.

All forms of public transport between Singaraja's Penarukan terminal and Amlapura will stop at Sangsit and Berdikari Cottages.

Jagaraga & Sawan

Jagaraga has an interesting **pura dalem**, with delightful sculpted panels along its front wall, both inside and out. On the outer wall look for a vintage car sedately driving past, a steamer at sea and an aerial dogfight.

Several kilometres inland from Jagaraga, Sawan is a centre for the manufacture of gamelan gongs. Around Sawan are **cold water springs** believed to cure all sorts of illnesses.

Regular bemos from Penarukan terminal in Singaraja stop at Jagaraga on the way to Sawan.

Kubutambahan

About 1km east of the turn-off to Kintamani is **Pura Maduwe Karang** (Temple of the Landowner). Like Pura Beji at Sangsit, the temple is dedicated to agricultural spirits, but this one looks after unirrigated land. This is one of the best temples in northern Bali, and is particularly noted for its sculpted panels, including the famous bicycle panel depicting a gentleman riding a bicycle with flower petals for wheels. Kubutambahan is on the Singaraja to Amlapura road, and there are regular bemos and buses.

Gitgit

About 11km south of Singaraja are the pretty – and pretty touristy – waterfalls of **Air Terjun Gitgit** (adult/child 3300/1600Rp) The well-signposted path (800m) from the main road in the village is lined with souvenir stalls and warung. The 40m falls are a good place for a picnic when it's not too busy, but litter can be an issue. There is another small waterfall, sometimes called **Gitgit Multi-Tier Waterfall** (donation 5000Rp) about 2km further up the hill from the main falls and about 600m off the main road.

Regular buses and minibuses travel between the main Sukasada terminal in Singaraja and Denpasar (Ubung terminal), via Bedugul, and stop at Gitgit.

LOVINA

☎ 0362

Lovina manages to exude a sedate charm even as the number of hotels and other tourist places grows. Almost merging into Singaraja to the west, the town is really a string of coastal villages – Pemaron, Tukad Mungga, Anturan, Kalibukbuk, Kaliasem and Temukus – that have taken on this collective name.

Lovina is a convenient base for trips around the north coast or the central mountains. The beaches are made up of washed-out grey and black volcanic sand, and they are mostly clean near the hotel areas, but generally unspectacular. Reefs protect the shore, so the water is usually calm and clear.

Orientation & Information

The Lovina tourist area stretches over 8km, but the main focus is Kalibukbuk, 10.5km west of Singaraja.

If you are planning a reading holiday in Lovina, come prepared. There's no decent place to buy a new book (there's lots of places for well-thumbed old bestsellers) and you can't buy a newspaper. The main post office is 1km west of central Kalibukbuk.

There are plenty of moneychangers around Lovina, especially in Kalibukbuk. There are ATMs on Jl Bina Ria and at the Jl Raya Lovina intersection.

Other facilities:

Police station (Jl Raya Lovina)
Spice Cyber (☎ 41305; Jl Bina Ria; per min 300Rp; 8am-midnight;) The best place for internet access, and it's air-conditioned.

Sights & Activities

BEACHES

A paved beach path runs along the sand in Kalibukbuk. It greatly eases a beach stroll – even if it is popular with scooters.

Otherwise, the best beach areas include the main beach east of the Dolphin Monument as well as the curving stretch a bit west. The cluster of cheap hotels in Anturan also enjoy a good beach.

DOLPHIN WATCHING

Sunrise boat trips to see dolphins are Lovina's much-hyped tourist attraction – so much so that a large concrete crowned **monument** has been erected in honour of

BALI

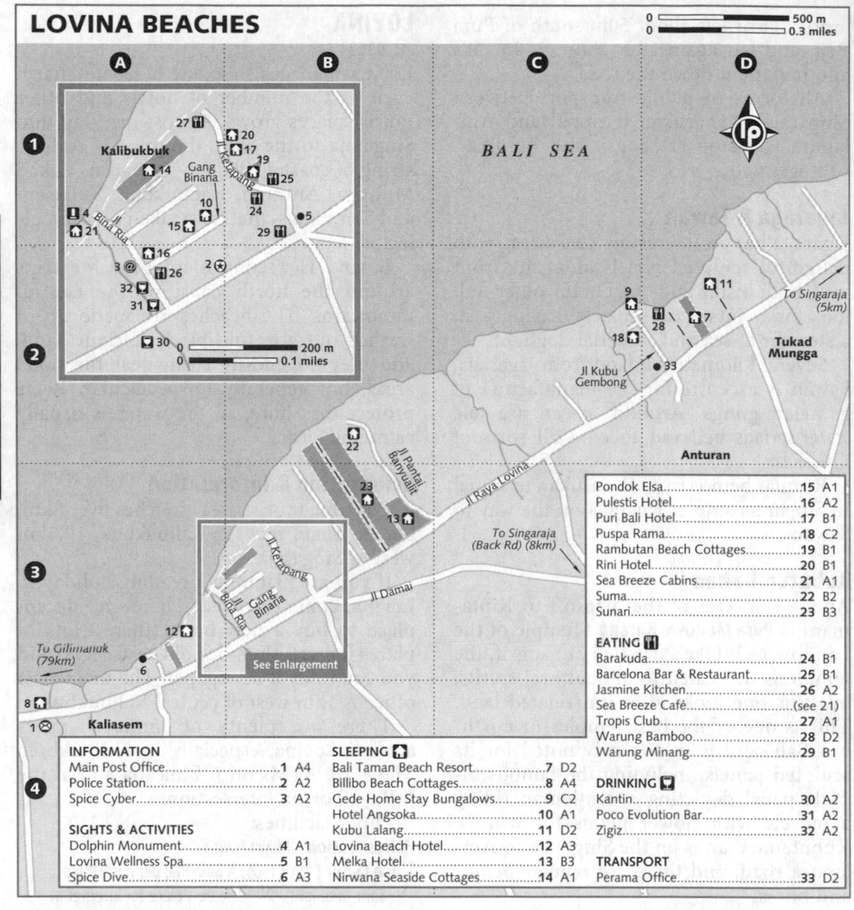

the over-touted cetaceans. Some days, no dolphins are sighted, but most of the time at least a few surface.

Expect constant hassle from your hotel and touts selling dolphin trips – and if you want to go, it's best to buy a ticket the day before. The price is fixed at 40,000Rp per person by the boat owners' cartel. Trips start at 6am and last two hours. Note that the ocean can get pretty crowded with loud and belching power boats and there's great debate about what all this means to the dolphins.

DIVING

Scuba diving on the local reef is better at lower depths, and night diving is particularly recommended. Many people stay here to dive off Pulau Menjangan (p357), a two- to three-hour drive west.

Spice Dive (☎ 41509; www.balispicedive.com) has the best reputation locally. It runs four-dive PADI open-water certificate courses for US$250. Spice Dive is based at the pleasant Café Spice, found at the end of the beach path.

SNORKELLING

Generally, the water is clear and some parts of the reef are quite good for snorkelling. The best place is to the west, a few-hundred metres offshore from Billibo Beach Cottages. Snorkelling gear costs about 20,000Rp per day.

MASSAGE & SPAS

Lovina Wellness Spa (☎ 0812 377 2046; Jl Ketapang; massage from 70,000Rp; 🕑 10am-7pm) offers Balinese, Ayurveda, and foot massage, as well as 'rebirthing' (for those who missed the fun the first time?).

Sleeping

Hotels are spread out along Jl Raya Lovina, and on the side roads going off to the beach. There are decent places to stay in every price range.

BUDGET

Singaraja to Anturan

Kubu Lalang (☎ 42207; http://kubu.balihotelguide.com; r 75,000-170,000Rp) The five bungalows here are designed in traditional rice-barn style. Edged in between rice fields, each one is different and exotically decorated, and has a modern open-air bathroom, some with hot water and tubs.

Anturan

A few tiny side tracks and one proper sealed road, Jl Kubu Gembong, lead to this lively little fishing village, busy with swimming locals and moored fishing boats. It's a real travellers' hang-out.

Gede Home Stay Bungalows (☎ 41526; Jl Kubu Gembong; r 50,000-120,000Rp; ❄) The friendly staff here win praise. Cheap rooms have cold water while better ones have hot water and air-con.

Puspa Rama (☎ 42070; Jl Kubu Gembong; s/d 60,000/70,000Rp) This is one of several cheap places on this street. The six rooms have hot water and are set in very lush grounds.

Anturan to Kalibukbuk

Jl Pantai Banyualit has a good selection of hotels, although the beachfront area is not very inspiring.

Suma (☎ 41566; Jl Pantai Banyualit; r US$10-30; ❄ 🏊) In a mannered stone building, Suma has views of the sea from its upstairs rooms. The pool is large and there's also a pleasant café.

Kalibukbuk

A little over 10km from Singaraja, the 'centre' of Lovina is the village of Kalibukbuk. Jl Ketapang is marginally quieter and more pleasant than Jl Bina Ria. There are small *gang* off both.

Hotel Angsoka (☎ 41841; www.angsoka.com; Gang Binaria; r 40,000-200,000Rp; ❄ 🏊) There's a large range of rooms here, from cold-water basic to large with air-con and hot water. All enjoy the benefits of the good-sized pool and quiet gardens.

Pondok Elsa (☎ 41186; Gang Binaria; r 65,000Rp, with air-con 90,000Rp; ❄) This two-storey heavily ornate building has seven clean, pleasant rooms.

Pulestis Hotel (☎ 41035; jokoartawan@hotmail.com; Jl Bina Ria; r 70,000-100,000Rp; ❄ 🏊) The 14 rooms here have funky exteriors, clean interiors and pebbled open-air bathrooms – some with hot water. The café overlooks an indigo pool.

Puri Bali Hotel (☎ 41485; www.puribalilovina.com; Jl Ketapang; r 80,000-180,000Rp; ❄ 🏊) The pool area is very attractive and has lush plantings. The better rooms, with hot water and air-con, are plain but comfortable.

Rini Hotel (☎ /fax 41386; rinihotel@telkom.net; Jl Ketapang; r 80,000-300,000Rp; ❄ 🏊) A super-clean 30-room place with a large saltwater pool. Cheaper rooms are basic but more expensive ones are huge, with air-con and hot water.

West of Kalibukbuk

Lovina Beach Hotel (☎ 41005; www.lovinabeachhotel.com; Jl Raya Lovina; r 75,000-250,000Rp, bungalows 250,000Rp; ❄ 🏊) Clean rooms in heavily detailed Balinese bungalows are set in pleasant grounds right on the beach. Better ones come with hot water; private bungalows have air-con and views.

Billibo Beach Cottages (☎ 41355; Jl Raya Lovina; r 125,000-200,000Rp; ❄) Located near one of the best spots for snorkelling, the cottages here are clean and comfortable and come with hot water and good access to the beach.

MIDRANGE

Anturan

Bali Taman Beach Resort (☎ 41126; www.indo.com/hotels/bali_taman; Jl Raya Lovina; r US$35-85; ❄ 🏊) Facing the busy road but extending down to the beach, the Bali Taman has 30 rooms that vary greatly. The best ones are bungalows with ocean views. The pool faces the ocean and is surrounded by leafy gardens. There's a spa.

Anturan to Kalibukbuk

Melka Hotel (☎ 41552; www.melkahotel.com; Jl Pantai Banyualit; r US$30-45; ❄ 🏊) Complete with its own animal menagerie (deer, snakes, birds etc), the Melka defines idiosyncratic. There is a range of rooms, from those with cold water and fan to those in a flash new addition with air-con, hot water, balconies with views and satellite TV. Plans to have dolphins in a tank may horrify some.

Kalibukbuk

Nirwana Seaside Cottages (☎ 41288; www.nirwanaseaside.com; bungalows 100,000-125,000Rp, deluxe r 210,000-300,000Rp;) On large and lovely beachfront grounds off Jl Bina Ria, the 58-unit Nirwana has a vast beachfront site. All bungalows have some character and hot water. Those with beach views are a great deal. A newer wing has hotel-style air-con rooms.

Sea Breeze Cabins (☎ 41138; r US$15, bungalows US$35-40;) An excellent choice in the heart of Kalibukbuk, off Jl Bina Ria, the Sea Breeze has lovely bungalows right on the beach, some with sensational views from their verandas.

Rambutan Beach Cottages (☎ 41388; www.rambutan.org; Jl Ketepang; r 300,000-500,000Rp;) The hotel, on a large area of land, features two swimming pools and charming gardens. The 48 rooms and villas are tasteful, with lashings of Balinese style. There are a few cold-water economy rooms for about 120,000Rp. The owner is a real Lovina booster.

TOP END

Anturan to Kalibukbuk

Sunari (☎ 41775; www.sunari.com; r US$85-130, villas US$240-360;) Off Jl Raya Lovina, the imposing entrance to this place leads to a large beachfront resort with redecorated rooms and good services. Villas come variously with private plunge pools, whirlpools and ocean views. Grounds are verdant with banana trees and a profusion of posies.

Eating

Just about every hotel has a café or restaurant. In addition, Kalibukbuk has food carts, warung, cafés and some fine restaurants. Many of the places listed here are also good for an end-of-the-day drink.

ANTURAN

Warung Bamboo (dishes 7000-30,000Rp; 4am-10pm) A small, open-fronted place, Bamboo faces a lively section of beach. It serves typical travellers' fare and cheapish beer and has a relaxed feel. To find it, walk east along the beach from the end of Jl Kubu Gembong.

KALIBUKBUK

Warung Minang (☎ 0812 393 0792; Jl Raya Lovina; dishes 6000-8000Rp) This stylish Padang-style café is a great find. Choose from numerous fresh dishes on display, then savour the local art on the walls.

Barcelona Bar & Restaurant (☎ 41894; Jl Ketepang; dishes 10,000-30,000Rp) This restaurant has a lovely, open-air, shady area out the back. The food is excellent, and includes *sate pelecing* (fish satay with Balinese spices).

Barakuda (Jl Ketepang; dishes 13,000-25,000Rp) Seafood is the speciality here. The prawns in many forms are excellent. On many nights you can get giant lobster for 135,000Rp. Balinese specialities can be ordered the day before.

Sea Breeze Cafe (☎ 41138; dishes 13,000-38,000Rp) Right by the beach off Jl Bina Ria, with an uninterrupted outlook. There's a range of Indonesian and Western dishes and good breakfasts. It's another spot for sunset drinks. The Sea Breeze Cabins here are good too (left).

Jasmine Kitchen (☎ 41565; Gang Binaria; dishes 15,000-30,000Rp) Enjoy excellent Thai fare in this elegant two-level restaurant. The menu is long and authentic; the staff gracious. Try the homemade ice cream for dessert amid the stylish surroundings.

Tropis Club (☎ 42090; Jl Ketepang; dishes 15,000-30,000Rp) The long menu at this beachside place includes wood-fired pizza, which may not transport you to Italy but may get you as far as Oman. It's an attractive place with a soaring roof.

Drinking

Lovina's social scene centres on Jl Bina Ria, which is happy-hour HQ and has several bar-restaurants.

Kantin (☎ 0812 460 7791; Jl Raya Lovina; dishes 6000-12,000Rp; 11am-2am) Funky open-air place where you can watch traffic by day and groove to acoustic guitar by night. It offers a long drinks list, fresh juices and coffees and a few local snacks.

Poco Evolution Bar (☎ 41535; Jl Bina Ria; dishes 12,000-18,000Rp; 11am-1am) At various times movies are shown and cover bands perform

PERAMA TOURIST SHUTTLE BUSES FROM LOVINA

Destination	Fare (Rp)
Candidasa	100,000
Kuta	70,000
Padangbai	100,000
Sanur	70,000
Ubud	30,000

at this popular place. There is an internet area off the bar. Classic travellers' fare is served.

Zigiz (Jl Bina Ria; small/large Bintang 6000/11,000Rp; 6pm-1am) This small place has walls covered in artwork and live music some nights. Other times you just keep hearing *'Play that funky music white boy.'*

Getting There & Away

BUS & BEMO

To reach Lovina from South Bali by public transport, you'll need to change in Singaraja (see p368). Regular blue bemos go from Singaraja's Banyuasri terminal to Kalibukbuk (about 6000Rp) – you can flag them down anywhere on the main road.

If you are coming by long-distance bus from the west, you can ask to be dropped off anywhere along the main road.

TOURIST SHUTTLE BUS

Perama buses stop at its office in front of **Hotel Perama** (☎ 41161; Jl Raya Lovina) in Anturan. Passengers are then ferried to other points on the Lovina strip (5000Rp). See the boxed text (above) for information on fares.

Getting Around

The Lovina strip is *very* spread out, but you can easily travel back and forth on bemos (2000Rp).

AROUND LOVINA

☎ 0362

There are some interesting sites in the slopes of the mountains behind the north coast.

Air Terjun Singsing

About 5km west of Kalibukbuk, turn left opposite Puri Singsing Hotel in Temukus village to reach this waterfall. It's about a 300m walk in, and the waterfall is not huge, but the pool underneath is good for swimming. The water isn't crystal clear, though it's cooler than the sea and very refreshing. You can clamber further up the hill to another waterfall (Singsing Dua), which is slightly bigger and has a mud bath that is supposedly good for the skin. This waterfall also cascades into a deep pool in which you can swim. Come in the wet season (October to March).

Air Panas Banjar

☎ 0362

Not far from Brahma Vihara Arama monastery, these **hot springs** (adult/child 4100/2000Rp, parking 1000Rp; 8am-6pm) are beautifully landscaped with lush tropical plants. You can relax here for a few hours and have lunch at the restaurant, or even stay the night.

Eight fierce-faced carved stone *naga* pour water from a natural hot spring into the first bath, which then overflows (via the mouths of five more *naga*), into a second, larger pool. In a third pool, water pours from 3m-high spouts to give you a pummelling massage.

It's only about 3km from the monastery to the hot springs if you take the short cut – go down to Banjar Tega, turn left in the centre of the village and follow the small road west, then south to Banjar village. From there it's a short distance uphill before you see the 'Air Panas 1km' sign on the left (on the corner by the police station).

Celukanbawang

Celukanbawang is the main cargo port for North Bali, and has a large wharf. Bugis schooners – the magnificent sailing ships that take their name from the seafaring Bugis people of Sulawesi – can sometimes be seen anchoring here.

West of Celukanbawang the road is sparsely populated.

PEMUTERAN

☎ 0362

This wonderfully isolated area, with limited facilities, has extensive, untouched coral reefs about 3km offshore, good snorkelling, and is handy for dive sites on Pulau Menjangan (p357) to the west.

The area is home to the Reef Seen Turtle Project, run by the Australian-owned **Reef Seen Aquatics** (☎ 93001; www.reefseen.com). Turtle eggs and small turtles purchased from locals are looked after here until they're ready for ocean release. More than 6000 turtles have been released since 1994. You can visit the small hatchery, see Boomer, the turtle who wouldn't leave, and make a donation to sponsor and release a tiny turtle.

Reef Seen also offers diving, boat cruises and horse riding. A PADI introductory dive costs US$55, and dives at Pemuteran/Pulau Menjangan are US$55/65 for two dives. Horse-riding treks pass through the local villages and beaches (250,000Rp for one hour). Simple accommodation (per room 150,000Rp) is available to dive guests and horse riders.

Pemuteran's hotels all have their own dive operations.

SLEEPING & EATING

Pemuteran is a delightful place to stay, with many midrange and top-end choices. There are several small warung along the main drag, otherwise all the hotels have good restaurants.

Jubawa Home Stay (☎ 94745; r 150,000-200,000Rp;) Not far from the Matahari, this cheery place is a good budget choice. The best rooms have hot water and air-con and guests have free internet access. The café serves Balinese and Thai food and there is a long list of cocktails. It's on the mountain side of the road.

Taman Sari Bali Cottages (☎ 288096; www.balitamansari.com; bungalows US$35-65, ste US$80-150;) Thirty-one rooms are set in gorgeous bungalows that feature intricate carvings and other traditional artwork. It's located on a long stretch of quiet beach. The resort is also involved in an off-shore reef restoration project – look for the wires snaking through the sand and water that provide low amounts of energy that stimulate growth.

Pondok Sari (☎ 92337; www.pondoksari.com; r US$38-45;) There are pleasant bungalows here with traditional rooms and lovely flower-filled open-air bathrooms. Snorkelling is possible off the beach. The restaurant (dishes 14,000Rp to 30,000Rp) features Western and Indonesian classics.

Matahari Beach Resort & Spa (☎ 92312; www.matahari-beach-resort.com; r US$169-440;) One of Bali's best hotels, the Matahari is an elegant place in an isolated location on the eastern outskirts of Pemuteran. Beautiful and traditionally furnished bungalows are set in attractive gardens, and the pool overlooks the black-sand beach. The most intriguing part of the resort, however, is the spa, which is like a grand water palace and is open to nonguests.

GETTING THERE & AWAY

Buses making the journey from Singaraja (12,000Rp) to the ferry port in Gilimanuk (8000Rp) pass Pemuteran. To reach South Bali, get a bus west and change in Cekik or Gilimanuk (p358).

Sumatra

Anchored tenuously in the deep Indian Ocean, this giant island is still as wild and unpredictable as the Victorian-era jungle-seekers dreamed. Millennia of chaos erupting from the earth's toxic core or from the fierce ocean waves create and destroy in equal measure. When the earth and sea remain still, the past's death and destruction fertilise a verdant future. The rugged mountains and fertile valleys are fed by near-constant rains colouring the jungles and the rice terraces many shades of green.

Sumatra is still visibly diverse, with more than 52 tribal languages and the full spectrum of societal organisation. In a few remaining pockets, hunter-gatherer tribes collaborate with the jungle for survival. Other tribes have sewn together the expectations of the outside world with their own customs. The Bataks of Danau Toba; the matrilineal Minangkabau of West Sumatra – each bus ride will deliver you to another tribal heartland.

Don't come looking for a holiday, that's Bali, or empire builders, that's Java. Sumatra is an adventure, the kind of demanding ride that requires a dusty knapsack and tough travelling skin. Climb up a smoking volcano, slog through muddy jungle paths, spot a wild orang-utan high up in the canopy, or scuba dive through a sculpted underwater landscape. Endure the Sumatran spin cycle and earn your rest amid a picturesque volcanic lake where you can slip into the morning mist and swim through the land before time.

HIGHLIGHTS

- Finding your inner Batak in laid-back **Danau Toba** (p399), where friends are forthcoming and days undemanding
- Checking out the orang-utan centre at **Bukit Lawang** (p390); it's better than Clint Eastwood's *Any Which Way But Loose* if you want encounters of the ape kind
- Sneaking a peek inside the gaseous volcano craters that ring the hill town of **Berastagi** (p394)
- Exploring underwater peaks and valleys at the dive sites around **Pulau Weh** (p422), a tropical island that hasn't sold out
- Casting off your city slicker in the scenic countryside around **Bukittinggi** (p441), where the matrilineal Minangkabau built soaring-roofed houses and the women told the men what to do

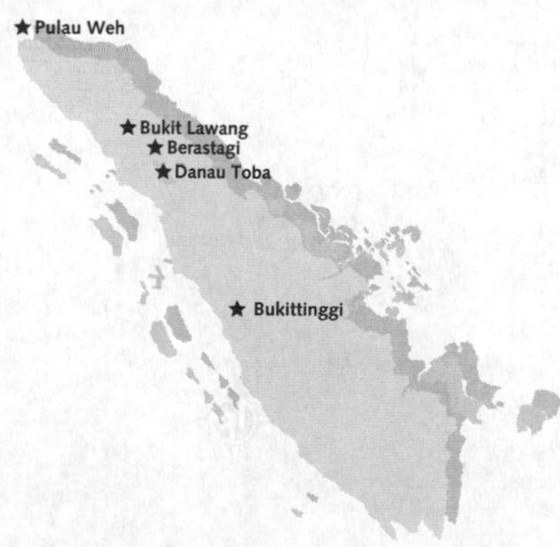

- POPULATION: 40 MILLION
- LAND AREA: 473,606 SQ KM (WORLD'S SIXTH-LARGEST ISLAND)
- HIGHEST PEAK: GUNUNG KERINCI (3805M)

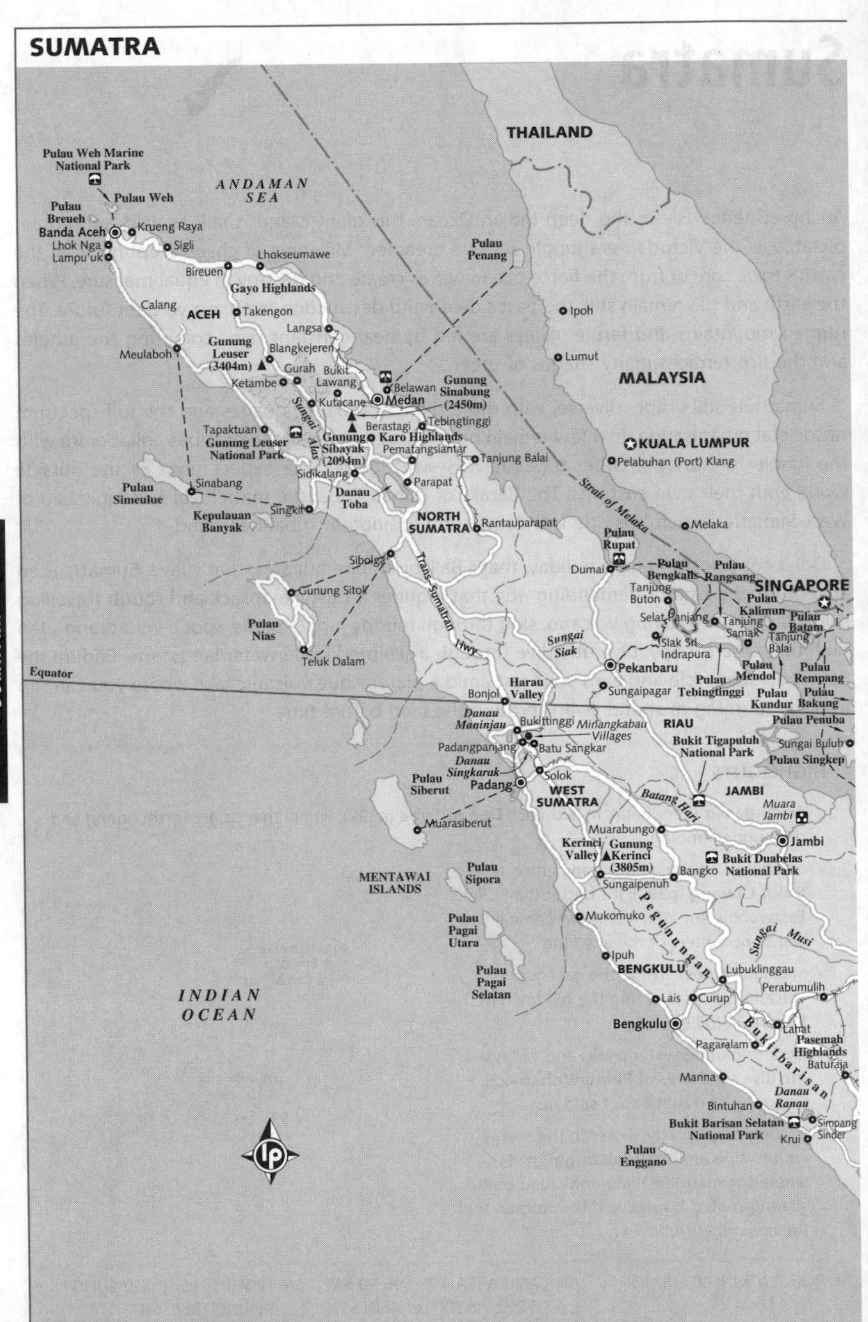
SUMATRA
THAILAND
Pulau Weh Marine National Park
Pulau Weh
ANDAMAN SEA
Pulau Breueh
Banda Aceh
Krueng Raya
Lhok Nga
Lampu'uk
Sigli
Pulau Penang
Lhokseumawe
Bireuen
Gayo Highlands
Calang
ACEH
Takengon
Ipoh
Langsa
Gunung Leuser (3404m)
Blangkejeren
Meulaboh
Lumut
Gurah
Ketambe
Bukit Lawang
Belawan
Gunung Sinabung (2450m)
MALAYSIA
Sungai Alas
Kutacane
Medan
Berastagi
Tebingtinggi
Tapaktuan
Gunung Sibayak (2094m)
Karo Highlands
Gunung Leuser National Park
Pematangsiantar
KUALA LUMPUR
Tanjung Balai
Pelabuhan (Port) Klang
Sidikalang
Parapat
Pulau Simeulue
Sinabang
Danau Toba
Strait of Melaka
Singkil
Kepulauan Banyak
NORTH SUMATRA
Rantauparapat
Melaka
Pulau Rupat
Sibolga
Trans-Sumatran Hwy
Dumai
Pulau Bengkalis
Pulau Rangsang
SINGAPORE
Gunung Sitoli
Tanjung Buton
Pulau Kalimun
Pulau Batam
Pulau Nias
Selat Panjang
Tanjung Samak
Tanjung Balai
Slak Sri Indrapura
Sungai Siak
Teluk Dalam
Pekanbaru
Pulau Mendol
Pulau Rempang
Equator
Harau Valley
Pulau Tebingtinggi
Pulau Kundur
Pulau Bakung
Sungaipagar
Bonjol
Danau Maninjau
Bukittinggi
Minangkabau Villages
RIAU
Pulau Penuba
Bukit Tigapuluh National Park
Sungai Buluh
Padangpanjang
Batu Sangkar
Pulau Singkep
Danau Singkarak
Solok
Pulau Siberut
Padang
WEST SUMATRA
Batang Hari
JAMBI
Muara Jambi
Muarasiberut
Muarabungo
Jambi
Kerinci Valley
Gunung Kerinci (3805m)
Bukit Duabelas National Park
MENTAWAI ISLANDS
Pulau Sipora
Bangko
Sungaipenuh
Pegunungan
Mukomuko
Pulau Pagai Utara
Sungai Musi
Ipuh
BENGKULU
Lubuklinggau
Pulau Pagai Selatan
Perabumulih
INDIAN OCEAN
Lais
Curup
Bengkulu
Lahat
Bukitbarisan
Pasemah Highlands
Pagaralam
Baturaja
Manna
Danau Ranau
Bintuhan
Bukit Barisan Selatan National Park
Simpang Sinder
Krui
Pulau Enggano

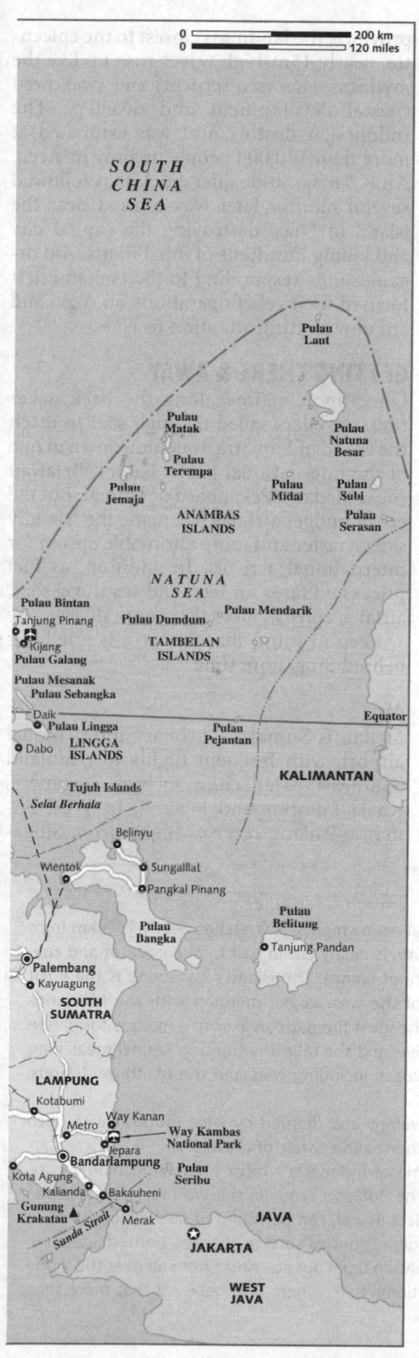

HISTORY

Pre-Islamic history is often more a matter of myth than fact, but archaeological evidence suggests that Sumatra was the gateway for migrating tribes from mainland Southeast Asia. Stone tools and shells unearthed north of Medan indicate that hunter-gatherers were living along the Strait of Melaka (Selat Malaka) 13,000 years ago. Two megalithic cultures appeared around 2000 years ago, one in the mountains of western Sumatra, and the other on Pulau Nias.

The Strait of Melaka, an important trade route between China and India, exposed the east coast of Sumatra to the regional superpowers and popular ideas of the day, such as Islam. The kingdom of Sriwijaya emerged as a local player at the end of the 7th century, with its capital presumably based near the modern city of Palembang. After Sriwijaya's influence waned, Aceh, in the northern tip of Sumatra, assumed control of trade through the strait. Aceh is presumably where Islam was first introduced to Indonesia by Muslim sea traders from Gujarat (western India). In the spirit of diplomacy and trade, the animist Acehnese adopted the faith of their visitors and continue to practise a more devout form of Islam than their neighbouring provinces. Aceh's control of the shipping route increased after its main rival, Melaka, fell to the Portuguese in 1511. The era of Aceh's sultanate prevailed until the beginning of the 17th century, when Dutch traders decided they wanted a piece of the spice trade.

The most influential port of the day, Samudra (meaning 'ocean'), near Lhokseumawe, eventually became the name that the traders used to refer to the entire island, alternatively referred to as Lesser Java. It was Marco Polo who corrupted the name to 'Sumatra' in his 1292 report on the area. In more poetic times, the island was known as Swarnadwipa (Island of Gold).

Throughout the colonial era, Sumatra saw almost every foreign power stake a claim in its resources: the Dutch based themselves in the West Sumatran port of Padang, the British ruled in Bencoolen (now Bengkulu), American traders monopolised pepper exports from Aceh, and the Chinese exploited tin reserves on the islands of Bangka and Belitung, east of Palembang. Oil and coffee were other prized Sumatran exports.

SUMATRA

In the early 19th century, the Dutch attempted to establish military control over all of Sumatra, a move met with resistance by the disparate tribes. In 1863, after three military expeditions, the Dutch finally established authority over Nias. Treaties and alliances brought other areas of Sumatra under Dutch rule, including Bengkulu, which the British willingly traded for Melaka.

A peace might have been brokered, but the Dutch were never welcomed in Sumatra, and the island contributed several key figures to the independence struggle, including future vice-president Mohammed Hatta and the first prime minister, Sutan Syahrir. Despite these liberators, Sumatra was as dissatisfied with Jakarta's rule as it was with the Dutch. From 1958 to 1961, rebel groups based in Bukittinggi and the mountains of South Sumatra resisted centralisation, resulting in clashes with the Indonesian military. Fiercely independent Aceh, though, proved to be Jakarta's most troublesome region. Aceh's separatist movement started in the late 1970s and continued until 2006 (see p414), with brief spells of quiet counterweighted with extreme repression by the Indonesian military.

No human conflict could compare to the destruction of the 2004 Boxing Day tsunami, in which a 9.0-plus-magnitude earthquake off the northwestern coast of Sumatra triggered a region-wide tsunami. In Aceh province, the landmass closest to the epicentre, nearly 15m-high waves rose up like the mythical *naga* (sea serpent) and swallowed coastal development and dwellers. The Indonesian death count was estimated at more than 170,000 people, mainly in Aceh. An 8.7-magnitude aftershock that followed several months later was centred near the island of Nias, destroying the capital city and killing hundreds of inhabitants. Aid organisations responding to the tsunami first focused their relief operations on Aceh and are now shifting attention to Nias.

GETTING THERE & AWAY

Once upon a time along the backpacker trail, travellers sailed the high seas to reach the island of Sumatra, touching down in one of the international ports: Batam, Belawan (near Medan), Pekanbaru or Dumai. But the era of budget airlines has made the friendly skies a faster and more affordable option for international arrivals. In addition, as fuel prices and fares for land and sea travel soar, airfares consistently take a nose dive.

Keep in mind that Sumatra is one hour behind Singapore time.

Air

Medan is Sumatra's primary international airport, with frequent flights to mainland Southeast Asian cities such as Singapore, Kuala Lumpur and Penang. In West Sumatra, Padang receives flights from Singa-

SUMATRA AU NATUREL

Sumatra's main superlatives come from its natural endowments: it stretches nearly 2000km from Banda Aceh in the north to Bakauheni in the south, is nearly cut in half by the equator and covers an area of 473,606 sq km, just shy of the size of France. The island's backbone is the Bukit Barisan range, which runs most of the length of the west coast, merging with the highlands around Danau Toba and central Aceh. Forming the most dramatic peaks are a military formation of almost 100 volcanoes; 15 of them are still active, and the tallest is Gunung Kerinci measuring in at 3805m. The string of islands off the west coast, including Nias and the Mentawai Islands, are geologically older than the rest of Sumatra.

The coastal lowlands on the east coast are swampy and drained by wide muddy rivers, such as Batang Hari, Siak and Musi, that empty into the shallow Strait of Melaka.

In the remaining forests, Sumatra boasts some of Indonesia's most interesting biodiversity. Flowers and primates top the naturalist's list. The *Rafflesia arnoldii*, the world's largest flower, and the *Amorphophallus titanum*, the world's tallest flower, can be found in pockets of the Bukit Barisan jungle. The island is also home to endangered species such as the two-horned Sumatran rhino, the honey bear, the elephant and the Sumatran tiger. But scientists from all over the world come to northern Sumatra's Gunung Leuser National Park, where it is believed that more than 5000 orang-utans still live in the wild.

VISA ON ARRIVAL

Regulations for visiting Indonesia are in flux. At the time of research, most nationalities could obtain a visa on arrival at the following international entry points, but check with an Indonesian consulate for the current situation.

- Pulau Batam: airport and the ports of Nongsa, Sekupang, Waterfront City (Teluk Senimba) and Batam Centre (p461).
- Pulau Bintan: ports of Tanjung Pinang, Bandar Bentan Telani Lagoi and Bandar Sri Udana Lobam in Tanjung Uban (p466).
- Medan: Polonia airport and Belawan port (p388).
- Pekanbaru: airport and port (p458).
- Padang: airport and Teluk Bayur port (p435).
- Dumai: Yos Sudarso port (p459) .
- Sibolga port (p406).

pore and Kuala Lumpur several times a week. In eastern Sumatra, Palembang is linked to Singapore. The primary international carriers include Garuda Indonesia, Malaysian Airlines, Lion Air, Tiger Airways, Air Asia, and Silk Air.

You can also hop on a plane from Jakarta to every major Sumatran city aboard Garuda, Merpati Nusantara Airlines, Jatayu, Adam Air, Mandala or Sriwijaya. Flights from Sumatra to other parts of Indonesia typically connect through Jakarta. One notable exception is Merpati's flight between Medan and Pontianak (Kalimantan).

Boat

Despite cheap airfares, many travellers still heed the call of the sea and enter Sumatra by ferry from Malaysia. Except for more remote islands, most destinations are more easily and affordably reached by air. There are two primary port options: Melaka (Malaysia) to Dumai (Indonesia) or Penang (Malaysia) to Belawan (Indonesia). If you don't have a lot of time to explore Sumatra, Belawan is your best option, as it is a short bus ride from Medan (see p388), which sits at the centre of most tourist attractions. Dumai is on Sumatra's east coast and is a five-hour bus ride to Bukittinggi; see p459 for more information.

From Singapore, ferries make the quick hop to Pulau Batam and Bintam, the primary islands in the Riau archipelago. These water routes are used mainly by Singaporean weekenders heading to the Riau islands' beaches and resorts.

From Batam, boats serve the following mainland Sumatran ports: Dumai, Palembang and Pekanbaru. Only a few backpackers use Batam as an entry into Sumatra because all but Dumai are a long way from postcard-worthy spots. See Pulau Batam (p462) or Pulau Bintan (p466) for more information on boat transfer between Singapore and beyond.

Ferries swim across the narrow Sunda Strait linking the southeastern tip of Sumatra at Bakauheni to Java's westernmost point of Merak. The sea crossing is a brief dip in a day-long voyage that requires several hours' worth of bus transport from both ports to Jakarta on the Java side and Bandarlampung on the Sumatran side. See p480 for more details.

Pelni-operated boats still paddle between Indonesia's islands, carrying freight and families. Except for more-remote islands, most destinations are more easily and affordably reached by air.

Check with local ticket agents for schedules and prices as both are subject to change.

GETTING AROUND

Most travellers bus around northern Sumatra and then hop on a plane to Java, largely avoiding the Third World conditions of Sumatra's highway system. Most of the island is mountainous jungle and the poorly maintained roads form a twisted pile of spaghetti on the undulating landscape. Don't count on getting anywhere very quickly on Sumatra.

On the other hand, Sumatra's airports are incongruously modern and numerous, providing a quick and cheap means of arrival or escape.

Air

An hour on a plane is an attractive alternative to what may seem like an eternity on a bone-shaking bus filled with chain smokers and cockroaches. For long-distance travel, airfares are competitive with bus and ferry fares, but routes within the island are limited. Medan to Banda Aceh and Medan to Gunung Sitoli are two popular air hops.

Domestic carriers include Merpati, Mandala, Jatayu, Adam Air, Lion Air and Sriwijaya. Sabang Merauke-Raya Air Charter (SMAC) flies to minor destinations that the bigger airlines don't bother with. See the Sumatra Airfares map (p380) for routes and sample fares.

All Sumatran airports charge an airport departure tax (between 15,000Rp and 30,000Rp) that is not included in your ticket. Ticket agents are located in the smallest of towns and typically charge 10% commission.

Boat

Most boat travel within Sumatra connects the main island with the many satellite islands lining the coast.

The most commonly used routes link Banda Aceh with Pulau Weh, Sibolga with

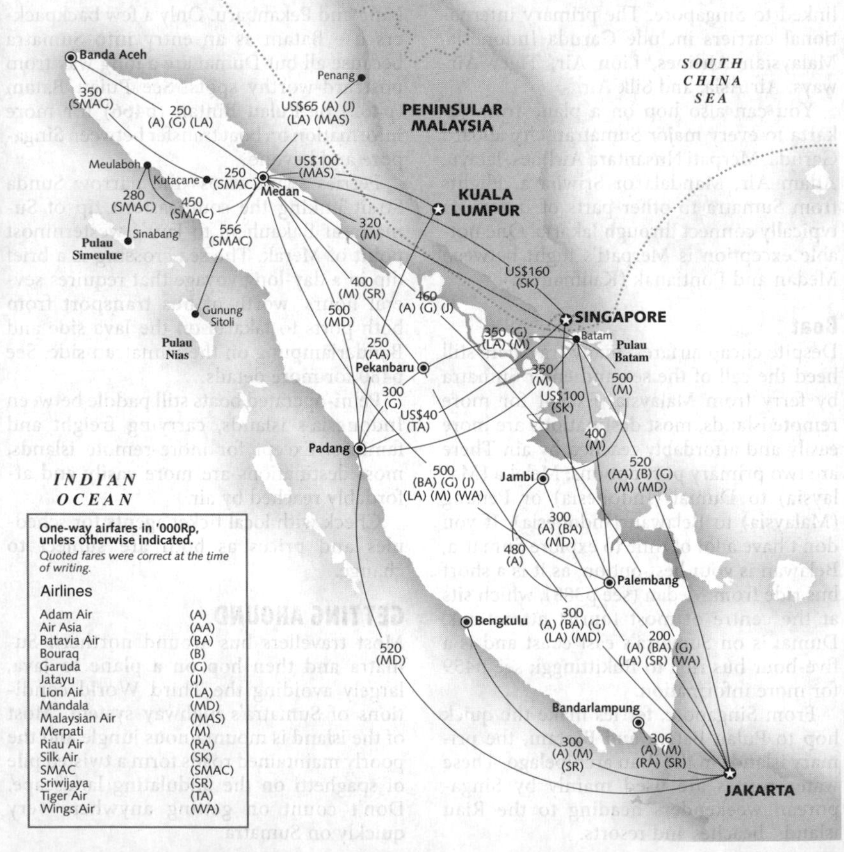

CULTURE IN A CAN

You could visit every tribal minority, hike every peak and read every anthropological study, but nothing puts you closer to 'Sumatra' than the economy buses. Grindingly slow, uncomfortable and thoroughly exhausting, economy buses are a cultural experience not to be missed.

Anything goes on economy: sacks of rice, chain-smoking, travelling cockroaches and unabashed littering. Often the roads are so twisty that drivers carry a stash of plastic bags for the weak stomachs. Welcome to the vomit route.

At various stops, young troubadours hop aboard and strum a few chords on the guitar. The collection hat is passed around and filled with spare cigarettes, snack food and wrinkled 1000Rp notes.

Then there are the tea and 'mystery' stops. Sometimes these stops are meal breaks at roadside cafés, other times they are prayer stops at local mosques. And still other times they are totally inexplicable and must surely be a quick visit by the bus driver to a clandestine girlfriend.

By and large, English isn't widely spoken in Sumatra, but occasionally the public bus is an exception. After circumnavigating the country, we found that all but two rides had a near-fluent passenger, usually a student or English-language graduate, and conversations meandered from their love of Kurt Cobain to the security of an Indonesian government job.

Pulau Nias, and Padang with Pulau Siberut (in the Mentawai Islands chain). In the less-visited areas of southeastern Sumatra, Jambi, Palembang and Pekanbaru are important towns for river transport. The Riau islands of Batam and Bintan are also linked to southeastern port towns by ferry.

Most long-distance ferries have several classes, ranging from filthy and crowded to filthy and less crowded. An upgrade in class might be a necessary luxury.

Bus

Bus is the most common mode of transport around Sumatra and in many cases is the only option for intercity travel. But it is far from efficient or comfortable. The primary thoroughfare is the Trans-Sumatran Hwy, which is little more than a jungle-bound animal track for beasts who eat petrol. Locals prefer a more affectionate term – 'chicken roads' – as the pavement inexplicably disappears, oncoming traffic must yield to one another and the potholes are as big as moon craters. It is not uncommon during the rainy season for mudslides to block the road or for bridges to wash out.

Most trips take extra long because of road conditions. At this laborious pace you have plenty of time to soak up the views: cascades of deep lush greens, terraced rice fields, mottled rushing rivers and isolated villages gathered around the communal well.

Buses range from economy sardine cans to modern air-con coaches. At the top of the class structure are super-executive buses with reclining seats, deep-freeze air-con, toilets, and an all-night serenade from Scorpions albums. Many passengers come prepared with winter hats, gloves and earplugs.

Bus terminals in Sumatra can range from modern and organised to run-down and abandoned. In some towns, you can go straight to the bus terminal to buy tickets and board buses, while other towns rely on bus company offices located outside the terminals. Ticket prices vary greatly depending on the quality of the bus and perceived gullibility of the traveller. It pays to shop around and to ask at your guesthouse about reliable companies; but do be aware that some accommodations act as booking agents and charge a commission for their services.

Local Transport

The usual Indonesian forms of transport – bemo/*opelet* (small minibuses), becak and *bendi* (two person horse-drawn carts) – are available for getting around towns and cities in Sumatra. The base rate for a bemo or *opelet* is 1500Rp to 2000Rp, while the minimum fare for becak and *bendi* is 5000Rp.

Establish a price for a becak ride before climbing aboard. For an *opelet*, you pay after you disembark.

Minibus

Back when Sumatra was crawling with backpackers, there were numerous tourist

TIPS FOR TOURISTS

- Spick-and-span cash – greenbacks and other foreign currencies might cross borders with ease but moneychangers in Sumatra want pristine bills. No rips, folds or pen marks. Some will even nit-pick over serial numbers.
- Bathroom fright night – you could be an old hand with the Asian sky bombers but toilets along the Sumatran bus route are sometimes a logistical challenge. That's the hole? Just wait till you get into the country and find that the hole is the river.
- Gratis? Never met him – when your economy is in the toilet, very few things are free. Hospitality without a tip? Try that trick in more prosperous times.
- Solo equals loco – forget language barriers, if you're travelling alone, especially women, you'll confuse the moustaches off Sumatrans. The West's appreciation of solo survival doesn't have a counterpart in Sumatran culture. And a woman with no male escort makes about as much sense as wearing a hot-dog costume.
- Happiness is an avocado shake – 'Hello mister' chases you through a fitful sleep until the 5am call to prayers. Everyone is a friend for hire. And you've started littering because garbage disposal seems so hopeless. Nothing puts a Wellbutrin glow on the day like an avocado shake.

minibuses that linked the major stops along the trail. These are long gone, but there are some locally used minibus services that can be more convenient than hustling out to the bus terminal. Some minibuses are in superb shape and provide door-to-door service, while others are a little rickety and shovel in more people than a clown car. Typically, tourists will end up paying more than the locals; negotiating a front seat ensures a little breathing room as the driver won't crowd his steering range. This way you get to look death head-on.

Train

The only useful train service in Sumatra runs from Bandarlampung (p480) to Palembang, and then on to Lubuklinggau. There are also less useful passenger trains from Medan to Pematangsiantar, Tanjung Balai and Rantauparapat.

NORTH SUMATRA

With surgical precision, most travellers make a delicate incision into North Sumatra's key attractions: orang-utans in Bukit Lawang, volcanoes in Berastagi, and hanging out in Danau Toba. Medan is the focal point of this circulation and sees new arrivals leave again in less than 24 hours.

North Sumatra stretches from the Indian Ocean to the Strait of Melaka and from sea to shining sea it is anything but homogenous. The rolling landscape varies from sweaty plains to cool highlands, while the houses of worship switch between the metal-domed mosques to the arrow-straight steeples of Christian churches. The coastal Malays, relatives of mainland Southeast Asia, live along the Strait of Melaka and are the largest ethnic group. In the highlands around Danau Toba are the delightful Batak, which are further subdivided into five classes. If you can name them all then you've either married into the clan or are destined to. Then there are the Pesisirs (central Tapanuli) along the Indian Ocean coastline and the megalithic culture of Pulau Nias (p407).

North Sumatra has a population of almost 12 million and is an economically robust province, producing more than 30% of Indonesia's exports. Oil, palm oil, tea and rubber are produced in large quantities and fine tobacco is grown in the rich soil around Medan.

MEDAN

☎ 061 / pop 2 million

Medan is the capital of North Sumatra and is the third-largest city in Indonesia. Depending on your perspective, you'll either love it or hate it. If you're coming from saner parts of mainland Southeast Asia, Medan will be everything that's wrong with an Asian city: choked with traffic, pollution and poverty. If you've worked your way north through Sumatra, Medan is thankfully modern, with air-con, internet and a middle class.

Most people only stay a night and grab transport out the next day. The city's major attraction is a graveyard of colonial buildings centred around Kesawan Square. For urban junkies, Medan has lots of confusing public transport to conquer.

History

Medan has had several major incarnations. The plains were once used as a battlefield between the kingdoms of Aceh and Deli (the word *medan* translates as 'field' or 'battlefield') from the end of the 16th century to the early 17th century.

But more importantly, Medan was a planter's trading post, a civilised district of tidy lanes and open-air cafés for society-deprived plantation owners. An enterprising Dutch planter named Nienhuys introduced tobacco to the area in 1865, which ushered in prosperity, imported Chinese labourers and investment in infrastructure. In 1886 the Dutch made it the capital of North Sumatra and by the end of Dutch rule the population had grown to about 80,000.

Once the Dutch were kicked out, Medan tossed off its starched uniform and grew as it pleased. A wealthy merchant class, mainly of ethnic Chinese, dominates the cosmopolitan side of town, while a handful of ethnic tribes from all over Sumatra make do in the run-down remainder. Animosity towards the Chinese erupted into violent rioting on Medan's streets on several occasions during the 1990s.

Orientation

The sprawling city of Medan radiates from the confluence of the Sungai Deli and Babura. Most backpackers head to the neighbourhood surrounding Mesjid Raya on Jl Sisingamangaraja (often abbreviated as 'SM Raja') for accommodation. North of this area is the city centre, organised around Jl Pandu and Jl Pemuda. The historic district occupies Jl Ahmad Yani around Lapangan Merdeka (Freedom Square). The manicured part of town is Polonia, west of Sungai Deli following the spine of Jl Imam Bonjol. Little India is sandwiched between Jl H Zainal Arifin, Jl Imam Bonjol and Jl Cik Ditiro.

Information

BOOKSHOPS

Finding English reading material in Sumatra is a hassle and Medan's slim pickings is a bumper crop compared to other stops on the road.

Gramedia bookshop Medan Mall (Jl Gajah Mada); Sun Plaza (Jl H Zainul Arifin) Good for maps and paperbacks.

INTERNET ACCESS

Internet access is available at most of the large shopping plazas and costs 5000Rp per hour.

Nusa Net (Jl SM Raja) Basement of Yuki Plaza.

Indo.net (Jl RH Juanda)

MEDICAL SERVICES

For an ambulance, dial ☎ 118.

Rumah Sakit Gleneagles (☎ 4566368; Jl Listrik 6) The best hospital in the city, with a 24-hour walk-in clinic and pharmacy, as well as English-speaking doctors and specialists.

MONEY

Medan has branches of just about every bank operating in Indonesia. Most banks are headquartered along the junction of Jl Diponegoro and Jl H Zainal Arifin.

SUMATRA IS BURNING

Every year smoke and haze from fires used to clear farmland and plantations choke the skies over the island and its neighbours, sometimes downing planes and closing schools as far away as Kuala Lumpur. Malaysia complains bitterly about its inconsiderate neighbour and promises are made by Indonesian officials that next year won't be as bad, until next year comes. As for Sumatra, fires are part of the family. In the evening, backyard burn piles are most communities' solution to a lack of municipal garbage collection. Mini fires follow people throughout the day as most Sumatrans, men and women, are chain smokers. These clove-smoking dragons are so comfortable with a cigarette that it often looks like an extra digit. Cigarettes are so much more than a habit or a hobby: they are a social lubricant, the accepted payment for a medicine man and an offering to the deceased. Perhaps it is the influence of the smoking volcanoes that encourages the Sumatrans to light up.

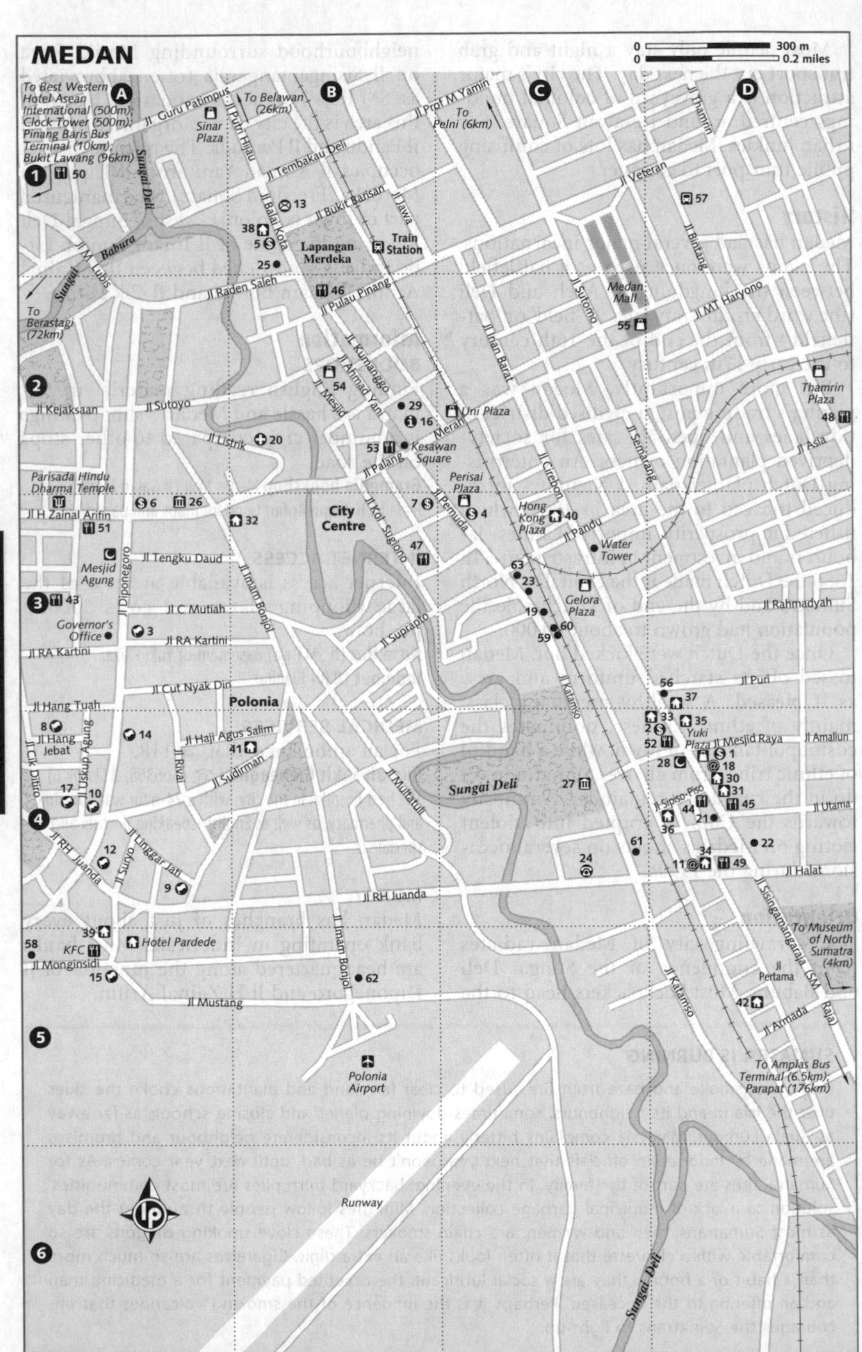
MEDAN
0 300 m
0 0.2 miles
A
B
C
D
1
2
3
4
5
6
To Best Western Hotel Asean International (500m); Clock Tower (500m); Pinang Baris Bus Terminal (10km); Bukit Lawang (96km)
To Belawan (26km)
To Pelni (6km)
To Berastagi (72km)
To Museum of North Sumatra (4km)
To Amplas Bus Terminal (6.5km); Parapat (176km)
Jl Guru Patimpus
Sinar Plaza
Jl Putri Hijau
Sungai Deli
Sungai Babura
Jl M Lubis
Jl Tembakau Deli
Jl Prof M Yamin
Jl Thamrin
Jl Veteran
Jl Bukit Barisan
Jl Balai Kota
Jl Jawa
Lapangan Merdeka
Train Station
Jl Raden Saleh
Jl Pulau Pinang
Jl Bintang
Medan Mall
Jl Sutomo
Jl MT Haryono
Jl Kumanggo
Jl Ahmad Yani
Jl Mesjid
Jl Inan Barat
Thamrin Plaza
Jl Kejaksaan
Jl Sutoyo
Jl Listrik
Uni Plaza
Kesawan Square
Jl Palang Merah
Jl Semarang
Jl Asia
Parisada Hindu Dharma Temple
Jl H Zainal Arifin
Perisai Plaza
City Centre
Jl Kol Sugiono
Jl Pemuda
Jl Cirebon
Hong Kong Plaza
Jl Pandu
Water Tower
Jl Tengku Daud
Mesjid Agung
Jl Diponegoro
Jl Imam Bonjol
Gelora Plaza
Jl C Mutiah
Governor's Office
Jl RA Kartini
Jl Suprapto
Jl Rahmadyah
Jl Cut Nyak Din
Jl Puri
Jl Hang Tuah
Polonia
Jl Katamso
Jl Hang Jebat
Jl Uskup Agung
Jl Haji Agus Salim
Jl Rivai
Yuki Plaza
Jl Mesjid Raya
Jl Amaliun
Jl Cik Ditiro
Jl Sudirman
Jl Multatuli
Sungai Deli
Jl Sipiso-Piso
Jl Utama
Jl RH Juanda
Jl Suryo
Jl Linggar Jati
Jl Halat
Jl Sisingamangaraja (SM Raja)
Hotel Pardede
KFC
Jl Monginsidi
Jl Mustang
Jl Pertama
Jl Armada
Polonia Airport
Runway
Sungai Deli
lp
1 2 3 4 5 6 7 8 9 10 11 12 13 14 15 16 17 18 19 20 21 22 23 24 25 26 27 28 29 30 31 32 33 34 35 36 37 38 39 40 41 42 43 44 45 46 47 48 49 50 51 52 53 54 55 56 57 58 59 60 61 62 63

SUMATRA

INFORMATION
ATM Complex....1 D4
ATM Complex....2 D4
Australian Consulate....3 A3
Bank....4 C3
Bank Indonesia....5 B1
BCA Bank....6 A3
BNI Bank....7 B3
Denmark Consulate....8 A4
Finland Consulate....(see 8)
German Consulate....9 A4
Gramedia Bookshop....(see 55)
Gramedia Bookshop....(see 51)
Hotel Danau Toba International....(see 32)
Indian Consulate....10 A4
Indo.net....11 D4
Japanese Consulate....12 A4
Main Post Office....13 B1
Malaysian Consulate....14 A4
Netherlands Consulate....15 A5
North Sumatra Tourist Office....16 B2
Norwegian Consulate....17 A4
Novotel Soechi Medan....(see 40)
Nusa Net....18 D4
Perdana Express....19 C3
Rumah Sakit Gleneagles....20 B2
Sukma Medan....21 D4
Tobali Tour & Travel....22 D4
Trophy Tours....23 C3
Wartel....24 C4

SIGHTS & ACTIVITIES
Balai Kota....25 B1
Bukit Barisan Military Museum....26 A3
Istana Maimoon....27 C4
Mesjid Raya....28 D4
Tjong A Fie Mansion....29 B2

SLEEPING
Deli Raya Hotel....30 D4
Hotel Alamanda....31 D4
Hotel Danau Toba International....32 B3
Hotel Garuda Citra....(see 35)
Hotel Garuda Plaza....33 D4
Hotel Raya....34 D4
Hotel Sumatra....35 D4
Hotel Zakia....36 D4
Ibunda Hotel....37 D3
Inna Dharma Deli....38 B1
JJ's Guesthouse....39 A5
Novotel Soechi Medan....40 C3
Polonia Hotel....41 B4
Sarah's Guest House....42 D5

EATING
Bollywood Food Centre....43 A3
Corner Café Raya....44 D4
Majestik Bakery & Cafe....45 D4
Merdeka Walk....46 B2
Pasar Buah Berastagi....47 B3
Pasar Ramai....48 D2
Rumah Makan Famili....(see 37)
Rumah Makan Sibolga....49 D4
Sumatera Vegetarian Restaurant....50 A1
Sun Plaza....51 A3
Taman Rekreasi Seri Deli....52 D4
Tip Top Restaurant....53 B2

SHOPPING
Arts & Crafts Shops....54 B2
Medan Mall....55 C2

TRANSPORT
Adam Air....(see 33)
Air Asia....56 D3
Buses to Singkil (Singkil Raya)....57 D1
Garuda....58 A5
Jatayu Airlines....59 C3
Karitika Air....60 C3
Malaysian Airlines....(see 32)
Merpati....61 C4
National Car Rental....(see 30)
Silk Air....(see 41)
SMAC....62 B5
Sriwijaya Air....63 C3

Bank Danamon (JL Pemuda)
Bank Indonesia (Jl Balai Kota)
BCA bank (Bank Central Asia; Jl H Zainal Arifin)
BNI bank (Bank Negara Indonesia; Jl Pemuda)

There are ATMs all over the city. Try the following:
ATM (Yuki Plaza, Jl SM Raja)
ATM (Hotel Garuda Plaza, Jl SM Raja)

Shop around, as exchange rates can differ significantly from bank to bank. Medan typically offers the best rates on the island.

Outside of banking hours (see p845), there are moneychangers on the corner of Jl Sipiso-Piso and Jl SM Raja, as well as at travel agencies on Jl Katamso.

POST
Main post office (Jl Bukit Barisan; 8am-6pm) Located in an old Dutch building on the main square; fax, photocopy and parcel services are available.

TELEPHONE
International calls can be made at several wartel around town. The following have Home Country Direct phones:
Hotel Danau Toba International (☎ 4157000; Jl Imam Bonjol 17)
Novotel Soechi Medan (☎ 4561234; Jl Cirebon 76A)

TOURIST INFORMATION
There is an information desk at the domestic arrivals terminal at the airport.
North Sumatra Tourist Office (☎ 4528436; Jl Ahmad Yani 107; 8am-4pm Mon-Fri) Brochures, maps and basic information.

TRAVEL AGENCIES
Jl Katamso is packed with travel agencies that handle air tickets and ferry tickets.
Perdana Express (☎ 4566222; Jl Katamso 35C) Sells Pelni and Penang ferry tickets.
Sukma Medan (☎ 7325418; Jl SM Raja 92A) Sells Penang ferry tickets.
Tobali Tour & Travel (☎ 7324472; Jl SM Raja 79C) For tourist buses to Danau Toba.
Trophy Tours (☎ 4155666; fax 451 1243; Jl Katamso 33D) Ticket agent for most of the airlines (1st floor), and tour operator (2nd floor).

Dangers & Annoyances
Use big-city common sense in Medan. Watch your bags, as snatch thieves are prevalent. To keep your sanity, remember that you don't have to speak to everyone who speaks to you. It is common practice in Indonesia for becak drivers to call out to pedestrians to solicit business. You'll get a 'Hello mister' or even a 'Hello, you like cigarette?' every few feet, but not responding is perfectly acceptable if you don't want to go

anywhere. Although this may seem rude, in Sumatra a response is an invitation.

Sights

ISTANA MAIMOON

The crumbling **Maimoon Palace** (Jl Katamso; admission by donation; ⏰ 8am-5pm) was built by the sultan of Deli in 1888. The building is badly in need of restoration and is a good introduction to what all of Sumatra looks like.

MESJID RAYA

Just around the corner from the palace is the unusual black-domed **Grand Mosque** (cnr Jl Mesjid Raya & SM Raja; admission by donation; ⏰ 9am-5pm, except prayer times), which was commissioned by the sultan in 1906. The Moroccan-style building has ornate carvings, Italian marble and stained glass from China.

Dress modestly when visiting the mosque – women are asked to cover their heads with the scarves provided.

MUSEUMS

The **Museum of North Sumatra** (☎ 7716792; Jl HM Joni 51; admission 1000Rp; ⏰ 8.30am-noon & 1.30-5pm Tue-Sun) has an extensive collection of dog-eared artefacts covering North Sumatran history and culture and some fine stone carvings from Nias.

Bukit Barisan Military Museum (Jl H Zainal Arifin 8; admission by donation; ⏰ 8am-1pm Mon-Thu & Sat), near the Hotel Danau Toba International, has a small collection of weapons, photos and memorabilia from WWII, the War of Independence and the Sumatran rebellion of 1958.

COLONIAL MEDAN

Ghosts of Medan's colonial mercantile past are still visible along Jl Ahmad Yani from Jl Palang Merah north to Lapangan Merdeka. Some are still stately relics, while others have been gutted and turned into parking garages, demonstrating the enduring friendship between Indonesia and its former coloniser.

Tjong A Fie Mansion (closed to public) is the former residence of a famous Chinese merchant; his home, which mixes Victorian and Chinese styles, is intentionally similar to his cousin's (Cheong Fatt Tze) home in Penang. Across the street is Tip Top Restaurant (see opposite), an historic spot for sipping colonial nostalgia. Further north is Lapangan Merdeka, a former parade ground surrounded by handsome Art Deco buildings, such as the Bank Indonesia, Balai Kota (Town Hall) and the post office.

For more information about Medan's colonial architecture, check out *Tours Through Historic Medan and its Surroundings* by Dirk A Buiskool, a longtime Medan resident. The author also operates **Tri Jaya Tour & Travel** (☎ 7032967; www.trijaya-travel.com), which offers historic city tours.

Sleeping

Medan's budget options aren't the best value in Sumatra and you'll get more for your money in the midrange category. The majority of accommodation is on or near Jl SM Raja.

BUDGET

Sarah's Guest House (☎ 7358729; Jl Pertama 12; d from 30,000Rp) A friendly, family-run place, tucked away on a quiet road.

Hotel Zakia (☎ 7322413; Jl Sipiso-Piso 12; d 40,000-45,000Rp) Most backpackers' default choice, Zakia seems great until you've been feasted on by bedbugs.

Hotel Alamanda (☎ 7343507; Jl SM Raja 59/81A; d 40,000-60,000Rp) Not much going for it but location.

Hotel Raya (☎ 73666601; Jl RH Juanda 53; d 45,000-75,000Rp; ❄) A bit of an improvement from the other SM Raja cheapies.

JJ's Guesthouse (☎ 4578411; www.guesthousemedan.com; Jl Suryo 18; s/d 75,000/145,000) In an old Dutch villa, JJ's has tidy boarding house–style rooms run by a mannerly Indonesian woman. The guesthouse is a quick becak ride to/from the airport (5000Rp), but they have a terrible time finding the place. It's across the street from the KFC and behind Hotel Pardede. Rates include breakfast and lots of chitchat.

MIDRANGE

Hotel tax and breakfast are included in the quoted rates.

Ibunda Hotel (☎ 7345555; fax 7358989; Jl SM Raja 31; d 150,000-200,000Rp; ❄) A cheery spot, with minty green walls and new tiled baths.

Hotel Sumatera (☎ 7321551; Jl SM Raja 35; d 180,000-200,000Rp; ❄) Add another zero to the price tag and rooms in Medan start to look a lot better.

Hotel Garuda Citra (☎ 7367733; fax 7360564; Jl SM Raja 27; d 200,000Rp; ❄) The rooms are better than the common space would suggest.

Hotel Danau Toba International (☎ 4157000; fax 4530553; Jl Imam Bonjol 17; d 269,000/300,000Rp;) A mini resort near the airport, Danau Toba International is starting to show its age, but Sumatra isn't youth-obsessed.

TOP END

Medan's best hotels all have the standard top-end facilities you'd expect such as fitness centres, swimming pools and 24-hour room service.

Hotel Garuda Plaza (☎ 7361111; fax 7364411; Jl SM Raja 18; r 300,000-900,000Rp;) Almost hip, Garuda Plaza is Medan's homage to Jakarta, with modern, corporate accents.

Hotel Deli River (☎ 7032965; Jl Raya Namorambe 129; r 400,000Rp;) Outside the city chaos, this family-run hotel is shaded by fruit trees and overlooks the Deli River. The hotel provides free transfers from the airport and rates include breakfast.

Polonia Hotel (☎ 4142222; fax 4538870; Jl Jend Sudirman 14; d from 400,000-500,000Rp;) Close to the airport, in the aristocratic section of Medan.

Some other international-standard hotels are:

Novotel Soechi Medan (☎ 4561234; Jl Cirebon 76A;)

Best Western Hotel Asean International (☎ 575 888; cnr Jl Gatot Subroto & Glugur bypass;)

Inna Dharma Deli (☎ 7744; Jl Balai Kota 2; r from 475,000;) Occupies the site of a colonial hotel, supposedly where Mata Hari was once bedded.

Eating

Medan has the most varied selection of cuisines in Sumatra, from basic Malay-style *mie* (noodle) and *nasi* (rice) joints, to top-class hotel restaurants.

For Chinese food, let your tummy do a tour of Medan's **night market** (Pasar Malam; Jl Semarang), east of the railway line, off Jl Pandu. Lots of simple warungs occupy the front courtyards of the houses in the little lanes around Mesjid Raya; the menu is on display with a few pre-made curries, coffee, tea and sometimes juices.

Majestik Bakery & Cafe (Jl SM Raja 71; pastries 2000Rp) Keep the munchies at bay during a long bus ride with sweets from this super-sized bakery.

Rumah Makan Famili (Jl SM Raja 31; dishes from 6000Rp) A well-known Padang spot, on the ground floor of Ibunda Hotel, for beef rendang with duck egg. The restaurant is a refreshing space drowning out traffic with an indoor waterfall and lots of high-flying businessmen meeting over lunch. You can also get the wacky meats: bowel, brain or heart simmered in coconut milk.

Rumah Makan Sibolga (Jl RH Juanda 65; dishes from 6000Rp) Near the travellers haunt, Sibolga can take good care of timid foreigners who pull up a chair.

Taman Rekreasi Seri Deli (Jl SM Raja; dishes from 8000Rp; evening only) For basic Malay food, this venue, opposite the Mesjid Raya, is a slightly upmarket approach to stall dining. But the *keropok* (cracker) sellers, blind beggars and spoon players might find you more of an oddity than vice versa.

Bollywood Food Centre (☎ 4536494; Jl Muara Takus 7; dishes from 10,000Rp) Lip-smacking Indian-style curries are a family affair at this blindingly bright restaurant in Little India (Kampung Keling). It also serves cold Bintang. Malay-Indian roti shops are located nearby.

Sumatera Vegetarian Restaurant (Jl Gatot Subroto 35; mains 10,000Rp) For vegetarians, this is the place to go when you just can't face another *gado gado* (dish with mixed vegetables and coconut sauce).

Tip Top Restaurant (Jl Ahmad Yani 92; dishes 10,000-15,000Rp) Only the prices have changed at this old colonial relic, great for a drink of bygone imperialism. The menu, with typewriter font and 1950s dishes, should be enshrined in a museum rather than used to sate hunger.

Merdeka Walk (Lapangan Merdeka, Jl Balai Kota; dishes 10,000-15,000Rp; 5-11pm) Inspired by Singapore's alfresco dining, this collection of outdoor cafés occupies Lapangan Merdeka and is anchored by one of the shiniest McDonald's you'll see outside the Soviet bloc.

Corner Café Raya (cnr Jl SM Raja & Sipiso-Piso 1; dishes 12,000-18,000Rp; 24hrs) A Western expat and his Indonesian wife run this home-away-from-home café, complete with breakfast fry-ups, cold beer, international TV and travellers' advice. There's talk of opening up some of the upstairs rooms for rent.

Pasar Ramai (Ramani Market; Jl Thamrin) The main fruit market, next to Thamrin Plaza, is a profusion of colour and smells, and has an impressive selection of local and imported tropical fruit.

Pasar Buah Berastagi (Berastagi Fruit Market; Jl Kol Sugiono) An upmarket, air-con shop more conveniently located to fruit lovers.

Sun Plaza (cnr Jl Ainul Arifin & Diponegoro) The whole city have flipped their wristwatches over this shiny new shopping centre, where there's a, get this, Starbucks, pan-Asian food court, European-style restaurants and a startling amount of affluence.

Shopping

Medan has a number of interesting arts and crafts shops, particularly along Jl Ahmad Yani. **Toko Asli** (No 62), **Toko Rufino** (No 56) and **Toko Bali Arts** (No 68) all have selections of antique weaving, Dutch pottery and carvings.

Clothes, shoes, jewellery, electrical goods and cosmetics can be found at any of Medan's multilevel shopping centres. Most also have well-stocked supermarkets.

Getting There & Away

Medan is Sumatra's main international arrival and departure point.

AIR

Medan's Polonia Airport is 2km south of the city centre. Remember that there is an airport tax for departing flights (see the boxed text on p871).

There are daily international flights from Medan to Singapore, Kuala Lumpur and Penang. Domestic flights connect Medan to Jakarta, Banda Aceh, Pekanbaru, Padang, Batam, Pontianak and Gunung Sitoli. See the Sumatra Airfares map (p380) for sample fares.

The following airlines have offices in Medan and serve the destinations as listed:

Adam Air (☎ 734999; www.flyadamair.com; Hotel Garuda Plaza, Jl SM Raja 18) Banda Aceh, Jakarta, Penang.

Air Asia (☎ 7331988; www.airasia.com; Jl SM Raja 19) Jakarta, Kuala Lumpur.

Garuda (Garuda Indonesia; ☎ 4147744) Jl Monginsidi 340 (Jl Monginsidi 340); Jl Balai Kota 2 (Inna Dharma Deli, Jl Balai Kota 2) Jakarta, Banda Aceh.

Jatayu Airlines (☎ 4528988; www.jatayuairlines.co.id; Jl Katamso 62A) Banda Aceh, Ipoh, Jakarta, Lhokseumawe, Padang, Penang, Surabaya.

Karitika Air (☎ 4522433; Jl Katamso 37) Banda Aceh, Batam.

Malaysian Airlines (☎ 4519333; www.malaysiaairlines.com; Hotel Danau Toba International, Jl Imam Bonjol 17) Kuala Lumpur, Penang.

Merpati (Merpati Nusantara Airlines; ☎ 321888; www.merpati.co.id; Jl Katamso 219) Batam, Gunung Sitoli, Jakarta, Palembang, Pekanbaru, Pontianak.

Silk Air (☎ 4537744; www.silkair.com; Hotel Polonia, Jl Sudirman 14) Singapore.

SMAC (☎ 4551888; Jl Imam Bonjol 59) Simeulue, Gunung Sitoli.

Sriwijaya Air (☎ 4552111; Jl Katamso 29) Pekanbaru.

BOAT

High-speed ferries (140/210 Malaysian ringgit one way/return; five hours; 10am daily) depart from the port of Belawan, 26km from Medan, to the Malaysian city of Penang.

There is a 30,000Rp surcharge for harbour tax and a bus transfer to Belawan from Medan; see the boxed text on below about transfer in the opposite direction. Tickets

THE WATERS OF FORGETTING: PENANG TO MEDAN

It must be difficult to mark time when each day looks the same. Every day tourists get off the boat at Belawan convinced that they've already paid for land transport to Medan and every day the same characters tell them that they are mistaken. Didn't we ask in Penang, the travellers ask each other? Shrugs, convictions, indifference. Tomorrow will be a repeat of today.

You see, the bus transfer to Medan, like all the great philosophical matters, is relative. In Malaysia, transfer from port to city is included. But cross the ocean and the answer is different.

That is, unless you have the key to uniformity: a separate bus ticket. If you received this crucial slip, then hold on to it until you're comfortably seated in a bus going somewhere within Medan's city limits.

Most buses picking up tourists are run by ticket agents in Medan and will deposit everyone at their office somewhere within the city limits. (Different agents, different buses, different offices.) All of this equals lots of potential for ripping off tourists.

If you want to skip all this nonsense, green *opelet* 81 runs between Belawan and Medan (7000Rp).

can be bought from agents on Jl Katamso or Jl SM Raja (see p385). Buses depart Medan at 8am.

Pelni ships sail to Jakarta and Batam. The **Pelni office** (☎ 6622526; Jl Krakatau 17A) is 8km north of the city centre, but it is much easier to buy tickets and check schedules from the agencies on Jl Katamso.

BUS

There are two major bus terminals in Medan: Amplas, serving southern destinations, and Pinang Baris, serving northern destinations. For long-distance travel, most people deal directly with the bus ticketing offices located outside of the terminals.

Amplas bus terminal is 6.5km south of the city centre along Jl SM Raja. Almost any *opelet* heading south on Jl SM Raja will get you to Amplas (3000Rp). Bus ticket offices line the street nearby at Km 6 and include the following:

ANS (☎ 7867603) Serves Bukittinggi (air-con/executive 110,000/190,000Rp, 20 hours).
ALS (☎ 7866685) Also serves Bukittinggi – same details as ANS.
Pelangi (☎ 7863026) Runs buses to Pekanbaru (air-con/super-executive 120,000/160,000Rp, 12 hours) and Banda Aceh (air-con/executive 100,000/170,000Rp, 13 hours).
Kurnia (☎ 7016417; Jl SM Raja, Km 6) Runs buses to Jambi (air-con 220,000Rp, 24 hours) and Palembang (250,000Rp, 36 hours).

There are frequent public buses to Parapat (30,000Rp, five hours), the jumping-off point to Danau Toba. Minibuses (80,000Rp) also leave from **Tobali Tour & Travel** (☎ 7324472; Jl SM Raja 79C).

Pinang Baris bus terminal (Jl Gatot Subroto), 10km west of the city centre, serves northern destinations. Get there by taxi (25,000Rp) or by *opelet* 24, 37 or 64 (5000Rp).

There are frequent public buses to both Bukit Lawang (8000Rp, three hours) and Berastagi (7000Rp, two hours) every half-hour between 5.30am and 6pm.

Although there are buses to Banda Aceh from here, it is easier to get to the Pelangi ticket agent near Amplas.

A minibus departs at 8pm daily for Singkil (70,000Rp, 10 hours), the departure point for boats to the Banyak Islands. Buses depart from **Singkil Raya** (☎ 081 26560739; Jl Bintan), past the caged bird warehouses. Take *opelet* 53 from Jl SM Raja to Medal Mall.

CAR

Chauffeur-driven car rental can be arranged through most of the major hotels. **National Car Rental** (☎ 4157744, ext 766; Deli Raya Hotel, Jl Balai Kota 2) rents self-drive cars for 100,000Rp per day within Medan city limits.

TRAIN

Rail services are very limited, with just two trains a day to Tanjung Balai (business class only, 30,000Rp). There are four trains daily to Rantauparapat (business/executive 50,000/70,000Rp).

Getting Around

TO/FROM THE AIRPORT

It is cheaper and less of a hassle to sail past the throng of taxi drivers to the becak queue at the airport gate (becak aren't allowed inside the airport). It should cost 7000Rp to 10,000Rp to reach the hotel district on Jl SM Raja. But if you like to haggle, a taxi ride should cost 20,000Rp.

PUBLIC TRANSPORT

Medan's got more *opelet* than you can shake a spoon player at. They cost 2500Rp for most in-town destinations. Here are a few helpful routes: white Mr X from Jl SM Raja to Kesawan Square, Lapangan Merdeka and train station; and yellow 64 from Maimmon Palace to Sun Plaza.

For becak, reckon on paying about 5000Rp for most destinations. But they'll ask you to pay more than double that.

BUKIT LAWANG

☎ 061 / pop 30,000

Imagine yourself a little hairier and better with your toes and you've got Bukit Lawang's main attraction: the orang-utan.

Bukit Lawang is one of the most accessible places to spot this reclusive primate, thanks to an orang-utan conservation programme that has been operating on the eastern edge of the Gunung Leuser National Park (p427) since the 1970s. The national park is one of the orang-utan's last remaining strongholds, with more than 5000 animals thought to be living in the wild.

Since the village is only 96km northwest of Medan, Bukit Lawang is also one of the easiest places from which to make the leap into the jungle, a diverse and rugged forest crisscrossed by clear, fast-flowing rivers.

SUMATRA

RED-HEADED COUSINS

Orang-utans, the world's largest arboreal mammal, once swung through the forest canopy throughout all of Southeast Asia, but are now found only in Sumatra and Borneo. Researchers fear that the few that do remain will not survive the continued loss of habitat to logging and agriculture.

While orang-utans are extremely intelligent animals, their way of life isn't compatible with a shrinking forest. Orang-utans are mostly vegetarians; they get big and strong (some males weigh up to 90kg) from a diet that would make a Californian hippie proud: fruit, shoots, leaves, nuts and tree bark, which they grind up with their powerful jaws and teeth. They occasionally also eat insects, eggs and small mammals.

And all of the forest is their pantry, requiring them to migrate through a large territory following the fruit season. But they aren't social creatures; they prefer a solitary existence foraging during the day and building a new nest every night high up in the trees away from predators.

Orang-utans have a long life span, often living up to 30 to 40 years old in the wild. They breed slowly and have few young. Females reach sexual maturity at about the age of 10 and remain fertile until about the age of 30, on average having only one baby every six years. Only the females raise the young, which stay with their mothers until reaching sexual maturity.

The 'orang hutan' (a Malay word for 'person of the forest') has an extremely expressive face that has often suggested a very close kinship with the hairless ape (humans). But of all the great apes, the orang-utans are considered to be the most distantly related to humans.

Many tourists slip-slide through the mud and undergrowth on multi-day treks and hobble back to the village to recuperate.

Bukit Lawang was extensively damaged by a flash flood in November 2003, which killed 280 people and destroyed much of the riverfront development. The essentials of the town and tourist infrastructure have been rebuilt but the community is still grieving for lost relatives and livelihoods.

Orientation & Information

The nearby village of Gotong Royong, 2km east of the river, has effectively become the new town centre. About a kilometre north of the bus stop begins the stretch of riverside accommodation.

There are no banks, but a local travel agent will change money. There is no post office here, but you can buy stamps from the shops and use a local post box. There is a market on Friday and on Sunday in Bohorok town, 15km away, where you will also find the nearest police station and clinic.

Bukit Lawang Visitors Centre (🕒 8am-3pm) Displays of flora and fauna found in Gunung Leuser National Park, plus a book of medicinal plants and their uses, and fashion shots of some of the rehabilitated orang-utans. Exhibits are decidedly faded but it is still worth a look. Past visitors often record reviews of guides in the sign-in book.

PHKA ranger station (🕒 7am-3pm) This office isn't too eager to receive visitors, although its sign suggests otherwise.

PHKA permit office (park entrance) Timed with the orang-utan feedings, the rangers open up this office to collect permit fees; don't bother arranging permits in town.

Bukit Lawang Guide Association (hours vary) Located across the street from the visitors centre, this place distributes a rate sheet for hikes and its touts will follow you around town until you sign up for a hike.

Dangers & Annoyances

The guide harangue starts on the bus before you've even left Medan. A friendly stranger hops aboard and makes a beeline to the nearest available seat. They are full of Bukit Lawang tidbits and just so happen to be going in the same direction, or, imagine that, they are guides. Then they'll escort you to a guesthouse, sit you down and sign you up for a trek. If you resist, the Indonesian fish boil begins: everyone starts to apply the pressure, and every greeting in the town is 'Are you trekking tomorrow?' It's enough to make you hop back on the bus and seek refuge in Medan, of all places. Before leaving in a huff, give Bukit Lawang a day or two to grow on you. After the initial blitz, the place can be quite charming.

Sights & Activities

ORANG-UTAN FEEDING CENTRE

Bukit Lawang's famous orang-utan centre was set up in 1973 to help primates readjust to the wild after captivity or displacement through land clearing. Much of the original duties of the centre have been moved to more-remote locations, but twice-daily feedings are still provided to semi-dependent orang-utans. These events are open to the public (no guide required) and provide one of the closest views of the forest ape outside the confines of a zoo.

During the centre's decades-long career, it has introduced 200 orang-utans into the jungle and many of them have successfully mated with the wild population. Before releasing the animals into the jungle, the centre teaches the orang-utans, many of whom have been kept as caged pets, how to forage for food in the wild, build nests, climb trees, and other essentials for survival. The orang-utans are also treated for diseases that they contracted during contact with humans.

Once the apes are on their own in the wild, the centre still provides feedings to supplement awkward transitions or demanding circumstances. The feedings provided by the centre consist of milk and bananas and are considered a fairly bland diet compared with the diversity of food found in the forest. The semi-wild apes who appear at the centre's 'welfare' platform are typically nursing or pregnant females in need of an extra source of nutrition.

There are two feeding times a day: 8.30am to 9.30am and 3pm to 4pm. These are the only times visitors are allowed to enter the national park without a guide.

The feeding platform is located on the west bank of Sungai Bohorok within the park boundaries, about a 20-minute walk from the village. The river crossing to the park office is made by dugout canoe. Perlindungan Hutan dan Konservasi Alam (PHKA; Directorate General of Forest Protection and Nature Conservation) permits are required to enter the park (20,000Rp, plus 500Rp insurance) and are available from the office at the foot of the trail to the platform.

Since 1996 the centre has been closed to new arrivals, as the park is considered saturated with orang-utans. A replacement quarantine centre, just outside Medan, opened in 2002 to carry on the rehabilitation efforts, but it is not open to the public. Originally funded by World Wildlife Fund and Frankfurt Zoological Society, the centre now falls under the management of the Indonesian government, which does not provide adequate budgetary resources.

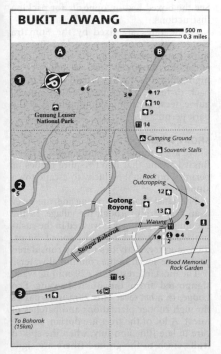

BUKIT LAWANG

INFORMATION
- Bukit Lawang Guide Association 1 B2
- Bukit Lawang Visitors Centre 2 B2
- PHKA Permit Office & Park Entrance 3 B1
- PHKA Ranger Station 4 B2

SIGHTS & ACTIVITIES
- Bat Cave 5 A2
- Orang-Utan Feeding Centre 6 A1
- Tubing Rental 7 B2

SLEEPING
- Bukit Lawang Eco Lodge 8 B2
- Garden Inn 9 B1
- Indrah Valley .... (see 9)
- Jungle Inn 10 B1
- Nora's Homestay & Restaurant 11 A3
- Wisma Bukit Lawang Indah 12 B2
- Wisma Leuser Sibayak 13 B2

EATING
- Open Air Cafe 14 B1
- Tony's Restaurant 15 B3

TRANSPORT
- Bus Station 16 A3
- Canoe to Park Entrance 17 B1

MONKEY BUSINESS

When out on a trek in Bukit Lawang, spotting an orang-utan won't be hard. In fact, some of the semi-wild apes will find you first in the hope of getting a hand-out. In the past, guides regularly broke park regulations and maintained their own feeding sites in the forests to ensure an orang spotting, but with the decline in tourism that practice seems to have subsided. What does remain are a few human-friendly apes that will follow trekking groups until a meal is delivered. Guides don't actively encourage the illegal feeding, but they don't discourage it either.

The obvious problems with these unsanctioned feedings are that the orang-utans often learn aggressive behaviour, which can range from shoving their outstretched hands in tourists' faces or grabbing backpacks. Touching an orang-utan is more dangerous for the animal than for you because human diseases can be passed through contact and then affect the whole orang community.

Park rangers are not paid in a timely fashion and permit money is sent directly to Jakarta. Despite having these problems, the rangers are dedicated to their jobs and often supplement their incomes and their hands-on experience by working with foreign researchers.

Outside Gunung Leuser National Park, orang-utans can be found in the Tanjung Puting and Kutai National Parks, in the Gunung Palung and Bukit Raja Reserves in Kalimantan, as well as in neighbouring Sarawak and Sabah in Malaysia.

For more information about Sumatran orang-utans try the Sumatran Orangutan Society (www.orangutans-sos.org) and the Sumatran Orangutan Conservation Programme (www.sumatranorangutan.com).

TREKKING

Treks into the Gunung Leuser National Park require a guide and can last anywhere from three hours to two days. Most people opt for two days so that they can spend the night in the jungle, which increases the likelihood of seeing orang-utans and other critters in the wild.

Despite the pressure, take your time in choosing a guide. Talk to returning trekkers and decide how much jungle time you really need.

If you've got serious flora or fauna curiosities, you should arrange a trek with one of the park rangers who often collaborate with foreign researchers.

If you just want a few souvenir pictures and stories, find a guide you like. People who trekked with guides from the village have mainly positive feedback, with the greatest kudos going to the nightly meals and campfire socials. Common complaints range from guides who don't know enough about the flora and fauna, bunching of treks together, and feeding of the orang-utans.

For experienced jungle hikers the trails around Bukit Lawang are overtrekked; you're better off to be based at Gurah (p428).

It is best to hike in a small group and to leave as early as possible, as this increases your chances of seeing wildlife. See the boxed text on opposite for packing instructions.

Guide rates are fixed by the Sumatra Guide Association: they are US$10 for a three-hour trek; US$25 for a day trek; and US$45 for a two-day trek, including overnight camping in the jungle and rafting back to town. Prices include basic meals, guide fees, camping equipment and the park permit.

SHORT WALKS

There are a number of short walks around Bukit Lawang that don't require guides or permits, but you'll be lucky to escape town alone.

The **canal** that runs alongside the river is an easy stroll through the village. In the evening everything gets washed in the rushing waters: frolicking kids, soiled bums, dirty laundry. Activities usually considered private are social in the communal waters.

The most interesting is a 20-minute walk, signposted from the Bukit Lawang Eco Lodge, to a **bat cave**. This 2km walk passes through rubber plantations and patches of forest. A lot of the trees are durian, so take care in late June and July, when the spiked fruits crash to the ground (there are signs warning people not to linger). You'll need a torch (flashlight) to explore the cave.

TUBING

A shed along the river en route to the orang-utan centre rents inflated truck inner tubes (7000Rp per day), which can be used to ride the Sungai Bohorok rapids. Don't underestimate the river though; currents are extremely strong and when the water is high, tubing is officially off limits, though few will tell you this. People have got into difficulties on the river, and life jackets aren't available.

Sleeping

The flood wiped out many of Bukit Lawang's family-run losmen and only a few have decided to rebuild. The following are listed in geographic order from south to north.

Nora's Homestay & Restaurant (☎ 081 3620706561; d from 20,000Rp) Big Mama Nora has a brood of bamboo huts built in a quiet corner between the main road and the rice fields. Ask the bus driver to drop you off 3km before the river.

On the western bank of the river are the following:

Bukit Lawang Eco Lodge (☎ 081 26079983; r 80,000-165,000Rp) The village's most upmarket lodging, Eco Lodge has a range of hotel-style rooms set back in the forest. There are many commendable attempts at ecofriendly business: an organic garden provides produce for the restaurant, a medicinal plant garden preserves the pharmaceutical aspects of the jungle and there is recycling.

Wisma Leuser Sibayak (☎ 4150576; r from 30,000Rp) Only a few rooms are open, while others are empty shells from the flood.

Wisma Bukit Lawang Indah (☎ 088 28643; d 30,000Rp) A little further upstream is this stereotypical budget spot.

On the eastern bank, another 10 minutes' walk from the visitors centre, are several peaceful riverine guesthouses.

Indrah Valley (d 20,000Rp) Two bamboo huts squat beside the river, with small balconies facing the forest and gangs of monkeys scampering across the rocks.

Garden Inn (d 30,000-50,000Rp) Immediately behind Indrah, Garden has basic rooms in a nondescript building.

Jungle Inn (d from 50,000Rp) Kitty-cornered to the park entrance, Jungle Inn has got personality. One room overlooks a cascading waterfall, while another incorporates the hill's rock face and the bathroom sprouts a shower from living ferns. Local woodworkers

---

JUNGLE KNOW-HOW

The Sumatran jungle is legendary for its terrain: steep slippery pitches and precipitous drops. The trails can be well-worn paths or barely visible breaks in the underbrush. This is no stroll through the park, you'll need to be responsibly fit, and well prepared, for any jungle wander.

Trekking Checklist

Bring along mosquito and leech repellent, sunscreen and lots of water. Wear long sleeves and long pants to protect against bugs and thorns, and sturdy shoes with good grip to combat gravity. A dry change of clothes and sandals for camp are a good idea.

The difference between the rainy season and the dry season is wishful thinking; paths are always slippery and rain is usually likely. Monsoon storms usually creep up in the afternoons and will undoubtedly unleash torrents on you. Travel with a lightweight rain jacket and a water-resistant bag that will keep electronics and passports dry (a plastic bag isn't going to work). A sarong is useful as a sleeping sheet or as a towel.

Responsible Trekking

Although the jungle seems indestructible, seemingly benign human activities can disturb the vulnerable communities who call this place home. Here are a few tips for being considerate in the forest.

Collect your trash, even fruit rubbish, and carry it out of the jungle with you for proper disposal.

Don't feed the animals. Giving away food to wild creatures robs them of their independence and creates aggressive behaviour.

SUMATRA

designed much of the carved railings and furniture from driftwood.

Eating

Most of the guesthouses have restaurants, where the guides camp out for new arrivals.

Tony's Restaurant (mains 15,000Rp) Although it looks closed, Tony's is still firing up pizzas. It is located directly behind the bus terminal.

Several **open-air cafés** along the river en route to the park entrance serve fruit salads, nasi goreng and a chill ambience.

Durian trees are abundant in and around Bukit Lawang. The fruit is as fresh and as cheap as you'll find anywhere and perfumes the whole place with its distinctive scent.

Getting There & Away

What should be a quick trip into the country is a four-hour rover mission on the surface of the moon. The road has crater-sized potholes, and buses have to yield to heavy vehicles overloaded with palm oil bundles from the local plantations.

There are direct buses to Medan's Pinang Baris bus terminal every half-hour between 5.30am and 5pm (8000Rp). Public minivans (10,000Rp) also leave for Medan throughout the day.

If you catch the first bus out of Bukit Lawang at 5.30am, you might be able to return to Medan in time to catch the boat to Penang, but the flexibility of time in Indonesia is unreliable in a crunch.

BERASTAGI

☎ 0628 / pop 600,000

You might have to pinch yourself upon arriving in Berastagi: the town is too busy with daily life to pounce on tourists. What a blissful relief from the guide overload you'll find elsewhere in Sumatra.

Berastagi has a healthy economy based on something other than tourism. As an agricultural trade centre, the town's markets are always humming with activity, and modern-day snake oil hawkers fill the sidewalks with 'big-city' amusements for isolated country folk. On sale are jungle miracle cures, second-hand shoes, and 20-years-behind pop music. On Sunday, the largely Christian community takes the babies and bibles out for worship.

Beyond the town are the lush green fields of the Karo Highlands, dominated by two volcanoes: Gunung Sinabung to the west and the smoking Gunung Sibayak to the north. These volcanoes are a day hike apiece, making them two of Sumatra's most accessible volcanoes, and the primary reason why tourists get off the bus in the first place.

Berastagi is at an altitude of 1300m, and the climate is deliciously cool, sometimes even cold.

Orientation

Berastagi is essentially a one-street town spread along Jl Veteran. The colourful Tugu Perjuangan (Combat Memorial), com-

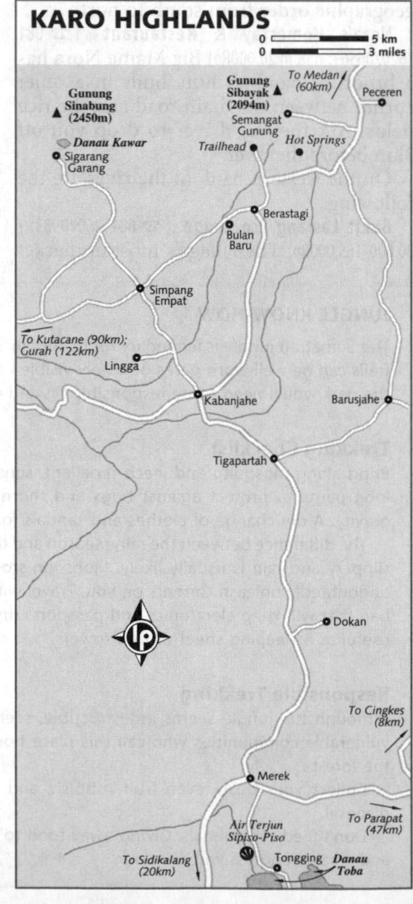

SUMATRA

memorating the Bataks' struggle against the Dutch in the 1800s, marks the centre of town. The hill to the northwest of town is Bukit Gundaling, a popular picnic spot.

Information

BNI bank (Bank Negara Indonesia; Jl Veteran) With ATMs.

BRI bank (Bank Rakyat Indonesia; Jl Veteran) With ATMs.

Post office (Jl Veteran) Near the memorial at the northern end of the street.

PT Pesiar Tour & Travel (Jl Veteran) Can book plane tickets.

Telkom wartel (Jl Veteran) Near the memorial at the northern end of the street is a 24-hour Telkom wartel, which has a Home Country Direct phone and internet.

Sights & Activities

Berastagi is under-utilised as an escape from Indonesia's intensity. Most people spend a couple of days here hiking and then tramp south to Danau Toba. But there is a lot of unhindered wandering you can do on foot and motorbike.

Because there aren't specific attractions within the town, the surrounding sights are listed here and can be found on the Karo Highlands map (p394).

Trails on both volcanoes are neither clearly marked nor well maintained and it is easy to get lost or lose your footing. During the wet season, paths can be extremely slippery or even washed out. The weather is variable and views from either mountain are far from guaranteed. Be prepared for abrupt weather changes (fog, cold temperatures and rain can sneak up during a clear day). Bring supplies such as food, drink, rain gear and a torch, in case you get caught out after dark. See the boxed text on p393 for other hiking necessities.

GUNUNG SIBAYAK

At 2094m, Gunung Sibayak is probably the most accessible of Indonesia's volcanoes.

If you've got a companion, the hike can be done without a guide. If travelling alone, it is recommended to hire a guide through the guesthouses; typical rates are 100,000Rp to 150,000Rp. The hike can be done in five hours and you should set out as early as possible.

There are three ways to tackle the climb, depending on your energy level. The easiest way is to take the track that starts to the northwest of town, a 10-minute walk past

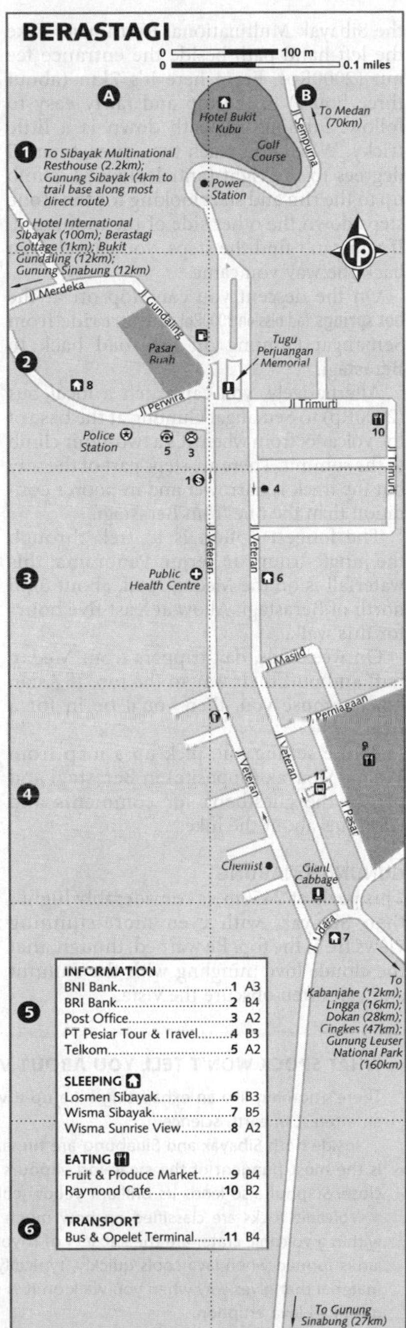

the Sibayak Multinational Resthouse. Take the left-hand path beside the entrance fee hut (2000Rp). From here it's 7km (about three hours) to the top and fairly easy to follow. Finding the path down is a little tricky. When you reach the crater, turn 90 degrees to the right (anticlockwise), climb up to the rim and start looking for the stone steps down the other side of the mountain. If you can't find the steps, you can also go back the way you came.

On the descent you can stop off at the **hot springs** (admission 3000Rp), a short ride from Semangat Gunung on the road back to Berastagi.

Alternatively, you can catch a local bus (2000Rp) to Semangat Gunung at the base of the volcano, from where it's a two-hour climb to the summit. There are steps part of the way but the track is narrower and in poorer condition than the one from Berastagi.

The longest option is to trek through the jungle from Air Terjun Panorama; this waterfall is on the Medan road, about 5km north of Berastagi. Allow at least five hours for this walk.

On weekends, day-trippers from Medan huff and puff their way to the top. If Asian hikers amuse you, then you'll be in for a treat.

Before setting out, pick up a map from Wisma Sibayak (opposite) in Berastagi and peruse the guestbook for comments and warnings about the hike.

GUNUNG SINABUNG

This peak, at 2450m, is considerably higher than Sibayak, with even more-stunning views from the top. Be warned, though, that the clouds love mingling with the summit and can often obscure the vista.

Most guesthouses recommend taking a guide, as hikers have gotten lost and died. The path up the mountain from Danau Kawar is fairly well trodden by locals, but relying on a guide takes the guesswork out of timing your return to town or reading changing weather conditions. The climb takes six to eight hours depending on your skill and the descent route.

To reach the trailhead, take an *opelet* to Danau Kawar (6000Rp, one hour). The entrance fee is 2000Rp. There is a scenic campground surrounding Danau Kawar if you're travelling with gear.

TRADITIONAL VILLAGES

There are some fine examples of traditional Karo Batak architecture in the villages around Berastagi. Most of the houses are no more than 60 years old – or possibly 100, but certainly not 400, as claimed by some guides.

Guesthouses in Berastagi can arrange guides who will be able to give cultural overviews of the Karo.

Kampung Peceren

On the northern outskirts of Berastagi, this village has a cluster of traditional houses, which are still occupied. Any *opelet* heading north can drop you there (2000Rp). There's a 2000Rp entry fee to the village.

Lingga

The best-known and most visited of these villages is **Lingga** (admission 2000Rp), a few kilometres northwest of Kabanjahe. There are about a dozen traditional houses with characteristic horned roofs. Some, such as the *rumah rajah* (king's house), are occupied and in good condition; others, including

WHAT SPOCK WON'T TELL YOU ABOUT VOLCANOLOGY

There's nothing like an exhausting hike up a volcano and a nervous peek into the pit to ignite an interest in earth science.

Inside both Sibayak and Sinabung are fumaroles, vents through which gases escape. Sulphur is the most pungent of the steaming vapours and causes difficulty in breathing if you get too close. Sulphur also lends its brilliant yellow colour to some of the surrounding rocks.

Volcanic rocks are classified on how much silica they contain. The easiest types to identify within a volcanic crater are the subsets of rhyolite: pumice and obsidian. The black glassy obsidian is formed when lava cools quickly, typically a result of effusive lava flows. The white porous material that gives way when you walk on it is pumice, which is the solidified version of a frothy, gas-filled lava eruption.

the *sapo ganjang* (the house for unmarried, young men), have almost collapsed.

There are regular *opelet* to Lingga from Kabanjahe (2000Rp).

Dokan

The charming little village of Dokan is approximately 16km south of Kabanjahe. Traditional houses are still in the majority and most are in good condition. Entry is by donation and you can get here by the occasional direct *opelet* from Kabanjahe (4000Rp).

AIR TERJUN SIPISO-PISO

These narrow but impressive **falls** cascade 120m down to the north end of Danau Toba, 24km from Kabanjahe and about 300m from the main road. It is fairly easy to get here by yourself; take a bus from Kabanjahe to Merek (8000Rp) and then walk or hitch a ride on a motorbike.

Sleeping

Jl Veteran sees extremely heavy traffic and many rooms in the centre of town are very noisy. Berastagi's best options are all sister properties of the Sibayak empire. Keep in mind that a hot shower might be a happy splurge after a long hike.

BUDGET

Wisma Sibayak (☎ 91104; Jl Udara 1; d 25,000-50,000Rp) Tidy and spacious rooms in the two-storey building have great views but lots of street noise. The restaurant is the closest Berastagi comes to a travellers haunt, with ageing comment books and knowledgeable staff.

Losmen Sibayak Guesthouse (☎ 91122; Jl Veteran 119; d 35,000-40,000Rp) Nice cheapies with a lot of Indonesian personality comprise the Sibayak enterprise's budget place.

Wisma Sunrise View (☎ 92404; Jl Kaliaga; d 50,000Rp) Perched on a little hill, Sunrise earns its namesake view and is just far enough outside of town to be a convenient stroll. Alternatively, you can catch a blue 'Bayu' *opelet* (1500Rp).

Sibayak Multinational Resthouse (☎ 91031; Jl Pendidikan 93; d 50,000-75,000Rp) Away from the town centre, Multinational has a manicured garden and straightforward rooms with hot shower. On weekends, Indonesian families stretch their lungs in the serene setting. The hotel is a short *opelet* ride north of town on the road to Gunung Sibayak.

MIDRANGE & TOP END

A number of three- and four-star hotels appeal to out-of-towners, but their price tags don't match their standards.

Berastagi Cottages (Jl Gundaling; d from 300,000Rp) Another quiet, out-of-town possibility with a range of stylish rooms. There are great garden views.

Hotel International Sibayak (☎ 91301; www.hotelsibayak.com; Jl Merdeka; d 700,000-900,000Rp; 🏊) Wooden floors, generous beds, read-the-newspaper toilets: there's a lot right about the International, except the price. If you can eek out a discount, then you'll earn a shiny frugal star. The hotel is on the road to Bukit Gundaling.

Eating & Drinking

The rich volcanic soils of the surrounding countryside supply much of North Sumatra's produce, which passes through Berastagi's colourful produce and fruit markets. Passionfruit is a local speciality, as is *marquisa Bandung*, a large, sweet, yellow-skinned fruit; and the *marquisa asam manis*, a purple-skinned fruit, makes delicious drinks.

Most of the budget hotels have restaurants, but head into town for more diversity. Along Jl Veteran there are a variety of evening food stalls, as well as simple restaurants specialising in *tionghoa* (Chinese food). Because this is a Christian community, you'll see a lot of *babi* (pork) on the menu. Another local favourite is *pisang goreng* (fried banana).

Cafe Raymond (Jl Veteran 49; 🕑 8am-midnight) Berastagi's local bohemians hang out at Café Raymond, a roots-reggae homage, serving fruit juices, beer and Western food.

Getting There & Away

The **bus terminal** (Jl Veteran) is conveniently located near the centre of town. You can also catch buses to Medan (8000Rp, 2½ hours), anywhere along the main street; buses run to and from Medan between 6am and 8pm.

To reach Danau Toba without backtracking through Medan, catch an *opelet* to Kabanjahe (2500Rp, 20 minutes) and change to a bus for Pematangsiantar

(12,000Rp, three hours), then connect with a Parapat-bound bus (10,000Rp, 1½ hours). It is a little bit of a pain but gets there in time.

Berastagi is the southern approach for visits to Gunung Leuser National Park. To reach the park, catch a bus to Kutacane (40,000Rp, five hours).

Getting Around

Opelet to the surrounding villages leave from the bus terminal. They run every few minutes between Berastagi and Kabanjahe (2500Rp), the major population and transport centre of the highlands. Local *opelet* are most easily waved down from the clock tower in town.

PARAPAT

☎ 0625

The mainland departure point for Danau Toba, Parapat has everything a transiting tourist needs: transport, lodging and supplies.

The commercial sector of the town clumps together along the Trans-Sumatran Hwy (Jl Sisingamangaraja, aka SM Raja). Branching southwest towards the pier, Jl Pulau Samosir passes most of Parapat's hotels. After 1km, a right fork (Jl Haranggaol) leads to the pier, another kilometre southwest. The bus terminal is 2km east of town, but most buses pick up and drop off passengers from ticket agents along the highway or at the pier.

Information

There is a string of moneychangers and a wartel along Jl Haranggaol.

BRI bank (Bank Rakyat Indonesia; Jl SM Raja) Has an ATM.

Planet Wisata (Jl Haranggaol) Internet access for 10,000Rp per hour.

Post office (Jl SM Raja)

Sleeping

You'll have to crash for the night if your bus gets in after the last boat to Samosir. Here are a few options:

Hotel Singgalang (☎ 41260; Jl SM Raja 52; r 25,000-50,000Rp) A big Chinese-run place with basic rooms and a downstairs restaurant.

Charlie's Guesthouse (☎ 41277; Jl Tiga Raya 7; d 30,000Rp) Beside the ferry dock, Charlie's is cheap and close; it's run by a local Toba music legend.

Mars Family Hotel (☎ 41459; Jl Kebudayaan 1; d 50,000-150,000Rp) On a quiet street near the waterfront, this place has a variety of unremarkable rooms from windowless boxes to more-expensive options with lake views.

Hotel Toba (☎ 41073; Jl Pulau Samosir 10; d 150,000-200,000Rp) If you're not in a hurry to get out of Parapat, Hotel Toba has breezy common spaces, a sandy beach and solid rooms.

Eating

The highway strip (Jl SM Raja) is well equipped to feed the passing traveller, with every variety of Indonesian cuisine. Mr Diamond is the entertaining and enterpris-

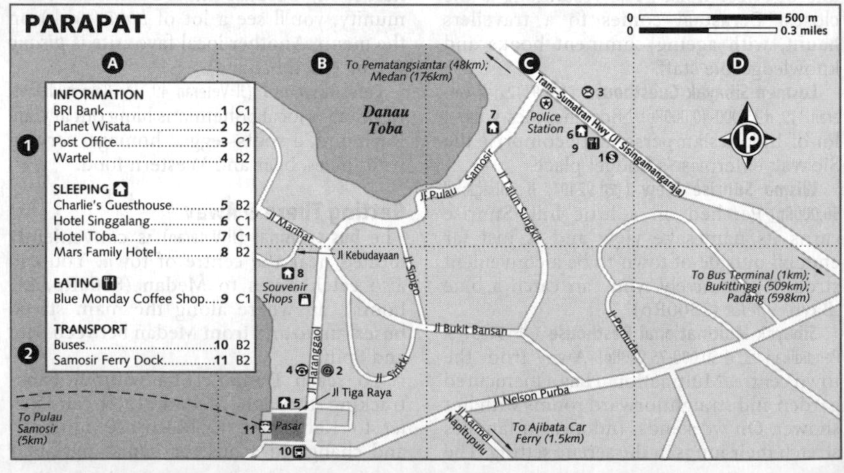

ing proprietor of **Blue Monday Coffee Shop** (Jl SM Raja; mains from 15,000Rp). In addition to a cup of coffee, he'll sell you a tour to the outlying countryside, sing a few old Western pop songs, book a bus ticket and, if you need accommodation, he's even got rooms (20,000Rp). Many of the ANS buses drop off foreigners here.

Getting There & Away

BOAT

For details of ferries to Samosir, see p406.

BUS

The **bus terminal** (Trans-Sumatran Hwy) is about 2km east of town on the way to Bukittinggi, but is not frequently used (so say the travel agents). Prices are highly negotiable, so shop around at the different ticket agents.

Buses to Medan (30,000Rp, five hours) are frequent, although services taper off in the afternoon. There are also minibuses (50,000Rp) that deliver passengers to Jl SM Raya in Medan. Other destinations include Sibolga (60,000Rp, six hours), Bukittinggi (economy/super-executive 160,000/200,000Rp, 15 hours) and Padang (economy/super-executive 170,000/200,000Rp, 17 hours).

If you're heading south to Bukittinggi, you get to experience the hazing ritual of travelling the Trans-Sumatran Hwy. The highway is more like a back road and the trip akin to the spin cycle. Now you know how your socks feel.

Getting Around

Opelet shuttle constantly between the ferry dock and the bus terminal (2000Rp).

DANAU TOBA

☎ 0625 / pop 517, 000

Toba gets touted as Sumatra's prettiest volcanic lake, a claim that detracts from its real appeal: the Batak people. Sure there is a backdrop of mountains and a cool, clear lake, but Toba's relaxed atmosphere remains intact even when the day is hazy or the shorefront overgrown with weeds. And the Batak culture has modernised with grace despite tinkering from missionaries and tourists.

A lot has changed in Toba since its heyday, when Bataks and backpackers found that their common interests of having a good time made a nice little cottage industry. The spring break–style partiers now howl at the moon in Thailand instead of Toba. On weekends money from Medan and Aceh comes to call and a few travellers still pop in with great expectations. But the numbers aren't enough to hide the obvious: tourism in Toba is almost dead.

This is all the more reason to come, not out of some sort of travelling philanthropy, but because the beaten trail is now off the beaten track. Nice hotel rooms go for a song, the outgoing Batak are genuinely glad to see you and the crowds that make travelling feel like child's play are being babysat somewhere else.

'*Horas*' is the traditional Batak greeting and it's delivered with great gusto, as are a few glasses of jungle juice (most Toba Batak are Christians) to warm up the pipes for the music-loving Batak.

Orientation

Danau Toba is the largest lake in Southeast Asia, covering a massive 1707 sq km. In the middle of this huge expanse is Pulau Samosir, a wedge-shaped island almost as big as Singapore that was created by an eruption between 30,000 and 75,000 years ago. Well, Bahasa Indonesia calls it an island, but those visiting the west of Toba will discover that Samosir isn't actually an island at all. It's linked to the mainland by a narrow isthmus at the town of Pangururan – and then cut again by a canal.

Directly facing Parapat is another peninsula occupied by the village of Tuk Tuk, which has Samosir's greatest concentration of tourist facilities. Tomok, a few kilometres south of Tuk Tuk, is the main village on the east coast of the island; Pangururan is the largest town on the west coast.

Information

The following facilities are all located in Tuk Tuk (p404). There is a small police station at the top of the road leading to the Carolina Hotel (p405).

BOOKSHOPS

Better load up on reading material in Toba, because the rest of Sumatra is a desert for the printed word. **Gokhon Library** and several other sundries shops nearby have used and rental books.

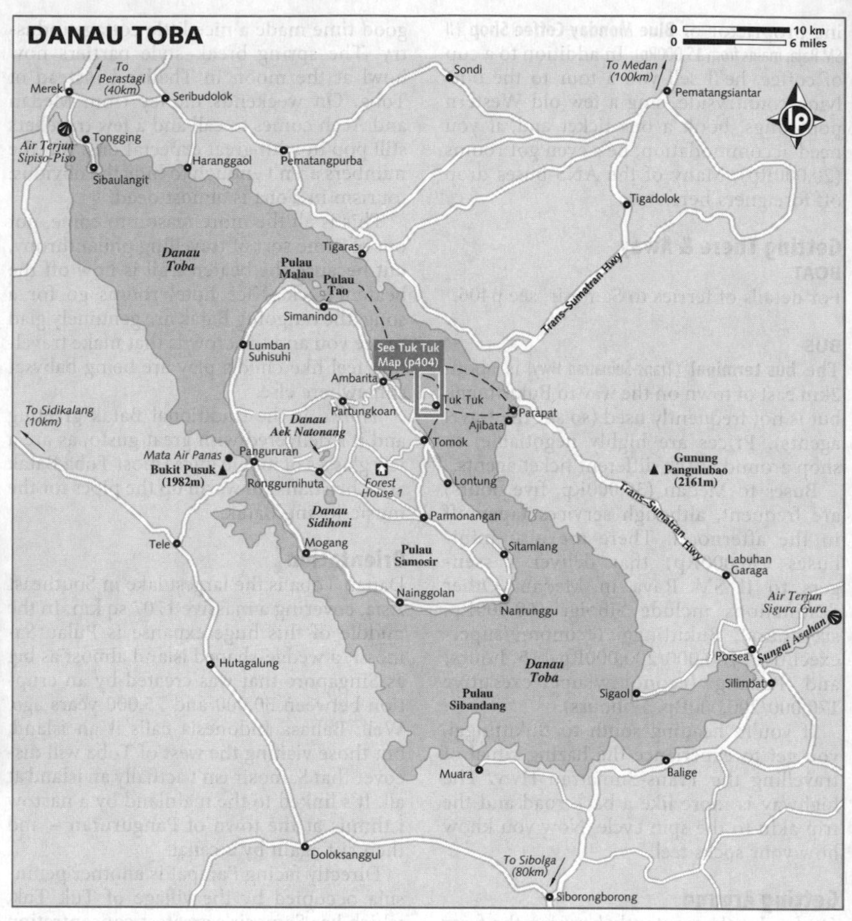

INTERNET ACCESS & TELEPHONE

Internet access (25,000Rp per hour) is available at Samosir Cottages (p404). A wartel is located across the street from Rumba Pizzeria & Homestay.

MEDICAL SERVICES

Health centre (☎ 451075) Small 24-hour place close to the turn-off to Carolina Hotel, at the southern end of the peninsula; is equipped to cope with cuts and bruises and other minor problems.

MONEY

Be sure to change your money before you get to Samosir. Exchange rates at the island's hotels and moneychangers are pretty awful.

POST

Samosir's only **post office** is in Ambarita, but several shops in Tuk Tuk sell stamps and have postboxes.

Sights & Activities

In Tuk Tuk, **Sunshine Beauty & Wellness** (☎ 451108, Tuk Tuk; ⏰ 10am-6pm) will turn beasts into beauties with affordable haircuts, facials, after-sun treatment and traditional massages.

You'll see more Christian paraphernalia in Toba than you will in the American Bible Belt. In Batak communities, homes are typically decorated with tapestries of a long-haired Jesus and gold cross necklaces adorn cleavage. The rice paddies and villages are cultivated around sober Protestant-style churches and tombs merging traditional Batak architecture and Christian crosses.

This was once the 'heart of darkness' from the perspective of the European and American missionaries and the first evangelists met their makers by the tips of spears. Good timing brought survival and fame to a German missionary named Nommenson. His arrival preceded a bumper crop and in return the Batak king traded in a few animistic beliefs for the lucky charm of Christianity.

The resulting blend of traditional culture and imported religion, observable in the Batak countryside, puts a realistic face to those exotic tales of mannered missionaries and cannibalistic natives.

The following sights and activities are located around Danau Toba (p400).

KING SIDABUTAR GRAVE

The Batak king who adopted Christianity is buried in Tomok, a village southeast of Tuk Tuk. The king's image is carved on his tombstone, along with those of his bodyguard and Anteng Melila Senega, the woman the king is said to have loved for many years without fulfilment. The tomb is also decorated with carvings of *singa*, mythical creatures with grotesque three-horned heads and bulging eyes. Next door in death is the missionary who converted the tribe, the career equivalent of boy band stardom. Next in the row is an older Batak royal tomb, which is used as a multilingual fertility shrine for childless couples, according to souvenir vendors.

The tombs are 500m up a narrow lane lined with souvenir stalls. Tomok is only 5km from Tuk Tuk and is an easy bike ride.

STONE CHAIRS

More traditional Batak artistry and legend is on view in Ambarita, 5km north of Tanjung Tuk Tuk.

The 300-year-old **stone chairs** (admission 2000Rp; 8am-6pm) is where village matters were discussed and wrongdoers were tried. A second set of megaliths in an adjoining courtyard was where the accused were bound, blindfolded, sliced and rubbed with chilli and garlic before being beheaded.

Guides love to play up the story and ask for volunteers to demonstrate the process. It is customary to pay a small fee for the tale, or risk meeting a savoury death (just kidding).

There is a small market in Ambarita on Thursday (7am to 10am) to the right of the T-junction.

MUSEUM HUTA BOLON SIMANINDO

At the northern tip of the island, in Simanindo, there's a fine old traditional house that has been restored and now functions as a **museum** (admission 5000Rp; 10am-5pm). It was formerly the home of Rajah Simalungun, a Batak king, and his 14 wives. Originally, the roof was decorated with 10 buffalo horns, which represented the 10 generations of the dynasty.

The museum has a small but interesting collection of brass cooking utensils, weapons, Dutch and Chinese crockery, sculptures and Batak carvings.

Displays of traditional **Batak dancing** are performed at 10.30am from Monday to Saturday (30,000Rp), if enough tourists show up.

The village of Simanindo is 15km from Tuk Tuk and is accessible with a hired motorbike.

SIMANINDO TO PANGURURAN

The road that follows the northern rind of Samosir between Simanindo and the town of Pangururan is a scenic ride through the Bataks' embrace of life and death. In the midst of the fertile rice fields are large multistorey **graves** decorated with the distinctive Batak-style house and a simple white cross. Reminiscent of Thai spirit houses, Batak graves reflect much of the animistic attitudes of sheltering the dead. Cigarettes and cakes are offered to the deceased as memorials or as petitions for favours. Typical Christian holidays, such as Christmas, dictate special attention to the graves.

In Pangururan, a simple **warung** (Jl Danau Toba; mains 10,000Rp), across from the police station, looks more like a bus stop than a restaurant, but it does a busy lunch-time trade of Batak dishes, such as *sassang* (stewed pork) and *nila* (fish stew).

SWIMMING

Danau Toba reaches a depth of 450m deep in places and is refreshingly cool. But only

THE BATAKS

British traveller William Marsden astonished the 'civilised' world in 1783 when he returned to London with an account of a cannibalistic kingdom in the interior of Sumatra that, nevertheless, had a highly developed culture and a system of writing. The Bataks have been a subject of fascination ever since.

The Bataks are a Proto-Malay people descended from Neolithic mountain tribes from northern Thailand and Myanmar (Burma) who were driven out by migrating Mongolian and Siamese tribes.

When the Bataks arrived in Sumatra they trekked inland, making their first settlements around Danau Toba, where the surrounding mountains provided a natural protective barrier. They lived in virtual isolation for centuries.

The Bataks were among the most warlike peoples in Sumatra, and villages were constantly feuding. They were so mistrustful that they did not build or maintain natural paths between villages, or construct bridges. The practice of ritual cannibalism, involving eating the flesh of a slain enemy or a person found guilty of a serious breach of *adat* (traditional law), survived among the Toba Bataks until 1816.

Today there are more than six million Bataks, divided into six main linguistic groups, and their lands extend 200km north and 300km south of Danau Toba.

The origins of the name 'Batak' are unclear; one theory suggests it could come from a derogatory Malay term for robber or blackmailer. Another claims that it was an abusive nickname, coined by Muslims, meaning 'pig eater'.

The Bataks are primarily an agricultural people and the rich farmlands of the Karo Highlands supply vegetables for much of North Sumatra, as well as for export.

Religion & Mythology

The Bataks have long been squeezed between the Islamic strongholds of Aceh and West Sumatra and, despite several Acehnese attempts to conquer and convert, it was the European missionaries who finally quelled the waters with Christianity.

The majority of today's Bataks are Protestant Christians, however, many still practise elements of traditional animist belief and ritual. Traditional beliefs combine cosmology, ancestor and spirit worship and *tondi* – the concept of the soul that exists near the body and from time to time takes its leave, which causes illness. It is essential for Bataks to make sacrifices to their *tondi* to keep it in good humour.

The Bataks believe the banyan to be the tree of life; they tell a legend of their omnipotent god Ompung, who created all living creatures by dislodging decayed branches of a huge banyan into the sea.

Architecture

The most distinctive element of Batak culture is traditional architecture. Batak houses are built on stilts, up to 2m from the ground with a hipped (Karo) or saddleback (Toba) roof ending in sharp rising points said to resemble buffalo horns. Houses are traditionally made of wood (slotted and bound together without nails) and roofed with sugar-palm fibre or, more often these days, rusting corrugated iron. The gables are usually extravagantly embellished with carvings of serpents, spirals, lizards and monster heads complete with bulbous eyes.

a few of the hotels in Tuk Tuk maintain weed-free swimming spots.

Across the isthmus, just before Pangururan, there are some *mata air panas* (hot springs) that the locals are extremely proud of. Most foreigners look around at the litter and decide that the waters are too hot.

TREKKING

If you don't fully succumb to Samosir's anaesthetising atmosphere, there are a couple of interesting **treks** across the island. The trails aren't well marked and can be difficult to find, but ask any of the guesthouses for a map. In the wet season (December to March) the steep inclines are

The space under the main structure is used for rearing domestic animals such as cows, pigs and goats. The living area, or middle section, is large and open with no fixed internal walls. A traditional village is made up of a number of such houses, similar to the villages of the Toraja people of central Sulawesi.

Culture

The strong Indian influence running through Batak culture is evident in the cultivation of wet-field rice, the type of houses, chess, cotton and even the type of spinning wheel.

A purely Batak tradition is the *sigalegale* puppet dance, once performed at funerals, but now more often a part of wedding ceremonies. The life-sized puppet, carved from the wood of a banyan tree, is dressed in the traditional costume of red turban, loose shirt and blue sarong. The *sigalegale* stand up on long, wooden boxes where the operator makes them dance to gamelan (percussion orchestra) music accompanied by flute and drums.

One story of the origin of the *sigalegale* puppet concerns a widow who lived on Samosir. Bereft and lonely after the death of her husband, she made a wooden image of him and whenever she felt lonely hired a *dalang* (puppeteer-storyteller) to make the puppet dance and a *dukun* (mystic) to communicate with the soul of her husband.

Whatever its origins, the *sigalegale* soon became part of Batak culture and was used at funeral ceremonies to revive the souls of the dead and to communicate with them. Personal possessions of the deceased were used to decorate the puppet, and the *dukun* would invite the deceased's soul to enter the wooden puppet as it danced on top of the grave.

Arts & Crafts

Traditionally, the Bataks are skilled metalworkers and woodcarvers; other materials they use are shells, bark, bone and horn. Their work is decorated with fertility symbols, magic signs and animals.

One particularly idiosyncratic art form developed by the Toba Bataks is the magic augury book, *pustaha*. These books comprise the most significant part of their written history. Usually carved out of bark or bamboo, the books are important religious records that explain the established verbal rituals and responses of priests and mourners. Other books, inscribed on bone or bamboo and ornately decorated at each end, document Batak myths.

Porhalaan are divining calendars – 12 months of 30 days each – engraved on a cylinder of bamboo. They are used to determine auspicious days on which to embark on certain activities, such as marriage or the planting of the fields.

Music

Music is as important to the Bataks as it is to most societies, but traditionally it was played as part of religious ceremonies rather than for everyday pleasure. Today the Bataks are famous for their powerful and emotive hymn singing.

Most of their musical instruments are similar to those found elsewhere in Indonesia – cloth-covered copper gongs in varying sizes struck with wooden hammers; a small two-stringed violin, which makes a pure but harsh sound; and a kind of reedy clarinet.

very muddy and slippery and can be quite dangerous.

The central highlands of Samosir are about 700m above the lake and afford stunning views of mist-cloaked mountains on a clear day. The top of the escarpment forms a large plateau and at its heart is a small lake, Danau Sidihoni. Samosir's vast tracts of jungle have long since vanished and the only forest you will pass through on either walk is pine, and even this is only in small areas. However, there are many interesting cinnamon, clove and coffee plantations and some beautiful waterfalls.

Most people opt for the short trek from Ambarita to Pangururan. It can be done in a day if you're fit and in a hurry, though it's best to stay overnight in one of the villages. The path starts opposite the bank in Ambarita. Keep walking straight at the escarpment and take the path to the right of the graveyard. The three-hour climb to the top is hard and steep. The path then leads to Partungkaon village (also called Dolok); here you can stay at **Jenny's Guest House** or **John's Losmen**. From Partungkaon, it's about five hours' walk to Pangururan via Danau Sidihoni.

The road between Tomok and **Forest House 1**, an interior guesthouse, is now paved and many visitors steer motorbikes up the escarpment to Danau Sidihoni.

Bring along wet-weather gear and some snacks. There are no warung along the way but you should be able to buy cups of coffee or even arrange accommodation at villages en route.

Festivals & Events

The week-long **Danau Toba Festival** is held every year in mid-June. Canoe races are a highlight of the festival, but there are also Batak cultural performances.

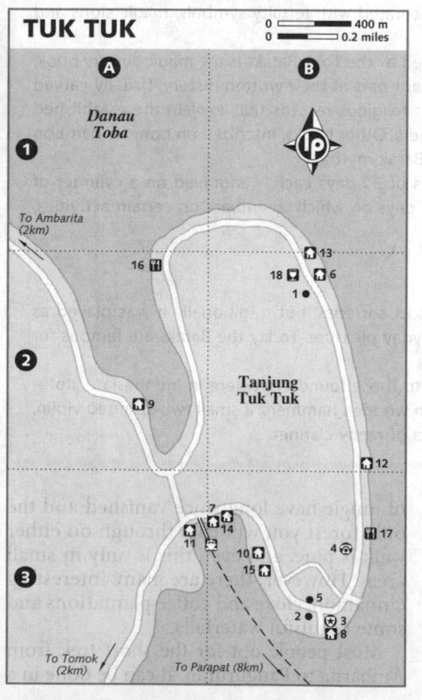

Sleeping

The eastward-facing coast of the Tuk Tuk peninsula is chock-a-block with more multi-storey hotels than there is demand, creating a near ghost town. Some people visit temple ruins, others prefer the solitude of tourism ruins. But if emptiness equals eeriness for you, you'll be better off on the north and south coasts, where little guesthouses are tucked in between village chores: washing the laundry on the rocks and collecting the news from neighbours.

All of the places listed here are located in Tuk Tuk (p404).

Vandu (d 10,000-20,000Rp) One of the cheapest on Tuk Tuk, and it shows.

Horas Chill Out Café & Homestay (d from 15,000Rp) A half-dozen birdhouse bungalows are perched on the cliff, with good views and a steep descent to the water below.

Christina's Guesthouse (☎ 451027; d 15,000-35,000Rp) Cheap and laid-back, Christina's is comfortable like a well-worn pair of jeans.

Bagus Bay & Restaurant (☎ 451287; dm 10,000Rp, d 20,000-50,000Rp) Next door to Tabo Cottages, Bagus is the recovering professional's choice, a bit more hip for midlife wanderers. Rooms in traditional Batak houses overlook avocado trees and a children's playground.

Samosir Cottages (☎ 451050; d from 25,000Rp) Travellers who get stranded in Parapet over-

INFORMATION
Gokhon Library....1 B2
Health Centre....2 B3
Police Station....3 B3
Wartel....4 B3

SIGHTS & ACTIVITIES
Sunshine Beauty & Wellness....5 B3

SLEEPING
Anju Cottages....6 B2
Bagus Bay & Restaurant....7 B3
Carolina Hotel....8 B3
Christina's Guesthouse....9 A2
Horas Chill Out Café & Homestay....10 B3
Liberta Homestay....11 A3
Romlan....12 B2
Samosir Cottages....13 B2
Tabo Cottages & Vegetarian Restaurant....14 B3
Vandu....15 B3

EATING
Bamboo Restaurant & Bar....16 A2
Rumba Pizzeria & Homestay....17 B3

DRINKING
Brando's Blues Bar....18 B2

night typically get escorted to Samosir Cottages, a package-type hotel that discounts its rooms to suit budget tastes. A nice sun and swim area keeps those travellers put.

Liberta Homestay (☎ 451035; d 25,000-50,000Rp) A chill universe is created here by a lazy-day garden and arty versions of traditional Batak houses. Crawling around the balconies and shortened doors of the rooms feels like being a deck hand on a Chinese junk. In the evening, Liberta is a local hot spot for guides and guitars.

Tabo Cottages & Vegetarian Restaurant (☎ 451318; d 40,000-145,000Rp) The professionals' choice, Tabo Cottages has modern rooms set in a beautiful garden. Lots of expats from Jakarta and Aceh bring the family here for a weekend getaway.

Carolina Hotel (☎ 41520; d 40,000-60,000Rp) Considered Tuk Tuk's swankiest (a relative term), Carolina is neat and orderly, perhaps too much so for dishevelled types. But its economy rooms are an eagle's eyrie with a hilltop perch in a polished Batak-style building. Carolina's swimming area is the best on the island.

Feel free to poke around what is not listed here, as there are often deep discounts for pioneers. If you've come for swimming, take a good look at the hotel's water access; everyone claims that they have great swimming holes but fail to mention the docking boats or drown-able weeds. Touts from various guesthouses often scoop up travellers at the Parapat pier, taking the guesswork out of the shelter search.

Some other perfectly comfortable options include:

Anju Cottages Waterfront complex.
Romlan (d 40,000Rp) Popular with a German clientele.

Eating

There are dozens of half-open restaurants, so surprised to see a customer that the neighbourhood kids have to fetch the proprietor. Vegetarian menus prevail, with homemade bread and *tempe sambal* (tofu with chilli sauce). We entrust you with the task of foraging for yourself in this wilderness.

The guesthouses tend to mix eating and entertainment in the evening. Most restaurants serve the Batak speciality of barbecued carp (often appearing as 'goldfish' on menus), sometimes accompanied by traditional dance performances.

> **PERFECT PHRASING**
>
> Phrasebooks will tell you that 'please' and 'thank you' are the most important passwords into a foreign culture. But phrasebooks get compiled in classrooms not bar rooms. In Toba Batak, the best phrase for ingratiating yourself is the foolproof *'Na sigareton'* ('Please have a cigarette').

The following restaurants are all located in Tuk Tuk (p404).

Bamboo Restaurant & Bar (☎ 451236; mains 10,000-25,000Rp) A stylish place to watch the sun slink away, Bamboo has cosy cushion seating, a down-tempo mood and a reliable menu.

Rumba Pizzeria & Homestay (☎ 451310; mains 10,000-25,000Rp) Sometimes Rumba's is full of energy cranking out Toba music and side dishes of cheerfulness. But even if it's deserted, the pizzas are divine after the monotony of nasi Padang.

Drinking

Brando's Blues Bar (Tuk Tuk) There are a handful of foreigner-oriented bars, such as this one in between the local jungle-juice cafés. The local tipple is palm wine, known as *tuak*.

Entertainment

Today the parties are all local – celebrating a wedding, new addition on a house or the return of a Toba expat. Invitations are gladly given and should be cordially accepted. On most nights, music and spirits fill the night air with the kind of camaraderie that only grows in small villages. The Toba Bataks are extremely musical and passionate choruses erupt from invisible corners.

Check around Tuk Tuk to see if any of the tourist restaurants are hosting Batak dancing.

Shopping

Samosir's souvenir shops carry a huge range of cheap and tacky cotton T-shirts. For something slightly more original, local Gayo embroidery is made into a range of bags, cushion covers and place mats.

Around Tuk Tuk there are numerous woodcarvers selling a variety of figures, masks, boxes and *porhalaan*, as well as some traditional musical instruments.

Getting There & Away

BOAT

Ferries between Parapat and Tuk Tuk (7000Rp) operate about every two hours from 9.30am to 7.30pm. Ferries stop at Bagus Bay; other stops are by request. The first and last ferries from Samosir leave at about 8.30am and 4.30pm; check exact times with your hotel. When leaving for Parapat, stand on your hotel jetty and wave a ferry down.

Five ferries a day shuttle vehicles and people between Ajibata, just south of Parapat, and Tomok. There are five departures per day between 8.30am and 8.30pm. The passenger fare is 3000Rp. Cars cost 150,000Rp, and places can be booked in advance at the **Ajibata office** (☎ 41194) or **Tomok office** (☎ 41157).

BUS

See Parapat (p399), the mainland transit point, for information on bus travel to/from Danau Toba.

On Samosir, Pangururan has a daily buses to Berastagi (30,000Rp) via Sidikalang, which is also a transfer point to Kutacane and Tapaktuan (on the west coast).

Getting Around

Local buses serve the whole of Samosir *except* Tanjung Tuk Tuk. A helpful service is the regular minibuses between Tomok and Ambarita (2000Rp), continuing to Simanindo (3000Rp) and Pangururan (10,00Rp). The road between the neck of the peninsula is a good spot to flag down these minibuses. Services dry up after 3pm.

You can rent motorcycles in Tuk Tuk for 70,000Rp a day. Bicycle hire costs from 25,000Rp a day.

SIBOLGA

☎ 0631 / pop 90,000

The departure point for boats to Nias, Sibolga is a west-coast port town with a reputation for hustling tourists. As tourist numbers decline, the hassles have diminished to a fish boil of touts when you step off the bus/boat – the usual port town bad manners. Watch your money, know how much things cost and have a healthy scepticism for unsolicited advice.

Information

BNI bank (Bank Negara Indonesia; Jl Katamso) It is advisable to change money here or use the ATM, as options are limited on Nias.

Post office (Jl Tobing; 8am-6pm) Internet access available (5000Rp per hour).

Telkom wartel (Jl A Yani 35) International phone calls can be made from here.

Dangers & Annoyances

Dragging around surf gear will invite inflated prices: either be willing to bargain hard or accept a degree of extra 'service'.

A more serious scam involves being detained on suspicion of carrying drugs. Some travellers have reported being searched and intimidated by groups of uniformed officials demanding exorbitant bribes before releasing travellers. Don't leave your bags unattended or with a 'helpful' guide.

Sights

Pantai Pandan is a popular white-sand beach at the village of Pandan, 11km north of Sibolga. A few hundred metres further on is **Pantai Kalangan** (admission 2000Rp). Both beaches get very crowded at weekends, but are good places to pass the time while you're waiting to catch a boat from Sibolga. *Opelet* run to the beaches all day (3000Rp).

Sleeping & Eating

If you get stuck overnight in Sibolga, try the following:

Hotel Pasar Baru (☎ 22167; cnr Jl Imam Bonjol & Raja Junjungan; d with fan/air-con 75,000/100,000Rp;) A decent enough place to sleep in a pinch.

Hotel Wisata Indah (☎ 23688; Jl Katamso 51; d from 180,000Rp;) The only upmarket hotel in town, Wisata Indah has a pool, comfortable rooms and sea views. It even has a day-use fee for the pool and showers.

There are plenty of Padang restaurants and coffee shops directly across the street from the harbour for pre- or post-departure nibbles.

Getting There & Away

BOAT

Ferries to Nias leave from the harbour at the end of Jl Horas. There are two port options for Nias: the capital city of Gunung Sitoli, which is in the north of the island and a three-hour bus ride from the surf break; or Teluk Dalam, which is in the south and a 15-minute ride away.

Boats to Teluk Dalam are the obvious choice but they don't run every day. **PT Simeulue** (☎ 21497; Jl Sultan Bustani) runs a ferry to Teluk Dalam (economy/cabin bed 60,000/90,000Rp, 11 hours), departing at 8pm on Sunday, Tuesday and Thursday. Economy class is two tiers of pallets in the hold of the boat; if you opt for this class, try to get a spot on the top level where it will be less claustrophobic. Cabin class at least affords privacy and a mattress, if not a higher degree of cleanliness.

If you arrive in Sibolga on any other day of the week, catch a Gunung Sitoli–bound boat (economy/air-con/cabin 43,000/63,000/120,000Rp, eight to 10 hours), which departs at 8pm every day but Sunday). **ASDP** (☎ 21752), in front of the harbour, runs a modern passenger and car ferry. The air-con class is the best value: seats recline, the room is fairly cool and generally quiet.

Ferries generally leave one to two hours late. If you arrive in Sibolga and are told you have just missed the boat it is often worth going to the harbour yourself to verify this.

You don't have to pay extra for surfboards on either service but you'll be lucky to get away without coughing up any cash to the local heavies.

BUS

Sibolga is a bit of a backwater as far as bus services are concerned and the route is windy and inordinately slow. The bus terminal is on Jl Sisingamangaraja, 2km from the harbour. You can ask the bus driver to drop you off at the harbour. A becak between the two should be 5000Rp.

There are frequent departures for Bukittinggi (70,000Rp, 12 hours), Padang (72,000Rp, 14 hours), Medan (70,000Rp, 11 hours) and Parapat (60,000Rp, six hours).

There are also minivan services that shuttle folks between Sibolga and Medan (80,000Rp) – prices are highly negotiable.

PULAU NIAS

As myth busters, we've got good and bad news about Nias. The 'wave' is superb and has deservedly kept this far-flung island on the international surfing circuit. The ancient megalithic monuments and traditional architecture are also incredible for cultural tourists.

But the island ambience is as razor sharp as the coral break. Maybe it is the surfers' fault; maybe it is the vast economic disparity between the islanders and the visitors; maybe it is Nias' warrior past or the devastating earthquake. Who knows. But one thing is certain, this is not laid-back island living.

Before launching into a laundry list of hassles, let's put things in perspective. Nias is almost the size of Bali but gets a whole lot less attention from the government. Development, economic opportunity and basic nutrition are sorely lacking. The tourist economy started drying up several years ago, and then the island got socked by the 2004 Boxing Day tsunami, which killed 122 people and destroyed rice crops. Three months later, the 28 March earthquake levelled the capital city and killed an estimated 400 to 500 people. Recovery efforts and aid have been slow and scattershot and temporary tents are still visible across the island. It would take the patience of Job to embrace wealthy visitors without expectations.

History

Local legend tells it that Niassans are the descendants of six gods who came to earth and settled in the central highlands. Anthropologists link them to just about everyone: the Bataks of Sumatra, the Naga of Assam in India, the aborigines of Taiwan and various Dayak groups in Kalimantan.

Nias history is the stuff of campfire tales in which an exotic people practised headhunting and human sacrifice long after the rest of the world started fainting at the sight of blood.

Traditionally, Niassan villages were presided over by a village chief, heading a council of elders. Beneath the aristocratic upper caste were the common people, and below them the slaves, who were often traded. Until the first years of the 19th century Nias' only connection with the outside world was through the slave trade.

Sometimes villages would band together to form federations, which often fought each other. Prior to the Dutch conquest, and the arrival of the missionaries, intervillage warfare was fast and furious, spurred on by the desire for revenge, slaves or human heads. Heads were needed for stately burials, wedding dowries and the construction of new villages.

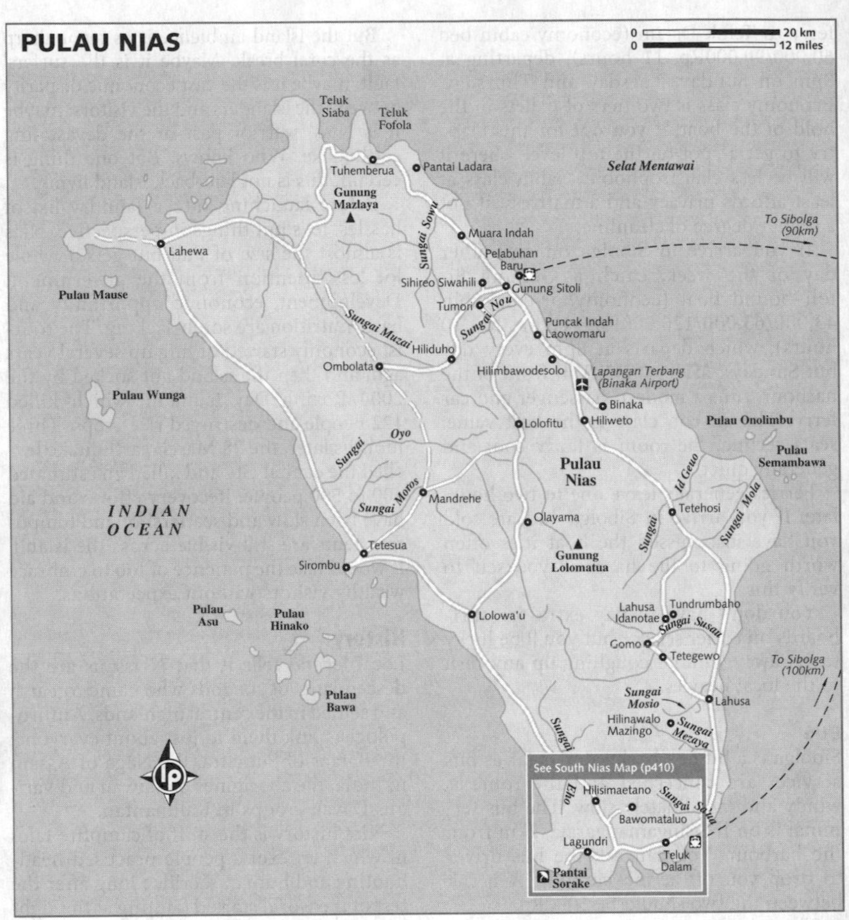

When they weren't warring, they were farming, a tradition that continues today. They cultivated yams, rice, maize and taro, despite the thick jungle, and raised pigs as a source of food and a symbol of wealth and prestige; the more pigs you had, the higher your status in the village. Gold and copper work, as well as woodcarving, were important industries.

The indigenous religion was thought to have been a combination of animism and ancestor worship, with some Hindu influences. Today the dominant religions on Nias are Christianity and Islam – overlaid with traditional beliefs.

The island did not come under full Dutch control until 1914. Today's population of about 639,000 is spread through more than 650 villages, most inaccessible by road.

Orientation & Information

For a place known to the outside world, Nias is surprisingly underdeveloped and the earthquake undid any minor steps forward. Don't expect rapid transport across the island, internet connection or reliable mobile phone coverage.

Gunung Sitoli, the island's biggest town, and Binaka, the only airport, are both in the north. The famous surf break is in the south at Pantai Sorake, accessible via the port town of Teluk Dalam. Some might refer to the surfing area as Teluk Lagundri, which is the bay that the waves barrel into.

Gunung Sitoli has two working ATMs, and there is one moneychanger in Teluk Dalam.

Dangers & Annoyances

Chloroquine-resistant malaria has been reported on Nias, so be sure you take appropriate precautions.

GUNUNG SITOLI

☎ 0639

Gunung Sitoli, on the northeastern coast of Nias, is the island's main town. It was badly destroyed by the 28 March 2005 earthquake and rebuilding has stalled at piling up rubble.

Orientation & Information

The port is about 2km north of the centre of town, and the bus terminal about 1.5km south, beyond the bridge. Businesses are clustered around the parade ground in the centre of town.

Bank Sumut (Jl Hatta) MasterCard-accessible ATM.

BRI bank (Bank Rakyat Indonesia; ☎ 21946; Jl Imam Bonjol; 🕑 8am-4pm Mon-Fri) ATM available.

Post office (cnr Jl Gomo & Hatta) Opposite the parade ground.

Public hospital (☎ 21271; Jl Cipto M Kusomo) For dealing with minor emergencies.

Sights

Museum Pusaka Nias (☎ 21920; Jl Yos Sudarso 134A; admission 2000Rp; 🕑 8am-noon & 1-5pm Tue-Sat, 2-5pm Sun) has a good collection of woodcarvings, stone sculptures and ceremonial objects. The garden has an interesting display of local plants and herbs and some models of traditional Niassan architecture.

If you're curious about viewing more examples of Nias' cultural heritage, see p411.

Sleeping & Eating

Accommodation options in Gunung Sitoli have not been rebuilt since the earthquake. If you need to stay on the north coast to catch a departing flight, try these options outside the town centre:

Wisma Soliga (☎ 21815; d with fan/air-con from 50,000/100,000Rp; ❄) Located 4km south of town, this is a friendly, well-managed place with clean and spacious rooms.

Miga Beach Bungalows (☎ 21460; d from 150,000-200,000Rp; ❄) Nearby, Miga sits right on a small beach with comfortable rooms.

To get to either hotel take an *opelet* from the bus terminal (2000Rp). A becak will cost about 10,000Rp. These hotels are 14km from the airport and can arrange transport for 50,000Rp per person.

There are lots of small **restaurants** along the main streets in Gunung Sitoli. **Bintang Terang** (Jl Sirao 10; mains 10,000Rp) has good seafood fried noodles.

TELUK DALAM

☎ 0631

The average European would practically tower over this squat port town, which is as loud and chaotic as much larger cities. You'll need to pass through Teluk Dalam for transit connections to the beach or to pick up provisions.

The **post office** (Jl Ahmad Yani) and **Telkom wartel** (Jl Ahmad Yani) are both near the harbour. There are lots of Indonesian banks, but none exchanges foreign currency. A **moneychanger** is across the street from the BRI bank.

PANTAI SORAKE & TELUK LAGUNDRI

☎ 0630

A fish-hook piece of land creates the perfect horseshoe bay of Lagundri and the surf break at Sorake, which is said to be the best right-hander in the world. The main surfing season is June to October, and in July and August waves can be more than 4m high. Folks refer to this area interchangeably as Sorake or Lagundri.

The Boxing Day tsunami destroyed many of the family-run guesthouses and restaurants on the beach. The businesses that could afford to rebuild are all located on Pantai Sorake, which is considered to be more protected from future disasters.

Dangers & Annoyances

Times are tough here – not that hardship is an annoyance, but it creates disparity between a tourist's expectations for a holiday and the locals' economic concerns. Many generous people who have had the means and relationship with Nias have sponsored the rebuilding of local houses and bungalows destroyed by the tsunami, ostensibly in exchange for free accommodation, but more importantly as true grassroots giving. By circumventing bloated aid organisations, many people can see tangible results from their disaster donations. The downside to this is that some locals view every new arrival here as a possible donor and the sales pitch can come from your losmen or from a stranger you meet on the beach, blurring the line between charity and con game. Unless you have a relationship with a family, it is not advisable to expect that your donation will be spent as promised.

Before the tsunami, many visitors left the island cursing about petty theft and incessant scams. In 2002, beach businesses had formed an association that had managed to curtail some of the bad behaviour: local kids are no longer torturing turtles so that tourists will pay a ransom.

Renting surf gear on the island is still a source of unexpected headaches. Be sure you pay a fair price; if it is too cheap, you'll pay for it at the end with inflated damage costs. There is still the usual gang of guys who hang out on the beach looking for the next greenhorn. Remember that trustworthy people are usually too busy during the day to meet and greet the tourists. It may sound alarmist, but single women should be cautious in accepting invitations to drink with the locals.

In general, you'll enjoy Nias a lot more if you choose your losmen carefully and keep a low profile.

Activities

SURFING NIAS

Sorake's famous right consistently unrolls between June and October. Access to the wave is a quick paddle from the Keyhole, a break in the coral reef that lies between the beach and the bay.

The March 2005 earthquake lifted the Sorake reef up by about 1m, a shift that has improved the wave, so they say.

Folks also claim that the off-season waves are good for beginners, a term frequently misinterpreted by nonsurfers. If you've never surfed before, you're better off learning in a place that is easier to get to and on a break with a sandy beach.

Most surfers arrive with their own gear, but you can rent equipment from **Key Hole Surf Camp**, in front of the Keyhole.

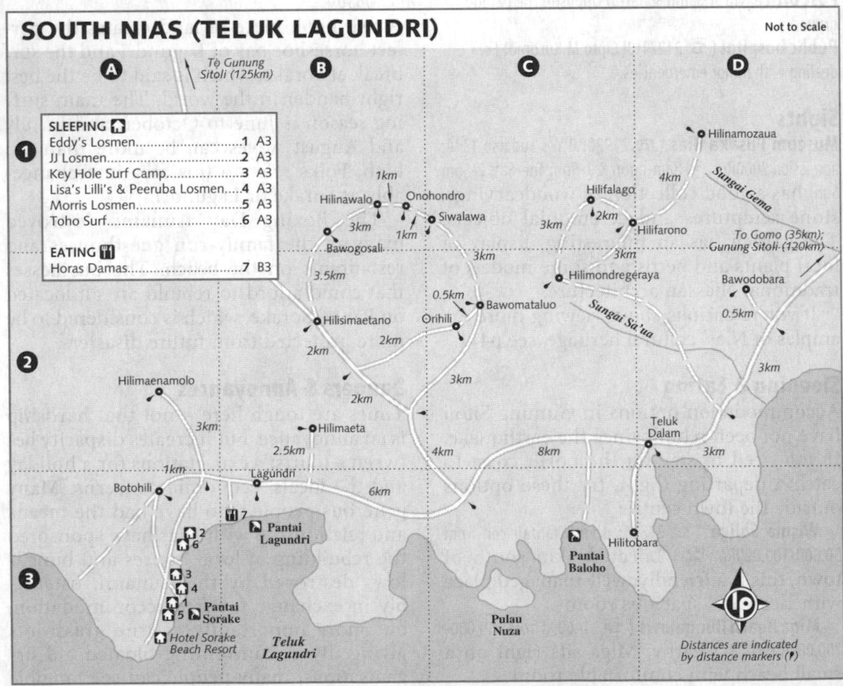

OFFSHORE SURFING

Popular surfing destinations off Nias include the islands of Asu, Bawa and Hinako. More exposed than Nias itself, the islands see bigger and more-consistent waves. With a left-hander at Asu and a strong right-hander at Bawa, good surf is almost guaranteed regardless of wind direction.

The risk of malaria is high on these islands, particularly Bawa, which has a large swamp in its interior. Visitors should take proper precautions.

Sirombu on Nias' west coast is the jumping-off point for the islands. There might be a public bus from Gunung Sitoli – no-one could say for sure; otherwise you can charter transport for about 500,000Rp.

From Sirombu there are cargo boats (50,000Rp). You can also charter boats (500,000Rp, maximum of 10 people) from local fishermen at Teluk Dalam and save yourself the hassle of getting to Sirombu.

Bawa has several simple losmen (50,000Rp per night), including one run by an Indonesian named German. Bring your own food.

Surfers on Nias are saying that the earthquake adversely affected the waves on Asu. Now the ride is good only if the swell is high. Tours can be organised through **Sumatran Surf Adventures** (www.sumatransurfadventures.com).

Pulau Tello, further south towards the Mentawai Islands, is another destination that can be reached by charter boat.

There are also other breaks within the bay under certain conditions and a few rides elsewhere on the island. Visit Surfing Sumatra (www.surfingsumatra.com) for a quick wave profile for Nias and nearby.

SWIMMING

A wide sandy beach starts just north of JJ Losmen and rounds the horseshoe bay all the way to the southeastern tip. A rind of dead coral separates Pantai Sorake from the water and swimming possibilities.

Sleeping & Eating

The western part of the bay, known as Pantai Sorake, is the primary location for lodging since the tsunami destroyed much of the construction elsewhere on the bay. Most surfers stay on the northern end so they can watch the waves. Accommodation is in basic beach bungalows run by local families and usually costs between 25,000Rp and 50,000Rp. Choose your losmen carefully as some families are extremely sweet and others will act hurt if you spend your money elsewhere or have their children begging for pens.

It is expected that you eat your meals, especially dinner, at your losmen, and inquiries of where you've eaten can range from curiosity to accusation. In general, the more expensive the lodging, the less likely your hosts will care where you spend your money. Food is quite expensive on the island, with dinner prices averaging between 35,000Rp to 50,000Rp for a plate of fish or chicken.

The following guesthouses run south to north:

Morris Losmen and **Eddy's Losmen** are next door to each other, a few minutes walk from the waves. **Lisa's**, **Lili's** and **Peeruba Losmen** are clumped together on a sunny patch of sand just on the edge of the action.

Key Hole Surf Camp (75,000Rp), right in the thick of things, charges a little more, giving you freedom to eat where you please. Next in line is **Toho Surf**, which has nice beachfront balconies. **JJ Losmen** is the last in the row, with freshly varnished wooden rooms.

The only development on this side of the bay is **Horas Damas**, an open-air restaurant with a view of the deep blue.

TRADITIONAL VILLAGES

For hundreds of years, Nias residents built elaborate villages around cobblestoned streets lined with rows of shiplike wooden houses. The traditional homes were balanced on tall wooden pylons and topped by a steep, thatched roof. Some say the boat motif was inspired by Dutch spice ships. Constructed from local teak and held together with hand-hewn wooden pegs, the houses are adorned with symbolic wooden carvings. The technology of traditional architecture proved quite absorbent and these structures fared better in the 2005 earthquake than modern concrete buildings.

Reflecting the island's defensive strategies, villages were typically built on high ground reached by dozens of stone steps. A stone wall for protection usually encircled the village. Stone was also used to carve bathing pools, staircases, benches, chairs and memorials.

Within the island there is geographic diversity in the traditional house building. In northern Nias, homes are freestanding, oblong structures on stilts, while in the south they are built shoulder to shoulder on either side of a long, paved courtyard. Emphasising the roof as the primary feature, southern Niassan houses are constructed using pylons and crossbeams slotted together without the use of bindings or nails.

Gomo & Around

The villages around Gomo, in the central highlands, contain some of the island's best examples of stone carvings and *menhirs* (single standing stones), some thought to be 3000 years old. Such examples can be found in the village of **Tundrumbaho**, 5km from Gomo, **Lahusa Idanotae**, halfway between Gomo and Tundrumbaho, and at **Tetegewo**, 7km south of Gomo.

Unfortunately, Gomo is virtually inaccessible. Getting to Tundrumbaho involves a tough two-hour uphill slog through the steamy jungle. From Lagundri, negotiate with the losmen owners for someone to take you there and back by motorcycle, or catch a bus to Lahusa and then hitch a ride. Getting to Tetegewo is possible, but it's a long trip – it's probably only worthwhile if you're interested in this type of architecture.

Hilinawalo Mazingo

One of only five such surviving buildings on the island, the **Omo Hada** (chieftain's house) is situated in the prestigious 'upstream' direction of the remote village, garnering the first rays of morning light. It still serves its traditional purpose as a meeting hall for seven neighbouring villages and is currently undergoing restoration work by a local conservation group, North Sumatra Heritage, with funding from World Monuments Fund and corporate sponsors. In order to repair damages from age and climate, villagers have been trained in traditional carpentry skills, in turn preserving crafts that were nearing extinction.

The area is known as Eri Mazino and is 18km from Lagundri between Teluk Dalam and Lahusa district. You can take a public bus to Simpang Oge and then hire an *ojek* (motorcycle that takes passengers) from there or arrange transport directly from Lagundri. The last 8km of the trip is arduous due to poor road conditions.

Bawomataluo

This is the most famous, and the most accessible, of the southern villages. It is also the setting for *lompat batu* (stone jumping), featured on Indonesia's 1000Rp note.

Bawomataluo (literally 'sun hill') is perched on a hill about 400m above sea level. The final approach is up 88 steep stone steps. Houses are arranged along two main stone-paved avenues that meet opposite the impressive **chief's house**, thought to be the oldest and largest on Nias. Outside are stone tables where dead bodies were once left to decay.

Although Bawomataluo is still worth exploring, tourism is in full swing here, with lots of eager knick-knack sellers.

There are also cultural displays of **war dances**, traditionally performed by young, single males, and **stone jumping**. The latter was once a form of war training; the jumpers had to leap over a 1.8m-high stone wall traditionally topped with pointed sticks. These days the sticks are left off – and the motivation is financial.

From Bawomataluo, you can see the rooftops of nearby **Orihili**. A stone staircase and trail lead downhill to the village.

Bawomataluo is 15km from Teluk Dalam and is accessible by public bus (5000Rp).

Hilisimaetano

There are more than 100 **traditional houses** in this large village, 16km northwest of Teluk Dalam. **Stone jumping** and **traditional dancing** are performed here during special events. Hilisimaetano can be reached by public transport from Teluk Dalam (5000Rp).

Botohili & Hilimaeta

Botohili is a small village on the hillside above the peninsula of Pantai Lagundri. It has two rows of **traditional houses**, with a number of new houses breaking up the skyline. The remains of the original entrance, **stone chairs** and paving can still be seen.

Hilimaeta is similar to Botohili and is also within easy walking distance of Lagundri. The stone-jumping pylon can still be seen and there are a number of **stone monuments**, including a 2m-high stone penis. A long pathway of stone steps leads uphill to the village.

GETTING THERE & AWAY

Air

SMAC (☎ 0639-21010; Jl Sudirman, Gunung Sitoli) has flights from Medan to Binaka airport, 17km south of Gunung Sitoli, several times a week (556,000Rp). Surfboards cost an extra 30,000Rp. Flights usually leave in the morning. SMAC operates a minibus between Binaka airport and Gunung Sitoli (30,000Rp). Ask a local travel agent if Merpati is operating flights from Binaka to Padang, a service that was in question at the time of writing.

Boat

There are boats every night except Sunday from Gunung Sitoli to Sibolga. In theory, all services leave at 8pm, but in practice they seldom set sail before 10pm. Ticket prices are 43,000/63,000/120,000Rp for economy/air-con/cabin. **ASDP** (☎ 0639-21554; Jl Yos Sudarso) has an office at the harbour in Gunung Sitoli.

Boats to Sibolga also leave from Teluk Dalam every Monday, Wednesday and Friday. Boat tickets to Sibolga can be bought at **PT Simeulue** (☎ 081 2167033; Jl Saunigaho). Tickets cost 60,000/90,000Rp for economy/cabin class.

GETTING AROUND

Getting around Nias can be slow. In Gunung Sitoli, the bus terminal is 1.5km south of the centre of town; an *opelet* from the pier costs 2000Rp.

From Gunung Sitoli, there are minibuses to the southern market town of Teluk Dalam (50,000Rp, three hours), which has transport to Lagundri, 13km away. You can also arrange transport directly to Sorake (75,000Rp). You will probably be charged extra to take a surfboard but always whittle the initial quote as low as a smile can get. Services dry up in the afternoon, so aim to leave before noon.

To get to Sorake and/or Lagundri from Teluk Dalam, catch a local bus from the town centre (5000Rp). Losmen will also hunt the town looking for new arrivals and usually charge 10,000Rp for motorbike transfer.

SUMATRA

SUMATRAN SUPERPOWER

As a global contender for the notorious title of 'superpower', Sumatra has as much control over world events as your average lawn vole. That is, until you tally up all the times that violent natural disasters on the island have literally shook the planet.

Take for instance the 1883 eruption of Krakatau in southern Sumatra. This volcanic explosion equalled the equivalent of 200 megatons of TNT and makes the A-bomb dropped on Hiroshima look like backyard fireworks. So much ash was hurled into the atmosphere that the sky was darkened for days and global temperatures were reduced by an average of 1.2 degrees Celsius for several years.

It is said that the blast that created Danau Toba some 100,000 years ago – before scientists were around to measure such rumblings – would have made Krakatau look like an after-dinner belch.

Then there was the 2004 Boxing Day earthquake, the world's second-largest recorded earthquake (recently upgraded from magnitude 9 to 9.3). The resulting tsunami hit more than a dozen countries around the Indian Ocean, leaving more than 300,000 people dead or missing and millions displaced. The force of the event is said to have caused the earth to wobble on its axis and shifted surrounding landmasses southwest by up to 36m.

In terms of movers and shakers, the same cannot be said for Bollywood's pop stars or even US foreign policy.

ACEH

Guess what, boys and girls: Aceh is the next best spot. Forget Laos, Cambodia and even beachy Thailand. Those are *so* 2002 and overrun by folks who would get spooked in the produce department back home. Aceh has white sands, coffee-growing highlands and minority tribes – all in one province. The best part is that you can earn your intrepid stripes: the name 'Aceh' will put a few worry lines on loved ones' faces, but the reality is a lot tamer than Saturday-night pub crawls.

After years of conflict with the Indonesian military and the devastating effects of the Boxing Day tsunami, Aceh is truly poised for a great regeneration. The province has a wealth of natural resources (gas, gold, copper and silver) and it has brokered enough autonomy to ensure that profits aren't entirely siphoned off by Jakarta. The presence of international aid organisations and accompanying charitable donations, even if partially squandered by corruption, is rebuilding what was lost and helping foster an already intelligent and ambitious workforce. About 40% of Acehnese live in poverty, but many are hopeful that the new-found peace and attention from the outside world will rebuild a stronger future.

The only thing missing in this devout Muslim land is hard-core boozing. But if your trip is timed with the Lenten season, you can abstain with a purpose or just sniff out the quiet pockets of appreciation.

Do remember though to monitor the news about the stability of the peace in Aceh. Indonesia is mercurial.

TRAVELLING TO ACEH

No special permit or permission is required to visit Aceh province. At one time foreign visitors were limited but since the 2004 tsunami these restrictions have been eased at the entry points into Aceh. Confusion does arise if you inquire with Indonesian embassies or outside of the island of Sumatra, as the Indonesian government has not yet disseminated an official decision on the matter.

History

In the days of sailing ships, Aceh competed with Melaka on the Malay Peninsula for control of the important spice trade route. Aceh was also the entryway into the archipelago for Islam, and Banda Aceh, the capital, was an important centre of Islamic learning and a gateway for Muslims making the pilgrimage to Mecca.

The influx of traders and immigrants and the province's strategic position contributed to Aceh's wealth and importance. The main exports were pepper and gold; others included ivory, tin, tortoiseshell, camphor, aloe wood, sandalwood and spices. Though Aceh's power began to decline towards the end of the 17th century, the province remained independent of the Dutch until war was declared in 1871. It was 35 years before the fighting stopped and the last of the sultans, Tuanku Muhamat Dawot, surrendered.

In 1951 the Indonesian government incorporated Aceh's territory into the province of North Sumatra. However, the prominent Islamic Party was angered at being lumped together with the Christian Bataks, and proclaimed Aceh an independent Islamic Republic in September 1953. Prolonged conflict ensued and in 1959 the government was forced to give Aceh 'special district' status, granting a high degree of autonomy in religious, cultural and educational matters. Despite this special status the government strengthened its grip on Aceh's huge natural gas reserves, pocketing the majority of profits and leaving the locals impoverished.

In December 1976 Gerakan Aceh Merdeka (GAM; Free Aceh Movement) was formed and began fighting for independence. In the early years of the struggle fighting was limited, but by 1989 GAM had gathered strength and launched a renewed attack on the Indonesian government.

By 1990 the area had been designated a 'special combat zone' and eight years of near-military rule followed. Years of army atrocities and human rights abuses perpetrated during this time only emerged after the fall of Soeharto in 1998. In the following years army massacres continued while GAM intimidated whole villages into giving the rebel forces support. Deaths, tortures, disappearances and arbitrary arrests

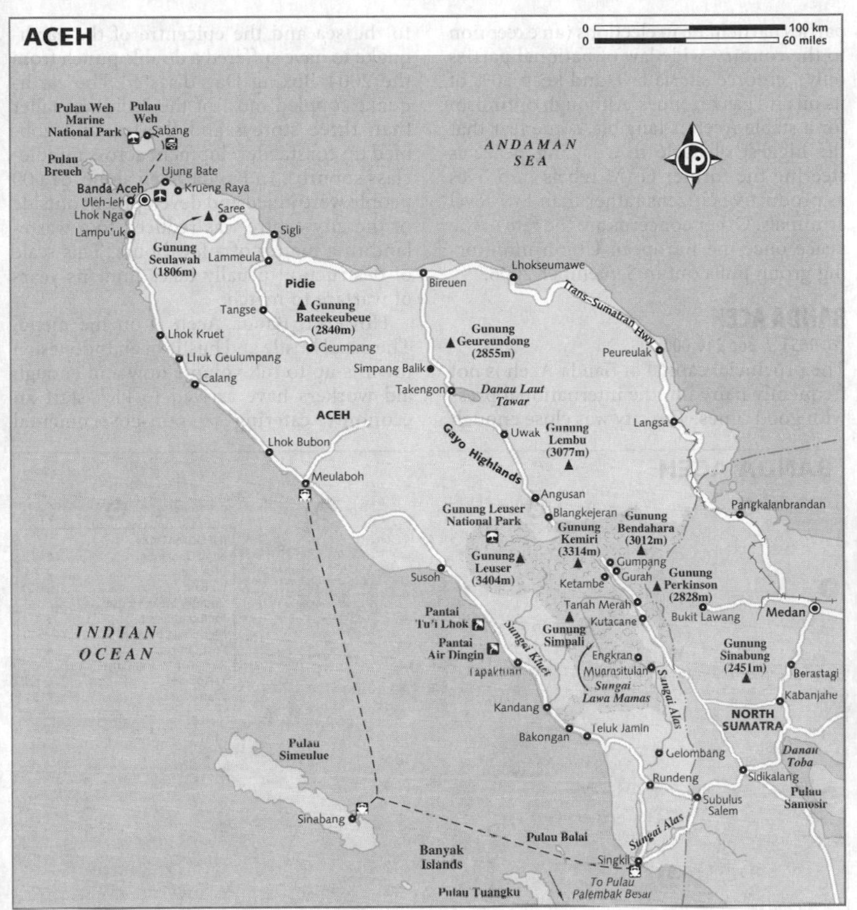

occurred on a daily basis, with each side blaming the other. The ordinary people of Aceh were the real losers: tens of thousands of them were displaced and living in fear of both sides.

At the turn of the millennium, several steps towards peace were made: a brief cease-fire was declared in 2000, and in 2002 Jakarta granted a 'special autonomy' law allowing the province to keep up to 70% of oil and gas revenues and implement Islamic (sharia) law. Peace talks were also initiated for the first time since the conflict began and progressed for a year and a half before crumbling. For two years afterwards, all of the progress toward normalcy was quickly reversed. Martial law was declared in 2003, paving the way for a full-scale military assault on the separatists – the biggest military operation in Indonesia since the 1975 invasion of East Timor.

The 2004 tsunami provided the necessary counterpoint to open up the sealed province to relief organisations and renew peace talks between Jakarta and the rebels. On 15 August 2005, a peace accord was signed in Helsinki and many of the important steps of the agreement have been met: GAM rebels successfully surrendered their weapons and the Indonesian troops have withdrawn from the province. On 11 July 2006, the Indonesian government ratified the political end of the bargain with legislation that allows Aceh to have local political parties participate in elections (an exception to the country-wide law of national parties only), enforce sharia law, and keep 70% of its oil and gas revenues. Although optimism for a stable Aceh is tangible, some fear that the biggest obstacle to a lasting peace is steering the former GAM rebels into lives as productive citizens rather than low-level criminals. Other concerns are the fate of the peace once the European Union monitoring group pulls out in September 2006.

BANDA ACEH

☎ 0651 / pop 210,000

The provincial capital of Banda Aceh is not frequently paired in the international press with good times. The city was close enough to the sea and the epicentre of the earthquake to have suffered a double punch from the 2004 Boxing Day disaster. The earthquake toppled most of the buildings taller than three storeys and the tsunami gobbled up coastal development across middle-class suburbs. In Banda Aceh alone, 61,000 people were killed and development outside of the city centre was reduced to a wasteland in a matter of a few hours. This scale of destruction usually takes humans years of warfare to match.

However, Banda Aceh is on the mend. The usual hustle and bustle of an Indonesian town is up to full volume now and enough aid workers have arrived to kick-start an economy catering to non-governmental

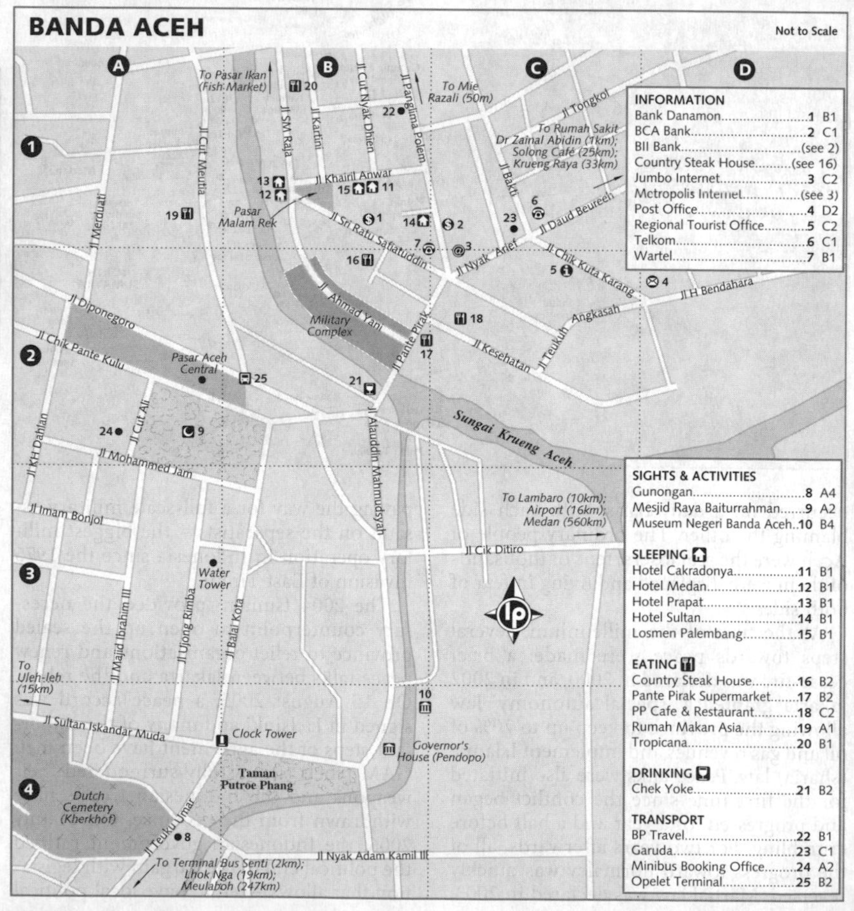

organisations (NGOs). Prices have swollen to soak up spendthrift per diems and bilingual Acehnese are finding handsome work as drivers and interpreters.

There is still grief and an obliterated landscape, but the city residents are blessed with courage. If at times being a tourist feels superficial, viewing the aftermath of the 2004 tsunami provides a necessary grounding in history and human drama. Residents will share their stories of loss and ask for nothing in return but an open heart.

What will Banda Aceh look like in a few years' time? After one year, the city had passed through the initial disaster phase: debris had been removed, the dead buried, and some businesses reopened. But rebuilding homes and infrastructure was moving at an imperceptible pace. Aid organisations anticipate being in the area until 2008, but no-one is sure if this is a realistic timeline.

What's certain, though, is that Banda Aceh will challenge any stereotypes you may have about Islam. In this devoutly Muslim city, the hassles are few and the people are friendly and easy-going. You'll see headscarfed policewomen directing traffic or sit next to a well-educated Muslim woman travelling without a male companion. Even when the city shuts down for important prayer times, locals use the afternoon break to visit with friends while the sermons are broadcast in the background.

Orientation

Banda Aceh is split in two by Sungai Krueng Aceh. In the southern part of the city is its best-known landmark, the Mesjid Raya Baiturrahman. Behind the mosque is the huge Pasar Aceh Central (central market), and adjoining the market is the main *opelet* terminal. Southwest of these landmarks are empty lots and rubble piles due to the earthquake. Rebuilding has been slow in this part of town.

The residential neighbourhoods in the southeast corner were largely unaffected by the disaster and many of the NGOs have rented the houses for their offices. The area is referred to as Geuceu Komplek.

North of the river is the city centre and where much of the rebuilding has been concentrated. The commercial spine is Jl Panglima Polem.

Information

INTERNET ACCESS & POST

The presence of internet-savvy NGOs means that Banda Aceh is firmly planted in the 21st century, unlike the rest of Sumatra. Rates are 5000Rp/hour.

Country Steakhouse Off Jl Sri Ratu Safiatuddin. This restaurant also has wireless access for laptops.

Jumbo Internet (Jl Panglima Polem 2)

Metropolis Internet (Jl Panglima Polem 8)

Post office (Jl Teukuh Angkasah; 8am-6pm) A short walk from the centre, there are also internet facilities here.

MEDICAL SERVICES

Rumah Sakit Dr Zainal Abidin (26090, 22606; Jl Nyak Arief) One of the best hospitals in town.

MONEY

There are lots of ATMs around town, mainly on Jl Panglima Polem and on Jl Sri Ratu Safiatuddin.

BCA bank (Bank Central Asia; Jl Panglima Polem)

BII bank (Bank Internasional Indonesia; Jl Panglima Polem)

Bank Danamon (Jl Sri Ratu Safiatuddin)

TELEPHONE

Telkom wartel (Jl Daud Beureeh) Home Country Direct phone.

Wartel (Jl Panglima Polem)

TOURIST INFORMATION

Regional tourist office (Dinas Parawisata; 23692; Jl Chik Kuta Karang 3) The regional tourist office is at the back of a government building. The staff are friendly and have free copies of an excellent guidebook to the province.

Sights & Activities

MESJID RAYA BAITURRAHMAN

With its brilliant white walls and liquorice-black domes, the **Mesjid Raya Baiturrahman** (admission by donation, headscarf required; 7-11am & 1.30-4pm) is a dazzling sight on a sunny day. The first section of the mosque was built by the Dutch in 1879 as a conciliatory gesture towards the Acehnese after the original one had been burnt down. Two more domes – one on either side of the first – were added by the Dutch in 1936 and another two by the Indonesian government in 1957. The mosque survived intact after the 2004 earthquake and tsunami, a sign interpreted by many residents as direct intervention from the divine. The best time to catch the mosque is during Friday afternoon prayers,

SUMATRA

THE ACEHNESE

Sitting at the far northern tip of Sumatra, Aceh was a gatekeeper for the Strait of Melaka, an important trade-winds route between India and China. So many nations passed within reach that modern-day Aceh is an ethnic blend of Indonesian, Arab, Tamil, Chinese and indigenous groups. Curiously, some of the tallest people in Indonesia live in the province. Ethnic groups include the Gayo and Alas in the mountains, the Minangkabau on the west coast, the Kluetin in the south, and Javanese and Chinese throughout.

Religion

Aceh is the most staunchly Muslim part of Sumatra, with Christians and Buddhists comprising only a small percentage of the population. In Banda Aceh, billboards remind visitors to travel globally, dress locally. Sharia law has been in place in the province since 2003.

Nevertheless, animism is also part of the everyday fabric of Acehnese life and there is a popular belief in the existence of spirits who dwell in old trees, wells, rocks and stones. Ghosts and evil spirits are said to be particularly malicious around dusk, when they can wreak havoc on all they come in contact with. *Dukun* are still called in to help solve grievances, cure illnesses, interpret dreams and omens and cast spells on enemies.

At significant times of the agricultural year, such as harvest, age-old rituals are still observed and, in some parts of Sumatra, pilgrimages are made to the tombs of Acehnese scholars and religious leaders.

Weapons

Metallurgy was learned early from Arab and Persian traders and, because of Aceh's continued involvement in wars, weapon-making became a highly developed skill. Acehnese blades can have both edges sharpened or just one, and can be straight, concave or convex. The handles of weapons are usually made of buffalo horn, wood or bone. They are carved in the form of a crocodile's mouth, a horse's hoof or a duck's tail and embellished with gold or silver. The sheaths are made of rattan, silver or wood and fastened with bands of sousa, a mixture of gold, brass and copper.

when the entire building and yard are filled with people.

GUNONGAN & KHERKHOF

All that remains today of Aceh's powerful sultanates are on view at **Gunongan** (Jl Teuku Umar). Built by Sultan Iskandar Muda (r 1607–36) as a gift for his Malay princess wife, it was intended as a private playground and bathing place. The building consists of a series of frosty peaks with narrow stairways and a walkway leading to ridges, which represent the hills of the princess' native land.

Directly across from the Gunongan is a low, vaulted gate, in the traditional Pintu Aceh style, which gave access to the sultan's palace – supposedly for the use of royalty only.

To reach Gunongan, take a *labi labi (opelet)* bound for Jl Kota Alam (3000Rp).

Not far from the Gunongan is the **Kherkhof** (Dutch Cemetery), the last resting place of more than 2000 Dutch and Indonesian soldiers who died fighting the Acehnese. The entrance is about 250m from the clock tower on the road to Uleh-leh. Tablets set into the walls by the entrance gate are inscribed with the names of the dead soldiers. The cemetery suffered some flooding from the tsunami.

To reach the Kherkhof take *labi labi* 9 or 10.

MUSEUM NEGERI BANDA ACEH

Take a tour of the province's treasured keepsakes at **Museum Negeri Banda Aceh** (Jl Alauddin Mahmudsyah 12; admission 1500Rp; 8.30am-4pm Tue-Thu, 8.30am-noon Fri & Sat). The museum has displays of Acehnese weaponry, household furnishings, ceremonial costumes, everyday clothing, gold jewellery and calligraphy.

In the same compound as the museum is the **Rumah Aceh** – a fine example of traditional Acehnese architecture, built without nails and held together with cord and pegs.

The best example of this art form is the *rencong*, a dagger that has a convex iron and *damascene* (etched or inlaid) blade with one sharpened edge. Less well-known Acehnese weapons are the *siwah* (knife) and *pedang* (pointed sword).

Jewellery

While there is a long tradition of fine gold and silver jewellery craft – stemming from the early days of the sultanate – there is almost no antique jewellery to be found in Aceh today. Much of it was sold to raise money for the war against the Dutch. Excellent gold and silver jewellery is still produced, but there is not much variation in design.

Weaving & Embroidery

Despite its long history and prominent reputation, Acehnese weaving is rapidly disappearing. On the other hand, embroidery is a vital art form. Areas around Sigli, Meulaboh and Banda Aceh are renowned for embroidery using *soedjoe* (gold-coloured metallic thread) on tapestry, cushions, fans and wall hangings. The main motifs are flowers, foliage and geometric designs. The finished work is decorated with mirrors, golden paillettes, sequins and beads, in an effect known as *blet blot*.

Mendjot beboengo is a kind of embroidery from the Gayo and Alas regions south of Takengon, traditionally done only by men. Stylised motifs of geometric flowers in red, white, yellow and green are embroidered on a black background.

Music

Typical instruments used by the Acehnese include the *arbab*, a three-stringed zither made from the wood of the jackfruit tree, with strings of bamboo, rattan or horsetail hair; and bamboo flutes (*buloh merindu*, *bangsi*, *tritit* and *soeling*). Gongs made of brass (sometimes dried goatskin) are also common, and come in three sizes: *gong*, *canang* and *mong-mong*, and are struck with padded wooden hammers.

It contains more Acehnese artefacts and war memorabilia. In front of it is a huge cast-iron bell, the **Cakra Donya**, said to have been a gift from a 15th-century Chinese emperor.

MARKETS

Market lovers will enjoy the colourful **Pasar Aceh Central**, which is just north of the Mesjid Raya between Jl Chik Pante Kulu and Jl Diponegoro.

Pasar Ikan (fish market; Jl SM Raja) defines freshness. Boats ease into the river and unload their cargoes of shark, tuna and prawns onto the vendor carts.

TSUNAMI LANDMARKS

It doesn't make for sunny postcard fodder, but travelling over oceans to mourn the dead is a profound gesture of sympathy. Seeing the place with your own eyes allows for personal and sacred memorials and helps feeble imaginations understand the scale of a disaster. Many of the most moving images of the tsunami will be erased in the coming years: the freighter ships deposited miles inland will be disassembled, the empty landscape will be rebuilt, the amputated families will form new connections. But what will remain is an ancient human custom: housing the dead so the living can remember.

There are four mass graves in and around Banda Aceh where the dead in the province were buried. The largest site is **Lambaro**, located on the road to the airport, where 46,000 unidentified bodies were buried. Other grave sites include **Meuraxa**, **Lhok Nga** and **Darusalam**, where another 54,000 bodies were interred. Families who wish to mourn the loss of unlocated relatives choose one of the mass graves based on possible geographic proximity; they have no other evidence of where to lay their prayers.

VOLUNTEERING OPPORTUNITIES

More than 1000 schools in Aceh were destroyed or damaged by the tsunami.

SUMATRA

Libraries were ruined, sports equipment swept out to sea, computer equipment lost. And then there's the human toll: some estimates claim that 2500 teachers were killed and a third of the tsunami deaths were children. Rebuilding lives in Aceh also means rebuilding educational facilities. The leading Indonesian organisation working with the schools is the philanthropic arm of the Sampoerna cigarette company. **Sampoerna Foundation** (☎ 636097; www.sampoernafoundation.org) has several projects working to restore classrooms, supplies and provide scholarships for orphaned children. The foundation is happy to meet with part-time volunteers and introduce them to partner schools.

Forum Bangum Aceh (FBA; ☎ 45204; www.fba.or.id) is the leading local NGO formed by Aceh residents to work directly and effectively with affected communities. The group has two ongoing projects: microeconomic packages to get businesses up and running, and educational outreach. Because FBA is a small organisation, it is more responsive to short-term volunteers than the larger

ANATOMY OF DISASTER RELIEF

Even in a climate of competing fashionable causes, no other natural disaster has galvanized the world's attention and support like the 2004 tsunami. Money poured in from all corners of the globe and every international aid organisation rushed to help and be seen helping. Both the disaster and the response were chaotic, causing public opinion to sour towards the well-known agencies, believing that their donations were better placed under the pillow for the disaster fairy.

With a few years under the bridge, what did the relief groups do right and what did they bungle?

The tsunami was an unprecedented disaster and in Aceh alone even a decades-long separatist movement couldn't achieve the level of destruction that the ocean accomplished in a few hours. According to figures from the United Nations Development Program (UNDP), Aceh was in a state of emergency from January to May 2005. During that time, basic shelter and nutrition were provided, families reunited, dead bodies were recovered and buried, 70,000 cubic metres of debris were removed and used in reconstruction efforts, and possible water-borne health epidemics were averted. Those could all be claimed as successes.

Now for the sore spots. Rebuilding of homes has been slow. By February 2006, the UN-managed construction teams had only completed 20,000 homes and, according to estimates, a total of 160,000 new or refurbished homes are needed. Access to materials is part of the problem: agencies bound by international standards can only use harvests from sustainable sources of timber. That's good news for Sumatra's protected forests, but being ecofriendly is a crummy consolation prize for someone stuck in a tent. Bricks are a possible alternative but the brick-making facilities in Aceh are not mechanised. An average worker can produce only 500 bricks per day. There's also a labour shortage: in 2006, Aceh needed 200,000 construction workers but only 40,000 were registered. Then there's the question of where to rebuild. Many land deeds were washed away, some property is now underwater, and disputes over ownership and inheritance are common.

The UNDP has targeted 2007 as the year that all displaced people will have housing. If reconstruction continues at the current rate, 2010 is a more likely target.

But what the aid organisations botched most was the public relations game. Banda Aceh is filled with sealed-off SUVs stamped with agency logos looking like princely chariots. Many communities are reluctant to cooperate with relief workers because of too many unfilled promises by inexperienced organisations, or cultural misunderstandings. The uniform of the relief workers, an agency badge and a memory stick in a breast pocket, has become something of a local joke. Then there's the counterattack. Aid workers complain that locals only work if they're paid and that they always want more. Casual observers, from a safe café distance away, accuse NGOs of being bloated bureaucracies, pointing to anecdotes about overpaid executives whose résumés comprise car washing. And everyone assumes that all that money is being poured down someone else's gullet. In reality, a portion might be wetting fat cats' whistles, and the rest of the money that was promised was never delivered. Natural disasters, like weddings, often bring out the worst and best in people.

NGOs. Whatever your area of expertise, FBA will find a place for you.

Sleeping

Only a few of Banda Aceh's hotels have reopened since the tsunami. Those that have are usually filled with aid workers and have increased their rates, but not their standards.

Losmen Palembang (☎ 22044; Jl Khairil Anwar 49; d with fan/air-con 50,000/150,000Rp; ❄) A basic place with dark and depressing rooms.

Hotel Prapat (☎ 22159; Jl Ahmad Yani 19; d with fan/air-con 100,000/200,000Rp; ❄) One of the more affordable spots, Prapat has motel-style rooms with Western toilet and clean sheets.

Hotel Medan (☎ 21501; Jl Ahmad Yani 15; d 180,000-250,000Rp; ❄) The freighter boat has been removed from the parking lot and many of the flooded rooms have been nicely renovated.

Hotel Cakradonya (☎ 33633; Jl Khairil Anwar 10; d with fan/air-con 330,000/500,000Rp; ❄) Has comfortable rooms that have seen better days.

Hotel Sultan (☎ 22469; Jl Panglima Polem 1; d from 500,000Rp) When the NGOs hit town, this was one of the only functional hotels and has been packed out ever since. The rates are ridiculously overpriced and the going joke in town is that this is a two-star hotel with five-star prices.

Eating

The square at the junction of Jl Ahmad Yani and Jl Khairil Anwar is the setting for the **Pasar Malam Rek**, Banda Aceh's lively night food market.

Rumah Makan Asia (☎ 23236; Jl Cut Meutia 37/39; mains 10,000Rp) Aceh's version of *masakan Padang* (Padang dish) has an array of zesty dishes, such as *ikan panggang* (baked fish).

Mie Razali (☎ 27148; Jl Panglima Polem 85) This local rice and noodle chain spins up an avocado–chocolate shake that tastes like ice cream after a romp through a green field.

PP Cafe & Restaurant (Jl Kesehatan 115; mains 12,000Rp) Has a good selection of Indonesian and some European food.

Pante Pirak supermarket (Jl Pante Pirak; 🕒 until 10pm) Good for stocking up on supplies or just watching the buying habits of Banda Aceh's middle class.

Country Steak House (☎ 081 1680012; Jl Sri Ratu Safiatuddin 45B; mains 60,000-100,000Rp; 🕒 10am-midnight) Wherever there are executives, rest assured there are steaks. Psst, there's beer here too.

Tropicana (Jl SM Raja; mains from 15,000Rp) One of two seafood restaurants in town where the NGOs go. Just look for the tell-tale SUVs parked out front.

Drinking

Because of sharia law, alcohol is not available as openly here as elsewhere in Indonesia, but Chinese restaurants, the Hotel Sultan and Country Steak House serve beer. As long as it is kept quiet, most of the locals don't mind.

If you'd like to see what life is like without the fermented juice, follow the locals to the brewed replacement. The teenagers in town sip and smoke at **Chek Yoke** (Jl Chik Pante Kulu), a coffee shop on the southern banks of the river.

Aceh's most famous coffee house is nicknamed **Solong Café** (Jasa Ayah Cafeteria; Sedia Bubuk Aceh, Ulee Kareng). One-pound bags of finely ground, locally grown coffee are on sale and make a delicious post-Indo gift. You'll need to take a taxi.

Getting There & Away

AIR

There are several flights a day from Banda Aceh to Medan (250,000Rp) on Garuda, Adam Air and Lion Air. The last flight leaves Banda Aceh at 5.30pm. **BP Travel** (☎ 32325; Jl Panglima Polem 75) is a helpful air ticket agent. **Garuda** (Garuda Indonesia; ☎ 32523; Jl Daud Beureeh 9) also has an office in Banda Aceh.

BOAT

After the tsunami, the port moved to Ulehleh, 15km northwest of Banda Aceh's city centre. The road to the port goes straight through the tsunami's path – once a two-car garage suburb, now an eerie, empty landscape. Bamboo barracks in places have replaced the fine homes, but otherwise there is very little evidence of the former communities: no roads, streetlights or clotheslines. See Pulau Weh for boat schedules and fare information (p424).

BUS

South of the city centre you'll find the **Terminal Bus Senti** (Jl Teuku Umar). There are numerous buses to Medan (economy/air-con

120,000/150,000Rp, nine to 13 hours). As long as the peace agreement holds, overland travel between Banda Aceh and Medan is safer now than in the past.

The west coast road from Banda Aceh to Meulaboh was destroyed by the 2004 tsunami. When land transport does resume, you'll have the option of public buses that depart from the bus terminal or minibuses that depart from offices behind the mosque on Jl Mohammad Jam.

South of Meulaboh, the road is in working order and can be accessed via the interior road through Aceh or from Medan.

Getting Around

Airport taxis charge 60,000Rp to 70,000Rp for the 16km ride into town. Rates have increased with the NGO presence. The unlikely bargaining chip of being a tourist and not an NGO can get you a cheaper price. A taxi from the airport to Uleh-leh port will cost 100,000Rp.

Labi labi are the main form of transport around town and cost 1500Rp. The **opelet terminal** (Jl Diponegoro) is that special breed of Indonesian mayhem.

For Uleh-leh (5000Rp, 30 minutes), take the blue *labi labi* signed 'Uleh-leh'. You can also reach Lhok Nga and Lampu'uk (15,000Rp).

Becak around town should cost between 5000Rp and 10,000Rp, depending on your destination. From the centre of town to Geuceu Komplek, a becak should cost about 10,000Rp.

PULAU WEH

☎ 0652 / pop 25,000

You are in for a real treat at Pulau Weh. The island's fingers grasp at the mighty Indian Ocean, forming vistas of alternating land and sea. Like the terrestrial landscape, the underwater geography is rugged and varied, creating the scuba version of hiking. Divers describe great walls of languid sea fans, deep canyons and rock pinnacles, plus a lot of big fish.

Hardly on the international radar of beach scenes, Weh is mellow and unconcerned with tourist dollars. Along the muddy island road are little villages with underwear-only kids playing in the yard, lazy cows tied up to a green patch of grass and scrappy goats looking for garden victims. The shops cater to the locals with communal TVs and coffee instead of souvenir kitsch.

Pulau Weh is shaped roughly like a horseshoe. On the northeastern leg is the port town of Sabang, where most of Weh's population lives. The primary tourist beaches are Gapang and Iboih, which are about 20km away heading towards the northwestern leg.

It's always a little rainy on Weh, with two monsoon seasons. November to January are the wettest, coolest months but are also the best times to see whale sharks.

Malaria has been reported on the island, so take the proper precautions.

The tsunami did give Weh a minor licking, but the island fared better than the mainland. Many of the coastal businesses that were bashed up have since rebuilt and the villagers banded together to repair roads, replant trees and fill in washed-out pockets of the beach.

Sabang

The island's main township is an interesting mix of traditional fishing village and old colonial villas. During Dutch rule, Sabang was a major coal and water depot for steamships, but with the arrival of diesel power after WWII it went into decline.

During the 1970s it was a duty-free port, but this status was eliminated in 1986 and Sabang once again became a sleepy fishing town. Today the only industry – other than fishing – is rattan furniture.

Most people pass through Sabang fairly quickly en route to the tourist beaches, but return to town for provisions.

The **post office** (Jl Perdagangan 66) is next door to the **telephone office** (🕑 24hr), which has a Home Country Direct phone.

BRI bank (Bank Rakyat Indonesia; Jl Perdagangan) changes travellers cheques and US dollars at terrible rates. It also has an ATM that only accepts MasterCard.

Alternatively, try your negotiating skills with the Chinese moneychangers scattered about town.

Sabang is surrounded by beautiful beaches. Just 10 minutes' walk away is **Pantai Paradiso**, a white-sand beach shaded by coconut palms. A little further on is **Pantai Kasih** (Lover's Beach), and about 30 minutes from town is **Pantai Sumur Tiga**, a popular picnic spot.

Other attractions around Sabang include **Danau Anak Laut**, a serene freshwater lake that supplies the island's water, and **Gunung Merapi**, a semi-active volcano, which holds boiling water in its caldera and occasionally puffs smoke.

SLEEPING & EATING

Few people choose to stay in town unless they get stuck.

Losmen Irma (☎ 21148; Jl Teuku Umar 3; s/d 40,000/60,000Rp) A local boarding house.

Losmen Pulau Jaya (☎ 21344; Jl Teuku Umar 17; d 60,000-75,000Rp; ❄) Another cheap spot across the road.

Hotel Holiday (☎ 21131; Jl Perdagangan 1; d 60,000-150,000Rp; ❄) A marked step up, Hotel Holiday is a Chinese-run hotel with solid, if not fashion-plate, rooms.

Samudera Hotel (☎ 21503; Jl Diponegoro; d with fan/air-con 60,000/150,000Rp; ❄) This old Dutch villa in a peaceful area up the hill is full of worn charm. Cheaper rooms are fairly simple but the more expensive options are bright and spacious.

There are plenty of restaurants along the main street, Jl Perdagangan, serving cheap Padang food. There's also a fruit market near the BRI bank.

Gapang

Occupying a sandy cove, Gapang is more social than Iboih, with little beachside cafés and front-door swimming. Some may try to argue that one beach is better than the other, but both have their charms.

SLEEPING & EATING

Gapang has the greatest variety of accommodation on the island, from pseudo resorts to cheapie huts. On the weekends, rates often increase by double or more because of short-term business from the NGOs based in Aceh. If you're staying longer than two days or arrive mid-week, you should be able to get the rates quoted here or cheaper. The hotels are listed here in geographical order from west to east.

Leguna Resort (☎ 22799; d 175,000-380,000Rp; ❄) A garden of generous-sized chalets, a handful of which have sea views. There is a small enclosed beach but the resort is a little weatherworn.

Flamboyan (☎ 081 360272270; d 250,000-400,000Rp; ❄) A large resort-type outfit with pleasant traditional-style rooms and a restaurant built on top of the rocky point.

Following the small road around the headland will lead you to Gapang's main hang-out.

Ohana (80,000Rp) Three basic wooden bungalows with *mandis* (common Indonesian bath, consisting of a large water tank from which water is ladled over the body) are planted on the hillside.

No-name Bungalows (20,000-40,000Rp) This bamboo barrack had just been built when we arrived and had not yet been christened. The rooms are basic and are a shoe-less stumble to the waves.

Ramadilla (50,000Rp) Past everything else, Ramadilla's cabins climb up the hill with a longhouse or two that commands a chieftain's view of the sea.

Beachside cafés, serving Western food, absorb the evening breezes and post-dive appetites. For lunch, head out to the main road, where a small warung does delicious *nasi bungus* (rice and curry served for takeaway in a banana leaf).

Iboih

More rustic than Gapang, Iboih follows a rocky headland with a string of simple bungalows along a woodsy footpath. The almost castaway feel is a foolproof backpacker magnet.

A small path leads through a stone gateway past the village well and up and over a small hill to the bungalow strip.

Opposite Iboih, 100m offshore, is **Pulau Rubiah**, a densely forested island surrounded by spectacular coral reefs known as the **Sea Garden**. It is a favourite snorkelling and diving spot. The coral has been destroyed in places but there is still plenty to see including turtles, manta ray, lion fish, tigerfish and occasional sharks.

If you are a strong swimmer it is possible to make your own way there. Beware of strong currents, especially at the southern tip of the island.

Adjacent to the Sea Garden is the **Iboih Forest nature reserve**. It has some good walks and coastal caves that can be explored by boat.

SLEEPING & EATING

Simple palm-thatch bungalows, many built on stilts and overhanging crystal-clear water, make up the majority of the accommodation here.

Most places are very similar, but do a wander before declaring a winner. If you arrive mid-week and stay for several days, you can negotiate 30,000Rp a night. If you're near the weekend when the NGOs arrive expect to pay 50,000Rp or more depending on how long you stay. Most places have shared bathroom facilities.

The following losmen are listed in geographic order as you'll approach them: **Arina**, **Fatimah**, **Oong's** and **Yulia's**.

Just off the main road are a few **shops** selling sundries, Indonesian lunches and coffee in front of a small beach. If you speak Bahasa Indonesia, this is where you can scoop up the village gossip.

Next door to Rubiah Tirta Divers is **Chill Out Café**, serving all three meals and a view of a small beach. **Norma's**, the restaurant portion of Oong's Guesthouse, does a nightly seafood dinner around a communal table and serves beer. Further down, **Yulia's** has shakes and light fare. Prices at these places tend to be around 25,000Rp for mains.

Long Angen

This secluded beach on the western side of the island is ideally located for spectacular sunsets. The beach itself only exists for six months of the year – the sand is swept away by the sea from November to May.

Activities

DIVING & SNORKELLING

People don't come to Weh for the nightlife or the bikinis. They come for the diving, which is considered some of the best the Indian Ocean has to offer. On an average day, you're likely to spot morays, manta rays, lionfish, and stingrays. During plankton blooms, whale sharks come to graze. Unlike other dive sites, the coral fields take a back seat to the sea life and landscapes. There are close to 20 dive sites around the island, most in and around Iboih and Gapang.

There are two dive operators on the island. At Iboih, **Rubiah Tirta Divers** (☎ 081 534020050; info@rubiahdivers.com) is the oldest dive operation on the island and charges US$30/54/72 for one/two/three dives.

At Gapang, **Lumba Lumba Diving Centre** (☎ 331133; www.lumbalumba.com) is the centre of activity with the comings and goings of wet-suit creatures. Ton and Marjan Egbers maintain a helpful website with detailed descriptions of dives and other need-to-know information. Rates are quoted in euros and start at €25/45/65 for one/two/three; you can pay with plastic. Padi diving courses are also available. The centre's shop has internet access (20,000Rp per hour).

Snorkelling gear can be hired almost anywhere for around 15,000Rp per day.

Getting There & Away

Sabang is the port town on Pulau Weh. Fast ferries to Sabang leave the mainland from Uleh-leh, 15km northwest of Banda Aceh, at 9.30am and 4pm (economy/cabin 60,000/70,000, two hours). Slow ferries leave at 2pm (12,000Rp, three hours). In the opposite direction, the slow ferry leaves at 8am and the fast ferry at 8.30am and 4pm. You should get to the port at least an hour before departure to get a ticket.

Getting Around

From the port, there are regular bemo to Sabang (10,000Rp, 15 minutes), and Gapang and Iboih (50,000Rp, 45 minutes). *Labi labi* run from Jl Perdagangan in Sabang to Gapang and Iboih (30,000Rp). The road from Sabang to the beaches is rough in patches, like all roads in Sumatra.

ACEH'S WEST COAST

Rounding the northwestern tip of Sumatra's finger of land is a string of little villages and endless beaches backed by densely forested hills. This is the perfect recipe for paradise, but several factors have conspired to keep the sands free of beach blankets: the unstable safety situation during the military occupation of Aceh, and the 2004 tsunami.

Lhok Nga & Lampu'uk

☎ 0656 / pop Lhok Nga 200, Lampu'uk 1000

These coastal weekend spots, only 17km from Banda Aceh, were levelled by the tsunami. In Lampu'uk the wave travelled some 7km inland, killing four out of every five people. One elementary school in the area went from a student population of 300 children to 35; nearly a generation wiped out. Many of the villagers are still living in temporary shelters.

Somewhat cruelly, the beach and ocean are just as beautiful as ever, perhaps more so. None of the beachside development, except for the now repaired cement company, has been rebuilt.

Joel's Beach BBQ (☎ 081 37528; per person 100,000-150,000Rp) organises group fish fries on the beach of Lampu'uk near where his beach bungalows used to be located. There are plans in the future for accommodation. Call in advance to make reservations.

Take *labi labi* 04 (15,000Rp) from the *opelet* terminal in Banda Aceh for both Lhok Nga and Lampu'uk.

Calang & Meulaboh

☎ 0655 / pop Calang 10,000, Meulaboh 80,000

Everything in the town of **Calang** was destroyed by the tsunami; the population was cut in half and infrastructure is gone.

Further south, **Meulaboh,** 240km from Banda Aceh, was the closest town to the earthquake's epicentre and is often referred to in the press as 'ground zero'. The town was completely destroyed and close to a third of the 120,000 population were killed.

The town has since been moved to a largely unaffected, northern suburb. **Meuligo Hotel** (Jl Iskandar Muda 35; 75,000Rp; ❄) survived the tsunami and is open for business.

Full recovery for these communities is many years away. Many survivors still remain in temporary camps and the only visitors going in and out are aid workers engaged in humanitarian relief.

Even accessing these towns to provide relief has been difficult. The west-coast road from Banda Aceh to Meulaboh was destroyed by the tsunami. USAID has contracted with Halliburton to rebuild parts of the road by 2008, but this target date had been previously moved forward due to logistical problems and may very well slide again.

There are currently no bus services to Calang or Meulaboh, but there are helicopter food missions arranged for aid workers. The airport is operational and SMAC runs twice-weekly flights between Meulaboh and Banda Aceh (281,000Rp).

There is currently a public ferry that goes from Uleh-leh to Calang (120,000Rp, six hours) four times a week.

Do also note that malaria can be a problem, so take precautions. Before going for a swim, be aware that some of the west-coast beaches have very strong currents.

Pulau Simeulue

☎ 0650 / pop 70,000

The isolated island of Simeulue, about 150km west of Tapaktuan, is a rocky volcanic outcrop blanketed in rainforest and fringed with clove and coconut plantations. Few visitors make it this far – though the surfing is said to be excellent along the west coast.

Simeulue suffered relatively minor damage from the 2004 tsunami. Many residents heeded ancestral knowledge and ran into the hills when the ocean started to recede. This resulted in a death toll of only nine people. The north coast was hit the worst, leaving villagers without homes, livestock or crops. The March 2006 earthquake also shook Simeulue, causing structural damage to concrete buildings, and three reported deaths.

The port of Sinabang and the airport are still operational. Along the main road in Sinabang is **Losmen Simeuleu** (30,000Rp) and **Losmen Lovya** (30,000Rp).

On the west coast is the surf camp **Baneng Beach Retreat** (☎ 081 362417692; www.simeulue.com; packages from US$80), also called 'Willy's Place'. Reef uplift from the earthquake has flattened out some of the famous surf breaks, but new spots are being discovered.

SMAC flies to Simeulue (450,000Rp) from Medan and Banda Aceh; inquire with the Medan **office** (☎ 4551888) or a local travel agent for ticketing and schedules.

Ferries run from the mainland ports of Singkil and Meulaboh to Pulau Simeuleu's port town of Sinabang. Until Aceh's west-coast road is restored, land connections are best made via North Sumatra (Medan or Parapat) instead of Banda Aceh.

Tapaktuan

☎ 0656 / pop 15,000

The sleepy seaside town of Tapaktuan, 200km south of Meulaboh, is the main town in South Aceh. It's very laid-back by Sumatran standards and, although it has few specific sights, it can be a pleasant place to hang out for a couple of days. Although its location would suggest otherwise, Tapaktuan was not noticeably affected by the tsunami. Many displaced people from other parts of Aceh have sought refuge here with relatives or friends.

Most places of importance are on the main street, Jl Merdeka, which runs along the coast. The town can be used as a base to explore the lowland **Kluet region** of Gunung Leuser National Park, about 45km south. Kluet's unspoilt swamp forests support the densest population of **primates** in Southeast Asia and are also good sites for **bird-watching**. It may be possible to hire guides through the national park office in Kandang, 38km south of Tapaktuan.

Pantai Tu'i Lhok and **Pantai Air Dingin**, about 18km north of Tapaktuan, are the best of several good beaches in the area. Opposite both beaches are waterfalls with natural plunge pools where you can cool off.

Gua Kelam (Dark Cave), 3km north of Tapaktuan, is a spectacular series of caves and tunnels that can be explored, but you'd be wise to take a guide. Don't worry about finding a guide – they'll find you.

Most of the places to stay are along Jl Merdeka. **Losmen Bukit Barisan** (☎ 21145; s/d 35,000/60,000Rp), in an old Dutch house, is a friendly place with basic rooms and a certain shabby charm; and **Hotel Panorama** (☎ 21004; d from 50,000Rp; ❄) is a large, modern hotel with a range of reasonable rooms.

Jl Merdeka is also a good place to find a bite to eat. Seafood is a speciality and there are several **restaurants** selling delicious grilled fish for about 10,000Rp. After dark, the **night market** by the main pier, opposite Hotel Panorama, kicks into action and is a lively place for a quick meal.

SUMATRA

GETTING THERE & AWAY

Until the west-coast road is repaired, Tapaktuan is better reached from Medan (90,000Rp, 10 hours) via Berastagi and Sidikalang. From Sidikalang it's possible to get a direct bus to Pangururan (40,000Rp, two hours) on the west coast of Danau Toba.

Singkil

☎ 0658 / pop 20,000

Singkil is a remote port at the mouth of Sungai Alas. It merits a mention only as the departure point for boats to the Simeulue and Banyak islands.

Catching a boat will mean spending a night at one of Singkil's very basic **losmen** (30,000Rp).

There are daily minibuses from Medan to Singkil (70,000Rp, 10 hours). If you're travelling from Berastagi, Danau Toba or Tapaktuan, you will need to change buses at Sidikalang and Subulus Salem.

Boats leave for Pulau Balai (25,000Rp, four hours) at 1pm on Wednesday.

BANYAK ISLANDS

pop 5000

The Banyak (Many) Islands are a cluster of 99, mostly uninhabited, islands, about 30km west of Singkil. The islands are very remote and see few casual visitors. The 2004 Boxing Day earthquake and tsunami, followed by the 2005 Nias quake, destroyed many coastal dwellings and contaminated freshwater wells. The main island of Pulau Balai was permanently see-sawed by the quake, causing the west coast to rise by about 70cm and the east coast to drop below sea level. The main town of Balai now experiences flooding at high tide.

Malaria has been reported on the islands, so take suitable precautions.

Inquire at the pier about accommodation on Pulau Balai. Lodging may also be available on Pulau Palambak Kecil, Pulau Rangit Besar, Pulau Panjang and Pulau Ujung Batu with local families; ask about meals when arranging a room.

There is one boat a week (Wednesdays at 1pm) between Balai and the mainland port of Singkil (one way 25,000Rp, four hours).

GAYO HIGHLANDS

As long as the peace lasts, the interior of Aceh is ripe for off-the-path picking. This is coffee country, cool and mountainous with spectacular vistas and the odd spotting of wild jungle critters. The road from Takengon to Blangkejeran, the main towns of the Gayo Highlands, is astoundingly picturesque and can be used as an alternative route to or from Berastagi.

Farming is the main occupation in the highlands and the principal crops are coffee and tobacco, followed by rice and vegetables. You'll know you're in Gayo country by the number of water buffalo, which replace the hump-necked *bentang* cattle preferred in the rest of the province.

The Gayo, who number about 250,000, lived an isolated existence until the advent of modern roads and transport. Like the neighbouring Acehnese, the Gayo are strict Muslims and were renowned for their fierce resistance to Dutch rule.

Before building an itinerary around the Gayo Highlands, watch the press for any unsettling developments in the peace accord. It is probably safe to assume that no news is good news.

Takengon

☎ 0643

Takengon is the largest town in the highlands, but retains a sleepy charm, with a spectacular setting and refreshing climate. The town is built on the shores of Danau Laut Tawar, a 26km-long stretch of water, surrounded by steep hills rising to volcanic peaks. Gunung Geureundong, to the north, rises 2855m.

Much of the town centre dates from the beginning of the 20th century, when the town was used as a Dutch base.

ORIENTATION & INFORMATION

All of the action is in the centre of town on Jl Lebe Kadir. You'll find the post office, Telkom wartel, police station and Mesjid Raya here. You can change US dollars (cash and travellers cheques) at **BRI bank** (Bank Rakyat Indonesia; Jl Yos Sudarso).

SIGHTS & ACTIVITIES

Takengon's main attractions are all natural. Admire the views, cruise around the lake in a *perahu* (dugout canoe) or explore caves, waterfalls and hot springs.

The best cave is **Loyang Koro** (Buffalo Caves), 6km from town, with some interesting stalagmites and plenty of bats. In the village of Kebayakan, just north of town, you can see the sole attraction made by humans in the area: the intricately **carved house** of the region's last traditional ruler. Further on, at Simpang Balik, about 15km north of Takengon, the sulphurous **hot spring** is said to cure skin diseases.

In the week following Independence Day (17 August), Takengon hosts a regional **horse-racing** carnival, held at the track to the west of town. It's a highly spirited affair, with 12-year-old jockeys from all over the highlands riding bareback in the hope of glory.

SLEEPING & EATING

Hotel Buntu Kubu (☎ 22254; Jl Malem Dewa; d from 50,000Rp) This place has a magnificent view over the lake. The hotel has a varied history: it was a former Dutch official residence, museum and Indonesian military post.

Hotel Renggali (☎ 21144; Jl Bintang; d from 150,000Rp) Perched on the lakeside 2km out of town, Renggali is set in beautiful gardens and has some hit-and-miss rooms.

Padang food and Chinese-style noodle dishes can be found all along Jl Lebe Kadir, Jl Pasar Inpres and around the bus terminal.

Delicious fresh Gayo coffee is available pretty much everywhere. A local speciality is *kopi telor kocok* – a raw egg and sugar creamed together in a glass and topped up with coffee.

SHOPPING

Takengon is the place to buy traditional-style Gayo/Alas tapestry, which is made into clothes, belts, purses and cushion covers. At the market, it's sometimes possible to buy highly decorated engraved pottery called *keunire*, which is used in wedding ceremonies.

GETTING THERE & AWAY

There are two buses a day to Medan: an economy bus (70,000Rp, 13 hours) and a 'deluxe' air-con bus (95,000Rp, 11 hours). Other destinations include Banda Aceh (60,000Rp, eight hours).

Heading south, there are regular buses to Blangkejeran (53,000Rp, seven hours) and Gurah/Ketambe (50,000Rp, nine hours). You would connect through these towns to reach Berastagi.

GETTING AROUND

Labi labi leave from the southern end of Jl Baleatu. Fares around town cost 1500Rp. *Perahu* for lake cruising can be hired at the pier at the end of Jl Laut Tawar.

Blangkejeran

Blangkejeran is the main town of the remote southern highlands. The area is recognised as the Gayo heartland and it's possible to hire guides to take you out to some of the smaller **villages**. Accommodation is available in several small guesthouses. There are regular buses north to Takengon and south to Gurah and Kutacane.

GUNUNG LEUSER NATIONAL PARK

☎ 0629

Gunung Leuser National Park is one of the world's most important and biologically

SUMATRA

diverse conservation areas. It is often described as a complete ecosystem laboratory because of the range of forest and species types.

Within the park's boundaries live some of the planet's most endangered species – tigers, rhinoceros, elephants and orang-utans. Although your chances of seeing these celebrity animals are extremely remote, you can be sure of encountering plenty of primates. The most common is the white-breasted Thomas Leaf monkey, which sports a brilliant, crested punk hairdo.

Habitats range from the swamp forests of the west coast to the dense lowland rainforests of the interior. Much of the area around Ketambe is virgin forest. Above 1500m, the permanent mist has created moss forests rich in epiphytes and orchids. Rare flora includes two members of the rafflesia family, *Rafflesia acehensis* and *Rafflesia zippelnii*, which are found along Sungai Alas.

More than 300 bird species have been recorded in the park, including the bizarre rhinoceros hornbill and the helmeted hornbill, which has a call that sounds like maniacal laughter.

The park faces a great number of challenges. Poachers have virtually wiped out the crocodile population and have severely reduced the number of tigers and rhinoceros. According to the Indonesian Forum for the Environment, a fifth of the park has been adversely affected by illegal logging and road construction. A highly controversial road project, called Ladia Galaska, has been on the government agenda for years and when completed will link the eastern and western coasts of the province through the park. The progress of the project has been slow and embattled.

This park receives a lot of rain throughout the year, but rain showers tend to lessen in frequency and duration from December to March.

Orientation & Information

Gurah, in the heart of the Alas Valley, is one of the main access points to Gunung Leuser National Park. Directly across the river is Ketambe, home to a world-renowned conservation research station, which is off limits to tourists (see the boxed text on below). Kutacane, 43km from Gurah, is the closest town of any note and is the place to go for transport, supplies and post and telephone facilities.

You are not allowed to enter the park without a permit and a guide. Both are available from the PHKA office in Tanah Merah, about 45 minutes from Gurah, and 15 minutes from Kutacane. Permits cost 20,000Rp (plus 500Rp insurance) per day. In theory you will need three photocopies of your passport but this is rarely required. Guides can be hired from the PHKA office or from any guesthouse in Gurah. If you have a certain plant or animal objective, ask around for the guides with that speciality.

Guide prices are fixed by the Sumatran Guide Association (US$15 for three hours, US$20 per day, US$40 for a two-day trek).

Trekking

For serious trekkers and jungle enthusiasts Gurah offers a much more authentic experi-

KETAMBE RESEARCH STATION

The Ketambe Research Station has been conducting extensive studies of the flora and fauna of Gunung Leuser National Park for almost 30 years.

In the early 1970s Ketambe was home to Sumatra's orang-utan rehabilitation programme, but the project was relocated to Bukit Lawang to allow researchers to study the Ketambe region without the disruption of tourists. Nowadays the station's primary concern is hard-core conservation, research and species cataloguing. Both the centre and the surrounding forest are off limits to almost everyone but the Indonesian and international researchers.

The 450-hectare protected area consists mainly of primary lowland tropical forest and is home to a large number of primates, as well as Sumatran tigers, rhinoceros, sun bears, hornbills and snakes. Despite its protected status, a third of the area has been lost to illegal logging since 1999.

For more information on Ketambe research activities, visit www.eu-ldp.co.id/16RMIDivx.htm or visit the website of the park's conservation and outreach organisation, Leuser Development Program (www.eu-ldp.co.id).

SUMATRA

ence than the trekking near Bukit Lawang. Be prepared for hordes of leeches, swarms of stinging insects and extreme terrain. The PHKA office in Tanah Merah has information about a variety of treks, from short walks to 14-day hikes through the jungle to the tops of the park's mountains. Here are a few options; guides can also tailor a trip to specific requests:

Gurah Recreation Forest The *hutan wisata* (recreation forest) at Gurah is a park within the national park. The forest's 9200 hectares have walking tracks and viewing towers; the most popular walk involves a two-hour (5km) hike from Gurah to hot springs by Sungai Alas. There's also a 6km walk to a waterfall.

Gunung Kemiri At 3314m, this is the second-highest peak in Gunung Leuser National Park. The return trek takes five to six days, starting from the village of Gumpang, north of Gurah. It takes in some of the park's richest primate habitat, with orang-utans, macaques, siamangs and gibbons.

Gunung Perkinson Allow seven days for the return trek to the summit of Gunung Perkinson (2828m), on the eastern side of the park. There are wild orchids, lady slipper and other flowers unique to Aceh, as well as a spectacular moss forest along this route.

Gunung Simpali The trek to Gunung Simpali (3270m) is a one-week round trip starting from the village of Engkran and following the valley of Sungai Lawe Mamas. Rhinos live in this area. The Lawe Mamas is a wild, raging river that joins the Alas about 15km north of Kutacane.

Gunung Leuser The park's highest peak is, of course, Gunung Leuser (3404m). Only the fit should attempt the 14-day return trek to the summit. The walk starts from the village of Angusan, northwest of Blangkejeran.

Sleeping & Eating

Accommodation is scattered along the only road through Gurah. Each guesthouse has its own small **restaurant**.

Pondok Wisata Ketambe (☎ 21709; d from 60,000Rp) Coming from the south, it is the first option with forest bungalows. More-expensive rooms have hot water.

Guesthouse Sadar Wisata (d 50,000-60,000Rp) Next door, this has a range of good-value bungalows from basic older models to newer, more comfortable rooms across the road.

Gurah Bungalows (r from 85,000Rp) The only upmarket option, 4km up the road. Clean, spacious rooms are set deep in the forest, right on the bank of the river.

If you arrive in Kutacane too late to reach Gurah, you might have to spend the night at **Wisma Rindu Alam** (Jl Besar; d from 50,000Rp).

Getting There & Around

SMAC flies from Kutacane to Medan and to Banda Aceh.

Long-distance buses leave from the terminal in Kutacane for Medan's Pinang Baris terminal (80,000Rp, six hours) and Berastagi (40,000Rp, five hours). Along the way there are fine views of Gunung Sinabung and the Alas Valley.

From Kutacane there are countless *labi labi* to Tanah Merah (5000Rp, 15 minutes) and Gurah (10,000Rp, one hour).

There are also buses heading north to Blangkejeran and beyond.

WEST SUMATRA

In West Sumatra the earth swells as mightily as an angry sea. Silent but deadly volcanoes stand alone on their pedestals, reminding the populous who commands the landscape. Roads daring to traverse the serpentine mountain ranges are more crooked than a politician, winding in and out of valleys sewn together by a patchwork of verdant, terraced rice paddies. Thanks to a combination of rich volcanic soil and ample rainfall the region is an excellent growing area and pockets of lush tropical rainforest survive.

The people who tamed the jungle are the Minangkabau, an ethnic group that has dominated the province's cultural and political identity. Their distinctive buffalo-horned buildings dominate West Sumatra's cities and villages, and their colourful wedding parades subdue the usual bustle of modern-day traffic.

But the Minangkabau influence isn't confined to the fertile highlands. Because of their traditional custom of *merantau* – travelling to find your fortune – the Minangkabau have filtered across Indonesia, exporting their cuisine *(nasi Padang)* and their language (a dialect of Malay which formed the basis for Bahasa Indonesia). They are regarded by their compatriots as an adaptable, intelligent people, and are one of the most economically successful ethnic groups in the country.

The hot, bustling city of Padang is the gateway to the province, but it's the pleasant hill town of Bukittinggi that headlines the tourist itinerary. An idyllic volcanic

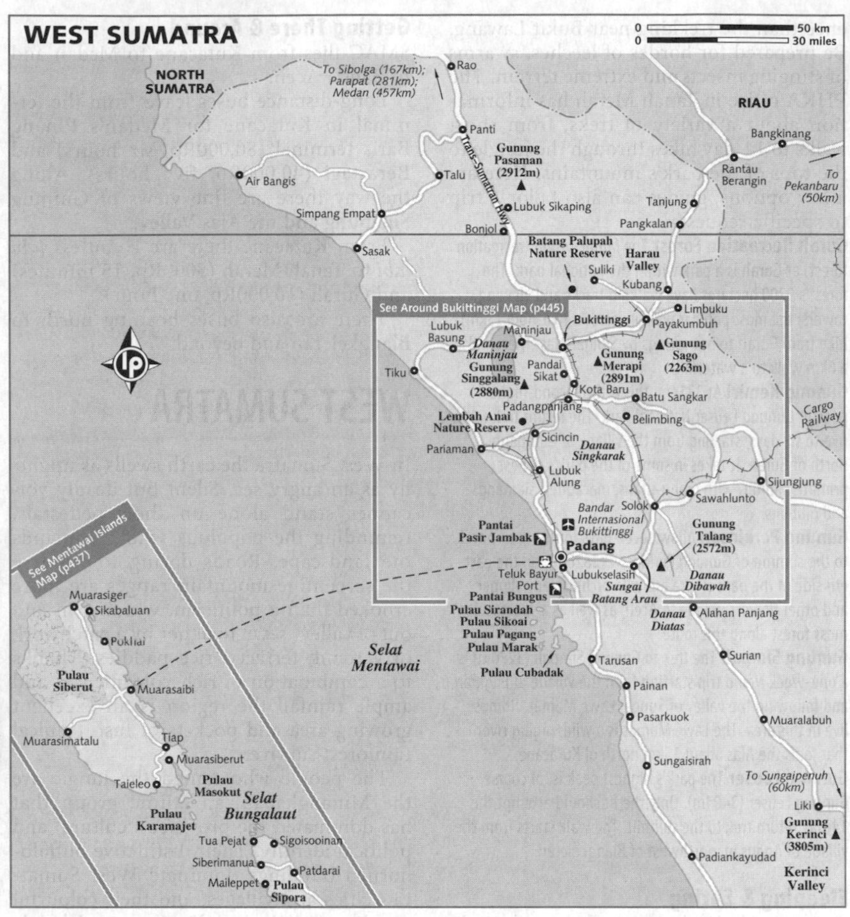

lake, Danau Maninjau resides peacefully close to perfection. Off the west coast, the Mentawai Islands, long isolated from mainland Sumatra, offer a fascinating glimpse of traditional tribal culture and rip-roaring surf breaks.

History

Little is known about the area's history until the arrival of Islam in the 14th century. However, the abundance of megalithic remains around the towns of Batu Sangkar and Payakumbuh, near Bukittinggi, suggest that the central highlands supported a sizable community some 2000 years ago.

After the arrival of Islam, the region was split into small Muslim states ruled by sultans and it remained this way until the beginning of the 19th century, when war erupted between followers of the Islamic fundamentalist Padri movement and supporters of the local chiefs, adherents to the Minangkabau *adat*. The Padris were so named because their leaders were haji, pilgrims who had made their way to Mecca via the Acehnese port of Pedir. They returned from the hajj determined to establish a true Islamic society and stamp out the pre-Islamic ways that dominated the ruling houses.

The Padris had won control of much of the highlands by 1821 when the Dutch decided to join the fray in support of the Minangkabau traditional leaders. The fighting dragged on until 1837, when the Dutch overcame the equator town of Bonjol, the stronghold of the Padri leader Imam Bonjol, whose name adorns street signs all over Indonesia. In today's Minangkabau society, a curious fusion of traditional beliefs and Islam is practised in West Sumatra.

PADANG

☎ 0751 / pop 880,000

Padang is typical of Sumatra's modern landscape: a sprawling noisy place circumnavigated by tripped-out *opelet* blasting squeaks-and-beeps techno music. As the capital of West Sumatra province, Padang might have once been a showpiece, but the economic depression that has followed the 1997 currency crash means that the city's infrastructure gets used but never renewed. Capital, more so than capability, feeds the modern machine.

Padang is an entry point into Sumatra to/from Jakarta, Singapore and Kuala Lumpur. Arriving in Padang after the relative comfort of mainland Southeast Asia makes for a rough landing. Padang has few tourist amenities and limited English. Despite the urge to hide from the smell of kerosene and diesel exhaust, you'll find that the locals are genuinely friendly and curious about the few foreigners who find their way into town.

Savvier travellers skip the heat and humidity and migrate to the beaches around

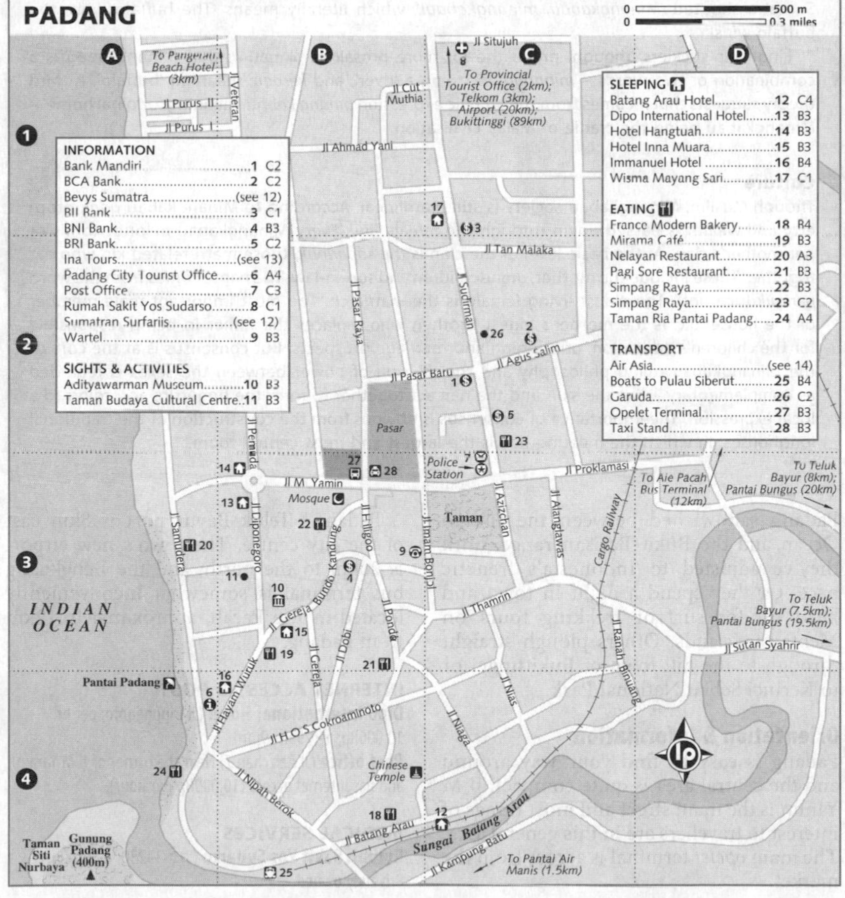

THE MINANGKABAU

Legend has it that the Minangkabau are descended from the wandering Macedonian tyrant Alexander the Great. According to the story, the ancestors of the Minangkabau arrived in Sumatra under the leadership of King Maharjo Dirajo, the youngest son of Alexander.

Anthropologists, however, suggest that the Minangkabau arrived in West Sumatra from the Malay Peninsula some time between 1000 and 2000 BC, probably by following Sungai Batang Hari upstream from the Strait of Melaka to the highlands of the Bukit Barisan mountains.

Even if they don't have Alexander's bloodline, the Minangkabau reflect his wanderlust and love of battle, albeit in the milder form of buffalo fighting. Their success in buffalo fighting is believed to have bestowed the people with their tribal name, and the horns of the beast is the focus of their architecture and traditional costumes.

The legend of how the 'Minangkabau' named themselves begins with an imminent attack by a Javanese king. Rather than pit two armies against each other, the Minangkabau proposed a fight between two bulls. When the time came, the West Sumatrans dispatched a tiny calf to fight the enormous Javanese bull, but the half-starved beast was outfitted with sharp metal spears to its horns. Believing the Javanese bull to be its mother, the calf rushed to suckle and ripped the bull's belly to shreds. When the bull finally dropped dead, the people of West Sumatra shouted *'Minangkabau, minangkabau!'*, which literally means 'The buffalo wins, the buffalo wins!'

Linguistic sticklers, though, prefer the far more prosaic explanation that Minangkabau is a combination of two words – *minanga*, meaning a 'river', and *kerbau*, meaning 'buffalo'. A third theory suggests that it comes from the archaic expression *pinang kabhu*, meaning 'original home' – Minangkabau being the cradle of Malay civilisation.

Culture

Though Muslim, Minangkabau society is still matrilineal. According to Minangkabau *adat*, property and wealth is passed down through the female line. Every Minangkabau belongs to his or her mother's clan. At the basic level of the clan is the *sapariouk*, those matri-related kin who eat together. These include the mother, grandchildren and son-in-law. The name comes from the word *periouk* (rice pot). The eldest living female is the matriarch. The most important male member of the household is the mother's eldest brother, who replaces the father in being responsible for the children's education, upbringing and marriage prospects. But consensus is at the core of the Minangkabau ruling philosophy and the division of power between the sexes is regarded as complementary – like the skin and the nail act together to form the fingertip, according to a local expression. The importance of consensus is obvious from the construction of the traditional longhouses, in which the meeting hall is the largest and most central room.

Padang sandwiched between the Indian Ocean and the Bukit Barisan range, until they've adjusted to Indonesia's frenetic pace. Or they spend a night in town and head off for surf or trekking tours on Mentawai Islands. Others plough straight through to the hill town of Bukittinggi or to Kerinci Seblat National Park.

Orientation & Information

Padang is easy to find your way around and the central area is quite compact. Jl M Yamin is the main street and most things of interest to travellers are in this general area. The main *opelet* terminal is across from the market.

Padang's Teluk Bayur port is 8km east of the city centre. The town's new airport is 20km to the north; and the Bengkuang bus terminal is somewhat inconveniently located in Aie Pacah, approximately 12km from Padang.

INTERNET ACCESS & POST

Dipo International Hotel (Jl Diponegoro; per hr 10,000Rp; 🕑 9am-9pm)

Post office (Jl Azizchan 7) Near the corner of Jl M Yamin and has internet access (10,000Rp per hour).

MEDICAL SERVICES

Rumah Sakit Yos Sudarso (☎ 33230; Jl Situjuh 1) Privately owned.

Arts & Crafts

West Sumatra has a reputation for exquisite, hand-loomed *songket* cloth, and fine embroidery. *Songket* weaving uses gold and silver threads (imitation these days) to create patterns on a base of silk or cotton. The designs are usually elaborate floral motifs and geometric patterns. One of the most popular designs, used in both weaving and embroidery, incorporates stylised flowers and mountains in an ornate pattern known as *gunung batuah*, or 'magic mountain'.

Weavers use another, unusually painstaking, technique called 'needle weaving'. The process involves removing certain threads from a piece of cloth and stitching the remaining ones together to form patterns. This cloth is traditionally used for ceremonial occasions only. The Minangkabau are also renowned for their fine embroidery.

Another highly developed art found in West Sumatra is silverwork. Filigree jewellery, as fine as spider webs, is a speciality. There are many handicraft villages around Bukittinggi.

Dance & Music

Dance is an important part of Minangkabau culture. Dances include the colourful *tari payung* (umbrella dance), a welcome dance about a young man's love for his girlfriend; the dramatic *tari piring* (plate dance), which involves the dancers leaping barefoot on piles of broken china; and the dazzling *tari lilin* (candle dance), in which female dancers are required to rhythmically juggle and balance china saucers – with burning candles attached to them – while simultaneously clicking castanets.

The most popular of the Minangkabau dances is the *randai*, a dance-drama performed at weddings, harvest festivals and other celebrations. The steps and movements for the *randai* developed from *pencak silat*, a self-defence routine, combined with themes from literature and *gamelan* music. Every village in West Sumatra has at least one all-male *randai* group of 20 performers. The traditional version tells the story of a woman so wilful and wicked that she is driven out of her village before she brings complete disaster on the community.

It is the custom for Minangkabau youths to spend some time in a *surau* (prayer house), where they are taught, among other things, how to look after themselves. This includes learning *pencak silat*. The style of *pencak silat* most often performed is the Mudo, a mock battle that leads the two protagonists to the brink of violence before it is concluded. It is a dramatic dance involving skilled technique, fancy footwork and deliberate pauses which follow each movement and serve to heighten the tension.

The percussion instruments used to accompany most of the dances are similar to those of the Javanese *gamelan* and are collectively called the *telempong* in West Sumatra. Two other instruments frequently played are the *puput* and *salung*, kinds of flute that are usually made out of bamboo, reed or rice stalks.

MONEY

Padang has branches of all the major Indonesian banks and there are ATMs all over town, including one at the post office. There's a 24-hour moneychanging service with reasonable rates at the Dipo International Hotel.

Bank Mandirir (Jl Bagindo)
BCA bank (Bank Central Asia; Jl Agus Salim)
BII bank (Bank Internasional Indonesia; Jl Sudirman)
BNI bank (Bank Negara Indonesia; Jl Bundo Kandung)
BRI bank (Bank Rakyat Indonesia; Jl Sudirman)

TELEPHONE

Telkom wartel (cnr Jl Ahmad Dahlan & Khatib Sulaiman; 24hr) Huge Minangkabau-style building located north of the city centre.

Wartel (Jl Imam Bonjol 15H; 24hr) It is much easier to use this wartel in the town centre to make international or collect calls.

TOURIST INFORMATION

Padang city tourist office (34186; Jl Hayam Wuruk 51; 7.30am-4.30pm Mon-Thu, 7.30-11.30am Fri) Tucked into a government office, busy with smoking and socialising, is a desk for basic tourist information.

West Sumatra provincial tourist office (55231; Jl Khatib Sulaiman 22) Located outside the centre of town.

Sights & Activities

Padang's **old quarter** along Jl Batang Arau is filled with old Dutch and Chinese warehouses overlooking the hardworking

SUMATRA

fishing boats eased into harbour for a day's rest. The **beachside promenade** along Jl Samudera is where locals go for sunset strolls or morning workouts.

Adityawarman Museum (Jl Diponegoro; admission 1500Rp; 8am-4pm Tue-Sun), built in the Minangkabau tradition, offers some less-appealing insights into Padang's past and has a small collection of antiques and objects of historical and cultural interest.

Taman Budaya Cultural Centre (Jl Diponegoro) stages sporadic dance performances as well as poetry readings, plays and exhibitions of paintings and carvings. Ask at the tourist office for details.

Tours

Padang is used as the mainland launching point for tours of the offshore Mentawai Islands, which are famous for a hunter-gatherer culture and world-class surfing. The various islands of the Mentawai chain are starting to sprout reclusive resorts if you're hunting for a holiday away from the crowds. See p440 for more information.

SUMATRA

Festivals & Events

A colourful annual boat race is held in Padang to commemorate Independence Day (17 August).

The highlight of the West Sumatran cultural calendar is the Islamic festival of Tabut, held at the seaside town of Pariaman, 36km north of Padang. It takes place at the beginning of the month of Muharam (based on the Islamic lunar calendar, usually January or February) to honour the martyrdom of Mohammed's grandchildren, Hassan and Hussein, at the battle of Kerbala.

Central to the festival is the *bouraq*, a winged horse-like creature with the head of a woman, which is believed to have descended to earth to collect the souls of dead heroes and take them to heaven.

Nearby villages create painted effigies of *bouraq* and adorn them with gold necklaces and other paraphernalia. The effigies are carried through the streets with much merriment, dancing and music, and are finally tossed into the sea. Spectators and participants then dive into the water and grab whatever remains of the *bouraq*, preferably the gold necklaces.

Padang hosts at least one major **horse-riding** event a year. Horses are ridden bareback and jockeys are dressed in the traditional costume of their region or village – the aim is to gain prestige for the district where the horse is bred and raised.

Sleeping

You are better off coughing up a few more rupiah for the midrange hotels than suffering in the budget holes. All quoted rates include breakfast and tax.

MIDRANGE

Wisma Mayang Sari (☎ 22647; Jl Sudirman 19; d from 86,500Rp;) Clean and acceptable economy rooms hang out in this modern villa in the north of town.

Immanuel Hotel (☎ 28560; Jl Hayam Wuruk 43; d from 125,000Rp;) As sweet as a tall glass of Fanta, Immanuel is a small, friendly place with comfortable air-con rooms and a cast of outgoing long-term boarders.

Hotel Hangtuah (☎ 26556; Jl Pemuda 1; d from 194,000Rp) Unchanged from the days of pillbox hats, Hangtuah is pleasantly retro, if a little noisy.

Dipo International Hotel (☎ 34261; dipo@pdg.vision.net.id; Jl Diponegoro 13; s/d 260,000/220,000Rp) Dipo has some handy tourist facilities with a 24-hour restaurant, moneychanger, a Home Country Direct phone and internet facilities. Oh yeah, and the rooms are overpriced.

TOP END

Batang Arau Hotel (☎ 27400; Jl Batang Arau 33; batangarau@yahoo.com; s/d 375,000/475,000Rp) If you've got the loot to spare, you'll like Padang a whole lot more from the vantage point of this refurbished Dutch bank building in the old colonial quarter. The four rooms are artfully decorated with black-and-white tiled floors, spa-sized baths and shady balconies overlooking the river and a shaggy hill.

Hotel Inna Muara (☎ 35600; natour-muara@padang_wasantara.net.id; Jl Gereja 34; d from 574,000Rp) Recently rehabilitated from sloppy to swanky, Inna Muara will tickle the bargain-hunters when promotional discounts are in full effect.

Eating

Padang is the birth mother of the cuisine that migrated across Indonesia. Even though everyone swears that Padang cuisine tastes better outside of Padang, pay homage to the native cooks with a visit to

MEET BREAKFAST, LUNCH & DINNER: PADANG CUISINE

Eating in a foreign land just got a whole lot easier thanks to Padang cuisine. Forget about pointing at a pot or snooping at your neighbour's meal. With Padang cuisine, you sit down and the whole kit and caboodle gets laid out in front of you. You decide which ones look tasty and push the others aside. You pay for what you eat – nibbling, sniffing and fondling included.

The drawback is that you never really know what you're eating, since there's no menu. If the dish contains liquid, it is usually a coconut milk curry, a major component of Padang cuisine. The meaty dishes are most likely beef or buffalo, occasionally offal or, less likely, even dog. Some of the fun of Padang-ing is identifying the mystery meat. Because most dishes are cooked slowly and thoroughly, the difference between chicken and certain types of fish isn't so obvious.

The most famous Padang dish is *rendang*, in which chunks of beef or buffalo are simmered slowly in coconut milk until the sauce is reduced to a rich paste and the meat becomes dark and dried. Other popular dishes include *telor balado* (egg dusted with red chilli), *ikan panggang* (fish baked in coconut and chilli) and *gulai merah kambing* (red mutton curry).

Most couples pick one or two meat dishes and a vegetable, usually *kangkong* (water spinach), and load up with a plate or two of rice. Carbs are manna in Padang cuisine. Vegetarians should ask for *tempe* or *tahu* (tofu), which comes doctored up in a spicy sambal. The orphan dishes are collected and returned to the display window protected from curious flies by a lacy curtain.

Before digging into the meal – and we mean this literally, as your right hand is your utensil – wash up in the provided bowl of water. Food and sauces should be spooned onto your plate of rice, then mixed together with the fingers. The rice will be easier to handle if it is a little wet. Use your fingers to scoop up the food, and your thumb to push it into your mouth. It is messy even for people raised on it.

Padang cuisine has an earthy spiciness that might need a little sweet tea or water as a chaser. There is usually a tumbler of lukewarm water (a sign that it has been boiled for sterilisation) on the table.

After you've slurped and sucked your plate clean, wash up, let out a burp (or don't be surprised if your neighbour does), and fire up a cigarette.

one of these famous franchises: **Pagi Sore** (Jl Pondok 143; mains 8000Rp) and **Simpang Raya** (☎ 27300; mains 8000Rp; Jl Bundo Kandung 3-5). There are also several Padang restaurants along Jl Samudera near Jl Purus.

France Modern Bakery (Jl Batang Arau; mains 2000Rp) If you're still easing into rice for every meal, break your fast at this local bakery within walking distance of Batang Arau Hotel.

Taman Ria Pantai Padang (Jl Samudera; mains 6000-8000Rp) After sunset this collection of stalls dishes up everyday eats and uncommonly good views of the sea.

Nelayan Restaurant (Jl Samudera; mains 25,000Rp) Further north, Nelayan is the place for serious seafood fans.

Mirama Cafe (Jl Hayam Wuruk 38; mains 25,000Rp) Padang goes stylish, so to speak, at this upmarket air-con spot for tidier versions of Indonesian standards.

Jl Niaga is lined with civil servant–friendly lunch spots and a night market dominates Jl Pondok near Jl Imam Bonjol.

Getting There & Away

AIR

Padang's new airport is the **Bandara Internasional Minangkabau** (off Jl Adinegoro), 20km north of the centre of town. The following airlines operate international and domestic flights – for fares see the Sumatra Airfares map (p380):

Air Asia (Hotel Huangtuah, Jl Pemuda 1) Flies daily to Kuala Lumpur, Malaysia.

Garuda (Garuda Indonesia; ☎ 30737; Jl Sudirman 2) Operates daily flights to Jakarta and thrice-weekly flights to Pekanbaru and Singapore.

Mandala (☎ 39737; Pangeran's Beach Hotel, Jl Veteran) Flies daily to Jakarta and Medan; located 3km outside the town centre.

Merpati (Merpati Nusantara Airlines; ☎ 444831; Pangeran's Beach Hotel, Jl Veteran) Flies daily to Batam, Jakarta and Gunung Sitoli.

Other airlines serving Jakarta include **Adam Air** (☎ 840999; Jl Pemuda 2), **Lion Air** (☎ 446100; Pangeran's Beach Hotel, Jl Veteran) and **Batavia** (☎ 28383; Jl Damar 36). **Tiger Airways** (book online at www.tigerairways.com) flies to Singapore.

BOAT

Boats to Siberut (the largest in the Mentawai Islands chain) leave from the harbour on Sungai Batang Arau, also known as Sungai Muara, just south of Padang's city centre.

The Teluk Bayar port is 8km from town and receives infrequent Pelni ships.

BUS

Padang's Bengkuang terminal is inconveniently located in Aie Pacah, about 12km from town. A purple *opelet* from the market to the terminal costs 4000Rp.

There are frequent local buses to Bukittinggi (10,000Rp, two hours), but most locals prefer the shared minivans that leave from Minang Plaza (15,000Rp). To reach Minang Plaza, take a white *opelet* (2000Rp) from Jl Hayam Wuruk.

If you're heading to Danau Toba, take a Parapat-bound bus (180,000Rp, 17 hours), which usually leaves in the evening.

Other destinations include Bengkulu (125,000Rp, 16 hours) and Sibolga (80,000Rp, 14 hours). To reach Kerinci Seblat National Park, take a Sungaipenuh-bound bus (70,000Rp, six hours).

For Medan and Jakarta, which both take a day or more travelling by land, it is cheaper and faster to fly.

Getting Around

Bandara Internasional Minangkabau airport is 20km north of the centre, on the Bukittinggi road. Airport taxis charge between 60,000Rp and 90,000Rp for the ride into town. The budget alternative is to take one of the two white Damri buses (15,000Rp) that do a loop through Padang. From the airport, tell the conductor the name of the street you're heading to and they'll sit you on the correct bus. Supposedly the Damri buses circle the city picking up passengers in time for departing flights, but locals were highly sceptical about this.

There are numerous *opelet* around town, operating out of the Pasar Raya terminal off Jl M Yamin. The standard fare is 2000Rp.

AROUND PADANG

The key to enjoying Padang is getting out of the central city and into the sunset-facing beaches.

Air Manis

The closest escape from Padang is the fishing village of Air Manis, just south of Sungai Batang Arau. Overlooking the river is a **Chinese cemetery** – from there it's a 10km walk to the village's dark-sand beach.

According to local mythology, the rock at the end of the beach is what remains of Malin Kundang, a seafarer who was transformed into stone when he returned to his village after making his fortune but refused to recognise his mother. His boat got the same treatment.

If Air Manis is where you'd rather bed, **Villa Puncak** (☎ 767888; www.mentawai.com; Jl Air Manis 88, Padang Selatan; s/d US$145/190), overlooking the beach, has a jungle-hidden stone-and-timber guesthouse where the only visible neighbours are monkeys and birds.

Blue *opelet* 402 goes from Padang to the bottom of the hill (2000Rp) and from there you can hire a motorcycle (5000Rp) to Air Manis. You can also turn it into a long stroll by taking the *perahu* across the river from Jl Batang Arau.

Beaches

To the north and south of Padang are several low-key beaches for a little surf and turf. **Pantai Bungus**, 20km south of Padang, is the staging point for outings to several offshore islands – the kind of places where you just sit and wait for the coconuts to fall. Folks say great things about the underwater world around Pulau Sikoai.

Losmen Carlos (☎ 751153; Pantai Bungus; r from 75,000Rp) can arrange snorkelling trips to the offshore islands. There are other nearby losmen, if you've had enough of our recommendations.

Hotel Pusako Sikuai (☎ 36333; Pulau Sikuai; r from 500,000Rp) is a jungle-clad resort with upmarket chalets.

To reach Pantai Bungus, take a blue *opelet* labelled 'Kabung Bungus' (8000Rp, 45 minutes).

Further south is **Pulau Marak**, which has a gibbon rehabilitation centre and miles of undisturbed sand, coral and wilderness. The island is accessible on a tour through **Mentawai Sanctuary** (☎ 767888; www.mentawai.com).

Pasir Jambak is the best of several beaches north of Padang. You can stay at **Uncle Jack's** (r per person with meals 75,000Rp). Jack can organise snorkelling trips to nearby Pulau Sawo.

Opelet 423 will get you there for 5000Rp. When leaving, taxis can be arranged to take you directly to the airport.

MENTAWAI ISLANDS

Although the distance between the mainland and the Mentawai Islands is not great, nature contrived to keep this island chain isolated. Strong winds, unpredictable currents and razor-sharp corals thwarted navigation and trade with the mainland.

As a result, the Mentawai people had very little contact with the outside world and remained one of the 'purest' indigenous societies in Indonesia until the 19th and 20th centuries.

Siberut is the largest island in the chain and is home to the majority of the Mentawai population. It is also the most closely studied and protected island in the archipelago. About 60% of Siberut is still covered with tropical rainforest and shelters a rich biological community that has earned it a designation as a Unesco biosphere reserve. The western half of the island is protected as the Siberut National Park.

The archipelago is thought to have broken off from the rest of Sumatra about 500,000 years ago, and the separation resulted in unique flora and fauna. Mentawai is ranked alongside Madagascar in terms of endemic primate population, with 60% of terrestrial mammals recorded as endemic. Four species of primate display a variety of primitive characteristics, making them particularly important in the study of the species' evolution. Of particular interest is *Siamang kerdil*, a rare species of black-and-yellow monkey usually called *simpai Mentawai* by the locals.

Change has come in a hurry to Mentawai. Tourism, logging, *transmigrasi* (government-sponsored scheme to encourage settlers to move from overcrowded regions to sparsely populated ones) and other government-backed attempts to mainstream the culture have separated the people from the jungle and whittled the jungle into profit. It isn't what it used to be, but it is a long way from being like everywhere else. And that keeps trekkers happily braving mud and bugs to visit the remaining traditional communities. Surfers comprise the other Mentawai-bound pilgrims, many of whom rank Mentawai right alongside Nias as a

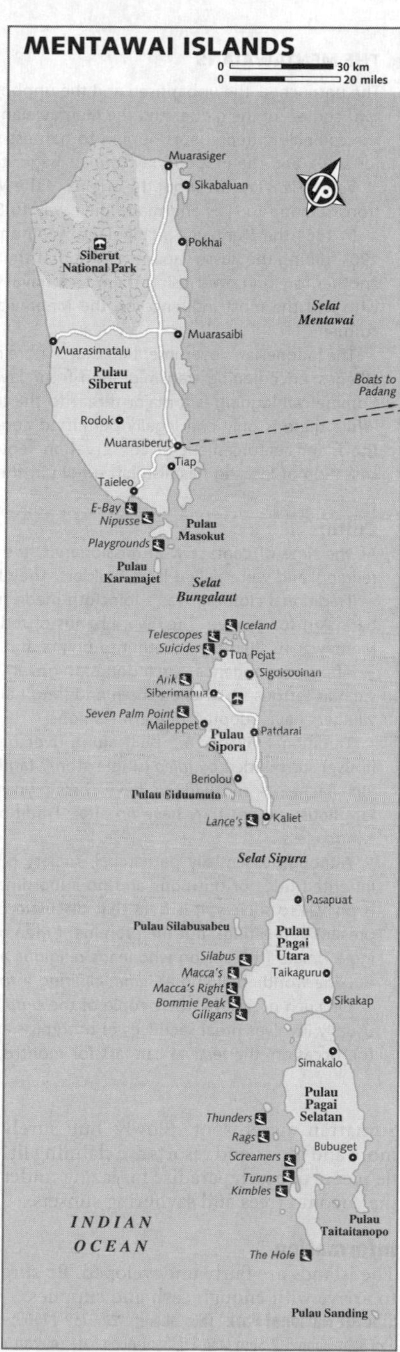

THE MENTAWAIANS

The untouched, the unbaptised and the unphotographed have long propelled Westerners to distant corners of the globe. And the Mentawaians have seen every sort of self-anointed discoverer: the colonial entrepreneurs hoping to harness the land for profit, missionaries trading medicine for souls, and the modern-day tourists eager to experience life before the machine.

Very little is known about the origins of the Mentawaians, but it is assumed that they emigrated from Sumatra to Nias and made their way to Siberut from there.

In 1864 the Mentawai archipelago was nominally made a Dutch colony, but it was not until 1901, during the Russo-Japanese War, that the Dutch placed a garrison on the islands to prevent another foreign power using them as a naval base. In subsequent years it was the missionaries who had the most influence on the Mentawai people, creating fundamental changes in their culture.

The Indonesian government enforced more changes by relocating Mentawaians to mainstream villages, encouraging transmigration from Java and opening up parts of the chain to logging. Commercial logging is a major threat to the longevity of the forest and the traditional culture. While there is only one legally permitted concession (and one pending petition) operating on the island, enforcement of conservation regulations lacks proper funding and oversight. The cessation of logging has also left a hole in the immature economy.

Culture

At the time of contact with missionaries, the Mentawaians had their own language, *adat* and religion, and were skilled boat builders. They lived a hunter-gatherer existence.

Traditional clothing was a loincloth made from the bark of the breadfruit tree for men and a bark skirt for women. They wore bands of red-coloured rattan, beads and imported brass rings. Mentawaians filed their teeth into points and decorated their bodies with tattoos.

After independence, the Indonesian government banned many of the Mentawaians' customs, such as tattoos, sharpened teeth and long hair. Although the ban has not been enforced, many villagers have adopted modern fashions.

Traditional villages are built along river banks and consist of one or more *uma* (communal house) surrounded by *lalep* (single-storey family houses). Several families live in the same building. Bachelors and widows have their own quarters, known as *rusuk*, identical to the family longhouse except they have no altar. Traditionally, the houses stand on wooden piles and are windowless.

Although essentially patriarchal, society is organised on egalitarian principles. There are no inherited titles or positions and no subordinate roles. It is the *uma*, not the village itself, that is pivotal to society. It is here that discussions affecting the community take place. Everyone is present at meetings, but the prominent men make most of the major decisions, including choosing a *rimata* (the person who leads religious affairs and is the community's spokesperson to the outside world), building an *uma*, clearing a forest or laying out a banana plantation.

On such occasions, the people of the *uma* carry out a religious festival known as *punen*. This usually involves ritual sacrifices of both pigs and chickens and, depending on the importance of the occasion, the festival can last for months, sometimes years. All kinds of everyday jobs and

Sumatran sweet spot. Slowly but surely more and more land resorts are claiming little pieces of beach paradise for lazing under the coconut trees and savouring sunsets.

Information

The islands are fairly undeveloped. Be sure to arrive with enough cash and supplies.

Siberut National Park (TNS; Siberut; ☎ 0759-21109; 8am-noon & 2-5pm Mon-Fri, 8am-noon Sat) You can arrange local guides at the park office, which is a 10-minute *ojek* ride from the Siberut harbour to the village of Maileppet. The park office also runs a simple guesthouse (50,000Rp) and a small library.

Activities

TREKKING

The main reason people come to Siberut is to visit the traditional villages of the interior.

activities become taboo; work in the fields is stopped and strangers are denied access to the *uma*, its isolation being marked by a cordon of palm leaves and flowers.

Religion

The native Sibulungan religion is a form of animism, involving the worship of nature spirits and a belief in the existence of ghosts, as well as the soul. The chief nature spirits are those of the sky, sea, jungle and earth. The sky spirits are considered the most influential. There are also two river spirits: *Ina Oinan* (Mother of Rivers) is beneficent, while *Kameinan* (Father's Sister) is regarded as evil. In addition, all inanimate objects have a *kina* (spirit), which gives them life.

The worship of the soul is of utmost importance, being vital to good health and longevity. The soul is believed to depart the body at various times during life before its ultimate escape at death. Sickness, for example, is the result of the temporary absence of the soul; dreams also signify that the soul is 'on vacation'.

When the soul leaves the body at death it is transformed into a *sanitu* (ghost). Mentawaians try to avoid these ghosts, whom they suspect of malevolently attempting to rob the living of their souls. To protect themselves, they place fetish sticks at every entrance to the village. This tactic is considered foolproof, provided no-one has committed a ritual sin or broken a taboo.

German missionary August Lett was the first to attempt to convert the local people, but he was not entirely successful: eight years after his arrival Lett was murdered by the locals. Somehow the mission managed to survive and 11 baptisms had been recorded by 1916. There are now more than 80 Protestant churches throughout the islands.

More than 50 years after the Protestants, Catholic missionaries moved in to vie for converts. They opened a mission – a combined church, school and clinic – in south Siberut. Free medicines and clothes were given to any islander who became a Catholic, and by 1969 there were almost 3000 converts.

Islam began to make inroads when government officials were regularly appointed from Padang during the Dutch era, and then to complicate religious matters further, the Baha'í faith was introduced in 1955. Today more than half the population claims to be Protestant, 16% Catholic, 13% Muslim, while the rest have no official religion.

Traditional Economy

Taro and banana are the staple crops of the Pagai islands and Sipora, while on Siberut, sago is also cultivated. Other crops include cassava and sweet potato.

Traditionally, women own the taro fields and are responsible for planting and maintaining them. The banana plantations belong to the men – some are worked by one or two families, others by an entire *uma*. In most cases the plantations operate on a subsistence level.

On Mentawai, especially Siberut, land is not cleared by fire, which is considered too disruptive to the forest.

Hunting is a major social activity for the men of the islands and is closely related to the traditional religions.

There is a lot of debate about how to trek responsibly: hiring a local Mentawai guide, rather than an outsider, is one obvious option. But transport costs can be expensive if you're travelling alone. More affordable, but not as directly beneficial to the local community, is to join an organised tour through a mainland operator. Most backpackers join a guided trip from Bukittinggi, but because fewer and fewer travellers are visiting Sumatra, collecting the minimum number of people (between five and six) means waiting around for a few days or more.

To cut out the waiting game, try posting your planned travel dates to Mentawai on Lonely Planet's Thorn Tree (http://thorntree.lonelyplanet.com) to connect with other interested parties. Otherwise, you might consider signing up with the more expensive online agents or Mentawai resorts (see Sleeping, right). Most trips to Mentawai last for 10 days (two of which are travel days from the mainland).

Prices in Bukittinggi start at US$200 for the full 10 days and include a guide, accommodation (at family homestays) and transport, but there will be lots of extra costs, as Indonesia has a culture of tipping. Ask up front about what other costs are involved. See p392 for information about hiring a guide.

Trekking Essentials

What should you expect on this trip? Well Siberut isn't Chiang Mai hill tribe country. Treks usually include plenty of slogging through mud, crossing furious ravines on slippery rotting logs and battling with insects. Chloroquine-resistant malaria is a concern and proper precautions should be taken. Sanitation is rudimentary, with the local river serving as the communal faucet and toilet.

May is generally the driest month, while October and November are the wettest – but it can rain on Siberut any time of year. The seas between Siberut and West Sumatra can get very rough in June and July, when it can be too dangerous to sail.

You'll want to travel light but well prepared. Carry trekking essentials: a mosquito net, rain gear, insect and leech repellent, torch (flashlight), water purification tablets and plastic bags for keeping things dry. You can buy most supplies in Muarasiberut, but they are much cheaper in Padang.

You will also need to bring things for barter and gifts. Cigarettes are the preferred gift, but pens, pencils and paper might sit lighter on the conscious. Talk to your guide about what is customary.

SUMATRA

SURFING

The Mentawai Islands have consistent surf year-round at hundreds of famous and not-so-famous breaks. But the best of the good waves can be found roughly between April and October (give or take a month).

In the past, charter boats were the primary means of reaching the top surfing spots, but beachside camps (many of which are affiliated with charter companies) have set down roots on the islands. Surf resorts also offer cultural tour treks into the interior of Siberut.

Tours & Charters

The following companies can arrange trekking tours and surf charters. Most have offices in Padang and a substantial online presence.

Bevys Sumatra (Map p431; ☎ 7517810835; bevyssumatra@yahoo.com; Hotel Batang Arau, Jl Batang Arau 33, Padang) A tour and ticket agent based in Padang, Bevys can arrange ferry tickets to Mentawai and organise a variety of mix-and-match tours from cultural trekking to dive trips.

Ina Tours (Map p431; ☎ 34262; Jl Diponegoro 13, Padang) Next door to Dipo International Hotel in Padang, this travel agent organises cultural tours to Mentawai Islands.

Mentawai Sanctuary (Map p431; ☎ 767888; www.mentawai.com; Villa Puncak, Jl Air Manis No 88) Surf charters (from US$1550 for a 10-day tour), as well as island and culture tours. There are also plans for a resort near Ebay surf break, south of Siberut.

Sumatran Surfariis (Map p431; www.sumatransurfariis.com; Hotel Batang Arau, Jl Batang Arau 33) An affiliated venture from the folks at Hotel Batang Arau, Sumatran Surfariis operates a variety of surf boat charters. Packages start at US$1600 for a 10-day tour.

Sleeping

Mentawai Islands is starting to open up as a resort destination. Many places are focused on the surf scene, but the white sands and natural surroundings are suitable for the average layabout. Lodging for ethno-treks is typically pre-arranged in family homes. Visit the individual resort's website for booking information in your home country.

Wavepark Resort (Pulau Siberut; www.wavepark.com; package US$140-160) The first land-based resort on Mentawai, Wavepark has a front-row view of Hideaways and a quick shuttle transfer to Wavepark.

Macaroni's Resort (Pulau Pagai Utara; www.macaronisresort.com; packages from US$150) Bamboo villas built over the water; quick speedboat transfer to Macaroni's and Macas Right.

Aloita Resort & Spa (Tua Pejat, Pulau Sipora; www.aloitaresort.com; packages from US$180) Seven bungalows occupy a private beach within shuttle's reach of Telescopes and Icelands. The resort also offers scuba diving and certification, as well as a spa.

Kandui Resort (Pulau Karamajet; www.mentawaiislands.com; packages from US$200) Lodging in traditional Mentawai lodges *(uma)* and transfer to surf spots.

Getting There & Away

The only airport is on Pulau Sipora, but there are only charter flights.

Boats leave from Padang to Siberut on Monday, Wednesday and Thursday (from 85,000Rp). The return trip to Padang leaves on Tuesday, Thursday, Friday and Saturday.

Mentawai Express operates a morning speedboat (from 85,000Rp, four hours) on Thursday; the return trip leaves Siberut on Friday. Sumber Rezeki Baru runs an overnight ferry (from 67,000Rp, 10 hours) from Padang to Siberut on Monday and Wednesday. The return trip leaves Siberut on Tuesday and Thursday. Beriloga, Mentawai Express and Sumber Rezeki Baru operate boats to other islands in the chain, such as Pulau Sipora and Pulua Pagai Utara.

Tickets can be bought from **Bevys Sumatra** (Map p431; ☎ 7517810835; Jl Batang Arau), a travel agent located at Hotel Batang Arau, which also acts as a ticketing agent.

BUKITTINGGI

☎ 0752 / pop 95,000

Welcome to a cool, lush landscape where fertility comes from volcanic destruction. Off in the distance are the blue circumcised mountains – the Merapi, Singgalang and the more distant Sago – that periodically belch out the earth's interior fury. A crown of puffy white clouds hides their naked tips, and at their feet unfold terraced rice fields made so fertile by the once toxic emissions that seasons don't matter. Sitting at 930m above sea level, Bukittinggi is a busy market town halfway between the heavens and the rice paddies, with spectacular views of both. The town's alternate name, Tri Arga, refers to the three majestic mountains that dictate the region's fortunes.

Bukittinggi was once a well-carved niche in the Southeast Asia trail but now only sees a trickle of travellers headed for hikes to the nearby volcanoes, rafflesia sanctuary or for culture tours into the Minangkabau heartland.

During the Padri Wars (1821–37), a civil war between the local chiefs and Islamic reformists, Bukittinggi was a Dutch stronghold (the Dutch sided with the chiefs in this conflict). After independence it was also here that Sumatran rebels declared an independent government in 1958 – one of a long list of separatist attempts in the archipelago.

Orientation

The town centre is conveniently compact and can easily be covered on foot. Jl Ahmad Yani was the tourist strip, now a depressing ghost town where far too many guides fish for too few customers. The town is much more interesting at the top of the hill around the clock tower, where the markets and the local sightseers promenade.

The bus terminal is south of the town centre, but accessible by public transport.

Information

INTERNET ACCESS & POST

Giganet (Jl Ahmad Yani; per hr 12,000Rp; ⏲ 10am-10pm) Very slow, but conveniently located.

Kantin.net (Jl Sudirman; per hr 5000Rp) Catch it at the right time and the connection just sails.

Post office (Jl Sudirman) South of town near the bus terminal; internet facilities (10,000Rp per hour).

MONEY

There are lots of banks and moneychangers along Jl Ahmad Yani.

BII bank (Bank Internasional Indonesia; Jl Ahmad Yani)

BNI bank (Bank Negara Indonesia; Jl Lenggogeni)

TELEPHONE

International calls can be made from dozens of wartel around town.

TOURIST INFORMATION

Tourist Office (Jl Sudirman; ⏲ 8am-4pm) Across from the clock tower; city maps distributed by sweet if limited English–speaking staff.

TRAVEL AGENCIES

Bukittinggi has plenty of travel agencies, most of them along Jl Ahmad Yani. It's a good idea to stroll along the street and compare what they offer.

Sights

Pasar Atas (btwn Jl Minangkabau & Yamin) is a large, colourful market crammed with stalls selling fruit and vegetables, second-hand clothing and crafts. It's open daily, but the serious action is on Wednesday and Saturday, when the stalls overflow down the hill and villagers from the surrounding area come to haggle and ogle.

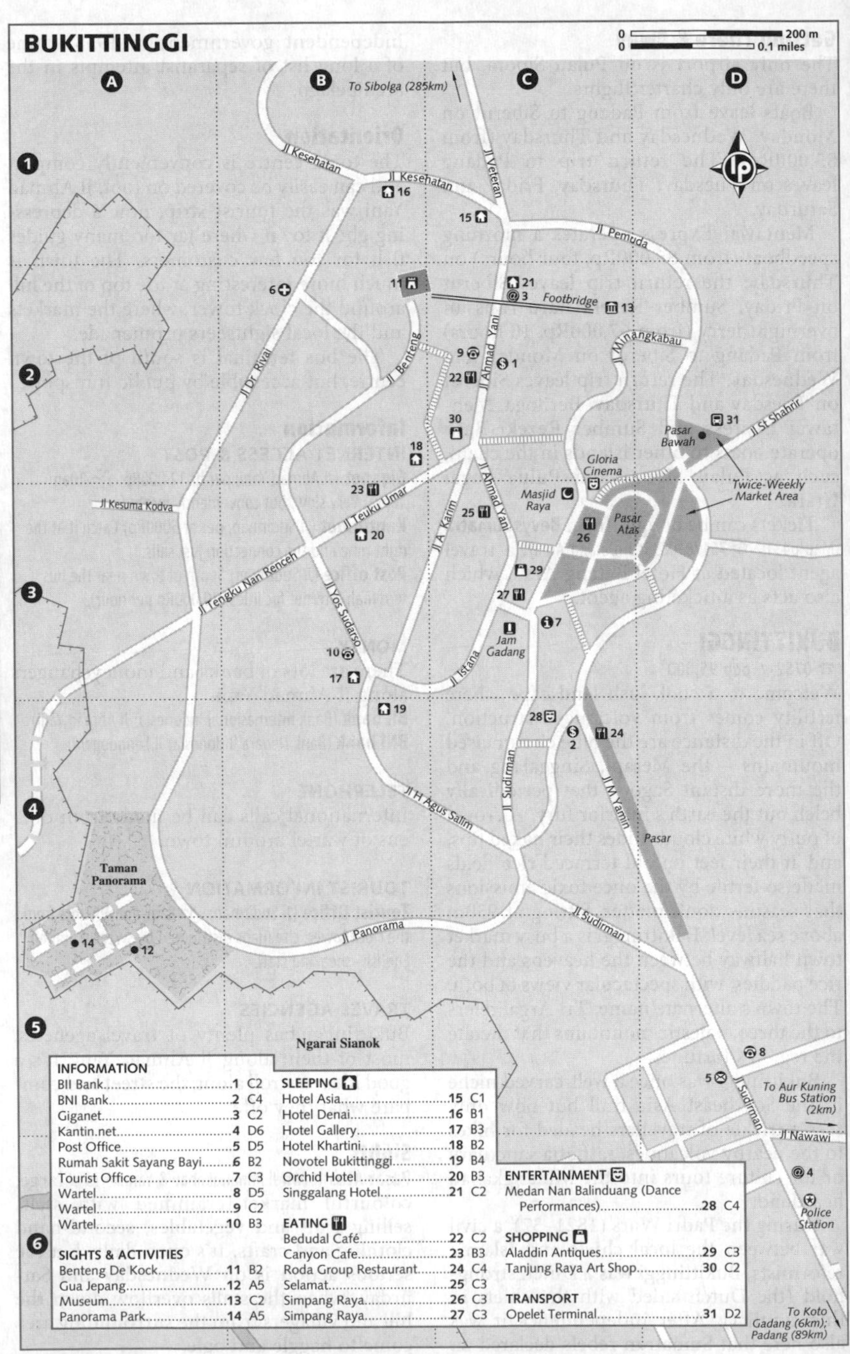
BUKITTINGGI
0 200 m
0 0.1 miles
A
B
C
D
1
2
3
4
5
6
To Sibolga (285km)
Jl Kesehatan
Jl Kesehatan
Jl Veteran
Jl Pemuda
Footbridge
Jl Minangkabau
Jl Dr Rivai
Jl Benteng
Jl Ahmad Yani
Jl St Shahrir
Pasar Bawah
Gloria Cinema
Twice-Weekly Market Area
Masjid Raya
Pasar Atas
Jl Kesuma Kodva
Jl Teuku Umar
Jl A Karim
Jl Ahmad Yani
Jl Tengku Nan Renceh
Jl Yos Sudarso
Jam Gadang
Jl Istana
Jl Sudirman
Jl H Agus Salim
Jl M Yamin
Pasar
Taman Panorama
Jl Panorama
Jl Sudirman
Ngarai Sianok
To Aur Kuning Bus Station (2km)
Jl Sudirman
Jl Nawawi
Police Station
To Koto Gadang (6km); Padang (89km)
INFORMATION
BII Bank 2 C2
BNI Bank 2 C4
Giganet 3 C2
Kantin.net 4 D6
Post Office 5 D5
Rumah Sakit Sayang Bayi 6 B2
Tourist Office 7 C3
Wartel 8 D5
Wartel 9 C2
Wartel 10 B3
SIGHTS & ACTIVITIES
Benteng De Kock 11 B2
Gua Jepang 12 A5
Museum 13 C2
Panorama Park 14 A5
SLEEPING
Hotel Asia 15 C1
Hotel Denai 16 B1
Hotel Gallery 17 B3
Hotel Khartini 18 B2
Novotel Bukittinggi 19 B4
Orchid Hotel 20 B3
Singgalang Hotel 21 C2
EATING
Bedudal Café 22 C2
Canyon Cafe 23 B3
Roda Group Restaurant 24 C4
Selamat 25 C3
Simpang Raya 26 C3
Simpang Raya 27 C3
ENTERTAINMENT
Medan Nan Balinduang (Dance Performances) 28 C4
SHOPPING
Aladdin Antiques 29 C3
Tanjung Raya Art Shop 30 C2
TRANSPORT
Opelet Terminal 31 D2

SUMATRA

Benteng de Kock (Benteng Fort; admission to fort & zoo 5000Rp) was built by the Dutch during the Padri Wars. Apart from the defensive moat and a few rusting cannons, very little remains of the original fortifications. It does, however, provide fine views over the town from its hilltop position. Clouds migrate over rusted tin roofs brought to life by the evening call to prayer.

A footbridge leads from the fort over Jl Ahmad Yani to Taman Bundo Kandung, site of the **museum** (admission 1000Rp) and **zoo**. The museum, constructed in 1934, is an example of Minangkabau architecture, with its small amphitheatre and colourful statues. It is the oldest museum in the province and has a dusty collection of Minangkabau historical and cultural exhibits. The zoo is just depressing.

Taman Panorama (Jl Panorama; admission 2000Rp), on the southern edge of town, overlooks the deep Ngarai Sianok (Sianok Canyon). This is especially scenic at sunset, when fruit bats swoop through the canyon. Guides will approach visitors under the auspices of friendship; don't get confused, this is how business works in Indonesia and payment is expected, even if an explicit price is never discussed. They'll lead you through **Gua Jepang** (Japanese caves), which was one of many feats of engineering that the Japanese accomplished with slave labour during WWII.

Jam Gadang (Big Clock Tower; btwn Jl Istana & Sudirman) is Bukittinggi's Big Ben and is the centre of the city's provincial activities: schoolchildren crowding under shade trees and day trippers smiling for photo opportunities. The tower was built in the 1920s to house the Dutch queen's clock gift. After independence, the European homage was refitted with a Minangkabau roof.

Tours

With the decrease in tourist numbers, a simple stroll through town leads directly into the guide gauntlet. Often the pitch for business precedes the usual Indonesian formalities of handshakes and introductions. If perchance you can't find any guides, try **Bedudal Café** (Jl Ahmad Yani) and **Canyon Café** (☎ 21652; Jl Teuku Umar 8). Take your time in finding a guide and be firm with a 'no' if you're just browsing.

Tours fall into two categories: culture or nature. There are day-long Minangkabau tours of the surrounding countryside, multi-day hikes to Danau Maninjau, and overnight volcano treks. If you're travelling solo, you'll have to wait a day or so for enough people to fill out the minimum requirement.

Sleeping

Good luck finding a hotel room well insulated from the pre-dawn call to prayers. If you aren't already conditioned to waking up with the muezzins, Bukittinggi will break you in.

Most hotel rates quoted here include a simple breakfast. Hotel tax is only applied to top-end options and inclusive rates can be negotiated. On holiday weekends rooms fill up with Indonesian visitors. Temperatures in Bukittinggi are relatively cool, making hot-water showers more of a necessary luxury than air-con.

SUMATRA

HIRING YOUR NEXT BEST FRIEND

In Indonesia, the line between business and socialising isn't as distinct as it is in the West. We expect printed prices and obvious sales tactics. Without a price tag, we assume that it is free or done out of friendship. On the other side of the cultural divide, Sumatrans prefer business to resemble friendship: a little chit-chat, a steady sales pitch, and a sort of telepathic understanding that payment is expected. They'd rather be helpful instead of entrepreneurial, but necessity dictates an income. The sluggish state of the Sumatran economy means that unemployment is high, with an overload of young resourceful men supporting themselves by guiding too few tourists.

Once you realise that nothing is gratis, ask about prices. Don't assume that the quoted price is all-inclusive. You are expected to buy lunch and drinking water for your guide. If transport isn't included in the initial price, you should pay for this as well. A tip at the end is also welcome. Most are smokers and a pack costs about 10,000Rp. If all this seems steep, keep in mind that the guides have a couple of crumpled rupiah to their name and not a lot of other opportunities.

BUDGET

Singgalang Hotel (☎ 21576; Jl Ahmad Yani 130; d 60,000-70,000Rp) For a basic cheapie, Singgalang has a surprisingly breezy atmosphere.

Orchid Hotel (☎ 32634; Jl Teuku Umar 11; d 60,000-75,000Rp) A basic multistorey number where backpackers hope to meet other backpackers to swap trail notes and work through no-tourist shell shock.

Hotel Khartini (☎ 22885; Jl Teuku Umar 6; d from 70,000Rp) Meticulously maintained hotel with a tidy grandmotherly lobby of potted plants and doilies. There's a comfy upstairs sitting area and clean rooms.

Hotel Gallery (☎ 23515; Jl H Agus Salim 25; d from 90,000Rp) Doesn't look like much from the outside, but after scrambling up and down mountain-like stairs, you'll find a pair of economy rooms worth every rupiah. The basic rooms have their own patio garnering a fully loaded view of Gunung Merapi.

MIDRANGE & TOP END

Hotel Asia (☎ 625277; Jl Kesehatan 38; d from 100,000-125,000Rp) When a little more comfort is needed, Hotel Asia delivers 'deluxe' without a self-absorbed price tag. Staff are friendly and the rooms pristine.

Hotel Denai (☎ 32957; Jl Dr Rivai 26; s/d from 325,000/520,000Rp) Quintessentially Sumatran: laid-back and comfortable, but sloppy and run-down.

Novotel Bukittinggi (☎ 35000; Jl Yos Sudarso; d from 650,000Rp;) Bukittinggi's only top-end hotel bears an international name but not quality. The curious Arab-/Moghul-style building has sumptuous public areas, a great view bar, but rather standard rooms. It's better to grab an evening drink with a view than stay the night.

Eating

In the evening, Jl Ahmad Yani fills up with **dinner stalls**.

Naturally enough, Padang food is plentiful. Locals disagree about which outpost does the best *nasi Padang* – you'll just have to try them all for yourself: **Roda Group** (Jl M Yamin), south of the clock tower; **Simpang Raya** (Jl Ahmad Yani), with another branch on Jl Minangkabau; and **Selamat** (Jl Ahmad Yani). Dishes start at 5000Rp.

For bread, beer and English menus, try **Bedudal Café** (Jl Ahmad Yani) or **Canyon Café** (☎ 21652; Jl Teuku Umar 8). They also prepare the local speciality, *dadiah campur*, which is a tasty mixture of oats, coconut, fruit, molasses and buffalo-milk yogurt.

Entertainment

Medan Nan Balinduang (Jl Lenggogeni; tickets 40,000Rp; ☎ 8.30pm Thu) If enough tourists show up, this culture centre presents Minangkabau dance performances.

West Sumatrans love a good **bullfight**, known locally as *adu kerbau*. The centres for bullfighting are the villages of Kota Baru and Batagak, between Padang and Bukittinggi. Bullfights are held irregularly, and most tours originate out of Bukittinggi; ask the local guides about upcoming events.

It bears no resemblance to Spanish bullfighting – there is no bloodshed (except by accident) and the water buffalo bulls are unharmed, save for their reputations. The showdown matches up two animals of roughly the same size and weight who are made to lock horns in a trial of strength. The winner is whichever one forces the other into a retreat. It often ends up with both beasts charging around a muddy paddock, scattering onlookers in all directions.

The original intention was to help develop buffalo breeding in the region, but as a spectator sport the main focus is betting. The host village will often kick off proceedings with a meeting of village elders, followed by a demonstration of *pencak silat*.

Shopping

Bukittinggi is a good place to go shopping for everyday necessities and otherwordly oddities: shiny headscarves, sarongs, false teeth, plastic sandals, interesting antiques, and curios. Box collectors can look out for a couple of Minangkabau versions. *Salapah panjang* (long boxes) are brass boxes used for storing lime and tobacco; *salapah padusi* are silver boxes for storing betel nut and lime.

Souvenir shops line Jl Ahmad Yani. Poke your head into **Tanjung Raya Art Shop** (☎ 23435; Jl Ahmad Yani 85) and **Aladdin** (☎ 33593; Jl Ahmad Yani 14).

The market shops are crammed with beautiful embroidered Minangkabau garments in rich reds and golds. Pillow cases and slippers are easy-to-carry souvenirs, as are ceremonial wedding sashes and gold hair adornments.

Getting There & Away

The Aur Kuning bus terminal is about 2km south of the town centre, but easily reached by *opelet* (1500Rp). Tell the driver you're going to Kampung China, where most of the hotels are located.

There are heaps of buses to Padang (12,000Rp, two hours), Danau Maninjau (6000Rp, 1½ hours) and Solok (9000Rp, two hours).

Bukittinggi is a stop for the north-/southbound buses on the Trans-Sumatran Hwy. Bussing to Jakarta (air-con/executive from 226,000/300,000Rp including ferry ticket, 29 hours) is more expensive than catching a flight from Padang. Medan-bound buses (air-con/executive 110,000/190,000Rp, 20 hours) also stop off at Parapat (air-con/executive 110,000/190,000Rp, 14 hours). En route, you'll cross the equator, just outside of Bonjol.

East–west buses shake, rattle and roll to Pekanbaru (35,000Rp for economy, five hours) and Dumai (economy/air-con 60,000/80,000Rp, 10 hours), where you can catch a boat to Melaka. There are a few buses to Bengkulu (80,000Rp), Jambi (75,000Rp) and Palembang (150,000Rp), but most services leave from Padang.

Getting Around

Opelet around Bukittinggi cost 1500Rp. *Bendi* cost from 5000Rp. A taxi from the bus terminal to Jl Ahmad Yani costs 15,000Rp.

AROUND BUKITTINGGI

While Bukittinggi is an interesting market town, visitors come to explore the Minangkabau countryside, hike up an active volcano or sniff the world's biggest, smelliest flower.

Handicraft Villages

Silver shops occupy the old Dutch houses of **Koto Gadang**, which is known for its handicraft tradition. The village is about 5km from Bukittinggi and can be reached by *opelet* from Aur Kuning bus terminal (400Rp). Alternatively, it is an hour's walk from Taman Panorama. The route is heavily worked by guides and only the bullheaded manage to go at it alone.

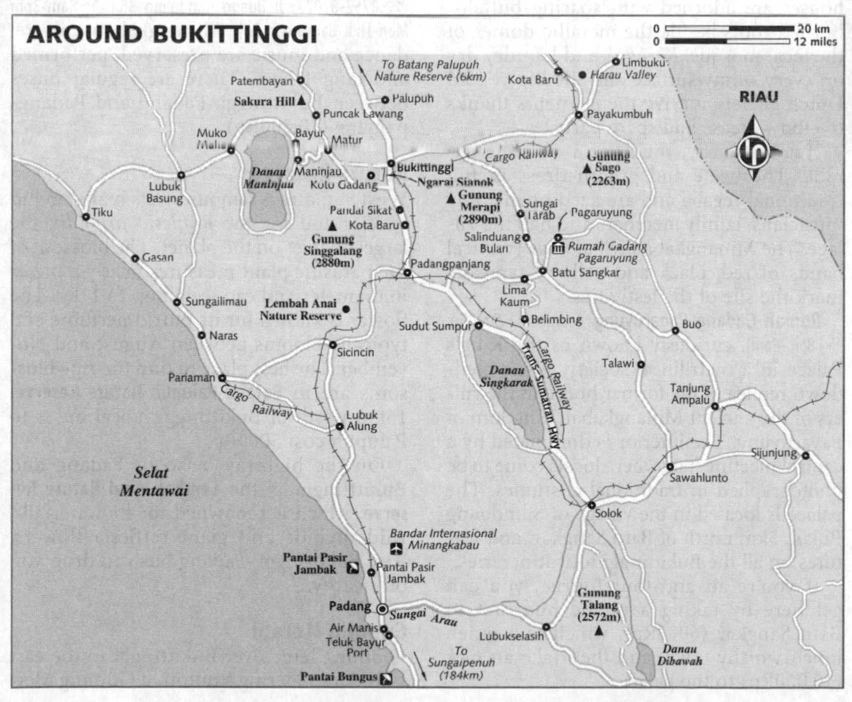

WHO LET THE DOGS OUT

Unlike other parts of Southeast Asia, Sumatra is not overrun with packs of stray dogs. In Islam, dogs are regarded as impure and contact with the animal is prohibited. Then what is all that barking, you might ask? Minangkabau culture makes an exception to some of the Islamic precepts, especially when it comes to protecting crops. The farmer's great nemesis is the wild boar, which will root up vegetable patches during overnight feasts. To combat the intruder, farmers keep very vocal hunting dogs, usually tied up on leashes or kept in pens. All that caged energy is then unleashed on boar-hunting days, assigned to various villages throughout the year. In other hunting traditions, the prey is usually retrieved for the owner, but because pigs are also haram (forbidden) in Islamic law, the dogs get the spoils instead of the scraps.

Famous for *songket* weaving and woodcarving, **Pandai Sikat** stays true to its name, which means 'clever craftsmen'. The village is only 13km from Bukittinggi and easily accessible by *opelet* (6000Rp) from Aur Kuning bus terminal.

Minangkabau Sights

The countryside around Bukittinggi is oh so charming. Terraced rice fields sprout makeshift scarecrows cradled in the palm of a jagged mountain range. In the villages, the Minangkabau traditional wooden houses are adorned with soaring buffalo-horned roofs beside the metallic domes of the local mosque. *Keropok* and laundry dry on every sunny surface and the hip-roofed Dutch chalets survive the elements thanks to elbow grease and spare parts.

If you're lucky, you'll see a wedding parade. The bride and groom dress in full traditional regalia and are accompanied by musicians, family members and half the village. The Minangkabau tribal flags (vertical bands of red, black and yellow) typically mark the site of the festivities.

Rumah Gadang Pagaruyung (admission 5000Rp; 8am-6pm), curiously known as the King's Palace in a matrilineal society, is a scaled-down replica of the former home of the rulers of the ancient Minangkabau kingdom of Payaruyung. The interior is dominated by a central meeting hall, where locals come to be photographed in traditional costumes. The palace is located in the village of Silinduang Bulan, 5km north of Batu Sangkar, and features on all the Bukittinggi tour itineraries.

If you're an anti-tour tourist, you can get here by taking a public bus first to Batu Sangkar (6000Rp), which is a quiet, lunch-worthy town, and then take an *ojek* (10,000Rp) to the palace.

Another popular tour stop is **Belimbing**, one of the largest surviving collections of traditional architecture in the highlands. Many of the homes are 300 years old and are in various geriatric states. In many cases the owners have built modern homes nearby and use the relics for ceremonial purposes. The mixing of the old and new makes it a more worthwhile stop than a preserved theme park.

For ethno-musicologists, the town of Padangpanjang, 19km south of Bukittinggi, is a major pilgrimage site because of the **Conservatorium of Traditional Music** (STSI; ☎ 0752-82077; Jl Bundo Kanduang 35; 8am-3pm Mon-Thu, 8am-noon Fri). Minangkabau culture, dance and music are preserved, performed and taught here. There are regular buses between Bukittinggi, Padang and Padangpanjang (10,000Rp).

Nature Reserves

West Sumatra is famous for its many orchid species and for the *Rafflesia arnoldii*, the largest flower on the planet. The blossom of the parasitic plant measures nearly a meter in diameter and can weigh up to 11kg. The flower is known for its putrid perfume and typically blooms between August and November. The best place to find the ripe blossoms are in **Batang Palupuh Nature Reserve**, 16km north of Bukittinggi. Local buses to Palupuh cost 5000Rp.

On the highway between Padang and Bukitttinggi is the **Lembah Anai Nature Reserve**, which is renowned for its waterfalls, wild orchids and giant rafflesia flowers. Any Bukittinggi–Padang bus can drop you off nearby.

Gunung Merapi

Looming large over Bukittinggi to the east is the smouldering summit of Gunung Merapi (2891m). Merapi is one of Sumatra's most restless volcanoes and is occasionally deemed too dangerous to climb. The last major eruption was in 1979, but ask locally for an up-to-date status report.

If Merapi isn't huffing and puffing, then visitors typically do an overnight hike in order to view sunrise on the summit. The climb begins at the village of Kota Baru (of bullfighting fame). It's a one-hour climb to the forestry station shelter then another four to the top. You'll need good walking boots, warm clothing, a torch, food and drink.

It's unwise to attempt the climb alone, and people are advised to take a guide or join a group. Travel agencies in Bukittinggi do guided trips to Merapi for US$20 per person.

Harau Valley

Following the emerald road of rice fields leads to the speck-sized village of Harau, a little one-lane road where automobiles have to yield to groups of schoolchildren and sauntering old men. Another 3km from the village rises spectacular 100m cliffs that enclose the verdant Harau Valley, 15km northeast of Payakumbuh.

Harau Valley is under-used by backpackers, most of whom zip in and out on tours to **Lemba Harau** (admission 1500Rp), a series of pooling waterfalls. A handful of self-sufficient rock-climbers base themselves here, within an echo's reach of the scalable heights. But Harau's rice fields, jungles filled with howling gibbons and easy pace is surely why people stumble through Sumatra instead of baking on the beaches in Bali.

Smack in the middle of the valley is **Echo Homestay** (☎ 7750306; Taratang Lb Limpato; d from 50,000Rp), one of Sumatra's most scenic places to stay. Slum it in the ewok-hut bungalows with shared bathroom or step up to the artsy wooden treehouses designed in traditional Minangkabau style.

There is no direct transport to the Harau Valley, but you can take a local bus from Bukittinggi to Payakumbuh (5000Rp) and then hire an *ojek* to take you the rest of the way (10,000Rp).

DANAU MANINJAU

☎ 0752

When viewed from the mountains above, Danau Maninjau looks as if a piece of the sky had grown weary with its eternal floating and crawled to earth for an afternoon nap. And the pace is just as sleepy: no jarring call to prayers, no overload of 'Hello mister' calls. Just the basic elements: land, sky and water.

This is a great place to evaporate a Sumatra session with early-morning swims or quiet afternoons watching the clouds wisp over the peaks and slither down the 600m crater walls. From the right vantage point you can outline Maninjau's crater lip, engulfing a diminutive lake measuring 17km long and 8km wide.

The final descent to Danau Maninjau, on the road from Bukittinggi, 38km west, is unforgettable. The road twists and turns

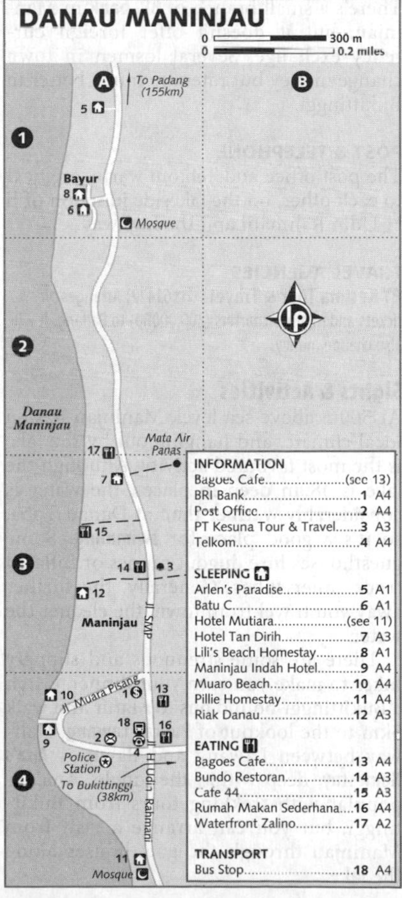

through 44 hairpin bends, and offers stunning views over the shimmering blue lake and surrounding hills.

Orientation & Information

The only village of any size is Maninjau, but most people stay near Bayur, 3km north. Tell the conductor where you want to stay and you'll be dropped off at the right spot.

In Maninjau village, most businesses centre around the junction of Jl H Udin Rahmani and the highway to Bukittinggi.

INTERNET ACCESS

Bagoes Cafe (per hr 20,000Rp; 10am-9pm) Slow and unreliable internet access.

MONEY

There's a small branch of **BRI bank** in Maninjau, but it doesn't offer foreign currency exchange. Several losmen in town change money but rates are much better in Bukittinggi.

POST & TELEPHONE

The post office and Telkom wartel are next to each other, on the lakeside junction of Jl H Udin Rahmani and the highway.

TRAVEL AGENCIES

PT Kesuna Tour & Travel (☎ 61422) Arranges air tickets and minibus charters (300,000Rp) to Padang. It will also change money.

Sights & Activities

At 500m above sea level, Maninjau has an ideal climate, and hanging out by the lake is the most favoured activity. Although the lake is 480m deep in places, the water is considerably warmer than at Danau Toba, so it's a good place for **swimming**. Some guesthouses hire dugout canoes or inflated truck inner tubes. Generally, the further away you travel from town, the cleaner the water.

There are some strenuous and slippery hikes to make you earn your dinner. Catch a Bukittinggi-bound bus to Matur and walk 5km to the lookout of **Puncak Lawang**. Halfway between Lawang and Bayur is **Ana's Homestay**, deep within the jungle. Ana's is popular with trekking tours from Bukittinggi, but you can arrange a visit from Maninjau through the guesthouses along the lake.

Festivals & Events

Rakik Rakik is celebrated on the night before Idul Fitri (the end of Ramadan) by building a platform to hold a replica Minangkabau house and mosque. The offering is then floated out onto the lake on canoes accompanied by fireworks and revelry.

Sleeping

Want to stay in a postcard-perfect setting? Then migrate to the guesthouses around Bayur, where you can watch the quiet industry of cultivating the land and lake. Fisherfolk paddle silently to the shore to ravel and unravel weighted nets and stoic coconut hunters command their trained monkeys to scale the towering palms and pluck out only the good fruit.

If you need more city-ish action, there is a louder heartbeat in Maninjau village, but the shorefront is dominated by small-scale fish ponds, making swimming less appealing.

MANINJAU

Riak Danau (☎ 081 9751706; d 20,000Rp) The best of a cluster of cheapies in town.

Pillie Homestay (☎ 61048; d 30,000Rp) South of Maninjau's main junction, Pillie's draw is the personality of the pleasant family: mama, papa and the girls.

Muaro Beach (☎ 61189; d 30,000-40,000Rp) Well hidden past the village schools along a twisty footpath, Muaro has basic numbers on the beach.

Hotel Mutiara (☎ 61049; d from 80,000Rp) Next door to Pillie, Mutiara is a breezy spot with clean, tiled rooms.

Maninjau Indah Hotel (☎ 61018; d from 165,000Rp) Of the hotels in town, Maninjau Indah has the best location: overlooking the lake far enough from road noise.

Hotel Tan Dirih (☎ 61263; r from 100,000Rp) Rooms here are better than at Maninjau Indah, but the location is lacking.

BAYUR

To get to the following from the main road, take the tiny tracks through the paddy fields to the lakefront.

Arlen's Paradise (☎ 081 535204714; d from 75,000Rp) From the front porches of Arlen's grown-up bungalows, you get a full shot of Maninjau's scenic beauty and enough privacy to swim in modern fashions.

SUMATRA

Further south is Bayur's primary clutch of bungalows. Some close for the season, some for good. These were the ones open during research:

Lili's Beach Homestay (d from 30,000Rp) A hardcore backpacker spot with bungalows just a notch above camping.

Batu C (d from 30,000Rp) Next door, Batu C has a bed-head vibe with basic huts on a nice beach, but the toilets are still terrible.

Eating

Most of the **guesthouses** serve basic meals such as *mie/nasi goreng*, some Western favourites and freshly caught fish. A few places in Maninjau village are also worth checking out.

Bagoes Cafe (☎ 61418; mains 10,000-12,000Rp) A tourist-friendly place with all the usual fare and a few local specialities. There are free movies on demand, and internet.

Cafe 44 (☎ 61238; mains 10,000Rp) Budget views of the lake, with a good selection of local food and a friendly atmosphere.

Waterfront Zalino (☎ 61740; mains 10,000-18,000Rp) A little classier than the rest of Maninjau, this waterfront restaurant does grilled fish with a perky attitude.

Rumah Makan Sederhana and **Bundo Restoran** (dishes 8000Rp) both serve a good selection of Padang food.

Getting There & Around

There are hourly buses between Maninjau and Bukittinggi (10,000Rp, 1½ hours). To reach Padang without backtracking to Bukittinggi, catch an *opelet* to Lubuk Basung (5000Rp, 20 minutes), then a bus to Padang (7000Rp, three hours). There is also an economy bus to/from Dumai (40,000Rp).

Several places rent out mountain bikes for 30,000Rp a day, motorcycles for 65,000Rp (including petrol) and canoes for 10,000Rp.

Buses travel throughout the day between Maninjau and Bayur – just stand by the road and hail one. Alternatively, you can take an *ojek* between the two (3000Rp to 5000Rp).

KERINCI VALLEY

☎ 0748 / pop 300,000

Kerinci is a stunning mountain valley tucked away high in the Bukit Barisan on Jambi's western border. Much of the cool, lush forests are protected as the Kerinci Seblat National Park. To the south is picturesque Danau Kerinci and a patchwork of rich farmland. The waxy-leafed bushes of Kerinci's profitable tea plantations transform the hilltops into rows of green corduroy. Much of the wealth in the valley is also from cinnamon plantations, which supply 40% of the world's market.

Dotting the valley are 200 villages, the majority being unmistakably Minangkabau West Sumatran, with the same matrilineal social structure. Kerinci is in Jambi province but appears in this section because of its geographic proximity to Padang.

Sungaipenuh

Sungaipenuh (Full River) is the largest town, the regional administrative centre and transport hub in the valley. It has a quiet, provincial atmosphere, with most places of importance near the large sports field in the centre of town.

This is where you'll be able to purchase supplies for hikes and entertain yourself once you emerge from the woods.

INFORMATION

BNI ATM (Bank Negara Indonesia; Jl Matadinata) Just off the main square; accepts MasterCard and Visa.

BNI bank (Bank Negara Indonesia; Jl Ahmad Yani) Exchange US dollars (cash and travellers cheques) here; opposite Hotel Matahari.

TNKS (Taman Nasional Kerinci Seblat; ☎ 323701; Jl Basuki Rahmat 11; 8am-2.30pm Mon-Thu, 8-11am Fri, 7.30am-12.30pm Sat) Park headquarters sell park permits and the informative booklet 'An Inside Look at the Secret Valley of Sumatra'.

Post office (Jl Sudirman 1)

Telkom wartel Around the corner from the post office, on the southern side of the sports field next to Hotel Aroma; also has internet access.

SIGHTS

Mesjid Agung Pondok Tinggi

This fine old **mosque** (Jl Sudirman; admission by donation 10,000Rp), with its pagoda-style roof, stands at the northern edge of Sungaipenuh in the village of Pondok Tinggi. Not a single nail was used when it was built in 1874 and, although it looks nothing special from the outside, the interior has elaborately carved beams and old Dutch tiles. You need permission to go inside and must be dressed in traditional attire. The mosque is west of the central square.

SUMATRA

SLEEPING & EATING

Accommodation options in Sungaipenuh are not plentiful or particularly affordable.

Hotel Yani (☎ 21409; Jl Murandi 1; d 65,000-100,000Rp) Next door to Minang Soto, Yani is one the town's better budget options.

Hotel Jaya (☎ 21221; Jl Martadinata; d 85,000-160,000Rp) The newest hotel in town, Hotel Jaya looks like a nouveau riche mansion, smuggling a little style into this backcountry.

Last-resort options include **Hotel Matahari** (☎ 21061; Jl Ahmad Yani 25; d 75,000Rp) and **Aroma Hotel** (☎ 21142; Jl Imam Bonjol 14; d 65,000R-150,000Rp).

Kerinci is known for the local speciality of *dendeng batokok*, charcoal-grilled strips of pounded beef. Street stalls pop up in the evening along Jl Teuku Umar, a block from the square. The fruit and produce market is at the southern end of Jl Diponegoro.

Minang Soto (Jl Muradi; dishes from 5000Rp) On the main street, Minang Soto is the town's favourite stop for Padang food.

Kersik Tua

Just beyond the tea plantations of the massive Kayo Aro estate, Kersik Tua is often used by Gunung Kerinci trekkers as a base, as the village is a 5km walk to the park entrance. The village is 43km north of Sungaipenuh on the road from Padang and can be reached via any Padang–Kerinci bus.

There are basic necessities available in Kersik Tua, including several basic homestays.

Subandi Homestay (☎ 357009; d 50,000Rp) is a family home with clean, simple rooms. The proprietor, Pak Subandi, is also a jack of all trades: rice farmer, jungle guide, keen birdwatcher and environmentalist.

The other homestays include **Wisma Paiman** (☎ 357030; d 25,000Rp) and **B Darmin** (☎ 357070; d 25,000Rp).

In front of the park entrance, 5km from Kersik Tua, **Losmen Pak Edes** (50,000Rp) has rooms with shared *mandis* and can arrange park permits and guides. Many people stay here before or after the trip to Danau Gunung Tujuh.

ORANG PENDEK: LITTLE BIG FOOT

Every culture that has lived among trees tells stories about elusive creatures that straddle myth and reality. Tales about leprechauns, fairies, and even Sasquatch have existed for so long that it is impossible to determine which came first: the spotting or the story. The Indonesian version of these myth makers is the *orang pendek*, which has been occasionally spotted but more frequently talked about in the Kerinci forests for generations.

Villagers who claim to have seen orang pendek describe the creature as being about 1m tall, more ape-like than human, but walking upright on the ground. The creature's reclusive habits made it a celebrity in local mythology. Common folk stories say that the orang pendek has feet that face backwards so that it can't be tracked through the forest or that it belongs to the supernatural not the world of flesh and blood. Others say that the first-hand accounts were only spottings of sun bears.

Scientists have joined the conversation by tramping through the forest hoping to document the existence of orang pendek. British researchers succeeded in making a plaster cast of an animal footprint that fits the orang pendek description and doesn't match any other known primate. Hair samples with no other documented matches have also led researchers to believe that there is merit to the local lore. Two members of Fauna & Flora International, a British-based research team, even reported separate sightings, but were unable to collect conclusive evidence. Researchers sponsored by the National Geographic Society have resumed the search by placing motion-sensitive cameras in strategic spots in the jungle. So little is known about this region and so many areas are so remote that researchers are hopeful that the orang pendek will eventually wander into the frame.

If nothing else, the orang pendek helps illuminate aspects of Sumatrans' linguistic and cultural relationship with the jungle. Bahasa Indonesia makes little distinction between man and ape, for example 'orang-utan' (forest man) or 'orang rimba' ('people of the forest', the preferred term for the Kubu tribe) may reflect a perceived blood tie between forest dwellers. This imprecision is often used for comic effect. A common joke is that the orang pendek (meaning 'short man') does indeed exist, followed by the punch line that the shortest person in the room is the missing link.

Kerinci Seblat National Park

This is the largest national park in Sumatra, covering a 350km swath of the Bukit Barisan range and protecting 15,000 sq km of prime equatorial rainforest spread over four provinces, with almost 40% of the park falling within Jambi's boundaries.

Most of the protected area is dense rainforest; its inaccessibility is the very reason it is one of the last strongholds of endangered species such as the Sumatran tiger and Sumatran rhinoceros. There have also been numerous reported sightings of the orang pendek (see the boxed text, opposite).

Because of the great range of elevation within the park, Kerinci has a unique diversity of flora and fauna. Many high-latitude flowers, like a type of edelweiss, grow in the forest. At lower altitudes, there are more familiar tropical flowers – orchids, rafflesia and the giant *Amorphophallus* (a Sumatran native and one of the tallest flowers on the planet).

As with many of Sumatra's protected areas, encroachment by farmers, illegal logging and poaching are all serious issues for Kerinci. Looking at satellite photographs of the park shows quickly disappearing forest cover. According to park estimates, between 2002 and 2004, a total of 23,000 hectares (230 sq km) of forests were destroyed.

Tourist infrastructure within the park is nonexistent and Kerinci sees very few visitors. Trekking opportunities typically focus on the northern region of the park, while the southern region is the traditional zone where local people are allowed to cultivate the land. Permits and guides are required to enter the park; both can be arranged at the TNKS office in Sungaipenuh (see p449) or through area losmen. There is a park office at the northern entrance, but it is rarely staffed. Surrounding the newly built office are the remnants of park-owned buildings that were torched by pro-logging interests.

Permits cost 15,000Rp and guide rates are highly negotiable, ranging from 50,000Rp to 150,000Rp per day. Be sure to clarify with your guide what the quoted rate entails. Camping gear, food and transport may be considered additional costs.

Kerinci's climate is very cool, and approaches cold as you gain altitude. Bring warm clothes and rain gear on treks. See the boxed text on p393 for additional instructions.

GUNUNG KERINCI

In the northern corner of the park is Gunung Kerinci (3805m), an active volcano and Sumatra's highest peak. It is said that from the summit you can see north all the way to Gunung Singgalang and Gunung Merapi on those rare clear days.

Summit treks typically start in the village of Kersik Tua and tackle the mountain in two stages. It takes approximately six hours to climb to a camping ground at about 3000m, where most people spend the night. The next day the final two-hour climb to the summit departs at dawn in order to be at the top for sunrise.

The volcano last erupted in 1934 and today you'll find a small greenish crater lake at the top. You'll also spot Javanese edelweiss and, if you're lucky, a few rare bird species, such as Schneider's pitta and red-billed partridge.

There are cave paintings in Gua Kasah on the lower slopes, 5km from Kersik Tua. On the way back down the mountain, you can stop at **Sungai Medang Hot Springs & Wisma** (day use 2000Rp, r 50,000Rp). The facility has overnight rooms and day-use rooms – both with hot-water *mandis*, a wonderful elixir from the jungle chills.

Although the path to the top of the mountain is clearly defined, parts are covered in scree, making it easy to slip, and weather conditions can change very suddenly. It is recommended to hire a guide who knows the terrain and weather patterns. You'll need to bring food, water, camping gear (which can be hired in Kersik Tua) and warm clothes, as it can get as low as 2°C at night.

Most people spend the preceding night at a homestay in Kersik Tua (opposite), where guides, permits and supplies can be arranged.

DANAU GUNUNG TUJUH

A much easier climb than Gunung Kerinci, this tranquil lake sits at 1966m, garnering it the superlative of being the highest volcanic lake in Southeast Asia. As the name suggests, seven scenic mountains encircle it.

It takes 3½ hours to climb to the lake from the village of Pelompek, 8km beyond Kersik Tua. An additional two-hour hike leads to a camping beach.

To reach the starting point, take a bus from Sungaipenuh to Pelompek (4000Rp) and hire an *ojek* (from 5000Rp) for the remainder of the trip to the park entrance.

The lake is within the park boundaries, so you need to get a permit either in Pelompek or from Losmen Pak Edes, near the park entrance.

DANAU KERINCI

Danau Kerinci, 20km south of Sungaipenuh, is a small lake nestled beneath Gunung Raja (2543m). There is a popular recreational park and an annual festival, typically held in July and displaying traditional Kerinci dance and music. **Stone carvings** in the villages around the lake suggest that the area supported a sizable population in megalithic times. The best known of these stone monuments is **Batu Gong** (Gong Stone), in the village of Muak, 25km from Sungaipenuh. It is thought to have been carved 2000 years ago.

To reach the lake, catch a public bus from Sungaipenuh to Sanggaran Agung (2000Rp). The last return bus leaves around 4pm.

SENGERING CAVES

The extensive network of caves outside the village of Sengering includes the celebrated **Gua Tiangko**. Obsidian-flake tools found in the cave show that it was occupied by some of Sumatra's earliest known residents some 9000 years ago. The caves are also known for their stalactites and stalagmites.

It is also locally believed that caves act as mediums for communicating with the supernatural and entrance into these sacred spaces requires a modest ritual. Hiring a guide helps both in the exploration of the physical and immaterial landscape of the caves.

Sengering is 9km from Sungai Manau, a village on the road to Bangko. Public buses leave from Sungaipenuh to Bangko in the mornings.

Getting There & Away

There is a regional airport but at the time of writing there was no contracted carrier.

Sungaipenuh doesn't have a bus terminal, but the bus companies all have offices near the market in the centre of town.

The shortest approach to Sungaipenuh is from the West Sumatran capital of Padang (70,000Rp, six to eight hours). Buses pass the village of Kersik Tua en route to Sungaipenuh; if you're staying in Kersik Tua, let the driver know, as it's easy to miss. **PO Cahaya Kerinci** (☎ 21421; Jl Diponegoro), **PO CW Safa Marwa** (☎ 22376; Jl Yos Sudarso 20) and **PO AYU Transport** (☎ 22074; Jl Cokroaminoto), all in Sungaipenuh, run Padang-bound services.

Other destinations include Dumai (200,000Rp, twice weekly), Bukittinggi (80,000Rp, 10 hours, twice weekly), Bangko (30,000Rp, four hours, daily) and Bengkulu (75,000Rp, 16 hours, daily).

Getting Around

You can get almost anywhere in the valley from the bus terminal in Sungaipenuh market. Sample destinations and fares are Danau Kerinci (2000Rp), Kersik Tua (5000Rp) and Pelompek (5000Rp).

BENGKULU

Cut off from its neighbours by the Bukit Barisan range, Bengkulu remains Sumatra's most isolated province – and nothing much seems to have changed here for years.

Few tourists make it this far, but those that do are rewarded with the simple pleasures of ordinary Indonesian life and an opportunity to learn Bahasa Indonesia without the crutch of bilingualism.

History

Little is known of Bengkulu before it came under the influence of the Majapahits from Java at the end of the 13th century. Until then it appears to have existed in almost total isolation, divided between a number of small kingdoms such as Sungai Lebong in the Curup area. It even developed its own cuneiform script, *ka-ga-nga*.

In 1685, after having been kicked out of Banten in Java, the British moved into Bengkulu (Bencoolen, as they called it) in search of pepper. The venture was not exactly a roaring success. Isolation, boredom and constant rain sapped the British will, and malaria ravaged their numbers.

The colony was still not a likely prospect in 1818 when Sir Stamford Raffles arrived as its British-appointed ruler. In the short time he was there, Raffles made the pepper market profitable and planted cash crops of coffee, nutmeg and sugar cane. In 1824 Bengkulu was traded for the Dutch outpost of Melaka and a guarantee not to interfere with British interests in Singapore.

From 1938 to 1941 Bengkulu was a home-in-domestic-exile for Indonesia's first president, Soekarno.

BENGKULU

☎ 0736 / pop 380,000

A quiet provincial capital, Bengkulu doesn't have much to do for tourists but chat up the locals, most of whom don't speak English. Alternatively, you could pass through as a UFO – unidentified foreign object.

Orientation

Although Bengkulu is by the sea, most of the town is set back from the waterfront, touching only near the fort, Benteng Marlborough. The coast is unexpectedly quiet and rural, just a kilometre or so from the town centre.

The commercial spine of Jl Suprapto and the nearby Pasar Minggu Besar are in the modern town centre, which is connected to the old town area around the fort by the long and straight Jl Ahmad Yani/Jl Sudirman.

Information

INTERNET ACCESS

Satelit Internet (Jl S Parman 9; per hr 5000Rp; 10am-8pm)

MONEY

There are plenty of ATMs around town.

BCA bank (Bank Central Asia; Jl Suprapto 150) The best place to exchange money.

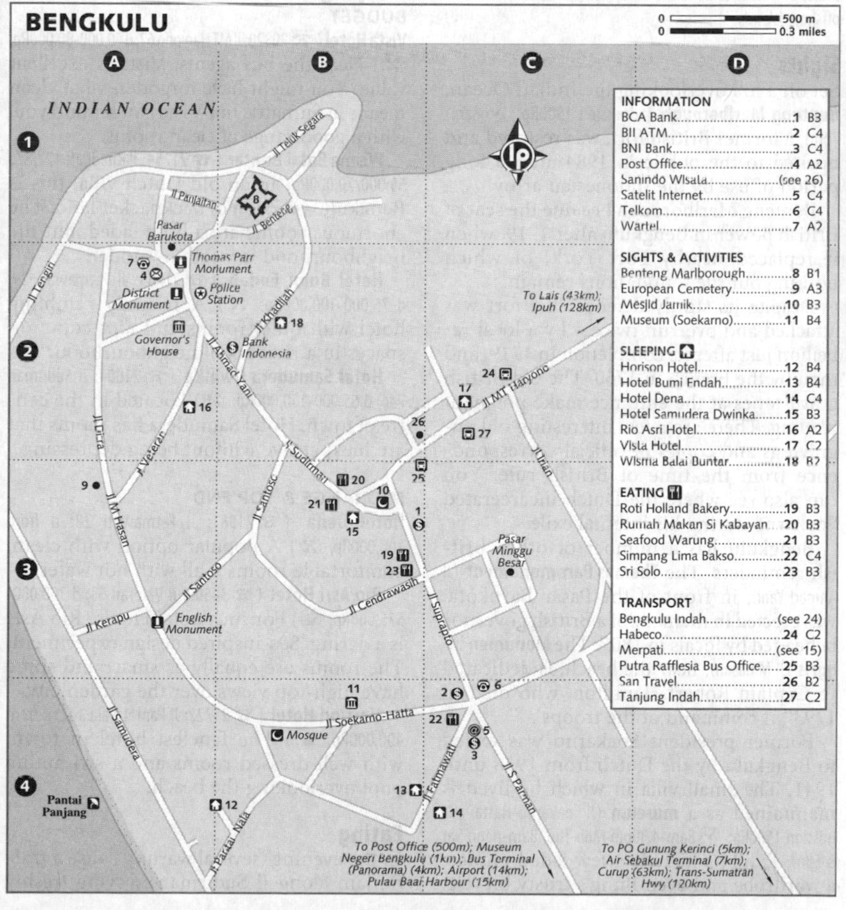

BII bank (Bank Internasional Indonesia; Jl Suprapto)
BNI bank (Bank Negara Indonesia; Jl S Parman) Travellers cheques and US dollars can be changed here.

POST

Main post office (Jl S Parman) South of town centre; also has poste restante.
Post office (Jl RA Hadi 3) More convenient, opposite the Thomas Parr monument.

TELEPHONE

Telkom wartel (cnr Jl Suprapto & Soekarno-Hatta; 7am-10pm) International calls can be made here.

TRAVEL AGENCIES

Sanindo Wisata Tours and Travel (27522; Jl Mt Haryono 73) Sanindo Wisata can arrange historical city tours, as well as tours to the Curup tea plantations and offshore islands.

Sights

Set on a hill overlooking the Indian Ocean, **Benteng Marlborough** (admission 1500Rp; 8am-7pm), a former British fort, was restored and opened to the public in 1984 after a long period of use by the Indonesian army.

Benteng Marlborough became the seat of British power in Bengkulu after 1719, when it replaced nearby Fort York, of which nothing but the foundations remain.

Despite its sturdy defences the fort was attacked and overrun twice – by a local rebellion just after its completion in 1719, and then by the French in 1760. The old British gravestones at the entrance make poignant reading. There are a few interesting old engravings and copies of official correspondence from the time of British rule. You can also see where the Dutch incarcerated Soekarno during his internal exile.

Bengkulu has a number of other British reminders. The **Thomas Parr monument** (Jl Ahmad Yani), in front of the Pasar Barukota, was erected in memory of a British governor beheaded by locals in 1807. The **Monumen Inggris** (Jl M Hasan), near the beach, is dedicated to Captain Robert Hamilton, who died in 1793 'in command of the troops'.

Former president Soekarno was exiled to Bengkulu by the Dutch from 1938 until 1941. The small villa in which he lived is maintained as a **museum** (Jl Soekarno-Hatta; admission 1500Rp; 8am-4.30pm Mon-Thu, 8am-noon Sat & Sun). Exhibits include a few faded photos, a wardrobe and even Bung's trusty bicycle. During his stay, Soekarno, who was an architect, designed the **Mesjid Jamik** (Bung Karno mosque; cnr Jl Sudirman & Suprapto).

Museum Negeri Bengkulu (32099; Jl Pembangunan; admission by donation; 8am-4.30pm Tue-Thu, 8am-noon Sat & Sun) has a poorly labelled collection of standard Sumatran fare. Bring your own light if you want to see anything. The graves in the **European cemetery** (Jl Ditra) behind the small church are testament to the colonialists' vulnerability to malaria.

Bengkulu's main beach, **Pantai Panjang**, although not the best in Indonesia, is clean, generally deserted and a good place for a walk. Strong surf and currents make it unsafe for swimming.

Sleeping

BUDGET

Vista Hotel (20820; Jl MT Haryono 67; d 40,000-80,000Rp;) Near the bus agents, Vista is excellent value. You might have forgotten what clean means in Sumatra, but Vista can remind you, with a good range of clean rooms.

Wisma Balai Buntar (21254; Jl Khadijah 122; s/d 55,000/70,000Rp) In an old Dutch villa, this is Bengkulu's version of backpacker land. The enormous rooms are a little faded, but the neighbourhood is worth a wander.

Hotel Bumi Endah (21665; Jl Fatmawati 29; d 75,000-100,000Rp;) A friendly rambling hotel with quiet rooms and airy common spaces in a residential neighbourhood.

Hotel Samudera Dwinka (21604; Jl Sudirman 246; d 65,000-100,000Rp;) Located in the centre of town, Hotel Samudera has rooms that are inexpensive without being depressing.

MIDRANGE & TOP END

Hotel Dena (21981; Jl Fatmawati 28; d from 100,000Rp;) A popular option with clean, comfortable rooms – all with hot water.

Rio Asri Hotel (34500; Jl Veteran 63; d 300,000-575,000Rp;) For such a staid town, Rio Asri is a daring '80s-inspired design experiment. The rooms are equally as smart and some have high-top views over the garden city.

Horison Hotel (21722; Jl Pantai Nala 142; d from 400,000Rp;) The fanciest hotel in town, with well-dressed rooms and a swimming pool overlooking the beach.

Eating

In the evening, several warung cause a traffic jam along Jl Sudirman, serving freshly

SUMATRA

grilled seafood and *martabak* (stuffed savoury pancake).

Roti Holland Bakery (Jl Suprapto 124; pastries 2000Rp; 8am-5pm) Chocolate doughnuts are wrapped thoughtfully in a cardboard box for those with self-control. The rest of us can tear into the pastries at the café tables.

Sri Solo (Jl Suprapto 118; mains 8000Rp; 10am-10pm) The equivalent of an ice-cream parlour, Sri Solo serves local families after church, gangs of schoolkids and courting couples plates of *ayam baker* (grilled chicken) and tasty fruit juices.

Rumah Makan Si Kabayan (Jl Sudirman 51; mains from 25,000Rp; 6-10pm) This is where Bengkulu entertains guests, with fitting VIP prices.

Simpang Lima Bakso (Jl Soekarno-Hatta; mains from 10,000Rp) Bengkulu is *bakso* (meatball and noodle soup) crazy and this simple warung does a thriving business beside the city's crazy five-way intersection.

Getting There & Away

AIR

Merpati, Sriwijaya and Adam Air operate daily flights to Jakarta. The **Merpati office** (☎ 27111; Jl Sudirman 246) is in the Hotel Samudera Dwinka. Other tickets can be purchased through **Sanindo Wisata Tours and Travel** (☎ 27522; Jl Mt Haryono 73).

BUS

Bengkulu has two bus terminals: Air Sebakul terminal, 15km east of town, serves long-distance destinations, while Panorama terminal, 7km east, is used by local buses.

However, it is much easier to go to the bus company offices on Jl MT Haryono, as almost all long-distance destinations can be reached from here.

To get to Air Sebakul take a yellow *opelet* (2000Rp) to Panorama and then a white one (2000Rp) to Air Sebakul.

Putra Rafflesia (☎ 20313; Jl MT Haryono 12) services Palembang (economy 80,000Rp, 15 hours) and Padang (air-con 125,000Rp, 16 hours). **Bengkulu Indah** (☎ 22640; Jl MT Haryono) services a wide range of destinations. **San Travel** (☎ 21811; Jl MT Haryono 73) goes to Bukittinggi (80,000Rp, 17 hours).

PO Gunung Kerinci (Jl Bali 36) runs buses up the coast to Sungaipenuh in the Kerinci Valley (75,000Rp, 18 hours). **Tanjung Indah** (Jl MT Haryono 108) runs minivans to Palembang (150,000Rp) and other destinations.

Habeco (Jl MT Haryono), at the northern edge of town, has daily buses along the coast road to regional destinations, such as Lais (8000Rp, two hours), Ipuh (20,000Rp, five hours) and Mukomuko (30,000Rp, eight hours).

Getting Around

Airport taxis charge a standard 60,000Rp to town. The airport is 200m from the main road south, from where there are regular *opelet* to town (2000Rp). Tell the driver where you want to stay or simply ask for the *benteng* (fort). *Opelet* and *ojek* also greet buses when they arrive at Jl MT Haryono/Jl Bali. *Opelet* fares to almost anywhere in town are 2000Rp, *ojek* 5000Rp.

There are no fixed routes for *opelet*; tell the driver your destination or general area and you might get a nod of approval. The city is roughly divided up into the Kampung (the area around Benteng Marlborough), Simpang Lima (the intersection of Jl Suprapto, Parman, Fatmawati and Soekarno-Hatta) and Minggu (the area around Pasar Minggu).

NORTHERN BENGKULU

The coast road (Jl Manusurai Pantai), running north from Bengkulu to Padang, offers a number of possibilities for travellers.

The road is sealed all the way and the journey takes about a mere 16 hours, a real quickie when measured by the Sumatran distance stick. However, in the wet season the coast road is prone to wash-outs and landslides, so the going can be much slower.

The journey can be done in a number of short hops, stopping off at a town along the way for the hell of it; each town has at least one losmen. The first town north of Bengkulu is **Lais**. There are reputed to be elephants further north near **Ipuh**, around the mouth of Sungai Ipuh. **Mukomuko**, 200km north of Bengkulu, is the largest community on this stretch of road and was the northern outpost of the British colony of Bencoolen.

Curup is a small market town in the foothills of the Bukit Barisan, halfway between Bengkulu and Lubuklinggau. There are several surviving traditional homes and the town itself is in a valley watered by the upper reaches of Sungai Musi, which eventually flows through Palembang. Curup is a good base for visits to the surrounding mountains, including volcanic **Gunung Kaba**, 19km east of town, which has two large smouldering craters surrounded by dense rainforest.

There's nowhere to change money in Curup, so come prepared. Curup has a mediocre losmen and hotel to choose from.

Getting There & Away

Padang–Bengkulu buses can stop off at the northern coastal towns. Curup can be reached by frequent connections to Bengkulu and Lubuklinggau.

PULAU ENGGANO

This remote island, 100km off the coast of southern Bengkulu, is so isolated that until the early 20th century some Sumatrans believed that it was inhabited entirely by women, who miraculously gave birth to children sired by the wind.

The island is featured on a map of Asia drawn in 1593. Enggano is Portuguese for 'deceit' or 'disappointment', which suggests that the Portuguese were the first Europeans to discover it. It wasn't until three years later that Dutch navigators first recorded it.

Enggano's original inhabitants are believed to have fled the Sumatran mainland when the Malays migrated there. Today the islanders live by cultivating rice, coffee, pepper, cloves and copra. Wild pigs, cattle and buffalo are abundant.

The island has an area of 680 sq km and there are no tourist facilities. **Malakoni** is the main harbour. The island is relatively flat (the highest point is Bua Bua, at 250m) and has a swampy coastline interspersed with some good **beaches** and **snorkelling**. Few tourists make it this far and you need to speak some Bahasa Indonesia in order to have any worthwhile contact with the local people.

It is best to report to the *kepala desa* (village chief) and seek advice for lodging.

Getting There & Around

In theory there are three boats a week from Bengkulu to Malakoni, but no-one in Bengkulu was able to vouch for this service. Alternatively, go to the small port of Bintuhan, about 225km south of Bengkulu, and ask at the harbour.

The villages on the island are connected by tracks originally made by the Japanese and not very well maintained since. The only way to get around is to walk.

RIAU

The landscape and character of Riau province is decidedly distinct from the northern and western rind of Sumatra. Rather than mountains and volcanoes, Riau's character was carved by rivers and narrow ocean passages. Trading towns sprang up along the important navigation route of the Strait of Melaka, across which Riau claims cultural cousins.

For the port towns, such as Pekanbaru, and the Riau islands, proximity to Singapore and Kuala Lumpur has ensured greater access to the outside world than the interior Sumatran jungle. The discovery of oil and gas reserves has also built an educated and middle-class populous within an otherwise impoverished island.

The interior of the province more closely resembles Sumatra as a whole: sparse population, dense jungle, surviving pockets of nomadic peoples (including the Sakai, Kubu and Jambisal) and endangered species, such as the Sumatran rhinoceros and tiger.

A strain of chloroquine-resistant malaria has been reported in Riau archipelago.

History

Riau's position at the southern entrance to the Strait of Melaka, the gateway for trade between India and China, was strategically significant.

From the 16th century, the Riau Islands were ruled by a variety of Malay kingdoms, which had to fight off constant attacks by pirates and the opportunistic Portuguese, Dutch and English. The Dutch eventually won control over the Strait of Melaka, and mainland Riau (then known as Siak) became their colony when the Sultan of Johor surrendered in 1745. However, Dutch interest lay in ridding the seas of pirates, so they could get on with the serious business of trade, and they made little effort to develop the province.

Oil was discovered around Pekanbaru by US engineers before WWII, but it was the Japanese who drilled the first well at Rumbai, 10km north of the city. The country around Pekanbaru is crisscrossed by pipelines connecting the oil wells to refineries at Dumai because ocean-going tankers cannot enter the heavily silted Sungai Siak.

PEKANBARU

☎ 0761 / pop 750,000

Before the Americans struck oil, Pekanbaru was little more than a sleepy river port on Sungai Siak. Today it is Indonesia's oil capital, with all the hustle and bustle of modern cities.

Pekanbaru's primary purpose for tourists is as a transit point between ferries from Singapore, but the increased affordability of air travel has curtailed the sea passage. Now only Western oil executives on business trips find themselves in Pekanbaru.

If you do decide to wander through, you'll spend most of your time accepting inexplicable gestures of kindness, from café conversations to instant friendships.

Orientation

The main street of Pekanbaru is Jl Sudirman. Almost everything of importance to travellers – banks, hotels and offices – can be found here or close by. Speedboats leave from the Sungai Duku port. The new bus terminal is 5km west of town.

Information

Most of the city's banks and ATMs are spread along Jl Sudirman. There are plenty of travel agencies around town that can

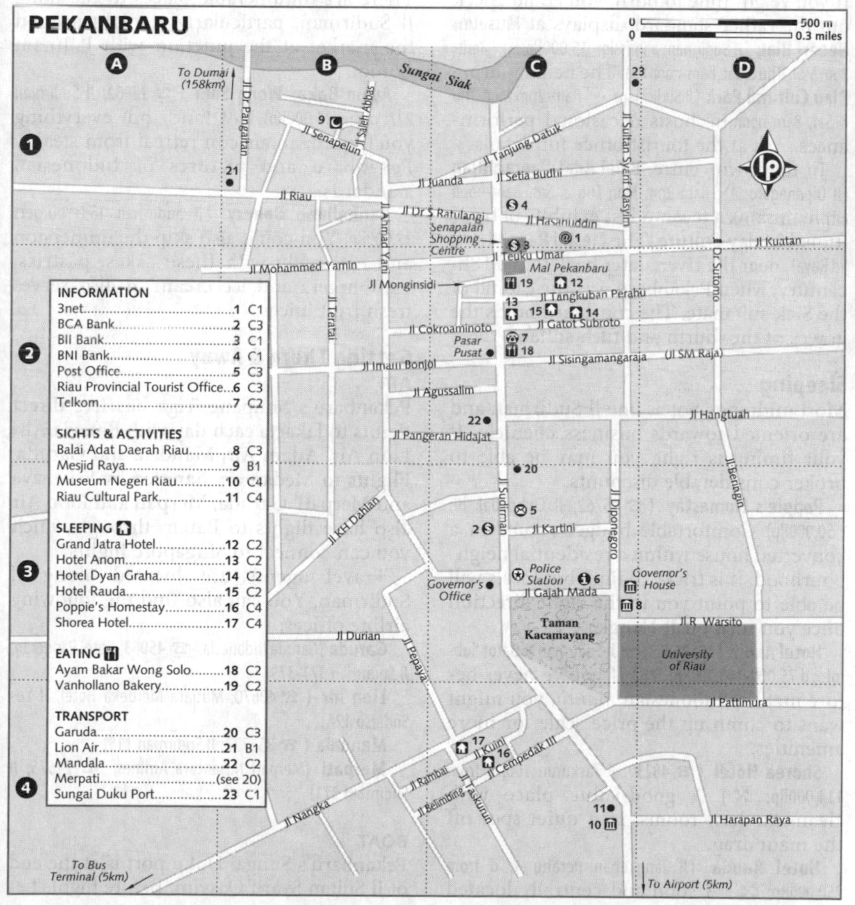

book plane and bus tickets as well as tours of the local area.

3net (Jl Teuku Umar 11; per hr 6000Rp; 9am-9pm) Internet café and travel agency.

BCA bank (Bank Central Asia; Jl Sudirman 448)

BII bank (Bank Internasional Indonesia; Jl Nangka 4) Changes US and Singapore dollars (cash and travellers cheques).

BNI bank (Bank Negara Indonesia; Jl Sudirman)

Post office (Jl Sudirman) Between Jl Hangtuah and Jl Kartini.

Riau provincial tourist office (31562; Jl Gajah Mada 200; 8am-4pm Mon-Thu, 8-11am Fri)

Telkom wartel (Jl Sudirman; 8am-9pm) About 1km north of the post office.

Sights

If you've got time to burn, you could check out the rather standard displays at **Museum Negeri Riau** (Jl Sudirman; admission 15,000Rp; 8am-2pm Mon-Thu & Sat, 8am-noon Fri). The neighbouring **Riau Cultural Park** (Jl Sudirman; 8am-2pm Mon-Thu & Sat, 8am-noon Fri) hosts occasional performances. Ask at the tourist office for details.

In the town centre, **Balai Adat Daerah Riau** (Jl Diponegoro; 8am-2pm Mon-Thu & Sat, 8am-noon Fri) maintains a few modest exhibits of traditional Malay culture. The **Mesjid Raya** (Jl Mesjid Raya), near the river, dates back to the 18th century, when Pekanbaru was the capital of the Siak sultanate. The courtyard holds the graves of the fourth and fifth sultans.

Sleeping

Most midrange hotels line Jl Sudirman and are oriented towards business clientele. If your timing is right, you may be able to broker considerable discounts.

Poppie's Homestay (45762; Jl Cempedak III; r 50,000Rp) Comfortable budget rooms in a converted house within a residential neighbourhood. It is tricky to find, but locals will be able to point you in the right direction once you turn off Jl Nangka.

Hotel Anom (36083; cnr Jl Sudirman & Gatot Subroto; d 75,000-140,000Rp) If you've never before met the Indonesian *mandi*, you might want to climb up the price scale for more amenities.

Shorea Hotel (48239; Jl Taskurun 100; d from 114,000Rp) A good-value place with clean, modern rooms, in a quiet spot off the main drag.

Hotel Rauda (Jl Tangkuban Perahu 4; d from 250,000Rp) A solid and centrally located midrange option. The rooms are nothing special and ultimately forgettable – a plus when it comes to all the things that could go wrong.

Hotel Dyan Graha (26600; www.dyangraha.co.id; Jl Gatot Subroto 7; d 585,000-800,000Rp) Conveniently central, this is one of Pekanbaru's upmarket options. The bathrooms are certainly a plus. Rates include breakfast and tax.

Grand Jatra Hotel (Komplek Mal Pekanbaru, Jl Tangkuban Perahu; d from 776,000Rp) Visiting oil executives stay at this brand-new spot, providing international standards and décor.

Eating

There are innumerable places to eat along Jl Sudirman, particularly at night around the market at the junction with Jl Imam Bonjol.

Ayam Bakar Wong Solo (32962; Jl Sudirman 227; mains 15,000Rp) Not fancy but everything you'll need: an air-con retreat from steamy Pekanbaru and pictures of Indonesian standards.

Vanhollano Bakery (Jl Sudirman 153; burgers 12,000Rp) You could also skip the immersion and eat safely with these cakes, pastries, hamburgers and ice cream. It also serves fresh fruit juices.

Getting There & Away

AIR

Pekanbaru's Simpang Tiga has five direct flights to Jakarta each day with Batavia Air, Lion Air, Adam Air, Mandala and Garuda. Flights to Medan are handled by Sriwijaya and Merpati. Garuda, Merpati and Lion Air also have flights to Batam through which you can connect to Singapore flights.

Travel agents are located along Jl Sudirman. You can also find the following airline offices:

Garuda (Garuda Indonesia; 45063; Hotel Pangeran, Jl Sudirman 371-373)

Lion Air (40670; Mutiara Merdeka Hotel, Jl Yos Sudarso 12A)

Mandala (856777; Jl Sudirman 115)

Merpati (Merpati Nusantara Airlines; 21575; Jl Sudirman 371)

BOAT

Pekanbaru's Sungai Duku port is at the end of Jl Sultan Syarif Qasyim. Before flights be-

SUMATRA

came so affordable, many travellers bounced between Pekanbaru and Batam's Sekupang port (economy/cabin 132,000/235,000Rp, six hours, 8am departure) en route to Singapore. When all the fares are tallied up, it is a long, expensive haul compared to the flying birds.

From Pekanbaru, boats also go to Melaka, Malaysia, three times a week (economy/cabin 215,000/365,000Rp; eight hours; 9am), Tanjung Pinang on Bintan (142,000Rp), Tanjung Balai on Karimun (200,000Rp) and Tanjung Samak on Pulau Rangsang (185,000Rp). It's also possible to go down Sungai Siak to Tanjung Buton (60,000Rp) and Selat Panjang (100,000Rp).

Ticket agents are located at the pier.

BUS

Pekanbaru's Terminal Nangka, 5km west of the town centre, is modern and uncharacteristically organised for Sumatra. There are posted prices and even staffed ticket booths within the terminal. If you don't want to be ripped off, buy tickets directly from the booths rather than the freelancers roaming the terminal. Destinations include Bengkulu (air-con 115,000Rp), Bukittinggi (economy 35,000Rp, five hours), Dumai (economy 7000Rp, five hours), Jambi (economy/air-con 75,000/150,000, 12 hours), Medan (economy 120,000Rp, 12 hours), and Padang (economy 51,000Rp, six hours).

Getting Around

Airport taxis charge 60,000Rp for the 10km trip into town.

Opelet around Pekanbaru cost a standard 2000Rp. From the port, catch a light-blue *opelet* to Pasar Pusat on Jl Sudirman. Green *opelet* on Jl Nangka shuttle between town and the bus terminal.

AROUND PEKANBARU

Some 120km downriver from Pekanbaru is **Siak Sri Inderapura**, site of the beautiful Asserayah el Hasyimiah Palace, built in 1889 by the 11th sultan of Siak, Sultan Adbul Jalil Syafuddin. It was the seat of the Siak sultanate until 1945. The palace was restored as a museum in 1989 but the best artefacts have been removed to Jakarta. The site also houses a dazzling white **mosque** with a silver dome.

You can stay at the basic **Penginapan Monalisa** (s/d 50,000Rp), by the dock in Siak.

To get there take the boat from the Sungai Duku port at 7.30am (economy/cabin 50,000/60,000Rp, four hours).

DUMAI

☎ 0765 / pop 180,000

Like most of Pekanbaru's oil, travellers enter and exit through the port of Dumai. Most are bound for the Malaysian port of Melaka. Although airfares between Malaysia and Sumatra are often more competitive, many travellers are still smitten with the idea of sailing the high seas.

If you get stuck in town, try the very basic **Wisma Hang Tua** (Jl Sudirman 431; d with fan from 50,000Rp); **Hotel Tasia Ratu** (☎ 31307; Jl St Syarif Kasim 65; d 100,000Rp), a tolerable midrange option; or **Royal Dumai Hotel** (☎ 34888; Jl Sudirman 58; d from 175,000-275,000Rp), Dumai's fanciest place.

Melaka-bound ferries depart from the Yos Sudarso port of Dumai three times a day at 8am, 10.30am and 1pm (170,000Rp, two hours). You must check in at the port two hours before departure in order to clear immigration. The port tax is 3500Rp.

Ferries travel daily to Batam (220,000Rp, seven hours). Two Pelni boats call at Dumai then Bintan en route to Jakarta.

There are frequent buses from Dumai to Padang (economy/air-con 70,000/100,000Rp, 12 hours), Bukittinggi (economy/air-con 50,000/80,000Rp, 10 hours) and Pekanbaru (economy 7000Rp, five hours). There are also minibus services timed with the arrivals of the boats from Batam.

RIAU ISLANDS

The Riau Islands are scattered like confetti across the South China Sea. The locals say there are as many islands as there are grains in a cup of pepper. That would be about 3214 islands in all, more than 700 of them uninhabited and many of them unnamed.

Pulau Batam and Bintam are practically suburbs of Singapore, with the attendant industry and recreation. In fact, the islands prefer to think of themselves as distinct from mainland Sumatra. Further away in the archipelago are the remote islands of Anambas, Natuna and Tambelan.

PULAU BATAM

☎ 0778 / pop 440,000

Nowhere in Sumatra is the pace of development more rapid than on Batam. With the

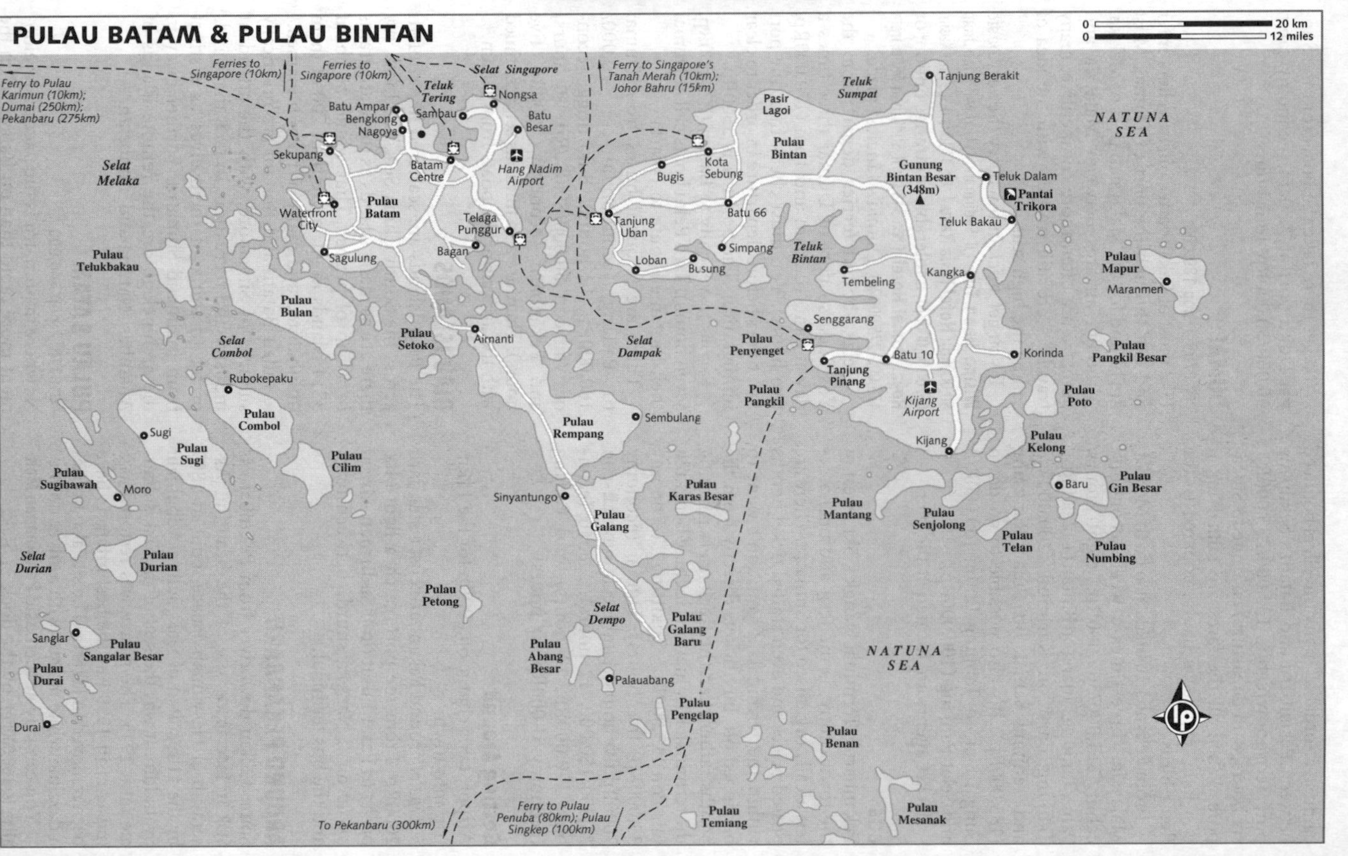
PULAU BATAM & PULAU BINTAN
0 20 km
0 12 miles
Ferry to Pulau Karimun (10km); Dumai (250km); Pekanbaru (275km)
Ferries to Singapore (10km)
Ferries to Singapore (10km)
Teluk Tering
Selat Singapore
Ferry to Singapore's Tanah Merah (10km); Johor Bahru (15km)
Nongsa
Batu Ampar
Bengkong
Nagoya
Sambau
Batu Besar
Sekupang
Batam Centre
Hang Nadim Airport
Selat Melaka
Waterfront City
Pulau Batam
Telaga Punggur
Bagan
Sagulung
Pulau Telukbakau
Pulau Bulan
Pulau Setoko
Airnanti
Selat Combol
Rubokepaku
Pulau Combol
Sugi
Pulau Sugi
Pulau Cilim
Pulau Sugibawah
Moro
Selat Durian
Pulau Durian
Pulau Petong
Sanglar
Pulau Sangalar Besar
Pulau Durai
Durai
Pasir Lagoi
Teluk Sumpat
Tanjung Berakit
Pulau Bintan
Bugis
Kota Sebung
Gunung Bintan Besar (348m)
Teluk Dalam
Pantai Trikora
Tanjung Uban
Batu 66
Teluk Bakau
Loban
Busung
Simpang
Teluk Bintan
Tembeling
Kangka
Senggarang
Selat Dampak
Pulau Penyenget
Tanjung Pinang
Batu 10
Korinda
Pulau Pangkil
Kijang Airport
Kijang
Pulau Rempang
Sembulang
Sinyantungo
Pulau Galang
Pulau Karas Besar
Selat Dempo
Pulau Galang Baru
Pulau Abang Besar
Palauabang
Pulau Pengelap
NATUNA SEA
Pulau Mapur
Maranmen
Pulau Pangkil Besar
Pulau Poto
Pulau Kelong
Baru
Pulau Gin Besar
Pulau Mantang
Pulau Senjolong
Pulau Telan
Pulau Numbing
NATUNA SEA
Pulau Benan
Pulau Mesanak
Pulau Temiang
To Pekanbaru (300km)
Ferry to Pulau Penuba (80km); Pulau Singkep (100km)

island's proximity to Singapore, Batam is the labour-intensive production leg of the Singapore–Johor Baru industrial triangle. Land and labour are cheaper here than in Singapore and many electronics companies have established production plants in the industrial park of Mukakuning. Much like the factory towns outside of Hong Kong, Mukakuning employs and houses mainly young women from impoverished areas of Indonesia. Hardly anyone living in Batam is a native and half the population is under 30 years old.

Higher up the economic food chain are the Western managers and executives who oversee the factories, as well as engineers employed by one of the island's largest multinationals, J Ray McDermott, which makes offshore oil rigs and pipelines.

In addition to industry, the island has made several unsuccessful bids at diversifying into a tourist destination. Because its miles of coastline are too close to Singapore's harbour to be swimmable, resorts have tried to distract tourists with golfing and gambling, a promising combination until the Indonesian government unplugged the casinos.

The next jackpot scheme is to develop the island as a retirement community for East Asians, Singaporeans and Jakarta-based Chinese. New housing complexes are going up faster than new factories.

Besides using Batam as a transit point for boats from Singapore to Sumatra, it is unlikely that a tourist would purposely come to Batam. The majority of foreigners here arrive on corporate assignments and find that the island has cultivated a bit of a boys club ambience. The main town of Nagoya has plenty of girlie bars to make the buttoned-down execs feel like studs.

Orientation & Information

Most travellers to Batam arrive at the northern port of Sekupang by boat from Singapore. Sekupang has an international and domestic terminal next door to each other and all the short-term necessities that new arrivals need: immigration desk and moneychangers. There are no ATMs at Sekupang, so arrive with cash to avoid a taxi to Nagoya.

The main town on the island is Nagoya, with hotels, banks and other necessities. To the south is the island's administrative centre, Batam Centre, which also has port facilities.

Waterfront City and Nongsa are the surviving resort areas that attract Batam expats on weekends and package tourists from elsewhere in Asia.

On Batam, Singapore dollars are as easy to spend as the Indonesian rupiah.

Nagoya

This is the original boom town, showing a lot more skin than you'll find in the rest of Sumatra. The heart of town is the Nagoya Entertainment District, where bars and massage parlours indulge male camaraderie with lap dances and take-home prizes. Although it ain't pretty, Nagoya is ultimately functional, with Western-geared food and entertainment sneaking in just under Singapore prices.

The city is divided up like Singapore into main avenues and tributary blocks and exhibits a certain Chinese industriousness similar to the city-state.

INFORMATION

Awal Brothers Hospital (☎ 431777; Jl Baloi) Western-trained doctors and international facilities, 7km south of Nagoya.

Barelang Internet (Komplek Batam Plaza 4; per hr 10,000Rp)

Bank Danamon (Jl Imam Bonjol) Across from Goodway Hotel.

Batam Tourist Promotion Board (☎ 322871; next door to Sekupang domestic terminal) It can help with local information and hotel bookings but keeps erratic hours.

Post office (Jl Imam Bonjol)

SLEEPING

The really cheap stuff isn't worth it in Nagoya, but the midrange numbers are luxury compared to mainland Sumatra. The majority of midrange hotels are in the small lanes behind Goodway Hotel.

There are a handful of top-end hotels where visiting corporates are housed. The top-end lobbies often suggest great expectations but don't deliver inside the rooms; we've listed here the ones that come close to international expectations. Rates include tax and service charge.

Hotel Bahari (☎ 421911; Komplek Nagoya Square, Block D; d 145,000-200,000Rp; ❄) Bahari I and II occupy the block, with comfy concrete boxes with hot and cold showers. Breakfast included.

SUMATRA

Goodway Hotel (☎ 42688; www.goodwayhotel.com; Jl Imam Bonjol; s/d from 480,000/540,000Rp;) Displaced gentleman are lucky to have this classic hotel in this far-flung corner of the world. The décor is subdued and the best rooms have balconies.

Planet Holiday (☎ 433555; www.planetholidayhotel.com; Jl Raja Ali Haji; d from 500,000Rp;) Service is crisp, the rooms are modern and as the tallest building in town there are views over squatty Batam.

EATING & DRINKING

Nagoya has a tasty mix of Indonesian and Chinese restaurants and warung.

Grill Bar (☎ 7013670; Goodway Hotel; Jl Imam Bonjol; mains from 50,000Rp; 10am-11pm) Chase away the rice blues with a manly meal of New Zealand Angus steaks at this cherished expat restaurant.

Kedai Kopi Indah (mains from 20,000Rp) A popular in-town stop for Chinese-style seafood dishes, such as pepper crab and fish claypot. Located behind Panorama Hotel.

Golden Prawn (Bengkong; mains from 50,000Rp) This famous *kelong* (open-air seafood restaurant) is considered one of the best on the island. Everything is charged by the kilo.

For local food, head to the **night market** (Jl Raja Ali Haji) or the big and raucous **Pujasera Nagoya** (food centre, opposite Hotel Sahid Rashinta).

Goodway Wine Bar (☎ 426888; Goodway Hotel, Jl Imam Bonjol) Through the wild-west saloon doors is a comfortable tap room for unwinding expats. Kenneth, the publican, once peddled his 'very British' demeanour in Hollywood, a role he plays today.

There are lots of other naughty nightlife options, but this information isn't a secret. Just drop into the Wine Bar and chat up the Benny Hill gang.

Waterfront City

Near the shipyards, Waterfront City's resorts are a strange occurrence: beachside resorts without beach activities. Instead they focus on resort diversions: swimming, spa-ing, golfing and organised activities. These resorts are heavily marketed to East Asians, mainly Koreans. Weekday discounts through travel agents might override the obvious drawbacks.

Harris Resort (☎ 381888; d S$115-135;) This fun-in-the-sun resort is targeted to families and folks of all ages.

Holiday Inn Resort (☎ 381333; d S$200;) Mainly a corporate hotel, Holiday Inn has classically decorated suites with balconies overlooking the pool. The internationally recognised spa is a fave for Singaporeans who don't want to spa-trek all the way to Bali.

Nongsa

Batam's prettiest, but still unswimmable, beach occupies the less-developed Nongsa peninsula. Casino resorts had provided the biggest draw for nearby Singaporeans, but the Indonesian government recently outlawed gambling, effectively drying up business.

Turi Beach Resort (☎ 310075; d from S$200;) Of the surviving resorts, Turi is the best and provides a close but delicious escape for Batam-bound visitors. The thatched-roof huts designed in the Balinese style have all the midlife comforts and a linen-suit ambience.

Golf courses in Nongsa offer attractive promotional packages (S$70-100) during the week; Singapore-based travel agents typically have the best rates. Nongsa's two courses are **Tering Bay** (☎ 778761; 818 Jl Hang Lekiu, Km 4), which was designed by Greg Norman, and **Palm Spring Golf Resort** (☎ 778761222; Jl Hang Leiku).

Nongsa's favourite *kelong* is the **Rezeki Kelong** (Batu Besar; mains from 50,000Rp).

Getting There & Away

AIR

Hang Nadim airport is on the eastern side of the island. Garuda, Merpati, Mandala, Bouraq and Air Asia operate to/from Jakarta. Merpati destinations also include Medan, Padang, Palembang, Jambi and Pekanbaru, as well as Pontianak in Kalimantan (650,000Rp). Jatayu also flies to Medan.

Most of the hotels in Nagoya have travel agencies.

BOAT

Batam has five ports and services between Singapore, the Sumatran mainland and other Riau Islands.

To Pulau Bintan

The ferry dock at Telaga Punggur, 30km southeast of Nagoya, is the main port for speedboats to Bintan. The departure tax is 3500Rp.

Boats to Bintan's Tanjung Pinang (one way/return 35,000/60,000Rp, every 30 minutes from 7.30am to 5.50pm) take 45 minutes. There are also boats to Bintan's Lagoi resort area (one way/return 100,000/170,000Rp, three times a day).

To Elsewhere in Indonesia

The main reason travellers come to Batam is its links to the Sumatran mainland. Dumai Express and Surya Gemilang Jaya are the best of the domestic carriers.

Boats leave from Batam's Sekupang terminal to Pekanbaru (210,000Rp, six hours, two morning departures). In order to make the connection without spending the night on Batam, you'll need to catch the first ferry from Singapore at 7.30am and assume that the Indonesian boats are running late as usual.

There are also two morning boats from Sekupang to Dumai (220,000Rp, six hours), one morning boat to Kuala Tungkal (231,000Rp) on the Jambi coast and three boats weekly to Palembang (305,000Rp, eight hours).

Other destinations from Sekupang port include Karimun (62,000Rp, one hour, every hour from 8am to 4pm) and Pulau Kundur (81,000Rp, two hours, every hour from 8am to 2.30pm).

Pelni ships pass through Batam to and from Belawan (the port for Medan) and Jakarta. The tickets can be bought at the domestic ferry terminal or at travel agencies in Nagoya.

Singapore

Frequent services shuttle between Singapore and Batam, taking between 25 minutes to 45 minutes depending on the pier. Tickets for all ferries to Singapore cost S$17/23 one way/return. There is a S$2 harbour departure tax leaving Batam and an hour time difference between Indonesia and Singapore. Penguin has the biggest and fastest ferries (25-minute crossing).

Sekupang is most widely used by tourists because the terminal that receives boats from Singapore's Harbourfront Centre is next door to the domestic terminal for transfer to the Sumatran mainland. The boats to Singapore run approximately every hour from 6am to 6.45pm, and to Batam from 7.30am to 8pm. Batam Centre and Waterfront City have services only to/from Singapore's Harbourfront Centre. The last boat to leave the island departs from Batam Centre at 9.30pm. Waterfront City's schedule is fairly limited, with only four departures per day. Ferries to Nongsa shuttle back and forth to Singapore's Tanah Merah, with eight departures per day between 8am and 8pm.

At Sekupang port don't buy a ticket from the many touts and refuse any offers of 'assistance' to see you through immigration.

Getting Around

Taxis are the primary way to get around. Sample fares are as follows: from Sekupang to Nagoya (50,000Rp, 45 minutes) and Batam Centre to Nagoya (30,000Rp, 30 minutes). From the airport, it will cost 90,000Rp to Sekupang, 70,000Rp to Nagoya and 60,000Rp to Batam Centre.

Blue-and-white bemo shuttle between Nongsa and Nagoya (13,000Rp). There's also a public bus from Telaga Punggur to Nagoya (10,000Rp).

PULAU BINTAN

☎ 0771 / pop 200,000

Just across the Selat Dampak from Batam, the island of Bintan is twice as large and a mirror opposite. Where Batam is a creation of imported workers, Bintan has a local community of ethnic Hakka and Indo-Malays.

On the west coast, Tanjung Pinang is a busy provincial city, while the high-end resorts in the north of the island around Lagoi do beach escapes right. For the working stiffs from Singapore, there are the more rustic beaches on the eastern end of the island around Pantai Trikora for affordable weekend escapes.

Although Bintan is under the influence of Singapore prices, it is a smidge cheaper, so the last bits in your wallet won't evaporate as quickly as in the metropolis.

Bintan is also the administrative centre of the Riau Islands, a title that has funnelled some much-needed development to the island.

Tanjung Pinang

The main port town on the island is a bustling mercantile centre with more ethnic diversity than most Sumatran towns. There is lots of provincial-style shopping and nibbling on Chinese and Indonesian specialities. Nearby are several traditional-style villages and temple attractions that tickle the culture-bone of weekending Singaporeans.

ORIENTATION & INFORMATION

The port, hotels, and other necessities are all within walking distance. There are plenty of ATMs around town and bank branches, mainly on Jl Teuku Umar.

Bank Mandiri (Jl Teuku Umar)
BCA bank (Bank Central Asia; Jl Ketapang)
BNI bank (Bank Negara Indonesia; Jl Teuku Umar)
Extreme Internet (Jl Mawar 9A; per hr 10,000Rp; 10am-10pm) On the 2nd floor of a wartel office.
Pinang Jaya Tour & Travel (☎ 21267; Jl Bintan 44) Air tickets.
Post office (Jl Merdeka) Near the harbour, on Tanjung Pinang's main street.
Tourist information centre (☎ 31822; Jl Merdeka 5; 8am-5pm) Behind the police station; the helpful English-speaking staff organise city tours
Wartel (Jl Bintan)
Wartel (Jl Merdeka)

SIGHTS & ACTIVITIES

You can stroll around Tanjung Pinang in a leisurely hour. The older part of town is found around the narrow piers near Jl Plantar II. The harbour hosts a constant stream of vessels, from tiny sampans to large freighters.

The following sites can be visited independently or through tour programs arranged through the tourist office.

Penyenget

A short hop across the harbour from Tanjung Pinang, tiny **Penyenget** was once the capital of the Riau rajahs. The island is believed to have been given to Rajah Riau-Lingga VI in 1805 by his brother-in-law, Sultan Mahmud, as a wedding present. Another historical footnote is that the Penyenget-based sultanate cooperated with Sir Stamford Raffles to hand over Singapore in exchange for British military protection in 1819.

The island is littered with interesting relics and can be walked in a couple of hours. The coastline is dotted with traditional Malay stilted houses, while the ruins of the **old palace** of Rajah Ali and the **tombs** and

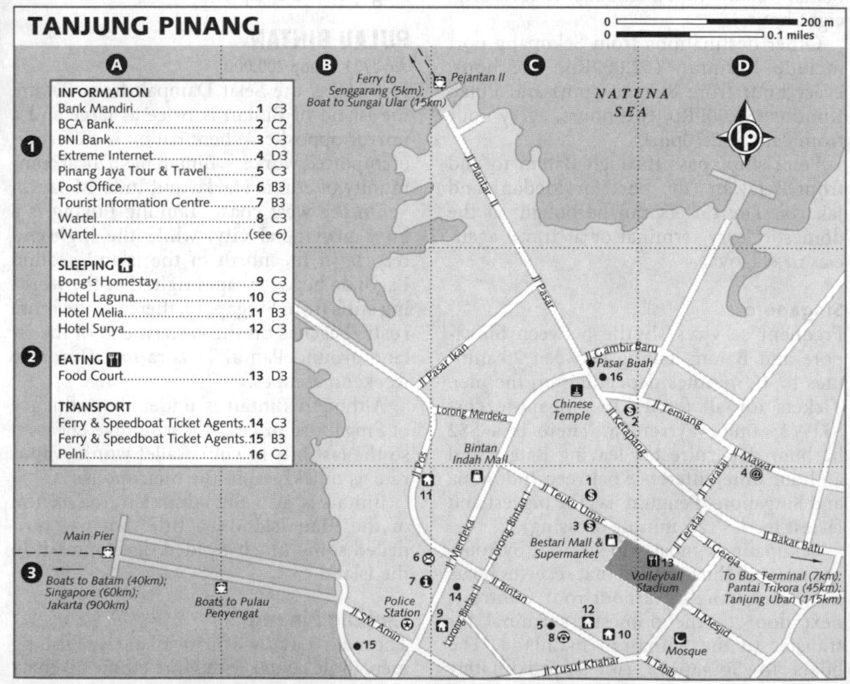

graveyards of Rajah Jaafar and Rajah Ali are clearly signposted inland. The most impressive site is the sulphur-coloured **mosque**, with its many domes and minarets. Dress appropriately or you won't be allowed in.

There are frequent boats to Pulau Penyenget from Bintan's main pier (4000Rp, from 7am to 5pm). There's a 2000Rp entry charge at weekends.

Senggarang

A fascinating village sits just across the harbour from Tanjung Pinang. The star attraction is an old **Chinese temple**, now suspended in the roots of a huge banyan that has grown up through it.

The temple is to the left of the pier, where boats from Tanjung Pinang dock. Half a kilometre along the waterfront, **Vihara Darma Sasana**, a complex of three temples, all said to be more than a century old, occupy a large courtyard facing the sea.

Boats to Senggarang (10,000Rp) leave from Pejantan II wharf.

Sungai Ular

Snake River swims through mangrove forests to **Jodoh temple**, the oldest Chinese temple in Riau Islands. The temple is decorated with gory murals depicting the trials and tortures of hell. You can charter a sampan (80,000Rp for five people) from Tanjung Pinang harbour.

SLEEPING & EATING

All of Tanjung Pinang's accommodation is within walking distance of the harbour.

Bong's Homestay (Lorong Bintan II 20; d 30,000Rp) A few basic rooms will make you feel like a stowaway. The family speaks English well and is good at US trivia.

Hotel Surya (☎ 318387; Jl Bintan 49; s/d 55,000/90,000Rp; ❄) Quality varies at this multistorey hotel. Fan rooms are basic concrete boxes, while some rooms have sunny windows and new paint.

Hotel Laguna (☎ 311555; Jl Bintan 51; d from 250,000Rp; ❄) Tanjung Pinang's corporate stay, with big beds and walk-in shower.

Hotel Melia (☎ 21898; Jl Pos 25; d from 350,000Rp) Bright and airy rooms and enormous suites with views over the harbour.

In front of the volleyball stadium on Jl Teuku Umar, an open-air **food court** (mains 8000Rp) whips up tasty snacks.

If you're looking for Padang food, there are several places on Jl Plantar II serving good fish or jackfruit curries.

The colourful *pasar buah* (fruit market) is at the northern end of Jl Merdeka. In the evening there are several food stalls scattered around town serving *mie bangka*, a Hakka-style dumpling soup.

GETTING THERE & AWAY

See p466 for details about how to get there and away.

GETTING AROUND

It is fairly easy to get around central Tangjung Pinang by catching one of the many *opelet* (2000Rp). The *opelet* don't have fixed routes, so tell the driver your destination and see if he agrees.

The bus terminal is inconveniently located 7km out of Tanjung Pinang, along the road to Pantai Trikora. But there aren't many services that leave from here.

To get to the outlying beaches is expensive. A taxi from Tanjung Pinang to Pantai Trikora is a long ride and will cost 100,000Rp. You can also fish around for share taxis, but most drivers won't want to cut a deal with a 'rich' foreigner. If you head out to the main highway, you can catch Barakit-bound public buses that pass through Trikora (20,000Rp).

Another not-so-affordable option is to rent a car, which gives you flexibility in exploring the beaches around the island. **Rico Rental** (☎ 315931; Jl Yos Sudarso 1) rents Kijang for 250,000Rp per day (not including petrol). Renting a car in Tanjung Pinang is cheaper than relying on the resorts in Lagoi.

Pantai Trikora & Around

Bintan's east coast is lined with rustic beaches and simple wooden bungalows. The main beach is **Pantai Trikora**, which is pretty enough at high tide but turns into miles of mud flats at low tide. The beaches to the north around Malangrupai have more consistent surf and turf. Regardless though, the area is relatively deserted: just you, the ocean and a few napping dogs. A group of small islands off Pantai Trikora are well worth visiting and there is good **snorkelling** outside the monsoon season (November to March).

SLEEPING & EATING

Accommodation at Trikora is outside the village of Teluk Bakau. The following can organise snorkelling trips to offshore islands (150,000Rp):

Shady Shack (☎ 081 364515223; www.lobo.kinemotion.de; d with breakfast 150,000Rp) A handful of weather-beaten shacks face directly to the sea. This is just a step above camping and is a good excuse not to shower or brush your teeth.

Gurindam Resort (☎ 26234; Telok Bakau, Km 35; weekday/weekend d with breakfast 150,000/210,000Rp) Designed like a Muslim fishing village with stilt-frame bungalows built over the water, this is a dream come true for down-to-earth family getaways. There's fishing in the attached fish ponds, a thatched-roof restaurant big enough for energetic tots, and a small swimming beach.

Lagoi

Bintan's resort area stretches along the northern coastline of the island along Pasir Lagoi, with acres of wilderness buffering the hotels from commoners to the south. Security is in full effect, with checkpoints at access roads and at hotel entrances. The beaches are sandy and swimmable, the resorts have polished four- and five-star service and there are water-sports activities and entertainment for all ages.

There are three golf courses in Lagoi designed by champion golfers: **Bintan Lagoon Resort Golf Club** (☎ 0770-691399), **Laguna Bintan Golf Club** (☎ 0770-693188) and top-rated **Ria Bintan Golf Club** (☎ 0770-692839; www.riabintan.com). Weekday promotional rates and packages range from S$55 to S$150.

SLEEPING

There are three resort compounds comprising several hotel clusters, private beaches and golf courses. Check with travel agents about weekday discounts, which can be as generous as 50%.

Of the three, we found the hotels within Laguna Bintan (Angsana Resort and Banyan Tree) and Nirwana Gardens (Nirwana Resort) compounds to be accommodating and well maintained.

Angsana Resort & Spa Bintan (☎ 0770-693111; www.angsana.com; packages S$320-480;) The more dressed-down companion to sophisticated Banyan Tree, Angsana is best suited to young professionals. The breezy common spaces are decorated in zesty citrus colours, with private rooms sporting a contemporary colonial style. The superior rooms are nice but the suites are super.

Banyan Tree Bintan (☎ 0770-693100; www.banyantree.com; packages S$480-650;) More private and privileged than Angsana, Banyan Tree has the famed spa facilities and a high-powered retreat deep in the jungle. The hotel shares the 900m-long beach with Angsana.

Nirwana Resort Hotel (☎ 0770-692505; www.nirwanagardens.com; d from S$320;) More targeted to local families, Nirwana is comfortable and unfussy, with sweet staff but not the best beach. The lagoon-style pool has a large baby pool area, but the grounds are little thirsty. The suites have sea views and huge bathrooms.

Getting There & Away

AIR

Kijang airport is currently used for cargo, not passenger, flights.

BOAT

Bintan has three ports and services to Batam, Singapore and other islands in the Riau archipelago.

Tanjung Pinang is the busiest harbour and the best option for folks planning to stay in Tanjung Pinang or Pantai Trikora. If you're bound for the resort area of Lagoi, the port at Kota Sebung is more convenient. Tanjung Uban is the third option.

To Batam

Regular speedboats depart from the main pier in Tanjung Pinang for Telaga Punggur on Batam (35,000Rp, 45 minutes) from 7.45am to 4.45pm daily. There are also boats that go from Lagoi to Batam's Telaga Punggur (one way/return 100,000/170,000Rp).

To Elsewhere in Sumatra

There are boats to Pekanbaru (300,000Rp, daily) and Dumai (275,000Rp, daily). Tickets for all of these destinations can be bought from agents on Jl Merdeka, just outside of the harbour entrance.

Daily ferries travel to other islands in the Riau chain, such as Pulau Karimum's Tanjung Balai (80,000Rp, 2½ hours), Pulau Lingga's Daik (57,000Rp, three hours), Sungai

Buluh on Singkep (60,000Rp, three hours) and Penuba (80,000Rp, three hours). The Anugra Makmur company runs boats every 10 days to the remote Natuna Islands.

Pelni sails to Jakarta weekly from the southern port of Kijang. Travel agencies in Tanjung Pinang can supply tickets and schedules.

To Malaysia

There are boats to Johor Bahru in Malaysia (140,000Rp, five departures) from Tanjung Pinanag. Tickets can be bought from agents on Jl Merdeka, just outside of the harbour entrance.

To Singapore

Boats from Tanjung Pinang go to Singapore's Tanah Merah (one way S$25) between 7am and 6.30pm. There are more frequent services on the weekend.

Bintan Resort Ferries (www.brf.com.sg) is the only company that handles transport between Lagoi and Singapore; ticket prices vary based on day of week but start at S$26.

Getting Around

For Lagoi-bound visitors, most resorts organise shuttle service between the harbour at Kota Sebong and the hotels as part of the package price or for an additional S$6.

OTHER RIAU ISLANDS

Few travellers reach the remote outer islands of Riau. Getting there is half the problem. Head to the better-serviced islands first, and you can usually organise to island-hop from there.

Pulau Singkep

Singkep is the third-largest island in the archipelago. Huge tin mines once provided most of the island's jobs, but since their closure much of the population has moved elsewhere and the island has reverted to being a sleepy backwater.

The main town, **Dabo**, is shaded by lush trees and gardens and clustered around a central park. A large **mosque** dominates the skyline. The fish and vegetable **markets** near the harbour are interesting, and Jl Pasar Lamar is a good browsing and shopping area. **Batu Bedua**, 4km from town, is a lovely white-sand beach fringed with palms.

There is accommodation available at the simple **Wisma Gapura Singkep** (☎ 077621136; Jl Perusalaan 41; d from 80,000Rp).

You can eat at the **markets** behind Wisma Sri Indah or try any of the warung on Jl Pasar Lama and Jl Merdeka. Food stalls and warung pop up all over the place at night.

There's one boat a day to Tanjung Pinang on Bintan (57,000Rp, three hours) and daily ferries to Daik on Pulau Lingga. Boats dock at Singkep's northern port of Sungai Buluh, from where there are buses to Dabo. Several shops in Dabo act as ticket agencies.

Pulau Penuba

Penuba is a small island wedged between Singkep and Lingga. It's an idyllic place to do little but swim, walk and read. There are some great beaches near the north coast village of **Tanjung Dua** and others near the main settlement, **Penuba**, on the southeastern coast.

Penuba is a sleepy village centred around the **Attaqwa Mosque**. Accommodation is available at the house next door – ask around for the caretaker – and you can eat at several warung along Jl Merdeka, the main street.

A daily boat travels to Penuba from Tanjung Pinang (80,000Rp, three hours) on Bintan, or you can charter a boat from Singkep for the half hour trip.

Pulau Lingga

Not much remains of the glory that was once the royal island of Lingga except a few neglected ruins. Today there are few creature comforts and little in the way of modern development. The island resembles a crown and rises sharply from the shore to form the three jungle-clad peaks of **Gunung Daik**. The central peak reaches 1163m and is the highest point in the archipelago. Locals maintain that it has never been climbed.

Daik, the main village and arrival point, is hidden 1km up a muddy river. The town itself is pretty much a single street, with some cargo wharves and about a dozen Chinese shops. It has a certain tropical, seedy charm and a very laid-back atmosphere.

The main site of historical interest is the modest ruin of the **palace** of Rajah Suleiman, the last rajah of Lingga-Riau. Next to the palace are the foundation stones of a building said to have housed the rajah's extensive harem. The palace was made of wood and little survives today, though the surrounding jungle hides overgrown bathing pools and squat toilets. The ruins are a two-hour walk from Daik and you'll need very clear directions or a guide to get you through the maze of overgrown forest paths.

On the outskirts of Daik the **Mesjid Sultan Lingga** houses the tomb of Rajah Mahmud I, who ruled in the early 19th century. A half-hour walk from town is the **Makam Bukit Cenckeh** (Cenckeh Hill Cemetery) on a hill overlooking the river. The crumbling graves of Rajah Abdul Rakhman (r 1812–31) and Rajah Muhammed (r 1832–41) are here. The remains of an old fort are nearby.

There is one basic **hotel** (d around 60,000Rp) in Daik, near the ferry dock on the main street. There are a few small **warung** on the main street.

There are daily boats for the two-hour trip from Daik to Dabo on Singkep (40,000Rp), and a daily service to Tanjung Pinang (50,000Rp, three hours) on Bintan.

Natuna Islands

These islands are right off the beaten track and difficult to reach.

The population of **Pulau Natuna Besar** is fairly small, although there's an extensive *transmigrasi* programme along Sungai Ulu, with settlers from Java growing cash crops such as peanuts and green peas.

The islands are noted for fine basket-weave **cloth** and various kinds of **traditional dance**. One particularly idiosyncratic local dance is a kind of *Thousand & One Arabian Nights* saga, incorporating episodes from Riau-Lingga history.

Ask in Tanjung Pinang on Pulau Bintan about infrequent boat services to Natuna.

JAMBI

For such a centrally located province, Jambi is not easy to reach and sees few foreign visitors. The province occupies a 53,435-sq-km slice of central Sumatra, stretching from the highest peaks of the Bukit Barisan range in the west, to the coastal swamps facing the Strait of Melaka in the east.

The eastern lowlands are mainly rubber and palm oil plantations. Timber is also big business, as is oil; Jambi's main field is southeast of the capital on the South Sumatran border.

In the western portion of the province is the Kerinci Seblat National Park, home to Sumatra's highest peak, Gunung Kerinci (3805m), Sumatran tigers (Jambi's faunal mascot) and rhinos. The park is covered in the West Sumatra section (see p451) because Padang has more convenient transit links than Jambi.

Most of the province is sparsely populated; many are migrants from Java and Bali. In the province's fast disappearing forests, the Orang Rimba are an endangered hunter-gatherer tribe.

History

The province of Jambi was the heartland of the ancient kingdom of Malayu, which first rose to prominence in the 7th century. Much of Malayu's history is closely and confusingly entwined with that of its main regional rival, the Palembang-based kingdom of Sriwijaya. The little that is known about Malayu has mostly been gleaned from the precise records maintained by the Chinese court of the time.

It is assumed that the temple ruins at Muara Jambi mark the site of Malayu's former capital, the ancient city of Jambi – known to the Chinese as Chan Pi. The Malayu sent their first delegation to China in 644 and the Chinese scholar I Tsing spent a month in Malayu in 672. When he returned 20 years later he found that Malayu had been conquered by Sriwijaya. The Sriwijayans appear to have remained in control until the sudden collapse of their empire at the beginning of the 11th century.

Following Sriwijaya's demise, Malayu re-emerged as an independent kingdom and stayed that way until it became a dependency of Java's Majapahit empire, which ruled from 1278 until 1520. It then came under the sway of the Minangkabau people of West Sumatra.

In 1616 the Dutch East India Company opened an office in Jambi and quickly formed a successful alliance with Sultan Muhammed Nakhruddin to protect its ships and cargoes from pirates. It also negotiated a trade monopoly with Nakhruddin and his successors. The major export was pepper, which was grown in great abundance. In

ORANG RIMBA

Jambi's nomadic hunter-gatherers are known by many names: outsiders refer to the diverse tribes collectively as Kubu, an unflattering term, while they refer to themselves as Orang Rimba (People of the Forest) or Anak Dalam (Children of the Forest). Descended from the first wave of Malays to migrate to Sumatra, they once lived in highly mobile groups throughout Jambi's lowland forests.

As sedentary communities began to dominate the province, the Orang Rimba retained their nomadic lifestyle and animistic beliefs, regarding their neighbours' adoption of Islam and agriculture as disrespectful towards the forest. Traditionally the Orang Rimba avoided contact with the outsiders, preferring to barter and trade by leaving goods on the fringes of the forest or relying on trusted intermediaries.

In the 1960s, the Indonesian government's social affairs and religion departments campaigned to assimilate the Orang Rimba into permanent camps and convert them to a monotheistic religion. Meanwhile the jungles were being transformed into oil palm and rubber plantations during large-scale transmigration from Java and Bali.

Some Orang Rimba assimilated and are now economically marginalised within the plantations, while others take the government hand-outs and then return to the forests. About 2500 Orang Rimba retain their traditional lifestyles within the shrinking forest. The groups were given special settlement rights within Bukit Duabelas and Bukit Tigapuluh National Parks, but the protected forests are as vulnerable to illegal logging and poaching as other Sumatran parks. In addition, areas once classified as restricted are frequently converted into production.

In the opinions of the NGO groups that work with the Orang Rimba, it isn't a question of *if* the tribes will lose their jungle traditions but *when*. In the spirit of practical idealism, the organisation WARSI (www.warsi.or.id) established its alternative educational outreach. Rather than forcing educational institutions on the Orang Rimba, teachers join the nomads that will accept an outsider and teach the children how to read, write and count – the equivalent of knowing how to hunt and forage in the settled communities.

1901 the Dutch East India Company moved its headquarters to Palembang and effectively gave up its grip on Jambi.

JAMBI

☎ 0741 / pop 490,000

The capital of Jambi is the city of the same name, a busy river port about 155km from the mouth of Sungai Batang Hari. Jambi is not known as a tourist destination, but those who have wandered the markets and watched the city in action have found that nowhere can be more fun than somewhere.

Orientation

Jambi sprawls over a wide area, a combination of the old Pasar Jambi district spreading south from the port, and the new suburbs of Kota Baru and Telanaipura to the west. Most of the banks, hotels and restaurants are in Pasar Jambi near the junction of Jl Gatot Subroto and Jl Raden Mattaher, while government buildings are out at Kota Baru.

Information

There are plenty of ATMs around town. Jl Dr Sutomo is the primary bank street.

Culture & Tourism Office (☎ 445056; Jl H Agus Salim, Kota Baru) The English-speaking staff are keen to promote the province and can organise city tours.

Main Telkom wartel (Jl Dr Sumantri) In Telanaipura.

Post office (Jl Sultan Thaha 9) Near the port.

Thamrin Internet (Jl Gatot Subroto 6; per hr 6000Rp; 🕑 11am-9pm) Internet access near Gloria Bookshop.

Wartel (Jl Raden Mattaher; 🕑 8am-9pm) More convenient than the main Telekom wartel; you can make international phone calls here.

Sights & Activities

Jambi is the starting point for excursions to the archaeological site of Muara Jambi (see p470).

Museum Negeri Propinsi Jambi (cnr Jl Urip Sumoharjo & Prof Dr Sri Sudewi, Telanaipura; admission 2000Rp; 🕑 8.30am-3pm Mon-Fri), one of the city's few attractions, is out in Telanaipura. It has a selection of costumes and handicrafts, as well as a small historical display. Take an *ojek* (2000Rp).

Nearby the museum is a **batik centre** that produces and sells traditional Jambi textiles featuring striking floral motifs. The centre also has a range of handicrafts from all over the province, including *songket* weaving and finely woven split-rattan baskets. The centre provides employment for local women.

Sleeping

Accommodation in Jambi isn't much of a bargain, so you should opt for convenience instead. The most social spot to base yourself is near the market, behind the Novotel, where you'll find a cluster of midrange and top-end hotels.

Lukman Language Exchange (l_tanjung@yahoo.com) Delightful Jambi resident Lukman can provide lodging in his home in exchange for a few appearances by an English native speaker at his weekly tutoring sessions.

Hotel Da'lia (☎ 50863; Jl Camar 100; d 70,000-90,000Rp; ❄) Basic and clean, this is the best you'll get in the budget range.

Hotel Jambi Raya (☎ 34971; Jl Camar 45; s/d 160,000/250,000Rp; ❄) Deluxe rooms are decorated in glam honeymoon style.

Hotel Abadi (☎ 25600; Jl Gatot Subroto 92; d 390,000-500,000Rp; ❄ 🏊) Otherwise average top-end rooms are decorated with Jambi batik bedspreads for a local flair. Junior suites have a tranquil balcony.

Novotel (☎ 27208; novotel@e-jambi.net; Jl Gatot Subroto 44; d from 500,000Rp) Currently the most expensive hotel in town but far from being worth it.

Eating

Saimen Perancis (Jl Raden Mattaher; pastries 2000Rp) An excellent bakery that also serves meals.

Simpang Raya (Jl Raden Mattaher 22; dishes 7000Rp) An old friend in the *nasi Padang* game.

Munri Food Centre (Jl Sultan Agung; mains 10,000Rp) More night-time eats set the night ablaze at this alfresco dining area.

Ancol (near Sungai Batang Hari) Just down from the Trade Centre, this is an evening destination for promenading and river breezes. Stalls sell local favourites, such as *nanas goreng* (fried pineapples) and *jagung bakar* (roasted corn slathered with coconut milk and chillis).

Pasar Makanan (Jl Sultan Iskandar Muda) Lots of regional Palembang specialities, which Jambi also claims as its own, get top billing at this busy market.

Getting There & Away

AIR

The Sultan Thaka Airport is 4km east of the centre. Adam Air, Batavia Air and Mandala fly to Jakarta daily. Merpati flies to Batam. Most tickets are available through travel agents, but **Mandala** (☎ 24341; Jl Gatot Subroto 42) also has an office.

BOAT

Ratu Intan Permata (☎ 60234; Simpang Kawat, Jl M Yamin) operates connecting services from Jambi to the coastal town of Kuala Tungkal (35,000Rp, two hours), from where there are speedboats to Batam (200,000Rp, five hours).

BUS

The highways to the south and north are in poor condition, making bus travel an arduous task. Bus ticketing offices occupy two areas of town: **Simpang Rimbo**, 8km west of town, and **Simpang Kawat**, 3.5km southwest of town on Jl M Yamin.

There are frequent economy buses to Palembang (40,000Rp, seven hours).

Ratu Intan Permata (☎ 60234; Simpang Kawat, Jl M Yamin) has comfortable door-to-door minibus services to Pekanbaru (150,000Rp, eight hours), Bengkulu (175,000Rp, 10 hours), Palembang (120,000Rp, six hours) and Padang (200,000Rp, 13 hours).

Safa Marwa (☎ 65756; Jl Pattimura 77) runs a similar service to Kerinci-Sungaipenuh (90,000Rp, 10 hours).

Buses from Jambi depart from the companies' offices.

Getting Around

Airport taxis charge a standard 60,000Rp for the 8km run into town. Local transport comprises the usual assortment of *ojek* and *opelet*. Rawasari *opelet* terminal, off Jl Raden Mattaher in the centre of town, is where all *opelet* start and finish their journeys. The standard fare is 2000Rp.

MUARA JAMBI

The large temple complex at Muara Jambi, 26km downstream from Jambi, is the most important Hindu-Buddhist site in Sumatra. It is assumed that the temples mark the location of the ancient city of Jambi, capital of the kingdom of Malayu 1000 years ago. Most of the temples, known as *candi*, date from the 9th to the 13th centuries, when Jambi's power was at its peak. However, the best of the artefacts have been taken to Jakarta.

For centuries the site lay abandoned and overgrown in the jungle on the banks of the Batang Hari. It was 'rediscovered' in 1920 by a British army expedition sent to explore the region.

Sights

It's easy to spend all day at **Muara Jambi** (admission by donation; 8am-4pm). The forested site covers 12 sq km along the north bank of the Batang Hari. The entrance is through an ornate archway in the village of Muara Jambi and most places of interest are within a few minutes' walk of here.

Eight temples have been identified so far, each at the centre of its own low-walled compound. Some are accompanied by *perwara candi* (smaller side temples) and three have been restored to something close to their original form. The site is dotted with numerous *menapo* (smaller brick mounds), thought to be the ruins of other buildings – possibly dwellings for priests and other high officials.

The restored temple **Candi Gumpung**, straight ahead of the donation office, has a fiendish *makara* (demon head) guarding its steps. Excavation work here yielded some important finds, including a *peripih* (stone box) containing sheets of gold inscribed with old Javanese characters dating the temple back to the 9th century. A statue of Prajnyaparamita found here is now the star attraction at the small **site museum** nearby.

Candi Tinggi, 200m southeast of Candi Gumpung, is the finest of the temples uncovered so far. It dates from the 9th century but is built around another, older temple. A path leads east from Candi Tinggi to **Candi Astano**, 1.5km away, passing **Candi Kembar Batu** and lots of *menapo* along the way.

The temples on the western side of the site are yet to be restored. They remain pretty much as they were found – minus the jungle, which was cleared in the 1980s. The western sites are signposted from Candi Gumpung. First stop, after 900m, is **Candi Gedong Satu**, followed 150m further on by **Candi Gedong Dua**. They are independent temples despite what their names may suggest. The path continues west for another 1.5km to **Candi Kedaton**, the largest of the temples, then a further 900m northwest to **Candi Koto Mahligai**.

The dwellings of the ordinary Malayu people have long since disappeared. According to Chinese records, they lived along the river in stilted houses or in raft huts moored to the bank.

Getting There & Away

There is no public transport to the park. You can charter a speedboat (300,000Rp) from Jambi's river pier to the site. You can also hire an *ojek* (35,000Rp).

SOUTH SUMATRA

Like Riau and Jambi provinces, the eastern portion of South Sumatra shares a common Malay ancestry and influence from its proximity to the shipping lane of the Strait of Melaka. Rivers define the character of the eastern lowlands, while the western high peaks of the Bukit Barisan form the province's rugged underbelly. The provincial capital of Palembang was once the central seat of the Buddhist Sriwijaya empire, whose control once reached all the way up the Malay Peninsula.

Despite the province's illustrious past, there aren't very many surviving attractions except for the hospitality that occurs in places where bilingual Indonesians don't get a lot of opportunity to practise their English.

PALEMBANG

☎ 0711 / pop 1.67 million

Sumatra's second-largest city, Palembang is reminiscent of Bangkok 30 years ago. This is a riverine culture that crawled to land to establish an equally free-flowing metropolis. It is chaotic and sprawling but still reverential of the central Sungai Musi.

The core industries of oil refining, fertiliser production and cement manufacturing scent the air with a distinctive odour you might first mistake as your own funk.

The town is also a major port, being only 80km from the mouth of Sungai Musi. When Sumatra's oil fields were discovered and opened in the early 1900s, Palembang quickly became South Sumatra's main export hub. As well as oil, the port handles exports from the province's seemingly endless rubber, coffee, pepper and pineapple plantations.

History

A thousand years ago Palembang was the centre of the highly developed Sriwijaya civilisation. The Chinese scholar I Tsing spent six months in Palembang in 672 and reported that 1000 monks, scholars and pilgrims were studying and translating Sanskrit there. At its peak in the 11th century, Sriwijaya ruled a huge slab of Southeast Asia, covering most of Sumatra, the Malay Peninsula, southern Thailand and Cambodia. Sriwijayan influence col-

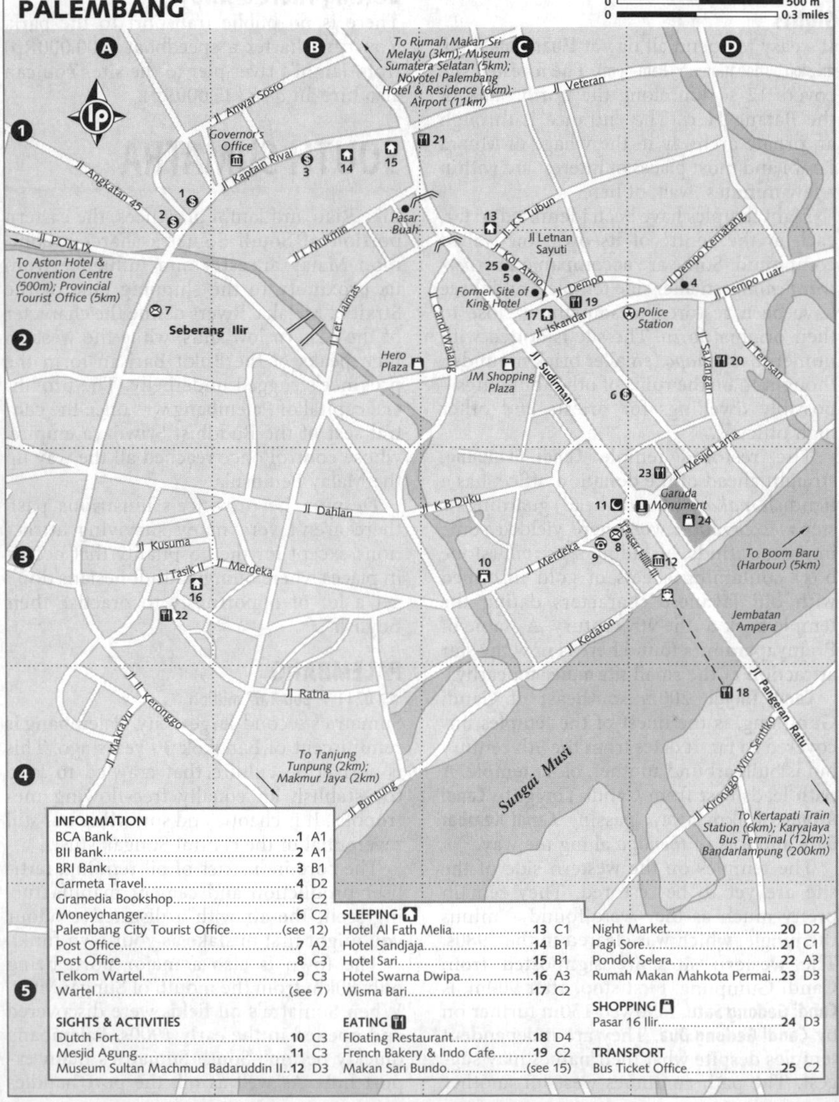

lapsed after the kingdom was conquered by the south Indian king Ravendra Choladewa in 1025. For the next 200 years, the void was partly filled by Sriwijaya's main regional rival, the Jambi-based kingdom of Malayu.

Few relics from this period remain – no sculpture, monuments or architecture of note – nor is there much of interest from the early 18th century, when Palembang was an Islamic kingdom. Most of the buildings of the latter era were destroyed in battles with the Dutch.

The city's name comes from two words: *pa* (place) and *limbang* (to pan for gold). The prosperity of the Sriwijayan city is said to have been based on gold found in local rivers.

Orientation

Palembang sits astride Sungai Musi, the two halves of the city linked by the giant Jembatan Ampera (Ampera Bridge). The river is flanked by a hodgepodge of wooden houses on stilts. The southern side, Seberang Ulu, is where the majority of people live. Seberang Ilir, on the north bank, is the city's better half, where you'll find most of the government offices, shops, hotels and the wealthy residential districts. The main street, Jl Sudirman, runs north–south to the bridge. The bus terminal and train station are both on the southern side.

Information

Palembang has branches of all the major banks and there are ATMs all over the city. Outside banking hours, the bigger hotels are a better bet than moneychangers.

BCA bank (Bank Central Asia; Jl Kapitan Rivai)

BII bank (Bank Internasional Indonesia; Jl Kapitan Rivai)

BRI bank (Bank Rakyat Indonesia; Jl Kapitan Rivai)

Moneychanger (Jl Kol Atmo)

Palembang city tourist office (☎ 358450; Museum Sultan Machmud Badaruddin II, Jl Pasar Hilir 3) A useful office at the Museum Sultan Machmud Badaruddin II, off Jl Sudirman; the staff can arrange trips down the Sungai Musi and handicraft tours.

Post office (Jl Merdeka) Close to the river, next to the Garuda monument. Internet facilities available.

Provincial tourist office (☎ 357348; Jl Demang Lebar Daun) Outside of the centre of town; a useful office.

Telkom wartel (Jl Merdeka; 🕑 8am-9pm) Next to the post office; international phone calls can be made here.

Wartel (Jl Kapitan Rivai)

Sights

Museum Sumatera Selatan (☎ 422382; Jl Sriwijaya 1, Km 5.5; admission 1000Rp; 🕑 8am-4pm Sun-Thu, 8-11am Fri) is well worth a visit. It houses finds from Sriwijayan times, as well as megalithic carvings from the Pasemah Highlands, including the famous *batu gajah* (elephant stone). There is a magnificent *rumah limas* (traditional house) behind the museum. The museum is about 5km from the town centre off the road to the airport.

Museum Sultan Machmud Badaruddin II (Jl Pasar Hilir 3; admission 1000Rp; 🕑 8am-4pm Mon-Thu & Sat, 8-11am & 1.30-4pm Fri) has a few dust-covered exhibits.

Other Palembang attractions include the imposing **Mesjid Agung** (Jl Sudirman), built by Sultan Machmud Badaruddin at the beginning of the 19th century.

The remains of a late-18th-century **Dutch fort**, occupied today by the Indonesian army, can be seen to the north of Jl Merdeka. Only sections of the fort's outside walls still stand.

Tours

Carmeta Travel (☎ 356653; Jl Dempo Luar 29/30) Agents can book city and river tours and trips to Bangka and Danau Ranau.

Festivals & Events

Palembang's annual tourist event is the **bidar race** held on Sungai Musi in the middle of town every 17 August (Independence Day) and on 16 June (the city's birthday). A *bidar* (canoe) is about 25m long, 1m wide and is powered by up to 60 rowers.

Sleeping

The midrange hotels in Palembang are typical Indonesian breeds: personality-less multistorey boxes with prices that make a backpacker wince. The upmarket business options are slowly but surely maturing to match international standards.

Hotel Al Fath Melia (☎ 370488; Jl KS Tuban 19; d from 100,000Rp; ❄) Set on a quiet street, this is a decent choice with fairly basic rooms.

Hotel Sari (☎ 313320; Jl Sudirman 1301; d 120,000-140,000Rp; ❄) On a noisy junction, this hotel has the best 'deluxe' you'll find for the money.

Wisma Bari (☎ 315666; Jl Letnan Sayuti 55; d from 150,000Rp; ❄) Well positioned in a quiet lane, the postmodern rooms are modest but tolerable.

Hotel Swarna Dwipa (☎ 313322; Jl Tasik II; s/d from 270,000/300,000Rp;) In a leafy area, this mini resort is filled with Indonesian bigwigs, but the rooms don't quite deliver.

Aston Hotel & Convention Centre (☎ 383838; Jl POM IX; d with breakfast from 400,000Rp;) The very modern Aston is decorated in the reigning trend of global minimalist. The business travellers stay self-contained here for conferences.

Hotel Sandjaja (☎ 362222; Jl Kaptain Rivai 6193; d from 450,000Rp;) This smart, upmarket hotel has rooms that match what you would get back home for the same price, plus a few more fingerprints. But when measured on the Sumatran scale, this is top-grade.

Novotel Palembang Hotel & Residence (☎ 369777; Jl R Sukamto 8A; d with breakfast from 800,000Rp;) Outside of the town centre, the Novotel is a stone fortress resort with chic rooms oriented around a central pool.

Eating

Palembang lends its name to the distinctive cuisine of southern Sumatra (including Lampung and Bengkulu) in the same way Padang lends its name to West Sumatran fare.

The best-known dishes are *ikan brengkes* (fish served with a spicy durian-based sauce) and *pindang*, a spicy, clear fish soup. Another Palembang speciality is *pempek*, also known as *empek-empek*, a mixture of sago, fish and seasonings that is formed into balls and deep fried or grilled. Served with a spicy sauce, *pempek* is widely available from street stalls and warung; you typically pay for what you eat.

Palembang food is normally served with a range of accompaniments. The main one is *tempoyak*, a combination of fermented durian, *terasi* (shrimp paste), lime juice and chilli that is mixed up with the fingers and added to the rice. *Sambal buah* (fruit sambals), made with pineapple or sliced green mangoes, are also popular.

Rumah Makan Mahkota Permai (Jl Mesjid Lama 33; dishes from 6000Rp) Near the junction with Jl Sudirman, this is a good place to try Palembang food.

Rumah Makan Sri Melayu (☎ 420468; Jl Demang Lebar Daun; mains 25,000-35,000Rp) For the full immersion of Palembang food and culture, visit this showpiece restaurant with polished wooden seating around a stylish coy pond.

Floating Restaurant (Seberang Ulu; mains 5000-20,000Rp; noon-10pm) Directly across the Sungai Musi from the museum are Palembang's favourite date restaurants, serving local specialities.

Pondok Selera (Jl Rambutan; mains from 5000Rp) Near the Songket Village, this open-air lunch spot pulls in the government workers for Palembang style *ayam baker* served with fresh vegetables and sambal.

French Bakery and Indo Cafe (Jl Kol Atmo; dishes 8000Rp) Near the bus ticket agents, this bakery and café offers all sorts of carb-loaded dishes and fancy coffee drinks.

The main **night market** (Jl Sayangan), to the east of Jl Sudirman, has dozens of noodle and sate stalls. Missing Padang food already? Load up at our old pals **Pagi Sore** (Jl Sudirman) and **Makan Sari Bundo** (Jl Kaptain Rivai).

Shopping

Tanjung Tunpung, 2km from the town centre, is the handicraft village where Palembang's local *songket* industry is based. Ground-floor showrooms display sarongs used in marriage ceremonies and traditional costumes, as well as more functional scarves and textiles. Above the storefront are the workshops where it takes the young weavers a month to weave one sarong and chest wrap as well as keep up with the daily soap operas.

Makmur Jaya (☎ 3553720; Jl Ki Gede Ing Suro 12) Beyond tourist-market selections of fine silk and batiks.

Pasar 16 Ilir (Jl Mesjid Lama; 6am-6pm) Near the river, just off Jl Pangeran Ratu, this market sells batik and other textiles from Sumatra and Java, as well as house wares.

Getting There & Away

AIR

Sultan Badaruddin II airport is 12km north of town. There are flights by Silk Air to Singapore three times a week (US$90-110). Garuda flies daily from Palembang to Yogyakarta (800,000Rp) and Surabaya (655,000Rp).

Garuda, Adam Air, Wings Air, Lion Air, Batavia Air and Sriwijaya all fly to Jakarta.

Merpati flies to Batam daily and Medan four times a week. Garuda, Wings, Lion, Merpati, Jatayu and Batavia also have flights to Medan. Batavia Air serves Jambi daily.

Carmeta Travel (☎ 356653; Jl Dempo Luar 29/30) can handle all of these ticketing arrangements.

BOAT

There are several services each day from Palembang's Boom Baru harbour to Mentok on Bangka (100,000Rp to 200,000Rp depending on class, four hours).

There are direct ferry services to Batam (VIP/business 305,000/255,000Rp, 10 hours). Boats depart from Boom Baru on Tuesday, Thursday and Saturday at 7.30am.

BUS

The **Karyajaya Bus Terminal** (cnr Jl Sriwijaya Raya) is 12km from the town centre.

Most of the bigger companies have ticket offices on Jl Kol Atmo, just near the former Hotel King. These agents are convenient for buying advance tickets and checking departure times, but it is recommended to catch the bus at the terminal instead of dealing with the extra transfer fee and extra wait time from the agents' offices.

Sample destinations and fares include Bukittinggi (air-con 165,000Rp, 18 hours), Medan (220,000Rp, 36 hours) and Jakarta (air-con 150,000Rp, 20 hours).

There are several companies on Jl Veteran offering door-to-door minibus services to Jambi (120,000Rp, six hours) and Bengkulu (150,000Rp, 15 hours).

TRAIN

On the south side of the river, Kertapati train station is 8km from the city centre. There are two daily train departures to Bandarlampung. The morning train has economy class only (28,000Rp); the evening train has executive (85,000Rp) and business (50,000Rp) class. The trip takes nine to 10 hours.

There are also two trains that go northwest to Lubuklinggau (economy/business 28,000/60,000Rp) with a stop at Lahat (for the Pasemah Highlands). It's four hours to Lahat and seven to Lubuklinggau, but the fares are the same.

Getting Around

Opelet around town cost a standard 2000Rp. They leave from around the huge roundabout at the junction of Jl Sudirman and Jl Merdeka.

Any *opelet* marked 'Karyajaya' (4000Rp) will get you to the bus terminal. Any *opelet* marked 'Kertapati' (4000Rp) will get you to the train station.

Taxis to the airport cost 50,000Rp to 70,000Rp. A taxi from the station to the town centre should cost around 30,000Rp.

DANAU RANAU

Remote Danau Ranau, nestled in the middle of the southwestern Bukit Barisan range, is one of the least accessible and least developed of Sumatra's mountain lakes. It's an extremely peaceful spot and an excellent place to just relax or, if you're feeling energetic, go hiking in the surrounding mountains. It's possible to climb Gunung Seminung (1881m), the extinct volcano that dominates the region. Temperatures at Ranau seldom rise above a comfortable 25°C.

The main transport hub of the area is Simpang Sender, about 10km northwest of the lake. At the northern tip is Banding Agung, the main settlement. There is no bank, so change money before you get there.

There are several small hotels in Banding Agung, including **Losmen Batu Mega** (Jl Sugiwaras 269; d 50,000Rp) and **Hotel Seminung Permai** (Jl Akmal 89; d 80,000Rp). Jl Akmal is the main street leading down to the lake.

The village of Pusri also has accommodation, including **Danau Ranau Cottages** and **Wisma Pusri** (d 60,000-100,000Rp).

South of Simpang Sender on the western shore is **Wisma Danau Ranau** (d 150,000-200,000Rp), an upmarket place popular with tour groups.

Padang food is about all you'll find in the restaurants.

Getting There & Away

Most routes to Danau Ranau go through the Trans-Sumatran Hwy town of Baturaja. There are two buses a day to Baturaja from the main bus terminal in Palembang (20,000Rp, four hours). The Palembang–Bandarlampung train line stops at Baturaja, which is about 3½ hours south of Palembang.

There are regular buses for the remaining 120km from Baturaja to Simpang Sender (10,000Rp, three hours), where you can pick up an *opelet* for the final 18km to Banding Agung (4000Rp). It's a good idea to arrive in Baturaja as early as possible to give yourself plenty of time to get a bus out again. If you do get stuck, there are dozens of uninspiring budget losmen to choose from.

KRUI

The quiet coastal village of Krui is an ideal base to explore the unspoilt western coastline. Well off the beaten track, it receives few visitors and there's little to do except enjoy small-town life and the magnificent scenery. Long, white-sand beaches with turquoise waters stretch north and south from Krui and can be explored by taking local *opelet* up and down the coast.

You can stay at **DWI Hotel** (☎ 51069; Jl Merdeka 172; d 1200,000Rp) in the town centre. **Hotel Mutiara Alam** (☎ 51000; 3km south of Krui; d 50,000Rp) is an out-of-town possibility right on the beach.

Backpackers might not pay much attention to Krui but surfers come for the unhindered swells that roar in off the ocean. Right in front of the scenic **Karang Nyimbor Beach Hotel** (☎ 086 812122115; www.sumatrasurfcamps.com; 10km north of Krui; surf packages per day from US$100) surf camp is a long reef break surfable during all tides. The proprietors also have accommodation near other breaks that line the southwestern coast.

There are daily buses to Krui from Bandar Lampung (50,000Rp, six hours) and Bengkulu (80,000Rp, eight hours). *Opelet* depart regularly for Liwa (6000Rp, one hour) and from there to Simpang Sender (for Danau Ranau).

PASEMAH HIGHLANDS

The highlands, tucked away in the Bukit Barisan west of Lahat, are famous for the mysterious megalithic monuments that dot the landscape. The stones have been dated back about 3000 years, but little else is known about them or the civilisation that carved them. While the museums of Palembang and Jakarta now house the pick of the stones, there are still plenty left *in situ*.

The main town of the highlands is Pagaralam, 68km (two hours by bus) southwest of the Trans-Sumatran Hwy town of Lahat.

The best source of information about the highlands is the Hotel Mirasa in Pagaralam. There's nowhere to change money, so bring enough rupiah to see you through.

Sights & Activities

MEGALITHIC SITES

The Pasemah carvings are considered to be the best examples of prehistoric stone sculpture in Indonesia and fall into two distinct styles. The early style dates from almost 3000 years ago and features fairly crude figures squatting with hands on knees or arms folded over chests. The best examples of this type are at a site called **Tinggi Hari**, 20km from Lahat, west of the small river town of Pulau Pinang.

The later style, incorporating expressive facial features, dates from about 2000 years ago and is far more elaborate. Examples include carvings of men riding, battling with snakes and struggling with elephants. There are also a couple of tigers – one guarding a representation of a human head between its paws. The natural curve of the rocks was used to create a three-dimensional effect, though all the sculptures are in bas-relief.

Sculptures of this style are found throughout the villages around Pagaralam, although some take a bit of seeking out. **Tegurwangi**, about 8km from Pagaralam on the road to Tanjung Sakti, is the home of the famous **Batu Beribu**, a cluster of four squat statues that sit under a small shelter by a stream. The site guardian will wander over and lead you to some nearby dolmen-style stone tombs. You can still make out a painting of three women and a dragon in one of them.

The village of **Berlubai**, 3km from Pagaralam, has its own **Batu Gajah** (Elephant Stone) sitting out among the rice paddies, as well as tombs and statues. There is a remarkable collection of stone carvings among the paddies near **Tanjung Aru**. Look out for the one of a man fighting a giant serpent.

GUNUNG DEMPO

This dormant volcano is the highest (3159m) of the peaks surrounding the Pasemah Highlands and dominates the town of Pagaralam. Allow two full days to complete the climb. A guide is strongly recommended as trails can be difficult to find. The lower slopes are used as a tea-growing area, and there are *opelet* from Pagaralam to the tea factory.

Sleeping

The best place to stay in the highlands is Pagaralam.

Hotel Mirasa (☎ 21484; Jl Mayor Ruslan; d from 60,000-80,000Rp) There is a range of rooms to choose from and the owner can organise transport to the sites or guides to climb Gunung Dempo. The hotel is on the edge of town, about 2km from the bus terminal.

Hotel Telaga (☎ 21236; Jl Serma Wanar; d from 60,000Rp) A basic place with simple but clean rooms and very little else.

If you get stuck in Lahat, there is **Hotel Permata** (☎ 21642; Jl Mayor Ruslam III 31; s/d 60,000/80,000Rp; ❄), conveniently close to both the bus terminal and the train station.

Getting There & Around

Every bus travelling along the Trans-Sumatran Hwy calls in at Lahat, nine hours northwest of Bandarlampung and 12 hours southeast of Padang. There are regular buses to Lahat from Palembang (35,000Rp, five hours), and the town is a stop on the train line from Palembang to Lubuklinggau. There are frequent small buses between Lahat and Pagaralam (10,000Rp, two hours).

There are *opelet* to the villages near Pagaralam from the town centre's *stasiun taksi* (taxi station). All local services cost 1500Rp.

PULAU BANGKA

☎ 0717 / pop 790,000

Bangka is a large, sparsely populated island 25km off Sumatra's east coast. Bangka has several white-sand beaches and a peaceful way of life but little in the way of alluring accommodation. Resort hotels were originally designed for wealthy visitors from Singapore and Malaysia, but they, like everyone else, have been spooked by security in Indonesia.

The island's name is derived from the word *wangka* (tin), which was discovered near Mentok in 1710. Tin is still mined on the island, although operations have been greatly scaled down in recent years.

There are only small pockets of natural forest left on Bangka with a large part of the land cleared for rubber, palm oil and pepper plantations.

Pangkal Pinang

Bangka's main town is Pangkal Pinang, a bustling business and transport centre with a population of about 140,000 people.

Most places of importance to travellers are close to the intersection of the main streets, Jl Sudirman and Jl Mesjid Jamik. The bus terminal and markets are nearby on Jl N Pegadaian.

SLEEPING

There are quite a few cheap losmen around the centre of town.

Penginapan Srikandi (☎ 21884; Jl Mesjid Jamik 42; d 35,000Rp) Simple and clean, and, best of all, cheap.

Bukit Shofa Hotel (☎ 21062; Jl Mesjid Jamik 43; d 70,000-90,000Rp; ❄) A large, modern place with a choice of decent rooms.

Sabrina Hotel (☎ 22424; Jl Diponegoro 73; d 100,000Rp; ❄) A midrange place with comfortable rooms on a quiet side street off Jl Sudirman.

EATING

There are lots of small restaurants in Pangkal Pinang, including plenty of places along Jl Sudirman and in the markets near the main junction.

Restaurant Asui Seafood (Jl Kampung Bintang; seafood from 20,000Rp) Behind the BCA bank, this is the place to go for seafood. *Gebung*, known locally as 'chicken fish' because of the firmness of its flesh, is worth trying.

Mentok

Mentok, on the northwestern tip of the island, is the port for boats to/from Palembang. Most people hop on a bus directly from the port to Pangkal Pinang.

In Mentok, there is little of interest other than a **memorial** to 22 Australian nurses shot dead by the Japanese during WWII.

If you get stuck, try **Tin Palace Hotel** (Jl Major Syafrie Rahman 1; s/d 50,000/70,000Rp; ❄).

Beaches

The best beaches are on the northeastern coast around the town of Sungailiat, the island's administrative centre.

Pantai Parai Tenggiri is one of the most popular and is monopolised by the **Parai Beach Hotel** (☎ 92335; Jl Pantai Matras; d from 400,000Rp; ❄). The deserted **Pantai Matras,** 5km further on, is even better.

Getting There & Away

Merpati flies three times a week to Jakarta (350,000Rp).

There are several services each day from Palembang's Boom Baru jetty to Mentok on Bangka (100,000Rp to 200,000Rp depending on class, four hours).

Pelni ships stop in at Mentok travelling to Bintan. The **Pelni office** (☎ 22743) is outside the port gates in Mentok.

Getting Around

There is regular public transport between Bangka's main towns, but most *opelet* stop running in the mid-afternoon. After that taxis are the only option.

Airport taxis charge 50,000Rp for the 7km run into Pangkal Pinang.

There are public buses from Mentok to Pangkal Pinang (15,000Rp, three hours) and Sungailiat (20,000Rp, 3½ hours).

LAMPUNG

At the very tip of this bow-shaped landmass is Sumatra's southernmost province, which was not given provincial status by Jakarta until 1964. Although the Lampungese have had a long history as a distinct culture, the most recent tug of Jakarta's gravitational force is altering Lampung's independence streak. Big-city TV news and fashions have crept across the Sunda Strait, as did Javanese settlers under the *transmigrasi* policies, designed to off-load excess population and turn a profit in the wilds of Sumatra.

Outside the provincial capital of Bandarlampung, the province's robust coffee plantations dominate the economy and the unclaimed forests, closely followed by timber and pepper. There are also large areas of rubber and palm oil plantation.

Today many Jakarta weekenders hop over to tour the Krakatau volcano or visit the elephants of Way Kambas National Park. The rugged western seaboard is ostensibly protected as the Bukit Barisan Selatan National Park.

History

Long before Jakarta became the helm of this island chain, there's evidence that Lampung was part of the Palembang-based Sriwijayan empire until the 11th century, when the Jambi-based Malayu kingdom became the dominant regional power.

Megalithic remains at Pugungraharjo, on the plains to the east of Bandarlampung, are thought to date back more than 1000 years and point to a combination of Hindu and Buddhist influences. The site is believed to have been occupied until the 16th century.

Lampung has long been famous for its prized pepper crop, attracting the West Javanese sultanate of Banten to the area at the beginning of the 16th century and the Dutch East India Company in the late 17th century.

The Dutch finally took control of Lampung in 1856 and launched the first of the transmigration schemes that sought to ease the chronic overcrowding in Java and Bali. Most migrants came to farm the fertile plains of eastern Lampung and today the area is something of a cultural melting pot.

BANDARLAMPUNG

☎ 0721 / pop 850,000

Perched on the hills overlooking Teluk Lampung, Bandarlampung is the region's largest city and its administrative capital. The fourth-largest city in Sumatra, it is the product of an amalgamation of the old towns of Telukbetung (coastal) and Tanjungkarang (inland).

Bandarlampung is the transport hub for stepping into Sumatra from Java and used to see a lot of coming-and-going foreigners. But plane travel now whisks backpackers away from more-northern latitudes. Today visitors come on package tours to Way Kambas or Krakatau arranged in Jakarta.

Orientation

Bandarlampung is something of an administrative creation and the now massive, sprawling city has no real heart. Most places of relevance to travellers are in Tanjungkarang, including the train station and the bulk of the hotels. The Rajabasa bus terminal is 10km north of the town centre; the airport is 24km away.

Information

All the major banks have branches in Bandarlampung, and there are ATMs all over town.

Arie Tour & Travel (☎ 474675; Jl Monginsidi 143) A helpful travel agent located outside the city centre.

BCA bank (Bank Central Asia) Jl Raden Intan 98 (Jl Raden Intan 98); Jl Kartini (Jl Kartini) Offers the best exchange rates.

SUMATRA

BCA bank (Bank Central Asia; Jl Kartini) Offers the best exchange rates.
BII bank (Bank Internasional Indonesia; Jl Kartini)
BNI bank (Bank Negara Indonesia; Jl Kartini)
FajaNet (Jl Raden Intan 61; per hr 5000Rp; 10am-10pm) Internet access.
Lippo bank (Jl Kartini)
Post office Main office (Jl KH Dahlan); central branch (Jl Kotaraja)
Provincial tourist office (☎ 266184; Jl Sudirman 29) A helpful centre centrally located.
Rumah Sakit Bumi Waras (Jl W Monginsidi)
Squid Net (Jl Raden Intan 88a; per hr 5000Rp; 10am-8pm) Internet access.
Telkom wartel (Jl Majapahit; 24hr) International and Home Country Direct calls can be made here.

Sights

The **Krakatau monument** (Jl Verteran, Telukbetung) is a lasting memorial to the force of the 1883 eruption and resulting tidal wave. Almost half of the 36,000 victims died in the 40m-high tidal wave that funnelled up Teluk Lampung and devastated Telukbetung. The huge steel maritime buoy that comprises the monument was washed out of Teluk Lampung and deposited on this hillside.

Lampung Provincial Museum (Jl Teuku Umar; 9am-4.30pm, closed Mon), 5km north of central Tanjungkarang, houses a dusty collection of bits and pieces – everything from Neolithic relics to stuffed animals. To reach the museum, catch a grey *opelet* (2500Rp).

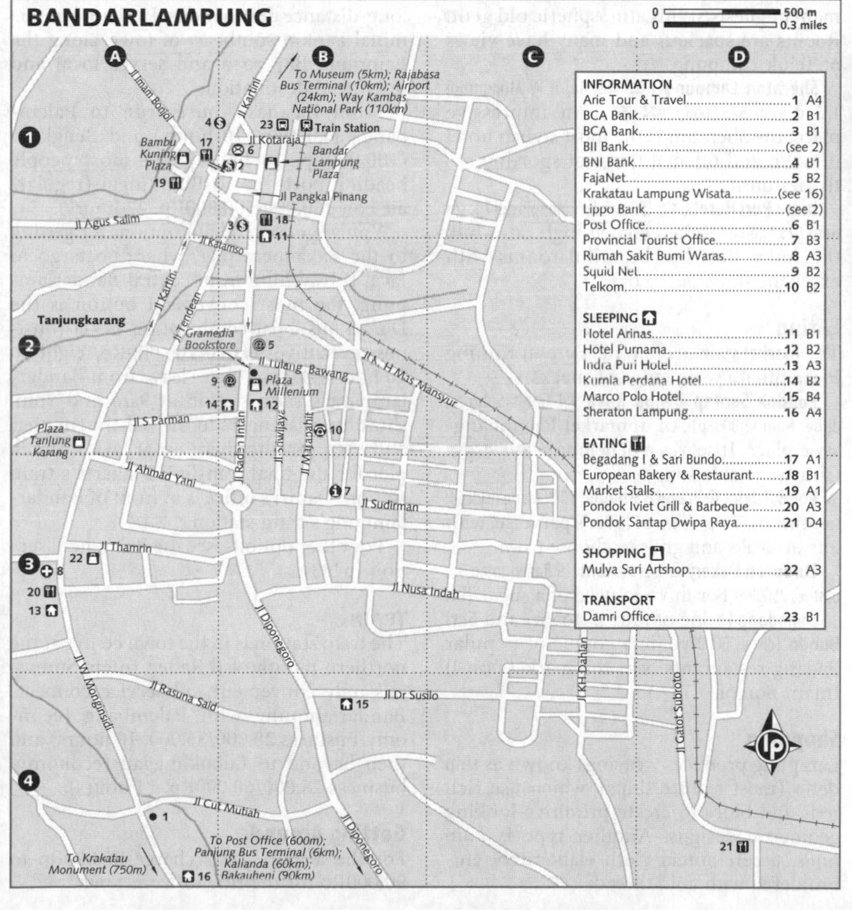

Sleeping

Bandarlampung has a nice selection of mid-range hotels that line Jl Raden Intan, within walking distance or a short *ojek* ride from the train station.

Hotel Purnama (☎ 261448; Jl Raden Intan 77; d 90,000-150,000Rp; ❄) The best option in this price range. It is well managed and maintained, with big comfortable rooms.

Kurnia Perdana Hotel (☎ 262030; Jl Raden Intan 114; d 95,000-125,000Rp; ❄) Clean, comfortable rooms with TV, but no charm.

Hotel Arinas (☎ 266778; Jl Raden Intan 35; d from 200,000Rp; ❄) Central with clean, comfortable, modern rooms, all with TV and hot water.

Marco Polo Hotel (☎ 262511; Jl Dr Susilo 4; d from 250,000Rp; ❄ 🏊) Loads of character are permanent guests at this atmospheric old gent. Rooms are spacious and many have views of Teluk Lampung.

Sheraton Lampung (☎ 486666; Jl W Monginsidi 175; d from 575,000Rp; ❄ 🏊) An impressive place, the Sheraton is the most stylish hotel in town and offers a range of sporting activities onsite.

Indra Puri Hotel (☎ 258258; Jl W Monginsidi 70; s/d from 625,500/687,500Rp) Perched high on a hill, the Indra Puri has beautiful rooms with excellent views of the bay.

Eating

The **market stalls** around the Bambu Kuning Plaza offer a wide range of snacks.

Pondok Santap Dwipa Raya (Jl Gatot Subroto; dishes from 15,000Rp) An upmarket Palembang-style place. It serves a delicious *sayur asam* (sour vegetable soup).

Pondok Iviet Grill and Barbeque (Jl W Monginsidi 64; steaks from 15,000Rp) A meat lover's paradise, with lots of steaks and grills to choose from.

European Bakery & Restaurant (Jl Raden Intan 35; pastries 2500Rp) For those in need of a sugar fix.

Begadang I (one of four in town) and **Sari Bundo** (dishes 6000Rp) are a couple of popular Padang restaurants near the markets on Jl Imam Bonjol.

Shopping

Lampung produces weavings known as **ship cloths** (most feature ships), which use rich reds and blues to create primitive-looking geometric designs. Another type is *kain tapis*, a ceremonial cloth elaborately embroidered with gold thread.

Mulya Sari Artshop (Jl Thamrin 85) A good collection of both ship cloths and *kain tapis* can be found here.

Getting There & Away

AIR

The airport is 24km north of the city. There are flights every day to Jakarta through Merpati, Sriwijaya, Adam Air and Riau Air. Riau also flies to Palembang twice a week. Do note that Merpati flies to Halim Perdanakusuma Airport not Soekarno-Hatta airport. Arie Tour & Travel (p478) is a helpful travel agent.

BUS

There are two bus terminals in Bandarlampung. The city's sprawling Rajabasa bus terminal is 10km north of town and serves long-distance destinations. Panjang bus terminal is 6km southeast of town along the Lampung Bay road and serves local and provincial destinations.

From Rajabasa, buses run to Palembang (80,000Rp, 10 hours) and Bengkulu (100,000Rp, 16 hours), but most people heading north go to Bukittinggi (regular/air-con 160,000/300,000Rp, 22 hours).

You've got several bus options for getting to the Bakauheni pier, where boats go to Java. If travelling from central Bandarlampung, the most convenient option is the Damri bus–boat combination ticket (business/executive 90,000/105,000Rp, eight to 10 hours). Damri buses leave from Bandarlampung's train station at 9am and 9pm, shuttling passengers to the Bakahueni pier, and then picking them up at Java's Merak pier for the final transfer to Jakarta's train station. Damri's office is in front of Bandarlampung's train station.

For other options, see the Bakauheni section (p483).

TRAIN

The train station is in the town centre at the northern mouth of Jl Raden Intan. Sumatra's only convenient rail service connects Bandarlampung with Palembang (economy/business 28,000/85,000, 10 hours) and then beyond to Lubuklinggau (economy/business 28,000/60,000Rp, 14 hours).

Getting Around

For the airport, taxis charge 80,000Rp to 90,000Rp for the ride to/from town.

SUMATRA

All *opelet* pass through the basement of the Bandar Lampung Plaza on Jl Raden Intan and the standard fare around town is 2000Rp.

To reach the Rajabasa bus terminal, take a green *opelet* (2000Rp). To reach the Panjang bus terminal, take a green *opelet* to Sukaraja and then transfer to a red *opelet* (2000Rp).

WAY KAMBAS NATIONAL PARK

This national park is one of the oldest reserves in Indonesia. It occupies 1300 sq km of coastal lowland forest around Sungai Way Kambas on the east coast of Lampung. What little remains of the heavily logged forests is home to endangered species of elephants, rhinos and tigers.

It is believed that close to 200 wild Sumatran elephants *(Elephas maximus sumatrensis)* live in the park, but reliable estimates are uncertain and poaching and development pressures are constant. The Sumatran elephant is a subspecies of the Asian elephant and is found only in Sumatra and Kalimantan. Another rare but endemic creature in Way Kambas is the Sumatran rhino, the only two-horned rhino of the Asian species. Its hide is red in colour with a hairy coat.

The area around Way Kanan, a subdistrict of the park, is frequently visited by bird-watchers. Of the most remarkable species, white-winged duck and Storm's stork get the binoculars fogged up.

For some time an elephant training centre operated in the park and served as a major tourism draw. The centre was created to rehabilitate wild elephants that were threatening farmer's crops. It was hoped that training the elephants for jobs in the logging or tourism industry would resolve the conflicts created by diminishing wild lands. But the elephants, like many of the island's human population, had a hard time finding work and caring for a large population of animals proved too costly after the monetary crisis. As a result many of the elephants have been moved elsewhere and the ones who remain are used to carry tourists on jungle treks.

Also operating in the park is the Sumatra Rhino Sanctuary, where four rhinos formerly held in captivity are introduced to more wild surroundings in the hopes of successful breeding. The Sumatran rhino is a solitary animal and its habitat in the wild is so fractured that conservationists fear the species will die out without intervention. Breeding centres for rhinos are a controversial component of species-protection campaigns as they are expensive to maintain and have reported few successful births. For more information, visit the website of the International Rhino Foundation (www.rhinos-irf.org), one of the lead organisations involved with the centre and anti-poaching patrols in the park.

Visiting the Park

For the average visitor not engaged in wildlife conservation, a visit to the park is a nice break from the concrete confines of Jakarta, but it's not a true wild safari. Most visitors are led through the forest on elephants or by canoes on the Sungai Way Kanan and surrounding waterways. The most commonly spotted animals on the tour include primates and birds. Herds of elephants are seen here from time to time but sightings of the Sumatran tiger are extremely rare.

A day trip to Way Kambas costs around US$50 per person for a minimum of two people and can be arranged through tour operators in Jakarta. Bandarlampung-based tour agents include **Arie Tour & Travel** (☎ 474675; Jl W Monginsidi 143) and **Krakatau Lampung Wisata** (☎ 263625, 486666; Sheraton Lampung).

You could visit the park independently, but transport is limited and expensive. To strike out on your own, hire an *ojek* from Rajabasalama to Way Kanan, where you can hire a guide (50,000Rp to 100,000Rp) and arrange transport.

Sleeping & Eating

Tourist facilities within the park are limited. About 13km from the entrance to the park is Way Kanan, where there are a collection of simple **guesthouses** (75,000Rp) on the banks of Sungai Way Kanan. **Food stalls** nearby cater for day-trippers and close after dark, so you'll need to bring food if you're staying the night.

Getting There & Away

The entrance to Way Kambas is 110km from Bandarlampung.

There are buses from Bandarlampung's Rajabasa bus terminal to Jepara (15,000Rp,

2½ hours). They pass the entrance to Way Kambas, an arched gateway guarded by a stone elephant, in the village of Rajabasalama, 10km north of Jepara. Alternatively, you can catch a bus to Metro (8000Rp, one hour) and then another to Rajabasalama (10,000Rp, 1½ hours).

From the park entrance, you can also hire a motorcycle to take you into the park and to pick you up.

KALIANDA

☎ 0727

Kalianda is a quiet little town overlooking Teluk Lampung 30km north of the Bakauheni ferry terminal. The main reason for passing through is to visit Krakatau, but the town can also be used as an alternative base to Bandarlampung. Nearby are pretty white-sand beaches and simple fishing villages. Jakarta weekend refugees fed up with Bali have begun small migrations to Kalianda.

Sights & Activities

Overlooking the town is **Gunung Rajabasa** (1281m), an easily scaleable volcano. Afterwards you can soak in the **hot springs** at Wartawan Beach, just beyond Canti. Beaches around Canti have relaxing sea breezes. An *opelet* to the beach costs 4000Rp.

Off the coast **Pulau Sebuku** and **Pulau Sebesi** have snorkelling and swimming. Cargo boats leave from Canti to these islands, or you can charter a tour from the local fishermen.

To reach Krakatau, stop in at Hotel Beringin and ask about organised tours or head down to the Canti harbour on weekends to pair up with local groups chartering boats.

Sleeping & Eating

Hotel Beringin (☎ 2008; Jl Kesuma Bangsa 75; d 50,000Rp) Close to the centre of town, this is an old Dutch villa with high ceilings and languid fans. The hotel has lots of information about local attractions and can arrange trips to nearby attractions.

Kalianda Hotel (☎ 2392; d from 80,000Rp; ❄) On the way into town from the highway, this is a more upmarket choice.

Laguna Helau (☎ 081 1727638; www.lagunahelau.com; Jl Sinar Laut 81, Ketang; cottages from 200,000Rp) Just outside town, this oceanside resort has cottages inspired by stilt-frame fishing villages nestled between a private beach and palm-fringed lagoon. Larger bungalows have four bedrooms and kitchen facilities.

The **food stalls** that appear in Kalianda's town centre at night are the best places to eat.

Getting There & Around

There are regular buses between Kalianda and Bandarlampung's Rajabasa bus terminal (8000Rp, 1½ hours). Most buses don't run right into Kalianda, but drop you on the highway at the turn-off to town. From there, simply cross the road and wait for an *opelet* into town (2000Rp). There are a few direct buses from the Bakauheni ferry terminal to Kalianda (10,000Rp), but it's usually quicker to catch any north-bound bus and get off at the junction for town.

There are regular *opelet* from Kalianda to Canti (4000Rp) and along the road that rings Gunung Rajabasa via Gayam and Pasuruan.

There are also cargo boats from Canti, a fishing village outside of Kalianda, to nearby Sebuku and Sebesi (12,000Rp). Canti can be reached by public bus.

GUNUNG KRAKATAU

Krakatau might have come closer than any other volcano in recent history to destroying the planet when it erupted in 1883. Tens of thousands were killed either by the resulting tidal wave or by the pyroclastic flows that crossed 40km of ocean to incinerate Sumatran coastal villages. Afterwards all that was left was a smouldering caldera where a cluster of uninhabited islands had once been. Perhaps peace had come, thought local villagers. But Krakatau, like all scrappy villains, re-awoke in 1927 and resulting eruptions built a new volcanic cone since christened Anak Krakatau (Child of Krakatau).

Tours to the island launch from West Java (see p126) or from Kalianda on the Sumatran coast. Organised tours typically cost US$90 per person. **Hotel Beringin** (left) in Kalianda might also be able to organise a tour.

You can also join up with weekenders chartering boats from Canti, a fishing village outside of Kalianda, or from Pulau Sebesi (see left). Charters usually cost 500,000Rp to 900,000Rp for 15 people.

BAKAUHENI

Bakauheni is the major ferry terminal between Java and southern Sumatra.

There are frequent ferries between Bakauheni and Merak, Java's westernmost port. A fast ferry runs between the two ports every 30 minutes from 7am to 5pm and costs 22,500Rp; the crossing takes 40 minutes. A slow ferry runs every 30 minutes, 24 hours a day and costs 6700Rp; the crossing takes two to three hours.

The journey between the two islands sounds like a snap until you factor in land transport between the ferry terminals and the major towns on either side. Bakauheni is 90km from Bandarlampung, a bus journey of about two hours. Buses to the port leave from the Bandarlampung town centre (see p480) or from the Panjang bus terminal (20,000Rp). A taxi to Bakauheni from Bandarlampung should cost 30,000Rp. In Java, the bus transfer from the port of Merak to Jakarta is another two-hour journey; see p116 for more information.

BUKIT BARISAN SELATAN NATIONAL PARK

At the southern tip of Sumatra, this national park comprises one of the island's last stands of lowland forests. For this reason the World Wildlife Fund has ranked it as one of the planet's most biologically outstanding habitats and is working to conserve the park's remaining Sumatran rhino and tigers. The park is also famous for many endemic bird species that prefer foothill climates, and several species of sea turtle that nest along the park's coastal zone.

Of the 365,000 hectares originally designated as protected, only 324,000 hectares remain untampered. The usual suspects are responsible: illegal logging and plantation conversion, and poachers are also at work.

Tourist infrastructure in the park is limited and most people visit on organised tours. The easiest access point into the park is through the town of Kota Agung, 80km west of Bandarlampung.

Kantor Taman Nasional Bukit Barisan Selatan (☎ 21064; Jl Raya Terbaya, Kota Agung; 8am-4.30pm Mon-Thu, 8am-noon Fri) sells permits into the park (5000Rp) and can arrange guides and trekking information.

Less-accessible access points are Sukaraja, 20km west of Kota Agung, and Liwa, the northernmost entry way.

Kota Agung has several **basic hotels** and there is a **campground** near Sukaraja.

There are frequent buses from Bandarlampung to Kota Agung (10,000Rp).

Nusa Tenggara

Indonesia's dazzling arc of eastern islands that stretches towards northern Australia is perhaps the most varied and rewarding part of the nation to explore. There are few regions of the world that can compete with Nusa Tenggara for sheer diversity – east of Hindu Bali are the largely Islamic islands of Lombok and Sumbawa, followed by predominantly Catholic Flores with its Portuguese heritage, while Timor and the Alor and Solor Archipelagos have Protestant majorities. On all of these islands, animist rituals and tribal traditions continue alongside the minarets, temples and chapels, particularly in rural areas. Though Bahasa Indonesia is a unifying tongue, each main island has at least one native language, which is often subdivided into dialects.

The spectacular terrain is almost as diverse: the fecund volcanic slopes and shimmering rice paddies of western Lombok contrast sharply with the arid hillsides of Komodo and Sumba, which turn dusty brown at the end of the long dry season.

If you've a thirst for adventure or nature, or if you surf, snorkel, hike or dive, the opportunities in Nusa Tenggara are almost limitless. Of the dozens of volcanoes, the sublime cone of Kelimutu – its summit crowned by three crater lakes of different hues – has to be the region's prime draw, though Lombok's towering Rinjani is a much more challenging ascent.

The cities and towns in this region are generally not places to linger long – with little in the way of cultural appeal and an excess of fumes, heat, noise and urban grime – though they are rarely threatening or dangerous; personal safety is not normally a great concern.

HIGHLIGHTS

- Gazing at the lunarlike landscape atop **Gunung Kelimutu** (p561), with its three astonishing crater lakes, each a different colour
- Trekking up the lush slopes of **Gunung Rinjani** (p519), the sacred volcano that dominates northern Lombok
- Coming face-to-face with the mother of all lizards in **Komodo** (p541) or **Rinca** (p543)
- Exploring the villages of **Sumba** (p590), characterised by their extraordinary rocket-roofed clan houses, and marvelling at the island's unique tribal culture, tombs and textiles
- Snorkelling or diving in coral reefs teeming with marine life around the **Gili Islands** (p511), **Labuanbajo** (p546) and **Komodo National Park** (p546)

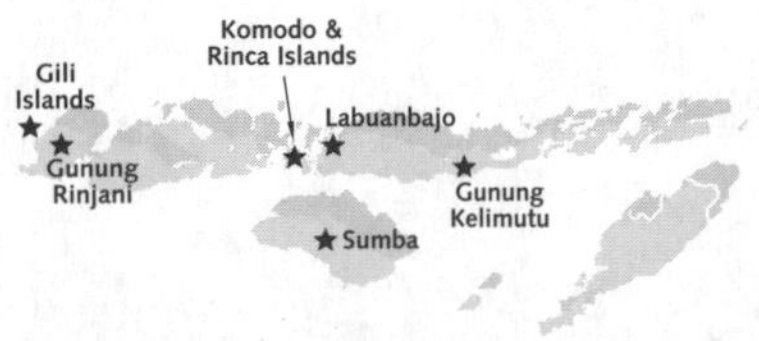

- POPULATION: 8.2 MILLION
- LAND AREA: 68,053 SQ KM
- HIGHEST PEAK: GUNUNG RINJANI (3726M)

HISTORY

The region of Nusa Tenggara has always been, and remains, remote. Before the 15th century, virtually the only external contact these islands had were sporadic visits from Chinese and Arab traders in search of sandalwood, spices and tortoiseshell. In 1512 the Portuguese first landed in (and named) Flores; they also named Timor and Solor and brought Christianity to all three islands soon after their arrival.

The Dutch began to muscle in on the region in the 17th century, taking control of Kupang in 1653 and later shunting the Portuguese off to East Timor. But, with few resources to tempt them, they devoted little attention to Nusa Tenggara, only really establishing firm control over the area in the 20th century by forming alliances with tribal rajahs.

Little changed after WWII, the vast majority of people continuing to make a living from fishing or subsistence farming. Periodic droughts could be devastating: famine killed an estimated 50,000 in Lombok in 1966, provoking the government to implement a *transmigrasi* programme that moved thousands of families from the island to other parts of the nation.

Today there remains very little industry in the region (apart from a colossal mine in Sumbawa), and many Nusa Tenggarans are forced to move to Java, Bali or Malaysia in search of work. It's also quite common for women to work as maids in the Gulf states, Singapore and Hong Kong. The potential for tourism remains vast, but, due to political instability, poor infrastructure and transport links, and low educational standards, Nusa Tenggara looks unlikely to profit much from this sector for some time yet.

WILDLIFE

The region's real trump card is the Komodo dragon (see p542), the world's largest lizard, which can easily be spotted on the islands of Komodo and Rinca. Small numbers also exist in western Flores.

The coral reefs of Nusa Tenggara are some of the richest in the world, and there's an incredible array of marine life, from tiny reef dwellers such as nudibranchs, sea snails and pipe fish to pelagic giants: manta and devil rays, pilot whales, and dolphins.

CLIMATE

On the islands east of Bali, seasonal differences are more pronounced. The driest months are August and September, and the wettest months are between November and February. However, the duration of the seasons varies from island to island. The seasons in Lombok are more like those in Bali, with a dry season from April to September and a wet season from October to March. Much the same applies to both Sumbawa and Flores. The duration of the dry season increases the closer you get to Australia – the rusty landscapes of Sumba and Timor contrast strongly with well-vegetated Flores. See also the climate chart for Kupang, p848.

At almost 10°S latitude, Timor is also the only island in Indonesia that is far enough from the equator to experience typhoons (cyclones), but these are rare. Nearby northern Australia is not so lucky.

GETTING THERE & AROUND

Overland travel is very arduous in many parts of mountainous Nusa Tenggara, particularly in Flores. Lombok, Sumbawa and Timor have fairly decent surfaced main roads and some comfortable bus services. Get off the highways and things slow down considerably, however. Ferry services have actually worsened in recent years, partly due to the downturn in tourism (and several sinkings). Fortunately, several airlines now cover the main inter-island routes, as few travellers who have endured the punishing long haul across Nusa Tenggara by surface transport are willing to repeat the experience.

Air

There are twice-weekly flights between Darwin in Australia and Kupang, jointly operated by Air North and Merpati (Merpati Nusantara Airlines). Mataram has the only other international airport in Nusa Tenggara, with twice-weekly connections to Singapore on Silk Air and daily connections to Kuala Lumpur (KL) on Merpati. Most visitors use Bali as the international gateway to Nusa Tenggara, as there are so many more connections available.

Several airlines operate within Nusa Tenggara, but the main two are Merpati and Transnusa (which mainly operates

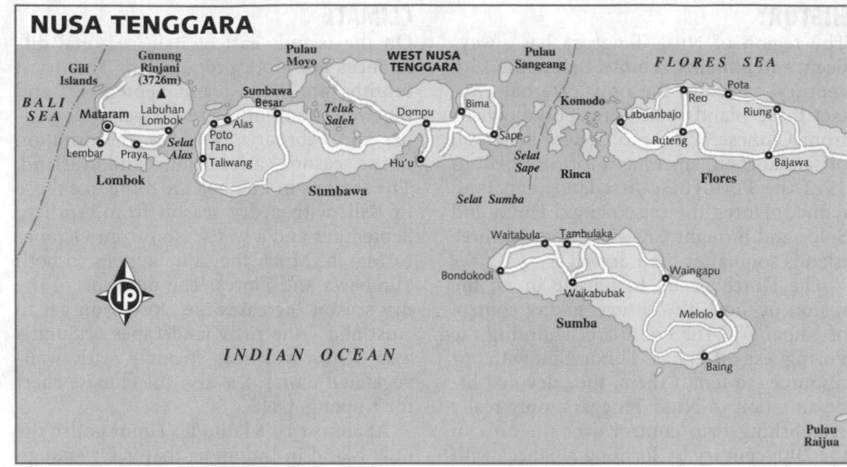

between the eastern islands). Other airlines, including Adam Air, GT Air, Lion Air, Batavia Air and Wings Air, concentrate on the main routes to/from Mataram and Kupang.

With Merpati, the delays or cancellations remain an inconvenience; however, it remains the best-connected airline in Nusa Tenggara. Transnusa is generally more reliable and punctual, but flight cancellations are common on all routes in Nusa Tenggara, particularly on the less popular (and less profitable) ones.

Nusa Tenggara is not well connected to other parts of Indonesia, and you'll have to travel via Bali to get to Sulawesi, Maluku and Papua.

It's wise to book early, and reservations are essential in the peak August tourist season. The most popular routes are to/from Bali and Flores (particularly Maumere–Denpasar). Overbooking often occurs, so make sure your booking is confirmed when buying the ticket, and always reconfirm. If a flight is 'full', it is worth going to the airport before departure, as there are often 'no-shows', which means last-minute seats are available.

Bicycle

Many people hire bicycles to get around the Gili Islands, but they are not a popular form of transport anywhere else in Nusa Tenggara. Long-distance cycling is an option on Lombok (though the roads are narrow and traffic can be quite heavy) and across the undulating terrain of Sumba and western Sumbawa. Cycling on volcanic Flores or mountainous Timor requires Tour de France levels of endurance, though some riders do travel across both islands using buses to get their bikes up the steepest inclines and freewheeling downhill.

Boat

Pelni's *Awu*, *Dobonsolo*, *Dorolonda*, *Kelimutu*, *Sirimau*, *Tatamailau*, *Pangrango* and *Tilongkabila* ferries all service Nusa Tenggara. Schedules are provided under individual town entries in this chapter. Pelni's more basic Perintis cargo ships cover many routes and are an option if you get stuck. Ask at the office of the *syahbandar* (harbour master) or at the shipping offices. Conditions are primitive, but you can often negotiate to rent a cabin.

Somewhat dilapidated, slow ferries also connect many of the islands. There are very regular sailings between Bali and Lombok, and Lombok and Sumbawa. Between Sumbawa and Flores there's a daily ferry, but it does not stop at Komodo.

Other ferry connections include twice-weekly services between both Kupang and Larantuka (Flores) and Kupang and Kalabahi (Alor). Boats also connect Ende (Flores) with Waingapu (Sumba); Larantuka (Flores) with Lembata and Kalabahi; and Kupang with Rote. There are plenty of other possibilities; see the relevant sec-

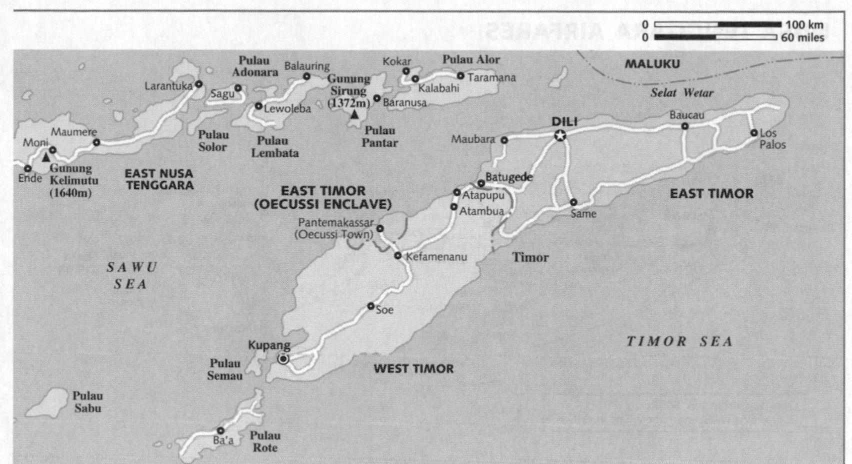

tions of individual town entries for more details.

A popular way of travelling between Lombok and Flores or vice versa is on a boat tour, stopping at Komodo and other islands along the way. See p516 for more information.

Bus

Travelling by bus is generally uncomfortable, hot and slow in Nusa Tenggara despite most main roads being sealed. However, some of the main cross-island truck routes are covered by air-con express coaches: Mataram–Labuhan Lombok; the trans-Sumbawa journey as far as Bima; and Kupang–Dili in Timor.

Elsewhere expect an oven-hot bus with near-zero legroom, betel-nut gobbing passengers, and an excess of clucking chickens and dried fish. Buses constantly stop to drop off and pick up passengers. In remote parts be prepared for endless loops around town at the beginning and end of each journey as the driver searches for, and later drops off, passengers – a maddening local practice called *keliling* that provokes curses and vitriol from many a traveller. Even if the road is sealed, it is usually narrow and winding, and there are usually sections under repair that will rattle the fillings. Don't underestimate journey times – a trip of only 100km may take up to four hours.

Flores' interminable switchbacks and mountain ranges mean that there is no comfortable way to cross the island by land unless you have all the time in the world and the patience of a saint.

Most buses leave in the morning between 6am and 8am, so be prepared for early starts. Where buses leave later in the day, they are less patronised, so they often spend longer looking for passengers. There are also night buses between Mataram and Bima. Long-distance buses usually meet the main ferries for those planning to travel straight through to other destinations.

Buying bus tickets for the right price can be a real hassle in Nusa Tenggara as foreigners routinely get overcharged. Touts are always around hotels and bus terminals, willing to 'assist', but this gets even more expensive. The same goes for many travel agents. The right price is only really available if buying from the actual bus company office or by finding out the correct tariff from fellow passengers. Good luck!

Car & Motorcycle

Self-drive cars can be found at very reasonable rates in Senggigi, Lombok (from 150,000Rp a day for a 4WD), though remember to inspect the car thoroughly first, as insurance is often extremely basic, and you'll usually have to pay for any damage. Consider hiring a car with a driver from 300,000Rp, including petrol. Elsewhere it's much more difficult and expensive to rent a car. Hotels are good contact points, but expect to pay 350,000Rp to 500,000Rp a

NUSA TENGGARA AIRFARES

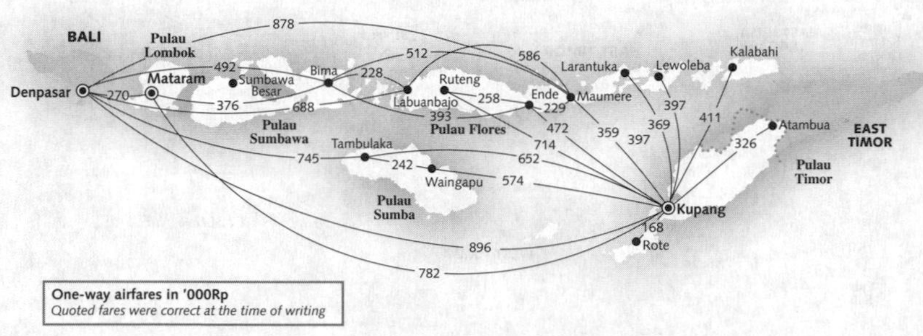

day, including driver and petrol. Bemos can be chartered for shorter trips.

If you are an experienced rider, motorcycling is great way to see Nusa Tenggara, and you can transport your bike on ferries between most of the islands. It's best to bring your own machine. Short-term hires are possible virtually anywhere (around 35,000-60,000Rp a day), though this usually amounts to a casual agreement between you and the bike owner and there is no paperwork involved. It's difficult to convince anyone to let you take their bike to another island.

Traffic is relatively light, even on the main highways, but the usual hazards of villages crowded with pedestrians, chickens and goats apply. Driving at night is not recommended, as many vehicles do not have lights.

LOMBOK

Lombok is the most popular destination in Nusa Tenggara, with the fabled Gili Islands drawing visitors for action both in and out of the water, mighty Gunung Rinjani luring trekkers, and the big breaks on the south coast a magnet for surfers.

The island of Lombok shapes up at about 80km from east to west and about the same from north to south, with lush evergreen landscapes and parts which are chronically dry. Droughts, particularly in the south and east, can last for months, causing crop failure and famine – though recent improvements in water management have made life in Lombok less precarious.

Rice is an important crop, though yields are lower here than on neighbouring islands. Tobacco, coconuts, coffee, kapok and cotton are also important crops, while cloves, vanilla, pineapple and pepper have also been introduced.

The indigenous Sasak (around 90% of the population) are Muslims but have a culture and language unique to Lombok. There's also a significant Hindu Balinese minority – a legacy of the time when Bali controlled Lombok.

History

In the early 17th century Lombok's Sasak princedoms were usurped by the Balinese, who took control of western Lombok, and the Makassarese, who invaded eastern Lombok. By 1750 the whole island was in Balinese hands.

In western Lombok, relations between the Balinese and the Sasaks were relatively harmonious, but in eastern Lombok the Balinese had to maintain control from garrisoned forts, and peasant rebellions were common.

The Dutch intervened in the late 19th century, and, after an initial defeat that cost 100 lives, overran Cakranegara. Here the last rajah families surrendered by *perang poepoetan* – men, women and children in white clothing throwing themselves at the perplexed Dutch, who kept shooting.

In the following years, the Dutch were able to maintain the support of the surviving Balinese and the Sasak aristocracy, and they controlled more than 500,000 people with no more than 250 troops.

Even after Indonesian independence, Lombok continued to be dominated by its Balinese and Sasak elite. In 1958 Lombok became part of the new province of Nusa Tenggara Barat (West Nusa Tenggara), and Mataram became its administrative capital. Following the attempted coup in Jakarta in 1965, Lombok experienced mass killings of communists and ethnic Chinese.

Under former president Soeharto's 'New Order', there was stability and some growth, but crop failures led to famine in 1966, and to severe food shortages in 1973. Many moved away from Lombok under the government-sponsored *transmigrasi* programme.

Tourism took off in the 1980s but was mostly developed by outside investors and speculators. As Indonesia descended into economic crisis and political turmoil in the late '90s, Lombok began to feel the pinch.

On 17 January 2000, serious riots engulfed Mataram. Christians and Chinese were the primary victims, but the agitators and provocateurs were from outside Lombok. Ultimately all Lombok suffered, and tourism has yet to recover, the situation compounded by the Bali bombs of 2002 and 2005.

AVOIDING OFFENCE

Most of Lombok is culturally conservative, and immodest dress and public displays of affection between couples can cause offence. Both men and women should dress appropriately away from Senggigi and the Gili Islands. Nude or topless bathing anywhere is very offensive.

Islamic law forbids drinking alcohol and, though booze is widely available throughout Lombok, public drunkenness is quite definitely frowned upon. It is particularly offensive to drink near a mosque. Ramadan is a time to be particularly sensitive about local cultural sensibilities – during this time there are no parties in Gili Trawangan.

Today Lombok's tourism potential remains strong, particularly with work starting on a new international airport in 2006. But with many Sasaks adopting a stricter practice of Islam, the cultural gulf between conservative Islamic and liberal Western values is acute.

Culture

Lombok has a population of just over three million. Almost 90% of the people are Sasak, about 10% are Balinese, and there are small numbers of Chinese, Javanese, Bugis and Arabs.

Originally hill people, the Sasaks are now spread all over Lombok and are generally much poorer than the Balinese minority. Virtually all Sasaks are Muslims, but many retain much less orthodox Wektu Telu beliefs (see p492) and ancient animist rituals. *Adat* (traditional law) is still fundamental to their way of life, particularly customs relating to birth, circumcision, courtship and marriage.

Sasaks show a fascination with heroic trials of strength, physical prowess and one-on-one contests. *Peresehan*, sometimes misleadingly called 'Sasak boxing', is a fight between two men using long rattan staves and small rectangular shields made of cowhide. *Lanca*, originally from Sumbawa, is another trial of strength, this time between men who use their knees to strike each other.

Most of Lombok's Chinese population lives in Ampenan or Cakranegara. The Chinese first came to Lombok with the Dutch as a cheap labour force, but after independence most stayed on and started businesses. In the aftermath of the 1965 purge, many of Lombok's Chinese were murdered en masse, along with the thousands that were killed throughout the country. Racism and economic jealousy resurfaced in early 1998 and January 2000, when the Chinese bore the brunt of protests and riots in Mataram.

Lombok's Balinese are concentrated in the Mataram region and the west of the island. Before the arrival of Islam in the 15th century, Hindu-Balinese culture dominated Lombok, alongside indigenous animist rituals. Today, the Balinese are a disproportionately powerful minority, particularly in the business and tourism sectors.

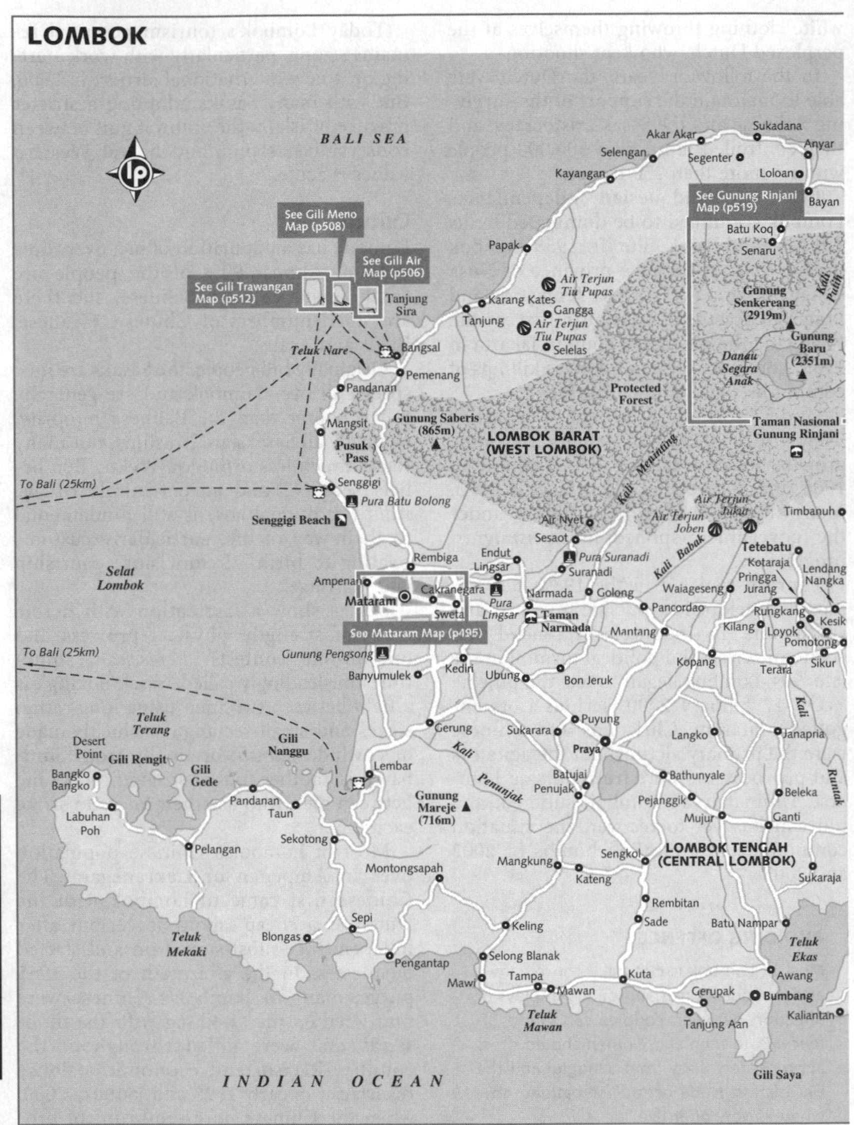

DANCE

Lombok has an indigenous music style and a number of traditional dances that are performed during seasonal or life-cycle ceremonies. Many are also performed during the Senggigi festival (held annually in late July).

The popular Cupak Gerantang, which originated in Java, tells the story of Panji, a romantic hero. A version of the Panji story, the Kayak Sando, in which the dancers wear masks is found only in central and eastern Lombok.

The Gandrung is about love and courtship, a social dance, usually performed by the young men and women of villages in Narmada, Lenek and Praya.

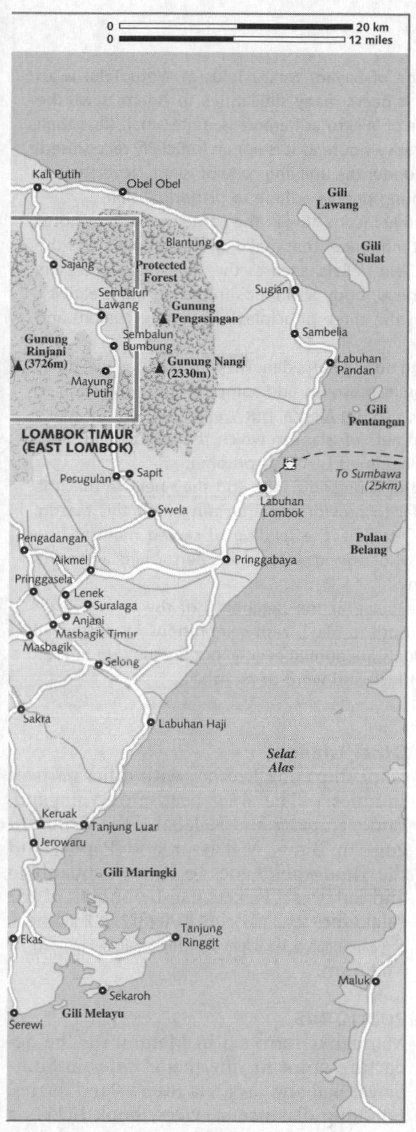

A former war dance, Gendang Beleq is performed to the beat of a *gendang beleq* (big drum). The Oncer is another war dance performed vigorously by men and young boys in central and eastern Lombok. Look out too for the Rudat, performed by men in pairs, backed by singers, tambourines and cylindrical drums called *jidur*.

MUSIC

The Tandak Gerok is an eastern Lombok performance which combines dance, theatre and singing to music played on bamboo flutes and on the two-stringed bowed lute called a *rebab*. A unique feature of the Tandak Gerok is that the vocalists imitate the sound of the gamelan (traditional Javanese and Balinese orchestra) instruments. It's usually performed after harvesting or other hard physical labour, but it's also staged at traditional ceremonies.

The Genggong involves seven musicians using a simple set of instruments, including a bamboo flute and a *rebab*; they accompany their music with dance movements and stylised hand gestures.

Getting There & Away

AIR

There are daily flights to/from Denpasar and Mataram on Merpati (seven daily), Wings Air (four daily) and GT Air (two daily). Merpati also has limited flights to Sumbawa Besar (from Mataram) and to Bima on Sumbawa (from Denpasar and Mataram).

Lion Air and Garuda both operate daily flights to Surabaya with connections to Jakarta. Silk Air has two flights a week to/from Singapore, and Merpati has daily flights to/from KL.

The departure tax is 10,000Rp for domestic flights and 100,000Rp for international flights.

Offices for the airlines currently represented in Lombok:

Garuda (Garuda Indonesia; ☎ 0370-638259, www.garuda-indonesia.com; Hotel Lombok Raya, Mataram)
GT Air (☎ 0370-634935) At the airport.
Lion Air (☎ 0370-629111; www.lionair.co.id; Hotel Sahid Legi, Mataram)
Merpati (☎ 0370621111; www.merpati.co.id; Jl Pejanggik 69, Mataram)
Silk Air (☎ 0370628254; www.silkair.com; Hotel Lombok Raya, Mataram)
Wings Air See Lion Air.

BOAT

Lombok has very regular boat connections with Sumbawa and Bali, and by Pelni ship to/from elsewhere in Indonesia.

Bali

Ferries travel between Padangbai (Bali) and Lembar (Lombok) every 90 minutes

NUSA TENGGARA

WEKTU TELU

Believed to have originated in the northern village of Bayan, Wektu Telu (or Wetu Telu) is an indigenous religion unique to Lombok – though it bears many similarities to Agami Jawi, the Javanese Islamic syncretism. Officially the number of Wektu adherents is quite small (less than 30,000), although this is almost certainly a conservative figure as it is not an 'officially recognised' religion, and Wektu traditions and rituals continue under the unifying code of Islam. Nevertheless, numbers have been steadily declining as more young people adhere to orthodox Islam.

In the Sasak language, *wektu* means 'result' and *telu* means 'three'. The name probably denotes the complex mixture of Hindu, Islamic and animist influences that make up this religion; and the concept of a trinity is embodied in many Wektu Telu beliefs, such as the sun, moon and stars (representing heaven, earth and water), and the head, body and limbs (representing creativity, sensitivity and control). Wektu laws are based on the three principles of religion, custom and governance.

The Wektu Telu observe only three days of fasting during Ramadan. They do not pray five times a day as laid down by Islamic law, they do not build mosques and some have no objection to eating pork. Their dead are buried with their heads facing Mecca, but Wektu Telu do not make pilgrimages there. In fact, the only fundamental tenets of Islam to which the Wektu Telu seem to hold firmly are the belief in Allah, and that Muhammed is Allah's prophet.

For the Wektu, death does not signify the end of a person's soul, and they believe that the departed return on important days in the calendar to provide ritual blessings. For this reason, much respect is paid to Wektu ancestors. Three rituals – the reading of sacred mantras, the offering of betel nut, and the placement of a bowl of spring water – are performed when the Wektu wish to invite their ancestors to a ceremony.

Most of the Wektu Telu religious festivals take place at the beginning of the rainy season (from October to December), or at harvest time (April to May), with celebrations in villages all over the island. Many of these ceremonies and rituals are annual events, but, as they do not fall on specific days, getting to see one is a matter of luck and word of mouth.

around the clock. Fares for foot passengers are 21,000Rp, for motorcycles 65,000Rp and for cars 450,000Rp. The trip takes four to five hours.

The luxury catamaran **Mabua Express** (☎ Lombok 0370-681225, Bali 0361-721212) connects the Pelni port at Lembar with Pelabuhan Benoa (Bali) but has a reputation for cancelling, and as the fare (from US$28) exceeds the price of many flights between the islands it's not popular. It's scheduled to depart Bali at 8.30am and Lombok at 2.30pm, and takes 2½ hours to complete the trip.

There's also a Perama shuttle bus and boat service (185,000Rp) from Padangbai, which now stops at all the Gili Islands (four to five hours) before heading on to Senggigi (five to six hours).

Sumbawa

Ferries travel between Labuhan Lombok and Poto Tano on Sumbawa every 45 minutes (passenger 12,500Rp, motorcycle 32,000Rp, car 253,000Rp). They run 24 hours a day and the trip takes 1½ hours.

Other Islands

Pelni ships link Lembar with other parts of Indonesia. The *Awu* heads to Waingapu, Ende, Kupang and Kalabahi; the *Kelimutu* goes to Bima, Makassar and Papua; and the *Tilongkabila* goes to Bima, Labuanbajo and Sulawesi. Tickets can be bought at the **Pelni office** (Map p495; ☎ 0370-637212; Jl Industri 1; 🕒 8am-noon & 1-3.30pm Mon-Thu & Sat, 8-11am Fri) in Mataram.

PUBLIC BUS

Mandalika terminal in Mataram is the departure point for the major cities in Sumbawa, Bali and Java, via inter-island ferries. For long-distance services, book tickets a day or two ahead at the terminal, or from a travel agency along Jl Pejanggik/Selaparang in Mataram. If you get to the terminal before 8am, there may be a spare seat on a bus going in your direction, but this is by no means a certainty.

Sample fares are Bima (economy/luxury 110,000/135,000Rp, 12 hours), Denpasar (luxury 110,000Rp, seven hours), Sumbawa

Besar (economy/luxury 60,000/77,000Rp, six hours), Jakarta (luxury 375,000Rp, 38 hours), Surabaya (luxury 179,000Rp, 20 hours) and Yogyakarta (luxury 272,000Rp, 30 hours).

TOURIST SHUTTLE BUS/BOAT

The Bali-based company **Perama** (www.peramatour.com) has tourist shuttle bus/boat services between the main tourist centres in Lombok (Senggigi, the Gili Islands and Kuta) and most tourist centres in Bali (Ubud, Sanur and the Kuta region). A few other companies offer similar services at similar prices. Tickets can be booked directly, or at any travel agency in Lombok or Bali, and include ferry charges.

Getting Around

There is a good road across the middle of the island, between Mataram and Labuhan Lombok. The Mataram–Praya–Kuta and Mataram–Senggigi–Anyar routes are also pretty decent sealed roads, though they're on the narrow side. Public transport is generally restricted to the main routes; away from these, you need to charter a bemo, *cidomo* (horse-drawn cart) or *ojek* (motorcycle taxi) – or walk. During the wet season, remote roads are often flooded or washed away, particularly around the foothills of Rinjani, and others become impassable because of fallen rocks and rubble.

BUS & BEMO

The main terminal, Mandalika, is at Bertais, 6km southeast of central Mataram; other regional terminals are in Praya, Anyar and Pancor (near Selong). You may have to go via one or more of these terminals to get from one part of Lombok to another. For main routes, fares are fixed by the provincial government, and a list should be displayed at the terminals. The bus and bemo drivers will still try to overcharge and touts will hassle endlessly. Most public transport becomes scarce in the afternoon and normally ceases after dark, often earlier in more remote areas.

Chartering a bemo can be convenient and reasonably cheap – about 175,000Rp per bemo per day (including petrol), depending on distance and road conditions. Some bemos are restricted to certain routes or areas – the yellow bemos that shuttle around Mataram cannot be chartered for a trip to Lembar.

CAR & MOTORCYCLE

Senggigi is by far the best place to organise car or motorcycle rental. Arrangements can be made in Mataram and other places, but rates are much higher. Hotels and travel agencies offer the most competitive rates; 'official' car-rental companies often have a wider range of vehicles but tend to be more expensive.

Jeep-style vehicles are best for Lombok's roads. Suzuki Jimnys cost from 150,000Rp per day, and Toyota Kijangs cost about 225,000Rp, excluding petrol. Discounts are offered for longer periods. Hiring a car with a driver is a very sensible and popular option as you won't be liable for any damage – expect to pay about 325,000Rp per day.

Motorcycles can be rented in Mataram and Senggigi for around 35,000Rp per day.

It's important to have an International Driving Licence – your rental agency may not request it, but police checks have become far more common in recent years, and you can expect a fine if you don't possess one.

Check your insurance arrangements carefully. Some small places do not offer any form of cover at all, and other agencies will only offer very basic cover – another good reason for hiring a car with a driver.

Bringing a vehicle from Bali is not very straightforward any more due to new insurance regulations. It is better to proceed to Lombok and arrange a rental in Senggigi.

If you'd rather someone else did the driving, contact **Ido Ado Dalmin** (☎ 0813-3956-2129), a reliable driver-guide who speaks fair English. He charges around 350,000Rp per day for a 4WD car (including petrol) and his services.

TOURIST SHUTTLE BUS

Lombok's main tourist centres are linked by a shuttle bus service. There's a two-person minimum for the bus to run. Currently, this service only links Mataram with Kuta, Senggigi, Bangsal and Tetebatu – so you can't travel from Kuta to Bangsal without changing shuttle buses in Mataram, but you can normally connect on the same day. From Senggigi there are also shuttle boats to the Gili Islands. **Perama** (www.peramatour.com) is the most established operator, with the widest network.

MATARAM

☎ 0370 / pop 320,000

The capital, and main city on Lombok is Mataram, although it's actually a conglomeration of several towns – Ampenan (port); Mataram (administrative centre); Cakranegara (business centre), which is often shortened to 'Cakra'; and Bertais-Sweta to the east, home to the bus terminal. It's not an unattractive city and it has some broad tree-lined avenues, but, as sights are thin on the ground and there are beaches close by at Senggigi, very few travellers choose to stay here.

Orientation

The four towns are spread along one main road that starts as Jl Pabean in Ampenan, quickly becomes Jl Yos Sudarso, then changes to Jl Langko, then Jl Pejanggik and finally travels through Sweta to Bertais as Jl Selaparang. It's a one-way street all the way, running west to east. A parallel one-way road, Jl Tumpang Sari–Jl Panca Usaha–Jl Pancawarga–Jl Caturwarga–Jl Pendidikan, brings traffic back towards the coast.

Information

EMERGENCY

Police station (☎ 631225; Jl Langko) In an emergency, dial ☎ 110.

Rumah Sakit Umum (☎ 622254; Jl Pejanggik 6; 8am-noon special service for tourists) The best hospital in Lombok and has English-speaking doctors.

IMMIGRATION

Kantor Imigrasi (☎ 632520; Jl Udayana 2; 7am-2pm Mon-Thu, to 11am Fri, to 12.30pm Sat)

INTERNET ACCESS

Most cybercafés are in the streets around Mataram Mall.

Deddy's (Mataram Mall; per hr 6000Rp; 9am-9pm)

MONEY

You'll find plenty of banks with ATMs scattered along Cakra's main drag; most of them will change cash and travellers cheques. Mataram Mall and the airport also have ATMs and moneychangers (which open longer than the banks).

POST

Main post office (Jl Sriwijaya 37, Mataram) Inconveniently located, but has internet and poste restante services.

Sub-post office (Jl Langko, Ampenan) Near the Nitour Hotel.

TELEPHONE

There are wartel on Jl Pejanggik and at the airport.

Telkom (☎ 633333; Jl Pendidikan 23, Mataram; 24hr) Offers phone and fax services.

TOURIST INFORMATION

West Lombok tourist office (☎ 621658; Jl Suprapto 20; 7.30am-2pm Mon-Thu, to 11am Fri, 8am-1pm Sat) Has some maps and leaflets, but it's not a particularly informative office.

West Nusa Tenggara tourist office (☎ 634800; Jl Singosari 2; 8am-2pm Mon-Thu, to 11am Fri, to 12.30pm Sat) Offers limited information on Lombok, but has better details and maps about Sumbawa.

Sights

MUSEUM NEGERI NUSA TENGGARA BARAT

This modern **museum** (☎ 632519; Jl Panji Tilar Negara 6; admission 1500Rp; 8am-2pm Tue-Thu & Sat & Sun, to 11am Fri) has exhibits on the geology, history and culture of Lombok and Sumbawa. If you intend to buy antiques or handicrafts, take a look at the kris, *songket* (silver- or gold-threaded cloth), basketware and masks for comparison.

MAYURA WATER PALACE

Built in 1744 this **palace** (Jl Selaparang; admission if requested 1000Rp; 7am-7.30pm) was once part of the Balinese kingdom's royal court in Lombok. It's a pleasant retreat, popular with fishermen (for its lake) and families, but in 1894 it was the site of bloody battles between the Dutch and Balinese. The complex contains a large artificial lake, with a modest replica of a *bale kambang* (floating pavilion) in its centre. The original pavilion was a court of justice.

The entrance to the walled enclosure of the palace is on the western side, just off Jl Selaparang.

PURA MERU

Opposite the water palace, this **temple** (admission by donation; 8am-5pm) is the largest in Lombok. Built in 1720 by a Balinese prince in an attempt to unite Lombok, it's

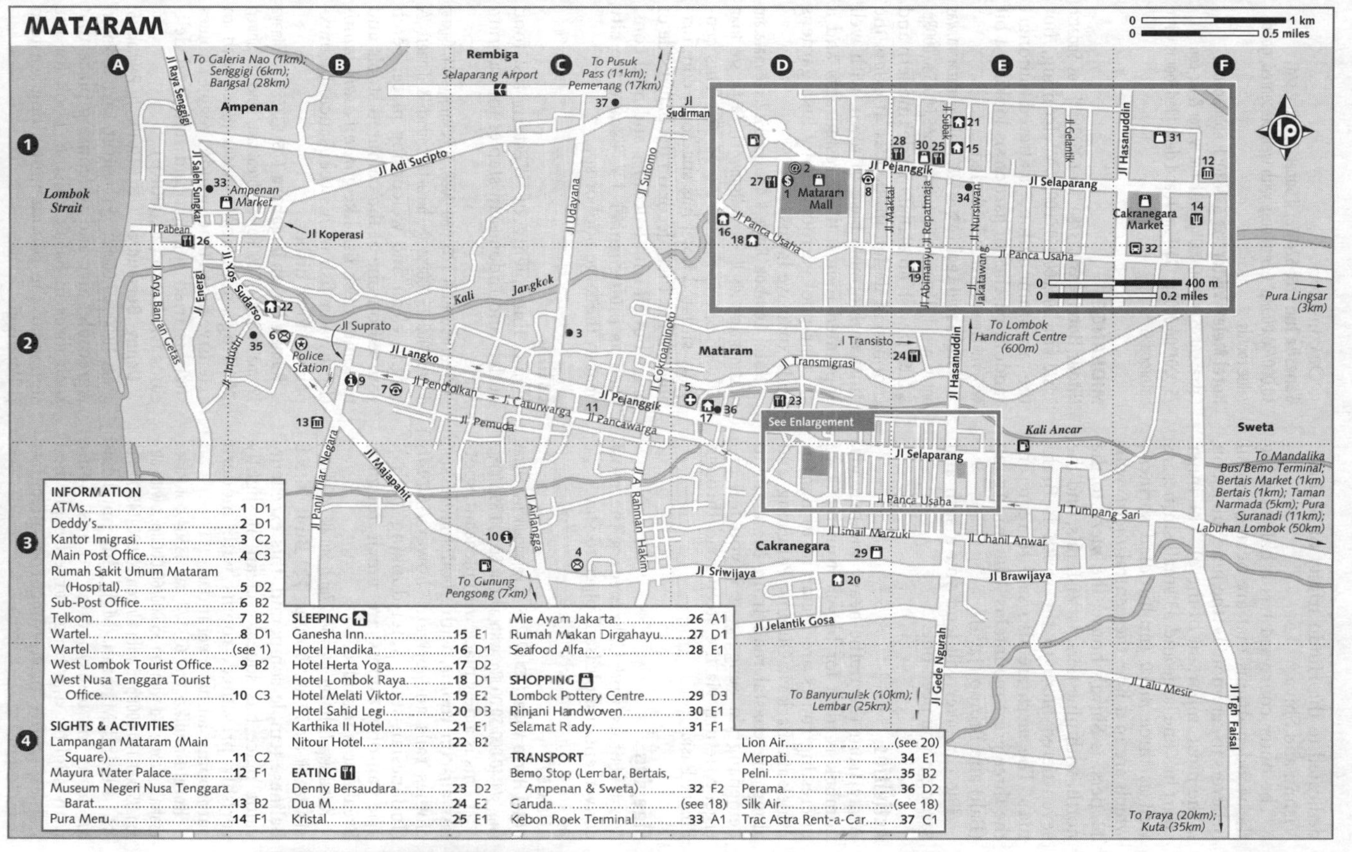

NUSA TENGGARA

dedicated to the Hindu trinity of Brahma, Vishnu and Shiva.

The outer courtyard has a hall housing the wooden drums that are beaten to call believers to ceremonies (the June full moon is the most important of these). The inner court has one large and 33 small shrines, as well as three *meru* (multiroofed shrines), which are in a line: the central *meru*, with 11 tiers, is Shiva's house; the *meru* to the north, with nine tiers, is Vishnu's; and the seven-tiered *meru* to the south is Brahma's. The *meru* are also said to represent the three great mountains: Rinjani, Agung (Bali) and Bromo (Java).

The caretaker will lend you a sash and sarong if you need one.

Activities

Away from the traffic-heavy main roads, Lombok is ideal for bicycle touring. Two interesting routes are Mataram to Banyumulek and back via Gunung Pengsong, and along the coastal road from Mataram to Pemenang via Senggigi – if you feel energetic, return via the steep road through Pusuk Pass.

Sleeping

Most visitors find Cakranegara the most convenient and pleasant place to stay.

BUDGET

Hotel Herta Yoga (☎ 621775; Jl Pejanggik 64, Mataram; s/d 40,000/50,000Rp, with air-con 80,000/85,000Rp; ❄) This is a new place with pleasant, spotless air-con rooms, with good mattresses, clothes rails and private showers/*mandis* (Indonesian-style water-dunking baths). The fan-only rooms are much rougher. Breakfast is included.

Karthika II Hotel (☎ 641776; Jl Subak 1, Cakra; r with fan/air-con 70,000/90,000Rp; ❄) Built like a Balinese temple compound, this excellent-value place has squeaky clean, if slightly garishly presented, rooms with modern bathrooms; all have verandas.

Hotel Handika (☎ 633578; fax 635049; Jl Panca Usaha 3, Cakra; s/d with fan 55,000/60,000Rp, s with air-con 85,000-130,000Rp, d with air-con 95,000-145,000Rp; ❄) Behind Mataram Mall, this hotel has an array of idiosyncratic rooms, some with slightly alarming carved-eagle bed frames, in five price categories. Breakfast is included.

Or consider:

Ganesha Inn (☎ 624878; Jl Subak 2, Cakra; s/d 30,000/40,000Rp) Guesthouse with well-presented, good-value rooms.

Hotel Melati Viktor (☎ 633830; Jl Abimanyu 1, Cakra; s/d 45,000/50,000Rp, with hot water & air-con 75,000/100,000Rp; ❄) Smart and clean tiled rooms with bathrooms.

MIDRANGE

Nitour Hotel (☎ 623780; fax 625328; Jl Yos Sudarso 4; s/d from 200,000/250,000Rp) Welcoming, but the accommodation, scattered amongst random patches of garden, is looking a bit worn. Breakfast is included.

Hotel Sahid Legi (☎ 636282; sahid@mataram.wasantara.net.id; Jl Sriwijaya 81; r/deluxe r 365,000/580,000Rp; ❄ 🏊) Swish hotel that marries modern and Indonesian design influences. It offers the most comfortable base in town, with well appointed rooms, three restaurants and a circular pool surrounded by lush gardens and expansive lawns.

Hotel Lombok Raya (☎ 632305; lora@mataram.wasantara.net.id; Jl Panca Usaha 11, Cakra; s/d from 390,000/525,000Rp plus 21% tax; ❄ 🏊) This centrally situated hotel has spacious, comfortable rooms, their décor on the bland side of beige but all with balconies and mod cons, such as multichannel TV. Escape the city heat in the large pool or spa.

Eating

You'll find plenty of Western fast-food outlets and Indonesian staples in Mataram Mall.

Seafood Alfa (☎ 660-0088; Jl Pejanggik 34, Cakra; dishes 8000-25,000Rp; 🕒 breakfast, lunch & dinner) A bright, clean and welcoming place; perch yourself on one of the coloured stools and tuck into fresh fish like *gurami asam manis* (freshwater fish with sweet sauce) or inexpensive local dishes.

Rumah Makan Dirgahayu (☎ 637559; Jl Cilinaya 19; mains 8000-30,000Rp; 🕒 breakfast, lunch & dinner; ❄) Huge, popular Makassar place with an extensive menu that includes veggie choices such as fried spinach and tofu, and delicious fried carp (20,000Rp).

Denny Bersaudra (☎ 633619; Jl Pelikan 6; dishes 10,000-27,000Rp; 🕒 breakfast, lunch & dinner) Agreeable, airy and welcoming place that specialises in Sasak cuisine. Look for the sign near the roundabout along western Jl Pejanggik.

Dua M (☎ 622914; Jl Transisto 99, Mataram; dishes 12,500-20,000Rp; ⏰ breakfast, lunch & dinner) Authentic Sasak food, including terrific *ayam goreng Taliwang* (Sumbawa-style spicy chicken). Try to bag the low table facing the garden and pond.

Other recommendations:

Kristal (☎ 627564; Jl Pejanggik 22, Cakra; dishes 6000-20,000Rp; ⏰ breakfast, lunch & dinner) Head here for Chinese cuisine and seafood.

Mie Ayam Jakarta (Jl Pabean; dishes 5000-12,000Rp; ⏰ breakfast, lunch & dinner) Scores for tasty, inexpensive Javanese food.

Shopping

For handicrafts try the many stores on Jl Raya Senggigi, the road heading north from Ampenan. At Sayang Sayang (2km north of Cakra) the Lombok Handicraft Centre has a wide range of crafts from across Lombok and Nusa Tenggara.

Galeria Nao (☎ 626835; Jl Raya Senggigi 234, Menintinq) Beautifully finished contemporary wooden furniture and artefacts that wouldn't look out of place in *Wallpaper* magazine.

Lombok Pottery Centre (☎ 640351; Jl Sriwijaya 111, Cakra) Offers a vast range of Lombok pottery, and prices here can be reasonably competitive.

Rinjani Handwoven (☎ 633169; Jl Pejanggik 44) You can see weavers in action at this workshop and buy their handiwork.

Selamat Riady (☎ 631196; Jl Tanun 10) Offers textiles, including ikat from Lombok, Flores and Sumba, and a few other crafts.

Getting There & Away

The sprawling, dusty Mandalika bus terminal in Bertais is the main bus and bemo terminal for the entire island and also for long-distance buses to Sumbawa, Bali and Java (see p487).

The terminal is fairly chaotic, so be sure to keep a level head to avoid the 'help' of the commission-happy touts. Long-distance buses leave from behind the main terminal building, while bemos and smaller buses leave from one of two car parks on either side.

Kebon Roek terminal in Ampenan has a bemo to Bertais (1500Rp) and services to Senggigi (3000Rp).

Perama (☎ 635928; www.peramatour.com; Jl Pejanggik 66) operates shuttle buses to popular destinations in Lombok (including Bangsal, Kuta and Tetebatu) and to Bali.

Getting Around

TO/FROM THE AIRPORT

Lombok's Selaparang airport is on the northern side of the city 5km from Cakra. A taxi desk sells prepaid tickets: 17,500Rp to anywhere in Mataram, 48,000Rp to Senggigi, 98,000Rp to Bangsal and Lembar, and 145,000Rp to Kuta. Alternatively, walk out of the airport to Jl Adi Sucipto and take one of the number seven bemos that run frequently to Ampenan.

BEMO

Mataram is *very* spread out, so don't plan on walking from place to place. Yellow bemos constantly shuttle between Kebon Roek terminal in Ampenan and Mandalika terminal in Bertais (10km away). These terminals are good places to charter bemos. Outside the market in Cakra is a handy bemo stop for services to Bertais, Ampenan, Sweta and Lembar. The standard fare is 1500Rp.

CAR & MOTORCYCLE

Most hotels can arrange rentals, but you'll almost certainly find a much better deal in Senggigi. Six hours' hire of a Toyota Kijang, including petrol and driver, is 425,000Rp through **Trac Astra Rent-a-Car** (☎ 626363; www.trac.astra.co.id; Jl Adi Sucipto 5, Rembiga Mataram). Self-drive costs 385,000Rp per day.

TAXI

For a metered taxi, call **Lombok Taksi** (☎ 627000).

AROUND MATARAM

☎ 0370

East of Mataram are some gorgeous areas with villages, rice fields and temples; they're reminiscent of some of the best landscapes and scenery that Bali has to offer.

Taman Narmada

Apparently designed as a scaled-down version of the summit of Gunung Rinjani and its crater lake, this **park** (Map pp490-1; admission 5000Rp; ⏰ 7am-6pm) was built in 1805. Though the rectangular main pool and manicured terraced gardens hardly look like a volcanic cone, the extensive grounds are a pleasant enough place to spend an hour or two (except perhaps on Sunday, when it gets packed). The temple, **Pura Kalasa**, is still in use, and the Balinese Pujawali celebration is held here every year (in November or December) in honour of the god Batara, who is said to dwell on Gunung Rinjani. There's also a large swimming pool (2000Rp extra) in the grounds.

Narmada is 6km east of Bertais, 100m south of Lombok's main east–west highway. Frequent bemos from Mandalika run to Narmada market, which is directly opposite the entrance to the gardens.

Pura Lingsar

This large **temple compound** (Map pp490-1; donation requested; 7am-6pm), built in 1714, is the holiest in Lombok. It combines the Bali Hindu and Wektu Telu religions in one complex. The compound was designed in two separate sections and built on two different levels: the Hindu temple in the northern half is higher than the Wektu Telu temple in the southern section.

The Wektu Telu temple is noted for its small enclosed pond devoted to Lord Vishnu and for the holy eels that can be enticed from their hiding places with hard-boiled eggs (available at stalls outside). You will be expected to rent a sash and/or sarong (or bring your own) to enter the temple, but not to enter the outer buildings.

A huge ritual battle, Perang Topat, is held here every year in mid-December. After a costumed parade, Hindus and Wektu pelt each other with *ketupat* (sticky rice in coconut leaves).

Pura Lingsar is 9km northeast of Mandalika. Take a bemo from the terminal to Narmada (2000Rp) and then another to Lingsar (2000Rp). Ask to be dropped off near the entrance to the temple complex, which is 300m down a well-marked path from the main road.

Pura Surandi

Set amidst gorgeous countryside, this **Hindu temple** (Map pp490-1; donation requested; 7.30am-6pm) is one of the holiest in Lombok. It's worth a visit for its lovely gardens, which have a bubbling, icy cold natural spring and restored baths with ornate Balinese carvings (plus the obligatory holy eels).

Just above the temple, **Losmen Jati** (☎ 6606437; r 30,000Rp) is a friendly and well-kept place, while the once-wonderful colonial atmosphere of the **Suranadi Hotel** (☎ 636411; fax 635630; r from 195,000Rp;) still has some faded charm, as well as a pool and tennis courts.

Several smart restaurants are dotted along the main road close to the temple, and there are plenty of cheap warungs in the neighbouring village of Suranadi.
The temple is 6km northwest of Narmada and served by frequent public bemos. Failing that, charter one.

Sesaot & Around

Some 4km northeast of Suranadi is Sesaot, a charming market town on the edge of a forest. There are some gorgeous picnic spots and you can swim in the river. The water is very cool and is considered holy, as it comes straight from Gunung Rinjani. There is regular transport from Narmada, and bites are available at the warungs along the main street.

Just further east, **Air Nyet** is another pretty village, with more options for swimming and picnics. Ask for directions for the unsigned turn-off in the middle of Sesaot. The bridge and road to Air Nyet are rough, but it's a lovely stroll (about 3km) from Sesaot; otherwise, charter a vehicle from Sesaot or Narmada.

Gunung Pengsong

This Balinese hilltop **temple** (Map pp490-1; admission by donation; 7am-6pm), 9km south of Mataram, has spectacular views across a green ocean of rice fields towards distant volcanoes and the sea. Japanese soldiers hid here towards the end of WWII, and remnants of cannons can be found, as well as plenty of pesky monkeys. It's a 15-minute walk up to the top of the temple complex from the entrance. Very little direct public transport comes here, so it's best visited with your own wheels.

Banyumulek

This is one of the main **pottery centres** in Lombok, specialising in decorated pots and pots with a woven fibre covering, as well as more traditional urns and water flasks. It's close to Mataram: head south of Sweta on the main road to Lembar, and after 6km take the turn-off on the right to Banyumulek, a couple of kilometres to the west.

LEMBAR & THE SOUTHWESTERN PENINSULA

Lembar

☎ 0370

Lombok's main port for Bali and Pelni ships is Lembar. Though the harbour itself, with azure inlets ringed by soaring green hills, has to be one of Indonesia's most beautiful, there's no reason to stay the night here given the transport connections with Mataram and Senggigi. But if you do somehow get stuck or need a bite to eat, the clean and very hospitable **Losmen Tidar** (☎ 681444; Jl Raya Pelabuhan; s/d with bathroom from 40,000Rp) 1km north of the ferry port is an excellent deal. It has neat rooms and cottages, one with its very own fish pond, and offers very hearty Indonesian meals (dishes from 8000Rp to 17000Rp). The rate includes breakfast.

Plenty of bemos shuttle between Lembar and the Mandalika terminal in Bertais (3500Rp), or you can catch one at the market stop in Cakra. See p491 for details of ferries and boats between Bali and Lembar.

Southwestern Peninsula

☎ 0370

The corrugated, beach-blessed coastline and tiny offshore islands west of Sekotong have long been hyped as Lombok's next big tourism destination, but while the odd pocket of development is ongoing here, for now it remains a tranquil, highly scenic region. The hump-shaped inland hills form rich pastureland in the rainy season; visit the area at this time and you'll hear cowbells clanking. The road that hugs the coast, passing white sandy coves, is narrow but sealed until Selegang. A track continues to the west past Bangko Bangko to Tanjung Desert, one of Asia's legendary surf breaks. There's no accommodation at Desert Point, so you'll need to bring camping gear.

Only a few of the beautiful offshore islands, fringed with coconut palm–studded sandy beaches and offering fine snorkelling, are inhabited. Currently, Gili Nanggu and Gili Gede have accommodation. The latter island has some Bugis villages, where locals make a living from boat building, and also some offshore pearl farms.

SLEEPING & EATING

Places to stay and restaurants are thin on the ground in this region, and some close in the rainy season. At the time of research, **Sundancer** (www.sundancerresort.com), a huge new hotel and resort with a PADI diving centre, was due to open in late 2006 just west of Pandanan.

Mainland

Putri Doyang (☎ 081 23752459; Jl Raya Pelangangi, Tembowong; s/d 25,000/50,000Rp) Simple, clean rooms and hospitable owners make this losmen, 2km north of Pelangan, a budget option worth considering.

Sekotong Indah Beach Cottages (☎ 6601921; r without/with air-con 55,000/85,000Rp; ❄) Basic, tiled and cleanish rooms with a great location opposite a sandy beach 2km west of Taun. There's also a restaurant (dishes 5000Rp to 20,000Rp; open breakfast, lunch and dinner).

Bola Bola Paradis (☎ 623783; batuapi99@hotmail.com; Jl Raya Bangko-Bangko; r 160,000-280,000Rp; ❄) Just west of Pelangan, this attractive place set on a fine stretch of sand has funky octagonal bungalows and comfortable air-con rooms. There is also a good restaurant (mains 20,000Rp to 55,000Rp; open breakfast, lunch and dinner) and a chic lounge area.

Nirvana Roemah Air (☎ 640107; www.lombokandbeyond.com/lombokhotels/nirvana.html; Jl Raya Medang, Sekotong Barat; villas US$150-250; ❄) Billing itself as a floating island resort, this luxurious place in a secluded mangrove-fringed location has stylish wood-panelled villas. Book online for substantial discounts in the quiet season. Prices include airport transfers.

Islands

Gili Nanggu Cottages (☎ 623783; www.gilinangu.com; cottages s/d 100,000/120,000Rp, bungalows 225,000/275,000Rp; ❄) A great choice, this island resort has a beachfront location and rustic two-storey *lumbung* (rice barn) cottages, plus less attractive but comfortable air-con bungalows. There is also a decent seafood restaurant (dishes 16,000Rp to 27,000Rp; open breakfast, lunch and dinner) here. Lifts from Lembar can also be organised.

Secret Island Resort (☎ 6613579; www.secretislandresort.com; r 200,000Rp, bungalows 250,000Rp, two bedroom villas 1,000,000Rp; ❄) This new resort on Gili Gede offers spacious, modern accommodation with CD players and fridges. All rooms have terraces and fine sea or mountain views. The bar-restaurant rustles up great seafood and barbecued meats. Check out the hot tub, and a spa, plunge pool and pool are planned. Kayak, snorkel and dive trips can be arranged.

GETTING THERE & AWAY

Bemos buzz between Lembar and Pelangan (1¾ hours, every 30 minutes) via Sekotong (25 minutes). West of Pelengan transport is less regular, but the route is still served by infrequent bemos until Selegang.

To reach Gili Nanggu, a return charter on a *prahu* (outrigger fishing boat) from Tuan costs 150,000Rp. Public boats connect Tembowong with Gili Gede and Gili Ringit (both 8,000Rp one way), leaving from Putri Doyong losmen, 2km north of Pelangan. Alternatively, you can charter boats here for about 60,000Rp one way or arrange a day trip around the islands for about 225,000Rp.

SENGGIGI

☎ 0370

Superbly positioned along a stretch of sweeping bays, Senggigi is Lombok's principal beach resort. Accommodation here is generally excellent value for money, as luxury hotels have slashed rates in an attempt to draw in tourists following several tough years. Unless you visit in peak season, expect quiet restaurants and empty shopping malls but plenty of attention from the street hawkers.

Senggigi has fine sandy beaches, and as the sun sinks all eyes turn west to take in the blood-red sunsets over Bali that can be enjoyed from one of the seafront restaurants. As it gets dark, the fishing fleet lines up offshore, its bright lanterns glinting like a floating village against the night sky.

North of Senggigi there is a succession of wonderful, near-deserted coves, where you can pretty much guarantee to have a beach to yourself, bar the odd fisherman and his net.

Orientation

The Senggigi area spans about 10km of coastal road. Most of the shops and other facilities, and a fair concentration of hotels, are on the main road, Jl Raya Senggigi,

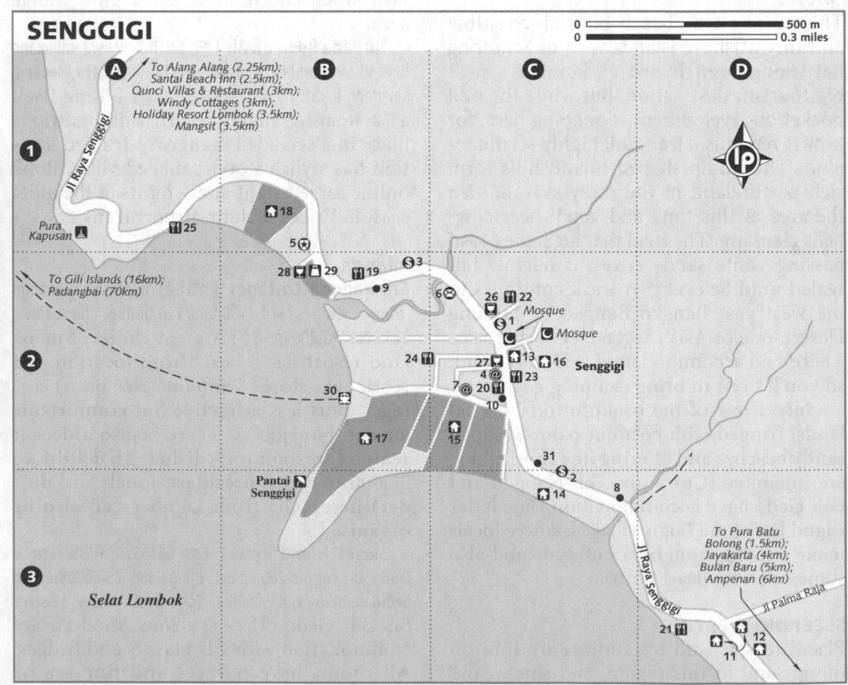

which starts about 6km north of Ampenan. Street numbers are not used.

Information

EMERGENCY

The nearest hospitals are in Mataram.

Police station (☎ 110) Next to the Pasar Seni (Art Market).

Senggigi Medical Clinic (☎ 693856) Based at the Senggigi Beach Hotel.

Tourist Police (☎ 632733)

INTERNET ACCESS & TELEPHONES

Most internet cafés on the main strip also double as wartels.

Millennium Internet Café (☎ 693860; Jl Raya Senggigi; per min 300Rp; 🕑 24hr)

Superstar (Senggigi Plaza A2; per min 300Rp; 🕑 24hr)

MONEY

There are several ATMs in central Senggigi. Bank Central Asia (BCA) and Bank Negara Indonesia (BNI) have branches on Jl Raya Senggigi where you can change cash and travellers cheques.

POST

Post office (Jl Raya Senggigi)

Sights

PURA BATU BOLONG

The small pagodas of this modest Balinese **temple** (admission by donation; 🕑 7am-7pm) cling to a rocky volcanic outcrop that juts into the sea about 2km south of central Senggigi. Crabs scuttle over statues, and families come here to snack and cool off at the beach below. It's oriented towards Gunung Agung, Bali's holiest mountain, and is a favoured spot to watch sunsets. The rock underneath the temple has a natural hole that gives it its name – *batu bolong* (literally, 'rock with hole'). For temple etiquette, see the boxed text, p489.

Activities

There's reasonable snorkelling off the point in Senggigi, in the sheltered bay around the headland, and in front of Windy Cottages, a few kilometres north of town. You can hire snorkelling gear (25,000Rp per day) from several spots along the beach near Senggigi Beach Hotel.

Diving trips from Senggigi normally visit the Gili Islands, so you may want to consider basing yourself there. Professional dive centres:

Blue Marlin Dive Centre (☎ 692003; www.dive-indo.com; Jl Raya Senggigi & Holiday Resort Lombok)

Dive Indonesia (☎ 639367; www.diveindonesiaonline.com; Galeria Mall, Jl Raya Senggigi)

Dream Divers (☎ 692047; www.dreamdivers.com; Jl Raya Senggigi)

If you're thinking of hiking Gunung Rinjani, you could drop by the local office of the **Rinjani Trek Club** (☎ 693202; rtc.senqqiqi@qmail.com; Jl Raya Senggigi) for information about routes and conditions.

INFORMATION		
BCA ATM	1	C2
BCA ATM	2	C3
BNI ATM	3	B2
Millennium Internet Café	4	C2
Police Station	5	B1
Post Office	6	C2
Senggigi Medical Clinic	(see 17)	
Superstar	7	C2
SIGHTS & ACTIVITIES		
Blue Marlin Dive Centre	8	C3
Dive Indonesia	9	B2
Dream Divers	10	C2
Rinjani Trek Club	(see 20)	
SLEEPING		
Batu Bolong Cottages	11	D3
Café Wayan	12	D3
Hotel Elen	13	C2
Lina Cottages	14	C3
Mascot Cottages	15	C2
Raja's Bungalows	16	C2
Senggigi Beach Hotel	17	B2
Sheraton Senggigi Beach Resort	18	B1
EATING		
Asmara	19	B2
Bumbu	20	C2
Café Alberto	21	D3
Cafe Wayan	(see 12)	
English Tea Room	22	C2
Papaya Café	23	C2
Sugar Café	24	B2
Warung	25	A1
DRINKING		
Club Tropicana	26	C2
Happy Café	27	C2
Office	28	B2
Papaya Café	(see 23)	
Sugar Café	(see 24)	
SHOPPING		
Asmara Collection	(see 19)	
Pasar Seni	29	B2
TRANSPORT		
Departure Point For Perama Boats	30	B2
Kotasi	(see 13)	
Perama	31	C2

Sleeping

Virtually everything is located on or just off the main drag, Jl Raya Senggigi.

BUDGET

Senggigi

Hotel Elen (☎ 693014; r without/with air-con 50,000/75,000Rp; ❄) A quadrangle of cheap if not very cheerful rooms. Prime yourself for an early morning wake-up call from the two very local mosques.

Raja's Bungalows (☎ 081 23770138; rajas22@yahoo.com; s/d 60,000/75,000Rp) A welcoming, bohemian guesthouse that's popular with travellers, Raja's has inviting, spotless rooms with high ceilings, bamboo furniture and zany outdoor bathrooms – this place has bathrooms with both *mandis* and showers. There's plenty of communal chilling space too.

Lina Cottages (☎ 693237; r with fan/air-con/sea view 60,000/75,000/150,000Rp; ❄) Occupying pole position right on the beach, Lina's is a good choice with a variety of rooms, the cheapies on the small side and fan only. There's an adjoining Indo-Chinese restaurant.

Café Wayan (☎ 693098; s/d incl breakfast 100,000/150,000Rp) At the rear of the café, these four stylish rooms, tastefully furnished with beautiful ikat fabrics and Balinese artefacts and with large bathtubs, enjoy a peaceful location overlooking a blossom-filled garden.

Mangsit

Santai Beach Inn (☎ 693038; www.santaibeachinn.com; lumbung s/d incl breakfast 70,000/80,000Rp, bungalows 95,000-200,000Rp) Set in a lush garden by the beach, this unusual place has a selection of rustic *lumbung* and spacious bungalows, constructed from local wood and bamboo. Inexpensive, healthy veggie and fish dishes (15,000/25,000Rp lunch/dinner) are eaten communally in a pleasant pavilion, and there's a book exchange.

Windy Cottages (☎ 693191; lidya@mataram.wasantara.net.id; cottages with cold/hot water 110,000/150,000Rp, r 140,000Rp; ❄) Charming, popular beachside place with decent snorkelling offshore (you can hire gear here for 15,000Rp per day). The attractive thatched cottages have verandas, many with sea views. Also has some air-con rooms and a restaurant (dishes 14,000Rp to 30,000Rp).

Bulan Baru (New Moon Hotel; ☎ 693786; r incl breakfast 200,000Rp; ❄ 🏊) Set in a lovely garden and a short walk from a fine sandy beach, this welcoming hotel has spacious, well-furnished rooms, all with minibars, air-con and bathrooms with hot water. The friendly Australian owners, and staff, are a mine of information about Lombok and local culture. Children aren't allowed.

MIDRANGE

Senggigi

Batu Bolong Cottages (☎ 693065; bbcresort_lombok@yahoo.com; inland/beachside bungalows 125,000/260,000Rp; ❄) This place has good-value, spacious rooms with fridges facing a lawned beachfront plot, with the waves just beyond. Its cheaper digs are looking a little tired, however. Breakfast is included.

Mascot Cottages (☎ 693365; fax 693236; bungalows s/d 200,000/275,000Rp; ❄) Undergoing renovation at the time of research, this place has air-con bungalows set in a garden that extends towards the beach.

Jayakarta (☎ 693048; www.indo.com/hotels/jayakartalombok; r US$38-43, ste from US$63; ❄ 🏊) This Indonesian chain hotel, in a beachfront setting 5km south of central Senggigi, offers competitive rates on its comfortable air-con rooms with sea views. There's also a large pool.

Mangsit

Holiday Resort Lombok (☎ 693444; fax 693092; holiday resort lombok; Jl Raya Senggigi; r from US$68, bungalows from US$140; ❄ 🏊) A well-designed luxury hotel with the full gamut of accommodation options, from rooms to large private bungalows. Also has a fine spa and scuba school, and a playground and day nursery for children aged two to 11.

TOP END

Senggigi and Mangsit have an excess of luxury hotels, so discounts on the rack rates listed here are usually available.

Senggigi

Senggigi Beach Hotel (☎ 693210; www.senggigibeach.aerowisata.com; r US$97, beach bungalows US$121-194 plus 21% tax; ❄ 🏊) These classy detached bungalows with spacious, comfortable rooms enjoy a beautiful setting in lush gardens set back from the beach, though only 105 and 106 have uninterrupted sea views. There's a large pool, a spa and tennis courts in the complex.

Sheraton Senggigi Hotel (☎ 693333; www.sheraton.com; r from US$178) Just north of the centre, this fine hotel has commodious rooms, most with timber floors, huge beds and decorative textiles, and a well-regarded spa and health club. Discounts can drop rates to around US$80 a night.

Mangsit

our pick Qunci Villas (☎ 693800; www.quncivillas.com; garden/ocean-view r US$85/109 plus 21% tax;) Lombok's hippest hotel, combining textbook minimalist design with Balinese and Japanese influence. The rooms are undeniably gorgeous (book room eight for the best sea view) and popular with moneyed Europeans and rich kids from Jakarta. There is a small pool at the ocean's edge and a very fine restaurant (see right). You'll find the staff are extremely well trained and welcoming. For the seriously wealthy, up in the hills behind the hotel are two villas (from US$325 a night) that come close to defining Lombok luxe.

Alang Alang (☎ 693518; www.alang-alang-villas.com; s/d bungalows US$80/110) Stylish bungalows, most are semidetached with commodious beds and Balinese wood furniture, but only bungalows 101 to 110 have decent sea views. The beach here consists of a narrow stretch of sand, and the pool is small.

Eating

Central Senggigi is an excellent place to eat out, there being a glut of cosmopolitan restaurants. Many offer free transport for evening diners – phone for a ride.

For authentic Indonesian street food, head to the hillside warungs on the route north to Mangsit, where sate sizzles and pots of noodles bubble.

SENGGIGI

Café Wayan (☎ 693098; dishes 9000-45,000Rp) Stylish Balinese-run place with an extensive menu of soups and salads, pizza, pasta dishes, seafood, and yummy freshly baked breads and cakes.

Bumbu (☎ 692236; mains 18,000-30,000Rp) Deservedly popular little restaurant on the main strip, come here for inexpensive Thai curries and Indo cooking served up on a narrow terrace. There's always a daily special.

Sugar Café (☎ 6194000; Plaza Senggigi; mains 22,000-44,000Rp;) Perhaps the most modern place in town, this chic little lounge bar-resto is highly atmospheric, with candlelit tables and creative, beautifully presented Indonesian and Asian fusion cuisine.

English Tea Room (☎ 692085; Blok A4, Senggigi Sq; dishes 21,000-65,000Rp; breakfast, lunch & dinner;) A civilised air-con retreat, this delightful place, located in a shopping plaza, offers a wide choice of salads and sandwiches as well as terrific cakes. The teas include Ceylon and Indonesian green and you'll find some interesting coffees too. There's a terrace table upstairs.

Papaya Café (☎ 693616; mains 28,000-50,000Rp;) Invitingly decorated, with rattan sofas and exposed stone walls, this enjoyable place has a tempting menu of Indonesian, Chinese and Japanese dishes and some of the best cocktails in town.

Café Alberto (☎ 693313; mains 30,000-85,000Rp) Occupying a large beachfront plot away from the road, feast on Italian (pizza and pasta) or Indonesian cuisine (the usual suspects in generous portions) at this enjoyable restaurant. Lunch at a table on the sand and then snooze it off on one of the sunloungers.

Asmara (☎ 693619; www.asmara-group.com; mains 18,000-75,000Rp;) Consistently recommended by expats, this comfortable, spacious and airy two-storey thatched restaurant offers fine European cuisine (try the Mediterranean herb-crusted fish fillet) plus Indonesian and international favourites. Children are well catered for, and there's a small pool and play area.

MANGSIT

Bulan Baru (☎ 693786; mains 24,000-48,000Rp) Head to this hotel restaurant for comfort food – think meaty bangers and creamy mash, or a juicy imported steak.

Qunci (☎ 693800; www.quncivillas.com; mains 46,000-64,000Rp) Abutting the beach, this terrific hotel restaurant (see left) has a modern menu with both Asian and European – think tuna balsamico and seafood risotto – dishes. Arrive before sunset and get the party started with two-for-one cocktails during happy hour (4pm to 7pm).

Drinking & Entertainment

Senggigi's after-dark action is pretty middle of the road, revolving around a handful of bars and a disco or two. All bars are on Jl

Raya Senggigi except one, and they close around 1am, or earlier if it's very quiet.

Happy Café (☎ 693984) This slightly staid but popular bar has a resident cover band playing reggae or pop tunes.

Papaya Café (☎ 693616) It's hardly cutting edge, but the Papaya also has live music of the *muzak* variety every night and is fine for a relaxed drink. Happy hour is from 4pm to 8pm.

Office (☎ 693162) Beachside bar with fine sunset views, a pool table and live sports events on the TV. Office is popular with middle-aged expats.

Sugar Café (☎ 081 23962206; Senggigi Plaza) Hip place with electronica and lounge music and a mixed gay and straight clientele. Also serves fine food.

Club Tropicana (☎ 693432; admission 25,000Rp; 11pm-2am) Old skool-style disco with slightly cheesy DJs.

Shopping

Senggigi's shopping malls are woefully under-occupied – many stores are vacant. The Pasar Seni (Art Market) has some handicraft stalls, and **Asmara Collection** (☎ 693619; Jl Raya Senggigi), in front of the restaurant, has fine weavings, tribal art and furniture.

The warehouses and craft shops along the main road to Ampenan are also worth a look.

Getting There & Away

BOAT

Perama (☎ 693007; Jl Raya Senggigi) operates a daily boat to the Gili Islands at 9am for 70,000Rp, which means you avoid having to deal with Bangsal. The dive schools (see p501) also operate speedboat shuttles (from 120,000Rp) to the Gilis most days; contact them in advance.

BUS

Regular bemos travel to Senggigi from the Kebon Roek terminal in Ampenan (3000Rp), some continuing north as far as Pemenang and Bayan. Overcharging tourists is common on this route.

Perama has several tourist shuttle bus and boat services daily between Senggigi and Bali, including Kuta, Bali/Bali airport (160,000Rp) and Ubud (160,000Rp), and other places within Lombok, including Tetebatu (80,000Rp) and Kuta (80,000Rp).

Getting Around

A prepaid taxi from the airport to Senggigi costs 48,000Rp. Very efficient and prompt **Bluebird taxis** (☎ 627000) will whisk you around the Senggigi area and beyond. Remember that many restaurants offer free lifts for diners; call for a ride.

Cars and motorcycles are readily available for hire in Senggigi; ask at any hotel or travel agent. **Kotasi** (☎ 693804; Jl Raya Senggigi) has motorcycles from 40,000Rp per day and jeeps from 175,000Rp per day (its insurance covers you for a maximum charge of US$500 in case of damage).

GILI ISLANDS

☎ 0370

Just off the northwestern coast of Lombok is a vision of tropical paradise – a trio of tiny coral-fringed islands, each with white sandy beaches and pellucid water teeming with a kaleidoscopic array of reef fish. For years the islands of Gili Air, Gili Meno and Gili Trawangan were a budget-priced stopover for travellers on the Asian trail, but in recent years accommodation options have diversified and now there are luxury villas and rustic-chic bungalows dotted between the simple bamboo-and-thatch huts for rent.

Delightfully free of cars and motorcycles, the Gilis are home to just the tinkling *cidomo* and the odd bicycle. Each island has professional scuba-diving centres, and the snorkelling is excellent too.

Each Gili has its own character and charm – Trawangan has a big party scene, Meno is very mellow and Air's atmosphere falls somewhere between the two. Note that, in most places in the Gili Islands, the water comes from wells and is a bit saline.

DANGERS & ANNOYANCES

There are no police on any of the Gilis, so report any theft to the island *kepala desa* (village head), or, if you are on Gili

> **GILI ISLANDS CURRENTS: WARNING**
>
> Currents between the Gili Islands are very strong. Take care when snorkelling offshore, and do not attempt to swim between the islands – this goes double after a night on the ale.

SURVIVING BANGSAL

Bangsal, a squalid little port, is the gateway for public boats to the Gilis. Frankly, it's a hole and has become so overrun with persistent small-time hustlers and would-be scammers that it's best to completely ignore anything that you're told here about boats being cancelled, or other tall tales. Keep calm, and head straight for the ramshackle boat terminal to get your ticket.

Public bemos to Bangsal actually stop in Pemenang on the main road, 1km from the port. Hiring a *cidamo* (around 3000Rp) to the port is money well spent as it'll save you an ear-bending from the hustlers on your way to the terminal.

It's quite possible to avoid Bangsal altogether by using the Perama boat service between Senggigi and the Gilis, or by booking a speedboat transfer (from US$12, 15 minutes) to/from Lombok via the Gili dive schools – these use the serene little bay of Teluk Nare to the south.

Trawangan, notify Satgas, the community organisation that runs island affairs via your hotel or dive centre. Satgas uses its community contacts to resolve problems or track down stolen property with a minimum of fuss.

Incidents are rare, but several foreign women have experienced sexual harassment and even assault while on the Gilis – it's best to walk home in pairs to the quieter parts of the islands. Each island has a gaggle of local gigolos who compete to impress and seduce visiting Western women, and they can get very territorial with other males that they see as competition.

Jellyfish are common when strong winds blow from the mainland, and they can leave a painful rash. See p885 for the best ways of treating jellyfish stings.

GETTING THERE & AWAY

From Bali, most people either use the Perama shuttle bus/boat service (185,000Rp, five hours from Padangbai), which now stops at all the Gili Islands before heading on to Senggigi, or fly to Mataram and travel on from there.

Coming from other parts of Lombok, you can travel via Senggigi (from where there is a direct Perama boat service to the Gilis) or Bangsal (the cheapest route). Alternatively, you can book a shuttle bus or speedboat: Blue Marlin and Manta Dive (p512) on Gili Trawangan can arrange transfers (125,000Rp to 250,000Rp per person, depending on destination and passenger numbers), which leave from the idyllic harbour of Teluk Nare, south of Bangsal.

Coming by public transport, catch a bus or bemo to Pemenang, from where it's about 1km by *cidomo* (3000Rp) to Bangsal harbour. Bangsal is a headache; see the boxed text, above for how best to deal with the inevitable hassle there. Boat tickets are sold at the Koperasi harbour office, where prices are displayed, but the public boats (roughly 8am to 5pm) don't leave until full (about 18 people). While it can take hours for the boat to Gili Meno to fill up, you shouldn't have to wait more than an hour for the other two islands. One-way fares are 5500Rp to Gili Air, 6800Rp to Gili Meno and 8800Rp to Gili Trawangan. Special charters can also be organised in Bangsal.

All boats pull up on the beach when they get to the Gilis, so you'll have to wade ashore with your luggage.

Island-Hopping

There's a twice-daily boat service that loops between all three islands, meaning you can spend the day snorkelling and exploring Meno and get back to Air or Trawangan for a sunset drink.

The morning boat leaves Air at 8.30am, stops by Meno at 8.45am, Trawangan at 9.30am and Meno again at 9.45am, and returns to Air at 10am. In the afternoons the boat leaves Air at 3pm, Meno at 3.15pm, Trawangan at 3.30pm, Meno at 4.15pm (having stopped there for half an hour) and gets back to Air at 4.30pm. Check the latest timetable at the islands' dock.

GETTING AROUND

The Gilis are flat and easy enough to get around on foot or by bicycle. For longer trips, hiring a *cidomo* for a clip-clop around an island is a great way to explore the terrain; a short trip costs around 7000Rp, or pay about 20,000Rp for a two-hour jaunt.

Gili Air

pop 1800

Closest to the mainland, Gili Air's easy-going appeal contrasts with party-boy Gili Trawangan and sedate Gili Meno. The island retains a distinctly rural character, its coconut grove–filled, flat landscape juxtaposed with dramatic views of Gunung Rinjani and, on a clear day, Gunung Agung in Bali. Its narrow white-sand beaches, turquoise water and laid-back atmosphere are the main draw, but in the high season the bar scene can get quite lively.

ORIENTATION

Boats stop at the southern end of the island, near the jetty, and the **Koperasi harbour office** (⏲ 8am-5.30pm) has a hut here with prices marked clearly outside. Virtually all accommodation and restaurants are on the eastern and southern coasts, which have the best beaches for swimming. The network of dirt tracks that crisscrosses the island can get quite confusing at times. To explore Air it's simplest to follow the coastal path around the island – it's a lovely walk that takes about an hour and a half.

INFORMATION

There's a small **Perama office** (☎ 637816) close to the Gili Indah Hotel. **Ozzy's Shop** (☎ 622179; per min 400Rp; ⏲ 8am-8pm) has pedestrian-paced internet access and a wartel and will change money, as will Hotel Gili Air, but exchange rates are poor. Blue Marlin charge 7% for cash advances on credit cards. There's a clinic in the village for medical services.

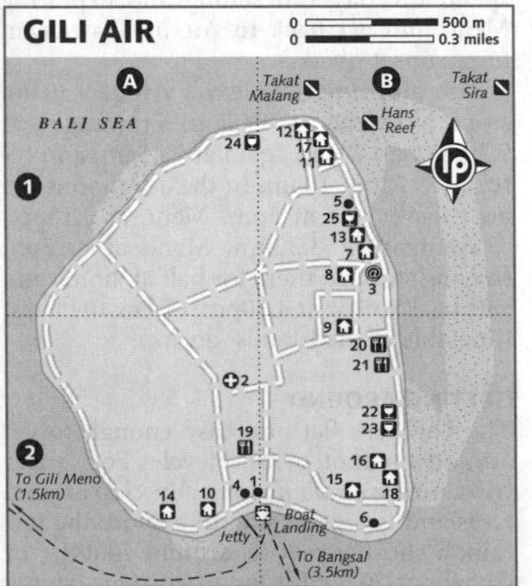

ACTIVITIES

Cycling

Ozzy's Shop has bikes for hire for 20,000Rp a day. Exploring the island by bike is a delight, though sandy tracks can make the going a bit tough, and you're sure to end up in someone's backyard at times due to the unmarked trails.

Snorkelling & Diving

You'll find diverse marine life **snorkelling** off the east coast, and easy beach access; gear can be hired from Ozzy's Shop for 15,000Rp a day. Check with dive centres first about currents, as sometimes they can be extremely strong. Ozzy's Shop also operates **glass-bottomed boat tours** (per person 40,000Rp, minimum four people) around all three islands.

There are several good **scuba diving** sites a short boat ride away. See the boxed text, p511 for more information. Gili Air has two

INFORMATION
Koperasi/Public Boat Office....1 A2
Medical Clinic....2 A2
Ozzy's Shop....3 B1
Perama....4 A2

SIGHTS & ACTIVITIES
Blue Marlin Dive Centre....5 B1
Dream Divers....6 B2

SLEEPING
Abdi Fantastik....7 B1
Coconut Cottages....8 B1
Gili Air Santay....9 B2
Gili Indah Hotel....10 A2
Gusung Indah....11 B1
Hotel Gili Air....12 B1
Kira Kira....13 B1
Lucky's....14 A2
Nusa Tiga Bungalows....15 B2
Pino Cottages....16 B2
Pondok Sandi....17 B1
Sunrise Cottages & Restaurant....18 B2

EATING
Abdi Fantastik....(see 7)
Blue Marlin....(see 5)
Coconut Cottages....(see 8)
Gecko Cafe....19 A2
Hotel Gili Air....(see 12)
Munchies....20 B2
Sasak Warung....21 B2

DRINKING
Chill Out Bar....22 B2
Gita Gili....23 B2
Legend Pub....24 A1
Star Bar....25 B1

dive schools, **Blue Marlin Dive Centre** (☎ 634387; www.diveindo.com) and **Dream Divers** (☎ 634547; www.dreamdivers.com).

SLEEPING

Prices quoted here are high-season rates – expect a discount of about 25% in low season. Breakfast is included in all the hotels listed, except Lucky's.

Budget

Gili Air Santay (☎ 641022; giliair_santay@yahoo.com; s/d 40,000/50,000Rp) Set back from the beach in a quiet coconut grove, these spacious bamboo-and-timber huts are just above the bog-standard category. All come with hammocks and fairly modern bathrooms.

Abdi Fantastik (☎ 636421; bungalows 75,000-80,000Rp) Enjoying unobstructed sea vistas, these neat – rather than 'fantastik' – thatched bungalows are just a few metres from the shore. They have verandas, and a hammock to swing in.

Sunrise Cottages & Restaurant (☎ 642370; s 50,000-75,000Rp, d 80,000-100,000Rp) A class above the real cheapies, this efficiently run place has rustic two-storey *lumbung*-style bungalows with bathrooms and separate living areas (with a day bed and hammock). The accommodation is well spaced apart and is at the rear of a pretty garden. There's a safe for valuables and a great beachside café-restaurant.

Kira Kira (☎ 641021; kirakira@mataram.wasantara.net.id; s 70,000-110,000Rp, d 80,000-125,000Rp) Stylish, well-presented thatched cottages, with rattan furniture, large ceiling fans, decent beds and hammocks, overlooking a small garden. The restaurant (open from 7am to 9pm) serves Japanese dishes such as tempura.

our pick **Coconut Cottages** (☎ 635365; www.coconuts-giliair.com; r 110,000-180,000Rp) A delightful, welcoming Indo-Scottish owned place with a selection of atmospheric accommodation spread around a fecund, well-tended garden. Some of the well-maintained cottages have shell-inlaid decorative detailing, and all have good-quality mattresses, bamboo furniture and bedside reading lights. There's a fine restaurant here too (see right).

Also worth considering:

Gusung Indah (☎ 081 23789054; r 70,000-100,000Rp) Facing a good stretch of beach, these simple bungalows with verandas are decent value. You pay more for a sea view.

Lucky's (☎ 081 23782156; bungalows 45,000Rp) Run by a friendly family, these basic bungalows enjoy a quiet location.

Nusa Tiga Bungalows (r 40,000-50,000Rp) Basic bamboo bungalows set in a coconut grove, inland from the east coast.

Pino Cottages (☎ 639304; r 60,000-80,000Rp) Set back from the beach, Pino has well-maintained and clean thatched cottages with hammocks.

Pondok Sandi (s/d 50,000/100,000Rp) Facing the sea, these spacious huts come with bathrooms.

Midrange

Gili Indah Hotel (☎ 637328; gili_indah@mataram.wasantara.net.id; bungalows 200,000-350,000Rp; ❄) Conveniently close to the jetty, the well-run Gili Indah has a variety of good, well-constructed bungalows. The best have air-con and huge front decks with expansive sea views.

Hotel Gili Air (☎ 634435; www.hotelgiliair.com; r US$17, with hot water US$33, with hot water & TV US$43-63; ❄ 🏊) Setting itself up as the island's 'proper' hotel, this place offers four classes of digs – from rustic-but-comfy huts to international hotel chain–style rooms, with marble bath and attractive wooden furniture; however, the pool is small and the gardens look neglected.

EATING

Dining out in Gili Air is a treat, with an array of simple places serving Indonesian and Western dishes, many located right by the sea – there's nothing fancy, though. Beware: service can be slow.

Abdi Fantastik (☎ 636421; dishes 10,000-25,000Rp) Come here for some of the best Sasak food on the island at fair prices; try the *kangkung pelecing* (spicy water spinach).

Santay (☎ 641022; dishes 12,000-20,000Rp) Perch yourself on a beachside table, soak up the views of Gunung Rinjani and tuck into dishes that include good pumpkin-and-coconut curry, or sate.

Gecko Café (☎ 641014; dishes 10,000-25,000Rp, Wed dinner from 35,000Rp; 🕑 lunch & dinner) This friendly caff is good for sandwiches, cake and coffee, or Indonesian snacks. The Wednesday night dinners – such as roast beef followed by apple crumble – are an island institution for homesick Divemasters.

Coconut Cottages (☎ 635365; dishes 10,000-28,000Rp) An inventively prepared menu that combines Western and Indonesian dishes;

you'll dine well in this pleasant hotel restaurant. Try the fantastic Sasak buffet, served every Wednesday night (40,000Rp per person) during the high season.

Blue Marlin (☎ 634387; dishes 15,000-35,000Rp) The best bet for Western food, the kitchen here serves up a mean burger, as well as pasta, sandwiches and stick-to-yer-ribs breakfasts.

Hotel Gili Air (☎ 634435; dishes 15,000-56,000Rp) Recommended by resident foreigners as the best venue for pizza and pasta on the island. It also serves Indonesian dishes and steaks. The service here is prompt.

Or try:

Munchies (dishes 7500-26,000Rp; lunch & dinner) Serves fine curries, fish and overflowing sandwiches.

Sasak Warung (mains 12,000-28,000Rp) Dine well here by the waves under pretty shell lanterns.

DRINKING & ENTERTAINMENT

Except for the odd party, Gili Air is generally pretty quiet at night.

Star Bar (3pm-late Thu-Tue) Next to the Blue Marlin, this little bar's trump card is Azam, its charismatic trickster barman.

Chill Out Bar (11-2am) Popular with visitors and locals, and has a good selection of spirits and cocktails.

Gita Gili (11-1am) A friendly bar, where on request you can watch a DVD while you sink a cold one.

Legend Pub (10am-11.30pm Thu-Tue, happy hour 5-7pm, party 10pm-2am Wed) Wednesday night is the big one here, especially in high season, with speakers bumpin' to (mainly) reggae bass lines.

Gili Meno

pop 300

Gili Meno is the quietest of the three islands, and it has the best beaches. With such a small permanent population, it's not hard to play Robinson Crusoe, should you so desire, along Meno's isolated shores.

ORIENTATION

Most accommodation is strung out along the eastern coast, near the widest and most picturesque beach. Inland you'll find homesteads, coconut plantations and a shallow lake that produces salt in the dry season.

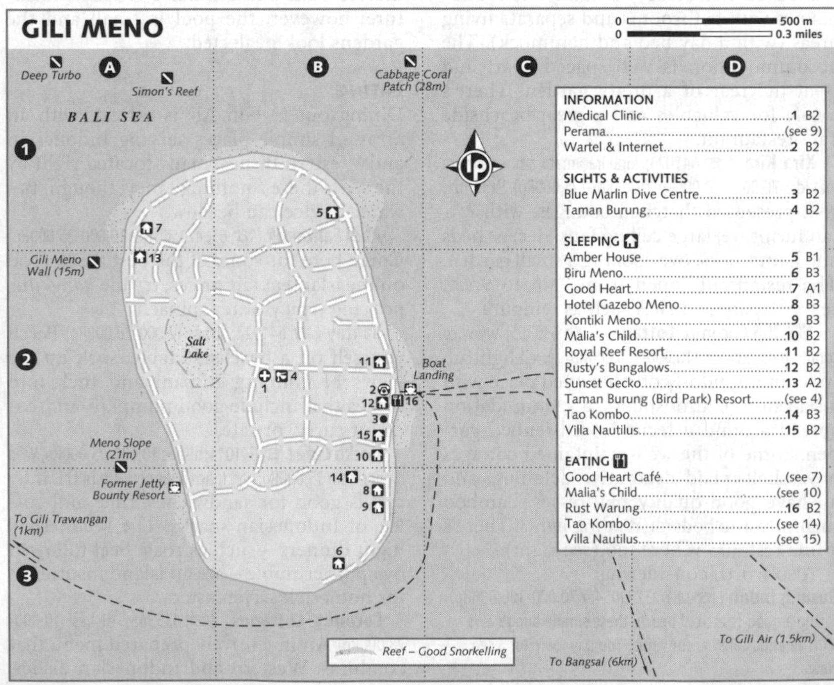

INFORMATION

There are a couple of minimarkets by the boat landing, so you will be able to locate most basic supplies. **Internet access** (per min 750Rp) and a wartel are available near the boat landing. Money can be exchanged at hotels, including the Gazebo Meno and Kontiki Meno, at poor rates. For tours and shuttle bus or boat tickets, the travel agent **Perama** (☎ 632824) is based at Kontiki Meno bungalows. The **medical clinic** (thegilimenoclinic@hotmail.com), near the bird park, has a resident nurse. Doctors are also on call in Mataram.

SIGHTS & ACTIVITIES

About 300m inland from the boat landing, the **Taman Burung Bird Park** (☎ 642321; admission 30,000Rp; 9am-5pm) has an impressive and well-cared-for collection of 300 or so exotic species from Asia and Australasia, as well as three kangaroos and a baby Komodo dragon. The birds are let out of their cages for three hours a day, when they fly around a large expanse covered by netting. Feeding times are also held. There's a bar, and accommodation is available (see p510).

Snorkelling trips (40,000Rp per person, minimum four people), sometimes in glass-bottomed boats, leave from the jetty – ask the fishermen there. There's good snorkelling off the northeast coast near the Amber House huts, on the west coast near Good Heart and also around the jetty of the (abandoned) Bounty Resort – gear is available for 20,000Rp per day (ask at your accommodation). Always ask about the state of the currents – Blue Marlin is the best place to go for this. **Blue Marlin Dive Centre** (☎ 639979; www.diveindo.com) offers fun dives and courses from Discover Scuba to Divemaster. For more on snorkelling and diving, see the boxed text, p511.

SLEEPING

Budget

Basic places are generally more expensive than equivalent lodgings on the other Gilis, and rates don't usually include breakfast. Prices quoted are high season – reductions of up to 25% are possible the rest of the year. In theory, all places have 24-hour power, but this is not very reliable.

Tao Kombo (☎ 081 23722174; tao_kombo@yahoo.com; platforms/bungalows 25,000/90,000Rp) About 200m inland, this mellow place has attractive, individually decorated bungalows scattered around a large garden, and some bamboo sleeping platforms (with mattresses, mosquito nets and safety boxes). There's a generator for 24-hour power, a chill out lounge and a bar-restaurant (see p510).

Biru Meno (☎ 081 33657322; bungalows 80,000-100,000Rp) A very welcoming place located in a tranquil spot south of the main strip. It has a selection of spacious sea-facing bungalows; the most expensive have big windows and coral walls. There's also a restaurant serving inexpensive local food.

Kontiki Meno (☎ 632824; bungalows with fan/air-con 90,000/150,000Rp;) Clean breeze-block bungalows, some with elaborately carved doorways. Book 1 or 2 for an uninterrupted sea view.

Malia's Child (☎ 622007; www.gilimeno-mallias.com; r 150,000Rp) Facing the sea, these attractive, orderly bamboo-and-thatch bungalows with fans, mosquito nets and Western toilets sit pretty on a well-raked stretch of sandy beach.

Good Heart (☎ 081 339556976; bungalows 150,000Rp) This excellent, friendly Balinese-owned place has a row of superb, newly-built twin-deck *lumbung*-like bungalows with coconut-wood roofs and beautiful freshwater bathrooms. Good Hart is opposite a narrow stretch of beach that faces Trawangan, and there's also a book exchange and a good restaurant (see p510). Discounts of around 40% are offered in the low season.

our pick **Sunset Gecko** (081 5766418; fircfrog11@hotmail.com; bungalows/house 150,000/350,000Rp) This new place, built by a multinational team to high ecostandards, has gorgeous A-frame bungalows and a stunning two-bedroom timber house – enjoy the best views on the island from its upper deck. All accommodation has excellent ventilation and plenty of natural light. It's in an isolated spot but next to a tranquil beach with some snorkelling. A restaurant serving Japanese, Indonesian and Western food is planned. Rates drop substantially off peak.

Other recommendations:

Amber House (☎ 643676; amber_house02@hotmail.com; s/d from 30,000/40,000Rp) Attractive bamboo bungalows in a flourishing garden with sea aspects.

Royal Reef Resort (☎ 642340; r 150,000Rp) Large and orderly bungalows overlooking the sea.

Rusty's Bungalows (Pondok Wisata; ☎ 642324; s/d 50,000/60,000Rp) Bog-standard but acceptable huts behind the boat landing.

Midrange

Taman Burung (Bird Park) Resort (☎ 642321; www.balipvbgroup.com; dm/deluxe r 30,000/300,000Rp; ❄) This place offers four comfortable air-con rooms with TV/DVD players and basic self-catering equipment, as well as a funky dormitory with three bunk beds. Check out the restaurant and Beatles-themed bar too.

Hotel Gazebo Meno (☎ /fax 635795; r with fan/air-con US$30/65; ❄ 🏊) Classy, spacious and stylish bungalows set in a coconut grove just off the beach. Bungalows with air-con have a distinctly colonial feel with parquet floors, desks and chaise lounges. There's a small saltwater swimming pool.

Top End

Villa Nautilus (☎ 642143; www.villanautilus.com; r US$75; ❄) Deluxe detached villas, beautifully finished in contemporary style with natural wood, marble and limestone. The design allows plenty of natural light to flood the lounge level, which has doors opening on to a decked terrace – book villa 1, 2 or 3 for sea views. Steps lead up to the bedroom/dressing room and down to the shower.

EATING & DRINKING

The beachfront restaurants near the boat landing all offer fine views for your meal, which is just as well as service can be slow.

Rust Warung (☎ 642324; mains 6000-28,000Rp; 🕑 breakfast, lunch & dinner) Simple *beruga* with low tables and a menu of Indonesian and Western favourites.

Good Heart Café (☎ 081 339556976; mains 7500-20,000Rp; 🕑 breakfast, lunch & dinner, happy hour 6-8pm) Perfectly primed for the sunset, Good Heart has a relaxed atmosphere, which is aided by bamboo wind chimes and shells decorating the trees. BBQs are held regularly and the bar has a variety of cocktails.

Tao Kombo (☎ 081 23722174; mains 9000-24,000Rp; 🕑 breakfast, lunch & dinner) Popular bar run by Frenchman Bob. It has a chilled vibe, lounge tunes, cocktails and a pool table. Tuck into fine Italian and Indonesian cuisine here too.

Villa Nautilus (☎ 642143; mains 15,000-27,000Rp; 🕑 breakfast, lunch & dinner) Come here for breakfast, a sandwich, pasta or a pizza from the wood-fired oven.

Malia's Child (☎ 622007; dishes 15,000-28,000Rp; 🕑 breakfast, lunch & dinner) You'll eat well here, with tasty Indonesian food and pizza served either on an upper level with fine views or on one of the seaside *berugas*.

Gili Trawangan

pop 1500

Trawangan has a reputation as a party island, a Shangri La for backpackers and hedonistic Indonesians that's awash with budget-priced digs and dive centres. Shoestring ravers do still flock here, but the island's increasingly upmarket facilities – a mushrooming lux-fest of lounge bars, sushi restaurants and boutique hotels – has meant that Jakartan hipsters and weekending Singaporeans are almost as common as rupiah-lite gap-year students. It's the one corner of Nusa Tenggara where tourism is really vibrant, and while there are still plenty of tranquil corners, the island's main strip buzzes every night until the early hours.

Unfortunately, environmental management has yet to catch up with the pace of development, and discarded garbage blots the landscape, particularly in the village just inland from the beach.

Diving is so critical to the local economy that the island's fishermen are paid by the scuba schools *not* to fish on Trawangan's reefs, a pioneering initiative that has resulted in greatly increased diversity, with turtles and top predators such as reef sharks frequently spotted here. Culturally, this moratorium is not without its difficulties, however, as the islanders are descended from Bugis fishermen who arrived in Trawangan 55 years ago.

ORIENTATION & INFORMATION

Boats dock on the eastern side of the island, which is also home to virtually all of Trawangan's accommodation and restaurants. The **Koperasi harbour office** (🕑 8am-5.30pm) has a hut at the boat landing, with prices clearly marked outside. The best stretch of beach is just north of the dock.

Several places will change cash or travellers cheques, but rates are poor. Dive shops give cash advances on credit cards for a hefty 7% commission.

There is no post office, but stamps and postcards are sold in the wartel and Pasar Seni (Art Market).

Emergency

Satgas A community organisation which controls security on the island. Contact it via your hotel or dive school.
Villa Ombak Clinic (9am-5pm) Just south of Hotel Villa Ombak.

Internet Access & Telephone

You'll find various places spread along the eastern waterfront. One option is **Lightening** (internet access per minute 400Rp), which also has a wartel.

Travel Agencies

Perama (638514; www.peramatour.com) Located just north of the jetty.

SIGHTS & ACTIVITIES

Boat Trips & Snorkelling

Glass-bottomed boat trips (40,000Rp per person, including snorkelling equipment) to coral reefs can be booked at many stores on the main strip.

UNDERWATER GILIS

The Gili Islands are a terrific dive destination. Though coral life above 18m is not generally in good condition – years of fish bombing and the El Niño phenomenon, which caused 'heatstroke' damage to the temperature-sensitive reefs back in the 1990s, have taken their toll – you'll find that marine life is plentiful and varied. Turtles and black- and white-tip reef sharks are common, and the macro life is excellent, with seahorses, pipe fish and lots of crustaceans. Around full moon, large schools of bumphead parrotfish appear to feast on coral spawns, while at other times of the year manta rays glide by dive sites.

Safety standards are high in the Gilis – there are no dodgy dive schools, and instructors and training are professional. Rates are fixed (no matter who you dive with) at US$25 a dive, with discounts for a package of 10 dives. A PADI Open Water course costs US$300, the Advanced course is US$225, Divemaster starts at US$650, and Nitrox and Trimex dives are offered by some schools. For contact details of dive schools, see individual island entries.

The Gili Eco Trust, a partnership between dive operators and the local community, aims to improve the condition of the reefs. All divers help fund the trust by paying a one-off fee of 30,000Rp with their first dive. Another initiative has seen the establishment of several reef growth accelerators called 'Biorock' – these use electrical currents to stimulate coral development. Two Biorock installations are located directly opposite Hotel Villa Ombak at a depth of 8m. For more information, consult www.biorock.net.

Surrounded by coral reefs and with easy beach access, the Gilis are superb for snorkelling too. Masks, snorkels and fins can be hired for as little as 20,000Rp per day. On Trawangan try the area right off the main beach, where turtles are often seen. Around Gili Meno, the pier by the (closed) Bounty Resort has prolific marine life, while over on Air the walls off the east coast are good.

Some of the best dive sites:

Deep Halik The canyonlike profile of this site is ideally suited to drift diving. Black- and white-tip sharks can often be seen at 28m to 30m.

Deep Turbo At around 30m, this site is ideal for Nitrox diving. It has impressive sea fans and catches the prevailing currents, so anything can come out of the big blue (including, very occasionally, mantas or even whale sharks).

Hans Reef Off the northeast coast of Gili Air. Great for macro life (small stuff), including frogfish, ghostfish, seahorses and pipe fish.

Japanese Wreck For experienced divers only (as it lies at 45m), this shipwreck of a Japanese patrol boat is another site ideal for Nitrox divers. Soft coral is prolific, and there are lots of nudibranchs, lionfish and frogfish.

Shark Point Perhaps the most exhilarating dive in the Gilis: reef sharks and turtles are spotted very regularly, as well as schools of bumphead parrot fish and mantas. Look out too for cuttlefish and octopuses. At shallow depths there can be a strong surge.

Simon's Reef The reef here is in excellent condition, schools of trevally can be seen and occasionally great barracuda and leopard sharks.

Sunset (Manta Point) The sloping profile of the reef here has good coral growth below 18m, including some impressive table coral. Large pelagic are frequently encountered and strong currents are rarely an issue.

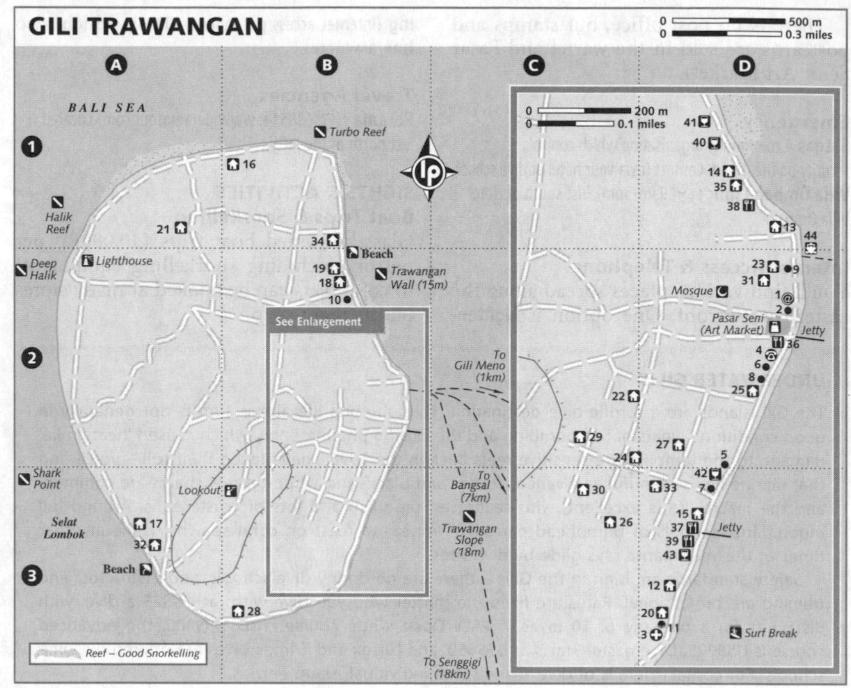

There's fair snorkelling off the beach north of the jetty, though there's plenty of coral damage in evidence here. Beware of strong currents further out from the shoreline. The reef is in better shape close to the lighthouse off the northwest coast, but you'll have to scramble over some low coral to access it.

Snorkel gear can be hired for around 20,000Rp per day from shacks near the jetty.

Diving

Trawangan is a veritable diver's delight with seven established scuba schools, no cowboys and inexpensive prices. For more information, see the boxed text, p511.

Professional dive centres operating from Gili Trawangan:

Big Bubble (☎ 625020; www.bigbubblediving.com)
Blue Marlin Dive Centre (☎ 632424; www.diveindo.com)
Dive Indonesia (☎ 642289; www.diveindonesianonline.com)
Dream Divers (☎ 634496; www.dreamdivers.com)
Manta Dive (☎ 643649; www.manta-dive.com)
Trawangan Diving (☎ 649220; www.trawangandive.com)
Villa Ombak Diving Academy (☎ 638531; gilidive@mataram.wasantara.net.id)

Surfing & Water Sports

Trawangan's fast right-hand wave breaks over a coral outcrop that isn't sharp. It's best at high tide and can be surfed all year long. You'll find it just south of Villa Ombok. **Fun Ferrari** (☎ 081 23756138; Horizontal Bar; water sports per 15 min incl tuition 150,000Rp, fishing US$50) offers water-skiing, parasailing, wakeboarding and sports fishing.

Walking & Cycling

Trawangan is perfect for exploring on foot or by bike. You can walk around the whole island in a couple of hours – if you finish your walk at the hill on the southwestern corner (which has the remains of an old Japanese gun placement) as the sun is setting, you'll have a terrific view of Bali's Gunung Agung.

Bikes can be hired from 15,000Rp a day from just south of the jetty.

INFORMATION		
Lightening	1	D2
Perama	2	D2
Villa Ombak Clinic	3	D3
Wartel	4	D2
SIGHTS & ACTIVITIES		
Big Bubble	5	D2
Blue Marlin Dive Centre	6	D2
Dive Indonesia	7	D3
Dream Divers	8	D2
Fun Ferrari	(see 41)	
Manta Dive	9	D2
Trawangan Diving	10	B2
Villa Ombak Driving Academy	11	D3
SLEEPING		
Beach House	12	D3
Beach Wind Bungalows	13	D1
Big Bubble	(see 5)	
Blue Beach Cottages	14	D1
Blue Marlin	(see 6)	
Creatif Satu	15	D3
Desa Dunia Beda	16	B1
Dewi Sri	17	A3
Dream Village	18	B2
Good Heart	19	B2
H Rooms	(see 41)	
Hotel Villa Ombak	20	D3
Kelapa Villas	21	A1
Lisa Homestay	22	C2
Manta	23	D2
Martas	24	C2
Pak Majid	25	D2
Pandian Wangi Cottages	26	C3
Pondok Lita	27	D2
Pondok Santai	28	B3
Pondok Sederhana	29	C2
Puri Hondje	30	C3
Sama Sama Bungalows	31	D2
Sunset Cottages	32	A3
Tir Na Nog	(see 43)	
Trawangan Cottages	33	D3
Villa Almarik	34	B1
Warna	35	D1
EATING		
Anna's	36	D2
Beach House	(see 12)	
Blue Marlin	(see 6)	
Horizontal	(see 41)	
Kayangan	37	D3
Reccy Living Room	38	D1
Ryoshi	39	D3
Tir Na Nog	(see 43)	
DRINKING		
Café Wayan	40	D1
Horizontal	41	D1
Rudy's Pub	42	D3
Tir Na Nog	43	D3
TRANSPORT		
Boat Landing & Koperasi	44	D1

SLEEPING

There are approaching a hundred places to stay in Gili Trawangan, from simple beach huts to private villas. Most of the very cheapest accommodation is in the village, and you'll pay more for a beachside address. Perhaps the hottest real estate is the area north of the harbour, where you can stumble out of your bungalow and flop on the beach, neutralising those (perhaps inevitable) hangovers with a morning dip.

Rates quoted are high-season prices, which drop by about 30% off peak. Breakfast is included unless stated otherwise.

Budget

Pandian Wangi Cottages (s/d 40,000/75,000Rp) Friendly place with simple, clean rooms with fans and mossie nets.

Sunset Cottages (☎ 081 23785290; s/d 50,000/60,000Rp) Friendly place on the southwest coast, opposite a little beach, with traditional-style huts that catch the afternoon breeze.

Pak Majid (r 60,000Rp) In the thick of the action, this place has clean concrete bungalows with plain furnishings. Breakfast is not included.

Pondok Sederhana (☎ 081 338609964; r 60,000Rp) Run by a house-proud and friendly Balinese lady, the spotless rooms here face a neat little garden.

Pondok Santai (s/d 60,000/70,000Rp) On the south coast, yet only a five-minute walk from the main strip, these simple, secluded thatched huts all have two beds and an attached *mandi*.

Dewi Sri (☎ 081 933145164; r 60,000Rp & 100,000Rp) A family-owned place with two classes of well-built bungalows scattered around a spacious beachside plot. There's good home cooking available.

Lisa Homestay (☎ 081 339523364; r 75,000Rp) Very friendly little place with light and airy tiled rooms that look over a garden.

Beach Wind Bungalows (☎ 081 23764347; s/d with fan 75,000/85,000Rp, with air-con 120,000/150,000Rp; ❄) Excellent-value, stylish, spacious rooms in a row just off the beach. All rooms have handsome bamboo-framed beds and a veranda; those with air-con have two beds. There's also ping pong, a book exchange and snorkel gear for hire.

Creatif Satu (☎ 634861; r with fan/air-con 75,000/125,000Rp; ❄) Right by the jetty, this place has large, clean, acceptable rooms.

Pondok Lita (r 80,000-100,000Rp) Nine good rooms around a garden, all with two beds, tiled floors and a clean bathroom. Also has a book exchange and laundry service.

Trawangan Cottages (☎ 623582; r without/with air-con 140,000/100,000Rp; ❄) Well-kept rooms with private bathrooms and verandas with nice seating. It's on the main strip.

Warna (☎ 623859; r 140,000Rp) Four well-priced, tasteful bungalows with large beds and attractive wooden furniture are ranged along a gorgeous narrow garden. It's just off the beach.

Puri Hondje (r 150,000Rp; ❄) Tucked away down a quiet village lane, these very stylish rooms overlook a small fish pond surrounded by bougainvillea and palms.

Blue Beach Cottages (☎ 623538; bbc@indo.net.18; r with fan/air-con 170,000/250,000Rp;) Representing good value for money, these attractive huts have high ceilings, rattan furniture, ikat wall hangings, hot water and reading lights. The huts are set alongside a blooming garden. But, best of all, you're just off the beach.

Midrange

Big Bubble (☎ 625020; www.bigbubblediving.com; r with fan/air-con US$22/30;) Right behind the diving school is this row of very stylish modern rooms, facing a beautiful garden. Built from natural materials, each room comes with hammocks and a front terrace. There's a wonderful pool and decked area out the front.

Blue Marlin (☎ 632424; www.diveindo.com; r US$25;) Decent air-con rooms, all with wardrobes and desks, hot water and baths, TVs and air-con, are set behind the Blue Marlin dive school.

Tir Na Nog (☎ 639463; tirnanog@mataram.wasantara.net.id; r US$25, villa US$125;) At the rear of this bar on the main strip, these huge rooms have been thoughtfully designed and decorated; most have spacious private terraces and swanky modern bathrooms. For real luxury, book the private villa which even comes with its own chef.

Sama Sama Bungalows (☎ 081 23763650; r with fan/air-con 250,000/350,000Rp;) Combining natural materials (logwood bed frames, timber flooring and coconut-wood furniture) with mod cons, including TV/DVD players, these rooms make a comfortable base. The place is set back a little from the beach.

Martas (☎ 081 23722777; martas_trawangan@yahoo.com; r/f 250,000/400,000Rp;) Representing exceptional value for money, these sumptuous detached two-storey air-con bungalows, owned by a helpful and welcoming English-Indonesian couple, are grouped around a lush garden and decorated in calming creams and beige. The family rooms sleep four.

Manta (☎ 643649; www.manta-dive.com; r 380,000Rp;) Eight delightful modern *lumbung*-style bungalows, each with twin or king-size beds, a safe, a fridge and wonderful screened outdoor bathrooms, with volcanic stone floor tiles. Prices are flexible during the low season.

Beach House (☎ 642352; www.beachhousegilit.com; r 300,000-400,000Rp, villas 2,500,000Rp;) Competitive pricing and the simple elegance of these understated modern rooms mean that this place is busy all year round. There's a freshwater plunge pool at the rear (and also a four-bedroom villa with its own pool).

Good Heart (☎ 081 22395170; r 100,000Rp, bungalows 350,000-500,000Rp;) A great choice with superb-value budget rooms, each with large beds, and a couple of very stylish thatched A-frame bungalows – these have all the mod cons, and pebble-floored open-air bathrooms.

our pick **Dream Village** (☎ 081 8546591; 500,000Rp;) A wonderful new place with contemporary *lumbung* bungalows, each extremely well finished, with teak floors and rattan chairs, fridges and gorgeous outdoor bathrooms. An Italian restaurant, a spa room and a small pool are in the pipeline.

Top End

Villa Almarik (☎ 638520; www.almarik-lombok.com; r US$70-75;) Huge, light, airy high-ceilinged bungalows with dining/living room area and contemporary bathrooms, TVs and minibars. The swimming pool is modestly sized though.

Hotel Villa Ombak (☎ 642336; www.hotelombak.com; r US$75-135 plus 21% tax;) Just south of the main drag, this very attractive resort occupies a leafy garden plot partly shaded by yuccas and palms. The faux-traditional two-storey A-frame bungalows are not that large for the price but do have real character, while the stunning superior rooms are more minimalist in design. Ombak has a great pool, a spa, a diving academy, a restaurant and a beach bar too.

our pick **H Rooms** (☎ 639248; somersguy@yahoo.com; villas US$100;) Redefining the mod-Asian look so prevalent in Bali, these remarkable villas behind the Horizontal bar can sleep four comfortably, with dividing walls separating sleek interiors complete with Japanese-style tatami matting, distressed coconut-wood walls and decked floors. Home-cinema equipment, huge Jacuzzis and gorgeous open-air bathrooms are all standard, while butler and personal DJ services can also be arranged.

Desa Dunia Beda (☎ 641575; www.desaduniabeda.com; US$110 plus 21% tax;) Out on their own in the north of the island, these absolutely astonishing Javanese Joglo bungalows command the biggest wow factor on Trawangan. Each has been decorated with classy furniture and boasts a four-poster bed, writing desk, sofa and back-to-nature open-air bathroom. The pool is smallish, though, and it is isolated up here.

Kelapa Villas (☎ 632424; www.kelapavillas.com; US$150-410 plus 21% tax;) Between the coasts, surrounded by coconut groves, these beautifully finished luxury villas boast full catering facilities, private pools and all the comforts of home, including TV/DVD players and freshwater bathrooms.

EATING

It's easy to munch your way around the world in Trawangan, which belies its size and offers everything from sushi to Irish stew.

Anna's (dishes 5000-8000Rp; breakfast, lunch & dinner) Tiny, friendly little warung with a very small menu. It serves up a mean *nasi campur* (rice with a choice of side dishes) and *soto ayam* (chicken soup).

Kayangan (dishes 7500-15,000Rp; breakfast, lunch & dinner) It may look a bit grubby, but the inexpensive Chinese and Indonesian dishes here are executed well.

Café Wayan (dishes 17,000-35,000Rp; breakfast, lunch & dinner) Hygiene standards are high, so this is a great venue for salads (try the papaya and chicken), as well as pasta and Thai and Indo faves. Leave room for the cakes, including death-by-chocolate and carrot.

Ryoshi (☎ 639463; dishes 17,000-48,000Rp, set menus from 37,000Rp; breakfast, lunch & dinner) Authentic, super-fresh sushi and sashimi at moderate prices served on Nippon-style low tables (though you can also eat your Eastern treats next door at the 'Irish bar' too).

Beach House (☎ 642352; dishes 17,000-50,000Rp; breakfast, lunch & dinner) Boasts one of the best beachside terraces and a menu that takes in everything from tasty baguettes through the usual Indonesian suspects to chargrilled sirloin steaks.

Tir Na Nog (☎ 639463; dishes 21,000-37,000Rp; breakfast, lunch & dinner) Ideal for enormous portions of comfort food like Irish stew and fish and chips, and puds such as banoffi pie.

Horizontal (☎ 639248; dishes 25,000-65,000Rp; breakfast, lunch & dinner) An achingly contemporary design which marries sexy seating with modish lighting, this place has an eclectic, to-die-for menu of pan-Asian and mod-European food.

Other recommendations:

Blue Marlin (mains 9000-35,000Rp) Offering mainly Western food, this place serves up some of the finest fish and seafood in Trawangan – choose yours from the iced streetside display.

Reccy Living Room (dishes 12,000-23,000Rp) Friendly place with *beruga* overlooking the beach that offers good Western food such as lasagna. Order the house special 'rice table' a day in advance.

DRINKING & ENTERTAINMENT

Despite its size, Trawangan punches way above its weight in the party stakes. Its rotating parties fire up around 11pm and go on until 4am or so (except during Ramadan). DJs from Bali and beyond mix techno, trance and house music, while Rudy's Pub (Friday) has a more eclectic musical policy.

Tir Na Nog (☎ 639463; 7am-2am Wed-Mon, 7am-4am Tue) Known to one and all as the 'Irish bar', it combines a sociable barnlike main room, where you can catch live sport on a big screen and play table soccer, and a superb beachside terrace. Snacks and meals can be ordered from Ryoshi restaurant next door. The big night here is Tuesday.

our pick **Horizontal** (☎ 639248; www.horizontalbar.com; 10am-2am) Adjacent to a gorgeous stretch of beach, this place offers a more sophisticated vibe than the usual drinking spots in Trawangan. Primarily a chill-out lounge, it's decorated in a contemporary style, with luxe scarlet lounges, decked floors and lots of funky details. Fantastic cocktails (try the raspberry margarita), a full menu (see left), Italian coffees and occasional DJ events.

Rudy's Pub (8am-4am Fri, 8am-11pm Sat-Thu) Run by the inimitable Joko, this bar is the best locally-owned place in town, and it hosts a terrific Friday-night party.

NORTH & CENTRAL LOMBOK

☎ 0370

The sparsely populated northern part of Lombok is remarkably beautiful, with a variety of landscapes, few tourists and even fewer facilities. Public transport is not frequent, nor does it detour from the main road. With a set of wheels, however, you

BOAT TOURS BETWEEN LOMBOK & FLORES

Travelling by sea between Lombok and Labuanbajo is a popular way to get to Flores, as you get to see far more of the region's spectacular coastline and dodge some seriously lengthy bus journeys and nonentity towns. Typical itineraries from Lombok take in snorkelling at Pulau Satonda off the coast of Sumbawa, a dragon-spotting hike on Komodo, and other stops for swimming and partying along the way. From Labuanbajo it's a similar story but usually with stops at Rinca and Pulau Moyo.

However, be aware that this kind of trip is no luxury cruise – a lot depends on the boat, the crew and your fellow travellers, whom you are stuck with for the duration. Some shifty operators have reneged on 'all-inclusive' agreements deals en route, and others operate decrepit old tugs without lifejackets or radio. The seas in this part of Indonesia can be extremely hazardous, especially during the rainy season when trips can be cancelled – and this journey is certainly not one to embark upon with some dodgy set-up.

For the safety concerns mentioned above, the well-organised tours on decent boats run by Perama (see Gili Trawangan, Mataram or Senggigi for contact details) are recommended. Current charges for cabin/deck are 1,500,000/1,050,000Rp for the three-day trip to Labuanbajo, and 1,000,000/700,000Rp for the two-day Labuanbajo–Lombok journey.

can explore the shore, waterfalls and inland villages. The main coastal road is narrow but sealed and in good condition.

Towering Gunung Rinjani is unquestionably the region's main attraction. But even if you don't attempt the cone itself, the southern slopes are well watered and lush, and offer scenic walks through rice fields and forest. Most villages in central Lombok are traditional Sasak settlements, and several of them are known for their handicrafts.

Bangsal to Bayan

The road from Senggigi to Bangsal is very scenic, slaloming around the contours of a succession of cove beaches. North of Bangsal public transport is less frequent. Several minibuses a day go from Mandalika terminal in Bertais (Mataram) to Bayan, but you may have to get connections in Pemenang and/or Anyar.

SIRA

This peninsula has a glorious sweeping white-sand **beach**, some snorkelling and Lombok's most luxurious hotel, the **Oberoi Lombok** (☎ 638444; www.oberoihotels.com; pavilions from US$240, villas from US$350 plus 21% tax;). The villas and pavilions here are beyond commodious, with lashings of marble, teak floors and astonishing garden-bathrooms with sunken bathtubs.

Close by, signposted on the road south to Bangsal, is the **Lombok Golf Kosaido Country Club** (☎ 640137; US$80 per round), an attractive 18-hole, 72 par course by the sea – **Manta Dive** (☎ 643649; www.manta-dive.com) in Gili Trawangan can organise discounted rates here.

GONDANG & AROUND

Just northeast of Gondang village, a 6km trail heads inland to **Air Terjun Tiu Pupas**, a 30m waterfall that's only really impressive in the wet season. Trails continue from here to other waterfalls, including **Air Terjun Gangga**, the most beautiful of all. A guide is useful to navigate the confusing trails in these parts. Speak to the owners of **Pondok Pantai** (☎ 081 23752632; bungalows 50,000-90,000Rp), a welcoming Dutch- and Indonesian-run beachside guesthouse with lovely thatched bungalows and tip-top food (dishes 9000Rp to 22,000Rp), 2km north of Gondang.

BAYAN

This northernmost part of Lombok is the birthplace of the Wektu Telu religion and also has some venerable **mosques**. One very fine example 2km east of Bayan, on the road to Laloan, is said to be the oldest in Lombok, dating from 1634. Built on a square platform of river stones, the structure has a pagoda-like upper section and inside there's a huge old drum.

Batu Koq & Senaru

These picturesque villages, merging into one another along a ridge with sweep-

NUSA TENGGARA

ing views to the east and south, are the main starting points for climbing Gunung Rinjani. If you've not got your volcano-climbing head on, they are still worth visiting, as there are some fine walking trails and dramatic waterfalls.

INFORMATION & ORIENTATION

The two villages are spread out along a single steep road that heads south to Rinjani. Batu Koq is about 3km south from Bayan, and Senaru is a further 3km uphill.

At the southern end of Senaru village, **Rinjani Trek Centre** (RTC; ☎ satellite 086812104132; www.info2lombok.com) has good information on Rinjani and the surrounding area.

SIGHTS & ACTIVITIES

Definitely visit **Air Terjun Sindang Gila** (2000Rp), a spectacular set of falls 20 minutes' walk from Senaru. The walk is partly through forest and partly alongside an irrigation canal that follows the contour of the hill, occasionally disappearing into tunnels where the cliffs are too steep.

A further 50 minutes or so up the hill is **Air Terjun Tiu Kelep**, another waterfall, where you can go swimming. The track is steep and tough at times, so it's a good idea to take a guide (15,000Rp).

Six kilometres south of Bayan is the traditional village of **Dusun Senaru**, where locals will invite you to chew betel nut (or tobacco) and show you around.

Community tourism activities that can be arranged through most guesthouses (such as Pondok Senaru) are a **rice terraces and waterfalls walk** (35,000Rp), which includes Sindang Gila, some stunning vistas and a bemo ride back, and the **Senaru Panorama Walk** (45,000Rp), which is led by female guides and takes in local lifestyles.

Head to Emy Café for a post-hike massage (25,000Rp).

SLEEPING & EATING

A few more comfortable rooms have been built in recent years, but most of the dozen or so losmen have basic rooms and shared cold-water *mandis*. As the climate is cooler here you won't need a fan. All these places are dotted along the road from Bayan to Senaru.

Bukit Senaru Cottages (r 40,000Rp; breakfast, lunch & dinner) Shortly before Dusun Senaru, this place has four well-constructed semi-detached bungalows overlooking a leafy garden. The bungalows have verandas, and bathrooms with Western-style toilets.

Pondok Indah & Restaurant (☎ 081 75788018; s/d 80,000/100,000Rp; breakfast, lunch & dinner) A well-run, friendly place with spacious accommodation in two blocks 3km south of Bayan. Many rooms share a communal balcony and have well-scrubbed showers and Western toilets. There's parking and a good restaurant (dishes 7000Rp to 18,000Rp).

Pondok Senaru & Restaurant (☎ 622868, 086812104141; r 150,000-300,000Rp; breakfast, lunch & dinner) Well set-up place 4km from Bayan with great easterly views of the valley from its recommended restaurant (dishes 11,000Rp to 21,000Rp) and a choice of spacious, spotless rooms – a little overpriced, but the most comfortable digs in town. The superior rooms have a TV, a minibar and a *hot* shower.

Also worth considering:

Bale Bayan (☎ 081 75792943; r 40,000Rp; breakfast, lunch & dinner) Opposite Dusun Senaru village, this place has rustic bungalows and a restaurant in a nice garden.

Pondok Segara Anak (☎ 081 75754551; r 40,000Rp; breakfast, lunch & dinner) Panoramic views and neat, clean, good-value rooms. It's 3km from Bayan.

Rinjani Homestay (☎ 081 75750889; s/d 35,000/40,000Rp; breakfast, lunch & dinner) A little further uphill, this place has plain, clean rooms and a restaurant with Western and Indonesian food (dishes 7000Rp to 25,000Rp).

Emy Café (dishes 5000-12,500Rp; breakfast, lunch & dinner) and **Galang Ijo** (dishes 5000-8000Rp; breakfast, lunch & dinner), both midway between Batu Koq and Senaru, do simple food and some Sasak specials.

GETTING THERE & AWAY

From Mandalika terminal in Mataram, catch a bus to Anyar (12,500Rp, 2½ hours). Bemos leave Anyar for Senaru (4000Rp) about every 20 minutes until 4.30pm. If you're coming from, or going to, eastern Lombok, get off at the junction near Bayan (your driver will know it), from where bemos go to Senaru.

Sembalun Lawang & Sembalun Bumbung

☎ 0376

High on the eastern side of Gunung Rinjani is the beautiful Sembalun Valley, whose inhabitants are descended from the Hindu Javanese. Sembalun Lawang is the other main point of departure for treks up Gunung Rinjani. The statue of an enormous garlic bulb in the village is indicative of the area's main crop, which is harvested in October.

Sembalun Bumbung, 3km south of Sembalun Lawang and just off the main road, is a sprawling and relatively wealthy village. It's often referred to simply as 'Sembalun'; 'Bumbung' is used to differentiate it from Sembalun Lawang. The latter is the more convenient place to stay for organising treks.

INFORMATION & ACTIVITIES

The staff at the **Rinjani Information Centre** (RIC; 6am-6pm; Sembalun Lawang) are well informed about hiking in the area and can arrange treks, including a not-too-demanding four-hour **village walk** (per person 100,000Rp, minimum 2 people). The more strenuous **wildflower walk** (per person for 2 people, incl guide, porters, meals & all camping gear 560,000Rp) is a delightful two-day trek inside Rinjani's National Park (Taman Nasional Gunung Rinjani), through flower-filled grasslands; costs decrease if there are more of you.

The RIC has also helped local women to revive traditional weaving in Sembalun Lawang. Follow the signs from the village centre to their workshops.

SLEEPING & EATING

Accommodation is more expensive in Sembalun Lawang than Senaru or Batu Koq, but the vistas here are more impressive.

Bale Galeng (s/d with shared bathroom 30,000/45,000Rp) These basic but serviceable *lumbung* cottages with shared *mandi*-style bathrooms are set in a rambling garden rich in shrubs and medicinal herbs. It's about 1km from the RIC.

Maria Guesthouse (r 50,000Rp) Homestay with two basic rooms and shared bathroom; rates include breakfast and dinner.

Losmen Lembah Rinjani (☎ 081 803620918; s/d with shared bathroom 60,000/80,000Rp, s/d 130,000/160,000Rp) Head down a side road near the information centre to find this well-run place. The more expensive rooms have Western-style shower and toilet; the cheaper rooms have less impressive volcano views. There is also a restaurant on site (dishes 8000Rp to 14,000Rp; open breakfast, lunch and dinner).

Sembalun Nauli (☎ 081 8362040; sembalunnauli@lycos.com; Sembalun Lawan; r 120,000Rp) These smart, spacious rooms with wonderful views of Rinjani are 3km before Sembalun Lawang on the road from Senaru. You can get good local food here (dishes 6000Rp to 17,000Rp; open breakfast, lunch and dinner).

GETTING THERE & AWAY

From Mandalika bus terminal, take a bus to Aikmel (8000Rp) and change there for Sembalun Lawang (9000Rp). Hourly pick-ups connect Lawang and Bumbung.

There's no public transport between Sembalun Lawang and Senaru, you'll have to charter an *ojek*, or a bemo for around 100,000Rp.

Roads to Sembalun are sometimes closed in the wet season due to landslides.

SAPIT

☎ 0376

On the southeastern slopes of Gunung Rinjani, Sapit is a tiny, very relaxed village with views across to Sumbawa. Tobacco-drying *open* (red-brick towers) loom above the beautifully lush landscape, and 'baccy' can be bought in blocks in the market.

Sights

Between Swela and Sapit, a side road leads you to **Taman Lemor** (Lemor Park; admission 1500Rp; 8am-4pm), where there is a refreshing spring-fed swimming pool and some monkeys. Further towards Pringgabaya, **Makam Selaparang** is the burial place of ancient Selaparang kings.

You can also visit some small waterfalls and hot-water springs near Sapit. Ask either homestay (following) for directions.

Sleeping & Eating

Hati Suci Homestay (☎ 081 8545655; www.hatisuci.tk; s 40,000-45,000Rp, d 75,000-85,000Rp) An efficiently run place with excellent budget bungalows in a fragrant garden. The accommodation and restaurant (dishes 8000Rp to 18,000Rp; open breakfast, lunch and dinner) both have stunning views of Sumbawa. Hikes to Rinjani can be organised here.

Balelangga B&B (☎ 22197; s/d with shared bathroom 30,000/50,000Rp) Offers simple, clean rooms with *mandi*-style shared bathroom and good home cooking (dishes 6000Rp to 18,000Rp; meals available breakfast, lunch and dinner). It's sometimes closed during the low season.

Getting There & Away

To reach Sapit, first catch a bus to Pringgabaya from the Mandalika bus terminal (13,000Rp) and then a bemo to Sapit (6000Rp). Occasional bemos also go to Sapit from the Sembalun Valley in the north.

GUNUNG RINJANI

Towering over the entire northern part of the island, the mighty Rinjani volcano is of immense cultural (and climatic) importance for Lombok's people, while climbing the peak is one of Indonesia's most exhilarating experiences. The great cone, which reaches 3726m, and its upper slopes were declared a national park in 1997.

Gunung Rinjani is the highest mountain in Lombok and the second highest in Indonesia. Its caldera contains a cobalt crescent-shaped lake, **Danau Segara Anak** (Child of the Sea), which is about 6km across at its widest point. The crater has a series of natural hot springs known as **Air Kalak**, whose waters locals take to blend with herbs to make medicinal treatments, particularly for skin diseases. The lake is 600m below the crater rim, and rising from its waters is a minor, newer cone, **Gunung Baru** (or Gunung Barujari), which only emerged a couple of hundred years ago. This ominously grey, highly active scarred peak erupted as recently as October 2004.

Both the Balinese and Sasaks revere Rinjani. To the Balinese, it is equal to Gunung Agung (p333), a seat of the gods, and many Balinese make an annual pilgrimage here. In a ceremony called *pekelan*, people throw jewellery into the lake and make offerings to the mountain spirit. Some Sasaks make several pilgrimages a year to the crater lake – full moon is their favourite time for paying respect to the mountain and curing their ailments by bathing in the hot springs.

The climb to the crater lake is not to be taken lightly and should only be undertaken as part of an organised trek, due to the active status of Gunung Baru and, sadly,

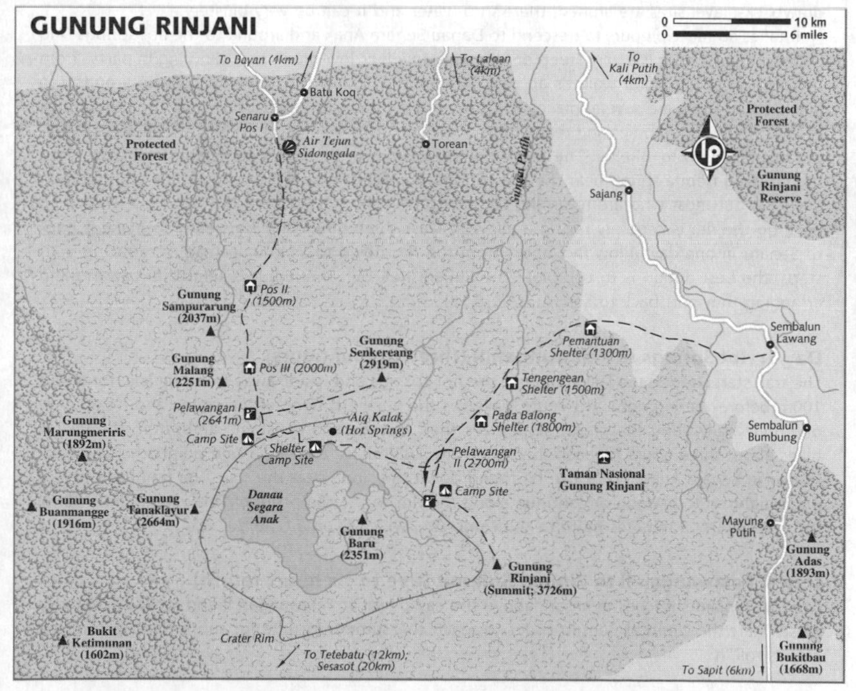

CLIMBING GUNUNG RINJANI

The most popular ways to climb Gunung Rinjani are the four- or five-day hiking expeditions (described below) that start at Senaru and finish at Sembalun Lawang, or a strenuous dash from Senaru to the crater rim and back. Independent hiking is not recommended at any time, due to safety and security concerns, but a guide is essential from the hot springs to Sembalun Lawang, as the path is indistinct. These treks are outlined on the Gunung Rinjani map (p519). Another good map is the one from the Rinjani Trek Centre – it is large, in full colour, glossy and easy to follow.

It's *often not possible* to climb Rinjani during the rainy season, particularly after heavy rainfall, when the trail around the lake is very dangerous due to the hazard of falling rocks.

Day 1: Senaru to Pos III (4½ to five hours)

At the southern end of the village is the RTC (Pos I, 601m), where you register and pay the park fee. Just beyond the post the trail forks – continue straight ahead on the right fork. The trail climbs steadily through scrubby farmland for about half an hour to the sign at the entrance to Gunung Rinjani National Park. The wide trail climbs for another 2½ hours until you reach Pos II (1500m), where there's a shelter. Water can be found 100m down the slope from the trail, but it should be treated or boiled.

Another 1½ hours' steady walk uphill brings you to Pos III (2000m), where there are another two shelters in disrepair. Water is 100m off the trail to the right but sometimes evaporates in the dry season. Pos III is the usual place to camp at the end of the first day.

Day 2: Pos III to Segara Anak & Hot Springs (four hours)

From Pos III, it takes about 1½ hours to reach the rim, Pelawangan I, at an altitude of 2641m. Set off very early for the stunning sunrise. It's possible to camp at Pelawangan I, but there are drawbacks: level sites are limited, there's no water and it can be very blustery.

It takes about two hours to descend to Danau Segara Anak and around to the hot springs (Aiq Kalak). The first hour is a very steep descent and involves low-grade rock climbing in parts. From the bottom of the crater wall it's an easy 30-minute walk across undulating terrain around the lake's edge. There are several places to camp, but most locals prefer to be near the hot springs to soak their weary bodies and recuperate. There are also some caves nearby, which are interesting but not used for shelter. The nicest camp sites are at the lake's edge, and fresh water can be gathered from a spring near the hot springs. Some hikers spend two nights or even more at the lake, but most who are returning to Senaru from here head back the next day. The climb back up the rim is certainly taxing – allow at least three hours and start early to make it back to Senaru in one day. Allow five hours from the rim down to Senaru. Instead of retracing your steps, the best option is to complete the Rinjani trek by continuing to Sembalun Lawang and arranging transport back to Senaru (see p518).

Day 3: Hot Springs to Pelawangan II (three to four hours)

The trail starts beside the last shelter at the hot springs and heads away from the lake for about 100m before veering right. The route traverses the northern slope of the crater, and it's an easy one-hour walk along the grassy slopes. It's then a steep and constant climb; from the lake it takes about three hours to reach the crater rim (2639m). At the rim, a sign points the way back to Danau Segara Anak. Water can be found down the slope near the sign. The trail forks here – go straight on to Lawang or continue along the rim to the camp site of Pelawangan II (2700m); it's only about 10 minutes more to the camp site, which is on a bare ridge.

Day 4: Pelawangan II to Rinjani Summit (five to six hours return)

Gunung Rinjani stretches in an arc above the camp site at Pelawangan II and looks deceptively close. Start the climb at 3am in order to reach the summit in time for sunrise and before the clouds roll in.

It takes about 45 minutes to clamber up a steep, slippery and indistinct trail to the ridge that leads to Rinjani. Once on the ridge, it's a relatively easy walk uphill. After about an hour heading towards what looks like the peak, the real summit of Rinjani looms behind and towers above you.

The trail then gets steeper and steeper. About 350m before the summit, the scree is composed of loose, fist-sized rocks – it's easier to scramble on all fours. This section can take about an hour. The views from the top are truly magnificent on a clear day. The descent is much easier, but again, take it easy on the scree. In total it takes three hours or more to reach the summit, and two to get back down.

Day 5: Pelawangan II to Sembalun Lawang (five to six hours)

After negotiating the peak, it's possible to reach Lawang the same day. After a two-hour descent, it's a long and hot three-hour walk back to the village. Head off early to avoid as much of the heat of the day as possible and make sure you have plenty of water. From the camp site, head back along the ridge-crest trail. A couple of hundred metres past the turn-off to Danau Segara Anak is a signposted right turn leading down a subsidiary ridge to Pada Balong and Sembalun Lawang. Once on the trail, it's easy to follow. It takes around two hours to reach the bottom.

At the bottom of the ridge (where you'll find Pada Balong shelter; 1800m), the trail levels out and crosses undulating to flat grassland all the way to Sembalun Lawang. After about an hour you will hit Tengengean shelter (1500m); it's then another 30 minutes to Pemantuan shelter (1300m). Early in the season long grass obscures the trail until about 30 minutes beyond Pemantuan. The trail crosses many bridges; at the final bridge, just before it climbs uphill to a lone tree, the trail seems to fork; take the right fork and climb the rise. From here, the trail follows the flank of Rinjani before swinging around to Lawang at the end. A guide is essential for this part of the trip.

Variations

Possible variations to the routes described above are outlined here:

- Compress the last two days into one (racking up a hefty 10 to 11 hours on the trail). On the plus side it's downhill all the way after the hard climb to the summit.
- Retrace your steps to Senaru after climbing to the summit, making a five-day circuit that includes another night at the hot springs.
- Another popular route, because the trail is well defined and (if you're experienced) can be trekked with only a porter, is a three-day hike from Senaru to the hot springs and back. The first night is spent at Pos III and the second at the hot springs. The return to Senaru on the final day takes eight to nine hours.
- For (almost) instant gratification (if you travel light and climb fast) you can reach the crater rim from Senaru in about six hours. You'll gain an altitude of approximately 2040m in 10km. Armed with a torch, some moonlight and a guide, set off at midnight to arrive for sunrise. The return takes about five hours.
- If you reach Pelawangan I early in the day, consider a side trip following the crater rim around to the east for about 3km to Gunung Senkereang (2919m). This point overlooks the gap in the rim where the stream from the hot springs flows out of the crater and northeast towards the sea. It's not an easy walk, however, and the track is narrow and very exposed in places – it would take around two hours to get there and back.
- Start trekking from Sembalun Lawang (a guide is essential), from where it takes six or seven hours to get to Pelewangan II. This is a shorter walk to the rim than from Senaru, with only a three-hour trek up the ridge.

because there have been (very) occasional attacks on hikers (see below). Climbing Rinjani during the wet season (November to March), when the tracks are often treacherously slippy and there's a real risk of landslides, is not at all advisable – the national park office usually forbids access to Rinjani for the first three months of the year. June to August is the only time you are guaranteed (well, almost) no rain or cloud, but it can still get *very* cold at the summit.

Senaru has the best services for trekkers, so most start their treks there. Those who want the fastest summit climb, however, should start from Sembalun Lawang on the eastern side.

Organised Treks

The best and most inexpensive way to organise a trip is to head to either the **RTC** (☎ satellite 08681210413 2; www.info2lombok.com) in Senaru or the **RIC** (🕑 6am-6pm) in Sembalun Lawang. Anyone passing through Senggigi can first contact the **Rinjani Trek Club** (☎ 693202; rtc.senggigi@gmail.com; Jl Raya Senggigi) office there. Funded by the New Zealand government, the centres use a rotation system so that all local trekking organisers get a slice of the hiking pie.

Whether you book through your losmen, or directly at the RTC, the RIC or the Rinjani Trek Club, the same trek packages (at the same prices) are offered. The most popular are four- or five-day treks from Senaru to Sembalun Lawang via the summit and include food, equipment, guide, porters, park fee and transport back to Senaru. The four-day trek costs 1,250,000Rp for two to four hikers and 1,050,000Rp for more than five. The deals are cheaper the more of you there are.

GUNUNG RINJANI SECURITY WARNING

Although there were incidents of armed robbery on Rinjani in 2000, in recent years safety was not an issue until a group was attacked in July 2005. While this is believed to be an isolated incident, we recommend that you seek safety advice locally before you set out.

There are plans to post police and mountain security guards inside the crater.

A number of agencies in Mataram, Senggigi and the Gili Islands can organise all-inclusive treks. Prices usually include everything outlined above, plus return transport from the point of origin. For example, **Perama** (www.peramatour.com), with offices in all of these locations, has a trekking package that leaves from any of the places above and goes via Senaru using RTC official guides for 1,600,000Rp per person (minimum of two people).

Guides & Porters

Hiking independently is not recommended, due to security and safety concerns; see the boxed text, left for more details.

If you don't want to do an all-inclusive trekking package with the RTC or the RIC, you can hire guides (100,000Rp per day) and porters (80,000Rp) from them independently, but make sure that you take a radio (10,000Rp per day). Contract your guides and porters directly from the centres in Senaru and Sembalun Lawang, as they are licensed for your security. Guides are knowledgeable and informative, but they won't carry anything for you, so take at least one porter. You also have to provide food, water and transport for them, and probably cigarettes as well.

Entrance Fee & Equipment

The entrance fee for the Rinjani National Park is 27,000Rp – register and pay at the RTC in Senaru or the RIC in Sembalun Lawang before you start your trek.

Sleeping bags and tents are essential and can be hired at either RTC or RIC. You'll also need solid footwear, layers of warm clothing, wet-weather gear, cooking equipment and a torch (flashlight), but these can also be hired from the RTC. Expect to pay about 50,000Rp a head per day for all your equipment.

Take a stove so you don't need to deplete the limited supply of firewood. Carry all rubbish out with you and make sure others in your party do the same.

Backpacks can be left at most losmen in Senaru or in the RTC for around 5000Rp per day.

Food & Supplies

Trek organisers at RTC and RIC can arrange food, or you can take your own. It's better to buy most supplies in Mataram or Senggigi, where it's cheaper and there's more choice, but some provisions are available in Senaru. Take plenty of water and a lighter.

Getting There & Away

For transport options from Sembalun Lawang to Senaru, see p518. If you've purchased a trekking package, transport back to the point of origin is usually included.

TETEBATU

☎ 0376

Tetebatu, nestling in the lower slopes of Gunung Rinjani, is an attractive rural retreat at an elevation just high enough (400m) to make the climate a tad more refreshing than down on the sticky coast. There are magnificent views across tobacco fields and rice paddies towards southern Lombok, east to the sea and north to Rinjani. The *open* that dot the landscape are used for drying tobacco, the major crop here. Tetebatu makes a fine setting for a few days' hiking to nearby waterfalls or visiting the surrounding handicraft villages.

Tetebatu is quite spread out, with facilities on roads north and east (nicknamed 'Waterfall Rd') of the *ojek* stop in the centre of the village. There's a **wartel** (🕑 9am-9pm) next to Salabuse Café.

Sights & Activities

A shady 4km track leading from the main road just north of the mosque heads into **Taman Wisata Tetebatu** (Monkey Forest) with black monkeys and waterfalls – you will need a guide to find them (ask at your losmen). Alternatively, you could take an *ojek* from the turn-off.

On the southern slopes of Gunung Rinjani National Park are two **waterfalls**. Both are accessible only by private transport or on a lovely 1½-hour walk (one way) through the rice fields from Tetebatu. If walking, even in a group, *be sure* to hire a reputable guide (ask at your losmen).

Locals believe that water from **Air Terjun Jukut** (Jeruk Manis, Air Temer; admission 2000Rp) will increase hair growth. The falls are a steep 2km walk from the car park at the end of the road.

Northwest of Tetebatu, **Air Terjun Joben** (Otak Kokok Gading; admission 2000Rp) is more of a public swimming pool, so it's less alluring.

Bicycles can be hired at Pondok Tetebatu, as well as other losmen, for 15,000Rp per day. The narrow country lanes around Tetebatu are a delight to explore by bike, particularly if you try to stick to east–west routes, which are far less challenging than the steep north–south inclines.

Sleeping & Eating

Most accommodation in Tetebatu has a rustic charm. Losmen on Waterfall Rd tend to be more funky.

Pondok Tetebatu (☎ 632572; s/d 30,000/45,000Rp) Just north of the intersection, this is a good choice. The two rows of neat, spotless rooms that face a pretty garden have Western toilets. There is also a simple roadside restaurant here offering tasty local food (dishes 8000Rp to 35,000Rp; open breakfast, lunch and dinner) here.

Losmen Hakiki (☎ 018 0803737407; cottages 50,000-70,000Rp) With a lovely aspect over rice fields, about 1km east of the intersection, this place has charming little *lumbung* with yellow window frames and serves tasty Indonesian and Sasak cuisine (dishes 7000Rp to 18,000Rp; open breakfast, lunch and dinner).

Cendrawasih Cottages (☎ 081 803726709; r 65,000Rp) Four gorgeous little *lumbung* cottages, with bamboo walls and showers/ *mandis,* facing a pond and garden. The elevated octagonal lounge and eating area (dishes 7000Rp to 22,000Rp; open breakfast, lunch and dinner) has sweeping views of the surrounding region. It's about 500m east of the intersection.

Wisma Soedjono (☎ 21309; r 75,000-150,000Rp, cottages 125,000Rp; 🏊) About 2km north of the intersection, these slightly soulless but functional rooms and lovely two-storey chalet-style cottages (with balconies and verandas) are scattered around a rambling family home. The large swimming pool is infrequently cleaned, however. There's also a fair restaurant serving loal and Western food (dishes 10,000Rp to 28,000Rp; open breakfast, lunch and dinner).

Salabuse Café (☎ 081 75731143; dishes 6000-17,500Rp; 🕑 breakfast, lunch & dinner) Cheery, cheap place serving Western, Indonesian and Sasak meals.

Getting There & Around

Buses go from Mandalika to Pomotong (7000Rp), which is on the main east–west highway. From there take a bemo to Kotaraja (2000Rp), then an *ojek* (3000Rp) or *cidomo* (4000Rp) to Tetebatu.

Motorcycles can be rented at Pondok Tetebatu, as well as other losmen, for 50,000Rp per day.

SOUTH OF TETEBATU

☎ 0376

It's best to rent or charter private transport from Tetebatu to visit the craft villages in the area.

The nearest market town to Tetebatu is **Kotaraja**, which is also the transport hub of the area. It's known for its skilled blacksmiths. There's a market on Monday and Wednesday morning.

Loyok is noted for its fine basketry and **Rungkang** is known for its pottery, made from a local black clay. You'll find workshops in both villages.

Masbagik is a large town on Lombok's east–west highway with a daily morning market, a huge cattle market on Monday afternoon, and an imposing new mosque with elegant minarets. There's an ATM opposite the mosque. **Masbagik Timur**, which is 1km east, is a centre for black-clay pottery and ceramic production.

Lendang Nangka is a Sasak village surrounded by picturesque countryside, 3km north of the highway. In and around the village you can see blacksmiths make knives, hoes and other tools using traditional techniques. A few silversmiths are also based here, and there's a excellent homestay, **Radiah's** (☎ 0376631463; per person incl meals 50,000Rp) run by English-speaker Radiah and his wife, Sannah, who make Western visitors very welcome and will explain Sasak traditions and all about local agriculture. Everyone knows their house in the village.

Pringgasela is a centre for traditional weaving on simple looms; the local textiles produced here feature coloured stripes. You can watch the weavers in action and buy sarongs and throws.

NUSA TENGGARA

SOUTH LOMBOK

☎ 0370

South Lombok is blessed with the island's best beaches, from dramatic cliff-backed coves to oceanic expanses that catch world-class waves. The region is noticeably drier than the rest of Lombok and more sparsely populated, with limited roads and public transport. Most visitors head for Kuta – the antithesis of its Balinese namesake – a tranquil, relaxed base for exploring the terrific southern coastline.

Praya

pop 35,000

Praya is the south's main town. It's a very spread out place, with tree-lined streets and a few old **Dutch buildings**. There's nothing of much interest to visitors here, however, except perhaps a couple of ATMs on Jl Jend Sudirman, but by 2008 Lombok's new international airport should open close by, boosting the local economy. Meanwhile, the bemo terminal, on the northwestern side of town, is the transport hub for the region.

Just up from the market, the **Dienda Hayu Hotel** (☎ 654319; Jl Untung Surapati 28; r 50,000-80,000Rp; ❄) has rooms with cold-water facilities that are in fair shape.

Around Praya

SUKARARA

The main street here is given over to touristy, commercial craft shops, but you may want to put up with the sales speak in order to see the various styles of weaving and see the weavers at work. **Darnia Setia Artshop** (🕑 7am-6pm) has the widest range of textiles, some coming from Sumba and elsewhere in Flores.

To reach Sukarara, take a bemo to Puyung (1500Rp) along the main road. From there, hire a *cidomo* (approximately 2500Rp) or walk the 2km to Sukarara.

Penujak

Penujak is well known for its traditional *gerabah* pottery, made from a local clay with the simplest of techniques. The pots are up to 1m high, and there are also various kitchen vessels and decorative figurines. The traditional pottery is a rich terracotta colour and hand burnished.

Penujak is on the main road from Praya to the south coast; any bemo to Sengkol or Kuta will drop you off (fares are approximately 2000Rp).

Rembitan & Sade

The area from Sengkol down to Kuta is a centre for traditional Sasak culture. Regular bemos cover this route.

Rembitan is on a hill just west of the main road. It's a slightly sanitised 'traditional' Sasak village but still boasts an authentic cluster of thatched houses and *lumbung*. On top of the hill is **Masjid Kuno**, an ancient thatched-roof mosque that's a place of pilgrimage for Lombok's Muslims, as one of the founding fathers of Islam in Indonesia is said to be buried here.

On the road between Rembitan and Sade are stores selling Javanese-style **batik paintings** (albeit painted by locals).

A little further south is **Sade**, another traditional, picturesque village that has been extensively renovated. It has informative guides who'll tell you about Sasak houses and village life. Donations are 'requested' by guides at both villages – 3000Rp to 7000Rp is enough, and expect to pay for photos too.

Kuta

Lombok's Kuta beach is a magnificent stretch of white sand and turquoise sea with rugged hills rising around it. Surfers are drawn here by the world-class waves, but the village has a languid charm of its own with some delightful hotels and a succession of dramatic bite-shaped bays nearby.

Despite long-slated plans for a succession of five-star resorts, these have failed to materialise, and this superb coast is still all but undeveloped, with far, far fewer facilities than the (in)famous Kuta Beach in Bali. Kuta comes alive during the annual **Nyale Fishing Festival** (in February or March; see right) and during the main tourist season (August), but for the rest of the year it's very quiet.

Tourism dominates the local economy, but locals also harvest seaweed for the cosmetic industry in the dry season.

INFORMATION & ORIENTATION

Several places change money, including Kuta Indah Hotel and Segare Anak Cottages, which is also a postal agency.

There's a small wartel in town and the Kuta Corner Internet café next to Matahari Inn also buys, sells and rents second-hand books. The local market fires up on Sunday and Wednesday at 7am. **Perama** (☎ 654846), based at Segare Anak Cottages, runs tourist shuttle buses to Mataram (75,000Rp) with connections to Senggigi and elsewhere.

> **NYALE FESTIVAL**
>
> On the 19th day of the 10th month in the Sasak calendar – generally February or March – hundreds of Sasaks gather on the beach at Kuta, Lombok. When night falls, fires are built and young people sit around competing with each other in rhyming couplets called *pantun*. At dawn the next day, the first *nyale* (wormlike fish) are caught, after which it's time for the teenagers to have fun. In a colourful procession, boys and girls sail out to sea – in different boats – and chase one another with lots of noise and laughter. The *nyale* are eaten raw or grilled, and are believed to have aphrodisiac properties. A good catch is a sign that the rice harvest will also be good.

Virtually everything in Kuta is on a single road that runs parallel to the beach, either east or west of the junction where the road from Praya hits town.

ACTIVITIES

Cycling

The guesthouse Mimpi Manis rents out bicycles for 20,000Rp a day. Pedal to the east to the Novotel and Pantai Segar. Westwards, there's an extremely steep hill leading to the Ashtari restaurant.

Surfing

Plenty of good waves break on the reefs, including 'lefts' and 'rights', in the bay in front of Kuta, and some more on the reefs east of Tanjung Aan. As the waves break a long way from shore, use local boatmen to tow you out for around 50,000Rp. About 7km east of Kuta is the fishing village of Gerupak, where there are several breaks on the reefs at the entrance of Teluk Gerupak (Gerupak Bay). There are plenty of breaks further out, but nearly all need a boat; the current charter rate is a negotiable 200,000Rp per day. Mawi also offers consistent surf.

Drop by the friendly **Kimen Surf** (☎ 655064; kimensurf@yahoo.com), just west of the junction, for swell forecasts, tips and information. Boards can be rented here (30,000Rp per day), repairs are undertaken, lessons are offered (310,000Rp for four hours), and day trips to Gerupak (240,000Rp) and Bangko Bangko (950,000Rp) are organised.

SLEEPING

Breakfast is included at all the places listed below. All accommodation is virtually on or just behind the beach, except one.

Budget

Segare Anak Cottages (☎ 654846; segareanakbungalows@yahoo.co.id; r 35,000-65,000Rp) Overlooking a pretty garden, the basic huts here have seen better days, but the newer concrete bungalows are a good deal and worth paying the extra for. Segare is around 800m east of the junction; it's also home to a moneychanger and the Perama office.

Melon Homestay (☎ 081 7367892; angela_grannemann@web.de; r 50,000Rp, apt 65,000Rp) A terrific deal, this place has two gorgeous apartments with lounges and self-catering facilities; one has sea views from its balcony. There are also a couple of smaller modern rooms with verandas and bathrooms. It's about 400m east of the junction.

Mimpi Manis (☎ 081 8369950; www.mimpimanis.com; s 50,000-90,000Rp, d 65,000-105,000Rp) An extremely welcoming English-and Balinese-owned guesthouse with two spotless, bright rooms and a two-storey house, each with a shower room and TV/DVD player. There's home-cooked Balinese and Western food (dishes 9000-22,000Rp), a darts board and plenty of good books to flick through. It's 2km inland from the beach, but the owners offer a free drop-off service.

Rinjani Bungalows (☎ 654849; s/d with fan 80,000/95,000Rp, with air-con 200,000/250,000Rp; ❄) Looking good, this well-run place is about 1km east of the junction. It has very clean bamboo bungalows with ikat bedspreads and bathrooms with Western toilets, and spanking-new spacious concrete bungalows, each with two double beds, hot water and hardwood furniture.

Surfers Inn (☎ 655582; www.lombok-surfersinn.com; r with fan 100,000-160,000Rp, with air con 180,000-500,000Rp; ❄ 🏊) A very smart, stylish and orderly place with five classes of modern rooms, each with huge windows and large beds, and some with sofas. The inn is about 600m east of the junction. Book ahead, as it's very popular.

Also recommended:

G'day Inn (☎ 655432; s/d 40,000/60,000Rp) This friendly, family-run place offers clean, recently renovated rooms, some with hot water, and a café. Located about 300m east of the junction.

Ketapang Bungalows (☎ 655194; s/d 30,000/40,000Rp) Has simple thatched-roof bungalows with verandas; it's 500m east of the junction.

Lamancha (☎ 655186; s/d 40,000/50,000Rp) Four simple but spotless semidetached huts with *mandis* and showers; it's 400m east of the junction.

Midrange

Matahari Inn (☎ 655000; www.matahariinn.com; r 180,000-550,000Rp; ❄ 🏊) This Balinese-themed hotel has an array of baroque rooms, each suffering somewhat from gaudy artefact overkill and an excess of reclining Buddhas and the like. Nevertheless, the garden, shaded by bamboo and palm trees, is gorgeous. It's just west of the junction.

Kuta Indah Hotel (☎ 653781; kutaindah@indonet.id; r US$17-30; ❄ 🏊) Set around a well-tended garden with a clipped lawn, these cottages are spacious but slightly tired-looking, though the pool's nice. It's about 400m west of the junction.

Tastura Beach Resort (☎ 655540; tastura@mataram.wasantara.net.id; bungalows US$25-30; ❄ 🏊) Bland government-owned hotel with 20 distinctly average bungalows in expansive grounds 600m east of the junction. Rooms could be much cleaner.

Top End

Novotel Lombok (☎ 653333; www.novotel-lombok.com; r without/with terrace US$120/140, villas US$235 plus 21% tax; ❄ 🏊) This attractive resort 3km east of the junction has contemporary-styled rooms with coconut-wood flooring and furniture and lovely thatched Sasak-style villas. The two pools face a superb beach, and there's a wonderful spa and a plethora of activities on offer, including catamaran sailing, fishing, scuba diving and even archery classes.

EATING & DRINKING

In addition to the places reviewed below, there are warungs along the esplanade.

Family Cafe (☎ 653748; mains 6000-30,000Rp; 🕑 breakfast, lunch & dinner) Large thatched restaurant with a tempting menu, including delicious *sate pusut* (served with coconut and chilli) and *urap urup* (mixed vegetables with sambal and coconut). It's just west of the junction. It also serves cocktails.

our pick **Astari** (dishes 8000-22,000Rp; 🕑 breakfast, lunch & dinner) Perched on a mountain top

2km west of town on the road to Mawan, this remarkable, mainly vegetarian lounge-restaurant has a to-die-for healthy menu that takes in winsome breakfasts, focaccia sandwiches and creatively assembled mains; there's always a daily special too. The view matches the cuisine, and it's easy to lose hours up here daydreaming, enjoying the music, browsing through magazines, playing backgammon and gazing out over Kuta's low hump-backed hills to the distant ocean rollers.

Ilalang (dishes 11,000-35,000Rp; breakfast, lunch & dinner) Right on the beach, this ramshackle-looking place scores for its fresh seafood.

Cafe Lombok Lounge (☎ 655542; dishes 12,000-30,000Rp; breakfast, lunch & dinner) Inexpensive Indonesian food, including *cumi cumi* (squid), and Western dishes like omelettes.

Mascot Pub (dishes 12,000-38,000Rp; 11-2am) This pub offers the only nightlife in town. Come here to see local bands most Friday and Saturday nights. Also serves Indonesian food.

Empat Ikan (Novotel Lombok; mains 75,000-175,000Rp; breakfast, lunch & dinner) For something more fancy, this beachside hotel restaurant is strong on fish and seafood.

GETTING THERE & AWAY

Kuta is a hassle to reach by public transport. From Mandalika terminal in Mataram you'll have to go via Praya (5000Rp), then to Sengkol (3000Rp) and finally to Kuta (2000Rp). You'll usually have to change buses at all these places. Many people opt for the Perama shuttle bus option from Senggigi or the Gili Islands to Kuta.

GETTING AROUND

Ojeks congregate around the main junction as you enter Kuta. Bemos go east of Kuta to Awang and Tanjung Aan (2500Rp), and west to Selong Blanak (3000Rp), or can be chartered to nearby beaches. The guesthouse Mimpi Manis rents motorcycles for 35,000Rp a day.

Around Kuta

Quite good roads traverse the coast to the east, passing a series of beautiful bays punctuated by headlands. There's public transport, but it's much easier by motorcycle.

Pantai Segar is about 2km east around the first headland, within walking distance of the town. The enormous rock of Batu Kotak, 2km further on, divides two glorious white-sand beaches. Continuing east, **Tanjung Aan** is a very fine beach with chalk-white powdery sand. Due to a spate of problems with stealing, there's a security guard keeping an eye on the place – even so, it's best not to bring valuables to the beach. The road continues another 2km to the fishing village and surfer's fave **Gerupak**, where there's a market on Tuesday and a restaurant on the beach. Alternatively, turn northeast just before Tanjung Aan and go to **Awang**, a busy fishing village with a sideline in seaweed harvesting. You could take a boat from Awang across to **Ekas** (a charter costs around 120,000Rp) or to some of the other not-so-secret surf spots in this bay.

West of Kuta are a succession of outstanding beaches that all have superb surf when conditions are right. It's possible that this region may eventually be developed when the new airport is completed near Praya, but for now it remains near-pristine and all but deserted. The road, which is potholed and very steep in places, doesn't follow the coast closely, so you'll need to detour slightly to find the beaches. **Mawan** (parking motorcycle/car 2000/4000Rp) is the most impressive, a bite-shaped bay backed by steep green hills with a fine sandy beach below. **Tampa** is similar but a little wilder – you will need to drive through rice fields along a grassy road and past a tiny village to get there. **Mawi** (parking motorcycle/car 2000/4000Rp), 16km from Kuta, is an absolutely stunning beach and surfing stronghold with a legendary barrel wave, but there can be a very strong riptide, so be extra careful. Sadly, thefts have been reported here. **Selong Blanak** is another wonderfully expansive stretch of sand.

From **Pengantap**, the road climbs across a headland to descend to another superb

> **SOUTH LOMBOK SECURITY WARNING**
>
> Tourists have been threatened and robbed at knifepoint on the back roads of south Lombok, in particular around Mawi. Ask around about the latest situation and do not leave vehicles unattended – find a local to watch it for a tip.

bay; follow this around for about 1km, then look out for the turn-off west to **Blongas**, a sheltered bay with relatively calm water and fine swimming. The road to reach it is very steep, rough and winding, but it has breathtaking scenery.

EAST LOMBOK

☎ 0376

All that most travellers see of the east coast is Labuhan Lombok, the port for ferries to Sumbawa, but the road around the north-eastern coast is in fair shape, and a round-the-island trip is quite feasible. Similarly, the once-remote southeastern peninsula is becoming more accessible, particularly to those with their own transport.

Labuhan Lombok

Labuhan Lombok, also known as Labuhan Kayangan, is the port for ferries and boats to Sumbawa. The town centre of Labuhan Lombok, 3km west of the ferry terminal, is a scruffy place but has great views of Gunung Rinjani.

Try to avoid staying overnight, as there's only one decent place, **Losmen Lima Tiga** (☎ 23316; Jl Raya Kayangan; r 55,000Rp). About 2.5km inland from the port on the main road, this is very clean family-run place with neat little rooms and spotless shared bathrooms. There are warungs in the town and around the ferry terminal.

GETTING THERE & AWAY

Bus & Bemo

Frequent buses and bemos travel between Labuhan Lombok and Mandalika terminal in Mataram (11,000Rp, two hours), and also head north from Labuhan Lombok to Anyar. Note that public transport to and from Labuhan Lombok is often marked 'Labuhan Kayangan' or 'Tanjung Kayangan'. Buses and bemos that don't go directly to Labuhan Lombok but just travel the main road along the east coast will only drop you off at the port entrance, from where you'll have to catch another bemo to the ferry terminal. Don't walk; it's too far.

Ferry

See p492 for details of ferry connections between Lombok and Sumbawa, and p497 for bus connections between Mataram and Sumbawa.

North of Labuhan Lombok

This road has limited public transport and becomes very steep and windy as you near Anyar. There are isolated black-sand beaches along the way, particularly at Obel Obel.

Leaving Labuhan Lombok, look out for the giant mahogany trees about 4km north of the harbour. From Labuhan Pandan, or from further north at Sugian, you can charter a boat to the uninhabited **Gili Sulat** and **Gili Pentangan**. Both islands have lovely white beaches and good coral for snorkelling, but no facilities.

Just before the village of Labuhan Pandan, 15km from Labuhan Lombok, the Swiss-run **Matahari Inn** (☎ 081 23749915; www.pondok-matahari.com; s/d 90,000/120,000Rp) is a beautifully peaceful place with clean, comfortable bungalows right on the beach and two rooms inland. There's good food (dishes 7000Rp to 26,000Rp), snorkelling and fun dives (US$31 per dive), and scuba-diving courses are offered by the instructor owners.

South of Labuhan Lombok

Selong, the capital of the East Lombok administrative district, has some Dutch-colonial buildings. The transport junction for the region is just to the west of Selong at **Pancor**, where you can catch bemos to most points south.

On the coast is **Labuhan Haji**, where the black sand is a bit grubby, but the water is OK for swimming. The basic, isolated bungalows at **Melewi's Beach Hotel** (☎ 621241; r 40,000Rp) are almost on the beach and have great views across to Sumbawa.

Tanjung Luar is one of Lombok's main fishing ports and has lots of Bugis-style houses on stilts. From there, the road swings west to **Keruak**, where wooden boats are built, and continues past the turn-off to **Sukaraja**, a traditional Sasak village where you can buy woodcarvings. Just west of Keruak a road leads south to **Jerowaru** and the southeastern peninsula. You'll need your own transport; be warned that it's easy to lose your way and the roads go from bad to worse.

A sealed road branches off west past Jerowaru – it gets pretty rough but eventually reaches **Ekas**, from where you can charter a boat to Awang across the bay.

NUSA TENGGARA

The only accommodation in this remote part of Lombok is the spectacularly sited **Heaven on the Planet** (☎ 081 23705393; www.heaventheplanet.co.nz; basic chalets 100,000-150,000Rp, villas 300,000-500,000Rp; 🅧), an ideal base for activity junkies, with surfing, diving and abseiling facilities. There are two restaurants and a well-stocked bar. The road here is terrible, so it's best to contact the hotel and get them to pick you up, or charter a boat from Awang (around 120,000Rp).

SUMBAWA

The rugged land mass of Sumbawa looms large between Lombok and Flores, separated from each by a narrow strait. Larger than Bali and Lombok combined, Sumbawa is a sprawling island of twisted and jutting peninsulas, with a coast fringed by precipitous hills and angular bights, and a mountain line of weathered volcanic stumps stretching along its length.

Though Sumbawa is an extremely scenic island, it's a poor one, and health and education is very much at the development stage in most parts. Few Western travellers venture here other than wave-seekers – there are surf camps at Sekongkang and Hu'u. Transport connections off the well-served cross-island road are infrequent and uncomfortable, so to explore the countryside it's best to charter transport or rent a motorcycle.

Culture

Sumbawa is roughly divided between two linguistically and, to some extent, ethnically distinct peoples: the Sumbawanese speakers, who probably reached the west of the island from Lombok, and the Bimanese speakers, who independently occupied the Tambora Peninsula and the east. The squatter, darker-skinned Bimanese are more closely related to the people of Flores, while the western Sumbawans are closer to the Sasaks of Lombok. Both languages have considerable variation in dialect.

Sumbawa is an overwhelmingly Islamic island; Christian missionaries didn't even bother to try here. But in remote parts *adat* (traditional indigenous and animist traditions) thrive under the veneer of Islam.

During festivals you may come across traditional Sumbawan fighting, a sort of bare-fisted boxing called *berempah*. Horse and water buffalo races are also held before the rice is planted.

History

Before the 17th century, Sumbawa had been subject to both Javanese Hindu and Islamic cultural influences, but the expansionist Makassarese states of Sulawesi gained control of the island by force and, by 1625, Sumbawa's rulers had converted to Islam.

Western Sumbawa held sway over much of Lombok and this brought it into conflict

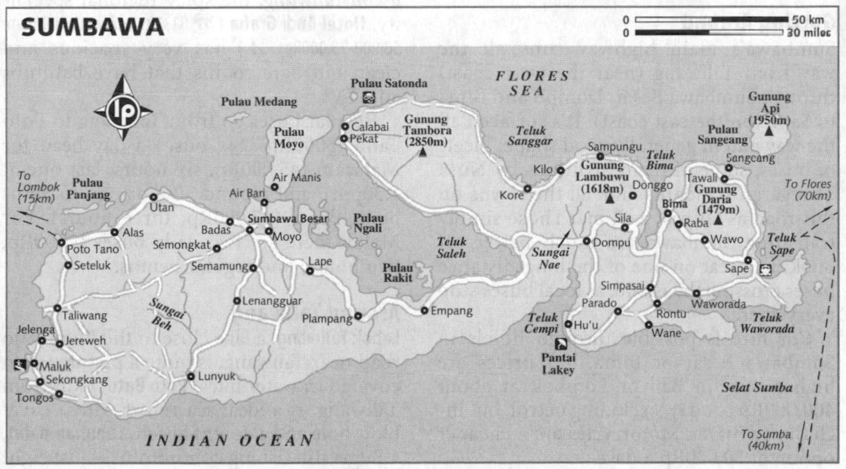

with the Balinese during the 18th century. Barely had the wars finished when Gunung Tambora in Sumbawa exploded in April 1815, killing tens of thousands. One of the most cataclysmic eruptions of modern times, it reduced a 4200m peak to approximately 2850m and devastated agricultural land. All around the globe, the following year was known as 'the year without a summer', due to the amount of volcanic ash in the atmosphere.

From the middle of the 19th century, immigrants repopulated Sumbawa, and the island's coastal regions have small numbers of Javanese, Makassarese, Bugis, Sasaks and other ethnic groups.

In 1908 the Dutch intervened to prevent the prospect of a war between the three states that made up western Sumbawa. The sultans kept a fair degree of their power under the Dutch, but after Indonesian independence their titles were abolished; now their descendants hold official power just when they are functionaries of the national government. The only traces of the old sultanates are the palaces in the towns of Sumbawa Besar and Bima.

Dangers & Annoyances

Most Sumbawans are incredibly friendly and hospitable, but you may encounter a degree of resentment against Western influence. Protestors destroyed a remote exploration camp belonging to mining giant Newmount in March 2006.

Getting Around

Sumbawa's main highway runs all the way from Taliwang (near the west coast) through Sumbawa Besar, Dompu and Bima to Sape (on the east coast). It's surfaced all the way and in generally good shape. Fleets of buses, some of them luxurious by Nusa Tenggaran standards, link all the towns on this road as far east as Bima. Those simply transiting Sumbawa are much better off booking a seat on one of the long-distance buses crossing the island, as local buses stop everywhere.

Car hire is possible through hotels in Sumbawa Besar or Bima, but prices are higher than in Bali or Lombok at about 400,000Rp per day, excluding petrol, but including a driver. Motorcycles are a cheaper option at 50,000Rp a day.

WEST SUMBAWA

☎ 0372

This relatively arid region is very sparsely populated, with the oceanic rollers of Maluk and Sekongkang drawing just a trickle of visitors.

At one time the name Sumbawa only applied to the western half of the island, which fell under the sway of the sultan of Sumbawa; the eastern half of the island was known as Bima.

Poto Tano

Poto Tano is the main port for ferries to/from Lombok, but there's absolutely no reason to loiter.

Ferries run every 45 minutes, 24 hours a day, between Labuhan Lombok and Poto Tano (12,500Rp, 1½ hours). The through buses from Mataram to Sumbawa Besar, Taliwang or Bima include the ferry fare.

Buses also meet the ferry and go to Taliwang (5000Rp, one hour) and Sumbawa Besar (9000Rp, two hours).

Taliwang

Though it's the regional capital, Taliwang is little more than an oversized village, 30km south of Poto Tano down a good, if narrow sealed road. It's a conservative place with a merchant class of Indonesians of Arab descent. The sale of alcohol is forbidden here.

If you need a bite to eat, head to **Rumah Makan Totang Raja** (☎ 81263; Jl Jendral Sudirman; dishes 6000-15,000Rp), where you can tuck into *ayam taliwang*, the spicy regional speciality. **Hotel Andi Graha** (☎ 81319; Jl Jendral Sudirman; 50,000-75,000Rp; ❄) has very spacious and clean but bare rooms that have bathtubs and TVs.

Regular buses go from Taliwang to Poto Tano (5000Rp). Six buses a day head for Mataram (45,000Rp, six hours, last one at 1.30pm), and around 30 a day go to Sumbawa Besar (17,000Rp, three hours). For Maluk there are two daily buses (7000Rp, two hours) and regular bemos.

Around Taliwang

Lebok Taliwang, a lake close to the Poto Tano road near Taliwang, is quite a picture when covered in water lilies. **Poto Batu**, 6km from Taliwang, is a local sea resort with a cave/blow hole and a decent beach. **Labuhan-balat**, a Bugis stilt fishing community of just eight houses on a very pretty bay, is 7km from Taliwang; take a truck or bemo here.

From Taliwang, bemos and trucks run 11km south over a good sealed road to Jereweh, from where it is 6km to the beach at **Jelenga**, popular with surfers for the offshore 'left' Scar Reef. **Jelenga Beach Bungalows** (bungalows 35,000Rp) has very basic accommodation that fronts the beach.

Maluk & Sekongkang

A key surfing destination, **Maluk** village is 30km south of Taliwang down a (mainly) sealed but potholed road. The superb beach has white sand framing turquoise-and-deep-blue waters. Its isolation had kept the number of visitors to a trickle, but a massive mining project near Maluk has driven a wave of development.

The open-cut gold mine about 30km inland is the biggest thing to hit Sumbawa since Islam. The Newmont mine employs about 4000 workers, extracting copper and gold, and though this had a huge impact on Maluk when it first opened, the expats and bars have now shifted to Townside, a nearby gated private enclave. Maluk has since reverted to type as a provincial, if prospering and bustling little place. There's a BNI bank with ATM on Jl Raya Maluk, and Wartel Jaya just off it has (pedestrian) internet access.

Fifteen kilometres further south, the spread out settlement of **Sekongkang** also has a fine surf beach and a scattering of upmarket accommodation options geared to attract the high rollers from the Newmont mine. The beach is at Sekongkang Bawah, 2km downhill from Sekongkang Atas, where some buses stop.

Of the famous surf spots, Supersuck is a powerful 'left' reef break near Maluk that can give 100m rides; Yo Yo's in Sekongkang Bawah offers two reliably consistent 'right' reef breaks.

SLEEPING & EATING

Kiwi Maluk (☎ 635166; Jl Pasir Putih, Maluk; r with fan/air-con 85,000/200,000Rp;) A surfers' inn where the fan-only rooms are pretty rough around the edges. The air-con options are clean and comfortable with good beds and bathtubs with hot water. The barnlike bar has a darts board and serves inexpensive Western and Indonesian faves (dishes 10,00Rp to 32,000Rp; open breakfast, lunch and dinner).

Hotel Trophy (☎ 635119; fax 635130; Jl Raya Maluk, Maluk; r incl breakfast 180,000-432,000Rp;) Offers four classes of rooms, quite excellent by Sumbawan standards. All are spotless and nicely designed, with big beds, reading lights and wardrobes, and some have sofas and minibars; however, the restaurant is pricey (mains 30,000Rp to 40,000Rp; open breakfast, lunch and dinner).

Yo Yo Resort (☎ 081 23951899; Sekongkang; r US$24-48;) Formerly a surf camp, this badly-run place has poor-value rooms – some even lack windows.

Tropical Beach Resort & Spa (☎ 289104; www.tropicalbeachresort.com; Sekongkang; r US$60-95, villas US$125;) On a fine sandy cove, this place has a huge pool. The rooms – quite elegant, though overpriced – are kitted out with quality wooden furniture, some with four-poster beds.

Rantung (Sekongkang; dishes 30,000-70,000Rp; breakfast, lunch & dinner) This expensive beach bar-restaurant has Western food, including club sandwiches and steaks, and it also serves some Chinese and Mexican dishes.

Masakan Padang (Jl Raya Maluk, Maluk; meals 8000-18,000Rp; breakfast, lunch & dinner) Has good, cheap Padang food and cold beer.

There are plenty of warungs along Jl Raya Maluk that serve up delicious *ikan bakar* (grilled fish).

GETTING THERE & AWAY

Two buses a day travel between Taliwang and Maluk (7000Rp, 1½ hours), but bemos cover the route hourly. Two buses leave Maluk for Sumbawa Besar (22,000Rp, 7½ hours) at 7am and 8.30am daily.

SUMBAWA BESAR

☎ 0371 / pop 55,000

Sumbawa Besar, often shortened to just 'Sumbawa' by locals, is the principal town of the western half of the island. It's a resolutely provincial, unexceptional place where horse carts called *benhur* still hold their own with bemos, and there are no attractions except for the old palace. A trip out to Pulau Moyo or to nearby villages can be rewarding, but they can be difficult to reach. For most travellers, Sumbawa Besar is just a rest stop on the journey across the island.

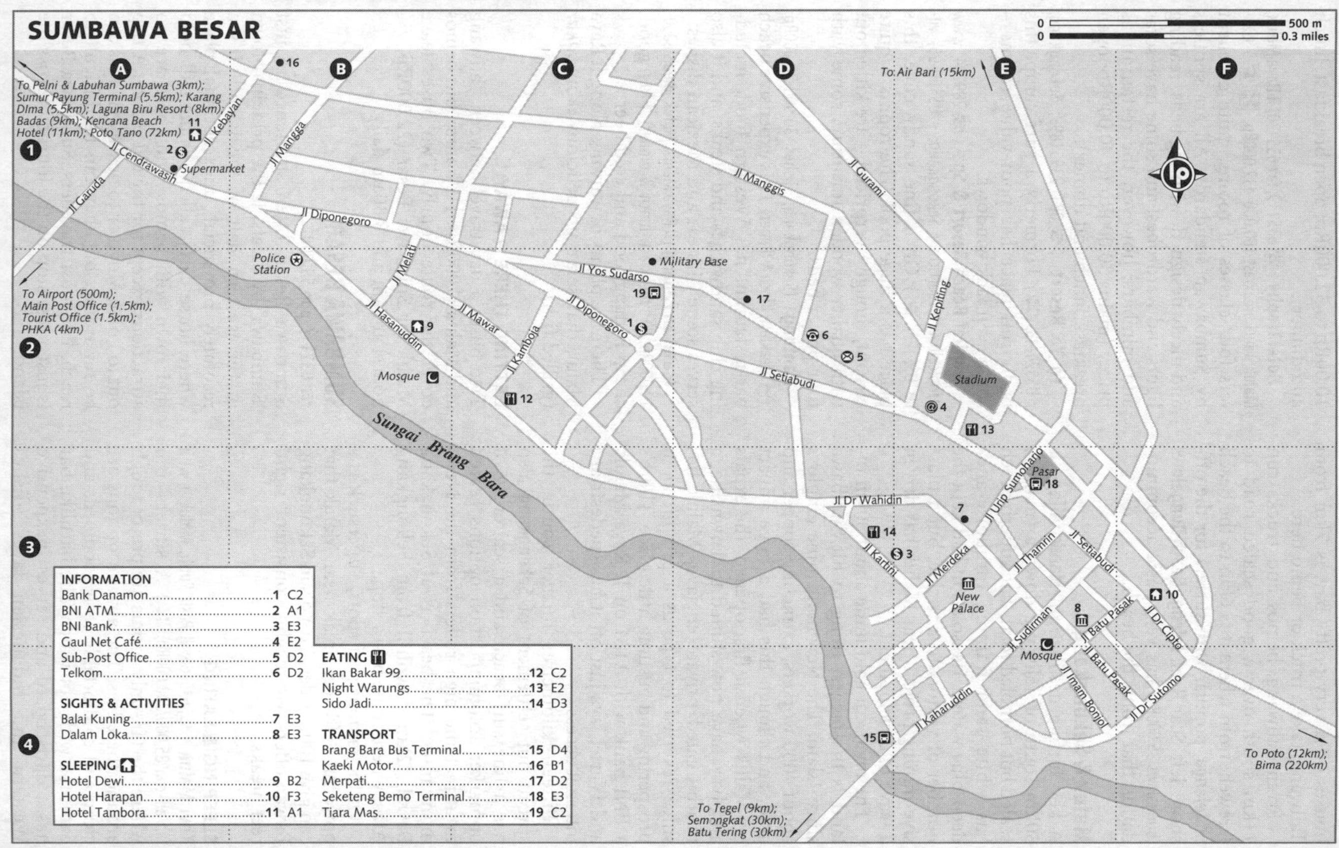
SUMBAWA BESAR
0 500 m
0 0.3 miles
A
B
C
D
E
F
1
2
3
4
To Pelni & Labuhan Sumbawa (3km); Sumur Payung Terminal (5.5km); Karang Dlma (5.5km); Laguna Biru Resort (8km); Badas (9km); Kencana Beach Hotel (11km); Poto Tano (72km)
To Airport (500m); Main Post Office (1.5km); Tourist Office (1.5km); PHKA (4km)
To Air Bari (15km)
To Tegel (9km); Semongkat (30km); Batu Tering (30km)
To Poto (12km); Bima (220km)
Jl Kebayan
Jl Cendrawasih
Jl Garuda
Supermarket
Jl Mangga
Jl Diponegoro
Police Station
Jl Melati
Jl Hasanuddin
Jl Mawar
Jl Kambola
Mosque
Sungai Brang Bara
Jl Yos Sudarso
Military Base
Jl Manggis
Jl Gurami
Jl Kepiting
Stadium
Jl Setiabudi
Jl Dr Wahidin
Jl Unp Sumoharjo
Pasar
Jl Kartini
Jl Merdeka
Jl Thamrin
New Palace
Jl Sudirman
Jl Batu Pasak
Jl Dr Cipto
Jl Imam Bonjol
Jl Dr Sutomo
Jl Kaharuddin
INFORMATION
Bank Danamon 1 C2
BNI ATM 2 A1
BNI Bank 3 E3
Gaul Net Café 4 E2
Sub-Post Office 5 D2
Telkom 6 D2
SIGHTS & ACTIVITIES
Balai Kuning 7 E3
Dalam Loka 8 E3
SLEEPING
Hotel Dewi 9 B2
Hotel Harapan 10 F3
Hotel Tambora 11 A1
EATING
Ikan Bakar 99 12 C2
Night Warungs 13 E2
Sido Jadi 14 D3
TRANSPORT
Brang Bara Bus Terminal 15 D4
Kaeki Motor 16 B1
Merpati 17 D2
Seketeng Bemo Terminal 18 E3
Tiara Mas 19 C2

Orientation

Sumbawa Besar is fairly small, making it navigable on foot, except maybe for trips to the main post office or tourist office, which are only a bemo or *benhur* ride away.

Information

Bank Danamon (Jl Diponegoro) Gives credit-card cash advances.

BNI bank (Bank Negara Indonesia; Jl Kartini 10; 8am-2.30pm Mon-Fri, 8am-noon Sat) Has currency exchange and an ATM. There's a second ATM next to Hotel Tambora.

Gaul Net Café (Jl Setiabudi 14; per hr 11,000Rp) Internet access here is not quick.

Main post office (Jl Garuda)

Perlindungan Hutan dan Konservasi Alam (PHKA; ☎ 23941; 8am-3pm Mon-Fri) The office of the national park service has information about Pulau Moyo and can occasionally offer transport to the island. It's about 4km southwest of town in the village of Nijang; take a bemo from the roundabout on Jl Garuda.

Sub-post office (Jl Yos Sudarso) This is nearer the town centre.

Telkom office (Jl Yos Sudarso; 24hr) The cheapest place to make international calls.

Tourist office (☎ 23714; Jl Bungur 1; 7am-2pm Mon-Thu, to 11am Fri, to 1pm Sat) Just off Jl Garuda, 100m south of the main post office on the edge of town. The staff try to be helpful, and brochures are available.

Sights

DALAM LOKA (SULTAN'S PALACE)

Constructed in 1885, the remains of this imposing palace, which covers an entire city block, had deteriorated until near dereliction by the 1980s. A rather shoddy subsequent renovation has left this once regal structure with an ignominious tin roof, which provides shelter to a few of the original pillars and carved beams that remain. The premises are locked, but if you loiter with intent on Jl Batu Pasak the caretaker, who speaks some English, should show up. Inside are a few illustrations, explanations in Bahasa Indonesia and an old palanquin, but otherwise it is empty. A small donation towards the upkeep is customary.

The descendants of the sultans now live in the **Balai Kuning** (Yellow House; ☎ 21101; Jl Dr Wahidin), a handsome Art Deco–style mansion with yellow shutters. There are numerous artefacts from the days of the sultanate here. Call first to take a look in their house. Again, a small donation is expected.

Sleeping

If you've come from Lombok or Bali be prepared for a quantum drop in quality. Budget rooms proliferate on Jl Hasanuddin, with a mosque nearby as a wake-up call for those early buses.

Hotel Harapan (☎ 21629; Jl Dr Cipto 7; s/d 25,000/35,000Rp) A family-run place with tiny, half-decent rooms with *mandis* and Western toilets around a courtyard.

Hotel Dewi (☎ 21170; Jl Hasanuddin 60; s/d 25,000/35,000Rp, with air-con 55,000-90,0000Rp;) Rambling place with a warren of rooms, all with bizarre 1970s-style furnishings, but at least they are good value. The 'VIPs' have hot water and air-con. There's a cheap restaurant here.

Hotel Tambora (☎/fax 21555; Jl Kebayan; s 45,000-209,000Rp, d 66,000-253,000Rp;) A once-popular hotel with an impressive lobby. It has a selection of unlovable rooms with mismatched décor highlighted by overhead strip lighting. Still, there are usually vacancies here.

Kencana Beach Hotel (☎ 22555; fax 22439; Poto Tano road km11; bungalows 90,000Rp, with air-con 180,000-300,000Rp;) By far the best choice in the area, this is a well-run and enjoyable place on a quiet, sandy cove. There's a selection of good timber bungalows, many right on the beach, a big pool, and tasty Western and Indonesian food in the restaurant. It's 11km west of town.

Laguna Biru Resort (☎ 23777; laguna_biru@telkom.net; Poto Tano road km8; d with shared/private bathroom 350,000/400,000Rp) Eight kilometres west of town, this place is geared to Japanese divers and has tatami mats and garish but comfortable rooms, though some lack a private bathroom (shared facilities are Western-style).

Eating

Ikan Bakar 99 (☎ 23065; Jl Hasanuddin; dishes 9000-17,000Rp; breakfast, lunch & dinner) Inexpensive place to eat fresh seafood, including tasty *kepitang rebus* (boiled crab) and the house special *ikan bakar*.

Sido Jadi (☎ 22398; dishes 12,000-32,000Rp; breakfast, lunch & dinner) Clean, popular restaurant offering large portions of Chinese favourites.

For a cheap feed make your way to the warungs in front of the stadium, where you'll find sate sizzling and *bakso* (meatball soup).

Getting There & Away

AIR

There are two flights a week with **Merpati** (☎ 22002; Jl Yos Sudarso 16) to/from Mataram, with connections to Denpasar. Departure tax is 6000Rp.

BOAT

Pelni's *Tilongkabila* calls in at the small port of Badas, 9km west of Sumbawa Besar, every month en route to Lombok, Bali, and Sampit, Kalimantan. The *Tatamailau* links Badas with Flores, Alor, Timor and Papua. The Pelni office is at Labuhan Sumbawa, the fishing port, 3km west of town on the Poto Tano road.

BUS

Sumbawa Besar's main long-distance bus terminal is the Sumur Payung terminal at Karang Dima, 5.5km northwest of town on the highway, although some morning buses to Bima leave from the **Brang Bara Terminal** (Jl Kaharuddin). Routes include Bima (45,000Rp, seven hours via Dompu, six daily between 7am and 8pm); Poto Tano (12,000Rp, two hours, very regularly until 5pm); Mataram (70,000Rp including ferry, seven hours, four daily between 7am and 10am); Denpasar (180,000Rp including ferries, around 12 hours, two daily). You can book tickets at **Tiara Mas** (☎ 21241; Jl Yos Sudarso). Cheaper buses without air-con leave for Mataram (55,000Rp) throughout the day.

Getting Around

TO/FROM THE AIRPORT

It's easy to walk into town from the airport, which is only 500m from Hotel Tambora. Turn to your right as you exit the airport terminal and cross the bridge. Alternatively, take a yellow bemo (1000Rp) or an *ojek* (2000Rp).

BEMO

The streets here, apart from the bemo speedway along Jl Hasanuddin, are relatively stress-free. Bemos and *benhur* cost 1000Rp for trips anywhere around town.

The local **Seketeng bemo terminal** (Jl Setiabudi) is in front of the *pesar* (market). For trips to villages around Sumbawa Besar, there are public bemos. Start early, as there are often only one or two bemos daily; after that it's necessary to charter.

CAR & MOTORCYCLES

One of the few places offering rental is **Kabeki Motor** (☎ 22710; Hotel Cirebon, Jl Kebayan 4). A Kijang is 350,000Rp per day, or 400,000Rp with a driver. Speak to the staff at Hotel Tamora, who can often fix you up with a motorcycle for 40,000Rp a day.

AROUND SUMBAWA BESAR

All these attractions are tricky to reach by public transport. Ask at Hotel Tambora if you want to hire a local guide, which is a good idea – they will arrange transport.

Pulau Moyo

Most of Pulau Moyo, an island off the coast just north of Sumbawa Besar, is a nature reserve, with coral reefs teeming with fish. Moyo rises to 648m; its centre is composed mainly of savannah with stands of forest. Moyo is inhabited by wild cattle and pigs, barking deer, and bird life that includes megapodes.

Accommodation on the island is limited to one basic operation and one indulgent resort. It is possible, but difficult, to visit Moyo independently on a day trip.

For transport, you may be able to hitch a ride with PHKA in Sumbawa Besar, which has good info and a map of Moyo. If not, head to Air Bari, which is on the coast north of Sumbawa Besar. Public bemos (5000Rp, one hour) run to Air Bari three or four times daily to no fixed schedule, starting at around 7am. They leave from the turn-off to Air Bari, at the far end of Jl Sudirman. Otherwise, charter a bemo.

From Air Bari, speedboats cost 60,000Rp per person (fishing boats and outriggers about half that) to the south coast of the island (3km away). Ask for Pak Lahi if you are having problems finding a boat. The boats can take you to snorkelling spots Air Manis, and Tanjung Pasir (the better of the two). Good reefs with a plunging wall can be found all around the island if you are prepared to charter a boat. Just northeast of Pulau Moyo is small **Pulau Satonda**, which also has good beaches, snorkelling and a saltwater lake in the middle of the island. It is three hours by boat from Air Bari.

If you want to dive Pulau Moyo, contact the **Laguna Biru Resort** (☎ 23777; laguna_biru@telkom.net), who run day trips for US$80 for two dives, including all gear. **Blue Mar-**

lin (☎ 632424; www.diveindo.com), based in Gili Trawangan, operates a five-day live-aboard trip to Moyo from Lombok that costs from US$550 per person. Some of the best diving is around **Pulau Medang**, off the northwest coast.

The seas around Moyo can get turbulent from December to March, so if the boat operators don't want to go to sea, they may have a good reason.

SLEEPING

Amanwana Resort (☎ 22233; www.amanresorts.com; all-inclusive jungle tents s/d US$725/800, ocean tents US$825/900 plus 21% tax; ❄) On Moyo's western side, Amanwana is the ultimate island hideaway. Famous former guests include Princess Di and Bill Gates. The luxurious tents are seriously lavish, though they don't have bathtubs. Pamper yourself with a 'jungle cove massage' or savour a bottle of wine in the Music Pavilion. There's a dive school here too. Most guests arrive by seaplane from Bali (US$550 return). Definitely nice, but what a price!

A forestry worker offers basic **bungalows** (per night incl simple meals 45,000Rp) in the south of Moyo. Arrange the return journey from Moyo with whoever takes you there. There are also four PHKA guard posts on Moyo – one at the southern end and the others in villages – where it should be possible to stay overnight for a donation, but take your own food and water.

Other Sights & Activities

Some of the best *songket* sarongs are made in **Poto** village, 12km east of Sumbawa Besar and 2km from the small town of Moyo. Traditional designs include the *prahu* (outrigger boat) and ancestor head motif. Modern Balinese-style ikat is also woven on handlooms; head to the village across from the football field and ask to see it being made.

The hills south of Sumbawa Besar are home to a number of **traditional villages** and offer **hiking** possibilities. One of the more interesting villages is **Tegel**, from where horses can be hired to venture higher into the forest.

Near **Batu Tering** are megalithic sarcophagi, carved with low-relief crocodile and human figures, believed to be the 2000-year-old **tombs** of ancient chiefs. Footprints in the stones are said to be those of the gods. Batu Tering is about 30km by bemo from Sumbawa Besar, via Semamung. Hire a guide in the village to visit the sarcophagi, which are 4km away.

Air Beling is a pretty waterfall in the southern mountains. Take the road south through Semamung a further 8km to Brangrea and then the turn-off to the falls, from where it is 6km along a rough road with many forks. It is nigh on impossible to find without a guide.

EAST SUMBAWA

☎ 0373

The contorted eastern half of Sumbawa has always been linguistically and culturally distinct from the west.

A trickle of travellers pass through this region bound for Komodo and Flores, but virtually no-one stays longer than a night or so, except in Hu'u, an attractive surf beach on the south coast.

Gunung Tambora

Looming over central Sumbawa is the 2850m volcano Gunung Tambora. Its 6km-wide caldera contains a two-coloured lake, and there are views as far as Gunung Rinjani (Lombok). It can be climbed from the western side: the base for ascents is the village of Pancasila near the town of Calabai, which is five hours by a very crowded bus from Dompu or an hour by speedboat from Sumbawa Besar. Guides can be arranged in Pancasila, but few people make the climb because it is a hard two-day trip, and there's the excruciating bus journey getting there and away. But at least you won't be bumping into fellow climbers on the summit.

Tambora's peak was obliterated in one of the greatest volcanic explosions of modern times, the eruption of April 1815 (see p530), but since then all has been quiet. The eruption buried the entire population of the state of Tambora. In 2004 investigations by University of Rhode Island and Indonesian vulcanologists unearthed bronze bowls and ceramic pots in a Pompeii-like buried village that indicate that the region had strong trading links with Vietnam and Cambodia.

Dompu

The seat of one of Sumbawa's former independent states, Dompu is now the third-biggest town on the island. There's a colourful market snaking through its back streets, but otherwise it's just a stopover with few lingerers.

Money can be changed at the **BNI bank** (Bank Negara Indonesia; Jl Nusantara; 7.30am-3pm Mon-Fri, 8.30am-noon Sat), which has an ATM.

The best hotel is the hospitable **Wisma Samada** (☎ 21417; Jl Gajah Mada 18; s/d 40,000/50,000Rp, with air-con 60,000/80,000Rp;), which has plenty of really decent, spacious rooms with attractive wooden beds and desks. Bathrooms have Western toilets and *mandis*. You'll enjoy your meal at **Rumah Makan Rinjani** (☎ 21445; Jl Sudirman; mains 5000-14,000Rp), a spotless, very orderly restaurant right opposite the main mosque where a terrific *nasi campur* is just 5000Rp.

GETTING THERE & AWAY

Daily buses run from Ginte main bus terminal, 2km from the centre, to Bima (9000Rp, two hours), Sape (15,000Rp, four hours) and Sumbawa Besar (35,000Rp, five hours). You can also get an air-con bus and ferry combined ticket through to Mataram (110,000Rp), but availability can make this difficult – several travel in convoy from Bima, passing by the terminal at 9pm.

Two buses leave the Lepardi local bus terminal on the southern side of town for Hu'u (7000Rp, 1½ hours) at 7am and 11am daily. At other times you'll have to charter a bemo or taxi.

Hu'u & Lakey Beach

Hu'u is best known as a stronghold of surf culture, and wave addicts come from around the world to take on Lakey Peak and pipe. Several attractive new and renovated places are now grouped on Lakey beach, 3km from Hu'u, and the sweeping stretch of sand makes a great beach destination even if you've no interest in riding the rollers – though swimming is only possible at high tide. The best surf is between June and August, though inexperienced surfers might find conditions intimidating as the waves break over a sharp, shallow reef.

INFORMATION

Most hotels will change US and Australian dollars at poor rates; it's best to bring enough rupiah with you or use the ATM in Dompu. There's a wartel at Balumba but currently no internet access in the area.

SLEEPING & EATING

Lakey's accommodation is mostly wedged together adjacent to the main surf breaks. Most places have their own restaurants – Aman Gati and Mona Lisa are two good choices. Prices do fluctuate a little depending on the season. Options are listed below in the order you reach them from Dompu.

Mona Lisa Bungalows (r with fan 35,000-50,000Rp, with air-con 90,000-100,000Rp;) A popular, long-running choice with 22 rooms, from economy options with outside shared or private *mandi* to comfortable bungalows in a verdant garden. Safety deposit boxes are available, and there's a good restaurant (open breakfast, lunch and dinner).

Balumba (☎ 21682; s/d 50,000/75,000Rp, with air-con 100,000/150,000Rp;) The cheaper rooms with simple private bathrooms are perfectly serviceable and set around a garden, while the air-con bungalows all have two beds but cold-water bathrooms. There's a store where you can buy beer and play ping pong, and a wartel.

Any Lestari (☎ 21684; r with fan 60,000Rp, bungalow with air-con 100,000-150,000Rp;) Offers a choice of clean, good-value accommodation, from simple rooms to very spacious bungalows with hot water. A large new restaurant was about to open when we visited. Rates include breakfast.

Alamanda Bungalows (☎ 623519; s/d 90,000/110,000Rp) An excellent choice, with dinky little detached cottages in grassy grounds, all with direct sea views, tasteful bamboo furnishings, verandas and smart bathrooms.

Hotel Aman Gati (☎ 623031; www.amangati.com; s/d with fan US$18/25, air-con US$30/40, high-season supplement US$10;) Well-run place in lovely grounds with plenty of tropical greenery right opposite Lakey Peak. Offers 10 slightly spartan but spotless fan-only rooms with Western-style bathrooms, and smart air-con rooms and bungalows with TVs and hot-water showers. The beachfront restaurant (open breakfast, lunch and dinner) has fine sea views and offers tasty Indonesian and Western food, including vegetarian choices.

GETTING THERE & AWAY

The 43km road from Dongu is sealed and in good condition.

From Dompu's Ginte main bus terminal take a bemo (1000Rp) or *benhur* to the Lepardi local terminal on the southern outskirts, from where there are two (slow) buses in the morning as far as Hu'u (7000Rp, 1½ hours). There are more frequent buses to Rasabau (5000Rp), from where you'll have to take a crowded bemo to the beach (2000Rp).

Try doing this with a surfboard and you'll soon see why so many people take a taxi from Bima airport (around 350,000Rp). Leaving Hu'u, there's one early-morning bus or infrequent bemos to Rasabau, or any of the hotels can arrange a taxi (200,000Rp to Dongu, 350,000Rp to Bima).

Donggo

From Sila, on the Dompu–Bima road, infrequent buses run to the village of Donggo. It is 4km along a good road, and then 10km on a rough road up the mountain. It may be possible to stay with the *kepala desa* in Donggo. The village has a few traditional houses and superb views. The Dou Donggo (Mountain People) living in these highlands speak an archaic form of the Bima language and may be descended from the original inhabitants of Sumbawa. Numbering about 20,000, they've adopted Islam and Christianity over their traditional beliefs in the last few decades, with varying degrees of enthusiasm; they're being absorbed into Bimanese culture and will probably disappear as a distinct group. The most traditional village is Mbawa where, at least until a few years ago, people still wore distinctive black clothes, and a few *uma leme* (traditional houses whose design was intimately connected with the traditional region) still stood.

BIMA & RABA

☎ 0374 / pop 70,000

Bima and Raba together form the major town in the eastern half of Sumbawa. Bima, Sumbawa's chief port, is a grubby run-down place that becomes mud-bound in the wet season and frazzled in the dry. You'll want to get out sharpish. Raba, a few kilometres east, is the much more orderly but dull administrative centre.

The Bima region has been known since the 14th century for its sturdy horses, which were exported to Java. Today, Bima is a conservative Islamic place with one mediocre sight – the former sultan's palace – though the *pasar malam* (night market) on Jl Flores is worth a wander.

Virtually everyone is here to take the ferry (or a flight if they're lucky) to Labuanbajo in Flores; they then head to Rinca or Komodo for a dragon-spotting session. Remember one thing: the ferry between Sumbawa and Flores no longer stops at Komodo, no matter what some hustlers may claim.

Information

INTERNET ACCESS

Komodo Explorer (Jl Sumbawa; per hr 11,000Rp)

MONEY

BNI bank (Bank Negara Indonesia; Jl Sultan Hasanuddin; 8am-2pm Mon-Fri) Has an ATM and changes foreign currency and travellers cheques. If you're heading east, this is the last ATM before Ruteng.

POST

Main post office (Jl Sultan Hasanuddin) A little way out.

TELEPHONE

Telkom office (Jl Soekarno Hatta; 24hr) Adjacent to the tourist office and has the best rates for international calls.

TOURIST INFORMATION

Dinas Pariwisata (☎ 44331; Jl Soekarno Hatta; 7am-3pm Mon-Fri, to 7am noon Sat) This visitor information office is next to the Kantor Bupati in Raba, about 2km from Bima. There are some keen and helpful English-speaking staff here.

TRAVEL AGENCIES

It's best to organise trips to Komodo and Rinca in Labuanbajo (Flores), but these operators may be able to hook you up with a boat heading east:

Doro Parewa Makmur (☎ 43440; Jl Sumbawa 16) Helpful Merpati and Pelni agent in the centre of town with some English-speaking staff.

Travel Lancar Jaya (☎ 43737; Jl Sultan Hasanuddin)

Tropic Island Expedition (☎ 43666; Jl Martidinata 59) Local outfit that operates regular trips to Komodo and further east.

Sights

SULTAN'S PALACE

The former home of Bima's rulers is now partly a **museum** (Jl Sultan Ibrahim; tourist admission 5000Rp; 8am-5pm Mon-Sat) with a grab-bag of dusty curios, including a royal crown, sedan chairs, battle flags and weapons. Built

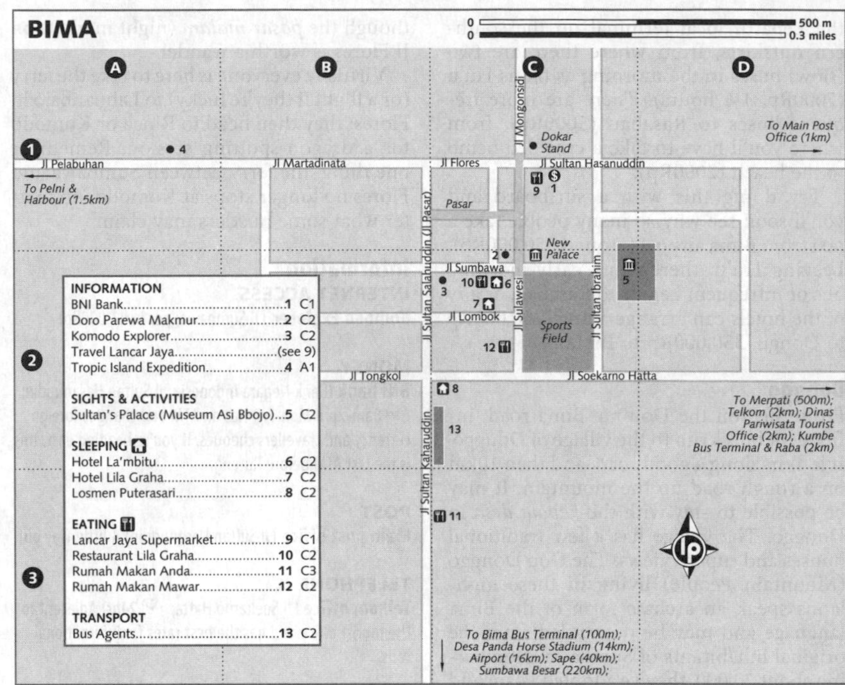

in 1927, the palace had fallen into complete disrepair by the late 1950s but has since been restored. Look out for the royal bedchamber and photos of the tombs of some early Bima rulers; the tombs still stand in the hills outside town.

Activities

Horse racing is held every Sunday throughout the dry season (May to October) at the Desa Panda horse stadium, 14km from town on the airport road. There's a large grandstand, a gaggle of warungs and plenty of cheering as boys on horses thunder around a dusty track. The height of the racing season is 17 August as independence fever kicks in.

Sleeping

Bima is compact, and most hotels are in the middle of town. There also a few very grotty, insecure cheapies.

Losmen Puterasari (Jl Soekarno Hatta 7; s/d 25,000/30,000Rp) No frills at all, so look before you (s)leep.

Hotel La'mbitu (☎ 42222; fax 42304; Jl Sumbawa 4; r with fan & hot water 50,000Rp, with air-con & hot water 75,000-105,000Rp;) This is as good as it gets in Bima. There's a choice of clean, well-appointed rooms on several floors that are bright and airy. Rates include a small breakfast.

Hotel Lila Graha (☎ 42740; fax 44705; Jl Lombok 6; s/d with fan 60,000-100,000Rp, with air-con 100,000-175,000Rp plus 10% tax;) A bizarre warren-like hotel with a staggering array of rooms. The economy rooms are poky, while some of those in the new wing have two beds, phones and hot water.

Eating

Rumah Makan Mawar (☎ 42272; Jl Sulawesi 28, mains 7000-19,000Rp; breakfast, lunch & dinner) A good choice for Indonesian food, including a mighty fine *nasi campur*.

Restaurant Lila Graha (Jl Sumbawa; mains 8000-22,000Rp; breakfast, lunch & dinner) Attached to the hotel of the same name, this is the best in town. It serves seafood and Chinese and Indonesian cuisine, with a few Western dishes thrown in.

Rumah Makan Anda (Jl Sultan Kaharuddin; breakfast, lunch & dinner) is also worth a look, and the *pasar* (market) has stalls selling interesting snacks. Self-caterers should scout the aisles at **Lancar Jaya Supermarket** (Jl Sultan Hasanuddin).

Getting There & Away

AIR

You can fly to Bima with **Merpati** (☎ 42697; Jl Soekarno Hatta 60), which has five flights a week to/from Denpasar and regular connections to Mataram, Ende and Maumere. The flight to Labuanbajo leaves on Monday only. Services to Tambulaka (Sumba) and Kupang may resume in the future. Note that some Sumbawa-bound planes from Lombok and elsewhere will not accept surfboards; always phone to check first.

Departure tax from Bima is 6000Rp.

BOAT

Travel agencies in town can organise tickets, since the **Pelni office** (☎ 42625; Jl Kesatria 2) is at Bima port. There are currently no fast ferries leaving Bima. *Tatamailau* travels monthly from Bima via Maumere and Timor to ports in West Papua, while the monthly *Kelimutu* connects Bima with Larantuka, Timor and Papau. *Tilongkabila* goes to Labuanbajo and Sulawesi one way, and Lembar and Benoa the other.

BUS

For most buses to/from the west, Bima bus terminal is a 10-minute walk south along Jl Sultan Kaharuddin from the centre of town, though you can buy a ticket in advance from bus company offices on Jl Sultan Kaharuddin.

The majority of buses heading west to Lombok leave in convoy (7pm to 7.30pm), but there are some daytime services too. Fares to Mataram range from 78,000Rp for normal services (without air-con) to 118,000Rp for the luxury, air-con buses that take about 11 hours. Tiara Mas has the best buses. Many continue to Denpasar, arriving at 11am the next morning, then Surabaya and Jakarta.

Destinations in Sumbawa are mostly serviced by smaller crowded buses that stop anywhere and everywhere. They run between 6am and 5pm. Destinations from Bima include Dompu (9000Rp, two hours) and Sumbawa Besar (45,000Rp, seven hours).

Buses east to Sape go from Kumbe bus terminal in Raba, a 20-minute (1500Rp) bemo ride east of Bima. Pick up a yellow bemo on Jl Sultan Kaharuddin or Jl Soekarno Hatta. Buses leave Kumbe terminal for Sape (9000Rp, two hours) from about 6am until 5pm. If you leave at 6am sharp you *may* just make it to Sape for the 8am ferry to Flores, which usually leaves a little late, but don't count on it. It's much safer to charter a bemo which will do the run in 1½ hours and cost around 130,000Rp.

Getting Around

The airport sits amid salt pans by the highway about 17km from the centre. You can walk out to the main road about 100m in front of the terminal and catch a passing bus there, though most will be very crowded. Alternatively, taxis meet arrivals, charging 60,000Rp to Bima or 350,000Rp to Hu'u.

A bemo around town costs 1000Rp per person; *benhur* are 2000Rp.

As there are no official rental agencies, try hiring a motorcycle through your hotel or one of the travel agencies; expect to pay around 60,000Rp per day.

Around Bima

On the main highway between Bima and Sape, the Wawo area is noted for its traditional houses, *uma lengge*. There are fine examples at the 'traditional' village of **Maria**, just off the highway – they can be seen from the bus on the way to Sape – and even more impressive three-storey houses at neighbouring **Sambori**.

The Wera region extends northeast of Bima and includes some impressive scenery of rice terraces, gorges and views of the active **Gunung Api** (1950m). In the Bugis village of **Sageang**, 10km north of Tawali, schooners are still built. Public transport is limited here and renting a motorcycle in Bima is the best way to explore the area.

SAPE

☎ 0374

Not a pretty place, Sape is a shambolic little port of tottering wooden houses, with a distinct odour caused by squid and cuttlefish drying under locals' houses and the extensive salt pans nearby. It has a reputation for being quite a hassle for travellers, though many of the hustlers seem to have moved on these days due to the downturn in tourism in Nusa Tenggara.

Sape has an excess of *benhur* – jingling buggies that don't look very much like Roman chariots, drawn by skinny, pom-pomed horses – and the drivers obviously think they're Charlton Heston as they race each other along the main street after dark.

There's a **PHKA Komodo Information Office** (8am-2pm Mon-Sat) 500m inland from the port with a few brochures and maps.

Luckily, there's one decent place to stay, **Losmen Mutiara** (71337; economy r 25,000Rp, standard 65,000Rp, with air-con 100,000Rp;), which is right next to the port gates and has tidy, clean rooms. It's nothing special but far better than the other squalid options in this town. Eat next door in the clean **Rumah Makan Arema** (71015; dishes 7000-12,000Rp), located inside a clothes store, which has good *kare* (curry) and rustles up a filling omelette for brekkie.

Getting There & Around

BUS

The ferries arriving at Sape are always met by buses, usually express services direct to Lombok or Bali.

For most destinations in Sumbawa it is necessary to get to Bima for an onward bus. Buses leave every half hour for Raba (9000Rp, two hours) until around 5pm. From Raba take a bemo to Bima (1500Rp, 20 minutes). Some buses also run straight through to Bima. Taxi drivers will no doubt claim buses have stopped running and you must charter their vehicle to Bima – ignore them.

BOAT

Regular breakdowns and heavy storms disrupt ferry services – always double-check the latest schedules first in Bima and Sape. The most reliable places to go for this information in Bima are Dinas Pariwisata (see p537), hotels and travel agencies; anyone in Sape should be able to point you in the right direction.

The ferries running to Labuanbajo (27,000Rp per person, 58,000Rp per motorcycle, eight to nine hours) no longer stop at Komodo. Ferries leave at 8am daily Wednesday to Monday and on Tuesday at 3pm. Tickets can be purchased at the pier about one hour before departure.

The rusty, ancient ferries blare out Indo metal from the top deck and screen kung fu movies inside.

It is possible to charter a boat to Komodo, but it's a much better idea to get to Labuanbajo and sort out a boat there, as many of the Sape-based vessels are not seaworthy and the seas around Komodo are notoriously treacherous – travellers have even had to swim to shore after being shipwrecked.

There is also a ferry service connecting Sape with Waikelo (32,000Rp, seven hours) in West Sumba. It leaves Sape at 5pm on Monday and returns from Waikelo on Tuesday at 9am.

KOMODO & RINCA ISLANDS

Komodo and Rinca are hilly and desolate yet beautiful islands, sandwiched between Flores and Sumbawa, that are home to gargantuan reptiles – the legendary Komodo dragon. The world's largest lizard, known locally as *ora*, it can reach over 3m in length, weigh up to 100kg and feed on animals as large as deer and buffalo.

These isolated islands are surrounded by some of the most tempestuous waters in Indonesia, fraught with riptides and whirlpools. From the sea they look a far more fitting habitat for monstrous reptiles than for the few hundred fishermen and their families who eke out a living in these parched lands.

Rinca receives just as many visitors as Komodo because it's nearest to the port of Labuanbajo in Flores – the main jumping-off point for trips to the Komodo National Park. A steady stream of visitors make their way here these days, but to understand how far off the beaten track it used to be, read *Zoo Quest for a Dragon* by naturalist and broadcaster David Attenborough, who filmed the dragons in 1956. Dragons also inhabit Pulau Padar and coastal areas of northwestern Flores.

Though there are hiking trails, it's not permitted to walk them without a guide as dragons have very occasionally attacked (and killed) humans – two villagers have died in the last twenty years. Dragons are

a docile bunch for the most part, but they could snap your leg as fast as they'll cut a goat's throat.

You're pretty much guaranteed to see dragons whichever island you visit, as they have an extremely keen sense of smell and there's usually one or two sniffing around the kitchens at the visitor camps.

Visiting Komodo National Park

This **national park** (www.komodonationalpark.org), a World Heritage site, encompasses Komodo, Rinca and several neighbouring islands, and their incredibly rich surrounding coral reefs, mangroves and seas.

The 40,000Rp park entrance fee and the conservation fee (US$15 for adults and US$7.50 for under 16s), collected on arrival by rangers, buy a three-day permit for both Komodo and Rinca.

Hiring a guide (30,000Rp) is both mandatory and very useful, as all speak some English and are very knowledgeable about the islands' flora and fauna. And they carry a big stick. A camera permit is another 25,000Rp.

Komodo is one of the driest corners of Nusa Tenggara, and heavy rains are not common. However, the seas are calmest between April and September.

KOMODO

Rugged Komodo, its gulley-ridden hillsides frazzled by the sun and drying winds to a deep rusty red for most of the year, is the largest of the islands in the national park. The accommodation camp of **Loh Liang**, run by PHKA, is on the east coast of the island. Various treks around the island can be organised with the PHKA office located here.

A half-hour walk south of Loh Liang is the fishing village of **Kampung Komodo**. It's a friendly Muslim Bugis village of stilt houses that's full of goats, chickens and children. The inhabitants are said to be descendants of convicts exiled to the island in the 19th century by one of the sultans in Sumbawa.

Activities

DRAGON SPOTTING

You're likely to see dragons all year at Banu Nggulung, a dry river bed about a half-hour

KOMODO DRAGONS

There were rumours of these awesome creatures long before their existence was confirmed in the West. Fishers and pearl divers working in the area had brought back tales of ferocious lizards with enormous claws, fearsome teeth and fiery yellow tongues. One theory holds that the Chinese dragon is based on the Komodo lizard. The first Dutch expedition to the island was in 1910; two of the dragons were shot and their skins taken to Java, resulting in the first published description.

The Komodo dragon is actually a monitor lizard. All monitors have some things in common: the head is tapered, the ear openings are visible, the neck is long and slender, the eyes have eyelids and round pupils, and the jaws are powerful. But the dragons also have massive bodies, powerful legs (each with five-clawed toes) and long, thick tails (which function as rudders but can also be used for grasping or as a potent weapon). The body is covered in small, non-overlapping scales; some may be spiny, others raised and bony.

The dragons' legs allow them to sprint short distances, lifting their tails as they run. When threatened they'll take refuge in their normal resting places – holes, trees (for the smaller ones) or water. They are dangerous if driven into a corner and will then attack even a much larger opponent. Komodos often rise up on their hind legs just before attacking and the tail can deliver well-aimed blows that will knock down a weaker adversary. Their best weapons are their sharp teeth and dagger-sharp claws, which can inflict severe wounds.

Komodos have a very keen sense of smell. All monitors feed on other animals – small ones on insects, larger ones on frogs and birds, and the *ora* (the local name for the dragon) on deer, wild pig and water buffalo. *Ora* can expand their mouth cavity considerably, enabling them to swallow prey as large as a goat. To tackle even bigger prey, they ambush their victim, bite it and wait for the potent bacteria their mouths contain to take effect – waiting around for up to two weeks for a buffalo to die – before tucking in. Mature dragons are also cannibalistic, and small *ora* live the first five years of their lives up in trees for safety, not moving to ground level until they are 1m in length.

Of all the monitors, the *ora* lays the largest eggs – around 90mm long and weighing around 200g. The female lays 15 to 30 eggs at a time and often buries them in the wall of a dry river. She then protects her cache for three months from predators. The incubation period is nine months.

Komodo dragons are *not* relics of the dinosaur age; they're remarkably versatile, hardy modern lizards, if not exactly sensitive and new age. Why they exist only on and around Komodo is a mystery, as is why males outnumber females by a ratio of 3.4 to one. Around 1300 *ora* live on Komodo, perhaps 1100 on Rinca and a small number (around 50) on the west coast of Flores.

The villagers of the region have never hunted Komodos, as they weren't as good to eat as the numerous wild pigs on the island – and for other reasons not too hard to imagine! Today the *ora* is a protected species.

walk from Loh Liang. The organised feeding of goats to dragons is a thing of the past, and dragons are now only fed here when the PHKA wants to do a head count. Banu Nggulung still attracts dragons, but since the feeding stopped fewer dragons are turning up.

A little 'grandstand' overlooks the river bed where the dragons gather. Spectators are fenced off from the dragons – don't expect to walk up to the dragons and have them say 'cheese'. A telephoto lens is handy but not essential. It is possible to spot dragons on some of the other walks, and a few 'pensioner' dragons (and lazy ones) can often be seen around the camp looking for food.

HIKING

Most visitors stay one night at Komodo and only visit Banu Nggulung, but Komodo has a number of other hikes on offer. All hikers must hire a guide to accompany them.

Walks from Loh Liang include the climb to Gunung Ara (538m), around 3½ hours return. The chances of seeing a dragon are slim, but there are expansive views from the top. Poreng Valley, 5.5km from Loh Liang, is another favourite dragon haunt and has a more out-in-the-wild feeling than Banu Nggulung; the trail continues to Loh Sebita. Even if you do not spot dragons, there's plenty of other wildlife, such as buffaloes, wild boar and some of Komodo's bird life.

SNORKELLING

Snorkelling can be arranged from Loh Liang; equipment costs about 50,000Rp and boat rental is 225,000Rp for four people. Good snorkelling can be found at Pantai Merah (Red Beach) and the small island of Pulau Lasa near Kampung Komodo.

RINCA

Rinca is slightly smaller than Komodo but nearer to Labuanbajo. Boats arrive at the sheltered dock of Koh Kima, where you'll probably find a dragon or two lurking. It's a five-minute walk to the PHKA camp at **Loh Buaya**, which has a ticket office and information centre, guides' office, wooden bungalows and a café. There's plenty of interesting material in the camp about the islands and their wildlife. Again, keep the entrance ticket if you're heading to Komodo.

Several guided walks are offered across Rinca. As temperatures will inevitably be furnace-hot, most people opt for an hour or so exploring the area close to the camp. But for those with the stamina, four-hour circular hikes can be organised.

There are no set dragon-feeding places on Rinca, but there are often a few monitors on the fringes of the camp at Loh Buaya. Finding dragons in the bush is not so easy, but the guides know spots where Komodos sun themselves. They'll show you dragon nests (the females dig huge burrows to lay their eggs, which they then guard for three months), cacti that have been ravaged by termites, and perhaps the huge webs of the nephilia spider, which can reach 15cm across and are strong enough to trap small birds. As wildlife is much more abundant than on Komodo, you may encounter long-tailed macaques, wild water buffaloes, Timor deer, horses or even wild boar. Bird life includes spangled drongos, fish eagles, bee eaters, megapodes and the orange-footed scrub fowl.

Sleeping & Eating

Both Komodo and Rinca **PHKA camps** (per person per night 45,000Rp) have large wooden cabins on stilts with balconies. Each cabin contains spartan rooms with well-weathered mattresses, a sitting area and a *mandi*. During the peak tourist season – around July-August – the rooms may be full, but extra mattresses will be rustled up so everyone is accommodated.

Both camps have restaurants with a limited menu of *nasi/mie goreng*, fish and other simple meals, plus drinks.

Getting There & Away

Ferries travelling between Sape and Labuanbajo have not been stopping at Komodo for several years now, so the only way here is by some sort of charter. One of the most popular ways to arrive is on a boat tour between Lombok and Flores – these stop at Komodo for a night or two. See the boxed text, p516, for the pros and cons of such trips.

Other than the boat tours, Labuanbajo is the main jumping-off point for Komodo and Rinca. It *is* possible to charter boats from Sape (see p540) in Sumbawa to Komodo, but be extremely cautious, as many boats here are barely seaworthy.

Chartering a boat to Rinca costs between 225,000Rp and 600,000Rp return from Labuanbajo, depending on the vessel. Boats usually leave at about 8am for the two-hour journey to the island and then return via snorkelling spots. You can book through your hotel or an agency, or start speaking to captains directly at the harbour, which will cut out the commission. **Captain Rudy** (☎ 085239054859) charges 500,000Rp for a well-organised trip on a twin-engined boat that can accommodate 10 people. Whoever you sail with, remember to check that the vessel has a radio and life jackets.

Komodo day trips start at around 600,000Rp from Labuanbajo, but as the journey takes about four hours each way the island is probably better suited to a longer trip. Two-day charter boat rates begin at around 1,200,000Rp for up to six people.

FLORES

A fascinating, mountainous and remarkably beautiful island, Flores has a volcanic topography that has longed shaped its destiny. A chain of cones stretches the length of this verdant island, provoking a

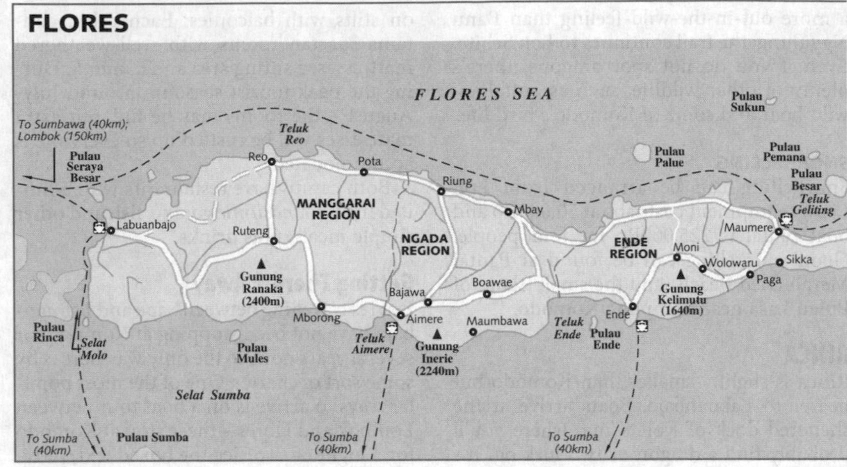

complicated relief of V-shaped valleys and knife-edged ridges – terrain that was near-impenetrable until recent years and that has separated the island into many distinct ethnic groups. Today, though Flores is overwhelmingly Catholic, rich indigenous cultures continue to thrive alongside mainstream religious beliefs.

Flores has the most remarkable sight in Nusa Tenggara – the sublime multihued crater lakes of Kelimutu – terrific beaches around Labuanbajo and east of Maumere, and idyllic offshore islands with fine snorkelling. The island attracts a steady flow of travellers but has nothing like the tourist scene in Bali or parts of Lombok.

The rugged nature of the island makes road construction difficult, and Flores' serpentine east–west road is impossible to traverse quickly, so you'll need to draw on extra reserves of patience when the going slows – though fortunately you'll always have remarkable natural beauty to wonder at along the way.

History

A startling recent find near Ruteng appears to indicate that a unique species of dwarf hominid lived in Flores until around 12,000 years ago (see the boxed text, p552), though the evidence for the existence of a unique species of 'Flores man' has not yet been accepted by all scientists.

Flores owes its name to the Portuguese, who called the island's easternmost cape Cabo das Flores, meaning 'Cape of Flowers'. It's thought that the island's diverse cultures developed from a common ancestry. Long before Europeans arrived in the 16th century, much of coastal Flores was firmly in the hands of the Makassarese and Bugis from southern Sulawesi. They brought gold, elephant tusks (used as currency), linen and copperware, and left with rubber, sea products, sandalwood, cinnamon, cotton and fabric. Bugis and Makassarese slave raids on the coasts of Flores were a common problem, forcing people to retreat inland. Eastern Flores came under the sway of Ternate in Maluku during the 15th and 16th centuries.

As early as 1512, Flores was sighted by the Portuguese navigator Antonio de Abreu. The Portuguese, drawn by the lucrative sandalwood trade, built fortresses on Pulau Solor and at Ende. Christianity was a successful import, and today a church is the centrepiece of almost every village.

In the 17th century, the Dutch kicked the Portuguese out of most of Flores, and by 1850 they had purchased Portugal's remaining enclaves in the area, including Larantuka.

The Dutch were near-constantly confronted with rebellions and inter-tribal wars. Unrest continued until a major military campaign in 1907 subdued most of the tribes of central and western Flores. Missionaries moved into the isolated western hills in the 1920s.

Today Flores is holding its breath for provincial status. This will be a huge de-

NUSA TENGGARA

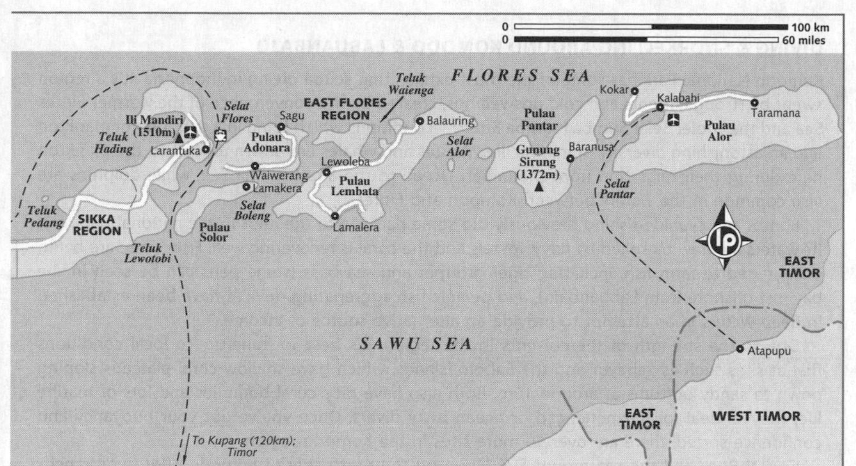

velopment for the island, as it is currently under the jurisdiction of Kupang and has only limited control over its own affairs.

Culture

The island's 1.8 million people are divided into five main linguistic and cultural groups. From west to east, these are the Manggarai (main town Ruteng), the Ngada (Bajawa), the closely related Ende and Lio peoples (Ende), the Sikkanese (Maumere), and the Lamaholot (Larantuka). In the more remote areas, some older people don't speak a word of Bahasa Indonesia, and their parents grew up in purely animist societies.

Physically, the people at the western end of the island are more Malay, while the other inhabitants of Flores are more Melanesian.

Around 85% of the people are Catholic, but in rural areas particularly, Christianity is welded onto *adat*. Animist rituals are still used for births, marriages and deaths and to mark important points in the agricultural calendar. Even educated, English-speaking Florinese still admit to the odd chicken, pig or buffalo sacrifice to keep their ancestors happy when rice is planted.

Muslims tend to congregate in fishing villages and coastal towns such as Ende (where they make up half the population).

Getting Around

What one Indonesian tourist leaflet charitably calls the 'Trans-Flores Hwy' spirals, twists and tumbles nearly 700km from Labuanbajo to Larantuka, at the eastern end of the island. It's sealed all the way, but buses are invariably small, cramped and overcrowded, and the road is narrow and tortuously winding. Floods and landslides in the rainy season are common. On the other hand, the stunning scenery certainly helps compensate.

It is best to break a trans-island journey at regular intervals so as not to get the bus passenger's version of road rage. Be warned that all the twists and turns make a lot of people sick on the buses – it isn't much fun sniffing the country air on a long ride.

Work started on an alternative route, the so-called 'Trans Northern Hwy' between Reo and Mbay, years ago but many sections are in a deplorable state these days.

For those with more money than time, car rental is available in Labuanbajo or Maumere. The trans-island rate is 450,000-500,000Rp per day, including driver and petrol. This is becoming a very popular option for small groups, as you can stop where you like to take in remote attractions or take a photo. See p549 and p567 for reliable transport fixers in the main arrival points of Labuanbajo and Maumere, respectively.

Motorcycling across the island is fantastic with the combination of roads and scenery, but it's only for experienced bikers, due to tough conditions and blind bends. A few superhuman cyclists with legs of steel manage to traverse the island too, using

DIVING & SNORKELLING AROUND KOMODO & LABUANBAJO

Komodo National Park has some of the most exhilarating scuba diving in Indonesia. It's a region swept by strong currents and cold upswellings, created by the convergence of the warmer Flores Sea and the cooler Selat Sumba (Sumba Strait) – conditions which bring in a rich soup of plankton and an astonishing diversity of marine life. Mantas and whales are drawn to feed on the plankton here during their migration from the Indian Ocean to the South China Sea, while dolphins are also common in the waters between Komodo and Flores.

Bomb- and cyanide-fishing previously did some damage to the reefs in the national park, but its waters are now patrolled by navy vessels and the coral is recovering well. Fishermen are being encouraged to farm fish, including tiger grouper and sea bass (some pens can be seen in the bay just offshore from Labuanbajo), and pelagic fish aggregating devices have been established in deep waters in an attempt to provide an alternative source of income.

Due to the strength of the currents in the region, it's best to 'tune-up' to local conditions first at sites such as Sebayur and the Sabolo islands, which have shallow coral plateaus sloping down to sandy bottoms at around 10m. Both also have nice coral bommies and lots of marine life; they're ideal for inexperienced or ocean-rusty divers. Once you've got your buoyancy and confidence sorted, there are over 50 more sites in the Komodo region.

Crystal Rock and the sea mount Full Moon on the north side of Komodo offer nudibranchs and seahorses, batfish and reef sharks. Dozens of mantas can sometimes be seen at Lankoi Bay and Pulau Tala (September to January is the best season), while whale sharks are occasionally spotted at Nusa Kode off the southern coast of Rinca.

For a real adrenalin surge, Gili Banta can throw up absolutely anything from huge schools of barracuda to hammerhead, bull and grey sharks. Batu Balong has long been a favourite with divers, but the currents can be ferocious here; sharks, Napoleon wrasse and turtles are seen regularly.

See opposite for recommended Labuanbajo-based dive schools. Several live-aboards from Bali and Lombok also pass through this area.

local buses to get up the worst hills and freewheeling down, but the topography of the island rules out cycling for all but Tour-de-France trainees.

LABUANBAJO

☎ 0385

A picturesque fishing community clinging to the western tip of Flores, Labuanbajo has an agreeably weathered, slightly ramshackle charm. It's the main jumping-off point for Komodo and Rinca, and with dozens of world-class dive sites and fine snorkelling nearby there's every reason to spend a few days here. The attractive harbour is scattered with outrigger fishing boats and is sheltered by the islands, giving the impression that you're standing on the shores of a vast lake.

Though there aren't any readily accessible walk-on-and-flop beaches, some of the small islands nearby have blissful white-sand bays and bungalow-style accommodation.

Information

INTERNET ACCESS

Prundi (per hr 5000Rp) It's quite a hike east of the centre.

MONEY

The one ATM in Labuanbajo at the time of writing only accepted local cards; the nearest alternatives are in Ruteng (or in Bima if you're heading west). Moneychangers will offer similar rates to the banks. Banks that accept travellers cheques and change dollars:

BNI (Bank Negara Indonesia; Jl Yos Sudarso; 🕓 8am-4.30pm Mon-Fri) Also offers credit-card cash advances.

BRI (Bank Rakyat Indonesia; Jl Yos Sudarso; 🕓 8am-3.30pm Mon-Fri)

POST

Post office (Jl Yos Sudarso; 🕓 7am-2pm Mon-Sat)

TELEPHONE

The Telkom office is 1km west of town but offers the best rates. The wartel near the waterfront just seems to pick high prices out of the air.

TOURIST INFORMATION

Dinas Pariwisata (☎ 41170; 🕓 7am-2pm Mon-Thu & Sat, to 11am Fri) About 1km out of town on the road to the airport.

PHKA information booth (☎ 41005; tnkomodo@indosat.net.id; Jl Yos Sudarso; 🕑 8am-2.30pm Mon-Thu, to 11am Fri) PHKA administers the Komodo National Park, provides helpful, practical information for Komodo and Rinca islands, and has a small gift shop.

Sights & Activities

ISLANDS

Boat trips to nearby islands make great day trips, offering the chance to snorkel or crash out on a deserted beach. Most hotels will offer to set you up with a boat to the uninhabited island of your choice, or you can get down to the dock and put your bargaining head on. A half-day trip to **Pulau Bidadari**, where there's coral and clear water, costs around 60,000Rp per person with four or more. Beaches worth lounging on are **Pantai Waecicu**, where the bungalows are now closed but there's snorkelling around the tiny offshore island of Kukusan Kecil, **Pulau Serayu** and **Pulau Kanawa** – the last two have accommodation and offer free transport if you stay there. Most boats leave from the shoreline at the northern end of the main street.

DIVING & SNORKELLING

With dive sites around the islands near Labuanbajo and the proximity of Komodo National Park, there are some excellent scuba and diving opportunities here; see opposite for a full rundown.

Local dive operators have their offices strung out along the seafront road:

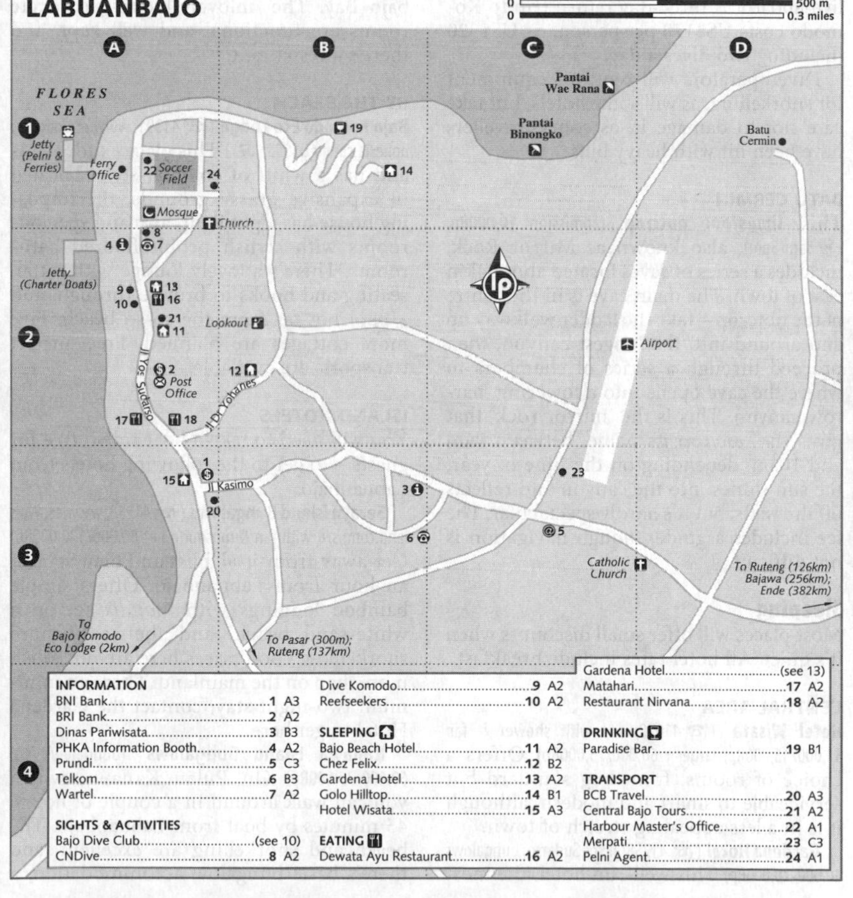

Bajo Dive Club (☎ 41503; www.komododiver.com)
CNDive (☎ 41159)
Dive Komodo (☎ 41354; www.divekomodo.com)
Reefseekers (☎ 41443; www.reefseekers.net)

It's best to have a chat with all the dive schools first and ask about their equipment and boats before you decide who to dive with. Reefseekers is very well informed about local conditions and has speedboats for fast transfer times. Condo of CNDive offers a 'manta guarantee'. Two dives cost between US$48 and US$75, including all gear and lunch; the further away the site is – say the northern side of Komodo – the higher the price.

Based in Labuanbajo, the **Feliana** (☎ 03617420995; emilbei@indo.net.id) is a beautiful teak sailing boat that operates as a dive live-aboard. A three-day return trip to Komodo costs US$170 per person, or US$320 including two dives a day.

Dive operators will rent out equipment for snorkelling, as will some hotels, but take care not to damage it, as some travellers have been hit with heavy bills.

BATU CERMIN

This **limestone outcrop** (admission 10,000Rp; 8am-5pm), also known as Mirror Rock, includes a series of caves located about 4km east of town. The main cave is in the centre of the outcrop – take the ladder walkway up and around into the longest canyon, then proceed through a series of chambers to where the cave opens into a towering, narrow canyon. This is the 'mirror rock' that gives the outcrop its name; between 9am and 10am, depending on the time of year, the sun shines into the canyon and reflects off the walls, but it's hardly spectacular. The fee includes a guide, though navigation is not difficult.

Sleeping

Most places will offer small discounts when it's quiet. All hotel rates include breakfast.

CENTRAL AREA

Hotel Wisata (☎ 41020; s/d with shower & fan 35,000/45,000Rp, larger r 60,000/75,000Rp) Offers a choice of rooms, from bog standard but serviceable to smart and modern, although it is in a less appealing stretch of town.

Gardena Hotel (☎ 41258; Jl Yos Sudarso; bungalows 40,000-70,000Rp) This well-run hotel, the most popular place in town, offers neat, well-spaced wooden bungalows. The bungalows are dotted around a leafy hillside plot and most have fine harbour views from their verandas. The restaurant here is excellent.

Bajo Beach Hotel (☎ 41008; r with fan & shower 65,000Rp) Set back off the road, these plain, tiled rooms have ceiling fans and bathrooms with Western toilets.

Chez Felix (☎ 41032; Jl Dr Yohanes; r 60,000-90,000Rp) Set in a quiet location above the bay and run by a friendly family who all speak good English, this is a good option, with neat, clean and comfortable rooms. Also has a restaurant.

Golo Hilltop (☎ 41337; s/d with fan 75,000/85,000Rp, with air-con 150,000Rp) Dutch-run place that enjoys a terrific location high above Labuanbajo Bay. The unlovely-looking concrete rooms are functional and well kept, and there's a restaurant.

BY THE BEACH

Bajo Komodo Eco Lodge (☎ 41391; www.ecolodgesindonesia.com; r US$55;) This place exudes class and has a whiff of colonial style. Located in expansive grassy grounds, the imposing house has eight light, airy and spacious rooms with stylish pebble-floored bathrooms. There's a lovely lounge with rattan seating and books to browse through, and a pool not far from the so-so beach. Five more cottages are planned. Free airport transports are available.

ISLAND HOTELS

You will need to take a boat ride – free for guests – to get to the following hotels from Labuanbajo.

Serayu Island Bungalows (☎ 41258; www.serayaisland.com; s/d with fan & mosquito net 80,000/100,000Rp) Get-away-from-it-all bliss on Pulau Serayu, an hour from Labuanbajo. Offers simple bamboo lodgings with *mandis* set on a white-sand beach, and there's offshore snorkelling. Food prices here are not much more than on the mainland. There's a minimum two-night stay; contact the Gardena Hotel to get here.

Kanawa Island Bungalows (bungalows s/d 60,000/75,000Rp) On Pulau Kanawa, which you can walk around in a couple of hours, 45 minutes by boat from Labuanbajo. The beach and snorkelling are excellent, and there's basic bungalow accommodation, a few hammocks and a restaurant. Contact the Kanawa office opposite the Gardena Hotel for a free ride.

Eating & Drinking

Labuanbajo has some extremely good-value restaurants, with fresh seafood and sizzling hot plates something of a local speciality; both are available at very reasonable prices.

Matahari (☎ 41083; Jl Yos Sudarso; dishes 10,000-23,000Rp; breakfast, lunch & dinner) Terrific views from the port-facing deck, particularly at sunset, and a menu that includes sandwiches, soups and hot plates.

Gardena Hotel (☎ 41258; Jl Yos Sudarso; mains 12,000-23,000Rp; breakfast, lunch & dinner) This enjoyable and very popular hotel restaurant is just high enough above the street to offer fine views of the bay. It's open-sided to catch the sea breeze and the portions are huge; gorge yourself on the house special, snapper hot plate (20,000Rp).

Dewata Ayu Restaurant (☎ 41304; Jl Yos Sudarso; mains 12,000-25,000Rp; breakfast, lunch & dinner) Intimate little restaurant with friendly staff and fine hot plates – try the beef steak or tuna.

Restaurant Nirvana (Jl Yos Sudarso; mains 13,000-28,000Rp; breakfast, lunch & dinner) It's looking a bit under-patronised these days, but this place, with panoramic harbour views, has tasty dishes such as tuna cooked with butter and garlic.

There's no real bar scene in Labuanbajo and most people are content to enjoy a beer or two with their meal. But at weekends the **Paradise Bar** (6pm-2am Fri & Sat), up a steep hill on the northern side of town, has live music and sells mixed spirit-based drinks.

Getting There & Away

AIR

Merpati has flights between Labuanbajo and Denpasar four days a week. The **Merpati office** (☎ 41177) is between Labuanbajo and the airport, about 1.5km from town.

GT Air has four direct flights per week between Denpasar and Labuanbajo. Its ticket agent is **BCB Travel** (☎ 41088; Jl Kasimo). At the time this book went to press, Transnusa had begun flying to Maumere (586,000Rp, four times a week).

Departure tax from Labuanbajo is 6000Rp.

BOAT

No ferries stop at Komodo. The ferry from Labuanbajo to Sape (27,000Rp, eight to nine hours) leaves at 8am daily. On Monday and Thursday it travels via Weikelo in west Sumba, making the journey time to Sape about 17 hours. Tickets for Sape can be purchased at the harbour master's office (in front of the pier) one hour before the vessel's departure. See p540 for Sape boat schedules.

The **Pelni agent** (☎ 41106) is easy to miss, tucked away in a side street in the northeast of town. The monthly Pelni ship *Tilongkabila* heads to Makassar and the east coast of Sulawesi, or to Bima, Lembar and Benoa. *Tatamailau* also travels monthly from Labuanbajo to Maumere, Timor and ports in West Papua.

Many travellers choose to take a boat trip between Flores and Lombok, stopping at Komodo and Sumbawa along the way for snorkelling and exploration. For more on this option, see p516. The local Perama boat contact is **Central Bajo Tours** (☎ 41289; fax 41490; Jl Yos Sudarso).

BUS & TRUCK

There is no bus terminal in Labuanbajo so most people book their tickets through a hotel or agency, which makes them more expensive than they should be. If you get an advance ticket, the bus will pick you up from your hotel.

There are buses to Ruteng (30,000Rp, four hours) every two hours, one to Bajawa (70,000Rp, 10 hours) at 6am daily, and three weekly to Ende (105,000Rp, 15 hours). Additional buses meet arriving ferries.

Passenger trucks also ply the route to Ruteng. If you travel this way, it's imperative to get a seat in front of the rear axle; the positions behind are good approximations of ejector seats.

Getting Around

The air field is about 1.5km from the town. Hotel reps meet flights and offer free lifts, or a private taxi is 10,000Rp to town.

Speak to transport supremo **Tarsi** (☎ 41649) about renting a Kijang (450,000Rp a day, including driver and fuel) or a 10-seater minibus (750,000Rp) for trips across Flores. Motorcycle rental is also possible; speak to your hotel.

RUTENG

☎ 0385 / pop 35,000

A market town and meeting point for the hill people of western Flores, Ruteng is the heart of Manggarai country, which extends to the west coast from north of Aimere. The town is surrounded by rice fields on gentle slopes beneath a line of volcanic hills.

Ruteng is a pleasantly cool town of broad streets, but it's spread out and not particularly atmospheric, though there are some interesting sights in the vicinity. Most people just spend a night here, stopping to break the interminable bus journey.

Ruteng's lively, sprawling **pasar** (Jl Kartini) is a meeting place for people from the surrounding hills.

Information

For information, the Merlin restaurant has good noticeboards. There's no internet access; go to Bajawa or Labuanbajo for a cyberfix.

BNI bank (Bank Negara Indonesia; Jl Kartini; 🕒 8am-3.30pm Mon-Sat) Changes cash and travellers cheques and has an ATM, though poor satellite connections mean that this can't be relied upon.

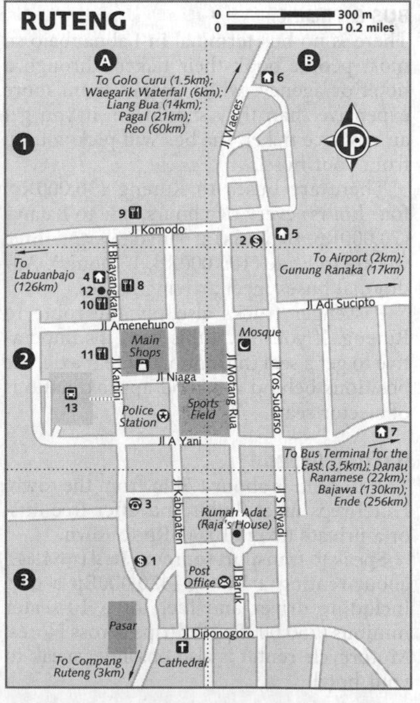

BRI bank (Bank Rakyat Indonesia; Jl Yos Sudarso; 🕒 7.30am-3pm Mon-Fri, 8am-1pm Sat) The ATM has a 500,000Rp withdrawal limit. The bank also changes US dollars.

Post office (Jl Baruk 6; 🕒 7am-2pm Mon-Sat)

Telkom office (Jl Kartini; 🕒 24hr)

Sleeping

Rima Hotel (☎ 22196; Jl A Yani 14; economy s/d/tr 50,000/60,000/75,000Rp, s/d/tr with bathroom 60,000/75,000/90,000Rp) This excellent little wooden hotel is a dead ringer for a Swiss chalet, and the service is pretty efficient and welcoming too. All the rooms are neat and tidy, some with bunk beds and the more expensive options with showers (the shared bathrooms have Western-style facilities). There's also a restaurant and bar area, and motorcycle hire can often be arranged through them.

Losmen Agung (☎ 21080; Jl Waeces 10; r 70,000Rp) It's a bit of a hike from the centre, but the rustic location, around rice paddies, is appealing, and the clean, well-maintained rooms have bathrooms.

Hotel Sindha (☎ 21197; Jl Yos Sudarso 26; economy r 40,000Rp, standard r 100,000Rp, VIP r 150,000Rp) Initial impressions are terrible here, with a real air of decay about the reception and corridors; however, the standard rooms at the rear are reasonable and have natural light, and the VIP rooms have hot-water showers. Avoid the economy options at all costs.

Hotel Dahlia (☎ 21377; Jl Bhayangkara; r 75,000-125,000Rp, VIP r 175,000-200,000Rp) There are four classes of rooms, none good value for money. The VIP rooms are spacious, if plain, and have hot water.

INFORMATION

BNI Bank	1	A3
BRI Bank	2	B1
Telkom	3	A3

SLEEPING

Hotel Dahlia	4	A2
Hotel Sindha	5	B1
Losmen Agung	6	B1
Rima Hotel	7	B2

EATING

Agape Café	8	A2
Lestari	9	A1
Restaurant Merlin	10	A2
Supermarket	11	A2

TRANSPORT

Agen Bus	12	A2
Bus Terminal	13	A2

> **THE MANGGARAI**
>
> The Manggarai hill people are perhaps the best known and most interesting of the many 'traditional' ethnic groups in Flores. They tend to be shy but friendly – you'll see many around Ruteng in their distinctive black sarongs, trailing black-haired pigs into market or herding beautiful miniature horses. The Manggarai language is unintelligible to the other people of Flores.
>
> Christianity now predominates among the upland Manggarai; traditional animist practices linger but are dwindling. In some villages you can still find the *compang*, a ring of flat stones on which offerings were placed, or you may be shown ritual paraphernalia used during sacrificial ceremonies.
>
> The *penti* ceremony, held during August between the rice harvest and the next planting, is the most important Manggarai event. It's a cleansing ceremony that honours the ancestors and involves the slaughter of buffalo and pigs. Trials of strength take place at this time, including *caci* fights between combatants wearing wooden masks like uptilted welder's helmets. One carries a rawhide oval shield and a 1m-long whip, and the other has a short, springy stick and a thick cloth wrapped around his forearm.

Eating

Warungs around the market serve Padang food, meatball soup and sate.

Agape Café (☎ 22561; Jl Bhayangkara 6-8; dishes 8000-30,000Rp; ⌚ breakfast, lunch & dinner) A very welcome new café, with friendly service, an espresso machine and cakes. It also serves breakfasts, Western and Indonesian cuisine, and Guinness and Bintang. Speak to the owner, Timotius, and he'll show you the substantial gas-fired coffee bean roasting machines at the rear. Local coffee is for sale here too.

Lestari (☎ 21393; Jl Komodo 2; dishes 10,000-15,000Rp; ⌚ breakfast, lunch & dinner) Head to this log cabin–styled resto for well-priced Indonesian food, including shrimp and fish dishes.

Restaurant Merlin (☎ 22475; Jl Bhayangkara 32B; mains 13,000-30,000Rp; ⌚ breakfast, lunch & dinner) Offers an extensive menu of Chinese – try the chicken with chilli sauce – and Indo dishes, though Merlin sure is pricey for the provinces.

Ruteng also has the biggest **supermarket** (Jl Kartini) between Bima and Ende.

Getting There & Away

AIR

The airport is 2km southeast of town, and flights are usually met by hotel reps offering free rides.

At the time of research **Transnusa** (☎ Kupang office 0380881256) was about to start flights from Ruteng to Kupang (four weekly) all via Ende. Check at your hotel or call Kupang for the latest schedule. Merpati offers two weekly flights to Kupang via Ende, though cancellations are frequent on this route.

BUS

The bus terminal for eastern destinations is located inconveniently 3.5km out of town. Bemos run here for 1000Rp. Local buses, trucks and those heading west still run from the central bus/bemo terminal near the police station.

There are regular buses and bemos to Reo, so these are an option if you're heading to Pagal (6000Rp, every 1½ hours). It's best to leave early from Ruteng and aim to be out of Pagal by 3pm. Buena Mas buses going to Bajawa (40,000Rp, five hours) and Ende (70,000Rp, nine hours) depart at 7.30am; there are also a couple of later services to each town. Buy your ticket in advance at **Agen Bus** (☎ 21302; Jl Bhayangkara 4) or your hotel. Buses to Labuanbajo leave about every two hours (30,000Rp, four hours) from the central bus/bemo terminal.

Getting Around

Bemos cost 1000Rp around town. Contact Rima hotel about motorcycle rental.

AROUND RUTENG

Compang Ruteng, a 'traditional' village 3km from Ruteng has a *compang*, a traditional ancestor altar composed of a raised stone burial platform of rocks and a couple of renovated *rumah adat* (traditional houses). One is the Mbaru Gendrang, a ceremonial meeting house that contains heirlooms, including a gold-and-silver *panggal*, the mask

THE FLORES 'HOBBIT'

The Manggarai have long told folktales of *ebo gogo* – hairy little people with flat foreheads who roamed the jungles during the times of their recent ancestors. No-one paid them much attention until September 2003, when archaeologists made a stunning find.

Excavating the limestone cave at Liang Bua, they unearthed at a depth of 6m a skeleton that was the size of a three-year-old child but had the worn-down teeth and bone structure of an adult. Six more remains appeared to confirm that the team had unearthed a new species of human, *Homo floresiensis*, which reached around 1m in height and was inevitably nicknamed the 'hobbit'.

Lab tests brought another surprise. The hominid with the nutcracker jaw and gangly, chimplike arms lived until 12,000 years ago, practically yesterday in evolutionary terms, when a cataclysmic volcanic eruption is thought to have wiped out the little people and devastated the island of Flores.

It seems that *Homo floresiensis* could represent the first ever example of human dwarfism, an evolutionary phenomenon that has been well documented in the animal world, particularly on islands. In Jersey, one of the British Channel Islands, red deer shrank to a sixth of their normal European size in just 6000 years, while California's Channel Islands were once home to the ultimate oxymoron of the animal world – a pygmy mammoth.

Flores is particularly rich in these evolutionary quirks of nature. It had mini elephants called 'stegodon' as well as examples of giantism (which tend to occur in the same locations as dwarfism), such as colossal rats and Komodo dragons.

But not all scientists are convinced about the origins of the Flores find. The prevailing school of thought argues that the Flores hominids are descendants of *Homo erectus*, a species that fled Africa around two million years ago and spread throughout Asia – though no DNA has yet been extracted to confirm this. Until recently it was thought that the arrival of *Homo sapiens* in Asia put paid to *Homo erectus* around 50,000 years ago, though Flores humans could indicate that the species survived in isolated places.

Anthropologists opposed to this suggest that the Flores find could represent *Homo sapiens* (who were known to be travelling between Australia and New Guinea 35,000 years ago) that suffered from microcephaly – a neurological disorder causing stunted head growth, and often dwarfism, that runs in families.

But the momentum still seems to be with the original theory, given that in 2005 a second large jawbone was found, of broadly similar dimensions to the first discovery. And with tools very similar to those found in Liang Bua reportedly unearthed in Timor, and possibly in Sulawesi, more little people could yet emerge from the evolutionary backwoods.

For details about visiting Liang Bua, see below.

shaped like a buffalo horn and used in ceremonial *caci* (a martial art in which participants duel with whips and shields).

Visitors are asked to sign in and make a sizable donation (about 15,000Rp). Ask around Ruteng for information on the ceremonies that are held further afield.

Golo Curu, a hill to the north of Ruteng, offers spectacular early-morning views of the hills, valleys, rice paddies, terraced slopes and distant mountain valleys. Walk down the Reo road and, when you're 20 minutes past the Hotel Karya, turn right at the small bridge. There's a derelict shrine on the hilltop with a statue of the Virgin Mary on a pedestal. Further north, 6km from Ruteng, near Cancar, is the **Waegarik waterfall**.

Manggarai sarongs are black with pretty embroidered patterns. They are sold in the main Ruteng market, or visit the weaving village of **Pagal**, 21km north of Ruteng on the main road to Reo. See p551 for transport information.

The 2400m **Gunung Ranaka**, an active volcano that erupted in 1987, can be reached by road from the 8km mark east of town past the airport. Views from the mountain are obscured by 3m regrowth – you'll be better off saving energy for a volcano climb elsewhere.

The limestone cave of **Liang Bua**, where the Flores 'hobbit' was found (see above), is about 14km north of Ruteng, down a very rough dirt track that is often not passable after periods of heavy rain. Archaeologists believe that the lip along the entrance permitted sediments to build up steadily as water flowed through the cave over millennia, sealing the remains of the humans and animals who lived and died there. There is not much to see at the 30m-wide cave, although some sticks mark the place where the little folk were found. It's best to travel here with a local guide, as the Liang Bua cave is considered sacred to locals – speak to the owners of the Dahlia or Rima hotels or the Agape Café about organising a trip here.

Danau Ranamese, a circular aquamarine lake 22km from Ruteng, is right next to the main Bajawa road. There are picnic spots here, and a couple of waterfalls tumble from the rear of the crater, flooding the rice paddies below. Trails loop around the lake and visitors centre, where you may be charged a 10,000Rp entrance fee. Any bus on the Bajawa–Ruteng route passes by the lake, and all will stop.

BAJAWA

☎ 0384

The attractive, relaxed hill town of Bajawa sits at an altitude of 1100m and is surrounded by forested volcanic hills, with Gunung Inerie (2245m) looming large to the south. It's something of an overgrown village with well-tended gardens bursting with blooms, its suburbs fusing gently with corn fields. The climate is mild and there's a good range of restaurants and accommodation, making it a popular place to spend a few days exploring the countryside.

Bajawa is the main trading centre of the Ngada people, one of the most traditional groups in Flores. Forays to visit Ngada villages or nearby hot springs (for many, their only hot shower in Flores!) are the original attractions, but the recently emerged volcano of Wawo Muda, with its Kelimutu-esque lakes, is also proving a hit.

Information

BNI bank (Bank Negara Indonesia; Jl Pierre Tendean; 8am-3pm Mon-Fri, to 12.30pm Sat) Has an ATM and exchanges dollars and travellers cheques.

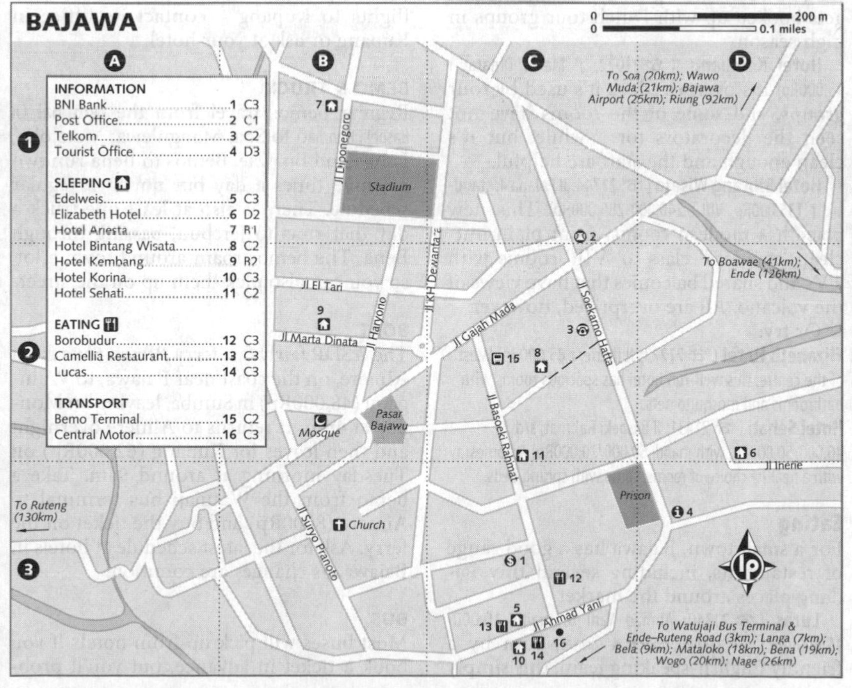

NUSA TENGGARA

Post office (Jl Soekarno Hatta; 8am-2pm Mon-Sat)
Telkom Office (Jl Soekarno Hatta; per hr 12,000Rp; 24hr, internet 8am-6pm) The cheapest place for international calls.
Tourist office (21554; Jl Soekarno Hatta; 8.30am-3pm Mon-Fri, 8.30am-1pm Sat) Has a few yellowing leaflets but not much practical advice.

Sleeping

There's a good choice of budget digs in Bajawa, though very little above this price bracket. All prices include breakfast.

Hotel Korina (21162; Jl Ahmad Yani 81; s/d 50,000/60,000Rp) A very tidy family-run place with large, clean rooms with decent mattresses and attached bathrooms with Western toilets and *mandis*.

Hotel Ariesta (21292; Jl Diponegoro; s/d with mandi 60,000/75,000Rp) A deservedly popular family guesthouse in the north of town with bright, clean rooms at the front or around the pleasant courtyard area at the back.

Edelweis (21345; Jl Ahmad Yani 76; s/d 65,000/75,000Rp) Opposite the Korina, this is another excellent family-owned place. It has clean, homely rooms with frilly bedding and pleasant light, airy living areas. It gets booked up with Dutch tour groups in high season.

Hotel Kembang (21072; Jl Marta Dinata; r 95,000Rp) It's overpriced, as it's used by tour groups, and some of the rooms have not seen the decorators for a while, but it's clean enough and the staff are helpful.

Hotel Bintang Wisata (21744; Jl Palapa 4; standard r 135,000Rp, VIP r 240,000-285,000Rp) This new place has modern rooms, from plain-but-clean 'standard' class to 'VIP' rooms with TVs and shared balconies that have views of the volcano. All are overpriced, however.

Or try:

Elizabeth Hotel (21223; Jl Inerie; r 85,000Rp) West of the centre, this well-run hotel has spacious rooms with bathrooms and mosquito nets.
Hotel Sehati (21431; Jl Basoeki Rahmat; s/d 40,000/50,000Rp, with mandi 60,000/70,000Rp) A homestay with a healthy choice of rooms, some with sprung beds.

Eating

For a small town, Bajawa has a good range of restaurants, including several tiny Padang places around the market.

Lucas (21340; Ahmad Yani 6; mains 10,000-15,000Rp; breakfast, lunch & dinner) Run by a friendly English-speaking team, this simply furnished tin-roofed place serves up fine pork sate and other local faves, including a fearsome if not unpalatable *arak*. Along with the Camellia, it's a good place to meet other travellers and local guides.

Camellia Restaurant (21458; Jl Ahmad Yani 74; most mains 15,000Rp; breakfast, lunch & dinner) A large, well-established Chinese-run place with a wide choice of local and Western dishes on the menu, including sandwiches and Swiss rosti.

Borobudur (21894; Jl Basoeki Rahmat; mains 10,000-23,000Rp; breakfast, lunch & dinner) Located in the front room of a suburban house, this clean place has steak, seafood, and Chinese and Indonesian grub.

Shopping

Big, busy and colourful, Pasar Bajawu (Bajawa Market) sells plentiful fruit that's of good quality. Lots of the local women wear ikat cloth, some of which is for sale.

Getting There & Away

AIR

Bajawa no longer has a reliable air service, but it's possible that Merpati may resume flights to Kupang – contact its office in Kupang or ask at your hotel.

BEMO & TRUCK

Regular bemos travel from the **terminal** (Jl Basoeki Rahmat) to Soa, Mangulewa, Mataloko, Langa and Boawae. Bemos to Bena run two or three times a day but not to a regular schedule. There is also at least one truck a day that runs to Jerebuu, passing through Bena. The bemos roam around town a lot, so you can also pick them up on the street.

BOAT

The ASDP fairly fast ferry *Perum* runs from Aimere, on the coast near Bajawa, to Waingapu (48,000Rp) in Sumba, leaving on Monday at 4pm. It returns to Aimere overnight and then leaves for Kupang (62,000Rp) on Tuesday morning at around 9am. Take a bemo from the Watujaji bus terminal to Aimere (8000Rp) and buy the ticket on the ferry. Ask for the latest schedule at hotels in Bajawa, as changes are common.

BUS

Most buses will pick up from hotels if you book a ticket in advance, but you'll prob-

THE NGADA

Over 60,000 Ngada people inhabit the upland Bajawa plateau and the slopes around Gunung Inerie. They were subdued by the Dutch in 1907, and Christian missionaries arrived in about 1920. Older animistic beliefs remain strong, and most Ngada practise a fusion of animism and Christianity.

The most evident symbols of continuing Ngada tradition are the pairs of *ngadhu* and *bhaga*. The *ngadhu* is a parasol-like structure about 3m-high, consisting of a carved wooden pole and thatched 'roof', and the *bhaga* is like a miniature thatched-roof house. You'll see groups of them standing in most Ngada villages, though in the less traditional ones some of the *bhaga* have disappeared.

The functions and meanings of *ngadhu* are multiple, but basically they symbolise the continuing presence of ancestors. The *ngadhu* is 'male' and the *bhaga* is 'female', and each pair is associated with a particular family group within a village. Some are said to have been built to commemorate people killed in long-past battles over land disputes, and they may be more than 100 years old. Periodically, on instruction from ancestors in dreams, a pair of *ngadhu* and *bhaga* is remade according to a fixed pattern, accompanied by ceremonies that may involve buffalo sacrifices.

The traditional Ngada village layout is two rows of high-roofed houses on low stilts. These face each other across an open space that contains *ngadhu* and *bhaga* and groups of human-sized vertical and horizontal stone slabs. The latter, which appear to be graves of important ancestors, have led to some exotic theories about the Ngada's origins.

Traditionally, the Ngada believe themselves to have come from Java and they may have settled here three centuries ago. But similar stone structures (megaliths) crop up in other remote parts of Indonesia – among them Pulau Nias, Sumatra's Batak highlands, parts of Sulawesi, Sumba and Tanimbar – as well as in Malaysia and Laos. The common thread is thought to be the Dongson culture, which arose in southern China and northern Vietnam about 2700 years ago, then migrated to Indonesia. Megaliths survived only in isolated areas that weren't in contact with later cultural changes.

In addition to *ngadhu*, *bhaga* and the ancestor worship that goes with them, agricultural fertility rites continue (sometimes involving gory buffalo sacrifices), as well as ceremonies marking birth, marriage, death and house building. The major annual festival is the six-day Reba ceremony at Bena, 19km from Bajawa, held in late December or early January, which includes dancing, singing, buffalo sacrifices and the wearing of special black ikat costumes. The highest god in traditional Ngada belief is Gae Dewa, who unites Dewa Zeta (the heavens) and Nitu Sale (the earth).

ably have to endure endless loops around town before the bus finally leaves from the main Watujaji terminal, 3km south of the centre just off the Ende–Ruteng road.

The bus to Labuanbajo (70,000Rp, 10 hours) leaves at 7am; buses to Ruteng (40,000Rp, five hours) are at 7am, 11am and noon; and buses to Ende (44,000Rp, five hours) go at 7am and noon. There are also buses to Riung (18,000Rp, three hours), along a tough, winding road, at 8am and noon.

You will pay a commission if you book your ticket through a hotel.

Getting Around

Yellow bemos (1000Rp) cruise around town, but it is easy to walk almost everywhere except the bus terminals. *Treks* (trucks) also serve remote routes, most leaving the villages in the morning and returning in the afternoon.

Motorcycles cost 75,000Rp a day, or a Kijang (with driver) is 350,000Rp at **Central Motor** (☎ 21242; Jl Ahmad Yani).

The airport (Map p556) is 25km from Bajawa and about 6km outside Soa. Bemos from the Pasar Bajawu cost 6000Rp, but don't get stranded in Soa.

AROUND BAJAWA

The main attraction of Bajawa is the chance to get out into the countryside and explore the traditional villages. It is certainly possible to visit the area alone, but you'll learn a lot more about the culture and customs (like the caste system) with a good guide, and some will organise meals in their home

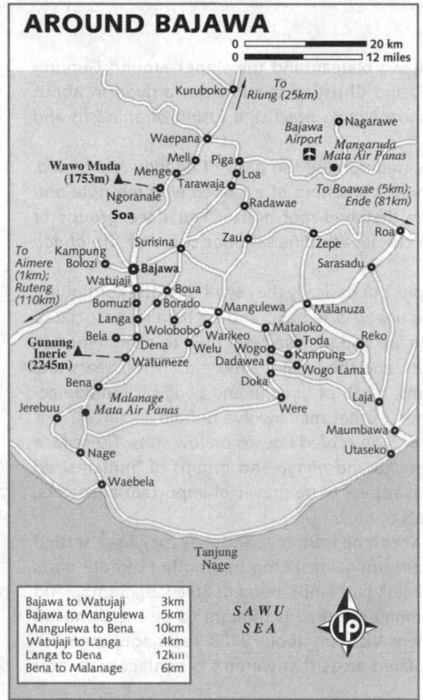

villages or treks across the countryside. The main difference is their proficiency in English (a few also know a little Dutch, German and/or French). You're likely to have prospective guides approach you in your hotel, or in the restaurants Camellia and Lucas.

Aim to pay around 100,000Rp a day for a guide, including bemo fares. For those wanting to cover ground at a faster pace, see p555 for motorcycle- and car-hire information.

The villagers are now quite used to tourists. If visiting, it is customary to sign the visitors' book and make a donation. Taking photos is usually OK, but ask first and remember that entering a village is like entering someone's home. Bena and Wogo are the most traditional and impressive villages, and Bena has the bonus of fine views.

Langa & Bela

There are totem pole–like *ngadhu* (dedicated to male ancestors) and *bhaga* (female ancestors) in Langa, which is 7km from Bajawa, but this village is fairly modern. Bemos travel here from Bajawa's bemo terminal. Bela is more interesting and traditional and is a couple of kilometres away, off the main road.

Bena

On the flank of the **Gunung Inerie** (2245m) volcano, 19km from Bajawa, Bena is one of the most traditional Ngada villages, and its stone monuments are a protected site. Houses with high thatched roofs line up in two rows on a ridge, the space between them filled with fine *ngadhu, bhaga* (which are smeared with blood after sacrifices) and strange megalithic tomblike structures. Most houses have male or female figurines on their roofs, while doorways are decorated with buffalo horns and jawbones – a sign of the family's prosperity.

A small Christian shrine sits on a mound at the top of the village and behind it a recently built lookout offers a spectacular view down a jagged valley to the sea – a two-hour walk away. Gunung Inerie can be climbed from Watumeze, between Langa and Bena, in about four hours.

Bena is the most visited village, and weavings and souvenir stalls line the front of houses. Although the village is crowded when tour buses arrive, traditional beliefs and customs are strongly followed, though all villagers are now officially Catholic and attend a local missionary school. Village elders still talk about a rigidly enforced caste system that prevented 'mixed' relationships, with those defying the *adat* facing possible death. If you can speak Dutch, the senior villager Yosef Rodja Gale will explain all.

Bena is 12km from Langa down a poor but (mostly) sealed road that's passable in a Kijang or motorcycle. There's one daily bemo to/from Bajawa (4000Rp); it leaves Bena at 7am and returns from Bajawa at 1pm.

Nage

Nage is a traditional village on a plateau about 7km from Bena, with great views of Gunung Inerie. A number of well-maintained *ngadhu, bhaga* and tombs lie between two rows of high-roofed houses. About 2km before Nage are the **Malanage Mata Air Panas** (hot springs), where a fast-flowing, hot and emerald-green river mixes with a cold-water stream, offering a warm power shower.

You can walk from Nage to Bena; just continue north on the sealed road through the village. Otherwise, one bemo in the morning and one in the afternoon runs from Bajawa via Bena and Mangulewa.

Wogo

Wogo is a large village with eight or nine sets of *ngadhu* and *bhaga*, ringed by traditional houses. This is one of the area's largest and most traditional villages, though a few mod cons have arrived, including electricity.

About 1km further on from Wogo, turn off at the Dadawea sign and follow the track to the left to Wogo Lama, where vast groups of jagged stones jut out from the ground. These megalithic **ancestor tombs** are still used in ceremonies.

Wogo is 1.5km from Mataloko, which is 18km from Bajawa on the Ende road and easily reached by bus or bemo – very regular bemos shuttle to Wogo from the highway at Mataloko (1000Rp). Mataloko is famous for its huge seminary, located on the highway.

Wawo Muda

Wawo Muda is the latest volcano to emerge in Flores, blowing its top in 2001 and leaving behind a sort of mini-Kelimutu, complete with several small lakes coloured a burnt orange inside its crater. Pine trees charred by the eruption stand in isolated patches like hairs on a balding pate, and there are spectacular views of the near-perfect cone of Gunung Inerie.

The volcano is best visited in the wet season from November to March, if the trails are not too sodden, as in the dry months the lakes usually evaporate. To get there take one of the regular bemos from Bajawa (5000Rp, 50 minutes) or an *ojek* to the village of Ngoranale, near Menge, and walk an hour up an easy-to-follow trail. Some *ojek* drivers may offer to take you the whole way up, as the path is doable on a motorcycle.

Soa

Soa, about 20km north of Bajawa, is a transitional cultural region whose people are related to the Bajawanese and Boawaenese. Interesting sites in this area include **Loa**, where traditional *sagi* fights with lumps of wood are held around June.

A more popular site is the developed **Mangaruda Mata Air Panas** (hot springs; admission 2500Rp), past the airport on the back road to Boawae. Unfortunately, there are lots of half-finished buildings, which detract from the atmosphere, but as you clamber beneath the small waterfall and wallow in the hot water it's easy to forget all that.

BOAWAE

Boawae is 41km from Bajawa on the highway to Ende and is the centre for the Nage-Keo people. It sits at the base of **Gunung Ebulobo**. This smoking volcano can be climbed with a guide hired in the village. It usually involves an overnight stop on the mountain, then a two-hour ascent early the next morning, but the hike may not be possible to do in the rainy season.

This is the source of most of the best Bajawa-area ikat. Gory buffalo sacrifice rituals take place here, and an equally messy form of boxing called *etu* is part of the May to August harvest festivities. The boxers wear garments made of tree bark that have been painted with animal blood. Their gloves may be studded with broken glass.

Few visitors bother to stop at Boawae, but **Wisma Nusa Bunga** (r from 25,000Rp), on the highway, has clean, simple rooms.

Hotel Sao Wisata (r 40,000Rp) is a better option than Wisma Nusa Bunga. To get here, take the road next to the Wisma Nusa Bunga and follow it for 1.5km down to the river and then around to the left near the church. In lush gardens by the river, this is a delightful guesthouse, and meals are available.

RIUNG

This quiet fishing village 72km from Bajawa lies opposite a scattering of offshore islands with white-sand beaches and excellent snorkelling over intact reefs. Though the area is known as the **Seventeen Islands Marine Park**, there are actually more than 21 islands, but the government authorities decided on the number as a convenient tie-in with Indonesia's Independence Day (17 August).

Riung itself is spread out and fairly nondescript, and it has a shoreline of mud-flats and mangroves that is home to a Muslim Bugis stilt-house community.

Information

The PHKA office on the main drag has information about the Riung area and accredited guides. Before going to the islands you must sign in and pay 10,000Rp per person (plus 5000Rp boat fee) at a separate booth by the dock.

There's a BNI bank, but it didn't offer any exchange facilities when we visited. Come with enough cash, or one of the guides may exchange greenbacks for rupiah. At the time of research a new phone mast was due to become operational in late 2006, providing mobile phone access to the village. Electricity is normally restricted to between 6pm and 8pm only.

Sights & Activities

Guides will appear at your hotel offering to organise **boat trips** to several of the islands, though there are few people in town outside the July-August high season, so sharing a boat is not easy. A day trip costs 250,000Rp (for up to six, not including lunch) if you use a guide, or perhaps 175,000Rp if you negotiate directly with the boat owners in the harbour. Renting snorkel gear is usually extra. Three or four islands are usually included in the boat trip, including Pulau Ontoloe, which has a massive colony of flying foxes. (These huge fruit bats blacken the sky around Riung at sunset as they head inland to feed).

It's also possible go **diving** in the islands with Awing Muhammed, an experienced Divemaster who trained in Timor. Two dives cost 600,000Rp to 750,000Rp, including all gear. You'll find Awing in the Bugis village at a former hotel known as Nur Iklas.

On the shore around Riung **giant iguanas** with yellow markings used to be an attraction, though they are now very rare indeed. **Komodo dragons** can still be seen occasionally. Hike up to **Watujapi Hill**, about 3km from Riung, for a magnificent view of the coast and the Seventeen Islands Marine Park.

Sleeping & Eating

There are several homestays scattered around town, though unfortunately standards have slipped with the downturn in tourism.

Hotel Florida (s/d 25,000/35,000Rp, with mandi 50,000/60,000Rp) The first place on the road into town. Its best days were many moons ago and there's an air of decay setting in, though the staff are informative about the region.

Homestay Madona (r 35,000Rp) Seven very basic rooms with *mandis* and verandas in a family house. A friendly old couple run the place and cook meals on request.

Liberty Homestay (r 40,000Rp) On the same stretch as Homestay Madona, Liberty has a nice balcony area and large rooms, plus the owners speak some English.

Nivana (bungalows 75,000Rp) A new place with six well-constructed detached bamboo bungalows with open-air bathrooms. It's jointly owned by a Swiss woman and her somewhat self-obsessed local partner.

Pondok SVD (s/d 90,000/150,000Rp, superior 275,000/300,000Rp) Clean as a whistle, this missionary-run place has absolutely spotless rooms with desks, reading lights and Western toilets. The superior-class rooms have an additional living area with a sofa and a TV. The staff couldn't be more friendly, but the food here is very pricey (dishes 15,000Rp to 20,000Rp, set meals 40,000Rp).

There are only a few eating places in Riung:

Rumah Makan Murah Muriah (mains 10,000-20,000Rp, large beer 15,000Rp; breakfast, lunch & dinner) Behind the market, this friendly place with gingham tablecloths offers tasty local grub and sells beer.

Rumah Soto Sate (dishes 6000-14,000Rp; breakfast, lunch & dinner) Small Javanese-style place that has good sate.

Getting There & Away

From Ndao terminal in Ende (26,000Rp, four hours), a bus leaves every morning at 6am. The only alternative is to take a bus at 1pm to Mbay and then a bemo to Riung. The road to Ende is narrow and bumpy but sealed. Buses from Bajawa (18,000Rp, three hours) leave at 8am and noon, and the wildly winding road is reasonable. The Riung–Ende bus leaves at 7am, and buses to Bajawa depart at 5am and 11.30am.

ENDE

☎0381 / pop 80,000

The port town of Ende is an important transport hub, with good sea and air connections to the other islands in Nusa Tenggara, though there's little to see in the town itself. Nevertheless, some fine mountain scenery surrounds the town, including the cones of Gunung Meja (661m) near the airport and larger Gunung Iya, occupying a promontory to the south.

The people gathered in south-central Flores, in and around Ende, have a mix of Malay and Melanesian features. The aristocratic families of Ende link their ancestors through mythical exploits and magical events to the Hindu Majapahit kingdom of Java. Today the population of Ende is evenly split between Christians and Muslims.

Orientation

Ende is at the neck of a peninsula jutting south into the sea. The old port and most of the shops are on the western side of the neck. The main port, Pelabuhan Ipi, is on the eastern side.

Information

INTERNET ACCESS & TELEPHONE

Telkom Office (Jl Kelimutu; 24hr) Has cheap international calls and also offers internet access (10,000Rp per hour).

MONEY

Hotel Ikhlas will exchange money after hours.

Bank Danamon (Jl Soekarno; 8am-3.30pm Mon-Fri, to noon Sat) Has an ATM and offers larger credit-card withdrawals.

BNI bank (Bank Negara Indonesia; Jl Gatot Subroto) Near the airport, this bank offers the best rates and has an ATM.

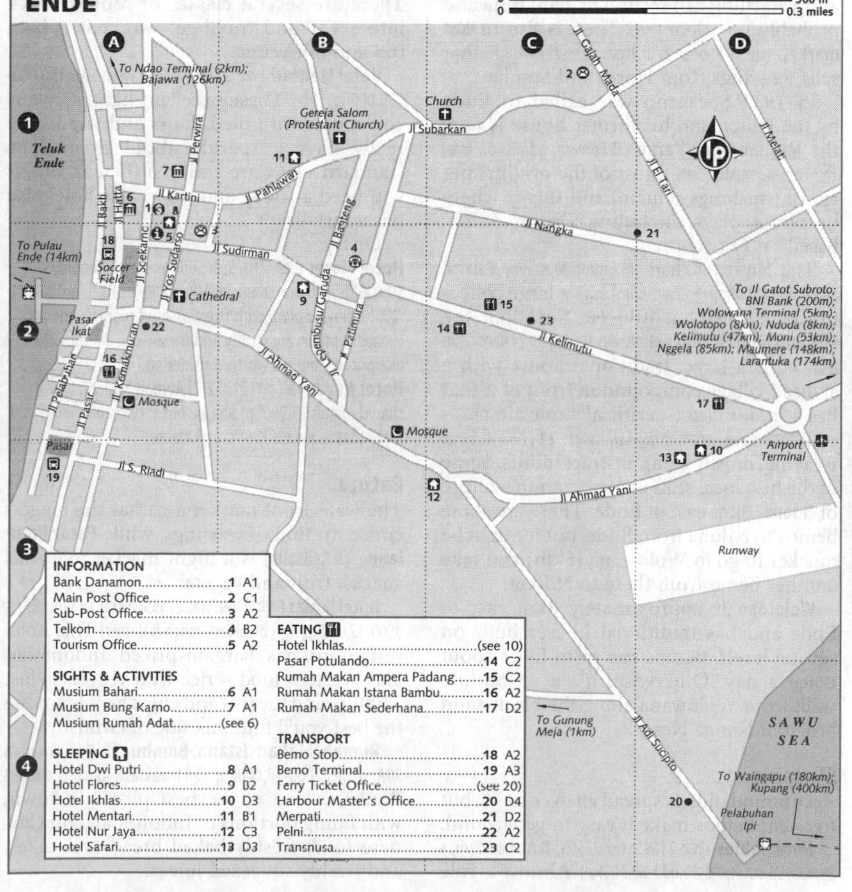

TOURIST INFORMATION

The owners of Hotel Ikhlas are very well informed about the latest transportation schedules.

Tourism Office (☎ 21303; Jl Soekarno 4) Dispenses up-to-date information and has enthusiastic staff.

POST

Main post office (Jl Gajah Mada) Out in the northeastern part of town.

Sub-post office (Jl Yos Sudarso) Sells stamps; it's opposite Hotel Dwi Putri.

Sights

Ende has a few sights of passing interest. The ramshackle **waterfront market** (Jl Pasar) is not a bad place to poke around, with pyramids of fruit, food, tea and clothes for sale and a startling fish section of giant tuna and probably a shark or two. There is also an **ikat market** (cnr Jl Pabean & Jl Pasar; 7am-4pm) that sells weavings from Flores and Sumba.

In 1933 Soekarno was exiled to Ende by the Dutch and his former house is now the **Musium Bung Karno** (Jl Perwira; admission free; 7am-noon Mon-Sat). Most of the original period furnishings remain, and this is where he wrote plays, including *Doctor Satan*, based on *Frankenstein*.

The **Musium Bahari** (Maritime Museum; Jl Hatta; admission 1000Rp; 7am-8pm) has a large collection of seashells but little else. Next door, the **Musium Rumah Adat** (admission 1000Rp; 8am-2pm Mon-Sat) is a large, traditional house with a stylised village compound in front of it that has a *tubu musu* (sacrificial stone altar).

The Ende area has its own style of ikat weaving, mostly using abstract motifs. Some of the best local stuff comes from the village of **Ndona**, 8km east of Ende. There are some bemos to Ndona from Ende, but it might be quicker to go to Wolowana (5km) and take another bemo from there to Ndona.

Wolotopo is approximately 8km east of Ende and has traditional houses built on several levels. Bemos run from Ende about twice a day. Otherwise, it's a 45-minute walk from Wolowana along the black-sand beach of Nanga Nesa.

Sleeping

Accommodation is spread all over town, but frequent bemos make it easy to get around.

Hotel Ikhlas (☎ 21695; fax 22555; Jl Ahmad Yani; s 25,000-50,000Rp, d 40,000-60,000Rp) Almost a role model for budget hotels, this very well-run place has plenty of tidy, neat little rooms at moderate prices – those at the rear around a sunny courtyard are the most desirable. The friendly, well-informed staff and management can provide travel information, and the food is great value (see below).

Hotel Safari (☎ 21997; Jl Ahmad Yani 65; economy s/d 50,000/60,000Rp, with air-con 100,000/150,000Rp;) Right next door to Hotel Ikhlas, this is a step upmarket and has a choice of spacious rooms, each with two beds and, from economy class to 'VIP', all overlooking a peaceful rear courtyard. Breakfast is included.

Hotel Dwi Putri (☎ 21685; Jl Yos Sudarso; r with fan 65,000-95,000Rp, with air-con 125,000-200,000Rp;) This almost elegant looking modern hotel has a classy façade but is under-patronised. There are several classes of rooms; check into a VIP and you'll get two beds, a bath tub and hot water.

Hotel Mentari (☎ 21802; Jl Pahlawan 19; r 150,000-250,000Rp;) These excellent light, airy air-con rooms with tiled floors and wardrobes really have a sparkle about them. The standard class are quite sufficient unless you need a fridge and a TV. The hotel also has a restaurant.

Or try:

Hotel Flores (☎ 21075; Jl Sudirman 28; economy r 50,000Rp, with air-con & TV 100,000Rp, VIP r 175,000Rp;) Unlovely place with five classes of rooms – the cheaper options are scruffy and the air-con doubles are overpriced –but it's worth considering.

Hotel Nur Jaya (☎ 21252; Jl Ahmad Yani 20; r with shared mandi 25,000Rp) Simple but serviceable family-run place that is always kept pretty clean.

Eating

The waterfront market area has the biggest concentration of warungs, while **Pasar Potulando** (Jl Kelimutu) is a night market that sells snacks, fruit and vegetables.

Hotel Ikhlas (☎ 21695; fax 22555; Jl Ahmad Yani; dishes 3500-12,000Rp; breakfast, lunch & dinner) This hotel restaurant has bargain-priced Indonesian and Western food – rice with veggies is just 3500Rp, and the fish and chips here is among the best you'll find this side of Grimsby.

Rumah Makan Istana Bambu (Jl Kemakmuran 30A; mains 7000-18,000Rp; breakfast, lunch & dinner) Ranks as one of the best places in town, with filling portions of Indonesian and Chinese food, freshly baked bread and cakes, and freshly squeezed juices.

Good Padang restaurants:

Rumah Makan Ampera Padang (Jl Kelimutu 31; most dishes 5000-8000Rp; breakfast, lunch & dinner)

Rumah Makan Sederhana (☎ 24481; Jl Kelimutu; dishes 4500-10,000Rp; breakfast, lunch & dinner)

Getting There & Away

AIR

Schedules change every few months in eastern Nusa Tenggara, so always check flight information in advance. At the time of research, **Transnusa** (☎ 24222; fax 23592; Jl Kelimutu 37) was very well connected, offering flights to Kupang (11 weekly, some via Maumere) with connections to destinations such as Waingapu and Alor. **Merpati** (☎ 21355; Jl Nangka) has three weekly flights to Kupang and two weekly to Bima.

Departure tax is 6000Rp.

BOAT

Ende is the major port for southern Flores and is well connected to other islands. Ships dock at Pelabuhan Ipi, which is the main port, 2.5km southeast from the town centre.

The following schedules change frequently. **ASDP** (☎ 22007) ferries to Waingapu (42,500Rp, six hours) leave Ende on Thursday night, before looping back again and heading to Kupang. Buy tickets at the harbour. There are also twice-weekly services to Kupang (58,000Rp, seven hours) on a small fast ferry, but this stops when conditions are rough.

Pelni's *Awu* and *Pangrango* stop in Ende every two weeks. *Awu* sails west to Waingapu, Lembar and Benoa, and east to Kupang, Kalabahi and Larantuka. The *Pangrango* sails from Ende to Waingapu, Badas and Surabaya and on the return route east to Sabu and Kupang. Visit the helpful **Pelni office** (☎ 21043; Jl Kathedral 2; 8am-noon & 2-4pm Mon-Sat).

Dharma Lautan Utama (☎ 21927; Jl Adi Sucipto) operates *Kirana II* between Kupang and Surabaya, calling at Ende. It runs roughly to a weekly schedule, but the day it leaves is impossible to define.

Other boats sail irregularly to these and other destinations; for details, ask at the harbour master's office at Pelabuhan Ipi.

BUS & KIJANG

It's about 5km from town to Wolowana terminal, where you catch buses for eastern Flores. Buses to Moni (14,000Rp, two hours) operate from 6am to 2pm. Buses to Maumere (37,000Rp, five hours) leave at 7am, 9am and 4pm. Maumere buses will drop you in Moni but charge the full fare through to Maumere. A bus to Nggela leaves at 7am, and a through bus to Larantuka leaves at 7am (nine hours).

Buses heading west leave from the Ndao terminal, 2km north of town on the beach road. Departures from Ende are to Ruteng (70,000Rp, nine hours) at 7.30am; Labuanbajo (105,000Rp, 15 hours) at 7am; Bajawa (44,000Rp, five hours) at 7am and 11am; and Riung (26,000Rp, four hours) at 6am.

Kijang jeeps that operate as shared taxis also leave Ende for Maumere (front/rear seat 60,000/50,000Rp, 4½ hours). There's at least one every day operated by **Simpati** (☎ 23777); call them first for a pick-up.

Getting Around

The airport is just east of the centre. Those planning on staying at hotels such as the Ikhlas and Safari can walk, but others heading further into town should take a taxi for around 15,000Rp.

Bemo run frequently to just about everywhere in town (even Pelabuhan Ipi) for a flat rate of 1000Rp. You can easily flag a bemo on the street; if not, pick one up at the bemo stop on Jl Hatta (near the old port).

KELIMUTU

Set in plunging craters at the summit of a volcano, the coloured lakes of Kelimutu are undoubtedly the most spectacular sight in Nusa Tenggara. Astonishingly, the lakes periodically change hue – on our visit the largest was an iridescent turquoise, its neighbour chocolate brown and the third lake dark green. A few years ago the colours were blue, maroon and black, while back in the 1960s the lakes were blue, red-brown and *café au lait*.

It's thought that the lakes' colours are in constant flux due to dissolving minerals, a process that can accelerate in the rainy season. The moonscape around the summit gives Kelimutu an ethereal atmosphere, especially when clouds billow across the craters and sun shafts add luminescent pinpoints to the lakes.

Kelimutu is sacred to local people, and legend has it that the souls of the dead go to these lakes: young people's souls go to the warmth of Tiwu Nuwa Muri Koo Fai (Turquoise Lake), old people's to the cold of Tiwi Ata Mbupu (Brown Lake) and those of the wicked to Tiwi Ata Polo (Black Lake).

The volcano has attracted sightseers since Dutch times, and today there's a sealed road up to the lakes from Moni, 13.5km away at the base of the mountain. Kelimutu's relative isolation means that surprisingly few visitors make it here outside of the July–August high season, and even then it's not too hard to find a peaceful spot to enjoy this natural wonder. Visit in the rainy season or in the afternoon and you may even have Kelimutu, in silence, to yourself.

There's a staircase up to the highest lookout, Inspiration Point, from where all three lakes are visible. It's not at all advisable to scramble around the fringes of the craters – the scree is loose and a couple of hikers perished here recently.

Pray for a sunny day – sunrise is stunning and the turquoise lake reaches its full brilliance in the sunlight. If the weather is not good, come back the next day – Kelimutu is really worth seeing at its best.

Enterprising locals sell coffee and snacks here.

Getting There & Away

Moni is the usual base for visiting Kelimutu. It's normally best to view the lakes in the early morning before the clouds move in. Local transport is timed to reflect this, with trucks or minibuses picking you up at 4am from your hotel; a ride can be arranged anywhere in Moni and costs 15,000Rp return per person. There's a PHKA post halfway up, where you have to pay 2000Rp per person. From the car park it's a 15-minute walk to the first of the crater lakes. The return journey to Moni is at 7am, which is too little time to see the sun bring out the lakes' full beauty – the rusty-red hues around the fringes of the brown lake and the startling turquoise of the biggest lake – so some prefer to linger and walk down later.

If the skies look particularly clear and you have, or hire, your own transport, it's well worth considering a trip to Kelimutu later in

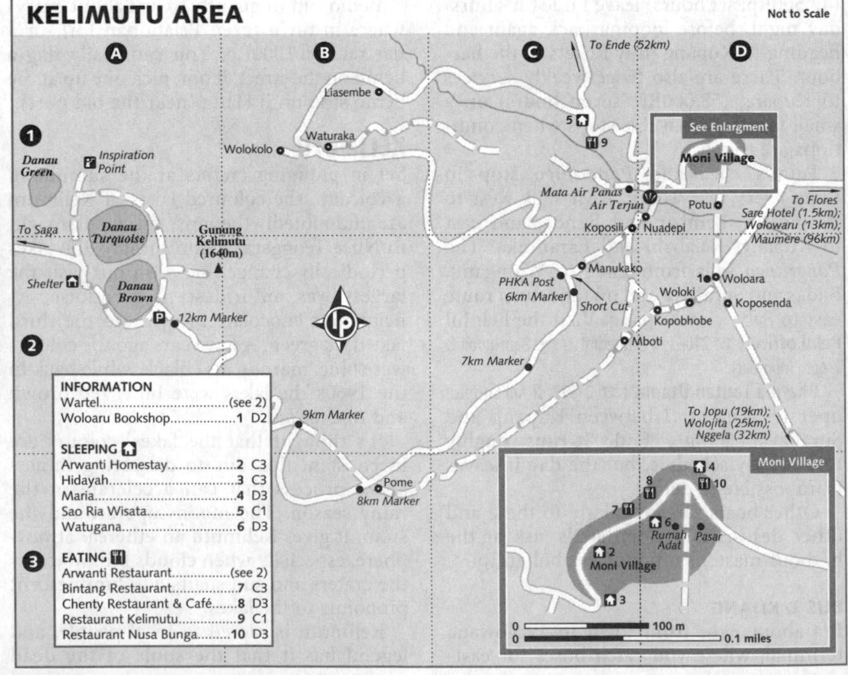

the day when everyone has gone – the silence of the mountain returns and the natural spectacle becomes even more moving.

The walk down takes about 2½ hours and isn't too taxing. A *jalan potong* (shortcut) leaves the road back to Moni at the PHKA post and reaches the highway about 750m from the centre of Moni. This cuts about 6km off the journey.

Another path branches off the shortcut at Koposili and goes via the villages of Mboti and Pome, reaching the Kelimutu road near the 8km marker, about 5.5km from the summit. This path is no shorter, but it passes through villages where locals serve drinks and breakfast.

MONI

Moni is a pretty village, nestled among soaring peaks, which serves as the gateway to Flores' main tourist attraction, Kelimutu. It is scenic, cooler than the lowlands and a good place for walks.

The village is strung alongside the Ende–Maumere road in the heart of the Lio region, which extends from east of Ende to beyond Wolowaru. Lio people speak a dialect of the Ende language and are renowned for their ikat weaving: pieces adorned with bands of blue and rusty-red. A colourful market spreads over the playing field in front of Moni's church every Monday morning. Cloth from the Nggela and Maumere regions can be bought here. You'll also find a few stalls along Moni's main street, as well as at the parking area for Kelimutu.

Information

There are no banks in Moni and the exchange rates on offer are appalling – come with cash. There's a wartel at Arwanti Homestay, but the rates are extortionate. Otherwise there are no phones in Moni.

Apart from the guesthouses, one of the best sources of information in the area is the Woloaru Bookshop, 1.5km from the centre of Moni. Dutch owner Mark leads birding trips and guided walks around the area from 50,000Rp per person, and sells and exchanges used books as well as Kelimutu postcards.

Sights & Activities

In the *kampung* (village) opposite the market, the high-thatched *rumah adat* serves as a cultural centre of sorts. **Traditional dance performances** (20,000Rp) are held in front of it during the peak season of July and August. Ask around at other times.

Apart from the trek to/from Kelimutu there are several other walks from Moni. About 750m along the Ende road from the centre of Moni, paths lead down to a 10m **air terjun** (waterfall), with a pool big enough for swimming and **mata air panas** (hot springs). This is the village *mandi* and visitors can also bathe here – men in the left pool, and women in the right. Another short walk is south past the church to **Potu** and **Woloara** (about 2.5km from Moni). From Woloara, continue on through several villages to **Jopu** (about 5km). Energetic types could walk on to **Wolojita** and **Nggela** or loop back to Wolowaru and catch a bus or truck back to Moni.

Sleeping

The downturn in tourist numbers in recent years has hit Moni hard, and prices are very reasonable. Accommodation is virtually all in the budget category and quite spread out along the highway. These places are listed in the order you approach them from Ende.

Sao Ria Wisata (small bungalows 75,000Rp, larger bungalows 125,000Rp) Government-owned place perched in splendid isolation on the hillside above Moni. It has well-maintained if overpriced detached bungalows with verandas; hot water is planned.

Hidayah (s/d 40,000/50,000Rp) Ramshackle bamboo huts next to a burbling brook and pretty rice fields.

Arwanti Homestay (s/d 75,000/100,000Rp) This place has three attractive spacious bungalows, each equipped with bamboo furnishings, two bedrooms, a sitting room, a bathroom with shower and a front veranda. Unfortunately, they could be cleaner, and the staff could certainly be a little more helpful.

Watugana (s/d 40,000/60,000Rp) Simple, clean rooms with big beds, mossie nets and a bathroom make this a popular place. Banana pancakes or fruit salad is the staple breakfast.

Maria (r 50,000Rp, bungalows 75,000Rp) Rooms and bungalows, some with attached bathrooms and Western toilets, are basic but clean. Breakfast is thrown in.

Flores Sare Hotel (☎ 038121075; r 100,000 & 165,000Rp) Viewed from the road it looks

NUSA TENGGARA

like a half-finished building site, but if you pass through the large adjoining restaurant there are some very spacious and surprisingly orderly rooms with high ceilings and big beds. Granny would lurve the flowery bedspreads.

Eating

The choice of restaurants is pretty good for such a tiny place.

Chenty Restaurant & Café (dishes 6000-17,000Rp; breakfast, lunch & dinner) Long-running, popular place above the main road in the centre of the village with a good selection of Indonesian food. The noise and action often gravitates here when Moni is busy.

Bintang Restaurant (dishes 6000-15,000Rp; breakfast, lunch & dinner) With an engaging owner and well-priced menu of the usual Indo suspects, this is probably the best place to eat in town. It's perched above the road in central Moni and has good views.

Restaurant Nusa Bunga (dishes 5000-15,000Rp; breakfast, lunch & dinner) Tiny place with cheap and cheerful Indonesian and Western food. Try the Moni cakes, a sort of spicy bubble and squeak.

Arwanti Restaurant (mains 11,000-18,000Rp; breakfast, lunch & dinner) It certainly looks the part, with stylish décor and a tempting menu, but the food is very plain, the service is slow and the staff are distracted.

Restaurant Kelimutu (dishes 9000-20,000Rp; breakfast, lunch & dinner) Right next door to Sao Ria Wisata, this attractive place with a thatched roof has Indo and Western food – though speedy the service ain't.

Getting There & Away

Moni is 53km northeast of Ende and 98km west of Maumere. For Ende (14,000Rp, two hours), buses start at around 7am, and there's a bus all the way to Labuanbajo at noon. Many additional buses and trucks leave on Monday, Moni's market day.

For Maumere (23,000Rp, three hours), the first buses from Ende start coming through at around 9am or 10am and then later in the evening at around 7pm.

As most of the buses stop midroute in Moni they can be crowded, and it's first come, first served for a seat. Sometimes you'll be sitting in the aisle on a sack of rice or even on a pig if you're lucky. Some of the homestays make 'bookings', which usually means they will hail a bus for you and charge you extra.

AROUND MONI

Wolowaru

The village of Wolowaru, straggling along the Maumere road just 13km southeast of Moni, is a handy base for the ikat-weaving villages of Wolojita and Nggela. There's a daily morning market that winds down at around 9am, except on Saturday, the main market day.

The **Hotel Kelimutu** (☎ 41020; s/d 10,000/15,000Rp) has simple rooms with shared facilities for ablutions. For authentic local food, **Rumah Makan Jawa Timur** (mains 6000-13,000Rp) is a popular place and is right next to Hotel Kelimutu.

All Maumere–Ende buses stop in Wolowaru. A few morning buses originate here – check schedules at the Jawa Timur – and most buses stop at this restaurant for a meal break.

The road to the following villages branches off from the main road in Wolowaru.

Nggela & Wolojita

Beautiful ikat sarongs and shawls can be found in these and other villages between Wolowaru and the south coast. Impromptu stalls often spring up before your eyes as you approach the villages.

Nggela is worth a visit for its hilltop position above the coast, but the chief attraction is the weaving, usually done by hand and still using many natural dyes. The weaving is among the finest in Flores, and you'll be able to watch the artisans at their work. In former times the size, colour and pattern of the ikat shawls of this region indicated the status of the wearer. Nggela ikat typically has black or rich dark brown backgrounds, with patterns in earthy red, brown or orange. Bargain hard and watch out for brighter synthetic dyes, which are becoming more common (you should pay less if the dyes aren't natural).

Homestay Nggela Permai (s/d 20,000/30,000Rp) is in Nggela for those visitors who want more of the authentic village experience than can be found in Moni.

Wolojita is about 7km inland from Nggela and has weavings of a similar quality, but not Nggela's fine location.

A road branches off the Ende–Maumere road at Wolowaru and heads to Wolojita

NUSA TENGGARA

(12km) and Nggela (19km). One bus per day leaves Ende at 6am for Nggela, passing Moni at about 9am and then Wolojita. Otherwise, it's a good half-day's walk to Nggela from Wolowaru. It's only 2km or 3km further from Moni via Woloara, so you could just as easily start from there. The volcano-studded scenery is beautiful, particularly on the downhill stretch of the road as it runs into Nggela.

From Wolojita to Nggela, either follow the road or take a short cut past the hot springs (ask for the *jalan potong ke Nggela*). It would be pushing it to do the return walk on the same day, but there might be a truck going back to Wolowaru.

MAUMERE

☎ 0382 / pop 50,000

The seaport of Maumere is a pretty forlorn place, but as it's one of the main gateways to Flores, and well connected with Bali and Timor, you may well end up here for a night. Its crumbling concrete buildings and air of decay brutally betray its recent history – in 1992 an earthquake and resulting 20m tsunami killed thousands here. The city authorities appear to have done little to help the town's recovery, however: mounds of rubbish line the streets, nibbled by marauding pigs and goats, which only compounds the postapocalyptic air that lingers on.

The town is the major centre of the Sikkanese language and culture, which extends east between central Flores and Larantuka. This area has been one of the chief centres of Catholic activity and missions in Flores since Portuguese Dominicans arrived some 400 years ago.

Some interesting trips can be made out of town to ikat-weaving villages and east to the once-legendary Maumere sea gardens, coral reefs which are steadily recovering after the tsunami. A string of beach bungalow resorts also line this coast, offering a temptingly accessible alternative to staying in town.

Information

Several travel agencies offer up-to-date transport information and can arrange car rental, tailor trip itineraries or just make bookings for planes and boats.

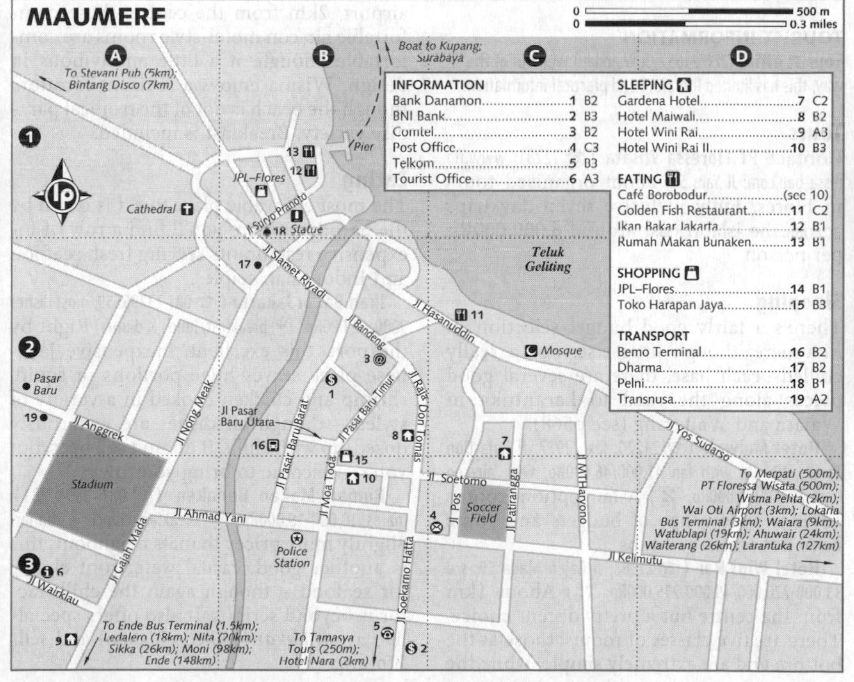

INTERNET ACCESS

Comtel (Jl Bandeng 1; per hr 10,000Rp;) The best internet connection in Flores, this place has a useful noticeboard too.

MONEY

Bank Danamon (Jl Pasar Baru Barat) Has an ATM and, with some persuasion, the staff will do credit-card cash advances – up to 5,000,000Rp with a 50,000Rp charge.

BNI bank (Bank Negara Indonesia; Jl Soekarno Hatta) Has the best rates in town an ATM.

POST

Post office (Jl Pos) Next to the soccer field.

TELEPHONE

Telkom office (Jl Soekarno Hatta; 24hr) Opposite BNI. Internet access is also available here.

TRAVEL AGENCIES

PT Floressa Wisata (22281; Jl Yani 50; www.floressa-bali.com) Next to the Merpati office, this efficient company can book boat and airline tickets and offers organised tours.

Tamasya Tours (21796; ignas_maumere@yahoo.com; Jl Tubin 35A) Run by the irrepressible Ignas, this is a reliable travel agency.

TOURIST INFORMATION

Tourist office (21652; Jl Wairklau) Well out of the way, this has limited literature and practical information.

Tours

Contact **PT Floressa Wisata** (22281; www.floressa-bali.com; Jl Yani 50) about organised tours in Flores. Fully inclusive seven-day trips across the island cost around 6,000,000Rp per person.

Sleeping

There's a fairly good budget selection in Maumere, though little else. For a really chilled beach base, there are several good places along the road to Larantuka in Waiara and Waiterang (see p568).

Hotel Maiwali (21220; fax 22977; Jl Raja Don Tomas 40; s/d with fan 41,000/46,000Rp, with air-con from 78,000/98,000Rp;) A fair option; rooms cover a wide range of budgets and some have hot-water bathtubs.

Hotel Wini Rai (21388; Jl Gajah Mada 50; s/d 33,000-220,000/49,000-275,000Rp;) About 1km from the centre but a pretty decent choice. There are five classes of rooms; those at the bottom end are extremely simple, while the best rooms are well appointed and spacious. It's close to the Ende (west) bus terminal. A second branch in the centre, the **Hotel Wini Rai II** (21362; Jl Soetomo) has near-identical room categories and prices.

Gardena Hotel (22644; Jl Patirangga; s/d with fan 50,000/60,000Rp, with air-con 100,000/120,000Rp;) First choice in central Ende, the Gardena is a very well run and hospitable place in a quiet street close to the centre. Even the fan-only rooms have sprung mattresses, and the en-suite bathrooms are clean and have Western-style bogs. English-speaking staff will help out with travel connections, and rates include breakfast.

Hotel Nara (22001; s/d with fan 50,000/60,000Rp, with air-con 100,000/120,000Rp;) Under the same efficient management as the Gardena, this new place has absolutely bargain-priced and very spacious rooms with good beds, wardrobes and TVs. The drawback is that it's about 2.5km from the centre, though *ojeks* and bemos pass by regularly. At the time of research a restaurant was under construction.

Wisma Pelita (21732; Jl Sudirman 33; s 175,000-215,000Rp, d 250,000-290,000Rp;) Near the airport, 2km from the centre, these comfortable air-con motel-style rooms are comfortable enough, if a little anonymous in design. Wisma enjoys a seafront location, though the beach is not of the tropical paradise variety. Breakfast is included.

Eating

The most enjoyable place to eat is down by the harbour, where you'll find a row of inexpensive restaurants serving fresh seafood and Indonesian staples.

Ikan Bakar Jakarta (081 23795559; most dishes 9000-12,000Rp; breakfast, lunch & dinner) Right by the port, this excellent, inexpensive Javanese place serves huge portions of squid, shrimp and chicken cooked in a variety of styles – though all dishes are generously dosed-up with chilli. It doesn't sell beer, but you're welcome to bring your own.

Rumah Makan Bunaken (081 339448814; mains 10,000-18,000Rp; breakfast, lunch & dinner) Slightly more pricey than its neighbour, this is another good, casual waterfront choice for seafood – though again the chilli factor is beyond serious. It also offers specials like *ayam bakar* (grilled chicken) and sells Bintang.

Café Borobodur (☎ 22858; Jl Soetomo 5; dishes 10,000-20,000Rp; ⏰ breakfast, lunch & dinner) Simple if scruffy place that's fairly well geared to Western tastes, with breakfasts (15,000Rp), jaffles, sandwiches, and Indonesian and Indo-Italian food. Diners might even linger for a coffee if management ever gets round to installing a fan. The café is next door to the Hotel Wini Rai II.

Golden Fish Restaurant (Jl Hasanuddin; large fish 35,000Rp; ⏰ breakfast, lunch & dinner) Pricey place that's famous for its fish and crab – choose your victim from the tank. It's on the coast, but the view is far from spectacular.

Entertainment

There's one disco in town, though it's usually empty, even on Saturday. Most nightlife is of the karaoke and imported Java girls variety.

Stevani Pub (⏰ 8pm-2am) The original karaoke place, this has some grooving most nights after midnight. It's 5km west of town, on the seafront.

Bintang Disco (⏰ 7pm-2am) Come here if you like dancing on your own, though the karaoke section next door is popular and it sells imported whisky. It's 7km west of town.

Shopping

Toko Harapan Jaya (Jl Pasar Baru Timur) Has a good stock of weavings, including some ikat from Flores, Sumba and other islands. Carvings and other artefacts are also on sale here, but bargain hard, as prices start high.

Getting There & Away

AIR

Maumere has good air connections. **Merpati** (☎ 21342; Jl Sudirman) has five flights a week to/from Kupang, four to/from Labuanbajo and five to/from Denpasar with connections to Jakarta. The signposted office is just off the main road to the airport.

Transnusa (☎ 21393; Jl Anggrek 2), by the stadium, has daily flights to Kupang; three days a week this flight goes via Ende (229,000Rp).

Departure tax is 6000Rp.

BOAT

Pelni's *Awu* sails fortnightly from Maumere to Makassar and Kalimantan to the west, Larantuka and Kalabahi to the east, and Kupang to the southeast. **Pelni** (☎ 21013; Jl Suryo Pranoto) is near the entrance to the port.

Dharma (☎ 21091; Jl Nong Meak 2) operates the fairly smart *Kirana* ship that connects Maumere with Surabaya (301,000Rp) and Kupang (115,000Rp). The day of departure depends on sea conditions, but there's usually one trip to each destination per week.

BUS & KIJANG

There are two bus terminals in Maumere. The departure times given below are certainly not precise – be prepared to wait around until there are sufficient passengers and the baggage has been loaded.

Buses to Larantuka (32,000Rp, four hours), and buses and bemos to Geliting, Waiara, Ipir and Wodong leave from the Lokaria (or Timur) terminal, approximately 3km east of town, at 7.30am and 3pm. Kijang shared taxis also leave from here to Larantuka (60,000Rp, three hours) at 7.30am, and sometimes later in the day too.

The Ende (or Barat) terminal 1.5km southwest of town is the place for buses west to Moni (23,000Rp, three hours) and Ende (37,000Rp, five hours), both at 7am and 3pm. Buses to destinations such as Sikka and Ledalero also depart from here. Kijang shared taxis also leave this terminal for Ende (50,000Rp per person, 4½ hours) at around 7.30am.

Getting Around

TO/FROM THE AIRPORT

Maumere's Wai Oti airport is 3km from town, 800m off the Maumere–Larantuka road. A taxi to/from town is 12,000Rp, or 50,000Rp from the beach hotels in Waiterang. It's about a 1km walk out of the airport to the Maumere–Larantuka road to pick up a bemo (1000Rp) into town.

BEMO

Bemos cost 1000Rp and run around town regularly.

CAR & MOTORCYCLE

Renting a car costs around 500,000Rp per day, including driver and fuel for trips around the Maumere region. Those organising road trips to Moni and further west should agree on an itinerary and a schedule of staggered payments before departure. The travel agency PT Floressa Wisata and the Gardena Hotel can both organise rental cars. Motorcycles (around 50,000Rp per day) can usually be arranged by your hotel.

AROUND MAUMERE

Ledalero & Nita

Many Florinese priests studied at the Roman Catholic seminary in Ledalero, which is 18km from Maumere on the Ende road. The chief attraction here is the **museum** (admission free), which houses a collection of historic stone implements and Florinese ikat, with designs and natural dyes that are either rare or no longer produced, including softly textured, pastel-coloured old Jopu sarongs. It's a good place to try to piece together the jigsaw of Florinese culture. It is customary to leave a donation.

Nita is 2km beyond Ledalero on the main road and has a Thursday market, where you should be able to purchase some extremely good-quality local ikat, made with imported cotton. A weavers' group, Kelompok Sentra Tenun Ikat Lepo Lorun, has helped improve and regulate standards here with help from INFID (International NGO Forum on Indonesian Development). Bemos to Ledalero and Nita leave from Maumere's Ende terminal.

Sikka & Lela

On the south coast 26km from Maumere, Sikka was one of the first Portuguese settlements in Flores. Its kings dominated the Maumere region until the 20th century. Today it's interesting mainly as the home of Sikkanese weaving; be prepared to be pounced on by a small army of lady ikat-wallahs as soon as you enter town. Sikka's beautiful church dates from 1899.

The road to Sikka leaves the Ende road 20km from Maumere. Regular bemos (3000Rp) run from Maumere to Sikka.

About 4km before Sikka is Lela, another weaving centre, which has a Catholic population. It has a few colonial buildings and a long and rocky black-sand beach.

Watublapi

Watublapi is in the hills 19km southeast of Maumere and is a large Catholic mission. From here, it is a pleasant walk to **Ohe**, for views over both coasts of Flores. **Bola** is a large village 6km from Watublapi, and 2km further on is the traditional coastal weaving village of **Ipir**. Market day in Ipir is Monday and bemos go there from Maumere (5000Rp, 1½ hours). On other days bemos usually finish at Bola. It may be possible to stay with villagers or the *kepala desa* in Bola or Ipir.

Waiara

Waiara is the jumping-off point for the Maumere 'sea gardens'. Once regarded as one of Asia's finest dive destinations, the 1992 earthquake and tidal wave destroyed many of the reefs. Though Mother Nature has been doing her bit, the marine life and reefs around Pulau Pemana and Pulau Besar are still in recovery mode.

Just off the Larantuka road 9km east of Maumere, Waiara has two resorts. The well-run **Flores Sao Resort** (☎ 21555; fax 21666; s 75,000-250,000Rp, d 100,000-350,000Rp;) has helpful staff, but the rooms, though clean, are looking dated – think 1970s sitcom décor. All accommodation is air-con and spacious: standard rooms are a bit bare, superior rooms have huge verandas, and deluxe rooms are built in a chalet style. The beach is so-so. Breakfast is included, and diving costs US$75 for two dives, including all gear. The attractive **Sea World Club** (Pondok Dunia Laut; ☎ 21570; www.sea-world-club.com; s/d from US$15/20, with air-con from US$20/25;) is run by missionaries. Standard rooms have nice ikat bedspreads and good comfort levels for the price, while the beach houses, some with two bedrooms, front the sandy beach and have big verandas. There's a good restaurant and scuba diving (US$50 for two dives including hire of scuba gear) here too.

To get to the hotels, catch any Talibura- or Larantuka-bound bus from Maumere to Waiara (2000Rp). Both hotels are signposted from the highway; Flores Sao Resort is about 500m further along the road. For a fee, the resorts can arrange drop-offs or pick-ups for guests from Maumere.

Ahuwair & Waiterang

Offering a wonderfully tranquil and relaxed alternative to staying in Ende, the narrow, coconut tree–shaded beaches Ahuwair and Waiterang are 24km to 26km east of Maumere, close to **Wodong** village. Three simple bungalow operations – all well set up for backpackers and one with a scuba school – make this a great base to seriously chill and hammock-swing away the bruising memories of road travel in Flores.

The variety of dive and snorkelling sites is impressive here, with plenty of marine life around Pulau Babi and Pulau Pangabaton, a Japanese wreck, and the 'muck' (shallow mud-flats) to explore. Mantas, reef sharks and fascinating macro life proliferate around dozens of dive sites in this region, but the snorkelling just off the beach in Waiterang is not that impressive. All the hotels can organise snorkelling trips to the islands for around 75,000Rp per person, including lunch and equipment, with a minimum of three people. Happy Dive, based at Ankermi, charges US$55 for two dives, including all gear and boat transfers. In November whale-watching trips are also offered.

All the following places are signposted from the highway and down side tracks 200m to 500m from the road; they are listed in the order you approach them from Maumere. There's no tourist trail in these parts, so it's normally very tranquil. Rates include breakfast.

our pick **Sunset Cottages** (sunsetcottages@yahoo.co.uk; Maumere–Larantuka rd km25; bungalows with mandi 40,000Rp) Extremely hospitable place managed by local villager Henry, who is very helpful, speaks good English and is switched on to travellers' needs. There are six simple, attractive bamboo-and-coconut-wood bungalows right on the beach, and great, imaginatively prepared food is served – order ahead for fresh fish. Snorkel gear is available for hire.

Wodong Beach Cottages (s/d bungalow with mandi 35,000/40,000Rp) Next up, 2km further on, these 10 simple wood-and-thatch bungalows with attached *mandis* are run by the friendly couple Siska and Sino, and there's a nice bar-restaurant area.

Ankermi (ankermi@yahoo.com; s/d 30,000/35,000Rp, two-storey bungalow 45,000Rp) A little further on, this Swiss- and Indonesian-owned place has simple, traditional wood-and-bamboo bungalows set back from the beach, safety boxes, excellent food, a library, the Happy Dive scuba school and lots of information about nearby attractions.

Wodong is on the Maumere–Larantuka road. Take any Talibura, Nangahale or Larantuka bemo or bus from the Lokaria terminal in Maumere (3000Rp). A bemo from Wodong to Waiterang costs 1000Rp. A taxi or chartered bemo from Maumere is around 50,000Rp. Through buses to Larantuka passing by are often hopelessly crowded; to get a seat it is better to first go to Maumere.

Around Waiterang

Nangahale, around 10km northeast of Wodong, is an interesting boat-building village that was settled by survivors from Pulau Babi after the 1992 earthquake. It's easily reached by bemo or bus from Waiterang. On the way to Nangahale, the road passes **Patiahu**, 33km from Maumere, which has the best white-sand beach on this stretch of coast.

The landscape southwest of Waiterang is dominated by smoking **Gunung Egon** (1703m). This active volcano can be climbed from Blidit in around three hours, slightly less coming down. There is little shade, so start early to avoid the heat of the day. It is a relatively easy climb apart from the final scramble to the top. Blidit is 6km from Waiterang – 25,000Rp by chartered bemo. Guides to take you up Egon can be arranged in Waiterang.

LARANTUKA

☎ 0383

A busy little port of rusting tin-roofed houses at the eastern end of Flores, Larantuka nestles around the base of **Gunung Ili Mandiri**, separated by a narrow strait from Pulau Solor and Pulau Adonara. Most folk choose not to linger here and quickly depart for the Solor Archipelago or Kupang by boat.

This corner of Indonesia, though always isolated, was one of the first to attract European interest, as it lay on sea routes used by the Portuguese seeking sandalwood from Timor. Forts and more than 20 Dominican missions were built by 1575. Portugal maintained a presence in Larantuka until the mid-19th century, and their descendents, called 'Topasses', are still a significant community in Larantuka today.

Easter is a particularly good time to be in town, when there are huge processions of penitents and cross-bearers.

Orientation & Information

Hotels, the ferry pier, shipping offices and the main bus terminal are in the southern part of town. Further northeast is the Islamic quarter, and the **tourist office** (8am-2pm Mon-Fri), post office, **Telkom office** (24hr) – which has internet access – and airport. The Kupang ferry pier is to the south. **BRI bank** (Bank Rakyat Indonesia; Jl Udayana) will change money and travellers cheques; it was rumoured to be opening an ATM when we were in town.

Sights & Activities

Catholicism flourishes in Larantuka. There's a large **cathedral**, and the smaller **Kapela Tuan Maria** (Holy Mary Chapel) contains Portuguese bronze and silver known as *ornamento*. On Saturday morning women say the rosary in Portuguese and Latin in this chapel.

Larantuka's **market** has some weaving – look for ikat from Lembata, Adonara and Solor.

Sleeping & Eating

Hotel Fortuna II (21383; s/d with mandi 32,000/49,000Rp, with air-con 82,000/118,000Rp;) Of the three Fortunas in town, this is the best option and has spacious rooms. The rooms with air-con, if not exactly business class, are the best in Larantuka.

Hotel Tresna (21072; Jl Yos Sudarso 8; s/d from 35,000/50,000Rp, with air-con 80,000/110,000Rp;) Has perfunctory, rather soulless rooms, but a nice little garden. If Rulies is full, it's a good alternative – it's virtually next door.

Hotel Rulies (21198; Jl Yos Sudarso 40; s/d/tr 40,000/60,000/80,000Rp) Popular and family-run, this is a decent budget hotel with clean rooms, some with private *mandi*, though some beds are saggy. The helpful English-speaking manager has the latest ferry schedules.

Rumah Makan Nirwana (Jl Niaga; dishes 5000-14,000Rp; breakfast, lunch & dinner) Larantuka's first choice, RM may be modest, but the Chinese and Indonesian dishes here come in filling portions and the fish is fresh.

Eating possibilities are limited, but a few warungs set up in the evening along Jl Niaga.

Getting There & Away

AIR

At the time of research Merpati had three flights a week between Larantuka and Kupang. There's no office in Larantuka, just a counter at the airport where you can buy tickets. To check the latest schedules, call its Kupang office on 0380833833.

BOAT

Boats leave from two piers in Larantuka, one in the centre of town and the other at Waibalun Port (4km south of town, 1500Rp by bemo). Double-check departure times in advance, especially in the rainy season, when schedules are more like suggestions. All boats get very crowded, so board early to get a seat. Bring some food and water.

Wooden boats to Lewoleba on Lembata (15,500Rp, four hours), all via Waiwerang (Adonara, 8000Rp) and Solor (Lamakera, 9000Rp), depart from the pier in the centre of town at 7.30am and 12pm.

Ferries leave Waibalun Port for Lembata on Friday and Monday at 2pm and continue to Baranusa (Pantar) and Kalabahi (42,500Rp, 20 hours). Sit on the upper deck unless you want to be soaked in sea spray. Heading to Kupang (39,500Rp, around 13 hours), ferries depart Monday and Wednesday at 1pm from Waibalun. Going the other way, ferries to Larantuka leave Kupang on Thursday and Sunday at around 4pm.

Several useful Pelni services call on Larantuka. *Awu* serves Kalabahi, Kupang, Lembar, Benoa and Makassar. *Sirimau* also goes to Kupang, Kalabahi and Makassar. *Kelimutu* connects direct with Kupang,

THE LAMAHOLOT

The Larantuka area has long had close links with the islands of the Solor Archipelago (Adonara, Solor and Lembata), including a language: Lamaholot. At some stage, probably before the 16th century, the Lamaholot area became divided between the Demon people, centred on Larantuka and the western parts of Solor island, and the Paji, who were linked to the Rajah of Adonara in the east. Ritualistic warfare to secure fertility and health periodically erupted. Today, though the head-hunting has ceased, people still know who is Paji and who is Demon. Animist rites to mark birth, name-giving, house-building, marriage, and agriculture survive.

while *Tatamailau* calls in at Larantuka on its way to West Papua. The **Pelni office** (☎ 21155; Jl Diponegoro) has details on all Pelni services, or try the **harbour master's office** (Jl Niaga) for other options.

BUS

The main bus terminal is 5km west of the town, about 1km from Waibalun, but buses also pick up in the centre of town – speak to your hotel staff about this. Coming into town, buses sometimes drop you at or near your hotel.

The touts at the ferry terminal and bus terminal are pushy. Buses to/from Maumere cost 32,000Rp and take almost four hours. You'll also find Kijangs waiting at the terminal; these speedy shared taxis cost 60,000Rp per person for an air-con three-hour ride to Maumere. Transport to Maumere is regular until around 5pm.

Getting Around

Bemos (1000Rp) run up and down Jl Niaga and Jl Pasar, and to outlying villages. *Ojeks* also run to the pier and bus terminal for about 3000Rp.

AROUND LARANTUKA

Six kilometres north of Larantuka is a white-sand beach at **Weri**; you can get there by bemo from the central bemo stop in Larantuka. **Mokantarak** is 10km from Larantuka on the road to Maumere and is a traditional village with a *rumah adat*.

SOLOR & ALOR ARCHIPELAGOS

A remote and, until recently, very inaccessible chain of volcanic and mountainous islands stretches out east of Flores, separated by swift and narrow straits. Adonara and Solor are where the Portuguese settled in the 16th century and are closest to Larantuka. Further east, Lembata is the main island of interest because of the traditional whaling village of Lamalera. These islands form the Solor Archipelago, which has close cultural links with the Larantuka area: together their people are known as the Lamaholot (see opposite).

Beyond Lembata are the main islands of the Alor Archipelago, Pantar and Alor, where some tribes were still head-hunting in the 1950s. Kalabahi (Alor) is the main town in this region, with excellent air and sea links to Timor.

The scenery is spectacular, all the islands produce distinctive ikat weaving, and there are some almost purely animist villages, despite the spread of Christianity and (to a lesser degree) Islam.

You'll definitely need at least some basic Bahasa Indonesia to get by in these parts, and, because foreigners are so few and far between, constantly being the centre of attention can get wearing. That said, the Lamaholot islanders are incredibly friendly

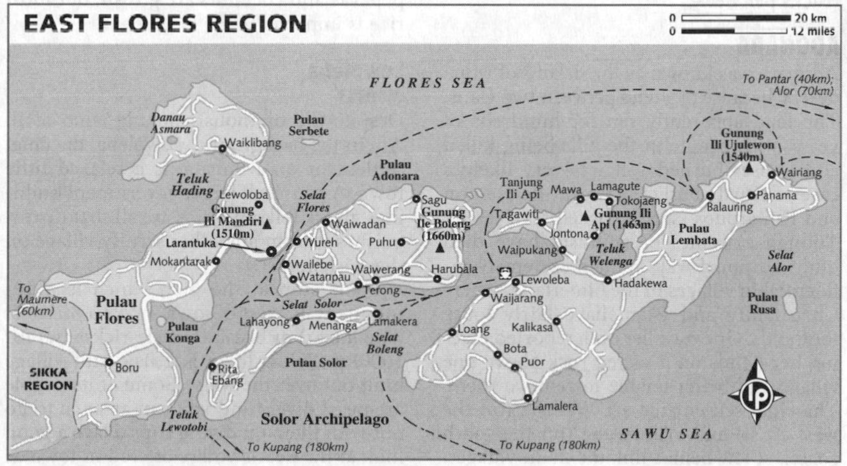

and interested in you and where you're from.

Food quality and general hygiene are not great away from the urban centres of Kalabahi and Lewoleba (Lembata). Bring plenty of money – there's only one ATM (in Kalabahi), and banks and moneychangers offer poor rates.

There's not much to see on the island of Solor itself. Most travellers in this region come to visit Lamalera village on Lembata, and dive the rich coral reefs off Alor.

History

European contact was made as early as 1522 when the only remaining ship of the explorer Magellan's fleet sailed through Selat Alor (Lembata-Pantar Strait). By the middle of the century, the Dominican Portuguese friar Antonio Taveira had landed on Solor to set about spreading Catholicism. The Solor mission became the base for extending Christianity to mainland Flores, and a fort was built to protect the converts from Muslim raids. The Portuguese were eventually forced out of Solor by the Dutch, but until the mid-19th century Portugal held on to Wurek (Adonara) and Pamakajo (Solor).

Getting Around

Alor and Lembata both have some bemos and ancient buses, but most of the islands have only one decent road, and transport to more isolated areas is limited to a few trucks per week.

ADONARA

Adonara was known as the 'Island of Murderers' because of a feud between two clans. The feud apparently ran for hundreds of years, with people in the hills being killed and houses burned – it was very likely a case of ritual conflict between the Demon and Paji groups (see the boxed text, p570). Though extremes of animism have died out, traditional ways remain extremely influential in villages in the hinterland, where Christianity and Islam have fairly loose footholds. One traveller even reported placing her hands on a sacred rock above one village and being unable to remove them. The chief settlements are Wailebe (on the west coast) and Waiwerang (on the south coast). A few bemos link the main villages.

Waiwerang

Waiwerang's markets on Monday and Thursday attract villagers from throughout the island and from Solor. Waiwerang has a post office, a wartel and a bank, but money cannot be changed.

Places to stay include **Hotel Ile Boleng** (Jl Pasar Baru), the best in town, where English is spoken and meals can be arranged. Rooms at the back have great views over the water. Hotel Asri is the second choice.

All the boats from Larantuka to Lewoleba (7000Rp, two hours) on Lembata call in at Waiwerang. Passenger ferries dock at the main wharf in the centre of town, but at low tide they may dock at the car-ferry port 1km west of town. The boat to Lamalera leaves on Friday evening at around 11pm.

Small boats run between Waiwerang and the towns of northern Solor (Lamakera, Menanga and Lahayong) on Monday and Thursday. Otherwise you can charter a boat to Solor for up to six people for around 200,000Rp.

LEMBATA

Lembata is a fascinating island that attracts a trickle of travellers – around 200 a year according to government stats. It's best known for the whaling village of Lamalera and for the volcano **Ili Api**, which towers over the main town of Lewoleba. As in the rest of the Lamaholot region, many Lembata villagers still use the slash-and-burn method of clearing land. Corn, bananas, papayas and coconuts are grown, but most rice is imported.

Lewoleba

☎ 0383

Despite the ominous smoking cone of Ili Api in the background, Lewoleba, the chief settlement on Lembata, is a relaxed little town. A couple of larger government buildings and a Telkom office are all that distinguishes it from any other scruffy village on these islands.

Boats stop at the pier, which is a 10-minute walk west of town – take a *mikrolet* (small taxi) or becak (bicycle-rickshaw) for 1000Rp. Below town is a Bajo stilt village built out over the water. Some of its people are pearl divers and you can arrange to go out with them on diving trips. Have a good look at the pearls you're offered in town as many are just shells. Locals can take you out by sampan to a sandbank off Lewoleba – it's the closest place to town for a swim, with beautifully clear water.

ORIENTATION & INFORMATION

The centre of Lewoleba is the market place, which comes alive every Monday, though there's not much of interest – unless you're a portrait photographer, that is.

The post office is off the main street near the southern side of the market. If you are stuck for cash, the Flores Jaya shop opposite the post office will change US dollars at dreadful rates. The **Telkom office** (7am-11pm) is 1km west of town.

SLEEPING & EATING

Lile Ile (s/d 30,000/45,000Rp) Long-running homestay owned by a Dutch-Indonesian called Jim. It has a row of simple but serviceable rooms with stunning views of Ili Api across the water. It's a popular place, as Jim is a mine of information about Lembata and has the best DVD collection this side of Bangkok's Khao San Rd. Home-cooked meals are served on a huge open deck.

Losmen Rejeki (41028; s/d 35,000/45,000Rp, with air-con 60,000/75,000Rp;) Opposite the market, this is run by the extremely hospitable Pak Tanto and has comfortable rooms, some with very efficient air-con. Generous portions of food are served up, including fresh fish, and there's a fridge full of Bintang. Pak provides good local info and can arrange a 4WD to Lamalera and elsewhere.

Hotel Lewoleba (41012; Jl Awololong 15; s/d 28,000/38,000Rp, with mandi 45,000/60,000Rp, with air-con 75,000/95,000Rp;) The upmarket lobby, complete with sofas, sets the tone in this fairly slick place. It has a selection of rooms – the cheapest are a tad rough, but those with air-con are a treat for this part of the world. It's down the road opposite the Losmen Rejeki, past the post office.

You'll find some simple warungs close to the market.

Rumah Makan Bandung (dishes 5000-7500Rp) Spicy Javanese-style cuisine.

Rumah Makan Hosana (meals 9000Rp) OK Padang food.

GETTING THERE & AWAY

Merpati operates one flight a week from Kupang every Tuesday, but it's a 12-seater plane, so book early.

Boat schedules in this part of Indonesia are subject to very frequent changes and cancellations. See p570 for boat connections from Larantuka, and p577 for connections from Kalabahi.

GETTING AROUND

Mikrolet run around town and to the ferry dock, and there are a few becak, which cost 1000Rp anywhere around Lewoleba.

There are no longer any ferries between Lewoleba and Lamalera; trucks (12,000Rp, 3½ hours) cover this route, leaving daily at around noon. The road is sealed for the most part but extremely rough, rutted and potholed. If you've missed the noon connection you could consider heading to Bota, which is served by more regular transport, and walking from there (it's about 2½ hours, mainly downhill, to Lamalera). Alternatively, consider chartering a ride in Losmen Rejeki's Kijang.

Buses to the east run to Hadakewa (5000Rp, 45 minutes) and direct to Balauring (12,000Rp, two hours). Infrequent trucks ply some of the rough back roads. Buses terminate next to the ferry dock, or you can find them in Lewoleba in front of the market.

Hiring a motorbike from a local costs around 75,000Rp per day. This is best arranged through your guest house.

Around Lewoleba

Lembata's best ikat, recognisable by its burgundy base and highly detailed patterning, comes from the villages on the slopes of Ili Api, 15km to 20km from Lewoleba. On the north coast, **Atawatun** and **Mawa** are two sources of fine weaving. At **Jontona**, on the eastern side of a deep inlet on Lembata's north coast, it's possible to stay with the *kepala desa*. An hour's walk from Jontona towards Ili Api is the **Kampung Lama** (Old Village), with many traditional houses. These contain sacred and prized objects, including a huge number of elephant tusks, but are occupied by villagers only for ceremonies such as the *kacang* (bean) festival in late September or early October. It is possible to climb **Ili Api** from Lama; it takes a full day to go up and down and is easiest with a guide (best arranged in Jontona).

Regular bemos from Lewoleba head to Waipukang (30 minutes), from where you can walk to Jontona in an hour. Infrequent bemos also run to Atawatun, Mawa and Lamagute, though this region is best explored with your own wheels.

Lembata has some good **beaches**. Take a *mikrolet* to Tagawiti and walk for 2km to the beach, where there's reasonable snorkelling out on the reef. The eastern bay on the way to Hadakewa also has some good snorkelling closer to shore. Sunbathing is difficult – the crowds of kids block out the sunlight. It certainly pays to be able to speak some Bahasa Indonesia if venturing further afield.

Lamalera

pop 1800

Like characters from *Moby Dick*, the men of Lamalera village on the south coast of Lembata hunt whales using nothing more than spears, wooden boats and a prayer to their ancestors. Because of the small numbers of whales taken – around 15 to 25 a year – these hunters have been deemed exempt from the international ban on whaling, and their extremely tough and hazardous livelihood continues. The whaling season is mainly from May to October, when the seas aren't too rough.

Lamalera itself is a tiny, fascinating, poor yet extremely welcoming little village that rises up steeply from a small volcanic sand cove. You won't find any phones, internet, or banks. There is electricity between 6pm and 9pm only. There's no escaping how the people live here – huge bones sit atop the shoreside boat shelters, giant ribs are littered in gardens, and if there's been a recent kill bits of whale meat hang from houses. There's some snorkelling in a little bay west of the village, or don a mask and snorkel and you'll come across discarded whale bones in the harbour.

On Saturday there's an interesting **barter-only market** at Wulandoni, about a 1½-hour walk along the coast from Lamalera. Another nice walk along the coast is to **Tapabali**, where you can see local weaving – the ikat has motifs of whales and mantas.

SLEEPING & EATING

There are four small homestays in Lamalera. Rates include all meals.

Guru Ben's (r 40,000Rp) A deservedly popular place, this schoolteacher's homestay has been welcoming travellers for over a decade. It's above the village, perched on a ridge overlooking the shoreline. Pak Ben speaks good English and is a gracious host.

White House (r 40,000Rp) Owned by Baba Yosef, this rental house is right on the point at the end of the beach directly above the shore. Someone will come in to cook meals on request.

Mama Maria's Homestay (r 40,000Rp) Just behind the main square. Maria Dasion and her daughter are terrific, very welcoming hosts. They are both good cooks and you'll have plenty of opportunity to practise your Bahasa Indonesia with them.

Abel Beding (r 40,000Rp) On the main path through the village, past the town square, this is another popular and enjoyable place to stay. Abel speaks some English, and will help with local information.

LAMALERA'S HERITAGE

Lamalera's inhabitants are thought to have originally fled from Lapan Batan, a island near Pantar, after it was devastated by a volcanic eruption. The villagers believe that their ancestors arrived in wooden boats that each clan has kept as the model for all future vessels – though one clan's folklore has it that they reached Lamalera on the back of a blue whale, which are never hunted for that reason. Though the original boats (called *tena*) have been repaired and extended over generations, the villagers consider them to be living beings and a physical link to their ancestors and the ancestral home.

The loss of a *tena* means the loss of an important part of their heritage. In March 1993 two boats from Lamalera sank after being dragged almost to Timor by a wounded whale. The crew of was later picked up by a third boat from the village, and the 36 men then drifted for several days before being rescued by a cruise ship.

The loss of the boats sent the village into a two-month mourning period during which no whaling was allowed. When the mourning period finished, a ceremony took place to 'let the boats go'.

LAMALERA'S WHALERS

'*Baleo*, *Baleo*!' the shout goes when potential targets are spotted in the waters off Lamalera. This is the last village on earth where humans still regularly hunt whales by hand, using bamboo-shafted harpoons. It's a hazardous, savage way of life that takes around 15 to 25 sperm whales from the ocean in an average year, a subsistence livelihood that conservation groups have determined does not threaten sperm whale numbers (estimated at over a million worldwide).

Be warned that if you accompany the whalers on a hunting trip it can be an extremely harrowing and bloody experience that can drag on for hours. However, your chances of seeing a whale hunt or the bloody business of butchering a whale are quite small. Note that, if a whale has been speared but is not dead, the hunters will not necessarily want to head for home as night approaches so you can get your evening meal – their food supply for the next few weeks is on the other end of the line.

The wooden whaling boats (called *tena*) are around 10m long and held together with wooden dowels and lashed twine. Some engine-powered boats are now being used in Lamalera for hunting dolphins and manta rays, but virtually all whaling vessels still carry a mast, a sail made from palm leaves and a crew who row furiously to bear down on a whale when one is spotted. As the gap between the boat and the whale narrows, the harpooner – balanced on a protruding plank – takes a harpoon and attempts to leap onto the back of the whale (using the force of his weight to drive home the harpoon). An injured whale will try to dive, dragging the boat with it, but cannot escape since it has to resurface. Often the whale will need to be speared with several harpoons before it weakens, the ocean becoming a blood bath as the hunters prod the great mammal with knives, attempting to speed up its death.

Every part of the sperm whale is used. The dark meat is shared according to traditional dictates, with most being reserved for the crew and portions going to virtually every family in the village. Spermacetu oil from the head (which was particularly prized by 19th-century whalers and used to burn lamps) is used for cooking. Innards are traded for fruit and vegetables in a barter-only market in the hills. Tourists buy the teeth.

The sperm whale is particularly prized, though other toothed whales (pilots and orcas) are occasionally taken. Baleen whales (plankton-eaters with sievelike feeding mechanisms) are never touched; see the boxed text, opposite. Mantas, dolphins, sharks (mainly hammerheads but also the odd whale shark) are hunted throughout the year – all are also caught using harpoons.

GETTING THERE & AWAY

From Lewoleba, a daily truck is scheduled to leave the market at noon (12,000Rp, 3½ hours) bound for Lamalera, though it's usually late and sometimes cancelled because of mechanical problems. Pak Tanto, the owner of Losmen Rejeki, also offers transport in his jeep. There's additional transport on market day (Monday), sometimes by boat – check at the harbour. Returning to Lewoleba, a daily truck leaves at 5am.

Balauring

This small town is predominantly Islamic and is on the peninsula at the eastern end of Lembata. Ferries linking Alor and Lembata call here, but there's no pressing reason to stay. There are wonderful views of Gunung Ili Api as you come into town.

Small buses (12,000Rp, two hours) run the 53km from Balauring over the sealed road to Lewoleba. Buses also run to **Wairiang** on the far eastern coast, a 45-minute journey.

ALOR

The final link of the island chain that stretches east of Java, Alor is a stunning volcanic island of remarkable cultural diversity. It's an extremely rugged place, the nature of the terrain and lack of roads serving to isolate the 170,000 inhabitants into some 50 tribes, and 14 languages are spoken (most of the Papuan family). The nearby island of Pantar is about as remote as it gets in the archipelago.

Although the Dutch installed local rajahs along the coastal regions after 1908, they had little influence over the interior, where people were still taking heads in the 1950s. The tribes had little contact with each other except during raids.

Alor today is around 75% Protestant and 20% Muslim (most of the latter live on the coast). However, indigenous animist traditions endure. Most islanders survive on subsistence farming (particularly of corn) but new cash crops, including vanilla, turmeric, candlenuts and cloves, are being grown, and the export of seaweed is increasing.

Though a network of roads now crosses the island, boats are still a common form of transport. Very few visitors make it here, but those who do are seduced by the warmth of the people, and the landscape. The diving can be world-class, with plenty of pelagics, including hammerheads, dogtooth tuna and Mola-Mola, as well as superb macro life.

Kalabahi

☎ 0386 / pop 42,000

Kalabahi is the chief town on Alor and is located at the end of a long and spectacular palm-fringed bay on the west coast. It's a clichéd tropical port – slow-moving and lazy, where the punishing heat is alleviated by occasional but very welcoming sea breezes.

Kalabahi is relatively prosperous, but outside the town living conditions are poor. There are a few interesting villages and beautiful beaches nearby, some with spectacular snorkelling and diving, but also with strong currents.

It's worth strolling around the Pasar Inpres, which has a huge variety of fruit as well as women weaving bamboo mats.

INFORMATION

It's best to bring plenty of cash to Alor as rates for US dollars and travellers cheques are poor, and the ATM at **BRI bank** (Bank Rakyat Indonesia; Jl Sutoyo; 7.30am-2pm), 300m east and 300 north of the harbour, is prone to tropical tantrums and accepts Mastercard/Cirrus cards only. The Toko Ombai shop on the road a block to the east will change foreign currencies, including US dollars, outside banking hours and often at better rates. There's a **Telkom** (Jl Soetomo; 24hr) and an internet connection at **Kantor PDE** (per hr 8000Rp), about 2km north of town.

SIGHTS & ACTIVITIES

Kalabahi's modest **museum** (Jl Diponegoro; 8am-3.30pm Mon-Sat), just west of the market, has some fine ikat, *moko* and assorted artefacts.

Scuba diving in Alor can be exceptional. La Petite Kepa (see p578) offers two dives for US$65, including all gear. Other scuba schools offering dives around the island include **Dive Alor** (www.divealor.com), based in Kupang, West Timor, and **Grand Komodo Tours** (www.komodoalordive.com), which runs liveaboards here from Bali.

SLEEPING

The most popular place to stay on Alor is La Petite Kepa Homestay (p578) on Pulau Kepa, near Alor Kecil.

Hotel Adi Dharma (☎ 21280; Jl Martadinata 12; r with fan & bathroom 35,000/50,000Rp, with TV & air-con 60,000/75,000Rp) A popular place with fine port views. The helpful owner, Ibu Inang, speaks English, has good travel information and can arrange transport. The hotel is about 200m west of the harbour, on the waterfront.

Hotel Melati (☎ 21073; Jl Soetomo; r 45,000Rp, with air-con 75,000Rp) Just west of the harbour, this place has functional clean rooms and a shady garden.

Hotel Pelangi Indah (☎ 21251; Jl Diponegoro 100; economy s/d 20,000/30,000Rp, r with air-con & shower 110,000/135,000Rp, ste 200,000) Out near the bus terminal, Pelangi Indah has five types of rooms, from claustrophobic economy-class cells through decent air-con rooms with *mandi* and veranda, to very spacious suites.

Hotel Nusa Kenari Indah (☎ 21119; Jl Diponegoro 11; r with fan & mandi 30,000Rp, with air-con 75,000Rp, ste 250,000Rp) Has clean and fairly comfortable air-con rooms; the suites here are modern and smart, with tiled floors and fancy furnishings. It's near the Pelangi Indah.

EATING

At night streetside warungs and *kaki lima* (food carts) set up near the harbour. Sate, *soto ayam* and other Javanese fare are on offer. This meagre collection is the closest thing to nightlife in Kalabahi, which otherwise closes down at around 8pm. Look out for *jagung ketama* (corn with green peas), a local speciality.

Rumah Makan Kediri (☎ 21146; Jl Martadinata; dishes 5000-8000Rp; breakfast, lunch & dinner) Centrally located near the pier on the waterfront, this popular Javanese-owned place serves the best *nasi campur* in town.

MOKO

Alor's chief fame lies in its mysterious *moko* – bronze drums about 50cm high and 33cm across, tapered in the middle like an hourglass and with four ear-shaped handles around the circumference. They sound a bit like a bongo when thumped. Thousands of them are scattered around the island – the Alorese apparently found them buried in the ground and believed them to be gifts from the gods, though they were probably brought by traders from India, China or Makassar.

Most *moko* have decorations similar to those on bronze utensils made in Java in the 13th- and 14th-century Majapahit era, but others resemble earlier Southeast Asian designs and may be connected with the Dongson culture that developed in Vietnam and China around 700 BC and then pushed its influence into Indonesia. Later *moko* even have English- or Dutch-influenced decorations.

Today, *moko* have acquired enormous value among the Alorese, and families devote great time and energy to amassing collections of them, along with pigs and land. *Moko* form an essential part of a bride's *belis* (dowry). In former times, whole villages would sometimes go to war in an attempt to win possession of a prized *moko*. The export of *moko* is restricted by the government.

There's a good collection in Kalabahi's museum.

GETTING THERE & AWAY

The airport is 9km from town. Transport schedules are subject to very frequent changes in this part of the nation.

Merpati (☎ 21041) has four flights a week to/from Kupang, some on a 12-seater Cassa plane that fills up quickly, so book ahead. The office is east of the harbour and up the road on the western bank of the river. **Transnusa** (☎ 21039; Jl Sudirman 100) flies the same route four times a week on a newer 48-seater plane.

Kalabahi is linked by passenger/car ferries to Kupang and Atapupu in Timor and Larantuka (Flores) via Baranusa (Pantar), Balauring, Lewoleba (Lembata) and Waiwerang (Adonara). These ferries leave from the ferry terminal 1km southwest of the town centre, a 10-minute walk or 1500Rp bemo ride.

To Kupang, ferries leave on Wednesday and Sunday at noon (42,000Rp, around 16 hours). For Atapupu, close to the border with East Timor, there's a Tuesday ferry at 8pm (22,700Rp, eight hours). It travels back from Atapupu on Monday at 10am.

Ferries depart Kalabahi for Larantuka (42,500Rp, around 20 hours) on Sunday and Thursday at 8am, passing through Baranusa, Balauring and Lewoleba (33,000Rp, 14 hours). For Larantuka departures, see p570. Bring plenty of food and water.

Pelni (☎ 21195) ships leave from the main pier in the centre of town (the Pelni office is opposite the pier). The *Awu* sails every two weeks between Kalabahi and Kupang, Ende, Waingapu, Lombok and Bali, or Larantuka and Sulawesi. In addition, the monthly *Tatamailau* sails to Kupang; ports in Papua, including Timika; and on to Ambon. Finally, the *Sirimau* connects Kalabahi with Kupang and Makassar.

Other small boats from the central wharf make their way to remote islands of the Alor Archipelago.

GETTING AROUND

Transport around town is by red bemo (1500Rp). It's possible to rent a motorcycle through the Hotel Adi Dharma for around 50,000Rp per day; for a car, speak to Pak Kris (☎ 21030). Jeeps called *pansars* leave from the Pasar Inpres to most parts of central Alor.

Around Kalabahi

Takpala is a traditional village about 13km east of Kalabahi. To get there take a Mabu bus (2000Rp) from the terminal at Kalabahi market. From where the bus drops you, walk about 1km uphill on a sealed road. There are several traditional high-roofed houses, and the view over the Flores Sea from the village is stunning. Bring some gifts of basic foodstuffs if you plan on exploring.

Nearby the villages of **Alor Kecil** and **Alor Besar** are good beaches with excellent snorkelling. The water here is wonderfully cool, but the currents are strong. Alor Kecil is the jumping-off point for Pulau Kepa, an offshore islet with a terrific place to stay, **La Petite Kepa** (☎ 081 338200479; www.la-petite-kepa.com; bungalows incl meals per person 75,000Rp), a French-run place in an idyllic spot with views of Alor and Pantar. It's well set up for travellers, with eight good bamboo-and-coconut-wood bungalows and fine, communally eaten local meals. Solar power provides night-time electricity. The owners offer scuba diving (US$65 for two dives, including equipment), and there's snorkelling on the western side of Pulau Kepa.

Buses and blue bemos to Alor Kecil (3000Rp, 30 minutes) and Alor Besar leave from the Kalabahi Pasar Inpres, or catch them on the harbourfront road. If you're heading to Kepa, stop by the pier and Pak Sere will ferry you across for a small fee.

Near the airport, at the northernmost tip of the island, is **Mali**, a lovely white-sand beach with good snorkelling. It's possible to rent a boat for a tour of the area and when the tide allows you can walk to **Pulau Suki**, off the beach at Mali. There's an old grave there, said to be that of a sultan from Sulawesi. It is usually possible to arrange to stay with a family in Mali.

Pantar

☎ 0386

The second-largest island of the Alor group, Pantar is about as far off the beaten track as you can get. Ferries between Larantuka and Alor stop at **Baranusa**; though it's the island's main town, it's a sleepy little place with a straggle of coconut palms and a couple of general stores.

Homestay Burhan (r 20,000Rp), Baranusa's only accommodation, is a friendly place with just three rooms; the price includes meals.

The main reason to visit Pantar is to climb **Gunung Sirung**, which is an active volcano with a huge and impressive smouldering crater. From Baranusa take a truck to Kakamauta, from where it is a three-hour walk to Sirung's crater. Bring water from Baranusa and stay with the *kepala desa* in Kakamauta.

The only other island of note is the sparsely populated **Pulau Pura**, sandwiched between Pantar and Alor. It is dominated by a towering, forested peak topped by a small crater lake.

WEST TIMOR

West Timor has never been much of a tourist destination, although it is very scenic, with rugged countryside and traditional villages that are well worth exploring. The combination of Indonesia's recent crises, visa restrictions, East Timor's harrowing struggle

EAST TIMOR VISA RUN

Hitting Dili in East Timor is an inexpensive way to renew your Indonesian visa from Nusa Tenggara. This visa run has generally been working smoothly for the last few years, though unrest in Dili did close the Indonesian consulate for a while in 2006 – check the current political situation before you cross the border. If you decide to go, be aware that East Timor is considerably more expensive than Indonesia and the return trip normally takes over a week by the time you've got to Dili, hung around for your visa and travelled back to West Timor.

Starting in Kupang, West Timor, book a **Timor Travel** (☎ 881543) bus from Kupang to Dili which will take you to the border at Motoain (150,000Rp, seven hours). Expect a bag search on both sides of the border, but travellers have not reported any extra hassles from customs or immigration officials. Once over the border, get your East Timor visa (available at the border for US$30) and you'll find your onward bus waiting for the 2½ hour trip to Dili. It's also possible to make your own way to the border from Atambua in West Timor; see p588).

Once in Dili, head to the Indonesian consulate for your visa (US$35), which all passport holders must have to re-enter West Timor. The consulate is near the Pertamina office on the western outskirts of Dili. Travellers have been issued with 60-day visas here on application, though 30 days is more usual. The visa takes five working days to issue, though some persuasive visitors have received theirs in just three days. Enjoy the delights of Dili and then run the route in reverse. You can buy your bus ticket for the return trip from **Ifau Travel** (☎ 7260019; queneno@yahoo.com; Rua Bemori, Culuhum).

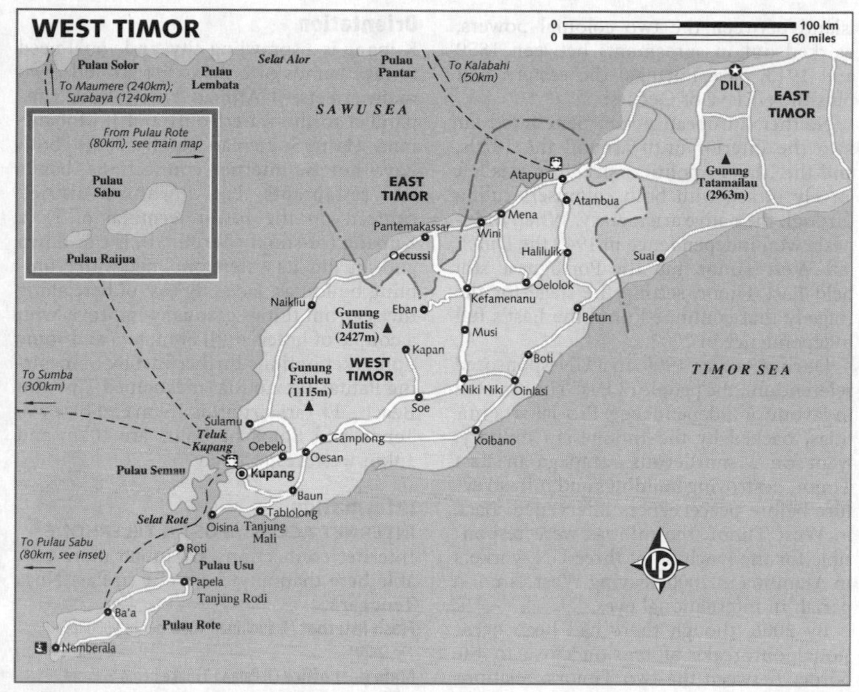

for independence and transport issues all but wiped West Timor from the tourism map for many years. But with twice-weekly Kupang–Darwin connections now back in operation and the proximity of East Timor offering an inexpensive visa run, visitor numbers are slowly increasing again.

Kupang is the main city and is very Indonesian, with its buzzing bemos and honking horns. Beyond Kupang, West Timor's landscape is captivating, with its spiky lontar palms, rocky soils and central hills dotted with villages of beehive-shaped huts. It also has some fantastic coastline, though there are no resorts, just empty beaches.

Aggravated by dry winds from northern Australia, the dry season is prolonged and results in food and water shortages. Maize is the staple crop, but coffee and dry rice are important.

Christianity is widespread, though in some rural areas animistic traditions endure. Many villagers still defer to their traditional chiefs, wear ikat, munch betel nut and down *tuak* (palm-sap liquor) with relish. Around 14 languages are spoken on the island, both Malay and Papuan types, though the native Tetum is understood in most parts. The population of West Timor is about 1.6 million.

West Timor offers excellent travel connections to other parts of Nusa Tenggara and Bali by boat and plane, including the remote islands of Alor and Rote.

History

The Tetum of central Timor are one of the largest ethnic groups on the island. Before Portuguese and Dutch colonisation, they were fragmented into dozens of small states. Conflict was all too common, with headhunting a popular pastime, although when peace was restored the captured heads were thoughtfully returned to the kingdom from which they came.

The first Europeans in Timor were the Portuguese, who prized its sandalwood trees. In the mid-17th century the Dutch occupied Kupang, beginning a long conflict for control of the sandalwood trade and leading to the Portuguese being pushed back to eastern Timor. The division of the island between the two colonial powers, worked out in agreements between 1859 and 1913, gave Portugal the eastern half plus the enclave of Oecussi.

Neither European power penetrated far into the interior until around the 1920s, and the island's political structure was left largely intact, with both colonisers ruling through the native aristocracy. When Indonesia won independence in 1949 the Dutch left West Timor, but the Portuguese still held East Timor, setting the stage for the tragedy that continued until the East's full independence in 2002.

During August 1999, in a UN-sponsored referendum, the people of East Timor voted in favour of independence. Pro-Jakarta militias, backed by the Indonesian military, went on a murderous rampage in East Timor, destroying buildings and infrastructure before peacekeepers intervened. Back in West Timor, the militias were responsible for the lynching of three UN workers in Atambua in 2000, leaving West Timor a pariah in international eyes.

By 2006, though there had been occasional outbreaks of tension close to the border between the two Timors, relations seemed to be stabilising and transport links by road and air were thriving. Kupang and most areas of West Timor are very safe and always have been.

KUPANG

☎ 0380 / pop 300,000

Kupang is all energy and commerce, a bustling city that's the capital of East Nusa Tenggara province (NTT), which includes West Timor, Rote, Sabu, the Solor and Alor Archipelagos, Sumba, Flores and Komodo. The city centre is scruffy and noisy, with streets patrolled by squadrons of Indonesia's most outrageous bemos, each kitted out with a bombastic sound system. Though Kupang is virtually bereft of cultural or architectural attractions, it's not a threatening or intimidating place. It's a reasonable base to linger for a few days if you're waiting for a flight or boat – English naval officer Captain William Bligh did after being cast adrift by the mutinous crew of the *Bounty* in 1789.

With the resumption of flights between Darwin and Kupang, a trickle of travellers have started to visit the city again.

Orientation

Kupang is a sprawling city, and you'll need to take bemos or *ojeks* to get around. Two main streets, Jl Ahmad Yani (which runs parallel to the waterfront) and Jl Mohammad Hatta/Sudirman to the south both have hotels, internet connections, banks and restaurants. The downtown district, centred on the bemo terminal of Kota Kupang (or simply Terminal), is run-down and squalid, its waterfront lined with crumbling buildings. Heading east of here along the seafront things gradually improve, with a couple of hotels on Jl Sumatera and some upmarket options further east by uninspiring Pantai Taman Ria (nicknamed Tim Tim Beach). El Tari airport is 15km east of town; Tenau and Bolok harbours are 10km and 13km west, respectively.

Information

INTERNET ACCESS, POST & TELEPHONE

Internet connections are much more reliable here than anywhere else in East Nusa Tenggara.

Flash Internet (Jl Sudirman 100A; per hr 9000Rp; 24hr)

Main post office (Jl Palapa 1) Take bemo 5. Poste restante mail comes here.

Telkom office (Jl Urip Sumohardjo 11; 24hr) Also has an ATM and offers internet connections between 8am and midnight at 8000Rp per hour.

MONEY

Kupang has plenty of banks and ATMs; however, they are not open on Saturday morning.

Bank Danamon (Jl Sumatera) Equipped with an ATM and offers cash advances of up to 5,000,000Rp.

BNI bank (Bank Negara Indonesia; Jl Sumatera) Has an ATM, as well as fair rates.

TOURIST INFORMATION

L'Avalon (Jl Sumatera) The bar looked on its last legs when we visited, but if it's open the ever-helpful owner Edwin Lerrick is extremely well informed about Timor and NTT.

NTT Tourist Office (☎ 21540; 7am-3pm Mon-Thu) Has maps and a few brochures, but little else. It's about 4km east of the centre; take bemo 10 or 7, get off at Jl Raya El Tari at the SMP5 secondary school and walk 200m east.

Pitoby Tours & Travel (☎ 832700; Jl Sudirman 136) You can check schedules and purchase flight and ferry tickets here.

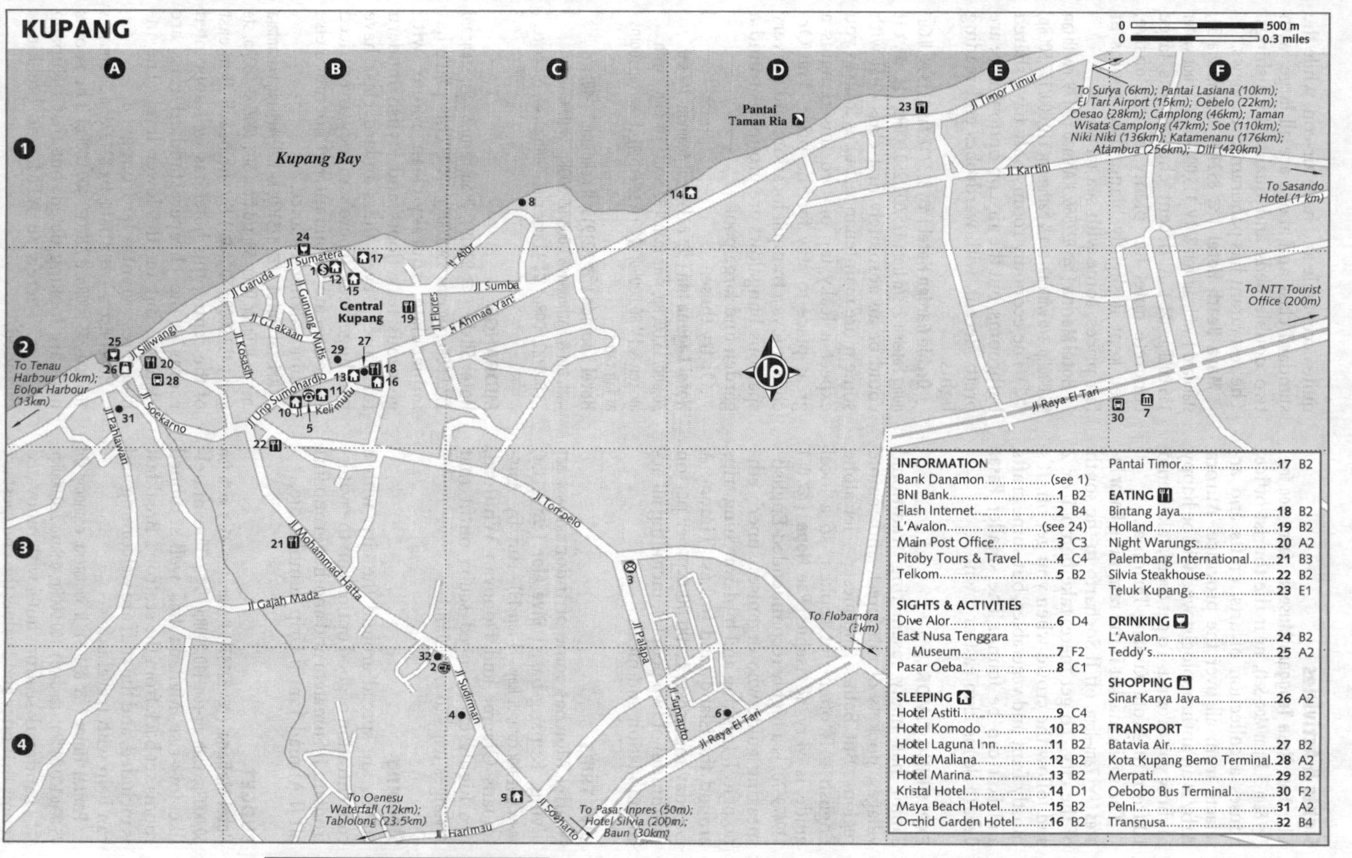
KUPANG
0 500 m
0 0.3 miles
Kupang Bay
Central Kupang
Pantai Taman Ria
To Surya (6km); Pantai Lasiana (10km); El Tari Airport (15km); Oebelo (22km); Oesao (28km); Camplong (46km); Taman Wisata Camplong (47km); Soe (110km); Niki Niki (136km); Katamenanu (176km); Atambua (256km); Dili (420km)
To Sasando Hotel (1 km)
To NTT Tourist Office (200m)
To Flobamora (3km)
To Pasar Inpres (50m); Hotel Silvia (200m); Baun (30km)
To Oenesu Waterfall (12km); Tablolong (23.5km)
To Tenau Harbour (10km); Bolok Harbour (13km)
Jl Timor Timur
Jl Kartini
Jl Raya El Tari
Jl Tompelo
Jl Palapa
Jl Suprapto
Jl Soeharto
Jl Sudirman
Jl Harimau
Jl Mohammad Hatta
Jl Gajah Mada
Jl Ahmad Yani
Jl Sumba
Jl Alor
Jl Flores
Jl Sumatera
Jl Gunung Mutis
Jl Garuda
Jl G Lakaan
Jl Kosasih
Jl Urip Sumohardjo
Jl Kelimutu
Jl Siliwangi
Jl Soekarno
Jl Pahlawan
INFORMATION
Bank Danamon (see 1)
BNI Bank 1 B2
Flash Internet 2 B4
L'Avalon (see 24)
Main Post Office 3 C3
Pitoby Tours & Travel 4 C4
Telkom 5 B2
SIGHTS & ACTIVITIES
Dive Alor 6 D4
East Nusa Tenggara Museum 7 F2
Pasar Oeba 8 C1
SLEEPING
Hotel Astiti 9 C4
Hotel Komodo 10 B2
Hotel Laguna Inn 11 B2
Hotel Maliana 12 B2
Hotel Marina 13 B2
Kristal Hotel 14 D1
Maya Beach Hotel 15 B2
Orchid Garden Hotel 16 B2
Pantai Timor 17 B2
EATING
Bintang Jaya 18 B2
Holland 19 B2
Night Warungs 20 A2
Palembang International 21 B3
Silvia Steakhouse 22 B2
Teluk Kupang 23 E1
DRINKING
L'Avalon 24 B2
Teddy's 25 A2
SHOPPING
Sinar Karya Jaya 26 A2
TRANSPORT
Batavia Air 27 B2
Kota Kupang Bemo Terminal 28 A2
Merpati 29 B2
Oebobo Bus Terminal 30 F2
Pelni 31 A2
Transnusa 32 B4

Sights & Activities

The **East Nusa Tenggara Museum** (admission free; 8am-3.30pm Mon-Sat), near the tourist office, houses a collection of arts, crafts and artefacts from all over the province. Aurora Arby is an anthropologist who will be happy to show you around. To get there, take bemo 10 from the Kota Kupang Terminal.

The main market is the rambling **Pasar Inpres** (7am-4pm) off Jl Soeharto in the south of the city. To get there, take bemo 1 or 2 and follow the crowd when you get off. It's mostly fruit and vegetables, but some crafts and ikat can be found. The smaller **Pasar Oeba** (Jl Alor) is 2km east of town.

EXPLORING TIMOR

Timor has many fascinating traditional villages, pockets of rainforest, and remote regions. But Bahasa Indonesia – let alone English – is often not spoken, so a local guide is very advisable. **Pae Nope** (081 339479670) is a highly recommended English-speaking guide who organises superb ethnological, trekking and bird-watching trips around the island (and to East Timor). A two-day tour costs 1,100,000Rp per person (minimum of two people), including all accommodation and meals.

DIVE TRIPS

Nearby Alor has some of Indonesia's best diving. Kupang-based **Dive Alor** (821154; www.divealor.com; Jl Raya El Tari 19), run by Australians Graeme and Donovan Whitford, is a highly experienced scuba outfit that arranges trips to the island.

NUSA TENGGARA

Sleeping

Hotels are spread around the city, with a concentration of good options on the waterfront on Jl Sumatera and another group just off Jl Ahmad Yani/Jl Urip Sumohardjo.

BUDGET

Hotel Maliana (821879; Jl Sumatera 35; r with fan 60,000Rp, with air-con 110,000Rp;) The motel-like low-rise Maliana has well-scrubbed rooms set back from the seafront. Breakfast is included, and the staff are welcoming and can help with travel info.

Pantai Timor (831651; Jl Sumatera; economy s/d 75,000/100,000Rp, standard r 160,000Rp, deluxe 220,000Rp;) Landmark seafront hotel with renovated rooms that offer good value: the cheapest are quite acceptable and have air-con, while the standard class and above are all large, with two double beds and quality furnishings. The restaurant has panoramic sea views.

Maya Beach Hotel (832169; Jl Sumatera 31; standard r with air-con & TV 115,000Rp, with hot water 135,000Rp;) A decent choice, this large concrete hotel has plenty of inoffensive, well-kept if slightly bland tiled rooms at fair prices, some with sea views.

Hotel Marina (822566; Jl Ahmad Yani 79; r with fan 55,000Rp, s/d with air-con & bathroom 110,000/137,500Rp;) The economy rooms only have shared bathrooms, but the air-con options here are pretty decent, with wardrobes and reading lights.

Orchid Garden Hotel (833707; fax 831339; Jl Gunung Fateleu 2; s/d from 175,000/250,000Rp;) It could be an absolutely first-class deal with some more maintenance, but as long as you expect a leaky tap or two this remains a great place to stay for the price. The Orchid enjoys a tranquil location, and the very spacious bungalows are grouped around a garden and large pool.

Or try these:

Hotel Laguna Inn (833559; Jl Kelimutu 36; s/d 30,000/35,000Rp, with mandi 37,500/45,000Rp, r with air-con & TV 80,000Rp;) A selection of spartan rooms at fair rates.

Hotel Komodo (821913; Jl Kelimutu 38-40; s/d with fan & bathroom 53,000/65,000Rp, with air-con 70,000/82,000Rp;) Large place with plenty of choice.

MIDRANGE

Hotel Silvia (825191; Jl Soeharto 51-53; standard 275,000Rp, superior 350,000Rp;) This place has immaculate, squeaky-clean rooms with gorgeous teak floors and stylish modern furniture – even the standard class have two huge beds. There's a fancy, overpriced in-house café-restaurant, but not much else within walking distance.

Kristal Hotel (825100; kristal@kupang.wasantara.net.id; Jl Timor Timur 59; s/d from 508,200/580,800Rp, ste from 1,452,000Rp;) By the beach 2km east of the centre, this hotel has well-appointed rooms – the cheaper standard class are identical but on the lower level. The in-house restaurant is far from good.

Hotel Astiti (821810; fax 831278; Jl Sudirman; s 165,000-275,000Rp, d 220,000-400,000Rp) The rooms here are looking dated, but that's Kupang all over. There's an ATM, and brekkie is included.

Eating

Despite the town's size there aren't very many enjoyable places to eat in Kupang, expect florescent striplights and zero effort on the atmosphere front. Culinary standards are decidedly average.

Bintang Jaya (Jl Ahmad Yani; meals 8000Rp; breakfast, lunch & dinner) The cleanest and best of several similar restaurants on this street, pick 'n' mix yourself a plateful of spicy Javan food from the large bowls in the window. Also sells beer.

Palembang International (☎ 822784; Jl Mohammad Hatta 54; dishes 6000-26,000Rp; breakfast, lunch & dinner) A busy, shabby-looking place with an inexpensive menu that includes mustard greens with chicken (8000Rp), noodles, and seafood specials, including giant prawns.

Silvia Steakhouse (Jl Beringin 3; dishes 12,000-29,000Rp; breakfast, lunch & dinner) This almost-stylish place with gingham tablecloths offers a long menu of Western dishes, including cognac steak and fish and chips. It also serves breakfast and fresh juices.

Teluk Kupang (☎ 833985; Jl Timor Timur; most dishes 15,000-38,000Rp; breakfast, lunch & dinner) Vast, kitsch, garishly decorated beachside place specialising in northern Sulawesi food – *ikan waku* (spicy fish) is the house special.

Holland (☎ 833367; Jl Irian Jaya 8; martabak 15,000-40,000Rp; dinner) Take-away place offering the gigantic *martabak*, the best in town.

Night warungs are located around the Terminal, try the *bubur kacang* (mung beans and black rice in coconut milk). Some of these warungs sell *rw* (dog meat).

Drinking

Gone are the days when the harbourfront was crammed with backpackers bound for Australia.

L'Avalon (Jl Sumatera) A rickety-looking shack above the 'beach' that was looking a spent force when we last called in. But, as the owner, Edwin, is quite a character and the best source of info in town, it may be worth stopping by to see if it's open.

Teddy's (Jl Siliwangi; noon-11pm) Open-sided place where the bar stools have great waterfront views, but it tends to be achingly empty these days.

Entertainment

Kupang's nightspots are uniformly seedy; most are little more than sleazy karaoke bars. **Surya** (6pm-2am), 6km east of town on the beach, and the bar at the **Sasando Hotel** (Jl Kartini 1; admission 25,000Rp; 7pm-1am) are dark places fitting this bill.

Shopping

For ikat and handicrafts there are some stores near the Terminal, and you may find ikat at the Pasar Inpres. Bizarre *ti'i langga* (conical hats) from Rote make a fun purchase, but try fitting one in your backpack.

Kupang's main shopping mall is the **Flobamora** (Jl Lamamentik) 3km southeast of town, take bemo 6 from the roundabout at Jl Beringin.

Sinar Karya Jaya (☎ 831473; Jl Siliwangi 94C) One of several places around here that sells artefacts and ikat.

Dive Alor (☎ 821154; www.divealor.com; Jl Raya El Tari 19) Has a huge selection of high-quality carvings and weavings from around Nusa Tenggara and some Chinese ceramics.

Getting There & Away

AIR

Kupang is the most important hub for air travel in Nusa Tenggara. **Merpati** (☎ 833833; Jl Ahmad Yani 66) flies to Denpasar (daily), Mataram (daily), Kalabahi (four times weekly), Waingapu (three weekly), Maumere (five weekly), Ende (three times weekly), Larantuka (three weekly), Lewoleba (one weekly), Atambua (two weekly) and Rote (Friday). Merpati/Air North fly to Darwin (Tuesday and Saturday).

Transnusa (☎ 822555; fax 832573; Jl Sudirman 68) has more modern planes, and flies to Denpasar (twice weekly), Kalabahi (four times weekly), Ende (four times weekly), Maumere (daily), Ruteng (four times weekly) and Waingapu (four times weekly).

Batavia Air (☎ 830555; Jl Ahmad Yani 73) flies daily to Surabaya and on to Jakarta. **Lion Air** (☎ 882119; El Tari airport) flies exactly the same route. Both operate flexi-fares, depending on how early you book.

Departure tax is 10,000Rp for domestic flights and 50,000Rp for international flights.

BOAT

Pelni ships depart from Tenau Harbour, 10km southwest of Kupang (4000Rp, bemo 12); ferries from Bolok Harbour, 13km southwest of Kupang (4000Rp, bemo 13). Expect to pay approximately 12,000Rp for a hotel drop when coming into town by bemo.

Boats are routinely late and schedules are regularly changed, particularly during the rainy season, when the seas are much rougher.

Pelni (☎ 824357; Jl Pahlawan 3; ⌚ 8.30am-3pm Mon-Sat, 9-11am Sun) is near the waterfront. Pelni's *Dobonsolo* runs every two weeks directly from Bali to Kupang, and on to Kota Ambon and Papua. The fortnightly *Awu* sails from Kupang to Ende, Waingapu, Lombok and Bali, or Kalabahi, Larantuka and Sulawesi. The fortnightly *Sirimau* sails between Kupang, Alor and Makassar. The fortnightly *Pangrango* sails from Kupang to Surabaya via Ende, Waingapu and Bima. The *Tatamailau* connects Kupang with Maumere, Bima, and Benoa, and on the return trip heads to Saumlake and Tual. The monthly *Kelimutu* links Kupang with Ende, Waingapu, Bima and Surabaya to the west, and Papua to the east. Finally, the monthly *Dorolonda* links Sulawesi and Papua via Kupang.

Two other ferries provide links to Surabaya: *Kirana II* (leaving Monday) via Maumere (125,000Rp), and *Dharma* (leaving Thursday) via Ende (115,000Rp). Book your tickets and check schedules first via a travel agent.

From Bolok Harbour, ferries sail to Larantuka (twice weekly), Kalabahi (Tuesday and Sunday at 2pm) and Ende on Wednesday. The Ende ferry continues on to Waingapu. There's also a weekly boat to Aimere in Flores on Thursday. For details of boats to Rote, see p590.

NUSA TENGGARA

BUS & BEMO

Long-distance buses depart from Oebobo terminal on the eastern side of town – catch bemo 10. Daily departures include Soe (22,000Rp, three hours) and Niki Niki (25,000Rp, 3½ hours) every hour or so from 5am to 6pm; Kefamenanu (36,000Rp, 5½ hours) and Atambua (52,000Rp, eight hours) at 7am, 9am, noon and 5pm.

Daily direct buses (150,000Rp one way, 11 hours) to Dili are operated by **Timor Travel** (☎ 881543). Call for a hotel pick-up, or they also pass by Oebobo terminal at 7am.

Bemos to villages around Kupang go from the central terminal, Kota Kupang.

Getting Around

TO/FROM THE AIRPORT

Kupang's El Tari airport is 15km east of the town centre. Taxis from the airport to town cost a fixed 50,000Rp. For public transport, turn left out of the terminal and walk 1km to the junction with the main highway, from where bemos to town cost 3000Rp. Going to the airport, take bemo 14 or 15 to the junction and then walk.

BEMO

A ride in one of Kupang's unique bemos (1500Rp) is one of the city's essential experiences. Windscreens are festooned with girlie silhouette stickers, Jesus of Nazareth and English premiership football stars, the bodywork is of the go-faster technicolour paint job, while banks of subwoofers unleash Indo rock, techno and hip-hop from beneath your seat. They stop running by about 9pm.

Kupang is too spread out to do much walking. The hub of bemo routes is the Kota Kupang terminal, usually just called Terminal. Useful bemo routes:

1 & 2 Kuanino–Oepura; passing many popular hotels.
5 Oebobo–Airnona–Bakunase; passing the main post office.
6 Goes to the Flobamora shopping mall.
10 Kelapa Lima–Walikota; from Terminal to the tourist information office and Oebobo bus terminal.
12 Tenau Harbour.
13 Bolok Harbour.
14 & 15 Penfui (useful for the airport).

CAR & MOTORCYCLE

It's possible to rent a car with a driver from 300,000Rp per day. Motorcycles cost around 50,000Rp per day. Ask at your hotel or a travel agent.

AROUND KUPANG

Islands

Pulau Semau to the west of Kupang has some decent sandy beaches and snorkelling. Irregular local boats go from Namosaen village, west of Kupang.

Pulau Kera (Monkey Island) is the blob of trees and sand that is visible from Kupang. This small, uninhabited island has sandy beaches and clear water. Access is by chartered boat only.

Beaches

Kupang's beaches are grubby and flotsam-strewn. **Pantai Lasiana**, about 10km east of town by bemo 17, is a fine sandy beach and a busy picnic spot at weekends, when food stalls and litter are the order of the day.

There are great beaches near Tablolong, 27km southwest of Kupang. From the village, head southwest around the headland and find your own deserted stretch of white sand, such as **Air Cina** – down a dirt track off the main road 3km before Tablolong. Bring plenty of food and water, and check when the last bemo goes back to Kupang.

Oenesu

This waterfall lies off the Kupang–Tablolong road. The turn-off is 13km from Kupang near Tapa village, which is serviced by regular bemos from Tabun. From the main road it's a 2.5km walk to the falls. Take the road to Sumlili; past the Imanuel church is the turn to the falls, which is 800m away along a rough road.

Baun

A small village 30km southeast of Kupang in the hilly Amarasi district, Baun is an ikat-weaving centre with a few Dutch buildings. You can visit the *rumah rajah*, the last rajah's house, which is now occupied by his widow. Market day in Baun is Saturday. From Baun to the south coast is a solid day's hike; there's a good surf beach down there.

To get to Baun, take a bemo from Kupang's bus terminal or Pasar Inpres.

Oebelo & Oesao

Oebelo, 22km from Kupang on the Soe road, has an interesting **workshop** (☎ 081 339242307) run by Pak Pah and his family – look for the faded Home Industri Sasando sign. Traditional 20-stringed Rotenese instruments, the *sasando* (featured on the 5000Rp note), are made here, along with electrified versions and the Rotenese lontar-leaf hat, *ti'i langga*. The family may treat you to a melodious singsong of Beatles tunes.

Oesau is another 6km down the road and has a war memorial dedicated to the 2/40th Australian Infantry Battalion.

CAMPLONG

A quiet hill town 46km from Kupang, Camplong has a small forest reserve, **Taman Wisata Camplong**, with some caves and a spring-fed swimming pool along with a caged Komodo dragon and a small croc. It's a tough 7km walk from here to **Gunung Fatuleu** (1115m), which attracts botanists interested in the unique montane flora found on its slopes.

Regular buses operate from Kupang's Oebobo terminal to Camplong (6000Rp, one hour) and on to Soe.

SOE

☎ 0388 / pop: 30,000

Soe, an important market town in central Timor, sits at 800m – nights are markedly less steamy here than on the coast. The town itself is a dull sprawl of modern houses, but it makes an excellent base for trips to traditional villages around the area.

Beyond Soe you'll see the beehive-shaped houses (*ume kebubu*, or *lopo*) that give the region its distinctive character. With no windows and only a 1m-high doorway, *lopo* are small and smoky, and the authorities have instituted a programme to replace them. The locals, however, consider their new houses unhealthy, as they're cold, so they construct new *lopo* behind the approved houses.

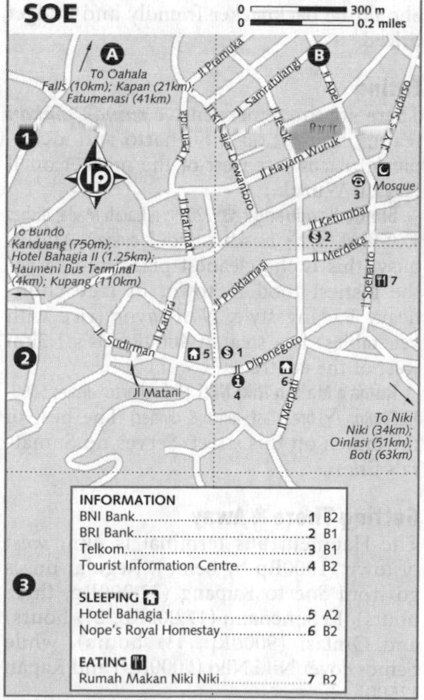

Information

The **tourist information centre** (☎ 21149; Jl Diponegoro) has good detail on the surrounding area and can arrange guides. Both **BNI** (Bank Negara Indonesia; Jl Diponegoro) and **BRI** (Bank Rakyat Indonesia; Jl Hatta) banks have ATMs, but exchange rates for cash and travellers cheques are poor.

Sleeping

Nope's Royal Homestay (☎ 21711; Jl Merpati 8; bungalows incl breakfast 75,000Rp) One very spruce and comfortable little bungalow with *mandi* in the grounds of the family home of a local rajah, Pae Nope. Pae speaks fluent English, is Timor's best guide, and lived in Darwin for years. More bungalows are planned.

Hotel Bahagia II (☎ 21095; Jl Gajah Mada 55; r 95,000-155,000Rp, cottages 210,000-397,000Rp) An excellent deal, this orderly, well-run hotel has a good range of rooms with ikat adorning the walls, and some with wrought-iron beds. It's 2km west of the centre.

Hotel Bahagia I (☎ 21015; Jl Diponegoro 72) The owners were planning to upgrade this place in the centre of town at the time of research. Should be backpacker-friendly and budget priced.

Eating

There are three inexpensive *rumah makan* (eating houses) on Jl Soeharto and a couple of places just west of the market on Jl Hayam Wuruk.

Bundo Kanduang (☎ 22079; Jl Gajah Mada; dishes 4000-18,000Rp; breakfast, lunch & dinner) Always busy, this is the cleanest place and serves the tastiest food in town, in true chilli-heavy Padang style. *Nasi sayur* (rice with vegetables) is a steal at 4000Rp. It's 1.5km west of the centre.

Rumah Makan Niki Niki (Jl Soeharto; dishes 5000-13,500Rp; breakfast, lunch & dinner) The best of the bunch on this street. Serves up Sumatra's finest.

Getting There & Away

The Haumeni bus terminal is 4km west of town (1000Rp by bemo). Regular buses go from Soe to Kupang (22,000Rp, three hours), Kefamenanu (17,000Rp, 2½ hours) and Oinlasi (9000Rp, 1½ hours), while bemos cover Niki Niki (5000Rp) and Kapan (2500Rp).

AROUND SOE

Oinlasi

Regular buses from Soe make the 51km trip along a winding mountain road to Oinlasi in around 1½ hours. Its Tuesday market is one of the biggest and best in West Timor and attracts villagers from the surrounding hill districts, many wearing their traditional ikat. Weavings, carvings, masks and elaborately carved betel-nut containers can be found, but get there early. The market starts early in the morning and continues until 2pm, but it's at its best before 10am. A direct bus from Kupang makes the trip in about four hours.

Boti

In an isolated mountain valley, 12km from Oinlasi along a recently improved mountain road, the traditional village of Boti is presided over by a charismatic young *kepala suku* (chief) called Benu, the youngest son of an elderly chief who died in 2005. Benu has vowed to maintain the strict laws of *adat*.

Only clothes made from locally grown cotton may be worn, and the villagers wear very special shirts, ikat sarongs and shawls made from handspun thread and coloured with natural dyes. Boti is one of the last remaining villages in Timor where men let their hair grow long (this is only after they are married). Indonesian education is largely shunned, and Boti's 300 or so villagers still follow ancient animist religious rituals, though another 700 neighbouring families who live in Boti's geographical realm of influence have adopted Protestantism.

The adherence to tradition has knock-on benefits, for the village attracts a trickle of visitors, including the occasional tour group, providing an additional source of income.

On arrival you will be led to the rajah's house, where, traditionally, betel nut should be placed in the tray on the table as a gift. It's possible to stay with the rajah in his house with all meals provided for 50,000Rp per person. Day trippers are also expected to contribute a sizable donation (about 15,000Rp).

The new chief will probably show you a treasure-trove of name cards and photos given to his father over the years. If you want to add to the collection, a business card or telephone card will suffice.

The Boti chief requests that you do not visit independently; bring a guide conversant with local *adat*. Soe is the best place to find a guide.

GETTING THERE & AWAY

From Oinlasi, take a bus south on the main road for 2km to the turn-off to Boti. It is then 9km on a rocky, hilly road that's passable by motorcycle or car – or it's a three-hour walk.

The road passes through the seven gates of Bele village. The system of gates and fences is designed to keep the animals in, for in these parts if a farmer catches an animal eating his crops he has the right to kill it. The amount of crop damage is then assessed, meat is distributed to the farmer as compensation, and the owner of the animal keeps the rest.

Bring water from Soe. A bemo charter from Soe is around 170,000Rp for a full-day trip to Boti.

Niki Niki

Niki Niki is 34km east of Soe along the Soe–Kefamenanu road and is the site of some old royal graves and two palaces, one imposing structure belonging to Rajah Nope. The village has a busy Wednesday market and a couple of restaurants, but no accommodation. Regular buses and bemos link Niki Niki and Soe.

Kapan

Kapan is 21km north of Soe and has an interesting market on Thursday, when the roads are blocked with stalls. The village is situated on steep slopes from where you can see **Gunung Mutis** (2470m). From Kapan, some trucks run to **Fatumasi**, which is 20km away and has even more spectacular alpine scenery, or you can take a bemo there from Soe. Mattheus Anin has a **homestay** (per person incl all meals 50,000Rp) here and leads guided walks up Gunung Mutis, pointing out plants and animals along the way.

On the way to Kapan are the **Oahala Falls**, 10km from Soe. The Kapan buses will drop you on the highway, from where it is a 2.5km walk to the falls.

Kolbano

The village of Kolbano is on the southern coast of the island 110km from Soe and has white-sand beaches and good surf between May and August. The easiest access is by bus from Noilmina on the Kupang–Soe road (about six hours over a decent road). From Soe, there are regular buses to Se'i along a twisting, dipping road that goes through isolated communities. Se'i buses sometimes continue to Kolbano.

KEFAMENANU

☎ 0388 / pop 30,000

Kefamenanu is a quiet hill town with some pleasant walks in the surrounding hills. The town was once a Portuguese stronghold; it remains devoutly Catholic and has a couple of impressive churches. Known locally as Kefa, it lies at the heart of an important weaving region and locals sometimes bring ikat to the hotels for visitors to haggle over.

Orientation & Information

Kefa is a sprawling place. It centres on the old market, *pasar lama*, which is around 2.5km north of the bus terminal.

Dinas Pariwisata (☎ 21520; Jl Sudirman) The tourist office is opposite the playing field north of the highway, and can help you find a guide.

Post office (Jl Imam Bonjol) Opposite the market.

Telkom office (Jl Sudirman; 🕑 7am-midnight)

Sleeping & Eating

Hotel Ariesta (☎ 31007; Jl Basuki Rachmat; r 45,000Rp, with bathroom 70,000Rp, with air con 90,000Rp; ❄) Well-run place that has good-value, clean accommodation and a decent restaurant (dishes 6000Rp to 18,000Rp; open breakfast, lunch and dinner).

Hotel Cendana (☎ 31168; Jl Sonbay; r with mandi & fan 40,000Rp, with air-con 95,000-150,000Rp; ❄) The most comfortable hotel in town, this welcoming place has good rooms and enjoys a quiet location. Staff can help you charter bemos and find a guide; they also rent out motorcycles.

Litani (Jl El Tari; dishes 8000-23,000Rp; 🕑 breakfast, lunch & dinner) The best in Kefa, a clean place with fresh seafood and Chinese delicacies.

Getting There & Away

Terminal Bus Kefa is a few kilometres south of the town centre. From here there are regular buses to Kupang (36,000Rp, 5½ hours) from 6am until about 4pm, and another at 8pm that leaves from the Rumah Makan

Minang Jaya, near the Hotel Cendana. Regular buses run to/from Soe (17,000Rp, 2½ hours) and Atambua (13,000Rp, two hours). Going to the enclave of Oecussi is now a pain, as an Indonesian visa is required to come back to West Timor – it's easier to visit Dili.

AROUND KEFAMENANU

Oelolok

Oelolok is a weaving village 26km from Kefa by bus and a further 3km by bemo. It has a Tuesday market. The Istana Rajah Taolin in Oelolok is a fine Dutch bungalow that served as the 'palace' of the local rajah.

Temkessi

A traditional village around 50km northeast of Kefa, Temkessi sees few travellers because of its isolation. Sitting high on a hilltop, its only entrance is a small passage between two huge rocks. The rajah's house sits on top of rocks overlooking the village. There's lots of weaving, but little Bahasa Indonesia is spoken, so a guide is very useful.

Regular buses run from Kefa to Manufui, about 8km from Temkessi. On market day in Manufui (Saturday), trucks or buses should run through to Temkessi. Otherwise, charter a bemo in Manufui.

ATAMBUA & AROUND

☎ 0389 / pop 36,500

Atambua is an anonymous-looking, scruffy town close to the border with East Timor that has hit the headlines for all the wrong reasons in the past few years. Large numbers of pro-Jakarta refugees and militias from East Timor – some with blood on their hands – settled around here, while three UN workers were murdered in Atambua in 2000. As there are now direct Dili–Kupang buses there's no reason to visit at all. If you do find yourself stuck here, be aware that though most locals are perfectly friendly you may encounter some anti-Western resentment; this is particularly true for Australians.

Atapupu is the port for Atambua, 25km north, but there's only one weekly ferry to Kalabahi, Alor (25,600Rp, seven hours), on Monday at 7am. **Betun** is a prosperous town 60km south, near the coast, which has a couple of hotels, including the recommended **Cinta Dama** (r 90,000Rp), and restaurants. A few intrepid travellers have visited the nearby villages of **Kletek**, **Kamanasa** and **Bolan** – you can see flying foxes and watch the sun set over the mountains at Kletek.

Information

There's a brochure-free **tourist office** (☎ 21483; Jl Basuki Rahmat 2) and a branch of **BNI bank** (Bank Negara Indonesia; 🕑 8.30am-3.30pm Mon-Fri), which exchanges foreign currencies.

Sleeping & Eating

Hotel Kalpataru (☎ 21351; Jl Gatot Subroto 3; s/d 25,000/40,000Rp) A centrally located colonial-style house which has simple, well-kept rooms. The owner, Pak Manik, speaks English and Dutch.

Hotel Nusantara Dua (☎ 21773; Jl Kasimo; r with bathroom 75,000Rp, with air-con 110,000Rp; ❄) The best in town, with comfortable rooms. It's close to the bus terminal but a fair walk from the centre.

Tuck in here:

Rumah Makan Estry (Jl Merdeka 11; 🕑 breakfast, lunch & dinner) Good for Chinese food.

Padang Raya (Jl Soekarno; 🕑 breakfast, lunch & dinner) For a point-and-eat spicy meal.

Getting There & Away

Merpati has two flights a week between Atambua and Kupang.

The bus terminal is 1km north of town (1000Rp by *mikrolet* 3 or 4). Destinations include Kupang (52,000Rp, eight hours) and Atapupu (4000Rp, 40 minutes). Bemos to the Motoain border with East Timor cost 5000Rp (40 minutes). Buses for Dili (US$3) leave from the other side when full. For more details about the trip over the border, see the boxed text, p578.

ROTE

The small, rain-starved island of Rote, between Timor and Sumba, is little visited but has a successful economy based on the majestic and nutritious lontar palm (see the boxed text, p590). There are some interesting indigenous cultures, a few beautiful coastal villages and some of Nusa Tenggara's best surf.

The slightly built Rotenese speak a language similar to the Tetum of Timor, though Bahasa Indonesia is almost universally understood.

In the late 17th century, after a bloody campaign, Rote became the source of slaves and supplies for the Dutch. Later the Rotenese began taking advantage of the Dutch presence, gradually adopted Christianity and, with Dutch support, established a school system that eventually turned them into the region's elite.

The Rotenese are open to outside influences, though there are still areas where people adhere to the old traditions. Ikat weaving on Rote today uses mainly chemical dyes, but the designs are complex: floral and *patola* (traditional geometric ikat design) motifs are typical. One tradition that hasn't disappeared is the wearing of the wide-brimmed lontar hat, *ti'i langga*, which has a curious spike sticking up near the front like a unicorn's horn (perhaps representing a lontar palm, or a Portuguese helmet or mast). Rotenese also love music and dancing; the traditional Rotenese 20-stringed instrument, the *sasando*, features on the 5000Rp note.

In recent years the island has become an important base for shark-fin fishermen who use speedboats to illegally fish in Australian waters just to the south.

Ba'a

Ba'a, Rote's main town, doesn't have a lot to offer travellers, though some houses have curious boat-shaped thatched roofs with carvings, which are connected with traditional ancestor cults. The coast from the ferry port at Pantai Baru to Ba'a is sparsely populated and has some superb coral beaches. Bring plenty of cash from Kupang, as exchanging money is difficult.

Just off Jl Pabean, **Pondok Wisata Karya** (Jl Kartini 1; per person 20,000Rp) has basic budget rooms. The manager speaks good English and changes money at ugly rates for the desperate.

Hotel Ricky (☎ 871045; Jl Gereja; s/d with fan 55,000/80,000Rp, with air-con 100,000/125,000Rp; ❄) is Ba'a's best hotel. It offers a variety of rooms, all with bathrooms, and has the best restaurant in town. Car hire at high rates can be arranged.

Both near the town centre, **Rumah Makan Karya** (Jl Pabean) and **Warung Makan Lumayah** (Jl Pabean) serve basic meals.

Shops sell the local delicacy, *susu goreng*, made from buffalo milk that's cooked until it becomes a brown powder. It doesn't look much, but it is sweet and very tasty.

Papela

This Muslim Bugis fishing village in the far east of Rote is set on a beautiful harbour. Every Saturday it hosts the biggest market on the island. There is one hotel, the **Wisma Karya** (Jl Lorong Asem), but a day trip is a better bet. Buses go to Papela from Ba'a and Pantai Baru over the best road on the island.

Nemberala

A surfers' secret for many years, Nemberala is a wonderful, relaxed little coastal village with white-sand beaches and a legendary 'left' between May and October, earning it the moniker T-land. Nemberala has some good accommodation and is the only real tourist centre on the island.

SLEEPING & EATING

Nemberala has a small selection of simple homestays. The prices quoted below rise a little in high season.

Mr Tomas Homestay (per person incl meals 35,000-50,000Rp) This popular place is run by a slightly eccentric, elderly and amusing ex-schoolmaster. It has worn rooms in the original house and a block of better rooms with shared *mandi*. As you come into Nemberala, the road swings around to the left; the homestay's near the corner.

Tirosa (per person incl meals 35,000-50,000Rp) Right near the beach. If you turn right at the corner near Mr Tomas and head north along the dirt road for 500m you'll reach it. Run by the *kepala desa* and his family, who speak good English.

Losmen Anugurah (☎ satellite 086812108916; rotisurf@yahoo.com; per person incl meals 35,000-50,000Rp) This surfers' favourite has cold beer and rooms with and without *mandi*. It's set back from the beach, but close to the main surf break.

Nemberala Beach Resort (www.nemberalabeachresort.com; ❄ 🅿) Right on the ocean, this newly renovated, tasteful resort has luxury stone-and-timber villas with porches and outdoor bathrooms. The restaurant specialises in seafood, including sashimi and lobster, with chocolate cake to round things off. A speedboat can whisk you out to other nearby surf breaks, and fishing trips for dog-toothed tuna and other fish

LONTAR PALM

With a dry season that's more pronounced than in other parts of Nusa Tenggara, and high population density, Rote is extraordinarily dependent on the drought-resistant lontar palm. The palm is extremely versatile; its tough yet flexible leaves are woven to make sacks and bags, hats and sandals, roofs, and dividing walls. Lontar wood is fashioned into furniture and floorboards. But it's the milky, frothy *nirah* (sap) tapped from the *tankai* (orange-stemmed inflorescences) that grow from the crown of the lontar that nourishes the islanders. Drunk straight from the tree the *nirah* is a refreshing, nutritious and energy-giving source of liquid (up to 600L can be tapped from one tree annually). If the *nirah* is left to ferment for hours it becomes *laru* (a palm wine), which is hawked around the lanes of Rote. With a further distillation the juice is distilled into a ginlike *sopi* – the power behind many a local fiesta.

can be arranged. Prices were not available at the time of going to press. Consult the website to make arrangements.

Around Nemberala

About 8km from Nemberala, **Bo'a** has a spectacular white-sand beach and good surf. It is possible to rent a motorcycle to Bo'a from Nemberala. Further east, **Oeseli** also has a superb beach but is more easily approached from Tudameda to the east.

The island of **Pulau Ndana** can be reached by boat from Nemberala. Legend has it that the island is uninhabited because the entire population was murdered in a revenge act in the 17th century and the small lake on the island turned red with victims' blood. Ndana has wild deer and a wide variety of birds. Its beaches are prime turtle-nesting territory.

Boni is about 15km from Nemberala, near the northern coast, and is one of the last villages on Rote where traditional religion is still followed. Market day is Thursday. To get here, rent a motorcycle in Nemberala.

Pulau Ndao is another ikat-weaving and lontar-tapping island, 10km west of Nemberala. The people here speak a language related to Sabunese and are renowned gold and silversmiths. It's possible to charter a boat to Ndao in Nemberala.

Getting There & Away

Merpati has a Friday connection between Rote and Kupang.

The Rote–Kupang ferry sank in 2006, with the loss of many lives. At the time of research the *Kandari Express* was the only regular link with Kupang (32,000Rp, 1½ hours), leaving Kupang at 8am daily and returning at noon. The service is sometimes cancelled due to rough seas.

Getting Around

A pack of buses and bemos greet boats at Pantai Baru and run to Ba'a (1½ hours), Nemberala (3½ hours) and other towns. Most bus transport around the island relies on the ferry timetable. Buses leave Ba'a for Pantai Baru around 10am to meet the ferry; otherwise connections around the island are limited.

Regular bemos run from Ba'a to Busalangga, and at least one bemo runs to Papela in the morning, while trucks service more remote locations. Otherwise *ojeks* will take you anywhere, including Nemberala.

The Hotel Ricky in Ba'a and the Nemberala Beach Resort in Nemberala can arrange a car and driver, but this will cost around 400,000Rp a day. Chartering a bemo is less, perhaps 180,000Rp. Motorcycle hire is also possible in Ba'a or Nemberala.

SUMBA

The dry, undulating island of Sumba has the richest tribal culture in Nusa Tenggara, centred on a religious tradition called *marapu*. It's one of the poorest but most fascinating islands to visit, with a decidedly off-the-beaten-track appeal courtesy of its thatched clan houses, colossal carved megalith tombs, outstanding hand-spun ikat and bloody sacrificial funerals.

Physically it looks quite different from the volcanic islands to the north, its countryside characterised by low limestone hills and fields of maize and cassava. Sumba's extensive grasslands made it one of Indonesia's leading horse-breeding islands. Horses are still used as transport in more rugged regions; they are a symbol of wealth and status and have traditionally been used as part of the bride-price.

Sumba's traditions remain particularly strong in its wetter, more fertile and more remote western half, which is home to about two-thirds of the island's 540,000 people. Though most islanders are now officially Protestant, *marapu* traditions and old conflicts are recalled every year at western Sumba's terrific, often-violent Pasola festivals, which involve ritual battles between teams of mounted horse riders.

These battles hint at deep-rooted tribal tensions, which periodically erupt between rival princedoms. As recently as 1998 around 3000 tribesmen clashed in Waikabubak, a battle that claimed 26 lives according to official figures (though many locals put the true number at over 100).

While some Bahasa Indonesia is spoken everywhere, Sumba has six main languages. Few travellers make it here, but it's a deeply rewarding place to explore and has fairly good transport connections with the rest of the region.

History

According to local legend a great ladder once connected heaven and earth. Down it clambered the first people on earth to Sumba, and they settled at Tanjung Sasar, on the northern tip of the island.

Fourteenth-century Javanese chronicles place Sumba under the control of the Majapahits. But Sumbanese history is more a saga of internal wars over land and trading rights between a great number of petty kingdoms.

Despite their mutual hostility, princedoms often depended on each other economically. The inland regions produced horses, timber, betel nut, rice, fruit and dyewoods, while coastal people concentrated on ikat production and trade with other islands.

The Dutch initially paid little attention to Sumba because it lacked commercial possibilities except some sandalwood trade. But in the early 20th century they finally decided to bring Sumba under their control and invaded the island.

In 1913 a civilian administration was set up, although the Sumbanese nobility continued to reign and the Dutch ruled through them. When the Indonesian republic ceased to recognise the native rulers' authority, many of them became government officials, so their families continued to exert influence. Today these ruling clans continue to exert hegemony by monopolising local government appointments.

The 1998 Waikabubak riots developed into a full-scale tribal conflict. The riots were initially sparked by demonstrations against the nepotism that saw applicants with the right connections getting local government jobs regardless of college grades.

Culture

IKAT

Sumbanese ikat is the most dramatic, and arguably best-executed in Indonesia. It's very highly prized by collectors, as natural dyes still predominate: earthy orange-red from the *kombu* tree bark, indigo blue, and yellow hues derived from *loba* leaves. Motifs form a pictorial history: a record of tribal wars and an age that ended with the coming of the Dutch – the skulls of vanquished enemies dangle off trees and mounted riders wield spears. A huge variety of animals and mythical creatures are also depicted.

Traditionally, ikat cloth was used only on special occasions; for example, to mark harvest rituals. Less than 90 years ago, only members of Sumba's highest clans and their personal attendants could make or wear it. The most impressive use of the cloth was at royal funerals, where dancers and the guards of the corpse were dressed in richly decorated costumes. The deceased was dressed in the finest textiles, then bound with dozens – sometimes hundreds – more, so that the corpse resembled a huge mound before burial.

The Dutch conquest broke the Sumbanese nobility's monopoly on the production of ikat and opened up a large external market, which in turn increased production. From the late 19th century ikat was collected by Dutch ethnographers and museums (the Rotterdam and Basel museums have fine collections), and by the 1920s visitors were already noting the introduction of nontraditional designs, such as lions, from the Dutch coat-of-arms.

A Sumbanese woman's ikat sarong is known as a *lau*. A *hinggi* is a large rectangular cloth used by men as a sarong or shawl.

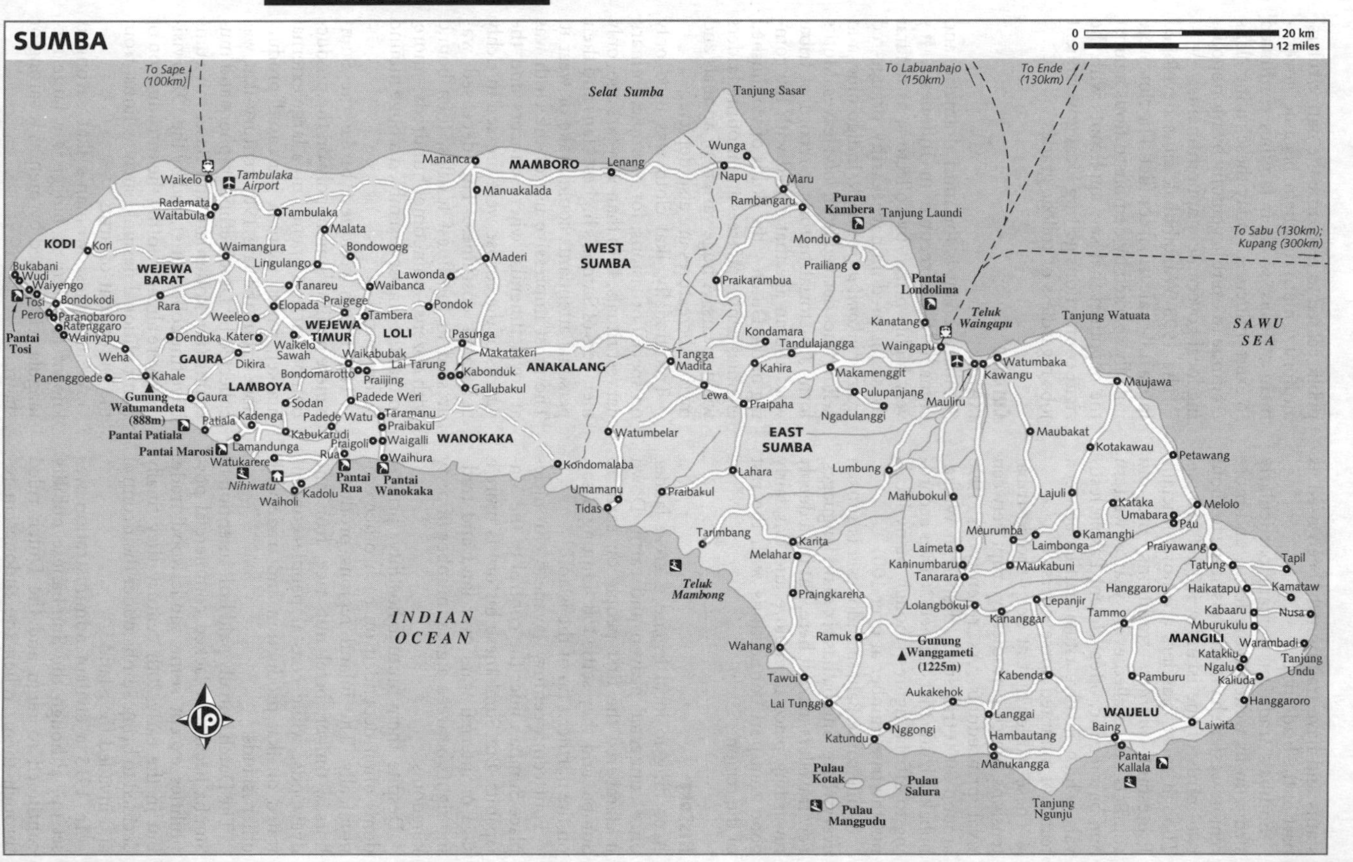
SUMBA
0 20 km
0 12 miles
To Sape (100km)
Selat Sumba
Tanjung Sasar
To Labuanbajo (150km)
To Ende (130km)
To Sabu (130km); Kupang (300km)
SAWU SEA
INDIAN OCEAN
KODI
WEJEWA BARAT
MAMBORO
WEST SUMBA
WEJEWA TIMUR
LOLI
GAURA
LAMBOYA
WANOKAKA
ANAKALANG
EAST SUMBA
MANGILI
WAIJELU
Waikelo
Tambulaka Airport
Radamata
Waitabula
Tambulaka
Malata
Bondowoeg
Kori
Waimangura
Lingulango
Bukabani
Wudi
Waiyengo
Tosi
Pero
Bondokodi
Paranobaroro
Ratenggaro
Wainyapu
Pantai Tosi
Rara
Tanareu
Waibanca
Lawonda
Elopada
Praigege
Pondok
Weeleo
Tambera
Denduka
Kater
Walkelo Sawah
Weha
Dikira
Waikabubak
Panenggoede
Kahale
Bondomarotto
Lai Tarung
Praiijing
Pasunga
Makatakeri
Kabonduk
Gallubakul
Gunung Watumandeta (888m)
Gaura
Sodan
Padede Weri
Padede Watu
Taramanu
Praibakul
Patiala
Kadenga
Kabukarudi
Praigoli
Waigalli
Pantai Patiala
Pantai Marosi
Lamandunga
Watukarere
Rua
Waihura
Pantai Rua
Pantai Wanokaka
Nihiwatu
Kadolu
Waiholi
Mananca
Manuakalada
Lenang
Maderi
Wunga
Napu
Maru
Rambangaru
Purau Kambera
Tanjung Laundi
Mondu
Prailiang
Praikarambua
Pantai Londolima
Teluk Waingapu
Kanatang
Tanjung Watuata
Kondamara
Tandulajangga
Waingapu
Tangga Madita
Kahira
Makamenggit
Watumbaka
Kawangu
Lewa
Praipaha
Pulupanjang
Ngadulanggi
Mauliru
Maujawa
Watumbelar
Maubakat
Kotakawau
Petawang
Kondomalaba
Umamanu
Tidas
Lahara
Praibakul
Lumbung
Mahubokul
Lajuli
Kataka
Umabara
Melolo
Pau
Meurumba
Laimbonga
Kamanghi
Praiyawang
Tarimbang
Karita
Melahar
Laimeta
Kaninumbaru
Tanarara
Maukabuni
Tatung
Tapil
Teluk Mambong
Praingkareha
Lolangbokul
Kananggar
Lepanjir
Hanggaroru
Haikatapu
Kamataw
Tammo
Kabaaru
Nusa
Mburukulu
Wahang
Ramuk
Gunung Wanggameti (1225m)
Warambadi
Katakliu
Ngalu
Kaliuda
Tanjung Undu
Tawui
Kabenda
Pamburu
Hanggaroro
Aukakehok
Lai Tunggi
Langgai
Nggongi
Katundu
Hambautang
Baing
Laiwita
Manukangga
Pantai Kallala
Pulau Kotak
Pulau Salura
Pulau Manggudu
Tanjung Ngunju

SUMABANESE TRADITIONS

Old beliefs fade, customs die and rituals change: the Sumbanese still make textiles but no longer hunt heads; 25 years ago the bride-price may have been coloured beads and buffaloes – today it might include a bicycle. Certainly, though, the bride dowry can still be high, and many Sumbanese men migrate just to find wives who don't expect a dowry.

Many Sumbanese men still carry their long-bladed knife in a wooden sheath tucked into their waistband. They wear scarves as turbans and wrap their brightly coloured sarongs to expose the lower two-thirds of their legs, with a long piece of cloth hanging down in front. A woman may have her legs tattooed after the birth of her first child as a mark of status; often it will be the same motifs that adorn her sarong. Another custom, teeth filing, has all but died out, but some older people have short brown teeth from the time when jagged white teeth were considered ugly.

Churches are now a common sight, and though in some areas traditions are dying, they continue to thrive in the west.

VILLAGES

A traditional Sumba village usually consists of two parallel rows of houses facing each other, with a square between. In the middle of the square is a stone with another flat stone on top of it, on which offerings are made to the village's protective *marapu* (spiritual forces). These structures, spirit stones or *kateda*, can also be found in the fields around the village and are used for offerings to the agricultural *marapu* when planting or harvesting.

The village square also contains the stone-slab tombs of important ancestors, usually finely carved, but nowadays virtually always made of cement. In former times the heads of slain enemies would be hung on a dead tree in the village square while ceremonies and feasts took place. These skull trees, called *andung*, can still be seen in some villages today and are a popular motif on Sumbanese ikat.

A traditional Sumbanese dwelling is a large rectangular structure raised on piles; it houses an extended family. The thatched (or nowadays often corrugated-iron) roof slopes gently upwards from all four sides before abruptly rising to a peak. In the loft are placed *marapu maluri* objects. For more details, see below.

Rituals accompanying the building of a house include an offering, at the time of planting the first pillar, to find out if the *marapu* agree with the location; one method is to cut open a chicken and examine its liver. Many houses are decked with buffalo horns or pigs' jaws from past sacrifices.

RELIGION

The basis of traditional Sumbanese religion is *marapu*, a collective term for all the spiritual forces, including gods, spirits and ancestors. At death the deceased join the invisible world, from where they can influence the world of the living. *Marapu mameti* is the collective name for all dead people. The living can appeal to them for help, especially their own relatives, though the dead can be harmful if irritated. The *marapu maluri* are the original people placed on earth by god; their power is concentrated in certain places or objects, much like the Javanese idea of *semangat*.

DEATH CEREMONIES

On the day of burial, horses or buffaloes are ceremonially killed and ornaments and a *sirih* (betel nut) bag are buried with the body. The living must bury their dead as richly as possible to avoid being reprimanded by the *marapu mameti* and to ensure the dead can enter the invisible world – which, some say, is accessed via a ladder from Tanjung Sasar.

Funerals may be delayed for up to 10 years (the body of the deceased sometimes stored in the loft of the family's house or given a temporary burial) until enough wealth has been accumulated for a full ceremonial funeral, accompanied by the erection of a massive stone-slab tomb. Often the dragging of the tombstone from outside the village is an important part of the procedure. Sometimes hundreds are needed to move the block of stone, and the family of the deceased feed them all.

When the Indonesian republic was founded, the government introduced a slaughter tax in an attempt to stop the destruction of hundreds of livestock. This reduced the number of animals killed, but it didn't alter basic attitudes. The Sumbanese believe you *can* take it with you.

VISITING VILLAGES

Many Sumbanese villagers are now accustomed to tourists, but many still have difficulty understanding the strange custom of Westerners who simply want to observe an 'exotic' culture. If you're interested in their weavings or other artefacts, the villagers put you down as a potential trader. If all you want to do is chat and look around, they may be puzzled about why you've come; and if you simply turn up with a camera and start putting it in their faces, they're likely to be offended.

On Sumba, giving *sirih pinang* (betel nut) is the traditional way of greeting guests or hosts. You can buy it at most markets in Sumba, or a few cigarettes will always be welcome. Offer your gifts to the *kepala desa* and to other village elders.

Many places also keep a visitors' book, which villagers will produce for you to sign, and you should donate a few thousand rupiah. Whatever the circumstances, taking a guide, at least to isolated villages, is a big help and some protection from getting into the wrong situation. A guide smooths over any language difficulties, and they will likely teach you enough about the behaviour expected of guests for you to feel confident visiting villages alone. No matter where you go, taking the time to chat with the villagers helps them to treat you more as a guest than a customer or alien. Remember that, when you enter a village, you're in effect walking into a home.

NUSA TENGGARA

WAINGAPU

☎ 0387 / pop 50,000

Waingapu is an enjoyable, dusty, spread-out town: urban enough to boast a few modest hotels and warungs, but so close to the countryside in spirit and location that roosters put paid to any chance of a lie in. It became an administrative centre after the Dutch military 'pacified' the island in 1906 and has long been Sumba's main trading post for textiles, much-prized Sumbanese horses, dyewoods and lumber.

Waingapu is the main entry point to Sumba by air or sea, but the island's principal attractions lie in the west and southeast. The town has a few ikat shops and workshops, and traders with bundles of textiles and carvings hang around hotels or walk the streets touting for custom.

Orientation & Information

Waingapu stretches between its small harbour in the north of town and the main centre, which is 1.5km southeast around the market and bus terminal. Freelance tour guides surface at hotels and are a useful bridge to traditional village life in Sumba – **Daniel Lanjamana** (☎ 62950) speaks English and is recommended.

At the time of research there was no internet access on Sumba, though rumour had it that a cybercafé was to open in the streets west of the market.

BNI bank (Bank Negara Indonesia; Jl Ampera) Has an ATM that accepts most cards in theory, though it's often not functioning. Usually has the best rates.

BRI bank (Bank Rakyat Indonesia; Jl Ahmad Yani) The ATM here only accepts Mastercard/Cirrus.

Post office (Jl Hasanuddin; 🕑 8am-4pm Mon-Fri) Close to the harbour.

Telkom office (Jl Tjut Nya Dien; 🕑 24hr)

Sleeping

Breakfast is included at all these places.

Hotel Lima Saudara (☎ 61083; Jl Wanggameti 2; s 25,000-50,000Rp, d 35,000-60,000Rp) Near the harbour, these slightly tired-looking rooms with *mandis* have little front porches.

Hotel Sandle Wood (☎ 61199; Jl Panjaitan 23; s/d 44,000/66,000Rp, with mandi 77,000/121,000Rp, with air-con from 121,000/143,000Rp; ❄) Offers a variety of pretty spartan rooms, some in need of a little more love and attention, but the location's quiet and the staff, aside from the owner, are friendly and helpful.

Hotel Elvin (☎ 61462; Jl Ahmad Yani 73; s/d with mandi 55,000/66,000Rp, with air-con 140,000/200,000Rp; ❄) A total renovation of one wing was nearly complete when we visited, meaning the blue-roofed Elvin should provide the best air-con rooms, all with verandas, in town. An older wing with much cheaper, spacious rooms with wardrobes and bathrooms is worth considering too.

Hotel Merlin (☎ 61300; Jl Panjaitan 25; s/d with fan 88,000/110,000Rp, with air-con & TV 110,000/132,000Rp, ste with hot water 154,000/176,000Rp; ❄) The rooms here are smart, clean and tiled, but most are directly opposite a fuel station on the noisiest street in Sumba. Your complimentary brekkie is served up on the 4th floor, from where Flores can be seen on clear days; access to the 4th floor is by some stairs built for a mythical breed of gigantic tourists.

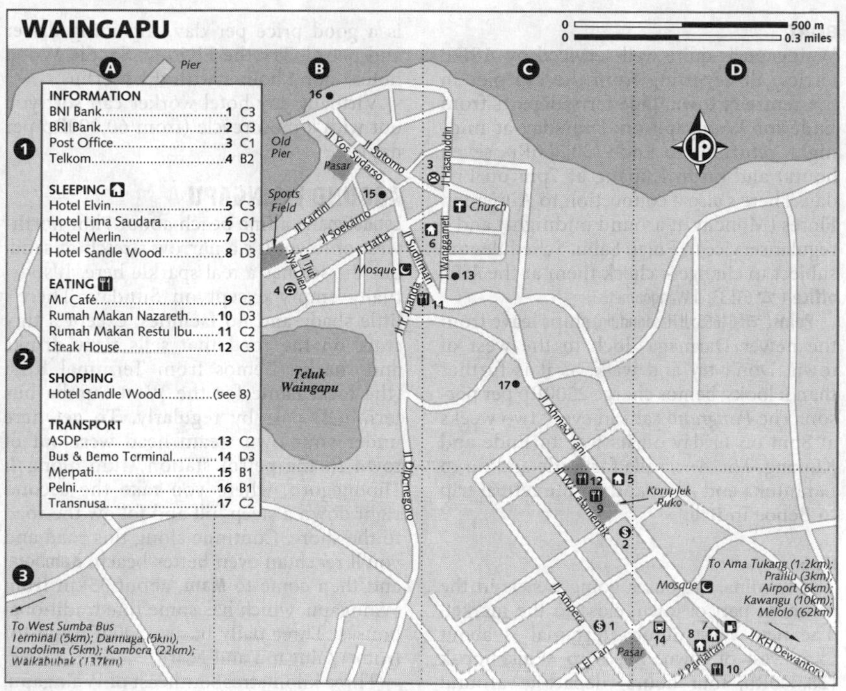

Eating

The new Komplek Ruko is an Indonesian-style food court with a row of inexpensive warungs – pick 'n' mix a dish or two.

Mr Café (☎ 62256; Komplek Ruko, dishes 7000-17,500Rp; ⏰ breakfast, lunch & dinner) Serves good sate and wonderful fresh mango juice.

Rumah Makan Restu Ibu (Jl Ir Juanda 1, dishes 8000-18,000Rp; ⏰ breakfast, lunch & dinner) Long-running place with a good-value line-up of Indonesian favourites.

Steak House (☎ 61751; Komplek Ruko; dishes 8000-25,000Rp; ⏰ breakfast, lunch & dinner) A great choice, with everything from T-bone steak and fish and chips to regular *nasi goreng*, roti and the like. Also has cappuccino and 'vodka' – though not of the triple-distilled variety.

Rumah Makan Nazareth (Jl WY Lalamentik; mains 13,000-24,000Rp; ⏰ breakfast, lunch & dinner) A varied menu of Chinese and Indonesian dishes, complemented by a few Western favourites.

Shopping

Waingapu has a few 'art shops' selling Sumbanese ikat and artefacts. Vendors also set up impromptu stalls in front of the hotels – some will squat there patiently all day. Prices in town can actually be very fair, and there's far more choice here than in the countryside.

Ama Tukang (☎ 62414; Jl Hawan Waruk) A good ikat workshop where you can see weavers in action, have the dying process explained and browse the extensive high-quality pieces for sale. To get there, head south of the bridge on the southern side of Waingapu and turn left after 400m into Jl Hawan Waruk. It's on the left about 800m along this road.

Hotel Sandle Wood (☎ 61199; Jl Panjaitan 23) Has a huge collection of ikat tucked away in a musty back room.

Getting There & Away

AIR

Merpati (☎ 61323; Jl Soekarno 4) has three flights a week to/from Kupang. There are more services to Denpasar from Tambulaka in West Sumba.

Transnusa (☎ 61489; Jl Ahmad Yani) has four flights a week to Kupang, two to Denpasar and one to Tambaluka.

BOAT

Waingapu is quite well serviced by ASDP ferries, all departing from the old pier in the centre of town. One ferry departs from Ende for Waingapu on Thursday at midnight, returning to Ende (30,800Rp, seven hours) and on to Kupang at 7pm on Friday. There's also a connection to Aimere in Flores (Monday at around midnight) and a regular service to Pulau Sabu. Schedules are subject to change – check them at the **ASDP office** (☎ 61533; Jl Wanggameti 3).

Pelni (☎ 61665; Jl Hasanuddin) ships leave from the newer Darmaga dock to the west of town. Don't try and walk, as it is further than it looks; bemos charge 2500Rp per person. The *Pangrano* calls in every two weeks at 8pm on Friday on its way to Ende and Kupang. The *Awu* sails for Ende and on to Larantuka and Alor, and on the return trip to Benoa in Bali.

BUS

The terminal for buses going east is in the southern part of town, close to the market. The new West Sumba terminal is about 5km west of town. Buses to Waikabubak (28,000Rp, four hours) depart at around 7am, 8am, noon and 3pm from the latter. The road is sealed but windy, and bridges are occasionally washed away in the wet season.

Buses head southeast to Melolo, Rende and Baing. Several travel through the morning and afternoon to Melolo, with a few continuing on to Rende, Ngalu and Baing. Most return to Waingapu on the same day.

There are also daily buses northwest to Prailiang and southwest to Tarimbang.

Getting Around

TO/FROM THE AIRPORT

The airport is 6km south of town on the Melolo road. A taxi into town costs about 15,000Rp, but the Merlin, Sandle Wood and Elvin hotels offer a free pick-up and drop-off service for guests.

BEMO

It's 1000Rp for a bemo ride to any destination around town, and 2500Rp to the western bus terminal.

CAR & MOTORCYCLE

Sumba has the highest car-hire rates in Nusa Tenggara. Even after bargaining, 450,000Rp is a good price per day, including driver and petrol. Try the Elvin or Sandle Wood hotels; don't bother with the Merlin.

Virtually any hotel worker can sort you out with a motorcycle (from 60,000Rp per day).

AROUND WAINGAPU

Londolima is a fine beach about 7km northwest of town. It's a narrow stretch of sand, but the sea has a real sparkle here. It's virtually empty except on Sunday. There's little shade and no facilities, except a tiny store on the road that sells fizzy drinks and snacks. Bemos from Terminal Kota (the local name for the West Sumba bus terminal) pass by regularly. To get here under your own steam head west out of town to the petrol station, 1km along Jl Diponegoro, where you take the second right down a steep hill and follow the road to the shore. Continue along this road and you'll reach an even better beach, **Kambera**, and then come to **Maru**, about 35km from Waingapu, which has some fine traditional houses. Three daily buses (5000Rp) go to/from Waingapu and Maru.

Three kilometres southeast of Waingapu, **Prailiu** is an ikat-weaving centre that's worth a quick look. Alongside some traditional thatched houses are some concrete tombs bearing carvings of crocodiles and turtles as well as empty graves that will be filled when the deceased's family can afford the funeral (see p593). Visitors to the village are asked for a cash donation. Bemos to Prailiu run from Waingapu's main bus and bemo terminal. Continuing southeast, it's a further 7km to **Kawangu**, which has some stone-slab tombs, located about 300m off the road to Melolo.

EAST SUMBA

Southeast of Waingapu are several traditional villages, some with striking stone ancestor tombs. The area produces some of Sumba's best ikat. Most villages are quite used to tourists – expect to have to pay to visit, and be prepared for plenty of attention from ikat vendors.

Melolo

The small town of Melolo, 62km southeast of Waingapu, is close to some interesting villages. There's no longer a losmen here, but resident Sony speaks some English and will put up guests for 25,000Rp per person. A short walk through mangroves from the village is a long, sandy beach, although the water is a bit murky.

The market is about 3km out of town on a lonely, dusty hill; Friday is the main market day, when some good textiles show up. Bemos run regularly from town to the market (1000Rp).

Buses to Melolo from Waingapu (8000Rp, 1½ hours) run hourly until around 4pm along a good sealed road.

Rende

Praiyawang is a traditional compound of Sumbanese houses and is the ceremonial focus of the village of **Rende**, located 7km south of Melolo. It has an imposing line-up of big stone-slab tombs and makes fine-quality ikat. You'll be shown some magnificent pieces, but the prices are high. Though Rende still has a rajah, other traditions have declined due to the cost of ceremonies and the breakdown of the *marapu* religion.

The largest tomb at Praiyawang is that of a former chief. It consists of four stone pillars 2m high, supporting a monstrous slab of stone about 5m long by 2.5m wide and 1m thick. Two stone tablets stand atop the main slab, carved with figures. A massive Sumbanese house with concrete pillars faces the tombs, along with a number of older *rumah adat*. It's possible to stay, but remember that these are members of a royal family, not hotel staff. Act accordingly!

Several buses go from Waingapu to Rende (9000Rp), starting at about 7am; otherwise, take a bus to Melolo, from where bemos and trucks run throughout the day. The last buses back to Waingapu leave at around 3pm.

Umabara & Pau

Like Rende, these two villages, about 4km southwest of Melolo, have traditional Sumbanese houses, stone tombs and weavings. At Umabara, the largest tombs, carved with images of crocodiles and turtles in deep relief, are for relatives of the present rajah, who speaks some English and is quite friendly. Villagers here will eagerly try to offload some ikat on you.

The turn off to the villages is on the main Waingapu–Melolo road, from where you head 1.5km down a side road until you come to a horse statue; here you can fork right for Umabara or left for Pau, both just a few minutes further on. A trail also links the two villages.

Mangili

The Mangili district, centred on the villages of **Ngalu** and **Kaliuda**, is famed for its fine weaving. Kaliuda ikat is reputedly the best in Indonesia and is noted for its rich natural colours and the fine lines of its motifs. Much of the best stuff has been made to order for traders and gets shipped off to Bali (and beyond), though you may see some ikat-weaving in action. Kaliuda also has some fine stone-slab tombs and a gaudy modern grave painted red, yellow and blue and decorated with animal figures and Christian crosses. Seven buses a day head here from Waingapu (12,500Rp; 2¾ hours), passing through Melolo and Ngalu. Kaliuda is a 3km walk from Ngalu towards the coast.

Baing

Thanks to the nearby beach of **Kallala**, Baing has emerged as the surf capital of east Sumba. Baing is the main village of the Waijelu district, 124km from Waingapu, but has little of interest. Kallala, 2km away on the coast, has a wide white-sand beach and big surf.

The renowned Mr David (as he is referred to throughout east Sumba) has lived in Sumba for over 30 years, is a mine of information and has set up two resorts in the region. **Mr David's** (fax 0387 61333; www.eastsumba.com; all-inclusive bungalows US$35), the Kallala resort, has simple, attractive beach bungalows that mostly attract surfers and a bar-resto with satellite TV. Game- and spear-fishing trips can also be arranged here.

The second resort is on the idyllic isle Pulau Manggudu, whose exquisite white-sand beaches are regularly visited by nesting sea turtles. The **Manggudu Island Resort** (fax 038761333; www.manggudu.com; all-inclusive bungalows US$35) has just four bungalows, superb surfing, snorkelling (mantas are common) and world-class fishing. Its remoteness simply adds to the appeal – contact Mr David first about travel to the island, which is a four-hour drive from Waingapu and then 40 minutes by boat.

Four buses a day go to Baing (28,000Rp, four hours), leaving Waingapu between 7am and 8am, and then again at around 11am and 1pm. The road is sealed all the way but is bumpy past Melolo. A dirt track with many branches runs from Baing to Kallala, but buses will drop you off at the beach if you ask.

SOUTH-CENTRAL SUMBA

This part of the island is little explored and difficult to access. Although there are daily buses from Waingapu to Tarimbang and trucks to Praingkareha, getting around may require a 4WD or motorcycle and, often, some hiking.

If you're looking for uncrowded waves, check out **Tarimbang**, around 88km southwest of Waingapu, where the gorgeous cove beach has terrific surf, some snorkelling, and rustic accommodation at Marthen's Homestay and the *kepala desa*'s six-room place. Both charge 50,000Rp per person including meals, but expect basic conditions and a repetitive diet. Daily buses to Tarimbang leave Waingapu in the morning (15,000Rp, four hours).

Praingkareha, 26km east of Tarimbang, has a majestic wet-season waterfall, the 100m-high **Air Terjun Laputi**. There's a pond with eels above the falls and a beautiful pool at its base. Tradition forbids women to look into the pool, but an exception is made for foreigners. The falls are about 3km from the village. If you walk via the valley, locals will offer to guide you there (this is recommended). Otherwise, follow the main road to a fork, take the old road to the left and walk down a steep path to the falls.

WAIKABUBAK

☎ 0387 / pop 18,000

A juxtaposition of thatched clan houses and a typical high street of concrete stores, administrative buildings and houses bristling with satellite dishes, Waikabubak is an odd but fascinating place. At about 600m above sea level, it's a little cooler than the east and a good base for exploring the traditional villages of western Sumba.

Though it seems an extremely tranquil place today, serious inter-tribal rioting occurred here in 1998; see p591 for details.

Information

There's no internet access.

BNI bank (Bank Negara Indonesia; Jl Ahmad Yani; 8am-3.30pm Mon-Fri) Changes most major currencies and has the best rates.

BRI bank (Bank Rakyat Indonesia; Jl Gajah Mada) Its ATM only accepts Mastercard/Cirrus cards.

Post office (Jl Sudirman; 8am-3.30pm Mon-Fri)

Telkom office (24hr)

Tourist office (☎ 21240; Jl Teratai 1; 8am-3pm Mon-Sat) On the outskirts of town, but the staff are helpful and informative about forthcoming funerals and cultural events.

BETEL NUT – THE PEACEKEEPER & PACEMAKER

Travel through Sumba and Timor and you can't avoid the random splodges of red residue that liberally decorate the pavements and bus aisles of this region, or the villagers' foaming, scarlet mouths. The substance behind the stain is betel nut, or *sirih pinang*, a mildly intoxicating stimulant that provides a nicotine-like or espresso-esque buzz and suppresses appetite. It's also carcinogenic – levels of mouth cancer are very high in societies that use the gear. The nut itself, which is large and oval-shaped, is actually the seed of the graceful betel palm tree.

Chewing betel is a statement of adulthood, and the three parts that make up the 'mix' that are chewed together have symbolic meaning. The green stalk of the *sirih* represents the male, the nut or *pinang* the female ovaries, and the lime *(kapor)* the sperm. It's the lime that causes the characteristic flood of red saliva in the mouth.

Betel nut traditionally played an important role in negotiation and discussion between different clans, and would always be offered to visitors as a gesture of welcome.

If you're offered betel nut, it's best not to refuse it – just put a little in your pocket, or give it a go. Unless you've been masticating *sirih* for years, it's highly likely you'll find it absolutely vile: its flavour is very bitter and its consistency gritty. Betel nut also creates an amazing amount of saliva, so get your gobbing head on as it's certainly not something that you'll want to swallow.

If you do make an effort, you'll find that *sirih*-chewing is a great way to interact with the locals, and you're sure to elicit cackles of delight from the old ladies.

Sights

TOMBS & TRADITIONAL KAMPUNG

Within the town are very traditional *kampung* with stone-slab tombs and thatched houses. Experienced guides are harder to find than in Waingapu, but you can probably get someone to go with you for about 40,000Rp per day.

Kampung Tambelar, just off Jl Sudirman, has very impressive tombs, but the most interesting *kampung* are on the western edge of town. It's only a short stroll from most hotels to **Prai Klembung** and then up the ridge to **Tarung** and **Waitabar**.

Kampung Tarung, reached by a path off Jl Manda Elu, is the scene of an important month-long ritual sequence, the *Wula Podhu*, each November. This is an austere period when even weeping for the dead is prohibited. Rites consist mainly of offerings to the spirits (the day before it ends, hundreds of chickens are sacrificed), and people sing and dance for the entire final day. Tarung's fine stone tombs are under official protection.

Other interesting *kampung* occupying ridge or hilltop positions outside town include **Praiijing** and **Bondomarotto**. Kampung Praiijing is especially scenic, perched on a hilltop about 4km from town, where there are five neat rows of traditional houses and large stone tombs. **Kampung Prairami** and **Kampung Primkateti** are also beautifully located on adjacent hilltops. You can take a bemo to the turn-off for Praiijing (1500Rp).

Another major *kampung* that is worth visiting is **Tambera**, 10km north on the road to Mamboro. It's serviced by the occasional bemo (4000Rp).

It is customary to give a cash donation (about 5000Rp to 8000 Rp), and you may be invited to chew betel nut.

Sleeping

Hotel Pelita (☎ 21104; Jl Ahmad Yani; economy s/d 30,000/35,000, superior 55,000/70,000Rp) Offers modern, clean, renovated rooms with bathrooms and some depressing last-resort economy options.

Hotel Aloha (☎ 21245; Jl Sudirman 26; r with mandi 45,000Rp, with TV 55,000Rp) Well-run with neat, clean rooms, good food and information. It moonlights as the Transnusa airlines agency and the town's wedding-cake supplier.

Hotel Artha (☎ 21112; Jl Veteran 11; s/d with mandi 30,000/60,000Rp, with fan & shower 60,000/80,000Rp) A tranquil spot with rooms set around a courtyard garden. The management is really on the ball here and can help out with anything from transport to information, making it a good choice.

Hotel Manandang (☎ 21197; fax 21292; Jl Pemuda 4; s/d 50,000/85,000Rp, s/d with bathroom 95,000/135,000Rp, with air-con 235,000/285,000Rp; ❄) This is another friendly place where the good-quality rooms overlook a peaceful garden, but it's overpriced. Some rooms have shared bathroom.

Eating

The choice is very limited. For cheap and cheerful basics, there are a few worthwhile warungs on the main road opposite the mosque.

Rumah Makan Fanny (☎ 21389; Jl Bhayangkara 55; dishes 10,000-20,000Rp; 🕑 breakfast, lunch & dinner) Justifiably the most popular place in town, this clean little eatery has gingham tablecloths and a winsome menu of tasty local grub, including *udang saos tiram* (prawns in oyster sauce) and *bakwan ikan* (Chinese-style fish soup).

Hotel Manandang (Jl Pemuda 4; meals 17,000-25,000Rp; 🕑 breakfast, lunch & dinner) Has a large, proper dining room and an extensive, though pricey, menu.

Shopping

Traders gather at hotels with ikat cloth from eastern Sumba, locally made bone, wood, horn and stone carvings, and jewellery.

Al Gadri (Jl Ahmad Yani) Souvenirs, including carvings and some ikat. The good stuff is hidden away at the back.

Getting There & Away

AIR

The **Merpati agent** (☎ 21051; Jl Ahmad Yani 11) is above a shop. The airline has two flights weekly from Tambulaka airport (42km northwest of Waikabubak) to Kupang and one to Denpasar. There's also the odd connection to Waingapu for those in a rush.

Transnusa (☎ 21245; Hotel Aloha, Jl Sudirman 26) Operates one weekly flight to Kupang and one to Denpasar.

Departure tax is 6000Rp.

BUS

The terminal in Waikabubak is central. Five daily buses run to Waingapu (28,000Rp, four hours) and throughout the day to Waitabula (4000Rp, one hour). There are frequent bemos to Anakalang, Wanokaka and Lamboya, and less frequent and less certain minibuses and trucks to other villages. To Kodi district, take a bus to Waitabula and catch a truck or bemo from there.

Getting Around

TO/FROM THE AIRPORT

Tambulaka, 42km northwest of Waikabubak, is the closest airport. The Bumi Indah bus is supposed to connect with flights, but it's not reliable. A bus to Waitabula and a bemo or *ojek* from there is the cheapest way for those with time. Most people get a taxi or charter a bemo (around 100,000Rp). Try checking flight lists at Merpati/Transnusa the day before; find out who is going and where they are staying and arrange to split the cost.

BUS

Bemos, trucks and minibuses service most other towns and villages in western Sumba; for details, see individual village entries. Generally, it's best to get them early, when they tend to fill up and depart more quickly.

CAR & MOTORCYCLE

Waikabubak is the place to rent a motorcycle for exploring west Sumba – you can expect to pay 60,000Rp a day. For car rental (around 450,000Rp with a driver), contact Hotel Manandang.

WEST SUMBA

☎ 0387

The traditional village culture of western Sumba is one of the most unblemished in Indonesia. *Kampung* of high-roofed houses are still clustered on their hilltops (a place of defence in times past), surrounding the large stone tombs of their important ancestors. Away from the towns, old women with filed teeth still go bare breasted, and men in the traditional turban and short sarong can be seen on horseback. The agricultural cycle turns up rituals, often involving animal sacrifices, almost year-round, and ceremonies for events like house building and marriage can take place at any time. Some *kampung* are unaccustomed to foreigners; taking betel nut and cigarettes is a good way to get a friendly reception.

Give yourself at least a few days around western Sumba. Once you have learned some basic manners as a guest arriving in a village – hopefully armed with some Bahasa Indonesia – it's possible to do without a guide.

Anakalang Villages

The Anakalang district east of Waikabubak has some exceptional stone megaliths and interesting traditional villages. Right beside the main road to Waingapu, 22km east of Waikabubak, **Kampung Pasunga** boasts one of Sumba's most impressive arrays of tombs. The grave of particular interest consists of a upright stone slab carved with images of a chief and his wife with their hands on their hips. This monument dates from 1926 and took six months to carve; 150 buffalo were sacrificed for the funeral ceremony. It is visible from the road. Pasunga's *kepala desa*, whose house has racks of buffalo horns, is friendly if you share some *sirih* or cigs with him. He will ask you to sign the visitors' book and may or may not ask for a donation. The village also has a huge drum 500m east of the tomb.

There are more interesting villages south of Pasunga. Cross the highway and you'll soon pass a market place (markets are held here on Wednesday and Saturday until about 1pm or 2pm); the road then continues to **Kabonduk**, home to Sumba's heaviest tomb, weighing in at 70 tonnes. It is said that 2000 workers took three years to chisel the tomb out of a hillside and drag it to the site.

From Kabonduk it is a very pleasant 15-minute walk across the fields and up the hill to **Makatakeri** and, five minutes further on, to **Lai Tarung**, the original ancestral village for the area, which has stunning views over the surrounding countryside to the coast and several tombs scattered around. There's also a government-built 'showroom' traditional house and some *marapu* houses. Lai Tarung comes alive for the Purungu Takadonga Ratu, a festival honouring the ancestors that's held every two years (in odd-numbered years), starting on July 10 and culminating on July 26.

At **Gallubakul**, 2.5km down the road from Kabonduk, the Umba Sawola tomb is a single piece of carved stone about 5m long, 4m wide and nearly 1m thick. At its eastern end is a separate upright slab with carvings of a rajah and queen, as well as buffalo and cockerel motifs. The grumpy *kepala desa* lives right by the tomb and will ask you to sign in and pay to take photos.

Regular minibuses run between Waikabubak and Anakalang (fewer after 1pm), or buses to Waingapu can drop you on the highway.

South of Waikabubak

The Wanokaka district south of Waikabubak has stunning scenery and several very traditional *kampung*. It's a very beautiful trip out of Waikabubak, taking a sealed but narrow road that splits after 6km at Pedede Weri junction, from where an azure ocean forms the distant horizon. After taking the left turn here, the road passes through the riverside settlement of **Taramanu** 4km further on, and then it's 2km or so downhill to **Waigalli**, which has fine tombs and is the scene of one of the March Pasola events (see p603). Just up a side road on the western side of valley from Waigalli, the Watu Kajiwa tomb in the deeply traditional and isolated village of **Praigoli** is one of the best in Sumba, with a striking symbol like the fleur-de-lys.

Returning to the Pedede Weri junction and heading southwest, you're not far from some very fine beaches. After 5km there's a side track south to **Rua**, with a wonderful stretch of sand, good surf and basic accommodation. Heading west again, the road passes through the villages of Kabukarudi and Kadenga before there's another turn-off south to the idyllic white sands of **Pantai Marosi**, 32km from Waikabubak, where you'll find a luxury resort.

The world-class surf spot known as Occy's Left that featured in the film *The Green Iguana* is on **Pantai Nihiwatu** east of Marosi. Surfers who have tried to ride the legendary waves here have been forced out of the sea by the luxury resort's security men.

SLEEPING & EATING

Ahong Homestay (r incl all meals 50,000Rp) Basic isolated beachside place in Rua popular with surfers.

Homestay Mete Bulu (r incl all meals 50,000Rp) Simple concrete rooms at Watukarere. Surfers should note that there's no longer any access to Pantai Nihiwatu, 1.5km away.

Sumba Nautil (☎ 038721806; www.sumbanautilresort.com; bungalows US$77-99, villas US$415, plus 21% tax;) Very stylish resort hotel set back from the shoreline on Pantai Marosi with beautiful ocean-facing accommodation and very fine cuisine (meals US$10 to US$13). The menu is overseen by the French owners. Dive trips and village visits can be organised. Rates include breakfast.

Nihiwatu Resort (www.nihiwatu.com; bungalows s/d US$200/300, villas from US$840, plus 21% tax;) Luxury hotel in extensive grounds, perched above idyllic Pantai Nihiwatu. The American hotel owner has restricted access to the beach itself, allowing only guests, tour groups and a few locals. Seven air-con bungalows and three villas all face the ocean and are fully equipped with modern amenities. Plenty of activities – fishing, surfing, diving, horse riding and mountain biking – are offered for additional costs. The minimum stay is five nights.

GETTING THERE & AWAY

Two daily buses run southeast to Waigalli from Waikabubak. Lamboya district buses cover the southwest towns and run through Padede Watu to Kabukarudi, Kadenga and Walakaka, but they don't usually run to the beaches. Buses leave roughly every hour throughout the day from Waikabubak.

By far the best way to visit the area is by car or motorcycle. Most roads are sealed and traffic is light. The hills south of Waikabubak are a very taxing ride for cyclists.

Kodi

Kodi is the westernmost region of Sumba, and the small town of Bondokodi, about 2km from the coast, is the centre of this district. The Kodi area offers plenty of attractions: villages with incredible high-peaked houses and unusual megalithic tombs; long white-sand beaches, with waves pounding over coral reefs; and the opportunity to see or buy some fascinating local wood, bone and horn carvings. If you're on foot you won't see much of the region unless you stick around for a few days.

The region's biggest **market** (held every Wednesday) is at Kori village; to get here, people from around the region hang off any vehicle they can get hold of, so it must be good. A couple of buses run from Bondokodi in the morning, before 8am. Watch out for pickpockets in the throng.

Kodi is a region with a reputation for lawlessness, and Sumbanese from other districts of the island are wary of Kodi people. Exploring with a guide is probably safest.

Pero

Pero is a friendly coastal village situated on spectacular coastline just a few kilometres from Bondokodi. It's a charming little place, which has a wonderfully end-of-the-earth appeal – west of here you won't hit land until Africa. There's a couple of surf breaks just offshore. The long-running **Homestay Stori** (per person incl all meals 50,000Rp) is run by a very hospitable family and has neat little rooms and absolutely delicious local food. At night an impromptu art shop of local bone, horn and wood carvings may be set up on the front porch. To visit traditional *kampung*, go north or south along the coastline.

To reach **Ratenggaro**, first cross the freshwater pool that runs to the coast below Pero. At low tide you can wade across; otherwise, locals will get you across in canoes for about 3000Rp per person. From the other side it's about 3km along Pantai Radukapal, a long stretch of white-sand beach, until you come to the fenced *kampung* of Ratenggaro. It is possible to stay with the *kepala desa* for a fee, and often visitors are asked for a hefty 20,000Rp just for visiting – to build toilets, allegedly.

The view from Ratenggaro along the coastline is breathtaking – coconut palms fringe the shoreline and the high roofs of Wainyapu peep out above the trees across the river. On the near side of the river mouth unusual stone tombs occupy a small headland. To get to **Wainyapu**, you'll probably have to wade across the river at low tide. The village chief here is locally famous for having 12 wives.

On the way to Ratenggaro, look out for the roofs of **Kampung Paranobaroro** through the trees, about 1km inland. The houses here have even higher roofs and stone statues, and there is an elaborate example with pig jaws and numerous buffalo horns hanging from its veranda. During the day only women and children are in the village – women are often weaving and happy to chat.

To reach **Tosi**, about 6km north and the scene of the Kodi Pasola in February, head north from Bondokodi market along the sealed road. Coming from Pero, it's a simple left at the T-junction. About 1km further on is a track on the left: follow it for 5km, past a series of tombs. Many people have reported aggression here, so bypass the village itself by taking a short walk to the beach, from where a track runs back to Pero.

From Waikabubak there are direct buses to Waitabula and frequent bemos and trucks from there to Pero.

Waitabula

☎ 0387

This sleepy market town, on the main highway between Tambulaka airport and Waikabubak, is a useful transport hub with frequent connections to Bondokodi/Pero, Waikelo and Waikabubak.

Project Hope – Sumba (☎ 24159) is a local organisation helping impoverished communities in the region. Visitors are welcome, and staff may be able to point you in the direction of knowledgeable local guides.

Hotel Ongko Cimpu (☎ 24055; s/d from 45,000/60,000Rp) is a well-kept and friendly place where the large rooms have attached *mandis*. Airport pick-ups and drop-offs can be arranged.

The alternative, **Losmen Anggrek** (s/d from 20,000/30,000Rp), was looking very run-down on our last visit.

Daily direct buses make the run all the way to Waingapu. Bemos or *ojeks* to the airport are 2000Rp.

Waikelo

☎ 0387

This small and predominantly Muslim town north of Waitabula is the main port for west Sumba and has a weekly connection with Sumbawa. The town has a superb beach and you can find relative solitude if you walk west around the bay.

Newa Sumba Resort (☎ 0215229117; www.newasumbaresort.com; s US$45, d US$60) is an upmarket resort with fine timber *kampung*-style bungalows on a spectacular white-sand beach. Meals cost about 48,000Rp. Regular buses and bemos travel between Waikelo and Waitabula, and a few continue to Waikabubak.

There is a weekly ferry service between Waikelo and Sape (Sumbawa). It departs from Sape for Waikelo on Monday at 5pm and returns to Sape (32,000Rp) at 9am on Tuesday, taking about seven hours.

PASOLA: LET THE BATTLES COMMENCE

A riotous tournament between two teams of spear-wielding, ikat-clad horsemen, the Pasola has to be one of the most extravagant, and bloodiest, harvest festivals in Asia. Held annually in February and March, it takes the form of a ritual battle – not so much a quarrel between opposing forces as a need for human blood to be spilt to keep the spirits happy and bring a good harvest. Despite the blunt spears that the combatants now use and the efforts of Indonesian authorities to supervise the events, few holds are barred; blood is spilt and sometimes deaths still occur.

The Pasola is part of a series of traditions connected with the beginning of the planting season. It takes place in four areas, its exact timing determined by the arrival on nearby coasts of a certain type of sea worm called *nyale*. Two days before the main events brutal boxing matches called *pajura* are held, the combatants' fists bound in razor-sharp local grasses.

Before the Pasola can begin, priests in full ceremonial dress must first wade into the ocean to examine the worms at dawn; they're usually found on the eighth or ninth day after a full moon. A prediction is then made as to how good the year's harvest will be, from the numbers and appearance of the *nyale*. Fighting begins on the beach and, later the same day, continues further inland, the opposing 'armies' drawn from coastal and inland dwellers. The riders gallop at each other, hurling their *holas* (spears) at rival riders (it's not permitted to use a spear as a lance).

In February, Pasola is celebrated in the Kodi area (centred on Kampung Tosi) and the Lamboya area (Kampung Sodan); in March it's in the Wanokaka area (Kampung Waigalli) and the remote Gaura area west of Lamboya (Kampung Ubu Olehka). Call hotels in Waingapu or Waikabubak to find out the approximate dates before travelling to Sumba, or contact a travel agent in Bali, Flores or Timor.

Kalimantan

Deep, dark and exotic, the very notion of Borneo rouses something in the subconscious. Summoning visions of mythical people and ancient forests, it tugs at the adventurer within. It's a romantic notion, but the world's third-largest island has managed to keep some of her secrets and most of them lie in the impenetrable interior of Kalimantan.

Occupying two-thirds of Borneo's primeval land mass, Kalimantan is one of Indonesia's least-visited provinces. A void on the tourist radar, it's a red flag to those hungry for the unknown. Mountains, forests and mighty rivers stretch across the interior, influencing the culture, history and livelihoods of villages throughout. Although the logging and mining industries have had a 30-year feeding frenzy, the fury of the chainsaw and the tide of wasteland is beginning to slow. But you need to be quick – Kalimantan's hidden world continues to diminish.

The once mysterious Sungai Mahakam is now a highway of river traffic, yet treacherous rapids still protect the customs of traditional Dayak villages. Even the urban jungle begs exploration. Dawn canoe rides to Banjarmasin's floating markets and dusk journeys through its enigmatic canals imbue travellers with a taste of modern culture.

You can trek in Kayan Mentarang National Park, the Apokayan Highlands, and around the eastern reaches of the vast Sungai Kapuas. And with little effort you can come face to face with orang-utans, macaques, proboscis monkeys, bird life and maybe even the odd sun bear.

HIGHLIGHTS

- Coursing Sungai Kumai in a *klotok* (motorised river canoe) and glimpsing the rust-red figure of an orang-utan in **Tanjung Puting National Park** (p631)
- Testing longboat limits; investigating Dayak villages beyond the rapids of **Sungai Mahakam** (p654)
- Discovering **Banjarmasin** (p635) at dusk and dawn from the canals of this animated city
- Trekking, rafting and exploring South Kalimantan's enigmatic **Pegunungan Meratus** (p644) around Loksado
- Going coastal in the tropical islands around **Pulau Derawan** (p663) and the isolated beaches north of **Pontianak** (p618)

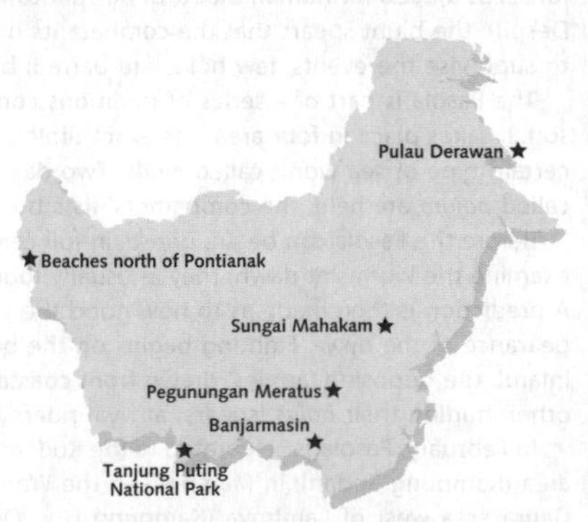

- POPULATION: 11.2 MILLION
- LAND AREA: 539,460 SQ KM
- HIGHEST PEAK: BUKIT RAYA (2278M)

HISTORY

Kalimantan's position on the India-China trade axis ensured strong influence from these two countries long before Europeans set foot on Borneo. By about AD 400, Hinduism arrived and Chinese settlements were established. As Islam spread east around the 15th or 16th century, coastal ports were converted and sultanates, such as Kutai and Banjarmasin, became major trading centres.

But it was ultimately the Europeans who colonised and shaped the province's modern history. In the early 17th century, Kalimantan became a scene of conflict between the British and the Dutch, ostensibly over the Brit's flourishing pepper trade. The conflict culminated in rebellion by 1701, and the British were evicted six years later. By the late 1820s the colonising Dutch had concluded treaties with various small west-coast states, including parts of the Banjarmasin sultanate.

In 1839 the establishment of a private colony in Kuching, Sarawak, by Englishman James Brooke, fuelled Dutch concerns to cement their commercial interests in Kalimantan. New coal mines in South and East Kalimantan were quickly developed and gradually the island gained commercial importance. The 1840s and 1850s brought several internal disputes, culminating in war between the Dutch and the Banjarmasin sultanate in 1859. The Dutch regained control after four years, but resistance continued until 1905.

By the end of the 19th century, Dutch commercial exploitation of the archipelago was at its peak. Rubber and oil markets were flourishing, and pepper, copra, tin and coffee plantations were developed. By the end of the century, oil was being drilled in East Kalimantan. In 1907, the British company Shell Transport & Trading merged with the Royal Dutch Company for the Exploitation of Petroleum Sources in the Netherlands Indies to form Royal Dutch Shell. By 1930 Shell was producing 85% of Indonesia's oil, and Kalimantan's fate as a stronghold was sealed.

The current division of Borneo between Indonesia and Malaysia originates from the British-Dutch rivalry. After WWII the Brooke family handed Sarawak over to the British government, at the same time that Sabah came under British administration, putting Britain in the curious position of acquiring a new colony at the time it was shedding others. Both remained under British control until 1963, when they joined with the Malay Peninsula – and, temporarily, Singapore – to form the nation of Malaysia.

East Kalimantan has been one of Indonesia's prime *transmigrasi* (transmigration) targets, a campaign which has had disastrous effects on the province. The transmigrants have settled on marginal lands, replacing diverse tracts of jungle with extensive monocultures of rubber and pulpwood trees. This practice is in direct discord with Dayak groups, whose indigenous land-use regimens and land rights are rarely recognised. Transmigrants have also provided mining and logging industries with a ready supply of cheap and young labour.

By the late '90s almost a fifth of the population were transmigrants, and brewing ethnic tension, particularly between Madurese migrants and the Dayaks and Malays, reached a bloody peak. During the 1997–98 upheaval hundreds died in violent clashes, most were Madurese. Dayaks returned to their traditional practice of head-hunting and the island seemed in a state of chaos. Calm was restored relatively quickly but the conflict flared again briefly in 2001. Again hundreds of people lost their lives and thousands of Madurese fled the island. Today tension between the Madurese and other ethnic groups is a mere simmer and most travellers will be oblivious to it. The pursuit of peace and progress have become common denominators for all groups.

CULTURE

The population of Kalimantan is more than 11 million. The three biggest ethnic groups are the recently arrived Malay Indonesians, who tend to follow Islam and live in settlements along the coasts and the main rivers; the Chinese, who have controlled trade in Kalimantan for centuries; and the Dayaks, the collective name for the indigenous inhabitants of the island. Individual Dayak tribes use their separate tribal names, such as Kenyah, Kayan, Iban and Punan.

The most striking feature of many of the older Dayak women is their pierced ear lobes, stretched with the weight of heavy gold or brass rings. This custom is increasingly rare among the young. Older Dayaks,

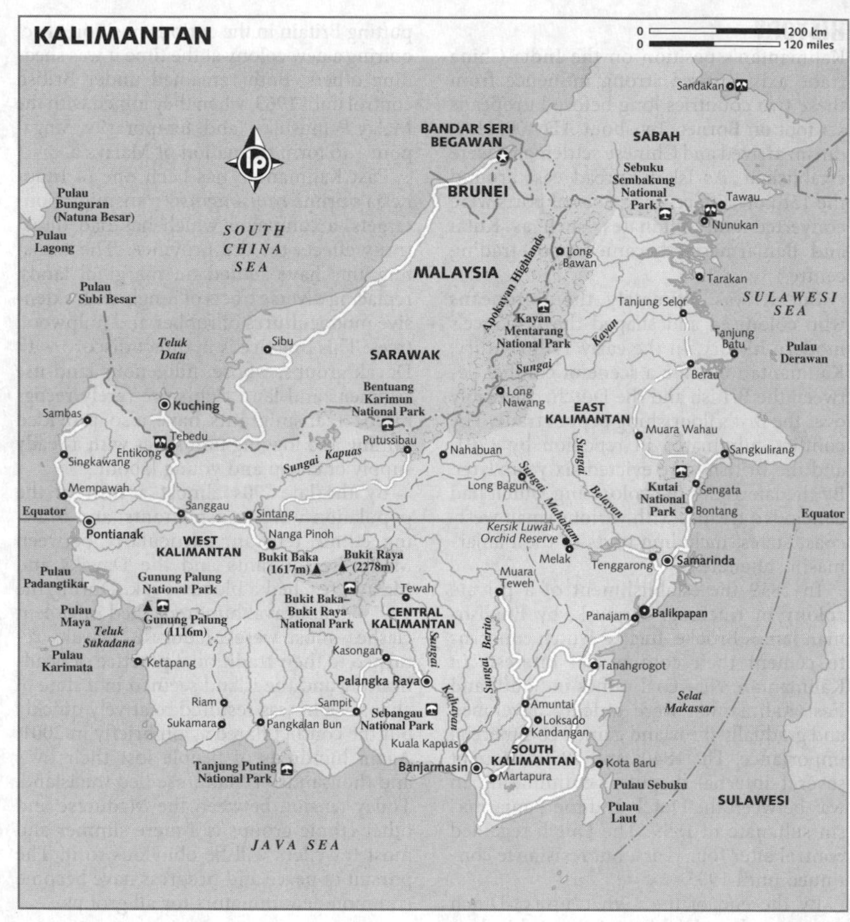

influenced by missionaries, often trim their ear lobes as a sign of conversion.

It was once the custom for all women to tattoo their forearms and calves with bird and spirit designs. Tattooing of young women has almost disappeared, except in tribes deep in the interior. It's still seen among men, although traditionally men in many Dayak cultures were expected to earn their tattoos by taking heads.

In the past, many Dayak tribes lived in large communal buildings, known as longhouses, which sit on tall posts above the ground, mainly for defence. But Dayak traditions and belief systems have taken a beating in the 20th century and this tradition has largely gone by the wayside in the last 50 years. Pressure from the Indonesian government, increasing development and Protestant missionaries also continue to weaken the backbone of Dayak tribal cultures.

WILDLIFE

Kalimantan's most celebrated inhabitant is the unbearably human-esque orang-utan. These rich amber–coloured primates with their soulful disposition are an undisputed highlight of the islands' fauna and an obvious magnet for tourists. Today, the few remaining orang-utan refuges are found in the national parks and reserves of Kalimantan. Camps in Tanjung Puting National Park in Central Kalimantan were the first such facilities, mainly dedicated to studying ex-captive orang-utans in order to reintroduce them into the wild. In East Kalimantan, the Wanariset Orang-utan Reintroduction Centre, which is closed to visitors, was established in the early 1990s with similar goals. Due to the lack of success with reintroducing orang-utans into the wild, in recent years the focus at these and other centres has shifted to behavioural studies, with an aim to promote a greater understanding of the need to protect orang-utans and the forest in which they live.

The easiest place to see orang-utans is Tanjung Puting National Park, where ex-captive and orphan feeding stations virtually guarantee close encounters, but spotting wild orang-utans is also possible. But the best place for wild orang-utans is Kutai National Park in East Kalimantan.

The deep waters of Sungai Mahakam in East Kalimantan are home to freshwater dolphins; there are proboscis monkeys, crab-eating macaques and crocodiles in the mangrove swamps; while the forest is the haunt of gibbons, clouded leopards, giant butterflies and hornbills, including the legendary black hornbill.

GETTING THERE & AWAY

Balikpapan's Seppingan is the only entry point in Kalimantan where Visas on Arrival (see p862) can be issued. For all other entry, whether by sea or air, you must have obtained a visa in advance.

Air

Malaysian Airlines flies between Pontianak and Kuching in Sarawak.

Balikpapan, Pontianak and Banjarmasin are the busiest airports, with connections throughout Kalimantan as well as Java and Bali. Due to turmoil in recent years, in addition to changes in government at the national and local levels, flights are in constant flux. The arrival of new airlines, coupled with fluctuating oil prices, has made competition stiff in recent years. As a rule, double check all flight times and prices with a local travel agency. See p607 for flight routes and fares in Kalimantan.

KALIMANTAN AIRFARES

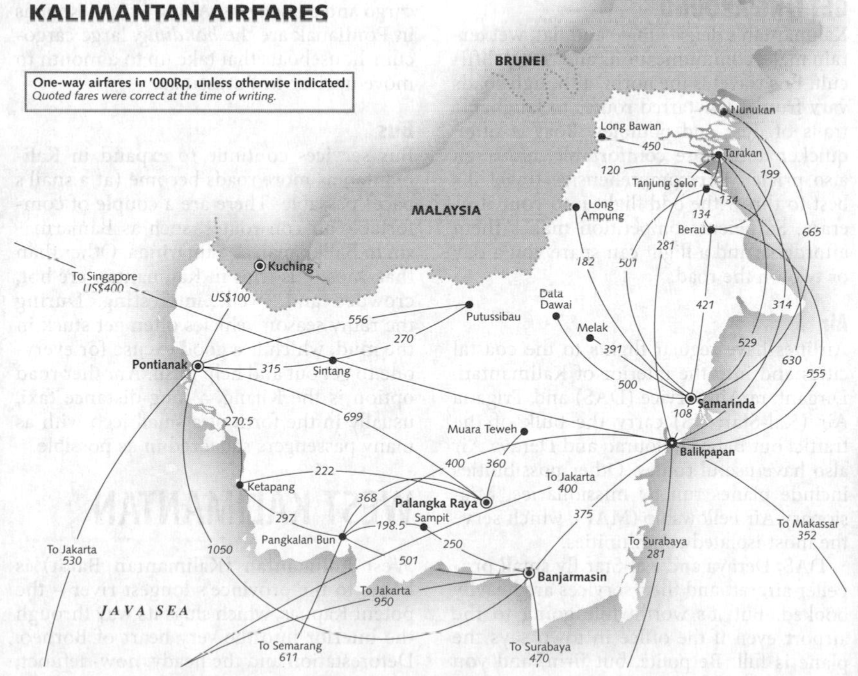

KALIMANTAN UN-VISA RUN

At the time of writing only residents of Sarawak were able to obtain visas from the Indonesian Honorary Consul in Kuching. This means of course that if you're in Sarawak or Indonesia and require a new visa, you'll need to fly to Singapore to apply for one at the Indonesian embassy there.

Boat

Speedboats depart frequently from Nunukan in East Kalimantan to Tawau in Sabah. Buy tickets on the dock on Tarakan.

There are ferry connections from Balikpapan, Samarinda, Banjarmasin, Pontianak and Kumai to Java and Sulawesi, with both Pelni and other companies. Hitching a ride on cargo ships is also possible in many ports.

Bus

Air-con buses from Pontianak to Kuching cost 140,000Rp to 200,000Rp and take about 10 hours. Bookings can be made at agencies around Pontianak and at some hotels.

GETTING AROUND

Kalimantan's dense jungle and flat, wet terrain make communications and travel difficult. Bus travel is the norm, although roads vary from a few tarred routes to laughable trails of dust and potholes. Boat is often quicker and more comfortable, although also pricier. For comprehensive travel it's best to throw the odd flight into your itinerary. Sufficient competition makes them affordable and a flight can spare you a day or two on the road.

Air

Airlines have regular flights to the coastal cities and into the interior of Kalimantan. Dirgantara Air Service (DAS) and Trigana Air (Kal-Star; KS) carry the bulk of the traffic, but Batavia, Bouraq and Deraya Air also have useful routes. Other possibilities include planes run by missionaries, Missionary Air Fellowship (MAF), which serve the most isolated communities.

DAS, Deraya and Kal-Star fly small propeller aircraft and their services are heavily booked. But it's worthwhile going to the airport even if the office in town says the plane is full. Be polite, but firm, and you may be surprised at what you can get away with. For travel on the smallest planes, passengers are weighed along with their luggage, so it doesn't help piling all your heaviest items into your hand luggage. The usual limit is 10kg, anything over will be charged accordingly.

Boat

The various river ferries have gone by the wayside these days as most public transport is by bus or Kijang (4WD vehicle used as a taxi). That said, one of Kalimantan's cultural highlights is to journey up Sungai Mahakam on a *longbot*, which, as the name suggests, is a longboat – a narrow vessel with two large outboard motors at the rear and bench seats in a covered passenger cabin. These still ply the river on a daily basis.

In rivers of all size throughout the province, *ces* (small motorised canoes) and speedboats are common modes of transport. The cost of fuel makes them pricey options, but they are easily the quickest way to get from A to B for locals and travellers alike. In some more remote areas you may find *taxi sungai* (river taxi), all of which carry both cargo and passengers. Along Sungai Kapuas in Pontianak are the *bandung*, large cargo-cum-houseboats that take up to a month to move upriver to Putussibau.

Bus

Bus services continue to expand in Kalimantan as more roads become (at a snail's pace) passable. There are a couple of comfortable air-con routes, such as Banjarmasin to Balikpapan or Samarinda. Other than that, most bus trips in Kalimantan are hot, crowded and…well…interesting. During the rainy season vehicles often get stuck in the mud, which is a good excuse for everyone to get out and help push. Another road option is the Kijang, a long-distance taxi, usually in the form of a small jeep with as many passengers squeezed in as possible.

WEST KALIMANTAN

West Kalimantan (Kalimantan Barat) is home to the province's longest river – the potent Kapuas, which slugs its way through the interior into the very heart of Borneo. Deforestation and the heady, now-defunct, days of water traffic may have robbed the Kapuas of much of its mystery, but its magnitude alone ensures remnants of untouched jungle and adventure. Eight hundred kilometres upriver, Dayak villages cling fiercely to tradition in scatterings around Putussibau.

North of Pontianak are water activities of an entirely different nature, on the tiny but magical beaches of Pasir Panjang and Tanjung Gundul. The transfrontier Bentuang Karimun National Park lies deep in the interior, sharing its border with the neighbouring Lanjak Entimau Wildlife Sanctuary in Sarawak, making it the largest conservation area in all of Borneo. Treks from Putussibau can also be made to the headwaters of Sungai Mahakam in East Kalimantan.

West Kalimantan is enriched by the highest concentration of ethnic Chinese in Indonesia. The proportion of Chinese residents is estimated to be 40% in Pontianak and 65% in Singkawang. Architecture, food, language and culture all have a distinct Chinese flavour, and even the major Islamic festivals are celebrated with Chinese firecrackers.

PONTIANAK

☎ 0561 / pop 460,000

Situated right on the equator, Pontianak lies astride the confluence of Sungai Landak and Sungai Kapuas. Some describe the city as

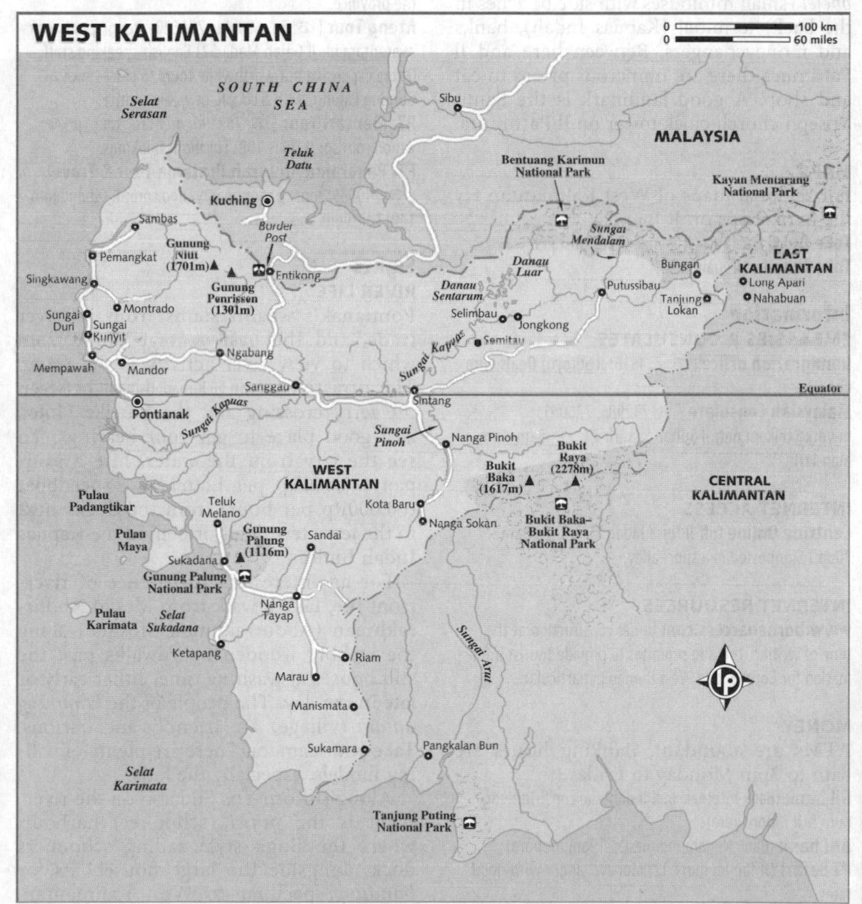

bustling…which it is in the wee hours. By midday, though, Pontianak churns with road, river and human traffic in various degrees of haste, all contributing their part in the urban din. The city itself sprawls over a vast area, with bus terminals and ramshackle suburbs creating mini-communities. Like Banjarmasin it really needs to be seen from the canals and riverside boardwalks. Charter a boat or walk over the Kapuas bridge from Jl Gajah Mada for a sweeping view of the river and brilliant orange sunsets.

Orientation

The commercial hub of Pontianak is in the north of town, particularly on Jl Rahadi Usman. Here you'll find markets, the main *opelet* (small minibuses with side benches in the back) terminal (Kapuas Indah), banks and moneychangers. Between here and Jl Pattimura there are numerous places to eat and shop. A good landmark is the Santo Yoseph church clock tower on Jl Pattimura.

MAPS

For regional maps of West Kalimantan try the bookshops on Jl Juanda:

Toko Buku Budaya (Jl Juanda 8-10) Upstairs.

Toko Juanda (Jl Juanda 32)

Information

EMBASSIES & CONSULATES

Immigration office (☎ 734516; Jl Sutoyo) Deals with visa issues.

Malaysian Consulate (☎ 732986, 736061; mwptk@telkom.net; Jl Sultan Syahrir 21, 🕑 8am-4pm Mon-Fri)

INTERNET ACCESS

Centrine Online (off Jl Nusa Indah III; 🕑 7.30am-10pm) Signposted in a short alley.

INTERNET RESOURCES

www.borneoaccess.com Under construction at the time of writing, this site promises to provide tourist information for Borneo, and West Borneo in particular.

MONEY

ATMs are abundant. Banking hours are 8am to 3pm Monday to Friday.

BII bank (Bank Internasional Indonesia; cnr Jl Tanjungpura & Jl Diponegoro)

BNI bank (Bank Negara Indonesia; Jl Tanjungpura)

PT Safari (Jl Tanjungpura 12) Moneychanger with good rates.

POST

Main post office (Jl Sultan Abdur Rahman 49; 🕑 7.30am-9.30pm Mon-Sat, 8am-2pm Sun) Poste restante.

TOURIST INFORMATION

City tourist office (☎ 732340; Jl Johar 1) Has some maps and information on Pontianak.

Kalimantan Barat tourist office (☎ 736172; fax 743104; Jl Sutoyo 17) Pa Iwan here can provide good advice on travel in West Kalimantan and he speaks English.

TRAVEL AGENCIES

Alex Afdhal (☎ 081 25768066; alexafdal@borneoaccess.com) Based at the Kartika Hotel on Jl Rahadi Usman, Alex speaks excellent English and is the general-secretary of the West Borneo Tour Guide Association; the most knowledgeable contact in town for trips throughout the province.

Ateng Tour (☎ 732683; fax 736620; ateng@pontianak.wasantara.id; Jl Gajah Mada 57) English-speaking staff. Offers expensive but worthwhile tours to places such as Gunung Palung, with a couple of weeks' notice.

PT. Mentari Tour (☎ 767196; mentari_tour_ptk@yahoo.com.sg; Jl Hijas 108) For flight bookings.

PT. Panorama Anugrah Pratama Tour & Travel (☎ 740545; tour_panorama@yahoo.com; Jl Diponegoro 149) For flight bookings.

Sights

RIVER LIFE

Pontianak's wealth stems from its river trade, and the best vantage point from which to view river activity is the water. The attractive **taman** (Jl Rahadi Usman), between the ferry crossing and the Kartika Hotel, is a good place to get your bearings. To see the city from the water, hire a sampan (35,000Rp per hour) or a speedboat (60,000Rp per hour) from the docks next to the ferry terminals or behind the Kapuas Indah Building.

For an interesting experience of riverfront life, take a walk from Mesjid Abdurrakhman (Abdurrakhman Mosque) along the wobbly wooden boardwalks past the stilt houses at washing time, either early or late in the day. The people of the *kampung dalam* (village) are friendly and curious. Take your camera. There are plenty of willing models, especially the kids.

Along Jl Kom Yos Sudarso on the riverfront is the *pinisi* (schooner) harbour, where the Bugis-style sailing schooners dock alongside the large houseboats, or *bandung*, peculiar to West Kalimantan.

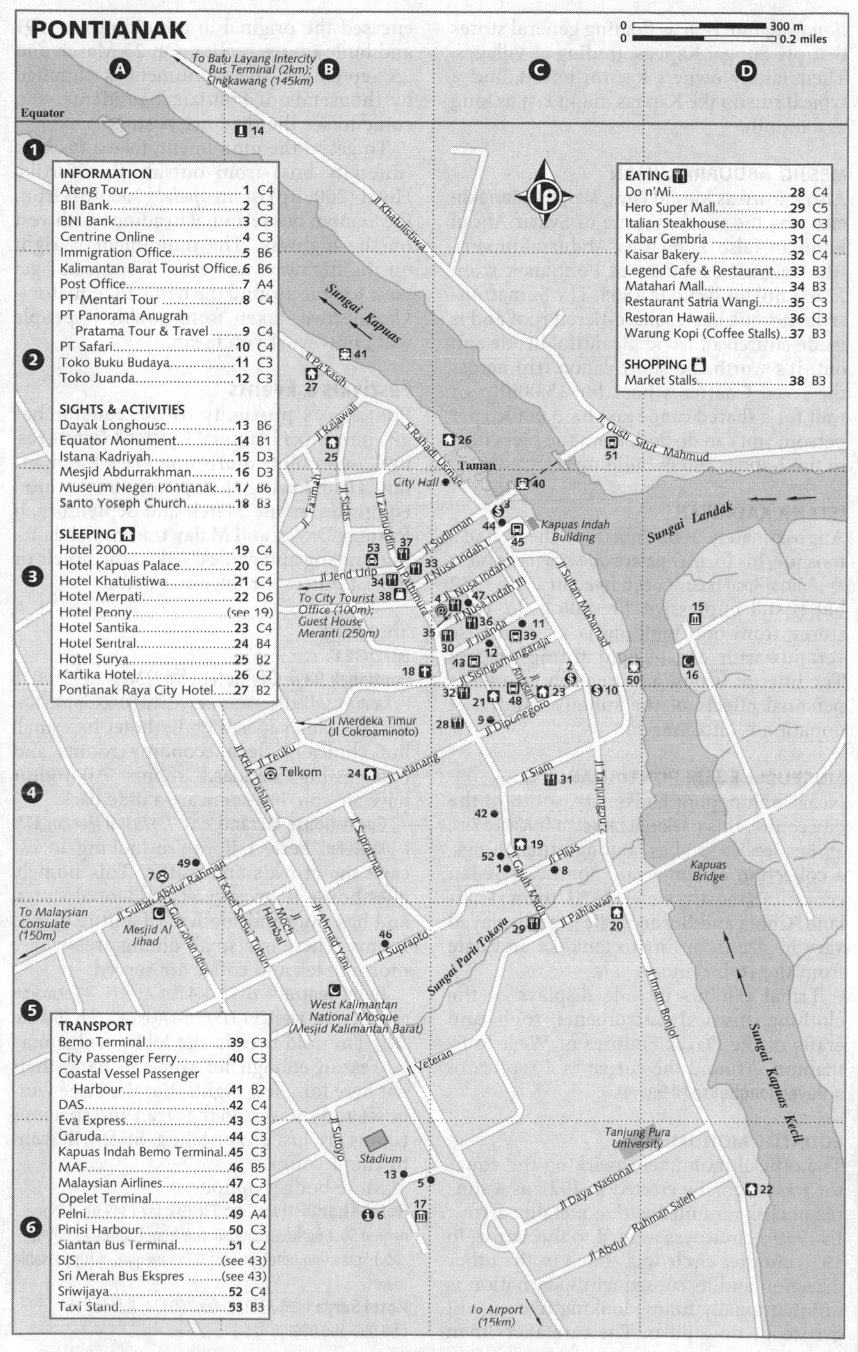
PONTIANAK
0 300 m
0 0.2 miles
A
B
C
D
1
2
3
4
5
6
Equator
To Batu Layang Intercity Bus Terminal (2km); Singkawang (145km)
INFORMATION
Ateng Tour....1 C4
BII Bank....2 C3
BNI Bank....3 C3
Centrine Online....4 C3
Immigration Office....5 B6
Kalimantan Barat Tourist Office....6 B6
Post Office....7 A4
PT Mentari Tour....8 C4
PT Panorama Anugrah Pratama Tour & Travel....9 C4
PT Safari....10 C4
Toko Buku Budaya....11 C3
Toko Juanda....12 C3
SIGHTS & ACTIVITIES
Dayak Longhouse....13 B6
Equator Monument....14 B1
Istana Kadriyah....15 D3
Mesjid Abdurrakhman....16 D3
Museum Negeri Pontianak....17 B6
Santo Yoseph Church....18 B3
SLEEPING
Hotel 2000....19 C4
Hotel Kapuas Palace....20 C5
Hotel Khatulistiwa....21 C4
Hotel Merpati....22 D6
Hotel Peony....(see 19)
Hotel Santika....23 C4
Hotel Sentral....24 B4
Hotel Surya....25 B2
Kartika Hotel....26 C2
Pontianak Raya City Hotel....27 B2
EATING
Do n'Mi....28 C4
Hero Super Mall....29 C5
Italian Steakhouse....30 C3
Kabar Gembria....31 C4
Kaisar Bakery....32 C4
Legend Cafe & Restaurant....33 B3
Matahari Mall....34 B3
Restaurant Satria Wangi....35 C3
Restoran Hawaii....36 C3
Warung Kopi (Coffee Stalls)....37 B3
SHOPPING
Market Stalls....38 B3
TRANSPORT
Bemo Terminal....39 C3
City Passenger Ferry....40 C3
Coastal Vessel Passenger Harbour....41 B2
DAS....42 C4
Eva Express....43 C3
Garuda....44 C3
Kapuas Indah Bemo Terminal....45 C3
MAF....46 B5
Malaysian Airlines....47 C3
Opelet Terminal....48 C4
Pelni....49 A4
Pinisi Harbour....50 C3
Siantan Bus Terminal....51 C2
SJS....(see 43)
Sri Merah Bus Ekspres....(see 43)
Sriwijaya....52 C4
Taxi Stand....53 B3
Jl Khatulistiwa
Sungai Kapuas
Jl Gusti Situt Mahmud
Sungai Landak
Jl Pak Kasih
Jl Kejawali
Jl Rahadi Usman
Taman
City Hall
Kapuas Indah Building
Jl Fatimah
Jl Sidas
Jl Zainuddin
Jl Sudirman
Jl Nusa Indah I
Jl Nusa Indah II
Jl Nusa Indah III
Jl Jend Urip
Jl Pattimura
To City Tourist Office (100m); Guest House Meranti (250m)
Jl Juanda
Jl Sisingamangaraja
Jl Antasari
Jl Sultan Muhamad
Jl Merdeka Timur (Jl Cokroaminoto)
Jl Diponegoro
Jl Teuku
Telkom
Jl Lelanang
Jl KHA Dahlan
Jl Siam
Jl Tanjungpura
Jl Hijas
Jl Gajah Mada
Kapuas Bridge
Jl Suprapman
To Malaysian Consulate (150m)
Jl Sultan Abdur Rahman
Jl Gusti Johan Idrus
Jl Kabel Satsui Tubun
Mesjid Al Jihad
Jl Moch Hambal
Jl Ahmad Yani
Jl Suprapto
Sungai Parit Tokaya
Jl Pahlawan
Jl Imam Bonjol
West Kalimantan National Mosque (Mesjid Kalimantan Barat)
Sungai Kapuas Kecil
Jl Veteran
Jl Sutoyo
Stadium
Tanjung Pura University
Jl Daya Nasional
Jl Abdul Rahman Saleh
To Airport (15km)
KALIMANTAN

Bandung function as floating general stores that ply Sungai Kapuas, trading at villages. Their family owners live on board, and a typical run up the Kapuas might last as long as a month.

MESJID ABDURRAKHMAN

Also known as Mesjid Jami, **Mesjid Abdurrakhman** was the royal mosque of Syarif Abdul Rahman (also known as Abdurrakhman), who reigned as Sultan of Pontianak from 1770 until his death in 1808. The Sumatran-style mosque has a square-tiered roof and is made entirely of wood. Beautiful inside and out, it's worth the short canoe trip across the river. Charter a boat for 15,000Rp or wait for a shared canoe taxi for 3,000Rp per person; you can do both from the piers next to the Kapuas Indah building.

ISTANA KADRIYAH

Approximately 100m north of the sultan's mosque, his former **palace** (admission by donation; 8.30am-4pm) hasn't been lived in since 1952 but is still impressive. Preceding the two-storey ironwood building is an immense veranda with ornate light fittings above. The interior is now a museum housing the personal effects of the sultan's family. A donation is encouraged.

MUSEUM NEGERI PONTIANAK

Near Tanjungpura University, south of the city centre, this national **museum** (Jl Ahmad Yani; 8am-3pm Tue-Sun) has, among other things, a collection of *tempayan:* Southeast Asian ceramics (mostly water jugs) from Thailand, China and Borneo. The jugs displayed vary in size from tiny to tanklike and date from the 16th century.

Tribal exhibits include displays of the clothing, musical instruments, tools and crafts of the Dayak cultures of West Kalimantan. Around the corner is a replica of a **Dayak longhouse** (Jl Sutoyo).

EQUATOR MONUMENT

The official monument marking the equator was originally erected in 1928 as a simple obelisk mounted with a metallic arrow. In 1930 a circle was welded to the arrow, in 1938 another circle was added in the other direction and its subsequent incarnation is unintentionally funny, looking like a giant gyroscope on a pillar. The caretakers then encased the original in a building in 1991 and built a huge replica. On 23 March and 23 September, the monument is engulfed by thousands of Pontianak residents who come to see the shadowless sun.

To get to the monument, take a *bis kota* (intercity bus) from outside the Kartika Hotel (2000Rp) or an *opelet* (3000Rp) from the Siantan bus terminal heading northwest on the highway. The monument is right on the highway, and even if you can't get your tongue around the name for equator – *khatulistiwa,* taken from Arabic – people will know what you mean.

Festivals & Events

Pontianak's proximity to the equator has given rise to a biannual **Equator & Culture Festival**, to promote tourism in West Kalimantan. Held during the spring and autumn equinoxes in late March and September, it features Dayak and Malay traditional dancing, singing and games. Ask at the hotels or tourist offices for the exact dates.

Sleeping

BUDGET

Pontianak Raya City Hotel (☎ 732496; fax 733781; Jl Pa'kasih 44; s/d incl breakfast from 70,000/80,000Rp plus 10% tax;) This super-friendly hotel has small but clinically clean economy rooms and twice-as-big 'standard' rooms. All rooms have air-con, but some are a little dark.

Guest House Meranti (☎ 731783; Jl Meranti 31A; r 100,000Rp) Perfect if you're looking to escape the crowds and traffic. This homely guesthouse is on a quiet residential street, and has snug and spotless (if a little bland) rooms. There is a small dining area where morning tea and coffee are served.

Hotel Sentral (☎ 737444; fax 734993; Jl Cokroaminoto 232; r incl breakfast 115,000-170,000Rp plus 10% tax;) The cold beer in the lobby fridge may be reason enough for some to hang their hat here for a few nights, but the large windows and showers in the clean and spacious rooms are just as appealing. Staff will want to adopt you.

More budget options:

Hotel Khatulistiwa (☎ 736793; fax 734930; Jl Diponegoro 56; r with/without air-con from 88,000/77,000Rp;) Sprawling hotel, just off Jl Diponegoro, with passable rooms.

Hotel Surya (☎ 734337; fax 760334; Jl Sidas 11A; r 80,000-100,000Rp;)

MIDRANGE & TOP END

Hotel 2000 (☎ 735061; fax 769039; Jl Gajah Mada 84; r 135,000-180,000Rp; ❄) Sandwiched between much pricier options, this compact, three-storey hotel has bare but cosy rooms, all with air-con, bath tubs and TVs. It's dirt-free, friendly and good value.

Hotel Merpati (☎ 745481; fax 762662; Jl Imam Bonjol 111; r 130,000-260,000Rp plus 10% tax; ❄) Another waterfront hotel but well south, this understated place has lovely rooms. The distance from the rest of Pontianak's action is something of a drawback, but easily worth the tranquil location and good night's sleep.

Kartika Hotel (☎ 734401; fax 738457; Jl Rahadi Usman; r incl breakfast 140,000-300,000Rp plus 21% tax; ❄) Overlooking the water, this concrete edifice has flagging but comfy rooms, all with loads of space, air-con, TV and private bathroom. The numerous facilities include a restaurant (mains 20,000Rp to 40,000Rp) serving breakfast, lunch and dinner, with floor-to-ceiling views of the Kapuas.

Hotel Peony (☎ 732878; hotel-peony@ptk.centrin.net.id; Jl Gajah Mada 86; r incl breakfast 220,000-450,000Rp; ❄) Modern, soft-lit rooms decorated in neutral tones and complete with luxury bathrooms put this small hotel a refreshing leap above much of the competition. Satellite TV and air-con are standard, and there's a bar, restaurant and smiling staff. As close to a boutique hotel as Kalimantan gets.

Hotel Kapuas Palace (☎ 736122; fax 734374; Jl Imam Bonjol; r from 350,000Rp plus 21% tax; ❄ 🏊) One of Pontianak's most posh hotels, the Kapuas Palace lavishes guests with plenty of creature comforts, including a fitness centre (perhaps not so comfortable), tennis court, bar and Western-style coffee shop, and a 100m pool. Rooms are *very* comfortable and the surrounding grounds are pleasant. Discounts are common year-round.

Hotel Santika (☎ 733777; www.santika.com; Jl Diponegoro 36; r incl breakfast 530,000-605,000Rp; ❄) Rivalling the Kapuas Palace in the quality stakes, Hotel Santika wins by a whisker with newer rooms and trendier décor. No expense has been spared to make guests as comfortable as possible, with little touches like 24-hour room service and a business centre.

Eating

Pontianak has excellent coffee and *warung kopi* (coffee shops) are central to its character, though they are generally frequented by male clientele. The best place to seek them out (the coffee shops, not the men!) is in the centre of town on the side streets between Jl Tanjungpura and Jl Pattimura.

our pick **Kabar Gembria** (Jl Siam 206; mains 10,000Rp; 🕑 breakfast & lunch) It doesn't look like much from the outside, but this small cafeteria-style diner serves a good spread of colourful and zesty vegetarian dishes, plus a few chicken and beef options for the carnivores. Dishes are diverse and inventive – think tempeh kebabs and roasted, curried eggplant. Diners help themselves from a long line of dishes and then pay for the contents of their plate. You can consume six variations plus a drink for under 10,000Rp, which makes it very popular with lunchtime office workers, although students and housewives fill the tables too. Die-hard health addicts will also appreciate the packaged goods on sale.

Legend Cafe & Restaurant (☎ 739260; Jl Pattimura 23; mains 15,000-35,000Rp; 🕑 breakfast, lunch & dinner) A smidge more global than your average Pontianak restaurant, Legend offers far-flung (for Kalimantan) delights including spaghetti bolognaise, and Singaporean laksa alongside Indonesian favourites. The restaurant's doors are left wide open, making it a breezy spot for a cold Bintang, and you may even dine to a lounge singer crooning Whitney Houston ballads.

Restaurant Satria Wangi (Jl Nusa Indah II; mains 15,000-35,000Rp; 🕑 lunch & dinner) This industrious restaurant serves Chinese-Indonesian fusion dishes of chicken, veggie and seafood, as well as excellent squid. The cool and calm interior is a perfect haven to escape the lunchtime heat, particularly when coupled with a fresh fruit juice. The homemade *sambal* (chilli sauce) may be the world's quickest solution to blocked sinuses.

Italian Steakhouse (☎ 736582; Jl Nusa Indah II 109; mains 15,000-40,000Rp; 🕑 lunch & dinner) Behind dim glass and polished doors, this Western-style restaurant cooks up hamburgers, pasta and steak, as well as Japanese-style hotpot at reasonable prices. Cool and elegant surrounds, and a good spot if you're sporting kids.

More options:

Restoran Hawaii (Jl Nusa Indah III 80; mains 15,000-25,000Rp; 🕑 lunch & dinner) Good Chinese food.

Matahari Mall (cnr Jl Jendral Urip & Jl Pattimura) The food court has a supermarket, and Western and Indonesian fast food.

Hero Super Mall (Jl Gajah Mada) For self-caterers.

Two bakeries serving cakes, bread and other goodies on Jl Pattimura are Do n'Mi and Kaisar Bakery.

Night warungs on Jl Sudirman and Jl Diponegoro dish up steaming plates of rice noodles, crab, prawns, fish and vegetables, and goat sate for under 10,000Rp.

Shopping

It's worth looking out for *kain songket* (material with silver or gold thread woven into it) from the town of Sambas. Various souvenir and material shops along Jl Nusa Indah I, II and III sell it, as do the market stalls lining Jl Pattimura. Prices are often cheaper than those at Sambas. Some of these shops also stock selections of old (and reproduction) trading beads, cheap bags of rough-cut gems and beautiful old Chinese and Dutch china and glassware.

Getting There & Away

AIR

Pontianak is well served by domestic airlines and the quickest way to get the cheapest fare is through a travel agent.

Batavia (☎ 734488; fax 736604; Jl Cokroaminoto 278), **Sriwijaya** (☎ 768777; Jl Gajah Mada), **Garuda** (☎ 734142; Jl Tanjungpura) and Adam Air have daily flights to Jakarta. **DAS** (☎ 731166; Jl Gajah Mada 67) and Kal-Star fly to Ketapang and DAS also flies to Putussibau. There are no direct flights to Balikpapan; you need to fly via Jakarta and at the time of writing Adam Air was the cheapest option.

Malaysian Airlines (☎ 737327; www.malaysiaairlines.com; Hotel Kini, Jl Nusa Indah III) flies to Kuching three times a week (US$100), with connections to Kuala Lumpur and Singapore.

MAF (☎ 733476; Jl Suprapto 50A) flies to various places in West Kalimantan; contact it for the most recent schedules. Fares for regular flights and charters are quite expensive. There's no sign on the office in Pontianak, but it's around the corner from the Malaysian Consulate.

Deraya connects Pontianak with Pangkalan Bun and Palangka Raya daily except Sunday.

BOAT

There are two **Pelni** (☎ 748124; fax 748131; www.pelni.co.id; Jl Sultan Abdur Rahman 12) ships sailing regularly between Pontianak and Java. The *Lawit* makes a weekly run to Jakarta (economy/cabin 170,000/600,000Rp, 36 hours) and also travels to Semarang for around the same price. Twice a month, the *Bukit Raya* goes from Pontianak to Surabaya (economy 170,000Rp, 40 hours).

The *Senopati Nusantara* is a private boat that sails to Semarang (economy 180,000Rp, 40 hours) about once a week. Another private boat, the *Kapuas Express,* sails to Jakarta (1st class/2nd class 400,000/300,000Rp, 20 hours) twice a week. Agents around town sell tickets for both of these. Daily jet boats go south along the coast to Ketapang (1st-class 135,000Rp, six to seven hours). All of these coastal boat services, including the Pelni ships, leave from the harbour area on Jl Pa'kasih north of the Kartika Hotel.

River boats up Sungai Kapuas have become a rarity as public buses have surpassed traditional river travel for speed and convenience. This is somewhat disheartening as the Western hustle and bustle leaves its mark; to truly get a taste of the local life in Kalimantan one must travel by its waterways. If time permits, seek out a *bandung* (cargo-cum-houseboat) and travel upriver with a family. The 800km journey from Pontianak to Putussibau could take anywhere from four days to a month. Families ply the river as a way of life, stopping to buy and sell along the way. Prices are completely negotiable, and for the right price there is always a more direct route. There is no organised way to arrange this and Bahasa Indonesia is essential for negotiations. Alex at the Kartika Hotel will be able to help you charter a boat.

BUS

Pontianak's intercity bus terminal is in Batu Layang, northwest of town. Take a ferry to Siantan (3000Rp) and a white *opelet* to Batu Layang (3000Rp), or take one of the *opelet* (3000Rp) that make the trip from the terminal on Jl Sisingamangaraja near the offices for buses to Kuching. From Batu Layang, buses go north along the coast to Singkawang (13,000Rp, 3½ hours) and Sambas (19,000Rp) and inland to Sanggau (22,000Rp) or Sintang (60,000Rp). Agents around the Kapuas Indah terminal also sell tickets for economy-class buses going to Putussibau (110,000Rp), but it's a gruelling 20-hour ride. All of these buses leave daily.

Virtually on top of each other on Jl Sisingamangaraja are numerous bus companies that run to/from Kuching on a daily basis (economy/executive 140,000/200,000Rp, 10 hours). Buses are relatively comfortable and generally depart Pontianak around 9pm, stopping at the border for several hours before it opens. Companies include:

Eva Express (☎/fax 743045; Jl Sisingamangaraja 143A)
SJS (☎ 734626; fax 744207; Jl Sisingamangaraja 155)
Sri Merah Bus Ekspres (☎ 733175; Jl Sisingamangaraja 137)

CAR & MOTORCYCLE

Renting a car and driver in Pontianak is the perfect way to see coastal West Kalimantan at your own pace. Travel agencies or your hotel can arrange a car for about 650,000Rp per day, plus petrol. You might get a better price by bargaining with the taxis that wait around the entrance to the Kapuas Indah *opelet* terminal, near the Garuda office. Motorcycles are an option for experienced riders only and cost around 100,000Rp a day.

Getting Around

TO/FROM THE AIRPORT

A counter at the airport sells tickets for taxis into town (60,000Rp). Alternatively, walk down the road in front of the terminal building to the main road into Pontianak, where you should be able to get an *opelet* for 3000Rp. It's a half-hour drive from the airport to the Kapuas Indah *opelet* terminal.

PUBLIC TRANSPORT

The main *opelet* terminals are in the middle of the city: the Kapuas Indah terminal

KALIMANTAN'S KILLING FIELDS

Mandor is a lush and sleepy settlement on the main road into West Kalimantan's interior. Diminutive in size, it's a place of overgrown jungle, subsistence farming and rice fields. But the serene demeanour is tainted by a tragic past; the town is also the burial ground of 21,037 West Kalimantan people who were murdered by Japanese troops during their three-year occupation of the area, a tragedy that has earned it the moniker of Kalimantan's Killing Fields.

When the Japanese navy arrived in Kalimantan in 1942, they entered a country readying itself for independence. Dutch authorities had returned home, leaving a leadership vacuum and an environment ripe for exploitation. The Japanese goal to incorporate Indonesia into its 'Great Asia' empire was no secret and they quickly established troops from Sambas to as far south as Ketapang. Treatment of the local population was shocking and although West Kalimantan's ethnic and cultural make-up was diverse, the desire to retain autonomy prompted a meeting of Dayak, Chinese, and Malay leaders as well as regional sultans. They journeyed from all over the province to meet secretly in Pontianak but were betrayed from within. With accurate information, the Japanese targeted influential leaders and brought them one by one to Mandor, where they were executed. To begin with, victims were restricted to sultans and their families, intellectuals and ethnic leaders, but before long the Japanese targeted anyone who posed a possible threat. This included most men over the age of 17 and any women who had the capacity to influence the local population.

The massacre spanned three years and went unrecognised until 1971, when a local man, Pak Sambad, presented the West Kalimantan governor with a report appealing for recognition. His efforts were successful, and by the end of the year sufficient funds were provided for a road to the site of the killings and a monument in the victims' honour.

Today Pak Sambad lives outside the gates of the memorial site and he is happy to talk about the area's history (in Bahasa Indonesia). The site itself contains 10 mass graves, one of which is a shrine to the slaughtered family of Sultan Abdul Hamid II. A carved stone storyboard also depicts the tragedy from the Japanese invasion to their departure. It is an exquisitely peaceful and reverent place, and the flourish of green and wildflowers are a fitting tribute to those who died. There's no official admission fee but Pak Sambad maintains the site and a donation of 20,000Rp or more is welcomed.

There are daily buses to Mandor (7,000Rp, two hours) from Pontianak's Batu Layang terminal. Buses heading to Ngabang will also stop at Mandor if you ask. The journey itself is beautiful, passing kilometres of rice fields, with forested hills and low-slung cloud hovering above.

near the waterfront, a terminal on Jl Sisingamangaraja and another one on Jl Antasari. There's a taxi stand outside Matahari Mall on Jl Jendral Urip, and becak (bicycle rickshaws) aplenty. A tour of the city and environs by taxi is 60,000Rp per hour, with a two-hour minimum.

The best and most fun way to get around is by public *opelet*. Rides cost 2000Rp to 3000Rp.

Motorised canoes depart from piers next to the Kapuas Indah building on the river. Crossing the river to the Istana Kadriyah and Siantan bus terminal is 2000Rp per person. A passenger ferry 100m downstream from the Kapuas Indah building takes passengers to the other side for 1000Rp.

SUNGAI KAPUAS

Pontianak is the launching point for trips along Indonesia's longest river. From the air, the many curves and oxbow lakes of the Kapuas basin make it a geographical spectacle; but at ground level, the primary attractions are the vessels and life on the river itself. As elsewhere in Kalimantan, take a slow boat to see and photograph the river activity.

Boats of all shapes and sizes journey the Kapuas, but these days it is mainly local traders. Even the road to Putussibau has improved to the point that buses have now replaced speedboats. Beyond Putussibau, however, or along tributaries, boats remain the dominant mode of moving people, though this usually means waiting around for enough people to fill a boat or chartering one yourself at considerable expense. In general, motorised canoes are less expensive (and slower) than speedboats, but still count on paying an average of 150,000Rp to 200,000Rp per hour for the journey.

Sintang

☎0565 / pop 25,000

Transmigrasi brought new farming families to the Sintang area in the early 1980s, and most now service the logging boom. During the rainy season, the streets of Sintang's waterfront are flooded. Don't be surprised if you have to wade knee-deep through the water or teeter on planks to get around.

The nearby **Gunung Kelam** monolith forms a 900m backdrop to Sintang and offers a challenging hike through the jungle. Butterflies, a waterfall *(air terjun)* and panoramic views of the surrounding countryside are to be enjoyed. Take a white *opelet* to Pasar Impres (2000Rp) and then a Kelam *opelet* to the base (6000Rp). A road circles the hill and you can be dropped off at the gaudy park entrance. The challenging path to the top has steel ladders on the more difficult rock faces.

Take a boat across the river (3000Rp) to visit the **Dara Janti Museum**. The former sultan's palace houses royal relics, Dayak artefacts, a gamelan orchestra and Portuguese cannons. Ask around to get the keeper to let you in and leave him a small donation. Boats congregate in front of the shops facing the river.

For excursions further afield seek the assistance of **Daniel Madu** (☎21815; Jl Sugiono 4), a local guide who speaks excellent English and local Dayak dialects. He specialises in trips down Sungai Pinoh to Central Kalimantan, across to the headwaters of the Mahakam in East Kalimantan and north to the lakes and rivers of Bentuang Karimun National Park. Contact him a month before your trip to arrange a trek.

SLEEPING & EATING

Sesean Hotel (☎21011; Jl Katamso 79; s/tw/d from 35,000/50,000/50,000Rp; ❄) On the waterfront, this is a friendly place with tiny singles, large twin rooms and doubles with air-con. The covered veranda facing the river is a great place to sit in the evening.

Sintang Permai (☎21053; Jl Supratman; r 55,000Rp) Run by the hard-working Mezeira Zain, this is a hotel in the style of a losmen (basic, often family-run, accommodation), and the newest and nicest spot to overnight in Sintang. It offers clean, no-nonsense but appealing fan-cooled rooms.

For eats, head to the waterfront area, where you'll find numerous warungs serving inexpensive *nasi* (rice), *ayam goreng* (fried chicken) and Padang food. Not far from Sintang Permai, **Bakso 33 Ripah** (☎21741; Jl Supratman 89; mains 7,000-15,000Rp; 🕑 lunch & dinner) serves good Indonesian food, and **Selera Kita** (mains 15,000-20,000Rp; 🕑 lunch & dinner) dishes up Chinese fare.

GETTING THERE & AWAY

At the time of writing there were no flights to Sintang, however DAS may recommence its schedule of flights here; check in Pontianak.

The road is partly sealed from Sintang to Putussibau, but heavy rains still create the odd mud hole that swallows up buses. The journey costs 65,000Rp and can take six to eight hours, depending on the weather. Buses to both Putussibau and Pontianak leave from the bus terminal in town. For buses south to Nanga Pinoh (5000Rp, one hour) head to Sungai Ukoi bus terminal, 10km southwest of Sintang (2000Rp by *opelet*).

River boats in Sintang stop by the dock in front of Jl Katamso. Speedboat charters are also available here.

Putussibau

☎0567 / pop 28,000

Putussibau is in a constant state of boom, owing to the increase of logging along the Indonesian-Malaysian border. On the Kapuas, a few kilometres upstream, are the traditional longhouse villages of **Melapi I** and **Sayut** (also known as Melapi II). Up Sungai Mendalam are **Semangkok I** and **Semangkok II**, which has a much older longhouse. You can charter a boat from the riverbank to go to the longhouses for about 150,000Rp per hour. A cheaper way to the Melapi longhouses is by public *opelet* for 7,500Rp, which leaves from the car park on the waterfront. The Melapi longhouses accept overnight guests, but payment for food is expected and it is customary to give gifts, such as pens, cigarettes (despite Western cries of horror) or bonbons. It's also polite to pay for any photographs you take.

Increasingly popular is the **Bentuang Karimun National Park** to the north, which offers good excursions to view indigenous flora and fauna in a pristine forest setting. There are also various adventure tours available, including rafting and trekking; ask the **Bentuang Karimun National Park office** (☎/fax 21773; Jl Komodor Yos Sudarso 130) for trip details and the best transport options.

SLEEPING & EATING

Losmen Harapan Kita (☎21157; Jl Pelita 3; s 25,000Rp, d 35,000-45,000Rp) Those on a tight budget are rudimentarily served at this simple losmen. The cheaper rooms have shared *mandis* (Indonesian-type bath).

MESS Pemda (☎21010; Jl Merdeka; r 90,000Rp; ❄) This ever-popular government hostel has clean rooms with air-con and a fairly raucous TV lounge.

Aman Sentosa (☎21691; Jl Diponegoro 14; r with/without mandi 100,000/50,000Rp; ❄) New and nice, Sentosa caters well to foreign travellers and is more likely to have availability than the cheaper options in town.

Tiara (Jl Melati 5; mains 5,000-12,000Rp; 🕑 lunch & dinner) Dishes up excellent sate, green vegetables, rice and mixed dishes.

Melati (Jl Diponegoro 7; mains 10,000-20,000Rp; 🕑 lunch & dinner) Has good food and beer; look for the prominent Guinness sign in front of the restaurant.

GETTING THERE & AWAY

DAS flies between Pontianak and Putussibau when there are sufficient passengers. A trip from Putussibau to the airport costs 35,000/30,000Rp by *opelet*/motorcycle.

From time to time MAF operates flights between Putussibau and Tanjung Lokan, although there's no guarantee. Make inquiries at the airport.

The bus to Pontianak from Putussibau is 110,000Rp and takes 20 hours.

To continue from Putussibau upriver to the village of Tanjung Lokan, it's necessary to charter a boat; ask at your hotel for local operators. The two-day trip costs around 3,000,000Rp.

Putussibau to Long Apari

The hardy, intrepid and wealthy (expenses are considerable) can begin a river and jungle trek eastwards from Putussibau, across the West-East Kalimantan border through the Muller Range to Long Apari at the headwaters of the Mahakam. It's dense and steamy going and only for highly experienced hikers, but there is prolific bird life and you may spot the odd snake or honey bear.

The first step is to find a knowledgeable guide, particularly for the trek from Tanjung Lokan to Long Apari. See the boxed text on p619 for information on guide etiquette and what to bring. Guide fees cost from 500,000Rp per day. See opposite for information on Sintang-based guide **Daniel Madu** (☎0565 21815; Jl Sugiono 4, Sintang). In Putussibau try **Jahari** (☎0567-21534). Alternatively the *bupati* (district head) in both towns can assist. Would-be guides will also find you; they will certainly be willing to take your cash, but may have little knowledge of the track and local languages. The village of **Tanjung Lokan** also has guides. *Do not* attempt the trip beyond Tanjung Lokan alone, as trails are not well marked.

In Putussibau charter a motorised canoe (1,800,000Rp) to make the one-day trip to Bungan. From there you must charter a smaller canoe for about the same amount for another day's travel to Tanjung Lokan. Fuel is *very* expensive.

From Tanjung Lokan eastwards, the rugged jungle trekking begins and you'll need six to seven days to reach Long Apari. A guide is essential as there are no villages along the way. This is a true adventure and your journey will take you into territory literally known as the 'Heart of Borneo', where the rainforest is pristine and thick in patches and the threat of the chainsaw is yet to arrive. From Long Apari, you have to charter a boat down the first part of the Mahakam. Regular public boat services begin at Long Bagun.

Mesra Tours (☎ 738787, 732772; fax 741017; www.mesra.com/tour), in Samarinda, offers tours of this trek going in the opposite direction.

SINGKAWANG

☎ 0562 / pop 104,000

This predominantly Hakka Chinese town boomed in the early 18th century, when mines from Sambas to Pontianak accounted for about one-seventh of the world gold extraction. Singkawang is also the site of Chinese ceramic workshops, making reproductions of the Ming dynasty water jars that, due to the Chinese influence on the island, featured prominently in the history of Kalimantan.

Apart from the ceramic workshops, Singkawang's main attractions are the nearby beaches of Pasir Panjang and Tanjung Gundul (see right).

The hotel precinct is at the northern end of Jl Diponegoro near the Chinese temple. **Hotel Khatulistiwa Plaza I** (☎ 631697; Jl Selamat Karman 17; r 40,000-80,000Rp; ❄) has a range of rooms in its three-storey shell, the nicest of which are on the lower floors. Air-con is an additional 10,000Rp. More upmarket is **Putra Kalbar III** (☎ 631551; Jl Diponegoro 27; r 95,000-120,000Rp; ❄), which has lovely midrange rooms, and the classy **Mahkota Singkawang Hotel** (☎ 631308; Jl Diponegoro 1; r 200,000-560,000Rp plus 21% tax; ❄ 🏊), which has four-star quality and a disco.

Chinese food is an obvious Singkawang speciality and one of the best places to sample it is **Rumah Makan Tio Ciu Selera** (Jl Diponegoro 106; mains 10,000-16,000Rp; 🕑 lunch & dinner). The seafood variations are fresh and unique and most are prepared in the savoury Chiu Chao (southern Chinese traditional) style. Cheap servings of noodles and *bakso* (meatball soup) can be had at **Bakso 68** (Jl Diponegoro; 🕑 lunch & dinner) and **Warung Dangau** (Jl Johan Godang; 🕑 lunch & dinner). A meal at either costs 8,000Rp to 14,000Rp.

Getting There & Away

There are frequent buses from Pontianak's Batu Layang terminal to Singkawang (13,000Rp, 3½ hours). From Singkawang to Gunung Poteng (see below), catch a Bengkayang bus east for the 12km trip (5000Rp). Let the driver know where you're going and he'll let you off at the foot of the hill.

Beyond Singkawang there are buses to Sintang (65,000Rp, nine hours) and Kijangs north to Sambas (13,000Rp, three hours), or south to Mandor (11,000Rp, three hours). The Singkawang bus terminal is in the southern part of town.

AROUND SINGKAWANG

The mountains surrounding Singkawang are lush and inviting. The slopes of **Gunung Poteng**, just 12km east of town, are a great place to search for the largest flower in the world, the rafflesia. Each flower only blooms once a year, but there is no season so you can see them year-round. Take a Kijang to Poteng and make the two-hour hike to the top.

On the highway just south of Singkawang is a series of **ceramic factories** that make huge Chinese jars with colourful motifs. The Semanggat Baru site, about 100m off the main road, 5km from Singkawang, has a long, ancient kiln and ceramics at various stages of manufacture. Prices are quite reasonable, ranging from 250,000Rp to over 1,000,000Rp, and if you like what you see, the factory can ship your purchase to Jakarta. Another kiln, the Sinar Terang, is 400m down the road.

Pasir Panjang & Tanjung Gundul

The jungle gives way to palm trees, white sand and crystalline water at two of the loveliest beaches in Kalimantan, both of which are easily reached from Singkawang.

About 12km south, **Pasir Panjang** is the better known of the two and teems with families on weekends and public holidays.

KALIMANTAN'S TOP JUNGLE ADVENTURES

Kalimantan has some spectacular jungle journeys for the intrepid traveller. The following require resilience, respect, Bahasa Indonesia and a keen sense of adventure; the reward is glimpses of ancient rainforests that may not be around for much longer.

Putussibau to Long Apari (p617)

The meek need not front up for this trek and river combo, which encompasses dense and magnificent jungle with all the primal trimmings. It involves two days of river travel and six or seven of trekking. Basic Bahasa Indonesia is essential in order to hire a guide.

Loksado & Around (p644)

This combo tour is easy to organise from Banjarmasin, but also simple enough to do on your own with some Bahasa Indonesia language skills. Bus from Banjarmasin to Loksado, take a few days to trek around Tanuhi and then return to the big smoke onboard a bamboo raft. The best fun you can have on floating foliage.

The Apokayan Highlands (p659)

A week's adventure with a flight into the interior and a five-day jungle trek through the Dayak villages of Long Uro, Lidung Payan and Long Sungai Barang. The highlands themselves are visually splendid and this trek requires a good level of fitness.

Long Bawan & Kayan Mentarang National Park (p660)

From Kalimantan's remote northern pocket you can travel by foot and motorised canoe into the 'Heart of Borneo', which encompasses some of the last pristine rainforest on this spectacular island. Forays into Kayan National Park reveal stunning flora and the chance to see clouded leopards.

What to Take?

They don't call it the jungle for nothing; Kalimantan's interior gets steamy and wet. Downpours are heavy and the humidity can keep your clothes somewhere between soggy and sopping for a frustratingly long time. A waterproof jacket is essential and layers of clothing are also recommended. For camping take a strong, waterproof material for shelter. Proper footwear is of course mandatory, not just for the terrain, but also to thwart entrepreneurial leeches and indignant fire ants. Basic medicines and iodine for drinking water are wise. Most importantly you want to pack this all up in as light a load as possible, in all likelihood you'll be carting your own gear.

Anything Else I Should Know?

All these treks require previous hiking experience and most of them also require a guide. Guide fees vary depending on the length and remoteness of the trek, but you should bank on paying 200,000Rp to 500,000Rp per day. On top of that you'll need to pay for food (allow around 50,000Rp per day) and transport costs.

Palapa Beach Hotel (☎ 633367; fax 633402; r 70,000-140,000Rp, cottages 160,000Rp; ❄) has clean twin rooms and small cottages with minibar fridges. The hotel manager, Ari Gu, can help organise overnight snorkelling tours to a tiny, deserted island called Pulau Randayan. Getting there can be as much as 800,000Rp and accommodation on the island is 100,000Rp for simple rooms. Snorkelling gear can also be organised.

From Singkawang take any *opelet* heading south on the highway from the Singkawang bus terminal (3000Rp, 20 minutes). Get off at the Taman Pasir Panjang (Long Beach Park) gate. There is a 2500Rp entrance fee to enter the park. It's a 500m walk to the beach. A motorcycle taxi from Singkawang is about 10,000Rp.

The **Kura Kura Resort** (☎ 085 822181173; www.kurakurabeach.com; Charlie@kurakurabeach.com; camping per tent 20,000Rp, r incl meals per person 100,000Rp, villa 600,000Rp) is much more isolated, about 3km from the village of Tanjung Gundul. The beach and surrounding hills here are unspoilt, a state that Charlie (the owner, who originally hails from Scotland) and his wife Siska are doing their best to maintain. The unobtrusive resort has no electricity or bright lights due to the interruption it would cause to turtles laying their eggs on the beach, and littering is against the rules. But the accommodation, which includes camping (tents supplied), homestay rooms and a villa sleeping up to seven people, is very comfortable. Meals are available with notice, as are a bevy of activities, including snorkelling, trekking, sailing and fishing.

To reach Kura Kura, call or email ahead to let Charlie and Siska know you're coming. They can meet you at Tanjung Gundul, which is 23km south of Singkawang and 5,000Rp by *opelet*.

SAMBAS

☎ 0562 / pop 56,000

Archaeological finds indicate Sambas had connections with the Sriwijaya kingdom and perhaps India in the 6th century, and became an important port city in its own right from the late 13th century. The Dutch established a warehouse for diamond trading in Sambas between 1608 and 1610, but showed little interest in colonising the area.

Palace ruins hint at the city's former prosperity, but Sambas is now better known for its *kain songket* (cloth with silver or gold thread woven through it). Check the prices in Pontianak before taking on the weavers or vendors at Sambas market. Prices might still be cheaper down south.

The market is at the end of the main street that runs north from the bus terminal towards the river. You can hire a canoe from the riverbank for about 10,000Rp and paddle the shortish distance on Sungai Sambas to visit **Keraton Sambas**, the former palace, now a museum, built by Sultan Mulia Ibrahim Tsjafioeddin in 1933. Both the architecture and the view of Sambas from the river are enchanting. It is only accessible by river.

Hotel Sejatra (☎ 91182; Jl Gusti Hamzah; r 50,000Rp; ❄), about 1km west of the market on the road from Singkawang, has spotless rooms. A good place to eat is **Restaurant Malayu** (Jl Pangaran); it serves the local speciality *bubur pedas* (a spicy vegetable rice porridge).

Buses to Sambas (13,000Rp, three hours) leave regularly from the Singkawang bus terminal.

GUNUNG PALUNG NATIONAL PARK

Home to several thousand wild orang-utans, Gunung Palung National Park has managed to cling onto pockets of untouched forest, despite the ugly intrusion of illegal logging. Long known as an area for research, the park is now being promoted for tourism as well. Facilities are simple and tourists are welcome to join the researchers at the Cabang Panti research site to view the orang-utans in small groups. A network of trails covers about 15 sq km of the park, traversing some of Kalimantan's most pristine tracts of swamp, and lowland dipterocarp, hill and mountain forest. Aside from the orang-utans, there is an amazing variety of wildlife, including gibbons, proboscis monkeys and hornbills.

Unless you visit Gunung Palung on an organised tour, patience, money and excellent Bahasa Indonesia are essential.

Orientation & Information

To get to Gunung Palung National Park the first order of business is to obtain a permit from the office of the **Unit Taman Nasional Gunung Palung** (UTN; Map p621; ☎/fax 0534-32720; Jl DI Panjaitan; 🕑 8am-2pm Mon-Fri, 8am-11am Sat) in Ketapang. It is best to fax the UTN office before arrival, so the staff can arrange a guide and begin processing a permit for the dates you plan to stay in the park. You will need to bring a copy of your passport to the office to process the permit and coordinate plans for departure with your guide. The fee is 1000Rp per person per day, with a 10,000Rp one-time processing fee.

Once you have the permit, stock up on food and provisions in Ketapang (get a list from the UTN office) and catch the bus (30km) north to Sukadana (40,000Rp, 1½ hours). The Cabang Panti research site can be reached by foot or boat. The latter is not recommended as accessibility depends on the river level – you may be required to drag the boat at low water. Additional time and money are also necessary to make arrangements for boat hire; UTN can help with the logistics.

It is mandatory to have a UTN guide with you on any ventures into the park. The people at the UTN office can help arrange one. The rate is 100,000Rp per day, plus your guide's food and transport costs. UTN guides don't necessarily know the terrain as well as local guides in and around Sukadana, so if you hire an additional guide for trekking you'll need to pay for their expenses (from 50,000Rp per day) too. In Tanjung Gunung ask for Nurual Hasan, who doesn't speak English, but knows the area well. The bus from Ketapang to Sukadana can drop you off at Tanjung Gunung, which is about 15km before Sukadana.

For more information on the research at Cabang Panti, contact Betsy Hill, field director at the **Gunung Palung Orang-utan Conservation Program** (GPOCP; Map p621; ☎ /fax 31150; Kotak Pos 144, Ketapang 78801, Kalimantan Barat).

KETAPANG

☎ **0534 / pop 30,000**

Tucked away on the far southwestern coast of Kalimantan, Ketapang has stayed somewhat isolated, even by Kalimantan standards. With no major roadways connecting the region, bar a hellish bus journey, the only way to get here is by boat or plane. Both options are quite feasible and relatively inexpensive. Most travellers only go to Ketapang to begin trips to the Gunung Palung National Park.

Information

Facilities in Ketapang include the following:

BNI bank (Bank Negara Indonesia; Jl Merdeka) Has an ATM.

Delta Pawan Family Travel (☎ 35206; Jl Diponegoro 20) Can book Pelni and other ferry tickets.

Post office (Jl Dr Sutomo)

Sleeping

Hotel Anda (☎ 32575; Jl R Suprapto; r 30,000-75,000Rp plus 10% tax;) The cheapest rooms at the two-storey Hotel Anda are basic shells with fans, TVs and shared *mandis*, but the 'VIP' rooms are significantly more pleasant with air-con and private bathrooms. It's in a good spot with plenty of eating options nearby.

Losmen Patra (☎ 32742; Jl Diponegoro 63; r 55,000Rp) A great budget option, this simple losmen has tidy, fan-cooled rooms with teeny but immaculate *mandis*. The rooms

can get a little steamy if it's a hot night, but the free drinking water, tea and coffee and friendly staff compensate.

Hotel Mess Graha (☎ 081 25746712; Jl Basuki Rachmad 15; r 60,000-85,000Rp; ❄) Clean rooms, reasonable prices and a central location attract local tourists and visiting businessmen by the truckload to Hotel Mess Graha. The downstairs TV lounge and lobby seem to be a meeting place for half of Ketapang.

Hotel Perdana (☎ 33333; fax 32740; Jl Merdeka 112; r 90,000-350,000Rp plus 10% tax; ❄) Down near the water, this is the most upmarket hotel in town. Rooms are carpeted and clean and the pricier options have showers. The hotel's best feature is its array of facilities – there's a restaurant downstairs and boat tickets can be arranged at the front desk. January to March attracts a 20% discount.

Eating & Drinking

Restaurant 99 (Jl R Suprapto; mains 15,000Rp; ⏰ lunch & dinner) Seafood is the speciality at this cheerful restaurant, and fans should sample the local prawns. Fresh fish is also sizzled up, as are the Indonesian and Chinese chicken and veggie dishes.

Pandan Wangi (Jl Basuki Rachmad) To cool off after a few days of hiking in the park, head to this juice bar serving tasty *es campur* (ice cubes with frozen fruit and syrup; 6000Rp), ice cream and other fresh local fruit blends. Highly recommended.

More eats:

Lambendang Restaurant (Jl R Suprapto 22; mains 10,000-20,000Rp; ⏰ lunch & dinner) Traditional Indonesian fare.

Kaisar Bakery (Jl R Suprapto; snacks 2,000-6,000Rp; ⏰ breakfast, lunch & dinner) Sweet and savoury baked goodies.

Almost side by side on Jl Diponegoro, Warung Kita and Warung Mentari both serve Padang-style lunch and dinner for around 10,000Rp a meal.

Getting There & Around

AIR

DAS, Kal-Star and Deraya have offices at the airport and fly to Pontianak and Pangkalan Bun.

BOAT

From the harbour north along Jl Gajah Mada, twice-daily jet boats head to Pontianak (1st class/economy 135,000/90,000Rp, six to eight hours depending on conditions). The upgrade to 1st class is recommended to get a reclining seat, and to avoid the crowds below, particularly when the seas get a bit choppy. Express ferries are also available to Semarang (150,000Rp, 10 hours) on Java. Inquire at Hotel Perdana or Delta Pawan Family Travel for more information.

BUS

The Ketapang bus terminal is on Jl Ahmad Yani, next to the Pasar Baru. Northbound buses go to Sukadana (17,000Rp, 1½ hours) and *ojeks* (motorcycles that take passengers) cost 50,000Rp. It is feasible to go overland to Pontianak, but the roads are so poor that it makes for an arduous, if not incredibly time-consuming, journey. For an adventure, it is also possible to go overland to Pangkalan Bun by combining bus, boat, minibus and a bit of trekking. This option is for those with loads of time, and the cost will depend on your bargaining abilities.

TO/FROM THE AIRPORT

A taxi to/from the airport costs 40,000Rp, or it's 15,000Rp by *ojek*. *Ojeks* can be hired at the park across from Hotel Perdana and charge 8,000Rp around town.

CENTRAL KALIMANTAN

Central Kalimantan province (Kalimantan Tengah, or Kal-Teng) was formed in 1957, after a Dayak revolt calling for greater autonomy from centuries of domination by Banjarmasin. It remains the only province with a predominantly Dayak population, mostly Ngaju, Ot Danum and Ma'anyan peoples. It's also the least populated province in Kalimantan, with just under two million people.

Central Kalimantan's northern reaches are mountainous, while the rest of the province is low, flat and poorly drained. Timber extraction has stripped much of the province of its forest cover, yet the interior offers some of the most fascinating journeys in Kalimantan. Climbing north, the rivers Kahayan, Lamandau and Balantikan consist of river rapids, jungle and Dayak villages, where longhouses, some several centuries old, remain intact. The province is also a magnet

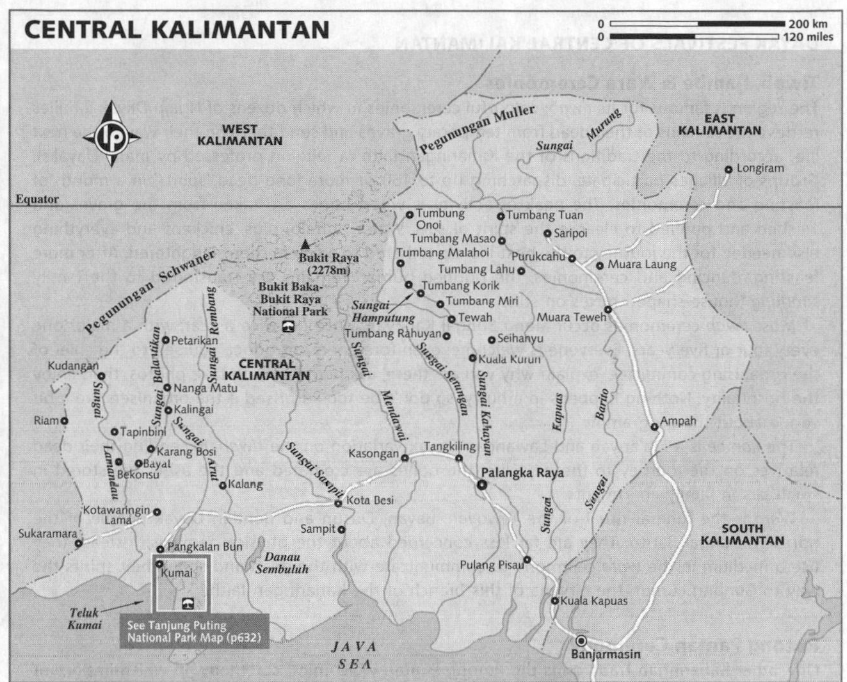

for wildlife lovers, owing to the celebrated Tanjung Puting National Park, home to Kalimantan's most accessible orang-utans.

PALANGKA RAYA

☎ 0536 / pop 186,500

Palangka Raya (Great and Holy Place) was built on the site of the village of Pahandut. During the Soekarno period it was considered for development as the capital city of Kalimantan. Today the city is a dusty swathe of streets with a seemingly endless supply of mechanics and shops selling merchandise in bulk. This makes it the perfect stopover en route to elsewhere (particularly if you have an ailing vehicle). If you find yourself here for a couple of days, veer off the main roads into the residential backstreets where life ambles at a warm and relaxed pace.

Information

There are several warnets about 2km down Jl Yos Sudarso with internet access for around 5000Rp per hour. Several banks on Jl Ahmad Yani have ATMs which accept international cards.

Bali Indah Photo (Jl Ahmad Yani 77) Sometimes has maps of Central Kalimantan.

Bank Mandiri (Jl Ahmad Yani; 🕑 7.30am-2.30pm Mon-Fri) The best place to change money.

Dinas Pariwisata regional tourist office (Km 5, Jl Cilik Riwut; 🕑 7am-2pm Mon-Fri) On the A taxi route; has a few brochures and may be able to suggest guides for travel into the interior.

Main post office (Jl Imam Bonjol; 🕑 7.30am-2.15pm) On the D taxi route.

Palangka Raya Guide Association – Yusuf Kawaru (☎ 32223341; Dandang Tingang Hotel, Jl Yos Sudarso 13) Can put you in contact with guides for trips into the interior.

PT Mulio Angkasa Raya (☎ 3221031; mulyo_plk@telkom.net; Jl Ahmad Yani 55) They can book flights and tours.

Sights

On the southern side of Jl Panjaitan, **Mandala Wisata** (Jl Panjaitan; admission free) is a model of a traditional longhouse that acts as an arts centre and venue for traditional dances and other performances when troupes are in town. For wandering around, try the lively **pasar malam** (night market; cnr Jl Jawa & Jl Halmahera).

DAYAK FESTIVALS OF CENTRAL KALIMANTAN

Tiwah, Ijambe & Wara Ceremonies

The region is famous for its *tiwah:* colourful ceremonies in which dozens of Ngaju Dayak families retrieve the remains of their dead from temporary graves and send them on their way to the next life, according to the traditions of the Kaharingan faith (a religion professed by many Dayaks). Groups of villages participate, dispatching up to 150 or more long-dead 'spirits' in a month of feasting and ceremonies. The peak of activity is when bones are taken from the graves and washed and purified to cleanse the spirit of sins. Water buffalo, pigs, chickens and everything else needed for the journey to the next life are tethered to a totem then slaughtered. After more feasting, dancing and ceremonies, the purified human remains are transferred to the family *sandung* (house-shaped boxes on stilts).

Most *tiwah* ceremonies occur along Sungai Kahayan, once or twice a year, with a major one every four or five years. Everyone is welcome, even foreigners. Introduce yourself to the chief of the organising committee, explain why you are there, ask permission to take photos, then enjoy the hospitality. Nothing happens in a hurry, so don't be too surprised if the organisers are a bit vague about the programme.

The *ijambe* is a Ma'anyan and Lawangan Dayak variation on the *tiwah*. In sending their dead relatives on the journey to the next life, the bones are cremated and the ashes are stored in small jars in family apartments.

Wara is the funeral ritual of the Tewoyan, Bayan, Dusun and Bentian Dayak people of the northern Sungai Barito. They are far less concerned about the physical remains; instead, they use a medium in the *wara* ceremony to communicate with the dead and show their spirits the way to Gunung Lumut, the nirvana of this branch of the Kaharingan faith.

Potong Pantan Ceremony

One other Kaharingan tradition is the Potong Pantan welcoming ceremony, in which important guests are met by the head of the village, offered a machete and invited to cut through *pantan* – lengths of wood that block the entrance to the village – to purge themselves of bad spirits. As they cut, guests introduce themselves and explain the purpose of their visit. *Tapung tawar* is an extension of the Potong Pantan, in which guests have their faces dusted with rice flour and their heads sprinkled with water to protect them from bad spirits and illness.

Museum Balanga (Km 2.5, Jl Cilik Riwut; donations welcome) opens when you knock on the door and provides a good glimpse into the indigenous cultures of the area. The main building has displays of Ngaju ceremonies, performed to celebrate the cycle of birth, marriage and death. The A taxi route goes past the museum.

The **Kalaweit Care Centre** (☎/fax 3226388; www.kalaweit.org; Jl Pinus 14) is a research and rehabilitation centre for ex-captive gibbons on their way into the wild. Gibbons face much the same problems as their more popular cousins the orang-utans and are just another reason these pockets of forests need to be protected. Tourists can call ahead to arrange a visit to the office to learn more about the work, but the gibbons are inaccessible as they are highly susceptible to disease. Kalaweit also takes on volunteers for one- to seven-week projects. Check its website for costs and details.

Sleeping

BUDGET

Hotel Melati Serasi (☎ 3223682; Jl Dr Murjani 54; s 22,000-44,000, d 33,000-60,500Rp; ❄) This quaint and friendly hotel is in a quiet spot and has a range of rooms. For next to nix, you can sleep in a basic shell with shared *mandis* or blow the budget on a comfy air-con room with private *mandi* and TV.

Hotel Virgo (☎/fax 3221265; Jl Ahmad Yani 13; r with/without air-con from 66,000/38,500Rp plus 21% tax; ❄) Pick of the budget bunch, Hotel Virgo has simple fan-cooled rooms with shared *mandis* and breezy 'VIP' rooms that rival the midrange options in town. It's spotless and exceedingly popular with local tourists.

Hotel Dian Wisata (☎ 3221241; fax 3223952; Jl Ahmad Yani 68; r 55,000-90,000Rp;) Edging closer to the hub, this inexpensive hotel has a pleasant interior with an atrium-like centre. Economy rooms (with shared *mandis*) are boxy and dank, but the standard and 'VIP' rooms are spacious, if a little ragged, and have air-con.

Two clean and friendly options in a quiet pocket of Jl Nias with similar standards are **Hotel Mahkota** (☎ 3221672; Jl Nias; s 33,000-66,000Rp, d 44,000-77,000Rp plus 21% tax;) and **Hotel Mina** (☎ 3222182; Jl Nias 17; s 30,000-55,000Rp, d 40,000-100,000Rp plus 21% tax;).

MIDRANGE & TOP END

Adidas Hotel (☎ 3221770; fax 3225328; Jl Ahmad Yani 90; r from 144,000Rp;) This friendly midsized hotel has slightly dank but sizeable 'deluxe' rooms with capacious beds. But the cheaper, standard rooms are bright and cheerful and much better value. There's also a small restaurant attached.

Hotel Lampang (☎ 3220003; hl@palangkaraya.wasantara.net.id; Jl Irian 2; s/d incl breakfast from 150,000/180,000Rp plus 21% tax;) Things look a little weary at the Lampang these days but it still fits the midrange bill – if for no other feature than the price. Some of the staff speak English.

Hotel Sakura (☎ 3221680; Jl Ahmad Yani 87; r incl breakfast 160,000-240,000Rp plus 21% tax;) The Sakura's best feature is its sizeable restaurant and central atrium. The rooms don't have quite the same flair. Nevertheless they contain the requisite TV, air-con, and shower head in the bathroom.

Dandang Tingang (☎ 3221805; dandang_tingang@yahoo.com; Jl Yos Sudarso 13; r 126,000-342,000Rp, ste 600,000Rp plus 21% tax;) On the outskirts of the main strip and laid across expansive green grounds, these are the nicest rooms in Palangka Raya. The wee, rustic (and comfortable enough) standard rooms don't quite fit the bill, but those in the middle of the five-tiered price bracket are well-kitted out. There's also a good restaurant, bar and disco.

Eating

Fabulous barbecued fish and freshwater crayfish are *the* dishes to tuck into in Palangka Raya.

KALIMANTAN

THE GREAT FIRES

In 1997 Kalimantan was ablaze, ravaged by fires that continued to burn for up to two years. Many were a result of the slash-and-burn agriculture practised by some of Kalimantan's indigenous peoples. Despite a 1997 presidential ban, this method is the fastest and cheapest way to clear land. Plantation companies also use fire to prepare land for planting. The ferocity of the fires was greatly exacerbated by the unusually dry conditions caused by El Niño. The catastrophe had a devastating impact on the environment, wildlife, human health and the region's economy.

With large areas of forest and peatland destroyed, wildlife and endangered species faced greater risk. The incidence of human respiratory disease rose dramatically in affected areas. Rain became dangerously acidic, causing damage to freshwater and marine ecosystems. Furthermore, biomass burning is a major source of gases in the atmosphere that contribute to global warming.

The Association of South East Asian Neighbours (Asean), along with other world nations have requested that Indonesia intensify efforts against slash-and-burn practices and encourage zero burning by the plantation industry. Although pockets of freshly burned land can be seen with relative ease, the type of large-scale destruction that fuelled the 1997–98 fires is now a thing of the past.

Toko Kue Lirissa (Jl Ahmad Yani; snacks 2000-5000Rp; ⌚ breakfast & lunch) Hotel Dian Wisata's next door neighbour is an excellent bakery selling a diversity of sweet and savoury roti, as well as fresh steamed dumplings and slices of cake.

Simpang Raya (☎ Jl Ahmad Yani; mains 10,000-18,000Rp; ⌚ lunch & dinner) Without a neighbour in sight, this restaurant serves decent Padang food, specialising in chicken and fish. It's all displayed in colourful marinades in the front window, and the large interior is bright, cool and clean.

Rumah Makan Melati (Jl Madura; mains 12,000-18,000Rp; ⌚ lunch & dinner) This welcoming corner restaurant has lovely 180-degree open doorways, street views and fat wooden bench seating, all of which endow it with a cosmopolitan air (well, Kalimantan-style anyway). Just about everything is barbecued, including spectacular *udang* (prawns) and a good spread of fish.

The lively *pasar malam* around Jl Halmahera and Jl Jawa has plenty of cheap noodle and rice stalls, plus a colourful range of seasonal fruit. For morning coffee, there are a few warungs on Jl Nias towards Rambang Pier.

More eating:

Supermarket (Jl Ahmad Yani) For self-caterers.
Depot Rizky (Jl Ahmad Yani; mains 6,000-10,000Rp; ⌚ lunch & dinner Mon-Sat) Simple and cheap.

Shopping

Central Kalimantan is best known for its skilful rattan weaving.

Souvenir shops (along Jl Madura) West of Jl Dharmasugondo, these have some nice baskets and mats from 70,000Rp up to 250,000Rp.

Pasar malam (cnr Jl Jawa & Jl Halmahera) Has tubular rattan or bamboo fish weirs for sale, just like the ones in the museum.

Citra Raya Plaza and the Barata Plaza on Jl Ahmad Yani both sell anything else you might need.

Getting There & Away

AIR

Between them Deraya, Kal-Star and DAS have daily flights to Pangkalan Bun, Ketapang, and Pontianak. DAS also flies to Muara Teweh three times a week. The best place to book tickets is **PT Mulio Angkasa Raya** (☎ 3221031; mulyo_plk@telkom.net; Jl Ahmad Yani 55).

BOAT

Speedboats head upstream along Sungai Kahayan to Tewah (300,000Rp, five hours, daily) from Garung Mas Pier.

BUS & KIJANG

Morning and evening buses depart for Pangkalan Bun (95,000Rp, 14 hours) and Banjarmasin (35,000, six hours) from the bus terminal, about 5km out of town on the D taxi route. There are also Kijang services to Banjarmasin, with eight people crammed into a 4WD for about 80,000Rp each; the Kijangs also take six hours. There has been an ongoing attempt to build a raised highway above the swamplands between Palangka Raya and Banjarmasin. The saga continues.

Getting Around

It takes a good 15 minutes to get to the airport. Taxis cost 60,000Rp.

Efficient taxi buses around town – marked A (heads northwest), B, or D (heads southwest) – cost 2500Rp. There's a taxi terminal on the corner of Jl Ahmad Yani and Jl Dharmasugondo in the Citra Raya Plaza.

Ojek hire is about 20,000Rp per hour. Becak drivers congregate around Rambang Pier and along Jl Halmahera at the *pasar malam*.

SEBANGAU NATIONAL PARK

South of Palangka Raya, this recent addition to Kalimantan's national parks is a peat swamp forest and home to an incredible diversity of **wildlife**, including more than 100 species of birds, 35 species of mammals and 6,900 orang-utans; one of the highest wild populations in Borneo. WWF-Indonesia has conducted a tireless campaign to establish protection for the area due to indications that the impact of illegal logging and palm oil plantations may have reduced the orang-utan population from as much as 13,000 since 1996.

Presently the park is inaccessible to tourists as it's maintained as a research reserve; however, there are ecotourism plans afoot. The best source of information is **WWF-Indonesia** (www.wwf.or.id).

SUNGAI KAHAYAN

It's tough going to explore Central Kalimantan's interior; it's so far off the tourist track the concept doesn't even exist. In its northern reaches is some of the least spoilt Dayak culture on the island. Isolation has limited the effects of modernity in the villages above Tewah and many don't see daily road or river traffic. Sadly much of the area has been logged, but pockets of forest still remain. If you go it alone, excellent Bahasa Indonesia is essential. Even if you do have language skills it's worthwhile seeking a guide through the **Palangka Raya Guide Association** (☎ 0536-32223341; Dandang Tingang Hotel, Jl Yos Sudarso 13, Palangka Raya). Be prepared for improvised, expensive and sometimes uncomfortable travel.

Below are some routes you could take, but they are suggestions only. This area is an opportunity for intrepid travellers to do their own thing and getting from A to B or X is going to be a similarly adventurous exercise whatever route you create. Some price estimates are given below but they fluctuate wildly.

One route is to take a speedboat from Palangka Raya to **Tewah** (300,000Rp), and then charter a *klotok* (motorised river canoe) to reach the Dayak villages north. First head to **Tumbang Miri** on Sungai Hamputung, via river rapids, and the longhouse settlement of **Tumbang Korik** (300,000Rp or more, six hours). It's possible to stay overnight in Tumbang Korik with a family and then trek to the Dayak village of **Tumbang Malahoi** (spending a night in the jungle). There are no official guides in Tumbang Korik but you may be able to recruit a local. From here charter a *klotok* to the historic village of **Tumbang Onoi** (200,000Rp, four hours). During the 1600s, the Dutch intervened here to stem fighting between rival tribes and the frequent incidence of headhunting. The peace was commemorated by a stone in the village, engraved with the names of all the village chiefs at the time. Tumbang Onoi also has a traditional longhouse still in use. You can spend the night in Tumbang Onoi, again with a family, and then head back downstream to Tewah by *klotok* (600,000Rp, 10 hours). Count on at least five or six days to do this trip.

Another, three-day option involves travelling by *ojek* from Tewah to Tumbang Miri, and then southwest to **Tumbang Rahuyan** or the gold-mining area near **Sungai Antai** (three hours). Then continue downriver by boat to **Tumbang Baringei** (three hours), on to **Tumbang Malahoi** (the site of a longhouse) by *ojek* and then by *klotok* or speedboat south to **Tangkiling** and on to Palangka Raya.

For a four- to five-day trip, take a speedboat from Palangka Raya as far as **Kuala Kurun** (200,000Rp, three hours) and travel by *ojek* north to **Seihanyu**. From here take a *klotok* to the upper reaches of the Kapuas to **Sungai Mendaun** and on to **Jarak Masuparia**. Hike from there to **Masuparia**, a gold-rush field in a natural depression in the jungle. Continue by *ojek* to **Tumbang Masao** then by *klotok* downstream to **Purukcahu** and **Muara Teweh** or continue from Tumbang Masao to Sungai Barito headwaters, past a series of rapids north of **Tumbang Tuan**. This territory, north of Muara Teweh has pockets untouched by logging, but in future years it is hard to say what will be left due to the voracity of the illegal logging operations. These last options are the most difficult and expensive, but well worth considering if you have the cash and the stamina.

MUARA TEWEH AREA

☎ 0519 / pop 37,500

Deep in the heart of logging country, Muara Teweh is the last river-boat stop on Sungai Barito, unless the water is high enough for boats to reach **Purukcahu**. From Purukcahu you can go further north by boat and hire Dayak guides to trek into the northeastern mountains and forest. Near Gunung Pacungapung, on the border of Central and East Kalimantan, a cement pillar marks the geographical centre of Borneo.

The main settlement of Muara Teweh is on the north bank of the Barito. The road parallel to the river, Jl Panglima Batur, is where you'll find most accommodation.

Muksin Hussein (☎ 3222342) is a teacher who speaks English and can help arrange guides. In Purukcahu, ask for Mahrani, a Siang Dayak who also speaks English and is a good person to ask about trips further inland.

In Muara Teweh you can rest your bones at **Barito Hotel** (☎ 3221080; Jl Panglima Batur 43; s/d/tr from 25,000/40,000/45,000Rp) or the very comfortable **Wisma Pacifik** (☎ 321231; Jl Panglima Batur 87; r from 120,000Rp; ❄), which also has a good restaurant.

There are a couple of warungs along Jl Panglima Batur west of Barito Hotel, one or two up the hill on Jl Surapati and also further along near the market.

In Purukcahu there are a couple of **losmen** (r around 20,000Rp), or you can also stay in the longhouse at Konut, about 10km from Purukcahu. Make a donation for your hosts' efforts.

Getting There & Away

AIR

DAS connects Muara Teweh with Palangka Raya three times a week. The airport is 5km north of town and costs 10,000/35,000Rp by *ojek*/Kijang or *opelet*.

BOAT

Cargo ships still ply Sungai Barito and it is possible to negotiate a ride. Another option is to charter a speedboat. Ask a local guide whom to contact.

BUS

The uncomfortable trip to Banjarmasin (55,000Rp, 12 hours) is served by daily (and nightly) buses. The bus terminal is 3km west of town across the bridge.

Opelet go to Purukcahu (50,000Rp, three hours) from the terminal on Jl Surapati.

MUARA TEWEH TO SAMARINDA

From Muara Teweh you can trek overland to **Long Iram** in East Kalimantan and then catch a boat down Sungai Mahakam to Samarinda. A number of different routes are possible, depending on whether you want to trek through the jungle or just follow logging roads – a depressing way to see the jungle. Logging roads head east from Muara Teweh or Muara Laung upriver. The trek takes up to two weeks and can be done on your own, or you can also try hitching rides if they come by. Be sure to take sun protection and iodine to purify your water. There are more interesting trails upriver from Purukcahu. Hire a guide along the way or bring one from Palangka Raya, Banjarmasin, Muara Teweh or Purukcahu.

PANGKALAN BUN

☎ 0532 / pop 39,500

If Kalimantan ran a 'Tidy Towns' contest Pangkalan Bun would leave the opposition in its dust, which it would have to import because it has none of its own. Largely used as a stopover en route to Tanjung Puting National Park, this is a surprisingly pleasant spot to hang the hat for a couple of days. Wide, ordered roads lined with processions of greenery, attractive residences and warm and friendly locals create a convivial and appealing atmosphere. There's also a neat waterfront market punctuated by gemshops and tidy warungs.

Information

Banks around town have ATMs.

BNI bank (Bank Negara Indonesia; Jl P Antasari) Will exchange US dollars and euro travellers cheques and cash at pitiful rates.

Borneo Holidays (☎ 29673; borneoholidays@planet-save.com; Jl HM Rafi'i Kompleks Beringin Rindang Gg J Ambu 25) Personalised guided tours to Tanjung Puting and Sungai Lamandau.

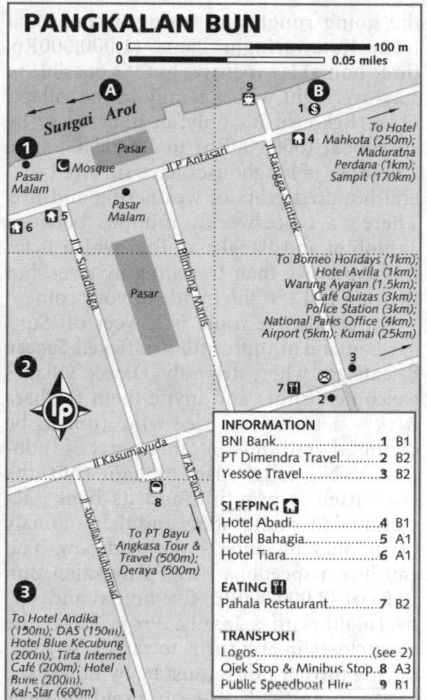

PT Bayu Angkasa Tour and Travel (☎ 22374; www.bayuangkasa.co.id; Jl Hasanudin 11/75) Tours to Tanjung Puting and elsewhere in Central Kalimantan.

PT Dimendra Travel (☎ 21170; Jl Kasumayuda) Air and boat tickets plus information about river trips and guides.

Tirta Internet Café (Jl Domba 23; per hr 9000Rp)

Yessoe Travel (☎ 21212) Books bus and air tickets and can suggest guides.

Sleeping

Hotel Bone (☎ 21213; Jl Domba 21; room r 35,000-84,000Rp) A decent budget hotel with fan-cooled rooms, Hotel Bone has clean and frugal economy rooms with shared *mandis*. The pricier 'VIP' rooms are more comfortable but not as good value.

Hotel Tiara (☎ 22717; fax 22721; Jl P Antasari 16; r from 45,000Rp; ❄) Big thumbs up! Hotel Tiara has ever-smiling staff and sparkling deluxe rooms with good beds and clinically clean *mandis*. The economy rooms are less fancy but still the best value in town. Breakfast is included, and tea, coffee and drinking water are free.

Hotel Andika (☎ 21218; fax 21923; Jl Hasanudin 20A; s/tw from 40,000/50,000Rp, d 70,000-85,000Rp; ❄) Modest but lovely rooms with miniporches sit on either side of a central atrium at this reliable hotel. Rates include breakfast and there is also a restaurant. Perfect for those on middle-of-the-road budgets.

Hotel Mahkota (☎ 21172; Jl P Antasari; r 138,000-270,000Rp; ❄) Hot water, air-con and plenty of room to stretch the toes are standards in every Mahkota room. Tariffs increase with the quality of the furnishings, and the 'Executive' is quite huge. Everything's spotless, but there is little direct sunlight.

Hotel Avilla (☎ 27710; fax 27711; Jl Pangeran Diponegoro 81; r incl breakfast 200,000-250,000Rp; ❄) Fresh and fine, Hotel Avilla has stylish and bright rooms, with glorious bathrooms, satellite TV and sinkable lounge chairs. Breakfast is served in the upstairs dining area before wide patio doors.

Hotel Blue Kecubung (☎ 21211; fax 21513; Jl Domba 1; s 186,500-285,500Rp, d 225,500-324,500Rp; ❄) The chandeliered-splendour of the shimmering lobby doesn't make it all the way to the rooms, and Blue Kecubung's a tad overpriced. The beds, however, are firm and the sizeable rooms all have air-con and satellite TV. There's also a restaurant, bar and fitness centre.

Also available:

Hotel Bahagia (☎ 21226; Jl P Antasari 100; r 50,000-170,000Rp; ❄) Central and spotless.

Hotel Abadi (☎ 21021; fax 21021; Jl P Antasari 150; r incl breakfast 65,000-125,000Rp; ❄) Decent value.

Eating & Drinking

Warung Ayayan (Jl Kasumayuda; mains 5,000-10,000Rp; 🕑 lunch & dinner) This wide and airy warung has a local fan club owing to excellent chicken and goat sate. The menu is mighty tasty and mighty cheap, and it's a great spot to make Pangkalan Bun pals.

Pahala Restaurant (Jl Kasumayuda; mains 5,000-12,000Rp; 🕑 lunch & dinner) A step up from the warung, this clean and breezy restaurant serves good iced drinks, *tempe* (fermented soya-bean cake), *nasi goreng* (fried rice) and the usual Indonesian fare.

Café Quizas (Jl Iskandar 63) If you're craving coffee, this spot with a beautiful garden setting in a traditional Indonesian building serves delicious blended hot and cold drinks. There is also a restaurant and disco playing music nightly.

You'll find barbecued chicken aplenty at the warungs around the *pasar* (market) by the waterfront, and small supermarkets on Jl P Antasari.

Getting There & Away

AIR

DAS (Jl Hasanudin), near Hotel Andika, **Kal-Star** (☎ 22824; Jl Hasanuddin 2) and **Deraya** (☎ 21224; Jl Antasari 55) connect Pangkalan Bun to Palangka Raya, Ketapang, Pontianak via Ketapang, Semarang and Sampit, and Banjarmasin and Surabaya, both via Sampit.

BOAT

Public speedboats leave from the dock near Losmen Selecta for Kotawaringin Lama (50,000Rp, two hours) up Sungai Lamandau. From there, 4WDs go to Sukamara (50,000Rp), from where you can take a speedboat to Manismata and further on up to Riam in West Kalimantan. You can continue up to Ketapang from Riam.

BUS

Numerous companies operate buses to Palangka Raya (95,000Rp, 14 hours), including **Yessoe Travel** and **PT Dimendra Travel** (☎ 21170; Jl Kasumayuda), **Maduratna Perdana** (☎ 22129; Jl P Antasari 17) and **Logos** (Jl Kasumayuda). Some also operate buses to Sampit (50,000Rp, six hours). Buses leave from their respective offices.

Getting Around

A taxi to/from the airport costs 45,000Rp. *Angkot* (minibus) to Kumai (7,500Rp) and *ojek* leave from near the roundabout on the hill leading up from Jl Kasumayuda.

SUNGAI LAMANDAU & SUNGAI BALANTIKAN

Snaking its way due north, Sungai Lamandau and its tributaries support a number of Dayak villages where longhouses and tradition are still intact. A guide is highly recommended and transport is irregular and expensive, but the route is ideal for experience-hungry travellers. Two hours north of Pangkalan Bun by speedboat (50,000Rp), the village of **Kotawaringin Lama** has a longhouse and a frail wooden palace, which was once occupied by the region's sultan. Continuing north, a peppering of small villages along the river leads to **Bekonsu**, also home to a number of longhouses, as well as traditional mausoleums. There are a series of rapids just south of Bekonsu that may make the going rough and hiring a speedboat from Kotawaringin Lama (1,000,000Rp, three hours) is expensive but it's possible to stay overnight with a family in the village. From Bekonsu it's only an hour or so by speedboat (500,000Rp) to **Tapinbini**, where a number of longhouses have survived several hundred years of weathering and fire. There's a twice-weekly minibus between Tapinbini and Pangkalan Bun which is far less expensive than travelling by river, but the ride will test the mettle of your spine.

An alternative route is to veer off Sungai Lamandau onto little-trafficked **Sungau Balantikan**, where friendly Dayak villages welcome visitors and invite them to share *tuak* – a traditional rice wine (not to be confused with *tuak* in other parts of Indonesia). No longhouses remain, but the river itself is beautiful and its banks accommodate orang-utans and that anomaly of Indonesian fauna – the wild cow. You can hire a speedboat from Pangkalan Bun to **Bayat** (2,000,000Rp, five hours) and stay overnight with a family. From Bayat the river closes in and turns to rapids, so journeying further north must be by motorised canoe. A particularly feisty rapid at **Nanga Matu** often forces people to haul their vessels along land for a kilometre or two. In two days you can explore the river all the way north to **Petarikan**, staying in villages along the way. Chartering a motorised canoe from Bayat will cost around 1,500,000Rp.

KUMAI

☎ 0532 / pop 23,000

Kumai is a small port town with freighters, and Bugis and Madura schooners tied up to the docks. It's the gateway for trips along Sungai Kumai to Tanjung Puting, and for boat travel further afield.

The main street, Jl HM Idris, runs parallel to the river, and most of the hotels are near the intersection with Jl Gerliya. At the southern end of Jl HM Idris is the Pelni office, shops, wartel and market. There are no money-changing facilities.

Anggun Jaya Travel Agency (☎ 61168; Jl Gerilya 383), near the Hotel Garuda can book airline, bus and Pelni tickets.

Sleeping

There's usually no problem getting a room in Kumai, *except* the night before a Pelni boat comes into town, when the town swells to bursting.

Losmen Aloha (☎ 61238; Jl HM Idris 465; s/d 25,000/35,000Rp) Conveniently placed near the wharf, this losmen has clean and basic fan-cooled rooms with shared *mandis*. It's at the intersection with Jl Gerliya.

Losmen Permata Hijau (☎ 61325; r from 50,000Rp;) This small and polished losmen is a sheer delight for budget travellers, with immaculate rooms, new beds, TVs and air-con. Even the shared *mandis* in the cheaper rooms glisten.

Hotel Garuda (☎ 61145; Jl Gerliya 377; r 110,000Rp;) A step up from the dosshouses, Hotel Garuda caters well to the comfort-needy, with clean rooms and friendly staff.

Eating

Aloha Rumah Makan (Jl HM Idris 465; mains 8,000-14,000Rp; lunch & dinner) Beneath Losmen Aloha, this corner restaurant has a pub aesthetic and serves filling and tasty Indonesian dishes. The fish is usually quite fresh, given that it's caught only a stone's throw away.

There are plenty of warungs serving noodles, sate, *bakso* etc, on Jl HM Idris towards the market. In the evening, vendors come out to sell *martabak* (pancakes), which are delicious.

Getting There & Away

Kumai is about 25 minutes away from Pangkalan Bun by *angkot* (7,500Rp); they depart from the hill on Jl Kasumayuda, just past the roundabout. Taxis from Pangkalan Bun airport to Kumai are 70,000Rp, including a stop to photocopy your passport and visa, a stop at the Pangkalan Bun police station for park registration and a check at the Tanjung Punting National Park and Conservation Office (PHKA) to enter the reserve. The trip by *ojek* costs 40,000Rp.

BOAT

Pelni ships connect Kumai with Semarang (150,000Rp) and Surabaya (170,000Rp) three times a week. The trip takes a full day and night to/from either city. The **Pelni office** (Jl HM Idris) is opposite the market, a short walk south from Losmen Aloha.

Private boats also run these routes on a daily basis – try the *Dharma Kencana I* and *II,* which can be booked at Hotel Garuda (150,000Rp to 300,000Rp). They take about the same time as the Pelni ships.

There are also private services offering a faster service to Java from Kumai. Contact **Anggun Jaya Travel Agency** (☎ 61168; Jl Gerilya 383) or **PT Dimendra Travel** (☎ 0532-21170; Jl Kasumayuda) in Pangkalan Bun.

TANJUNG PUTING NATIONAL PARK

Tanjung Puting National Park is one of Indonesia's highlights, and not just because of the enigmatic primates living in its maniacal forest. Coursing the river at a leisurely pace aboard a *klotok* or in a motorised canoe is as much a part of the experience. Walls of pandanus fringe the water's edge, beyond which proboscis monkeys and

ON THE FRONT LINE FOR KALIMANTAN'S FORESTS

Things have been looking up for the forests of Kalimantan in recent years, well at least in theory that is. The federal government's (relatively) progressive ideas about conservation have decelerated the fervour of the corporate chainsaw. But Kalimantan's vast interior is its own worst enemy. Providing the perfect cover, it enables illegal logging to run rampant. Local operations exploit government disorganisation to make quick cash. Corruption and payoffs are common as government officials often fold under their own economic pressures.

In the fight to save the few remaining areas of primary jungle, Kalimantan's national parks have become the only benchmark against which to measure what remains of the forest. Fortunately some tangible progress is also being made. Greater cooperation between some of the parks (most notably Tanjung Puting in Central Kalimantan) and surrounding villages has resulted in environmentally sustainable practices and a more equitable dispersal of the tourism dollar. A greater slice of the pie of course means that people don't necessarily need to fell trees to feed their families. The consequence is that protection of the forests in national parks is more than a warm and fuzzy concept. For this plan to work on a grand scale, however, there still needs to be much stricter enforcement of the laws protecting all parks, and this is an ideal yet to be realised.

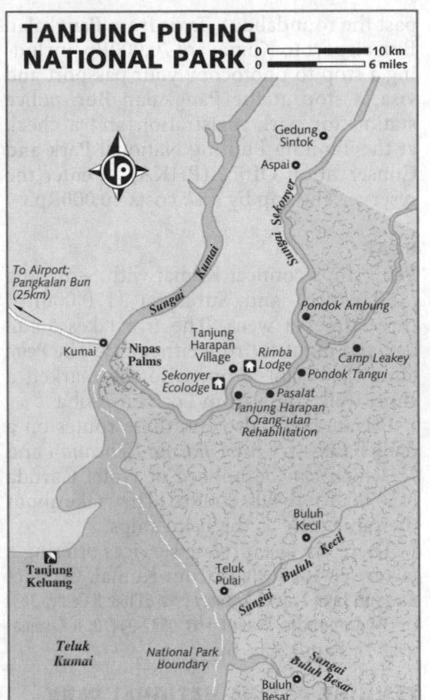

impudent macaques leap across the forest canopy. Joining them in less ostentatious fashion are sun bears, wild boars, clouded leopards, pythons, gibbons, porcupines, Sambar deer, crocodiles, the Giant Bornean butterfly and a wealth of bird life.

Small and unsullied tributaries branch off Sungai Kumai, their tannin-tinted water the colour of rich, black tea. In low season you can chug for hours without seeing another soul. Best of all the park maintains a tight grip on the impact of tourism – only a handful of trails provide access past the research centres, leaving the jungle untamed and teeming.

One of the park's seldom talked-up treats is the nightly spectacle of **fireflies**. From dusk till the wee hours they dance in the pandanus palms, lighting them up like Christmas trees.

Most visitors head straight to the research camps to get a glimpse of an orang-utan in the wild. **Camp Leakey**, the primary site, was established in 1971 when Canadian researcher Dr Biruté Galdikas – known locally as '*ibu* (mother) professor' – began taking in rescued orang-utans with the assistance of the Leakey Foundation, the US philanthropic foundation.

The orang-utans in Borneo and Sumatra are the only great apes outside Africa, and Dr Galdikas probably knows more about them than anyone. In the early days of her research, she would spend weeks tracking wild orang-utans and was the first to document, for instance, that the birth interval for orang-utans is about once in every eight years, making them vulnerable to extinction. Originally these camps were established to study and reintroduce orphaned or rescued orang-utans into the wild. Under the supervision of researchers, juvenile orang-utans learn to live in the forest, spending longer and longer away from the camps. However, being accustomed to human contact, as adults they never fully kick old habits and usually return for an afternoon feeding. In more recent years it has been discovered that these great apes can never be completely wild again. What the camp does provide is a sanctuary for these primates, and a unique place to study their behaviour. The knowledge acquired from Camp Leakey's research continues to be important to the survival of the orang-utan.

Today there are a number of research camps where you can witness orang-utans socialise and eat at specific feeding times. The bananas and condensed milk sessions are designed to supplement the diets of ex-captives, but inquisitive wild orang-utans sometimes watch from a distance. Feeding at **Tanjung Harapan** is at 3pm, at **Pondok Tangui** it's at 9am and at **Camp Leakey** it's at 2pm. Reaching feeding stations from each camp involves a short walk through jungle, which can be a slippery exercise if there has been recent rain. Boots or enclosed shoes are recommended as is a vat of insect repellent. There's also an excellent information centre at Camp Leakey and some of the knowledgeable rangers speak English. A fourth camp has been established at **Pondok Ambung**, but it's restricted to research and inaccessible to visitors.

Pasalat is a reforestation camp where saplings of sandalwood, hardwood and other trees are being reintroduced to the area to combat the devastating effects of logging, mining and the 1997–98 fires. It's worthwhile stopping in to see the impressive work the local rangers do, and to appreciate their dedication to the conservation of the park.

For additional information about the orang-utan research in Tanjung Puting contact the **Orangutan Foundation International** (OFI; ☎ +1-323-938 6046; www.orang-utan.org; 4201 Wilshire Blvd, Suite 407, Los Angeles, CA, USA 90010). The OFI also publishes *A Guidebook to Tanjung Puting National Park*, written by Drs Biruté Galdikas and Gary Shapiro.

The dry season in the park is May to September, and reduced rainfall will make your journey more enjoyable. On the other hand the river is higher during the wet season and this enables better access to smaller tributaries, albeit with more rain.

Orientation & Information

A trip into the park begins at the Pangkalan Bun police station, where you must register. Make sure you have photocopies of your passport and visa.

Then head to the **PHKA office** (national parks office; Map p629; ☎/fax 23832; Km 1.5 Jl HM Rafi'I; 7am-2pm Mon-Thu, 7am-11am Fri, 7am-1pm Sat) on the way into Pangkalan Bun from the airport. Registration costs 70,000Rp per person per day and 5000Rp a day for a *klotok* 'parking' fee or 15,000Rp for a speedboat. You must provide a copy of your police letter from Pangkalan Bun and a photocopy of your passport. The park office will give you two letters: one for you and one for the ranger at Camp Leakey.

Lastly head to Kumai, where you can arrange transportation upriver.

For more information contact the Director of Tanjung Puting National Park, at the PHKA office. For updates concerning what is being done in the local conservation effort, contact the director Pak Bayu at the **Friends of the National Park Foundation** in Bali (FNPF; ☎ 081 1398025; www.fnpf.org) or Wisnu at **Conservation International** (CI; ☎ 24858).

Guides

At the time of writing park management planned to make guides mandatory for all tourists. In Kumai, freelance guides will track you down and it can get a bit annoying after a while – patience is an asset. Guide fees are 150,000Rp to 200,000Rp per day. **Borneo Holidays** (☎ 0532-29673; borneoholidays@planet-save.com; Jl HM Rafi'i Kompleks Beringin Rindang Gg J Ambu 25, Pangkalan Bun) is run by Harry Purwanto and his guide Danson – who spent three years working inside the camp as a researcher. Danson's knowledge of the park and its wildlife is profound. They can arrange tours that cater to individual plans and budgets. **Suyono Majit**, who works on the *Satria* boat can also recommend guides. Another option is to hire a PHKA guide when you register. Some speak English and their knowledge of the park is an obvious asset.

Rules & Conduct

The park has certain rules of conduct that are imperative for the health of the ecosystems and their inhabitants. Unfortunately some visitors disregard them for the sake of a photo. Always go with a ranger or guide on the trails in the park. The orang utans are ex-captives and unafraid of humans. No matter what the boat crew or rangers do, don't succumb to the temptation to feed the orang-utans or initiate contact with them. The younger ones especially are *very* hard to resist picking up and cuddling, but they are highly susceptible to human diseases and you may be inflicting a great deal of harm.

The orang-utans look cute, but they are strong animals who will grab your camera, bag or anything else that is hanging off your body.

Another word of warning is do not swim in the river anywhere in the park. Especially at Camp Leakey; it may be tempting to take a dip to cool off, but there are plenty of crocodiles lurking in the murky waters. Several years ago a British volunteer worker was killed when taking a swim just off the Tanjung Puting dock. Stay on the dock during your *mandi*.

Klotok Hire

By far the best way to see the park is by hiring a *klotok* for a few days (or more). It serves as your transportation, accommodation and restaurant. At night the crew moor the boat well away from settlements, allowing passengers to enjoy the sunsets, fireflies and wildlife in peace. Sleep on mattresses on the upper or lower deck, wake to the haunting cries of gibbons at dawn and watch for the telltale splash of big crocodiles.

You can wash from the dock at the river pool at Camp Leakey, but avoid contact with the contaminated waters of Sungai Sekonyer. Mercury used in the gold mining upstream at Aspai is dumped directly into the river.

Plan for at least three days on the river. That way you can work your way slowly up the river to the various stations. Allow time to explore the forest reserves around the rehabilitation camps and plan your river movements for dawn or dusk, when various primates come down to the river's edge.

Numerous *klotok* operate from Kumai. They're identified by their boat names: *Harapan Mina III* and *Rosalia* (operated by Pak Muliadi and Pak Housni), *Cahaya Purnama* (operated by Pak Emeng), *Everedy* (operated by Pak Ari), *Garuda I* and *Garuda II* (both operated by the Bakso family), *Satria I* and *Satria II* (operated by Surono Majit), *Omega* (operated by Anung Emen), *Britania* (operated by Jen Joan) and *Spirit of the Forest* (operated by Herry Rostaman). At the time of writing, the standard price was 400,000Rp to 450,000Rp a day. Food is generally an additional 50,000Rp per day. Decide beforehand with the captain whether you are paying for their food as well, which is usually the case. If there's a cook on board that's also an additional 50,000Rp per day.

You can book a *klotok* beforehand with tour agencies in Pangkalan Bun (see p628) and Banjarmasin (p636). Boats are in high demand in July and August and around school and public holidays, but outside these times hiring a *klotok* on your own once you're in Kumai is a simple matter – operators will generally find you. The boats vary in standard and size so head to the docks to shop around. The operators of your accommodation in Kumai will also be able to assist.

Sleeping

our pick **Rimba Lodge** (☎ bookings 0532-6707083; www.rimbalodge.com; r $US45-85; ❄) Tucked behind a wall of forest, this comely ecolodge is Kalimantan's answer to the African safari camp. Devoid of glossy lighting and mod cons, it is constructed out of timber, in tune with the surrounding environment. A network of boardwalks connect clusters of rooms, and rich foliage provides privacy and entertainment; at night sleepy macaques compete with birds for space. Rooms are split into three categories – fan-cooled Ruby and Sapphire rooms and air-con Emerald rooms. The latter two also have hot water and immense beds. All rooms have mosquito nets and private bathrooms. The restaurant (mains 20,000Rp to 35,000Rp) serves Chinese and Indonesian fare and is open for breakfast, lunch and dinner.

Sekonyer Ecolodge (fax 22991; r 400,000Rp) Downstream and directly across from the Tanjung Harapan dock, this lodge is managed by locals and has comfortable rooms with private bathrooms and mosquito nets. It's not as classy as Rimba but a good option for those seeking a little more comfort than the *klotok*. There's also a restaurant attached serving simple fare (mains around 15,000Rp, open for lunch and dinner).

Four families in Tanjung Harapin Village offer simple **homestays** (incl dinner 150,000Rp) which provide an excellent opportunity to add a cultural bent to your experience of the park. Accommodation is in solid rooms behind each house, all with private *mandi*. This is a good cooperative effort for the village to earn income from the park's tourism and to be involved in its preservation.

Getting There & Around

Other than *klotok*, you can also hire wooden canoes at some of the stations for about 30,000Rp per day. This is a better way to explore Sungai Sekonyer and its shallow tributaries. The canoes are also much quieter so you're likely to see more wildlife, including crocodiles if you're lucky – or unlucky, depending on your viewpoint. Bring an umbrella or hat and lots of drinking water.

Speedboats from Kumai cost about 400,000Rp per day but this should be a last resort. It takes less than two hours to reach Camp Leakey but the trip is nowhere near as comfortable, the din of the motors chases away wildlife and the propellers wreak havoc on fish and crocodiles.

SOUTH KALIMANTAN

Dwarfed by its neighbours, South Kalimantan (Kalimantan Selatan, or Kal-Sel) may be the smallest province but it compensates by having Kalimantan's largest city and a tightly compacted diversity of geography and culture. Covering an area of just

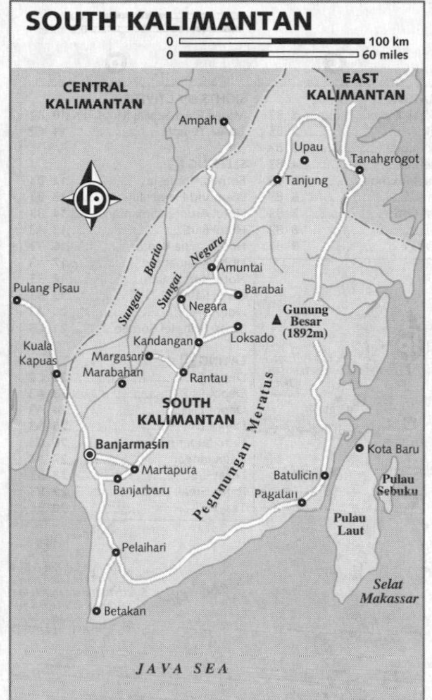

37,660 sq km, it squeezes in a population of over three million, with plenty of wild interior to spare. This means detours from the urban swell are relatively accessible and it's the easiest spot to find organised treks, rafting and other activities.

In the mountainous northeastern interior of South Kalimantan are groups of Dayaks said to be descendants of the original Banjar race. *Balai* (communal houses) accommodate up to 30 or more families and serve as a ritual centre for these mountain villages.

The province also has 10,000 sq km of wetlands, including 2000 sq km of tidal marshland and 5000 sq km of freshwater swamp. Although their very rich reserves are heavily exploited, their sheer size still makes them a valuable refuge for wildlife.

Kal-Sel is also the centre of Banjarese culture, which leaves its distinctive mark on every aesthetic. Traditional Banjarese clothing is made from *kain sasirangan,* cloth produced by a striking tie-dyeing process. The traditional Banjar-style house is the 'tall roof' design and the best examples can be seen in the town of Marabahan, 50km north of Banjarmasin on Sungai Barito.

BANJARMASIN

☎ 0511 / pop 810,000

Kalimantan's largest and most beguiling city rests gingerly over a labyrinth of canals, its taped-together mosques and houses perched on stilts or bundles of floating logs, and its residents up to their floorboards in water. Beyond, Banjarmasin's terra firma is a furore of traffic and trade, but the façade is wafer thin and the city's charm will envelop you quicker than the dust kicked up by the two-millionth *ojek*. A spread of attractions in and around the city can occupy several days, and absorbing Kalimantan's best urban culture in the markets both on and offshore is a must.

Orientation

Banjarmasin is big, but just about everything you might need is packed into the city centre around Pasar Baru. Most of the big banks are along Jl Lambung Mangkurat. Travellers arriving by ship at the port can catch small yellow *taxi kota* (city minibus) direct to Jl Hasanuddin (2000Rp), but most minibuses terminate at Central Antasari Plaza, a few hundred metres east of the city centre.

MAPS

Maps of South and Central Kalimantan are available at these places:

Toko Buku Merdeka (Jl Hasanuddin 44)
Gramedia bookshop (Jl Veteran 55-61)

Information

INTERNET ACCESS

Daissy Net (Jl Haryono MT; per hr 8000Rp) Upstairs from a wartel.

MONEY

The major banks have plenty of ATMs.

BNI bank (Bank Negara Indonesia; Jl Lambung Mangkurat)
Lippo Bank (Jl Pangeran Samudera; ⌚ 8am-3pm Mon-Fri) Can change up to US$500.

POST

Main post office (cnr Jl Pangeran Samudera & Jl Lambung Mangkurat)

TELEPHONE

Telkom office (Jl Lambung Mangkurat 4) For long-distance phone calls.

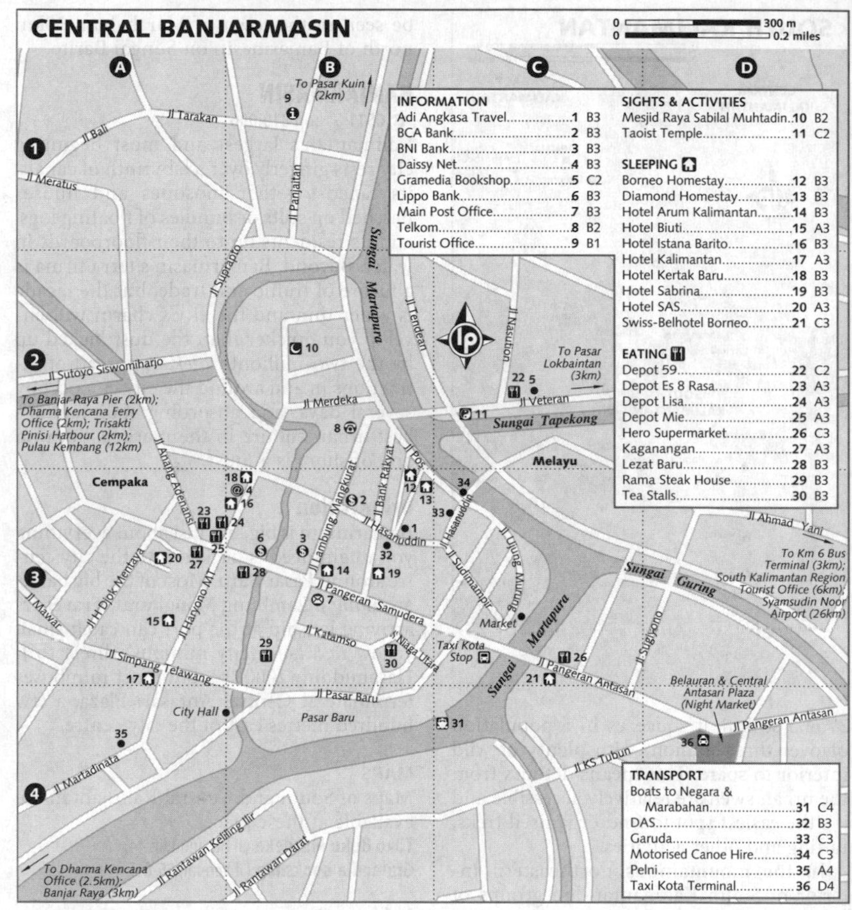

TOURIST INFORMATION

There's an information counter at the airport.

South Kalimantan regional tourist office (☎ 264510; fax 264512; Jl Pramuka 4; 🕑 7.30am-2.30pm Mon-Thu, 7.30am-11.30am Fri) On the way to the airport. Helpful staff can contact guides from the South Kalimantan Tourist Guide Association.

TRAVEL AGENCIES

See p638 for information about local guides and tours in the area.

Adi Angkasa Travel (☎ 4366100, 3352920; fax 4366200; Jl Hasanuddin 27) English-speaking staff; can arrange local tours and trekking trips into the interior, as well as flights.

Arjuna Satrya Wisata Putra (☎ 3365235; Ground fl, Arjuna Plaza, Jl Lambung Mangkurat) Can book domestic flights and tours in South and East Kalimantan. Also operates Amandit River Lodge in Loksado.

Sights & Activities

MESJID RAYA SABILAL MUHTADIN

A far cry from its ornate and reverent counterparts found elsewhere in Kalimantan, this enormous and modern **mosque** (Jl Sudirman) looks a bit like a landed mother ship. The copper-coloured dome and minarets with lids and spires have a sci-fi quality to them, but the vast interior is elegant. It's one of the largest mosques in the country and that's reason enough to visit. Proper attire is essential; visitors must wear long pants or skirts and suitable shirts.

FLOATING MARKETS

Banjarmasin's floating markets are a colourful exhibition of the area's fresh produce and an insight into the art of trading. The 5.30am wake up call is well worth it to see vessels laden with bananas, shrimp, fish, yams, spinach, coconut, incandescent spices and chillies, buckets of fuzzy rambutan and whatever else is in season. Sole traders in small canoes travel from as far as Negara, leaving at 2am to arrive on time. Manoeuvring their boats with dexterity and precision, they exchange goods and money and the frenzy is usually over by 9am. For breakfast, pull up beside the canoe café and, using a bamboo pole with a nail pushed through the end, spike your choice from the generous smorgasbord.

There are several markets in the area – one of the best and busiest is **Pasar Kuin** at the junction of the Kuin and Barito rivers. East of the town centre, another floating market, **Pasar Lokbaintan**, takes longer to get to, but is also worthwhile.

CANAL TRIPS

Another water bound way to scratch beneath Banjarmasin's surface is an afternoon canoe tour through its canals. With the sun on its descent, residents pour from houses lining the narrow waterways to wash clothes, children and themselves. You'll find yourself a spectacle to gleeful kids who follow the boat from the banks, gathering in numbers a la pied piper. A demure '*selamat sore*' (*sel*-amat *sor*-ay, meaning 'good day'), wave and the universal language of the high five will all be warmly received.. The wall to wall houses range in stature from veritable mansions with wide verandas to tiny shacks on the verge of capsizing. A glimpse inside, however, will reveal spotless interiors and proud residents. Some of the canals are tiny, particularly in dry season when the water level is low, and rubbish and vegetable matter is a constant.

The easiest way to see the canals is on a tour or with a guide (see p638). If you have sufficient Bahasa Indonesia you can organise a motorised canoe yourself. They congregate near the Jl Hasanuddin bridge and charge from 20,000Rp per hour.

PULAU KEMBANG

Home to a large tribe of long-tailed macaques who congregate at a decrepit Chinese temple, Pulau Kembang is an island 20 minutes from the city centre by boat. You can organise a boat from near the Jl Hasanuddin bridge; they cost from 20,000Rp per hour. On Sunday, Chinese families bring along gifts of eggs, peanuts and bananas for the monkeys. The temple is a decidedly minor attraction and, if you've fed monkeys before, it can be safely dropped from your itinerary. Otherwise, proceed with caution and *don't* touch the monkeys. Macaques can be quite aggressive when they're feeling peckish.

WALKING & CANAL TOUR

Begin your exploration of Kalimantan's largest city at the **Mesjid Raya Sabilal Muhtadin** (**1**; opposite), marvelling at its sci-fi exterior from the grassy grounds that surround it. Delve inside to see the contrasting and intricately adorned interior. After circumnavigating the mosque, make your way to Jl Merdeka and head across the bridge, over Sungai Martapura, to the Melayu area. Residences outnumber businesses on Banjarmasin's eastern bank, and it has the appearance of an endless village. Just after the bridge you'll pass a splendid **Taoist temple (2)** painted in vivid colours with gold inlay. The doors are often open and you can peer into the polished dark wood and candle-lit interior. If you're lucky you may also catch the drum maestros at work. Continue along Jl Veteran and take in the modest houses, some with haphazard picket fences, lining Sungai Tapekong. Stop at **Gramedia Bookshop** (**3**; Jl Veteran 55-61), Indonesia's answer to Borders, where you're likely to find a few foreign-language publications. Afterwards pop next door and cool off with a rich fruit juice or grab a bite to eat at **Depot 59** (**4**; p640).

Cross back over the river and head down busy Jl Lambung Mangkurat, past the imposing geometric architecture of **City Hall (5)** to the southern banks of Sungai Martapura. Walk east along the Jl Pasar Baru and amble through the bustling **Pasar Baru (6)**, where you might pick up a one-of-a-kind hat or exquisite *kain sasirangan* (tie-dye batik). Wander past tea stalls in the streets next to the market and make your way along Jl Ujung Murung. At the Jl Hasanuddin bridge flag down a motorised canoe and negotiate a tour of the canals and a trip to **Pulau Kembang** (**7**; left). If it's late enough

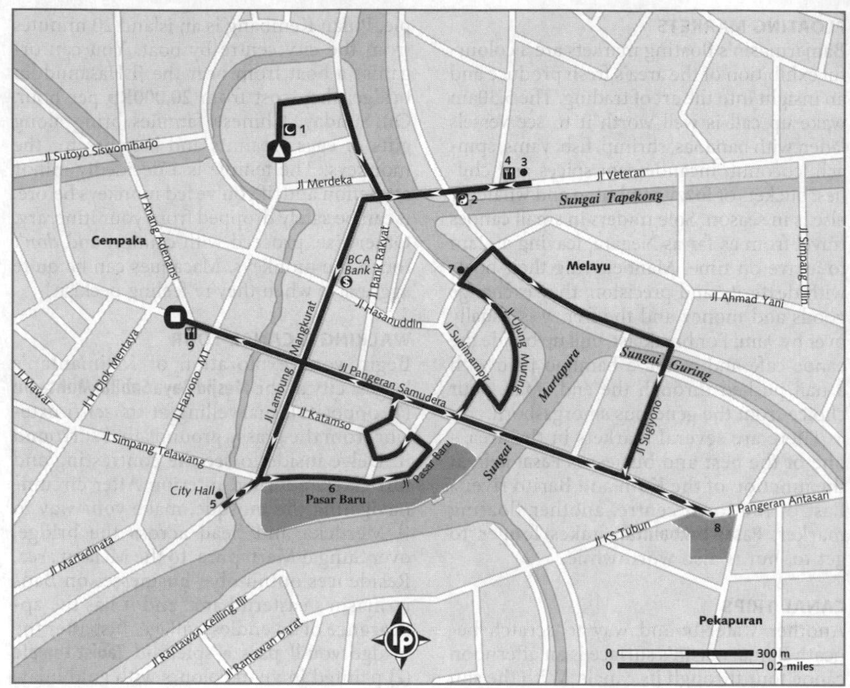

WALK FACTS

Start Mesjid Raya Sabilal Muhtadin
Finish Kandangan
Distance 5km
Duration Three hours

make your way past the shops and eateries along the eastern bank of Sungai Guring to the **belauran (8)**, where traders sell colourful produce alongside street snack vendors and tiny warungs. If you have the energy and hunger, take yourself to **Kandangan (9**; p642**)** for a well-earned dinner.

Tours

Local travel agents can organise tours of the city, canals and Pegunungan Meratus (Meratus Mountains) with English speaking guides. The best independent guide in the city is **Tailah** (☎ 4366100/3271685) who is based at Diamond Homestay. Friendly, fluent in English and utterly genuine, he also leads excellent tours to Loksado and the Pegunungan Meratus. Borneo Homestay offers similar tours, but make sure you're getting what you paid for. The going rate for a guide is about 75,000Rp for canal tours and 85,000Rp for floating-market tours, including all transport costs. Combined tours including a trip to Pulau Kaget will cost more. Guide fees for jungle tours to Loksado are about 100,000Rp per day, plus food, accommodation and transport.

Festivals & Events

Independence Day Banjarmasin celebrates 17 August with boat races on Sungai Martapura, and celebrations throughout.

Pasar Wadai (cake fair) During Ramadan dozens of stalls sell South Kalimantan's famous Banjarese pastries near Mesjid Raya or at Pasar Baru near City Hall.

Sleeping

Banjarmasin's accommodation generally leaps from budget to top end, skipping anything in between.

BUDGET

Diamond Homestay (☎ 4366100; fax 4366200; Jl Hasanuddin 58; s/d 30,000Rp/40,000Rp) Disregard the locked and forbidding exterior, this dirt-cheap option has a spacious and fan-cooled (but rustic) dorm, as well as smaller rooms. All have shared *mandis*. Your rupiah buys plenty of friendly attitude here. The homestay is on a nameless alley just off Jl Hasanuddin.

Borneo Homestay (☎ 4366545; borneo@banjarmasin.wasantara.net.id; Jl Hasanuddin 33; r 45,000-55,000Rp) This narrow, labyrinthine lodge caters to backpackers with friendly, English-speaking staff, rudimentary rooms and discount rates. City and further-afield tours can be arranged here but readers have provided mixed reviews of the quality. On the top floor is an abandoned bar with open windows, which is a nice spot to watch the sunset, but it feels like the homestay's heyday has passed. It's located just off Jl Hasanuddin.

Hotel Biuti (☎ 3354493; fax 4369884; Jl Haryono MT 21; r with/without mandi 75,000/60,000Rp, with air-con 100,000-150,000Rp; ❄) The economy rooms at this busy spot are a little cell-like, but the larger rooms with private *mandi* and air-con are amenable and come with TVs. The range of rooms is good, tea and coffee are included in the price and it's in a quiet location.

Also available:

Hotel Sabrina (☎ 3354721; fax 3354442; Jl Bank Rakyat 5; s 60,000-105,000Rp, d 70,000-125,000, ❄) Central and reliable.

Hotel Kalimantan (☎ 3354483; Jl Haryono MT 106; r from 25,000Rp) For the broke and brave.

MIDRANGE & TOP END

Hotel Kertak Baru (☎ 3354638; Jl Haryono MT 1; r 85,000-120,000Rp, ste 165,000Rp; ❄) You'll have to beat the local travellers to the reception desk at this extremely popular hotel if you want to spend the night. Decent rooms, the cheapest of which have private *mandis*, peel off a small corridor. It's the bottom end of midrange but a good step up from the backpacker haunts.

our pick Hotel SAS (☎ 3353054; fax 3365967; Jl Kacapiring Besar 2; r with fan 72,000Rp, with air-con 140,000-165,000Rp, ste/f 175,000/195,000; ❄) The best midrange place in Banjarmasin, Hotel SAS has a broad spectrum of rooms. The pick of the bunch is the 'Mandiangin', with an enclosed front patio, spotless bathrooms (with tub!), cool interiors and satellite TV – for those in need of some lazy R&R. Economy rooms on the ground floor are more basic but just as roomy and the furnishings and class increase with the price. Staff are friendly and some speak a little English. Breakfast is included and it's in a quiet spot on a small street just off Jl H Djok Mentaya. Mind the early morning calls to prayer from the mosque though.

Hotel Istana Barito (☎ 4367300; fax 3352240; Jl Haryono MT 16-20; r from 450,000Rp plus 21% tax; ❄ 🏊) On the downhill run from its glory days, the Istana Barito's lobby has the atmosphere of an underground car park. But the facilities are reasonable and the rooms still pass for lovely. Staff are gracious and walk-in discounts can be haggled.

Hotel Arum Kalimantan (☎ 4366818; fax 4367345; arumbjm@indo.net.id; Jl Lambung Mangkurat; r 450,000-676,000Rp, ste from 1,929,000Rp; ❄) A fine top-end hotel; walk past the smudged-concrete exterior into the fresh and renovated interior. The plush rooms are very comfortable, with colourful décor and pool or city views. Breakfast in the open ground-floor restaurant is included.

Swiss-Belhotel Borneo (☎ 3271111; www.swiss-belhotel.com; Jl Pangeran Antasari 86A; r from 480,000Rp; ❄) This flashy and upscale hotel has doormen in heavily adorned uniforms and an elegant array of rooms with all the creature comforts. Those at the cheaper end of the scale don't fare as well as the Hotel Arum Kalimantan's though. There's also a lounge bar and a good restaurant.

Eating

Banjarmasin's excellent array of *kueh* (cakes) includes deep-fried breads – some with delicious fillings – and sticky banana rice cakes, both cheap but tasty options for breakfast at the tea stalls. Local specialities include *ayam panggang* (chicken roasted and served in sweet soy sauce), fish and freshwater crayfish.

our pick Kaganangan (☎ 4364203; Jl Pangeran Samudera 8; mains 12,000-20,000Rp; 🕑 breakfast, lunch & dinner) A Banjarmasin institution, Kaganangan distinguishes itself from the bevy of similar eateries with a colourful interior, high-backed chairs, spotless table settings and walls of packaged snacks and supplies in choreographed display. Served in all manner of marinades, the fish here is fab and the rest of the menu boasts local specialities. It's also a nice spot if you're just hankering for a thick, sweet coffee and some fan-cooled respite.

Depot 59 (Jl Veteran 59; mains 6000-12,000Rp; breakfast, lunch & dinner) Tucked off the road, this popular diner is a weekend favourite with families, who feast on thick, lurid fruit juices and crowd-pleasing chicken. The *nasi pecel* (similar to *gado gado*) is also tasty, as is the chocolate *roti bakar* (baked bread).

Depot Es 8 Rasa (Jl Anang Andenansi; mains 8000Rp; lunch & dinner Mon-Sat) Another popular spot, you can fill up on excellent Indonesian food and juices and savour the social buzz here. Dishes don't win creativity awards but they go down easily without denting the wallet.

Depot Lisa (Jl Haryono MT; mains 14,000Rp; lunch & dinner) This neat, cheap and clean little eatery serves a good spread of fish and chicken dishes, plus *udang* when they've got them. It's fan-cooled, tidy and sheltered from the dust of the main road.

Rama Steak House (Arjuna Plaza, Jl Lambung Mangkurat; mains 45,000Rp; lunch & dinner Mon-Sat;) The name says it all – steaks in large quantities are served to middle-class locals and foreigners looking for a change from *sambal* and *ayam*. The surrounds are suitably refined.

More eating options:

Lezat Baru (3353191; Jl Pangeran Samudera; mains 15,000-25,000Rp; lunch & dinner;) Good Chinese restaurant.

Hero Supermarket (Jl Pangeran Antasari) For self-caterers.

Depot Mie (cnr Jl Haryono MT & Jl Pangeran Samudera; mains 5000Rp; lunch & dinner Mon-Sat) Hot and cheap noodles and rice.

For a taste of street culture, eat at the tea stalls along Jl Niaga Utara near Pasar Baru. Kalimantan's version of the night market is called *belauran*. Banjarmasin's is a huge affair at the Antasari terminal, where you will find more cheap eateries.

Shopping

The city is famous for its *kain sasirangan*, a kind of colourful tie-dye batik. A few stalls in the market near the Jl Antasari bridge sell *sasirangan*, but mostly as material. Clothes are sold in stores at Km 3.7, Jl Ahmad Yani. Large sizes may be difficult to find.

Getting There & Away

AIR

Several airlines including **Garuda** (3359065; fax 3359066; 2nd fl, Jl Hasanuddin HM 31) operate flights to Jakarta. There are also services to Balikpapan and Surabaya. **DAS** (52902; Blok 4, Jl Hasanuddin 6) and Kal-Star both have daily flights to Pangkalan Bun and the latter also flies to Pontianak. As with all airfares you'll get the best deal at a travel agent; see p636 for listings.

BOAT

River boats from the wharf at Pasar Baru travel twice a week to Negara (20,000Rp, 12 hours) and daily to Marabahan (10,000Rp, four hours). The seemingly impenetrable market is at the intersection of Jl Niaga Utara and Jl Pasar Baru. Walk through to the river.

Pelni (3353077; Jl Martadinata 10) boats travel to Surabaya (from 180,000Rp, 18 hours, weekly), Semarang (from 232,000Rp, 24 hours, twice weekly) and Jakarta (from 354,000Rp, 20 hours, weekly) from Trisakti Pinisi Harbour. Take a *taxi kota* from the terminal on Jl Pangeran Antasari for 2000Rp. The route passes by the harbour master's and various ticket offices, but the best place for updated Pelni information is its office.

The air-con **Dharma Kencana** (3351419) ferry to Surabaya (seat/economy 170,000/130,000Rp, 20 hours) docks at Jl Yos Sudarso 8 near the Trisakti Pinisi Harbour. It leaves every other day in the afternoon. There is a cafeteria on board. Buy tickets at Dharma Kencana's office.

BUS

Orange Colts and other buses depart frequently from the Km 6 terminal for Martapura (16,000Rp, 30 minutes) and Banjarbaru (16,000Rp, 45 minutes). There are also Colts to Kandangan (23,000Rp, three hours), Negara (35,000Rp, four hours), Barabai (38,000Rp, four hours) Margasari (25,000Rp, three hours) and Pagatan (40,000Rp, five hours). Frequent economy buses travel to Muara Teweh (60,000Rp, 12 hours), Balikpapan (75,000Rp, 15 hours) and Samarinda (90,000Rp, 17 hours). For the latter two destinations you can opt for a more comfortable air-con night bus: Balikpapan (110,000Rp, 12 hours), Samarinda (135,000Rp, 14 hours).

One bus leaves daily to Marabahan from Km 6, but it's easier to go to Kayu Tani Ujung in the northern part of Banjarmasin.

Colts leave frequently from there for Marabahan (6000Rp), a journey of about two hours. There's an extra 500Rp charge for the short ferry crossing. Take a *taxi kota* to Kayu Tani Ujung (1000Rp) from the Jl P Antasari terminal.

Getting Around

TO/FROM THE AIRPORT

Banjarmasin's Syamsudin Noor airport is 26km from town. Take a *taxi kota* from Pasar Baru or the terminal at Jl P Antasari to the Km 6 terminal. From there catch a Martapura-bound Colt, get off at the branch road leading to the airport and walk the 1.5km to the terminal. From the airport to the city, walk through the car park, turn left and head to the Banjarmasin-Martapura highway. From there pick up one of the frequent Colts to Banjarmasin. A taxi to/from the airport costs 60,000Rp.

PUBLIC TRANSPORT

It is possible to hire a boat operator to navigate the canals near Jl Hasanuddin bridge. Expect to pay 20,000Rp to 25,000Rp per hour without a guide.

Onshore, the area around Pasar Baru is small, central and easy to walk around. Taxis are 400,000Rp a day or 50,000Rp per hour, with a minimum of two hours. There are also plenty of becak, *ojek* and *bajaj* (three-wheeled motorised taxis). A *bajaj* from the city centre to Banjar Raya pier is around 10,000Rp; by *ojek* it costs about 10,000Rp.

The yellow minibuses are called *taxi kota* and they go to various parts of town, including the Km 6 terminal. The standard fare is 2000Rp. The taxi kota terminal is on Jl Pangeran Antasari near the night market, just east of the city centre.

AROUND BANJARMASIN

About 30km southeast of Banjarmasin are three towns that make interesting day trips from Banjarmasin.

Banjarbaru

In Banjarbaru, the **Museum Lambung Mangkurat** (☎ 0511-92453; Jl Ahmad Yani 36; ⏰ 8.30am-2.30pm Tue-Thu & Sun, 8.30am-11am Fri, 8.30am-1.30pm Sat) has a good collection of Banjar and Dayak artefacts, and some fascinating items excavated from the sites of Hindu temples in Kalimantan. The museum is on the Banjarmasin–Martapura road. Ask the Colt driver to drop you.

Martapura

Martapura is a little further east of Banjarbaru. With the diamond, gold and agate mines closed on Friday, the **market** swells with locals on their day off. This can be a photographer's paradise, with every type of food on sale and lots of colourfully dressed Banjar women. If crowds are not your thing, come on another day to shop and see the mines in Cempaka.

You can't miss the recent addition to the market area: a brilliant-white building with blue roofing built in traditional style. The choice of uncut gems, silver jewellery and trading beads – both strung and unstrung – are excellent, but be prepared to bargain hard. The old market is behind the new building. The old **Kayu Tangi diamond-polishing factory** (Jl Sukaramai) behind the market is open to visitors as a tourist shop. Colts leave frequently for Martapura (16,000Rp, 45 minutes) from the Km 6 terminal in Banjarmasin.

Cempaka

The Cempaka diamond fields are a short detour off the Banjarmasin-Martapura road. It's a good place to see some of the smaller diamond and gold digs and the conditions people are willing to endure in the hope of finding treasure lying within the soil. The diggers at the bottom of the shaft can spend the day up to their necks in water, passing up baskets full of silt that is washed away in the search for gold specks, diamonds or agate.

There are records of 20-carat diamonds from these fields as far back as 1846 – a 106.7-carat monster in 1850 and, the biggest of all, the 167.5-carat Tri Sakti (Thrice Sacred) found in August 1965. Most diamonds are a fraction of that size, but the hope of another big find keeps the miners focused on the job.

Diggers usually work in teams of 10 to 15, digging one day, sluicing the next. Typically, a 'chief' pays the miners 2500Rp a day lunch money to work the claim. If there's a find the team gets to divide about 50% of its value, after payments to the land owners, chief, pump operator and wood cutter are subtracted. The activity on the fields tends to follow the big finds. There are touts aplenty to show you the way and sell you polished stones. It's customary to give a 2000Rp tip to these 'guides'.

To get to Cempaka, take a Banjarmasin–Martapura Colt and ask to get off at the huge roundabout just past Banjarbaru. From there take a green taxi to Alur (2000Rp) and walk the last 1km along a dirt road off the main road to the diamond digs. The diamond mines and polishing centres are closed Friday.

MARABAHAN & MARGASARI

For a glimpse of river life, take a boat 65km up the Barito from Banjarmasin to Marabahan, a small town with some old, traditional Banjar-style wooden houses. The losmen on the river, such as the **Hotel Bahtera**, have adequate accommodation with rooms from 30,000Rp, with shared *mandis*.

From Marabahan you can charter a boat to Margasari, a handicraft village, which produces lots of rattan and bamboo products, such as fans, hats and maps. Colts from there to Banjarmasin (25,000Rp, daily) take about three hours. Boats leave daily from the Pasar Lima pier in Banjarmasin for Marabahan (10,000Rp) and take four hours.

KANDANGAN

☎0517

A transit town and launching point for exploration into the Meratus interior, Kandangan has a remarkable old marketplace built in the colonial era, and is a good spot to overnight and stock up.

Bangkau Hotel (☎21455; Jl Suprapto 2; r from 40,000Rp; ❄), around the corner from the central minibus terminal, has excellent accommodation in fan-cooled and air-con rooms. Cheaper digs can be found at **Losmen Loksado** (☎21352; Jl Suprapto; r 25,000-30,000Rp), about 100m up the street.

Food stalls at the minibus terminal have excellent *nasi bungkus* (takeaway rice parcels) with chicken or liver, but the best thing to eat in Kandangan is *ketupat,* a delicious local speciality that features sticky rice triangles and broiled *harawan,* a river fish, covered in coconut sauce and a squeeze of lime. Warung Ketupat Kandangan, about 1km northwest of the minibus terminal on the road to Barabai, is a good place to eat.

There are frequent Colts from Banjarmasin's Km 6 terminal (23,000Rp, three hours). There's a bus terminal 2km east of Kandangan where night buses stop each evening on the way from Banjarmasin to Balikpapan and Samarinda, usually at around 7pm. To get to the terminal, catch a minibus (5000Rp) heading to Negara, or take an *ojek* for 30,000Rp.

NEGARA

Northwest of Kandangan, the town of Negara is propped up on stilts along Sungai Negara. A wetland area during the rainy season, Negara is surrounded by water, making the city look like a very waterlogged island. The only land above water is the road, but even that disappears occasionally – in a fog of mosquitoes if not because of rain.

One amazing Negara custom is the raising of water-buffalo herds on wooden platforms. They are released daily for grazing and drinking, swim up to 5km and are herded home by 'canoe cowboys'. The wetlands are also remarkable for their prolific fish and bird life, the occasional snake and plenty of ducks.

Tour the town by boat – it may be as much as 50,000Rp for half a day, depending on your bargaining skills. Back on land, ask to see the sword-making. The local craftsmen forge beautiful swords, machetes and kris (daggers) in a variety of styles, complemented by remarkably decorative sheaths.

Surprisingly for such a large town, Negara has no hotel. You might manage to find a homestay, but it's probably better to stay in Kandangan. There are a few small warungs that serve *ketupat* and *ayam panggang.*

Colts from Banjarmasin to Negara (35,000Rp, four hours, daily) leave from the Km 6 terminal. From Kandangan to Negara there's the option of public minibus taxi (7000Rp), shared Japanese sedan with four people (per person 35,000Rp), chartered taxi (one way or return 350,000Rp) or *ojek* (40,000Rp). Twice-weekly boats leave from the Pasar Lima pier in Banjarmasin for Negara (20,000Rp) and take 12 hours.

LOKSADO

About 40km east of Kandangan in the Pegunungan Meratus, Loksado is the largest of some 20 villages spread over 2500 sq km between Kandangan and Amuntai to the

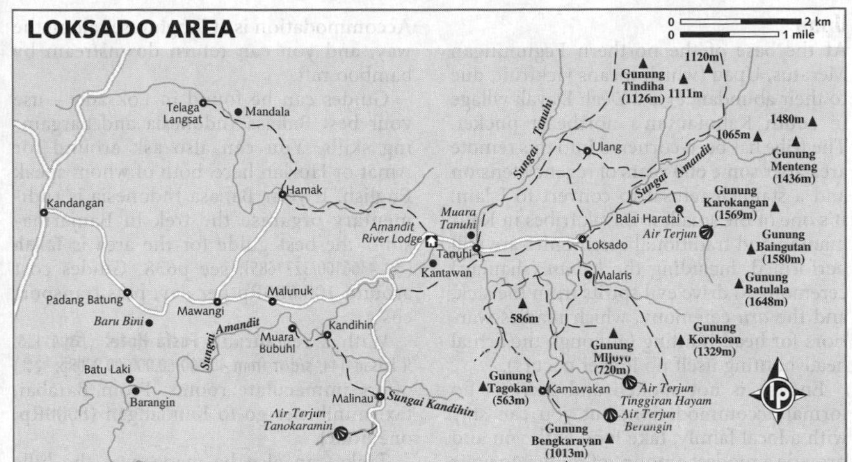

west and the South Kalimantan coast to the east. It's an important market village accessible by road and a good base for trekking in the area.

The small island on the river running through Loksado has basic accommodation available at **Loksado Kotek** (r 35,000Rp); ask for Amat who can arrange your stay.

Amandit River Lodge (s/d from US$45/50) is just off the road before arriving in Loksado. Those looking for a little luxury in this neck of the woods should check it out. The pleasant rooms are fan-cooled and there's a garden and a coffee shop. **Arjuna** (☎ 3365235; Ground fl, Arjuna Plaza, Jl Lambung Mangkurat) in Banjarmasin takes reservations.

Eateries along the main lane from the suspension bridge are basic and close shortly after dusk. The best breakfast is *roti* (bread) from the wok at a warung about 20m from the bridge.

Getting There & Away

Pick-ups leave the Kandangan minibus terminal for Loksado (12,000Rp, 1½ hours) in the afternoon, and leave Loksado for Kandangan early in the morning, departing from the main bridge.

Coming back from Loksado, many travellers charter a bamboo raft and pole down Sungai Amandit. The usual drop-off point is Muara Tanuhi, two hours downstream (80,000Rp), where there are also **hot springs** (have your bathing suit ready). Continuing on to Muara Bubuhi a few more hours downstream is feasible and there are some exciting rapids, but it costs a lot more. From the nearby road at Muara Bubuhi, minibus taxis and *ojek* go back to Kandangan. It's also possible to raft the whole way from Loksado to Kandangan; it takes about a day. There are tours to the area from Banjarmasin (see p638).

AROUND LOKSADO

From Loksado there are hundreds of paths through mountain garden plots to other villages over the hills, many crossing streams via suspension bridges. Follow the path upstream on Sungai Amandit for three hours (8km) to a series of **air terjun** just past Balai Haratai. It's easy enough to find the first waterfall, but local knowledge is handy if you want to climb to the middle and top falls, and find the nearby cave. Ask at Haratai or get someone from Loksado to tag along in exchange for some English practice or at least make it clear whether you will pay them or not.

Malaris

A 30-minute walk (1500m) or 10-minute *ojek* ride through a bamboo forest southeast of Loksado brings you to Malaris village. Until recently 32 families (about 150 people) lived in a large *balai*. There are now separate houses built for new families as the village begins to modernise. Ask to speak to the *kepala balai* (village head) about staying the night (including tea and coffee 30,000Rp).

Upau

At the base of the northern Pegunungan Meratus, Upau (which means jackfruit, due to their abundance) is a Deah Dayak village in south Kalimantan's northeast pocket. The tribe has been cornered into this remote area after some 600 years of regency tension and a staunch refusal to convert to Islam. It's one of the smallest Dayak tribes in Kalimantan and traditional ceremonies are still performed, including the *balian* (shaman) ceremony to drive evil spirits from the sick, and the *aru* ceremony, which readies warriors for head-hunting (although the actual head-hunting itself no longer occurs).

English is not spoken and there is no formal accommodation, but you can stay with a local family; take food with you and provide a modest amount of money to your hosts. You can stock up on supplies in Tanjung or at Upau's weekly market, which takes place on Friday.

Pegunungan Meratus is about 2km from the village, making it a good access point for treks. Two Upau locals who know the mountains very well and can act as guides are Aman and Dudang – ask around for them when you arrive. It's possible to do a moderate one-day trek from the village, but you can also trek for two or three days. The terrain is rough in parts and trekking experience is required.

To get to Upau catch a public minibus taxi from Negara (40,000Rp, two hours) to Tanjung. You can also catch a Colt directly from Banjarmasin's Km 6 terminal to Tanjung (70,000Rp, six hours). From Tanjung take a red and yellow *angkot* to Upau (6,000Rp, 1½ hours).

Treks

An excellent three-day trek begins at the village of **Tanuhi**, 2km from Loksado. Here you'll trek for a few hours through secondary agricultural forest and various isolated mountain villages, crossing suspended bamboo bridges along the way. On day two go through the primary forest of **Pegunungan Meratus** where the ancient forest provides a tranquil yet awe-inspiring spectacle. The ancient forest trees tower above the canopy, holding beehives suspended seemingly out of reach. But for the local Dayak and the rarely spotted honey bear, no obstacle is too great to get a taste of this divine nectar. Accommodation is at longhouses along the way, and you can return downstream by bamboo raft.

Guides can be found in Loksado – use your best Bahasa Indonesia and bargaining skills. You can also ask around for Amat or Horlan here, both of whom speak English. If your Bahasa Indonesia is rudimentary organise the trek in Banjarmasin – the best guide for the area is **Tailah** (☎ 4366100/3271685); see p638. Guides cost around 100,000Rp per day, plus transport costs.

With a restaurant, **Fusfa Hotel** (☎ 41136; Jl Hasan 144; s/d/tr from 40,000/60,000/90,000Rp; ❄) offers immaculate rooms. From Barabai, taxi minibuses go to Kandangan (8000Rp, one hour).

Treks can also be made over the hills from Loksado to the coast. The trek to **Kota Baru** on Pulau Laut takes three or four days by a combination of foot, minibus and boat, passing through hillside gardens, forests and over Gunung Besar, the province's highest peak at 1892m. You can return to Banjarmasin by bus (55,000Rp, six hours, daily).

SOUTH COAST

An alternative route between Banjarmasin and Balikpapan is the coastal route via **Pagatan** and **Batulicin**. Buses to Batulicin (45,000Rp) take six hours. From Batulicin, Pelni boats go to Makassar in Sulawesi.

Pagatan is known for its Bugis community and tradition of building the beautiful schooners that ply Indonesian waters. On 17 April each year, local Bugis make offerings to the sea. The ceremony known as the **Mapan Retasi**, literally 'giving the sea food', takes place at the end of week-long celebrations.

From Banjarmasin's Km 6 terminal, Colts to Pagatan take five hours and cost 40,000Rp.

EAST KALIMANTAN

East Kalimantan (Kalimantan Timur, or Kal-Tim) is the daddy of Kalimantan's provinces, covering 202,000 sq km. For decades the oil, mining and logging industries have gorged on the province's feast of natural resources, pumping prosperity into

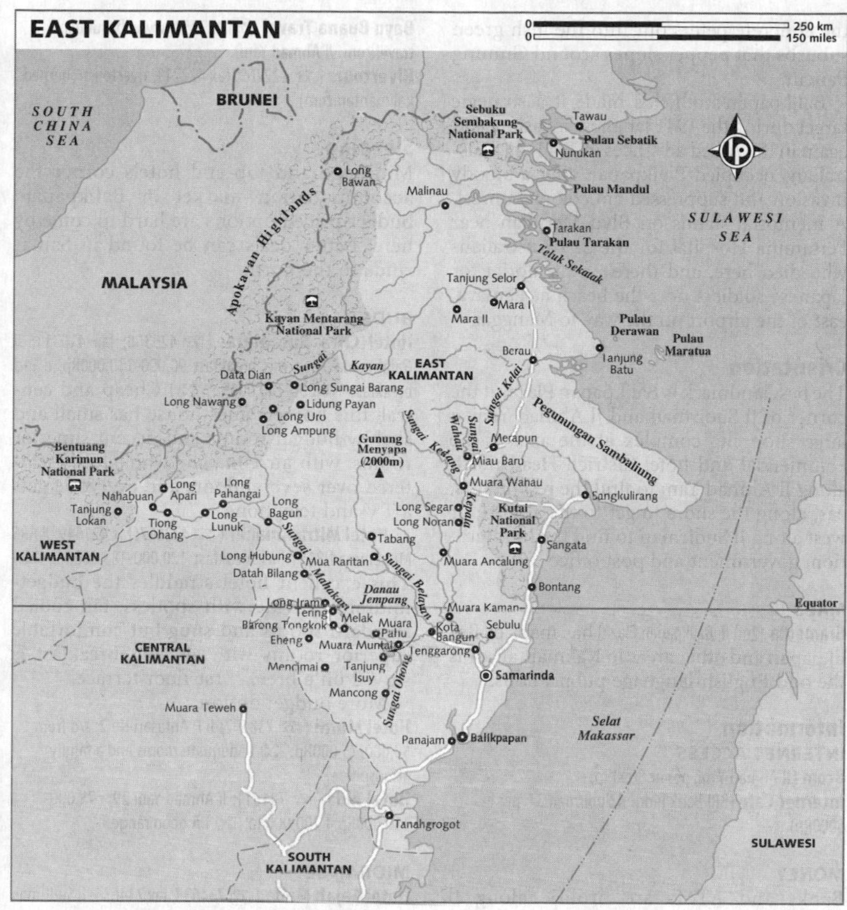

the cities and leaving scarred and battered footprints on the landscape. Thousands of hectares have been reduced to poor-quality grassland. The fires of the early '80s and late '90s also exacted their toll. Yet chunks of the terrain remain resilient, posing geographic obstacles in the form of river rapids, impenetrable forests and mountains to stem the ugly tide. With time and planning, intrepid travellers in search of a true adventure can still enjoy pockets of wilderness and reach places that rarely see a foreign face. Those looking for an easier route can exploit the commercial activity and infrastructure of the southern coastline and the mighty Sungai Mahakam. Dayak villages on the wider banks of this mighty river have confronted dramatic change, but modernisation's touch is muted once the jungle and waterways close in.

BALIKPAPAN

☎ 0542 / pop 450,000

Black gold pumps through Balikpapan's veins, from the endless stream of traffic, to the concrete, glass and steel business blocks competing for attention along the main drag. The huge oil refinery dominates the city and, when flying in, you can see stray tankers and offshore oil rigs.

For travellers it's best enjoyed for a bout of air-con and Western pleasantries. Industrious strips of traders, eateries and hotels line the waterfront, and climbing the hills, the concrete peters out into the lush green suburbs that pepper slopes around Gunung Pancur.

Balikpapan's oilfields made it a strategic target during the 1941 Japanese invasion, and again in the Allied advances in 1944–45. Australians occupied Balikpapan after a bloody invasion and suppressed anticolonial unrest. A memorial stands on Blvd Meridian near Pertamina Hospital for the 229 Australians who died here, and there's a memorial for Japanese soldiers near the beach at Lamaru, east of the airport on the way to Manggar.

Orientation

The best landmark is Balikpapan Plaza, at the corner of Jl Sudirman and Jl Ahmad Yani, a large shopping complex at the axis of the commercial and hotel district. Head north along Jl Ahmad Yani to find the restaurants, east along the shore to get to the airport, or west along Jl Sudirman to find the immigration, government and post office.

MAPS

Gramedia (2nd fl, Balikpapan Plaza) has maps of Balikpapan and other areas in Kalimantan, plus the odd English-language publications.

Information

INTERNET ACCESS

Bcom (Jl Ahmad Yani; per hr 8000Rp)
Internet Cafe (BRI Bank Bldg, Jl Sudirman 37; per hr 5000Rp)

MONEY

Banks and ATMs are prolific along Jl Sudirman.

BNI bank (Bank Negara Indonesia; cnr Jl Ahmad Yani & Jl Sudirman)
BRI bank (Bank Rakyat Indonesia; Jl Sudirman 37)
PT Haji La Tunrung Star Group (Jl Ahmad Yani 51)

TELEPHONE

Telkom office (Jl Ahmad Yani 418) Has facilities for local, national and international phone calls.

TRAVEL AGENCIES

PT Agung Sedayu (☎ 420601; fax 420447; Jl Sudirman 28) Sells airline and Pelni tickets.

Tours

Tours along Sungai Mahakam and into the Apokayan Highlands can be booked with the following:

Bayu Buana Travel (☎ 422751; www.bayubuanatravel.com; Jl Ahmad Yani)
Rivertours (☎ 422269; fax 422211; rivertours@borneokalimantan.com)

Sleeping

Midrange and top-end hotels corner the accommodation market in Balikpapan; budget-priced options are hard to come by here. Better deals can be found in Samarinda to the north.

BUDGET

Hotel Citra Nusantara (☎ 425366; fax 410311; Jl Gajahmada 76; s incl breakfast 90,000-110,000Rp, d incl breakfast 120,000-140,000Rp;) Cheap and central, this homely guesthouse has small and shabby budget rooms and decent superior rooms, with air-con. The whole lot is scattered over several floors and everyone gets a TV and telephone.

Hotel Mitra Amanni (☎ 422857; fax 421649; Jl ARS Muhammad 31; r incl breakfast 120,000-185,000Rp;) This excellent hotel straddles the budget-midrange divide with spotless, fan-cooled standard rooms and snug but comfortable superior rooms with air-con. Breakfast is served on a breezy, 1st-floor terrace.

More budget options:

Hotel Murni (☎ 738692; Jl P Antasari No 2; s/d from 50,000/75,000Rp;) Adequate rooms and a family atmosphere.
Hotel Aida (☎ 731011; Jl Ahmad Yani 29; r 75,000-150,000Rp, f 200,000Rp;) A good range.

MIDRANGE

Hotel Gajah Mada (☎ 734634; fax 734636; Jl Sudirman 14; s 95,000-235,000Rp, d 135,000-285,000Rp plus 10% tax;) Boasting three room categories, the Gajah Mada caters to budget and midrange travellers with glistening rooms off a cool, wide corridor. The cheapest versions are fan-cooled and the nicest are upstairs with river views.

Miramar Hotel (☎ 412442; miramar@indonet.net.id; Jl Pranoto 16; r incl breakfast 265,000-450,000Rp plus 21% tax;) In two separate buildings Miramar has a host of rooms, all with Western bathrooms, air-con and TVs. They could do with a touch-up but the facilities are good, the breakfast excellent and there's a pub attached.

Hotel Pacific (☎ 750888, 750345; www.hotelpacificbalikpapan.com; Jl Ahmad Yani; r incl breakfast from 350,000Rp, ste from 610,000Rp;) This glitzy new number treats guests to stylish rooms with tasteful Southeast Asian furnishings and first-class service. Onsite is a 24-hour restaurant and coffee lounge. Wireless internet access is also available.

More in the midrange bracket:

Bintang Hotel (☎ 735908; bintangh@indosat.net.id; Jl Sudirman Blok B, 31-34; r 190,000-245,000Rp, f/ste 315,000/445,000Rp plus 10% tax;) Good service and decent rooms.

Hotel Budiman (☎ 736030; fax 423811; Jl Ahmad Yani 34; r from 220,000Rp, ste 305,000Rp plus 20% tax;) Central and reasonable.

TOP END

Dusit Balikpapan (☎ 420155; dusitbpn@dusit.com; Jl Sudirman; r incl breakfast from 650,000Rp, ste incl breakfast from 1,740,000Rp plus 20% tax;) Sprawled over a huge area like a luxury colony, the Dusit has indulgent and appealing rooms, a fitness centre, tennis courts, restaurants and a cruisy lounge bar. It's as comfortable as Kalimantan gets.

Hotel Gran Senyiur (☎ 0800 1 226677, 820211; hgs@senyiurhotels.com; Jl ARS Mohammad 7; r/ste incl breakfast from 1,100,000/1,700,000Rp;) Balikpapan's classiest downtown digs require deep pockets but you get English-speaking staff, a choice of smoking or nonsmoking floors, facilities galore and stylish rooms. 'Superiors' are crisp and simple with polished bathrooms, and deluxe rooms have oodles of room, day beds and enormous bathrooms.

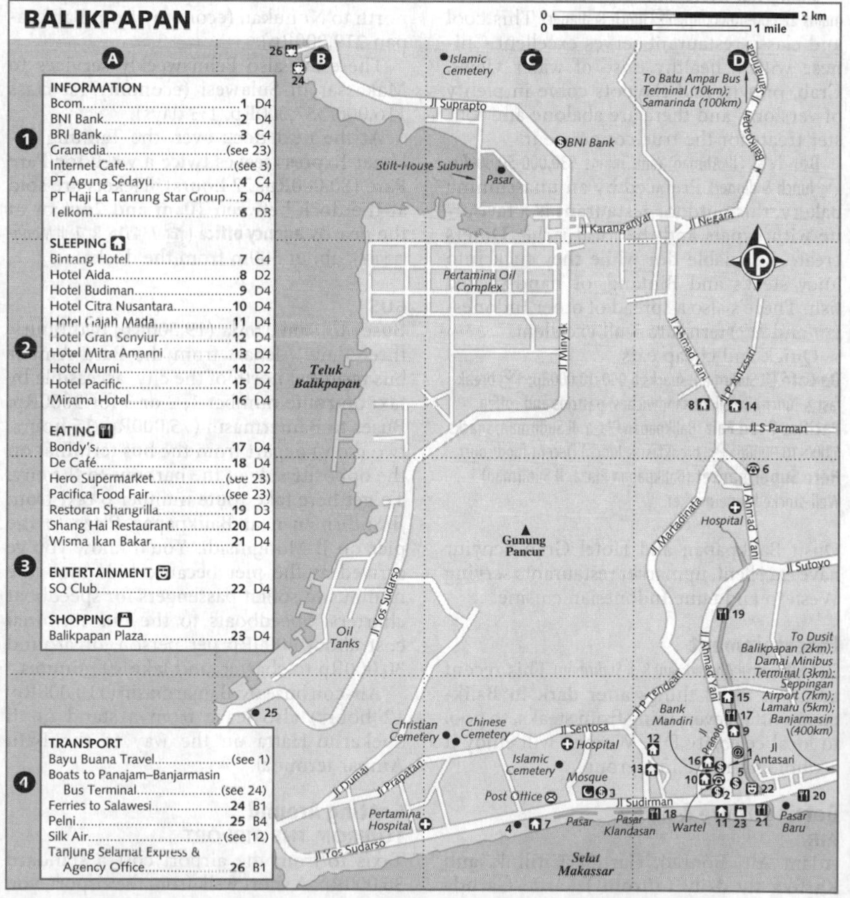

Eating & Drinking

There are plenty of cheap warungs near the water, particularly around Pasar Klandasan.

Wisma Ikan Bakar (Jl Sudirman; meals 11,000-28,000Rp; lunch & dinner) It looks like any other hole in the wall, but this little seafood restaurant sizzles fresh fish (which you hand pick) and dishes it out with equally fresh *sambal* and salad. It's fan-cooled, fuss-free and great value.

Restoran Shangrilla (Jl Ahmad Yani 29; mains 14,000-25,000Rp; lunch & dinner) A favourite with the locals, this family-run restaurant serves over 30 prawn dishes, plus tame and daring versions of clams, duck, beef, frog, chicken and literally pages of seafood. It's bright, cheerful and reasonably priced.

Shang Hai Restaurant (☎ 422951; Jl Sudirman; mains 22,000-40,000Rp; lunch & dinner) This cool and classy restaurant serves excellent Chinese with a healthy dose of water views. Crab, prawns and claypots come in plenty of versions, and there are abalone and lobster treats for the true connoisseur.

Bondy's (Jl Ahmad Yani; mains $30,000-50,000Rp; lunch & dinner) Prefaced by an unassuming bakery, this outdoor restaurant is a favourite with expats and the local riche. Diners create a sociable din while they tuck into juicy steaks and Bintang, or hand-picked fish. There's also a spread of other Indonesian and Western fare – all excellent.

Quick and cheap eats:

De Café (Jl Sudirman; snacks 6,000-10,000Rp; breakfast & lunch) Excellent sandwiches, pastries and coffee.
Pacifica Food Fair (Balikpapan Plaza, Jl Sudirman; snacks 5,000-10,000Rp; breakfast & lunch) Decent food court.
Hero Supermarket (Balikpapan Plaza, Jl Sudirman) Well-stocked supermarket.

Dusit Balikpapan and Hotel Gran Senyiur have excellent, upmarket restaurants serving Western and tame Indonesian cuisine.

Entertainment

SQ Club (cnr Jl Ahmad Yani & Jl Sudirman) This recent addition to all things after dark in Balikpapan offers everything from steaks, to pool to local celebrity DJs. Women will enjoy it a whole lot more in a group.

Getting There & Away

AIR

Adam Air, Bouraq, Garuda Citilink, and Kartika fly daily to/from Jakarta. Garuda Citilink and Kartika also fly daily to/from Surabaya, and Merpati has daily flights between to Makassar. There are daily flights to Tarakan.

Kal-Star and DAS fly to/from Berau, and DAS flies to Pangkalan Bun several times a week. Batavia flies to/from Banjarmasin.

Silk Air (☎ 730800; www.silkair.com; Hotel Gran Senyiur) flies to Singapore (US$480) daily.

BOAT

Pelni (☎ 424171; Jl Yos Sudarso 76) ships travel fortnightly to Pare Pare (economy 180,000Rp) in Sulawesi and then onto Surabaya (economy 300,000Rp) in Java. The *Dobonsolo* travels fortnightly to Toli Toli in Sulawesi (economy 130,000Rp) and then back to Tarakan (economy from Balikpapan 157,000Rp) and north to Nunukan (economy from Balikpapan 219,000Rp).

There are also Pelni weekly services to Makassar in Sulawesi (economy/1st class 116,000/357,000Rp, 1½ days).

At the next dock over, the Tanjung Selamat Express leaves twice a week for Pare Pare (80,000Rp, 22 hours). Tickets are sold at the dock between 10am and 2pm or at the nearby **agency office** (☎ 734516; Rt 1, Jl Monginsidi 4), about 500m from the docks.

BUS

Buses to Samarinda (19,500Rp, two hours, three daily) depart from the Batu Ampar bus terminal north of the city, accessible by taxi on route number 1, 2 or 3 for 3000Rp. Buses to Banjarmasin (75,000Rp, 15 hours, two daily) depart from the bus terminal on the opposite side of the harbour to the city. To get here take route number 6 taxi from Jl Sudirman near Balikpapan Plaza to the pier on Jl Monginsidi. You'll know you've arrived at the pier because kids mob the minibus to solicit passengers for speedboat charters. Speedboats to the bus terminal cost about 6000Rp per person, or around 30,000Rp to charter, and take 10 minutes.

Air-con buses to Banjarmasin (110,000Rp, 12 hours) also leave from a stand on Jl Soekarno-Hatta on the way to the Batu Ampar terminal.

Getting Around

TO/FROM THE AIRPORT

Taxis to/from the airport cost a standard 35,000Rp. A short walk from the airport, you can catch route number 7 taxis on the highway going to the Damai minibus terminal. Transfer to a route number 1 or 3 taxi to get into town (1500Rp).

TAXI MINIBUS

Damai, along Jl Sudirman towards the airport, is the main minibus terminal in town. The usual price within town is 1500Rp, but watch out for overcharging.

For more personalised service at a budget price, *ojek* cost between 6000Rp and 8000Rp per ride.

SAMARINDA

☎ 0541 / pop 600,000

The mighty Sungai Mahakam skirts Samarinda like a giant muddy flood. Here the river is a highway in its own right, peppered with houseboats and fishing vessels, boats lugging timber and tugs pulling demonic loads of coal. Along the banks, the city follows the water via a green esplanade, with two spectacular mosques dominating the view. Although it's another important trading port, Samarinda has retained far more of its Indonesian character than Balikpapan, and visitors will get a dose of East Kalimantan culture in between the business blocks. Meandering through the stalls of the lively Citra Niaga market will fill the nostrils, ears and eyes with all the heady activity of Southeast Asia. Samarinda city maps and regional maps can be found in the Gramedia bookshop in the Mesra Indah shopping centre.

Information

INTERNET ACCESS

Internet Cafe (Jl KH Khalid 1, Hotel MJ; per hr 10,500Rp)
Wartel Helma (Jl Basuki Rahmat 22; per hr 8000Rp)

MONEY

There are plenty of ATMs about town. For foreign exchange:

BCA bank (Bank Central Asia; Jl Sudirman)
BNI bank (Bank Negara Indonesia; cnr Jl P Sebatik & Jl Panglima Batur)

POST

Main post office (cnr Jl Gajah Mada & Jl Awang Long)

TOURIST INFORMATION

Tourist office (☎ 736850; cnr Jl Sudirman & Jl Awang Long) Decent information about the city and surrounds with some English-speaking staff.

TRAVEL AGENCIES

Many of Samarinda's travel agencies offer tours upriver.

Angkasa Express (☎ 200281; fax 200280; Plaza Lembu Swana)
Mesra Tours (☎ 738787, 732772; fax 741017; www.mesra.com/tour; Jl KH Khalid 1, Hotel Mesra) Excellent tours along Sungai Mahakam, treks to West Kalimantan, the Apokayan Highlands, Loksado in South Kalimantan and tours to Tanjung Puting National Park in Central Kalimantan. The manager Lucas Zwaal speaks fluent Dutch, English and Bahasa Indonesia.
Travel Waperisama (☎ 743124; Jl Diponegoro 7) Good for domestic flights.

Sights

Samarinda is a pleasant place to stroll around and the main attraction is seeing the city in action. There are two striking mosques on the waterfront, the oldest of which is **Mesjid Raya Darussalam** (Jl Niaga Selatan). It's possible to enter the mosque as long as it's not during Friday prayers. Visitors should dress respectfully, which means long pants and sleeves. About 3km west, the largest mosque in Southeast Asia is being constructed and its spires and gilded domes are suitably dramatic.

Every Sunday at 2pm traditional ceremonies incorporating dance and singing are held in the Kenyah Dayak village of **Pampang**, around 26km west of Samarinda. These are not made-for-tourist performances and the ritual is unadulterated. Inhabitants of the village still adorn their hands, feet, arms and legs with traditional tattoos and the women's earlobes are stretched by their characteristic earrings. The ceremonies are performed inside and around a longhouse. If you are taking photographs it's polite to make a small donation. Yellow public minibuses head to Pampang from Samarinda's Segiri long-distance bus terminal for around 7000Rp per person one way.

During the day the area between Jl Panglima Batur and **Citra Niaga** is bustling with vehicles, gold merchants, food-stall operators and fruit sellers.

On the south side of Sungai Mahakam, in the part of town called **Samarinda Seberang**, you can visit cottage industries where Samarinda-style sarongs are woven. The traditional East Kalimantan wraparound is woven from *doyo* leaf.

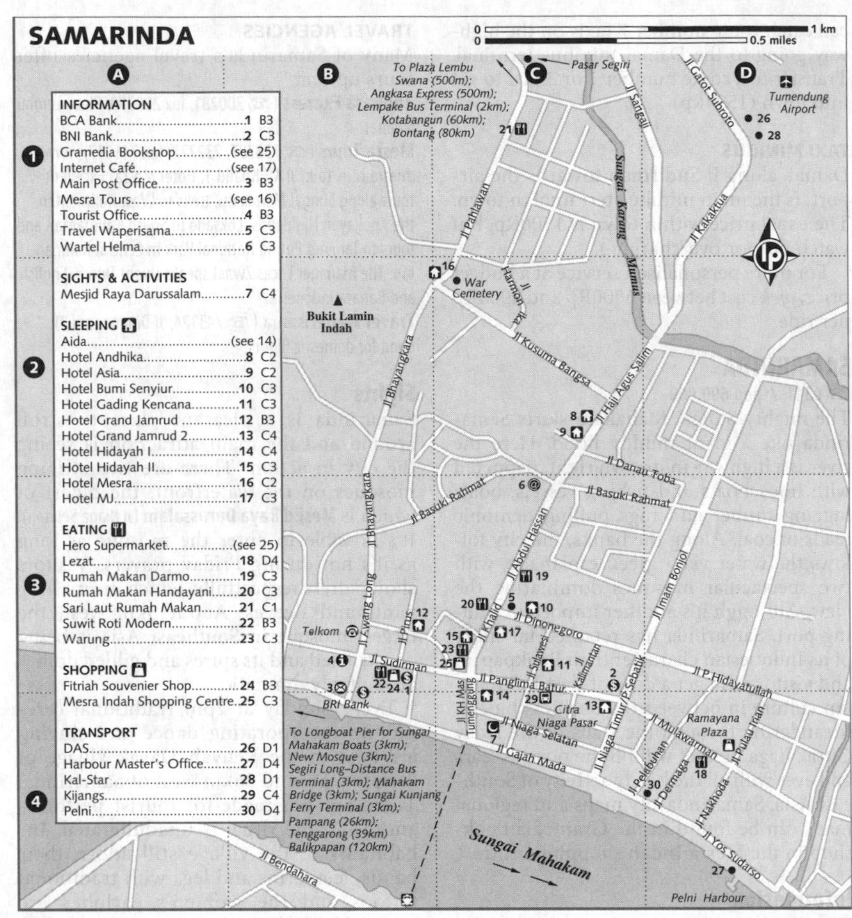

Sleeping

Budget hotels far outweigh midrange and top end options in Samarinda.

BUDGET

Hotel Asia (☎ 731013; fax 746426; Jl Haji Agus Salim 33; r from 52,000Rp; ❄) It doesn't waste much energy on the aesthetics but Hotel Asia's sheets are crisp and the surfaces clean. Skip the dismal economy rooms and splurge a few rupiah on the standard or medium ones, which have hot water and working flyscreens.

Hotel Hidayah I (☎ 731210/7311261; fax 737761; Jl KH Mas Temenggung; s 100,000-155,000Rp, d 125,000-190,000Rp; ❄) Aiming high, the efficiently run Hotel Hidayah I hits the mark with dependable budget rooms, showers, air-con options, a good restaurant and a balcony bar. It's also right in the thick of Citra Niaga, so there's a constant (noisy) buzz of activity.

Cheap as chips:

Hotel Hidayah II (☎ 741712; Jl Khalid 25; s from 50,000Rp, d 100,000-125,000Rp; ❄) Pleasant but windowless rooms.

Hotel Pirus (☎ 741873; fax 735890; Jl Pirus 30; r from 50,000Rp; ❄)

Aida (☎ 742572; Jl KH Mas Tumenggung; r incl breakfast from 95,000Rp; ❄) Low fuss and plenty of room types.

MIDRANGE

Hotel Gading Kencana (☎ 731512, 741043; fax 731954; Jl Sulawesi 4; r incl breakfast 115,000-187,500Rp;

) Possibly the only hotel in Indonesia where a Harley Davidson greets you in the foyer, the Gading Kencana has tidy and spacious rooms with air-con and private *mandi* or bathroom. Some of the cheaper versions have far more sunlight than their better-bedded upgrades.

Hotel MJ (747689, www.mjhotel.com; Jl KH Khalid 1; r 198,000-475,000Rp plus 21% tax;) Behind a bank-like façade, Hotel MJ has comfortable, sunlit rooms with bland but inoffensive décor. The beds are beautifully oversized and the ground floor has a restaurant, travel agent, internet café and boutique.

Hotel Grand Jamrud 2 (731233; fax 736096; Jl Panglima Batur 45; r incl breakfast 200,000-389,000Rp;) Emulating a Western chain, this sparkling hotel has austere but spotless rooms and pristine Western bathrooms. All have air-con but hot water costs a little extra. There are smiles aplenty from staff and breakfast is ample for lunch and dinner too.

Also available:

Hotel Grand Jamrud (743828; fax 743837; Jl Jamrud 34; r 160,000-315,000Rp;) Cool and comfortable.

Hotel Andhika (742358; fax 743507; Jl Haji Agus Salim 37; r incl breakfast 110,000-215,000Rp;) Pokey economy rooms but lovely 'medium' versions.

TOP END

Hotel Mesra (732772; www.mesra.com/hotel; Jl Pahlawan 1; r 320,000-630,000Rp, cottage 850,000Rp, ste 1,648,000Rp;) Presiding over town from an elevated position with plenty of greenery, Hotel Mesra has indulgent rooms and lovely cottages. Extras include tennis courts, a large pool, restaurants and bars.

Hotel Bumi Senyiur (741443; www.senyiur.co.id; Jl Diponegoro 17-19; r from US$85, ste from US$150 plus 21% tax;) Glitzy and modern, this luxury hotel has more brass than class but the rooms are lovely and the wealth of facilities excellent.

Eating

Samarinda's chief gastronomic wonder is the brilliant orange *udang galah* (giant river prawn) found in all the local warungs.

Rumah Makan Handayani (732452; Jl Abdul Hassan 7; mains 7,000-15,000Rp; lunch & dinner) A fat photo album illustrates every dish on the Indonesian-flavoured menu at this quiet and clean restaurant. You can wolf down tasty *gado gado* (mixed vegetables and peanut sauce) and *nasi goreng* (fried rice), or linger over more refined chicken, seafood and pigeon.

Rumah Makan Darmo (737287; Jl Abdul Hassan 38; mains 12,000-20,000Rp; lunch & dinner) If you pass by this Chinese-cum-Indonesian restaurant early enough, you may see them unloading the day's live crab and fresh seafood. The menu is exhaustive and there's a bright sea of spotless tables upstairs.

Sari Laut Rumah Makan (735848; Jl Pahlawan; mains 25,000-40,000Rp; dinner) It's worth the small journey north to tuck into the best *udang galah* in town. Super fresh and served in sizzling fragrant, spicy or Padang style, these dishes lure Javanese tourists by the car load.

Quick eats, bakeries and self-catering:

Suwit Roti Modern (Jl Sudirman 8; snacks 4,000Rp; breakfast & lunch) Sticky pastries and bread.

Warung (Jl Khalid; snacks 2,000-5,000Rp; breakfast, lunch & dinner) Excellent and nameless, near Mesra Indah Shopping Centre.

Hero supermarket (Mesra Indah Shopping Centre)

Shopping

Rattan goods, *doyo*-leaf cloth, carvings and other forest products are available from a string of souvenir shops west along the riverfront on Jl Slamet Riyadi and Jl Martadinata. Mesra Indah Shopping Centre is a large, glossy mall with a food court and Western-style clothing shops.

Fitriah Souvenir shop (Jl Sudirman 10) Catering to tourists, this shop sells high-quality items with price tags to match.

Getting There & Away

AIR

DAS (735250; Jl Gatot Subroto 92) flies to Melak, Long Ampung Data Dawai and Tanjung Selore several times a week. A month's advance booking is generally necessary to secure a seat. DAS and **Kal-Star** (742110; Jl Gatot Subroto 80) also fly to Tarakan, Berau and Nunukan.

BOAT

Pelni (741402; Jl Yos Sudarso 76) boats travelling between Balikpapan and Nunukan, and Balikpapan and Surabaya often take passengers in Samarinda (see p648). Fares vary depending on the boat; your best option is to check at the office for updated information.

The *Teratai* is a private boat that leaves every second day for Berau (150,000Rp,

27 hours). Ticket sellers hang around on Jl Yos Sudarso outside the harbour passenger terminal.

For information on which boat leaves when, check at the **harbour master's office** (Kantor Administrator Pelabuhan; Jl Yos Sudarso 2), about 200m east of Jl Nakhoda.

For daily passenger boats heading up Sungai Mahakam, take a green A route taxi to get to Sungai Kunjang ferry terminal, southwest of the town centre. Get to the pier by 6am, as boats leave at 7am. The journey to Melak (upper deck 120,000Rp) takes 19 hours and to Long Iram one day and a night (upper deck 150,000Rp). If conditions permit it's another 12 hours to Long Bagun (upper deck 200,000Rp). Most boats have a sleeping deck upstairs, as well as a sleeping deck and simple canteen on the lower level.

BUS

From Samarinda you can head northwest to Tenggarong or south to Balikpapan. The long-distance bus terminal is adjacent to the river-boat terminal at Sungai Kunjang, on the north side of the river a couple of kilometres upstream from the Mahakam bridge. Take a green A taxi from the centre of town (2500Rp). There are daily buses to Balikpapan (19,500Rp, two hours) and frequent buses to Kota Bangun (20,000Rp, three hours).

There are also Kijangs to Sebulu (8000Rp, 45 minutes) from Citra Niaga or Tenggarong (8000Rp, one hour) from Harapan Baru, the terminus for the orange G taxi, which leaves from Citra Niaga.

Buses to Bontang (20,000Rp, three hours, daily) and Berau (135,000Rp, 16 hours, daily) leave from the Lempake terminal north of the city, at the end of the B taxi route (5000Rp), which you can hail on Jl Bhayangkara.

Getting Around

Taxis from Tumendung airport are 35,000Rp. Alternatively, walk 100m down to Jl Gatot Subroto, turn left and catch a reddish-brown B taxi – all the way to the waterfront (3000Rp).

City minibuses, called taxis, run along several overlapping routes, designated A, B and C. Route C goes past Hotel Mesra and the university area. Most short runs cost 2500Rp.

KUTAI NATIONAL PARK

One of East Kalimantan's most underrated pockets of wilderness, Kutai National Park holds excellent opportunities to see wild orang-utans and prolific bird life. Sadly sizeable chunks of the park remain damaged due to fire, logging and entrepreneurial farmers, but the remaining forest teems with wildlife. Access to Kutai from Samarinda is easy, and if you're heading north it's a great way to break up the journey.

To get here catch a yellow bus from Samarinda's Lempake terminal to Bontang (20,000Rp, three hours), where you need to register at the **National Park office** (PHKA; Jl Mularman 236; ⏲ 7.30am-4pm Mon-Thu, 8am-noon Fri). Registration is free, but you must provide photocopies of your passport. Technically you don't need a guide to enter the park but finding orang-utans without one can be difficult. PHKA staff can act as guides for around 50,000Rp (or 100,000Rp for trekking) per day, plus transport costs. It's possible to charter a boat from the PHKA office into the park for around 200,000Rp.

A more intrepid alternative is to continue your bus journey from Bontang north to Sangata (10,000Rp). Ask the driver to drop you off at the main street rather than the bus terminal and walk several hundred metres to the right to **Hotel Kutai Parmai** (r 100,000Rp) and a small market. From the banks near the market you can pay local fishermen to take you to Camp Kakap in the park for around 200,000Rp one way. A cheaper way to do this is to catch a yellow local bus from Sangata's main street to Kabo Jaya, a small fishing settlement just west of the town. Charters from here only cost around 90,000Rp but they may be harder to come by.

Inside the park you can stay overnight at one of the basic guesthouses at Camp Kakap research centre, or at Sangkima for around 100,000Rp per night. Facilities are rudimentary and you must bring your own food. Staff at the office in Bontang will be able to provide updated information about staying overnight.

TENGGARONG

☎ 0541 / pop 75,000

A surprising pocket of urban finery, comely Tenggarong sits about 40km from Samarinda on the banks of Sungai Mahakam.

Once the capital of the mighty sultanate of Kutai, the town's regal air is today buoyed by the colour and flair of government investment. An elegant esplanade sidles up to the river before giving way to an ordered grid of streets and tidy buildings. Tenggarong is a pleasant place to explore on foot and there's enough to keep you here for a day or two. It's also a beautifully laid-back alternative to Samarinda.

Orientation & Information

Lippo Bank (Jl Sudirman) Has an ATM.
PT Duta Miramar (☎ 661184; Jl Kartini 35) Flight bookings.
Tourist office (☎ 661042; fax 661093; Jl Diponegoro) Information on the Erau Festival, the main cultural attraction at Pulau Kumala.

Sights

Tenggarong's **Mulawarman Museum** (Jl Diponegoro; admission 2500Rp; 10am-2pm Tue-Sun) is a tribute to the sultanate history of the area. The building is the former palace, although this version was built by the Dutch in 1936 after the more aesthetic original was destroyed by fire. The ground floor holds a modicum of artefacts and belongings of the 19 sultans who reigned here, including an elaborate Balinese puppet theatre complete with musical instruments, which was a gift from the Sultan of Yogyakarta. There are centuries-old statues, an opulent bedroom setting and some exquisite *doyo* cloth woven by Dayak women. Open only on Sunday, the basement holds the sultan's magnificent porcelain collection, which includes Yuan, Ming and Qing dynasty Chinese water jars.

Behind the museum the 'new' **Kedaton Kertanegara** (Sultan's Palace) is a photographer's delight. Huge but uninhabited, the building boasts beautifully crafted wooden balconies and magnificent stained-glass windows.

Across the banks of the river, **Pulau Kumala** (admission 10,000Rp; 9am-5pm) is a kitsch fun park occupying a chunk of the island by the same name. Littered with tame rides and activities, it's aimed squarely at young families. Unfortunately it was constructed at the expense of a once lush forest. Water taxis to the island leave from the pier at the end of Jl Imam Bonjol and cost 20,000Rp one way.

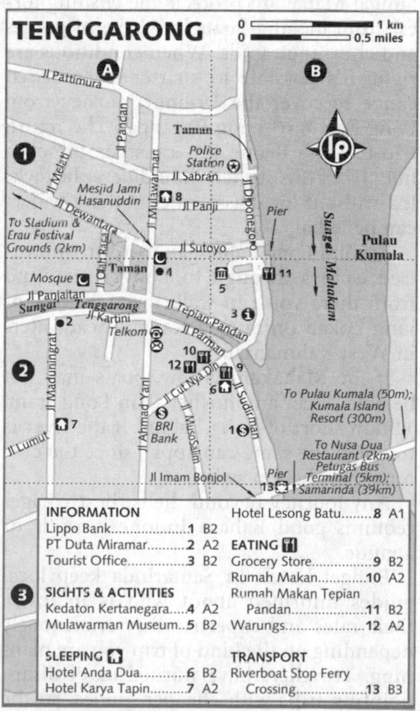

Festivals & Events

Once a year, Dayak people travel to Tenggarong from various points in Kalimantan to celebrate the **Erau Festival**. Although the festival is somewhat touristy, it's a good opportunity to see the Dayaks in their traditional finery perform tribal dances and ritual ceremonies and a fabulous excuse for a huge inter-tribal party. The festival is usually held the last week in September and lasts for one to two weeks. Contact the tourist office in Tenggarong or Samarinda for the exact dates.

Sleeping

Hotel Anda Dua (☎ 661409; Jl Sudirman 65; r 60,000-125,000Rp;) Basic, fan-cooled rooms with shared *mandis* occupy the rustic front section of this friendly hotel, and there is a splendid timber building out the back with comfortable air-con rooms containing private bathroom. Tea and coffee are served for these guests on the wide and gracious veranda.

Hotel Karya Tapin (☎ 661258; Jl Maduningrat 29; r incl breakfast 175,000-200,000Rp;) The décor and bedspreads are a tad faded, but the rooms at this small hotel come with high ceilings, TVs, showers in the bathrooms and spotless interiors. Service is exuberant.

Kumala Island Resort (☎ 6690277; fax 7069296; Pulau Kumala; r from 400,000Rp, ste 1,500,000Rp;) Planted on the southern tip of Pulau Kamala, this resort has a splendid timber interior and comfortable, generic rooms with private balconies. There are also lovely cottages plus a pool, spa, bar and restaurant.

Hotel Lesong Batu (☎ 663499; www.kutaikartanegara.com/lesongbatu; Jl Panji 1; r incl breakfast 532,000-602,000Rp, ste 2,108,000Rp;) Tenggarong's finest hotel has a lobby big enough to park a plane in, in fact several vintage cars reside in it. Opulent and brassy, it offers indulgent rooms and first-class service. There's a good café serving Indonesian and Western fare, and a classy piano lounge.

Eating

Rumah Makan Tepian Pandan (Jl Diponegoro 23; mains 10,000-20,000Rp; lunch & dinner) Another waterside restaurant, Tepian Pandan serves a good spread of dishes, leaning towards Chinese and Indonesian flavours. The atmosphere is relaxed and the views across the river to the island are lovely.

Rumah Makan (☎ 663087; Jl Cut Nya Din; mains 10,000Rp-20,000Rp; breakfast, lunch & dinner) This friendly option serves fresh and tasty Padang food, displayed in the front window, as well as great tea and coffee in the morning. The interior is ordered and spotless.

Nusa Dua Restaurant (Jl Bukit Biru; mains 20,000-30,000Rp; lunch & dinner) Tenggarong's classiest restaurant is a couple of kilometres south of the centre but worth the small trip. Excellent Chinese and Indonesian cuisine is complemented by great service and even better views.

A number of warungs are on Jl Cut Nya Din, near the intersection with Jl Sudirman, and a **grocery store** (Jl Sudirman) near the same corner is well stocked with food and cold drinks.

Getting There & Away

Kijangs to Tenggarong from Samarinda take one hour and cost 10,000Rp. They deposit passengers at the Petugas Bus terminal on the outskirts of Tenggarong, about 5km from the centre of town. From here *taxi kota* go to the centre of Tenggarong for 1500Rp. *Ojek* will take you for 5000Rp. Kijangs from the Petugas Bus terminal also go to Kota Bangun (15,000Rp, two hours).

SUNGAI MAHAKAM

Carving a mighty swathe through Borneo's southern pocket, Sungai Mahakam dominates the landscape and culture of southeast Kalimantan. Much of the towering forest that once flanked its 523km length has been reduced to flat and lonely scrub, but detouring onto small lakes and shallow tributaries rewards voyagers with Amazonian scenery. Here silence is punctuated by the chatter of impish macaques, the hoot of indignant proboscis monkeys and the flash of verdant kingfishers. Many of the towns and villages along the Mahakam are built over wooden walkways to keep them above water during the wet season. Some abodes are grand ironwood affairs with floor-to-ceiling glass fronts and sweeping balconies, while others are decaying shacks tucked neatly behind the 'Jones'.

Daily passenger boats ply the river from Samarinda all the way to Long Bagun. Here Sungai Mahakam protects the ensuing forest from logging boats by virtue of gorges and churning rapids. When conditions are right, it's possible to charter a motorised canoe to cover the 18-hour journey from Long Bagun to Long Pahangai. The return trip to Long Bagun takes just six or seven hours, but this stretch should *never* be tackled without local assistance – these waters can be lethal.

Beyond Long Pahangai, there are motorised canoes through to Long Apari, and from there you can walk through to Tanjung Lokan on Sungai Kapuas headwaters in West Kalimantan.

If the Mahakam is low, boats may not be able to get any further than Long Iram, 114km short of Long Bagun. If the river is too high the same can apply, since the currents may be too swift.

Any journey beyond the earliest villages requires good Bahasa Indonesia skills or a guide.

Budget hotels in Samarinda keep local guides informed about who is in town; their rates and expertise vary enormously depending on the kind of trip you are planning. Travellers have warned us of disappointing trips with cheaper guides, so the

A CES BY ANY OTHER NAME

The most common form of transport off Sungai Mahakam's beaten waterway is the *ces* – a motorised canoe with a long propeller shaft. These innovations only came to the area in 1990 when an entrepreneurial soul attached a 21/1HP engine to the back of his boat. The name (pronounced chess) comes from the sound made when starting the engine. It stuck and became as good a moniker as any. Coursing the river with all the power of a lawnmower must have been heavy going but the engines you'll encounter today are more likely to be 20HP.

rule of thumb is you get what you pay for, however Bahasa Indonesia-language skills will of course reduce the risk substantially. For real adventure, don't expect anything in the way of a bargain.

Suryadi (☎ 081 64598263; surya57@hotmail.com) is a reliable and friendly guide and a mine of information on treks upriver. He can organise customised trips along the Mahakam, across into West Kalimantan or into the Apokayan Highlands, at reasonable rates. If you can't reach him by phone, leave a message at **Hotel Hidayah I** (Jl Mas Tumenggung). **Rajim Rustam** (☎ 081 25854915, 0541-735641) is another English-speaking, knowledgeable and reliable guide operating out of Samarinda.

Kota Bangun

Kota Bangun is a dusty stop at the start of the Mahakam lake country, about three hours by bus from Samarinda along a sealed road. The only reason to stop here is to hire a *ces* (motorised canoe) and elude the main river via Muara Muntai, Tanjung Isuy and Mancong. Once off the main drag, pockets of forest climb maniacally, opening up for small villages populated by friendly and curious locals. You'll have to bargain for a *ces*, but it should be around 200,000Rp to Muara Muntai (one hour), 400,000Rp to Tanjung Isuy (three hours) and 600,000Rp to Mancong (six hours). Maskur, a local schoolteacher in Kota Bangun, speaks good English and offers his services as a guide.

If you get stuck here, you can overnight at **Losmen Muzirat** (☎ 081 25532287; Jl Mesjid Raya 46; s/d 20,000/40,000Rp), directly opposite the main mosque. It has basic rooms with shared *mandis* and abrupt staff.

There are eight buses a day to/from Samarinda (20,000Rp, three hours) between 7am and 4pm.

Muara Muntai

Muara Muntai is a colourful Kutai market town built over mud flats in the heart of the Mahakam's lake country. Wide, sturdy boardwalks act as streets, and dwellings range from cobbled-together shacks to two-storey timber houses. Check out the Bappeda's (Agency for Regional Development) fine, old wooden abode and huge portico, straight ahead from the dock. Things shut down during afternoon prayers but the population fills the boardwalks after dusk, particularly when the weekly night market takes place, although it changes regularly so pinning down a day is futile.

Penginapan Adi Guna (☎ 0541-205871, 081 545 146 578; tw 50,000Rp) is a clean and friendly losmen with simple, fan-cooled rooms and roomy shared *mandis*. There's a balcony overlooking a patch of boardwalk, and tea and coffee are served at all times. To get here follow the boardwalk from the dock and turn right.

An alternative is **Penginapan Tiara** (☎ 081 347 376 794; s/d 30,000/50,000Rp), a smaller affair left of the docks, also with simple fan-cooled rooms and shared *mandis*. It's not as breezy as Adi Guna but there's a good balcony out the front where you can watch Muara Muntai's world go by.

The warung between the two losmen serves *sop Muara Muntai*, a filling soup with rice, chicken, noodles, cabbage and a squeeze of lime. Several warungs opposite the Nita Wardana sell fried rice, noodles etc.

A longboat to/from Samarinda costs 70,000Rp and takes about 12 hours. But you can reach the village in around five hours by bussing from Samarinda to Kota Bangun and hiring a *ces* from there (200,000Rp, two hours). You can also charter a *ces* in Muara Muntai for a full day on the lakes for about 500,000Rp.

Tanjung Isuy

Tanjung Isuy, on the shores of Danau Jempang, is the first Dayak village on the Mahakam. This is Banuaq Dayak territory, but don't anticipate traditional dress and tattoos.

Modernisation has introduced stereos, televisions and the ubiquitous motorcycle, all of which are welcomed by those who can afford them. The transformation is largely skin deep, though, and the sense of community remains intact. The most popular night-time entertainment is still chewing the fat with locals on their front verandas, the rooster cacophony still calls the 5am alarm and the all-pervading river remains the focus of activity.

Tour groups stop at Tanjung Isuy for an 'authentic' Dayak experience. Most arrive in speedboats from Samarinda, mob the souvenir stalls in the longhouse, watch a mix of Dayak dancing and zoom back. Activity focuses on the **Louu Taman Jamrout**, a longhouse vacated in the late 1970s, and rebuilt by the provincial government as a craft centre and tourist hostel.

Despite the commercial nature of the pay-by-the-hour performances in the Louu Taman Jamrout, they are lively, rhythmic and loads of fun for the whole town. The mix of Kenyah, Kayan and Banuaq dancing is confusing, but very entertaining. Solo travellers could commission a dance for about 350,000Rp.

A *ces* journey from Muara Muntai to Tanjung Isuy traverses spectacular wetlands, shallow lakes and **Jantur**, a Banjar village built on a flooded mud flat. Jantur's **mesjid** stands alone on a bend in the river, accessible only by boats and high gangplanks. Beside it is the cemetery, the highest point in town but still just 20cm above the water level at the end of the wet season. Bodies buried here must be anchored in their watery graves to prevent them bobbing to the surface.

There are two good losmen in Tanjung Isuy (both have shared *mandis*). About 500m from the jetty, **Losmen Wisata** (Jl Indonesia Australia; s/d 35,000/50,000Rp) has rooms with double beds leading off a central dining area. The common space has breezy, wall to wall windows and a lengthy conversation-inducing table. Just next door is **Louu Taman Jamrout** (Jl Indonesia Australia; per person 60,000Rp), where the Dayak performances are held. Both losmen have mosquito nets to keep the ravenous bugs at bay, although the equally prolific geckos keep the numbers down. At night macaques scramble over the buildings' exteriors like cheeky stowaways.

Warung Makan Arema (Jl Taman Siswa; mains 7,000Rp; lunch & dinner) dishes up fragrant servings of *sop ayam* (chicken soup), tofu, veggies and chicken with large bowls of rice. It also sells everything from bottled water to iced coffee in a carton. From the jetty turn right and follow the main street. Take the first street on the left; the warung is about 200m along.

There are some nice *doyo* weavings and *mandau* (machetes) with carved handles (as well as a lot of junk) available in the craft centre next door to the Louu Taman Jamrout, at reasonable prices. Back down the road towards the dock, there's a house across from the first intersection that also sells carvings and weavings.

GETTING THERE & AWAY

Longboats from Samarinda don't schedule stops to Tanjung Isuy because it's well off the main route. The easiest way to get here is to hire a *ces* from Muara Muntai (200,000Rp, 1½ to two hours). There are also public *ces* to Muara Muntai leaving daily in the early evening (from 60,000Rp, depending on the number of passengers), but check at the dock. You can charter a *ces* direct to Kota Bangun (400,000Rp), then catch a bus and be in Samarinda or Balikpapan that night.

Mancong

The scenic area heading south to Mancong is a highlight of Sungai Mahakam and well worth the time and money it incurs to explore. The journey by *ces* takes you along Sungai Ohong, where the gorgeous stretch of riverside jungle is home to flocks of magnificent water birds. Hornbills sail above the canopy, electric blue kingfishers skim close to the water, and proboscis monkeys fling themselves from one branch to the next. Near villages and towns on the water, large ibis hang around the house docks hoping for an easy feed.

Mancong itself is a small village of only 500 or so people, but it provides one of the best impressions of how life on the Mahakam was before the era of logging, coal and oil. One side of the village is backed by towering trees and thickets of forest. The other was cleared long ago for cash crops of oil palm, which went up in smoke in the '97 fires. The main attraction is a grand,

FANCY MEETING YOU HERE

Tanjung Isuy sits in the southwest corner of **Danau Jempang** (Jempang Lake), a 15,000-hectare body of water fed by the tributaries of the Mahakam. The wetlands of Danau Jempang are crucial breeding and migration grounds for approximately 90 bird species as well as the critically endangered **Irrawaddy dolphin**, also known as the Pesut Mahakam. It is estimated that only 70 remain in the Mahakam and although they are protected by law, their habitat is not. Traffic along the Mahakam poses the greatest threat; collisions with fishing vessels, entanglement in nets, water and noise pollution from giant coal tugs and chemical waste from the mining industry have all taken their toll.

The good news is that a local nongovernment organisation – **Yayasan Konservasi RASI** (Conservation for Rare Aquatic Species of Indonesia; www.geocities.com/yayasan_konservasi_rasi/index.html) is making headway in the conservation of the Pesut Mahakam. Based at Muara Pahu, where the dolphins are most likely to be spotted, the organisation has researched and monitored the dolphins since 2000, raised awareness among the local population and worked with local fishermen to reduce specific dangers to the species. Their efforts have paid off and between 2003 and 2006 the number of dolphins rose from 65 to 70.

In conjunction with **Mesra Tours** (☎ 738787, 732772; fax 741017; www.mesra.com/tour), RASI promotes ecotours of the area, providing accurate information about where to best sight the dolphins and how to do so in a nonobtrusive manner. If travelling independently you can visit RASI's headquarters at Muara Pahu, which has information displays about the region's biodiversity importance. Staff here can also advise which tributaries to visit, and there are volunteer opportunities if you'd like to turn it into a real adventure.

From Muara Pahu you can hire a *ces* for a scenic river tour down **Sungai Bolowan** – a favourite stomping ground of the dolphins. The roundtrip takes about two hours and costs around 200,000Rp.

two-storey **longhouse** built with government assistance in 1987 after the original collapsed. With its demise went the last of the traditional longhouse-living in Mancong as families moved into new, separate dwellings. Today only one family occupies the new longhouse, making it the cleanest of its kind in all of Borneo. The building is still used for ceremonial purposes, including folk dances. A dozen or so totem statues grace the front, each marking a buffalo slaughtered for a feast. It's possible to stay in the longhouse for around 60,000Rp per person but be prepared for no electricity, bedding or food. Bahasa Indonesia is needed in order to ask permission from the family inside or whoever is manning the souvenirs in the white shack by the jetty.

To get to Mancong hire a *ces* from Tanjung Isuy (about 250,000Rp for the round trip) early in the morning. You'll need to go slowly to appreciate the scenery along the way and it should take about three hours in each direction. You can reduce the cost by returning to Tanjung Isuy by *ojek* for 100,000Rp. The trip takes about half an hour.

THE UPPER MAHAKAM

Melak & Around

Melak is the largest town on the Mahakam and the dusty activity here is a far stretch from the fishing villages you will have encountered along the way. Its ever expanding streets are filled with 4WDs and the constant thud and chatter of construction, but Melak is a good supply stop for trips further north and the surrounding area is worth visiting. There's a colourful weekly market every Tuesday, where giant catfish and *udang galah* dwarf earthly sized chickens and fuzzy bunches of rambutan.

About 30km inland from Melak, the tiny settlement of **Eheng** is home to one of the last operating longhouses in East Kalimantan. Built in 1960, its crumbling façade is held together by new planks of hardwood. About 30 families occupy the interior but they're only here in force on Monday night – market day eve. This is when most of the inhabitants who have been gathering rattan reeds or tending rice fields come home to prepare produce for the next day and indulge in a bout of socialising and gambling. The inhabitants are happy for people to have a look inside their home but Bahasa Indonesia is essential here, as a mark of respect more than anything else. It's also possible to stay overnight but you need to take bedding and food. It's also polite to offer money for your stay, but this will vary on who you speak to and how many of you there are. If you're just visiting during the day take a small gift with you – cigarettes and bonbons are favourites (despite the health implications).

From Melak a public minibus goes to Barong Tongkok then continues on to Eheng (12,000Rp, one hour), or you can hire an *ojek* in Melak for about 75,000Rp a day, or charter a 4WD for 300,000Rp.

Mencimai has an excellent **museum** (admission by donation; Mon-Fri) with detailed explanations in English and Bahasa Indonesia of the local systems of shifting agriculture. It explains the Banuaq systems of land use, methods for collecting wild honey, traps for pigs and monkeys, and bark-cloth production. It also has relics, including excellent old *mandau* and rattan ware.

In Melak **Penginapan Setiawan** (☎ 0545-41437; Jl Dr Sutomo; r 50,000Rp) is the newest losmen in town and has nine spacious rooms off a bright, open corridor. Tea and coffee are free, as is boiled drinking water. Next door, **Penginapan Blue Safir** (☎ 0545-41098; Jl Dr Sutomo; r 50,000Rp), has similar, if more dated rooms. About 100m closer to the jetty, **Warung Banjar** (Jl Dr Sutomo; mains 10,000Rp; lunch & dinner) serves good barbecued catfish with a side of soup and rice.

Souvenir shops are scattered around town and you can pick up great rattan bags, hats, baskets etc for 25,000Rp to 50,000Rp, depending on size and quality. You might find a few old *mandau* as well.

Boats leave daily for the 325km trip to Samarinda between 11am and 2pm (120,000Rp, 19 hours). A *ces* to/from Tanjung Isuy costs 500,000Rp and takes around four hours.

There is also a daily bus to Samarinda (100,000Rp, nine hours) but it's an exceedingly uncomfortable ride on unsealed roads. Regular public minibuses operate between Melak and Tering (9,000Rp, one hour).

Tering & Long Iram

A pleasant, quiet village with a few colonial buildings, Long Iram is often the end of the line for many would-be explorers because of river conditions or lack of time. It's an easy walk through market gardens to **Tering**, a congregation of three villages straddling the Mahakam at a point where the river begins an ascent north. Go north along Jl Soewondo, turn right at the path to the police station and walk on over pretty bridges to **Danau Gap**, 3km away.

On the northern bank of the river, **Tering Lama** is a Bahau Dayak village where traditional tattoos and elongated earlobes are still visible. The village also has four wooden statues carved in traditional Bahau Dayak style. There is also a magnificent church at the eastern end of town. **Tering Seberang** and **Tering Baru** are the busier counterparts on the southern side of the river. A *ces* between Long Iram and Tering takes about 40 minutes and will set you back around 60,000Rp.

When you arrive in Long Iram, get off at the floating café on the east bank, climb to the main road, turn right and wander down to **Penginapan Wahyu** (Jl Soewondo 57; r with breakfast per person 60,000Rp); look for the tiny sign opposite the two-storey shops. It has clean rooms.

Down the road Warung Lestari is the place to go for the best food on the Mahakam. Ignore the menu. Dinner is whatever's on the stove.

Long Iram is 1½ days' travel by longboat from Samarinda (lower/upper deck 110,000/150,000Rp).

Datah Bilang to Muara Merak

If conditions allow you to ferry upriver beyond Long Iram, places of interest include Datah Bilang, where there's a Protestant community of **Kenyah** and **Bahau Dayaks** who moved here from the Apokayan in the 1970s. The older women have the traditional long earlobes and will charge 15,000Rp to 20,000Rp per photograph. **Long Hubung**, 45 minutes north of Datah Bilang by motorised canoe (100,000Rp), is another Bahau Dayak village that has a basic **losmen** (r 50,000Rp).

Just 25km downstream is Muara Merak, a **Kenyah** settlement. Intrepid and experienced trekkers with good knowledge of Bahasa Indonesia may like to tackle some of the country here. It's possible to reach Tabang from Muara Merak by following Sungai Merah to the northeast. It's a seldom journeyed route and will take around six days to conquer. Good equipment, food and a Kenyah guide are essential. Unfortunately the latter can be difficult to come by but it's worth asking in Datah Bilang, Muara Merak and Long Hubung. Expect to pay at least 250,000Rp a day for their assistance. From Tabang you can journey down back to Kota Bangun along Sungai Belayan (see right).

Long Bagun to Long Apari

The end of the line for regular longboat services from Samarinda is Long Bagun, a small settlement with an abandoned longhouse, reasonably stocked shop for supplies and the utterly rudimentary **Penginapan Artomorow** (r 40,000Rp). It takes between three to six days by longboat from Samarinda, and the journey costs 150,000/180,000Rp for upper/lower deck. The rapids and shallow water here are prohibitive to large vessels and this turn of Mother Nature's hand has kept the forests eastwards safe from harm. Travel from this point onwards is more arduous and demanding, but it's where the real Borneo jungle lies.

The longboat journey from Samarinda to Long Bagun (200,000Rp, three days) stops overnight in Long Iram. Navigation can be tricky this far upriver and the crew uses the opportunity to sleep.

From Long Bagun you must charter motorised canoes from village to village or trek through the forests. River conditions must be optimal because of river rapids between Long Bagun and the next major settlement, **Long Pahangai**. Under normal conditions, it's a one- or two-day canoe trip from Long Bagun to Long Pahangai, then another day to Long Apari. **Long Lunuk**, between Long Pahangai and Long Apari, is a good place from which to visit Kenyah villages or alternatively, stay at **Tiong Ohang**, two hours upstream from Long Lunuk.

Long Apari is the uppermost longhouse village on the Mahakam and is beautiful. The longboat trip from Long Lunuk takes five to six hours. Dinner in Long Apari, if you're lucky, is often greasy pig and bony fish – tasty supplements from the city make welcome presents, not to mention a necessary break from the daily rice and noodles. The village is the stepping off point for treks to West Kalimantan.

GETTING THERE & AWAY

To start your trip from the top, fly to Data Dawai, an airstrip near Long Lunuk. DAS flies from Samarinda (500,000Rp, Wednesday, Friday and Saturday), but you need to book a month in advance. From there you can work your way downriver back to Samarinda, or trek overland to the Apokayan Highlands.

SUNGAI KEDANG KEPALA

There are regular longboat services up the Kedang Kepala, which branches north off the Mahakam near **Muara Kaman**; from Samarinda to **Muara Wahau** takes three days and two nights, and goes via the Kenyah and Bahau villages of **Tanjung Manis**, **Long Noran** and **Long Segar**. This trip is best for those looking to explore untouristed territory; the villages themselves are fairly isolated and many inhabitants have moved to more convenient destinations. Nearby caves were the site of 5th-century Sanskrit finds, now in the museum at Tenggarong.

An alternative route from Samarinda to Berau is to take a boat north from Muara Wahau to **Miau Baru** and try hitching a ride to the Dayak village of **Merapun**, two hours away. From Merapun, take a 12-hour boat ride down the Kelai to Berau.

SUNGAI BELAYAN

Another adventurous trip that offers a more cultural approach is up Sungai Belayan to **Tabang**. The Belayan branches northwest off the Mahakam at Kota Bangun, and chartered longboats take two nights and three days to reach Tabang from Samarinda (250,000Rp). You could also hire a *ces* in Kota Bangun to reach Tabang. The journey would only take about a day but expect to pay 1,000,000Rp plus for the expediency.

Tabang can also be reached on foot from the town of Muara Merak on the Mahakam. Hire a Punan guide in either Tabang or Muara Merak to lead you through the extensive rainforests that are nomadic Punan territory.

SUNGAI KAYAN & THE APOKAYAN HIGHLANDS

South of Tarakan is **Tanjung Selor** at the mouth of the mighty Sungai Kayan. Regular longboat services go up the Kayan as far as the Kenyah villages of **Mara I** and **Mara II**, but a long section of rapids – Kalimantan's wildest white water – prevents boats from reaching the headwaters of the Kayan in the Apokayan Highlands.

The Apokayan Highlands has some good trekking; you could also trek overland to the Mahakam headwaters from Long Ampung in about a week with a guide from Long Ampung. Guides in Samarinda lead easy or vigorous treks to Dayak longhouses from Long Ampung.

A most picturesque tour by **Suryadi** (☎ 081 64598263; surya57@hotmail.com), see p655, consists of the following itinerary: first a flight from Samarinda to Long Ampung on DAS, then a 2½-hour easy walk to stay overnight at the longhouse of **Long Uro**. The next day there's a 45-minute walk to the longhouse of **Lidung Payau** where you catch a boat back to Long Ampung for the flight back to Samarinda. Hardy travellers may include a difficult five-hour jungle walk from Lidung Payau to **Long Sungai Barang**. Nights are cold and longhouse verandas can be hard, so pack a sleeping bag.

DAS flies from Samarinda to Tanjung Selor (501,500Rp, daily except Friday and Sunday).

LONG BAWAN

Further north in the interior is the picturesque area around Long Bawan. Like the Apokayan, it's too far above the rapids to be of much interest to logging companies – yet. Also like the Apokayan, there's a noticeable military presence and prices are high, even for the simplest commodities. Any presents from the city will be welcome – cigarettes, toys, salt, sugar etc. DAS flies daily to Long Bawan from Tarakan for 450,000Rp. **Penginapan Agung Raya** (☎ 086 812105064; 60,000Rp) is a small, simple and clean hotel where you can overnight.

There is excellent trekking around Long Bawan, including forays into **Kayan Mentarang National Park**. Bordering Malaysian Sarawak to the west, this park holds the largest remaining block of rainforest in Kalimantan and boasts some of the most pristine tropical mountain ecosystems in the world. The rare clouded leopard, Malaysian sun bear and *banteng* (wild ox) are some of the spectacular fauna found in the area. The World Wildlife Fund (WWF) promotes ecotourism and a close relationship with the local communities to ensure sustainable development. With cloud forests reaching 2000m above sea level, you get the sense that you are the first to explore this rare and mystical landscape.

Treks in the area take several days, depending on your stamina and how long you want to hike for. A guide is essential and you should be able to secure one in Long Bawan for around 70,000Rp per day; ask Penginapan Agung Raya to get in contact with Alex Balang, who speaks English. Porters charge slightly less: 60,000Rp per day. Homestays in the area's villages cost between 60,000Rp and 90,000Rp, with meals included. Some of your journey may require the use of a motorised canoe, which will be your greatest expense at around 200,000Rp per hour.

For more information about visiting the park, contact the tourist offices in Samarinda (p649) or **Tanjung Selor** (☎ 0552-22321). For other information, including conservation, contact **Yayasan WWF Indonesia Kayan Mentarang Project** (☎ 0451-34661; fax 37242; Jl Gatot Subroto Rt 49, 53, Samarinda, Kalimantan Timur).

East of Kayan Mentarang lies the proposed **Sebuku Sembakung National Park**. The WWF is appealing to the Indonesian and Malaysian governments to establish the park as part of a network of protected areas, in order to conserve the remaining rainforests of the 'Heart of Borneo'. The proposed area for Sebuku Sembakung National Park is a pristine ecosystem that encapsulates 4000 sq km of all major habitats in Kalimantan, especially lowland hills composed of limestone outcrops. This area is home to the only known population of elephants in Kalimantan. Establishment of the park will be contingent on cooperation between the Malaysian and Indonesian governments and access is likely to remain poor for many years. The best source of information for progress is the **WWF website** (www.wwf.or.id).

BERAU

☎ 0554 / pop 52,000

Perched at the confluence of the Kelai, Berau and Segan rivers in Kalimantan's northeast corner, Berau is an ambling town with a sociable disposition. Inquisitive locals warm to new faces here and the place hums with a proud mood of self-sufficiency. The streets are sleepy during the day, but activity picks up after dusk when whole families pile onto *ojeks* and join the crowds at the nocturnal warungs.

People use the names Berau and Tanjung Redeb interchangeably. Strictly speaking, Tanjung Redeb is the spit of land between the Segan and Kelai rivers, whereas Berau refers to the whole urban area.

Information

ATMs are plentiful on Jl P Antasari and Jl Maulana.

BNI bank (Bank Negara Indonesia; Jl Maulana) US-dollar foreign exchange.

HG Computer (Jl Durian II; per hr 9,000Rp) Internet access.

Sights

Berau was once the seat of two minor kingdoms, Gunung Tabur, with its *kraton* (palace) on the banks of the Segan, and Sambaliung, with a *kraton* on the Kelai. The *kraton* face each other across Tanjung Redeb. Gunung Tabur's moment in history came towards the end of WWII when the *kraton* was mistaken for a Japanese military post and flattened by Allied bombers. The Sambaliung *kraton* was untouched, supposedly because of the spiritual power of two cannons.

The Gunung Tabur *kraton* was rebuilt, belfry and all, and is now **Museum Batiwakkal** (8am-2pm Mon-Sat; admission by donation). It contains a few relics, including an old cannon found in the jungle by the very first rajah; however, its spiritual powers have been in doubt since the Allied bombing. Canoe ferries cross the river regularly (1000Rp).

Sambaliung kraton is not a museum but has some relics of the last nine rajahs. The *kraton* has no strict opening hours but you should be able to access it between 10am and 3pm on weekdays. Get there by canoe (10,000Rp), or walk across Sungai Kelai by the bridge near the bus terminal. Just across the bridge on the right, the Hindu temple **Pura Agung Giri Natha** is worth a look as well.

At the bustling *pasar* by the bridge across Sungai Kelai you can purchase bunnies, birds, breakfast and just about everything in between, accompanied of course by the ubiquitous 'Hello Mister'.

The vivid green domes of Berau's monolithic **Mesjid Agung Baitul Hikmah** (Jl Mualana)

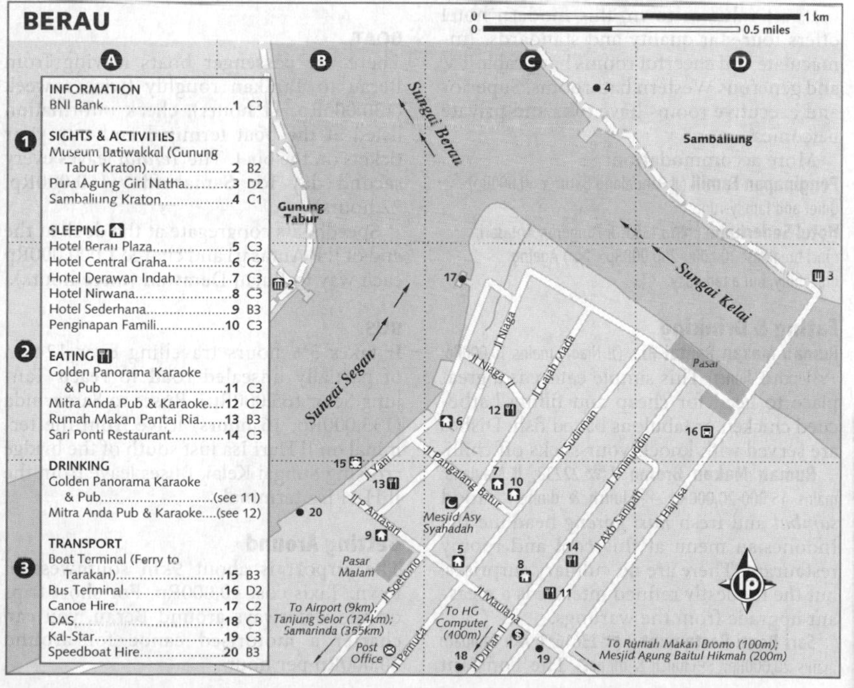

rise above the skyline and flicker with fairy lights at night. Inside the grounds are a polished oasis of brass and pillars.

Sleeping

Hotel Central Graha (☎ 22580; Jl Yani; r 30,000-100,000; ❄) The tidiest of Berau's cheap digs, this waterside hotel has snug and spartan fan-cooled rooms with shared *mandis*, which go for a song. If you're in need of a little more comfort opt for an air-con room with private *mandi*.

Hotel Nirwana (☎ 21893; Jl Aminuddin 715; s 60,000-100,000Rp, d 65,000-110,000Rp; ❄) The rooms here are snug but spotless and appealing, and even the simplest come with TV. In the cooler months, the fan-cooled options are great value. Breakfast is included.

Hotel Berau Plaza (☎ 23111; Jl P Antasari; r incl breakfast 140,000-190,000Rp; ❄) In a good central location, this long-standing hotel has reasonable accommodation, all with air-con and private bathrooms. The cheaper versions have small bathrooms and dim lighting but the place has a warm and efficient buzz.

Hotel Derawan Indah (☎ 24255; Jl Panglima Batur 396; r 250,000-350,000Rp plus 21% tax; ❄) Easily the best value in town, this modern hotel offers four-star quality and standards. Immaculate and cheerful rooms have cable TV and generous Western bathrooms. Superior and executive rooms have tubs and private balconies.

More accommodation:

Penginapan Famili (Jl Pangalang Batur; r 60,000Rp) Quiet and family-run.

Hotel Sederhana (☎ 21353; Jl Pangeran Antasari; r incl breakfast 200,000-280,000Rp; ❄) Ageing gracefully, but a tad dirty.

Eating & Drinking

Rumah Makan Pantai Ria (Jl Niaga; mains 10,000Rp; ⏰ lunch & dinner) This simple eatery is a great place to head for cheap and filling barbecued chicken or fabulous baked fish. Dishes are served with knock-your-socks off chilli.

Rumah Makan Bromo (☎ 22238; Jl Maulana; mains 15,000-20,000Rp; ⏰ lunch & dinner) Good *sambal* and fresh *nasi goreng* headline the Indonesian menu at this cool and roomy restaurant. There are no culinary surprises, but the modestly refined interior is a pleasant upgrade from the warungs.

Sari Ponti Restaurant (☎ 23616; Jl Akb Sanipah; mains 20,000Rp; ⏰ lunch & dinner) The constant stream of Chinese patrons proves how well the menu fares at this industrious restaurant. Chicken (cooked to perfection), seafood, beef, pigeon and plenty of veggie options are served in all manner of Chinese flavours, and the fruit juices are thick and fresh.

Both the following have restaurants next door serving the usual Indonesian fare plus a few Western dishes:

Mitra Anda Pub & Karaoke (Jl Gajah Mada) Cold beer and entertainment.

Golden Panorama Karaoke & Pub (Jl Akb Sanipah) Live music on weekends.

Wall to wall warungs spring up at night along Jl P Antasari, and you can tuck into barbecued shrimp, chicken and fish for under 10,000Rp.

Getting There & Away

AIR

DAS (☎/fax 21965; Jl P Durian II 26) and **Kal-Star** (☎/fax 21007; Jl Maulana 17) fly to Tarakan, Tanjung Selor and Nunukan daily between them. Kal-Star also flies to Balikpapan and Samarinda.

BOAT

There are passenger boats leaving from Berau to Tarakan roughly twice a week (130,000Rp, 11 hours); check information listed at the boat terminal and buy your tickets on the boat. The *Teratai* leaves every second day for Samarinda (150,000Rp, 27 hours).

Speedboats congregate at the dock at the end of Jl P Antasari and charge 1,000,000Rp each way to Pulau Derawan (three hours).

BUS

It takes 3½ hours travelling over 124km of partially unsealed road to reach Tanjung Selor (65,000Rp). Buses to Samarinda (135,000Rp, 16 hours) leave from the terminal on Jl Hari Isa just south of the bridge crossing Sungai Kelai. Buses leave from the Jl Hari Isa terminal.

Getting Around

The airport is about 9km southwest of town. Taxis cost 40,000Rp. For short trips on the waterways around Berau, you can charter a motorised canoe for around 50,000Rp per hour.

PULAU DERAWAN & AROUND

☎ 0551

Anchored in the Sangalaki Archipelago, a marine reserve off Tanjung Batu, Derawan is a beautiful tear-shaped speck of land with a village around the fringe, spotless white-sand beaches, coconut plantations in the centre and a good supply of fresh water. Schools of *tongkol* (tuna fish) surround the island and cause feeding frenzies near the surface where birds dive for spoils. Rare green turtles lay eggs on the beach near the Derawan Dive Resort. The area has some of the best snorkelling and diving in Indonesia and addicts happily pay the expensive transport out here for several days of bliss.

There are no cars, just a couple of motorcycles, and electricity generators run for only a few hours in the evening. The main entertainment is the volleyball and badminton matches in the early evening, and satellite TV.

Other islands in the group with accommodation include **Nabucco** and **Sangalaki**, which is home to manta rays and green turtles. Nearby are the islands of **Karaban**, which has an ecologically intriguing lake in its centre, caves with swallows' nests and a population of huge coconut crabs; and **Maratua**, which has a population of 2100 in four villages, set around a lagoon.

Activities

Pulau Derawan's main attractions, snorkelling and diving, are conducted from the Derawan Dive Resort. Individual dives cost around US$35, including tank and equipment hire. Dives off Pulau Sangalaki and other outer islands cost more. Renting snorkelling equipment is US$6 a day. You can also try hiring boats in the village; readers have recommended a captain named Agil for trips to the outer islands.

Sleeping & Eating

Losmen Ilham (Pulau Derawan; r 30,000-50,000Rp) This small and simple losmen has clean rooms with fans (when the electricity is on) and shared *mandis*. An additional 75,000Rp per person includes three meals a day.

Losmen Danakan (☎ 0868 121 6143; Pulau Derawan; r incl meals 75,000Rp) Next door to the Derawan Dive Resort, this warm, welcoming and immaculate homestay has just five rooms, all with shared *mandis*.

Derawan Dive Resort (☎ 0542-7072615; www.divederawan.com; Pulau Derawan; 5-nights all inclusive per person from US$970; ❄) This classy resort treats guests to comfortable accommodation in timber cottages and good buffet meals of Western and Indonesian dishes served in a floating restaurant. Packages include transport to the island and three dives per day. A minimum of two people is required.

Sangalaki Dive Resort (☎ 608 8242336; www.sangalaki.net; Pulau Sangalaki; r per person US$250; ❄) The most exclusive resort in the area has 12 beachfront chalets with private verandas. They're elevated to allow nesting turtles clear access to the rest of the beach. The central complex includes a restaurant that serves excellent seafood, a bar and satellite TV. Rates include meals and three dives per day.

More accommodation options:

Penginapan Yos Mas (Pulau Derawan; s/d with fan & shared mandi 40,000/60,000Rp) Near the public pier at the northern end of the island.

Nabucco Island Resort (☎ 0542-420258; www.nabuccoisland.com; Pulau Nabucco; s/d/t US$120/180/250; ❄) Isolated and indulgent resort. Rates include meals and snorkelling.

There are a couple of warungs in the village on Pulau Derawan. It's a good idea to bring along fruit and snacks from Berau or Tarakan for variety.

TANJUNG BATU

This is a fishing village with a couple of warungs and a losmen. If you are stuck here waiting for a boat, **Losmen Famili** (r 30,000Rp) has rooms with shared *mandis* (no fan).

Getting There & Away

The twice-weekly boats between Berau and Tarakan drop passengers at Tanjung Batu, from where you can hire a speedboat to Pulau Derawan (200,000Rp, one hour). A speedboat directly from Berau (1,000,000Rp, three hours) is far more expensive. Boats between Derawan, Sangalaki and Nabucco cost from 400,000Rp.

TARAKAN

☎ 0551 / pop 100,000

Although it's conveniently close to the Sabah border and a stepping stone to other places, Tarakan offers little of cultural interest. It was the site of bloody fighting between Australians and Japanese at the end of WWII.

Information

BNI bank (Bank Negara Indonesia; Jl Yos Sudarso) Foreign exchange and an ATM.

Immigration office (☎ 21242; Jl Sumatra) For visa regulations related to crossing between Indonesia and Malaysia.

PT Angkasa Express (☎ 51789; fax 23326; Jl Yos Sudarso, THM Plaza, Blok D-5) Air and boat tickets.

PT Sampurna Andal Mandiri (☎ 21975; Jl Yos Sudarso) Also air and boat tickets.

Sights

There's a **memorial** *(kuburan Australia)* to the Australian soldiers on the grounds of the Indonesian military barracks, right in front of their volleyball courts. A **gravesite** *(kuburan Jepang)* lies in the hills nearby

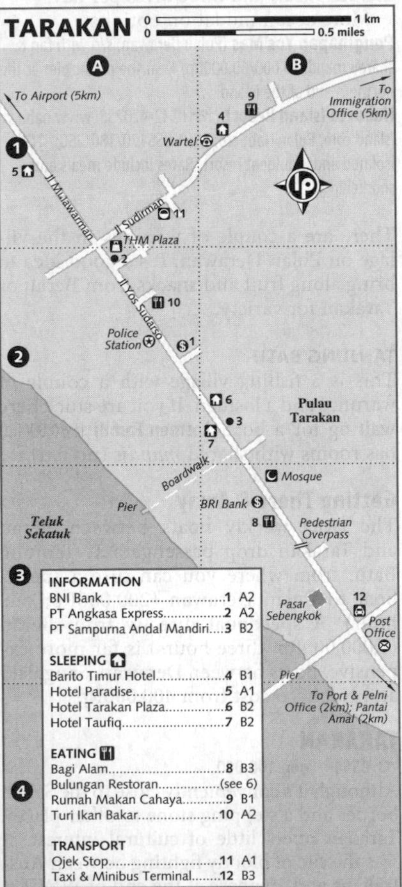

for the Japanese who were killed, alongside old bunkers.

Pantai Amal is a swimming beach outside of town. Get there by public minibus (3000Rp) or charter a taxi for 10,000Rp.

Sleeping & Eating

Hotel Taufiq (☎ 21347; fax 25940; Jl Yos Sudarso 26; s 45,000-100,000Rp, d 55,000/110,000Rp; ❄) This is a great budget option, although the pricier air-con rooms could take on any midranger. Spotless and friendly to boot.

Barito Timur Hotel (☎ 21181; Jl Sudirman 133; r 170,000-220,000Rp; ❄) A lovely midrange option, the Barito Timur as pleasant rooms and a sweet breakfast of cake, tea and coffee.

Hotel Tarakan Plaza (☎ 21870; fax 21029; Jl Yos Sudarso 1; s/d from 250,000/280,000Rp; ❄) The English-speaking staff here may be a bonus for some and although the rooms are ageing, they're lovely. There's a good restaurant (mains 20,000 to 30,000Rp) serving Indonesian fare and seafood, and a bar downstairs.

Hotel Paradise (☎ 22999; fax 32668; Jl Mulawarman 21; s/d from 240,000/260,000Rp; ❄) Tarakan's nearest version to high-end accommodation, the Hotel Paradise has reasonable rooms with a tad more comfort than other options in town. Inside, the Bulungan Restoran (mains 15,000-25,000Rp) is a comfortable retreat serving delicious Chinese, Western and Indonesian food for breakfast, lunch and dinner.

Rumah Makan Cahaya (Jl Sudirman; mains 10,000Rp; ⏲ breakfast, lunch & dinner) This eatery is a wee upgrade from the simple warungs around town, and serves steamy and spicy seafood, *nasi goreng* and Chinese dishes.

Tarakan is blessed with an abundant supply of fresh fish and plenty of warungs serve excellent *ikan bakar* (barbecued fish). On Jl Yos Sudarso try Turi Ikan Bakar or Bagi Alam.

Getting There & Away

AIR

Garuda Citilink and Kartika fly to Balikpapan. DAS and Kal-Star fly to Samarinda, and Kal-Star also flies to Tanjung Selor. DAS flies to Long Bawan.

BOAT

Pelni (☎ 51169; Jl Yos Sudarso) is at the main port. The *Dobonsolo* travels fortnightly to/from Toli Toli in Sulawesi (economy

140,000Rp) and north to Nunukan (economy 60,000Rp).

Private passenger boats head to Berau roughly twice a week (130,000Rp, 11 hours) from the other pier, located about halfway between the Pelni office and the THM Plaza. There are also daily speedboats (except Sunday) between Tawau in Sabah and Tarakan (150,000Rp); you can catch these at the pier the private passenger boats leave from.

Getting Around

A taxi to/from the airport is 35,000Rp, though you might be able to bargain for a cheaper ride. Alternatively walk out about 200m to the highway and try catching a public minibus. The standard price for public minibuses is 3000Rp. There are also *ojek* for hire at various street corners.

The best spot to catch a taxi, *ojek* or minibus is the terminal on Jl Yos Sudarso.

Sulawesi

The first thing everyone notices about Sulawesi is its strange shape. There must have been some serious tectonic action in this region to produce an island so bizarre. But bizarre is beautiful and in its contortions are its character, with an incredible diversity of people, cultures and landscapes spread across its length and breadth. Great seafarers like the Minahasans and the Bugis helped to shape modern Indonesia as they took to the seas in trade and conflict, but it is the land-locked cultures of the island that are most mysterious. Tana Toraja is spellbinding, home to a proud people hemmed in by magnificent mountains on all sides. The scenery of volcanoes and rice fields is stunning. However, the Toraja's elaborate death rituals are something else. Cave graves, *tau tau* (carved wooden effigies of the dead), a buffalo cult, houses shaped like boats and the dead treated like the living – a visit here is out of this world.

Known to the Portuguese as the Celebes, the island's most popular overland route is Makassar–Tana Toraja–Danau Poso–Togean Islands–Manado–Bunaken, and there are also plenty of rewarding side trips to be made throughout the region. Sulawesi is full of natural attractions. The leading national parks see few visitors and include such diverse draws as ancient megaliths in Lore Lindu and bug-eyed tarsiers in Tangkoko. However, it is the waters of Sulawesi that harbour its real treasures. Just offshore is some of the best diving and snorkelling in Indonesia, if not the world. Pulau Bunaken and the Lembeh Strait take top billing, but for those prepared to venture off the trail, there are the beautiful beaches of the laid-back Togean Islands in Central Sulawesi and the incredible Wakatobi Marine National Park in the far southeast.

HIGHLIGHTS

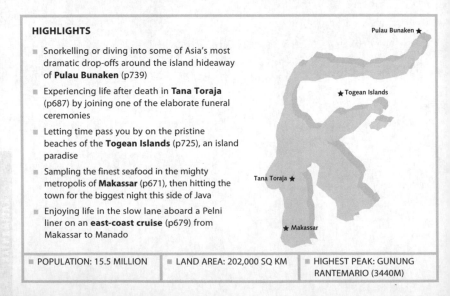

- Snorkelling or diving into some of Asia's most dramatic drop-offs around the island hideaway of **Pulau Bunaken** (p739)
- Experiencing life after death in **Tana Toraja** (p687) by joining one of the elaborate funeral ceremonies
- Letting time pass you by on the pristine beaches of the **Togean Islands** (p725), an island paradise
- Sampling the finest seafood in the mighty metropolis of **Makassar** (p671), then hitting the town for the biggest night this side of Java
- Enjoying life in the slow lane aboard a Pelni liner on an **east-coast cruise** (p679) from Makassar to Manado

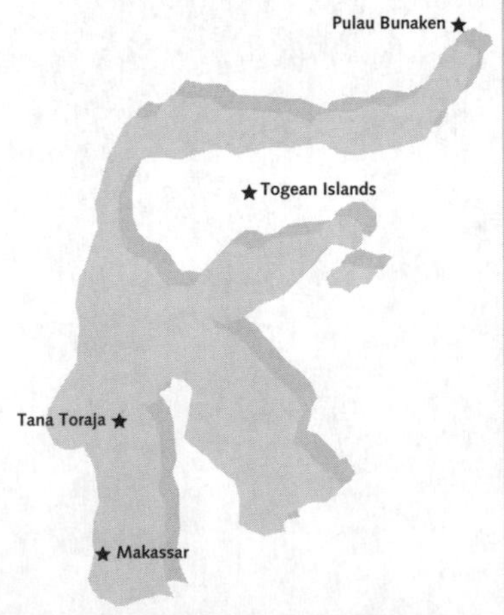

- POPULATION: 15.5 MILLION
- LAND AREA: 202,000 SQ KM
- HIGHEST PEAK: GUNUNG RANTEMARIO (3440M)

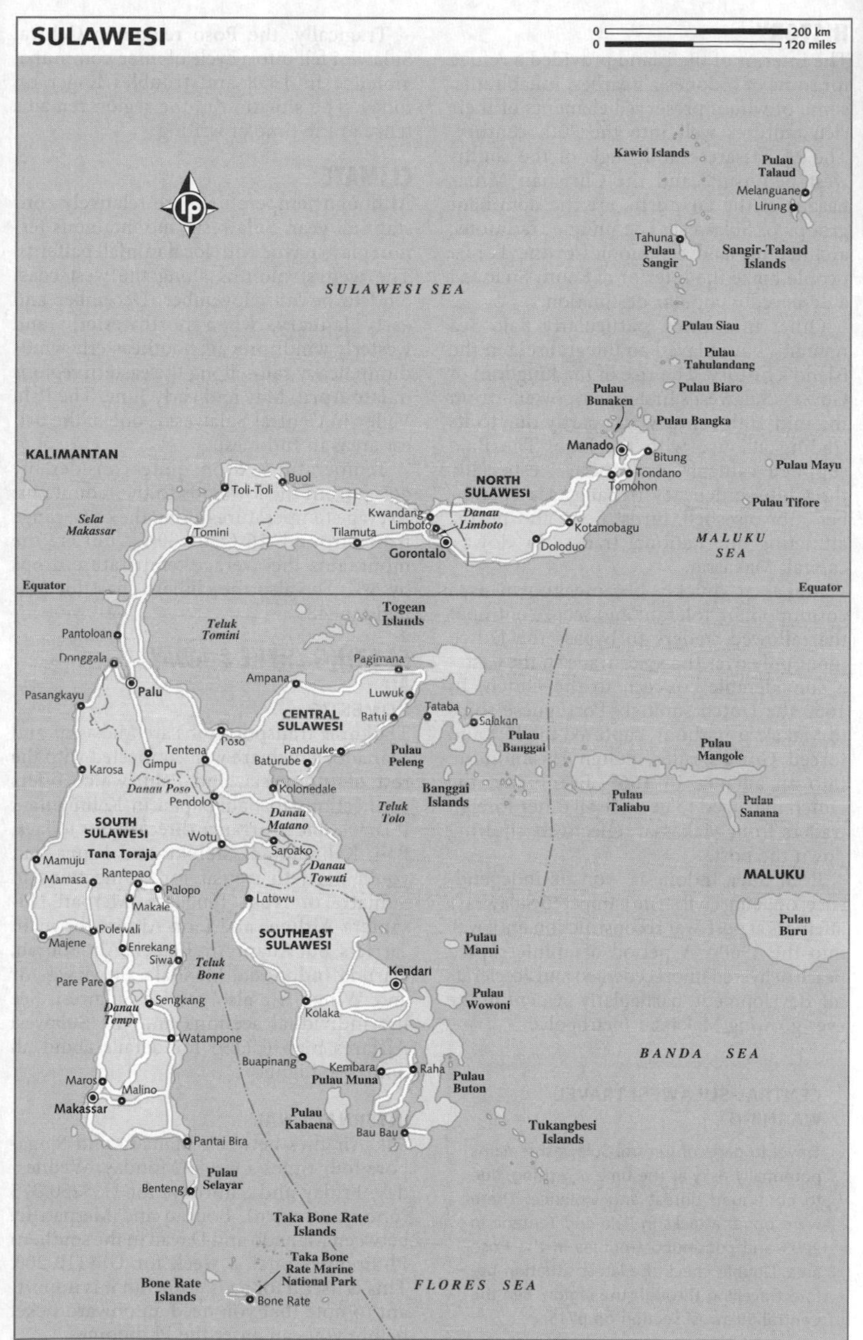
SULAWESI
0 200 km
0 120 miles
SULAWESI SEA
Kawio Islands
Pulau Talaud
Melanguane
Lirung
Tahuna
Pulau Sangir
Sangir-Talaud Islands
Pulau Siau
Pulau Tahulandang
Pulau Biaro
Pulau Bunaken
Pulau Bangka
Manado
Bitung
Tondano
Tomohon
Pulau Mayu
Pulau Tifore
KALIMANTAN
Buol
Toli-Toli
NORTH SULAWESI
Selat Makassar
Tomini
Kwandang
Limboto
Danau Limboto
Tilamuta
Gorontalo
Kotamobagu
Doloduo
MALUKU SEA
Equator
Equator
Togean Islands
Teluk Tomini
Pantoloan
Donggala
Palu
Pagimana
Ampana
Pasangkayu
Luwuk
CENTRAL SULAWESI
Batui
Tataba
Salakan
Pulau Banggai
Pulau Mangole
Poso
Tentena
Gimpu
Pandauke
Baturube
Pulau Peleng
Karosa
Danau Poso
Kolonedale
Banggai Islands
Pulau Taliabu
Pulau Sanana
Pendolo
Danau Matano
Teluk Tolo
SOUTH SULAWESI
Wotu
Saroako
Mamuju
Tana Toraja
Danau Towuti
MALUKU
Mamasa
Rantepao
Palopo
Makale
Latowu
Pulau Buru
Polewali
SOUTHEAST SULAWESI
Majene
Enrekang
Pulau Manui
Siwa
Teluk Bone
Kendari
Pare Pare
Pulau Wowoni
Sengkang
Kolaka
Danau Tempe
Watampone
BANDA SEA
Buapinang
Kembara
Raha
Pulau Muna
Pulau Buton
Maros
Malino
Makassar
Pulau Kabaena
Bau Bau
Tukangbesi Islands
Pantai Bira
Pulau Selayar
Benteng
Taka Bone Rate Islands
Taka Bone Rate Marine National Park
Bone Rate Islands
Bone Rate
FLORES SEA

HISTORY

The interior of the island provided a refuge for some of Indonesia's earliest inhabitants, some of whom preserved elements of their rich cultures well into the 20th century. The Makassarese and Bugis of the southwest peninsula, and the Christian Minahasans of the far north, are the dominant groups of Sulawesi. The unique traditions, architecture and ceremonies of the Toraja people make the interior of South Sulawesi a deservedly popular destination.

Other minorities, particularly Bajo Sea nomads, have played an integral role in the island's history. The rise of the kingdom of Gowa – Sulawesi's first major power – from the mid-16th century was partly due to its trading alliance with the Bajo. The Bajo supplied valuable sea produce, especially the Chinese delicacy trepang (sea cucumber), tortoiseshell, birds' nests and pearls, attracting international traders to Gowa's capital, Makassar.

Makassar quickly became known as a cosmopolitan, tolerant and secure entrepôt that allowed traders to bypass the Dutch monopoly over the spice trade in the east – a considerable concern to the Dutch. In 1660 the Dutch sunk six Portuguese ships in Makassar harbour, captured the fort and forced Gowa's ruler, Sultan Hasanuddin, into an alliance in 1667. Eventually, the Dutch managed to exclude all other foreign traders from Makassar, effectively shutting down the port.

Even after Indonesia won its independence, ongoing civil strife hampered Sulawesi's attempts at post-war reconstruction until well into the 1960s. A period of uninterrupted peace delivered unprecedented and accelerating development, particularly evident in the ever-growing Makassar metropolis.

CENTRAL SULAWESI TRAVEL WARNING

Travel to parts of Central Sulawesi remains potentially risky at the time of writing, due to continued unrest and violence. There were bomb attacks in Palu and Tentena in 2005 and continued troubles in the Poso area. Double check the latest situation before travelling through the region. See the Central Sulawesi section on p715.

Tragically, the Poso region in Central Sulawesi fell into a cycle of inter-communal violence in 1998 and troubles linger on today. The situation in the region remains tense at the time of writing.

CLIMATE

Although temperatures are relatively constant all year, Sulawesi's mountainous terrain plays havoc with local rainfall patterns. The wettest months along the west coast tend to be late November, December and early January, when northwesterly and westerly winds prevail. Southeasterly winds dump heavy rains along the eastern regions in late April, May and early June. The Palu Valley in Central Sulawesi is one of the driest areas in Indonesia.

Temperatures drop quite considerably going from the lowlands to the mountains. Average temperatures along the coast range from around 26°C to 30°C, but in the mountains the average temperature drops by 5°C. See also the climate chart for Manado, p848.

GETTING THERE & AWAY

Air

DOMESTIC

The three transport hubs are Makassar and Manado, which are well connected with the rest of Indonesia, and Palu, which offers connections to Balikpapan in Kalimantan. It is possible to arrange direct flights to Java, Bali, Kalimantan, Maluku and Papua, but you'll need to transit for connections to Sumatra or Nusa Tenggara. Merpati Nusantara Airlines and Lion Air are the main carriers, but Adam Air, Batavia Air, Bouraq, Garuda Indonesia, Mandala, Sriwijaya Air and Wings Air also service Sulawesi. See the individual sections and the Sulawesi Airfares map (p669) for details about all domestic flights.

INTERNATIONAL

Silk Air flies between Manado and Singapore four times a week (Monday, Wednesday, Friday and Saturday) for US$250/375 (one way/return). Bouraq and Merpati fly between Manado and Davao in the southern Philippines once a week for US$110/200. This is useful for a visa run, but it is important to note that you need an onward ticket before you can enter the Philippines.

SULAWESI AIRFARES

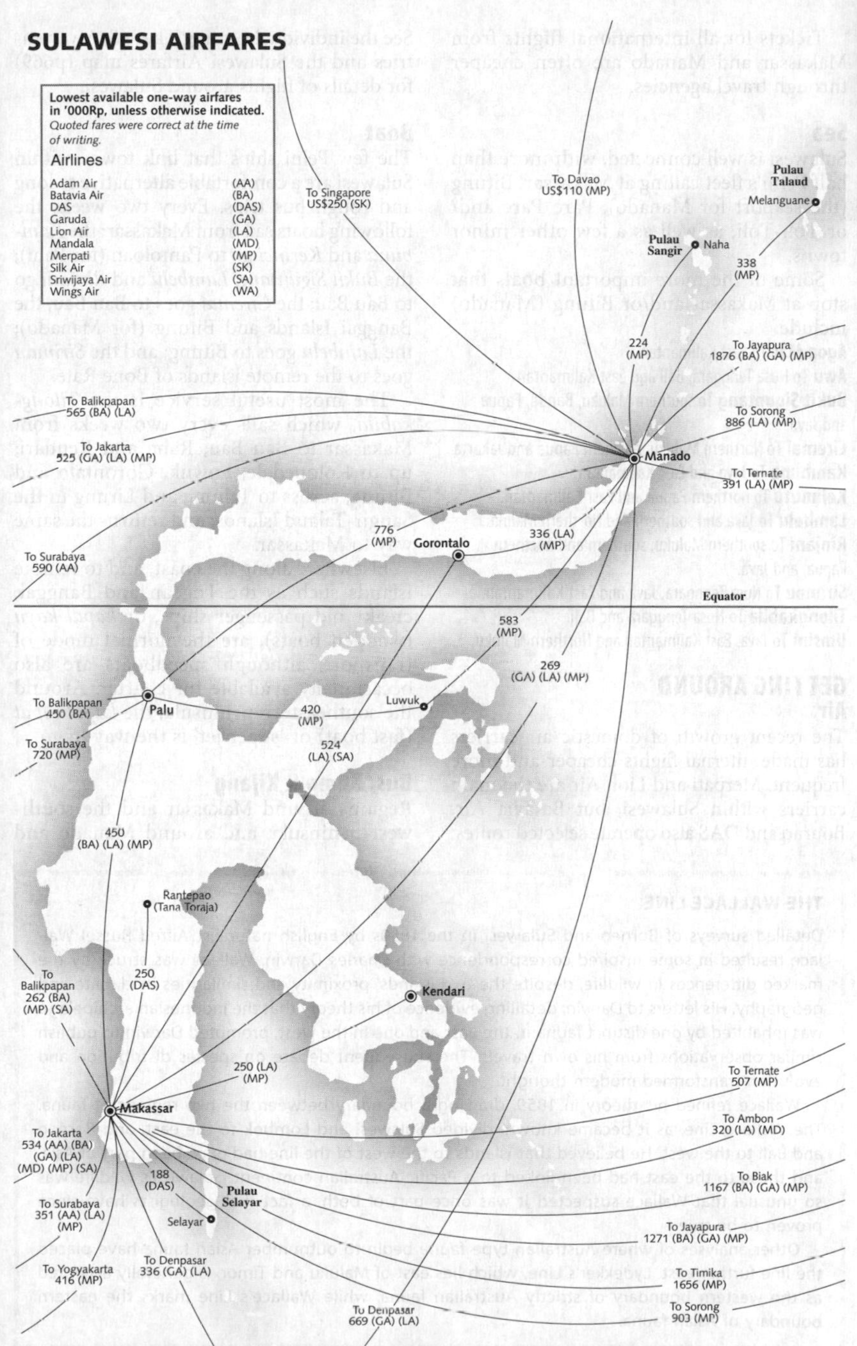

Tickets for all international flights from Makassar and Manado are often cheaper through travel agencies.

Sea

Sulawesi is well connected, with more than half Pelni's fleet calling at Makassar, Bitung (the seaport for Manado), Pare Pare and/or Toli-Toli, as well as a few other minor towns.

Some of the more important boats that stop at Makassar and/or Bitung (Manado) include:

Agoa Mas To East Kalimantan.
Awu To Nusa Tenggara, Bali and East Kalimantan.
Bukit Siguntang To southern Maluku, Banda, Papua and Java.
Ciremai To Northern Maluku, northern Papua and Jakarta
Kambuna To Java and East Kalimantan.
Kelimutu To northern Papua and East Kalimantan.
Lambelu To Java and southern and Northern Maluku.
Rinjani To southern Maluku, southern and northern Papua, and Java.
Sirimau To Nusa Tenggara, Java and East Kalimantan.
Tilongkabila To Nusa Tenggara and Bali.
Umsini To Java, East Kalimantan and Northern Maluku.

GETTING AROUND

Air

The recent growth of domestic air carriers has made internal flights cheaper and more frequent. Merpati and Lion Air are the main carriers within Sulawesi, but Batavia Air, Bouraq and DAS also operate selected routes. See the individual Getting There & Away entries and the Sulawesi Airfares map (p669) for details of flights around Sulawesi.

Boat

The few Pelni ships that link towns within Sulawesi are a comfortable alternative to long and rough bus trips. Every two weeks the following boats sail from Makassar: the *Kambuna* and *Kerinci* go to Pantoloan (for Palu); the *Bukit Siguntang, Lambelu* and *Rinjani* go to Bau Bau; the *Ciremai* goes to Bau Bau, the Banggai Islands and Bitung (for Manado); the *Lambelu* goes to Bitung; and the *Sirimau* goes to the remote islands of Bone Rate.

The most useful service is the *Tilongkabila,* which sails every two weeks from Makassar to Bau Bau, Raha and Kendari; up to Kolonedale, Luwuk, Gorontalo and Bitung; across to Tahuna and Lirung in the Sangir-Talaud Islands; and returns the same way to Makassar.

Elsewhere along the coast, and to remote islands such as the Togean and Banggai, creaky old passenger ships, or *kapal kayu* (wooden boats), are the normal mode of transport, although speedboats are also occasionally available for charter. Around the southeastern peninsula, the *kapal cepat* (fast boat) or 'super-jet' is the way to go.

Bus, Bemo & Kijang

Regions around Makassar and the southwest peninsula, and around Manado and

THE WALLACE LINE

Detailed surveys of Borneo and Sulawesi in the 1850s by English naturalist Alfred Russel Wallace resulted in some inspired correspondence with Charles Darwin. Wallace was struck by the marked differences in wildlife, despite the two islands' proximity and similarities in climate and geography. His letters to Darwin, detailing evidence of his theory that the Indonesian archipelago was inhabited by one distinct fauna in the east and one in the west, prompted Darwin to publish similar observations from his own travels. The subsequent debate on species distribution and evolution transformed modern thought.

Wallace refined his theory in 1859, drawing a boundary between the two regions of fauna. The Wallace Line, as it became known, divided Sulawesi and Lombok to the east, and Borneo and Bali to the west. He believed that islands to the west of the line had once been part of Asia, and those to the east had been linked to a Pacific-Australian continent. Sulawesi's wildlife was so unusual that Wallace suspected it was once part of both, a fact that geologists have since proven to be true.

Other analyses of where Australian-type fauna begin to outnumber Asian fauna have placed the line further east. Lydekker's Line, which lies east of Maluku and Timor, is generally accepted as the western boundary of strictly Australian fauna, while Wallace's Line marks the eastern boundary of Asian fauna.

the northeast peninsula, have good roads and frequent, comfortable buses (and less comfortable bemo, known in Sulawesi as *mikrolet* or *pete-pete*). Elsewhere, roads are often rough, distances are long, and public transport can be crowded and uncomfortable. Allow plenty of time to travel overland in Central Sulawesi, especially in the wet season. On the southeast and southwest peninsulas, sharing a Kijang (a type of 4WD taxi) is a quick, but not necessarily more comfortable, way of getting around.

SOUTH SULAWESI

Long the gateway to Sulawesi, the south is home to the island's only metropolis, Makassar, as well as one of Indonesia's most memorable destinations, timeless Tana Toraja. Makassar may not be the most charming city in the country, but it is sophisticated and self-confident and a good place to hit the town before heading into the interior. Tana Toraja is beautiful and beguiling, and home to some of the most elaborate ceremonies in Indonesia. Cliff graves littered with skulls and bones, puppet effigies of the deceased, dead people that are treated like the living and mass buffalo sacrifice; this isn't a movie, but real life for the warm and welcoming people of Toraja. Beyond these two great destinations lie some fine beaches on the southern tip and some quiet country backwaters where the land is lush and the people warm and friendly.

The province of South Sulawesi (Sulawesi Selatan; often shortened to Sul-sel) is a lush, mountainous region of caves, waterfalls and large lakes. Irrigated-rice agriculture is widely practised, and coffee, cotton and sugar cane are also important crops.

The estimated nine million inhabitants include the Bugis (who make up two-thirds of the population), the Makassarese (a quarter) and the Toraja. The Makassarese are concentrated in the southern tip, mainly around Makassar. The Bugis (centred around Watampone) and Makassarese have similar cultures; both are seafaring people who for centuries were active in trade, sailing to Flores, Timor and Sumba, and even as far afield as the northern coast of Australia. Islam is the dominant religion, but both retain vestiges of traditional beliefs.

History

The leading powers of the south were long the Makassarese kingdom of Gowa (around the port of Makassar) and the Bugis kingdom of Bone. By the mid-16th century, Gowa had established itself at the head of a major trading bloc in eastern Indonesia. The king of Gowa adopted Islam in 1605 and Bone was soon subdued, spreading Islam to the whole Bugis-Makassarese area.

The Dutch United East India Company (Vereenigde Oost-Indische Compagnie; VOC) found Gowa a considerable hindrance to its plans to monopolise the spice trade. They found an anti-Gowa ally in the exiled Bugis prince Arung Palakka. The Dutch sponsored Palakka's return to Bone in 1666, prompting Bone to rise against the Makassarese. A year of fighting ensued, and Sultan Hasanuddin of Gowa was forced to sign the Treaty of Bungaya in 1667, which severely reduced Gowa's power. Bone, under Palakka, then became the supreme state of South Sulawesi.

Rivalry between Bone and the other Bugis states continually reshaped the political landscape. After their brief absence during the Napoleonic Wars, the Dutch returned to a Bugis revolt led by the queen of Bone. This was suppressed, but rebellions continued until Makassarese and Bugis resistance was finally broken in the early years of the 20th century. Unrest lingered on until the early 1930s.

The Makassarese and Bugis are staunchly Islamic and independent minded – revolts against the central Indonesian government again occurred in the 1950s. Makassar and Pare Pare are still the first to protest when the political or economic situation is uncertain.

MAKASSAR

☎ 0411 / pop 1.6 million

Gateway to eastern Indonesia for centuries, Makassar is the most important city in Sulawesi. Like many of the nation's dynamic metropolises, Makassar might appear oversized and out of control at first glance. However, linger a little and you will be rewarded with some of the best seafood anywhere in the archipelago, the liveliest night scene this side of Surabaya and some striking sunsets from the seafront.

From Makassar, the Dutch controlled much of the shipping that passed between

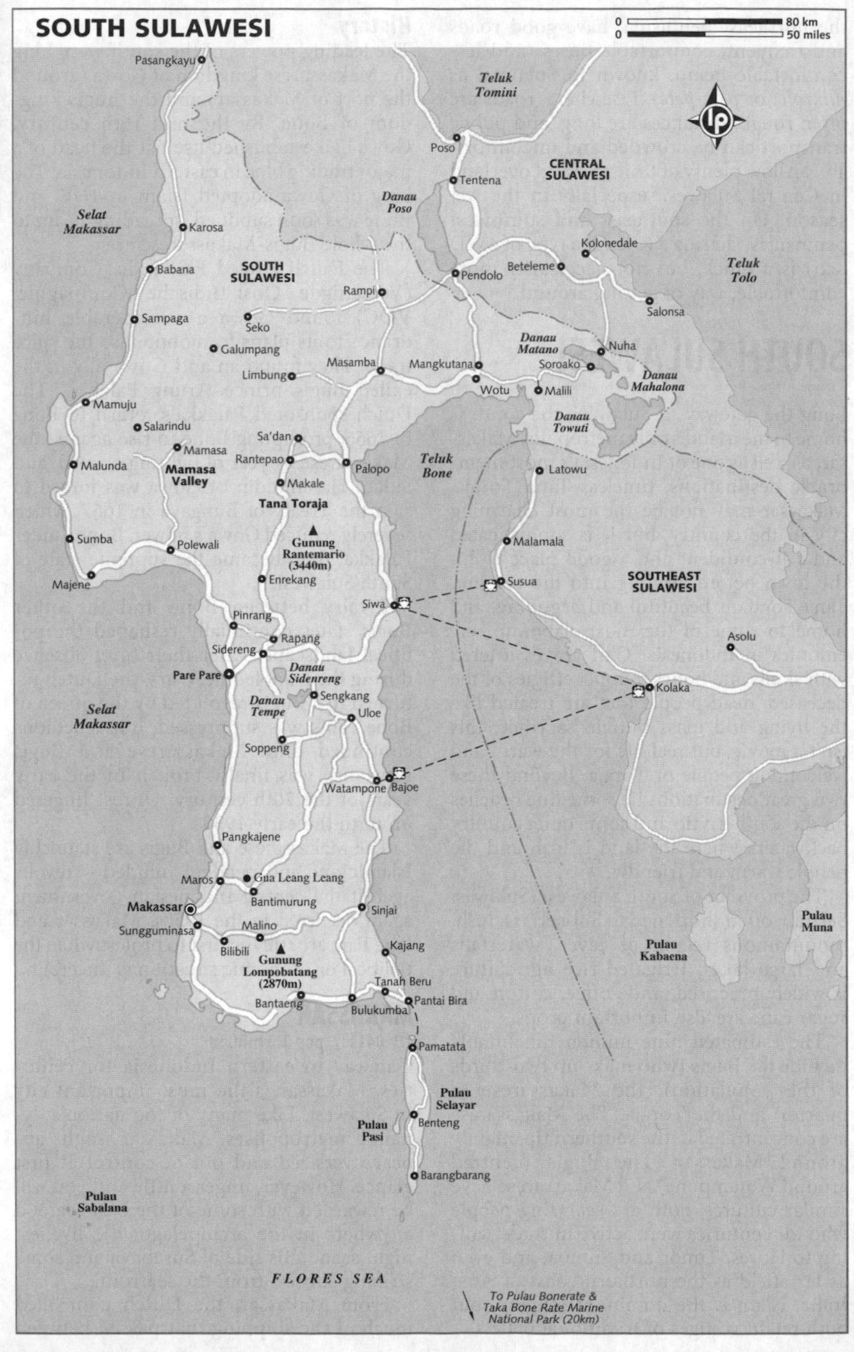

SOUTH SULAWESI
0 80 km
0 50 miles
Teluk Tomini
Pasangkayu
Poso
Tentena
CENTRAL SULAWESI
Danau Poso
Selat Makassar
Karosa
Kolonedale
Teluk Tolo
Babana
SOUTH SULAWESI
Pendolo
Beteleme
Rampi
Salonsa
Sampaga
Seko
Galumpang
Danau Matano
Nuha
Masamba
Mangkutana
Soroako
Limbung
Wotu
Malili
Danau Mahalona
Mamuju
Danau Towuti
Salarindu
Sa'dan
Mamasa
Teluk Bone
Rantepao
Palopo
Malunda
Mamasa Valley
Makale
Latowu
Tana Toraja
Gunung Rantemario (3440m)
Sumba
Malamala
Polewali
Majene
Enrekang
Susua
SOUTHEAST SULAWESI
Siwa
Pinrang
Asolu
Rapang
Sidereng
Pare Pare
Danau Sidenreng
Kolaka
Sengkang
Danau Tempe
Selat Makassar
Uloe
Soppeng
Watampone
Bajoe
Pangkajene
Maros
Gua Leang Leang
Bantimurung
Makassar
Sinjai
Sungguminasa
Malino
Pulau Muna
Pulau Kabaena
Bilibili
Kajang
Gunung Lompobatang (2870m)
Tanah Beru
Bantaeng
Bulukumba
Pantai Bira
Pamatata
Pulau Selayar
Benteng
Pulau Pasi
Barangbarang
Pulau Sabalana
FLORES SEA
To Pulau Bonerate & Taka Bone Rate Marine National Park (20km)

western and eastern Indonesia, and today the city is still a thriving port and important transport hub. The impressive Fort Rotterdam stands as a reminder of the Dutch occupation. Walk inside its walls and you have a little slice of old Amsterdam. Makassar is also the last resting place of Sultan Hasanuddin and of the Javanese prince Pangeran Diponegoro.

But that is old Makassar and today the city is expanding in every direction with new suburbs everywhere. Tanjung Bunga looms large on the horizon to the southwest of the city and may well become the new centre one day. To the east is Pannakukkang and its mighty malls.

In the area surrounding Makassar are the palace of the Gowanese kings, waterfalls where the naturalist Alfred Wallace collected butterflies, and cave-paintings left by the first inhabitants of Sulawesi.

Orientation

Makassar is *huge*, but you'll only need to venture into the eastern suburbs to catch a bus or go to the airport. The port is conveniently located in the northwest part of the city; Fort Rotterdam is in the centre of the older commercial hub; and the Hotel Makassar Golden dominates the beachfront. If you get disoriented, remember that the sun sets over the ocean, or look for two major landmarks: the Monumen Mandala (Mandala monument) and the Marannu Hotel.

Information

BOOKSHOPS

Gramedia (Ratu Indah Mall) The best place to pick up English-language books, newspapers and magazines.

EMERGENCY

Police station (☎ 110; Jl Ahmad Yani)

> **WHAT'S IN A NAME?**
>
> From the early 1970s until 1999 the official name of Makassar was Ujung Pandang, then during his final days as president, Habibie made the popular decision to change the name back to Makassar. In reality both names are still used, as they have been for centuries, and neither title is politically charged. It seems people preferred the name Makassar for its historical resonance.

IMMIGRATION

Immigration office (Jl Tentara Pelajar) Near the port.

INTERNET ACCESS & POST

Internet centres are springing up across the city, most charging 7000Rp per hour.

Cybernet (cnr Jl Kajaolalido & Jl Ahmad Yani) Above Pizza Ria, boasts almost 50 terminals.

Main post office (Jl Slamet Riyadi; 🕒 8am-9pm) Has a poste restante service, a Telkom office and an internet centre.

MEDICAL SERVICES

Rumah Sakit Pelamonia (☎ 324710; Jl Jendral Sudirman) The most convenient and well-equipped, hospital.

MONEY

Lapangan Karebosi is literally surrounded by banks with ATMs that accept all major credit cards, including Bank Negara Indonesia (BNI), Bank Central Asia (BCA), Bank Internasional Indonesia (BII), Lippo Bank and Bank Mandiri. Most are on Jl Ahmad Yani. These places can also change cash and travellers cheques. At the airport, several moneychangers offer slightly lower rates than in the city and some of the ATMs there accept credit cards.

TELEPHONE

Wartel are everywhere, so it is easy enough to make calls from almost anywhere in town. There are international telephones at the airport.

TOURIST INFORMATION

Sulawesi Tourism Information Centre (☎ 872336; cnr Jl Sam Ratulangi & Jl Sungai Saddang; 🕒 8am-4pm) There is not much on offer here, but the staff are helpful and friendly. Take any red *pete-pete* (a type of mikrolet or bemo) travelling south along Jl Jendral Sudirman to get here.

TRAVEL AGENCIES

Losari Holidays Tours & Travel (☎ 5063884; www.losari-tours.com; Jl Mappanyukki 1) The agent for Operation Wallacea projects in Sulawesi (see p714). Ticketing, car hire and a good source of information on travelling to the remote Tukangbesi Islands which make up Wakatobi Marine National Park.

Nell Tours (☎ 852445; www.nelltours.com; Jl Cendrawasih 103) A long-running travel agency specialising in trans-Sulawesi trips. Car hire, guides and full itineraries from Makassar to Manado and all points in-between.

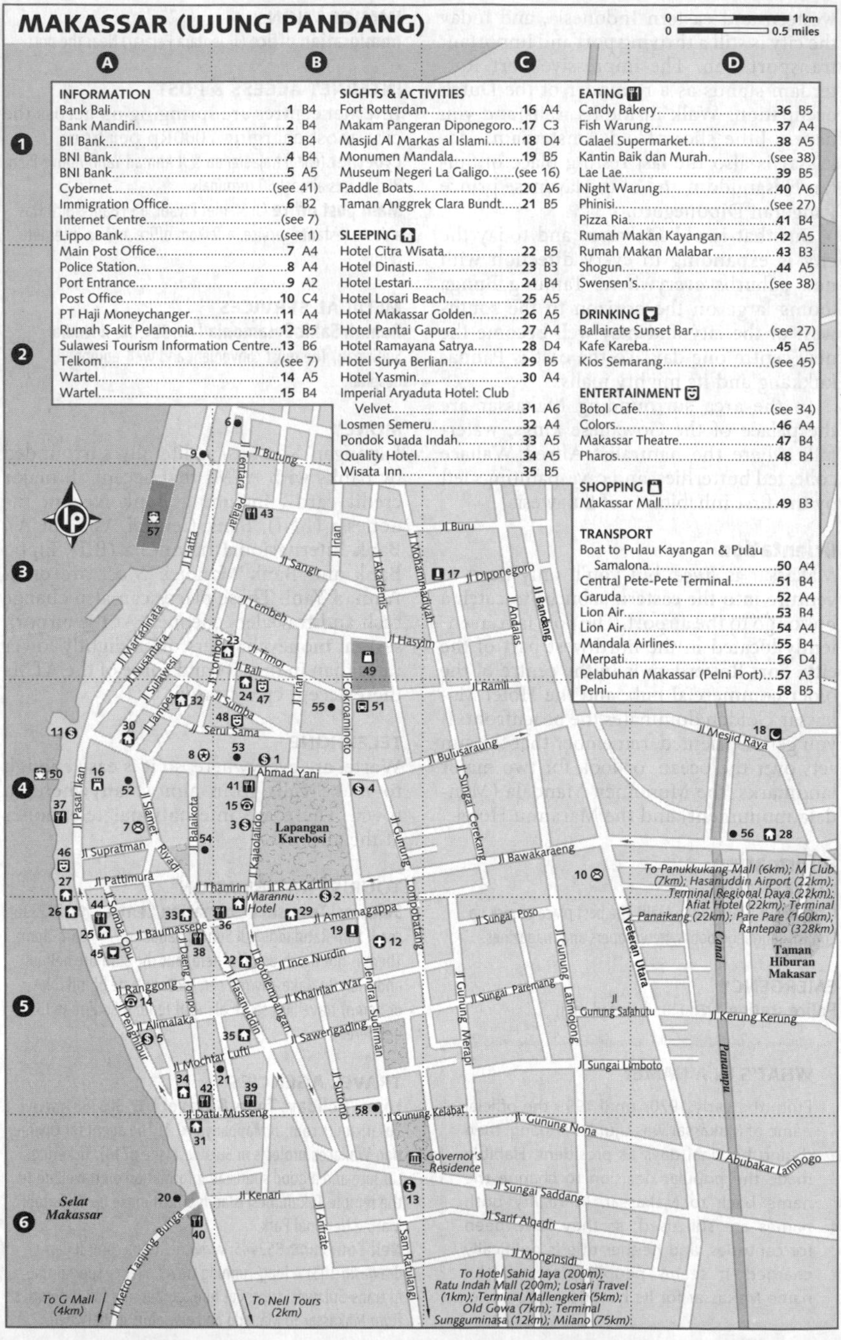

MAKASSAR (UJUNG PANDANG)

0 — 1 km
0 — 0.5 miles

INFORMATION
- Bank Bali ... 1 B4
- Bank Mandiri ... 2 B4
- BII Bank ... 3 B4
- BNI Bank ... 4 B4
- BNI Bank ... 5 A5
- Cybernet ... (see 41)
- Immigration Office ... 6 B2
- Internet Centre ... (see 7)
- Lippo Bank ... (see 1)
- Main Post Office ... 7 A4
- Police Station ... 8 A4
- Port Entrance ... 9 A2
- Post Office ... 10 C4
- PT Haji Moneychanger ... 11 A4
- Rumah Sakit Pelamonia ... 12 B5
- Sulawesi Tourism Information Centre ... 13 B6
- Telkom ... (see 7)
- Wartel ... 14 A5
- Wartel ... 15 B4

SIGHTS & ACTIVITIES
- Fort Rotterdam ... 16 A4
- Makam Pangeran Diponegoro ... 17 C3
- Masjid Al Markas al Islami ... 18 D4
- Monumen Mandala ... 19 B5
- Museum Negeri La Galigo ... (see 16)
- Paddle Boats ... 20 A6
- Taman Anggrek Clara Bundt ... 21 B5

SLEEPING
- Hotel Citra Wisata ... 22 B5
- Hotel Dinasti ... 23 B3
- Hotel Lestari ... 24 B4
- Hotel Losari Beach ... 25 A5
- Hotel Makassar Golden ... 26 A5
- Hotel Pantai Gapura ... 27 A4
- Hotel Ramayana Satrya ... 28 D4
- Hotel Surya Berlian ... 29 B5
- Hotel Yasmin ... 30 A4
- Imperial Aryaduta Hotel: Club Velvet ... 31 A6
- Losmen Semeru ... 32 A4
- Pondok Suada Indah ... 33 A5
- Quality Hotel ... 34 A5
- Wisata Inn ... 35 B5

EATING
- Candy Bakery ... 36 B5
- Fish Warung ... 37 A4
- Galael Supermarket ... 38 A5
- Kantin Baik dan Murah ... (see 38)
- Lae Lae ... 39 B5
- Night Warung ... 40 A6
- Phinisi ... (see 27)
- Pizza Ria ... 41 B4
- Rumah Makan Kayangan ... 42 A5
- Rumah Makan Malabar ... 43 B3
- Shogun ... 44 A5
- Swensen's ... (see 38)

DRINKING
- Ballairate Sunset Bar ... (see 27)
- Kafe Kareba ... 45 A5
- Kios Semarang ... (see 45)

ENTERTAINMENT
- Botol Cafe ... (see 34)
- Colors ... 46 A4
- Makassar Theatre ... 47 B4
- Pharos ... 48 B4

SHOPPING
- Makassar Mall ... 49 B3

TRANSPORT
- Boat to Pulau Kayangan & Pulau Samalona ... 50 A4
- Central Pete-Pete Terminal ... 51 B4
- Garuda ... 52 A4
- Lion Air ... 53 B4
- Lion Air ... 54 A4
- Mandala Airlines ... 55 B4
- Merpati ... 56 D4
- Pelabuhan Makassar (Pelni Port) ... 57 A3
- Pelni ... 58 B5

To Panukkukang Mall (6km); M Club (7km); Hasanuddin Airport (22km); Terminal Regional Daya (22km); Afiat Hotel (22km); Terminal Panaikang (22km); Pare Pare (160km); Rantepao (328km)

To Hotel Sahid Jaya (200m); Ratu Indah Mall (200m); Losari Travel (1km); Terminal Mallengkeri (5km); Old Gowa (7km); Terminal Sungguminasa (12km); Milano (75km)

To G Mall (4km)

To Nell Tours (2km)

Sights

FORT ROTTERDAM

One of the best-preserved examples of Dutch architecture in Indonesia, **Fort Rotterdam** (Jl Pasar Ikan; entry by donation, suggested 10,000Rp; 7.30am-6pm) continues to guard the harbour of Makassar. A Gowanese fort dating back to 1545 once stood here, but failed to keep out the Dutch. The original fort was rebuilt in Dutch style after the Treaty of Bungaya in 1667. Parts of the crumbling wall have been left untouched, and provide an interesting comparison to the restored buildings.

Inside the fort, **Museum Negeri La Galigo** (admission 1700Rp; 8am-12.30pm Tue-Sun) has an assortment of exhibits, including rice bowls from Tana Toraja, kitchen tools, musical instruments and various costumes. It's hardly riveting, but at this price who can complain? In practice, the museum seems to keep the same hours as the fort.

MAKAM PANGERAN DIPONEGORO

Prince Diponegoro of Yogyakarta led the Java War (1825–30), but his career as a rebel leader came to a sudden halt when he was tricked into going to the Dutch headquarters to negotiate peace, was taken prisoner and then exiled to Sulawesi. He spent the last 26 years of his life imprisoned in Fort Rotterdam. His tomb and monument can be seen in a small **cemetery** (Jl Diponegoro; entry by donation).

OLD GOWA

Remnants of the former kingdom of Gowa, 7km from town on the southeastern outskirts of Makassar, include **Makam Sultan Hasanuddin** (Jl Pallantiang, off Jl Sultan Hasanuddin), which memorialises the ruler of Gowa in the mid-17th century. Outside the tomb compound is the **Pelantikan Stone**, on which the kings of Gowa were crowned.

Benteng Sungguminasa (Jl Kh Wahid Hasyim; admission free; 8am-4pm), a fort that was once the seat of the Sultan of Gowa, is 5km further south at Sungguminasa. The former royal residence, now known as **Museum Balla Lompoa**, houses a collection of artefacts, including gifts from Australian Aborigines of Elcho Island, who have a history of trade with the Bugis. Although the royal regalia can be seen only on request, the wooden Bugis-style palace itself is the real attraction.

To go to Old Gowa and Sungguminasa, take a red *pete-pete* marked 'S Minasa' from Makassar Mall to the turn-off for the 1km walk to the tomb. A becak (bicycle-rickshaw) from there to the fort should cost around 8000Rp. Another becak will take you to Mallenkeri Terminal, from where *pete-pete* return to central Makassar; the *pete-pete* should cost about 3000Rp.

OTHER SIGHTS

Pelabuhan Paotere (Paotere Harbour; admission 500Rp), just a short becak ride north of the city centre, is where the Bugis sailing ships berth. There is usually lots of activity on the dock, and in the busy **fish market** a few streets south.

Taman Anggrek Clara Bundt (Clara Bundt Orchid Garden; Jl Mochtar Lufti 15; entry by donation) is a sanctuary hidden behind the Bundt family home. It contains exotic hybrids (some up to 5m high). There's also a verdant fruit orchard and an extensive shell collection.

The towering **Monumen Mandala** (Jl Jendral Sudirman; admission 5000Rp; 8am-4pm) is a smaller version of Jakarta's Monas (National Monument), and celebrates the 'liberation' of Irian Jaya (now known as Papua).

Activities

Top-end hotels such as Hotel Pantai Gapura and Imperial Aryaduta Hotel have **swimming pools** the public can use for 20,000Rp, although they get crowded on Sundays. Comedic fish-shaped **paddle boats** (15,000Rp per hr; 11am-9pm) are available to hire near the night warungs (food stalls) for a sunset paddle.

Makassar may not be as famous as other parts of Sulawesi when it comes to diving, but the small islands off the coast do offer abundant corals, a range of marine life and some of the largest wrecks off the Sulawesi coast, including a submarine, a gunship and cargo boat, all accessible to advanced divers. For more details, contact **Marlin Dive** (☎ 858762; www.marlindive.com).

Sleeping

Pickings are slim at the budget end of the spectrum. Life at the top can be good, however, as the smarter hotels in town are aggressive discounters.

BUDGET

A couple of budget favourites have closed in recent years, but there are some cheap hotel deals if you shop about. Some of the midrange hotels also offer budget fan rooms.

Losmen Semeru (☎ 318113; Jl Jampea 28; r 45,000Rp; ❄) This long-running budget stalwart still offers the best-value cheapies in town. The rooms are on the somewhat small side but include TV and air-con that (through creative carpentry) is shared between the rooms.

Hotel Ramayana Satrya (☎ 442478; fax 442479; Jl Bawakaraeng 121; economy 60,000Rp, VIP s/d 120,000/132,000Rp; ❄) Despite being a fair walk from the action, this hotel is quite popular for its range of rooms. The fan rooms are basic, but those with air-con are a good deal and the VIP rooms are like little suites with a sofa set. Breakfast is extra.

Afiat Hotel (☎ 553024; Jl Bandara Hasanuddin 1; r 65,000-120,000Rp; ❄) Strategically located on the corner of the airport access road, this hotel is a little on the shabby side. Even the so-called diamond and emerald rooms hardly sparkle. However, it might do at a push for those with an early flight out of Makassar.

Hotel Lestari (☎ 327337; Jl Savu 16; r 110,000-176,000Rp; ❄) Up near the port end of town, this unassuming façade in the backstreets conceals some of the best-value rooms in town. All have satellite TV, minibar, hot water and air-con, while the deluxe rooms from 150,000Rp include – get this – a DVD player.

Hotel Surya Berlian (☎ 327208; fax 331252; Jl Amannagappa 7; s/d 156,000/168,000Rp; ❄) It promises the finest service and familiar staff. Not the finest service and the staff are only likely to be familiar if you have stayed here before, but it's good value, with air-con, TV, fridge and 'bath tube'.

MIDRANGE

The choice of midrange hotels in Makassar is excellent. All rooms have air-con, satellite TV and include breakfast, unless otherwise stated.

Pondok Suada Indah (☎ 317179; fax 312856; Jl Sultan Hasanuddin 12; s/d from 114,000/138,000Rp; ❄) If Makassar ever becomes popular enough to justify a boutique hotel, this could be it. Set in a gracious, spacious old colonial-era house, it feels a long way from the modern metropolis right outside. All rooms are a decent size and the more expensive options include hot water and bath tubs.

Wisata Inn (☎ 324344; fax 312783; Jl Sultan Hasanuddin 36; s/d from 175,000/205,000Rp; ❄) This central hotel is deservedly popular thanks to a good-value range of rooms and the friendly staff. Rooms come in all shapes and sizes, including some bargain fan-cooled rooms from just 50,000Rp. The air-con rooms are large and include TV and hot water showers.

Hotel Citra Wisata (☎ 311018; fax 325154; Jl Botolempangan 28; s/d from 180,000/216,000Rp; ❄) Another central option set along a tree-lined boulevard, the Citra deserves recognition for not raising its rates much over the years. All rooms include hot water.

Hotel Dinasti (☎ 325657; fax 325758; Jl Lombok 30; r from 280,000Rp; ❄) Tucked away in the back streets near the port area is a little slice of China. Enter through the temple doorway and 'feel the oriental touch' as they say. Rooms are well equipped and include satellite TV and fridge. There is also a whirlpool hot tub available for guests.

Hotel Losari Beach (☎ 326062; los-htl@indosat.net.id; Jl Penghibur 10; s/d from 309,000/329,000Rp) Boasting a great location overlooking the seafront, this modern business hotel has good-value rooms featuring all mod cons. Prices rise rapidly for a premium sea view.

Hotel Yasmin (☎ 328329; fax 328283; Jl Jampea 5; r from 336,000Rp; ❄) Located near the main Jl Ahmad Yani strip, this three-star business hotel is popular with Indonesian sales folk. Rooms feature a tidy trim and 40% discounts are possible if you forgo the forgettable breakfast.

TOP END

There are plenty of top-end hotels in town and discounts are available on published rates, although not quite the bargains of years gone by.

Hotel Makassar Golden (☎ 333000; mghupg@indosat.net.id; Jl Pasar Ikan 50; r from 500,000Rp; ❄ 🏊) A short stroll south of the Hotel Pantai Gapura, this hotel is an old landmark with a similar mix of rooms and cottages with sea or city views. Discounts of 25% are common.

Hotel Sahid Jaya (☎ 875757; www.sahidhotels.com; Jl Sam Ratulangi 33; r from 650,000Rp; ❄ 🏊) Another contender for best hotel in Makassar, this 220-room place is a little way south of the action, but convenient for the nearby Ratu Indah Mall. With a swimming pool, fitness centre, and wi-fi internet access, the only drawback compared with the Imperial is the lack of a sea view.

Quality Hotel (☎ 333111; www.qualityhotel makassar.com; Jl Somba Opu 235; s/d with ocean view 800,000/900,000Rp;) Built as a Radisson, the rates have plummeted in the years since the chain pulled out. It's a good deal for its sea views and central location.

Hotel Pantai Gapura (☎ 325791; www.pantai gapura.com; Jl Pasar Ikan 10; r 650,000Rp, cottages from 1,000,000Rp,) It looks pretty forlorn from the front, but venture through to the back and this is one of the most atmospheric properties in town. Forget the rooms and make a date with a cottage, built on a series of solid walkways over the sea. Sea views cost more, but make sure you negotiate on any room. There is also a popular swimming pool, a lush garden, a sunset bar and kitsch boat-shaped restaurant.

Imperial Aryaduta Hotel (☎ 870555; www.aryaduta.com; Jl Somba Opu 297; r from 1,200,000Rp;) The leading address in town, the 230 rooms are equipped to an international four-star standard. All rooms include a safety deposit box and wi-fi internet access. There is a plush pool, a fitness centre and several bars. Discounts available.

Eating

For many it's the food that makes Makassar a great destination. There's an abundance of delicious seafood, excellent Chinese dishes, local 'specialities' such as *coto makassar* (soup made from buffalo innards), and a few international surprises.

Scoring a spectacular own goal, Makassar's famous seafront dining strip was shunted south onto Jl Metro Tanjung Bunga. The 'world's longest restaurant', as we once famously called it, is sadly no more. Nevertheless the hundreds of night warungs serve up fresh and cheap Indonesian and Chinese meals for around 15,000Rp, and you can still (just about) see Makassar's famous sunset.

A string of makeshift fish warung set up every night on the foreshore opposite Fort Rotterdam and serve some of the tastiest, cheapest seafood in town (about 15,000Rp per fish baked or fried). Roaming buskers provide tableside entertainment.

Jl Timor, in the heart of the Chinese quarter, is where you'll find restaurants serving delicious *mie pangsit* (wonton soup).

Most of the hotels have restaurants that are popular with well-to-do locals.

Kios Semarang (Jl Penghibur; mains 15,000-35,000Rp; lunch & dinner) The closest thing to a Makassar institution, keep on climbing the stairs to the 3rd floor where you will be rewarded with a rowdy crowd, good seafood and cheap beer. Start with a sunset and a Bintang or two before trying the fresh squid or shrimp.

our pick **Lae Lae** (☎ 334326, Jl Datu Musseng 8; fish from 15,000Rp; lunch & dinner) Quite simply, *the* spot in town for fresh fish and seafood. If you approach from the seafront, no, don't worry, it's not closed; keep walking and enter via the sizzling barbecue. Peer into the huge ice boxes and enter fish heaven. The staff can recommend something if the choice is overwhelming. The décor may be simple, but the fish with *cobek-cobek* (sauce made with chilli, lime and shrimp paste) is anything but.

Rumah Makan Kayangan (☎ 325273; Jl Datu Musseng 20; fish from 20,000Rp; lunch & dinner) Along the same street as Lae Lae, Kayangan is a slightly more upmarket affair with tablecloths and air-con, the latter particularly welcome at lunchtime. The fish is fresh, the service swift and the Bintangs are ice-cold. What more could you want?

Rumah Makan Malabar (☎ 319776; Jl Sulawesi 264; curry 20,000Rp; lunch & dinner) Run by a second-generation Keralan, Malabar is a little slice of the subcontinent, serving up flaky naan and tender *kare kambing* (goat curry). The choice is limited but the flavours more than make up for it.

Pizza Ria (cnr Jl Kajaolalido & Jl Ahmad Yani; pizzas from 20,000Rp; lunch & dinner) It's not quite as much of a chain as Pizza Hut, so is worth a dip if you are craving cheese.

Shogun Restaurant (☎ 324102; Jl Penghibur 2; sushi & sashimi platters from 60,000Rp; lunch & dinner) The only authentic Japanese restaurant in town is right next door to Hotel Losari Beach. The prices are high for Makassar, but very reasonable compared with the average Japanese bill. Makassar's abundant fish makes sashimi an excellent choice.

Club Velvet (Imperial Aryaduta Hotel, Jl Somba Opu 297) An evening jazz lounge that offers sumptuous platters for two with all sorts of flamboyant flavours.

Phinisi Restaurant (Hotel Pantai Gapura, Jl Pasar Ikan 10) Shiver me timbers, this is set aboard a full-size schooner. It's kitsch, but so is the menu, with international favourites such as 'Chicken Gordon Blue'.

Candy Bakery (Jl Baumassepe) Just around the corner from the massive Marannu Hotel, this little bakery has a good range of basic cakes and pastries.

If the hot weather is just too much, duck into Swensen's for an ice-cream, although be warned it doesn't taste like the real deal. Upstairs in the same food court above the well-stocked **Galeal Supermarket** (Jl Sultan Hasanuddin) is Kantin Baik dan Murah turning out good, cheap Indonesian food at an affordable price.

Drinking

A lot of the bars around the port area are little more than brothels disguised as karaoke bars and are best avoided by all but the proverbial drunken sailor. You really want to know how bad it is? Locals call it Vagina St.

Further south on Jl Penghibur, there are several lively places. The aforementioned Kios Semarang is definitely *the* watering hole in town. On Friday, the small band of Hash House Harriers gather here to eat, drink and be merry before their Saturday fun run.

Kafe Kareba (Jl Penghibur) On the corner opposite the Losari Beach Hotel, this outdoor beer garden features live bands and the drinks flow. They also have a pretty extensive menu of food for those wanting entertainment while they eat.

Ballairate Sunset Bar (Pantai Gapura Hotel) Built on stilts over the sea, this is the best located bar in town. Walk right through the hotel to discover draft Bintang by the pitcher and a perfect view of the sunset. Sundays are a bad idea as the Makassar jet-ski crowd strut their stuff on the water here.

Entertainment

NIGHTCLUBS

Drinking at nightclubs can be prohibitively expensive, as this is how they rake in the cash. It is best to warm-up at a bar before delving into the dance zone. Most of the clubs rumble on until about 3am.

Many of the top-end hotels house nightclubs with pricey drinks and bands playing MTV hits. Entry costs 30,000Rp to 50,000Rp, which usually includes a soft drink or beer.

Colors (Jl Pasar Ikan; admission variable) Housed in the old Benteng Theatre, this is currently the 'in' club in town. DJs and bands from Jakarta, ladies night on Wednesday and expensive drinks all round, this is where the hipsters hang out.

Pharos (Jl Nusakam Bangan 2; admission free for foreigners) Another Egyptian-themed club, which were all the rage in Asia a few years ago, this place is a veritable labyrinth. Wander through the video arcade and a maze of corridors and you'll find yourself in the hard house world of the new Indonesia.

M Club (admission incl 1st drink from 25,000Rp) On the edge of town, this warehouse club is one of biggest in Sulawesi. The music is tech-no prisoners and the lighting strobe-heavy, but if you want the Makassar experience, this is an essential stop. Foreigners often get in free. It's on the east side of town – all taxi drivers know the place. A taxi there should cost about 25,000Rp.

Botol Cafe (Quality Hotel, Jl Somba Opu 235) By far the most popular of the hotel nightclubs, this is tucked away rather uninvitingly in the basement car park.

CINEMAS

There are several modern multiscreen cinemas showing current Western films in their original language (with Indonesian subtitles):

Studio 21 (Jl Sam Ratulangi) On the top floor of the Ratu Indah Mall complex.

Makassar Theatre (Jl Bali) Hidden away in the back streets near the port.

Shopping

Jl Somba Opu has plenty of shops with great collections of jewellery, 'antiques' and souvenirs, including crafts from all over Indonesia, such as Kendari filigree silver jewellery, Torajan handicrafts, Chinese pottery, Makassarese brass work, and silk cloth from Sengkang. Shopping centres are the place to be for most Makassarese:

G Mall The massive centrepiece of the new Tanjung Bunga development, it is still finding its feet, as it's a fair way from town.

Makassar Mall The oldest in town, a sprawling mess and more like a market than a mall.

Panukkukang Mall Bigger than an Indonesian village, this is a popular mall in the affluent eastern suburbs.

Ratu Indah Mall (Jl Sam Ratulangi) The best of the more central malls, this could be anywhere in the world.

Getting There & Away

AIR

Makassar is well-connected to the rest of Indonesia, as many flights between Java and the easternmost islands call here en route. Shop around and check for the current prices with airlines and agents. For details on current fares, see the airfares map, p669.

Adam Air (☎ 4660999; Jl Andi Pangeran Pettarani 33) flies daily to and from Jakarta and Surabaya.

Batavia Air (☎ 3655255; Jl Ahmad Yani 35) flies daily to and from Palu, Balikpapan, Jakarta, Biak and Jayapura.

DAS (☎ 555774; Hasanuddin Airport) makes the scenic trip to and from Rantepao every Tuesday and Friday. It also serves Palau Selayar on Monday and Friday.

Garuda (Garuda Indonesia; ☎ 3654747; Jl Slamet Riyadi 6) flies directly to and from Manado, Denpasar, Jakarta, Jayapura and Biak every day of the week.

Lion Air (☎ 327038; Jl Ahmad Yani 22) flies daily to and from Manado, Kendari, Gorontalo, Palu, Jakarta, Surabaya, Denpasar and Ambon.

Mandala Airlines (☎ 322947; Jl Cokroaminoto 7) flies daily and directly to and from Jakarta and Ambon.

Merpati (Merpati Nusantara Airlines; ☎ 442892; Jl Bawakaraeng) connects Makassar and Jakarta, Balikpapan, Kendari, Surabaya, Biak, Jayapura, Manado, Palu, Ternate and Timika. There is also a handy Yogyakarta service four times a week.

Sriwijaya Air (Hasanuddin Airport) flies to Jakarta and Gorontolo.

BOAT

More than half the Pelni fleet stops in Makassar, mostly on the way to Surabaya and Jakarta, East Kalimantan, Ambon and Papua.

Useful services include the *Umsini* and *Kelimutu* to Balikpapan (economy/1st class 116,000/357,000Rp); the *Awu* and *Sirimau* to Kupang in Nusa Tenggara (249,000/786,000Rp); and the *Tilongkabila* to Bau Bau and then up the east coast to Kendari (131,000/405,000Rp), Kolonedale, Luwuk, Gorontalo and Manado.

The **Pelni office** (☎ 331401; Jl Sam Ratulangi; 8am-2pm Mon-Sat) is efficient and computerised. Tickets are also available at any Pelni agency around town. The chaotic Pelabuhan Makassar port, which is used by Pelni boats, is only a becak ride from most hotels.

BUS & KIJANG

Makassar has numerous terminals but three are most useful. Terminal Panaikang is in the eastern suburbs on the road to the airport, where there are regular buses to all points north, including Pare Pare (22,000Rp, three hours), Sengkang (33,000Rp, four hours) and Rantepao (45,000Rp, eight hours). **Litha Bus** (☎ 324847) has a twice daily VIP air-con service to Rantepao (75,000Rp) at 10am and 10pm. This is the bus of choice to Tana Toraja, as it offers better leg room than business class seats on an aeroplane, no kidding. There are also Kijang services to towns across South Sulawesi and buses to the rest of Sulawesi. To get to Panaikang (2000Rp, 30 minutes), catch any blue *pete-pete* marked 'Daya' from Makassar Mall or from along Jl Bulusaraung.

Terminal Mallengkeri is about 10km southeast of the city centre. From here, buses and Kijangs go to places southeast of Makassar, including Bulukumba (28,000Rp, three hours) and Pantai Bira (35,000Rp, four hours). For Pantai Bira, you may have to change in Bulukumba.

Terminal Sungguminasa has regular *pete-pete* services to Malino (10,000Rp, 1½ hours). To get to Mallengkeri or Sungguminasa, take a red *pete-pete* marked 'S Minasa' from Makassar Mall or from along Jl Jendral Sudirman. Ask to be dropped at Mallengkeri, or continue on to Terminal Sungguminasa.

Buses run all day but are most frequent in the morning so it's good to get to the terminals no later than 8am.

Arriving by plane, buses to Pare Pare, Toraja and all points north can be flagged down on the Makassar–Maros road, 300m from the terminal, saving a trip into town. However, you may need to wait a while for an empty seat.

Getting Around

TO/FROM THE AIRPORT

Hasanuddin Airport is 22km from the centre of Makassar. Prepaid taxis are easy to arrange at the airport booth outside arrivals. There are three fares from 64,000Rp to 86,000Rp, depending on the destination, but most hotels are in the centre which costs 75,000Rp. There is also a small toll fee of 1500Rp for the short cut. To the airport, a metered taxi is about 70,000Rp.

Pete-pete from Makassar Mall to Maros (4000Rp) pass the airport. The Damri bus to Maros (see right) also passes the entrance to the airport (which is 500m from the terminal).

Pete-pete and Damri buses *to* the city stop outside the main gate, although you may need to change to another *pete-pete* at Terminal Daya or Panaikang to get to the centre.

PUBLIC TRANSPORT

Makassar is hot, so using a becak, *pete-pete* or taxi can be a relief. The friendly old crooks that are the becak drivers like to kerb-crawl, hoping you'll succumb to their badgering and/or the heat. They want anything from 10,000Rp and up; locals pay about 5000Rp around town. The main *pete-pete* terminal is at the Makassar Mall, and the standard fare around town is 2000Rp. Air-conditioned taxis have meters and are worth using; it works out at about 4000Rp a kilometre and can be cheaper, and much faster, than becaks.

AROUND MAKASSAR

Pulau Samalona

A tiny speck just off Makassar, Pulau Samalona is popular for fishing and snorkelling, particularly on Sunday. Otherwise, there's nothing much to do – it takes a full two minutes to walk around the island. If you ask around, you can buy cold drinks and fresh fish meals. Snorkelling gear is also available. Compared to Makassar harbour, the water's pretty clear!

To get here you will have to charter a boat for about 200,000Rp one way or return from the special jetty in Makassar and prearrange to be picked up later. On Sunday you can probably share a boat with some day-trippers.

Pulau Kayangan

This tiny island is cluttered with strange tourist attractions and is not great for swimming (although plenty of locals do). It's very busy on Sunday, but almost completely empty for the rest of the week. Some of the restaurants around the island are positioned over the water, and many are perfect for sunsets. If you feel like staying here, **Wisata Bahari Pulau Kayangan** (☎ 0411-315752; r 150.000-350,000Rp) has somewhat overpriced rooms, although the deluxe options are huge and include satellite TV and air-con.

Boats travel from the special jetty in Makassar every 15 minutes (per person return 10,000Rp; on Sunday 15,000Rp) until 10pm – perfect for a sunset cruise followed by a meal on the island.

Bantimurung

Air Terjun Bantimurung (admission 10,000Rp), 42km from Makassar, are waterfalls set amid lushly vegetated limestone cliffs. Looking up, it's straight out of Jurassic Park, but then you scan the ground level and it's a classic *objek wisata* (tourist object). That translates as crowded with day-trippers on weekends (get your photo taken with strangers!), and peppered with litter and creative concrete, but it remains a wonderful and picturesque retreat from the heat of Makassar. Upstream from the main waterfall, there's another smaller waterfall and a pretty, but treacherous, pool. However, you will need a torch to make it through the cave en route. Bantimurung is also famous for its beautiful **butterflies**. The naturalist Alfred Wallace collected specimens here in the mid-1800s. However, numbers are plummeting as locals trap them to sell to visitors, so try not to encourage the trade.

Catch a Damri bus or *pete-pete* (5000Rp, one hour) to Maros from Makassar Mall in Makassar, and a *pete-pete* to Bantimurung (3000Rp, 30 minutes).

Gua Leang Leang

A few kilometres before Bantimurung is the road to these caves, noted for their ancient paintings. The age of the paintings is unknown, but relics from nearby caves have provided glimpses of life from 8000 to 30,000 years ago. There are 60 or so known caves in the Maros district, as the limestone karsts here have more holes than a Swiss cheese.

Catch a *pete-pete* from Maros (see above) to the 'Taman Purbakala Leang-Leang' turn-off on the road to Bantimurung, and then walk the last couple of kilometres. Alternatively, charter a *pete-pete* from Maros, and combine it with a trip to Bantimurung.

Malino

☎ 0417

Malino is a hill resort once famous as the meeting place of Kalimantan and East Indonesian leaders who endorsed the Netherlands' ill-fated plans for a federation. More recently, peace agreements have been struck for Maluku and Poso in the Resort Celebes. There are many scenic walks, and **Air Terjun Takapala** is a spectacular waterfall set amid rice fields 4km east of town. Look for the 'Wisata Alam Lombasang Malino' sign as you come into town for the waterfall turn off.

Resort Celebes (☎ 21300; Jl Hasanuddin 1; r from 254,000Rp) is a must for those with a sense of history, as many an important political agreement has been hammered out here. All rooms include satellite TV and hot water. It's a very peaceful place.

Hotel Pinang Mas (☎ 21173; Jl Karaeng Pado; r from 126,000Rp) is the place for huge views, but the prices are equally huge given the standard of the rooms. It's on the main road about 150m above the muddy market.

Both of the hotels have popular restaurants; otherwise you can eat at hole-in-the-wall warungs.

Terminal Sungguminasa has regular *pete-pete* services to Malino (10,000Rp, 1½ hours). Make sure you leave early before Malino's infamous rain sets in.

PANTAI BIRA

☎ 0413

Bira is the number one beach destination in South Sulawesi, but fear not, this is a world away from costa del Kuta in Bali. Fishing, boat building and weaving are the primary commercial activities here, but the powdery white-sand beaches are drawing some travellers off the main Makassar–Tana Toraja tourist trail. Divers are also discovering the area in small numbers, as Bira offers some rich rewards for the experienced. During the week Pantai Bira is a relaxed spot, where goats outnumber vehicles and, more often than not, tourists.

Orientation & Information

Almost everything is located along a small section of the road into Pantai Bira, Jl Kapongkolang. Foreign tourists must pay 5000Rp per person at the toll booth when they first enter 'town'. The Bira Beach Hotel has a wartel, which also acts as a postal agency, Pelni agency and moneychanger. Internet is available at **Muhlis Warnet** (Jl Kapongkolang) at a hefty 20,000Rp per hour. Electricity and the connection aren't that reliable, so it is best to wait until Makassar.

Sights

Boat builders use age-old techniques to craft **traditional ships** at Marumasa near Bira village and at Tanah Beru on the road to Bulukumba. Boats of various sizes can be seen at different stages of construction.

Weavers gather under raised houses to work and gossip. You can hear the click-clack of their looms as you walk along the streets in Bira village. There is a small **market** (*pasar* Bira) held in the village every two days.

A short hike from the road near Pantai Timur takes you to the top of **Pua Janggo**, a small hill with great views. Near the Pantai Bira hotels there are some **caves** with plenty of frisky monkeys; ask for directions from hotel staff.

Activities

DIVING & SNORKELLING

Experienced divers say that the diving around Pantai Bira is impressive, but as the currents are often strong, the emphasis really is on experience. The waters off Bira are particularly popular with sharks, rays and huge groupers, plus there is superb coral at several drop-offs. The best spots are around Pulau Selayar, Marumasa, northern Pulau Lihukan, and southern and eastern Pulau Betang.

The main dive centre in Bira is **South Sulawesi Diver** (☎ 82125; www.south-sulawesi-diver.com), based at Anda Bungalows. Run by a German instructor who has been exploring the waters for a few years, 10-dive packages start from €300. Fun dives are available, but the price depends on numbers. Diving is also available through the Bira Beach Hotel, but nobody was able to give us any information during our stay.

Snorkelling is also impressive off Bira, but it is worth chartering a boat to get to the best spots. A trip around Pulau Lihukan and Pulau Betang will cost about 150,000Rp per day. The beach in front of Bira View Inn is good, but don't venture too far because the currents can be surprisingly

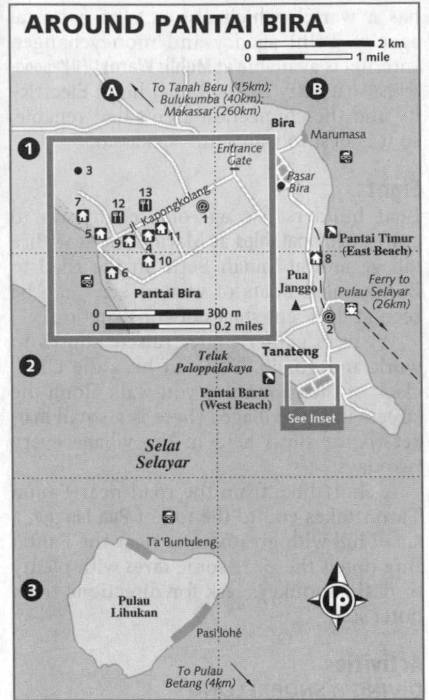

INFORMATION
Moneychanger........(see 5)
Muhlis Warnet........**1** A1
Pelni Agency........(see 5)
Postal Agency........(see 5)
Wartel & Internet Office........**2** B2
Wartel........(see 5)

SIGHTS & ACTIVITIES
Dive Centre........(see 5)
Monkey Caves........**3** A1
South Sulawesi Diver........(see 4)

SLEEPING
Anda Bungalows........**4** A1
Bira Beach Hotel & Restaurant........**5** A1
Bira View Inn........**6** A2
Hotel Sapolohe........**7** A1
Kaluku Kafe........**8** B2
Nusa Bira Indah Cottage........**9** A1
Riswan Guesthouse........**10** A2
Salassa Guesthouse........**11** A1

EATING
Rumah Makan Melati........**12** A1
Rumah Makan Sederhana........**13** A1

TRANSPORT
Harbour........(see 2)

strong and people have drowned. Equipment can be rented for about 40,000Rp per day from several hotels, including Riswan Guesthouse, Bira View Inn and Bira Beach Hotel.

SWIMMING

The tides can be severe, but **Pantai Barat** (West Beach) is a perfect stretch of beach, about 100m northwest of Bira Beach Hotel. You can hire huge inflatable rubber tyres, and enjoy the serenity – except on Sunday, when the place is usually crawling with day-trippers from Makassar. **Pantai Timur** (East Beach) is more your serene, coconut-fringed affair. Bear in mind that the locals are fairly conservative around here, so topless bathing for women should be considered a no-no.

Sleeping

Most accommodation is in small cottages with private bathrooms and verandas, but it pays to shop around, as some places are showing their age. Very few have genuine sea views and many are cluttered around 'gardens' of dead coral. Other places are set back from the beach, clustered around the only road in town.

Bira View Inn (☎ 82043; fax 81515; cottages 100,000-200,000Rp; ❄) The best rooms here are set in wooden cottages on a cliff overlooking the bay. Each has its own porch with a genuine sea view and they are in a slightly better state of repair than the nearby Bira Beach. This is the only hotel to really exploit its location.

Bira Beach Hotel (☎ /fax 83522; bungalows 125,000-200,000Rp; ❄) One of the first hotels here, it needs a bit of tender loving care to bring it up to speed. 'Sea view' is a somewhat abstract notion here, as the design of the cottages means the balcony faces the garden. Rooms are large, if threadbare, and air-con bungalows start from 150,000Rp. The restaurant here is one of the best in Bira.

Hotel Sapolohe (☎ /fax 82128; r 125,000-250,000Rp; ❄) The best of the beachfront hotels, few of the rooms take advantage of the sea view. The more expensive deluxe rooms are set in an elegant wooden stilt house and are veritable suites, with decent bathrooms, satellite TV and air-con. Cheaper rooms are in clean, comfortable bungalows out the back. Rates go through the roof during holidays.

Salassa Guesthouse (r 40,000-60,000Rp) A small, family-run place that has been recommended for its homely atmosphere. Two cheaper rooms have shared *mandi*, while two more include attached bathroom. The owners have a good knowledge of the local area and meals are available on request.

Riswan Guesthouse (☎ 82127; r incl all meals 70,000Rp) Set in a dominant position on a bluff overlooking the sea, this rambling old stilt house is the most welcoming home in town. Host Riswan is friendly and knowledgeable and all meals are taken communally. The rooms are basic and include shared facilities (shower and squat toilet), but touches such as a private locker show some thought.

Kaluku Kafe (www.kalukukafe.com; d in bungalow/cottage 120,000/280,000Rp) The only choice on Pantai Timur, Kaluku Kafe has a pristine setting amid palm trees. There is one bungalow, and the owner has recently added a cottage that can take up to six people. There is also a beachfront restaurant and craft shop, making it easy to lose days here.

Nusa Bira Indah Cottage (☎ /fax 0411-83519; r with fan/air-con 100,000/175,000Rp; ❄) The large rooms here are in better shape than some and the air-con options include a breezy porch. However, the location is a letdown with no views to soak up and not much of a garden.

Anda Bungalows (☎ 82125; fax 85033; bungalows with fan/air-con 150,000Rp/300,000Rp; ❄) The smartest rooms in town are found at the Anda…if only it had a beachside setting. All the bungalows are set around a lush garden and the new air-con bungalows are creatively decorated. The bathroom is almost Balinese style, with a separate sink and the place smacks of attention to detail, something that can't be said for the competition.

Eating

Most of the hotels have simple restaurants, but only the Bira Beach Hotel and Bira View Inn offer sunset views over the sea. Both serve seafood, a range of Indonesian and Western dishes and, mercifully, cold beer. The restaurant at the Nusa Bira Indah is well regarded and breezy. The restaurant at Anda Bungalows is the cleanest of the lot and has more of a Western selection than most. Most of the places charge around 20,000Rp for a main course.

There are a couple of local Indonesian restaurants along the main drag for cheap eats, including Rumah Makan Melati and Rumah Makan Sederhana.

Opposite the Bira Beach Hotel there is a cluster of food and drink stalls and a couple of nameless warungs serving cheap Indonesian fare and freshly grilled fish.

Getting There & Away

BOAT

The harbour at Pantai Timur services Pulau Selayar. Twice a month, there is a direct boat to Labuanbajo (92,000Rp) in Flores, but it's a slow ride, taking almost two days.

BUS, BEMO & KIJANG

From Makassar (Terminal Mallengkeri), a few Kijang go directly to Pantai Bira for 35,000Rp.

SULAWESI SEAFARERS

The Bugis are Indonesia's best-known sailors, trading and carrying goods on their magnificent wooden schooners throughout Indonesia.

The Bugis' influence expanded rapidly after the fall of Makassar, resulting in a Diaspora from South Sulawesi in the 17th and 18th centuries. They established strategic trading posts at Kutai (Kalimantan), Johor (north of Singapore) and Selangor (near Kuala Lumpur), and traded freely throughout the region. Bugis and Makassarese *pinisi* (schooners) are still built along the south coasts of Sulawesi and Kalimantan, using centuries-old designs and techniques. You can see boats being built at Marumasa and Tanah Beru, both near Bira.

The Bajau, Bugis, Butonese and Makassarese seafarers of Sulawesi have a 500-year history of trading and cultural links with the Australian Aborigines and their ships are featured in pre-European Aboriginal cave art in northern Australia. British explorer Matthew Flinders encountered 60 Indonesian schooners at Melville Bay in 1803; today many more still make the risky (and illegal) journey to fish reefs in the cyclone belt off the northern coast of Australia.

Many Minahasans of North Sulawesi, relative newcomers to sailing folklore, work on international shipping lines across the world. Like their Filipino neighbours, the Minahasans' outward-looking culture, plus their language and sailing skills, make them the first choice of many captains.

Alternatively, catch a Kijang or bemo to Bulukumba, and another to Pantai Bira (transport from Bulukumba to Pantai Bira stops at around 3pm).

Direct Kijangs from Pantai Bira to Makassar (40,000Rp) should be booked through your hotel the day before; otherwise get a *pete-pete* from Pantai Bira to Bulukumba (8000Rp) and take a Kijang to Makassar (28,000Rp) from there.

PULAU LIHUKAN & PULAU BETANG

Weavers at **Ta'Buntuleng** make heavy, colourful cloth on hand looms under their houses. On the pretty beach west of the village there is an interesting old **graveyard**, and off the beach there are acres of sea grass and coral, but mind the currents and sea snakes. To see the best coral, which is further out, you'll need a boat. In fact, you'll need to charter a boat to visit Lihukan and the nearby, uninhabited Pulau Betang, also known as Pulau Kambing.

PULAU SELAYAR

☎ 0414

This long, narrow island lies off the southwestern peninsula of Sulawesi and is inhabited by the Bugis, the Makassarese and the Konjo. Most reside along the infertile west coast and in **Benteng**, the main town. Like Pantai Bira, Selayar's long coastline is a repository of flotsam from nearby shipping lanes, perhaps accounting for the presence of a 2000-year-old Vietnamese Dongson drum, kept in an annexe near the former **Benteng Bontobangun** (Bontobangun Fort), a few kilometres south of Benteng.

Selayar's main attractions are its sandy **beaches** and picturesque scenery. The snorkelling near small **Pulau Pasi**, opposite Benteng, is good, but you will have to bring your own equipment (or rent some in Pantai Bira) and charter a boat.

Hotel Berlian (☎ 21129; Jl Sudirman, Benteng; r with fan 44,000Rp, with air-con & private bathroom 65,000-125,000Rp; ❄) offers the beds of choice for most visitors, thanks to a range of decent rooms and a reliable restaurant. The highest prices deliver satellite TV and hot water.

Ferries (2½ hours) leave Pantai Bira harbour for Pamatata (17,000Rp) around 10am and 3pm and from Pamatata around the same times. Hotels should know the current schedules. Buses leave Terminal Mallengkeri in Makassar each morning to link with the ferry from Pantai Bira.

TAKA BONE RATE

Southeast of Pulau Selayar, and north of Pulau Bone Rate, is the 2220-sq-km Taka Bone Rate, the world's third-largest coral atoll. The largest, Kwajalein in the Marshall Islands, is just 20% bigger. Some of the islands and extensive reefs in the region are now part of **Taka Bone Rate Marine National Park** (Taman Laut Taka Bone Rate), a marine reserve with a rich variety of marine and bird life.

There is no official accommodation on the islands, but if you manage to get here you can stay with villagers if you ask the *kepala desa* (village head) at Bone Rate on Pulau Bone Rate. Alternatively, take a tent and camp on a beach. Boats leave irregularly from Selayar. Most visitors are divers travelling on liveaboard trips.

WATAMPONE

☎ 0481 / pop 84,000

Known more simply as Bone (bone-eh) by locals, Watampone is a small town with a good range of hotels, but few foreigners end up staying here. Watampone was the capital of Bone, a semi-autonomous state under the overlordship of Gowa, the strongest anti-Dutch power in the East Indies. The authoritarian ruler Prince Arung Palakka and his followers returned from exile in 1666 and rallied the local Bugis for a long overland campaign, forcing Gowanese sultan Hasanuddin to cede territory, including Watampone.

Information

BNI bank (Bank Negara Indonesia; Jl Sukawati) One of the only ATMs in town.

Main post office (Jl Thamrin; 🕑 8am-9pm)

Prima Warnet (Jl Sukawati) Internet access at 15,000Rp per hr.

Telkom office (Jl Monginsidi)

Sights & Activities

A statue of Prince Arung Palakka dominates the square. South of the town centre is **Pusat Kebudayaan Bola Soba** (Jl Sukawati), a huge Bugis house built in 1881 and now used sparingly for cultural events.

Museum Lapawawoi (Jl Thamrin; admission free; 🕑 7am-4pm) is a former palace housing one of Indonesia's most interesting regional collections, including an odd array of court memorabilia and dozens of photographs of state occasions.

Sleeping & Eating

Wisma Bolaridie (☎ 21412; Jl Merdeka 6; small r 35,000Rp, s/d 50,000/70,000Rp) Believe it or not, this is a former royal residence, built in the Dutch colonial style. The cheaper rooms are rather small and located out the back, while in the main building there are huge, charming, yet dusty rooms.

Hotel Wisata Watampone (☎ 21362; fax 22367; Jl Jendral Sudirman 14; r from 120,000Rp; ✖ 🏊) The best hotel in town, the big rooms have satellite TV, hot water and air-con. There is a large swimming pool at the back of the hotel, but the water isn't that inviting.

Rumah Makan Ramayana (Jl Ponggawae; meals 10,000-25,000Rp; 🕑 breakfast, lunch & dinner) The best place in town, with spicy barbecued chicken one of the leading lights on the local menu.

Dynasty Restaurant (Jl Thamrin; meals 15,000-30,000; 🕑 breakfast, lunch & dinner) A short stroll southeast of the museum, the massive menu here is longer than its karaoke song list and that is saying something in Sulawesi. Chinese is king here, but there are a few Indonesian favourites.

There is a cluster of simple *rumah makan* (eating houses) in the market area, and night warung and Padang *rumah makan* (eating houses serving Padang food) along the main shopping street, Jl Ponggawae.

Getting There & Away

BOAT

Four ferries ply the route between the nearby port of Bajoe and Kolaka in Southeast Sulawesi (see right).

BUS & BEMO

Watampone is not a major transport junction, but several Kijangs and buses travel to Bulukumba (25,000Rp, three hours) for connections to Bira, and Makassar's Terminal Panaikang (30,000Rp, five hours). Buses also run to Palopo and Pare Pare. Try to get to the inconvenient and oversized terminal early to avoid long waits. It's 2km west of town, so take an *ojek* (motorbike taxi) or bemo from Jl Sulawesi. Kijangs to Sengkang (18,000Rp, two hours) leave from Jl Mangga in the centre of Watampone.

If you're heading to Rantepao (45,000Rp), get a connection in Palopo. Several bus agencies along Jl Besse Kajuara, either side of the bus terminal, sell tickets for the through trip to Kendari (95,000Rp).

AROUND WATAMPONE

Bajoe

Bajoe is the major regional port, 8km from Watampone, for connections to Kolaka.

Three ferries (eight hours) leave every evening at 5pm, 8pm and 11pm from Bajoe for Kolaka, the gateway to the southeastern peninsula. All departure and arrival times are for the benefit of those travelling to/from Makassar or Kendari. Tickets are 40,000/50,000Rp for deck/business class.

From Watampone, bemos go to Bajoe every few minutes from a special stop behind the market. From the bus terminal at the end of the incredibly long causeway in Bajoe, buses head off to most places, including Makassar and Rantepao, just after the ferry arrives. Get off the ferry and jump on an *ojek*, bus or bemo to Watampone.

SENGKANG

☎ 0485

Sengkang is a small riverside town with a nearby scenic lake, a traditional handwoven silk industry and several good hotels. **BNI bank** (Bank Negara Indonesia; Jl Ahmad Yani) has an ATM and can change money. For telephone calls, there is a Telkom Office on Jl Pahlawan.

Sights & Activities

DANAU TEMPE

Danau Tempe is a large, shallow lake fringed by wetlands, with floating houses and magnificent birdlife. Geologists believe the lake was once a gulf between southern Toraja and the rest of South Sulawesi. As they merged, the gulf disappeared and geologists believe the lake will eventually disappear too…silt from deforestation is speeding up the process.

There are no organised boat tours, so make for the longboat terminal (at the end of a laneway marked 'Setapak 7', opposite a sports field along Jl Sudirman) and charter a boat for about 40,000Rp for two hours (80,000Rp with a guide), in which time you can speed along **Sungai Walanae**, visit **Salotangah village** in the middle of the lake, go across to **Batu Batu village** on the other side, and come back. A boat trip is particularly charming at dusk. Staff at the hotels can also arrange trips and recommend places to visit.

SILK WEAVING

Sengkang's other attraction is its *sutera* (silk) weaving industry. You can visit the **silk workshops**, but most are located in remote villages, with little or no reliable public transport. Ask the staff at your hotel to recommend some workshops, and charter a *pete-pete* from the terminal. Alternatively, just walk around the **market** in Sengkang, where silk scarves and sarongs are on sale.

Sleeping & Eating

Hotel Al Salam II (☎ 21278; fax 21893; Jl Emmi Saelan 8; r 50,000-100,000Rp) Tucked away just off the Jl Sudirman main drag, this hotel has a range of reasonable rooms. It also has an informal restaurant and bar and this is pretty much the only eatery serving Bintang in town.

Pondok Eka (☎ /fax 21296; Jl Maluku 12; s/d with fan 50,000/65,000Rp, with air-con from 125,000/175,000Rp; ❄) Set around an attractive courtyard, this friendly, family-run place has well-tended rooms. The deluxe rooms include satellite TV and hot-water showers.

Hotel Apada (☎ /fax 21053; Jl Nangka 9; r 100,000-125,000Rp; ❄) Formerly owned by a princess, this large, rambling hotel has smart rooms that include attached bathrooms.

Restoran Tomudi (☎ 21885; Jl Andi Oddang 32; mains 15,000-25,000Rp; 🕐 breakfast, lunch & dinner) One of the few real restaurants in town, there is a hearty menu of Indonesian and Chinese staples. It doesn't serve alcohol, like most restaurants in Sengkang.

Getting There & Away

Sengkang is readily accessible from Pare Pare (15,000Rp, two hours) by bus or Kijang. If you're travelling to/from Rantepao (six hours), you may need a connection in Palopo. There are plenty of buses and Kijangs along the road to Watampone (18,000Rp, two hours) and Bajoe, and very regular buses to/from Terminal Panaikang in Makassar (33,000Rp, four hours).

Bemos to local destinations leave from the bus terminal behind the market on Jl Kartini. Agencies for long-distance buses, Kijangs and Pelni boats are a few metres south of the terminal.

PARE PARE

☎ 0421 / pop 114,000

Pare Pare is a smaller, greener version of Makassar, and a quiet stopover between Tana Toraja or Mamasa and Makassar. It's also the second-largest port in the region, with many Pelni services and boats to Kalimantan.

Orientation & Information

The town is stretched out along the waterfront. At night, the esplanade turns into a lively pedestrian mall with warungs and stalls. Most of what you need is on the streets running parallel to the harbour. The major banks change money.

Haji La Tunrung moneychanger (Jl Sultan Hasanuddin) Competitive rates.

Main post office (Jl Karaeng Burane) Has internet access.

Sleeping & Eating

Hotel Gandaria I (☎ 21093; Jl Bau Massepe 395; s/d with fan 40,000/70,000Rp) A friendly, family-run spot which has good-value rooms.

Hotel Gandaria II, (☎ 21093; Jl Samporaja 4; s/d with fan 40,000/70,000Rp) This is the Hotel Gandaria I's second location.

Hotel Kenari Bukit Indah (☎ 21886; Jl Jendral Sudirman 65; s/d from 163,000/200,000Rp; ❄) This hotel is a little way out of town, but for those with transport it is worth it for the superb sea views and a well-regarded restaurant. The rooms are some of the most comfortable in Pare Pare, with air-con, TV and hot water.

Restaurant Asia (Jl Baso Daeng Patompo; meals 10,000-25,00Rp; 🕐 breakfast, lunch & dinner) A monster menu of Chinese and Indonesian food, plus a wide selection of delicious seafood.

Warung Sedap (Jl Baso Daeng Patompo; meals 15,000-30,000Rp; 🕐 lunch & dinner) Next door to Restaurant Asia, this warung specialises in *ikan bakar* (baked fish), but check the price before you order your fish.

There are several small *rumah makan* along Jl Baso Daeng Patompo, in the vicinity of Hotel Siswa. At night, warungs line the esplanade, each with exactly the same choice of rice and noodle dishes.

Getting There & Away

BOAT

The main reason to come to Pare Pare is to catch a ship to East Kalimantan. Every two weeks, **Pelni** (☎ 21017; Jl Andicammi) runs the *Agoa Mas* to Nunukan in Kalimantan; *Kerinci* to Balikpapan and the *Binaiya* to

Samarinda. The *Awu* goes to Tarakan and on to Nunukan.

Every one or two days, several decent passenger boats travel between Pare Pare and Samarinda and Balikpapan (both 112,000Rp, 22 hours) and Nunukan (236,000Rp, two nights). Details and bookings are available from agencies near the port and just north of Restaurant Asia.

BUS

Pare Pare is on the main road between Makassar and Rantepao, and plenty of buses and Kijangs go to Terminal Panaikang in Makassar (22,000Rp, three hours) and Rantepao (25,000Rp, four hours). Most buses travel through Terminal Induk several kilometres south of the city, but it's often easier to hail a bus as it flies through town. Kijangs to Polewali (18,000Rp, two hours) leave from Terminal Soreang, 3km northeast of town.

PALOPO

☎ 0471 / pop 93,000

This Islamic port on the east coast of the peninsula is the administrative capital of the Luwu district. Before the Dutch, it was the centre of the old and powerful Luwu kingdom. The former palace is now the tiny **Museum Batara Guru** (Jl Andi Jemma), which is opposite the police station, and contains relics of the royal era. On the waterfront is a **Bugis village**, and a long pier where you can get a closer look at the fishing boats.

Palopo is a sprawling town with an inordinate number of becak. There is no reason to come here except to catch public transport. Vehicles regularly leave from just outside Terminal Bolu in Rantepao for the *very* winding trip to Palopo (20,000Rp, two hours). Plenty of buses and minibuses go from Palopo's organised terminal to Rantepao, Pare Pare, Makassar and Watampone. The road between Palopo and Watampone (six hours) is initially good, but disappears into huge potholes for the last two hours.

TANA TORAJA

Tana Toraja is quite simply unique. A cultural island, hemmed in by mountains on all sides, the Toraja prove there is life after death with their elaborate ceremonies. Take the beauty of Bali, the houses of the Bataks in Sumatra and the megalithic cultures of Sumba and you're still not even close. Cave graves, hanging graves, *tau tau* (life-sized wooden effigies) of the dead and buffalo carnage every summer; it's macabre but mesmerising. This is a world unto itself.

Tana Toraja is undoubtedly the most popular destination in Sulawesi. It's a vast, pretty and mostly unspoilt area of traditional villages, unique architecture and fascinating cultures. The funeral season is usually during July and August (see p691), when Toraja working throughout Indonesia return home for celebrations, tourists come in numbers and Rantepao hotel prices peak. However, in recent years, visitor numbers have been pretty low, so it doesn't hurt to time a visit with the funeral season to see the elaborate ceremonies in full swing.

RANTEPAO

☎ 0423 / pop 45,000

Rantepao is the most popular base for exploring the stunning countryside around Tana Toraja. It is in striking distance of most of the major sites and has a good range of accommodation and restaurants. It is the largest town and commercial centre of Tana Toraja and a far better option than the provincial capital of Makale. Rantepao has cool evenings and rain throughout the year – even in the dry season.

Information

INTERNET ACCESS & POST

Post office (Jl Ahmad Yani; 8am-4pm Mon-Sat) A small place in town.

Warnet Petra (Jl Andi Mappanyukki 46; per hr 8000Rp; 8am-7pm) Rantepao's only internet centre.

MAPS

If you're doing some serious hiking, pick up a copy of the detailed *Tana Toraja* (1:85,000) map, published by Periplus.

MEDICAL SERVICES

Rumah Sakit Elim (☎ 21258; Jl Ahmad Yani) The main hospital in town. If anything serious should befall you in Toraja, make for Makassar, as facilities here are basic.

MONEY

The best rates of exchange are available from moneychangers.

Bank Danamon (Jl Diponegoro) Has an ATM; also offers heftier cash advances.

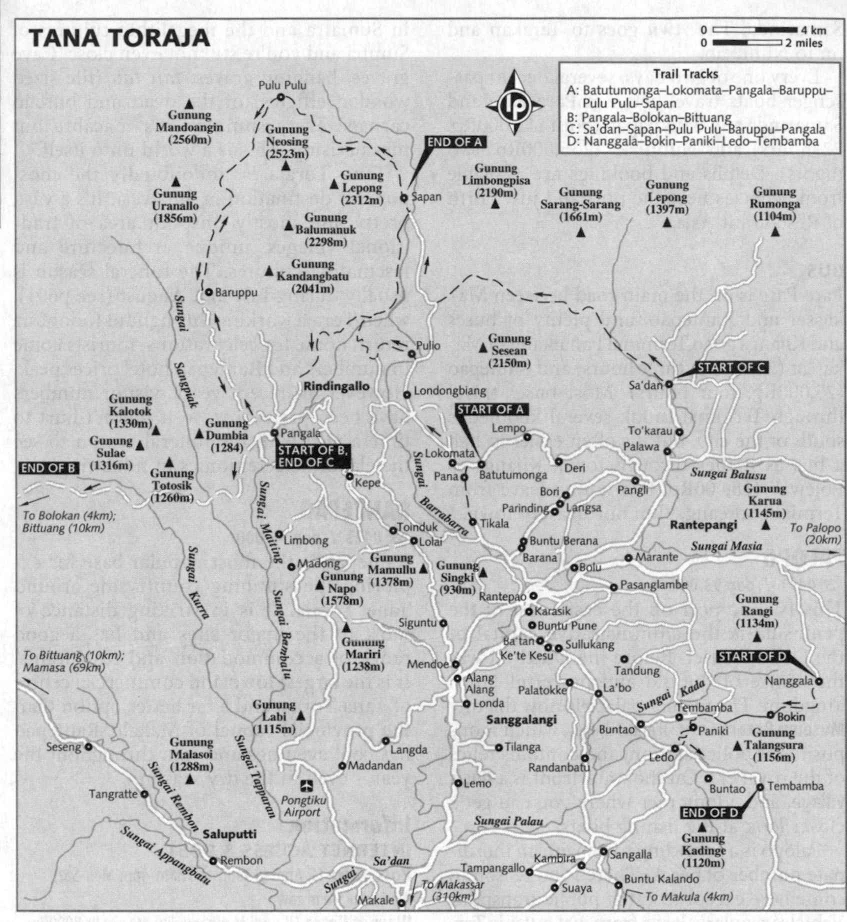

BNI bank (Bank Negara Indonesia; Jl Diponegoro) Another popular ATM.

Marazavalas (Jl Diponegoro) Moneychanger with reasonable rates.

TOURIST INFORMATION

Government Tourist Office (☎ 21277; Jl Ahmad Yani 62A) The friendly staff here can provide accurate, independent information about local ceremonies, festivals and other activities. But there is little in the way of handouts. It's just south of the hospital.

TELEPHONE

There are several wartel in town and many hotels offer international calls from rooms.

Telkom office (Jl Ahmad Yani; 24hr) Next door to the post office.

Sights

Rantepao's main **market**, *pasar* Bolu, is held every six days (but operates in a reduced capacity daily). The main market is a very big, social occasion that draws crowds from all over Tana Toraja. The commerce is lively, but incidental to the real business of the day – endless coffee, *kretek* (clove cigarettes) and gossip. Ask around Rantepao for the exact day, or seek out other markets in the area. There is a 10,000Rp charge to enter the livestock market, where the leading lights from the buffalo community are on parade. Many cost more than a small car. *Pasar* Bolu is 2km northeast of town, and easily accessible by bemo.

Activities

Most of the activities lie in the hills beyond and are covered on p702. However, most of the hotels that have **swimming pools** allow nonguests to swim for a fee of about 10,000Rp.

Tours

There are numerous travel agencies in Rantepao, offering a range of services, including organised tours of the region. Several reliable, long-running agencies in Rantepao, which can arrange tours (including trekking and cultural tours), vehicles and guides:

Indosella (☎ 25210; www.sellatours.com; Jl Andi Mappanyukki 111)

JET Tourist Service (☎ 21145; fax 23227; Jl Pontingku 31)

Toraja Permai (☎ 21785; fax 21236; Jl Andi Mappanyukki 10)

Sleeping

Rantepao has a wide range of cheap hotels and comfortable homestays, but prices usually rise in the tourist season (June–August), when some private homes also accept guests. Most budget and midrange places include breakfast in their prices, but they don't offer air-conditioning or a fan, as the nights are cool. Guides will sometimes say a hotel is closed because it doesn't offer a commission; check for yourself.

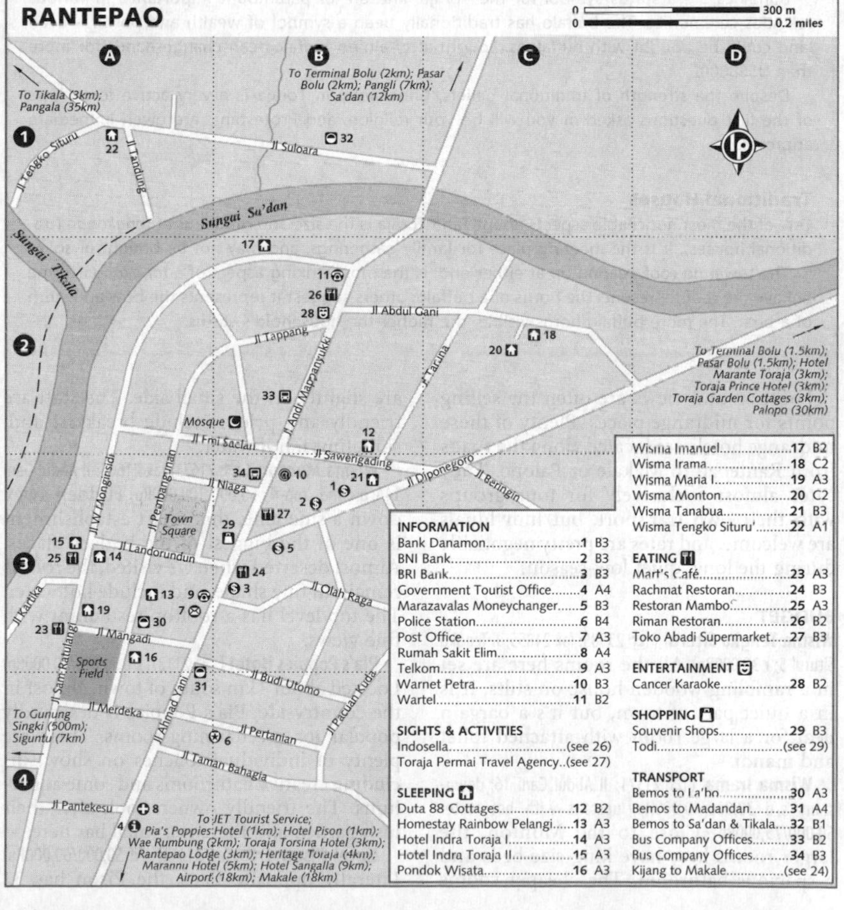

THE TORAJA

Inhabiting the vast, rugged landscape of the South Sulawesi highlands are the Toraja, a name derived from the Bugis word *toriaja* that had negative connotations similar to 'hillbilly' or 'bumpkin'.

Torajan life and culture for centuries had survived the constant threat from the Bugis from the southwest, but in 1905 the Dutch began a bloody campaign to bring Central Sulawesi under their control. The missionaries moved in on the heels of the troops, and by WWII many of the great Torajan ceremonies (with the exception of funeral celebrations) were disappearing.

Beliefs

Prior to the arrival of Christianity, the Toraja believed in many gods, but worshipped Puang Matua as the special god of their family, clan or tribe. Christianity undermined some traditional Torajan beliefs, but the ceremonies are still a vital part of life.

Torajan mythology suggests that their ancestors came by boat from the south, sailed up Sungai Sa'dan (Sa'dan River) and dwelled in the Enrekang region before being pushed into the mountains by the arrival of other groups.

Buffaloes are a status symbol for the Toraja, and are of paramount importance in various religious ceremonies. The buffalo has traditionally been a symbol of wealth and power – even land could be bought with buffaloes. Sought-after albino buffalos can change hands for more than US$8000.

Despite the strength of traditional beliefs, Christianity in Toraja is a very active force. One of the first questions asked of you will be your religion, and Protestants are given immediate approval.

Traditional Houses

One of the most noticeable aspects about Tana Toraja is the size and grandeur of *tongkonan* (traditional houses). It is the meeting place for family gatherings, and may not be bought or sold.

The towering roof, rearing up at either end, is the most striking aspect of a *tongkonan*. Some believe the roof represents the horns of a buffalo; others suggest it represents the bow and stern of a boat. The more buffalo horns visible, the higher the household's status.

Location and views are often the selling points for midrange places. Plenty of these midrange hotels are located along the roads from Rantepao to Makale or Palopo. They cater almost exclusively for tour groups with their own transport, but individuals are welcome, and rates are pretty negotiable during the long, quiet low-season.

BUDGET

Wisma Tengko Situru' (☎ 23985; fax 21855; Jl Tengko Situru' 5; r 30,000Rp) All the rooms here are set in a rambling wooden house on stilts. It is in a quiet part of town, but it's a bargain deal for a large room with attached toilet and mandi.

Wisma Irama (☎ 21371; Jl Abdul Gani 16; downstairs s/d 30,000/40,000Rp, upstairs with hot water 50,000/75,000Rp) Close to the Monton, the larger rooms here have king-size beds and a spacious bathroom. The cheaper rooms are slightly on the small side. The staff are friendly and prices include breakfast and, sometimes, hot water.

Wisma Monton (☎ 21675; fax 21665; Jl Abdul Gani 14A; ground-/top-fl r 50,000/100,000Rp) Hidden away down a side lane, this smart establishment is one of the biggest of the budget places. Almost deserted when we visited, the rooms remain in fine shape, and include hot water. The top level has a rooftop restaurant with fine views.

Pia's Poppies Hotel (☎ 21121; s/d 50,000/60,000Rp) Located about 1km south of town, almost in the countryside, Pia's Poppies is deservedly popular for its charming rooms. There are plenty of individual touches on show, including creative bathrooms and some aquariums. The friendly owners look after their lush garden and there is a small bar here.

Hotel Pison (☎/fax 21344; s/d 50,000/60,000Rp) Literally opposite Pia's, the Pison has 32

Funerals

Of all Torajan ceremonies, the most important is the *tomate* (funeral; literally 'deceased'). Without proper funeral rites the soul of the deceased will cause misfortune to its family.

The Toraja generally have two funerals, one immediately after death and an elaborate second funeral after preparations have been made. This is usually scheduled during the dry months of July to September.

Before the second funeral, the deceased remains in the family house. An invitation to visit the deceased is an honour. If you accept, remember to thank the deceased and ask permission of the deceased when you wish to leave… as you would a living host.

The second funeral can be spread over several days and involve hundreds of guests. Torajans believe that the souls of animals should follow their masters to the next life, hence the importance of animal sacrifices.

Visitors attending a funeral should wear black or dark coloured clothing.

Graves & Tau Tau

The Toraja believe that you can take possessions with you in the afterlife, and the dead generally go well-equipped to their graves. Since this led to grave plundering, the Toraja started to hide their dead in caves.

These caves were hollowed out by specialist cave builders. Coffins go deep inside the caves, and sitting on balconies in the rock face in front of the caves are *tau tau* – wooden effigies of the dead.

You can see *tau tau* carvers at work at Londa. There are many *tau tau* at Lemo and a few elsewhere, but it's becoming increasingly difficult to see them in Tana Toraja. So many have been stolen that the Toraja now keep them in their homes.

Books

In the souvenir shops and supermarkets in Rantepao there are a few decent locally produced guides: *A Guide to Toraja* by AT Marampa is available in English, German and French, and lists dances, ceremonies and some local walks. *Toraja – An Introduction to a Unique Culture* by LT Tangdilintin and M Syafei is written in their unique style. *Life and Death of the Toraja People* by Stanislaus Sandarupa is readable and informative.

rooms, each with a clean bathroom and mini-balcony with mountain views. All the rooms come with hot water, but some are showing their age more than others.

Wisma Maria I (☎ 21165; Jl Sam Ratulangi 23; s/d 45,000/70,000Rp, with hot water 95,000/110,000Rp) The well-tended rooms here are set around a large garden. It's a friendly set-up, rates include breakfast and it's a stone's throw from the popular Mart's Café. Don't try testing the stone theory, as you might get barred.

Wisma Imanuel (☎ 21416; Jl W Monginsidi 16; r 80,000Rp) Set in a large house overlooking the river, the rooms here are a generous size and include hot-water showers. Big balconies out front offer views over the garden and street action beyond.

Duta 88 Cottages (☎ 23477; Jl Sawerigading 12; r 80,000Rp) All the cottages here are *tongkonan*-style (in the style of a traditional Torajan house), set around a verdant little garden. The rooms are atmospheric and good value, as all come with hot water and satellite TV. Rates include breakfast.

If times are busy during the summer season, there are several other recommended options:

Homestay Rainbow Pelangi (☎ 21753; Jl Pembangunan 11A; r 70,000Rp) Amiable place offering basic rooms with attached bathroom.

Pondok Wisata (☎ 21595; Jl Pembangunan 23; r 60,000Rp) Smart, clean rooms with bathroom and good views to the mountains beyond.

Wisma Tanabua (☎ 21072; Jl Diponegoro 43; r from 50,000Rp) A friendly, central spot that doubles as a beauty salon.

MIDRANGE

Many of the midrange places are strewn throughout the buffalo-infested valleys, which is great for those with transport, but not so straightforward for those without. To get to these places, either hop in a bemo or take a becak.

Toraja Garden Cottages (☎ 23336; fax 25397; cottages incl breakfast 100,000Rp) Almost opposite the Toraja Prince Hotel, these wooden cottages are very good value. The thoughtful design includes a veranda with countryside views and both TV and hot water are available. Next door is the abandoned Toraja Cottages, a sad statement on the tourism slump.

Marannu Hotel (☎ 22221; fax 22028; Jl Pongtiku 116; r from 150,000Rp;) Located on the road to Makale, the rooms here are a little threadbare these days, but the large swimming pool is refreshing.

Toraja Torsina Hotel (☎ 21293; s/d 120,000/180,000Rp;) Set in the rice fields near the turn-off to Ke'te Kesu, the rooms here are clean and comfortable and worth the rupiah given the swimming pool.

Rantepao Lodge (☎ 23717; fax 21248; r 150,000-250,000Rp;) A sprawling compound near the Toraja Torsina Hotel, the deluxe rooms are the draw here. They have private balconies with an aspect over the rice fields, TV, fridge and hot water. The standard rooms are pretty basic for the money. There is also a swimming pool here.

Hotel Indra Toraja (☎ 21163; fax 21547; Jl Landorundun 63; standard/deluxe 180,000/216,000Rp) The only midrange option in the centre of Rantepao, the Indra has two annexes opposite each other. The rooms are similar in both, but most guests prefer the riverside option. Deluxe rooms include bath tubs and satellite TV, and all are set around a blooming garden. The riverside restaurant is not bad and features a singer most nights.

Hotel Sangalla (☎/fax 24485; r 250,000Rp) Located on the road to Makale, the rooms here are all set in Torajan *tongkonan* houses. Bamboo and wood furnishings predominate and the bathrooms are spotlessly clean. Check the rates before you commit, as US$85 is the optimistic walk-in price.

Toraja Prince Hotel (☎ 21430; www.torajaprincehotel.com; s/d 300,000/360,000Rp;), A few kilometres from town on the road to Palopo, the Prince is arguably the best-value midrange option on offer. All rooms feature a smart three-star trim and there is a small swimming pool. Published rates are more like US$70 and up, so check that discounts are available.

TOP END

Hotel Marante Toraja (☎ 21616; www.martantetoraja.com; deluxe r US$60, cottages US$78;) Another huge hotel, this time on the road to Palopo. The cottages have smarter bathrooms, but are slightly smaller than rooms in the main building. All are well-kitted out and overlook the swimming pool.

Heritage Toraja (☎ 21192; www.torajaheritage.com; r from US$85;) The swankiest hotel in Tana Toraja, this striking property was first built as a Novotel during the boom years. Most rooms are set in huge Torajan *tongkonan*-style houses in a lush garden with a lagoon-like pool. Facilities include satellite TV, minibar and safety deposit box. It's an atmospheric place, but all too often empty. It's about 3km from town towards Ke'te Kesu.

Eating

Going to ceremonies or local restaurants offers a great opportunity to sample Torajan food. The best-known dish is *pa'piong* (meat stuffed into bamboo tubes along with vegetables and coconut). If you want to try it in a restaurant, order several hours in advance because it takes time to cook – order dinner while having lunch. Less popular with the average visitor is dog, which is eaten in some parts of Tana Toraja. The following places are all open for breakfast, lunch and dinner.

Two of the longest-running restaurants are near the Hotel Indra Toraja on Jl Sam Ratulangi.

Mart's Café (Jl Sam Ratulangi 44; dishes 15,000-25,000Rp) This little restaurant has a good mix of Torajan specialities, Indonesian favourites and some simple Western fare. Good guacamole is available here, with prawn crackers. It's a cheap and sometimes lively place for a Bintang, but be prepared for a lot of local guides trying to sell their services.

Riman Restoran (Jl Andi Mappanyukki 113; mains from 15,000Rp) This centrally located eatery has a good mix of local delicacies and Asian favourites. This is a good place for white-water rafters to trade tales, as it is right next door to the Indosella office.

Restoran Mambo (Jl Sam Ratulangi; dishes around 20,000Rp) Just up the road from Mart's Café, this little canteen punches above its weight when it comes to the menu, including Torajan, Indonesian, Chinese and Western fare.

(Continued on page 701)

JERRY ALEXANDER

Fine dining in Senggigi (p500), Lombok

Tropical drinks (p84)

JERRY ALEXANDER

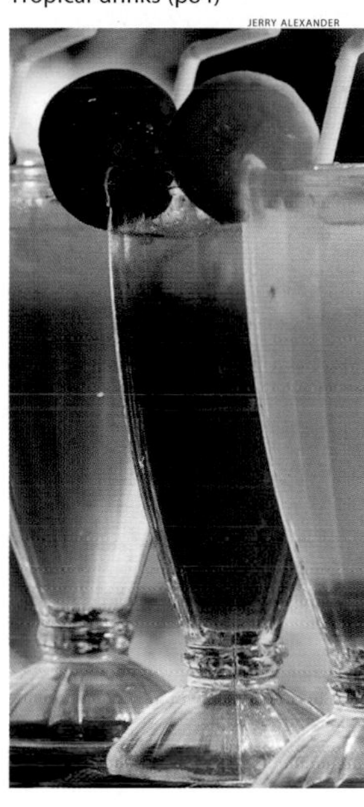

PETER HENDRIE

Sweet banana

Nasi goreng (p81), an Indonesian favourite

JERRY ALEXANDER

JAMES L

Danau Segara Anak and Gunung Baru, in the Gunung Rinjani region (p519), Lombok

PETER PTSCHELINZEW

Komodo dragon, Komodo National Park (p541)

Turquoise Lake, Kelimutu (p561), Nusa Tenggara

TONY WHE

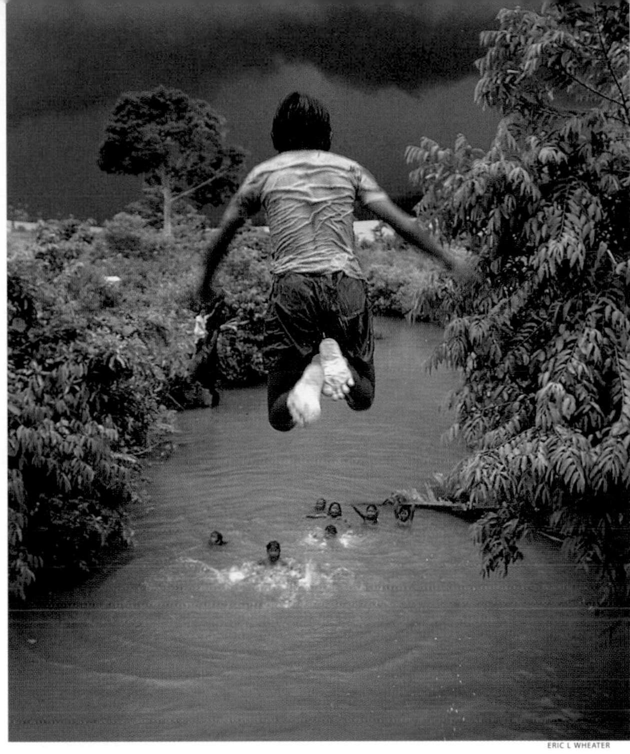
ERIC L WHEATER

Local kids playing in a river, Kalimantan (p604)

ANDREW BROWNBILL

Orang-utan in Tanjung Puting National Park (p631), Kalimantan

River trip near Banjarmasin (p635), Kalimantan

PETER PTSCHELINZEW

SIMON CHARLES ROWE

Tana Toraja (p687), Sulawesi

Tana Toraja funeral festival (p691), Sulawesi

SIMON CHARLES ROWE

Pulau Togean (p729) in the Togean Islands, Sulawesi

GREG

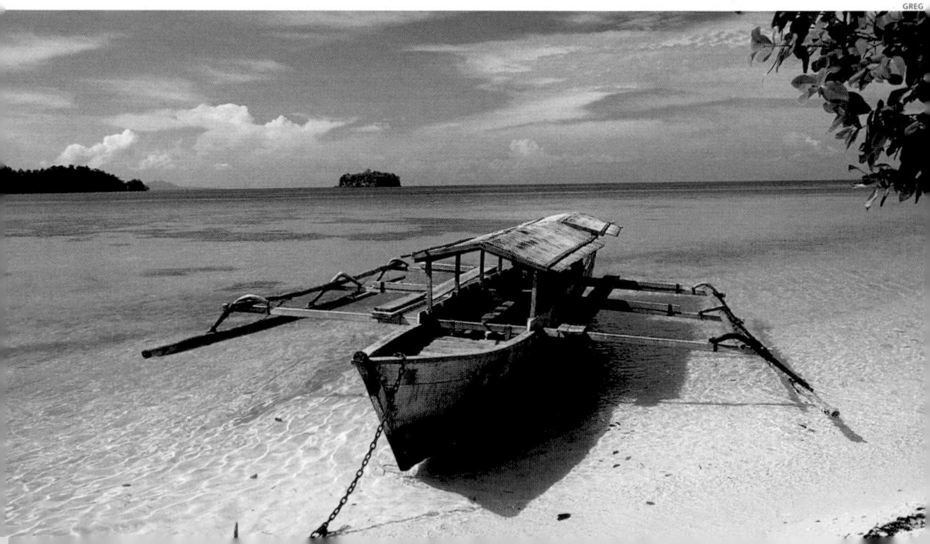

MICHAEL AW

Fishing off Pulau Ambon (p752), Maluku

ALISON WRIGHT

Malukan man (p751) in traditional village, Maluku

A shelter on the arduous trek through Manusela National Park on Pulau Seram (p762), Maluku

ANDREW MARSHALL& LEANNE WALKER

STEPHANE VICTOR

Luxury-hotel spa, Ubud (p307), Bali

Massage oils and towels, Bali (p266)

JERRY ALEXANDER

STEPHANE VICTOR

Spa bath, Ubud (p307), Bali

Hot springs of Air Panas Banjar (p373), Bali

JERRY ALEXA

GREGORY ADAMS
Young boy wearing a traditional kris (dagger; p73) during a temple ceremony

Indonesian street festival (p854)
PETER PTSCHELINZEW

Classical Legong dance (p273), Bali
GREGORY ADAMS

LIZ THOM

Dani tribesmen (p817), Baliem Valley, Papua

KARL LEHMANN

Mummy in a Dani village, Baliem Valley (p816), Papua

Hiking in the Baliem Valley (p818), Papua

KARL LEH

(Continued from page 692)

NEVER MIND THE BALOKS

Rantepao and Makale markets have whole sections devoted to the sale of the alcoholic *balok* (palm wine, also known as *tuak* and toddy). *Balok* is sold in huge jugs around town and comes in a variety of strengths, colours (from clear to dark red, achieved by adding bark) and flavours (sweet to bitter).

Coffee is Toraja's other famous brew, an excellent antidote to a night of *balok*-tasting.

Rachmat Restoran (Jl Ahmad Yani; mains around 20,000Rp) This huge restaurant blows hot and cold, as it traditionally caters to tour groups. That means it's busy for a few months and quiet the rest of the time. The menu has an impressive selection of Indonesian, Chinese and Asian greatest hits.

Wae Rumbung (Jl Pongtiku; mains around 25,000Rp) Set in a wooden pavilion overlooking the rice fields, this restaurant is popular with visiting Indonesians. The menu includes something for everyone and cold beers are available. It is right opposite the turn-off for Ke'te Kesu.

Toko Abadi (Jl Andi Mappanyukki) For trekkers and self-caterers, this is the best-stocked supermarket in town, although for fruit and veg, make for the market.

Entertainment

Errr…what entertainment? The only options are some pretty dire karaoke bars that double up as local pick-up joints. The woefully named **Cancer Karaoke** (Jl Andi Mappanyukki), near Riman Restaurant, is a good example of how bad these places can be, but if you still want more, there are plenty on the road to Makale.

Shopping

Woodcarving, weaving and basketry are the main crafts of Tana Toraja – some villages are noted for particular specialities, such as Mamasan boxes (used to store magic, salt, betel nuts), huge horn necklaces and wooden figurines. Woodcarvings include trays, panels and clocks, carved like the decorations on traditional houses. The carvers at Ke'te Kesu and Londa are renowned for the quality of their work.

The hard part is separating the quality from the tat. Artefacts sold in souvenir shops, especially around the market building in town, include mini replicas of Torajan houses with exaggerated overhanging roofs; Toraja weaving (especially good in Sa'dan); and the longer cloths of the Mamasa Valley. Necklaces made of seeds, chunky silver, and amber or wooden beads festoon the gift shops, but the orange-bead necklaces are the authentic Torajan wear. Black-and-red velvet drawstring bags are popular with tourists, much to the amusement of locals who use them for carrying betel nuts to funerals.

Todi (Jl Andi Mappanyukki 25) The leading ikat (cloth in which the pattern is produced by dyeing the individual threads before weaving) gallery in Tana Toraja. The stunning showroom is upstairs and there are some fine pieces available. Prices are high and an optimistic sign says no bargaining.

Getting There & Away

AIR

Flying – especially *into* Tana Toraja – provides a dramatic look at the landscape and architecture of traditional villages. The only carrier, DAS, flies from Makassar at 10.30am on Tuesday and Friday for 250,000Rp, returning around 11.40am. However, most locals consider this an unreliable service. Tickets can be booked through **Toraja Permai** (☎ 21785; Jl Andi Mappanyukki 10) or at hotels around town.

BUS & BEMO

Most long-distance buses leave from bus company offices along, or just off, Jl Andi Mappanyukki. The most comfortable buses (with slightly higher prices to match) are Litha, Batutumonga and Alam Indah. Try to book the ticket a day or so in advance.

There are plenty of buses heading north to Pendolo (70,000Rp, eight hours), Tentena (90,000Rp, 12 hours), Poso (110,000Rp, 13 hours) and Palu (135,000Rp, 20 hours). Even more buses head south to Pare Pare (25,000Rp, five hours). To Terminal Panaikang in Makassar (45,000 to 75,000Rp, eight hours), buses often run at night, and prices vary according to speed and the level of comfort and space. Various companies also have services to Mamuju via Polewali, from where there are connections to Mamasa. The only direct bus between Tana Toraja and Mamasa leaves from Makale, see p707.

From Terminal Bolu, 2km north of Rantepao, there are regular vehicles to Palopo. From outside Rachmat Restoran, Kijangs leave every minute to Makale (4000Rp, 20 minutes). See Around Tana Toraja (right) for more details about transport between Rantepao and other places in Tana Toraja. Plenty of bemos travel between Rantepao and Terminal Bolu.

Getting Around

From the airport, squeeze into whatever vehicle is available – usually a Kijang (20,000Rp per person), which goes to Rantepao, via Makale, and will drop you off anywhere in between. To the airport, tee up transport with the Toraja Permai office when you reconfirm your flight or charter a bemo or Kijang.

Rantepao is small and easy to walk around. Becak should cost around 4000Rp in town.

MAKALE

☎ 0423

Makale is the administrative capital of Tana Toraja, but has very few of the amenities of Rantepao. It's a small town built around an artificial lake and set amid cloud-shrouded hills. The town also boasts whitewashed churches sitting atop each hill and a busy market. Makale is well connected to most of Tana Toraja by bemo.

Sights

Makale's **market** (Jl Pasar Baru) is a blur of noise and colour. On the main market day, held every six days, you'll see pigs strapped down with bamboo strips for buyers' close inspection, buckets of live eels, piles of fresh and dried fish, and a corner of the market is reserved just for *balok* sales.

Sleeping & Eating

In all honesty, it is far more sensible to stay in Rantepao, which has a good selection of hotels to suit every budget.

Rumah Makan Idaman (Jl Merdeka; meals 5000-20,000Rp; breakfast, lunch & dinner) The only real restaurant in town is a small, friendly place that serves the usual Indonesian fare, as well as tasty baked fish. It is next door to Makale's *mesjid* (mosque).

When the market's pumping, you'll find local dishes for sale at warung, such as *pa'piong*, seasonal fruit and *kueh* (cakes).

Getting There & Away

See p701 for information about flights to Tana Toraja.

Every minute from dawn to dusk, Kijangs race between Rantepao and Makale (4000Rp, 20 minutes) – just flag one down. Most of the bus companies based in Rantepao also have offices near the corner of Jl Merdeka and Jl Ihwan Rombe in Makale. Buses will pick up pre-booked passengers in Makale for any destination from Rantepao (see p701). The only direct bus connection between Tana Toraja and Mamasa is with Disco Indah several times a week (80,000Rp, 10 hours).

See Around Tana Toraja (below) for regional public transport details from Makale.

AROUND TANA TORAJA

Stunning scenery, cascading rice fields, precipitous cliff graves, other-worldly *tau tau*, hanging graves, soaring *tongkonan* and colourful ceremonies – this is the wild world of Tana Toraja and it lies just a short walk or ride away from Rantepao.

Most of the places in this section can be reached on day trips from Rantepao, but longer trips are possible, staying overnight in villages or camping out. Public transport, organised tours, motorbike or mountain-bike rental, vehicle rental with a driver-cum-guide or, best of all, walking – anything is possible. The roads to major towns, such as Makale, Palopo, Sa'dan, Batutumonga, Madandan and Bittuang, are paved, but many other roads around Tana Toraja are constructed out of compacted boulders – vehicles don't get stuck, but your joints get rattled loose. Walking is often the only way to reach the remote villages.

GUIDES

In this region, many guides hold a government-approved licence, obtained by undertaking a course in culture, language and etiquette, and being fluent in the local language. Nevertheless, there are competent guides with no certificate (and incompetent licensed guides). The best way to choose a guide is to sit down and talk through a trip before committing.

Guides are useful if you have a common language, but if you have a sense of direction, a decent map (see p687 for map recommendations), know a few relevant phrases of Bahasa Indonesia and are not going too far off the beaten track, you won't go too wrong travelling without one. The main purposes of guides are facilitating visits to remote and traditional villages, and working as an informative and culturally sensitive go-between. Official licensed guides costs from 200,000Rp per day – plus their transport, food and accommodation. A car should cost 300,000Rp per day, perhaps 350,000Rp for a newer air-con vehicle. Official and unofficial guides and porters can be hired around Rantepao (you'll definitely be approached in the street and in restaurants); from the tourist office and agencies in Rantepao; from hotels; or ask around villages along the way. For a list of agencies in Rantepao offering organised tours of the region, see p689.

ACTIVITIES

Trekking

This is the best way to reach isolated areas and to really get a feel for the countryside and people. Always take good footwear; a water bottle and food, a strong torch (flashlight) in case you walk at night, stay in villages without electricity or want to explore caves; and an umbrella or raincoat – even in the dry season, it's more likely than not to rain. If you take advantage of Torajan hospitality, bring gifts or pay your way.

If you prefer a professional trekking company, contact **Indosella** (☎ 0423-25210; www.sellatours.com; Jl Andi Mappanyukki 111, Rantepao). Shorter hikes are mentioned in the individual sections later in this chapter, but a few of the popular longer treks include the following:

Batutumonga–Lokomata–Pangala–Baruppu–Pulu Pulu–Sapan Three days.
Bittuang–Mamasa Three days; see p708.
Pangala–Bolokan–Bittuang Two days; a well-marked trail.
Sa'dan–Sapan–Pulu Pulu–Baruppu–Pangala Three days; tough and mountainous.

For an overview of these trekking routes, check out the Tana Toraja map (p688).

Rafting

Sungai Sa'dan has 20 rapids, including a few that are Class IV (read pretty wild). Rafting trips, including transport to/from your hotel (anywhere in Tana Toraja), equipment, guide, insurance and food, cost €50 for one day on Class II to III rapids, or €155 for two days on Class III to IV rapids, with an overnight stay in local rest huts. Contact **Indosella** (☎ 0423-25210; www.sellatours.com; Jl Andi Mappanyukki 111, Rantepao) for more details.

ENTRANCE FEES

Most of the tourist sites around Tana Toraja have an entry fee of 10,000Rp. There is usually a ticket booth at each place, complete with the odd souvenir stall…or 10 in the case of Lemo and Londa. Sometimes there is no one about, but someone will usually track you down in the end and ask you to enter your name in the visitor book.

GETTING AROUND

Motorbikes and mountain bikes are available through hotels and some agencies. Remember that roads out of Rantepao and Makale are good, but often windy, steep and narrow, so they are more suitable for experienced bikers. Bikes can be used along some walking trails, but the trails are often too rocky.

Local public transport leaves from central Rantepao and Makale, as well as from the scruffy and muddy Terminal Bolu east of Rantepao; there are regular bemos and Kijangs to all main villages, but the vehicles are poorly signed so you may have to ask around the terminal. See the Rantepao map (p689) for where to catch bemos in central Rantepao heading to La'bo, Madandan, Sa'dan and Tikala.

Some of the more useful services head to the following destinations from Rantepao and Makale:

Bittuang For treks to Mamasa, only leaves from Makale.
La'bo Via Ke'te Kesu.
Lempo Useful for hiking up to Batutumonga.
Pangala Via Batutumonga.
Sa'dan Usually via Tikala.
Sangalla Only leaves from Makale.

Batutumonga

Batutumonga occupies a dramatic ridge on the slopes of Gunung Sesean, with panoramic views of Rantepao and the Sa'dan

Valley, and stunning sunrises. Located about 20km north of Rantepao via Deri, it is possible to stay here, or day trip from Rantepao for some hiking and a local lunch.

SLEEPING & EATING

The first two places are on the only road through Batutumonga.

Mentirotiku (☎ 081 1422260; r per person 60,000Rp, r with views 170,000Rp) With commanding views across the valley below, this place has crash-pad dorms with mattress in traditional *tongkonan,* as well as large rooms with bathroom. Prices are absurdly high for such a basic place. Try halving them! The restaurant has basic meals, including a 30,000Rp set dinner.

Mama Rina's Homestay (r incl breakfast & dinner per person 60,000Rp) This simple family affair has great views. The accommodation is just a mattress on the floor in a *tongkonan,* but the setting is superb.

Coffee Shop Tinimbayo (Bintang 20,000Rp) Located a few kilometres east of Batutumonga, this little café has a killer location, perched on a hairpin bend with infinite views over the cascading rice fields. Basic meals are possible, but cold drinks are easier to arrange.

GETTING THERE & AWAY

Simply take a bemo (8000Rp) to Lempo from Terminal Bolu in Rantepao, and walk 2km (uphill); sometimes the bemo goes through to Batutumonga, but if you're out of luck the walk from Lempo to Batutumonga is pleasant.

North of Rantepao

From Batutumonga, a scenic walk west takes you to **Lokomata**, a village with cave graves hewn into a rocky outcrop, and outstanding scenery. Backtrack and take the well-marked trail down the slopes to **Pana**, with its ancient hanging graves, and some baby graves in nearby trees. You can see tiny villages with towering *tongkonan,* women pounding rice, men scrubbing their beloved buffalo and children splashing happily in pools. The path ends at **Tikala** and, from there, regular bemos return to Rantepao.

Alternatively, backtrack through Lempo to **Deri**, the site of rock graves, walk down to the Rantepao–Sa'dan road and catch a bemo back to Rantepao. This is a very pleasant downhill walk (five hours) through some of the finest scenery in Tana Toraja.

At 2150m above sea level, **Gunung Sesean** is not the highest peak on Sulawesi, but one of the most popular for trekking. The summit is accessible via a trail from Batutumonga. The return trip to the summit takes five hours. A guide is a good idea if you're inexperienced or speak no Bahasa Indonesia.

Beyond Gunung Sesean, the sleepy village of **Pangala** (35km from Rantepao; 17,000Rp by bemo) is noted for its fine dancers, as is nearby **Baruppu**.

Losmen Sando (r per person 70,000Rp), Pangala's main accommodation, is a surprisingly elegant place with comfortable rooms, and a spacious restaurant overlooking a coffee plantation. Staff offer good advice about local trekking.

The traditional village of **Palawa**, east of Batutumonga, is similarly attractive but less popular than Ke'te Kesu, and has *tongkonan* houses and rice barns. In the dry season you can walk southwest, fording a river and walking through rice fields to **Pangli**, with its *tau tau* and house graves and then to **Bori**, the site of an impressive *rante* (ceremonial ground) and some towering megaliths. About 1km south of Bori, **Parinding** has *tongkonan* houses and rice barns. From here you can walk back to Rantepao or on to Tikala. The walk is easy enough to do without a guide – just ask for directions along the way.

Further north is the weaving centre of **Sa'dan** (12km north of Rantepao; take a bemo from Terminal Bolu for 5000Rp), where local women set up a market to sell their woven cloth. It's all handmade on simple looms, but not all is produced in the village.

West of Rantepao

About 2km west across the river from Rantepao, **Gunung Singki** (930m) is a steep hill. There's a slippery, overgrown hiking trail to the summit, which has panoramic views across Rantepao and the surrounding countryside. Return to the road to **Siguntu** (7km from Rantepao), which offers more superb views of the valleys and Rantepao.

The walk (3km) from Siguntu to the Rantepao–Makale road at Alang Alang is also pleasant. Stop on the way at the traditional village of **Mendoe**. From Alang Alang, where a covered bridge crosses the river, head to Londa, back to Rantepao, or remain on the western side of the river and continue walking to the villages of **Langda** and **Madandan**.

South of Rantepao

On the outskirts of Rantepao, just off the road to Makale, is **Karasik**, with traditional-style houses arranged around a cluster of megaliths. The houses may have been erected some years ago for a single funeral ceremony, but some are now inhabited.

Just off the road to Ke'te Kesu is **Buntu Pune**, where there are two *tongkonan* houses and six rice barns. According to local legend, one of the two houses was built by a nobleman named Pong Marambaq at the beginning of the 20th century. During Dutch rule, he was appointed head of the local district, but planned to rebel and was subsequently exiled to Ambon (Maluku), where he died. His body was returned to Tana Toraja, and buried at the hill to the north of Buntu Pune.

About 1km further along from Buntu Pune is **Ke'te Kesu** (5km from Rantepao), renowned for its woodcarving. The village has been preserved for visitors thanks to its traditional *tongkonan* and rice barns and offers some great photo opportunities. One of the houses in the village has several *tau tau* on display. On the cliff face behind the village are some cave graves and very old hanging graves. The rotting coffins are suspended on wooden beams under an overhang. Others, full of bones and skulls, lie rotting in strategic piles.

From Ke'te Kesu you can walk to **Sullukang**, which has a *rante* marked by a number of large, rough-hewn megaliths, and on to **Palatokke**. In this beautiful area of lush rice paddies and traditional houses, there is an enormous cliff face containing several cave graves and hanging graves. Access to the caves is difficult, but the scenery makes it worthwhile. From Palatokke, there are trails to **La'bo** and **Randanbatu**, where there are more graves, and on to Sangalla, Suaya and Makale.

Londa (6km south of Rantepao) is a very extensive burial cave at the base of a massive cliff face. The entrance to the cave is guarded by a balcony of *tau tau*. Inside the cave is a collection of coffins, many of them rotted away, with the bones either scattered or heaped in piles. Other coffins hold the bones of several family members – it's an old Toraja custom that all people who have lived together in one family house should also be buried together in a family grave. A local myth says that the people buried in the Londa caves are the descendants of Tangdilinoq, chief of the Toraja when they were pushed out of the Enrekang region and forced to move into the highlands.

Kids hang around outside the Londa caves with oil lamps to guide you around (about 20,000Rp). Unless you've got a strong torch, you really do need a guide with a lamp. Inside the caves, the coffins and skulls have been placed in strategic locations for the benefit of sightseers. If you're thin, and don't suffer from claustrophobia, squeeze through the tunnel connecting the two main caves, past some interesting stalactites and stalagmites. Londa is also famous for its wood carvers. A bemo between Rantepao and Makale will drop you at the turn-off, about 2km from the cave. Visit in the morning for the best photos.

Further south, 2km (east) off the Rantepao–Makale road, is **Tilanga** (10km from Rantepao), a lovely, natural cool-water swimming pool. You can swim in the pool, but don't be surprised if some friendly eels come to say hello.

Lemo (10km south of Rantepao) is the best-known burial area in Tana Toraja. The sheer rock face has a whole series of balconies for *tau tau*. According to local legend, these graves are for descendants of a Toraja chief who reigned over the surrounding district hundreds of years ago and built his house on top of the cliff into which the graves are now cut. Because the mountain was part of his property, only his descendants could use it. The chief himself was buried elsewhere because the art of cutting grave caves had not yet been developed. The biggest balcony has a dozen figures with white eyes and black pupils and outstretched arms like spectators at a sports event. It's a good idea to go before 9am for the best photos. A Rantepao–Makale bemo will drop you off at the turn-off to the burial site, from where it's a 15-minute walk to the *tau tau*.

East of Rantepao

Marante is a fine traditional village, just north of the road to Palopo. Near Marante there are stone and hanging graves with several *tau tau,* skulls on the coffins and a cave with scattered bones. From Marante you can cross the river on the suspension bridge and walk to pretty villages, set in rice fields.

About 7km off the Palopo road to the south is the traditional village of **Nanggala** (16km from Rantepao); take a bemo from Terminal Bolu for 3000Rp, but you may have to walk from the Palopo Rd. The village has a particularly grandiose traditional house and an impressive fleet of 14 rice barns. The rice barns have a bizarre array of motifs carved into them, including soldiers with guns, Western women and cars. Keep an eye out for a colony of huge black bats hanging from trees at the end of the village.

From Nanggala you can walk south to **Paniki**, a tough hike (five hours) along a dirt track up and down the hills. The trail starts next to the rice barns, and along the way are coffee-plantation machines grinding away. From Paniki walk (two hours) to Ledo and **Buntao** (15km from Rantepao), which has some house graves and *tau tau*. Alternatively, catch a bemo from Paniki to Rantepao. About 2km from Buntao is **Tembamba**, which has more graves and is noted for its fine scenery.

East of Makale

Sangalla has the simple **Homestay Kalembang Indah** (r per person 70,000Rp); rates include meals. South of Sangalla are the hot springs at **Makula**, well signposted from the Rantepao-Makale road. At Makula, you can stay at the upmarket **Hotel Sangalla** (☎ 24112; r from 125,000Rp;). The public can use the hot springs swimming pool for 10,000Rp.

There are more than 40 *tau tau* at **Tampangallo**, between Sangalla and Suaya. The graves belong to the chiefs of Sangalla, descendants of the mythical divine being Tamborolangiq, who is believed to have introduced the caste system, death rituals and agricultural techniques into Torajan society. The former royal families of Makale, Sangalla and Menkendek all claimed descent from Tamborolangiq, who is said to have descended from heaven on a stone staircase. Take a Kijang from Makale to Sangalla, get off about 1km after the turn-off to Suaya, and walk a short distance (less than a kilometre) through the rice fields to Tampangallo.

MAMASA VALLEY

Another area of outstanding natural beauty in Sulawesi, the Mamasa Valley is often referred to as West Tana Toraja, but this overplays the connection between Mamasa and Tana Toraja. Mamasan *tongkonan* have heavy, wooden roofs, which are quite different from the exaggerated boat-shaped bamboo roofs to the east. Torajan ceremonies and funerals survive in the Mamasa Valley, but on the whole these are far less ostentatious affairs than those around Tana Toraja.

Mamasans have embraced Christianity with unfettered enthusiasm: choir groups regularly meet up and down the valley, flexing their vocal chords in praise of God. *Sambu* weaving is a craft that still thrives in the hills around Mamasa village. These long strips of heavy woven material are stitched together to make blankets, which are ideal insulation for the cold mountain nights.

Like Tana Toraja, the best way to explore the valley is on foot. The paths tend to follow the ridges, giving hikers stunning views of the mountainous countryside. There are few roads, and many paths to choose from, so you'll need to constantly ask directions, or hire a guide. The other source of confusion is that village districts, such as Balla, cover broad areas and there are few villages within them. Even centres within the village area, such as Rante Balla, Balla Kalua and Buntu Balla, are very spread out.

MAMASA

Mamasa is the only large village in the valley. The air is cool and clean, and the folk are hospitable. The rhythm of life has a surreal, fairytale quality for those used to the hustle of Indonesia's big cities. The highlight of the week is the market every Monday, where hill people trade their produce. Look for locally made woven blankets, a must for those cold mountain nights. While walking through hill villages, trekkers will also be offered plenty of fine-looking blankets direct from weavers, so take money or gifts, such as condensed milk, chocolate, sugar or *kretek,* to barter with.

Sleeping & Eating

Losmen Mini (Jl Ahmad Yani; s/d 50,000/65,000Rp) A sort of creaky old mountain lodge in the heart of town, the rooms upstairs are a lot brighter than the dark offerings down below.

Mantana Lodge (Jl Emmy Saelan 1; s from 46,000Rp, d 87,000-120,000Rp) The most sophisticated digs in town, the rooms are bright and have attached bathroom. The restaurant here is arguably the best in town, with cold beer. You might catch a spirited church service downstairs.

Mamasa Cottages (s/d US$40/46) Built over hot springs at Kole, 3km north of Mamasa. It offers lovely rooms for a negotiable price. Hot spring water flows to every bathroom.

Other options:

Mamasa Guest House (just off Jl Buntu Budi; r 60,000Rp) Tucked away down a side street but offers good views.

Guest House Gereja Toraja (Jl Demmatande 182; r 60,000Rp) Reasonable rooms in an old house.

There aren't any real restaurants in Mamasa and most visitors end up chowing down in their guesthouse. Basic supplies are available in local shops, and there's a good selection of fresh produce in the market.

Getting There & Away

On a map, Mamasa looks tantalisingly close to Rantepao, but there's no direct transport because the road is so bad. You can travel from Makale to Bittuang by Kijang or bemo, but from Bittuang you'll have to walk (see p708). A new road is under construction, but due to the tough terrain it may take several

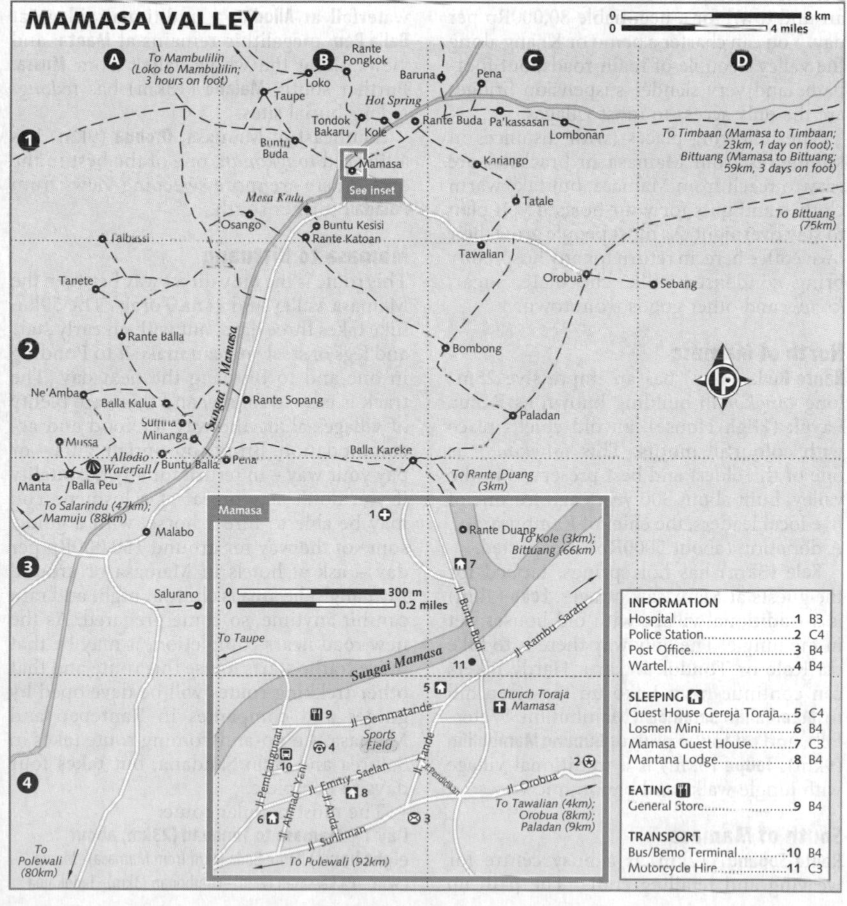

years to complete. Currently, jeeps are running from Mamasa to Ponding for 60,000Rp every day, where you can hook up with a horse on to Bittuang for about 150,000Rp.

The only direct connection between Tana Toraja and Mamasa is the bus (80,000Rp, 10 hours), three times a week from Disco Indah Bus in Makale. Otherwise, from Tana Toraja (or anywhere else), catch a bus towards Majene or Mamuju and get off at Polewali. From here lots of creaky minibuses go to Mamasa (30,000Rp, three hours) along a rough road, often prone to mudslides. Start early as services dry up in the afternoon.

AROUND MAMASA

The countryside surrounding Mamasa is strikingly beautiful. You can hire motorbikes around town for a negotiable 80,000Rp per day. You can charter a bemo or Kijang along the valley's couple of main roads, but footpaths and very slender suspension bridges are the only access to most villages.

The following places (with distances in kilometres from Mamasa in brackets) are easy to reach from Mamasa, but take warm clothes and gifts for your hosts if you plan to stay overnight. As most people grow their own coffee here, in return for any hospitality bring condensed milk, chocolate, sugar, *kretek*, and other goods from town.

North of Mamasa

Rante Buda (4km) has an impressive 25m-long *tongkonan* building known as Banua Layuk (High House), an old chief's place with colourful motifs. This *tongkonan* is one of the oldest and best preserved in the valley, built about 300 years ago for one of five local leaders, the chief of Rambusaratu. A donation (about 5000Rp) is expected.

Kole (3km) has hot springs, tapped for the guests at Mamasa Cottages. **Loko** (4km) is a traditional village with old houses, set in the jungle. The only way there is to hike via Kole or Tondok Bakaru. Hardy hikers can continue from Loko up the steep hill to **Mambulilin Sarambu** (Mambulilin Waterfall), and on to the peak of **Gunung Mambulilin** (9km). **Taupe** (5km) is a traditional village with jungle walks and panoramic views.

South of Mamasa

Rante Sopang (12km) is a busy centre for weaving and retailing crafts. The path up the hill from the roadside craft shop leads to a few workshops, where women weave long strips of heavy cloth for Mamasa's distinctive, colourful blankets.

Osango (3km) is the site of *tedong-tedong* (burial houses), supposedly up to 200 years old. There are lots of paths and the village is *very* spread out, so ask for directions along the way. **Mesa Kada** (2km) are hot springs, which are suitable for a swim.

Tanete (8km) has mountain graves under a cave. Tanete and nearby **Taibassi** are also centres for traditional weaving and carving. **Rante Balla** (12km) has big beautiful *tongkonan*, and woven blankets and baskets.

Buntu Balla (15km) has beautiful views, traditional weaving and *tedong-tedong* burial sites. Close to Buntu Balla there's a waterfall at **Allodio**; a traditional village at **Balla Peu**; megalithic remains at **Manta**; and views along the whole valley from **Mussa**. Further south, **Malabo** (18km) has *tedong-tedong* burial sites.

Southeast of Mamasa, **Orobua** (9km) has a fine old *tongkonan*, one of the best in the area. There are more sweeping views from **Paladan** further south.

Mamasa to Bittuang

This route is the only direct way between the Mamasa Valley and Tana Toraja. The 59km hike takes three days, but with an early start and legs of steel you can make it to Ponding in one and to Bittuang the next day. The track is easy to follow, and there are plenty of villages along the way for food and accommodation. Bring appropriate gifts – or pay your way – in return for any hospitality if you don't stay or eat at a losmen. You may be able to hire a horse, with a guide, some of the way for around 150,000Rp per day – ask at hotels in Mamasa or around Bittuang. The area is chilly at night and rain can hit anytime, so come prepared. As the new road nears completion, it may be that more traffic starts to use this route and that other trekking routes will be developed by guides and companies in Rantepao and Mamasa. An up-and-coming route takes in Salurea and Bulo Sandana, but takes four days to complete.

The most popular route:

Day 1 – Mamasa to Timbaan (23km, about eight hours) Rante Buda (4km from Mamasa)–Mama (3km)–Pa'kassasan (2km)–Lombonan (3km)–Tadokalua summit (4km)–Timbaan (7km). The walk is easy uphill but rises sharply at Lombonan. Tadokalua at the summit offers great views across both valleys. There's a simple stall here serving gritty coffee and packet noodle soup. The trail then winds its way down to Timbaan, where there are three losmen offering beds and meals for around 50,000Rp.

Day 2 – Timbaan to Paku (20km, about six hours) Mawai (4km from Timbaan)–Tabang (4km)–Ponding (5km)–Paku (7km). The path undulates its way past rice fields, through villages and over rivers. At Ponding you can stay at Homestay Papasado; or continue to Paku and stay at Mountain Homestay, both for 50,000Rp (with meals).

Day 3 – Paku to Bittuang (16km) It's easier to walk (three hours), but there is an irregular jeep service from Ponding and Paku to Bittuang for 20,000Rp, which will shake your fillings loose. There are three simple losmen at Bittuang, but you're better off catching a bemo or Kijang to Makale (15,000Rp, two hours), from where there are Kijangs to Rantepao.

SOUTHEAST SULAWESI

Few visitors make it to Southeast Sulawesi, but the handful of travellers that are prepared to venture a little off the beaten track will find themselves rewarded with some striking scenery and hospitable cultures, and surprisingly good transport links. The top attraction here is Wakatobi Marine National Park, located in the remote Tukangbesi Islands off the southern tip, offering some of Indonesia's best snorkelling and diving.

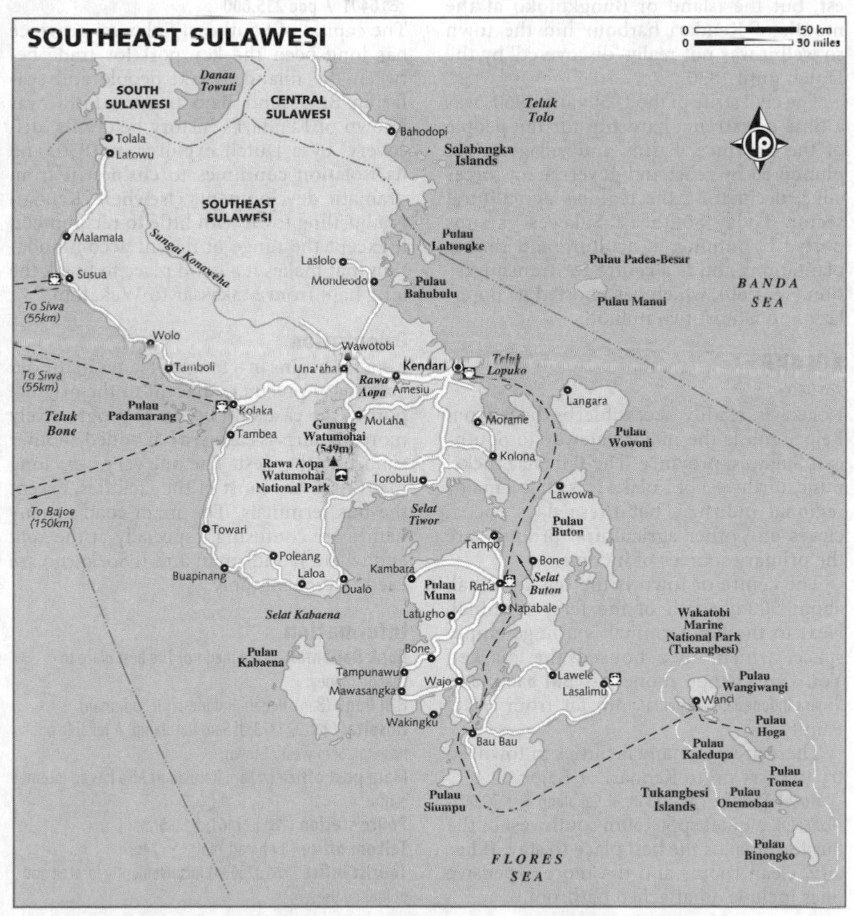

History

Some of the earliest records of life in Southeast Sulawesi are depicted in prehistoric paintings on the walls of caves near Raha. The red ochre paintings include hunting scenes, boats and warriors on horseback.

The region's most powerful pre-colonial kingdom was Buton, based at Wolio, near Bau Bau. Its control and influence over other regional states was supported by the Dutch colonialists. Buton came under direct Dutch rule after the fall of Makassar in 1669, and was granted limited autonomy in 1906.

Other local trading centres maintained a low profile, probably for reasons of self-preservation. Kendari was one of the busiest, but the island of Bungkutoko at the mouth of Kendari harbour hid the town so well it was not really 'discovered' by the Dutch until 1830.

The civil strife of the 1950s and 1960s was a time of extreme hardship for the people of the province. Farms and villages were plundered by rebel and government forces alike, decimating the region's agricultural sector. Today Southeast Sulawesi is supported by mining, agriculture and timber plantations and is a centre for transmigration (see p60), which has boosted its population to almost two million.

KOLAKA

☎ 0405

Kolaka is readily accessible by boat from Bajoe, and is the major gateway to Southeast Sulawesi province. The Pomalaa nickel mine northwest of Kolaka was once a major regional industry, but these days cocoa, cloves and other agricultural produce are the primary sources of income.

The centre of town is the bus terminal, about 500m north of the ferry terminal. Next to the bus terminal is a huge empty space, which once housed the market. You can change money at **BNI bank** (Bank Negara Indonesia; Jl Repelita), not far from Hotel Family.

There are not many facilities in town, so try to carry on to Kendari or Bajoe.

Hotel Family (☎ 21350; Jl Cakalang 6; r 30,000-40,000Rp), a quiet spot 150m southwest of the bus terminal, is the best place to stay. It has airy, clean rooms and the more expensive ones include an attached bathroom.

Getting There & Away

All day and night, plenty of buses, bemos and Kijangs travel between Kolaka and Kendari (45,000Rp, six hours). While you are on the ferry you may be able to find a spare seat on a bus going directly to Kendari or Makassar – just check with the bus drivers.

Three ferries travel overnight from Kolaka to Bajoe (40,000/50,000Rp deck/business class, eight hours), the main port on the eastern coast of the southwest peninsula. The ferries leave at 5pm, 8pm and 11pm, and are all timed to connect with services for a convenient arrival in Makassar.

KENDARI

☎ 0401 / pop 235,000

The capital of Southeast Sulawesi province has long been the key port for trade between the inland Tolaki people and seafaring Bugis and Bajo traders. Little was known of Kendari's history before its 'discovery' by a Dutch explorer in 1830, and its isolation continues to cushion it from dramatic developments elsewhere. Kendari is a bustling town with little to recommend it except the range of decent accommodation that makes it a good place to break the long haul from Makassar to Wakatobi.

Orientation

Kendari begins in a tangle of lanes in the old *kota* (city) precinct adjacent to the original port in the east, and becomes progressively more modern as each era has added another suburb to the west. The one very, *very* long main road has most of the facilities, except the bus terminals. The main road's many names are confusing, especially at the *kota* end where Jl Sudirman and Jl Soekarno are used interchangeably.

Information

Bank Danamon (Jl Diponegoro) The best place to change money.
BNI bank (Bank Negara Indonesia; Jl Sudirman)
Hospital (☎ 321773; Jl Sam Ratulangi) A reliable public hospital, 6km west of town.
Main post office (Jl Sam Ratulangi) Also has an internet centre.
Police station (☎ 321461; Jl Sudirman)
Telkom office (Jl Ahmad Yani; 🕑 24hr)
Tourist office (☎ 326634) Inconveniently located and of limited use.

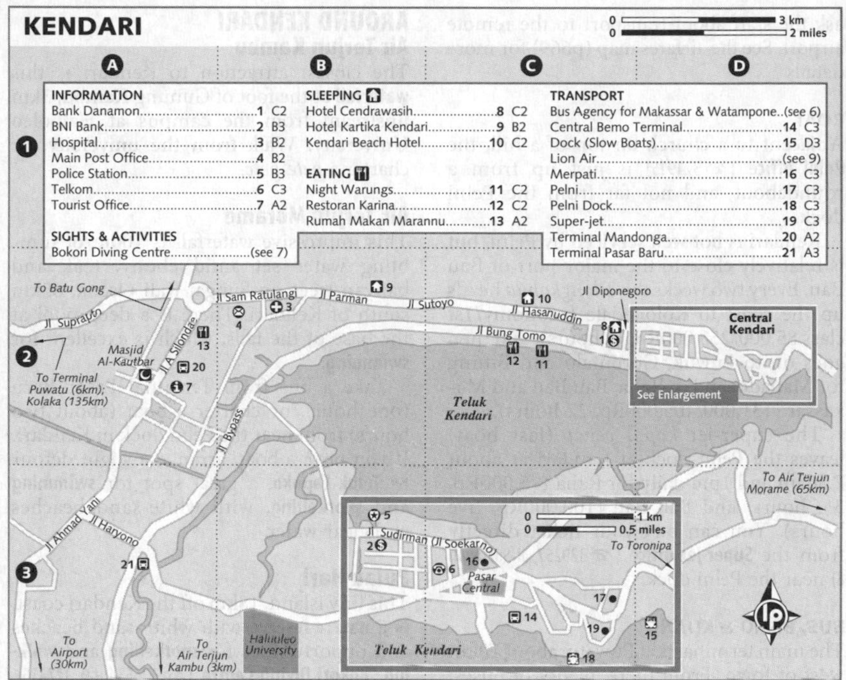

Festivals & Events

Festival Teluk Kendari (Kendari Bay Festival) is held each April and is the highlight of the social calendar, with dragon-boat races, traditional music and plenty of partying.

Sleeping

Hotel Cendrawasih (☎ 321932; Jl Diponegoro 42; r with fan/air-con 66,000/110,000Rp; ❄) A long-running place, just off the main road, with friendly staff and good service. The fan rooms are ageing these days, but have a balcony. The air-con rooms are in better shape.

Kendari Beach Hotel (☎/fax 321988; Jl Hasanuddin 44; r 100,000-150,000Rp; ❄) This is located on a small hill; take advantage of the private balcony to enjoy the views and breezes. All rooms have satellite TV, while the more expensive options come with hot water and better views. There is also a restaurant overlooking the bay with an extensive menu at affordable prices.

Hotel Kartika Kendari (☎/fax 321484; Jl Parman 84; r from 160,000Rp; ❄) This large hotel has smart rooms with satellite TV and hot water. You may have to pester staff to get the hot water working. Discounts available.

Eating

The night warung lining the esplanade along Jl Bung Tomo are a popular hang-out in the evening. They offer cheap Indonesian food, and excellent (free) views of the bay. Another group of warung about 200m further west specialise in tasty baked fish.

Restoran Karina (Jl Bung Tomo; mains 20,000Rp; ⏲ breakfast, lunch & dinner) Near the warungs, this eatery is good value for such a desirable location and has a good range of Indonesian food's greatest hits.

Rumah Makan Marannu (Jl A Silondae; mains 25,000-40,000Rp; ⏲ breakfast, lunch & dinner) Some of the best Chinese food in town, but watch the weight on the seafood, as it adds up quickly.

Getting There & Away

AIR

Merpati (Merpati Nusantara Airlines; ☎ 322242; Jl Sudirman) and **Lion Air** (☎ 329911; Jl Parman 84) connect Kendari and Makassar. Don't forget to ask the staff about transport to the remote airport. See the airfares map (p669) for more details.

BOAT

Adjacent to a church on top of a hill, the **Pelni office** (☎ 321915) is just up from a roundabout, and not far from the Pelni dock.

Kendari is not well serviced by Pelni, but is relatively close to the major port of Bau Bau. Every two weeks the *Tilongkabila* heads up the coast to Kolonedale (economy/1st class 85,000/258,000Rp, 12 hours), and then goes on to Luwuk, Gorontalo and Bitung for Manado; and to Raha, Bau Bau and Makassar (131,000/405,000Rp, 22 hours).

The super-jet *kapal cepat* (fast boat) leaves the Pelni dock at Kendari at about 7.30am and 1pm daily for Raha (75,000Rp, 3½ hours) and Bau Bau (100,000Rp, five hours). You can buy your ticket directly from the **Super-jet office** (☎ 329257; Jl Sukowati 8) near the Pelni dock.

BUS, BEMO & KIJANG

The main terminal is at Puwatu, about 10km west of town. From there, plenty of buses, Kijangs and bemos go to Kolaka (45,000Rp, six hours). It's more convenient to book a ticket (and board the bus) at one of the agencies in town. Most buses leave Kendari at about 1pm to link with the 8pm ferry (which means arriving in Bajoe at about 4am). The fare to Watampone/Makassar is 95,000/120,000Rp, and includes the ferry trip in deck class, but you can upgrade to business class.

Getting Around

Contact the airline office about transport to the airport, which is 30km southwest of Kendari – both airlines usually run a bus with certain pick-up points in town. From the airport, you can jump in a shared vehicle or if you don't mind the extra cost, charter one.

Kendari is *very* spread out. For short distances, take a becak; for anything along the main road, take a *pete-pete;* to anywhere else, catch an air-conditioned taxi. *Pete-pete* link the *kota* end of town with Terminal Mandonga and the market every few seconds, and many continue on to Terminal Puwatu.

AROUND KENDARI

Air Terjun Kambu

The closest attraction to Kendari is this **waterfall** at the foot of Gunung Kambu, 3km upstream from the campus at Haluoleo University. Walk from the university, or charter a *pete-pete*.

Air Terjun Morame

This impressive waterfall is 100m of tumbling water set amid ebony, teak and banyan trees on Sungai Kali Osena, 65km south of Kendari. There is a deep pool at the base of the falls, which is excellent for **swimming**.

Take a bus from Terminal Pasar Baru (one hour), or charter a boat (about two hours) from near the Pelni dock in Kendari. If you have a boat, arrange a slight detour to **Teluk Lapuko**, a great spot for **swimming** and **snorkelling**, with white-sand beaches and clear water.

Pulau Hari

This tiny island, 18km off the Kendari coast, is a **nature reserve** with white-sand beaches and opportunities for **snorkelling** and **walking**. **Bokori Diving Centre** (☎ 326634; fax 327435), based at the tourist office in Kendari, runs diving and snorkelling trips to Hari and other nearby islands. Alternatively, get a group together, and charter a boat from near the Pelni dock in Kendari. It should cost about 150,000Rp for the day, but bring your own snorkelling gear.

RAHA

☎ 0403

Raha, the main settlement on Pulau Muna, is a quiet backwater about halfway between Kendari and Bau Bau. Raha is famous for its horse fighting, cave paintings and lagoons. You can change money at **Bank Danamon** (Jl Sutomo) and **BNI bank** (Bank Negara Indonesia; Jl Sukawati), but don't (ahem) count on it.

Sleeping & Eating

Hotel Alia (☎ 21218; Jl Sudirman 5; r from 65,000Rp) Convenient for its proximity to the causeway, this quiet hotel has basic but clean rooms or you can become a VIP for just 125,000Rp. There is also a small restaurant that is open to all comers.

Hotel Ilham (☎ 21070; Jl Jati 16; r with fan 66,000Rp, with air-con 175,000Rp; ❄) One of the few places in town to offer an air-con escape during the hot season, this is a friendly operation.

Hotel Permata Sari (☎ 21164; Jl A Yani 67; s/d 65,000/75,000Rp) Conveniently located opposite the bus/bemo terminal, and still reasonably quiet. It has large, clean rooms.

Rumah Makan Cahaya Pangkep (Jl Sudirman; meals 10,000-25,000Rp; breakfast, lunch & dinner) The best option in Raha, with excellent baked fish, but bear in mind this is not the culinary capital of Indonesia.

Getting There & Away

Raha is the only stop between Kendari and Bau Bau on the fast super-jet. Purchase tickets the day before departure from the **Super-jet office** (☎ 22018; Jl Dewantara) in Kendari. These boats are scheduled to leave for Kendari (75,000Rp, 3½ hours) at 8.30am and 1.30pm; and for Bau Bau (50,000Rp, 1½ hours) at about 10am and 3.30pm. Be ready for the onboard scramble to claim a seat.

Every two weeks the Pelni liner *Tilongkabila* stops at Raha on its way up (via Kendari) and down (via Bau Bau) the east coast of Sulawesi. The Pelni office is at the end of the causeway.

AROUND RAHA

Napabale

Raha's main attraction is Napabale, a pretty lagoon at the foot of a hill. The lagoon is linked to the sea via a natural tunnel, so you can paddle through when the tide is low. It is a great area for **hiking** and **swimming**, and you can hire boats to explore the lake. Napabale is a scenic ride (15km) from Raha. You can reach it by *ojek*, or by regular *pete-pete* to Lohia village, from where the lagoon is another 1.5km walk, at the end of the road. There are usually a couple of food stalls, and often a few more on Sunday, when it's generally crowded. On other days you may have this idyllic place to yourself.

Pantai Melerua

Not far from Napabale, Melerua beach has superb scenery and unusual rock formations. Although you can swim and snorkel (bring your own gear), there isn't a sandy beach as such. Take the regular *pete-pete* towards Lohia and ask the driver to drop you off at the unmarked turn-off. From here, walk (or take an *ojek*) about 7km until the very rough path finishes.

Gua Mabolu

The solid 10km walk from Mabolu village to Gua Mabolu (Mabolu Caves), through plantations and pretty walled gardens, is probably more interesting than the caves themselves. The caretakers can take you to a selection of the best caves, starting with **Liang Metanduno**, which has paintings of a horse with two riders, headless warriors and some boats.

It is 12km from Raha to Mabolu village, so catch (or charter) a *pete-pete* to Mabolu and ask the driver to drop you off at the path to the caves. The paths are not clear, so you'll need someone from Mabolu to show you the way to the caves, and to the caretakers who live nearby.

Latugho

Festival Danau Napabale is held each June at the village of Latugho, 30km inland from Raha. The festival features horse combat, as well as the more gentle spectacle of kite flying. Horse fighting is a Muna tradition with a robust following – it's not for the tender-hearted.

BAU BAU

☎ 0402 / pop 83,000

Pulau Buton's prosperous main town, Bau Bau was the seat of the former sultanate of Wolio, which reigned over scattered settlements on Buton and neighbouring islands. With comfortable accommodation options, great views from the unusually well-preserved citadel walls and some decent beaches within easy *ojek* range, Bau Bau is a great place to await a boat connection to Maluku, North Sulawesi, or the diving paradise of Tukangbesi.

Orientation & Information

The terminal, main mosque and market are about 500m west of the main Pelni port, along Jl Kartini, which diverges from the seafront esplanade, Jl Yos Sudarso. Jl Kartini crosses a bridge then curves south past the post office towards the *kraton* (walled city palace).

The best internet café is a block inland from the main mosque. Around 1.5km east of the main port is a second harbour, with the offices for the **tourist department** (☎ 23588), Telkom and Pelni. The **BNI bank** (Bank Negara Indonesia; Jl Kartini) has an ATM that shouldn't be relied upon, as well as exchange.

Sights & Activities

Banking steeply behind the town centre is the **Kraton**, the Wolio royal citadel with impressively long and well-preserved 16th-century walls that offer great views over the town and its north-facing bay. Amid trees and flowers within the walls are timeless semi-traditional homes and the old royal mosque. Some 500m beyond the citadel's south gate is **Pusat Kebudayaan Wolio**, a cultural centre and museum in a restored old mansion-palace, which is the focal point of Bau Bau's **Festival Kraton** each September. Eleven kilometres southwest of Bau Bau, the nearest white-sand beach is the attractively palm-lined **Pantai Nirwana**, though there is a certain amount of rubbish. Locals prefer **Pantai Batauga**, 10km beyond, for swimming.

Sleeping & Eating

Hotel Lilyana (☎ 21197; Jl Kartini 18; r 95,000Rp) One of the smarter central hotels, it was given a facelift a few years ago and is still in good shape.

our pick **Hillhouse Resort** (☎ 21189; r with breakfast 100,000Rp) This little place has one of the most spectacular settings anywhere in Sulawesi. It's about half a klick above Pusat Kebudayaan Wolio, set amid a hilltop flower garden with outstanding panoramic views of the bay and beyond. The rooms are simple, with mosquito nets and shared bathroom. Be sure to call ahead to alert staff of your arrival and to order any meals (35,000Rp) in advance; there are no shops or eateries nearby.

Hotel Ratu Rajawali (☎ 22162; Jl Sultan Hasanuddin 69; r from 195,000Rp; ❄ 🏊) Right opposite the Pelni office, 2km east of the port, this hotel is a real gem. The well-appointed rooms include air-con and TV, plus small balconies that overlook the gardens and swimming pool towards the sea beyond. This is the preferred hotel of the Operation Wallacea teams (see right) when transferring to and from Pulau Hoga in Wakatobi.

You'll find restaurants and warungs (many set up at night) along the esplanade, a few hundred metres west of the port.

Getting There & Away

BOAT

The fast super-jet boat takes 1½ hours to Raha (55,000Rp) and five hours to Kendari (100,000Rp), and leaves at 7am and 12.30pm daily. Demand can often be greater than supply, so book ahead (from 5pm the day before) at the **Super-jet office** (☎ 22497), which is opposite Warung Pangkep, about 500m west of the port.

Every two weeks the Pelni liners *Bukit Siguntang, Ciremai, Lambelu, Rinjani* and *Kelimutu* link Bau Bau with Makassar (economy/1st class 92,000/285,000Rp), and most also go to Ambon, southern Maluku and/or Papua. Every two weeks the *Tilongkabila* goes up and down the east coast of Sulawesi, stopping off at Kendari and Bitung (for Manado), among other places.

TUKANGBESI ISLANDS

According to Jacques Cousteau, the Tukangbesi Islands offered 'possibly the finest diving in the world' when he surveyed the area in the 1980s. Most of the islands are now part of **Wakatobi Marine National Park** (Taman Laut Wakatobi). Positioned remotely off the far southeast coast, the islands are difficult to reach, but they do offer superb snorkelling and diving, a blaze of corals and marine life, isolated beaches and stunning landscapes.

The only place really geared up to travellers is Pulau Hoga. **Island Garden Resort** (bungalow per person 100,000Rp) has four bungalows here. For more details, contact **Hillhouse Resort** (☎ 0402-21189) in Bau Bau. It is also possible to arrange informal homestays on the island for about 50,000Rp including meals. Some basic snorkelling equipment is available, but bring your own if you want to be sure.

The British-based NGO, **Operation Wallacea** (www.opwall.com), organises 'volunteer' programmes for those interested in marine conservation. The public are welcome, but trips must be pre-booked and are expensive. The organisation has a study centre on Pulau Hoga and may be able hook people up with a homestay during busy periods.

Be aware that prices for charter boats and the like are higher on Hoga, as the locals have got used to working with Operation Wallacea.

The only other option is **Wakatobi Dive Resort** (www.wakatobi.com) on Pulau Onemobaa. This ultra-exclusive hideaway offers beautiful bungalow accommodation and one of the most celebrated house reefs in Indonesia. One-week packages including diving, full board and charter flights from Bali start at about US$2000. It is also the base for the elegant liveaboard the **Pelagian** (www.pelagian.wakatobi.com).

Getting to Hoga is the big headache. Unless you are fortunate enough to be staying at the Wakatobi Dive Resort, then it takes about two days in each direction to Makassar. From Bau Bau, take the daily boat to Wanci on Pulau Wangiwangi, which usually leaves in the evening and arrives very early the next day. Wait around for another boat, or more likely charter one, to Hoga. The smoothest option is to time your arrival with the Pelni liner *Tilongkabila* from Makassar.

CENTRAL SULAWESI

The leading lights in this region are the megaliths around Bada and Besoa Valleys and the tranquil Danau Poso, but the rugged landscape and hospitable highland cultures throughout Central Sulawesi make a detour worthwhile. Few other places in Indonesia can boast such an interesting and accessible pick 'n' mix of nature, culture, history and landscapes. Most of Central Sulawesi's population lives in the province's coastal towns; as a result, the 63,000-sq-km hinterland is sparsely populated. But it's these mountains, lakes and valleys that attract most visitors, though numbers have

CENTRAL SULAWESI TRAVEL WARNING

Travel to Palu, Poso and the surrounding districts remains potentially risky at the time of writing. Violent incidents continue to occur, including a bomb in Tentena in May 2005 which killed 22 people and a bomb in Palu on Christmas Day 2005 which killed eight. Add to that the random beheading of three schoolgirls in October 2005 and things are far from stable. While violence against foreigners is unlikely, travellers should double check the latest situation before travelling through the area and avoid crowded public places like bus terminals and markets. Police checkpoints are common and travelling by private vehicle is considered safer than by public transport.

been hard hit by the violence around the region and once-popular places are now very quiet.

History

Undated remains from a cave near Kolonedale indicate a long history of human settlement. The most spectacular prehistoric remains are the Bronze Age megaliths found throughout Central Sulawesi, but no one knows who was responsible for their creation. The highest concentration is along Sungai Lariang in the Bada Valley, and there are others throughout the region, down to Tana Toraja in South Sulawesi.

Since 1998, the Poso district has suffered from unpredictable violence. Drawn along religious lines, the violence has left more than 1000 people dead and many more displaced. Many buildings were destroyed during the clashes, which have since died down, but random bombings remain a real concern.

DANAU POSO

Indonesia's third-largest lake, Danau Poso, covers an area of 32,300 hectares and reaches an average depth of 450m. The lake is 600m above sea level – so the evenings are pleasantly cool without being too cold.

Danau Poso is the main reason to stop at Tentena or Pendolo. You can hike in the countryside around the lake, or take boat trips, but chartering boats is surprisingly hard to arrange in either town. There's a handful of narrow beaches around Tentena, but these disappear when the tide is high. The beaches near the jetty at Pendolo are better.

Sights

The lake is famous for its wild orchids, especially in **Taman Anggrek Bancea** (Bancea Orchid Garden). It is accessible on foot (about 11km), by chartered vehicle, or by irregular bemos to Taipa from Pendolo.

Air Terjun Salopa, near Tentena, is a crystal-clear series of pools, cascades and falls amid unspoilt forest. A path to the left of the falls leads to upper levels and some pristine swimming holes. Take a bemo heading west across the bridge from Tentena, ask to be dropped off at the turn-off and walk 3km through rice fields. A chartered bemo from Tentena will cost around 80,000Rp return.

Air Terjun Sulewana is a sunken gully of steaming white water, 10km from Tentena. Take any bemo heading north from Tentena and walk 3km west from the sign.

Festivals & Events

The undisputed highlight of Central Sulawesi's social calendar is the annual **Festival Danau Poso** held in Tentena in late August. Villagers from far afield gather for a colourful celebration of culture, with dancing, songs and traditional sports.

PENDOLO

Pendolo is a sleepy village on the southern shore of Danau Poso. It is a charming spot, and the beaches around the jetty are great for swimming, but Pendolo has far fewer facilities than Tentena.

Sleeping & Eating

Pendolo Cottages (Jl Ahmad Yani 441; r 50,000Rp, bungalow s/d 40,000/60,000Rp) Right next to the boat landing, about 1km east of the village centre, this rustic place has proved popular over the years. The bungalows are a better option than the rooms, but both include a hearty breakfast.

Homestay Masamba (r from 60,000Rp) Located at the end of Jl Pelabuhan, overlooking the lake, this place has a great reputation. Rooms are large and clean, plus there's an old jetty for some sun action.

Mulia Poso Lake Hotel (Jl Pelabuhan Wisata 1; r from 100,000Rp, cottages from 150,000Rp) Just to the east of Pendolo Cottages, the Mulia is the smartest place in Pendolo. Once popular with tour groups, hard times can mean generous discounts. There is also an elegant restaurant with reasonable prices.

Getting There & Away

BOAT

Most people take the Pendolo–Tentena boat (25,000Rp, three hours) to enjoy the views and fresh air – but it's no fun in rough weather. The boat leaves Pendolo daily at 8am from the jetty, near the Mulia Poso Lake Hotel, and is more reliable and scenic than the bus.

BUS & BEMO

Pendolo is on the main Palopo–Poso highway, but there is no bus terminal as such. Getting onward transport is normally a matter of hailing down a passing bus, but many are full. Between Pendolo and Tentena, take the boat; if heading further north, take the boat to Tentena, from where there are regular buses to Poso and Palu. See the Tentena Getting There & Away section (right) for more details.

From Rantepao you could charter a bemo for about 500,000Rp. Split among a few people, this is not unreasonable – it cuts hours off the journey, and you can see the mountains of the pretty Wotu–Pendolo stretch in daylight hours.

TENTENA

☎ 0458

Tentena, at the northern end of the lake, is larger and prettier than Pendolo, and is surrounded by clove-covered hills. Tentena has excellent accommodation and a varied cuisine, but lacks Pendolo's fine beaches. The Festival Danau Poso is held here in late August.

Information

Organised treks to Lore Lindu and Morowali parks can be arranged in Tentena. Most hotels double as local tour operators and trekking agencies: Pondok Wisata Ue Datu and Hotel Victori are reliable for providing good guides for Morowali, and travel advice about Lore Lindu and the Togean Islands. **PT Wisata Gautama Putra Indah** (☎ 21356), near Natural Cottages, is somewhere to meet guides and mull over trekking itineraries.

Sights & Activities

Tentena's pretty, covered 210m bridge marks where the lake ends and Sungai Poso begins its journey to the coast. V-shaped **eel traps** north of the bridge snare the 2m monsters for which Tentena is famous. Live specimens are available for inspection and sale at warungs in the centre of town.

Sleeping

Hotel Victori (☎ 21392; Jl Diponegoro 18; r 65,000-150,000Rp; ✖) A popular option, it offers big, breezy rooms, although not even the more expensive ones have air-con and hot water. There is also a book exchange, advice and guides for local tours and trekking, and a relaxed outdoor sitting area.

Hotel Intim Danau Poso (☎ 21345; fax 21488; Jl Yos Sudarso 22; s/d 125,000/150,000Rp) Probably the smartest hotel in town, it also boasts the best lake views. The economy rooms are good value and some have lake views. The more expensive rooms have 'mountain' and 'sea' views and are a good size.

Hotel Pamona Indah Permai (Jl Yos Sudarso 25; r 100,000-200,000Rp) Conveniently located next to the jetty, the more expensive rooms have satellite TV, fan and hot water.

Eating

The local speciality is *sugili* (eel). You could buy a few to take home, but it's a little easier to try it at local restaurants. You can buy tasty *pisang molen* (banana fried in a sweet pastry) at stalls in front of the eastern part of the bridge.

Hotel Pamona Indah Permai (meals 15,000-35,000Rp; ⏰ breakfast, lunch & dinner) Has a restaurant offering lake views and breezes, and fresh baked fish as well as plenty of other dishes. It's the best place to have lunch while waiting for the boat.

Getting There & Away

BOAT

Every day at 11am a boat chugs across the lake to Pendolo (25,000Rp, three hours) from Tentena. The boat is more scenic and reliable than the bus for travel between Tentena and Pendolo.

BUS & BEMO

There are plenty of buses and bemos that make the bumpy run to Poso (15,000Rp, two hours) and Palu. They leave from the terminal at the fork of the roads to Pendolo and Poso (2km north of Tentena), and sometimes from the market in central Tentena on Jl Yos Sudarso. For longer distances, such as the trip to Rantepao, you can also book tickets at the bus offices around Tentena.

JEEP

The availability and price of jeeps to Gintu in Lore Lindu National Park depends on the condition of the road. The price should be around 80,000Rp per person by public jeep, and up to 500,000Rp to charter one.

POSO

☎ 0452 / pop 47,000

Poso is the main town, port and terminal for road transport on the northern coast of Central Sulawesi. For most travellers it's a transit point and somewhere to change money. Many folk head for the beaches or continue to Ampana to catch the boat to the Togean Islands. Poso has been hit hard by internal conflict, the scars of which will remain for a long time.

Orientation & Information

The northern part of Poso, around Jl Haji Agus Salim, is more like a small village – it has limited shops and restaurants. Most facilities are along, or near, Jl Sumatera.

Poso has a friendly **tourist office** (☎ 21211; Jl Kalimantan 15), but limited resources. Poso is the last chance for Togean- and Tentena-bound travellers to change money; the best option is BNI bank, with an ATM, near the port.

Sleeping & Eating

Losmen Alugoro (☎ 21336; Jl Sumatera 20; s/d 40,000/55,000Rp, d with air-con 110,000Rp; ❄) One of the smarter losmen in town; the cheapies are quite pokey, but the air-con rooms are worth the money.

Losmen Lalang Jaya (☎ 22326; Jl Yos Sudarso; r 65,000Rp) Some rooms have ocean views, which gives the place more atmosphere than most. Conveniently located next to the port. It also has a good restaurant built over the sea.

Rumah Makan Pelangi (Jl Tadulako; meals 10,000-25,000Rp; ⏲ breakfast, lunch & dinner) One of the most reliable restaurants in the older part of town.

Every afternoon, night warung are set up along the breezy esplanade, Jl Pattimura, east of the port.

Getting There & Away

From the bus terminal, about 800m north of the post office, there are regular buses to Ampana (five hours), Kolonedale (eight hours), Rantepao (13 hours, 110,000Rp) and Manado (30 hours). From the terminal, minibuses also regularly go to Tentena (two hours, 15,000Rp).

Most buses for Palu (six hours), leave from offices along Jl Sumatera. It's worth paying a little more for the executive-class buses, as the stretch from Toboli to Palu is *very* rough. From the terminal, next to the market, bemos go to nearby villages and beaches.

AROUND POSO

There are plenty of good places for swimming and snorkelling around Poso. **Pantai Madale** is a snorkelling spot 5km east of Poso; **Pantai Matako** is a white-sand beach about 20km further east; and **Pantai Toini**, 7km west, has a few *rumah makan* for great seafood. All three can be reached by bemo from the terminal near the market in Poso.

Lembomawo, 4km south of Poso, is renowned for its ebony carving. Take a bemo from the terminal at the market in Poso.

LORE LINDU NATIONAL PARK

Covering an area of 250,000 hectares, this large and remote national park has been barely touched by tourism. It's a wonderful area for trekking – the park is rich in exotic plant and animal life, including butterflies larger than a human hand, impressive hornbills and shy tarsiers. It's also home to several indigenous tribes, and famous for its megalithic remains – giant freestanding stones around Gintu and Doda.

Information

The main national park office, rangers station and visitors centre are about a 1km walk from Kamarora village. You can buy permits here (20,000Rp), as well as at the small field offices (which have no accommodation) at Kulawi and Wuasa, and the **Balai Taman Nasional Lore Lindu office** (☎ 0451-457623; Jl Tanjung Manimbayan 144, Palu) where you can ask the staff questions and check out the detailed map on the wall.

Sights

Attractions in the park include ancient megalithic relics, mostly in the **Bada**, **Besoa** and **Napu Valleys**; remote peaks, some more than 2500m; bird-watching, including hornbills, around **Kamarora**; and the 3150-hectare lake, **Danau Lindu**.

Activities

For **trekking**, the rangers at Kamarora can show you the start of several short trails, which don't require a guide – such as the 10m-high **waterfall** about 2km from Kamarora, and the hot water springs at **Kadidia** (3km), where you can bathe. To reach the summit of the 2355m **Gunung Nokilalaki** (6km), you'll need a guide.

Other longer hikes (with a guide) include Rachmat to Danau Lindu (six hours one way) and Sadaunta to Danau Lindu (four hours one way). An exciting alternative is to go on horseback; horses and handlers are available from 100,000Rp per day at Watutau and Gimpu.

The main trekking trail is Tonusu to Gimpu, via Tuare and Moa, or Doda and Hangirah – or vice versa. Unless you're planning to return to your starting point, send all nonessential gear ahead by car or bus – get a taxi driver to deliver it, or put it on a bus and pick it up from the bus office. To start, take a public (or chartered) bemo to Tonusu or Gimpu, and then tackle the trail like this:

Tonusu–Gintu From Tonusu, walk for two days, sleeping under covered bridges. You'll need to carry food and water-purification tablets. You could shorten the hike, and charter a motorbike to Peatua (26km) and walk to Malei bridge (six hours). The next day, hike from Malei to Bomba (18km), and look for the Bomba, Bada and Sepe megaliths. At Bomba, stay at the friendly Ningsi Homestay. From there it's about 10km to Gintu, where you can stay at Losmen Merry.

Gintu–Moa It's an easy three-hour walk to Tuare, where you can stay with the *kepala desa*. Moa is four hours further on, over two difficult rivers. Moa's *kepala desa* also takes guests. There is a path from Gintu to Doda, a lesser centre for megalithic remains, where you can stay at the Losmen Rindu Alam.

Moa–Gimpu It's a strenuous eight-hour hike over two rivers with poor bridges, to Gimpu, where you can stay at the pleasant Losmen Santo. From Gimpu you can hike into the Besoa Valley, or travel back by public (or chartered) transport to Palu.

GUIDES

For long-distance trekking, a guide is compulsory, and also necessary if you're intent on finding the megaliths. You can organise a guide in Tentena or Pendolo, but agencies prefer to sell all-inclusive trips. An organised trek from Tentena will cost around 600,000Rp to 1,000,000Rp and up per person (depending on group size) for four to five days, including food, transport and accommodation.

If travelling independently, arrange a guide at the visitors centre (Kamarora); the two field offices (Kulawi or Wuasa); the tourist office in Poso; or the tourist office or national park office in Palu. Guides start at 200,000Rp per day.

Food is readily available in the villages, but it's wise to bring other necessities, such as mosquito repellent and sunblock lotion, plus gifts to repay any hospitality. If trekking, you may have to sleep under roofs of covered bridges, which can get cold. Conversely, during the day it can get very hot, so the wildlife will be resting in the forest and is often difficult to spot. See p843 for more information on safe and responsible trekking.

Getting There & Away

There are three main approaches to the park. Firstly, there's the trekking trail from Tonusu to Gintu. Secondly, there's the road from Palu to Gimpu (100km) – charter a vehicle or take the twice-daily bus from Terminal Masomba (p722). The road between Palu and Gimpu is paved, but deteriorates into a muddy track south of Gimpu. Lastly, there's the paved road (with irregular public transport) from Palu to Betue, via Rachmat, Kamarora, Wuasa, Sedoa and Watutau. Be warned that south of Betue, the road is terrible.

Roads within the park consist chiefly of mud and holes, and transport is by jeep, horseback and foot. Some of the walking trails have recently been overused by motorbikes, as locals criss-cross the park.

PALU

☎ **0451 / pop 282,000**

Palu, the capital of Central Sulawesi, only came to prominence during the Japanese occupation in WWII. Situated in a rain shadow for most of the year, it's one of the driest places in Indonesia. Generally the days are hot, and the nights are tolerably cool. Most travellers don't detour to this part of Sulawesi unless they're trekking in Lore Lindu National Park or heading on to Tanjung Karang.

Information

EMERGENCY

Police station (☎ 421015; Jl Sam Ratulangi)

INTERNET ACCESS, POST & TELEPHONE

Golden Computer Internet (Jl Wahidin) Central internet access.

Main post office (Jl Prof Muhammed Yamin SH 161) Inconveniently located, but does have a small internet centre.

Telkom office (Jl Ahmad Yani) Conveniently located and the staff are efficient.

MEDICAL SERVICES

Rumah Sakit Umum Propinsi Undata (☎ 421270; Jl Suharso) Large and reasonably well-equipped hospital.

MONEY

Most banks are represented in Palu, and a few have ATMs. BNI bank is the best and most convenient for changing money.

TOURIST INFORMATION

Balai Taman Nasional Lore Lindu office (☎ 457623; just off Jl Tanjung Manimbayan) For permits, maps and information about Lore Lindu.

Tourist office (☎ 455260; Jl Dewi Sartika 91) For brochures and city maps. It is also a good place to get independent information about Lore Lindu National Park.

Sights

The large **Museum Negeri Propinsi Sulawesi Tengah** (☎ 422290; Jl Sapri 23) features interesting traditional art, and other geological and archaeological items, but it is inconveniently located.

Sleeping

Purnama Raya Hotel (☎ 423646; Jl Wahidin 4; s/d 30,000/40,000Rp) The most memorable of the otherwise forgettable cheapies. The rooms are clean and include a bathroom. The knowledgeable manager also doubles as a local guide.

Hotel Dely Baru (☎ 421076; Jl Tadulako 17; s/d 80,000/85,000Rp; ❄) In a quiet neighbourhood, rather a long way from the action, this hotel is known for its service. The 1st-class rooms come with air-con, satellite TV and hot water.

Hotel Sentral (☎ 422789; fax 422418; Jl Kartini 6; r from 115,000Rp; ❄) Large, efficient and aptly named. All rooms have satellite TV. Deluxe rooms include hot water and a fridge. The cheaper rooms are quite pokey, however.

Rama Garden Hotel (☎ 429500; fax 429300; Jl Monginsidi 81; s/d from 110,000/160,000Rp) The rooms here are quite smart and the amenities rise with the price. The outdoor seating area downstairs is an attraction.

Palu Golden Hotel (☎ 421126; fax 423230; Jl Raden Saleh 1; r from 218,000Rp; 🏊) One of Palu's top addresses; the rooms are well-appointed. The swimming pool makes this a worthwhile investment.

Eating

There are plenty of night warung along the breezy seafront esplanade, Jl Raja Moili.

Golden Bakery (Jl Wahidin) This is the venue for scrumptious cakes, local burgers, reliable Indonesian food and fresh fruit juices.

Depot Citra (Jl Hasanuddin II; mains 15,000Rp; 🕑 breakfast, lunch & dinner) This friendly little spot is a good place to enjoy the bounty of the sea, including tasty baked fish.

Restaurant New Oriental (Jl Hasanuddin II; mains 20,000Rp; 🕑 breakfast, lunch & dinner) A popular Chinese-Indonesian restaurant with a never-ending menu, including pigeon and frog.

Restoran Marannu (Jl Setia Budi; mains 20,000-40,000Rp; 🕑 breakfast, lunch & dinner) One of the smarter spots in town, the menu here includes tasty seafood and Chinese cuisine.

Getting There & Away

AIR

There are flights to Makassar and Balikpapan with **Batavia Air** (☎ 428888), **Merpati** (Merpati Nusantara Airlines; ☎ 423341; Jl Monginsidi) and **Lion Air** (☎ 428777; Jl Raden Saleh 1). Merpati also flies from Palu to Luwuk and Manado several times a week, as well as to Surabaya. See map p669 for more details.

BOAT

Travelling by boat is one way to avoid long and uncomfortable bus rides through Central Sulawesi. Palu is also well connected to East Kalimantan.

Every two weeks, the Pelni liners *Kambuna*, *Nggapulu* and *Kerinci* sail to Balikpapan; the *Tidar* and the *Agoa Mas* sail to

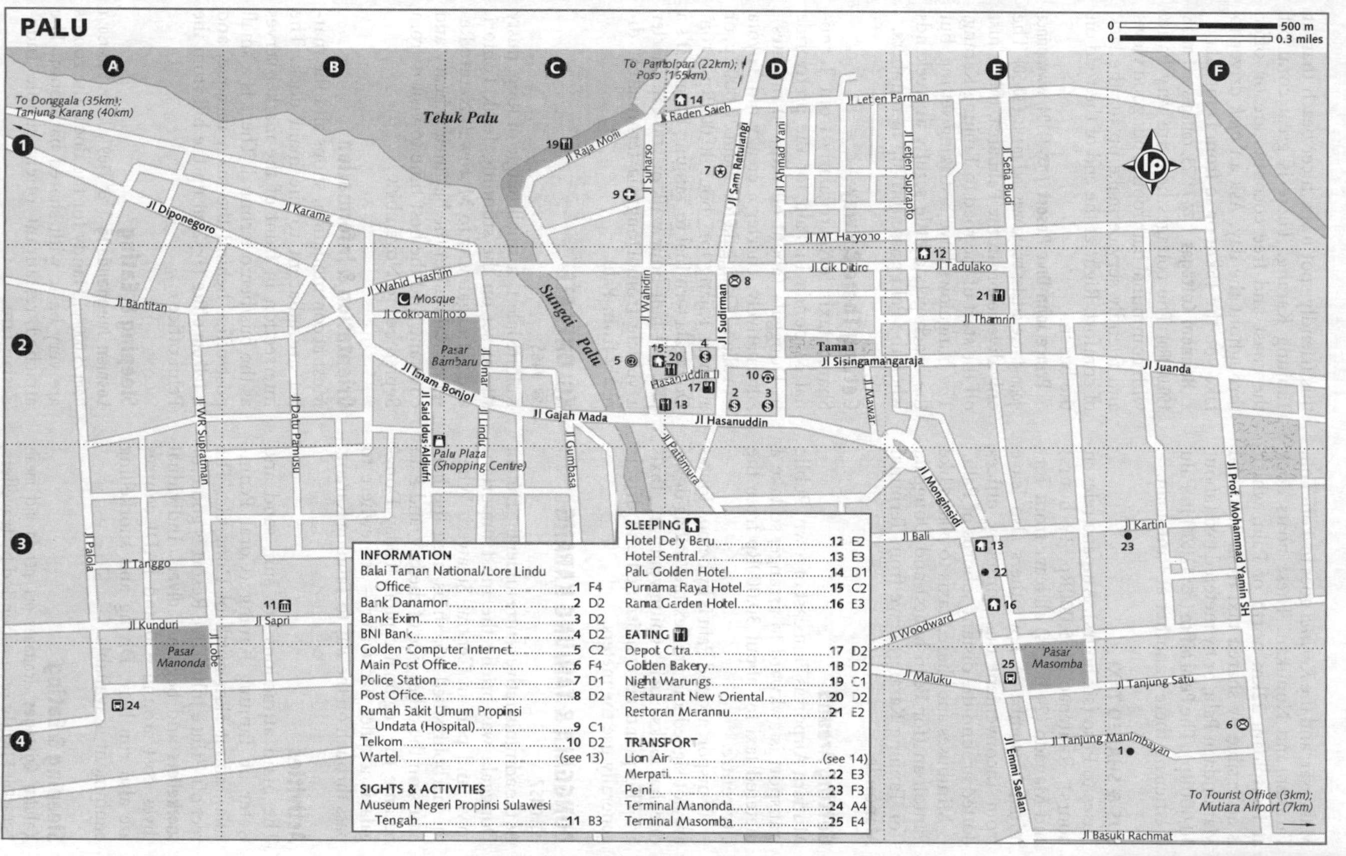

PALU
0 500 m
0 0.3 miles
To Donggala (35km); Tanjung Karang (40km)
To Pantoloan (22km); Poso (155km)
To Tourist Office (3km); Mutiara Airport (7km)
Teluk Palu
Sungai Palu
Pasar Bambaru
Pasar Manonda
Pasar Masomba
Palu Plaza (Shopping Centre)
Mosque
Taman
Jl Raja Moili
Jl Raden Saleh
Jl Let en Parman
Jl Letjen Suprapto
Jl Setia Budi
Jl Juanda
Jl Prof. Mohammad Yamin SH
Jl MT Haryono
Jl Cik Ditiro
Jl Tadulako
Jl Thamrin
Jl Sisingamangaraja
Jl Ahmad Yani
Jl Sam Ratulangi
Jl Sudirman
Jl Suharso
Jl Wahidin
Jl Hasanuddin II
Jl Hasanuddin
Jl Mawar
Jl Monginsidi
Jl Pattimura
Jl Gajah Mada
Jl Gumbasa
Jl Umar
Jl Lindu
Jl Imam Bonjol
Jl Said Idus Aldjufri
Jl Wahid Hashim
Jl Cokroaminoto
Jl Karama
Jl Diponegoro
Jl Bantitan
Jl Datu Pamusu
Jl WR Supratman
Jl Tanggo
Jl Kunduri
Jl Lobe
Jl Sapri
Jl Palola
Jl Kartini
Jl Bali
Jl Woodward
Jl Maluku
Jl Emmi Saelan
Jl Tanjung Satu
Jl Tanjung Manimbayan
Jl Basuki Rachmat
INFORMATION
Balai Taman National/Lore Lindu Office 1 F4
Bank Danamon 2 D2
Bank Exim 3 D2
BNI Bank 4 D2
Golden Computer Internet 5 C2
Main Post Office 6 F4
Police Station 7 D1
Post Office 8 D2
Rumah Sakit Umum Propinsi Undata (Hospital) 9 C1
Telkom 10 D2
Wartel (see 13)
SIGHTS & ACTIVITIES
Museum Negeri Propinsi Sulawesi Tengah 11 B3
SLEEPING
Hotel Dely Baru 12 E2
Hotel Sentral 13 E3
Palu Golden Hotel 14 D1
Purnama Raya Hotel 15 C2
Rama Garden Hotel 16 E3
EATING
Depot Citra 17 D2
Golden Bakery 18 D2
Night Warungs 19 C1
Restaurant New Oriental 20 D2
Restoran Marannu 21 E2
TRANSPORT
Lion Air (see 14)
Merpati 22 E3
Pelni 23 F3
Terminal Manonda 24 A4
Terminal Masomba 25 E4

Makassar; and the *Kerinci* goes to Toli-Toli, Tarakan and Nunukan. These boats dock at Pantoloan, 22km north of Palu, which is accessible by shared taxi from Terminal Manonda in Palu, or by metered taxi (about 30,000Rp). The **Pelni office** (☎ 421696) in Palu is efficient; there's another at Pantoloan.

BUS & SHARED TAXI

Buses to Poso (six hours), Ampana (eleven hours), Rantepao (135,000Rp, 19 hours) and Manado (24 hours) all leave from Terminal Masomba. A few others also leave from inconvenient bus company offices dotted around the distant suburbs of Palu.

Minibuses and shared taxis to places like Pantoloan (for Pelni boats) and Donggala (for Tanjung Karang) leave from Terminal Manonda.

Getting Around

Mutiara Airport is 7km east of town. Public transport is awkward to arrange, so take a metered taxi for about 30,000Rp from the city centre.

Transport around Palu is by bemo. Routes are not signed and are flexible, so flag down one that looks like it's going your way. Taxis are cheap and air-conditioned and drivers generally use the meters.

DONGGALA & TANJUNG KARANG

☎ 0457

As the administrative centre under the Dutch, Donggala was briefly the most important town and port in Central Sulawesi. When the harbour silted up, ships used the harbours on the other side of the bay, and Palu became the regional capital. Today Donggala is a quiet backwater – somewhere to pass through on the way to Tanjung Karang.

Activities

The main attractions are sun, sand and water at Tanjung Karang (Coral Peninsula), about 5km north of Donggala. The reef off Prince John Dive Resort is good for **snorkellers** and beginner **divers**. Individual dives cost around €30 and PADI courses are also run here. Diving and snorkelling equipment is available.

Sleeping & Eating

Kaluku Cottages (cottages per person incl meals 75,000Rp) Highly recommended by travellers, this friendly spot has a nicer beach than at Tanjung Karang. There is great coral off the coast and free coconuts are on offer throughout the day. Ask an *ojek* driver to take you the 15km or so from Donggala.

Harmoni Cottages (☎ 71573; cottages incl meals 150,000Rp) The cottages here are very basic, with communal bathrooms, but good views and friendly service make up for the lack of comfort. Right at the end of the road on the beach.

Prince John Dive Resort (☎ 71104; www.prince-john-diveresort.de; bungalows incl meals €30-50) The only dive resort in the Palu area, this is just off the start of the road to Tanjung Karang. The bungalows have a striking setting, but the beach gets a little scruffy at weekends when the Palu posse turn up in numbers.

Getting There & Away

Shared taxis leave regularly from Terminal Manonda in Palu for the pretty ride to Donggala (about 6000Rp, 30 minutes). Alternatively, charter a creaky old Toyota Corolla to Donggala for about 30,000Rp, or a newer Kijang for about 40,000Rp. From Donggala terminal to Tanjung Karang it's a pleasant half-hour walk or you can charter a vehicle from Donggala terminal or directly from Palu.

KOLONEDALE

☎ 0465

Kolonedale is a small tangle of long, dusty streets set on the stunning Teluk Tomori, and is the gateway to Morowali Nature Reserve. Rainfall in the bay area is heavy and constant, and the best time to visit is from September to November.

Orientation & Information

Most accommodation, shops and the market are adjacent to the main dock. The intersection in front of the market serves as the bus/bemo terminal. There is a small post office behind the main mosque, and a **Telkom office** (24hr) up the hill from the Pelni office.

Sleeping & Eating

Losmen Jungpandang (☎ 21091; Jl Yos Sudarso; r from 25,000Rp) Handy for the dock, the rooms are very basic with shared bathroom. The attached restaurant offers simple Indonesian fare.

Penginapan Sederhana (☎ 21124; Jl Yos Sudarso 64; r 20,000-115,000Rp) Formerly just another basic budget crashpad, this little guesthouse has added several smarter rooms in the past few years, making it the best all-rounder in town. It is managed by the local environmental group, Sahabat Morowali (Friends of Morowali), so has top information on Morowali Nature Reserve.

There are basic warungs around the bus terminal and market.

Getting There & Away

Several buses a day travel between Kolonedale and Poso (eight hours), via Tentena. You may also find a Kijang in Kolonedale going as far as Poso. From the south, cross Danau Matano by boat from Soroako to Nuha, rent a motorbike or jeep to Beteleme, and then wait for a bus to Kolonedale.

The Pelni liner *Tilongkabila* stops at Kolonedale about once a week on its way to Luwuk (economy/1st class 37,000/119,000Rp, eight hours) or Kendari. *Perahu* (traditional outrigger boats) leave the main dock most days at about 11pm for the overnight trip east to Baturube and Pandauke, from where there are buses to Luwuk (five hours).

TELUK TOMORI

Most visitors to Kolonedale head straight to Morowali, so they miss much of the stunning beauty of the islands and inlets around Teluk Tomori, where limestone cliffs plunge into emerald waters, and unbroken forests cover islands and surrounding hills. To properly explore the bay, rent a boat from Kolonedale: for around 100,000Rp or so per day, you can charter a small 'Johnson' (dugout canoe with an outboard motor), or for about 300,000Rp, a larger boat holding up to 10 people.

Sights include a **limestone cliff** across the water from Kolonedale with faint painted outlines of prehistoric handprints and fossils embedded in the rock; the oddly shaped '**mushroom rock**'; tiny **fishing villages**; and some fine **beaches** on uninhabited islands at the mouth of the bay. There are also **coral reefs** with plenty of marine life, but the visibility can be poor.

MOROWALI NATURE RESERVE

This 225,000-hectare nature reserve was established in 1980 on the northern shore of Teluk Tomori after Operation Drake, a British-sponsored survey of the endangered species in the area. The reserve includes islands in the bay, accessible lowland plains and densely vegetated peaks up to 2421m high.

Morowali is home to about 5000 Wana people who live mostly by hunting and gathering, and through shifting agriculture. The park is rich in wildlife, such as *anoa* (pygmy buffalo), maleo birds, *babi rusa* (wild deer-like pig) and the world's tiniest bat, but dense jungle is often all you'll see.

Trekking

You will need at least four days to properly visit the park, plus a few extra to get there and back, and the going is tough. Treks can be organised through travel agencies in Tentena (p717) for about 600,000Rp and up per person (depending on group size), including transport, food and accommodation, for a five- to six-day trek.

However, if you want to travel independently, and you need a guide (which is necessary to see the wildlife), wait until you reach Kolonedale. In Kolonedale, guides may approach you in the street; or you can organise one through your hotel; or visit the KSDA (National Parks) office – where you must register and buy a permit (20,000Rp per day). A good source of independent advice, and a good place to organise guides, is **Friends of Morowali** (☎ 0465 21125; Penginapan Sederhana, Jl Yos Sudarso 64), a local environmental group based in Kolonedale.

From Kolonedale it's a two-hour boat trip across Teluk Tomori and up Sungai Morowali to drop-off points for hikes to **Kayu Poli**, a small Wana settlement. You can stay in a local home there or at another village, and spend some time with the Wana

THE MALEO

One of Sulawesi's endemic, and most endangered, birds is a local chicken. The maleo *(Macrocephalon maleo)* has a black-and-white crest and an orange beak, but otherwise it is the same size, and has the same characteristics, as an ordinary chicken. The maleo lay huge eggs in nests in the ground near hot springs, but the eggs are often collected by locals for ceremonies and food.

people. West of Kayu Poli (three hours) is the eerily silent **Danau Rahu**, which takes about five hours to cross by canoe. You can leave the park via Sungai Rahu, and return to Kolonedale by boat.

LUWUK

☎ 0461 / pop 48,000

Luwuk is the biggest town on Sulawesi's isolated eastern peninsula, and the stepping-off point for the remote Banggai Islands. Nearby attractions include **Air Terjun Hengahenga**, the 75m-high waterfall 3km west of Luwuk; and the **Bangkiriang Nature Reserve**, which is 80km southwest of Luwuk and home to Central Sulawesi's largest maleo bird population.

Ramayana Hotel (☎ 21502; Jl Danau Lindu; s/d from 75,000/90,000Rp) is the best of the town's few hotels. The rooms are clean and the seaside restaurant attracts a breeze. VIP rooms run to 325,000Rp if you are feeling very important.

Maleo Cottages (☎/fax 324068; www.maleo-cottages.com; Jl Lompobattang; r incl breakfast 100,000Rp, cottages incl breakfast 120,000Rp) is by far the best place to stay in the Luwuk area, about 16km from town. There are rooms in the main house and three atmospheric cottages. Meals are available at 35,000Rp. This is the base for **Wallacea Dive Cruise** (www.wallacea-dive-cruise) so is a good place to arrange diving in the Banggai Islands or liveaboards to the Togean Islands.

Merpati (Merpati Nusantara Airlines; ☎ 21523; Jl Sam Ratulangi 50) has daily flights to/from Manado and several flights a week to Palu. See map p669 for more details.

Every week the Pelni liner *Tilongkabila* links Luwuk with Kolonedale (economy/1st class 37,000/119,000Rp, eight hours) or Gorontalo (134,000/45,000Rp, 11 hours), and is an excellent way to travel to this remote part of Sulawesi. There's a **Pelni office** (☎ 21888; Jl Sungai Musi 3) in town.

There are also buses to Pagimana, Poso and Bunta for connections to Ampana.

BANGGAI ISLANDS

With a *lot* of time and patience you can visit the wild and remote Banggai Islands. It's a superb area for **swimming**, **diving** and viewing **marine life** such as whales and dugongs. Alfred Wallace called the area 'the mother of all living coral reefs'. Boats can be chartered from most villages, but it is easiest to arrange diving and snorkelling trips through Maleo Cottages near Luwuk.

The largest and most populous island is **Pulau Peleng**, with the main settlements at Tataba and Salakan. There is still no accommodation on the islands, but you can stay at a local home in any village if you check with the *kepala desa* first.

There is a daily ferry between Luwuk and Tataba. The Pelni liner *Ciremai* links Tataba with Makassar or Bitung (for Manado).

TANJUNG API NATIONAL PARK

The 4246-hectare Tanjung Api (Cape Fire National Park) is home to *anoa, babi rusa*, crocodiles, snakes and maleo, but most people come to see the burning coral cliff fuelled by a leak of natural gas. To get here you need to charter a boat around the rocky peninsula from Ampana. It's more interesting at dusk.

AMPANA

☎ 0464

The main reason for travellers to come to Ampana is to catch a boat to/from the Togean Islands, but it's a laid-back, pleasant town and a good stopover while you recover from, or prepare for, an assault on the Togeans.

Orientation

The main Poso–Luwuk road goes through Ampana, and is called Jl Hatta. Many hotels are along Jl Kartini, which heads towards the sea from Jl Hatta. The main dock, market and bus terminal are all close to Jl Kartini.

Sleeping & Eating

Losmen Irama (☎ 21055; Jl Kartini; s/d 40,000/55,000Rp, with air-con 110,000Rp; ❄) A reliable cheapie, this place has been around for a long time. It offers comfortable, if uninspiring, rooms.

Oasis Hotel (☎ 21058; Jl Kartini; dm 30,000Rp, r 70,000-115,000Rp; ❄) Run in conjunction with the Kadidiri Paradise Resort in the Togeans, this is the best choice in town. Cheap dorms and a good range of rooms keeps the punters happy. The most expensive rooms include air-con and hot water.

Marina Cottages (☎ 21280; cottages 77,000Rp) Perched on a very rocky beach, the cottages boast a seafront setting and friendly service, and are in a perfect location for boats to Bomba. They are in Labuhan village, a 10-minute *bendi* (horse-drawn cart) ride from Ampana. The restaurant is worth visiting for the sunsets alone.

Rumah Makan Ikan Bakar (Jl Kartini; mains 15,000Rp) A good place for some cold beer and baked fish.

Getting There & Away

Ampana is on the road between Poso and Luwuk. Several buses travel each day to Poso (five hours), often continuing to Palu (11 hours). To get to Luwuk, catch a bemo from the terminal, opposite the main dock in Ampana, to Bunta and then another to Luwuk.

Boats to Poso, Wakai on the Togeans and beyond leave from the main boat terminal at the end of Jl Yos Sudarso, in the middle of Ampana. Boats to Bomba on Pulau Batu Daka leave from a jetty in Labuhan village, next to Marina Cottages.

TOGEAN ISLANDS

If you dreamt of an Indonesia with blissful beaches, plentiful coral and a place to live the life of a lotus eater, the Togean Islands fit the bill. This archipelago of beautiful coral and volcanic isles in the middle of Teluk Tomini is a riot of blue, gold and green. The undisturbed jungle shelters a variety of wildlife. The islands' reefs support a rich diversity of marine life, and the people of the seven or so ethnic groups sharing this place are hospitable. Although the islands are difficult to reach, and the facilities are basic, many travellers fall in love with the Togeans and their lifestyle – and often end up staying a lot longer than they anticipated. However, like many parts of Indonesia, the coral has suffered at the hands of local fisherfolk over the past decade.

Most of the rooms on the islands are in wooden cottages, on or near a beach. Most have a mosquito net but no fan because the sea breezes keep everything cool. Bathroom facilities range from communal and rustic to private and porcelain. All prices quoted are per person, and all rates include local meals. It is a good idea to bring along some snacks and treats. Beer, soft drinks and mineral water are available from shops and homestays.

Some of the local homestays are in a perpetual state of hibernation, as they see few visitors. They may not be inclined to open for just one or two guests, so ask around before committing yourself to one of the more remote islands.

Information

The Togeans were the *in-place* to be in the late 1990s, but the downturn in tourists that has affected much of Sulawesi has slowed the pace of development in recent years, probably a good thing for the fragile ecosystem here. There are bungalow resorts

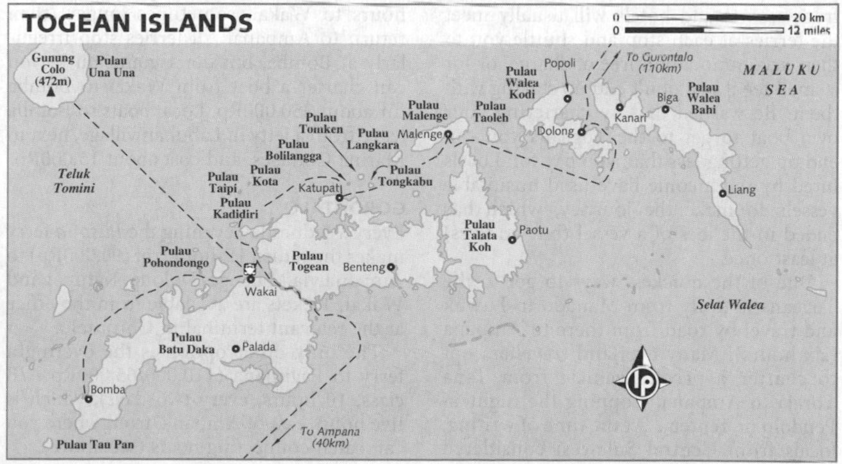

DIVING & SNORKELLING AROUND THE TOGEANS

The Togeans are the only place in Indonesia where you can find all three major reef environments – atoll, barrier and fringing reefs – in one location. Two atolls and their deep lagoons lie to the northwest of Pulau Batu Daka. Barrier reefs surround many islands at the 200m depth contour (5km to 15km offshore), and fringing reefs surround all of the coasts, merging with the sea grass and mangroves. There is also a sunken WWII B-24 bomber plane, which is a 30-minute trip by speedboat (or one hour by normal boat) from Kadidiri.

The mix of coral and marine life is spectacular and unusually diverse, although many reefs have sadly been badly damaged by bomb and cyanide fishing. The more conspicuous residents include brightly marked coral lobsters, a colony of dugong, schools of a hundred or more dolphins, the occasional whale, commercially important species of trepang (sea cucumber), and natural pearls.

Snorkelling gear is available at most homestays for about 25,000Rp, but it's always better to bring your own. **Diving** can be arranged at a number of places, including **Black Marlin** (p728) and **Kadidiri Paradise** (p728) on Pulau Kadidiri, **Island Retreat** (opposite) near Bomba and the upmarket **Walea Dive Resort** (p729) on Pulau Walea Kodi. Prices start from US$25 per dive and PADI courses are also available.

and homestays spread throughout the islands and nobody knows where they all are. The best source of current information about homestays, transport and activities is obviously other travellers, but it's also worth asking staff at hotels in Ampana and Gorontalo. Bring plenty of cash, as there are no banks on the islands.

Take care not to leave valuables in the room, as break-ins have been known to occur, particularly when people are out diving all day.

Getting There & Away

The Togeans are better serviced from Ampana than from Gorontalo. Representatives from resorts and hotels will usually meet the ferries at each stop and shuttle you to their accommodation free of charge, or for a small fee if you don't end up staying with them. Be warned that by chartering your own boat to get to the Togeans you can end up getting less than you pay for. Locals lured by the income have used unsuitable vessels to make the journey, which has ended in the loss of a vessel (but no lives) at least once.

One of the quickest ways to get to the Togeans is to fly from Manado to Luwuk and travel by road from there to Ampana (six hours). Many overland travellers opt to charter a private vehicle from Tana Toraja to Ampana, stopping the night in Pendolo or Tentena. At the time of writing, locals from Central Sulawesi considered travelling by public transport around Poso to be risky.

AMPANA

The *Puspita* ferry travels between Ampana and Gorontalo once a week, but the schedule often chops and changes, so don't plan flight connections around it. Every Monday morning it makes the 15-hour journey from Ampana to Gorontalo via Wakai (45,000Rp, four hours); Katupat (one hour from Wakai); Malenge (45 minutes); Dolong (one hour); then through to Gorontalo (90,000Rp, nine hours from Dolong).

Local boats depart 'almost daily' at 10am as far as Wakai (25,000Rp, three to five hours to Wakai, sometimes longer) then return to Ampana. All ferries stop irregularly at Bomba, but don't count on it; you can charter a boat from Wakai to Bomba for about 250,000Rp. Local boats to Bomba leave from a jetty in Labuhan village, next to Marina Cottages, and cost about 15,000Rp.

GORONTALO

Every Wednesday evening the *Puspita* ferry makes the return 15-hour trip (90,000Rp) to Ampana via Malenge, Dolong, Katupat and Wakai. Tickets are available from the office at the relevant terminal in Gorontalo.

The only other option is the overnight ferry to Pagimana (110,000/65,000Rp A/B class, 10 hours, every two days), which is five hours east of Ampana, from where you can catch connecting boats (see above).

MARISA

Anyone who is loaded with rupiah (about 1,500,000Rp) can charter a speedboat between Marisa (about 150km west of Gorontalo) and Wakai or Kadidiri. Both Black Marlin Dive (p728) and Kadidiri Paradise (p728) can arrange boat charters.

BUNTA

This is the key link in the fastest route to the Togeans. Take a morning flight from Manado to Luwuk, charter a car to Bunta (500,000Rp, four hours) and then charter a boat to Kadidiri (800,000Rp). It quickly adds up, but is not a bad option for a small group.

Getting Around

Allow plenty of time to get around, because transport within the Togeans is infrequent. Regardless of where you stay, you need boats to get there and away and to reach swimming and snorkelling spots. Schedules for public boats bend and break, so chartering something is a good way to get around.

Charters are not hard to arrange in Wakai, Bomba and Kadidiri, but are far more difficult to arrange in smaller settlements because there are simply not many boats around. You'll often have to accept anything that's available, from a nifty speedboat to a ponderous wooden trawler. The rates should be negotiable but are often fairly standard among the cartel of local operators (250,000Rp from Wakai or Kadidiri to Bomba on a speedboat).

Ask your homestay, or anyone around the village, about the current timetables for boats to other islands, or further on to Ampana and Gorontalo. The locals rely heavily on these boats, so they always know what is going where and when.

PULAU BATU DAKA

The largest and most accessible island is Pulau Batu Daka, which is home to the two main villages, Bomba and Wakai.

Bomba

Bomba is a tiny outpost at the southwestern end of the island, which most travellers sail past on the way to and from Wakai (for Pulau Kadidiri). Bomba is an appealing alternative to Kadidiri, as the coral is in much better shape here and it sees fewer visitors.

It's a pleasant walk to the **bat caves** in the hills behind Bomba, but you'll need a guide and a torch (flashlight).

In the village, **Losmen Poya Lisa** (r 90,000Rp) is easy to spot, as it is built over the water, but the rooms are pretty basic.

Poya Lisa Cottages (cottages 80,000-120,000Rp) is located on a pretty beach on its own little island, and is a friendly place that has proved popular with travellers over the years. No electricity, but bathrooms have been added.

ourpick Island Retreat (www.togian-island-retreat.com; r per person US$10-22) is set on the beautiful beach at Pasir Putih and has 20 cottages. The cheaper cottages have shared bathrooms, so it is worth the extra money to have a sea view and attached ablutions. There is good international food, including Mexican and pizzas. Diving is available here, plus

CONSERVATION OF THE TOGEANS

The Togean Islands are pristine and popular, but are under threat from local fishing practices and pearl farms, not to mention by-products of tourism such as rubbish and sewage.

The fishing of valuable Napoleon fish (for foreign Chinese restaurants) has resulted in a catastrophic increase in the number of crown-of-thorns starfish, which are destroying the coral around the Togeans at an alarming rate. Add to this extreme fishing methods like the use of explosives and cyanide, and in some places like Pulau Kadidiri the coral is really suffering.

Japanese pearl farms in the region have reduced access to traditional fishing areas and have not compensated local fishermen, nor provided grants to promote local community development, as initially promised.

Various groups have been lobbying the Indonesian government to declare the Togeans a protected marine national park over the years, but the wheels of bureaucracy turn slowly. Attention is now switching to secure local marine reserve status, which would allow much more local control over development and revenues. The money could be used to finance conservation activities, rubbish disposal, education programmes and the policing of illegal fishing practices.

THE BAJO

Nomadic Bajo 'sea gypsies' still dive for trepang, pearls and other commercially important marine produce, as they have done for hundreds, perhaps thousands, of years. The Bajo are hunter-gatherers who spend much of their lives on boats, travelling as families wherever they go.

There are several permanent Bajo settlements around the Togean Islands, and even some stilt villages on offshore reefs, but the itinerant character of Bajo culture still survives. Newlyweds are put in a canoe and pushed out to sea to make their place in the world. When they have children, the fathers dive with their three-day-old babies to introduce them to life on the sea.

The rare intrusions from the outside world can sometimes result in tragedy. When Bugis and Chinese traders introduced air compressors to enable the Bajo to dive longer and deeper for trepang, the lethal nature of caisson disease (the bends) was rarely explained properly. Around 40 men were killed, and many more crippled, in one area alone. These days the Bajo divers' only concessions to modernity are goggles fashioned from wood and glass, and handmade spear guns. Land-loving Indonesians tend to look down on the Bajo, in much the same way Gypsies were discriminated against in Europe.

snorkelling gear. Boat charters can be arranged from Ampana and Marisa.

Wakai

The largest settlement in the Togeans, Wakai is mainly used as the departure point for boats to Pulau Kadidiri, but there are several well-stocked general stores. A small **waterfall**, a few kilometres inland from Wakai, is a pleasant hike – ask directions in the village.

PULAU KADIDIRI

Long considered the place to be in the Togeans, the beach on Pulau Kadidiri is just a short boat trip from Wakai. It offers a perfect strip of sand; a good range of accommodation; snorkelling and swimming only metres from the door; and superb diving beyond. However, a word of caution: the reefs off Kadidiri have been severely damaged by bomb and cyanide fishing in the past decade and aren't what they once were.

A short walk west of the beach brings you to a series of craggy coral cliffs, home to coconut crabs the size of small footballs. Put your hand into any hole in the sand and you may never see it again!

Activities

Kadidiri is the most popular destination in the Togeans, and a range of activities are on offer. Apart from diving, snorkelling gear can be rented for about 25,000Rp per day and hikes around the island can be arranged with staff at the resort. There are treks around Pulau Una Una and boat hire for about 150,000Rp per day to visit the nearby islands, and for snorkelling. Many places have a small book exchange, which is just as well because you'll do a lot of reading.

Sleeping

Black Marlin Cottages (Gorontalo ☎ 0435-831869; www.blackmarlindive.com; cottages 85,000-150,000Rp) The base for popular British-run dive outfit Black Marlin Dive, these attractive cottages occupy a prime strip of beachfront. The smarter cottages include Western-style bathrooms. Visa and MasterCard are accepted, so you can bundle your accommodation in with your dives.

Pondok Lestari (cottages 125,000Rp) One of the oldest places in the area, it has recently upgraded its cottages and it occupies a fine stretch of sand, making it pretty good value.

Kadidiri Paradise Resort (☎ in Ampana 0464-21058; www.kadidiri-paradise.com; r per person US$10-25) On the same stretch of beach as Black Marlin, although there is no love lost between the two places, this attractive resort has 25 cottages. The cheaper rooms have shared bathroom or a mandi, while the pricier options have Western-style bathrooms and beachfront balconies. A friendly place with a good reputation.

Getting There & Away

The public boats sail tantalisingly close to Kadidiri, but don't stop, so you must go to Wakai first (see p726). Hotel representatives will usually meet the ferry and take you to Kadidiri for free. Once or twice a day a boat delivers fresh water and supplies to Kadidiri from Wakai; ask your homestay in Kadidiri or Wakai about the schedules. You can also charter a boat between Wakai and Kadidiri for about 50,000Rp one way.

PULAU UNA UNA

The Togeans are part of an active volcanic belt. Pulau Una Una, which consists mostly of **Gunung Colo** (472m), was torn apart in 1983 when the volcano exploded for the first time in almost 100 years. Ash covered 90% of the island, destroying all of the houses, animals and most of the crops. Thankfully, Una Una's population had been safely evacuated. These days you can trek to the top of the volcano (three hours), and admire the awesome lava landscapes all around the island.

A public boat leaves Wakai about twice a week, but there is nowhere to stay on Una Una. Black Marlin and Kadidiri Paradise on Pulau Kadidiri can organise guided treks up the volcano, plus snorkelling stops along the way.

PULAU TOGEAN

The main settlement on this island is the very relaxed Katupat village, which has a small market and a couple of shops. Around the island there are magical **beaches**, and some decent **hikes** for anyone sick of swimming, snorkelling and diving.

Losmen Melati (r 90,000Rp), near the boat jetty in Katupat, offers the traveller simple accommodation.

PULAU TOMKEN & PULAU BOLILANGGA

These two islands are a five-minute boat ride from Katupat. **Fadhila Cottages** (cottages from 125,000Rp) on Pulau Pangempa offers excellent food and superb snorkelling. The friendly family are happy to arrange a local dance for guests. **Bolilangga Cottages** (cottages from 80,000Rp) on Pulau Bolilangga is similarly good.

PULAU MALENGE

Malenge is remote and secluded, with wonderful **snorkelling** just offshore from the village. Some locals, with the aid of nongovernmental organisations, have established excellent **walking trails** around the mangroves and jungles to help spot the incredibly diverse fauna, including macaques, tarsiers, hornbills, cuscus and salamanders.

Near the jetty in Malenge village, **Malenge Indah** (cottages 70,000Rp) is attractively situated over the water.

> **COCONUT CRABS**
>
> Coconut crabs, the world's largest terrestrial arthropods, once lived on islands throughout the western Pacific and eastern Indian oceans, but unsustainable human exploitation has reduced stocks to a handful of isolated islands, including the Togeans. Mature crabs weigh up to 5kg, and their large-clawed legs can span 90cm.
>
> Despite popular myth, there is little evidence to support stories of crabs climbing trees to snip off coconuts, removing the husk and then carrying the nut up again to drop from a great height. However, there is evidence that humans are eating these crabs to the edge of extinction, so please make a more sustainable choice from the menu.

PULAU WALEA KODI

Dolong is a busy fishing village, and the only settlement on the island. Facilities are basic, transport is limited, and the island doesn't offer the picturesque beaches and snorkelling found elsewhere.

On an island just off Walea Kodi is the Italian-run **Walea Dive Resort** (www.walea.com). Package deals, including cottage, three meals (including Italian cuisine), transport and three dives a day, start from US$120 per person per day.

NORTH SULAWESI

North Sulawesi is world famous for its underwater action. Pulau Bunaken has an amazing array of marine life just a stone's throw from the shore and for more experienced divers, there is the lure of the Lembeh Strait. However, there is life above the water as well, with secluded bays and beaches around the Manado peninsula and some spectacular volcanoes brooding in the background. Make for the highlands if the heat gets too much and explore the beautiful countryside.

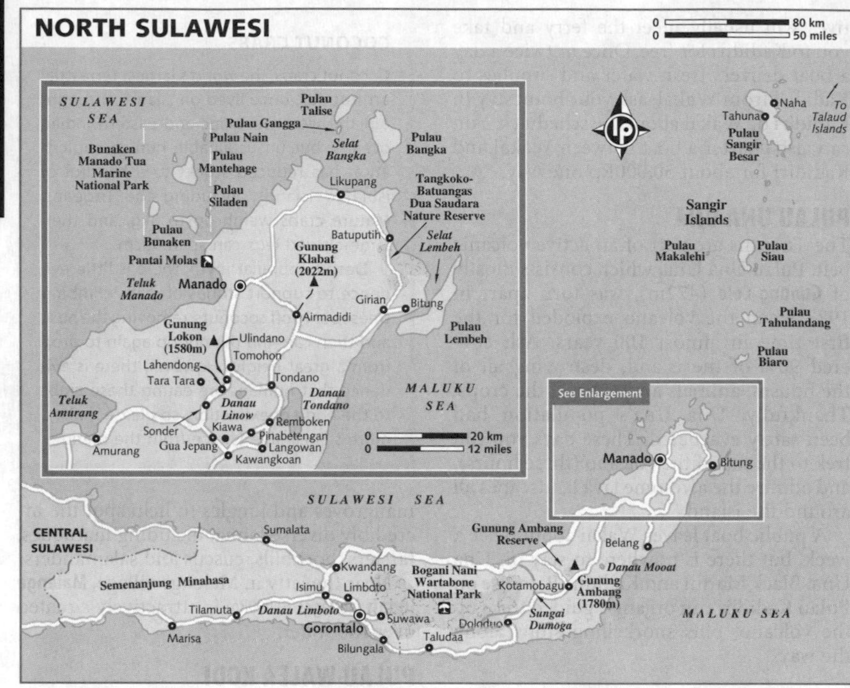

North Sulawesi is the most developed province on the island, and its people have a long history of trade and contact with the outside world. The Sangir-Talaud Island group forms a bridge to the Philippines, providing a causeway for the movement of peoples and cultures. As a result, the language and physical features of Filipino peoples can be found among the local Minahasans.

The two largest distinct groups in the region are the Minahasans and Sangirese, but there are many more dialects and subgroups. The kingdoms of Bolaang Mongondow, sandwiched between Minahasa and Gorontalo, were also important political players.

The Dutch have had a more enduring influence on this isolated northern peninsula than anywhere else in the archipelago: Dutch is still spoken among the older generation, and well-to-do families often send their children to study in the Netherlands.

History

A group of independent states was established at a meeting of the linguistically diverse Minahasan peoples around AD 670 at a stone now known as Watu Pinabetengan (near Kawangkoan).

At the time of the first contact with Europeans in the 16th century, North Sulawesi had strong links with the sultanate of Ternate (Northern Maluku) and Bugis traders from South Sulawesi. In 1677 the Dutch occupied Pulau Sangir and, two years later, a treaty with the Minahasan chiefs saw the start of Dutch domination for the next 300 years.

Although relations with the Dutch were often less than cordial, and the region did not actually come under direct Dutch rule until 1870, the Dutch and Minahasans eventually became so close that the north was often referred to as the '12th province of the Netherlands'.

Christianity became a force in the early 1820s, and the wholesale conversion of the Minahasans was almost complete by 1860. Because the school curriculum was taught in Dutch, the Minahasans had an early advantage in the competition for government jobs and positions in the colonial army.

The Minahasan sense of identity became an issue for the Indonesian government after independence. The Minahasan leaders declared their own autonomous state of North Sulawesi in June 1957. The Indonesian government then bombed Manado in February 1958, and, by June, Indonesian troops had landed in North Sulawesi. Rebel leaders retreated into the mountains, and the rebellion was finally put down in mid-1961.

GORONTALO

☎ 0435 / pop 150,000

The port of Gorontalo has the feel of an overgrown country town, where all the locals seems to know each other and everyone is super-friendly. The town features some of the best-preserved Dutch houses in Sulawesi and still retains a languid colonial feel.

Gorontalo's local hero is Nani Wartabone, an anti-Dutch guerrilla, and there is a large statue of him in Lapangan Nani Wartabone adjacent to the Melati Hotel.

Orientation & Information

Although spread out, most of the hotels, shops and other life-support systems are concentrated in a small central district. Many streets are ambiguously named, which can cause confusion. The main post office is a useful landmark.

Bank Danamon (Jl Jend Ahmad Yani) ATM machines, plus cash advances.

Black Marlin (☎ 831869; Jl Kasuari 9A) The office for Black Marlin on Pulau Kadidiri in the Togean Islands. A good place for travel information.

BNI bank (Bank Negara Indonesia; Jl Jend Ahmad Yani) ATM and currency exchange.

Telkom office (Jl Parman; 24hr) Efficient.

W@rsinet (Jl Jend Ahmad Yani 14A) Internet access available.

Activities

Diving is now available in the Gorontalo area with **Miguel's Diving** (www.miguelsdiving.com), but it is only seasonal from November to April. It's a good way to pass some time if stuck waiting for a boat to the Togean Islands.

Sleeping

Hotel Saronde (☎ 821735; Jl Walanda Maramis 17; s/d 55,000/88,000Rp, r with air-con & satellite TV 132,000Rp;) Just across the field from the Melati, this hotel is great value, and offers some useful travel information in the foyer. The newer wing houses the smarter, more expensive rooms.

Melati Hotel (☎ 822934; avelberg@hotmail.com; Jl Gajah Mada 33; r 60,000-140,000Rp;) The friendly Melati has been extending a warm welcome to travellers for many years now. It's based around a lovely old home, built in the early 1900s for the then harbourmaster (current owner Pak Alex's grandfather). The rooms in the original house are basic but atmospheric; the newer rooms are set around a pretty garden and are well furnished.

Yulia Hotel (☎ 828395; fax 823065; Jl Jend Ahmad Yani 26; s/d from 181,500/203,500Rp;) One of the smartest hotels in town with a good central location. All rooms have satellite TV and hot water.

Eating & Drinking

The local delicacy is *milu siram*, which is a corn soup with grated coconut, fish, salt, chilli and lime. You'll find it at the stalls around the market at night, or try it at **Cikia** (Jl Tribata 37; meals 10,000-20,000Rp), a no frills eatery well known for its local cuisine. The night market has a vast number of warung selling cheap and tasty food.

If you're craving a sweet treat, head to Rumah Makan Brantas on Jl Hasanuddin for the best selection of cakes and pastries this side of Manado.

Just off Jl Gajah Mada, Rumah Makan Viva is handy to some hotels, and turns out reliable Indo favourites like *gado-gado* and fried chicken.

If heading directly to the Togean Islands by boat, stock up on life's necessities at either the Santika or Citra supermarkets, both on Jl Parman.

Sasando Cafe (Jl Panjaitan) is one of the many karaoke cafés that have sprung up in town. Save the nightlife until Manado or Makassar!

Getting There & Away

AIR

You can travel to/from Manado with **Merpati** (Merpati Nusantara Airlines; ☎ 828397; Yulia Hotel), which has services three times a week. **Lion Air** (☎ 830035; Jl Rachmat 15) flies to Gorontalo once a week for a similar price, as well as to

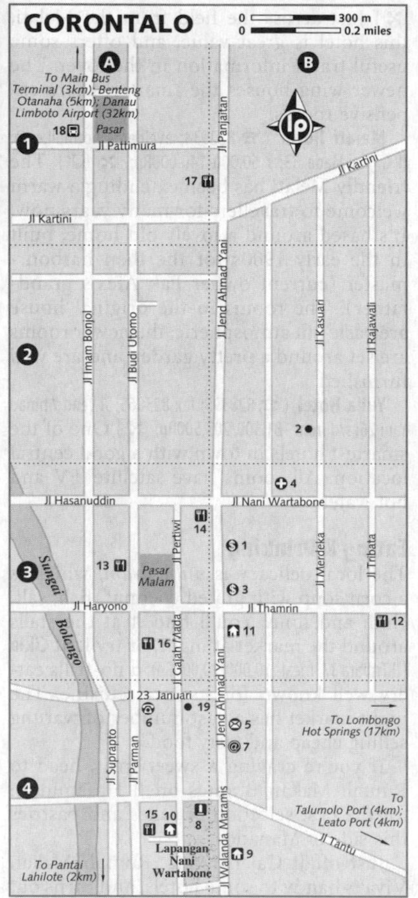

INFORMATION
Bank Danamon.......1 B3
Black Marlin Office.......2 B2
BNI Bank.......3 B3
Hospital.......4 B3
Post Office.......5 B4
Telkom.......6 A4
W@rsinet.......7 B4

SIGHTS & ACTIVITIES
Nani Wartabone Statue.......8 A4

SLEEPING
Hotel Saronde.......9 B4
Melati Hotel.......10 A4
Yulia Hotel.......11 B3

EATING
Cikia.......12 B3
Citra Supermarket.......13 A3
Rumah Makan Brantas.......14 A3
Rumah Makan Viva.......15 A4
Santika Supermarket.......16 A3
Sasando Cafe.......17 A1

TRANSPORT
Merpati.......(see 11)
Mikrolet Terminal.......18 A1
Pelni.......19 A4

Makassar. Sriwijaya Air also flies to Makassar. All airlines have offices at the airport, or tickets can be bought at agencies around town. See the map on p669 for prices.

BOAT

Gorontalo has two ports, both about 4km from the town centre: Talumolo port for the Togeans and Leato port for Pagimana and Pelni ferries. Both are easily accessible by *mikrolet* (small taxi) along Jl Tantu. Tell the driver your boat's destination and he'll drop you at the right place.

Every two weeks the Pelni liner *Tilongkabila* links Gorontalo with Bitung (for Manado). The **Pelni office** (☎ 821089; cnr Jl 23 Januari & Jl Gajah Mada) is efficient and convenient.

Every two days a large, stable ferry crosses the gulf from Gorontalo to Pagimana (A/B class 55,000/38,000Rp, 10 hours) and returns the next day. It leaves both places at about 9.30pm, and arrives at about 6am. This ferry is a more comfortable and regular (but more time-consuming) way of travelling between Gorontalo and the Togean Islands.

Direct boats also connect Gorontalo to the Togeans; see p726 for more details. You can book tickets at the office for **Black Marlin** (☎ 831869; Jl Kasuari 9A).

BUS

The main bus terminal is 3km north of town, and accessible by bemo, *bendi* or *ojek*. There are direct buses to Palu (90,000Rp, 17 hours) and Manado (normal/air-con 60,000/75,000Rp, 10 hours), departing every hour.

From the terminal, next to the market, *mikrolet* go in all directions to regional villages.

Getting Around

The airport is 32km north of Gorontalo. For 40,000Rp a share-car can be booked at the taxi desk inside the terminal, and you'll be taken to your requested address. To get to the airport, book the same service through the airline, travel agency or your hotel.

AROUND GORONTALO

On the outskirts of Gorontalo, on a hill at Lekobalo, overlooking Danau Limboto, is **Benteng Otanaha**. The fort was probably built by the Portuguese and supposedly used by Gorontalo kings as a bastion against the Dutch when relations soured. Today there are the remains of just three towers. Take a *bendi* or *mikrolet* from the *mikrolet* terminal to a path at the foot of the hill.

Pantai Lahilote is a white sandy beach 2km south of Gorontalo, and accessible by *bendi* or *mikrolet*. **Lombongo hot springs**, 17km east of Gorontalo, at the western edge of Bogani Nani Wartabone National Park, has a swimming pool filled with hot spring water. A nicer spot is the **swimming hole** at the foot of a 30m waterfall, which is a 3km walk past the springs. To get to the springs, take the *mikrolet* marked 'Suwawa' from in front of the hospital in Gorontalo.

KOTAMOBAGU

☎ 0434

Kotamobagu (or 'Kota') was once the seat of power for the pre-colonial Bolaang Mongondow kingdoms, but is now a prosperous market town in a fertile valley of towering coconut plantations. There's little to do, but it's a useful stopover between Manado and Gorontalo, and the gateway to the Bogani Nani Wartabone National Park.

Orientation & Information

The main road from the Bonawang bus terminal is Jl Adampe Dolot. This turns into Jl Ahmad Yani through the centre of town, and has several well-stocked supermarkets and a BNI branch (which changes money).

Bogani Nani Wartabone National Park office (☎ 22548; Jl AKD) Along the road to Doloduo, about 5km from central Kotamobagu. Permits, maps and helpful trekking tips.

Tourist office (Jl Ahmad Yani 188) Not much in the way of spoken English or handouts.

Sleeping & Eating

Hotel Ramayana (☎ 21188; Jl Adampe Dolot 50; s/d 38,000/55,000Rp) This hotel has clean, quiet accommodation, and is the best all-rounder in town.

There aren't all that many contenders, but Rumah Makan La Rose is probably the nicest restaurant in town.

Getting There & Away

The main Bonawang bus terminal is a few kilometres from Kotamobagu, in the village of Monglonai, and accessible by *mikrolet*. There are regular buses to Manado (three hours) and Gorontalo (eight hours).

From the central Serasi **bemo terminal** (Jl Borian), Kijangs go to Manado and bemo head to Doloduo.

BOGANI NANI WARTABONE NATIONAL PARK

About 50km west of Kotamobagu, this national park (193,600 hectares) has the highest conservation value in North Sulawesi, but it's mostly inaccessible. The park (formerly known as Dumoga-Bone) is at the headwaters of Sungai Dumoga and is a haven for rare flora and fauna, including black-crested macaque *(yaki)*, and a species of giant fruit bat only discovered in 1992. Finding rare fauna requires patience and luck, but you should see plenty of hornbills and tarsiers.

Visit the **Bogani Nani Wartabone National Park office** (☎ 0434-22548; Jl AKD), on the road to Doloduo, about 5km from central Kotamobagu. At this office you can buy permits (20,000Rp per visit), pick up useful tips, look at decent trekking maps and ask lots of questions. You can also enter the park, and buy a permit at Limboto, near Gorontalo, but this is a long way from the main hiking trails.

You could day trip from Kotamobagu with private transport, but it's best to base yourself in the park in order to appreciate the scenery and spot wildlife while hiking at dawn and/or dusk. The area around the park entrance at Kosinggolan village has several trails, lasting from one to nine hours, and there are various options for overnight jaunts through the jungle if you have camping equipment.

To Kosinggolan, take a regular *mikrolet* to Doloduo from the Serasi terminal in Kotamobagu. Then walk about 2km west (or ask the *mikrolet* driver to continue) to the ranger station at Kosinggolan, just inside the park, where you must register and pick up a compulsory guide for 40,000Rp per short hike (more for longer trips).

MANADO

☎ 0431 / pop 500,000

In 1844 Manado was levelled by earthquakes, so the Dutch redesigned it from scratch. Fourteen years later the famous naturalist

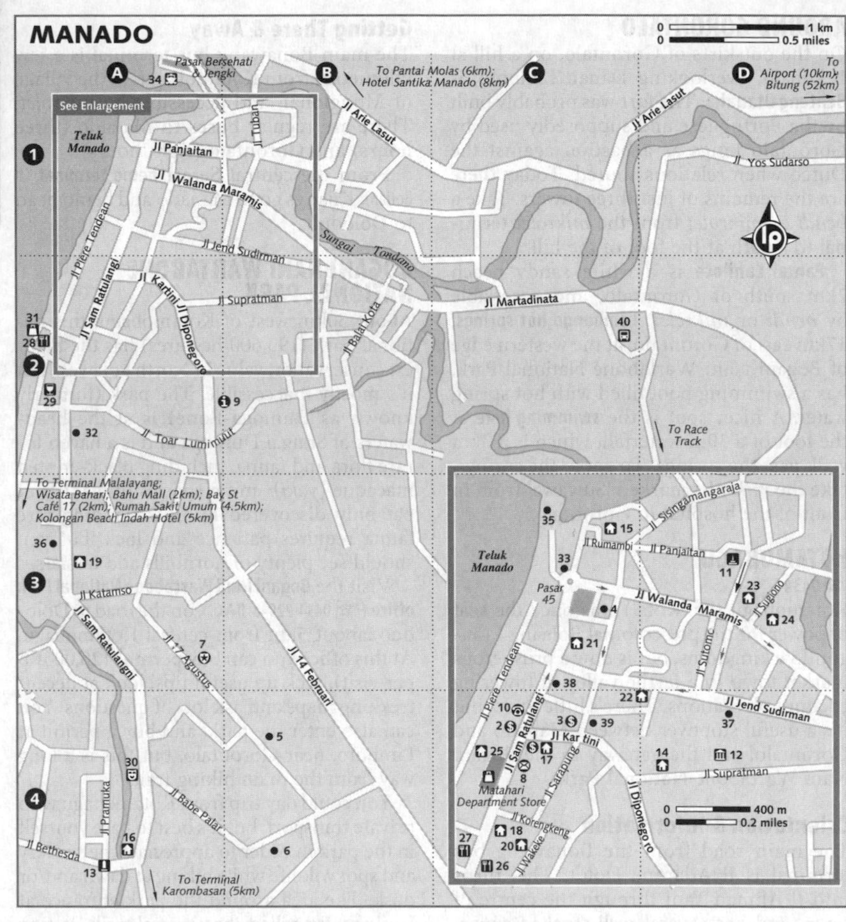

Alfred Wallace visited, and described the city as 'one of the prettiest in the East'. That was 150 years ago and time hasn't been kind to the place. Vestiges of the colonial period have succumbed to a swarm of *mikrolet* and the superb coast has been swallowed by shopping malls. Unattractive though it may be, Manado is a well-stocked base from which to visit the surrounding Minahasan region and islands to the north. It boasts the best wining and dining in North Sulawesi and locals hit the town on weekends.

History

Rice surpluses from Minahasa's volcanic hinterland made Manado a strategic port for European traders sailing to and from the 'Spice Islands' (Maluku). The Dutch helped unite the diverse Minahasan confederacy. By the mid-1800s, compulsory cultivation schemes were producing huge crops of cheap coffee for a Dutch-run monopoly. Minahasans suffered from this 'progress', yet economic, religious and social ties with the colonists continued to intensify. Elsewhere, Minahasan mercenaries put down anti-Dutch rebellions in Java and beyond, earning them the name *anjing Belanda* (Dutch dogs).

The Japanese occupation of 1942–45 was a period of deprivation, and the Allies bombed Manado heavily in 1945. During the war of independence that followed, there was bitter division between the nationalists and those favouring Dutch-sponsored

INFORMATION	
BCA	1 C4
BII Bank	2 C4
BRI Bank	3 C4
City Square	4 C3
Cybernet Café	(see 8)
Immigration Office	5 B4
KSDA (National Parks) Office	6 B4
Main Police Station	7 A3
Main Post Office	8 C4
North Sulawesi Tourism Office	9 B2
Telkom	10 C4
SIGHTS & ACTIVITIES	
Kienteng Ban Hian Kong	11 D3
Museum Negeri Propinsi Sulawesi Utara	12 D4
Sam Ratulangi Monument	13 A4
SLEEPING	
Biteya City Hotel	14 D4
Celebes Hotel	15 C3
Gran Puri Hotel	16 A4
Hotel Anggrek	17 C4
Hotel Central Manado	18 C4
Hotel Minahasa	19 A3
Hotel New Queen	20 C4
Hotel Sahid Kawanua	21 C3
Manado Bersehati Hotel	22 D4
New Angkasa Hotel	23 D3
Rex Hotel	24 D3
Ritzy Hotel	25 C4
EATING	
Dolphin Donats	26 C4
Rumah Makan Green Garden	27 C4
Seafood Warungs	28 A2
DRINKING	
Gacho	29 A2
ENTERTAINMENT	
Ha Ha Café	(see 31)
Studio 21 Cinema	30 A4
SHOPPING	
Mega Mall	31 A2
TRANSPORT	
Adam Air	32 A2
Batavia Air	(see 31)
Boat Ticket Offices	33 C3
Boats to Pulau Bunaken	34 A1
Garuda	(see 31)
Lion Air	(see 31)
Manado Port	35 C3
Mandala	36 A3
Merpati	37 D4
PT Virgo Ekspres	38 C3
Silk Air	39 C4
Terminal Paal 2	40 C2

federalism, and the city was bombed by Indonesian troops in 1958.

Today, the development of Bitung's deep sea port, and direct air links with the Philippines and Singapore, have helped to promote Manado's trade and tourism.

Orientation

Along Jl Sam Ratulangi, the main road running north–south, there are upmarket restaurants, hotels and supermarkets. The 'boulevard', Jl Piere Tendean, is a monstrous thoroughfare with hotels and half-finished shopping malls; it has limited coastal access.

Information

EMERGENCY

The emergency number for ambulances is ☎ 118.

Main police station (☎ inquiries 852162, emergencies 110; Jl 17 Agustus)

IMMIGRATION

Immigration office (☎ 863491; Jl 17 Agustus)

INTERNET ACCESS & POST

Cybernet Café (🕑 8am-10pm) Internet access at the main post office.

Informatics (🕑 8am-10pm) Fastest access in town; on the 4th floor of the Mega Mall.

Main post office (Jl Sam Ratulangi 23; 🕑 8am-7.30pm Mon-Fri, 8am-6pm Sat & Sun)

MEDICAL SERVICES

Rumah Sakit Umum (☎ 853191; Jl Monginsidi; Malalayang) The general hospital is about 4.5km from town and includes a decompression chamber.

MONEY

Manado is overflowing with banks, and it's the best place in the region to exchange money. ATMs can be found at the banks along Jl Sam Ratulangi, plus out at the airport.

BCA bank (Bank Central Asia; Jl Sam Ratulangi) Probably has the best rates, and quickly provides cash advances of up to 3,000,000Rp on Visa and MasterCard. ATMs available.

BII bank (Bank Internasional Indonesia; Jl Sam Ratulangi) Accepts Visa, MasterCard, Alto and Cirrus cards for cash advances, and has an ATM.

BNI bank (Bank Negara Indonesia) ATM and cash advances available at the airport.

TELEPHONE

Numerous wartel around town offer competitive long-distance rates.

Telkom office (Jl Sam Ratulangi; 🕑 24hr)

TOURIST INFORMATION

KSDA office (National Parks office; ☎ 862688; fax 864296; Jl Babe Palar) For informative brochures and advice about trekking in Tangkoko-Batuangas Dua Saudara Nature Reserve, visit this national parks office.

North Sulawesi Tourism Office (☎/fax 852723; Jl Diponegoro 111; 🕑 8am-2pm Mon-Sat) You can get a map and sign the guest book, but that's about it.

Tourist information counter Out at the airport, this is far more useful, with good maps on the wall, and plenty of hotel brochures with current rates.

Sights

Most of the main sights lie beyond the city, however the **Museum Negeri Propinsi Sulawesi Utara** (☎ 870308; Jl Supratman; admission 1000Rp;

SULAWESI

IN THE BEGINNING...

The original Minahasans are said to have descended from Lumimuut, who rose from the sea and gave birth to Toar. After many years' separation, mother and son met again. Not recognising each other, they married and their descendants populated the region. Minahasan lands and languages were divided by the god Muntu Untu at Watu Pinabetengan (Dividing Stone), a carved rock near Kawangkoan.

8am-3.30pm Mon-Thu, 8am-noon Fri) is a possible diversion. It features a large display of traditional costumes and housing implements, with captions in English.

The 19th-century **Kienteng Ban Hian Kong** (Jl Panjaitan) is the oldest Buddhist temple in eastern Indonesia and has been beautifully restored. The temple hosts a spectacular festival in February (dates vary according to the lunar calendar).

Activities

For relief from the incessant heat or an escape from the buzz of *mikrolet*, nonguests can use the **swimming pool** at Hotel Sahid Kawanua for 10,000Rp. There is also a **Superbowl** on the top floor of the Mega Mall for those looking to strike out.

Festivals & Events

Minahasans love an excuse to party. Watch out for these main festivals:

Tai Pei Kong festival Held at Kienteng Ban Hian Kong in February.

Pengucapan Syukur A harvest festival that can take place any time from June to August.

Traditional horse races Second week of August.

Sleeping

Manado has a good range of accommodation to suit all budgets, although most people push on through to Pulau Bunaken or dive resorts in the Manado and Lembeh area – see the Pulau Bunaken entry (p739) or the boxed text on p740 for more details.

BUDGET

Rex Hotel (☎ 851136; fax 867706; Jl Sugiono 3; s 55,000-70,000Rp, d 65,000-85,000Rp;) This small, friendly hotel is not too far from the action. It is worth paying a couple of bucks extra for smarter rooms with TV and bath tub.

Manado Bersehati Hotel (☎ 855022; fax 857238; Jl Sudirman 20; s/d from 42,500/67,500Rp, r with air-con & TV from 95,000Rp;) Signposted from bustling Jl Sudirman, this Minahasan-style building has a big range of small rooms. The self-proclaimed VIP rooms are larger. The hotel flyer includes a handy pocket-sized map of Manado.

Hotel Anggrek (☎ 851970; Jl Kartini 5; r 80,000-120,000Rp;) The most central of the budget places in town, it is far enough from Jl Sam Ratulangi to deliver a peaceful sleep. It is worth investing in the air-con as the rooms can heat up.

Other reliable budget options:

New Angkasa Hotel (☎ 864062; Jl Sugiono 10; r with fan 50,000Rp, with air-con from 75,000Rp;) Some of the best-value budget beds in town.

Biteya City Hotel (☎ 866598; Jl Supratman 11; r with fan/air-con/ste 55,000/100,000/185,000Rp;) Comfortable hotel near the museum with large, well-furnished rooms.

MIDRANGE

Hotel Minahasa (☎/fax 862559; minahasahotel@hotmail.com; Jl Sam Ratulangi 199; r with fan from 100,000Rp, with air-con from 180,000Rp;) This friendly, family-run hotel sprawls up the hillside, with large air-con rooms set around a flourishing garden. TV is not satellite, but the rooms include hot water. Work was underway on a swimming pool and spa during our stay, so prices may rise.

Celebes Hotel (☎ 870425; hotelcelebesmdo@yahoo.com; Jl Rumambi 8A; r 120,000-230,000Rp;) Towering over the port area, ask for a room on the 4th or 5th floor for big vistas over the water. All rooms are spotlessly clean and include air-con and hot water. A word of warning, however, make sure you are clear about the type of room you are getting, as the morning we were here another traveller was caught out when the price changed at check-out time. There are also some budget rooms with shared bath for just 50,000Rp. The rooftop restaurant has great views over the action below and is a fine spot for a sundowner.

Kolongan Beach Indah Hotel (☎/fax 853001; Jl Walter Monginsidi; r 160,000Rp;) Out in Malalayang, this is a quiet, attractive alternative to Manado, and is very handy to the Malalayang bus terminal, about 100m away. The smart rooms have air-con, hot water and satellite TV, and the restaurant is a good spot to wait for a bus.

Hotel Central Manado (☎ 864049; Jl Sam Ratulangi 33; s/d from 150,000/170,000Rp; ❄) Formerly the Jeprinda Hotel, this property has had a recent makeover. The standard rooms lack hot water, but the deluxe rooms from 180,000Rp are a good deal with air-con, satellite TV and a hearty breakfast.

Hotel New Queen (☎ 855551; fax 853049; www.newqueen-manado.com; Jl Wakeke 12; s/d from 192,000/264,000Rp; ❄) This hotel is very proud of the fact that it once won the Governor's trophy for 'cleanest midrange hotel in Manado'. Regularly full, thanks to well-appointed rooms and solid service.

Hotel Sahid Kawanua (☎ 867777; sahidkawanua@telkom.net.id; Jl Sam Ratulangi 1; s/d from 300,000/350,000Rp; ❄ 🏊) This hotel was built in the '70s and the rates here reflect the ageing interior. Popular for conferences, it's not bad value and has a large swimming pool.

TOP END

Gran Puri Hotel (☎ 822888; www.granpuri.com; Jl Sam Ratulangi 458; s/d from 450,000/500,000Rp; ❄ 🏊) The other contender for leading business hotel in Manado. The location is not great, but the rooms are sophisticated. The GPs Club is a popular basement bar.

Hotel Santika Manado (☎ 858222; www.santika-manado.com; r from 600,000Rp; ❄ 🏊) Part of the Santika chain, this major resort has luxurious rooms, a large swimming pool and walkway access through mangroves to the sea. Just 8km from town, this place feels like a world away from Manado. It is also the base for the Thalassa Dive Centre (www.thalassa.net).

Ritzy Hotel (☎ 855555; www.ritzymanado.com; Jl Piere Tendean; s/d from 550,000/605,000Rp; ❄ 🏊) This immense landmark was originally built as a Novotel. The four-star rooms are good value at these discounted prices. Request a sea view.

Kima Bajo Resort (☎ 860999; www.kimabajo.com; r from US$135; ❄ 🏊) The leading boutique resort in the Manado area, Kima Bajo offers indulgent rooms in a choice of bungalows and villas. The Mayana Spa is the place to unwind after a week of diving.

Eating

Adventurous Minahasan cuisine can be found around Manado, especially at the stalls that open up at night on Jl Piere Tendean. Get a taste for *rica-rica,* a spicy stir-fry made with *ayam* (chicken), *babi* (pork) or *r.w.* (pronounced air weh – dog!). *Bubur tinotuan* (corn porridge) and fresh seafood are local specialities worth looking out for.

Most of the malls have extensive food courts on their upper floors. Best are those at Mega Mall and Bahu Mall, but even the smaller shopping centres have cheap eats. Choose from Indonesian, Chinese, Italian and more.

Hidden behind the massive Mega Mall on Jl Piere Tendean is an excellent stretch of seafood warungs that kicks off every night. The price, variety and sunsets are unbeatable. Not all serve alcohol, so shop around if you are in the market for a drink with dinner.

There is a similar stretch of warungs behind the Bahu Mall, Jl Walter Monginsidi, just south of the town centre. Live bands sometimes play on a stage here, so it is better to choose a stall at a safe distance.

Bay St Café 17 (meals 10,000-30,000Rp; 🕑 lunch & dinner) Has some of the best pork ribs in Sulawesi, as well as good selection of fresh fish and cold Bintang.

Rumah Makan Green Garden (Jl Sam Ratulangi; mains 15,000-30,000Rp; 🕑 breakfast, lunch & dinner) This Chinese-Indonesian restaurant is popular for its lengthy seafood menu. However, the seafood's not fresh but frozen, which is a tad disappointing. There are also lots of cheap noodle-based dishes which make a good lunch or snack.

Dolphin Donats (Jl Sam Ratulangi 5; meals 15,000-35,000Rp; 🕑 breakfast, lunch & dinner) Almost opposite the Green Garden, this place predictably specialises in doughnuts and cakes, but there's a surprisingly large range of Indonesian, Chinese and Western food, such as steaks and burgers. Staff are friendly and service is swift.

Wisata Bahari (Jl Wolter Monginsidi; mains 20,000-50,000Rp; 🕑 lunch & dinner) Right next to the Bahu Mall is this huge restaurant built on stilts over the sea. Seafood is priced by weight and it's popular with high rollers from Manado.

Drinking

The drinks of choice are *saguer,* a very quaffable fermented sago wine, and Cap Tikus (literally, Rat Brand), the generic name for distilled *saguer*. Cap Tikus is sold as No 1, No 2 or No 3, referring to its strength (No 1 is the strongest!). It is best diluted and served over ice…with fresh fruit juice for a DIY cocktail.

There aren't many out and out bars in Manado. The best option for a sunset drink is to head to one of the seaside warungs behind the Mega Mall. Stick around and sink some drinks here, as the price rises rapidly in the clubs.

As the evening wears on, the most popular option for locals are the pool bars opening up all over town.

Gacho (Jl Piere Tendean) One of the best of the pool bars, just south of Mega Mall. Pitchers of Bintang are steep at almost 100,000Rp, probably to help subsidise the live band.

Styx (Bahu Mall) Even more sophisticated, and straight out of New York or London.

Corner (Bahu Mall) A couple of floors above Styx, this is a huge sports bar, but it is pretty quiet during the week, only picking up late on Saturdays. Bands from Jakarta sometimes play here and attract a cover charge of 25,000Rp or more. A glass of Bintang costs 25,000Rp.

Be very wary of places promoting karaoke. These are usually dark dens of iniquity, with overpriced drinks and working girls. Regular ruses include sitting at your table for five minutes and adding a hefty charge to the bill.

Entertainment

Music is a way of life for the Minahasans. They love jazz, and there are always small concerts and backroom gigs happening, so ask around.

NIGHTCLUBS

Ha Ha Café (entry incl 1 drink 50,000Rp) The leading club in town, this place is on the top floor of the Mega Mall. It is so vast that it looks like an aircraft hangar and only really fills up on Wednesdays, Fridays and Saturdays. Once the smuggled flasks of Cap Tikus are drained, the crowds loosen up and mob the dance floor.

CINEMA

Studio 21 Cinema (Jl Sam Ratulangi; entry 17,500Rp) The most sophisticated cinema in Manado, it features recent Western releases with Indonesian subtitles.

Getting There & Away

AIR

Manado is well-connected by air with other parts of Indonesia. See map p669 for a guide to prices for flights listed below.

Merpati (Merpati Nusantara Airlines; ☎ 842000; Jl Sudirman 111) has daily flights to Jakarta and Luwuk, and also Jayapura via Sorong; four flights a week to/from Gorontalo, as well as Makassar; three per week to/from Ternate; three a week to Palu; and twice weekly to the Sangir-Talaud islands towns of Melanguane and Naha.

Garuda (Garuda Indonesia; ☎ 877737) flies daily to/from Makassar, with same-day connections to Denpasar and Jakarta.

Adam Air (☎ 8880999) flies daily to/from Surabaya.

Lion Air (☎ 8880022) flies daily to/from Makassar, Jakarta, Denpasar, Ternate and Sorong, and once a week to/from Gorontalo.

Batavia Air (☎ 3864338) offers daily flights to/from Balikpapan and Jakarta.

Tickets for domestic flights often cost slightly less at travel agencies, and agencies often sell international tickets at substantial discounts.

See p668 for details about international flights to/from Manado on Bouraq, Merpati and **Silk Air** (☎ 863744). The international departure tax is 100,000Rp.

BOAT

All Pelni boats use the deep-water port of Bitung, 55km from Manado. Several of the Pelni liners call by once or twice every week: the *Umsini* goes to Balikpapan (economy/1st class 376,000/1,173,000Rp) and Pantoloan; the *Lambelu* goes to Ternate (111,000/317,000Rp) and Ambon (173,000/517,000Rp); the *Kelimutu* to Sorong (228,000/695,000) and Fak Fak; and the *Tilongkabila* to Luwuk (128,000/372,000Rp) and other ports along the southeastern coast.

There is no longer a Pelni office in Manado; the nearest one is in Bitung. However, **PT Virgo Ekspres** (☎ 858610; Jl Sam Ratulangi 5) is a reliable Pelni agent for checking information and purchasing tickets.

Every Monday, Wednesday and Friday afternoon the **Ratu Maria** (☎ 855851) makes the overnight trip to Pulau Siau (55,000Rp) and Tahuna (93,000Rp) in the Sangir-Talaud Islands.

Small, slow and uncomfortable boats leave Manado every day or two for Tahuna and Lirung, also in the Sangir-Talaud Islands; and to Mangole, Sanana, Tobelo and Ambon in Maluku. Tickets are available from the stalls outside the port. From Bitung, four overnight ferries a week also travel to Ternate in Northern Maluku.

BUS

There are three reasonably orderly terminals for long-distance buses and the local *mikrolet*.

From Terminal Karombasan, 5km south of the city, buses go to Tomohon (4000Rp), Tondano (5000Rp) and other places south of Manado. From the far southern Terminal Malalayang, very regular buses go to Kotamobagu (17,000Rp) and Gorontalo (60,000Rp, eight hours).

From Terminal Paal 2, at the eastern end of Jl Martadinata, varied public transport runs to Bitung (5500Rp) and the airport (2000Rp).

Getting Around

TO/FROM THE AIRPORT

Mikrolet from Sam Ratulangi International Airport go to Terminal Paal 2 (2000Rp), where you can change to a *mikrolet* heading to Pasar 45 or elsewhere in the city, for a flat fee of 1500Rp. Fixed-price taxis cost 70,000Rp from the airport to the city (13km).

PUBLIC TRANSPORT

It seems that Manado's *mikrolet*, if put bumper to bumper, would wrap around the city 75 times. On the bright side, finding one with a spare seat is a matter of waiting a second or two. They're not too hard to work out: look for the sign on top of the vehicle, check the direction it's going in and double-check the tiny sign on the window. *Mikrolet* heading south on Jl Sam Ratulangi with 'Wanea' on the window sign will go to Terminal Karombasan. Most *mikrolet* heading north go through Pasar 45 (with a few traffic jams along the way), and past the Pasar Jengki fish market, but some go directly to Terminal Paal 2 along Jl Sudirman. *Mikrolet* heading to Terminal Malalayang go down Jl Piere Tendean. The fare for any destination around town is 1500Rp.

Private taxis circle the city and the air-conditioning can be a relief on a hot day. However, very few drivers are willing to use the meter, so negotiate before setting off.

PULAU BUNAKEN

☎ 0431

The incredible shapes and colours of the fringing coral off the small island of Bunaken have earned it celebrity status among divers and snorkellers around the world. The marine biodiversity here is extraordinary, with more than 300 types of coral and 3000 species of fish. Drift along the reefs and enjoy the ultimate underwater epic. The 808-hectare island is part of the 75,265-hectare **Bunaken Manado Tua Marine National Park** (Taman Laut Bunaken Manado Tua), which includes: Manado Tua (Old Manado), the dormant volcano that can be seen from Manado, and climbed in about four hours; Nain and Mantehage islands; and Pulau Siladen, which has some more accommodation options.

The nearby city of Manado is both a blessing and a curse for Bunaken. It's a blessing as it has an airport offering connections with Singapore and most parts of Indonesia and is the supply base for the island, but ultimately it is proving a curse, as huge amounts of garbage are generated by the city and westerly winds often sweep mounds of the stuff onto Pantai Liang, turning the picturesque tropical beach into a refuse heap overnight.

Most of Pulau Bunaken's residents live in Bunaken village at the southern tip. The scarcity of fresh water has limited the island's development, and villagers must import their drinking water from Manado. Washing water is drawn from small, brackish wells. Pantai Liang is the most developed part of the island for tourism, but the rubbish problem means that many prefer to stay around Pantai Pangalisang on the east side of the island. There is a concrete path connecting Pangalisang and Liang, about a 30-minute walk, and both beaches are also connected by path to Bunaken village. The best beach is actually just to the north of Bunaken village, close to MC Homestay.

Many of the tourists who come to dive around Bunaken are on short vacations from Europe and elsewhere. This tends to mean higher prices on Bunaken than the mainland when it comes to things like Bintang beer. It also means some of the resorts

DIVING & SNORKELLING AROUND PULAU BUNAKEN

Bunaken boasts some of the world's most spectacular and accessible coral drop-offs, caves and valleys, full of brightly coloured sponges and fish – it is also common to see turtles, rays, dolphins and sharks. The most accessible site is the flat coral off Pantai Liang, which takes a dramatic 90-degree turn less than 100m offshore, plummeting from 1m to 2m depths into dark oblivion.

The best snorkelling and diving sites are marked on maps in most homestays on Bunaken, and any decent boatman will know where to take you. **Pantai Liang** and **Pantai Pangalisang** are good, accessible spots for those not chartering a boat. Well-worn snorkelling equipment can be rented from most homestays on Bunaken for about 40,000Rp per day, but it is often worth paying a little more to rent some quality equipment from one of the dive centres. The snorkelling is effortless, as currents carry you along the reef. A good option is to put in near Lorenso's Beach Garden and exit at Two Fish. The only disappointment for snorkellers is the sheer number of plastic bags floating by; just as you think you have seen a graceful ray, damn, it's another bag. Divers are at a real advantage, as they can leave behind any surface scum.

The rates for dive trips do vary, but it's obviously very important to use a qualified centre with well-maintained equipment. Trips around Bunaken and nearby islands, including most equipment, transport, lunch and a guide, will cost about US$60 for two dives; US$20 for subsequent dives; and US$300 to US$400 for PADI courses. Some places charge in euros rather than US dollars.

It is worth checking whether companies are members of the **North Sulawesi Watersports Association** (NSWA; www.divenorthsulawesi.com), which promotes conservation activities and local community initiatives. This organisation has almost 20 members and keeps on growing.

There are several reliable dive centres based on Pulau Bunaken and it is possible to shop around before committing.

Bastiano's (☎ 853566; www.bastianos.com; Pantai Liang) Caters mainly to European dive tourists on packages.

Bunaken Divers (☎ 3306034; www.bunakendivers.com; Pantai Pangalisang) Friendly Australian-run outfit that has been around a while.

Cha Cha Divers (☎ 081 24301356; www.bunakenchacha.com; Pantai Pangalisang) Small dive operator with the emphasis on a personal touch.

Froggies Dive Centre (☎ 850210; www.divefroggies.com; Pantai Liang) Pioneers of the famed lazy dive where the current does the work.

Living Colours (☎ 081 24306063; www.livingcoloursdiving.com; Pantai Pangalisang) One of the newer centres which has quickly made a name for itself.

Sulawesi Dive Quest (☎ 863023; www.sulawesi-dive-quest.com; Pantai Liang) Another operator concentrating on short-stay dive tourists from afar.

Two Fish Divers (☎ 081 1432805; www.twofishdivers.com; Pantai Pangalisang) Popular English-run operation that operates small groups and with no time limits.

There are also several operators based at resorts on the mainland and other islands that offer fully inclusive dive packages for five days or more:

Barracuda (☎ 854279; www.barracuda-diving.com) Based at their own bungalow resort on Pantai Molas, northeast of Manado.

Celebes Divers (☎ 826582; www.kudalaut.com) Operating from Italian-run Mapia Resort, about 8km south of Manado.

Eco Divers (☎ 824445; www.eco-divers.com) Based at the charming Tasik Ria Resort about 20km south of Manado.

Lumba Lumba Diving (☎ 826151; www.lumbalumbadiving.com) Promoting personal service, this homely dive centre has a loyal following. It's about 20km south of Manado.

Murex (☎ 826091; www.murexdive.com) One of the longest-running dive operators in the area, with a resort to the south of Manado and liveaboards roving further afield.

Nusantara Diving Centre (☎ 863988; www.ndcmanado.com) The daddy of dive operators around Bunaken, with its own impressive resort on Molas Beach, northeast of Manado.

Odyssea Divers (☎ 860999; www.odysseadivers.com) Based at the luxurious Kima Bajo Resort on the mainland.

For more on diving the Lembeh Strait, see p743.

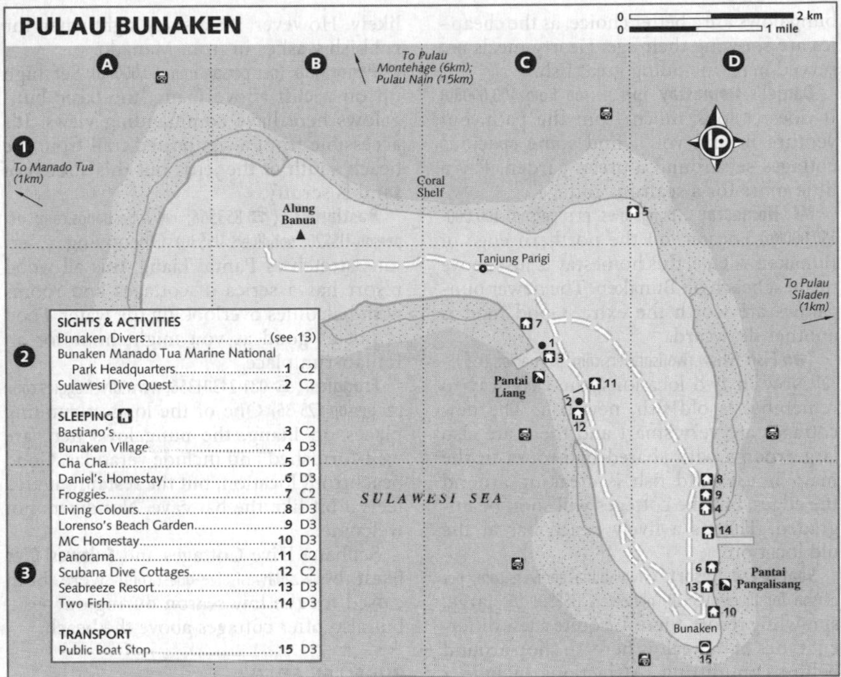

actively discriminate against nondivers, either by charging higher accommodation prices or turning them away. Diving is where the real money is made on this island.

Information

In an attempt to finance conservation activities, rubbish disposal, mangrove rehabilitation, local education programmes and the policing of any illegal fishing practices, an entrance fee system has been introduced for visiting Bunaken Manado Tua Marine National Park. The fee is 50,000Rp per day or 150,000Rp for one year, payable at the national park headquarters just off Pantai Liang on Bunaken or through tourism operators. The permit, in the shape of a plastic tag, should be worn while within the park boundaries.

Activities

BOAT TRIPS

For those with less time and more money, some of the dive operators and hotels can organise day trips to Bunaken on yachts, glass-bottom boats and pseudo-submarines.

Sleeping & Eating

There are more than a dozen resorts scattered around Bunaken and all prices quoted include three meals per day. There are plenty of budget and midrange resorts, but no luxurious hideaways, so if you want serious comfort, stick with the mainland resorts or try Pulau Siladen. Most rooms include at least a fan and a mosquito net and most places throw in transfers to and from the jetty in Bunaken village, in some cases to the mainland. Consider bringing some snacks and treats from the mainland, as there is not much available on the island beyond the set meals.

PANTAI PANGALISANG

The homestays at Pantai Pangalisang mostly overlook the mangroves, but are only metres from some extraordinary snorkelling sites and are very close to the island's best beach at Bunaken village.

Lorenso's Beach Garden (www.lorenso-bunaken.com; bungalows 80,000-120,000Rp) Run by lifelong islander Lorenso, these basic bungalows have a nice setting by the water. The bigger bungalows are a better choice, as the cheapies are showing their age. Hearty meals are served here, including great fish.

Daniel's Homestay (per person from 100,000Rp) It doesn't look much from the path, but venture in and you'll find some spacious cottages set around a green garden. Pay a little more for a seafront cottage.

MC Homestay (bungalows per person 100,000-150,000Rp) Located on the northern edge of Bunaken village, this homestay is just above the best beach on Bunaken. The newer bungalows are worth the extra. Good food is another drawcard.

Two Fish (www.twofishdivers.com; per person US$15-30) Now in two locations, the easy way to remember is old fish, new fish. The new cottages are very smart and there are also large rooms with shared bathroom in the main house. Old fish is creaking around the edges, but the cottages will soon be upgraded. There's a lively beach bar at the old location.

Seabreeze Resort (www.bunakendivers.com; per person for divers US$20, nondivers US$30) A large, sprawling resort, there are quite a few different types of bungalow here, so shop around before committing. Attractions include a verdant garden, good beach access and very cold beers thanks to the Ozzie owner.

Bunaken Village (www.bunakenvillage.com; cottages from €20;) A small, new place with very well-appointed cottages. The Western bathrooms are a delight and there is even a small swimming pool for a cooling dip.

our pick **Living Colours** (www.livingcoloursdiving.com; per person €25;) The bungalows here are beautifully set on a hillside above the sea. Tasteful furnishings include coconut wood beds, rattan chairs and Balinese drapes, and the bathrooms are spotless. The best all-rounder on the island.

Cha Cha (www.bunakenchacha.com; per person from US$50) In splendid isolation on the north-eastern tip of the island, 'The Last Resort' as it is sometimes nicknamed, has an intimate atmosphere thanks to just six bungalows. The menu is more varied than most, with Italian and Japanese to complement the local meals.

PANTAI LIANG

The homestays at Pantai Liang are closer together on a good stretch of sand, which means impromptu beach parties are more likely. However, it's a sorry sight when the rubbish washes in from Manado.

Panorama (per person from 80,000Rp) Set high up on a cliff above Liang, the basic bungalows here have commanding views. It's accessible from a signposted trail from the beach south of the jetty, but this stretch of sand is scruffy.

Bastiano's (☎ 853566; www.bastianos.com; per person US$20, nondivers US$30) Occupying a serious stretch of Pantai Liang, this all-wood resort has a series of cottages and rooms with balconies overlooking the water. Food is not as good as you might hope for an Italian-run place.

Froggies (☎ 081 24301356; www.divefroggies.com; per person €25-35) One of the longest-running places on Liang, the bungalows here are well-furnished and include verandas. Good beachfront location, but the restaurant area feels a bit like the bat cave. Nondivers not welcome.

Scubana Dive Cottages and **Sulawesi Dive Quest** (www.sulawesi-dive-quest.com) were both closed for the low season during our visit, but also offer cottages above the beach.

PULAU SILADEN

Pulau Siladen Martha Homestay (r 80,000Rp) Located in the fishing village in nearby Pulau Siladen, it offers a basic but friendly alternative to Bunaken.

Siladen Resort & Spa (www.siladen.com; r from US$120) A beautiful new resort on Siladen, the 15 cottages here are sumptuously furnished. Facilities include a lagoon pool, an indulgent spa and dive centre.

Getting There & Away

Every day at about 3pm, except Sunday, a public boat (25,000Rp, one hour) leaves the harbour, near Pasar Jengki fish market in Manado, for Bunaken village and Pulau Siladen. The boat doesn't normally stop at Liang or Pangalisang, so you'll have to walk from the boat landing in Bunaken village (near the huge church) to your homestay, or charter something directly from Manado to the jetties at Liang or Pangalisang beaches. The boat leaves Bunaken between 7am and 8am daily (except Sunday), so it's not possible to day-trip from Manado using the public boat.

Most travellers charter a boat. Boatmen will approach you when you walk along the

DIVING THE LEMBEH STRAIT

Lembeh has emerged as the critter capital of Indonesia. For the uninitiated, welcome to an alien world on our very own planet. Critters are the weird and wonderful creatures that inhabit the murky depths and are much admired by underwater photographers. However, this is muck diving and not for beginners thanks to strong currents. If it is coral you are after, you are better off around Bunaken. As Lembeh's fame grows, so do the number of dive resorts catering to visitors. All are set in their own secluded bays, but without transport it is nigh on impossible to travel between them. Packages usually include accommodation and meals, all dives and transfers from and to Manado airport. Some popular resorts:

Divers Lodge (☎ 081 24433754; www.diving-on-sulawesi.com) One of the more affordable options in the Lembeh area.

Gangga Island Resort (☎ 082 4313809; www.ganggaisland.com) OK, so it's not really Lembeh, but midway between here and Pulau Bunaken, but it deserves a mention. Elegant bungalows, a beautiful pool, clear seas – it's a real paradise.

Kungkungan Bay Resort (www.divekbr.com) The first resort to open in the Lembeh area, it has recently been renovated with a pool added. Diving with Eco Divers.

Lembeh Resort (☎ 0438-30667; www.lembehresort.com) Expensive Balinese-style resort in a private bay on Pulau Lembeh. Diving with Murex (see p740).

Two Fish Divers (☎ 081 1432805; www.twofishdivers.com) Affordable new resort, run by the popular Bunaken dive operator Two Fish (see p740).

road towards Pasar Jengki; in Bunaken, ask around the beach or your homestay. Prices vary based on the size of the boat. Cheapest are the outriggers, but these aren't that stable on choppy waters. Expect to pay 100,000 to 150,000Rp. Next are the small covered speedboats that can take four to six people and these are around 200,000 to 250,000Rp one way. Finally there are bigger boats able to take a dozen or more people that cost about 350,000 to 400,000Rp. Bear in mind that conditions are sometimes too choppy for any boats to make the crossing.

TOMOHON

☎ 0431 / pop 30,000

Tomohon is a pleasant, cool respite from Manado, with a stunning setting below Gunung Lokon volcano. It's popular with city folk on weekends; for travellers, it's a possible alternative to Manado, and an ideal base from which to explore the many nearby attractions. Tomohon's market offers a culinary adventure.

Sleeping

There are several excellent budget homestays clustered together at the foot of Gunung Lokon volcano. To get to Lokon Valley Homestay, Happy Flower Homestay or Volcano resort, catch the Manado–Tomohon bus, and get out at 'Gereja Pniel', a few kilometres before Tomohon. There is a sign pointing to Lokon Valley Homestay.

Lokon Valley Homestay (☎ 354262; r 80,000Rp) This super-friendly homestay has some of the best traveller information on offer anywhere in Sulawesi. The rooms are clean and include Western bathroom. The family enjoy promoting local cuisine; meals should be ordered in advance as all food is freshly prepared.

Happy Flower Homestay (☎ 352780; cottages 85,000Rp) Set in a pretty garden, the bungalows here were recently renovated and include hot water and a balcony. There is a central dining area on stilts, plus a pool table under the main house.

Volcano Resort (☎ 352988; cottages 85,000Rp) The cottages are great value, as they are virtual suites with a big bed, sofa and Western bathroom. There are also some budget rooms with shared bathroom at 40,000Rp.

Kawanua Cottages (☎ 352060; cottages from 110,000Rp; 🏊) Set around an immaculate garden with a swimming pool, the bungalows here are well equipped but beginning to show their age. It's about 4km south of Tomohon, on the road to Sonder.

Hotel Wawo (☎ 352449; r 165,000Rp) On the road to Uluindano, this three-room hotel is more like a homestay. Rooms come with hot water and satellite TV and the family suite is a virtual house in itself.

Highland Resort (☎ 353333; www.highlandresort.info; r from US$20) Located about 5km outside Tomohon near the road to Manado, this all-wooden resort has a healthy selection of bungalows. Amenities include satellite TV and hot water.

Gardenia Retreat (☎ 353333; gardenia@indosat.net.id; r from US$58, chalets from US$84) An oasis in beautifully manicured gardens, the chalets here are like a Balinese hideaway. Discounts available.

Eating

Minahasa's extraordinary cuisine is served in a string of restaurants on a cliff overlooking Manado, just a few kilometres before Tomohon. The food at **Pemandangan** (meals 15,000-45,000Rp) is as impressive as the spectacular views, with great seafood plus Indonesian staples. The bus from Manado to Tomohon will drop you off at any restaurant, but buses back to Manado are often full. Some of the hotels in Tomohon have restaurants open to the public, and there are plenty of simple *rumah makan* around town, especially at Tomohon's market.

Getting There & Around

Mikrolet and minibuses regularly travel to Tomohon (4000Rp, 40 minutes) from Terminal Karombasan in Manado. From the terminal in Tomohon, based around an abandoned petrol station along the main road, buses go to Manado, and *mikrolet* go to Tondano and various other towns.

There are a few *bendi* around town, but a good way to see local sights in quick time is to charter a *mikrolet*, or a more comfortable, but expensive, taxi. The taxis line up opposite the *mikrolet* terminal.

AROUND TOMOHON

Gunung Lokon volcano (1580m) contains a constantly simmering crater lake of varying hues, which takes about three hours to reach (and another hour to the peak) from Tomohon. Before climbing any volcano in the area, report to the **volcanology centre** (Kantor Dinas Gunung Berapi; ☎ 351076; Jl Kakashashen Tiga) in Tomohon. The centre can provide advice about the hike, and it also has spectacular photographs of other volcanoes. Lokon Valley Homestay in Tomohon can help arrange this, and other hikes in the area, for guests.

There are numerous other places to explore from Tomohon, and all are accessible by *mikrolet*. **Danau Linow**, a small, highly sulphurous lake that changes colours with the light, is home to extensive birdlife. Take a *mikrolet* to **Sonder**, get off at **Lahendong** and walk (1.5km) to the lake. From Danau Linow, you can also hike (8km) to Danau Tondano, but you'll need to ask directions.

DANAU TONDANO

This lake, 30km south of Manado, is 600m above sea level. It's a beautiful area for **hiking**, and is popular with Manado's upper class, who flock here for Sunday lunch. Just before Remboken village, along the road around the lake, **Objek Wisata Remboken** has a swimming pool, a wonderful restaurant overlooking the lake and some gardens to wander around. There are also several decent restaurants along the road around the lake, where fresh fish is, naturally, the speciality.

Mikrolet regularly leave for Tondano village (5500Rp) from Terminal Karombasan in Manado, or you can get there by *mikrolet* from Tomohon (2000Rp). From Tondano, catch another *mikrolet* to Remboken, and get off anywhere you like along the road around the lake.

AIRMADIDI

Airmadidi (Boiling Water) is the site of mineral springs. Legend has it that nine angels flew down from heaven on nights of the full moon to bathe and frolic here. One night a mortal succeeded in stealing a dress belonging to one of the angels – unable to return to heaven, she was forced to remain on earth.

Airmadidi's real attraction is the odd little **pre-Christian tombs** known as *waruga*. Corpses were placed in these carved stone boxes, in a foetal position, with household articles, gold and porcelain, but most have been plundered. There's a group of these tombs at Airmadidi Bawah, a 15-minute walk from the Airmadidi *mikrolet* terminal.

Mikrolet to Airmadidi leave from Terminal Paal 2 in Manado (3000Rp), and there are connections between Airmadidi and Tondano and Bitung.

GUNUNG KLABAT

Gunung Klabat (2022m) is easily the highest peak on the peninsula. The obvious path to the crater at the top starts behind the police station at Airmadidi, where you must register and take a guide. The climb (about four hours to the top, two for the descent) goes through rainforest where you can see superb flora and fauna, but it's a tough hike.

It's best to camp overnight near the top and be there for the sunrise and the stupendous views across the whole peninsula. Your guide should be able to provide a tent. Try to avoid Sunday, when the mountain can be surprisingly crowded with local hikers. This area was the last hideout for the anti-Indonesian rebels in the late 1950s and early '60s, and it's easy to see how they evaded capture for so long.

BITUNG

☎ 0438 / pop 137,000

Sheltered by Pulau Lembeh, Bitung is the chief regional port, and home to many factories. Despite its spectacular setting, the town is unattractive, so most travellers make for Manado or beyond as soon as possible.

Regardless of what time you arrive by boat in Bitung, there will be buses going to Manado, but if you need to leave Bitung by boat early in the morning it may be prudent to stay overnight. Be vigilant around the docks, as plenty of pickpockets turn up to greet the Pelni liners.

Hotel Nalendra (☎ 32072; Jl Samuel Languyu 5A; r from 120,000Rp) has been recommended by readers who have been stranded in Bitung over the years. The clean rooms include hot water, TV and air-con.

There are plenty of basic *rumah makan* in the town centre and near the port.

Getting There & Away

Bitung is connected to other towns by a surfaced racetrack along which *mikrolet* drivers often attempt to break land speed records. All sorts of vehicles leave regularly from Terminal Paal 2 in Manado (5500Rp, one hour). The driver stops at Terminal Mapalus, just outside Bitung, from where you have to catch another *mikrolet* (10 minutes) to town or the port.

See p738 for details about boats to Bitung. The port is in the middle of Bitung, and the **Pelni office** (☎ 35818) is in the port complex.

TANGKOKO-BATUANGAS DUA SAUDARA NATURE RESERVE

Tangkoko is one of the most impressive and accessible nature reserves in Indonesia, and includes some coastline and coral gardens offshore. About 30km from Bitung, the 8800 hectares are home to black macaques, cuscus and tarsiers, maleo birds and endemic red-knobbed hornbills, among other fauna, and rare types of rainforest flora. Tangkoko is also home to a plethora of midges, called *gonones,* which bite and leave victims furiously scratching for days afterwards. Always wear long trousers, tucked into thick socks, and take covered shoes. Sadly, parts of the park are falling victim to encroachment by local communities.

To enter the park, you need a permit from the KSDA (National Parks) field office in Batuputih, which costs 20,000Rp. The office can organise knowledgeable guides to lead you along designated hiking trails (about 6km each) to view wildlife, and boat trips to nearby islands to see the preserved nesting grounds of maleo. The **KSDA office** (National Parks office; ☎ 0431-862688; fax 864296; Jl Babe Palar) in Manado is a good source of information, and worth visiting before heading to Tangkoko.

TARSIERS

If you're visiting Sulawesi's Tangkoko-Batuangas Dua Saudara Nature Reserve or Lore Lindu National Park, keep your eyes peeled for something looking back at you: a tiny nocturnal primate known as a tarsier. These creatures are recognisable by their eyes, which are literally larger than their stomachs, so big in fact that they cannot rotate them within their sockets. Luckily their heads can be rotated nearly 360 degrees so their range of vision isn't compromised. Tarsiers also have huge sensitive ears, which can be retracted and unfurled, and disproportionately long legs, which they use to jump distances 10 times their body length. They use their anatomical anomalies to catch small insects. Tarsiers live in groups of up to eight, and communicate with what sounds like high-pitched singing. They are found only in some rainforests of Indonesia and the Philippines.

You could take a day trip from Manado with your own transport, but it's worth staying in, or near, the park so you can hike at dawn and/or dusk – easily the best times to see the wildlife. There are several basic losmen in Batuputih village – the best is probably **Mama Roos** (mamaroos@eudoramail.com; r incl meals 100,000Rp). Inside the park you can stay at **Ranger Homestay** (r 75,000Rp). If you have a tent, you can camp on the black-sand beach.

The **Pulisan Jungle Beach Resort** (☎ 0431-838185; www.pulisanresort-sulawesi.com; s/d bungalows incl meals from €27/35), located just to the north of the Tangkoko nature reserve, is an idyllic base to explore the region, dive into pristine waters, go bird-watching, hike or just take it easy. Boat trips to the national park are available and there is a beautiful stretch of sand here.

The main entrance is at Batuputih. From Manado, take a bus to Bitung, get off at Girian and catch a *mikrolet* to Batuputih. Some of the dive centres and hotels in and around Manado also run day trips to the park.

SANGIR-TALAUD ISLANDS

☎ 0432

Strewn across the sea between Indonesia and the southern Philippines are the volcanic island groups of Sangir and Talaud. There are 77 islands, of which 56 are inhabited. The main islands in the Sangir group are Sangir Besar and Siau; the main islands in the Talaud group are Karakelong, Salibabu and Kaburuang. The capital of the group is Tahuna on Sangir Besar; the other major settlement is Lirung on Pulau Salibabu.

There's a **tourist office** (☎ 22219; Jl Tona) in Tahuna.

Sights

The islands offer dozens of unspoilt sandy beaches; a few crumbling **Portuguese forts**; several **volcanoes** to climb; many caves and waterfalls to explore; and some superb **diving** and **snorkelling** (bring your own gear). But like most wonderfully pristine places, the islands are not easy to reach.

Sleeping & Eating

Rainbow Losmen (r 55,000Rp) Located further south along the coast from Tahuna in nearby Tamoko, this is a simple, friendly establishment in a pretty village.

Hotel Nasional (☎ 21185; Jl Makaampo 58; Tahuna; s/d with fan 50,000/75,000Rp, with air-con from 90,000/120,000Rp; ❄) Head here for a range of decent rooms, plus the best restaurant in Tahuna.

Hotel Victory Veronica (☎ 21494; Jl Ramenusa 16; Tahuna; r with fan/air-con 60,000/90,000Rp; ❄) The smartest place anywhere on the islands. It also has the decent Deniest Coffee Shop.

Penginapan Chindy (s/d around 30,000/45,500Rp) and **Penginapan Sederhana** (s/d around 30,000/45,500Rp) are both on Lirung, but don't expect too much luxury or privacy.

Getting There & Away

AIR

Twice a week, Merpati flies from Manado to Naha, which is about 20km from Tahuna; and on to Melanguane, which is near Lirung in the Talaud group. There's a **Merpati office** (Merpati Nusantara Airlines; ☎ 21037; Jl Makaampo) in Tahuna.

BOAT

Travelling by boat will give you a look at the stunning set of volcanic islands along the way. From Bitung (near Manado), the Pelni liner *Tilongkabila* stops at Tahuna and Lirung once every two weeks. Pelni boats are far more comfortable than the other options, such as the *Pulo Teratai* and the *Agape Star*, which sail between Manado and Lirung (15 hours), often stopping in Tahuna (11 hours), every one or two days. Book at the boat offices near the port in Manado.

Every Monday, Wednesday and Friday afternoon the **Ratu Maria** (☎ 0431-855851) makes the overnight trip from Manado to Siau (55,000Rp) and Tahuna (93,000Rp).

Also from Manado, small, slow and uncomfortable boats leave every day or two for Tahuna and Lirung. Tickets are available from the stalls outside the port.

The seas can get quite rough during the high wind of October to April.

Maluku

Formerly known as 'the Moluccas', these petite little morsels of paradise are a dream-come-true for seekers of superb snorkelling and picture-perfect white-sand beaches. Protected from mass tourism by distance and a (now outdated) reputation for civil unrest, this is one corner of the world where dreamy desert islands remain remarkably hospitable and inexpensive. In Maluku everything still moves delightfully slowly, except perhaps the lilting sound of Poco Poco, the home-grown answer to line dancing. With rustic but acceptable facilities and not another tourist for miles, this is somewhere to wind down a few gears, to learn Bahasa Indonesia and to revel in a tropical discovery that seems almost too good to be true.

Maluku also offers a thrill for history buffs. The Moluccas were the original 'Spice Islands'. Indian, Chinese, Arab and, later, European adventurers all came here in search of cloves and nutmeg. Until the 16th century such spices were worth their weight in gold and grew nowhere else. Thus in Maluku money literally 'grew on trees'. Today it's incredible to reflect that the search for this wealth began the whole process of European colonialism.

Maluku is remote and timetables aren't always convenient. Nonetheless, with regular flights into the region, and some flexibility and planning once here, it's possible to snorkel the brilliant Bandas, explore the beach strewn Kei Islands, survey North Maluku's mesmerising volcano-islands and explore ruined Dutch fortresses all within the limits of a one-month visa.

HIGHLIGHTS

- Snorkelling some of the world's finest accessible coral gardens in the historically fascinating **Banda Islands** (p765)
- Unwinding at **Ohoidertawun** (p777) or **Pasir Panjang** (p778), two stunning yet virtually undiscovered sweeps of the purest white sand
- Dining at **Floridas** or **Teratai** (p786) on Pulau Ternate as the sunset burnishes golden highlights onto the jungle-furred volcanic cone of neighbouring **Pulau Tidore** (p787)
- Being amongst the first tourists for a decade to explore the sleepy villages of the **Lease Islands** (p760) or **northern Seram** (p764)
- Discovering a desert island all for yourself off **Tobelo** (p789) on Halmahera

- POPULATION: 2 MILLION
- LAND AREA: 85,728 SQ KM
- HIGHEST PEAK: GUNUNG BINAYA (3027M)

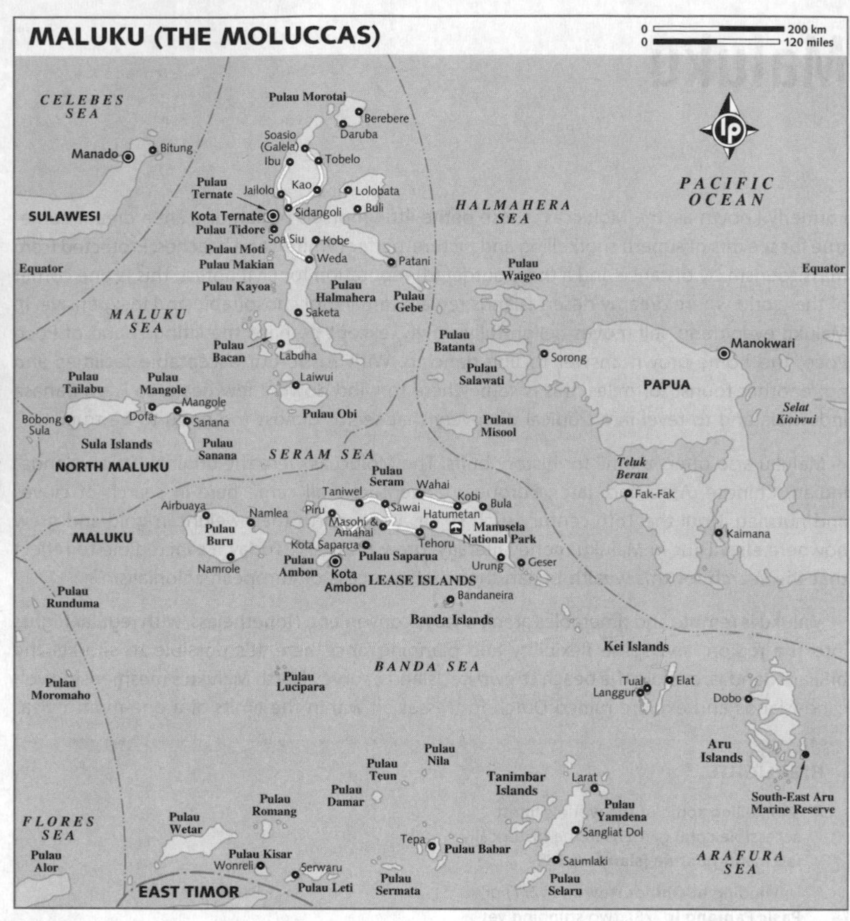

HISTORY

Precolonial Times

The name Maluku probably originated as *Jazirat-al-Muluk* (Land of Many Kings). The 'kings' in question ruled Ternate, Tidore, Bacan and other Maluku 'spice islands'. Their majestic fleets of *kora-kora* war-canoes policed empires that sometimes extended as far afield as Sulawesi and Papua. Their fabulous wealth came from a global monopoly of clove and other spice production. Spices preserved food in a world without refrigerators. And they complemented leeches to offer the best available medical hope against an array of medieval ailments. By the 1st century AD, Maluku spices were reaching Europe via tortuous and risky caravan routes through India and the Persian Gulf. This made them vastly expensive. Eventually Europeans figured out that they could save money by seeking the source of the spices for themselves.

The Portuguese

The Portuguese showed up in 1510. Their intercontinental expedition incurred awful losses of lives and ships but still managed to prove financially profitable. The Portuguese cheekily tried to reduce their costs by demanding a trade monopoly. Without any intention to respect such terms, Ternate's sultan agreed to a Portuguese clove monopoly in return for help against arch-enemy Tidore. Tidore responded by enlisting Spanish military assistance. Consistently committing cultural blunders, the Europeans soon outstayed their welcome and, having failed to monopolise the local clove trade, the Portuguese 'retired' south to trade from Ambon, Seram and the Banda Islands after 1795.

The Dutch

In the late 16th century the Dutch arrived with better guns and greater financial backing. Their bigger ships could use faster, direct sea routes from South Africa that were operable year round. This trumped their Hispanic competitors who stuck to slower, seasonal coastal routes via India. While seeing off new English rivals, the Dutch repeated many of the same cultural faux pas that had brought down the Portuguese. However, their determination to control a spice monopoly was brutally enforced, most infamously in the Banda Islands where uncooperative islanders were simply massacred. They were replaced by more compliant Dutch-owned slaves.

Fights to subjugate Ternate and Ambon took longer but, by the 1660s, the Dutch had wiped out all local opposition to their rule in Maluku and had evicted the last Spanish garrisons from Ternate and Tidore. The spice monopoly made a fortune for Holland over the next century. However, without competition, the operation became increasingly inefficient. It eventually collapsed into bankruptcy in 1795 and the Dutch East India Company (VOC) was nationalised. A year later, with Holland suffering the aftermath of the French Revolution, the British occupied Maluku. Politically this was a short episode. But commercially it spelt disaster for the Moluccas. The British smuggled out precious spice-tree seedlings to plant in their colonies in Malaya (Malaysia) and Ceylon (Sri Lanka). Within decades Maluku was becoming economically irrelevant as its spices could now be produced cheaply elsewhere.

After Independence

After WWII it soon became apparent that Indonesia was heading for independence as a unified single republic. This would inevitably be mainly Muslim and Javanese controlled. Predominantly Christian southern Maluku panicked and tried to break away in 1950 by proclaiming the Republik Maluku Selatan (RMS). Indonesian republican troops steadily retook the islands and by November the RMS 'government' had fled Ambon. However in the Seram jungles, armed RMS opposition rumbled on until the mid-1960s.

Christian Ambonese and Kei Islanders had been a major element in the Royal Netherlands Indies Army (KNIL). Several thousand KNIL troops in Java had stayed loyal to the Dutch during the independence tussles. Once the Dutch decided (under American pressure) to accept Indonesian independence, some 12,000 Malukans were

SPICY CENGKEH & PALA

Cloves were the ancient world's cure for toothache, halitosis and sexual disinterest. Today they're popular in mulled wine and cooking, and used in the manufacture of chewing gum, perfumes, toothpaste and distinctive Indonesian *kretek* cigarettes. They're the unopened flower buds of the *cengkeh* tree, originally native to Ternate, Tidore and Bacan. Today, however, cloves are also grown on Seram and Ambon and as far afield as Tanzania, Malaysia and Sri Lanka.

Nutmeg *(pala)* was once unique to the Banda Islands. It too has 'escaped' around the world and is now so important in Grenada that it features on that island's national flag. Nutmeg trees thrive in slightly elevated locations near the sea, especially when shaded by canopies of towering *kenari* trees which themselves produce a delicious almond-like nut.

The globular, pale-yellow nutmeg fruits split in half upon ripening to reveal a brown-black nut wrapped in surreally brilliant 'flames' of scarlet filigree. When dried and processed these nuts yield nutmeg spice, which was historically used as a hypnotic medicine – it shares a common chemical ingredient with the rave drug ecstasy. The dried, discoloured filigree is known as mace.

Today, both nutmeg and mace are used mostly in fruitcakes, seafood sauces and liqueurs. Nutmeg fruits are popular locally despite an aroma that is mildly reminiscent of parquet-floor cleaner.

resettled 'temporarily' in the Netherlands while tempers cooled. However as most were RMS sympathisers, sending them back to Maluku later proved unacceptable: it might have led to their massacre. So the Malukans stayed and today around 40,000 of their descendants remain in Holland. The dream of an independent 'South Moluccas' lived on in the Netherlands, culminating in two Maluku-related train hijacks there in the mid-1970s. However, after that there was negligible RMS activity…at least until 1999.

The Troubles

The year 1999 was one of unique tensions. Indonesia's economy was in tatters, elements of the army were disaffected with the new democratic government, and people were no longer afraid to speak their minds after the Soeharto years of terror-inspired silence. On top of this, Christmas and Idul Fitri (end of Ramadan) happened to coincide. Meanwhile the unexpected breakaway of East Timor may have rekindled the hopes of RMS agitators. And there was more. Maluku was to be split into two separate provinces, each with augmented regional powers. Especially in Ambon, where the Muslim-Christian ratio was finely balanced, each religious community could see the political benefits of frightening away members of the other. The area was ready to explode.

The spark was a petty dispute between a Christian bus driver and a Muslim youth. It rapidly spilled over into intercommunal riots. Ironically, Maluku society had long been a model of peaceful Christian-Muslim coexistence, strengthened by *pela gandong*, a unique form of inter-village bonding that predates religious affiliations. Muslim and Christian 'brothers' famously used to help each other even in building churches and mosques. Yet in the madness of 1999, these brothers were set against each other as riots turned to massacres.

Almost every island suffered some disturbances with villagers killed, buildings burnt and atrocities committed by both sides. In Tobelo (Halmahera) and Ambon, Muslims were widely perceived to be the initial victims. In response, Laskar Jihad, a fundamentalist Islamic group, set sail from Java to 'protect' these local Muslim minorities. However, their 'holy war' soon appeared to degenerate into thinly disguised revenge attacks on Christian communities, particularly against perceived RMS sympathisers. Fighting spiralled ever further out of control, especially on Ambon. Churches, mosques and thousands of houses were torched, with whole villages displaced and hundreds of thousands left homeless. When attempts at reconciliation were made, Laskar Jihad activists rushed to threaten negotiators whom they denounced as traitors.

Maluku Today

Tempers began to cool in February 2002 with the Malino II agreement which called for mutual respect and disarmament. Things improved markedly in October when Laskar Jihad suddenly disbanded and left Ambon. This was probably thanks to pressure on Indonesia as part of America's anti-terrorism sabre-rattling following the 11 September 2001 New York attacks. Although a few riots re-erupted during 2004 in Kota Ambon, recovery has been remarkably swift. Pockets of wrecked buildings are still visible but reconstruction is in full swing. The economy is booming with reconstruction funds creating an unprecedented air of optimism. Some refugees have returned home though some regions are now de facto segregated into distinct Christian and Muslim areas. With the dust settled, locals wonder how they were ever duped into the destructive spiral. Both sides

MALUKU TRAVEL WARNINGS & REALITIES

Some websites and even certain Indonesian embassies claim that you need a special permit to visit Maluku. In our experience this is totally untrue. Local tourist offices confirm that there are no longer any general travel restrictions. The only permits still required are for exploring parts of Seram (p763). Nonetheless you'd probably be prudent *not* to mention any plans to visit Maluku when applying for your Indonesian visa. To keep up to date, www.maluku2000.org carries news reports while www.websitesrcg.com/ambon has lots of background on 'the accident'.

believe that the bloodbath was deliberately stirred by outside *agents provocateurs,* and with poignant understatement the troubles are now commonly labelled 'the accident'.

CULTURE

Maluku's people have very mixed blood. To Malay and Melanesian precursors have been added Indian, Arab, Chinese and Portuguese genes, with more recent additions of Bugis (from Sulawesi seafarers) and Javanese (from transmigrants). Melanesian features are strongest on the Kei Islands. Tribal communities of Nua-ulu still inhabit the interior of Seram. But unlike in neighbouring Papua, you won't see people in Maluku wearing tribal garb. Only their red, bandana-like headscarves distinguish Nua-ulu men from other Malukans and their headhunting antics are graciously now relegated to folklore. Not all thatched, primitive villages that you see are 'traditional' – you might be looking at the make-do dwellings of those whose 'real' homes were burnt in 1999. Incredibly the region has over 130 distinct traditional languages, though some have now blended with Bahasa Indonesia to form the pidgin dialect of Ambonese Malay (lingua franca in central Maluku). Learning key words in each regional tongue is a great way to break the ice.

Muslims are more numerous in most of north Maluku. Christians form majorities in some central and southern areas.

TOP BUDGET CHILLOUTS

Watch the waves and unwind at these delightful, yet very inexpensive, little Maluku retreats:

- Savana Cottages, Ohoidertawun, Kei Islands (p777)
- Vita Guest House, Bandaneira (p769)
- Penginapan Seroja, Tidore (p787)
- Penginapan Lisar Bahari, Sawai (p764)
- Penginapan Lease Indah, Kota Saparua (p761)

GETTING THERE & AWAY

Air

Ambon and Ternate are the region's air hubs. Both have twice-daily connections to Jakarta via Surabaya, Makassar and/or Manado (Sulawesi). There are limited connections to Papua from Ambon and Langgur (Kei Islands). See map on p752.

Sea

Several Pelni liners stop in Maluku. Every two weeks *Bukit Siguntang* and *Ciremai* link Surabaya, Makassar and Bau Bau (Sulawesi) to Tual (Kei Islands) via the Banda Islands and Ambon. *Bukit Siguntang* returns via Kupang (Timor). *Lambelu* links Ternate to Ambon, Bau Bau and Makassar continuing to Surabaya and Tanjung Priok. Returning it loops to Bitung (Sulawesi) between Ambon and Ternate. *Sinabung* and *Nggapulu* both stop in Ternate between Bitung and Sorong on their odysseys between Jakarta and northern Papua.

The infamously variable *Kelimutu* and *Tatamailau* often serve Malukan ports on monthly loops and the relatively small *Sangiang* circles from Bitung to Ternate around Halmahera then back to Bitung (or vice versa) somewhat irregularly.

Non-Pelni vehicular ferries or slow 'motor' boats from North Sulawesi (Bitung or Manado) run to Ternate, Tobelo (Halmahera) and Sanana (Sula Islands). Highly uncomfortable Perintis cargo ships run between several Papua and Maluku ports and arc down to Kupang in Timor once every three weeks.

GETTING AROUND

Air

Merpati and Trigana Air weave a surprisingly impressive web of regional flights around Maluku. However with only four little planes between them for the whole network, engine trouble, bad weather or one-off charters can (and will) throw out the schedules for days. You can generally buy only one-way tickets booked from the departure point. Getting the return can be hit and miss: call the local airline agent or try asking a hotel to make a booking for you. Then pay on arrival. Smaller planes have 10kg baggage limits. See the map on p752 for price and route details.

Bus, Kijang, Bemo & Ojek

Maluku is mountainous and relatively undeveloped. The few roads that do exist are often potholed and narrow. The only

MALUKU AIRFARES

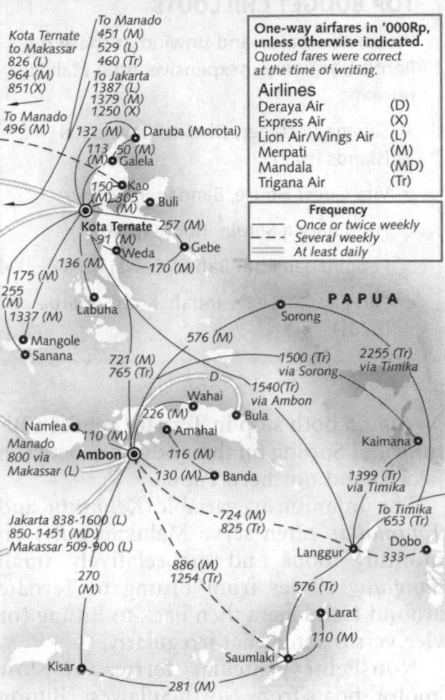

MALUKU FERRIES

long-distance buses are on Seram or Ambon-Seram routes. Especially on Halmahera and in rural Seram, shared Kijangs (fancy seven-seater overgrown Toyotas) are more common and comparatively pricey. Shorter routes are operated by bemo usually known as *mobil*. Renting an *ojek* (motorbike taxi) is usually very reasonable and the most pleasant way to travel if the rain holds off.

Boat

Pelni services *within* Maluku are patchy and the only direct boat link from Ternate to Ambon is its fortnightly *Lambelu* (southbound only). Some medium-range hops are served by uncomfortable ASDP ferries or by wooden boats known as *motor*. The latter have limited sweaty, wooden-board 'bed' spaces but tickets aren't always numbered so to secure one you might need to arrive many hours before departure. Perintis cargo boats are bigger but not designed with passengers in mind. Bring waterproofs. They generally run on roughly three-weekly loops via a string of smaller intermediate ports that are way off any tourist route. Ask at relevant harbours for departure details and always be prepared for uncertainty and rough conditions.

Speedboats link nearby islands and roadless villages. Locals use very specific terms for boat types: so don't be immediately put off if told that there isn't a *spid* (covered multi-engine speedboat) to your destination. There might still be a *Johnson* (outboard-powered longboat) or a *ketinting* or *lape-lape* (smaller, short-hop motorised canoes). Speedboats generally depart when there are sufficient passengers, usually very early in the morning when seas are calmest. Choice is better on major market days. In several cases chartering your own boat is worth considering: smaller or diesel powered boats will be much cheaper than multi-engined petrol ones.

PULAU AMBON

Manageably small yet offering plenty of contrasts, Maluku's most prominent island is lush and gently mountainous, indented with two great hoops of bay. Close to Kota Ambon, the main town, villages merge into a long suburban ribbon but further out light sparkles brilliantly through alluring flower gardens and swaying tropical foliage. Religiously divided, the island was the epicentre of the 1999–2002 troubles. But recovery has been amazingly swift. Don't be fooled by old reports of dangers or civil unrest: Ambon is back in business and is now the ideal hub for visiting some of Indonesia's most delightful yet utterly undiscovered gems: the Lease, Banda and Kei Islands.

History

Until 1512 Ambon was ruled by Ternate. The sultans brought the civilising force of Islam to the island's north coast and developed Hitu Lama as a major spice-trading entrepôt. The Ternateans were later displaced by the Portuguese who found the less developed, un-Islamicised south more receptive to Christianity and developed a fortress around which Kota Ambon would eventually evolve. In 1599 the Dutch renamed this fort *Victoria* and made Kota Ambon their spice-trade base. Despite a 1817 uprising in the Lease Islands (see the boxed text, p761), Dutch rule survived until WWII, when Kota Ambon became a Japanese military headquarters and prisoner-of-war camp. The result was extensive Allied bombing which destroyed most of its once-attractive colonial architecture. In 1950 Ambon was briefly the centre of the South Malukan independence movement. This was extinguished within a few months by Indonesian military force with a last stand at Passo village.

From 1999 until mid-2002, Ambon was ripped apart by Christian-Muslim intercommunal violence. In Kota Ambon the first wave of attacks came in January 1999 with a largely Christian mob assault on the city's main markets. A July 1999 reprisal torched predominantly Chinese businesses in the city centre. Island and city alike became polarised into Muslim and Christian zones. By late 2001, battered Kota Ambon looked like 1980s Beirut. During 2002 things improved markedly and the last significant disturbances were riots in 2004, though occasional provocations continue, including occasional sniping between police and army

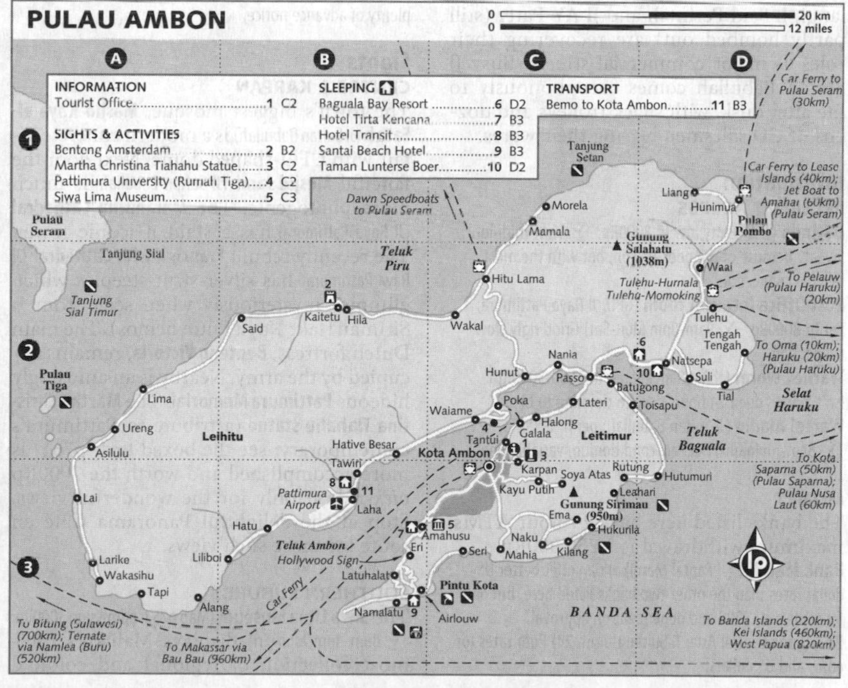

forces. Some burnt-out ruins remain, notably around Pattimura University in Rumah Tiga, but these are rapidly being rebuilt or swallowed by insatiable tropical weeds. By 2006 the island seemed gripped with a great optimism and visible economic resurgence. It's as though everyone suddenly awoke from a bad dream to find themselves back in their busy little south-sea paradise.

KOTA AMBON

☎ 0911 / pop 368,000

By the region's dreamy tropical standards, Maluku's capital is a dusty, throbbing metropolis. But compared to 'real' cities elsewhere, Kota Ambon retains a languid charm emphasised by a perfect arc of bay and its lushly mountainous backdrop. Sights are minimal and architecture wins no prizes but the scars of the 1999–2002 civil war are quickly healing and the town has regained its role as the regional transport hub.

Orientation

Almost all public road transportation emanates from the traffic-clogged markets of Mardika and Batu Merah. Jl Dr Sam Ratulangi, Jl Said Perintah and Jl AY Patty (still partly bombed out) are recovering their roles as major commercial streets. Busy Jl Sultan Babullah comes cacophonously to life after dusk, with snack trolleys and dozens of CD salesmen blaring their wares.

Information

INTERNET ACCESS

@stindo (Jl AY Patty; per hr 8000Rp; 🕑 9am-midnight) Sweaty because of the poor air-con, but with the most reliable connection.

Post Office Internet room (GPO, Jl Raya Pattimura; per hr 8000Rp; 🕑 9am-8pm Mon-Sat) Grindingly slow connection.

Warnet Worm (Jl AM Sangaji; per hr 3500-5000Rp) Isn't always open 24 hours despite claiming to be.

Wartel Aladin (Jl Sultan Babullah; per hr 6000Rp; 🕑 8am-midnight) Best air-conditioning, variable line.

MONEY

The banks listed here have 24-hour ATMs; maximum withdrawal is 1,250,000Rp.

Bank Mandiri (Jl Pantai Mardika) Can offer better US-dollar rates than the other two banks listed here, but only for sums over $200 and dependent on approval.

BCA (Bank Central Asia; Jl Sultan Hairun 24) Poor rates for euros and US dollars.

BNI (Bank Negara Indonesia; Jl Said Perintah 12) Near BCA; same poor rates.

Souvenir Asmat (☎ 349069; Jl Dr Sam Ratulangi) Friendly; a tiny, eccentric everything-shop run by an English-speaking ex-mariner who can sometimes change money at decent rates given a few phone calls.

TOURIST INFORMATION

Likes Tour (☎ 310296; Jl Tulukabessy; 🕑 8.30am-5pm Mon-Sat) Staff speak English and offer free, basic city maps. They coordinate very occasional group eco-tours to northern Seram (www.indonesia-parrot-project.org).

Souvenir Asmat (☎ 349069; Jl Dr Sam Ratulangi) Ask for Marwizar Bahri, an English-speaking helper, fixer and collector of almost anything.

Tourist Office (Maluku Provincial Tourist Bureau; Map p753; Dinas Parawisata; ☎ 312300; Jl Jenderal Sudirman, Tantui; 🕑 8am-4pm Mon-Fri) Offers fistfuls of colourful free brochures but the decent city map (20,000Rp) is cheaper bought from Abdulalie Hotel. The office has lovely bay views but getting here by vehicle requires a 4km one-way loop (use Tantui bemos passing the Commonwealth War Graves then doubling back). Getting back to town is less than 1km.

Yoh Syaranamual (☎ 351765; Gang da Silva 99) Experienced if ponderously slow-moving tour-guide speaking English and Dutch. Can arrange diving equipment given plenty of advance notice.

Sights

CENTRE & KARPAN

The town's biggest mosque, **Masjid Raya al-Fatah** (Jl Sultan Babullah) is a modern concrete affair with UFO-shaped dome. Next door the fanciful **Mesjid Jami** (Jl Sultan Babullah) is much more photogenic. The **Maranatha Cathedral** (Jl Raya Pattimura) has a staid if iconic tower. The recently rebuilt **Francis Xavier Cathedral** (Jl Raya Pattimura) has silver-strut steeples which glimmer mysteriously when seen from Jl Sirimau (take Kayu Putih bemos). The main Dutch fortress, **Benteng Victoria**, remains occupied by the army. Nearby is an amusingly hideous **Pattimura Memorial**. The **Martha Christina Tiahahu statue** (a tribute to Pattimura's contemporary; see the boxed text, p761) is more accomplished and worth the 7000Rp *ojek*-ride if only for the wonderful views. Stop at the delightful Panorama Café en route for more such views.

SOUTHERN SUBURBS

The **Siwa Lima Museum** (Map p753; admission 3000Rp; 🕑 8am-4pm Mon-Fri) displays Maluku's foremost collection of regional and colonial

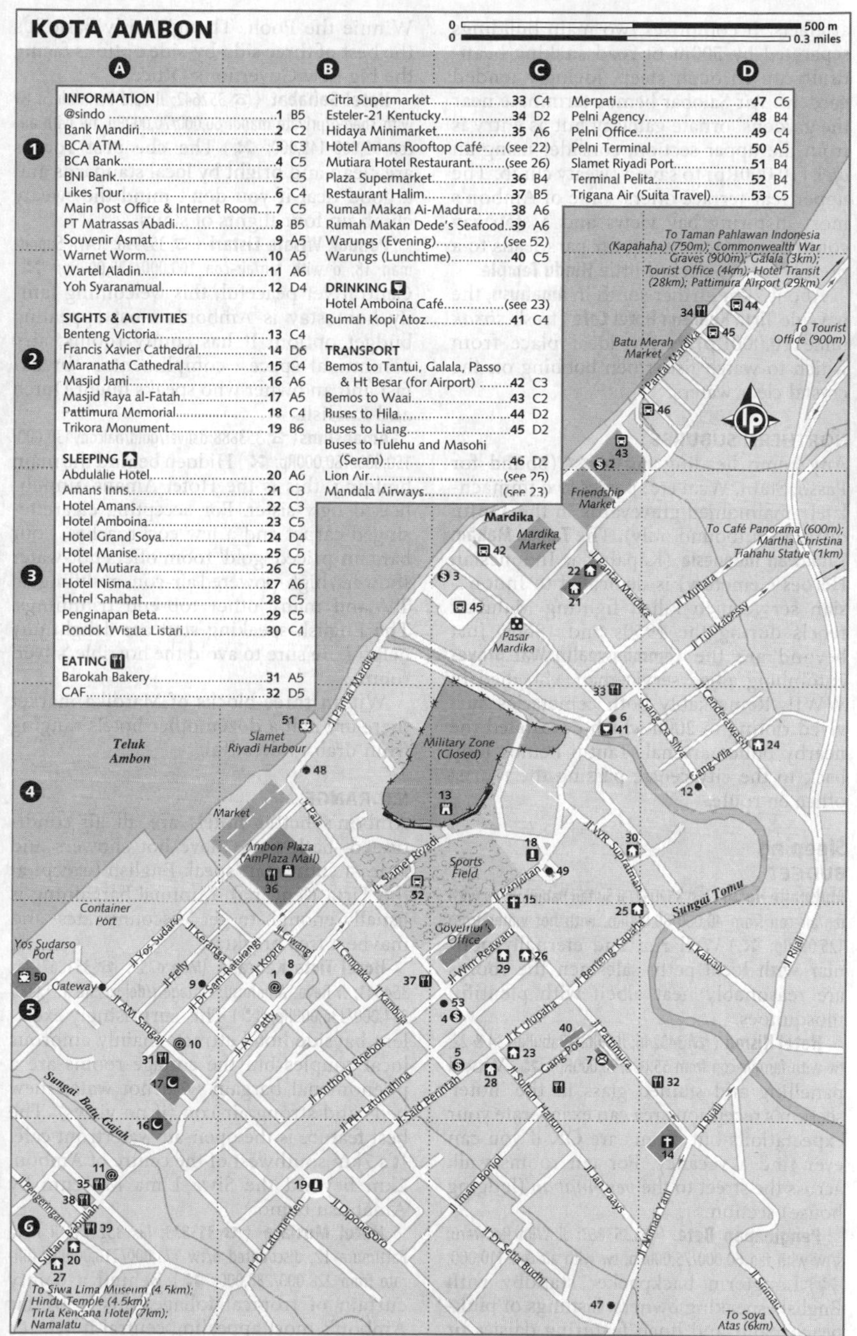
KOTA AMBON
0 500 m
0 0.3 miles
A
B
C
D
1
2
3
4
5
6
INFORMATION
@sindo 1 B5
Bank Mandiri 2 C2
BCA ATM 3 C3
BCA Bank 4 C5
BNI Bank 5 C5
Likes Tour 6 C4
Main Post Office & Internet Room 7 C5
PT Matrassas Abadi 8 B5
Souvenir Asmat 9 A5
Warnet Worm 10 A5
Wartel Aladin 11 A6
Yoh Syaranamual 12 D4
SIGHTS & ACTIVITIES
Benteng Victoria 13 C4
Francis Xavier Cathedral 14 D6
Maranatha Cathedral 15 C4
Masjid Jami 16 A6
Masjid Raya al-Fatah 17 A5
Pattimura Memorial 18 C4
Trikora Monument 19 B6
SLEEPING
Abdulalie Hotel 20 A6
Amans Inns 21 C3
Hotel Amans 22 C3
Hotel Amboina 23 C5
Hotel Grand Soya 24 D4
Hotel Manise 25 C5
Hotel Mutiara 26 C5
Hotel Nisma 27 A6
Hotel Sahabat 28 C5
Penginapan Beta 29 C5
Pondok Wisata Listari 30 C4
EATING
Barokah Bakery 31 A5
CAF 32 D5
Citra Supermarket 33 C4
Esteler-21 Kentucky 34 D2
Hidaya Minimarket 35 A6
Hotel Amans Rooftop Café (see 22)
Mutiara Hotel Restaurant (see 26)
Plaza Supermarket 36 B4
Restaurant Halim 37 B5
Rumah Makan Ai-Madura 38 A6
Rumah Makan Dede's Seafood 39 A6
Warungs (Evening) (see 52)
Warungs (Lunchtime) 40 C5
DRINKING
Hotel Amboina Café (see 23)
Rumah Kopi Atoz 41 C4
TRANSPORT
Bemos to Tantui, Galala, Passo & Ht Besar (for Airport) 42 C3
Bemos to Waai 43 C2
Buses to Hila 44 D2
Buses to Liang 45 D2
Buses to Tulehu and Masohi (Seram) 46 D2
Lion Air (see 25)
Mandala Airways (see 23)
Merpati 47 C6
Pelni Agency 48 B4
Pelni Office 49 C4
Pelni Terminal 50 A5
Slamet Riyadi Port 51 B4
Terminal Pelita 52 B4
Trigana Air (Suita Travel) 53 C5
To Taman Pahlawan Indonesia (Kapahaha) (750m); Commonwealth War Graves (900m); Galala (3km); Tourist Office (4km); Hotel Transit (28km); Pattimura Airport (29km)
To Tourist Office (900m)
Batu Merah Market
Jl Pantai Mardika
Friendship Market
Mardika
Mardika Market
To Café Panorama (600m); Martha Christina Tiahahu Statue (1km)
Jl Mutiara
Jl Tulukabessy
Pasar Mardika
Jl Cenderawasih
Gang Da Silva
Gang Vila
Military Zone (Closed)
Slamet Riyadi Harbour
Teluk Ambon
Market
Jl Pala
Ambon Plaza (AmPlaza Mall)
Jl Slamet Riyadi
Sports Field
Jl Panjaitan
Jl WR Supratman
Sungai Tomu
Container Port
Yos Sudarso Port
Gateway
Governor's Office
Jl Yos Sudarso
Jl Keranga
Jl Dr Sam Ratulangi
Jl Kopra
Jl Cwang
Jl Felly
Jl Cempaka
Jl Kambola
Jl Wim Reawaru
Jl Benteng Kapaha
Jl Kakialy
Jl Rijali
Jl AM Sangaji
Jl AY Patty
Jl Anthony Rhebok
Jl PH Latumahina
Jl Said Perintah
Jl K Ulupaha
Gang Pos
Jl Pattimura
Jl Sultan Hairun
Sungai Batu Gajah
Jl Pengeringan
Jl Sultan Babullah
Jl Dr Latumenten
Jl Diponegoro
Jl Imam Bonjol
Jl Dr Setia Budhi
Jl Jan Paays
Jl Ahmad Yani
Jl Sinimau
To Siwa Lima Museum (4.5km); Hindu Temple (4.5km); Tirta Kencana Hotel (7km); Namalatu
To Soya Atas (6km)
MALUKU

artefacts. It comprises two main buildings separated by 500m of road snaking beautifully up through steep, lovingly tended gardens. Air Salobar bemos terminate near the gardens' ornate gateway but as entry is from the upper section, consider using an *ojek* (10,000Rp) to save a sweaty climb. The upper rear terrace offers some of Ambon's most inspiring bay views and a stairway continuing from the top car park leads to a prettily flower-decked little **Hindu Temple**.

About 2km further south in **Amahusu**, the bayside **Tirta Kencana Hotel Café** (fresh *sirsak* juice 10,000Rp) is the ideal place from which to watch fishermen bobbing on the crystal clear waters.

NORTHERN SUBURBS

Any bemo heading northeast (bound for Passo, Stain, Waai etc) passes two immaculately maintained graveyards in the Tantui district (outbound only). The **Taman Makam Pahlawan Indonesia** (Kapahaha; Indonesian Heroes Cemetery) is dedicated to Indonesian servicemen killed fighting Malukan rebels during the 1950s and 1960s. Just beyond are the **Commonwealth War Graves** entombing allied servicemen who died in WWII. Remarkably both cemeteries survived rioting in 2000 which devastated the nearby police arsenal. Tantui bemos loop back to the city centre passing the tourist office en route.

Sleeping

BUDGET

Abdulalie Hotel (☎ 352057; Jl Sultan Babullah; tw with fan/air-con from 40,000/80,000Rp, with hot water from 125,000Rp; ❄) Well run and eternally popular with local petty salesmen the rooms are reasonably neat albeit with plentiful mosquitoes.

Hotel Nisma (☎ 343246; Jl Sultan Babullah 34 & 22; tw with fan/air-con from 55,000/90,000Rp; ❄) Wood panelling and stained glass in the 'hotel' section's reception area can exaggerate your expectations but rooms are OK if you can ever find a vacancy. For fan rooms walk across the street to the *penginapan* (lodging house) section.

Penginapan Beta (☎ 353463; Jl Wim Reawaru; s/tw with fan 60,000/75,000Rp, tw with air-con 110,000; ❄) Longterm backpacker standby with English-speaking owners, lashings of pink-peach paint and linen featuring daisies or Winnie the Pooh. Though fairly basic it's the best of three side-by-side options facing the big new Governor's Office.

Hotel Sahabat (☎ 352642; Jl Said Perintah 5; tw with shared/private mandi 60,000/70,000Rp, tw with air-con 95,000-145,000; ❄) The cheapest rooms are clean and bright by local standards and a good deal if you don't mind the sweaty climb up four flights of stairs.

Pondok Wisata Listari (☎ 355596; Jl WR Supratman 18; d with fan/air-con 100,000/125,000Rp; ❄) Central yet peaceful, this welcoming family homestay is Ambon's most appealing budget option. It has comfy rooms, airy communal spaces, complimentary breakfast and an owner who speaks fluent Dutch and English.

Amans Inns (☎ 353888; d silver/gold/balcony 130,000/150,000/180,000Rp; ❄) Hidden behind the main building, this is the Hotel Amans' unpublicised ugly sister. For accepting cigarette-singed carpet and a few cockroaches, your bargain-priced 'gold' room offers hot-water showers, high-powered air-con, multilingual TV and many other top-end trimmings. The English-speaking staff are delightfully helpful. Be sure to avoid the horrible 'silver' rooms.

Within three blocks of Mardika market there are half a dozen other hotels ranging from drab to dreadful.

MIDRANGE

Ambon's better hotels are all air-conditioned, bathrooms have hot showers and at least some staff speak English (except at the Tirta Kencana). Minimal bargaining is usually enough to get 'discount rates' and maybe a free breakfast.

Hotel Tirta Kencana (Map p753; ☎ 351867; fax 354841; Jl Raya, Amahusu; cottage r/deluxe/ste 121,000/244,000/336,000Rp; ❄) This surprisingly excellent bayside hotel attracts mainly amorous local couples but the cottage rooms are a phenomenal bargain with hot water, new beds and strong air-con (if no views). The best feature is the open-air waterfront café. It's 7km southwest of the centre of Ambon, 2km beyond the Siwa Lima Museum by Amahusu bemo.

Hotel Mutiara (☎ 353873; fax 352171; Jl Raya Pattimura 12; discounted d/tw 171,000/216,000Rp, full-rate from 228,000/288,000; ❄) Behind a dainty curtain of tropical foliage, this is by far Ambon's most appealing central hotel. It's cosy, tastefully executed and has a welcoming European atmosphere spiced with framed ikat (cloth in which the pattern is produced by dyeing the individual threads before weaving) and local fabrics. Rooms are to international standards with blindingly clean bathrooms. Keeping the new carpets as clean will be a challenge.

Hotel Amans (Ambon Manise; ☎ 353888; fax 354492; Jl Pantai Mardika 53A; tw from 200,000Rp; ❄) Ideally placed for public transport, the Amans is undergoing major reconstruction. Sensibly they've started with the guest rooms which are vastly better than you'd guess from the tired-looking corridors. Discounted 'deluxe rooms' at 240,000Rp are good value.

Hotel Grand Soya (☎ 312095; Jl Cendrawasih 20; discount/full-rate tw from 203,000/290,000; ❄) Locals adore the chintzy décor and *faux* marble. Rooms are slightly less tacky but already show signs of wear.

Hotel Amboina (☎ 355515; fax 355723; Jl Kapitan Ulupaha; d standard/executive/ste from 250,000/305,000/400,000Rp; ❄) Reception is stylishly minimalist and a soothing cream colour scheme prevails. However, most standard rooms are windowless while the much more attractive suites tend to suffer from oppressive road noise.

Hotel Manise (☎ 354144; fax 341054; Jl WR Supratman; discounted d/tw from 336,000/384,000Rp; ❄) Quite undeservedly considered Ambon's top hotel, the Manise has surprisingly unimpressive rooms, many windowless and some with ripped carpets. Credit cards accepted.

Airport

Hotel Transit (☎ 315095; d 275,000Rp; ❄) The airport is nearly an hour's drive from Kota Ambon but just 1.3km from this rather ragged hotel. The Transit is steeply overpriced with dodgy plumbing but those afraid to miss early flights seem prepared to stump up the cash.

Eating

Cheap warungs abound especially near Batu Merah market, on Jl Ahmad Yani, along Gang Pos (beside the post office, mainly lunchtimes) and on Jl Sultan Babullah and at Terminal Pelita (evenings).

Rumah Makan Ai-Madura (Jl Sultan Babullah 34/1; meals 6,000-12,000Rp; ⏰ breakfast, lunch & dinner) Dowdy but clean local eatery with excellent *nasi ikan* (rice and fish set meal) and good *gado-gado* (vegetables with peanut sauce). Great value despite un-priced menus.

Café Panorama (☎ 351884; Jl CM Tiahahu; mains 12,000-45,000Rp, fruit juices 9000Rp, beer 20,000Rp; ⏰ breakfast, lunch & dinner) Open-sided terrace café with ethnic designs, fabulous views and a few Western menu options. Karpan bemos drive past.

Restaurant Halim (☎ 352177; Jl Sultan Hairun; mains 22,000-55,000Rp plus rice; ⏰ dinner Mon-Sat; ❄) Partially decorated with varnished sago-stem walls and Nua-ulu artefacts, this long-standing favourite remains a-tinkle with old-fashioned oyster-shell lamps and serves beautifully cooked Chinese seafood meals.

Rumah Makan Dede's Seafood (☎ 356188; Jl Sultan Babullah; meals 25,000Rp; ⏰ 5pm-10pm Mon-Sat) Bustling, efficient, brightly unsophisticated place serving Ambon's best *ikan bakar*. Choose your fish and it arrives accompanied by five great sauces, dips, rice and salad. Sometimes opens midday.

For Western food try the quiet **Hotel Amans rooftop café** (meals 15,000-40,000Rp; ⏰ 7am-9pm) or the very pleasant **Hotel Mutiara Restaurant** (meals 22,000-55,000Rp; ⏰ breakfast, lunch & dinner). **CAF** (Jl Raya Pattimura; meals from 11,700Rp; ⏰ 9am-9pm) is Ambon's best-known place for fast food, but similar fried chicken tastes better for half the price at **Esteler-21 Kentucky** (Istana Gizi; Jl Pantai Mardika), an ultrasimple waterfront shack.

SELF-CATERING

Mardika and Batu Merah are vast markets. Useful stores:

Barokah Bakery (Jl AM Sangaji; ⏰ 6.30am-6pm) Try the great cheese buns (*roti keju*) here.

Citra supermarket (Jl Tulukabessy; ⏰ 8.30am-8.30pm Mon-Sat, 10am-6pm Sun)

Hidaya Minimarket (Jl Sultan Babullah)

Plaza supermarket (Ambon Plaza Mall, Jl Yos Sudarso; ⏰ 8am-8pm)

Drinking

Hotel Amboina Café (Jl Kapitan Ulupaha; beers 25,000Rp; ⏰ 24hr) Jazz themes and some deep-cushioned settees make for Ambon's most convivial informal meeting place.

Rumah Kopi Atoz (Jl Tulukabessy; coffee from 2500Rp; ⏰ 8.30am-6pm Mon-Sat) Simple coffee house occupying the only traditional-style pavilion for miles around.

Getting There & Away

AIR

Mandala (☎ 344206; www.mandalaair.com; Hotel Amboina, Jl Kapitan Ulupaha; 🕑 8am-5pm Mon-Fri, 8am-2pm Sat & Sun) flies to Jakarta daily via Makassar. Bookings are possible online: you don't pay till you collect the tickets (at least four hours before departure) and there's no penalty for cancelling. **Lion Air** (☎ 342566; Hotel Manise, Jl WR Supratman; 🕑 9am-5pm Mon-Fri, 9am-2pm Sat & Sun) has two flights daily to Jakarta via Makassar and/or Surabaya with connections to Manado and beyond to Ternate. Prices vary wildly according to demand. If you trust their 'City check-in' (2pm the day before flying), you can head to the airport without baggage. Their midnight flight *from* Jakarta arrives at 7am due to stops and time-zone changes. **Trigana Air** (☎ 355797; Suita Travel, Jl Anthony Rhebok) offers five weekly connections to Langgur (Kei Islands) and one weekly direct hop to Ternate. Ironically this leaves the same day (out Tuesday, back Wednesday) as the weekly Ambon–Ternate flights with **Merpati** (☎ 352481; fax 353272; Jl Ahmad Yani 19; 🕑 8am-noon & 1pm-4.30pm Mon-Fri, 9am-2pm Sat, Sun & public holidays) who operate a whole web of local weekly hopper flights (see the airfares map on p752). **Deraya Air** (☎ 323802; Pattimura Airport) flights to Bula (Seram) are normally limited to oil-company employees. AdamAir has proposed but not yet started Ambon services.

PT Matrassas Abadi (☎ 311111; Jl AY Patty; 🕑 8am-7pm) is Ambon's best-organised travel agency for domestic tickets (bookings stop at 5pm). Some English is spoken.

BOAT

Pelni

From Yos Sudarso harbour *Lambelu* heads to Bitung (northern Sulawesi; 172,000Rp, 22 hours) via Namlea (Buru, 56,000Rp) returning via Ternate (115,000Rp). *Ciremai* and *Bukit Siguntang* head east to Papua via Bandaneira (Banda Islands; 70,000Rp, seven hours) and Tual (Kei Islands; 177,000Rp). *Dorolonda* and the westbound *Bukit Siguntang* link to Surabaya via Kupang (28 hours). Other westbound boats head for Surabaya via Makassar (Sulawesi; 262,000Rp, 36 to 48 hours) and Bau Bau (Pulau Buton; 205,000Rp). The *Kelimutu* sometimes heads to Tual (233,000Rp) via Saumlaki (Tanimbar Islands, 182,000Rp) but its timetables are being revised. The glass-faced office of **Pelni** (☎ 348219; 🕑 8am-noon) is opposite the Pattimura Memorial: head down, around the back then upstairs again to buy tickets. Alternatively use one of many agencies around the port (minimal commission). One such handy agency faces Slamet Riyadi Harbour.

Other boats

Much less comfortable boats from **Slamet Riyadi Harbour** serve north and east Seram, Sanana (Sula Islands) and far southeast Maluku. From the ferry jetty in **Galala**, north of Tantui, the KMP *Danaurana* car ferry departs daily to Namlea (Buru) at 5pm (adult/child 55,000/40,000Rp, nine hours). Services to the Lease Islands and southern Seram use Passo, Tulehu or Hunimua ports (opposite).

BUS & BEMO

Frequent bemos and most of the rare buses start from a variety of points along Jl Pantai Mardika in Mardika and Batu Merah markets. However buses for just a few destinations in Seram depart from **Terminal Pelita** (Jl Slamet Riyadi), a lay-by beside the central sports field. These include 5am **Jaya Saka** (☎ 345507) and **Mulia Express** (☎ 341805) buses to Saka (for Sawai).

Getting Around

TO/FROM THE AIRPORT

From Pattimura Airport central Kota Ambon is 30km around the bay. Chartered bemos are sometimes cheaper than taxis (150,000Rp, 45 minutes). With minimal luggage you can take an *ojek* from the airport gate (3000Rp, 1km) to the east end of the runway and continue by regular Ht Besar bemo to Kota Ambon (5000Rp, one hour). If ferry departures oblige it is sometimes faster to take an *ojek* to the Poka jetty in Rumah Tiga (20,000Rp, 15 minutes) then cross by ferry to Galala (1500Rp, eight minutes, up to four per hour, from 6am to 6pm). From Galala take any bemo into town (2000Rp, 10 minutes).

BEMO

For the city centre ultra-frequent LinIII bemos (*mobils*) usefully head southwest from Pasar Mardika down Jl Pantai Mardika and Jl Dr Sam Ratulangi or Jl AY Patty, swinging around the Trikora monument onto Jl Dr Latumenteri. After 2km they loop back again via Jl Sultan Babullah and Jl Yos Sudarso. For any bemo ride consider getting on/off at least 200m away from the main market where vehicles typically jostle for ages through chaotic traffic jams.

AROUND PULAU AMBON

Soya Atas

An easy *ojek* trip to escape from the heat of Kota Ambon takes you to **Soya Atas** village, sitting way up on the high slopes of **Gunung Sirimau** (950m). The convincingly rebuilt **Soya Atas church** has risen from the ashes after being torched during the intercommunal strife of 2002. Across the road a tacky **St Francis Xavier statue** recalls the original Jesuit's Christianising mission here in 1546. A quick scramble beside the statue brings you to a quietly attractive viewpoint. A series of much longer steep footpaths lead to Ema and other villages beyond.

Southern Leitimur

Some of Ambon's most appealing coastal scenery is along the very accessible road southwest of Amahusu. Look for the amusing **Hollywood sign** painted in giant letters on the sea-defences at **Eri**. Thereafter the road wiggles across a pass from Latuhalat to **Namalatu**, a 'resort' of rock-pools that's famous for its **musical becaks**, each pedal-trishaw competing to blast its customers with a few decibels more than his competitor. Around 3km east, backing a less than idyllic pay-beach (admission 2000Rp) the **Pantai 'Santai Beach' Hotel** (Map p753; ☎ 323109; d 150,000Rp; ❄) offers eight sea-facing rooms with king-sized beds, comical toilets and curtained parking so that amorous couples can maintain anonymity. Further east are two attractive **Pintu Kota** 'recreation parks', perched atop attractive meadows which end in cliffs plunging towards the crashing waves below. Beyond a limpid bay, the increasingly bumpy road finally dead-ends at the forgotten little fishing village of **Seri** where outriggers and drying cloves lie quietly beneath the giant *ketapang* trees.

ACTIVITIES

Ambon offers some terrific **scuba diving** possibilities. Professional, American-owned **Maluku Divers** (☎ 323882; www.unexploredadventures.com) in Namalatu specialise in live-aboard odysseys but also offer one-day options with three dives. The standard cost per person is US$120 plus $30 for equipment rental, based on groups of five. However one traveller (without group) reports bargaining this to $110 for two boat-dives including equipment and accommodation (the company has a quietly stylish private guesthouse albeit with shared bathrooms). Although snorkelling is possible off Namalatu, there's much more underwater action around **Pulau Tiga** (which makes a brilliant lunch stop) and **Tanjung Sial Timur** (superb shoals of black snapper and surgeon fish). **Pinta Kota** is somewhat over-hyped but the **Hukurila** underwater archway is a marvel if you can handle depths of more than 40m.

Eastern Leihitu

The market town of **Passo** is one of Ambon's busiest. Beyond at Waitatiri is **Baguala Bay Resort** (Map p753; ☎ 362717; fax 362716; www.BagualaBayResort.com; Jl Raya; deluxe/cottage/ste 363,000/423,000/726,000Rp; ❄ 🏊), set in a lovely waterfront palm-garden. There's no beach but it's the only hotel on the whole island to have a decent swimming pool. The traditionally styled but fully equipped 'cottage' rooms are the best option. Although 17km east of central Kota Ambon, this could make a good alternative to staying in Kota Ambon with Waai bemos passing right outside every few minutes till mid-evening. The resort's **Waterside Café** (juice 8000Rp, snacks from 10,000Rp) serves good-value Western and local food including curious imitations of pizza.

A cheaper accommodation alternative with its own idyllic beach is the comfortable if slightly degenerating **Taman Lunterse Boer** (Map p753; ☎ 361366; d 150,000Rp; ❄). It's on the main road yet easy to miss, just 300m west of the over-busy **Natsepa pay-beach** (admission 2000Rp, parking 2000Rp).

Tulehu has a trio of useful ports. Use the jetties behind Tulehu market for speedboats to Haruku village. Use Tulehu-Momoking jetty for speedboats to Pelauw (Haruku Island) and Saparua Island. Use Tulehu-Hurnala for bigger ferries to the Lease Islands and Amahai (Seram).

Waai is famous for its 'lucky' **Bulut** (Moray eels). Spotting them supposedly augurs good luck. The cost of this good fortune is 10,000Rp paid to a waiting gentleman who will tempt the eels out of their dark recesses by feeding them raw eggs. The concrete **carp pond** (Jl Air Waysilaka) in which the eels lurk doubles oddly as the village washing pool. The experience is not exactly dramatic yet somehow it's intriguingly off-beat enough to amuse. Take a Waai bemo, get off just before the 'Margreet Salon' sign and walk two blocks inland to find the pond.

A spur off the main Liang road leads to **Hunimua** which has some pretty, uncommercialised **beaches** and is the departure jetty for car-ferries to Waipirit (near Kairatu, Seram), departing every two to three hours.

Bemos are very frequent till mid-evening on the Kota Ambon-Natsepa-Waai route (per hop 2000Rp). Liang buses are rare.

Northern Leihitu

The north coast is peaceful and little visited though several sleepy village stalls sell smoked fish to occasional passing *ojeks*. **Hitu Lama** has a rather scenic setting and a dawn speedboat service to western Seram. But the nearest thing to a tourist attraction is the 1649 **Benteng Amsterdam** in quietly attractive **Hila**. That Hila should be renowned for a Dutch fort is somewhat ironic considering it was originally the power base of anticolonial Ambon. The four-sided waterfront fort has a uniquely complete central keep, though the tiled roof is getting a little dilapidated. Five minutes' walk inland from the fort, then across a school football field, seek out Kaitetu's pretty little thatch-roofed **Mesjid Wapaue**. Originally built in 1414 on nearby Gunung Wawane, the mosque was transferred to the present site in 1664. According to a local legend, supernatural powers did the moving.

Hila is reached from Hunut by relatively rare bemo (5000Rp) or by *ojek* (30,000Rp). Continue on foot for five minutes beyond the eye-catching **Mesjid Besar** to find the fort.

LEASE, SERAM & BURU

LEASE ISLANDS

☎ 0931

Pronounced 'leh-*a*-say', these conveniently accessible yet delightfully calm islands have a scattering of fascinating olde-worlde villages, lovely bays and snorkelling possibilities (bring your own equipment). Sleepy Kota Saparua makes the most convenient base.

Most access is by speedboat from Tulehu or Passo on Pulau Ambon. Additionally, five days weekly the 9am *Layur* car ferry from Tulehu-Hurnala (☎ 0911-361435) visits Wae Riang (near Kabauw, Haruku, 5000Rp), Pelauw (Haruku, 9000Rp), Ume Putih (near Kulur, Saparua, 13,000Rp) and finally Wae Rae (Seram). It returns the same afternoon.

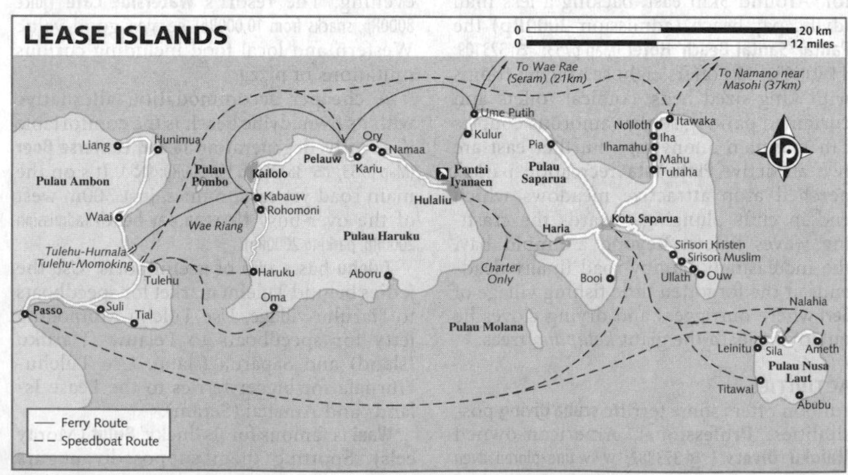

PATTIMURA & TIAHAHU

In 1817 the Dutch faced a small but emotionally charged uprising led by Thomas Matulessy, who briefly managed to gain control of Saparua's Benteng Duurstede. He killed all the fortress defenders but spared a six-year-old Dutch boy. For this minor 'mercy' Matulessy was popularly dubbed Pattimura ('big hearted'). The rebels were rapidly defeated and dispatched to the gallows but have since been immortalised as symbols of anticolonial resistance. Today their statues dot the whole of Maluku and Pattimura even features on Indonesia's 1000Rp banknotes. A much-romanticised heroine of the same saga is Martha Christine Tiahahu, whose father supported Pattimura. After daddy's execution on Nusa Laut, Martha was put on a ship to Java but grief-stricken she starved herself to death. Her remains were thrown into the sea but her memory lingers on.

Pulau Haruku

Pulau Haruku has no formal accommodation so visits are easiest as day trips from Ambon or in linking Ambon with Pulau Saparua. The Christian village of **Haruku** is famous for its November **Sasi Lompa festival**, marking the end of the annual prohibition (see boxed text, p777) on catching *lompa* flying-fish. The village is quietly quaint and relatively isolated down 8km of narrow bike-track from bigger **Rohomoni** where you'll spot Maluku's most impressive **thatch-roofed mosque**.

Pelauw, Pulau Haruku's main village, has a tacky **Cakalele monument** celebrating the island's other major festival. About 300m east of the port the one-wall ruin of **New Hoorn fort** is barely worth stopping to see. A relatively lonely road leads to the village of **Hulaliu** at the western end of which is **Pantai Iyanaen**, a narrow, sandy beach with some lovely sweeps of view towards Saparua and Seram.

GETTING THERE & AWAY

Speedboats leave when full (regularly till afternoon) from behind Tulehu market to Haruku and Oma villages (10,000Rp, 15 minutes), and from Tulehu-Momoking jetty for Pelauw (15,000Rp, 25 minutes). From Hulaliu it's relatively easy to charter a speedboat to Haria (Saparua) for 100,000Rp and continue by *ojek* (5000Rp) or bemo (3000Rp) to Kota Saparua. The car ferry from Pelauw to Ume Putih (Kulur) departs around 11am. Returning to Tulehu-Hurnala via Wae Riang it departs at around 2.30pm. No service on Tuesdays or Fridays.

GETTING AROUND

Rare bemos run between Pelauw and Kailolo. *Ojeks* from Kailolo cost 5000Rp to Rohomoni but a whopping 40,000Rp to Haruku. Pelauw to Hulaliu *ojeks* charge 20,000Rp.

Pulau Saparua

KOTA SAPARUA

The island's main village hosts the 1676 **Benteng Duurstede**, famously besieged by Pattimura in 1817 (see boxed text, above). The outer walls are renovated with mouldering grey concrete showing its original form and displaying several old cannons. When the gate appears locked, just pushing it open often works! Opposite the entrance a seemingly abandoned museum still displays models depicting Pattimura's exploits, but bring a torch as there's no light inside. Behind the museum is a popular sandy swimming beach backed by **Penginapan Duurstede** (☎ 21099; d 50,000Rp) with seven clean but fan-less rooms. The more comfortable **Penginapan Lease Indah** (☎ 21040; Jl Muka Pasar; unrenovated/renovated d 60,000/70,000Rp; ❄) has a pleasant garden culminating in a pair of bay-view seats amid bougainvillea. Further along Jl Muka Pasar are a few *rumah makan* (eating houses), the market and a Telkom building, directly behind which (on parallel Jl Belakang) is the small bemo terminal.

SOUTHEAST SAPARUA

A twisting lane leads through war-battered **Sirisori Kristen** and photogenic **Sirisori Muslim** to **Ullath** where the traditional-style *baileu* (meeting pavilion; see boxed text, p790) is overshadowed by the tall Protestant church tower. Beyond this, the road dead-ends at **Ouw**, famous for its elegantly simple **pottery** (*sempe*). None is obviously on show, but ask any local and you'll usually be led to a workshop where 5000Rp is a reasonable donation to watch the artist build up a typical bowl on an unpowered spindle device.

MALUKU

NORTHEAST SAPARUA

Arguably Saparua's most intriguing village is **Nolloth**, which retains a uniquely impressive traditional *baileu* and a fine 1860 church with an extraordinary chalice-shaped wooden pulpit. A curious selection of colourfully gaudy new Christian statuettes dot the town. Nolloth merges into **Itawaka**, where the village chief, known in Lease as *raja* (king) rather than *kepala desa* (village head), is building the five-room Penginapan Toholau Indah on a beach 10 minutes' walk around the headland. There's supposedly excellent snorkelling offshore here.

GETTING THERE & AWAY

At 5am the **Satu Nusa speedboat** (☎ 0852 18344222) leaves Kota Saparua for Passo on Ambon, returning at around 9am (40,000Rp, one hour). From Itawaka, 5am speedboats run to both Tulehu (Ambon) and to a muddy beach at Namano near Masohi (Seram, 35,000Rp), returning at around 7.30am.

GETTING AROUND

Bemos from Kota Saparua run occasionally to Haria (3000Rp) and Itawaka (5000Rp), very rarely to Ouw (5000Rp) and Kulur (8000Rp). *Ojeks* cost twice the bemo fare but are much more pleasant for sightseeing.

Pulau Nusa Laut

Sila village is the closest to Pulau Saparua. Its attractive **Ebenhaezer Church** is the oldest in Maluku (1719). Nearby is the small, overgrown but reasonably well preserved ruin of 1654 Dutch fort **Benteng Beverwyk**. Between the two, the friendly local English teacher offers a no-frills family **homestay** (House 15; 50,000Rp; ⌚ from 3pm). Nusa Laut has no roads but there's an easy-to-follow trail from Sila to Ameth (1¾ hours' walk) via picturesque **Nalahia**, where you descend a staircase to a sweep of opalescent bay. **Ameth** has an unusual if not especially beautiful octagonal church and some very fine coral gardens 300m offshore. Their marine life is 'protected' by a *sasi* (see boxed text, p777) and before snorkelling here you'll need to pay 100,000Rp to the village *raja*. Ameth's brand new **Penginapan Pari Musar** (☎ 21499; Jl Pendidikan; s/d 50,000/70,000Rp) has en suite bucket *mandis* and clean squat toilets. It's the bright pink house just beyond the tiny wartel booth facing the football pitch at Ameth's easternmost end.

GETTING THERE & AWAY

On Wednesday and Saturday public speedboats from each Nusa Laut village shuttle across to Kota Saparua market (20,000Rp each way), returning around lunchtime. At other times you'll usually need to charter: *from* Nusa Laut that's easy enough and cheapest if you head for Ouw (ex-Sila from 100,000Rp, ex-Ameth 150,000Rp). *To* Nusa Laut, however, finding a suitably powerful boat for the choppy seas can be very tough and relatively expensive as no such boats are moored in Ouw. Your best hope is to keep asking around at Kota Saparua market. Most Tuesdays and Friday mornings direct speedboats head from Ameth and Sila to Passo on Ambon (50,000Rp to 75,000Rp) returning next morning.

PULAU SERAM

☎ 0914

Some Malukans call Seram 'Nusa Ina' (Mother Island), believing that all life sprang from 'Nunusaku', a mythical peak ambiguously located somewhere in the island's western mountains. The best known of Seram's indigenous minority tribes, the Nua-ulu ('upper-river') or Alifuro people, sport red bandana headgear and were headhunters as recently as the 1940s. Seram's capital and main town is Masohi-Amahai, but the greatest attraction is Teluk Sawai on the northern coast. Seram's wild, mountainous interior has thick forests alive with cockatoos and colourful parrots but seeing them usually requires a punishingly masochistic trek into the remote Manusela National Park for which you'll need guides and extra permits.

GETTING THERE & AWAY

Air

From Amahai, **Merpati** (☎ 22231; Jl Martha Tiahahu) flies to Ambon via Banda on Mondays. Ambon-Wahai flights operate on Thursdays.

Boat

From Tulehu-Hurnala (Ambon) to Amahai, comfortable jet-boats (75,000Rp, 2½ hours) run daily except Sundays at 8am

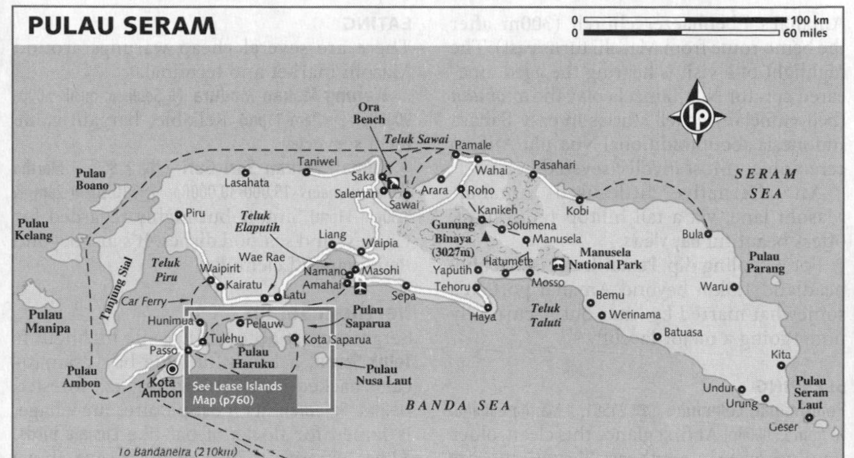

and 4pm, returning at 8am and 2pm. On Sundays there's a morning speedboat from Masohi instead. Car ferries link Waipirit (near Kairatu) to Hunimua (Ambon) six times daily (adult/child 11,500/8500Rp, 1½ hours) and Wae Rae to Ume Putih (near Kulur, Pulau Saparua) five days weekly. Daily speedboats from Namano cross to Itawaka (Saparua) at around 7.30am, returning at 5am (35,000Rp, 1¼ hours).

Bus

Cramped, direct buses perfumed with durian and sweat operate from Kota Ambon to various Seram towns. They use the Hunimua-Waipirit ferry for which you might have to wait a couple of hours. Generally it's more comfortable to take the jet-boat to/from Amahai and continue from Masohi.

GETTING AROUND

Masohi is Seram's main road-transport hub. Bemos are hyper-frequent on the Masohi-Amahai run. Buses or Kijangs to other destinations are rare especially after noon. By 10am you've probably missed the last service north to Saka for Sawai.

Masohi, Namano & Amahai

Predominantly Muslim Masohi is the spacious purpose-built capital of Central Maluku. Its wide streets are pleasant, and though there's not much to do it's not a bad place to wait out an almost inevitable day of missed connections and bureaucracy – technically signing in with the police here remains an obligation. The main street of Jl Soulissa heads southwest from the terminal/market/Masohi Plaza shopping mall. It becomes Jl Martha Tiahahu in the Christian suburbs, continuing for 6km through Namano village into predominantly Christian Amahai. Here, just before the main port, the larger road turns 90 degrees, passing the museum and dinky airport a kilometre beyond.

INFORMATION

Local police still require tourists to register in Masohi before travelling around Seram. Bring several photocopies of your visa and passport to police headquarters. Laboriously typing out your Surat Tanda Melapur (STM letter, 20,000Rp) takes an hour or two. On Saturdays ask the tourist office.

BRI ATM (Masohi Plaza shopping mall) More convenient than the banks strung along Jl Soulissa.

Central Maluku Tourist Office (Dinas Kebudayan & Parawisata; ☎ 21462; Jl Imam Bonjol; 🕑 8am-2pm Mon-Sat) Near the steep-roofed *Bupati* office in Masohi. Some staff members speak English, but while friendly they are of minimal practical help.

Police HQ (Jl Dr Siwabessy; 🕑 9am-2.30pm Mon-Fri)

SuperOjek (☎ 0813 43063684) Max Dopeng is an obliging English-speaking guide cum *ojek*-driver.

Telkom (Jl Geser 2; 🕑 24hr) Beside the *Bupati* office.

SIGHTS

The minuscule **Sangar Budaya Seram Museum** (☎ 22102; Soahuku; admission/photo-permit 10,000/10,000Rp; 🕑 8am-8pm, hours vary) is opposite

Amahai's Ebenhaezer church (300m after the bemo route from Masohi turns east). The highlight of a visit is hearing the aged, one-eared curator Nus Tamaela play the *totobuan* (bell-gamelan) or tell stories in easy Bahasa Indonesia about traditional Nua-ulu/Alifuro ceremonies. Most involve severed heads.

An alternative little-used Amahai-Masohi lane, via a tall hilltop radio mast, offers beautiful **bay views**.

For a cooling dip, **Pantai Kuako** is a pebbly headland 1.5km beyond Amahai port. It's somewhat marred by litter but is currently undergoing a major facelift.

SLEEPING

Penginapan Lelemuku (☎ 21581; Jl Martha Tiahahu; tw from 55,000Rp) At first glance this clean, older family house in southern Masohi appears basic and somewhat jerry-built. However, the new VIP rooms behind (twin rooms are 137,000Rp) are vastly nicer with rattan seats facing a garden that's a curious blend of real and artificial foliage.

Penginapan Irene (☎ 21238; Jl Martha Tiahahu; s/d/tw with fan from 45,000/66,000/88,000Rp, with air-con from 100,000/110,000/125,000Rp; ❄) Friendly, quiet and good value, the best rooms are 'cottages' (130,000Rp) at the rear with balcony seats facing a little ornamental garden. Pronounced 'ee-reh-neh', the *penginapan* is at the southern end of Masohi at the first bend beyond the petrol station: easily accessible by Amahai-bound bemos.

Lounusa Beach (☎ 21379; main road, Namano; d 100,000-150,000Rp; ❄) Owners speak Dutch and limited English and plan to construct two stilt rooms and a waterfront restaurant on their patch of mangrove bank (despite the name, there's no beach). Hopefully these will improve upon the somewhat lacklustre existing accommodation.

Hotel Tiara (☎ 22354; Jl Soulissa; d with fan/air con 77,000/125,000Rp; ❄) Tiara is excellent value with clean new rooms, 400m east of Masohi Plaza.

Hotel-Restaurant Isabella (☎ 22637; fax 21542; Jl Manusela 17; s/d from 80,000/185,000Rp; ❄) The two 'executive' rooms (265,000Rp) are Masohi's best options with hot-water showers, king-sized beds and Guns'n'Roses posters. However, other rooms are very disappointing, especially the windowless 'deluxe' (230,000Rp) and space-wasting 'presidential' (375,000Rp) ones.

EATING

There are several cheap warungs around Masohi market and terminal.

Warung Makan Madura (Jl Soulissa; meals 5000-9000Rp; 🕑 7am-11pm) Reliable, bargain-value local servery.

Rumah Makan Sari Guri (☎ 22809; Jl Martha Tiahahu; mains 15,000-30,000Rp; 🕑 10.30am-2pm & 5.30pm-11pm) Simple but highly regarded for Chinese and seafood dishes. It's just beyond Penginapan Lelemuku.

Northern Seram

Seram's most accessible scenic highlight is **Teluk Sawai**, a beautiful wide bay dramatically backed by cliffs and rugged, forested peaks. **Saleman**, its most picturesque village, is famed for flocks of bat-like **Lusiala birds**. These emerge at dusk from a cave above the village, supposedly bearing the souls of human ancestors. Saleman has no accommodation but, across the bay, tempting **Ora Beach** has marvellous spongy, white sand where the stilt bungalows and pavilion restaurant of **Ora Beach Hotel** are currently under reconstruction: for details check with Ambon's Baguala Bay Resort (p759).

Further round the bay is the photogenic stilt-house village of **Sawai**. It's a possible base for jungle hikes and *lape-lape* rides to Pulau Raja where bats *(kelelawar/uniki)* appear at sunset. There's great snorkelling in the offshore coral gardens (bring your own gear). The only hotel, **Penginapan Lisar Bahari** (Ali's Place; per person 150,000Rp) has creaky bamboo walls and very dim lamps but the terrace is idyllic for watching moonlight on the bay and doing nothing much of anything. Being perched over the water, rooms are predictably somewhat damp (bring a sleeping mat) and showers in the basic en suite bathrooms are rather salty. Costs include brilliant fish dinners, assorted snacks and endless tea.

East of Sawai, lethargic little **Wahai** was once Seram's main Dutch fort but a small, cannon-topped mound of stones is all that remains. There's inexpensive accommodation but little reason to visit.

GETTING THERE & AWAY

Tickets for the weekly Wahai–Ambon flight are only sold from Wahai airfield (no telephone). Masohi–Wahai buses (155,000Rp, five hours) bypass Sawai completely. Until the road extension to Saleman is finished, all access to Teluk Sawai is by boat from the tiny port of **Saka**. From here Kijangs to Masohi (50,000Rp, two hours) and two buses to Ambon (125,000Rp, seven to nine hours) all depart around 8.30am. Chartering longboats from Saka to Ora Beach/Sawai costs about 100,000/200,000Rp. Every morning boats from Sawai's central jetty depart to Wahai at 6.30am (45,000Rp) and Saka at 7am (20,000Rp, 40 minutes), though the Penginapan Lisar Bahari might claim otherwise, hoping you'll charter their longboat. Twice a week an uncomfortable slow boat runs from Sawai to Ambon (235,000Rp, 30 hours).

PULAU BURU

☎ 0913

Following the political chaos of 1965, this large island west of Ambon became the home-in-exile of communist suspects making it a sort of Indonesian anti-Siberia. Authorities remain somewhat suspicious of visitors. Despite tales of giant eels and 'flowers of longevity', mystical mountain lake **Danau Rana** is rather underwhelming, with boggy banks that don't offer ideal hiking conditions.

BANDA ISLANDS

☎ 0910

This tiny and historically fascinating cluster of 10 picturesque islands is Maluku's most tempting travel destination. Particularly impressive undersea drop-offs are vibrantly plastered with multicoloured coral gardens offering superlative snorkelling. Outlying Hatta, Ai and Neilaka each have utterly undeveloped picture-postcard beaches. And the central main islands, Pulau Neira (with the capital Bandaneira) and Pulau Banda Besar (the great nutmeg island) curl in picturesque crescents around a pocket-sized tropical Mt Fuji (Gunung Api). Were they more accessible, the Bandas might be one of the world's top tourist spots. Yet for now you'll have these wonderful islands almost entirely to yourself. Hurry – this can't last!

History

In the 15th century, the Banda Islands supplied all the world's quality nutmeg, then in great global demand (see boxed text, p749). Producing nutmeg takes knowledge but minimal effort so the drudgery of manual labour was virtually unknown here. Food, cloth and all necessities of life could be easily traded for spices with the Arab, Chinese, Javanese and Bugis merchants who queued up to do business. Things started to go wrong when the Europeans arrived, the Portuguese in 1512, then the Dutch from 1599. These strange barbarians had no foodstuffs to trade, just knives, impractical woollens and useless trinkets of mere novelty value. So when they started demanding a trade monopoly, the notion was laughable nonsense. However, since the Dutch were dangerously armed, some *orang kaya* (elders) signed a 'contract' to keep them quiet. Nobody took

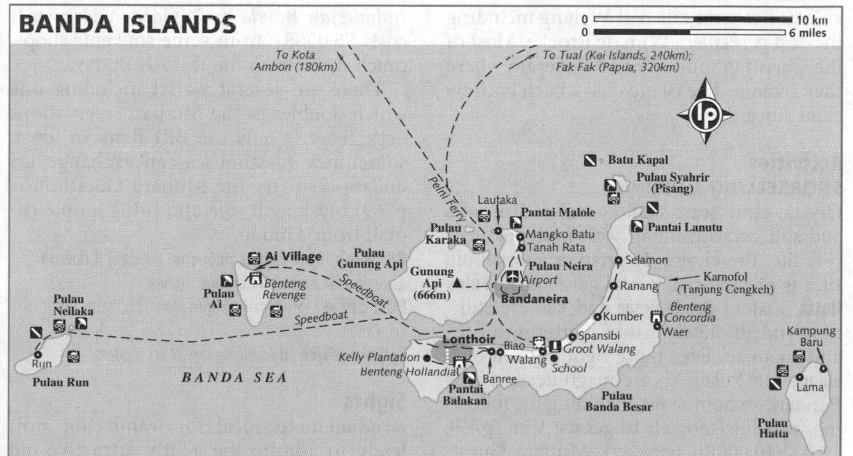

it at all seriously. The Dutch disappeared in their ships and were promptly forgotten. But a few years later they were back, furious to find the English merrily trading nutmeg in Pulau Run and Pulau Ai. Entrenching themselves by force, the dominant Dutch played cat and mouse with the deliberately provocative English, while trying ever unsuccessfully to enforce their mythical monopoly on the locals. Jan Pieterszoon Coen, the ruthless new governor general of the VOC (Dutch East India Company), reacted in 1621 by ordering the virtual genocide of the Bandanese. Just a few hundred survivors escaped to the Kei Islands.

Coen returned to Batavia (now Jakarta) and announced that the VOC would accept applications for land grants in the Bandas. The odd-ball Dutch applicants were provided with slaves, but had to settle permanently on the islands and produce spices exclusively for the company at fixed prices. They became known as *perkeniers*, from the Dutch word *perk* ('ground' or 'garden'). Nearly 70 plantations were established, mostly on Banda Besar and Ai.

This system survived for almost 200 years, but corruption and gross mismanagement meant that the monopoly was never as profitable as it might have been. By the 1930s Bandaneira was a place of genteel exile for better-behaved, anti-Dutch dissidents, and during WWII the islands were largely ignored by the Japanese.

In April 1999 there was a brief flare-up of violence when churches were burnt and at least five were killed at Walang including the 'last *perkenier*', Wim de Broeke. Most of the Christian minority fled to Seram where they remain. The islands have been entirely calm since then.

Activities

SNORKELLING & DIVING

Crystal-clear seas, shallow-water drop-offs and soft corals teeming with multicoloured reef life: the choice of pristine snorkelling sites is phenomenal. Coral gardens off **Pulau Hatta**, eastern **Banda Besar** and **Run** are stunning and absolutely justify chartering a boat and boatman. Even those right in front of **Ai village** (on Pulau Ai) are magnificent. Some Bandaneira homestays, including the following, rent fins/snorkels to guests: Vita (p769; 10,000/10,000Rp per day), Mutiara Guesthouse (p769; 15,000/15,000Rp) and Delfika (p769; 25,000/25,000Rp). Bandaneira's Hotel Maulana is the Bandas' only diving operation but charges US$90 to US$110 per double dive and has relatively aged equipment.

SWIMMING

There are beaches on the south coast of Banda Besar near **Lonthoir**, but for superb stretches of white sand the best places are **Ai**, tiny **Pulau Neilaka** (beware of currents) and especially the north coast of **Hatta** though shallow coral can impede swimming at low tide.

PULAU NEIRA & BANDANEIRA

Little Bandaneira has always been the Bandas' main port and administrative centre. In the Dutch era, the townsfolk virtually bankrupted themselves maintaining a European lifestyle and competing with their neighbours to build and furnish their spacious mansions – and to rebuild them every time Gunung Api's billows of volcanic ash burnt them down again. Today Bandaneira is a charmingly friendly place with many late-colonial houses still standing. The sleepy, flower-filled streets are so quiet that two becak count as a traffic jam.

Information

There's no tourist office but several guesthouses have helpful English-speaking owners. Delfika (p769) gives its guests a free, basic island map and a souvenir video-CD (VCD): it hopes to have internet access eventually. For great historical background, read *Indonesian Banda* by Willard A Hanna. It costs 75,000Rp from some souvenir shops, much more from the Rumah Budaya.

There are several wartel including one which doubles as the Merpati reservations desk. There's only the BRI Bank in town; sometimes guesthouses can exchange US dollars cash (try the Mutiara Guesthouse, p769) but play it safe and bring ample rupiah from Ambon.

BRI Bank (Bank Raykat Indonesia; Jl Kujali) It doesn't have an ATM and won't change money.

Post office (🕑 8am-12.30pm Mon-Thu, 8am-11pm Fri) Dinky.

Telkom office (Jl Asidiqin; 🕑 24hr) Modern.

Sights

Bandaneira is ideal for wandering aimlessly to admire the gently attractive old villas, ponder various mouldering ruins and count up the historic cannons that still lie as though dropped casually at random. It's lovely to just gaze at the cloudscapes and watch the sunset colours changing over Gunung Api.

FORTRESSES

In 1608, Dutch Admiral Verhoeven ordered the building of **Benteng Nassau** on foundations abandoned by the Portuguese in 1529. This was against the most express wishes of local island leaders and triggered a spiral of violent hostilities. The Bandanese were so incensed that they ambushed and executed some 40 Dutch 'negotiators' including Verhoeven himself. The Dutch retaliated in 1621 with the infamous beheading and quartering of 44 *orang kaya* within the fortress followed by the virtual genocide of the Bandanese population.

Ironically, the fort was in an indefensible lowland position and had to be augmented three years later by the more commanding **Benteng Belgica** (admission by 'donation' 20,000Rp), built at massive expense on the hill above. Named Belgica for Governor General Pieter Both's native Flanders, it's a five-pointed star fort in classic Vauban style. The massive cannon-deflecting bastions, over-engineered for the relatively easy task of keeping out lightly armed villager-intruders, were clearly designed to withstand English naval bombardment. Thus in 1796 it caused quite a scandal

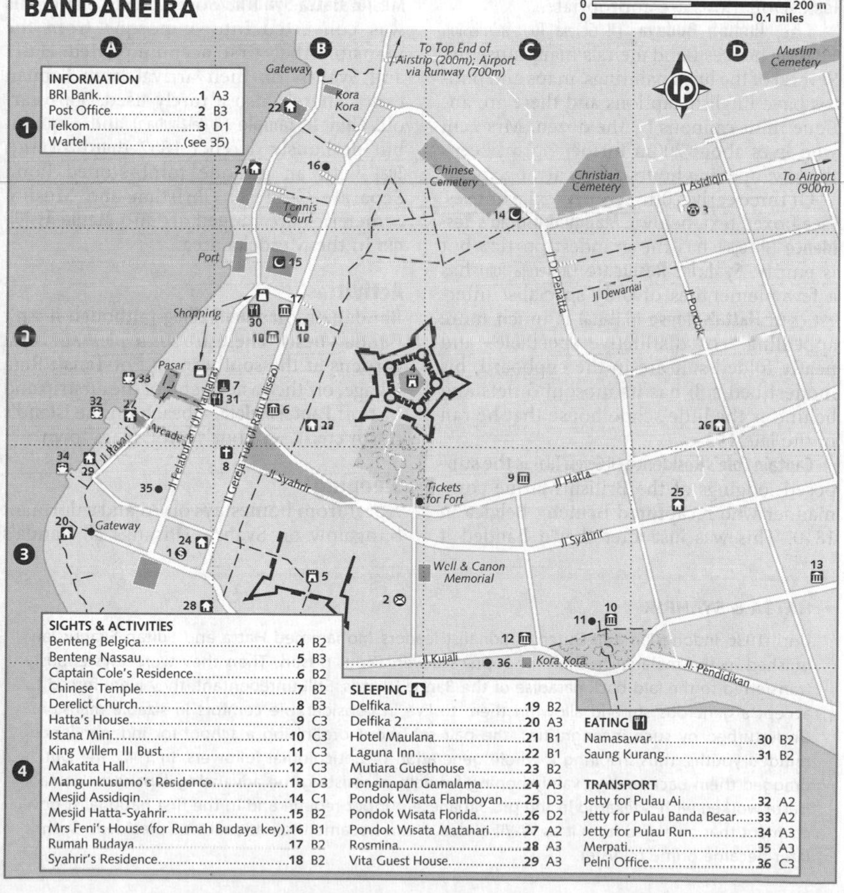

in Holland when the Brits managed to seize it (albeit briefly) without firing a shot.

From the 1860s both fortresses lapsed into ruin. Benteng Nassau remains largely overgrown, but Benteng Belgica was extensively restored in the 1990s. To reach the upper ramparts (great views) take the second arch on the left from the central courtyard.

HISTORIC HOUSES

Several historically significant Dutch-era buildings have been restored, a few hosting mini-museums. If you manage to gain access at all (knock and hope!) much of the fun of a visit is hearing the fascinating life stories of the septuagenarian caretakers, assuming your Bahasa Indonesia is up to the task. Donations are appropriate.

The **Rumah Budaya** (Jl Gereja Tua; admission 10,000Rp) houses Bandaneira's main museum. Several of the lurid paintings, maps and photos have English captions and there are antique mini-cannons by the dozen. Mrs Feni who lives about 200m further north, keeps the key; opening hours are by arrangement.

Of three early-20th-century 'exile houses' (see boxed text, below), **Mangunkusumo's Residence** (Jl Kujali) has the grandest portico but is empty. **Syahrir's Residence** (Jl Gereja Tua) has a few mementoes of only specialist interest, but **Hatta's House** (Jl Hatta) is much more appealing. His distinctive spectacles and neatly folded suit are in the cupboard, his modest bed still has its mosquito nets and behind is the little schoolhouse that he ran in the late 1930s.

Captain Cole's Residence (Jl Gereja Tua) is the supposed lodgings of the British Marine commander who recaptured Benteng Belgica in 1810. This was just after they'd handed it back to the Dutch having grabbed it in 1796! Closed to the public.

The grand but eerily empty 1820s **Istana Mini** (Jl Kujali) was a later residence for the Bandas' Dutch governors. It's usually unlocked. A haughty, medal-spangled bust of Dutch King Willem III rusts quietly in the side-garden.

Also empty is **Makatita Hall** (Jl Kujali) on the site of the former Harmonie Club (aka 'the Soc'), which once boasted seven snooker tables and was the focus of colonial-era social events. It is still used for special occasions. Lively caretaker Paman Bahalwan has plenty of WWII yarns to spin.

RELIGIOUS BUILDINGS

Behind the main port is the eye-catching **Mesjid Hatta-Syahrir**. Some locals claim this was converted into a mosque from the mansion that first accommodated Hatta and Syahrir on their arrival from Papuan exile. There's also a rarely used, 300-year-old **Chinese Temple** (Jl Pelabuhan) and a quaint but perilously derelict 1852 **church** (Jl Gereja Tua) with an antique tomb-stoned floor. Separate Chinese, Christian and Muslim cemeteries are ranged around **Mesjid Assidiqin** in the Merdeka area.

Activities

Bandaneira has **snorkelling** (although it isn't Banda's best). There are some pleasant coral gardens at the southern end of Tanah Rata village, off the eastern end of the airstrip and just off **Pantai Malole**, a beach on the island's north coast, an hour's stroll from town.

Sleeping

Apart from homestays on Ai and a dormant bungalow on Syahrir (Pisang) all Banda's

HATTA & SYAHRIR

Until 1936 Indonesian anti-Dutch nationalist leaders Mohammed Hatta and Sultan Syahrir languished in the malarial hellhole of Papua's Boven Digul prison. Then they were mysteriously transferred to the laid-back paradise of the Banda Islands. Still unrepentant, they were forced to accept a generous stipend allowing them to live in considerable comfort in sizable mansions. Unperturbed by such incongruities, the pair set about organising a school for independence-minded youths, thus inspiring a whole generation of anticolonial followers. In 1942 the Dutch dragged them back to Java vainly hoping for help in resisting the advancing Japanese. Instead, Hatta worked with Soekarno in the pro-Japanese puppet regime and in the first nationalist government that emerged from it as WWII ended. Hatta became the national vice president. Syahrir later became prime minister.

accommodation is in Bandaneira. Over a dozen family homes offer simple but clean rooms. Homestay prices here are roughly standardised at 60,000Rp for a single room and 75,000Rp for a double (both with fan). Typically add around 40,000Rp for air con (where available) should you choose to use it. Less popular places might knock off 10,000Rp, while you can expect to pay 10,000Rp to 20,000Rp extra for views or bigger rooms. Prices usually include frequent cups of tea and a light breakfast.

Vita Guest House (☎ 21332; Jl Pasar; ❄) Four comfortable rooms face a waterfront garden whose wonderful wooden jetty area is ideal for admiring the cone of Gunung Api over a cold beer (20,000Rp). Alan, the English-speaking owner, is very obliging and can arrange boat rentals at competitive rates. There's a useful communal kitchen and fridge.

Mutiara Guesthouse (☎ 21344; ❄) The Mutiara has superb-value new rooms and classically styled wooden furniture. Elements suggest nouveau riche suburban America, but the curious melange includes parrots, an artificial waterfall, a luridly colourful fish-tank, a spice garden and a veritable museum of local collectables. Enthusiastic English-speaking owner 'Abba' also sells pearls. Bicycle rental is 40,000Rp per day.

Delfika 2 (☎ 21127) Four neat rooms with *mandis* of which two have glimpses of volcano-view (best from room 101). The quiet roof terrace offers one of Bandaneira's best all-round viewpoints. When unstaffed, enquire at Delfika.

Delfika (☎ 21027; Jl Gereja Tua; ❄) Entered through an old-world sitting room with bags of atmosphere, most rooms are recently renovated and accessed off a lovely courtyard garden. Bahri speaks English.

Pondok Wisata Matahari (☎ 21050; Jl Pasar) Three of the slightly lacklustre rooms look out across the water towards Gunung Api.

Pondok Wisata Flamboyan (☎ 21233; Jl Syahrir) Fairly ordinary rooms around a central *jambu* tree, but renowned for good home cooking.

Penginapan Gamalama (☎ 21053; Jl Gereja Tua; ❄) Functional, relatively large rooms beyond some gratuitous tree-effect concrete pillars.

Pondok Wisata Florida (☎ 21086; Jl Hatta) This atmospherically ageing old home is full of old ceramics and lamps. Guest rooms have antique bedsteads but are somewhat basic and underlit.

Rosmina (☎ 21145; Jl Kujali) Rather basic with small if clean rooms, though the unkempt yard behind has great potential. Manager 'Bob' speaks rather frenetic English.

Hotel Maulana (☎ 21022; fax 21024; standard/deluxe/ste US$50/60/75; ❄) The strong point of this pseudo-colonial-style palace hotel is its lovely veranda overlooking the waterfront between palms and shaggy *ketapang* trees. Top-floor suites have the best views (no elevators). However, windows don't appear to be regularly washed and although there is hot water (unique in Banda), bathrooms show signs of rust and wear. Laguna Inn, the Maulana's cheaper annex on Jl Pelabuhan, shares similar pros and cons but you might be able to bargain them down to US$25 plus tax for fundamentally similar rooms.

Eating

Several homestays offer inclusive full-board deals or cook dinner by arrangement (typically 20,000Rp to 30,000Rp according to ingredients). This is the best way to taste Banda specialities like eggplant stuffed with *kenari*-almond paste or fish in nutmeg-fruit sauce. Especially when ships are in port, vendors sell dried nutmeg fruit slices and *kenari*-almond cakes. In December try *anggur* fruit, which look like black olives but taste like mildly astringent grapes.

Half a dozen eateries lie a bone's throw from Bandaneira's port and market. **Rumah makan Saung Kurang** (Jl Pasar; meals 5000Rp) is a basic shack serving decent *nasi ikan* at lunchtime. **Namasawar** (Jl Pelabuhan; gado-gado 10,000Rp, nasi ayam 15,000Rp) has good food and the nicest décor. **Delfika** (Jl Gereja Tua) serves seasonal fruit juices (7500Rp), disappointing ice cream (10,000Rp) and better banana pancakes (7500Rp). Only **Vita Guest House** (Jl Pasar) appears to serve beer (normally to guests only).

Shopping

Several souvenir shops on Jl Pelabuhan sell a small variety of souvenirs, postcards, 'antiques', pearls, contrived artefacts and genuine local snacks.

Getting There & Away

AIR

Merpati (☎ 21060; Jl Pelabuhan) flies from Bandaneira's cute little airport to both Ambon and Amahai (Seram) on Mondays. The Bandaneira office is in a wartel. Book well ahead or ask your guesthouse to book for you. Be aware that the flight sometimes gets cancelled.

BOAT

Pelni's *Ciremai* and *Bukit Siguntang* arrive at Bandaneira from Makassar (from 268,000Rp, 47 hours) via Bau Bau (Sulawesi) and Ambon (70,000Rp, seven hours). Both continue to Tual (Kei Islands; 96,000Rp, 11 hours) and Papua. On the way back both return to Ambon but the *Bukit Siguntang* then loops south via Kupang (Timor) to Surabaya, missing Bau Bau and Makassar.

The **Pelni office** (☎ 21122; Jl Kujali; 🕑 8am-1pm Mon-Sat) occupies a picturesque if bizarrely inconvenient location near Istana Mini.

Perintis cargo ships cross to southeastern Seram roughly every three weeks.

Getting Around

The island is walkably small but *ojeks* and becaks save sweat at 2000Rp per hop, 5000Rp to the airport or 15,000Rp to Malole Beach (*ojek* only). A couple of guesthouses rent bicycles and several offer free airport pick-ups.

PULAU GUNUNG API

This devilish little 666m volcano has always been a threat to Bandaneira, Lonthoir and anyone attempting to farm its fertile slopes. Its most recent eruption in 1988 killed three people, destroyed over 300 houses and filled the sky with ash for days. Gunung Api's historical eruptions have often proved to be spookily accurate omens of approaching intruders.

The volcano can be climbed for awesome sunrise views, but the 'recommended' route (around 90 minutes up) is surprisingly arduous and involves a scramble up frighteningly loose scree. Take much more drinking water than you expect to need, stashing some halfway for your return. Easier routes exist but are 'closed' due to the possibility of poisonous gas vents. Guides (from 50,000Rp) are prepared to accompany hikers: reassuring, though not strictly necessary.

Around Gunung Api are several attractive coral gardens, home to lurid purple-and-orange sea squirts. Good for snorkelling are the submerged north-coast lava flows and areas off little Pulau Karaka's handkerchief of beach. A motorised outrigger from Bandaneira should cost from 50,000Rp per short-day charter with various stops.

PULAU BANDA BESAR

pop 6000

The largest island of the group, Banda Besar was the most important historical source of nutmeg. It's more hilly than Neira and every bit as charming.

Walang, Biao and Lonthoir

Boats shuttle regularly from Bandaneira to **Walang** (to charter 3000Rp, or 15,000Rp, 15 minutes) where the school's friendly English teacher is keen for volunteer travellers to meet her students. Around 1km east of the jetty, the de Broeke family's **Groot Waling** estate was the last intact *perkenier* plantation house. However, its old nutmeg-drying barns are all that survived a murderous attack during the 1999 troubles. *Ojeks* (5000Rp) run via **Biao** village (home to a comical if scraggy pet cassowary) to **Banree**. From here coastal and ridge-climbing footpaths lead swiftly to **Lonthoir**, the island's sleepy main village. Lonthoir is steeply layered from waterfront to ridge-top through lush tropical foliage. Of several beautiful glimpsed views, the most idyllic is from **Benteng Hollandia**. Built in 1624, this was once one of the biggest Dutch fortresses in the Indies. Until shattered by a devastating 1743 earthquake, it covered most of the hilltop. Walking west along the ridge from here you'll pass a dinky green-and-white *masholah* (mosque), hidden behind which a newly concreted path descends steeply to **Pantai Balakan** (aka Laerkoey Beach), a pleasant sandy bay dotted with fishing boats. Alternatively continue west along the ridge-top past a 1884 Dutch grave towards **Kelly Plantation**. Here centuries-old, buttressed *kenari* trees still tower protectively over the nutmeg grove.

Eastern Banda Besar

The Biao–Walang road becomes a narrow path at Kumber and peters out after Selamon. Points beyond are only accessible by boat. Charters are often cheapest from Bandaneira. **Waer** village on the east coast, is fronted by **Benteng Concordia**, an unreconstructed but impressive star fortress with three of its four corner bastions intact. **Karnofol** (aka Tanjung Cengkeh) offers snorkellers very rich sea life, including reef sharks, though the visibility is somewhat poorer than at Hatta or Ai. **Pantai Lanutu** towards the island's diveable northeastern tip is a pleasant beach stop should you be passing, though not worth a special journey.

PULAU SYAHRIR (PISANG)

pop 40

This chunk of uplifted limestone has almost sheer, undercut 'walls' and a single sandy bay on the southwestern coast. The sunset views towards Gunung Api are better than the snorkelling here which, while good, is unexceptional by Banda's elevated standards thanks to extensive anchor scarring. Nearby **Batu Kapal** ('ship rock') does indeed look a little like a shipwrecked hulk, but heavy currents make diving around it a little overexciting. Some of its purple 'coral' formations look more like a Klingon skin disease.

Homestay Mailena is a simple, bougainvillea-draped cottage complex that could offer a magical do-nothing getaway. It's currently dormant but might be prepared to open by arrangement for longer stays. Ask at your guesthouse.

A chartered boat from Bandaneira costs from 100,000Rp (40 minutes), though a stop in Pisang is easy to tack onto your wish list for a multistop day of snorkelling.

PULAU HATTA

pop 800

Formerly known as Rozengain, this isolated island had no nutmeg. Thus its only historical relevance was a comical episode where eccentric English Captain Courthope raised a flag merely to enrage the Dutch. Today there are two small settlements with no facilities whatever. Yet Hatta has Banda's clearest waters and richest reefs, with coral holes and utterly splendid white-sand beaches lining its northern coast. One of the most eye-boggling, coral-crusted vertical drop-offs anywhere sits mere metres off tiny Lama village. Even if you can't find anyone else to share the cost, it's worth chartering a stable, covered craft from Bandaneira (diesel/petrol boat per day from 300,000/600,000Rp). Smaller boats are too slow or vulnerable in case of bad weather. Charters will usually allow several stops en route, including Pisang and Karnofol.

PULAU AI

pop 1000

Accessible Ai ('Ay') has brilliant snorkelling with pristine coral and great drop-offs just a flipper's flap from attractive beaches and rustic homestays. It was here that English agents trained local fighters to resist a 1615 Dutch attack. The islanders stunned the astonished Dutch with an unexpected counter-attack, inflicting some 200 casualties. A year later the humiliated Dutch prepared to make a revenge attack. A small British fleet appeared in the nick of time apparently prepared to defend their Ai comrades. But after a few volleys of cannon fire the English commander changed tactics. Instead he invited his Dutch opponent for a cup of tea. After a little chat the Dutch offered the Brits nominal trading rights and sovereignty in Pulau Run. Suitably bribed, the duplicitous Brits sloped off to Seram. When they returned almost all the Ai islanders had been massacred or had fled. The Dutch repopulated the island with slaves and prisoners.

Sights & Activities

From the main jetty a concrete path leads 50m up to Jl Pelabuhan. Turn left to see the underwhelming 1875 **Matalenco Gateway** and a pair of champion **kora kora boats** used each December for the *Pertandingan* races. Or turn right, past the **Mesjid Nur Ay**, to find the four-pointed star fortress **Benteng Revenge**. Originally built by the English, it was captured in 1616 and renamed by the bloodthirsty Dutch conquerors in 'revenge' for their humiliating defeat the previous year.

Just beyond are a few remnant walls of the **Welvaren plantation house**, whose nutmeg *perken* once covered almost one-third of the island. A stepped underwater drop-off, about 50m offshore roughly opposite this point offers some of the best snorkelling in Banda. A little inland is a ruinous **Dutch graveyard**.

Sleeping & Eating

None of the six homestays have signs. All prices are per person including three meals. Please be very careful not to waste water: Ai has no springs and all needs are provided

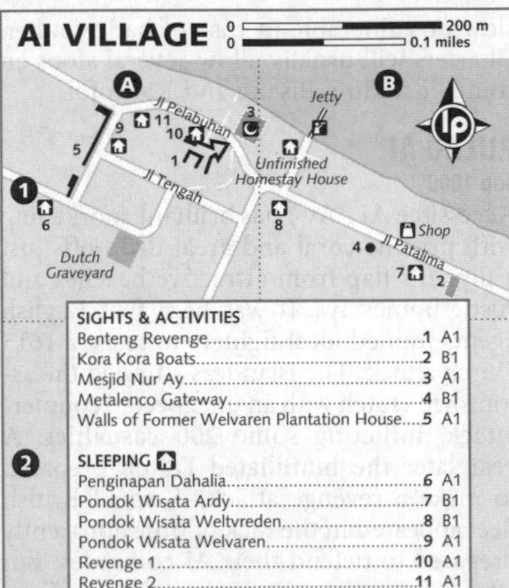

by collecting rainwater, or by laboriously transporting purchased water from Bandaneira when supplies run out. There are no restaurants here.

Revenge 2 (Jl Pelabuhan; 75,000Rp) Two rooms in a new house, with an enthusiastic English-speaking young owner and excellent food.

Penginapan Dahalia (75,000Rp) Pink and yellow house with shared squat toilet in the covered yard. Toy plane and machine gun above one bed.

Pondok Wisata Ardy (Jl Patalima; 100,000Rp) Marginally Ai's most comfortable option with clean, tiled floors and one room that even has a private rainwater-shower. Lacks the family atmosphere of some homestays.

Other options:

Pondok Wisata Weltvreden (75,000Rp) Near the jetty.

Pondok Wisata Welvaren (75,000Rp) Behind the rarely functioning wartel window.

Revenge 1 (75,000Rp) Creaky.

Getting There & Away

Two or three passenger longboats (10,000Rp, one hour) leave Ai daily when full, generally departing between 6am and 7am. They return from Bandaneira between 10.30am and 1pm. If you want to do a day trip *from* Bandaneira you'll have to charter (diesel/petrol boat 200,000/300,000Rp, 90/50 minutes).

PULAU RUN (RHUN)

pop 1000

The main attraction here is diving or possibly snorkelling the deeper-water drop-off which runs 70m to 150m off the island's northwestern coast (access by boat). Alternatively beach yourself briefly on the picture-perfect islet of Neilaka.

After the 1616 Dutch ravaging of Ai, the English initially rushed to defend their trading post on Run and built an 'impregnable' fort on the tiny, waterless islet of Neilaka, where they became increasingly besieged. The same eccentric Captain Courthope, who had taunted the Dutch on Rozengain (now Hatta), put honour above death in a preposterously futile last stand, refusing even the most reasonable offers to leave. Somehow British sovereignty was maintained even after the 1621 Dutch atrocities, during which all of Run's nutmeg trees were systematically destroyed. That left the English with an economically worthless scrap of land, which they finally swapped with Holland in 1667 for a then equally useless North American island. That island was Manhattan – not a bad deal, as it turned out.

GETTING THERE & AWAY

Most mornings there's a single public boat (15,000Rp, two hours) running from Run to Bandaneira, returning around noon. However, since there's no accommodation in Run you're better off chartering a boat from Ai (from 250,000Rp per day) or even Bandaneira. You'll need a boat anyway to reach Neilaka and Run's best drop-offs.

Run Village

Today Run village is an appealing little network of steps and floral concrete paths backed by vine-draped limestone cliffs. No identifiable historic buildings remain but there are nice views from between the tamarind trees at a probable castle site at the top of Jl Eldorado (which becomes Jl Rumalatur as the steps degenerate into a muddy scramble).

Pulau Neilaka

Some of Banda's finest white sand encircles picturesque **Neilaka**, an isle so small you can saunter around it in 10 minutes. All that's left of the English fort are a few scattered coral pebbles hidden within a pandanus thicket in the islet's centre. Swimming is safest from the eastern shore, while snorkelling is better off the northern point, but currents there are treacherous.

KEI ISLANDS & BEYOND

☎ 0916

Stunning white-sand beaches and extraordinary if mostly invisible cultural traditions make the Kei Islands one of Indonesia's most under-rated gems. Fortunately for those who adore the islands' genuine hospitality and complete lack of commercialism, they remain way off the tourist radar. Access is through the twin towns of Langgur (with the airport) and Tual (with the Pelni port). Although they're on separate islands (Pulau Kei Kecil and Pulau Dullah respectively), they're linked by a bridge into a single unit. Accommodation is available in either, plus on a couple of beaches. You could also stay in Elat on Pulau Kei Besar, a bigger, more attractively rugged island that locals call Nuhu Yut. In the unique Kei language *bokbok* means good. *Hanarun (li)* means (very) beautiful.

TUAL & LANGGUR

These twin towns hold almost all the Kei Islands facilities. While pleasant enough, neither has any real sights. Tual's most atmospheric quarter is **Kyonbawa**, a semi-island with narrow lanes, some stilt houses and a small raised **graveyard** with views across to Pulau Fa-ir. The **Un Tower** (not UN) at Tual's highest point looks like a white minaret balanced on a pile of dishes. Tual's

MALUKU

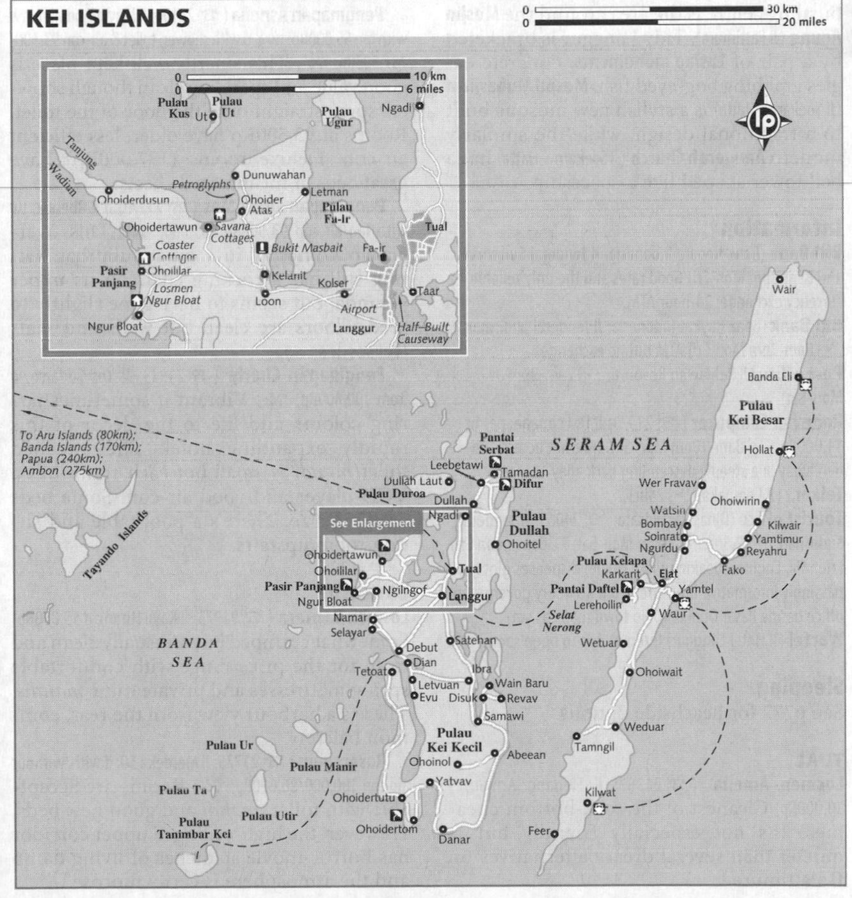

KEI CULTURE & MARRIAGE

Kei culture is vibrant and distinctive (see 'Sasi Savvy' boxed text, p777), but can make finding a life partner rather awkward. Kei islanders should marry within their caste. There are only three castes and the rule's no sweat for the majority who belong to the middle *renren* group. It's much more awkward for *melmel* (top caste) or *iri* (who were traditionally their servants) whose numbers are relatively tiny.

As with other Maluku islands, a *pela* system links pairs of villages into a virtual family to help one another at times of shortage. However marriage between *pela* families is a taboo considered akin to incest.

Once a potential partner has been found, the next hurdle is the thorny question of the bride-price. This a groom must pay in *lela* (*zad-zad*). A *lela* isn't a sum of money but a distinctive and highly expensive ceremonial minicannon. These are supposedly of 16th-century Portuguese origin. In fact, some believe that *lela* are being quietly and profitably produced by the smithies of Banda Eli.

Not surprisingly there are quite a few frustrated bachelors.

bustling centre is the area around the **Mesjid Agung** (Jl Pattimura). Tidy Langgur is bracketed by a pair of **Lusiap monuments**: concrete eagles grabbing bog-eyed fish. **Mesjid Muharjirin** (Jl Soekarno-Hatta) is a stylish new mosque built to a traditional design, while the similarly modern **Anugerah Church** (Jl Soekarno-Hatta) has a bell tower shaped like a spaceship.

Information

BNI Bank (Bank Negara Indonesia; Jl Jenderal Sudirman; 8am-3pm Mon-Fri) Good rates and the only reliable currency exchange; 24-hour ATM.

BRI Bank (Bank Raykat Indonesia; Jl Jenderal Sudirman; 8am-3pm Mon-Fri) ATM but no exchange.

Post office (Jl Pahlawan Revolusi; 7am-2pm Mon-Sat)

Ronevan Computer (21371; Jl Dr Leimana; per hr 11,000Rp; 8am-10pm Mon-Sat) Internet access; hidden away in a steeply descending back alley.

Telkom (Jl Cempaka; 24hr)

Tourist office (Dinas Parawisata; 24063; Jl Jenderal Sudirman; 7.30am-2.30pm Mon-Sat, 7.30am-noon Fri) Friendly, English-speaking Vicky (male) dispenses glossy, passingly informative brochures from a sweaty government office beside Pasar Ohoijang. No town maps as yet.

Wartel (Jl Hotel Langgur) Internet due to open soon.

Sleeping

See p777 for beachside options.

TUAL

Losmen Amelia (21387; Jl Fidnang Armau; s 30,000Rp) Cleanest of the rock-bottom cheapies. It's not especially friendly but is quieter than several dreary alternatives on Jl Pattimura.

Penginapan Asnolia (22106; Jl Mayor Abdullah; tw with fan 55,000Rp; tw & d with shower, toilet & air-con 93,500-137,500Rp;) This smartly well-kept place is good value and sparkling clean though showers spray straight onto the floor of the toilet. Rooms at 93,500Rp have older, less efficient air-con. Deluxe rooms (137,000Rp) have great beds, if mismatched sheets.

Penginapan Linda Mas (21271; Jl A Rhebok; tw with fan/air-con 93,500Rp/165,000;) This overgrown homestay in a quiet suburban setting still has a rocking chair on its upper veranda, but seems to have gone slightly to seed. Floors are clean but walls and mattresses less so.

Penginapan Charly (21923; Jl Yos Sudarso; d from 100,000Rp;) Vibrant if sometimes jarring colours add life to the décor of this rapidly expanding hotel. The attached toilet/*mandi* is small but each room has a VCD player and good air-con. Some beds are king size. There's a pool table and sitting room upstairs.

LANGGUR

Losmen Bahtera (21973; Jl Kayu Hitam; d 55,000Rp) Somewhat cramped but unusually clean and fresh for the price range with comfortable spring mattresses and private mini-*mandis*. There's a harbour view from the rear, common balcony.

Rosemgem (21775; Jl Merdeka 50; d with/without air-con 100,000/80,000Rp;) Rooms are acceptable with toilet, *mandi* and good new beds. However, the high-ceilinged upper corridor has horror-movie splotches of living damp and the atmosphere is eerily morose.

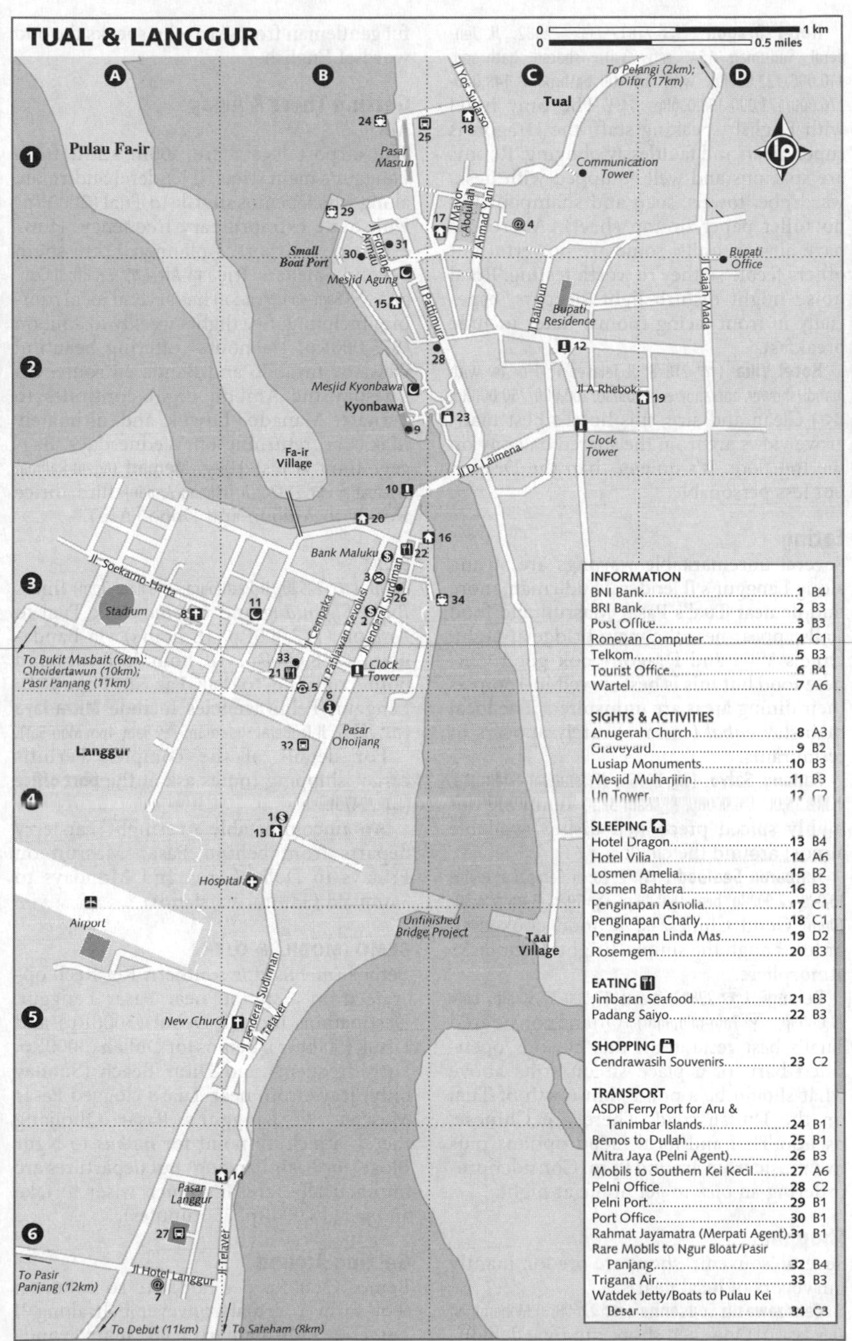

INFORMATION

BNI Bank	1	B4
BRI Bank	2	B3
Post Office	3	B3
Ronevan Computer	4	C1
Telkom	5	B3
Tourist Office	6	B4
Wartel	7	A6

SIGHTS & ACTIVITIES

Anugerah Church	8	A3
Graveyard	9	B2
Lusiap Monuments	10	B3
Mesjid Muharjirin	11	B3
Un Tower	12	C2

SLEEPING

Hotel Dragon	13	B4
Hotel Vilia	14	A6
Losmen Amelia	15	B2
Losmen Bahtera	16	B3
Penginapan Asnolia	17	C1
Penginapan Charly	18	C1
Penginapan Linda Mas	19	D2
Rosemgem	20	B3

EATING

Jimbaran Seafood	21	B3
Padang Saiyo	22	B3

SHOPPING

Cendrawasih Souvenirs	23	C2

TRANSPORT

ASDP Ferry Port for Aru & Tanimbar Islands	24	B1
Bemos to Dullah	25	B1
Mitra Jaya (Pelni Agent)	26	B3
Mobils to Southern Kei Kecil	27	A6
Pelni Office	28	C2
Pelni Port	29	B1
Port Office	30	B1
Rahmat Jayamatra (Merpati Agent)	31	B1
Rare Mobils to Ngur Bloat/Pasir Panjang	32	B4
Trigana Air	33	B3
Watdek Jetty/Boats to Pulau Kei Besar	34	C3

Hotel Dragon (☎ 21812; fax 22082; Jl Jenderal Sudirman 154; s/tw with shared bathroom 110,000/122,000Rp, with private bathroom 148,000-176,000/171,000-198,000Rp; ❄) The only hotel with English-speaking staff, the Dragon is super-clean and faultlessly obliging. Rooms are spacious and well equipped with desk, wardrobe, towels, soap and shampoo (but no toilet paper or top sheet). All rooms have air-con units: some are powerful but others feeble so they're worth testing. Road noise might disturb light sleepers, especially in front-facing rooms. Rates include breakfast.

Hotel Vilia (☎ 21878; Jl Telaver 1; d or tw with mandi/shower/hot shower 150,000/200,000/250,000Rp; ❄) Clean and airy, this hotel's best mangrove views are from the shared balcony on the top floor. It's quieter than the Dragon but less personable.

Eating

Several unremarkable warungs are strung along Langgur's Jl Jenderal Sudirman, more huddle near Tual's Pasar Masrun and food stalls appear near the main bridge at night. Hotels Vilia and Dragon cook good Chinese food but this is best served in-room as their dining areas are uninspired. The local mainstay *enbal* (cassava) rarely appears in restaurants.

Padang Saiyo (☎ 21951; Jl Jenderal Sudirman; mains 15,000-20,000Rp; 🕑 8am-5am) Tempting but highly spiced precooked dishes available almost around the clock.

Jimbaran Seafood (☎ 22620; Jl Cempaka; mains 16,000-22,000Rp, beer 16,000Rp; 🕑 10am-3pm & 4.30-10pm) Good Chinese-style food cooked to order though the simple, bright décor lacks atmosphere.

Pelangi (☎ 22802; mains 17,500-37,500Rp, beer 27,000Rp; 🕑 7am-midnight) Often considered Tual's best restaurant, this curious open-sided barn of a place sit on stilts above what should be a pond 3km north of Tual on the Dullah road. There are Chinese, pseudo-Thai and local menu options plus live music from around 9pm. Consider pre-ordering an *ojek* to get home at night.

Shopping

Several 'souvenir' shops are predominantly purveyors of local pearls.

Cendrawasih Souvenirs (☎ 22608; Jl Mohammad Amir Tamher) One such shop; run by a delightful gentleman from Aru who speaks the odd word of English.

Getting There & Away

AIR

The airport is a mere 300m stroll from Langgur's main street, Jl Jenderal Sudirman, along which bemos shuttle to Tual (2000Rp) with quite extraordinary frequency. However a new airport is planned 12km south beyond Satehan. **Trigana Air** (☎ 22780; Jl Cempaka; 🕑 8am-4pm Mon-Sat) has several local routings including five flights weekly to Ambon (875,000Rp, 1½ hours) offering beautiful views of Tayando and Banda en route. On Tuesday the Ambon flight continues to Ternate, Manado, Luwuk and ultimately Makassar, returning on Wednesdays. Baggage limit is just 10kg. **Merpati** (Agent Rahmat Jayamatra; ☎ 21376; Jl Fidnang Armau) flies thrice weekly to Ambon and Dobo (Aru).

BOAT

Pelni (☎ 22520; Jl Pattimura; 🕑 8am-2pm) liners *Bukit Siguntang* and *Ciremai* link Tual to Ambon (177,000Rp, 18 hours) via Bandaneira (128,000Rp, 10 hours). Eastbound both continue to Fak-Fak in Papua. In Langgur, Pelni agencies include **Mitra Jaya** (☎ 22392; Jl Jenderal Sudirman; 🕑 8am-4pm Mon-Sat).

For details of the complex Perintis cargo- shipping routes ask at the **port office** (☎ 22475).

An uncomfortable overnight car-ferry departs from behind Pasar Masrun on Fridays to Dobo (Aru) and Mondays to Saumlaki (Tanimbar Islands).

BEMO (MOBIL) & OJEK

Bemos (*mobils*) for southern Kei Kecil operate from a station near Pasar Langgur. Destinations include Debut (3000Rp) and Disuk (5000Rp). Bemos for Dullah (3000Rp, fairly frequent) and Difur Beach (Sunday only) leave from near Tual's clogged Pasar Masrun. At Langgur's Pasar Ohoijang there's a pick-up point for *mobils* to Ngur Bloat (for Pasir Panjang) but departures are impractically rare. It's much wiser to take an *ojek* (15,000Rp, 25 minutes).

Getting Around

Bemos (2000Rp per hop) are so common they form a virtual conveyer belt along Jl Jenderal Sudirman to Tual, many wind-

SASI SAVVY

Call it 'magic' or 'earth knowledge', Maluku experiences many hidden undercurrents of almost voodoo-esque beliefs, beautifully described in Lyall Watson's book *Gifts of Unexpected Things*. And the Kei group with its three castes, its gun-for-dowry customs and its holy trees is particularly rich in powerful superstition.

There's widespread Malukan belief in the idea of *sasi* as a 'prohibition' – a kind of 'spell' to protect property and prevent trespass. Physically the only barrier is a *janur* palm frond. But few would dare to break a *sasi* for fear of unknown 'effects'. For countless generations *sasi* have worked very well to prevent the theft of coconuts or to ensure that fish aren't caught during the breeding season. However, recently Kei Islanders have been using *sasi* as a cunning economic weapon. During late 2003, traditional landowners decided to put a *sasi* on the Tual-Langgur bridge, the only road link between the two towns. All bemo traffic stopped. Nobody dared to walk across. The result was a bonanza for boatmen. This silly situation lasted months till the authorities paid for a *sasi* removal ceremony. Other jokers made a *sasi* across the access route to the government offices so workers couldn't get to work. The 21st-century *sasi* seems to have become a unique version of the protection racket.

ing around via the Un Tower. Southbound from Tual, 'Langgur' bemos pass Hotel Vilia and terminate at Pasar Langgur. 'Perumnas' bemos divert to the area around the Anugerah church.

Ojeks cost 5000Rp per hop but renting per hour (15,000Rp) or day (50,000Rp) is remarkably good value. Folks at Hotel Dragon can organise self-drive *ojek*-bikes for similar rates.

PULAU KEI KECIL & PULAU DULLAH

Northern Kei Kecil

BUKIT MASBAIT

With great views over Langgur, the island's highest point is an important Easter pilgrimage site especially for Catholics. It's dominated by an open-armed Christ statue topping a globe and tower, surrounded by various scenes from the crucifixion. Notice the strikingly Asian features of the Roman centurion. Access up steps takes 10 minutes from an unmarked pass on the road to Letman just beyond Kelanit village.

OHOIDERTAWUN

The charming village of **Ohoidertawun** surveys a lovely bay that becomes a vast white sand flat at low tide. Craftsmen sit in the palm shade carving out canoes with adzes. An elfin Elim Church and pyramidal mosque coexist harmoniously. A footpath through the beachfront coconut grove passes Savana Cottages, a highly recommended four-room traveller retreat. The path continues to a stairway that leads up to Ohoider Atas village. But at low tide you can strike out across the sand from beside the bottom of the steps. Splashing through streams you pass small caves cut in the limestone cliffs, some containing human bones. And after around 25 minutes you'll find a series of red and orange **petroglyphs** painted on the cliff-faces. Although some designs look new, many are antique and their origin baffles archaeologists.

Sleeping

our pick **Savana Cottages** (☎ SMS only 0813 43083856; d 100,000Rp) For pure narcotic serenity, few budget guesthouses in Indonesia can beat Savana Cottages. Watch the changing moods of nature, the swooping curlews and the tide retreating in the moonlight while sipping an ice-cold beer or swinging from the hammock between sighing casuarinas. Locals believe that a particular holy tree beside the Savana Cottages has the power to enforce peace or bind relationships. And it seems to work an intangible magic on guests who are frequently mesmerised by this wonderful place's simple charms. Airy double-bedded cottage-style rooms come with rattan balcony chairs and towels for the shared bathrooms. There's a sweet little four-table café with tinkling wind-chimes (dinner 25,000Rp). When not away in Holland, English-speaking owner Gerson offers a variety of interesting excursions and explanations to some of the bizarre intricacies of Kei social life. Mosquito nets available on request.

PASIR PANJANG

The Kei Islands' most famous tourist draw is **Pasir Panjang**, 3km of white sand so powdery it feels like flour. Coconut palms curve across it obligingly for your photographic delectation. Yet despite the brochure-cover beauty, the beach is almost entirely deserted except at weekends. Amid the palms around 400m north of Ngur Bloat (aka Pasir Panjang village) are a handful of Saturday-night karaoke shacks, two offering accommodation.

The basic but more reputable **Losmen Ngur Bloat** (d incl breakfast 60,000Rp) has four rooms. Two have narrow new beds, the other have bigger but off-puttingly aged mattresses. There are private *mandis* and some beds have mosquito nets (essential here). You can hear but not see the waves from the rickety terrace. Keys are available from Evlyn Dresubun whose house is near the main junction in Ngur Bloat village.

There's nicer accommodation at the beach's reputedly haunted north end, 700m beyond Ohoililar village. **Coaster Cottages** (tw/apt 75,000/200,000Rp) has two slightly ageing rooms with a lovely porch plus a brand new apartment in a swish new house with double bed, big sitting room and curious scalloped *mandi*. Keys are available from Pedro Letsoin in Ohoililar village. Just beyond, the unmarked **Wisata Café** (meals 12,000-25,000Rp) is as yet little more than a house but the owners will cook for you on request and sometimes rent out one of their dishevelled rooms (150,000Rp).

Southern Kei Kecil

From **Debut** outrigger ferries cross to Tetoat from which a rough road continues to the impressive **Ohoidertutu Beach**. Also from Debut, daily speedboats cross to **Pulau Tanimbar Kei**, the most traditional and isolated of all the islands. There's no way back till next morning (unless you charter at around 2,000,000Rp!) and with no formal accommodation you'll have to arrange a bed through the *kepala desa*.

About 4km south of Debut between Dian and Letvuan, an unmarked track to the right leads down steps to **Gua Lian Hawan** – a pair of cave pools with ice-blue water and lots of butterflies. The road ends at **Evu**, source of Kei Kecil's fresh water and an unexpectedly popular weekend picnic spot thanks to its artificial splashing pool behind a monument displaying a *lela* (minicannon). In Evu's upper village, the older of two **St Antonius churches** is a photogenically ramshackle Dutch-era chapel.

Pulau Dullah

Dullah is famous as the starting point for October **Belang Races** using traditional *kora-kora* rowing boats. The races haven't run since 1998 but were slated to restart in 2006. A potholed kilometre beyond Tamadan is a beachless headland called **Pantai Serbat** with attractive distant views across limpid turquoise waters towards Kei Besar. For blinding white sand visit **Difur** which is idyllic on weekdays but over-run by strollers, motorbikes and food vendors on Sundays.

PULAU KEI BESAR

Scenic Kei Besar is a long ridge of lush, steep hills dotted with several picture-perfect beaches (better for photos than for swimming) and some of Maluku's most picturesque villages. Expect intense curiosity from locals and take your best *kamus* (dictionary) as nobody speaks English.

GETTING THERE & AWAY

Two daily passenger boats between Watdek (Langgur) and Elat (15,000Rp, 2½ hours) leave at 10.30am and 2.30pm in either direction, passing a series of *bagang* (fishing platforms). When demand is high, faster speedboats (25,000Rp, 80 minutes) occasionally double the routes, departing at the same times.

GETTING AROUND

Mobil are very rare; most road transport is by *ojek*. Be sure to book a return ride; Elat is the only place that you can reliably find an *ojek* and it's easy to get stranded in traffic-less outer villages.

Roadless settlements on the east coast are served by two multistop *Johnson* longboats. These depart daily from Yamtel around 1.30pm, awaiting passengers off the 10.30am ferry from Langgur. The longboats return next morning from Bandar Eli and Kilwat respectively, so day trips *from* Yamtel are impossible unless you charter (hugely expensive). Take sandals for wading through rock-pools to the boats. Sunscreen and rain protection are also important as the craft are uncovered.

Elat & Around

Kei Besar's main village and port is Elat, attractively set on a bay facing a handful of islets. Tempting **Pulau Kelapa** has a sandy beach just 10 minutes away by motor-canoe. There's a fine vista on the mountain-road descent towards Elat from the picturesque village of **Yamtel**.

An easy *ojek*-ride up the west coast north of Elat are several charming villages with island glimpses, bay views, stone stairways and rocky terraces. Most notable are **Ngurdu** (3km from Elat), **Soinrat** (4km), curiously named **Bombay** (7km) and **Watsin** (8km). Beyond, settlements are newer and less attractive. At **Wer Fravav** (12km) the road ends, but adventurous hikers could follow a (usually dry) riverbed through cacophonously exotic birdsong to a relatively intact stand of mountain forest.

SLEEPING & EATING

Elat has Kei Besar's only accommodation. Neither of these places have signs or fans. Both have shared toilets and *mandis*.

Penginapan Sanohi (☎ 23013; Jl Pelabuhan; r per person 20,000Rp) Sanohi has new sheets on very aged mattresses and some damp patches on the walls. The location is odd – the two floors above the BRI bank office. To get the key find Mrs Sanohi at the shop three doors back towards the port.

Penginapan Sederhana (Jl Uver; s/tw 30,000/40,000Rp) This is the neater option with cleanly tiled if rather stuffy rooms. It's the white-colonnaded bungalow with red trim at the northern end of the tiny park, one house uphill from the market on the road towards Yamtel.

Elat has a market and three rice-and-fish *rumah makan*. All close by dusk, so eat early or snack on biscuits from the few tiny evening shops.

Pantai Daftel

Southwest of Elat a steep, super-narrow road passes **St Josef's**, an unusual half-timbered hospital with lovely bay views glimpsed through palm fronds and bougainvillea. **Pantai Daftel**, a superb white-sand beach starts where the road reaches the coast (6km from Elat) at minuscule **Karkarit**. It stretches 1.8km to **Lerehoilin**, where a tiny waterside mosque faces a tidal island topped with ancient graves. The main access point is between these two hamlets at Daftel where there's a handful of picnic shelters on the beach behind a rusty Dalek-shaped mosque. The waving palms are superbly photogenic though the water is generally too shallow for swimming. You'll probably have it all to yourself except on Sundays when snack stalls open to cater to local picnickers.

Ojeks ask 20,000Rp return from Elat.

South of Elat

The main road south roller-coasters down the island's central spine and is asphalted as far as **Ohoiwait**. Though there are few glimpses of sea, it's worth venturing at least as far as **Waur** (6km from Elat). A Lourdes-style Madonna lurks in a grotto behind Waur's oversized wooden church, the 1927 **Gereja Hati Kudus Jesus**. Two hundred metres beyond, a **VOC cannon** points curiously at the church's front door from beside the **woma** (see boxed text, below).

East Coast

The eastern coastline has attractive tidal rock-pools but no beaches. Villages are comparatively isolated, steeped in superstitious traditions and tend to speak the local Kei language rather than Bahasa Indonesia. From Elat it takes at least an hour to reach Kilwair (21km away) via **Reyahru**, within whose high forests is hidden a mysterious **batu kapal** (stone boat). Straight-faced locals will assure you this was once a Portuguese shipwreck that somehow became petrified and ran up the mountain! Some 10 minutes' walk along the beach from **Kilwair**, Anderius Uwaubun is happy to show off his private turtle pool. Walk five minutes further to find the triple-arched **Kuel Rock**, site of local fairy tales in which a woman turned into a Kuel fish.

Well beyond the road's end, **Banda Eli** is home to many Bandanese. These are the

WOMA

The spiritual centre of every Kei village is marked by an open-air shrine known as a *woma*, into whose offering dish superstitious people drop coins for good luck. Many modern *woma* are tackily painted concrete monstrosities. But in Waur you can find a rare original one in the form of an unembellished five-legged stone altar.

MALUKU

descendants of survivors that fled the Banda Islands during the Dutch-led massacres of 1621 (see p765). The Bandanese language, now extinct in the Banda Islands, is still spoken here and the people are renowned for goldsmithing.

SOUTHERN MALUKU

Of many very isolated island Maluku island groups, perhaps the most interesting are the **Tanimbars** (Saumlaki is the capital). Known for wild orchids, their one real tourist attraction is at **Sangliat Dol,** around 1½ uncomfortable hours from Saumlaki. Here a 30m-high staircase leads up from the beach to an intricately carved 18m-long boat-shaped stone platform. The mostly flat **Aru** island group (Dobo is the capital) is famed for its pearls. Both capitals are served by flights from Langgur and by weekly car-ferries from Tual. A comparatively arid arc of southern islands swings back around towards Timor. These are of much more interest to geologists than to tourists and most are accessible only by rare Perintis cargo boats, though little **Pulau Kisar** has an airport. In early 2006 the Maluku government announced plans to develop infrastructure on **Pulau Wetar** hoping one day to develop transport links to East Timor, just 56km to the south.

PULAU TERNATE

☎ **0921**

A string of perfect volcanic cone islands lurk off the western coast of crazy-K shaped Pulau Halmahera. Of these, Pulau Ternate and its neighbour Pulau Tidore are the most populous, visually dramatic and historically significant. Both islands are ancient Islamic sultanates with a long history of bitter rivalry. As the world's only major producers of a globally important product (cloves), their sultans became the most powerful rulers in the medieval Indies, wasting much of their wealth fighting each other. At certain times both sultans could claim nominal influence that spread as far afield as Ambon, Sulawesi and Papua.

In 1511 the Portuguese were the first Europeans to settle in Ternate. Tidore's then ruler quickly responded by inviting in the Spaniards. Both sultans found their

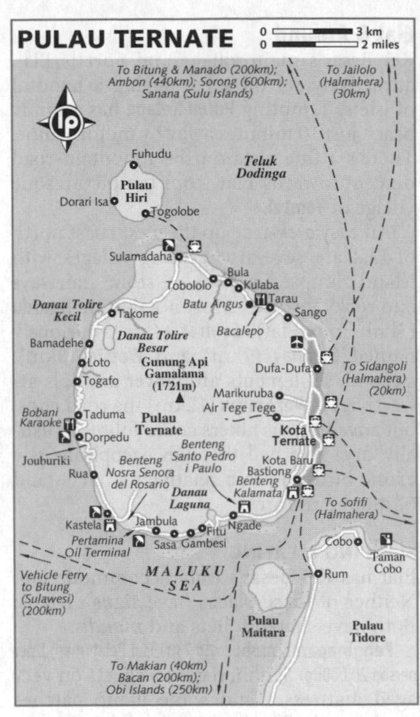

hospitality rapidly exhausted as the Europeans tried to dominate the islands, corner the spice market and preach Christianity. Ternate's Muslim population, already offended by the European's imported pigs and heavy-handed 'justice', were driven to rebel when Sultan Hairun (Khairun) was executed and his head exhibited on a pike in February 1570. The besieged Portuguese held out in their castle till 1575 when the new Ternatean sultan took it over as his palace. Five years later he entertained the English pirate-adventurer Francis Drake. After an amicable meeting, Drake astounded his host by his almost total disinterest in buying cloves. In fact, Drake's ship *Golden Hind* was so full of stolen Spanish-American gold that he simply couldn't carry any cloves.

The Spaniards and Dutch were the next to make themselves unpopular. In a history that is as fascinating as it is complicated and Machiavellian, they played Ternate off against Tidore as well as confronting one another for control of an elusive clove monopoly. The Dutch prevailed eventually, though the sultanates continued almost uninterrupted for most of the period and remain well-respected institutions today.

Ternate saw some violence in 1999–2000, but is now rebounding with major construction programmes. A proposed geothermal power station between Kastela and Rua should one day end the island's regular power cuts, but as yet there's only a collapsed signboard at the site.

KOTA TERNATE

Clinging to the volcanic cone of dramatic Gamalama, Kota Ternate offers some lovely glimpses of neighbouring islands but is mainly useful as a base for exploring North Maluku. There are a couple of partly restored forts and a palace to visit. For now most other architecture looks rather drab and haphazard, spiced painfully in some suburbs by occasional ruins of churches gutted in 1999. However a massive land-reclamation and building programme seems set to transform the city over coming years. Several fine new mosques are already under construction.

Orientation

Areas within the city are still called 'villages' but in reality, Kota Ternate is one long sprawl stretching around 10km from the airport to beyond Bastiong port. The commercial centre is on and around Jl Pahlawan Revolusi, known at its southern end as 'Swering', an eternally popular promenade for afternoon strolls and evening snacking. The main north–south through-road has different names at different points: Jl Sultan Khairun, Jl Merdeka, Jl Mononutu, Jl Hasan Esa and eventually Jl Raya Bastiong.

Information

INTERNET ACCESS

Chamber Internet (Jl Hasan Esa; per hr 10,000Rp) Sporadic opening hours.

Muara C@feNet (☎ 328412; Jl Pahlawan Revolusi; per hr 10,000Rp; 🕑 8am-midnight) Decent connection and a great central location but subject to power cuts and mosquitoes. It's in the Muara Hotel lobby, upstairs above the Nirwana Elsh Hotel.

Warnet Gamalama.net (Jl Pattimura; per hr 8,000Rp; 🕑 24hr; ❄) Comfy chairs, air-con, power-supply backup and OK connection. Within the Telkom Building.

Warung Internet Anteronet (Jl Sultan Khairun 125; per hr 6000Rp) Sporadic opening hours.

MONEY

Bank Mandiri (Jl Nukila) ATM for Visa and Delta but not MasterCard; withdrawals of up to 1,250,000Rp. There's also a branch on Jl Mononutu.

BNI Bank (Bank Negara Indonesia; Jl Pahlawan Revolusi; 🕑 7.30am-3pm Mon-Thu, 7.30-noon Fri) The only bank to change money: only US-dollar cash with a minimum $100 exchange.

Danamon Bank (Jl Pahlawan Revolusi) ATM is 24-hour and allows withdrawals up to 1,500,000Rp on most cards.

TELEPHONE

Strangely Ternate phone numbers can have five, six or seven digits. Expect rationalisation in coming years.

Telkom (Jl Pattimura & Jl Pahlawan Revolusi; 🕑 24hr)

TOURIST INFORMATION

Despite ample ranks of under-employed staff and reasonable spoken English these offices seem to serve little useful purpose. Between them they can't even muster an accurate map of Ternate City.

North Maluku Tourist Office (☎ 327396; Jl Kamboja 14; 🕑 8am-4pm Mon-Fri) Some passingly informative brochures are available if the boss hasn't walked off with the store-room key.

Ternate City Tourist Office (☎ 22760; Jl Kamaluddin 7; 🕑 8am-2pm Mon-Fri) Friendly staff can help you find a guide to climb Gamalama. Possibly.

Sights

KERATON (ISTANA KESULTAN)

Built in 1796 and restored in semi-colonial style, the Sultan's Palace is still a family home. However there is a **museum section** (donation) containing a small but interesting collection of Portuguese and Dutch helmets, various swords and armour, plus memorabilia from the reigns of past sultans. Notice the genealogy of the Ternatean royal family dating back to 1257. The airy veranda offers wide views towards Halmahera. First step in a visit is signing in at the **Sekretariat kiosk**

HELLO MISTER

Few places in Indonesia have so many ultra keen English-language students desperate to help tourists in return for conversation practice. They pop up everywhere. This can result in delightful friendships or infuriating feelings of being pestered, depending on your outlook (and good fortune).

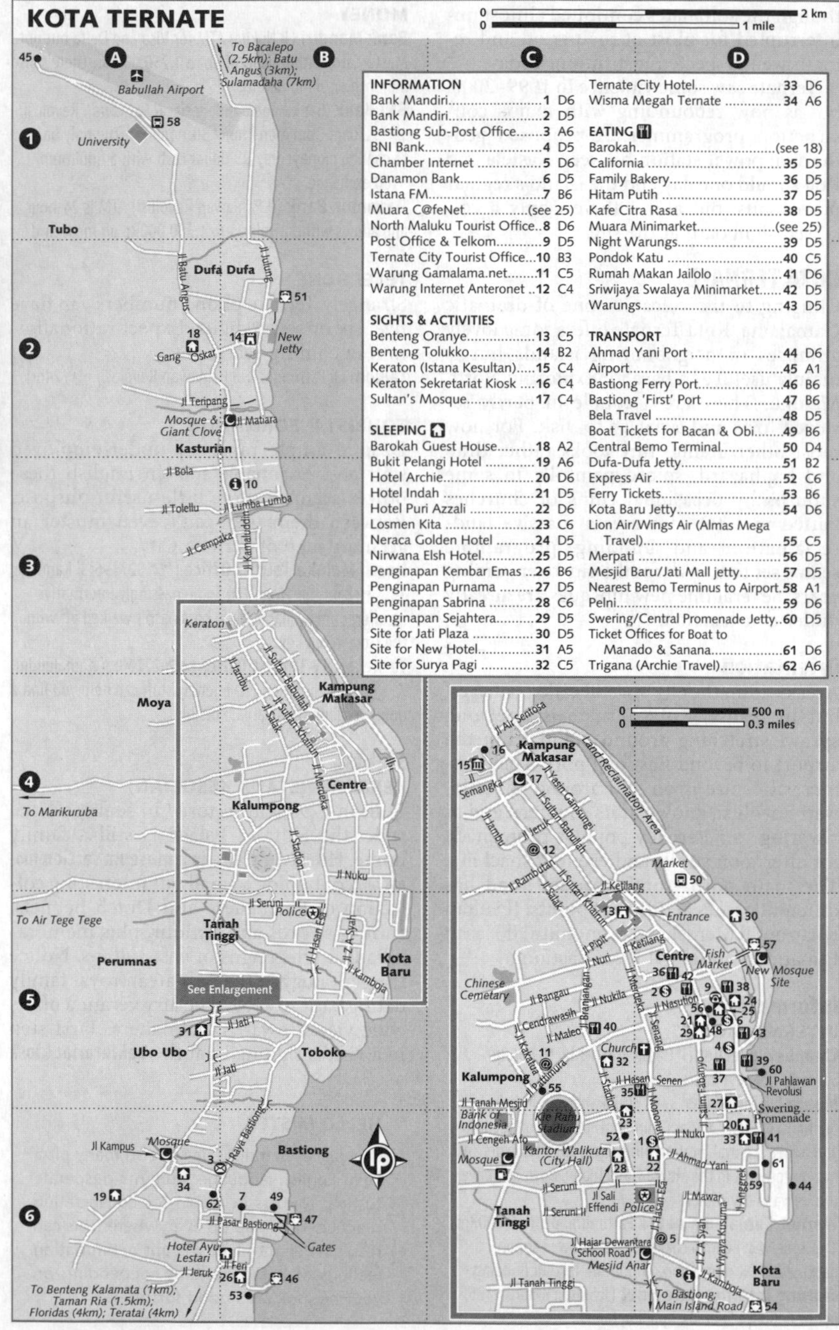
KOTA TERNATE
0 2 km
0 1 mile
INFORMATION
Bank Mandiri 1 D6
Bank Mandiri 2 D5
Bastiong Sub-Post Office 3 A6
BNI Bank 4 D5
Chamber Internet 5 D6
Danamon Bank 6 D5
Istana FM 7 B6
Muara C@feNet (see 25)
North Maluku Tourist Office 8 D6
Post Office & Telkom 9 D5
Ternate City Tourist Office 10 B3
Warung Gamalama.net 11 C5
Warung Internet Anteronet 12 C4
SIGHTS & ACTIVITIES
Benteng Oranye 13 C5
Benteng Tolukko 14 B2
Keraton (Istana Kesultan) 15 C4
Keraton Sekretariat Kiosk 16 C4
Sultan's Mosque 17 C4
SLEEPING
Barokah Guest House 18 A2
Bukit Pelangi Hotel 19 A6
Hotel Archie 20 D6
Hotel Indah 21 D5
Hotel Puri Azzali 22 D6
Losmen Kita 23 C6
Neraca Golden Hotel 24 D5
Nirwana Elsh Hotel 25 D5
Penginapan Kembar Emas 26 B6
Penginapan Purnama 27 D5
Penginapan Sabrina 28 C6
Penginapan Sejahtera 29 D5
Site for Jati Plaza 30 D5
Site for New Hotel 31 A5
Site for Surya Pagi 32 C5
Ternate City Hotel 33 D6
Wisma Megah Ternate 34 A6
EATING
Barokah (see 18)
California 35 D5
Family Bakery 36 D5
Hitam Putih 37 D5
Kafe Citra Rasa 38 D5
Muara Minimarket (see 25)
Night Warungs 39 D5
Pondok Katu 40 C5
Rumah Makan Jailolo 41 D6
Sriwijaya Swalaya Minimarket 42 D5
Warungs 43 D5
TRANSPORT
Ahmad Yani Port 44 D6
Airport 45 A1
Bastiong Ferry Port 46 B6
Bastiong 'First' Port 47 B6
Bela Travel 48 D5
Boat Tickets for Bacan & Obi 49 B6
Central Bemo Terminal 50 D4
Dufa-Dufa Jetty 51 B2
Express Air 52 C6
Ferry Tickets 53 B6
Kota Baru Jetty 54 D6
Lion Air/Wings Air (Almas Mega Travel) 55 C5
Merpati 56 D5
Mesjid Baru/Jati Mall jetty 57 D5
Nearest Bemo Terminus to Airport 58 A1
Pelni 59 D6
Swering/Central Promenade Jetty 60 D5
Ticket Offices for Boat to Manado & Sanana 61 D6
Trigana (Archie Travel) 62 A6
To Bacalepo (2.5km); Batu Angus (3km); Sulamadaha (7km)
Babullah Airport
University
Tubo
Dufa Dufa
New Jetty
Gang Oskat
Mosque & Giant Clove
Kasturian
Moya
Kampung Makasar
Keraton
Centre
Kalumpong
Tanah Tinggi
Kota Baru
To Marikuruba
To Air Tege Tege
Perumnas
See Enlargement
Ubo Ubo
Toboko
Bastiong
Mosque
Gates
Hotel Ayu Lestari
To Benteng Kalamata (1km); Taman Ria (1.5km); Floridas (4km); Teratai (4km)
0 500 m
0 0.3 miles
Land Reclamation Area
Market
Entrance
Fish Market
New Mosque Site
Chinese Cemetary
Church
Kie Raha Stadium
Bank of Indonesia
Kantor Walikuta (City Hall)
Police
Mesjid Anar
Swering Promenade
To Bastiong; Main Island Road

(☎ 21166; ⏰ 6am-6pm) to find when a guide is available. If you're lucky you might even be granted an audience with the sultan's enchanting sister Ibu Rini, and hear tales (in fluent English) of the royal family's amazing life sagas.

Only groups with the Sultan's permission (arranged well ahead) may see the **mahkota** (royal crown). Topped with cassowary feathers, it's worn only at coronations and supposedly has magical powers including growing 'hair', which needs periodic cutting. Some claim it has the more impressive ability to stop Gamalama from erupting.

All northbound bemos pass the grassy square that the Keraton overlooks.

SULTAN'S MOSQUE

Just south of the palace, the royal mosque has a traditional multi-tiered pyramid form. Beneath the corrugated red roof the heavy interior timberwork is impressive. There are big expansion plans. The mosque is the focus of *Laila Tulqadr* celebrations on the 27th evening of Ramadan when a mass of flaming torches welcomes the Sultan's procession.

BENTENG ORANYE

Almost hidden in the market-melee right at the centre of town are three re-concreted walls and four cannon-topped bastions. That's all that remains a massive 1607 **fort** that was headquarters of the entire Dutch VOC operation before it moved to Batavia (Jakarta) in around 1619. The fort later became the residence of the Dutch governors in Ternate.

BENTENG TOLUKKO

Built by the Portuguese in 1512 and restored by the Dutch in 1610, this dinky little 'womb-shaped' fort (also known as Benteng Hollandia) was the first European stronghold on Ternate. For a donation the lady living beside the entrance can let you in and show you photos of the extensive 1996 renovations. Take any bemo bound for Dufa-Dufa (2000Rp, 3km from town centre).

BENTENG KALAMATA

At the southernmost end of town, this small, heavy-handedly renovated fort is about 1km south of Bastiong. Once known as Benteng Kayu Merah (Red Wood Fort), it was built in 1540 by the Portuguese, and rebuilt by the Dutch in 1610. Waves lap right up to its angled walls and there are great views across to Tidore. Take a Rua, Sasa or Jambula bemo (2000Rp).

GUNUNG API GAMALAMA

This 1721m volcano *is* Pulau Ternate. Gamalama erupted in 1840, destroying almost every house on the island. Although it has blown its fiery nose as recently as 1980, 1983 and 1994 it is not considered imminently dangerous. A volcanology unit keeps careful watch from Marikuruba village. There are pleasant, short, clove-grove hikes from Air Tege Tege village (near the transmitter tower). The going is very steep and climbing above the tree line is both strenuous and hazardous. Reaching the often cloud-shrouded summit takes around five hours and requires a guide. At least two foreign visitors have disappeared in the attempt; some claim this was because they broke taboos (eg not urinating above a certain elevation) or failed to say requisite prayers en route. The tourist offices can help locate guides.

Sleeping

You'll probably value a powerful new air conditioner given the oppressive heat and sauna-like humidity. Even the nicest existing places often have a little peeling paint, damp patches, a slimy *mandi* and a hint of dysfunction. However at least five great-looking new hotels are under construction, including the almost-finished Surya Pagi (Jl Stadion), what looks a major construction in Ubo Ubo and the three-star waterfront Jati Plaza, part of the big new mall development.

BUDGET

Budget accommodation under 150,000Rp is plentiful but very often abysmal, notably between Ahmad Yani Port and Jl Kamboja. There are a few exceptions.

Taman Ria (☎ 22124; d 75,000-100,000Rp) Set in a waterfront garden 4km south of the centre beyond Benteng Kalamata, the best room (8A) is new and very pleasant with views of Tidore. Others are high-ceilinged boxes.

Penginapan Sabrina (☎ 25896; Jl Sali Effendi; s/d with fan 65,000/90,000Rp, d with air-con 150,000Rp; ❄)

MALUKU

Friendly, relatively clean family homestay in a quiet backstreet.

Hotel Indah (☎ 21334; Jl Bosoiri 3; s/tw with fan 66,000/77,000Rp, with air-con 93,500/110,000Rp, with air-con & hot water 137,500/154,000; ❄) Modest but eternally popular.

Nirwana Elsh Hotel (☎ 23257; Jl Pahlawan Revolusi; tw/ste 115,000-170,000/275,000Rp; ❄) Perfectly central, this is a rambling warren of acceptable all-air-con rooms. Though none is especially charming, they're recently renovated and reasonable value. From 170,000Rp you get hot water, at least when there's electricity (there isn't a generator).

Neraca Golden Hotel (☎ 21668; Jl Pahlawan Revolusi; s/tw from 99,000/126,500Rp; ❄) Once considered Ternate's best hotel, today the Neraca is looking pretty worn. Rooms are dreary and even the 165,000Rp junior suites have bucket *mandis* and non-flushing loos. However a crucial plus is that air-con rooms stay cool during inevitable city power-cuts thanks to the Neraca's earth-shaking generator. Supercentral.

Losmen Kita (☎ 21950; Jl Stadion; tw with cold/hot showers 150,000/200,000Rp; ❄) Rambling low-rise bed-factory with nearly 50 clean, bland rooms.

Ternate City Hotel (☎ 22555; fax 22630; Jl Nuku 1; standard s/d 143,000/187,000Rp, superior s/d 198,000/242,000Rp; ❄) All rooms are air-conditioned and most are reasonably bright though some are windowless and showing signs of wear. Superior rooms are similar but with hot water and fewer stairs to climb.

If money-saving is all that matters:

Penginapan Kembar Emas (☎ 3110750; Jl Feri, Bastiong; s/d 50,000/60,000Rp, d with fan 70,000Rp) Good value, clean cheapie facing Bastiong ferry port from behind a low wall. Clientele mostly male.

Penginapan Purnama (☎ 24297; Mohajarin Falajawa; per person 30,000Rp) Four survivable rooms without fan or bathroom in a slightly grubby family home with lots of old Chinese porcelain.

Penginapan Sejahtera (☎ 21139; Jl Salim Fabanyo 298; s/d from 38,000/70,000Rp) Tiny, very basic box-rooms but comparatively clean and repainted.

MIDRANGE

Barokah Guest House (☎ 23120; Gang Oskar; d/tw 175,000-220,000/220,000Rp; ❄) Well-appointed air-con rooms with minibar, TV, VCD-player and hot-water shower are ranged above the eccentric Barokah restaurant. Bridge-balconies have decent views of Gamalama. Some new doubles have amusing tiger-striped linen.

Wisma Megah Ternate (☎ 327989; Jl Raya Bastiong Dusun; s/d 150,000/250,000Rp; ❄) Creamy-coloured new air-con rooms have good beds and satellite TV in a nouveau-riche suburban house. Contemplate lovely wide views from bamboo chairs on the 3rd-floor terrace.

Bukit Pelangi Hotel (☎ 22180; fax 327077; Jl Jati Selatan 338; executive d from 330,000Rp; ❄) The Bukit Pelangi rises like a minor colonial palace high above Bastiong. Its best features are a terrace with a wonderful view and the big, sparse sitting room with grandfather clock. Rooms are comfortable but stylistically a very mixed bag. Most are painted in sickly pastel colours: look at several before choosing. There are a couple of cheaper options under 300,000Rp but those are particularly disappointing.

Hotel Archie (☎ 3110555; Jl Nuku 6; s from 258,000-286,000, tw from 286,000-313,500, d from 286,000-357,500Rp; ❄) Modern, floral rooms and attentive service, partly in English. Some better rooms have bathtubs entered between theatrical columns.

Hotel Puri Azzali (☎ 21959; Jl Mononutu 275; d 385,000, ste 440,000-495,000Rp; ❄) Bright, stylishly minimalist mini-hotel tastefully appointed with orchids and framed fabrics. Strangely, given the pricing, the small bathrooms don't have hot water, but otherwise the bedrooms were the most agreeable in Ternate at the time of research.

Eating

For cheap eats there's an almost limitless number of warungs, notably around the markets and on the 'Swering' promenade (Jl Pahlawan Revolusi).

The island's most appealing upmarket eateries are outside the city in Terau and Ngade (see p786).

Rumah Makan Jailolo (Jl Pahlawan Revolusi 7; meals 6,000-10,000Rp; 🕑 10am-10pm) Bright, reliable place for inexpensive point-and-pick rice-and-fish meals.

Hitam Putih (☎ 327423; Jl Hasan Senen; snack meals 6,600-11,000Rp, fresh juices 7700Rp; 🕑 7.30am-6pm & 7.30pm-11pm) Decent light snacks and excellent juices in a hoedown taverna with fish tanks and dinky lanterns. There's karaoke but the atmosphere is oriented towards couples and families, unlike many buy-a-girl places around town.

Kafe Citra Rasa (☎ 328420; Jl Pahlawan Revolusi; mains 8500-13,000Rp; 9am-10pm) Looks dowdy by day but at night it's fairly charming in the swaying wicker lamplight. Popular with couples and very affordable despite unpriced menus.

Barokah (☎ 23120; Gang Oskar; mains 14,300-66,000Rp; breakfast, lunch & dinner) An artificial goblin glade serving Japanese, European and local dishes that are tasty if somewhat greasy. The live music is relatively mellow.

California (☎ 311 0076; Jl Hasan Senen; burgers 10,200Rp, meals from 16,000Rp; 10am-10pm) Ternate's chicken fast food palace struggles valiantly with power cuts to produce very tasty 'chicken steaks' (9700Rp) as well as bird-burgers and Kentucky-style drumsticks.

Pondok Katu (☎ 327332; Jl Branjangan 28; mains 25,000-37,000Rp; 10am-10pm) This refreshingly air-conditioned oasis has high-beamed ceilings and is popular for seafood lunches and good Chinese food.

For self-catering try the **Sriwijaya Swalaya** (Jl Bosoiri) or **Muara** (Jl Pahlawan Revolusi) mini-markets. **Family Bakery** (Jl Nukila; 8am-7pm) has a selection of fresh bread and pastries.

Entertainment

In Ternate most entertainment revolves around dining or karaoke. Alternatively a couple of days per month you could turn out to cheer for Persiter, Ternate's major-league football team who play at the often overfull, unshaded Kie Rahu stadium. For afternoon games bring plenty of water, sun protection and a fan.

Getting There & Away

AIR

Lion Air/Wings Air (Almas Mega Travel; ☎ 55555; Jl Pattimura; 8am-8pm) flies twice daily to Manado with connections to Makassar, Jakarta and Surabaya. Prices are load-weighted so book ahead.

Express Air (☎ 328484; Jl Stadion; 8am-6pm Mon-Fri, 8am-2pm Sat & Sun) flies three times weekly to Jakarta via Makassar using a relatively fast Boeing 747, taking only five hours.

Trigana Air (Archie Travel; ☎ 328484; Jl Raya Bastiong; 8am-5pm Mon-Sat) provides a useful Ternate–Ambon–Tual link (out Wednesdays, returning Tuesdays) and hops once weekly to Makassar via Manado and Luwuk.

Merpati (☎ 21651; Jl Bosoiri; 8am-4pm Mon-Sat, 9am-noon Sun) flies daily except Mondays to Jakarta via Makassar, four times weekly to Manado and three times weekly to Yogyakarta via Makassar. It also operates two small planes buzzing to a wealth of North Maluku destinations. See the map on p752.

Bela Travel (☎ 25470; fax 25364; Jl Bosoiri; 9am-noon & 2-5pm Mon-Fri, 9am-3pm Sat) can book various onward flights ex Manado or Jakarta.

BOAT

Ternate is the shipping hub for North Maluku. Ahmad Yani port is the passenger harbour for **Pelni** (☎ 21434; 8am-4pm Mon-Sat) liners. The irregular *Sangiang* loops round Halmahera. *Nggapulu* and *Sinabung* both stop at Ternate between Sorong (Papua; 137,500Rp, 14 to 16 hours) and Bitung (northern Sulawesi, 97,500Rp, seven hours). The *Lambelu* links Ternate with Ambon (115,000Rp, 19 hours) via Namlea (Buru) eastbound only.

Non-Pelni slow boats *RM Theodora/Intim Teratai* both sail to Manado (145,000Rp, 21 hours) on Saturdays/Thursdays and to Sanana (Sula Islands, 210,000Rp, up to two days) on Tuesdays/Thursdays.

Other jetties:

Bastiong ferry port Vehicle ferries daily to Rum (Tidore, 3800Rp, 7am) and Sidangoli (Halmahera; 14,900Rp, 8am) and overnight to Bitung (North Sulawesi, 66,000Rp, 10am Wednesdays and 5pm Saturdays).

Bastiong 'first' port Speedboats to Rum (Tidore), and all boat services to Makian, Bacan (80,000Rp, 8pm) and Obi.

Dufa-Dufa jetty Speedboats to Jailolo (Halmahera).

Kota Baru jetty Twice daily speedboats to Sofifi (Halmahera) from where *mobils* connect to Weda.

Mesjid Baru/Jati Mall jetty Speedboats to Sidangoli (Halmahera).

Swering/Central Promenade jetty Daily speedboats to Goto (Tidore, 10,000Rp, 4pm) and to Sofifi (Halmahera, 30,000Rp, 10am).

Getting Around

Taxis want an outrageous 35,000Rp for the 6km hop from Babullah Airport into the centre of town. Sometimes *ojeks* will accept 15,000Rp from just beyond the gate. Alternatively walk 10 minutes to the university from where very frequent bemos cost 2000Rp to the central bemo terminal. Bemos continue from here in all directions (2000Rp) but within the centre, *ojeks*

(3000Rp per short hop) are much more convenient.

AROUND PULAU TERNATE

The places in this section are covered anticlockwise from Kota Ternate.

Facing the crashing waves in Terau, **Bacalepo** (☎ 21724; mains 25,000-90,000Rp, juices 13,800-16,500; ⏰ 10am-midnight) is one of Ternate's most appealing cafés, with a hint of Balinese style and a stepped waterfront terrace. Just beyond, **Batu Angus** (Burnt Rock) is a spiky 300-year-old lava flow, not a type of steak.

At the top of the island, **Sulamadaha** has a popular if somewhat scruffy black-sand beach just beyond the simple but acceptable **Hotel Pantai Indah** (d with fan 50,000Rp). From a cove some 800m east, occasional public longboats (3000Rp per person) buzz across to the offshore volcanic cone of **Pulau Hiri**. Hiri was last step of the Sultan's family's 1945 *Sound of Music*–style escape from Ternate. Snorkelling off Hiri is relatively good by Ternate standards and there are plans for a dive-shop in Sulamadaha – ask Riko at **Istana FM** (☎ 0812 4450304) near Bastiong 'First' port.

Beyond some nutmeg plantations and the village of **Takome**, the main road returns to the coast beside small, muddy Danau Tolire Kecil. Less than a kilometre further, a paved side-lane (2000Rp fee) climbs to the rim of **Danau Tolire Besar**. Startlingly sheer cliffs plummet down to the lugubriously green, crocodile-infested waters of this deep crater lake. Local children offer guide services should you want to descend (1½ hours return on foot).

Jouburiki beach, reached by a footpath from the southern edge of **Dorpedu**, was the spot where Ternate's very first sultan was supposedly crowned in 1257. More picturesque black-sand beaches are found at **Rua** and at **Kastela**. The latter village is named for the 1522 Portuguese fort of **Benteng Nosra Senora del Rosario**, whose ruins have recently received some ham-fisted partial renovations. Beside it, topped with a giant clove, a concrete monument graphically reminds you that the Portuguese murdered Sultan Hairun in 1570 then got their comeuppance five years later.

At Ngade the stubby fort remnant of **Benteng Santo Pedro i Paulo** was once Ternate's main line of defence against a 1606 Spanish attack.

our pick Floridas (☎ 24430; mains 11,000-250,000; ⏰ breakfast, lunch & dinner) Across the road from the fort, Floridas is a terraced restaurant with splendid views across the bay to the superimposed cones of Tidore and Maitara. They serve quite outstanding *ikan woku kenari* (fish in hot almond sauce roasted in a banana leaf).

Teratai (☎ 327445; mains 16,500-300,000; ⏰ 8am-11pm) Near Floridas, Teratai has similarly lovely views shared by two comfortable **guest rooms** (d 250,000Rp, ❄). Teratai's terrace has slightly more atmosphere than Floridas' but suffers more from karaoke noise.

Danau Laguna, a pleasant, spring-fed bowl-lake with a lushly forested perimeter is the last green space before reaching Kota Ternate again near **Benteng Kalamata**.

Getting Around

Most of the paved round-island road is served by public bemos from Kota Ternate's central terminal. They are remarkably frequent as far as Sulamadaha (3000Rp anticlockwise) and Kastela (2000Rp clockwise). Although no single bemo goes right around, some north-route vehicles drive as far as Togafo (4000Rp). From there it's a pleasantly windy 2km walk to Taduma, where the longest south-route bemos start.

A better alternative is to charter an *ojek* for the afternoon (around 30,000Rp per hour, negotiable).

SADDAM & OSAMA *Mark Elliott*

'Saddam is hero of the World' says a Bush-bashing signboard in Ternate. In Sidangoli the old Iraqi dictator's face co-decorates a public bench seat along with Osama bin Laden. There are plenty more like these. And Osama features widely on popular T-shirts. But don't assume that this implies deep-seated radical Islam. It's rather like a Che Guevara poster on a British student's wall: a trendy image that's highly unlikely to imply actual involvement with revolutionary communism. 'So who is this Osama chap on your chest?' I asked one bin Laden shirt wearer. She giggled embarrassedly. After consulting with some friends she finally replied: 'He's a friendly Arab who likes to help the poor'.

MALUKU

PULAU TIDORE

☎ 0921

Charming Tidore makes a refreshing contrast to the bustle of Ternate, its neighbour and implacable historical enemy. Tidore, also a great spice producer, was an independent Islamic sultanate from 1109 until abolished in the Soekarno era. The 36th sultan was reinstated in 1999. The island's proud volcanic profile looks magnificent viewed from Bastiong in Ternate, while the finest views of Ternate are from the Maftutu–Rum and Gurabunga–Lada-Ake roads on Tidore.

Getting There & Away

Twelve-seater speedboats from Bastiong 'First' port in Ternate depart very frequently until dusk (6000Rp, seven minutes). These arrive at Rum from where bemos run to Tidore's capital Soasio (7500Rp, 30 minutes) via the south coast road. There's also a Bastiong–Rum car ferry (3800Rp, 7am), and one direct speedboat from Goto to Kota Ternate's 'Swering' jetty at 7am.

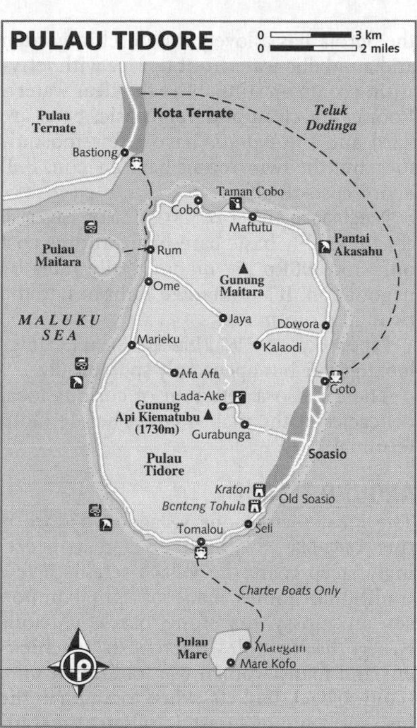

Getting Around

Bemos shuttle very frequently from Goto market terminal to old Soasio (2000Rp, 10 minutes), with most continuing to Tomalou (4000Rp) and some to Rum (7500Rp, 30 minutes). On the northern road no bemo goes beyond Maftutu from Soasio/Goto. Bemos to Gurabunga (8500Rp) leave infrequently except for busy Tuesday, Friday and Sunday market mornings. *Ojeks* want 50,000Rp return from Soasio to Lada-Ake via Gurabunga and a similar fee for the rough but appealing Soasio–Maftutu–Rum run.

SOASIO

Tidore's very modest historical heart is at the southernmost edge of Soasio, overlooked by **Benteng Tohula**. The overgrown remnants of this 17th-century Spanish fort sit on a low ridge reached by a new stairway. Barely a minute's walk north is the flower-decked Penginapan Saroja where it's worth having a gritty coffee (2000Rp) on the idyllic rear waterfront terrace even if you don't stay the night. Just beyond is the **Sonyine Malige Sultan's Memorial Museum**, displaying the sultan's sedan chair and giant spittoons, plus the royal crown topped with cassowary feathers. The crown is considered as magical as the Ternate equivalent. Opening hours are by arrangement; finding the museum's curator, Umar Muhammad, can be an amusing palaver: mornings try the DIKNAS office in the Dinas Pendidikan dan Kebudayan building, 2km north. Or try his home in the Gamatufgange area. Umar has been known to demand rather outrageous fees (up to 100,000Rp!) and isn't always keen to bargain.

One block inland from the museum, all that remains of the original **kraton** royal citadel (Istana Sultan) are the sturdy if overgrown whitewashed-base bastions. However, a new blue-roofed palace-villa is slowly taking shape here which might one day be rather grand.

Helpful English teacher **Muhlis Sehe** (☎ 0813 56027457) is ultra keen to meet English speakers.

Sleeping & Eating

Penginapan Seroja (☎ 61456; Jl Sultan Hassanuddin; s/tw 75,000/150,000Rp ❄) By far Soasio's most picturesque accommodation option,

MALUKU

the Seroja has a lovely little orchid garden and an idyllic waterfront terrace with jetty-sitting room on stilts above the clear waters. Rooms are clean and very basic, beds are hard and the *mandis* have a few mosquitoes, but the twin-rooms have air-con. Full board costs double.

Penginapan Sibu (☎ 62413; Jl Sultan Hassanuddin) Incredibly basic bare-board rooms cost only 150,000Rp *per month*. Daily rates by negotiation. It's unmarked right beside the two tall radio-masts.

Pondok Eky (☎ 61168; Jl Tana-apa) An appealing-looking café but opens only sporadically.

There's also a selection of curious local delicacies at the main market beside Goto terminal.

AROUND TIDORE

The most picturesque village in Tidore is tiny **Lada-Ake**. Set high up a disconcertingly steep road, the village retains a few traditional homes made of split bamboo set on mossy dry-stone bases. Curious *guwige* basket-poles offer nests to chickens and many women use traditional *saloi* (conical back-baskets) when foraging in the lush surrounding forest. Locals use the traditional Tidorean language in which *sukur dofu* means 'thank you', *saki* means 'delicious' and *sterek* (*lau*) means '(very) good'. Glimpsed views of Ternate are inspiring from the approach road.

The nicest coastal views are between Maftutu and Cobo where **Taman Cobo** is a popular little park with a two-room hut-hotel under construction.

Most other Tidorean villages are simply strips of homes on either side of the round-island coast road. None of these are outstanding, though several have small ribbons of beach. **Pantai Akasahu** north of Dowara is popular if underwhelming and a little grubby: notice its natural hot-water pool. From here to **Rum** the road is quiet and beautiful (best anticlockwise) but poorly maintained. A three-minute speedboat hop from Rum is **Pulau Maitara**, with clear blue waters for snorkelling and swimming, better than anything Ternate or Tidore proper can offer.

In **Tomalou**, just beyond the blue house-like **Mesjid Darussalam**, there is a jetty where you could attempt to charter a boat across to **Pulau Mare**, famed for its attractive, no-frills pottery.

OTHER ISLANDS OF NORTH MALUKU

None of these islands has any real history of tourism so visits will be often prove something of an adventure.

PULAU HALMAHERA

Maluku's biggest island is eccentrically shaped with four mountainous peninsulas, several volcanoes and dozens of offshore islands. Sparsely populated and hard to get around, its history has been largely shaped by events over in tiny but dominant Ternate. Although usually subservient to Ternate, Jailolo would occasionally break away as an independent sultanate, generally ruled by a deposed or renegade branch of the Ternate (or sometimes Tidore) royal family, or by loyalists regrouping to resist European incursions on Ternate. Religiously, the island is predominantly Muslim, although there are Christian majority villages in several areas of the more developed northern pen-

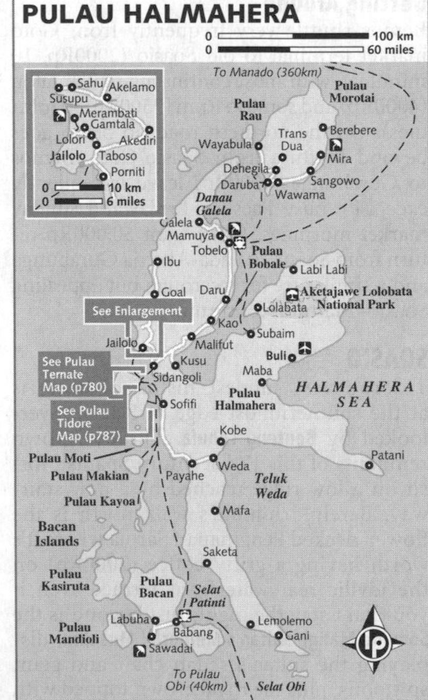

insula. Halmahera suffered severely from fighting in 1999–2002 and although now peaceful, many shockingly ruined churches remain visible especially in Galela and Sidangoli. Halmahera has few roads but a building programme currently underway, along with several new air routes and various boat links, means there are now several areas where you could be the first foreigner to visit in generations. One such place might be the remote new Aketajawe Lolobata National Park, which offers a slight hope of spotting the exceedingly rare Wallace's standard-wing bird of paradise, known locally as *burung bidadari*.

GETTING THERE & AWAY

Merpati has air links to Kao (for Tobelo), Bacan, the gold-mining town of Buli, Gebe via Weda and Morotai via Galela. Pelni's *Sangiang* loops around Halmahera once or twice a month from Ternate and/or Bitung (Sulawesi). There's also a weekly Tobelo–Manado boat. But by far the most popular access is by speedboat from Ternate. For the northwestern coast head for Jailolo. For Tobelo, Galela and the east cross initially to Sidangoli. For Weda take a speedboat to Sofifi from either Kota Ternate or from Goto in Tidore (25,000Rp, twice daily).

Jailolo

☎ 0922

Famed for its fragrant durians, attractive little Jailolo port steams gently amid the mangroves at the base of a lush volcanic cone. Before being incorporated by Ternate, Jailolo was an independent sultanate, though be aware that medieval historians used the term Jailolo (Gilolo) to refer to the whole island of Halmahera. Today, not even a stone remains of Jailolo's former *kraton* (palace), abandoned in the 1730s. However with two simple but acceptable hotels, Jailolo is a possible base for exploring some traditional villages in the surrounding area. **Penginapan Camar** (☎ 21100; Jl Gufasa; d 60,000-87,500Rp) is clean with shared *mandis*. The recently renovated **Penginapan Nusantara** (☎ 21305; d with fan/air-con 82,500/137,500Rp; ❄) has private bathrooms in some rooms. Both are just beyond the market, five minutes' walk from the long jetty where regular morning speedboats arrive from Dufa Dufa in Ternate (27,000Rp, one hour).

Around Jailolo

An easy but very pleasant *ojek* excursion takes you to **Merambati**, a long black-sand beach. En route are some distinctive churches and the floral villages of **Taboso**, **Lolori** and **Gamtala**. Each maintains its traditionally thatched *rumah adat* meeting hall (see p790). At the calmer, far-northern end of Merambati beach **Susupu** is a picturesque volcano-backed village that's reached via Akelamo on a longer, entirely different road.

Just 3.5km east of Jailolo, **Porniti** village has another traditional *rumah adat*. It's beside the narrow, partly potholed roller-coaster road to Sidangoli (50,000Rp, one hour by *ojek*).

Sidangoli

☎ 0921

Speedboats pulling in from Ternate (15,000Rp, 40 minutes, frequent before 11am) are met by a comical melee of porters and transport touts trying to lure you to their Tobelo-bound Kijangs (75,000Rp, three hours). These depart when (nearly) full from a 'terminal' just three minutes' walk away from the jetty. However, with no queuing system, guessing which car will be first to leave is very hit and miss. Most have finally departed by 11.30am.

You can see Sidangoli's few vaguely picturesque stilt houses and dramatically ruined church in five minutes. However, if rough water makes speedboat passage back to Ternate unsafe, **Penginapan Handayani** (☎ 328 471; Jl Cendani; d 60,000Rp) is quiet and friendly, 300m northwest of the terminal. In the opposite direction, the bearable **Penginapan Sidangoli Indah** (☎ 0813 40344905; s/d with fan & mandi 70,000/80,000Rp) has tiled floors and a peaceful if viewless terrace.

Tobelo

☎ 0924

Surrounded by coconut palms and fronted by a jigsaw of islands, Tobelo is northern Halmahera's only 'town', although it's little more than the one main Kao–Galela road (Jl Kemakmuran, also called Jl H Simange). That's roughly bisected just north of the market/terminal by Jl Pelabuhan (aka Jl Haven) which leads quickly to the main port. In contrast to most of North Maluku, Tobelo is majority Christian, so you can

RUMAH ADAT

Known as a *baileu* in the Lease Islands, a *rumah adat* is the nearest a Malukan village is likely to come to having a 'traditional' building. The most attractive are airy open-sided thatched structures doubling as village meeting places and general hang-outs. Some even have a communal TV. Many have disappeared, perhaps burnt in the 1999–2002 troubles or tastelessly modernised. However, in the Christian villages north of Jailolo, many fine thatched examples still stand, some dating from the villages' foundation (1910 at Lolori). In this area, each *rumah adat* displays a pair of *sasadu,* hairy balls hung from palm pennants at the end of an elongated apex beam. Rather than crude innuendo, their intended symbolism is as the 'feet' (representing stability) of the community. Tucked away into the palm-woven beams you may spot a *sie-sie* (bamboo pipe-cup). *Segera* (distilled palm wine) is quaffed from these cups, but only on special occasions.

get lunch, and even beer, during Ramadan (Muslim month of fasting). Just don't drink it in public.

INFORMATION

BNI Bank (Bank Negara Indonesia; Jl Kemakmuran; 7.30am-2pm) Opposite the market; 24-hour ATM but no currency exchange.

SLEEPING & EATING

Penginapan Asean Jaya (21051; Jl Pelabuhan; s/tw with fan 40,000/65,000Rp) Basic but neat and well kept by Anis, the delightful English-speaking owner.

Penginapan Alfa Mas (21543; Jl Kemakmuran; no fan/fan/air-con d 55,000/66,000/110,000Rp) Hidden in an off-road garden; cheap rooms are rather rough and the staff are comically camp.

Penginapan Meraksi Flower (22449; Jl Bhayangkara; d & tw with fan 66,000, with air-con 110,000-135,000Rp) The best rooms in the new section of this family homestay are Tobelo's top option. The building is 50m inland from the very over-rated Hotel President.

Villa Hermosa II (21887; Jl Parahyangan; d with air-con 150,000Rp;) Half of the rooms are excellent and brand new, albeit with screamingly gaudy pink sheets. The peaceful, semi-rural setting is 1.5km southwest of the centre, accessed by a track from near the petrol station.

Wisma Slasabila (22389; Jl Kemakmuran; d 150,000-200,000Rp;) Lemon-and-lime rooms around a narrow pond. Clean, fresh and friendlier than the next door **Penginapan Regina** (21149; Jl Kemakmuran; d with fan/air-con 95,000/165,000Rp;).

Rumah Makan Orion (21520; Jl Kemakmuran; meals 7500-12,500Rp; 9.30am-10pm Mon-Sat) Its theatrical *kangkung* hotplate (10,000Rp) has subtle tangs of garlic and ginger. It's diagonally opposite the Hotel President.

GETTING THERE & AWAY

Tobelo has no airport but **Merpati** (21167; fax 22322; Jl Kemakmuran; 8am-4pm Mon-Sat) flies three times weekly from both Ternate and Manado to Kao, linked with road transfers to/from Tobelo (35,000Rp, 70 minutes).

The *KM Elisabet II* sails to Manado (265,000Rp, 21 hours) on Wednesdays, returning Mondays. Pelni's *Sangiang* loops round Halmahera from Bitung (Sulawesi) on a Ternate–Babang (Bacan)–Gebe–Buli–Tobelo–Bitung route, or the same in reverse. The schedule is somewhat variable. Tobelo–Bacan costs 62,000Rp, Tobelo–Bitung 91,000Rp.

For Morotai there are daily speedboats (30,000Rp, two hours) from the main port. On Monday and Wednesday mornings the *Inerie* ferry (15,000Rp, four hours) also serves Morotai from Pelabuhan Penyebangan, 6km north of Tobelo.

Virtually all Kijangs to Sidangoli (75,000Rp, three hours) leave antisocially between 3.30am and 4am. Book ahead and they'll pick you up at your hotel. Bemos are fairly frequent to Galela (15,000Rp, one hour) but relatively rare to Kao.

Tobelo's Offshore Islands

Picturesque and with snorkelling potential, **Pulau Kumo** is just a 10-minute ride by shared outrigger (2000Rp) from Tobelo port. With a chartered boat you can head for an uninhabited coral-fringed island all of your own. Most have golden sandy beaches, but you'll need your own drinking water. Don't steal the coconuts! Sandy **Pulau Bobale Island**, accessed from **Daru**, is reputed to have great snorkelling and diving. Tobelo's Villa Hermosa II lends snorkels without charge, but only to guests.

Galela Area

☎ 0924

With a lush volcanic backdrop, plenty of bullock carts and fishermen on bamboo rafts, **Danau Galela** (Danau Duma) is the main attraction of the gently attractive Galela area. It's 25km north of Tobelo, 1.5km beyond Soasio (aka Galela town). The Galela district suffered especially during the 1999–2002 troubles, but today the road blocks have mostly gone and quick-growing tropical foliage has softened the ruins of burnt out churches and mosques. A 16km loop of asphalt road goes right around the lake but the best views are along the 4km of north-bank road nearest Soasio. On the south bank, **Penginapan Talaga Maloha** (☎ 611349; Jl Raya Soakonora; d 100,000Rp) is a three-room family homestay behind the Wartel Dua Putera 150m east of the oddly bulbous domed Igobul Mosque. Its narrow rear terrace looks directly out over the lake.

There's also acceptable accommodation in central Soasio, where **Penginapan Daloha** (☎ 611221; tw fan/air-con 100,000/150,000; ❄) is the unmarked pink house opposite Sumber Baru shop.

Galela has its own language in which *daloha* means 'good', *sukur dala dala* means 'thank you' and *to-tagi tagi* rather than *jalan jalan* is the ideal answer to the eternal question, 'Where are you going?'.

Merpati (☎ 611008) has bargain Wednesday flights to Morotai (50,000Rp) and Ternate (113,800Rp) from Galala's airfield. The Merpati lady lives in a totally unmarked house in central Soasio, just off the main road where it swings inland towards the lake.

PULAU MOROTAI

☎ 0923

Off Halmahera's northern tip, this sparsely populated island became a minor Japanese base during WWII. It leapt to importance when it was captured by the Allies and used to bomb Manila to bits – the sad fulfilment of General MacArthur's 'I will return' pledge to retake the Philippines. Among the Japanese defenders that retreated to Morotai's crumpled mountain hinterland was the famous Private Nakamura: only in 1973 did he discover that the war was over. Bunkers and rusty bullet-cases are visible at overgrown WWII battle sites near **Trans Dua**. That's 35 muddy minutes by *ojek* from Morotai's village capital **Daruba** where a rusting US amphibious lander *(amfibi)* lies hidden in a coconut plantation. Daruba fishing smacks can take you to **Pulau Sum Sum**, a beautiful desert island that was MacArthur's temporary WWII command base. It has delightful spongy, white sand and is littered with giant clam shells and the odd WWII bullet.

Berebere, famous for its lobsters (per kilogram from 50,000Rp), has surfing potential but there's no road from Daruba and boats from Tobelo are sporadic.

Daruba has two simple *penginapan* and six sometimes-open *rumah makan*. Tourists are very rare.

Getting There & Away

Merpati (☎ 21063, Daruba) operates flights between Ternate and Daruba via Galela. Otherwise access is by ferry or speedboat from Tobelo. Ferries to Tobelo (12,500Rp, four hours) depart Tuesday and Thursday. Twice a day, overloaded minibuses stagger along the rough roads to Mira and Wayabula but *ojeks* are much more comfortable for exploring.

PULAU MAKIAN

Moored off Halmahera's west coast, spiky-topped **Pulau Makian** is an impressive, 1357m volcano with a photogenically huge gash in the cone's northern flank. Its eruptions are rare but deadly, killing over 2000 people in 1760 and causing a full-scale evacuation in 1988. Although now resettled, Pulau Makian has no formal accommodation and many Makian islanders remain in Kota Ternate, where they're reckoned to be disproportionately powerful in the administration. Speedboats leave daily to Bastiong in Ternate (45,000Rp, two hours), returning the next morning.

PULAU KAYOA & PULAU GURAICI

The low-slung, reptilian ridge of **Pulau Kayoa** is not especially impressive above water. However it reportedly has some of North Maluku's best snorkelling, notably off the small islet of **Pulau Guraici** where the *kepala* *desa* reputedly maintains two basic cottages in case visitors show up.

PULAU BACAN

☎ 0927

Pleasant **Pulau Bacan**, whose laid-back capital **Labuha** curls almost imperceptibly around a languid west-facing bay, is a sleepy getaway from Ternate. It has a selection of modest guesthouses and features a small, exaggeratedly fortified Portuguese-Dutch fort, **Benteng Barnevald**, lying overgrown behind a stagnant moat.

The island's sights are fairly pitiful, but offer excuses to go wandering. **Air Panas** is a patch of ferric-orange pebbles discoloured by volcanic bubbling. The site is in sea shallows off **Kupal** village, in an achingly beautiful bay of fishing boats and swaying palms. It's 15 minutes by *ojek* from Labuha. The best place for a swim is the pebble beach off picturesque **Sawadai** village, 35 minutes by bemo from Labuha. Locals reckon **Air Belanda** (Dutch Water) is a tourist attraction. However viewing this small 'waterfall' is about as exciting as watching your *mandi* overflow.

Sleeping & Eating

Penginapan Borero Indah (☎ 21024; Jl Pasar 2; s/d with bathroom 50,000/100,000Rp; ❄) Near Labuha's central market, this clean, bright place has an orchid garden and staff so obliging they compete to bring you tea. Some of the doubles have air-con.

Pondok Indah (☎ 21048; Jl Oesman Syah; s/d with fan 55,000/77,000Rp; d with air-con 100,000Rp; ❄) In a family home, this is also pleasant, if slightly more dingy.

Half a dozen miniature *rumah makan* serve simple rice-and-fish dinners.

Getting There & Away

Labuha's airport is 4km east of town. **Merpati** (☎ 21603) has weekly flights to Ternate. Overnight boats (80,000Rp, eight hours) run daily from Bastiong (Ternate) to Babang, 16km east of Labuha. These arrive antisocially early (around 4am) but bemos await. Although boats continue to Jikotamu (near Laiwui, Obi Islands) there is no regular onward connection to Ambon without backtracking to Ternate.

SULA ISLANDS

Southwest of the Bacan Islands, the **Sula Islands** are remote, forested and sparsely populated. **Sanana** has a basic *penginapan* and a decrepit Dutch fort near the port. Twice-weekly flights or boats from Ternate to Sanana could be combined with the slow Sanana–Ambon boat as an adventurous way to link north and central Maluku. But seas are rough, boats very slow and the area is infamous for treacherous whirlpools.

MALUKU

Papua

Papua's mystique piques the imagination of the explorer, naturalist, anthropologist, politician and traveller in you. What about Papua (formerly known as Irian Jaya) would not intrigue? The diversity in lifestyle and culture of the indigenous people, who speak more than 250 languages, is matched only by Papua's biodiversity and geography. The terrain covering half of New Guinea, the planet's second-largest island, ranges from the misty peak of Puncak Jaya (5050m) – which features permanent snowfields and small glaciers – to the steamy island groups of Biak and Raja Ampat, just shy of the equator. Endemic wildlife gracing this vast expanse of jungle, mountain, swamp and sea include such weird and wonderful creatures as cassowaries, dugongs, showy *cenderawasih* (birds of paradise), egg-laying echidnas and tree-dwelling monitor lizards.

Though much of the region is covered by impenetrable jungle, most inhabitants live in and around coastal towns. Almost all visitors head to the Baliem Valley, home to some of the most remarkable traditional cultures on earth, while others are drawn to the art of the Asmat region, or the bird life and coral reefs of the northern coast and islands.

With its limited infrastructure, administrative sloth, political strife that continually keeps hot spots off-limits to foreigners, and an equatorial clime that puts siesta time in effect between 1pm and 5pm, Papua poses a few travel challenges. To those willing to accept, the rewards flow with a generosity as life-sustaining as Papua's brown tributaries ribboning through its thick, enigmatic jungle canopy.

HIGHLIGHTS

- Trekking through the sweet-potato terraces, thatch hut villages and unique culture of the **Baliem Valley** (p816)
- Setting out for a chance glimpse of the rare *cenderawasih* or seeking out spectacular diving in the **Raja Ampat Islands** (p802) off the coast of Sorong
- Discovering white-sand beaches and dive sites around **Pulau Biak** (p809), a resting place for WWII wrecks and relics
- Cruising magnificent **Danau Sentani** (p835) by longboat, or hiking its undulating shoreline
- Exploring the indigenous lowland culture and Australian-looking flora and fauna of **Wasur National Park** (p837)

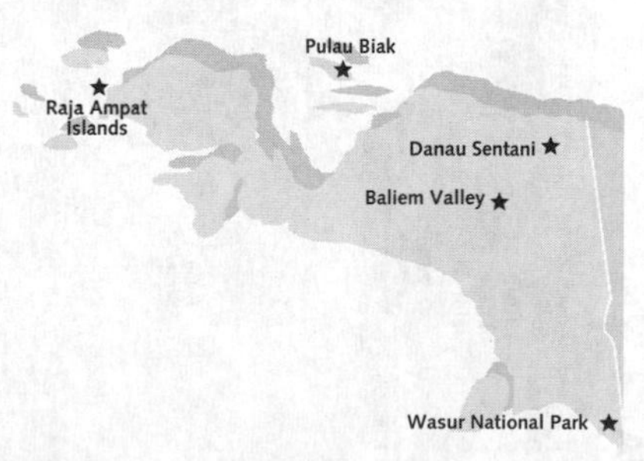

- POPULATION: 2.7 MILLION
- LAND AREA: 421,981 SQ KM
- HIGHEST PEAK: PUNCAK JAYA (5050M)

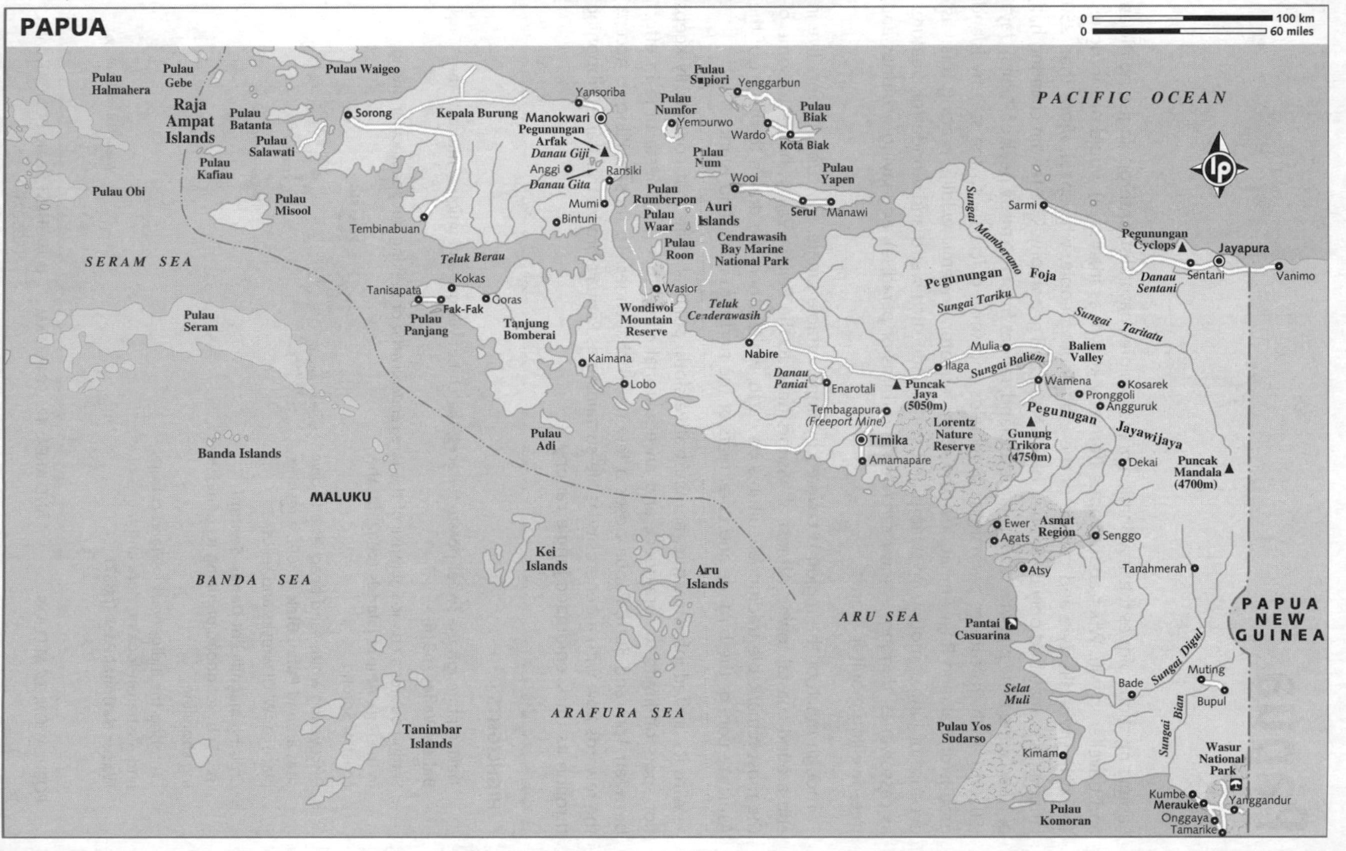
PAPUA
0 100 km
0 60 miles
PACIFIC OCEAN
Pulau Halmahera
Pulau Gebe
Raja Ampat Islands
Pulau Waigeo
Pulau Batanta
Pulau Salawati
Pulau Kafiau
Pulau Obi
Pulau Misool
Sorong
Kepala Burung
Tembinabuan
Manokwari
Yansoriba
Pegunungan Arfak
Danau Giji
Anggi
Danau Gita
Ransiki
Mumi
Bintuni
Pulau Supiori
Yenggarbun
Pulau Numfor
Yemburwo
Pulau Biak
Wardo
Kota Biak
Pulau Num
Wooi
Pulau Yapen
Serui
Manawi
Pulau Rumberpon
Auri Islands
Pulau Waar
Pulau Roon
Cendrawasih Bay Marine National Park
SERAM SEA
Teluk Berau
Kokas
Tanisapata
Fak-Fak
Goras
Pulau Panjang
Tanjung Bomberai
Wasior
Wondiwoi Mountain Reserve
Teluk Cenderawasih
Pulau Seram
Kaimana
Lobo
Nabire
Danau Paniai
Enarotali
Pulau Adi
Banda Islands
MALUKU
BANDA SEA
Kei Islands
Aru Islands
Tanimbar Islands
ARAFURA SEA
ARU SEA
Sarmi
Sungai Mamberamo
Pegunungan Foja
Sungai Tariku
Sungai Taritatu
Pegunungan Cyclops
Jayapura
Danau Sentani
Sentani
Vanimo
Mulia
Ilaga
Sungai Baliem
Baliem Valley
Puncak Jaya (5050m)
Wamena
Kosarek
Pronggoli
Angguruk
Tembagapura (Freeport Mine)
Lorentz Nature Reserve
Pegunungan Jayawijaya
Gunung Trikora (4750m)
Timika
Amamapare
Dekai
Puncak Mandala (4700m)
Ewer
Agats
Asmat Region
Senggo
Atsy
Tanahmerah
PAPUA NEW GUINEA
Pantai Casuarina
Sungai Digul
Bade
Muting
Bupul
Selat Muli
Sungai Bian
Pulau Yos Sudarso
Kimam
Wasur National Park
Kumbe
Merauke
Yanggandur
Onggaya
Tamarike
Pulau Komoran

IRIAN JAYA OR PAPUA?

When the Portuguese first sighted the island now shared by Papua and Papua New Guinea (PNG) in 1511 they called it *Ilhas dos Papuas* (Island of the Fuzzy Hairs), from the Malay word *papuwah*. Later, Dutch explorers called the island New Guinea, because the black-skinned people reminded them of the inhabitants of Guinea in Africa – and named the western half Dutch New Guinea. When sovereignty was transferred to Indonesia, the province was renamed Irian Barat (West Irian) and then Irian Jaya; *jaya* means 'victorious' in Bahasa Indonesia and *irian* means 'hot land rising from the sea' in the Biak language.

To placate the growing separatist movement, the Indonesian government agreed to rename the province Papua on 26 December 2001. To add to the confusion, many Papuan activists, and some international nongovernmental organisations (NGOs), refer to it as West Papua. And at the time of writing, Papua was divided into two provinces: Papua and Irian Jaya Barat (or 'Irjabar').

HISTORY

Dutch Rule

In 1660 the Dutch recognised the Sultan of Tidore's sovereignty over New Guinea island and, because the Dutch held power over Tidore (the Sultan's territory), New Guinea theoretically became Dutch. The British unsuccessfully attempted to establish a settlement near Manokwari in 1793, but by 1824 Britain and the Netherlands agreed that the western half, Dutch New Guinea, would become part of the Dutch East Indies.

In 1828 the Dutch established a token settlement in Lobo (near Kaimana) but it also failed miserably. About 27 years later the first missionaries, Germans, established a settlement on an island near Manokwari. The Dutch didn't try to develop the province again until 1896, when settlements were set up in Manokwari and Fak-Fak in response to perceived Australian ownership claims from the eastern half of New Guinea island. The province continued to be virtually ignored, except by mining companies from the USA and Japan, which explored the rich oil reserves during the 1930s.

WWII

After the bombing of Pearl Harbor, the Dutch declared war on Japan, so the province, as part of the Dutch East Indies, inevitably assumed importance in the battle for the Pacific. (Some Indonesians welcomed the Japanese as Asian liberators who would eradicate the hated Dutch colonialists.)

In early 1944 a four-phase push, led by US army general Douglas MacArthur, was launched from what is now Papua New Guinea (PNG) to liberate Dutch New Guinea from Japanese occupation. The Allies were far from optimistic: this part of the world was almost completely undeveloped, inhospitable and unchartered.

Phase one, the capture of Hollandia (Jayapura), was the largest amphibious operation of the war in the southwestern Pacific and involved 80,000 Allied troops. (Numerous WWII monuments and relics in and around Jayapura are testament to this event.) The second phase, to capture Sarmi, saw strong resistance from the Japanese. The third phase was the capture of Pulau Biak (primarily to control the airfield) and nearby Pulau Numfor, on the way to Sorong. Several hard battles were fought on Biak, exacerbated by Allied intelligence severely underestimating the Japanese strength. The fourth and final phase was the successful push to the Japanese air bases on Pulau Morotai, off northern Halmahera, and then towards the Philippines.

Along the south coast, the Allies fought for control of Merauke because of fears that it would be used as a base for Japanese air attacks against Australia.

Indonesia Takes Over

In 1945 the Dutch wrenched back the territory from the Japanese and used it as a place of exile. The infamous Boven Digul camp (in Tanahmerah) was established as a prison for Indonesian nationalists.

Following international pressure, the Dutch were forced to withdraw from the Dutch East Indies (which became Indonesia) after WWII, but still clung to Dutch New Guinea. In an attempt to stop Indonesia from gaining control, the Dutch encouraged Papuan nationalism and began

PAPUA

building schools and colleges to train Papuans in professional skills, with the aim of preparing them for self-rule by 1970.

Following WWII most Indonesian political factions claimed that Dutch New Guinea, like the rest of the former Dutch East Indies, should be part of Indonesia. Throughout 1962 Indonesian forces infiltrated the province, but with little success. The Papuan population failed to welcome the Indonesians as liberators and either attacked them or handed them over to the Dutch. However, US pressure eventually forced the Dutch to capitulate abruptly in August 1962.

A vaguely worded agreement in that year, under UN auspices, required that Indonesia allow the Papuans to determine, by the end of 1969, whether they wanted independence or to remain within the Indonesian republic. So in 1969 an 'Act of Free Choice' was 'supervised' by the UN. The Indonesian government, however, suddenly declared that it would use the procedure of *musyawarah*, by which a consensus of 'elders' would be reached.

In July 1969 the Indonesian government announced that the assemblies in the Merauke, Jayawijaya and Paniai districts had unanimously decided to become part of Indonesia. And West Irian, as it was then known, became Indonesia's 26th province.

Papuan Opposition

Even before the 'Act of Free Choice', the Indonesians faced violent opposition from the Papuans. In 1969 rebellions broke out on Pulau Biak and at Enarotali in the western highlands. Between 1977 and the mid-1980s occasional conflict erupted in the mountains around the Baliem Valley, at Tembagapura (site of the US-run Freeport mine), and in remote areas of the Paniai district.

After a short lull, anti-Indonesian activity recommenced. In 1995 members and sympathisers of the major independence group, the Free Papua Movement or Organisasi Papua Merdeka (OPM), stormed the Indonesian consulate in Vanimo, just over the border in PNG, and took to the streets in Tembagapura and Timika. In 1996 about 5000 Papuans rioted for several days and burned Pasar Abepura market in suburban Jayapura, resulting in several deaths. In the same year, several European and Indonesian researchers were kidnapped in a remote part of the Baliem Valley. The Europeans were released unharmed four months later, but two Indonesian hostages were killed by the OPM.

By late 1998 the post-Soeharto government indicated a willingness to listen to separatists and reduced the military presence in the province. In December 2001 the province was officially renamed Papua and significant concessions were offered by Jakarta: increased autonomy and a reinvestment of 80% of the revenue from Papua into the province.

But most separatists still want total independence and demilitarisation by Indonesia. Papuans are also still angry because the Indonesian government continues to sell off parts of the province for logging, mining and other commercial purposes without compensation or consultation. And they resent the occasional brutal responses of the Indonesians to political dissent.

Transmigrasi

The Indonesian policy of *transmigrasi* is also one of the reasons for continuing unrest in Papua. Over one-third of Papua's population originates from outside the province, mainly from Java, Bali and Sulawesi. Most of the transmigrants live in settlements near the main towns of Jayapura, Merauke, Manokwari, Nabire and Sorong.

As Papua represents about 22% of Indonesia's total territory, but only about 1% of its population, the Indonesian government continues to move thousands of people to Papua from other, overcrowded islands. Poor locations and lack of planning for many existing settlements indicate that the main thrust of *transmigrasi* is less for the benefit of the transmigrants than to make the province truly 'Indonesian'.

CLIMATE

Generally the best (driest) time to visit Papua is between May and October, though it can – and does – often rain anywhere, anytime. (Rain falls in Kota Biak about 25 days a month.) Strong wind and rain are more common along the north coast from November to March. Along the south coast, however, it can get quite wet and windy from April to October – but this is the dry season in Merauke, the only part of Papua with distinct seasons. The best time to visit the Baliem Valley is between March and August when the days are drier and cooler, though nights are usually cold year-round. Coastal towns are generally hot and humid, while it's often cooler in the highlands. See also the climate chart for Jayapura (pp848–9).

WILDLIFE

About 75% of Papua is forest, so it's no surprise that its flora is as varied as its geography. The usual lush collection of Asiatic species lie in the transition zone between Asia and Australia, postulated as the Wallace Line. The south coast's vegetation includes mangroves and sago palms, as well as eucalypts, paperbarks and acacias in the drier southeastern section. Highland vegetation ranges from alpine grasslands and heath to unique pine forests, bush and scrub. Papua boasts over 2500 species of orchids.

Animals are largely confined to marsupials, such as bandicoots, ring-tailed possums, pygmy flying phalangers, large cuscuses, tree kangaroos and wallabies. Reptiles include snakes both poisonous and not, crocodiles and frill-necked lizards. Papua is also home to about 800 species of spiders, 200 types of frogs and 30,000 kinds of beetles, while Pegunungan Arfak is renowned for its colourful butterflies.

Despite large-scale plunder, Papua's exquisite bird life is still a popular attraction for serious twitchers. Among the province's 600 species are thriving populations of cassowaries, bowerbirds, cockatoos, parrots, kingfishers and crowned pigeons. The acclaimed and elusive *cenderawasih* inhabit parts of Kepala Burung and Pulau Yapen.

CULTURE

The interior is predominantly populated by indigenous Papuans, while coastal towns are inhabited by descendants of intermarriages between Papuans and Melanesians and Indonesians, as well as transmigrants from western Indonesia.

Dani from the Baliem Valley live in compounds of huts made from trees and mud, raising their precious pigs. They still often use stone implements to farm their dietary/agricultural staple, the sweet potato. See p817 for more information about the Dani.

Less accessible are the Manikom and Hatam people who live near the Anggi Lakes, and the Kanum and Marind near Merauke. Other inhabitants of the southeast are the Asmat people, who are renowned for their carvings (see p838). Further inland from the Asmat region, the Kombai and Korowai live in truly extraordinary tree houses, sometimes up to dozens of metres above ground, to avoid tides, wild animals and tribal invasion. Incredibly, the Indonesian media reported in mid-1998 that two 'new tribes' that use sign language to communicate had been 'found' in very remote parts of the interior.

Churches of all denominations are found throughout Papua, but (despite claims by fervent missionaries) indigenous people enjoy a combination of traditional beliefs and Christianity. Officially, 99% of the Papuan population is Christian, but this seems difficult to believe given the number of

PAPUAN EDEN

In early 2006, a team of American, Australian and Indonesian biologists made international news when they reported on their foray into an isolated area of Pegunungan Foja (the Foja mountain range) in northern Papua. In this very remote jungle, the team found a stunning wealth of wildlife, discovering at least 20 new species of frog, a tree kangaroo formerly believed to exist only on one mountaintop in PNG, and the first new species of bird (the orange-faced honeyeater) discovered on the island of New Guinea since 1940. They also spotted the six-wired bird of paradise, until then believed to be extinct. None of the animals showed any fear of humans, evidence that they'd had no exposure to our own dangerous species.

To date, 40% of Indonesia's forests have been destroyed. For now, Papua's Pegunungan Foja is a protected conservation area, although it remains to be seen if the Indonesian government will make the long-term committed effort to protect this museum of biodiversity from poachers and logging interests.

TOP FIVE READS

- *Throwim' Way Leg* by Tim Flannery (2000) – a mammologist's travelogue of sorts, detailing his research years in Papua and PNG – full of lovely, funny observations and wonderful insights into the people and environment.
- *Under the Mountain Wall* by Peter Matthiessen (1987) – chronicles his daily life among the Kurulu tribe of the Baliem Valley in 1961.
- *The Lost World of Irian Jaya* by Robert Mitton (1983) – compiled from his letters, diaries, maps and photographs after his death in 1976; criticises the reckless way that Papuans have been forced into the modern world.
- *Poisoned Arrows* by George Monbiot (1989) – details a remarkable journey to the wilds of Papua with the objective of uncovering the truth about *transmigrasi* and the nature of anti-Indonesian resistance.
- *The Open Cage* by Daniel Start (1997) – first-hand experience of a hostage taken by the OPM (Free Papua Movement); he creates a commendably thorough backdrop of the Papuan context leading to his situation.

transmigrants from Muslim-dominated Java and Sulawesi.

Estimates of the number of languages spoken in Papua range from 200 to over 700 (there has been very little study about the linguistics of the province). There is no doubt though, that Papua and neighbouring PNG, with a combined population of only a few million, speak an inordinately high percentage of the world's languages. Sadly, some of these languages are slowly and permanently disappearing.

TRAVEL PERMIT

For increasingly obscure political and bureaucratic reasons, foreigners must obtain a travel permit known as a *surat keterangan jalan* – commonly known as a *surat jalan* – before they can visit some places in Papua, particularly the interior.

At the time of writing, you could visit Jayapura, Sentani, Manokwari, Pulau Biak and Sorong without a *surat jalan*. Depending on the whim of the local police, you may need one for Pulau Biak, Nabire and Manokwari; however, you can get one easily after you arrive at these towns. For other areas, such as Merauke, the Asmat region, Pulau Yapen, Timika, Fak-Fak, and the Baliem Valley (including Wamena; see also p817), you *must* have a *surat jalan* before arrival. At the time of writing, foreigners were not permitted to go to Gunung Trikora (Trikora Mountain), the Paniai district, Danau Habbema (Lake Habbema) or Sungai Mamberamo (Mamberamo River). For anywhere else not mentioned here, it's safe to assume that you'll need a *surat jalan*.

The permit lasts from one week to one month depending on the amount of time you request, the expiry date of your visa and the mood of the police. If you have a 30-day tourist visa, you can apply for a *surat jalan* at a local police station *(polres)*. If you have a business visa or any other type of visa, you'll have to visit a branch of the provincial police force *(polda)*, probably in Jayapura. Permits are normally available at any district capital, and are particularly easy to get in Kota Biak and Jayapura, where the staff are used to foreigners. Some police stations may be reluctant to issue a *surat jalan* allowing you to visit a more remote area of another district, so you may have to apply for a separate permit at the relevant district capital.

When you apply for the permit, supply the police with two passport-size photos and a big smile, and then tell them all the towns/places you may possibly travel to. It will take about one hour to type up for which an 'administration fee' is required (5000Rp is enough). The whole process may sound overwhelming, but don't be concerned: the police are invariably helpful and friendly, and as bored with the paperwork as you are. To save time and hassle, a travel agent or hotel in Papua may be able to arrange the permit for a negotiable fee. If you're on an organised tour, the permit should be arranged by your travel agency.

In places where a *surat jalan* is needed, your hotel or guide will request a photocopy of your permit to bring to the local police for registration and stamping. If not, you'll have to report to the police station yourself, preferably as soon as you arrive; certainly within 24 hours. In remote areas, including the Baliem Valley, you'll need to report and show your permit to the police or village authorities wherever you stay overnight. Always keep a few photocopies of your permit handy to give to local authorities.

GETTING THERE & AWAY

Most visitors fly straight to Jayapura through Biak and/or Makassar (Sulawesi) for a connection to Wamena in the Baliem Valley, but there are a number of other interesting ways to enter Papua. You could fly to Port Moresby (capital of PNG), and on to Vanimo before chartering a boat or crossing on foot to Jayapura; take a Pelni liner to Timika or Merauke and fly to Jayapura; take a boat or plane between Sorong or Fak-Fak and other Indonesian islands; or take a boat and/or plane along the north coast to Jayapura, stopping at Manokwari, Biak, Nabire and/or Serui.

Air

Unless you have lots of time, flying is the best way to get to and around Papua. Merpati Nusantara Airlines regularly links Papua's main regional centres (Sorong, Biak and Jayapura) with major cities elsewhere in Indonesia, such as Makassar and Jakarta. Garuda Indonesia airlines also links Biak and Jayapura with western Indonesia.

Current fares for flights to and around Papua are shown in the Papua Airfares map (p800), while information about schedules is included in the relevant sections later in this chapter.

Boat

Several Pelni liners, notably the *Tatamailau, Ciremai, Doro Londa* and *Nggapulu,* link the north and south coasts of Papua with Maluku, Sulawesi and Java every two or four weeks. See p872 for more information

TRAVELLING BETWEEN PAPUA & PNG

Though there are no flights between Papua and PNG, crossing the border by land or sea is fairly straightforward.

Boats leave daily at 6am from Hamadi port near Jayapura, but they only operate in good weather. Another option is to charter a boat between Jayapura and Vanimo for a negotiable 350,000Rp per person one way (minimum of three passengers). Ask around the port at Hamadi near Jayapura, or check with the travel agency PT Kuwera Jaya (p829) in Jayapura.

It's also possible to cross to the PNG border from Jayapura by land. Taxis head for the border from both Hamadi market and Yotefa market in Abepura, the latest leaving around 2pm. If none are available, you can charter one yourself for a negotiable 250,000Rp. It's a 2½-hour trip to Wutung, the village nearest the border. You'll have to cross the border itself on foot; once in PNG, you can hire a car to take you to Vanimo (about 10 kina/US$2.50).

Most visitors to PNG need a visa; the 60-day, garden-variety tourist visa (US$25) can be obtained at the **Consulate of PNG** (Map p834; ☎ 0967-531250; congenpng@yahoo.com.id; Jl Raya Argapura; 🕑 8am-4pm Mon-Thu, 8am-2pm Fri) in Jayapura. This usually takes two days, although they'll rush-process it for you in a few hours if you show up early and ask nicely. You can get a tourist visa without a ticket out of PNG, but you must show this visa to the airline company or travel agency when you buy an airline ticket out of Vanimo, the nearest town to Jayapura in PNG. Air Niugini currently flies between Vanimo and Port Moresby on Monday, Wednesday and Friday.

It is *very* important to note that you cannot get an Indonesian visa at the border if you're coming from Vanimo; you must obtain one beforehand. Indonesian tourist visas (valid for 30 days, nonextendable) are available in Vanimo or Port Moresby. If you're travelling to/from Jayapura by boat, visit the **Immigration office** (☎ 0967-521647; Jl Percetakan 15; 🕑 8am-4pm Mon-Fri) in Jayapura to make sure you have the correct entry/exit stamp(s) in your passport. If departing on an early-morning boat, you'll have to stop by the Immigration office the day before in order to get a back-dated exit stamp – for which you may have to pay a small convenience fee.

about Pelni schedules, while the relevant sections later in this chapter list some fares for major routes.

A few Perintis boats regularly link the north coast of Papua with Sulawesi and northern Maluku, and connect the south coast of Papua with southeast Maluku.

GETTING AROUND

Very few roads have successfully crossed the seemingly impenetrable terrain of Papua. Roads between Jayapura and Wamena, and Sorong and Manokwari, have been started, but are unlikely to be completed in the next few years – if ever! Boats are slow, infrequent and often uncomfortable, so flying is the best, and sometimes only, option.

Air

The hubs for internal flights around Papua are Sorong for the northwest; Biak for the Teluk Cenderawasih (Cenderawasih Bay) region; Jayapura for the Baliem Valley; and Merauke for the southeast coast. Some flights on the main carrier, Merpati, are over-booked, while others are cancelled through a lack of passengers. Garuda, which flies between Timika, Biak and Jayapura, is more reliable.

Merpati offices in Fak-Fak, Serui, Yemburwo (Pulau Numfor), Anggi, Senggo, Ewer and Manokwari are not computerised, so you can only book a flight *from* these towns at the relevant Merpati offices. This results in double-bookings and utter chaos at the offices, and a telephone reservation before arrival is usually worth diddly-squat. So, if you're flying with Merpati, always allow plenty of time and be prepared for delays and cancellations. Merpati planes to smaller destinations have a 10kg baggage limit per person, though this is usually ignored if you're a few kilograms over.

Between Sentani (Jayapura) and Wamena, planes are also operated by the cargo carrier **Trigana Air Service** (☎ Wamena airport terminal 0969-31611, Sentani airport terminal 0967-594383), Protestant-run **Mission Aviation Fellowship** (MAF; Wamena; ☎ 0969-31263; Jl Gatot Subroto; Sentani; ☎ 0967-91109; Jl Misi Sentani) and the Indonesian army. The MAF and the Catholic-run **Associated Mission Aviation** (AMA; ☎ 0967-591009; amasentani@jayapura

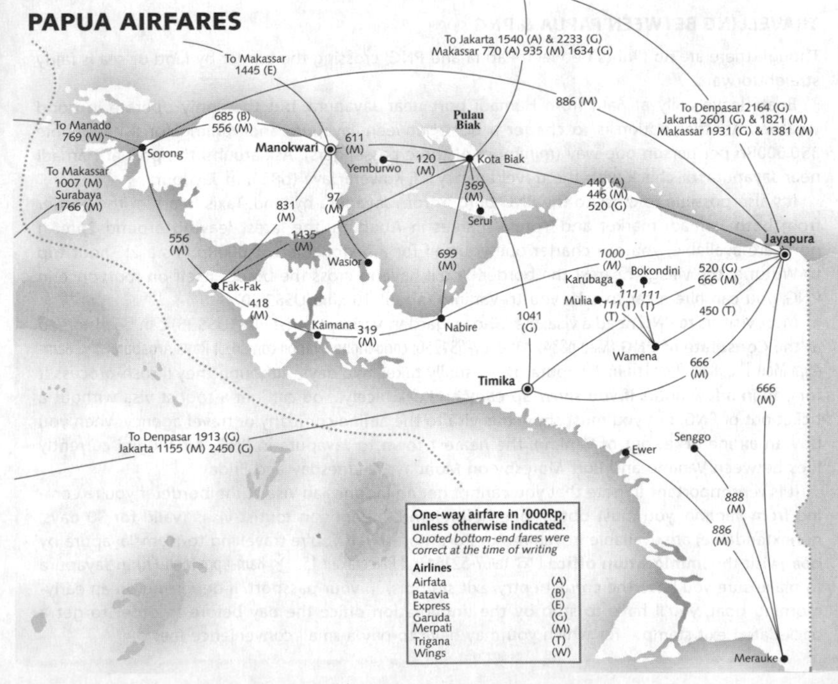

PAPUA TRAVEL WARNING

Outbreaks of civil unrest and violence are not uncommon in Papua, but they should not dissuade you from visiting the province. Sporadic riots have been flaring up with increasing frequency since 2000 in the Jayapura and Sentani region; in early 2006 three policemen and one military guard were beaten to death at a clash at Cenderawasih University near Jayapura. In 2002, two American schoolteachers were murdered in Timika, a city not noted for tourism but for a large percentage of resident expats. Papua is so huge that civil unrest tends to be localised, so be sure to stay abreast of current events.

.wasantara.net.id; Jl Misi Sentani, Sentani) also fly from Sentani (Jayapura) and/or Wamena to a dozen or more remote villages in the central and western highlands. These organisations sometimes accept tourists, but their primary concern is missionary business. You can also often charter their planes – at exorbitant rates. Make sure you book at least one week in advance. **Airfast** (☎ 021-5200696; www.airfastindonesia.com) planes, based in Jakarta, can also be chartered to/from Timika.

Current fares for flights around Papua are listed on the Papua Airfares map (p800), while information about schedules is included in the relevant sections later in this chapter.

Boat

Travelling around Papua by boat will take some time as well as planning. Four big Pelni liners – the *Ciremai, Dobonsolo, Doro Londa* and *Nggapulu* – stop at major towns along the north coast every two weeks. The *Sangiang* plies the south coast every two weeks, while the *Tatamailau* and *Kelimutu* also crawl along the south coast every four weeks. The Transport chapter (p872) has more information about Pelni schedules, while the relevant sections later in this chapter list some fares for major routes.

The next best option is a Perintis boat along either coast, but they are less comfortable and slower than Pelni liners. Many other basic boats sail along certain smaller sections of both coasts, and as far inland as the enormous rivers will allow. See relevant sections for more details.

No boat regularly links the north coast of Papua with the south coast.

WESTERN PAPUA

The western part of Papua offers outstanding diving and trekking, deserted beaches, remote islands, traditional cultures and easy-going towns. Travel around western Papua, however, is hindered by limited, costly and time-consuming transport, as well as annoying government regulations.

Conservationists continue to take an interest in the area: parts of Pegunungan Arfak (home to over 300 species of birds and 320 types of butterflies) are protected under the Arfak Mountains Wildlife Preservation (Capa) programme, with assistance from the World Wide Fund For Nature (WWF).

Activities

TREKKING

Pegunungan Arfak and Wondiwoi Mountain Reserve offer unlimited trekking opportunities, but you'll have to arrange everything yourself; there are no organised tours. The **Manokwari tourist office** (☎ 0986-212030; Jl Merdeka; 🕑 7.30am-2pm Mon-Fri) can provide useful information about trails, guides and permits, but this often depends on who you talk to. Otherwise, contact the **WWF office** (☎ 0986-222493; Jl Rendani, Wosi) or the **Cenderawasih Bay Marine National Park office** (☎ 0986-222356, 212303; Jl Rendani, Wosi) in Manokwari.

Guides/porters around western Papua cost about 80,000/45,000Rp per day. You can buy food in villages, and often stay in local houses for about 35,000Rp per person per night, but bring your own cooking and camping equipment, as well as wet-weather gear.

SORONG

☎ 0951 / pop 130,000

Though basically an oil, logging and district administration centre, Sorong makes a decent base for diving, trekking and birdwatching tours in western Papua. The city offers no compelling reason to linger, unless you're waiting for a plane or boat bound for

BIRDS OF PARADISE

Over 40 different species of *cenderawasih* (bird of paradise) are found in small areas of northern Papua and southern Maluku, as well as PNG.

Cenderawasih were first taken to Europe following colonial exploration around the Dutch East Indies. Their feathers fetched remarkable prices as fashionable accessories, so the birds soon faced extinction. Because traders often removed the birds' legs and wings to highlight their beautiful plumage, Europeans originally thought that the birds had no feet and spent their entire lives in flight.

The male bird is usually more brightly coloured than the female and displays its magnificent plumage during mating, often hanging upside down from branches to show off its colours. *Cenderawasih* usually nest in open parts of a tree, feed on fruit and insects, have remarkable thin, curled 'tail-wires' up to 30cm long with colourful tips, and make loud screeching noises.

These birds are scarce and elusive, but with lots of patience, time and a knowledgeable guide, it may be possible to spot some. Finding them will require chartering boats, organising guides and carrying camping equipment, as their territories are remote: Waigeo, Misool, Batanta and Salawati islands (off the coast of Sorong); along sections of the aptly named Teluk Cenderawasih; around the north coast of Pulau Yapen; and in the Aru Islands (southeast Maluku).

Organised bird-watching tours can be arranged through travel agencies in Sorong, Manokwari, Biak and Jayapura.

PAPUA

points beyond. Sorong is the jumping-off point for diving in Raja Ampat islands.

Orientation & Information

Sorong is quite spread out, so to visit banks, government and airline offices, as well as the main port and *angkot* (minibus) terminal, take a public/chartered *angkot*.

Bank Mandiri (Jl Ahmad Yani 99) Probably the best place to change money.

Police station (☎ 323210; Jl Basuki Rahmat) Will issue a *surat jalan* for travel to the interior or to any island off the coast of Sorong.

Sarana Solusi Informatika (SSI; Jl Yos Sudarso; per hr 8000Rp; 9am-8pm Mon-Sat, 3-8pm Sun) Internet access is charged in one-hour blocks, so watch that clock. About 100m west of Hotel Tanjung.

Tourist office (☎ 323070; Jl Burung Mambuk Remu Utara) Mildly useful.

Sights & Activities

Pantai Kasuari (Cassowary Beach) is ideal for swimming and snorkelling (bring your own gear) and accessible by public *angkot* from the terminal. A walk (40 minutes) around **Pulau Doom** is appealing, but be prepared: there are more 'hello misters' here per second than anywhere else in Indonesia! You can reach Doom (!) by public/chartered boat (2000Rp return) from the small harbour near Hotel Indah.

From the same harbour, you can also rent a boat (about 700,000Rp per day) to the nearby **Raja Ampat** islands, one of the world's most diverse reef systems. The islands include **Pulau Batanta** (for bird life and sandy beaches), **Pulau Waigeo** (hiking, swimming and snorkelling among shipwrecks) and **Pulau Kofiau** (diving).

The tiny islands around **Pulau Misool** boast some of the best coral and marine life in Indonesia. The area is fairly sheltered, and diving is possible year-round.

Sorong's long-established major operator is **Papua Diving** (☎ 0411-401660; fax 325274; www.papua-diving.com; Jl Gunung Gamalama 3), which runs a range of professional diving, trekking and bird-watching trips. This outfit concentrates on pre-booked, multiday tours rather than day trips, specialising in diving holidays in the Raja Ampat. The website contains details about tours, current costs and some of the local marine life.

Sleeping

Hotel Indah (☎ 321514; Jl Yos Sudarso 4; r 65,000-120,000Rp;) The best deals at the breezy Hotel Indah are on the 2nd floor, with air-con, ocean views and a tiled terrace. Sweet tea is the sole item offered for breakfast.

Hotel Tanjung (☎ 323782; Jl Yos Sudarso; r 75,000-200,000Rp;) Situated on the waterfront near the local market, Hotel Tanjung has a range of acceptable rooms. Though the cheaper ones don't have an attached *mandi* (Indonesian-style bath), all rooms come with a breakfast voucher for the oceanview restaurant upstairs.

Hotel Waigo (☎ 333500; Jl Yos Sudarso; r 165,000-300,000Rp; ❄) Playfully decked out in pink paint, psychedelic tile and stylised murals, Hotel Waigo is a superb deal – especially if you can snag one of the few oceanview rooms. Rates include breakfast and afternoon tea, served on the open-air terrace on the 4th floor.

Hotel Mariat (☎ 323535; Jl Ahmad Yani; r 466,000-1,060,000Rp, ste 1,101,000-2,371,600Rp; ❄ 📺) Though it's Sorong's pinnacle of luxury, the underwhelming accommodations don't quite merit these exorbitant prices. Still, if you're stranded in town, a standard room could be worth the splurge – the hotel boasts the only swimming pool in western Papua, as well as a full bar.

Eating

Every evening, warungs set up shop along the waterfront.

Rumah Makan Ruta Sayang (Jl Yos Sudarso; mains from 15,000Rp; 🕑 lunch & dinner) A few doors down from Restoran Tanjung, pick up the scent of meat on the grill at this hot spot.

Restoran Tanjung (Jl Yos Sudarso; mains around 30,000Rp; 🕑 breakfast, lunch & dinner) For spectacular sunsets and delectable baked fish, head upstairs from Hotel Tanjung's lobby.

Getting There & Away

Within Papua, Merpati flies daily from Sorong to Jayapura (with onward connections to Biak twice a week) and to Manokwari four times a week. Flights also leave daily for Jakarta, Makassar and Surabaya, while Wings flies to Manado once a week. Shop around for the best deals at the airline counters at the airport.

Sorong is the hub for all boat travel along the southern and northern coasts. Every two weeks, the *Rinjani* sails to Fak-Fak and Maluku (to Ternate 1st/economy class 323,000/149,000Rp), the *Sangiang* plies the south coast, the *Umsini* links Sorong with Sulawesi (to Makassar 1,247,000/575,000Rp), and the *Ciremai, Nggapulu, Dobonsolo* and *Doro Londa* connect Sorong with Sulawesi and/or Bali. The **Pelni office** (☎ 321716; Jl Ahmad Yani) also handles bookings for the Perintis boats. The **port** (Jl Ahmad Yani) is inconvenient, but accessible by *angkot*.

Getting Around

Gone are the days of schlepping 20km out to the Jefman Island airstrip to catch your flight; Sorong's new Domine Eduard Osok airport is conveniently located on the mainland, about 5km east of town.

Yellow *angkot* travel frequently along the main roads; from the airport, you'll have to transfer at the *angkot* terminal to one marked 'A' or 'B' to get into town. Airport taxis into town will cost 50,000Rp, while *ojek* (motorbike taxis) go for 10,000Rp.

FAK-FAK

☎ 0956

Wherever you turn in Fak-Fak – and yes, it *is* pronounced *that* way – your eyes will alight on picturesque views of the town's hills, trees and sparkling sea. But this quaint colonial town, built on coastal foothills, doesn't just have a pretty façade. While it was the first successful Dutch settlement in Papua, it retains some mystical local allure and lore. Ask around about the purported giants' bones found in the area, or venture northward to marvel at the rock-art sites along the coast.

Fak-Fak is accessible from Pulau Ambon and the Banda Islands (both in Maluku) by sea, and Sorong by air, so it's an enticing place to start and/or finish a visit to Papua.

Orientation & Information

Many facilities are along the main street, Jl Izaak Telussa, in the downtown area called Kota. As it snakes along the coast, this street leads to the tidy Pasar Tamburani (Tamburani Market) and the Tamburani *mikrolet* (minibus) terminal, facing the inlet. The steep roads climbing above Kota lead to the hillside quarters known as Wagom and Puncak, where you'll find the tourist office and Telkom office, respectively.

Alfa (Jl Cenderawasih; 🕑 9am-2pm & 5-10pm Mon-Sat, 5-10pm Sun) If this warnet in Puncak looks closed during opening hours, try knocking at the shop next door.

Bank Mandiri (Jl Izaak Telussa 26) Change cash and travellers cheques, but be prepared to wait.

Police (☎ 22200; Jl Tamburani) Once you arrive, report to this low-key police station, opposite Hotel Sulinah.

Post office (Jl Letjen Haryono)

Telkom (Jl Cenderawasih; 🕑 24hr)

Tourist office (☎ 22828; Jl Nuri 1; 🕑 7.30am-2pm Mon-Fri) Stop by for tips from the helpful staff, or a peek at the spectacular view from its balcony.

Sights & Activities

The best excursion is to **Pulau Tubir Seram** in the harbour. This tiny, uninhabited island is crossed with short **walking trails**, a huge monument dedicated to former German missionaries with a **museum** underneath, and superb views. The two-room **guesthouse** offers absolute seclusion. Before setting out, contact the tourist office about the status of the museum and guesthouse; at the time of writing, both were closed due to lack of funding and interest. You can charter a longboat (about 150,000Rp return) to the island from Danaweria village, just east of Fak-Fak.

About one hour by chartered boat from Terminal Tamburani, **Pulau Panjang** features the 1km-long, sandy **Pantai Wajob**.

Sleeping & Eating

The hotels listed below are all along, or just off, Jl Izaak Telussa.

Hotel Tembagapura (☎ 22136; Jl Izaak Telussa 16; r 65,000-165,000Rp; ❄) It's central, quiet and often full, and rates include breakfast.

Hotel Sulinah (☎ 22447; Jl Tamburani 93; r 80,000Rp) At the western end of the main street, this small family-run place offers clean rooms with shared *mandi* and the sounds of the call to prayer from the hill above. Breakfast and afternoon tea are included.

Fak-Fak Hotel (☎ 23196; Jl Suprapto 9; s 95,000-187,000Rp, d 105,000-220,000Rp; ❄) Priciest rooms have hot water, minibars and balconies with sweet 180-degree ocean views. Breakfast is not included, but you can order meals from the inhouse restaurant.

Hotel Marco Polo (☎ 22537; Jl Izaak Telussa 63; r 110,000Rp; ❄) This clean, friendly place is down a steep laneway opposite a mosque. Breakfast is included.

For ocean breezes and excellent *ikan bakar* (grilled fish) or *ayam lalapan* (fried chicken with chilli), head for the spit in the inlet known as Jl Baru or Jl Reklamasi. The waterside warungs are open in the evenings only and are most easily reached from the Terminal Tamburani side of the reclaimed road.

Getting There & Away

Merpati flies four days a week to Sorong, and twice a week to Nabire and Biak. The **Merpati office** (☎ 71275; Jl Izaak Telussa 57) is open irregularly.

Every two weeks, the Pelni liner *Rinjani* sails to Sorong and Ambon (1st/economy class 247,000/125,000Rp), the *Doro Londa* conveniently links Fak-Fak with the north coast of Papua, and the *Sangiang* sails down the south coast of Papua. Every four weeks, the *Tatamailau* and *Kelimutu* also ply the south coast of Papua and sail the ocean blue to Ambon.

Perintis boats stop at Fak-Fak every two or three weeks during their crawl along the south coast and around southeast Maluku. The port is centrally located at the eastern end of Jl Izaak Telussa, but the **Pelni office** (☎ 23371; Jl DI Panjaitan) is not – take a *mikrolet*.

Getting Around

Tiny Torea airport is on a hillside about 7km from town. From the airport, a chartered *mikrolet* might cost 25,000Rp if there's no one to share it with you; to the airport, you can usually catch one from Terminal Tamburani or charter one from town. The streets of Fak-Fak are extremely steep, so use *mikrolet* if you're straying beyond Kota to the hillside neighbourhoods.

AROUND FAK-FAK

Around the village and beach at **Kokas**, on the north coast of the peninsula, there is a plethora of Japanese WWII cannons, tunnels and shipwrecks, and a mosque built in 1870. With permission from the tourist office in Fak-Fak, you can stay in the guesthouse at Kokas, but watch out for the huge coconut crabs! *Mikrolet* travel the road from Fak-Fak to Ubadari, from where you can charter a boat to Kokas.

You should also charter a boat from Fak-Fak or Ubadari to inspect the ancient **rock paintings** along the coast as far as **Goras**, to explore the **Ugar Islands** (for diving) or to admire the magnificent **Air Terjun Madedred** (Madedred Waterfalls).

Those with bronze ambitions can take *mikrolet* to beaches starting about 1km west of town: **Pasir Putih I, II & III** all have white sands, azure waters and no crowds on weekdays.

MANOKWARI

☎ 0986 / pop 55,000

The first place in Papua to be settled by missionaries, Manokwari ('Old Village' in the Biak language) is a mellow base from which to explore Teluk Cenderawasih. The town is easy to roam around and provides most facilities.

Orientation & Information

Except for the suburb of Wosi to the west, most of Manokwari hugs Teluk Doreri. The eastern side of the bay, simply known as Kota, is a more convenient base than the western (Sanggeng) side.

Bank Mandiri (Jl Yos Sudarso)

BNI bank (Bank Negara Indonesia; Jl Merdeka 44) Also has a 24-hour ATM for Visa and MasterCard.

Cenderawasih Bay Marine National Park office (☎ 222356, 212303; Jl Rendani, Wosi) About 3km west of town, towards the airport.

Flashlink.net (Jl Merdeka 46; 🕑 9am-1pm & 5-9pm Mon-Sat) Slow internet connection tempered by soothing air-con.

Main post office (Jl Siliwangi 28) Opposite the port; serves your basic needs.

Police station (☎ 211359; Jl Bhayangkhara) About 200m east of the port, a *surat jalan* for surrounding areas is easy to obtain from here.

Telkom Wartel (cnr Jl Merdeka & Jl Kota Baru) Cushy booths in the most convenient place to make a telephone call.

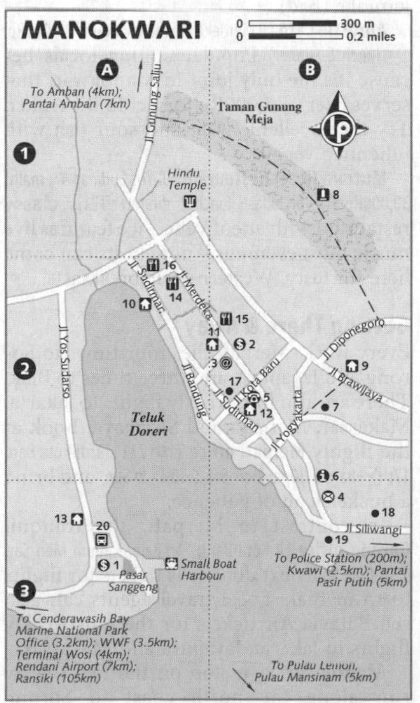

Tourist office (☎ 212030; Jl Merdeka; 🕑 7.30am-2pm Mon-Fri) Worth visiting, especially if you plan to trek around Pegunungan Arfak.

WWF (☎ 222493; Jl Rendani, Wosi) Good source of information about Cenderawasih Marine National Park and Pegunungan Arfak.

Sights & Activities

A reasonably flat 2.5km path crosses picturesque **Taman Gunung Meja** (Table Mountain Park), a protected forest with plenty of bird life and butterflies. Take a taxi to Amban (a pleasant university town) from Terminal Sanggeng, and ask the driver to let you off at the unsigned start to the well-marked trail. The **Tugu Jepang** (Japanese Monument), 1km before the end of the trail, offers great views, and the path ends behind Hotel Arfak.

Gua Jepang (Japanese Cave) is more of a series of tunnels that was built by the Japanese in WWII. The entrance, which you can look at but not really explore, is along the stone steps leading to Hotel Arfak, between two tennis courts.

Two German missionaries settled on **Pulau Mansinam** in 1855 and became the first in Papua to spread 'The Word'. This picturesque island, set majestically in a bay under

INFORMATION

Bank Mandiri	1 A3
BNI Bank	2 B2
Flashlink net	3 B2
Main Post Office	4 B3
Telkom Wartel	5 B2
Tourist Office	6 B2

SIGHTS & ACTIVITIES

Gua Jepang	7 B2
Tugu Jepang	8 B1

SLEEPING

Billy Jaya Hotel	(see 15)
Hotel Arfak	9 B2
Hotel Maluku	10 A2
Hotel Mokwam	11 B2
Losmen Apose	12 B2
Mutiara Hotel	13 A3

EATING

Abressio Café	14 A2
Billy Café	15 B2
Hawai Billy Bakery & Coffee Shop	16 A2
Mutiara Hotel Restaurant	(see 13)

TRANSPORT

Garuda	17 B2
Merpati	(see 17)
Pelni	18 B3
Port	19 B3
Terminal Sanggeng	20 A3

PAPUA

Pegunungan Arfak, is home to a small village, the ruins of an **old church**, a **memorial** to the missionaries, and a pleasant **beach**. It's best to report to the *kepala desa* (village head) before wandering around too far.

Nearby, **Pulau Lemon** boasts some more **beaches**, **WWII wrecks** and spots for **snorkelling** (bring your own gear), but is smaller, and less enticing and accessible, than Mansinam. A passenger boat (one way 3000Rp) from the jetty at Kwawi (accessible via the Pantai Pasir Putih taxis from Terminal Sanggeng) goes to Mansinam three or four times a day. It's more fun, however, to ask someone in Kwawi to take you in his canoe (about 100,000Rp return to both islands).

About 5km east of the town centre, **Pantai Pasir Putih** is a curved bay of white sand and clear water, ideal for **swimming** and **snorkelling** (bring your own gear). It's a little unkempt in parts, but quiet – except on Sunday when half of Manokwari invades the beach. The other half visits **Pantai Amban**, 3km north of Amban village and 7km north of Manokwari. This black-sand beach is perfect for **surfing** and watching the sunset. Taxis leave regularly from Terminal Sanggeng to both Pantai Pasir Putih and Amban village (from where you'll probably have to walk to the beach).

Tours

The only travel agency in Manokwari is **Arfak Paradigalla Tours & Travel** (☎ 0815-27004054; yoris_tours@yahoo.com). This effusive, one-man outfit offers tours around Manokwari, as well as bird-watching trips and treks around Pegunungan Arfak and the Anggi lakes.

Sleeping

All hotels listed below include breakfast (and some throw in afternoon tea) in their rates.

Losmen Apose (☎ 211369; Jl Kota Baru 4; s with shared mandi 50,000Rp, d with private mandi 150,000Rp) This is a friendly place opposite the Merpati agency. Rooms vary in quality, so view a few before deciding.

Billy Jaya Hotel (☎ 215787; Jl Merdeka 51; r 151,250-302,500Rp; ❄) Upstairs from Billy Café and its attached travel agency, the clean, cosy, lower-end rooms here are a terrific deal. Woven rattan ceilings, TVs and minibars add to the atmosphere and comfort.

Mutiara Hotel (☎ 217777; fax 211222; Jl Yos Sudarso 41; r 235,950-326,700Rp; ❄) All rooms at the Mutiara have bathroom and satellite TV, and are comfortably outfitted. Garden-view rooms at the back are quieter and actually cheaper than those facing the busy boulevard.

Other accommodation options:

Hotel Arfak (☎ 213079; fax 211293; Jl Brawijaya 8; r 50,000-150,000Rp; ❄) Its decaying colonial shell could use some work, but some rooms are OK for the prices.

Hotel Maluku (☎ 211948; Jl Sudirman 52; r 115,000-140,000Rp; ❄) Central and quiet, and better maintained than the Arfak, but with only squat toilets.

Hotel Mokwam (☎ 211403; Jl Merdeka 49; r 186,000-270,000Rp; ❄) A step up in price and quality is the spacious, friendly Mokwam.

Eating

Hawai Billy Bakery & Coffee Shop (☎ 212189; Jl Sudirman 100; mains 15,000Rp; 🕑 breakfast, lunch & dinner) An arm of the Billy empire, this relaxed spot serves espresso and pizza and features a wall of house-baked pastries.

Billy Café (☎ 211036; Jl Merdeka 51; mains around 25,000Rp; 🕑 lunch & dinner) The English menu details a few Western selections like hamburgers, but you're better off with the Indonesian or Chinese food. The main dining room blasts air-conditioning (good) and karaoke (bad).

Abressio Café (Jl Merdeka 87; mains around 30,000Rp; 🕑 lunch & dinner) Popular among locals because it's the only joint in Manokwari that serves beer – 15,000Rp for a cold Bir Anker. Try the excellent sweet-and-sour fish with julienned veggies.

Mutiara Hotel Restaurant (Jl Yos Sudarso 41; mains 30,000Rp; 🕑 breakfast, lunch & dinner) This classy restaurant with attentive service features live music most evenings – nonguests can come here for tasty, Western-style breakfasts.

Getting There & Away

Every week, Merpati flies four times to Sorong and Jayapura, and three times to Biak. There are also four weekly flights to Jakarta, Makassar, Manado and Surabaya. Book at the flighty **Merpati office** (☎ 211133; Jl Kota Baru 17; 🕑 8am-3.30pm Mon-Sat, 5.30-8pm Sun) and bring a bucket-load of patience.

In contrast to Merpati, the tranquil **Garuda office** (Jl Kota Baru; 🕑 8am-3.30pm Mon-Sat, 5.30-8pm Sun) next door sells tickets for flights to/from Biak. Local travel agents can also sell Batavia Air tickets for the four-weekly flights to Jakarta, Jayapura and Makassar.

Manokwari is a stop on the two-weekly run along the north coast to Sorong

(1st/economy class 394,000/182,000Rp), Biak (182,000/88,000Rp) and Serui (354,500/171,500Rp) on the Pelni liners *Ciremai, Dobonsolo, Doro Londa* and *Nggapulu*. Opposite the port, the **Pelni office** (☎ 215167; Jl Siliwangi 24) sells tickets for all major boats.

Getting Around

Rendani airport is a 10-minute drive west of the town centre. Charter a taxi (about 25,000Rp) or *ojek* (10,000Rp). Otherwise, walk straight outside the airport terminal and catch a public taxi to Terminal Wosi, another to Terminal Sanggeng and, if necessary, another to your hotel.

From Terminal Wosi, about 4km west of Manokwari, public taxis regularly leave for the airport and larger towns, such as Ransiki. From Terminal Sanggeng (in Manokwari), taxis link both sides of Teluk Doreri every nanosecond, and regularly depart for nearby beaches.

Yellow-helmeted *ojek* drivers hang around the taxi terminals and scoot along the main streets.

PEGUNUNGAN ARFAK & ANGGI LAKES

In Pegunungan Arfak, at an elevation of 2030m, are the Anggi Lakes: **Danau Giji** (29 sq km) and **Danau Gita** (24.5 sq km). These clear and deep lakes offer exquisite scenery and wildlife, as well as excellent **hiking** and **swimming**. Another reason to visit is to meet the traditional Manikom and Hatam people.

The two- or three-day trek to the lakes from Ransiki follows Sungai Momi to Siwi, and involves some climbing and hiking along muddy trails. A guide is essential – ask the district office in Ransiki. You can sleep in local huts along the way (per person about 30,000Rp), or the district office in Anggi can arrange accommodation (per person 40,000Rp). You should bring your own food, though you can buy vegetables along the way.

This trek can be done independently (with a guide), though **Arfak Paradigalla Tours & Travel** (☎ 0815-27004054; yoris_tours@yahoo.com) in Manokwari also can organise treks between Ransiki and the lakes.

RANSIKI

Crowded taxis (35,000Rp, three hours) leave every hour or so from Terminal Wosi in Manokwari for the pleasant *transmigrasi* town of Ransiki. It's a rough trip – and often impassable during the wet season (November to March) – but the scenery through the jungle, along the coast and among traditional villages is superb. Even if you're not going to the Anggi lakes, the trip to Ransiki is still worthwhile.

There's a small **guesthouse** (per person 50,000Rp) next to the Telkom office in Ransiki, which is especially useful if you're trekking to the Anggi lakes or visiting Pulau Rumberpon.

CENDERAWASIH BAY MARINE NATIONAL PARK

This reserve (Taman Laut Teluk Cenderawasih) consists of 18 islands and 500km of coastline, and at 14,300 sq km is the largest of its kind in Indonesia. It's home to endangered species of giant clams, turtles and dugongs, and offers some of the best **trekking**, **diving** (130 types of coral) and **bird-watching** (150 bird species) imaginable. Like most of Papua, however, exploration is severely hindered by government travel regulations and a lack of transport.

The larger inhabited islands in the area are Rumberpon, Mioswaar, Roon and Angrameos. You can explore the coastline or islands by speedboat from either Nabire or Ransiki for about 250,000Rp per day, or base yourself on Pulau Rumberpon or at Wasior (though neither is strictly within the park). Otherwise, organise a tour with **Arfak Paradigalla Tours & Travel** (☎ 0815-27004054; yoris_tours@yahoo.com) in Manokwari.

Before venturing into the reserve independently, permission and advice should be obtained from the **Cenderawasih Bay Marine National Park office** (☎ 0986-222356, 212303; Jl Rendani, Wosi) in Manokwari.

Pulau Rumberpon

This island offers **snorkelling** among superb coral and marine life, and outstanding **hiking**. It's also worthwhile chartering a boat to nearby islands such as **Pulau Wairondi**, with its untouched population of **turtles**, and **Pulau Auri**.

If you ask the village head on Rumberpon, you should be able to camp on the beach for a few days (bring your own tent and cooking gear) or stay in a village hut. It's also worth checking with the tourist office in Manokwari about other accommodation possibilities on the island.

Public speedboats (about two hours) leave Ransiki for Rumberpon most days.

Wasior

From Wasior, you can charter a boat to islands in the marine reserve or organise a trek in the **Wondiwoi Mountain Reserve** (Taman Pegunungan Wondiwoi), home to more than 100 species of birds. There's no official accommodation in Wasior, but finding somewhere to stay should not be any problem. Check with the tourist office in Manokwari that your *surat jalan* covers this area. Merpati flies twice a week to Wasior for about the same cost as the overnight ferries (100,000Rp) that travel daily between the Manokwari port and Wasior.

CENTRAL PAPUA

The centre for transport, commerce and tourism in Central Papua is Pulau Biak (1898 sq km), scene of many horrific WWII battles between the Allies and Japanese. The island has a great deal to offer and is a worthy stopover, especially if you're a WWII buff or into diving. Kota Biak is the principal centre, while Nabire (on the southern shore of Cenderawasih Bay) and Serui (on Pulau Yapen) are also appealing towns from which to explore the Teluk Cenderawasih region.

PULAU BIAK

Kota Biak

☎ 0981 / pop 57,500

Kota Biak is a relaxed town from which to explore attractions around Pulau Biak and the general Teluk Cenderawasih region. There is no accommodation elsewhere on the island, and transport is limited in the north, but most places of interest on Pulau Biak can be visited on day trips from the here.

Only one degree south of the equator, Biak is always hot and humid. So it's a good idea to start your day early and hibernate like the locals between 1pm and 4pm (when a lot of shops and offices are closed anyway).

In mid-August, Pulau Biak's **Munara Festival** features fire-walking, traditional dancing and boat races. Ask at the tourist office for more information.

ORIENTATION

Kota Biak is compact. A lot of what you'll need is along Jl Ahmad Yani (which joins Jl Prof M Yamin from the airport), Jl Sudirman (which heads past the port) and Jl Imam Bonjol, all of which intersect at the Bank Mandiri building. The majority of places to stay and eat are around this area, but a few offices, as well as the taxi (minibus) terminal and main market, are a short taxi ride away.

INFORMATION

A *surat jalan* is not required to visit anywhere on Pulau Biak, but Kota Biak is a handy place to obtain one for Pulau Yapen and the Baliem Valley.

Bank Mandiri (cnr Jl Imam Bonjol & Jl Ahmad Yani) Offers the best rates for cash and travellers cheques, and a 24-hour ATM.

BNI bank (Bank Negara Indonesia; Jl Imam Bonjol 23) Has an ATM that accepts Visa and MasterCard.

diBiak.com (Jl Sudirman 4; per hr 9000Rp; 🕑 9am-9pm) Popular internet centre housing plenty of PCs in heavenly air-conditioned comfort.

Main post office (Jl Prof M Yamin 59; 🕑 8am-2pm Mon-Fri, 8am-1pm Sat) A short taxi ride (take a taxi marked 'Ambroben') along the road to the airport; has a poste restante service.

Police station (☎ 21005; Jl Diponegoro) The friendly guys at the 'intel' section will need two photographs and an administrative fee of about 5000Rp to provide a *surat jalan*.

Rumah Sakit Umum (☎ 21294; Jl Sri Wijaya) The general hospital is 2.5km northwest of Hotel Sinar Kayu.

Telkom (Jl Yos Sudarso 1; 🕑 24hr) The mammoth office is at the split in the road, 500m southeast of the Bank Mandiri building.

Tourist office (☎ 21663; Jl Prof M Yamin 56; 🕑 7.30am-3pm Mon-Fri) Has helpful staff, just opposite the main post office. If you're in town in mid-January, stop by to find out if anything's on for Papua Tourism Week.

SIGHTS & ACTIVITIES

Cenderawasih Museum

This **museum** (Jl Sisingamangaraja) offers a dusty collection of shells, implements and WWII weapons, as well as a few Japanese war relics in the garden. Although touted by the local tourist office as a major attraction, this museum could be *far* better. If you're interested, find the caretaker (who lives on the grounds) and slip him a donation (per person 5000Rp) to open it up.

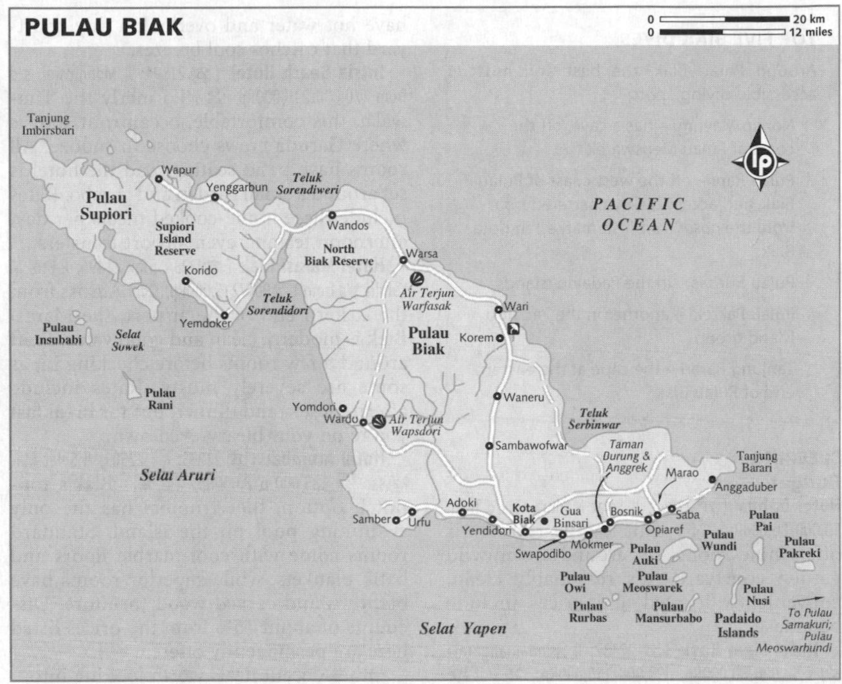

Diving

The underwater attractions around Pulau Biak and Teluk Cenderawasih have the potential to compete with northern Sulawesi, with the added bonus of being cheaper and less overrun by tourists. However, some local fishermen blithely continue their practice of dynamite and cyanide fishing, so you may find spots that are slightly less stunning than others.

The diving industry in Biak is small but growing, and there's nowhere else in Central Papua to organise diving/snorkelling trips or rent equipment. **Biak Diving** (☎ 26017; diving@biak.wasantara.net.id; Jl Ahmad Yani 39). This well-established agency charges 900,000Rp per person for two boat dives (or 750,000Rp for two beach dives). A single beach night-dive costs 750,000Rp, while overnight packages including food and basic accommodation on an island start at 1,150,000Rp. All rates include equipment and transport, and are for a minimum of two people. Full diving equipment can be rented for 300,000Rp per day.

It also offers all-day snorkelling and sightseeing tours for 600,000Rp per person (minimum of two, including equipment and transport) around Pulau Biak. Alternatively, you can just hire a snorkel, mask and fins for 70,000Rp per day.

Other Activities

Kota Biak is really the only base for organising bird-watching tours between Sorong and Jayapura. Check out Biak's two travel agencies for help with arranging regional tours. Independent guides who hang around the airport, like ecology-minded Matheus Rumbarar, can also customise bird-watching and island-hopping tours in the area.

Janggi Prima Tours & Travel (☎/fax 22973; Jl Pramuka 5) This impressive one-man show offers a wide range of trekking, bird-watching and diving tours around Biak and Yapen islands. The manager speaks good English.

PT Biak Paradise Tours & Travel (☎ 23196; paradise@biak.wasantara.net.id; Hotel Arumbai, Jl Selat Makassar 3; 8am-4pm Mon-Fri) The friendly manager Pak Benny speaks excellent English and is a valuable source of local information. He can arrange everything from bird-watching tours around the Biak island group to treks around Manokwari, the Baliem Valley and the Asmat region.

PAPUA

TOP FIVE BIAK DIVES

Around Pulau Biak, the best and most accessible diving spots:

- Noriko Mayumi – has a cave, off the coast of Pulau Meoswarek
- Pulau Rani – off the west coast of Pulau Biak, and accessible by chartered boat from the *pasar ikan* (fish market) in Kota Biak
- Pulau Rurbas – in the Padaido Islands
- Pulau Pakreki – another in the Padaido Island group
- Tanjung Barari – the cape at the eastern end of Pulau Biak.

SLEEPING

Budget

Hotel Dahlia (☎ 21851; Jl Selat Madura 6; s/d from 50,000/80,000Rp; ❄) This family-run affair offers nine rooms set around a semiwild garden courtyard. It's reasonably clean, conveniently located and prices include breakfast.

Hotel Sinar Kayu (☎ 22137; Jl Sisingamangaraja 89; s 50,000-80,000Rp, d90,000-150,000Rp; ❄) The many rooms here mean you'll almost always find a place to sleep. But the cheap quarters are fanless with outside *mandis*, while the nicer air-con rooms have only squat toilets.

Hotel Maju (☎ 21841; Jl Imam Bonjol 45; s/d 60,000/80,000Rp; ❄) Still Biak's best budget option, this place is often full. The rooms are smallish and nothing special, but they're clean (the ones at the back are far quieter). All rooms come with a simple breakfast.

Midrange & Top End

All places listed below offer rooms with private bathrooms, and all rates include breakfast (exception noted).

Hotel Irian Biak (☎ 21939; fax 21458; Jl Prof M Yamin 4; r 125,000-275,000Rp; ❄) Opposite the western side of the airport, this vast old place has lots of good-value, wood-floored rooms. The priciest real estate here is in the quiet oceanfront rooms, with private balconies and tiled floors.

Hotel Nirmala (☎ 22005; fax 24660; Jl Selat Madura 13; s/d 160,000/230,000Rp; ❄) Excellent value, with three meals and afternoon tea included in room rates, the clean and tidy rooms here have hot water and overlook a tidy courtyard that catches cool breezes.

Intsia Beach Hotel (☎ 21891; Jl Monginsidi; s/d from 170,000/210,000Rp; ❄) Formerly the Titawaka, this comfortable, oceanfront spot is where Garuda crews choose to snooze. All rooms have patio seating, and the hotel is set around a small garden and gazebo. Rates include three home-cooked meals per day, afternoon tea and even airport transfers.

Hotel Marasi Biak (☎ 22345; fax 21496; Jl Prof M Yamin; s/d from 175,000/215,000Rp; ❄) Across from the eastern end of the airport, the Marasi Biak is modern, clean and good value. Sniff around a few rooms before checking in, as some are severely musty. Rates include afternoon tea and dinner, but for breakfast you're on your bleary-eyed own.

Hotel Arumbai (☎ 21835; fax 22501; Jl Selat Makassar 3; r 185,000-618,000Rp; ❄ 🏊) Biak's top-notch option, the Arumbai has the only swimming pool on the island. Standard rooms come with cool marble floors and batik blankets, while superior rooms have bathtubs and carved wood furniture. Discounts of about 15% from the prices listed here are permanently offered.

Other decent deals worth looking into:

Padaido Hotel (☎ 22144; Jl Monginsidi 16; r from 180,000Rp; ❄) Also rents out a handful of immaculate, cheery little rooms.

Basana Inn (☎ 22281; fax 22343; Jl Imam Bonjol 46A; s 159,000-205,000Rp, d 200,000-240,000Rp; ❄)

Hotel Mapia (☎ 21383; Jl Ahmad Yani 23; s 95,000-145,000Rp, d 120,000-170,000Rp; ❄).

EATING

Barapen cuisine is food cooked under hot rocks, on which some of the braver (and possibly more intoxicated) guests attempt some impromptu fire-walking. To sample some traditional *barapen* cooking, you will have to be invited to a party in a village or arrange this through a local travel agency.

Padaido Café (☎ 21346; Jl Monginsidi 16; mains 15,000-25,000Rp; 🕑 lunch & dinner Mon-Sat) With its large outdoor patio, it's the only waterfront eatery in town. The friendly owners offer a few Western-style meals along with delish fish dishes.

Rumah Makan Rindu Alam (☎ 23039; Jl Imam Bonjol 22; 🕑 lunch & dinner) A cool, clean Padang place where the curries are spicy and the service fast and friendly.

PAPUA

Rumah Makan Nirwana (☎ 21506; Jl Sudirman 22; snacks from 2500Rp; ⌚ breakfast, lunch & dinner) *The* spot for cold soft drinks, pastries and assorted *kue-kue* (cakes).

The following restaurants provide menus with items listed in English:

Rumah Makan 99 (☎ 21450; Jl Imam Bonjol; mains 33,000Rp; ⌚ lunch & dinner) Small and friendly place with an extensive menu – your bill will have an unadvertised 10% service charge tacked on.

Rumah Makan Umum Jakarta (☎ 21969; Jl Imam Bonjol 10; mains 15,000-50,000Rp; ⌚ lunch & dinner) As clean and charmless as the 99, serving Chinese and Indonesian meals.

The best of the cheap warungs are in and around the markets, **Pasar Inpres** (Jl Erlangga) and **Pasar Lama** (Jl Selat Makassar).

DRINKING

During the late afternoon, a drink in the seaview garden of Hotel Irian Biak is very pleasant indeed. Even better is a sunset Bintang on the outdoor terrace of Padaido Café – but don't forget the mosquito repellent.

SHOPPING

There's an art shop and two general markets:

Iriani Art Shop (☎ 21457; Jl Imam Bonjol 40; ⌚ 8am-2pm & 5-9pm) This wonderful shop carries an enticing selection of Papuan art, carvings and jewellery at reasonable fixed prices.

Pasar Lama (Jl Selat Makassar) This market sells locally made items such as batiks, carvings and souvenirs made from shells, as well as Asmat and Baliem carvings (most of which are authentic imitations).

Pasar Inpres (Jl Erlangga) Market next to the taxi/bus terminal, mainly selling food and clothing, if you need to stock up.

GETTING THERE & AWAY

Air

Biak is the major centre for air travel throughout Papua. Merpati flies a few times per week to Fak-Fak, Jayapura, Manokwari, Nabire, Serui, Sorong and Timika. The same airline also flies regularly to Makassar (on the way to Jakarta, Manado and Surabaya), as well as to Yemburwo in Pulau Numfor. Stop by the **Merpati office** (☎ 21213;

PAPUA

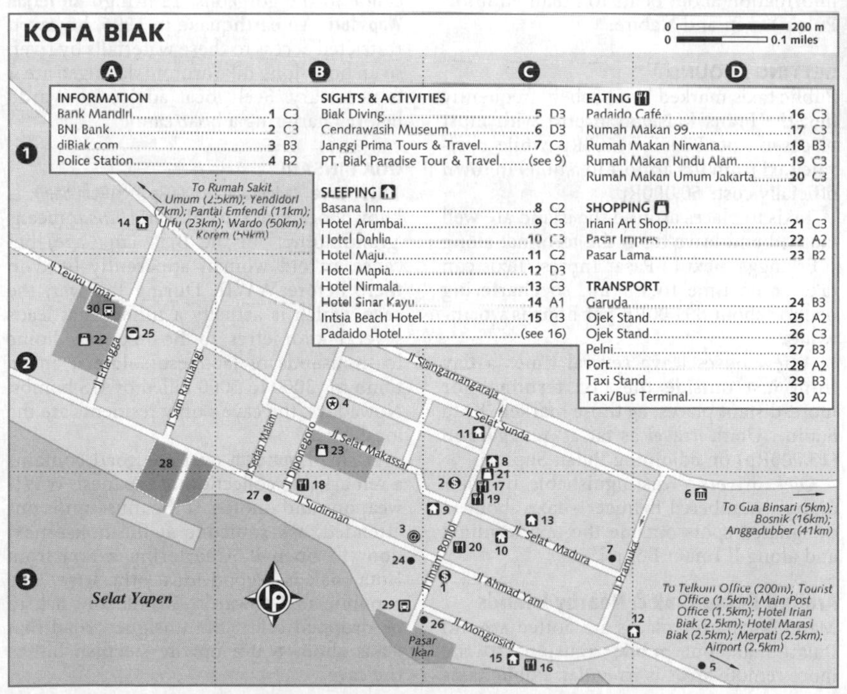

bikkmz@merpati.co.id; Jl Prof M Yamin; 8am-5pm), across the road from the airport, for current schedules.

Garuda (25737; bikdmga@garuda-indonesia.com; Jl Sudirman 3; 8am-9pm Mon-Fri, 8am-noon & 5-9pm Sat & Sun) flies six times per week to Jakarta, Jayapura and Makassar; book tickets at its air-conditioned, computerised office.

Boat

Every two weeks, the *Dobonsolo*, *Nggapulu* and *Sinabung* stop at Biak on the way to Manokwari (1st/economy class 182,000/88,000Rp) and Jayapura (376,000/177,500Rp). You can book tickets at the **Pelni office** (23255; Jl Sudirman 37; 9am-noon & 2-5pm Mon-Fri, 9am-1pm Sat, 10am-5pm Sun), though it's worth paying a little extra for a ticket from one of the agencies that spring up from nowhere around the port when a boat is due, rather than wait in line at the Pelni office for hours.

Perintis and a few other boats also stop at Biak. Tickets and current schedules are available at the port.

Refer to the relevant sections later for information about boats to Pulau Numfor, Pulau Yapen and Nabire.

GETTING AROUND

Public taxis marked 'Ambroben' frequently link the Frans Kaisiepo airport with most places in Kota Biak for 1500Rp, while a private taxi from the airport to a hotel in town officially costs 50,000Rp.

Taxis to places around the island are well marked and leave from the terminal along Jl Erlangga, next to Pasar Inpres. Taxis can take some time to fill up, so chartering one for about 50,000Rp per hour is worthwhile.

A few buses leave several times a day from just outside the taxi terminal for more-distant places, eg those marked 'Kota Supiori Utara' travel as far as Yenggarbun (15,000Rp) on adjoining Pulau Supiori.

Ojek drivers – distinguishable by their orange, numbered helmets – laze about at designated spots outside the taxi terminal and along Jl Imam Bonjol.

Around Pulau Biak & Nearby Islands

Many fascinating places are dotted around Pulau Biak, but public transport to the more remote areas is irregular. Public taxis and/or buses ply the rough roads to Samber (west of Kota Biak), Marao (to the east), Wardo (to the northwest), and Yenggarbun (in the far north). To places north of Wardo, and around most of Pulau Supiori, trucks, boats and feet are the main forms of transport.

Remember that villages on the island may look biggish on a map, but none is really more than a handful of huts with no accommodation or food for travellers.

URFU & SAMBER

Past Adoki, a side road continues for another bumpy 20 minutes to Urfu, surrounded by amazing **rock formations**. Along the beach to the pretty fishing village of Samber are some **relics**, reminders of a seemingly forgotten Dutch colonial past and of the Japanese occupation during WWII.

WARDO

At the end of the potholed road northwest of Kota Biak is Wardo, set on a picturesque bay. From Wardo (Biak for 'deep water'), you used to be able to charter a boat or canoe to the gorgeous, 12m-high **Air Terjun Wapsdori**. An earthquake in 1996, however, restricted access to these waterfalls by river, so an hour-long hike around damaged areas is necessary. Seek local advice in Wardo before chartering a boat/canoe.

GUA BINSARI

This **cave** (admission 20,000Rp; 7am-5pm) is known locally as Gua Binsari (*binsar* means 'grandmother' in the Biak language) because an old woman apparently lived in there before WWII. During the war, the cave, which is actually a tunnel that leads several kilometres to Bosnik, was home to thousands of Japanese soldiers, and a tomb for 3000 to 5000 killed by US bombs. Nowadays, the cave's only residents are the local bats.

A small **museum** over the road contains a remarkable collection of Japanese WWII weapons and photos. If the museum is unattended, ask someone at the house next door to open it. Chartering a taxi from Kota Biak is a good idea; otherwise, take a public taxi towards Bosnik and ask to be dropped off at the unsigned road that leads about 800m up the steepish hill to the cave.

TAMAN BURUNG & ANGGREK

About 4km east of Mokmer is the **Orchid & Bird Garden** (admission 10,000Rp; 7.30am-3pm). These large, serene gardens contain 72 species of orchids and about 50 types of caged birds, including strikingly-coloured lories, hornbills and *cenderawasih* (which is probably as close as you'll ever get to one). Several semi-tame cassowaries roam freely around the park, so keep your eyes peeled. Except for busy Sundays, there's often no-one around – so just walk through the gate and pay your admission fee if or when someone runs after you.

BOSNIK & BEYOND

Bosnik was the Dutch capital of the island and a landing site for the Allies in WWII. Badly destroyed during the 1996 earthquake and tidal wave, it is still home to some **WWII relics** along the sandy **beach**, and a small, busy, early-morning **market** every Wednesday and Saturday. Bosnik is also the place to charter a boat to the enticing Padaido Islands.

The eastern road continues past **Opiaref**, renowned for its wood carvers, and **Saba**, where you can explore the ruins of an ambitious – but ultimately abandoned – four-star resort and its quiet beach. Opiaref also has a pleasant **beach** and an enticing **cave** with underground pools; ask for directions. A trail continues along the coast about 10km past more charming, deserted beaches until you reach the village of **Anggaduber**.

PADAIDO ISLANDS

This stunning cluster of 36 reefs and islands (of which only 13 are inhabited) are wonderful for **swimming**, **diving** and **snorkelling**. The most appealing islands to visit are Pulau Owi (for its powder-white beach and WWII relics) and Pulau Nusi (snorkelling).

Owi and Auki Islands are the most populated and the closest to Pulau Biak, so you're likely to find a passenger boat to these islands from Bosnik and be able to stay in a local hut. Passenger boats also travel between Bosnik and several inhabited islands on Bosnik's market days (Wednesday and Saturday). It's also possible to charter a boat from Bosnik, or the *pasar ikan* (fish market) in Kota Biak, to remote islands – but work out a price beforehand and be sure to bargain.

KOREM

On the north coast of Pulau Biak, Korem was mostly destroyed by an earthquake and subsequent tsunami in 1996. The village has been rebuilt on the western side of the main road, but the **beach** is still delightful. Most locals refuse to visit the beach because of the number of people who died there in 1996. Ask the taxi driver to drop you off at the turn-off to the beach, and wait for a lift or walk (about 30 minutes).

NORTH BIAK RESERVE

At the northern end of Pulau Biak is Taman Biak Utara, 110 sq km of dense wilderness and pristine beaches. One highlight in the general area is **Air Terjun Warfasak**, a broad waterfall that plunges into a small lake, near Warsa. The best way to get around the reserve is on foot with an experienced local guide. Tours and guides can be organised by one of the travel agencies in Biak (p809).

PULAU SUPIORI

Separated from Pulau Biak by a narrow channel, most of Supiori Island is designated as the **Supiori Island Reserve** (Taman Pulau Supiori), an area of mangroves and montane forests with endemic species of parrots and cockatoos. If the bridge over the channel is broken, a pontoon with an ingenious pulley system takes passengers and even vehicles across the water.

The main road on Supiori continues as far as Wapur, though buses stop at Yenggarbun. If you have time, soaking up the scenery by public (or chartered) taxi/bus from Kota Biak to the channel and back is worthwhile. One of Biak's travel agencies (p809) can arrange local guides, and accommodation in Wapur and Yenggarbun should you wish to stay.

PULAU NUMFOR

This irresistible, unspoilt and undeveloped island is about half-way between Biak and Manokwari. Dozens of unexplored **snorkelling** and **swimming** spots are scattered around the island, such as **Pantai Asaibori** in the west and **Pantai Pakreki** to the south. From Kameri on Numfor, you can charter a boat (20 minutes) to the heavenly **Pulau Manem**, where there's no shortage of **bird life**, sandy **beaches** and Japanese **WWII wrecks**.

PAPUA

There is no official accommodation on Numfor, but you can stay with a local family if you contact the *kepala desa* in the main villages of Yemburwo (on the north coast), Kameri (a little further west) and Namber (west coast).

Merpati flies between Biak and Yemburwo twice weekly. The *Padmos* boat leaves from the main port in Kota Biak every week for a circular route to Numfor (12 to 15 hours), Manokwari and Ransiki, before returning to Biak via Numfor. Ask at the port for more details. Also, unscheduled public speedboats (which can be chartered) leave the *pasar ikan* in Kota Biak (eight to 10 hours), while other boats leave from Andie, near Yemburwo, for Kota Biak and Manokwari (five to six hours).

PULAU YAPEN

☎ 0983

This elongated mountainous island south of Pulau Biak offers bird life around its northern shores and superb **snorkelling** in several spots.

The only town of any size is the district capital, Serui. A *surat jalan,* which is needed for anywhere on the island, can be easily obtained in Kota Biak. **Bank Mandiri** (Jl Diponegoro) will reluctantly change US dollars cash.

Sights & Activities

To find some of the few **cenderawasih** still surviving in the north of the island, charter a boat (holding about 10 people) from Serui for about 300,000Rp per day. A guide (about 90,000Rp per day) will arrange for you to stay in local villages (around 45,000Rp per person). A 'protection fee' of 100,000Rp is levied on each group looking for the birds. To save the hassle of organising things yourself, **bird-watching** tours can be arranged with the travel agencies listed in the Biak (p809) and Jayapura (p829) sections.

Less than one hour south of **Serui**, the district capital, **Pulau Arumbai** offers superb **snorkelling** (bring your own gear) among coral reefs and dolphins, and is home to thousands of cockatoos and hornbills. There are also decent beaches at **Pantai Mariadei** and **Pantai Ketuapi**, and the scenery around **Danau Sarawandori** is delightful. You must charter a boat to Arumbai from Serui, but the beaches and lake are accessible by public taxi from Serui.

Public transport goes as far as Wooi in the west and Manawi in the east, but is infrequent, so chartering a taxi (about 50,000Rp per hour) is a quicker way of getting around. All roads on Yapen are rough and the terrain is mountainous, so allow plenty of time to get around.

Sleeping & Eating

The only three hotels on the island are all in Serui. Each offers rooms with a fan and bathroom, and the rates include three meals.

Merpati Inn (☎ 31154; Jl Yos Sudarso; s/d from 75,000/100,000Rp; ❄) Though it's a bit noisy, this is Serui's best place to stay – staff are cluey about chartered boats and Merpati schedules.

For rather unremarkable, but clean, hotel accommodation:

Bersaudara Hotel (☎ 31123; Jl Jendral Sudirman 56; r per person 70,000Rp)

Marina Hotel (☎ 31062; Jl Wolter Monginsidi; r per person 75,000Rp)

If you tire of hotel food, try a warung or *rumah makan* serving Padang food in the port area.

Getting There & Away

Merpati flies between Biak and Serui three times a week. Find the **Merpati office** (☎ 31620; Jl Yos Sudarso) next to (you guessed it) Merpati Inn.

Every two weeks, Pelni liners *Doro Londa, Nggapulu* and *Sinabung* stop on their way to Biak (1st/economy class 172,000/83,500Rp), Jayapura and Nabire. The overnight ferry *Teluk Cenderawasih I* makes the journey to Nabire and Biak twice a week. Tickets for all boats are available at the **Pelni office** (☎ 32347; Jl Diponegoro).

An adventurous alternative is to charter a boat from the *pasar ikan* in Kota Biak to the northern edges of Pulau Yapen, from where you'll have to wait around for public transport to Serui.

NABIRE

☎ 0984 / pop 45,000

Although travellers often pass over the capital of the Paniai district, Nabire is a pleasantly low-key town with wide streets, and nearby beaches and islands to explore.

PAPUA

FIRST CONTACT

Papua's last tracts of true wilderness likely secrete a few more undiscovered species, and possibly a few isolated tribes that have not yet made contact with outsiders. It's unknown how many groups, if any, remain uncontacted – or whether they wish to be – but there are certainly people actively trying to find them, and those purporting to sell such an experience.

'First contact' tours, intentions aside, are of questionable authenticity at best, and dangerous at worst – possibly for both the seekers and the sought. The possibility of introducing disease to a vulnerable population, or of forcing contact with a world that such a population may not be prepared to meet, makes these expeditions ethically insupportable.

Orientation & Information

Jl Pepera has a few important buildings, including the Telkom office and Bank Mandiri. Along nearby Jl Yos Sudarso (parallel to the waterfront) are the main post office, taxi terminal and most shops. The airport is walking distance (ask directions) from the hotels.

You can pick up a *surat jalan* for Nabire and/or trips into the interior at the **police station** (☎ 21110; Jl Sisingamangaraja) in Nabire.

Sights & Activities

Like most of Papua, the accessibility of nearby attractions is limited by irregular transport, rough roads and travel restrictions. For wonderful hiking and swimming, you can charter a boat to islands such as **Pulau Moor**, **Pulau Papaya** and **Pulau Nusi** (where it may be possible to stay in a hut, but bring your own food). Boats to these and other islands usually leave from the **MAF Beach** at the end of Jl Sisingamangaraja. Or perhaps charter a taxi to the **hot springs** near the port, or take a public taxi to **Pantai Wahario**, the best place for swimming and snorkelling (bring your own gear) in the area.

Sleeping & Eating

Anggrek Hotel (☎ 21066; Jl Pepera 22; r 80,000Rp) The second-best option, the Anggrek is set around a lovely garden. All rooms share *mandis*.

Hotel Nusantara (☎ 21180; Jl Pemuda 147; r from 125,000Rp; ❄) The best of a limited choice, this hotel has friendly service, a charming setting and a large range of rooms; prices include meals.

The most appealing of the cheap eateries around the taxi terminal are Rumah Makan Sari and Rumah Makan Kebun Sirih. For some of the most mouth-watering baked fish in Papua, try any of the warungs opposite the taxi terminal.

Getting There & Away

From Nabire, Merpati flies most days to Biak, and less frequently to Jayapura and Fak-Fak. Book as soon as you can at the **Merpati office** (☎ 21591; Jl Trikora), near Hotel Nusantara – as usual, be prepared for delays.

Every two weeks, the Pelni liners *Doro Londa* and *Nggapulu* stop at the Samabusa port near Nabire on the way to Serui (1st/economy class 77,500/36,500Rp) and Manokwari (210,000/65,000Rp). Perintis boats also crawl along the north coast and stop in Nabire every week or so, and *Teluk Cenderawasih I* heads to Serui (Pulau Yapen) and Kota Biak twice a week.

Samabusa port is about 20km east of Nabire; taxis are frequent when boats arrive and depart. The **Pelni office** (☎ 22350; Jl Sam Ratulangi 14) is behind the taxi terminal.

TIMIKA

☎ 0901 / pop 85,000

Timika exists almost entirely to service the Freeport copper and gold mine in Tembagapura, approximately 60km to the northeast. Although well connected to most cities in Papua, there are several reasons to avoid Timika: visiting the mine is not possible unless you've been officially invited by a Freeport employee; you will need a *surat jalan* before you can enter Timika; and, even more expensive than Wamena, Timika has little of interest to travellers.

Losmen Amole Jaya (☎ 22125; Jl Pelikan; d with fan & bathroom 120,000Rp) is the best – and about the only – budget-priced option. Meals are available to guests.

Serayu Hotel (☎ 321777; Jl Achmad Yani 10; d with bathroom 215,000Rp; ❄) The Serayu is a solid, reliable midrange option, a five-minute drive from the airport.

Timika serves as a useful entry point to Papua. Merpati and Garuda flights connecting Jakarta or Denpasar with Biak or Jayapura often detour through Timika.

FREEPORT & FREE PAPUA

In the southern highlands, PT Freeport Indonesia (a subsidiary of the massive US company, Freeport-McMoRan) operates the third-largest copper mine and the largest gold mine in the world. Since the opening of the mines in the 1960s, Freeport has built the modern town of Tembagapura (Bahasa Indonesia for 'Copper Town') and a staggering complex of tunnels and private roads carved through the rugged mountain range.

From the outset, however, there have been serious concerns. For example, many are troubled about the adequacy of the consultation with, or compensation for, the displaced Amungme and Kamoro people; Freeport employs about 18,000 people (easily the largest private employer in the province), but only about 30% are Papuans; copper tailings cause enormous environmental damage and affect the health of villagers through contamination of sago palms and drinking water; to undertake further mining, Freeport moves entire villages with thousands of indigenous people from their homelands; and the Indonesian military presence in the area has resulted in instances of human rights abuses.

Yet Jakarta is likely to remain unmoved. Freeport is Indonesia's largest foreign taxpayer; it has paid about US$3.9 billion in taxes and dividends between 1992 and 2005 and contributed about US$40 billion to the Indonesian economy during that same period.

Because the mines make a *profit* of more than US$1 million per day, local Papuan activists have made several demands: scholarships and other employment schemes for local youths; 1% of profits for local community projects; and changes to local Freeport and Indonesian security and community-development personnel.

Anger and frustration have resulted in sporadic riots and acts of sabotage by Papuan activists in Tembagapura and the nearby service town of Timika. The tragic Timika murders of one Indonesian and two American schoolteachers in 2002 remains unsolved; though 12 Indonesians were arrested in early 2006 in connection with the murders, it is still unclear whether Papuan extremists or the Indonesian army were responsible. (The Indonesian army has conducted similar atrocities in Papua.)

To its credit, Freeport spends around US$20 million each year on local community development. Jakarta, meanwhile, is happy to collect the huge taxes and allow Freeport to act as a quasilocal government responsible for community development and welfare.

Book flights at the **Merpati office** (☎ 323362; Jl Cenderawasih 28) and **Garuda office** (☎ 323456; Jl Cenderawasih SPII). From the air, you can see the awesome Freeport mine and the snow-capped Puncak Jaya (Carstenz Pyramid), Papua's highest mountain.

Every two weeks, the Pelni liner *Sangiang* stops at the nearby Amamapare port on its way to Merauke (1st/economy class 416,500/129,000Rp), Agats and southeast Maluku. Every four weeks, the *Kelimutu* and *Tatamailau* stop on their way to Merauke and southeast Maluku.

THE BALIEM VALLEY

The Baliem Valley is easily the most popular destination in Papua and the most accessible place in the interior. While the Dani people who inhabit most of the inner valley have adopted some Western conveniences, and the main town, Wamena, has a few modern facilities, the valley remains one of the last truly fascinating, traditional areas in the world.

The first white men chanced upon the valley in 1938, a discovery that came as one of the last and greatest surprises to a world that had mapped, studied and explored its remotest corners.

WWII prevented further exploration, so it was not until 1945, when a plane crashed in the valley and the survivors were rescued, that attention was again drawn to the region.

The first Dutch missionaries arrived in 1954, and the Dutch government established a post in Wamena two years later. These days, Indonesia has added its own brand of colonialism, bringing schools, police, soldiers, transmigrants and shops to the valley, though the local culture has in many ways proved resilient.

The 1272-sq-km Baliem Valley is about 60km long and 16km wide, with Wamena at its centre. Running through the valley, the mighty Sungai Baliem drops about 1500m in less than 50km on its way to the south coast.

Climate

The best time to visit is the drier months between March and August, when the days are fine (up to 26°C) and the evenings are cool (about 12°C). This coincides with the European summer, however, so the Baliem Valley is often busy in the middle of the year (especially August). During the wet season (September to February), trekking is often unpleasant and some trails will be impassable.

In any case, be prepared for rain *anytime* (on average, it rains 16 days every month in the valley), and always take cold-weather gear for higher areas, such as Danau Habbema (Lake Habbema).

Travel Permit

Enforcement of regulations get less stringent each year, but it's still prudent to get a *surat jalan* for Wamena and the Baliem Valley. You must obtain a *surat jalan* before arriving in Wamena; see p798 for more general information about the *surat jalan*.

The tiny police office in Wamena airport should be open when you arrive; if not, report to the **police station** (☎ 0969-31972; Jl Safri Darwin) yourself within 24 hours. It's painless, but necessary.

THE DANI

Several tribes around the Baliem Valley are grouped together under the name 'Dani', a rather pejorative term given by neighbouring tribes. Each tribe within the Dani group, however, is distinguishable by language, physical appearance, dress and social customs. The Dani are friendly, but can be shy. Long handshakes allowing time to really feel the other's hand are common.

Most Dani speak Bahasa Indonesia, but appreciate a greeting in their own language. Around Wamena, a man greeting another man says *nayak;* if greeting more than one man, *nayak lak*. When greeting a woman, a man says *la'uk,* or *la'uk nya* to more than one. Women also say (to men or women) *la'uk* to one person and *la'uk nya* to more than one. The northern and western Dani groups speak a dialect of Dani distinct from that spoken in the Wamena area.

Dani men often wear a penis sheath *(horim)* made of a cultivated gourd, the shape and size of which varies greatly from group to group. Many Dani, particularly in more remote areas, wear pig fat in their hair and cover their bodies in pig fat and soot for warmth. Traditionally, men wear no other clothing apart from ornamentation such as string hair nets, *cenderawasih* feathers and cowrie-shell necklaces. Unmarried women usually wear grass skirts, while married women traditionally wear skirts of fibre coils or seeds strung together, hung just below the abdomen. Dani women often carry string bags around their heads, usually heavily laden with vegetables, or even babies or pigs.

Dani men and women sleep apart in traditional Dani houses called *honai* (circular thatched-roof huts). The men from one compound sleep tightly packed in one hut, while women and children sleep in other huts. After a birth, sex is taboo for the mother for two to five years, apparently to give the child exclusive use of her milk. As a result, the average Dani life expectancy is 60 years, which is relatively high among traditional people, but this practice also contributes to polygamy and a high divorce rate. Despite pressure from the numerous missionaries around the valley, many Dani have maintained their polygamous marriage system – a man may have as many wives as he can afford. A man must give four or five pigs to the family of the girl he wishes to marry; his social status is measured by the number of pigs and wives he has.

One of the Dani's more unusual (and now prohibited) customs is to amputate one or two joints of a woman's finger when a close relative dies – you'll see many older women with fingers missing up to their second joint. Dani women will also often smother themselves with clay and mud at the time of a family death.

Throughout the region, locals request 1000Rp to 3000Rp or a cigarette or two if you want to take their photo, but they'll sometimes ask for up to 10,000Rp if they're decked out in feathers or ceremonial costumes.

HIKING & TREKKING IN THE BALIEM VALLEY

Papua's premier trekking destination and its strongest drawcard for foreign visitors, the Baliem Valley remains a fascinating area to visit. The rugged slopes of the Baliem Gorge, etched with its rocky patchwork of sweet potato terraces and thatch-roofed village compounds, are a testament to the resilience of the people who live here. Venturing even further over the valley walls brings trekkers to ever more diverse populations, from the Dani to the Yali and Lani people. Even short treks into the valley are well worth the effort.

The only half-decent map of the valley is the *Tourist Map* (25,000Rp), available from the Nayak Hotel (p822) in Wamena. However, do *not* use it as a substitute for a knowledgeable guide: the map is not completely accurate, nor is it detailed enough for trekking.

What to Bring

Everything is comparatively expensive in Wamena, so stock up in Sentani or Jayapura or bring your own supplies from home. Take a torch (flashlight) for exploring the caves in the area. Nights are always cold and usually wet, so bring warm clothes and waterproof gear if you're camping.

There is nowhere to rent hiking, camping or cooking equipment in Wamena, Jayapura or Sentani, so if you're trekking independently you'll have to bring your own gear. This will add considerable weight to your limited luggage allowance on the flights to/from Wamena, but you can avoid this by staying in village huts and eating local food – conditions will be basic but unforgettable. If you book a trek through an agency, it will provide all equipment except a sleeping bag.

Some larger villages have small kiosks selling biscuits, canned drinks, noodles and rice. The final reliable supplies are at Manda on the northeast side of the valley; Kimbim on the northwest; and Kurima to the south. You can buy sweet potatoes along the way, as well as some other vegetables and eggs at local markets. Your guide should know where to find drinking water, but you should bring tablets, filters or cooking equipment to purify it. If you bring your own bottled water, pack the empties out with you so they don't end up littering the trails.

Accommodation

Guides will know which villages around the valley still maintain Dani-style guest huts (50,000Rp per person). If you're trekking independently and aren't toting a tent, your best options are to ask for a bed in the house of a teacher (35,000Rp to 50,000Rp per person). Otherwise, ask at the village police station or the *kepala desa* where you can stay.

Sleeping on the floor of a Dani home is a last resort; and make sure you've been invited before entering a compound or hut. Dani huts are havens for all sorts of pesky insects; one traveller reported being badly bitten by fleas (from the pigs) and she was still madly scratching flea bites two months later.

Guides can make temporary shelters from trees and rocks, but this is not the lowest-impact way to go.

Guides & Porters

If you're travelling off the main roads or paths, a guide is essential. There are no decent maps of the valley, and a guide can help decide where to go, facilitate communication with locals, find or create places to stay, explain the local customs and ecology – plus, you'll get to know a local person.

Depending on the season and the number of tourists in town, guides will latch onto you as soon as you arrive in Wamena (and even in Sentani). An unfortunately common problem is that some guides, porters and/or cooks refuse to finish the trek until they're paid more than initially agreed. To avoid this, grill your fellow travellers for recommendations, or seek advice at the Wamena airport police office. The local police know the trustworthy local guides from the ones who've cheated past clients. And for what it's worth, if anything goes amiss you'll have someone to complain to.

When organising a trek yourself, allow a couple of days in Wamena to arrange things, and bargain long and hard. Expect to pay anywhere from 100,000Rp to 300,000Rp per day (around 200,000Rp is the usual speed) for an experienced guide who truly knows the area, and who speaks English and perhaps some of the local languages. Consider 'test-driving' a guide on a day hike before committing to anything longer term.

Porters are a very good idea and cost about 60,000Rp per day. On longer treks you may need two per trekker: one for a backpack and another for camping and cooking gear and food. A cook (if your guide or porter doesn't cook) costs another 120,000Rp per day. You will have to provide enough food for all guides, porters and cooks, and anything left over at the end should be distributed among the crew. A 10% tip at the end of a trek is also expected for each member of staff.

Day Hikes Without a Guide

Follow designated paths and/or roads, you can easily enjoy the short hikes listed below without a guide.

- Aikima–Suroba–Dugum–Mulima (three hours) – follow the foothills from Aikima to Dugum, then head back to the main road
- Elagaima–Ibele (three hours) – just follow the main road, and take a taxi one way
- Kimbim–Pummo (three hours) – mostly flat countryside, but only possible in the dry season when the Baliem River isn't too high
- Manda–Bugi (1½ hours) – a short, pleasant stroll
- Sugokmo–Kurima (two hours) – follow the main road/path; there's somewhere to stay in Kurima

Day Hikes With a Guide

Only a few of the many possible day hikes are listed below – your guide will know many more. For these hikes, you will need a guide to find the best and most direct paths and bridges. You can hire a guide in Wamena, or possibly a more knowledgeable one at the village you start from.

- Assologaima–Meagaima (four to five hours) – in Assologaima, Indonesian Independence Day (17 August) is marked with pig feasts, and traditional dancing and cooking
- Bolokme–Tagime–Kelila (seven hours) – consider staying in Kelila
- Kurima–Hitugi (three hours) – there's a place to stay in Kurima
- Meagaima–Manda-Bugi-Wolo (four hours)
- Meagaima–Manda–Munak–Pyramid (four hours) – can be combined with Pyramid-Pummo-Meagaima (3½ hours)
- Sugokmo–Tangma (five hours)
- Wolo–Ilugua (three hours) – two thirds of the way, a track to the right leads around a huge sinkhole and down to Gua Yogolok and Goundal, a village on the floor of an awesome canyon

Organised Treks

Depending on your bargaining skills, the number of fellow trekkers in your group, and the company you deal with, using a travel agency may not be much more expensive than organising a trek yourself. However, budget-priced trekking companies based in Wamena have trouble staying afloat (though they may reopen if and when tourism picks up again), so those listed below are upmarket agencies based in top-end resorts in the Baliem Valley or located in Jayapura. Agencies generally arrange special events like mock tribal fighting and pig feasts during stays in the local villages.

Advindo Tours (☎ 537777; aroel_advindo@yahoo.co.id; Jl Percetakan 17; 🕑 8am-5pm) This Jayapura agency offers a solid selection of package tours around the Baliem Valley for up to 14 days. Five-day/four-night Baliem Valley trekking trips cost around US$395 per person (minimum of two).

Baliem Valley Resort (☎ 32240; www.baliem-valley-resort.de) From the most upscale resort in the Baliem Valley come the priciest tours: five-day/four-night packages (including day treks, all transfers, accommodations and meals) cost a whopping US$900 per person (minimum of two). Unless you're staying at the relatively isolated resort, make tour inquiries before arriving in Wamena.

Papua Adventure Tours & Travel (☎ 586755; www.papuaadventure.com; Komplek Kotaraja, Jl Raya Abepura; 🕑 8am-5pm) Specialising in multiday trekking trips in the Baliem Valley and the Asmat, this agency (near the provincial tourist office) offers five-day/four night treks for around US$575 per person (minimum of two, excluding airfare).

In the countryside, you should show your *surat jalan* to police stations or village authorities if you *stay* (ie not visit on a day trip) anywhere outside Wamena. Reporting to the police is often unnecessary (and sometimes impossible) if you're trekking to remote areas, but still try to report to village authorities as you go along.

Some more remote areas in the region may be off limits to foreigners; the police in Wamena will let you know about the current situation.

Getting There & Away

Flying into Wamena is the only way to access the Baliem Valley; see p824 for details of flights and carriers.

Getting Around

Trekking is certainly the best way to explore the landscape, witness special ceremonies and visit traditional people, but if you don't have the time, money or inclination to trek, don't be put off coming to the Baliem Valley. It is possible to see some traditional people, villages and customs, as well as mummies, markets, hanging bridges and wild pigs, on day trips by public/chartered taxi from Wamena – and it will be far cheaper and easier than arranging a trek.

PUBLIC TAXI

Hopelessly overcrowded taxis head out from Wamena as far north on the western side of the valley to Pyramid (35km, two

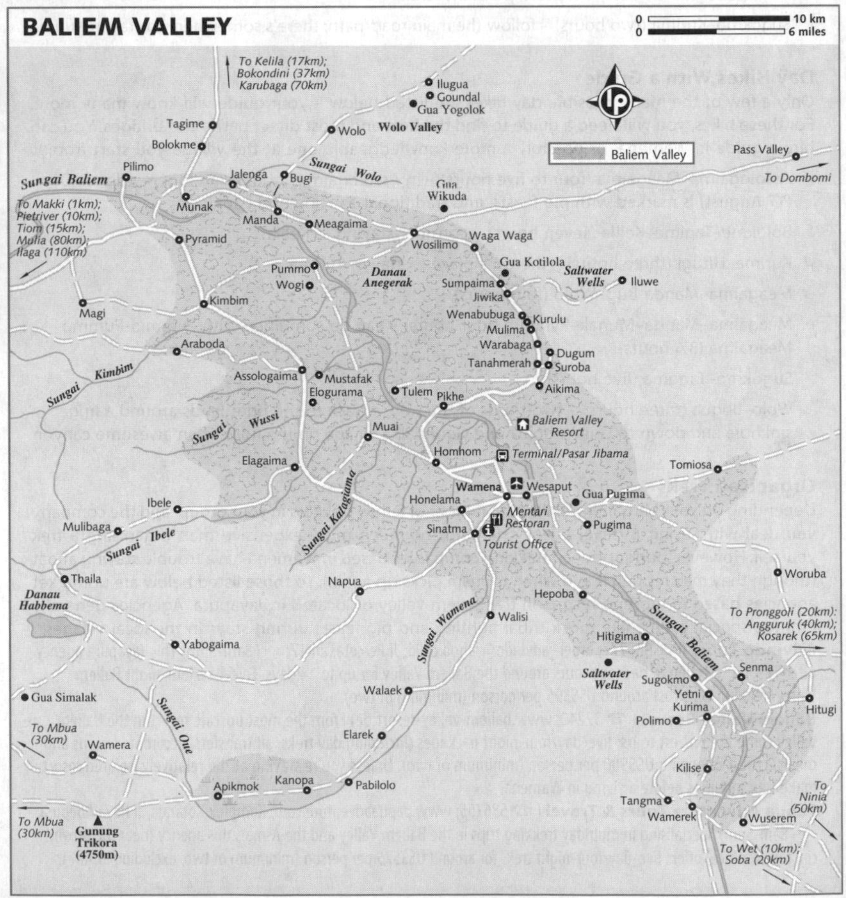

TOURISM IN THE BALIEM

Tourism in the Baliem Valley has been through several troughs and peaks: in 1988, only 758 foreigners visited, but by 1995 that figure had risen to over 6000. Then in 2002, only about 1000 came.

Regardless of numbers, the impact of tourism is still substantial. Wamena struggles to dispose of sewage and rubbish, and pollution from public transport is unacceptable. Gua Wikuda, near Wosilimo in the east, has been developed by indigenous people (with profits returning to them), but generally the tourist and transport industries, with the exception of guides, are run by non-Papuans.

There are ways for visitors to minimise the impact of tourism and improve the standard of living for indigenous people (see p58).

However, tourism can sometimes benefit indigenous people. Interest in the valley, for example, and travel within it, ensures that the Indonesian government does not mistreat indigenous Papuans. Also, traditions are often maintained, if only for the sake of tourist dollars, and some money does trickle back to help local community development.

hours); and north on the eastern side to Tagime (44km, 2½ hours). Public transport tends to slow down to a trickle all around the valley after 3pm and is less plentiful on Sunday. Almost no village or tourist attraction is signposted, so ask your taxi driver (or guide) to let you know when to get off.

All taxis are coded with numbers and/or letters, but knowing which one to take and from where it departs in Wamena is a tad confusing:

Around Wamena Taxis marked 'A3' leave for Wesaput (3000Rp) from along Jl Timor (opposite the main post office) in Wamena, and travel via Jl Gatot Subroto.

Baliem Valley – East The following taxis all leave from Terminal Jibama in Wamena. Taxis marked 'MM' go to Aikima (4000Rp), via Pikhe (3000Rp); 'SL' depart for Pikhe only; 'TM' and 'KL' head to Manda (8000Rp), via Jiwika (5000Rp) and Wosilimo (7000Rp); and 'BT' leave for Bolokme (10,000Rp) and Tagime (13,000Rp). Taxis that are marked, or claim to go to, 'Kurulu' actually start/finish at Jiwika. (Kurulu is the name of the local district based in Jiwika.)

Baliem Valley – South From the southern terminal, colloquially known as the 'Misi' terminal (Jl Ahmad Yani), taxis marked 'SG' or 'SK' go to Sugokmo (7000Rp). Those marked 'HM' stop at Hitigima (5000Rp).

Baliem Valley – West Taxis marked 'KMP' go to Kimbim (8000Rp) and Pyramid (10,000Rp), but you may need to get a connection in Kimbim for Pyramid. Taxis marked 'A1' go to Sinatma (2000Rp) from the corner of Jl Trikora and Jl Timor in Wamena. Those marked 'IB' leave for Ibele (6000Rp) from Sinatma.

CHARTERED TAXI

It is worth considering charter of a taxi for about 50,000Rp/400,000Rp per hour/day (a lot more for remote and rougher roads) in order to avoid the sardine-cans-on-wheels or to reach more remote places. Paying for empty seats will always hurry up your departure – and make you very popular with other impatient passengers.

WAMENA

☎ 0969 / pop 8500

The main town in the Baliem Valley, and the capital of the Jayawijaya district, Wamena is dusty and sprawling. Although there's not much to do in the town itself, it really is the only base from which to explore nearby villages and organise treks. Wamena is expensive compared to the rest of Indonesia, but this is understandable because *everything* – from doors to floors, and a whole lot more – has to be shipped to Jayapura, trucked to Sentani, and then flown to Wamena.

Orientation

Many hotels, restaurants and other important buildings are along (or close to) Jl Trikora, only one block from the airport. While the main street is not especially attractive, just a few blocks to the west some lovely, quiet streets, such as Jl Thamrin, are worth wandering around. Take a torch (flashlight) at night, because there are few street lights anywhere.

Information

Unless you plan on extracting cash from the ATMs (which all banks in town now have), you're well advised to stock up on rupiah before coming to Wamena, as the exchange

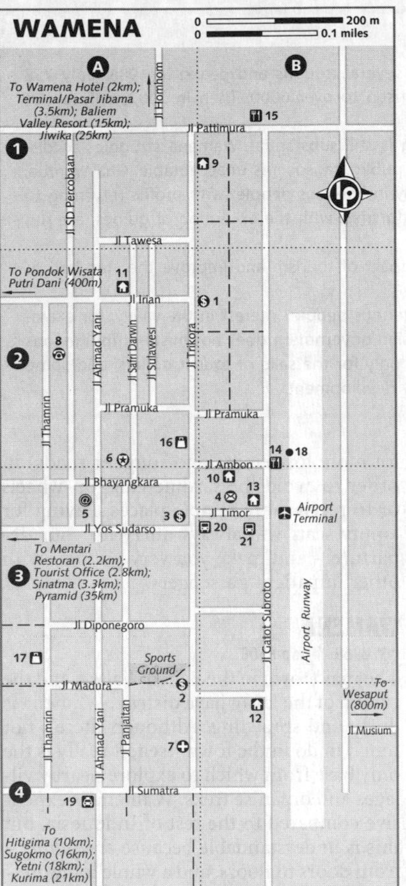

INFORMATION
Bank Mandiri..........1 B2
Bank Papua..........2 A4
BRI Bank..........3 A3
Main Post Office..........4 B3
Papua.com..........5 A3
Police Station..........6 A2
Rumah Sakit Umum..........7 A4
Telkom..........8 A2

SLEEPING
Baliem Pilamo Hotel..........9 B1
Hotel Anggrek..........10 B3
Hotel Srikandi..........11 A2
Hotel Syah Ria Makmur..........12 B4
Nayak Hotel..........13 B3
Pondok Wisata Mas Budi..........(see 15)

EATING
Kantin Bu Lies..........14 B2
Rumah Makan Mas Budi..........15 B1

SHOPPING
Papua Glory..........16 A2
Silimo Jaya..........17 A3
Souvenir Shops..........(see 16)

TRANSPORT
MAF Office..........18 B2
Misi Taxi Terminal..........19 A4
Taxi to Sinatma..........20 B3
Taxis to Wesaput..........21 B3

rates are *at least* 15% lower than those in Jayapura. There's nowhere else in the valley to change money. Wartel, aside from the Telkom office, are located along Jl Trikora.

Bank Mandiri (Jl Trikora 92) Will only change US dollars cash.

Bank Papua (Jl Trikora 45) Has lousy rates and endless lines.

BRI bank (Bank Rakyat Indonesia; cnr Jl Yos Sudarso & Jl Trikora)

Main post office (Jl Timor; 8am-2pm Mon-Thu & Sat, 8am-11am Fri) Reasonably efficient.

Papua.com (Jl Ahmad Yani 49; per hr 9000Rp; 8am-10pm Mon-Sat, noon-10pm Sun) Surprisingly fast connections in this efficient little internet café.

Rumah Sakit Umum (31152; Jl Trikora) You're better off getting sick or injured elsewhere, but if you need a hospital you'll get the bare minimum of care here.

Telkom office (Jl Thamrin; 24hr)

Tourist office (31365; Jl Yos Sudarso 73; 8am-3pm Mon-Fri) This office is barely worth recommending, as the disinterested staff have very little on-the-ground knowledge of the area. If you go, the unsigned office is about 3km from the BRI building; look for the Indonesian flag outside the red-and-white brick building on the left as you come from Wamena.

Sleeping

Though most hotels in Wamena don't have water heaters, staff can usually bring a bucket of freshly boiled water for guests who don't fancy a frigid bath.

BUDGET

Hotel Syah Rial Makmur (31306; Jl Gatot Subroto 45; r 80,000-160,000Rp) The cheapest place in Wamena. Each room is different – so check out a few before deciding on one – most are simple, with squat toilets. It's only a three-minute walk from the airport.

Nayak Hotel (31067; Jl Gatot Subroto 63; s/d/tr 100,000/125,000/150,000Rp) Directly opposite the airport, this has plenty of rooms that include breakfast, TV and phone. The cheaper rooms facing the road and airport are a little noisy, but they're large, tidy and good value.

Pondok Wisata Putri Dani (☎ 31223; Jl Irian 40; r 150,000-175,000Rp) About 600m past Hotel Srikandi, this little place offers spotless, comfortable rooms in a family home. The friendly owners provide breakfast, as well as endless tea and coffee. It's often full, so book ahead.

Hotel Srikandi (☎ 31367; Jl Irian 16; s/d from 150,000/190,000Rp) Friendly and tidy, with afternoon tea included – but no breakfast. However, the rooms are small, the bathrooms have a squat toilet, and it's noisy when there are numerous guests or the TV at reception is cranked up loud.

Wamena Hotel (☎ 31292; Jl Homhom 61; r 150,000-200,000Rp) Worth considering for some peace, seclusion and greenery, but the basic rooms surrounding the garden badly need some renovation. Breakfast is included here. The hotel is about 2km north of Jl Pattimura, an easy trip by becak or taxi.

MIDRANGE & TOP END

Hot water can be prepared for you if water heaters are not available, and breakfast is included in rates at these hotels.

Pondok Wisata Mas Budi (☎ 31214; Jl Pattimura; r 180,000-240,000Rp) Attached to the restaurant of the same name, this family-run hotel offers a few large, clean and modern rooms (some with squat toilets). The serenity may be shattered if the karaoke machine winds up next door, but you won't have to walk far for a bite to eat.

Hotel Anggrek (☎ 31242, 0812-4850610; Jl Ambon 1; r from 187,000Rp) Immaculate, convenient and comfortable, this guesthouse is one of the few hotels in central Wamena that offers hot water. The warm, family-style atmosphere and homemade jams and house-roasted coffee (!) could explain why it's often full.

Baliem Pilamo Hotel (☎ 31043; fax 31798; Jl Trikora; r 276,000-414,000Rp) Tropical-garden kitsch might justify the otherwise exorbitant prices; some bathrooms have delightful fake-lava walls adorned with plants. If you can live without TV, the low-end rooms here are a decent deal, but make sure you stay away from the noisy road. There's also a restaurant here.

Baliem Valley Resort (☎ 32240; www.baliem-valley-resort.de; r US$125) A majestic three-star resort set in 12 sq km of pristine countryside a 10km drive north of Wamena. The guest rooms are designed in the style of traditional *honai* (huts), with stone-walled showers, wood floors and spectacular views. Lunch is US$10 and dinner US$15. The German proprietor runs his own expensive tours from here and has a wealth of expertise on the area. Charter a taxi from the airport, as hotel transfers cost a staggering 750,000Rp.

Eating

The local specialities are goldfish (*ikan mas* in Bahasa Indonesia) – far larger than the variety found in your goldfish bowl – and prawns *(udang)*, which are more like crayfish. Both are expensive and in short supply, however. The restaurants listed below, except for Kantin Bu Lies, offer menus with items listed in English.

Kantin Bu Lies (☎ 31346; Jl Gatot Subroto; meals 10,000-15,000Rp; ⏰ lunch & dinner) Next door to the airport, this spot is recommended for simple Indonesian food, though prices can be steep. It's the best place to wait for your flight.

Mentari Restoran (Jl Yos Sudarso 47; mains 15,000-50,000Rp; ⏰ lunch & dinner) A delightful spot with genuine charm. It's unsigned (look for the 'fork-and-spoon' sign along the road), a 30-minute walk up from the BRI bank building (or a short taxi ride towards Sinatma).

Rumah Makan Mas Budi (☎ 31214; Jl Pattimura; mains around 20,000Rp, seafood 50,000-75,000Rp; ⏰ lunch & dinner) The food and service here is commendable, and the place is deservedly popular. The bad news is that the karaoke machine inevitably cranks up most evenings.

Wamena is strictly designated a 'dry' area, so no alcohol should be brought into the capital by travellers. Your bags will be checked at the airport for contraband. Some hotels sell beer for discreet, pricey consumption.

Shopping

The Dani are fine craftspeople, so potential souvenirs can be found all over the valley. Generally, it's cheaper to buy directly from the Dani in the villages, but they often strike a hard bargain, so it's also wise to check out prices in the shops and markets. Traders will approach you on the streets of Wamena or hang around the doorways of popular hotels and restaurants. Bartering is also acceptable.

The cost of stone axe blades (*kapak* in the Dani language) depends on the size and the labour involved; blue stone is the hardest and considered the finest material and is more expensive, from 45,000Rp to 500,000Rp (for something large and authentic). *Sekan* are thin, intricately handwoven rattan bracelets which cost from 5000Rp. *Noken* are string bags made from the inner bark of certain types of trees and shrubs, which is dried, shredded and then rolled into thread. The bags are coloured with vegetable dyes, resulting in a very strong smell; patterns vary according to their origin. *Noken* cost from 10,000Rp to over 50,000Rp.

Other handicrafts include: various head and arm necklaces *(mikak)* of cowrie shells, feathers and bone; grass skirts *(jogal* and *thali)*; assorted head decorations *(suale)*, made entirely of cassowary feathers or topped off with the tusks of a wild pig, for up to 100,000Rp; woven baskets for around 35,000Rp; carved spears and arrows for about 15,000Rp each; and woven place mats for about 15,000Rp. Asmat woodcarvings, shields and spears are also available in the souvenir shops, but be wary of price and quality.

Of course, the most popular souvenir is the penis gourd, held upright by attaching a thread to the top and looping it around the waist or chest. These are priced from 5000Rp to 60,000Rp depending on size (!), quality of materials, craftsmanship and your bargaining ability.

Silimo Jaya (Jl Thamrin 2) Worth supporting if you can find something appealing, this genuine cooperative of Dani people makes and sells traditional crafts. Unfortunately, it suffers from neglect and has only a few pots on offer.

Papua Glory (☎ 32058; Jl Trikora 3) This shop is one of several souvenir merchants near the corner of Jl Trikora and Jl Ambon. Here, the young proprietor stocks an interesting selection of Papuan and PNG art and handicrafts.

Getting There & Away

Since flying is the only way in and out of the valley, flights are often heavily booked, especially during the peak season (August). Always allow a couple of days' leeway for inevitable delays when travelling into or out of Wamena.

Trigana Air Service is the main carrier into and out of Wamena, with four flights a day. The fare from Wamena to Sentani (450,000Rp) is a bit less than the Sentani to Wamena fare (494,000Rp), when the planes are jam-packed with cargo. Trigana also flies from Wamena to Mulia, Karubaga and Bokondini. Book at the **Trigana office** (☎ Wamena airport terminal 31611, Sentani airport terminal 967-594383).

The missionary service, MAF, also flies between Sentani and Wamena once or twice a day, but the flights are almost triple the cost of Trigana's. MAF also flies to more obscure destinations around the highlands, such as Ilaga and Enarotali. Schedules are posted outside the **MAF office** (Wamena ☎ 31263; Jl Gatot Subroto; Sentani ☎ 0967-91109; Jl Misi Sentani).

The Indonesian army (TNI) also offers several cheap flights a day from Wamena to Sentani (only). These are primarily for locals and the military, but it is another possibility. Inquire at the TNI office inside the airport terminal in Wamena.

Getting Around

Most hotels in Wamena are within walking distance of the scruffy airport. For longer trips around town, take a becak. The official price for a becak is about 1500Rp per kilometre, but foreigners are always charged more. Any trip around town should cost 3000Rp to 5000Rp, and about 8000Rp to Wesaput. Becak can be hailed from along any street, but they don't run at night and they're not allowed along Jl Yos Sudarso at any time. They also evaporate when it rains!

Refer to p820 for details about minibus taxis around the valley. Those marked 'A2' and 'A3' (1000Rp) head up Jl Trikora to the 'pasar', officially called Terminal Jibama, several kilometres north of Wamena. It's a short walk to the 'Misi' taxi terminal on Jl Ahmad Yani.

AROUND WAMENA

Wesaput

Almost a suburb of Wamena, Wesaput is just across the other side of the airport. It's only accessible by becak (about 8000Rp) or public taxi (1500Rp); paths across the runway have been blocked by a large fence.

A decrepit stone clock marks the start of Jl Musium, the road through Wesaput.

At the end of Jl Musium, 800m past the clock, is the **Palimo Adat Museum** (8am-4pm Mon-Sat). It offers a small but interesting collection of Dani clothing, decorations and instruments, and is worth a look if only because it's the sole museum in the valley. A donation of about 5000Rp is expected. It does keep erratic hours, so it's best to visit before noon.

At the back of the museum is the nearest **hanging bridge** to Wamena. Strung across Sungai Baliem, it's 90m long and unstable at times. A tiny, impromptu Dani **market** is often set up by the bridge.

Pugima

The path from the other side of the bridge in Wesaput leads to Pugima, which has a few Dani compounds (past the huge church). Although Pugima is not particularly interesting, the one-hour, flat trail (with one small hill) from Wesaput provides an easy and convenient glimpse of Dani farms, villages and people, and of the magnificent scenery. Halfway along, behind a small lake, **Gua Pugima** is an eerie cave.

Sinatma

At the end of Jl Yos Sudarso, about 3.5km past the BRI bank building, is the 'suburb' of Sinatma, where there's a taxi terminal and a large, busy **market** (open daily). From the terminal, head right as you face Wamena and easy **walking trails** lead you to the raging Sungai Wamena, some pretty Dani compounds and dense woodlands. Near the small hydroelectric power station further up the hill you can cross the river on a treacherous **hanging bridge**.

MARKET DAYS

Mingling at highland markets is a great way to meet locals in a relaxed, quotidian setting. You'll find souvenirs like the colourful *noken* (bark-string bags) that women sling over their foreheads, or pick up bundles of veggies for the next leg of your trek.

There are daily markets at Sinatma and Pasar Jibama (next to the taxi terminal), as well as weekly markets in other locations.

Village	Market days
Bolokme	Mon & Fri
Jiwika	Sun
Kelila	Tue, Thu & Sat
Kimbim	Tue & Sat
Kurima	Tue & Fri
Manda	Mon & Thu
Pyramid	Sat
Tagime	Tue & Fri
Wosilimo	Mon

BALIEM VALLEY – SOUTH

The area south of Wamena, hugging Sungai Baliem, boasts the most dramatic mountain scenery in the valley.

About 10km from Wamena, **Hitigima** has a school and mission. A sign on the right as you head south, a few hundred metres past the church, indicates the path (2km) to some **saltwater wells** (*air garam* in Bahasa Indonesia), similar to the ones near Jiwika.

Near the bridge in **Sugokmo**, 6km further on, is a small **memorial** to a Japanese tourist and his Dani guide who drowned when a hanging bridge collapsed. Another 2km brings you to **Yetni**, the primary site of the Baliem Festival (p826).

The main road finishes near Yetni, from where it's a 45-minute walk to **Kurima**. (The hike to Kurima does involve crossing a river that's often waist-deep during the wet season.) Kurima is a charming village and a perfect base for **hikes** around the southern valley. If you ask around, someone will almost certainly be able to find you a bed (about 50,000Rp per person).

BALIEM VALLEY – EAST

The main road heading north along the eastern side of the valley is paved most of the way, and public transport continues as far as Tagime. The area near the bridge in **Pikhe** is excellent for short **hikes**.

Aikima

About 8km north of Wamena as the crow flies (but about 13km by road), just to the east of the road to Jiwika, is Aikima. This nondescript village is famous for its 270-year-old **Werapak Elosak mummy** (admission 20,000Rp; daylight hours), but the one near Jiwika is more accessible and in better condition. To see the Aikima mummy, ask at the large, round hut slightly up a hill on the left-hand side of the road as you come from Wamena.

PAPUA

BALIEM FESTIVAL

To coincide with the busiest time for tourism (and the European summer holidays), a festival is held in the Baliem Valley between about 9 and 14 August each year. Check with the tourist office in Wamena for current details, though the dates and activities vary little from year to year.

With the encouragement of the Indonesian government and local missionaries, the highlight of the festival is mock 'tribal fighting', where men from villages dress up in full traditional regalia. The festival also features plenty of traditional dancing by men and women, as well as Dani music. Pig races are also a lot of fun – for the guests, not the pigs, which usually end up roasted on a spit. Other attractions include a festival of flowers, exhibitions of traditional archery, and foot and bicycle races.

The festival is usually held at Yetni, between Sugokmo and Kurima. Although it is set up for tourists, and there's no shortage of foreigners watching the main events, the festival is a magical (and very photogenic) time to visit.

Suroba & Dugum

Just off the main road, the pretty villages of Suroba and Dugum are worth exploring. Ask the taxi driver to let you off at the nearest spot along the main road. Then walk (15 minutes) along the path through some of the nicest scenery you'll see around Wamena, and over two fascinating and intricate **hanging bridges** – one for locals and another more stable one for timid foreigners. At a clearing nearby, traditional **pig feasts** and **dancing** can be prearranged at substantial cost, mainly for packaged tours. If you ask around either village, there's a good chance you'll be offered some basic accommodation in a **Dani hut** (per person 50,000Rp).

Jiwika

Jiwika (pronounced Yiwika) is a local administrative centre, a pleasant base from which to explore the eastern valley, and a cheap, quiet alternative to Wamena. Ask around and you may be able to arrange a **mock fighting ceremony** between villagers for about 200,000Rp.

At Iluwe, about one hour up a steep path (with some scrambling at the top) from Jiwika, are some **saltwater wells** (admission 5000Rp; daylight hours). To extract the salt, banana stems are beaten dry of fluid and put in a pool to soak up the brine. The stem is then dried and burned, and the ashes are collected and used as salt. If a local boy in Jiwika doesn't offer his services as a guide, ask one to show you the way and to find out if anyone is working at the wells. Start the hike from Jiwika before 10am.

At the turn-off to Iluwe in Jiwika is **Lauk Inn** (r 90,000Rp), the only proper accommodation outside Wamena, and a lovely spot to boot. It offers basic but clean rooms (as opposed to Dani-style huts), and decent **meals** (10,000-20,000Rp) are available for guests if preordered. If the place looks closed, just rattle the gate loudly or ask at the shop next door.

Sumpaima, just north of Jiwika (look for the blue sign), is home to the 280-year-old **Wimontok Mabel mummy** (admission 20,000Rp, photos 2000Rp; daylight hours). It is the best and most accessible of its kind near Wamena.

Gua Kotilola

The road between Jiwika and Wosilimo is flanked by rocky hills in which some of the valley's 50 listed **caves** are located. At the back of an attractive Dani compound, **Gua Kotilola** (admission 5000Rp; 8am-4pm Mon-Sat) apparently contains the bones of victims of a past tribal war. It's on the right as you head north from Jiwika, about 22km from Wamena. Ask the taxi driver to drop you off outside the compound and yell for someone to open the gate.

Wosilimo

Wosilimo (or 'Wosi') is a major village with a few shops. **Gua Wikuda** (admission incl tour 10,000Rp; 8am-4pm Mon-Sat), along the road to Pass Valley, is nearly 900m long and boasts stalagmites over 1000 years old. The cave has been developed by some Dani people who will take you for a tour, though you can't see much without a lamp (another 15,000Rp).

One hour southwest from Wosi on foot, along a small path behind the church and over a hanging bridge, is **Danau Anegerak**.

This lake is another delightful area for **hiking**, and **fishing** is also available (locals rent out basic fishing equipment). You should be able to stay near the lake in a Dani-style **hut** (per person incl meals about 25,000Rp).

Pass Valley

A rough road continues from Wosilimo to Pass Valley. There is no public transport along this road, but Pass Valley is a popular place for **trekking**.

Manda

This enticing village has a shop and market, as well as loads of friendly people to meet, and wonderful scenery to admire and landscapes to hike around. Ask if the authentic **Dani-style huts** are open. They're not signposted, but easy to find just behind the market.

Wolo Valley

This is one of the most spectacular side valleys of Sungai Baliem. Inspired by a resolute strain of Evangelical Protestantism, **Wolo** is a nonsmoking village with lovely flower gardens. There is plenty of great **hiking** to be done in the area.

BALIEM VALLEY – WEST

The western side of the valley isn't as scenic for hiking or as interesting for day trips by taxi from Wamena; in fact, the road from Wamena to Pyramid (a six-hour walk) is comparatively dull.

Kimbim is a pleasant administrative centre with a few shops and a busy **market**. You should be able to find somewhere to stay if you ask at the police station or district office. About one hour on foot from Kimbim (ask directions), **Araboda** is home to the 250-year-old Alongga Huby **mummy** (admission 5000Rp; erratic opening hours).

About 7km past Kimbim is **Pyramid**, a graceful missionary village with a theological college, sloping airstrip and bustling **market**. Some taxis from Wamena go directly to Pyramid, but you may have to get a connection in Kimbim.

DANAU HABBEMA

This lake (3450m above sea level) is a wonderful **trekking** area and home to unique flora (including orchids). Also nearby are several caves, such as **Gua Simalak**.

The lake is sometimes off limits to foreigners (as it was at the time of writing) because of the nefarious activities of the Free Papua Movement (OPM). In any case, always check with the police in Wamena before visiting the lake and make sure your *surat jalan* includes 'Danau Habbema'. One reader has reported that some locals he encountered on the way to the lake demanded money from him to cross 'their land'.

There are two usual ways to reach the lake: trek from Elagaima, via Ibele (accessible by public taxi from Sinatma) and Thaila; or trek from Sinatma, via Walaek. (This road is sometimes accessible by vehicle as far as Pabilolo.) For both treks, you'll need a guide. Private camping is tolerated in the region, or ask to sleep in a local hut along the way. Some basic Dani-style accommodation is also available along the northern side of the lake.

GUNUNG TRIKORA

Gunung Trikora (4750m) is just 300m shy of Puncak Jaya, Papua's highest peak. Mountain-climbing experience, sturdy equipment and a knowledgeable guide are essential for climbing Trikora. Also required is a special permit, which can only be obtained from the army headquarters in Jakarta. Given plenty of notice, the tour agencies listed in the Jayapura section later may be able to organise trips.

LANI COUNTRY (WESTERN DANI)

West along Sungai Baliem and upstream from Pyramid is the home of the Western Dani who call themselves Lani. One accessible Lani village is Magi, about 1½ hours on foot from Kimbim or Pyramid.

Further west, between Sungai Pitt and Kuyawage, the Baliem disappears underground for 2km. **Ilaga**, about 60km west of Kuyawage, beyond the western Baliem watershed, is accessible by missionary flights from Nabire, Sentani and Wamena, but make sure your *surat jalan* allows you to travel this far.

YALI COUNTRY

East and south of the Baliem Valley are the Yali people. They live in rectangular houses, and the men often wear 'skirts' of rattan hoops, with penis gourds protruding from underneath. The Indonesian presence is thinner here than in the Baliem Valley, so missionaries provide much of the infrastructure, such as schools and transport. Bordering the Yali to the east are the Kim-Yal people, who practised cannibalism up until the 1970s.

Reaching Yali country on foot involves plenty of tough hiking along steep trails. **Pronggoli**, the nearest centre from Wamena as the crow flies, is a three-day slog by the most direct route, with camping necessary along the way. From Pronggoli to **Angguruk** takes another day. It's then relatively easy trekking from Angguruk to nearby villages, such as **Panggele**, **Psekni**, **Tulukima** and **Tenggil**.

An easier but longer (about seven days) option is the southern loop through Kurima–Tangma–Wet–Soba–Ninia, and then north on to Angguruk village. Another popular trek is Kosarek–Serkasi–Telambela–Membahan–Helariki–Angguruk (about six days). You can cut this tough trek by taking a missionary flight (more likely if you're on an organised tour) from Wamena to Kosarek or Angguruk. You can usually rely on a hut belonging to a local family or a teacher's house for somewhere to stay in the area, but bring all your own food.

EASTERN PAPUA

Many travellers come to this part of Papua just to get a connection to Wamena in the Baliem Valley, but Sentani, Jayapura and the surrounding areas, as well as the interior near Merauke, have a lot to offer. Adventurous travellers with *loads* of time and money also trickle down to the remote, swampy Asmat region, with its unique culture.

JAYAPURA

☎ 0967 / pop 195,000

Although Jayapura is dominated by non-Papuans and looks similar to most medium-sized Indonesian cities, it is pleasantly situated around Teluk Yos Sudarso and surrounded by steep hills. There's little reason to stay in Jayapura, because Sentani is more pleasant and convenient, but you may have to visit to book air or boat tickets, collect a

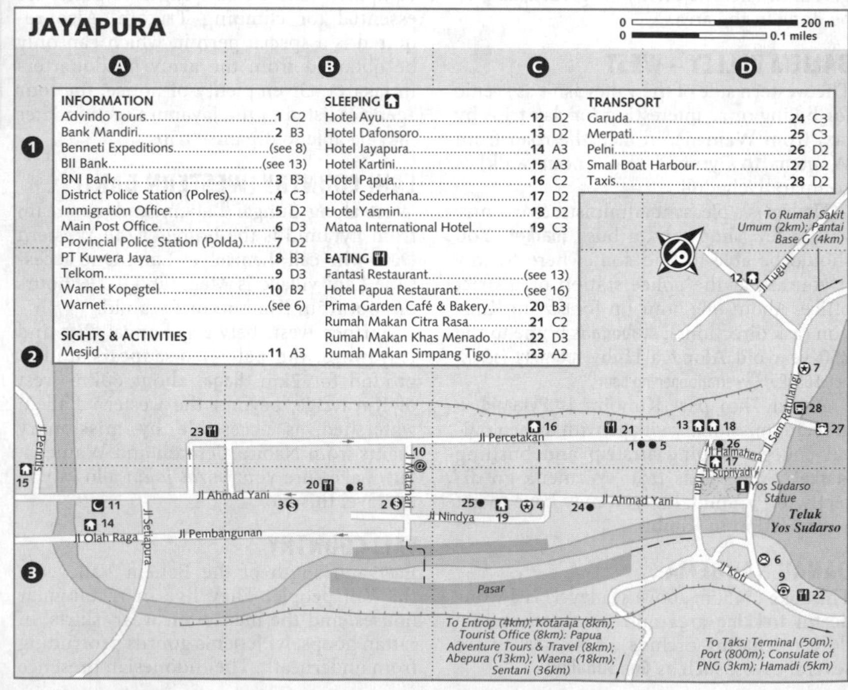

surat jalan for the Baliem Valley, or cash in travellers cheques.

See p833 for sights and activities around Jayapura.

Orientation

Just about everything you'll need is confined to the parallel main streets of Jl Ahmad Yani and Jl Percetakan. Along the waterfront, Jl Koti heads east to Hamadi, while Jl Sam Ratulangi goes north towards Tanjung Ria. Most government buildings are in the sprawling southern suburbs of Kotaraja, Abepura and Waena.

Information

EMBASSIES & CONSULATES

Consulate of Papua New Guinea (Map p834; ☎ 531250; congenpng@yahoo.com.id; Jl Raya Argapura; 8am-4pm Mon-Thu, 8am-2pm Fri) The friendly folks at this consulate issue visas to PNG. See p799 for details. To get to the consulate – about 3km east of downtown – catch a green B2 taxi (2000Rp) from along Jl Percetakan in Jayapura.

EMERGENCY

District police station (Polres; ☎ 531027; Jl Ahmad Yani; officially 7am-3pm Mon-Fri) Go to the 'Satuan IPP' office upstairs to arrange your *surat jalan;* expect to pay a 5000Rp administrative fee.

Provincial police station (Polda; ☎ 533861; Jl Sam Ratulangi 8) May keep longer hours, if you find the district police station closed.

Rumah Sakit Umum Pusat (☎ 533616; Jl Kesehatan) The city's public hospital is in the northern foothills.

IMMIGRATION

Immigration office (☎ 521647; Jl Percetakan 15; 8am-4pm Mon-Fri) If you travel between Jayapura and Vanimo (in PNG) by boat, stop by this office to get the proper Indonesian entry/exit stamps in your passport.

INTERNET ACCESS

Warnet Kopegtel (☎ 533891; Jl Ahmad Yani 18; per hr 9000Rp; 8am-midnight) Jayapura's smokier, more centrally located internet centre.

MONEY

All banks should be able to change rupiah into PNG *kina* (and vice versa); otherwise, try the reception desk at the Matoa International Hotel.

Stock up on rupiah before heading to the Baliem Valley, as the banks in Wamena offer woeful exchange rates. There are no exchange facilities at the Sentani airport.

Bank Mandiri (Jl Ahmad Yani) There's a 24-hour ATM, and you can exchange travellers cheques here if rates at the other banks are poor.

BII bank (Bank Internasional Indonesia; Jl Percetakan 22) Next to Hotel Dafonsoro, offers the same services and the best cash exchange rates in town.

BNI bank (Bank Negara Indonesia; Jl Ahmad Yani) BNI changes cash and travellers cheques, gives cash advances, and has an ATM for Visa and MasterCard.

POST & TELEPHONE

Main post office (Jl Sam Ratulangi; 8am-9pm) Has a warnet centre next door.

Telkom (Jl Sam Ratulangi; 24hr) Near the post office.

TOURIST INFORMATION

Tourist office (Map p834; ☎ 588765; www.papua.go.id; Komplek Kotaraja, Jl Raya Abepura; 7.30am-3pm Mon-Fri) The Papua provincial tourist office is barely worth visiting; but if you go, ask the taxi driver to let you off at the 'Kantor Dinas Daerah Otonom' building along the road between Jayapura and Abepura.

Tours

A few local travel agencies still offer a range of tours around Jayapura and Sentani (as well as tours to the Baliem Valley and Asmat region).

Advindo Tours (☎ 537777; aroel_advindo@yahoo.co.id; Jl Percetakan 17; 8am-5pm) Advindo Tours runs a range of package tours to the Baliem Valley, the Asmat region and elsewhere around Papua.

Benneti Expeditions (☎ 573323, benneti_travel@yahoo.co.id; Jl Ahmad Yani 39) Upstairs from PT Kuwera Jaya, independent Benneti can also arrange custom tours with English-speaking guides.

Papua Adventure Tours & Travel (☎ 586755; www.papuaadventure.com; Komplek Kotaraja, Jl Raya Abepura; 8am-5pm) This agency, near the provincial tourist office, offers a variety of tours around Papua, but specialises in multiday trekking trips in the Baliem Valley and Asmat region.

PT Kuwera Jaya (☎ 531583; Jl Ahmad Yani 39) This efficient company can book flights on airlines serving Jayapura – or for a small fee, Pelni tickets heading west.

Festivals & Events

Papua Tourism Week Held around mid-January, you may find a smattering of displays and events showcasing traditional culture as part of this promotion. Check in at the tourist office for more information.

Jayapura Cultural Festival During the first week of August, the city hosts an array of dance and music performances from around Papua.

Sleeping

Although hotels are scattered throughout Jayapura, staying in the city centre is most convenient for settling travel arrangements and reaching the city's services.

BUDGET

Hotel Jayapura (☎ 533216; Jl Olah Raga 4; s/d 30,000/40,000Rp) What's it like to sleep in a chicken coop? Find out here. Ceilings in the fanless, steambox rooms slope down to windows covered in chicken wire (for real!). All rooms share *mandis*. Breakfast is not included.

Hotel Ayu (☎ 534263; Jl Tugu II 1; s 45,000-85,000Rp, d 75,000-100,000Rp; ❄) Being the best cheap choice in Jayapura, this place is often full, and no wonder – it's snug and bright, with breakfast included and a pleasant common hall. Fan-only rooms have shared *mandis*, while air-con rooms have attached *mandis*.

Hotel Kartini (☎ 531557; Jl Perintis 2; s 55,000Rp, d 66,000-77,000Rp) Rooms are small and noisy at this family-run spot. It's just over the bridge and to the right at the top end of Jl Ahmad Yani. All rooms come with fan and breakfast.

Hotel Sederhana (☎ 531561; Jl Halmahera 2; d 93,500-209,000Rp; ❄) Central and clean, but fairly unremarkable and noisy. Despite the inflated rates, it's often full. Breakfast is included.

MIDRANGE & TOP END

Unless otherwise noted, rates include breakfast at the following hotels.

Hotel Dafonsoro (☎ 531695; fax 534055; Jl Percetakan 20; s 198,500Rp, d 253,000-300,000Rp; ❄) Central and friendly, this spotless hotel has quiet, characterless rooms with hot water and air-con. Traditional-style carvings decorate the marble halls of this unpretentious place.

Hotel Papua (☎ 535800; fax 533700; Jl Percetakan 78; r 350,000-450,000Rp, ste 500,000Rp; ❄) Along with bonuses like hot water, satellite TV and bathtubs in superior rooms, this place goes the extra decorating mile with mismatched murals and elaborately carved furniture. It's predictably overpriced, but a comparatively attractive deal.

Hotel Yasmin (☎ 533222; fax 536027; Jl Percetakan 8; d from 365,000Rp; ❄) A classy but pretentious place offering small, well-furnished rooms, with satellite TV. Save a little cash by asking for rates quoted in rupiah rather than US dollars.

Matoa International Hotel (☎ 531633; fax 531437; Jl Ahmad Yani 14; r from 366,000Rp; ❄) The flashest place in town charges accordingly. The guest rooms are most certainly comfortable (with satellite TV, fridge and hot water), but overpriced.

Eating & Drinking

Prima Garden Café & Bakery (☎ 532038; Jl Ahmad Yani 28; pastries around 6000Rp; 🕑 breakfast, lunch & dinner Mon-Sat, dinner Sun; ❄) Relax upstairs with some scrumptious pandanus cake and diner coffee.

Rumah Makan Khas Manado (Jl Koti; meals about 12,000Rp; 🕑 lunch & dinner) Has sea views, but surprisingly little fish. Most of what is available is simply a variation of the ubiquitous *nasi campur* (rice 'with the lot').

Rumah Makan Cita Rasa (☎ 534450; Jl Percetakan 66; meals 12,000-25,000Rp; 🕑 lunch & dinner) A clean and friendly place that serves the usual range of Indonesian and Chinese food.

Rumah Makan Simpang Tigo (Jl Percetakan; meals 20,000Rp; 🕑 lunch & dinner) Probably one of the better Padang-style places in town because it does offer other types of food. But the warbling diners at the karaoke machine are likely to limit any conversation.

Among the hotel restaurants downtown, the following are the best places for range, price, service and setting – plus, they will serve you a cold beer.

Fantasi Restaurant (Hotel Dafonsoro; mains around 30,000Rp; ❄)

Hotel Papua Restaurant (Hotel Papua; mains around 30,000Rp; ❄)

At night along Jl Ahmad Yani and around the waterfront, warungs serve cheap and tasty *gado gado* (vegetables with spicy peanut sauce) and *nasi campur*. Plenty of food stalls along Jl Nindya also sell delicious, filling *nasi campur* and baked fish from 5000Rp. Jayapura is 'dry', but alcohol is served here and there.

Getting There & Away

AIR

Jayapura is well connected to the rest of Indonesia. Every day, Merpati flies between Jayapura and Jakarta, via Biak, Timika and/or Makassar, and from Jayapura to Merauke. It also flies four times a week to Nabire.

Book at the efficient **Merpati office** (☎ 533111; djjgmmz@merpati.co.id; Jl Ahmad Yani; 7.30am-noon & 1-7pm). Refer to p824 for details about flights between Jayapura and Wamena.

Garuda also flies between Jayapura and Jakarta every day but Wednesday, via Biak and Makassar or Timika and Denpasar. Tickets are available at the **Garuda office** (☎ 522222; djjdmga@garuda-indonesia.com; Bank Papua Bldg, Jl Ahmad Yani 4-7; 9am-6pm Mon-Sat, 9am-3pm Sun).

The missionary service **AMA** (Map p832; ☎ 591009; amasentani@jayapura.wasantara.net.id; Jl Misi Sentani, Sentani) regularly flies to Ilaga, Nabire, Timika, Mulia and Enarotali, but not to Wamena. **MAF** (Map p832; ☎ 591109; Jl Misi Sentani, Sentani) can arrange charter flights.

All flights leave from the airport in nearby Sentani.

BOAT

Of course, all boats head west from Jayapura. Every two weeks, the Pelni liners *Sinabung, Nggapulu* and *Dobonsolo* travel to Biak (1st/economy class 356,500/115,500Rp), while the *Doro Londa* stops at Serui and Nabire (but not Biak).

The port is 800m east of the post office and accessible by any taxi to Hamadi. Tickets for all major boats are available at the **Pelni office** (☎ 531053; Jl Halmahera 1; 8.30am-6pm Mon-Sat) or for an extra fee at tour operator PT Kuwera Jaya.

Perintis boats also leave Jayapura every week or so for Serui, Nabire, Biak and Manokwari. These boats, and the other smaller ones that ply the north coast, normally leave from the **small boat harbour** (Jl Sam Ratulangi).

See p799 for details about crossing by boat from Jayapura to Vanimo.

Getting Around

A private taxi from Sentani airport to Jayapura will cost a whopping 100,000Rp. Try rounding up other passengers, or take a cheap, efficient public taxis. See p833 for details about catching public taxis between Sentani and Jayapura.

Public taxis to most places in and around Jayapura leave every second or two from designated stops along Jl Percetakan, Jl Ahmad Yani and Jl Sam Ratulangi. Trips around town cost 1500Rp. A ride on an *ojek* is a quick and easy way to get around the city centre.

SENTANI

☎ 0967

Sentani, 36km west of Jayapura, is a small town that services the airport. Built near the shores of the magnificent Danau Sentani, it's quieter, cooler and more convenient than Jayapura and has most of the facilities you'll need. But Sentani has lost some of its appeal: during riots by Papuan separatists between 1998 and 2002, many buildings, including offices and hotels, were destroyed, abandoned and/or looted. While some businesses have gotten back on their feet, others have been left to decay.

The only attraction is the unimpressive memorial-cum-cemetery, grandly named in English as the **Papua Freedom & Human Rights Abuses Memorial Park** (Jl Kemiri Sentani Kota). It contains the grave of the Papuan independence leader, Theys Eluay, who was murdered in November 2001 (by soldiers of the Kopassus special forces). See p833 for sights and activities around Sentani.

Information

You'll have to venture into Jayapura to change travellers cheques.

Airport information office (5am-5pm) At the airport terminal, it's useful for general inquiries, though it's not a tourist office.

Bank Mandiri (Jl Kemiri Sentani Kota) You can change cash here, or withdraw rupiah from its 24-hour ATM.

BNI bank (Bank Negara Indonesia; Multi Jaya Shopping Centre; Jl Kemiri Sentani Kota) About 3km west of the post office, this bank changes cash and has an ATM.

District police station (Jl Raya Hawai 97) Conveniently, you can now get your *surat jalan* at this station 5km east of Sentani.

Duta Computer (Jl Kemiri Sentani Kota; 2-9pm) Slow internet access has hit Sentani.

Main post office (Jl Kemiri Sentani Kota; 8am-5.30pm Mon-Sat) Has a poste restante.

Police station (Polres; ☎ 591105; Jl Airport) For local questions and complaints only; you cannot get a *surat jalan* here. The district police station issues the *surat jalan*.

Telkom office (Jl Eluay II; 24hr)

Sleeping

Since airport access is so easy from here and the town is so low-key, most visitors base themselves in Sentani rather than in Jayapura. All places listed below offer rooms with attached bathroom, and all rates include breakfast.

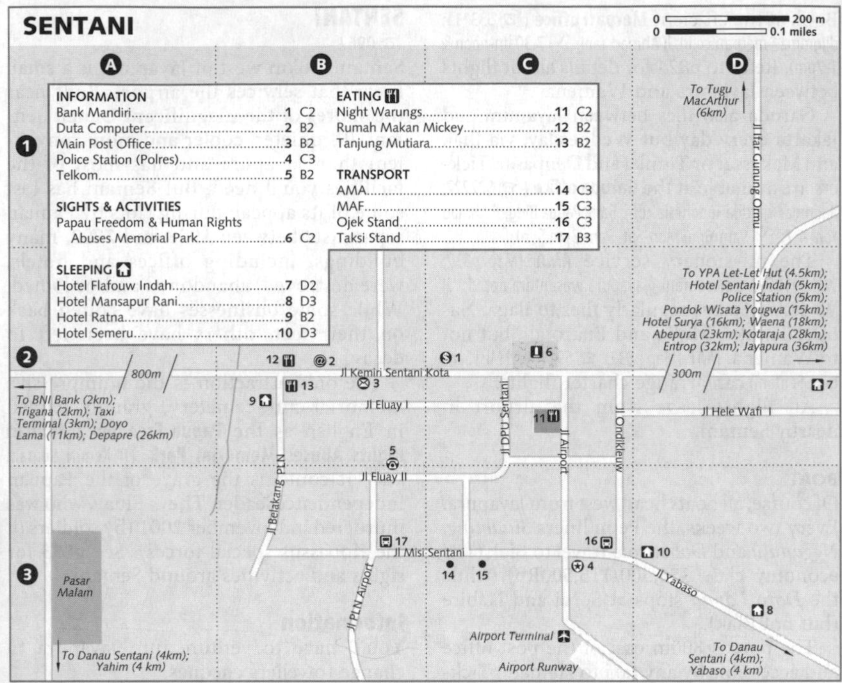

Hotel Semeru (☎ 591447; fax 591964; Jl Yabaso; s 100,000Rp, d 120,000-150,000Rp; ❄) The most convenient and best-value option in town. The basic rooms are slightly worn, but they are clean and comfortable. Breakfast is do-and-brew-yourself.

Hotel Flafouw Indah (☎/fax 591478; Jl Raya Sentani Kota; r 110,000-165,000Rp; ❄) Offers largish, cleanish rooms, but most are dark and noisy from the main road traffic. It's about 800m east of the post office.

Hotel Mansapur Rani (☎ 591219; Jl Yabaso 113; r 150,000-250,000Rp; ❄) Priced more for its potential than for what you actually get, 'ekonomi' rooms here are dingy and dank, while the 'deluxe' rooms at the back are slightly larger and brighter. Upsides include the garden setting, complete with flowers and roving ducks, and its proximity to the airport.

Hotel Ratna (☎ 593410; fax 592640; Jl PLN 1; r 165,000-330,000Rp; ❄) The Ratna's rooms are clean, green and comfortable, with cable TV and homey touches. Most staff speak English, and the standard is probably the best in Sentani for the price.

Hotel Sentani Indah (☎ 591900; fax 592828; Jl Raya Hawai; r from 455,000Rp; ❄ 🏊) Along the road to Jayapura is this incongruous monstrosity about 5km from Sentani. It has a fitness centre, pool, café, and lots of rooms that aspire to luxury but look a little worn and weary.

Eating

Tanjung Mutiara (☎ 591355; Jl Kemiri Sentani Kota; mains around 8000Rp; ⏰ lunch & dinner) Tasty Padang food in an immaculate, airy setting.

Rumah Makan Mickey (Jl Kemiri Sentani Kota 49; mains around 20,000Rp; ⏰ lunch & dinner) Mickey remains the most popular place for travellers and expats. The menu (written in English) has reasonably priced Indonesian and Western-style selections.

At the corner of Jl Airport and Jl Eluay I, several night warungs serve basic meals from late afternoon. A few nondescript *rumah makan* (eating houses) are dotted along the main road (the better ones are between Hotel Flafouw Indah and the turn-off to Tugu MacArthur). Sentani is another 'dry' town, though if you ask around, you can find a shop or two that sells cold beer.

Shopping

YPA Let-Let Hut (☎ 591372; Jl Raya Hawai; 8.30am-4pm Mon-Fri, 8.30am-noon Sat) Featuring an imaginative array of fair-trade souvenirs and handicrafts, this (thankfully, air-conditioned) shop is 4.7km east of Sentani, along the road to Jayapura. A portion of the shop's profits is funnelled back to the craftspeople's communities.

Getting There & Away

Several airline offices are conveniently located in the departure area of the airport terminal, including **Merpati** (☎ 591788), **Air Efata** (☎ 592030) and **Trigana** (☎ 594383).

Refer to p830 for details about travelling by plane from Sentani and by boat from Jayapura.

Getting Around

A private taxi from the airport to most hotels in Sentani costs about 10,000Rp, but you can easily walk (or hop on a public taxi).

Travelling by public transport between Sentani and Jayapura requires a change of taxis. First, catch a taxi to Abepura (4000Rp, 30 minutes) from anywhere in Sentani and disembark near the turn-off to the right for the Abepura terminal (look for the white church called Jewaat Elim). Then board one of the awaiting buses or taxis to Jayapura (2500Rp). From Jayapura, catch a taxi to Abepura from the waterfront terminal near the main post office, and get off at the roundabout in Abepura (the driver will probably kick you off here before returning to Jayapura). From here, catch another taxi to Sentani. If in doubt, check with the driver. Taxis stop running at about 8pm.

A convenient way to get around Sentani is by *ojek*. Drivers can take you to all the local sites, such as Yabaso (p835), Danau Sentani (p835) and Tugu MacArthur (p835), as well as to the taxi terminal in western Sentani – all for a negotiable fare. The most convenient *ojek* stand is on the corner of Jl Ondikleuw and Jl Misi Sentani.

AROUND JAYAPURA & SENTANI

☎ 0967

Several interesting places around Jayapura and Sentani can be easily visited on day trips from either town. Chartering a taxi for about 50,000Rp per hour is a painless way to reach more remote places or to see a few sights in one day.

Museums

Museum Loka Budaya (Cultural Museum; Jl Abepura, Abepura; admission by donation; 7.30am-4pm Mon-Fri) contains a fascinating range of Papuan artefacts, including the best collection of Asmat carvings outside of Agats, as well as a small souvenir shop. It's in the grounds of the Cenderawasih University (in the closest building to Jayapura, on the right-hand side of the road from Sentani). To get to the museum take the Sentani-Abepura taxi, almost as far as the turn-off to the Abepura terminal.

The **Museum Negeri** (State Museum; Jl Abepura, Waena; admission 750Rp; 8am-4pm Tue-Sat, 11am-4pm Sun) includes a marginally interesting collection of carvings, costumes, boats and artefacts from all over Papua, as well as historical items from Dutch colonial times. The museum is often closed; when open, a small shop inside sells souvenirs and books. The museum is easy to reach by taxi along the Sentani–Abepura road.

Next door, **Taman Budaya** (Cultural Park; Jl Abepura, Waena; admission free; 8am-4pm Tue-Sat, 10am-4pm Sun) is a collection of traditional houses, each representing a district of Papua – including the 'other district': the PT Freeport mine in Timika (!). The state of dilapidation of this park is a sad reflection of the general decline of Papua.

Pantai Base G

Made famous by General MacArthur, Base G Beach (also known locally as Pantai Tanjung Ria) is wide and desolate – except on Sunday when locals come in droves for a picnic and walk. Taxis marked 'Base G' regularly head north along Jl Sam Ratulangi in Jayapura for the pleasant trip to Tanjung Ria; ask to be dropped off at the beach, which is a 10-minute walk down the hill.

Depapre

Set under the dramatic mountain ranges of Pegunungan Cyclops, the pretty village of Depapre is an enjoyable day trip. From the village jetty you can charter boats or canoes to explore the sheltered Teluk Tanah Merah and enjoy some **snorkelling** (bring your own gear). A track (7km) from the back of the village leads to the secluded **Pantai Amai**.

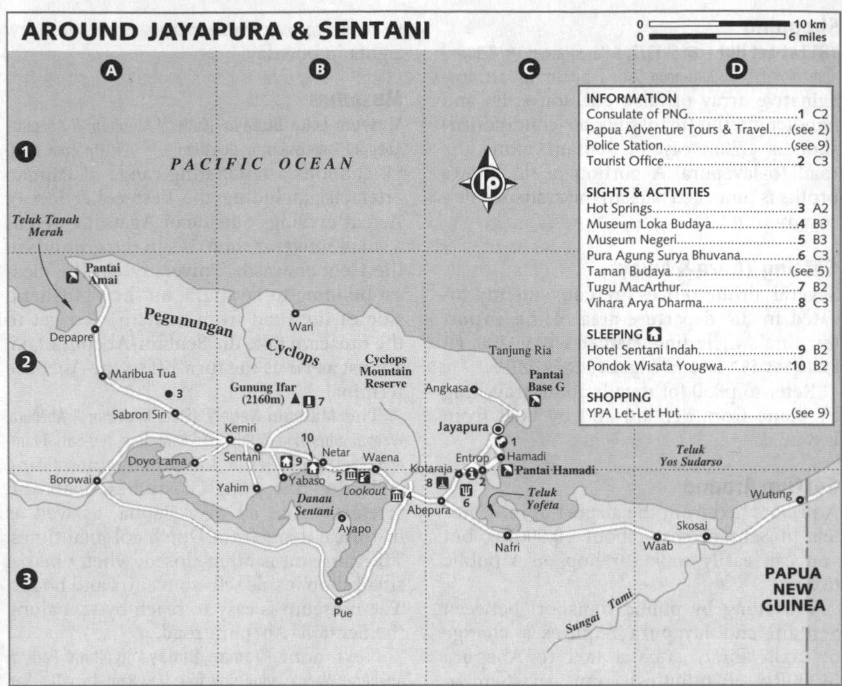

Taxis for Depapre (one hour) leave about every hour from the taxi terminal, 4km west of the post office in Sentani. You can easily stop along the way at other charming villages, such as **Maribua Tua**, and the hot springs at **Sabron Siri**.

Hamadi

Hamadi's bustling but down-at-heel daily **market** is one of the most fascinating in the region. Several shops along the main road also sell souvenirs, including tacky mass-produced Asmat and Dani art (but you'll find better stuff in Wamena).

Pantai Hamadi, the site of a US amphibious landing on 22 April 1944, is another two minutes' drive past the market. The beach is pleasant, if a little dirty, however, it contains some rusting **WWII wrecks** and a **WWII monument**. At the start of the trail to the beach, you'll have to report to the military barracks with a copy of your *surat jalan*.

Hamadi is also the place to charter a boat to nearby islands and to Vanimo in PNG (see the boxed text, p799).

Mahkota Beach Hotel (☎ 532997; fax 534537; Jl Hamadi Tanjung 1; r 160,000Rp; ❄) is, according to its brochure, 'a place where the Pacific Wave Singing'. Check out a few rooms here before settling on one, as some are in better repair than others. The breezy, seaside **restaurant** (meals 15,000-40,000Rp) offers tasty seafood, and live music most evenings. The hotel-restaurant is 500m down from the first bend in the road as you approach from Jayapura.

Taxis head to Hamadi from along Jl Koti in Jayapura every few seconds; you can also catch one directly to Hamadi from the terminal at Entrop.

Temples

Halfway along the Abepura–Entrop road, it's worth stopping for a look around two huge temples – if only for the magnificent views of Teluk Yofeta. The Buddhist temple, **Vihara Arya Dharma** (Jl Kotaraja; admission free; 🕑 daylight hours), was not built in any classical style, but the setting and views are worth the short, steep climb.

About 300m further down towards Jayapura, on the other side of the road, the

Hindu temple, **Pura Agung Surya Bhuvana** (Jl Kotaraja), is also fairly standard, but again the vistas are more than enough reason to visit.

Danau Sentani

This magnificent lake (96.5 sq km) is in itself worth a trip to Jayapura and/or Sentani. If you fly to Sentani, you will soar across the lake and see its 19 islands, as well as numerous fishing villages full of wooden houses precariously raised on stilts above the water. No organised tours of the lake are available, so you'll have to travel around independently, but it's certainly worth the effort. The lake is particularly attractive and photogenic at dusk and dawn.

SIGHTS & ACTIVITIES

Boating

A trip by boat across the lake is the best (and sometimes only) way to visit some of the islands and villages. From Yahim, 4km south of the *pasar malam* (night market) in Sentani by taxi, motorboats (for five people) can be rented for about 85,000Rp per hour, but you may have to spend some time looking for a solid boat and willing driver. Canoes cost considerably less, but obviously can't go far.

The most convenient and reliable option, especially if you're in a group, is to charter a motorboat from Pondok Wisata Yougwa (right). A sturdy boat (for nine people), with a knowledgeable driver-cum-guide, can be hired for a reasonable 150,000Rp per hour. From the same hotel, a *sepeda air* (paddle boat) costs from 15,000Rp per hour.

By boat, you can visit simple, friendly villages such as **Doyo Lama**, renowned for the manufacture of impressive, large **woodcarvings**, and for unexplained **rock paintings** nearby. Public transport to Doyo Lama also leaves from the taxi terminal in western Sentani two or three times a day (except Sunday). Alternatively, take a regular taxi (from the same terminal in Sentani) to Kemiri, along the main road to Depapre, and walk about 4km to Doyo Lama.

Hiking

Another way to explore the lake is to stroll for 40 minutes along Jl Yabaso from Hotel Mansapur Rani in Sentani. The road (then path) goes through **Yabaso** village and continues around the lake for another few kilometres past several villages. At the end of the path (90 minutes from Sentani), look for a public boat (or charter one) across the lake to a point close to Pondok Wisata Yougwa.

Between the Museum Negeri and Taman Budaya in Waena, another path (800m) leads to a decrepit lakeside recreational park, simply signposted as 'Danau Wisata'. After the boatman regains his composure from seeing a foreigner, he may agree to take you out on the lake.

Gunung Ifar

For breathtaking views of Danau Sentani, visit **Tugu MacArthur** on top of Gunung Ifar (2160m). Here, according to legend, MacArthur sat and contemplated his WWII strategies. A plaque on the monument reads: 'Here stood the Headquarters of General Douglas MacArthur and Task Force Reckless during the Pacific War'.

The very steep road (6km) to the top starts about 500m east of the corner of Jl Ondikleuw and Jl Kemiri Sentani Kota in Sentani. Taxis are irregular, except on Sunday when the hilltop is a popular picnic spot, so charter a taxi from Sentani or an *ojek* from the bottom of the access road, Jl Ifar Gunung Ormu. Just before you reach the monument, you may have to report to the local military office with a copy of your *surat jalan*.

SLEEPING & EATING

Along the Sentani–Abepura road, the charming **Pondok Wisata Yougwa** (☎ 571570; Jl Raya Sentani; r 180,000-220,000Rp; ❄) overlooks the lake. The sparkling rooms have bathrooms, and balconies with lake views, but the serenity is shattered by the traffic (which does quieten down at night). The breezy **restaurant** (fish meals from 30,000Rp) provides wonderful views and delicious fish. The hotel/restaurant is unmarked, about 15km from Sentani; ask the taxi driver to drop you off.

MERAUKE

☎ 0971 / pop 50,460

Merauke is a quite prosperous, orderly and clean town, renowned in Indonesia as the most eastern settlement in the country. There is very little to do, but it's an obvious

PAPUA

starting point for trips to the interior, particularly the Asmat region.

Information

Merauke has no town centre, so virtually everything you'll need is along Jl Raya Mandala, which stretches about 7km between the airport and port.

Bank Mandiri (Jl Raya Mandala 1) At the western end of the main road, not far from Hotel Asmat, changes US dollars cash and travellers cheques and has an ATM.

BNI bank (Bank Negara Indonesia; Jl Raya Mandala 168) Next to Hotel Megaria and has a 24-hour ATM for Visa and MasterCard.

Police station (☎ 321706; Jl Raya Mandala 48) North of Hotel Nirmala about 300m; handles extra permits for the interior.

Tourist office (☎ 322588; Jl Ahmad Yani 3; 8am-3pm Mon-Thu, 8-11am Fri) Along a street off the top end of Jl Raya Mandala; has a simple brochure, but no maps of town.

Sights & Activities

On Sundays when the tide is out, catch the motorcycle drag races along **Pantai Lampu Satu** – if you get there before the cops do. The beach is 5km along Jl Nowari, which starts southwest of the Bank Mandiri building in Merauke. If you don't mind an audience, splash around in the **hot springs** (Jl Yos Sudarso; admission free; 24hr), about 200m south of Hotel Asmat.

The peak of Merauke's dry season comes in October, the first week of which brings with it the **Asmat Art & Culture Festival** – also held in Agats (p838) – which features displays of Asmat woodcarving and traditional dancing. During the first week of November, the traditional festival of **Kimam** is celebrated with boat races, dancing and woodcarving, held on Pulau Yos Sudarso near Merauke (first week of November).

Sleeping & Eating

Hotel Nakoro (☎ 322287; Jl Irmasu 96; s/d from 145,000/175,000Rp) This sweet spot is on a quiet road and has a home style sort of feel. All rooms come with breakfast, and the smaller ones upstairs have pleasant views of banana trees below. Prices include breakfast.

Hotel Megaria (☎ 321932; Jl Raya Mandala 166; r from 150,000Rp;) Set back from the road and commendably quiet, the Megaria has a good selection of large, clean and well furnished rooms. Breakfast is not included, but the staff will bring you tea or coffee.

Hotel Asmat (☎ 321065; Jl Trikora 3; r 290,000-350,000Rp;) Just off the western end of Jl Raya Mandala, Hotel Asmat offers comfortable, quiet rooms (all with breakfast and amenities like satellite TV), as well as excellent service.

Kantin Mesaran (Jl Raya Mandala; meals from 10,000Rp; lunch & dinner) Just around the corner from Hotel Asmat, this place is run by deliriously cheery people who pile huge amounts of tasty eats on your plate.

Sandra Café (Jl Raya Mandala 125; meals from 15,000Rp; lunch & dinner) Set in a quasijungle garden opposite Hotel Megaria, Sandra Café looks appealing but offers the usual fare.

Javanis Café & Resto (☎ 321515; Jl Raya Mandala; meals from 15,000Rp; lunch & dinner) About 100m west of Hotel Megaria, this is another friendly restaurant serving typical Indonesian meals. The traffic outside is a bit noisy, but the atmosphere inside is pleasant enough.

Getting There & Away

Merpati flies daily from Merauke to Jayapura, and less regularly to regional centres such as Ewer and Senggo. Book tickets at the **Merpati** office (☎ 321242; mkqdmmz@plasa.com; Jl Raya Mandala 226; 8am-4.30pm Mon-Fri, 9am-2pm Sat, 11am-2pm Sun).

Every four weeks, the Pelni liner *Kelimutu* links Merauke with Timika (1st/economy class 416,500/129,000Rp) and southeastern Maluku, while the *Tatamailau* sails from Merauke to Timika, Fak-Fak and Sulawesi (1,801,500/558,000Rp). Also, every two weeks the *Sangiang* stops at Agats, Timika and Fak-Fak.

Perintis boats are the next best option. Other uncomfortable wooden boats also make fortnightly runs up and down the coast to Kimam (Pulau Yos Sudarso), Bade, Agats, and – incredibly – as far inland as Tanahmerah.

Tickets for Pelni and Perintis boats are available at the **Pelni office** (☎ 321638; Jl Sabang 318), about 200m south of Hotel Asmat.

Getting Around

Mopah airport is about 7km from Hotel Asmat. Take a private taxi for about 20,000Rp or a *mikrolet* outside the airport for 2500Rp. Yellow and red *mikrolet* hurtle up and down the main road, between the airport and port, every nanosecond (per trip 1500Rp).

AROUND MERAUKE

Wasur National Park

This **park** (admission 10,000Rp) is the joint project of the Indonesian Directorate of Forest Protection & Nature Conservation and the indigenous people (mainly the Kanum and Marind) who contribute to, and benefit from, the park and its management. The 4138-sq-km park (Taman Nasional Wasur) backs onto the PNG border, and features termite mounds, wetlands, traditional villages and extensive bird life (74 endemic species). Wildlife includes cuscus and kangaroos (including 27 endemic species), but animals are often very difficult to see. The best time to visit is during the dry season (July to January); access during the wet season (February to June) is often only possible to Yanggandur and Onggaya villages.

Before visiting, the **Wasur National Park office** (Balai Taman Nasional Wasur; ☎ 322495; info@wasur.com; Jl Garuda Leproseri 3; 🕑 8am-2.30pm Mon-Thu, 8-11am Fri, 8am-1pm Sat) asks that all travellers register with them to receive a travel permit. It is about 5km south of Merauke. It can arrange guides (150,000Rp per day) and organise transport. The park office at the Wasur entrance has a helpful **information centre** (🕑 8am-5pm).

Activities include **hiking** around the wetlands near Yanggandur, **horse-riding** around Rawabiru, and wildlife-viewing from the **observation tower** at Ukra.

It's possible to stay in various villages by checking in at the military posts and/or with the *kepala desa*, with a courtesy payment of around 50,000Rp per person. Visitors can also bring their own tents.

Public buses barrel over the park's dirt roads to the villages around the park only once or twice a day; otherwise, you'll have to charter a *mikrolet* from Merauke (about 50,000Rp per hour) or hire one of the knowledgeable, amiable park rangers to be your guide (recommended). The travel agencies listed on p829 can also arrange (expensive) tours around Wasur.

Sungai Bian & Muting

As an alternative to the comparatively overrun Baliem Valley, there are several regions near Merauke that are worth exploring. The most accessible is an area 170km by winding road north of Merauke (mainly around Muting and other villages strung along Sungai Bian). In this region there are probably enough rainforests, wildlife and traditional people to keep most visitors happy.

Foreigners are not permitted to visit this area independently, however, so all visits must be arranged with **Yapsel** (☎ 323204; Jl Misi) in Merauke, a local indigenous-run organisation.

THE ASMAT REGION

The Asmat region is a massive area of mangroves, pandanus and rivers with huge tides. It remains almost completely undeveloped and one of the few truly unexplored regions left in the world. The Asmat people are justifiably famous for their woodcarvings and less so for their past head-hunting exploits. They are seminomadic and their lives are dictated by the rivers, a necessary source of transport and food.

To appreciate what the Asmat region has to offer definitely takes a *lot* of time and a *lot* of money. Independent travellers with a limited budget and no real interest in the regional culture may be very disappointed with how little they can see. And Agats and the Asmat region is nowhere near as developed or accessible as Wamena and the Baliem Valley.

The travel agencies listed on p829 can arrange expensive trips to the Asmat region and to inland areas where the Kombai and Korowai people live in extraordinary tree houses. Expect to pay about US$150 per person per day, plus airfares.

Agats

☎ 0971 / pop 1350

Facilities in the Asmat region are very limited and almost nonexistent outside Agats, which has two hotels, limited electricity and precious little fresh water. Due to the extraordinary tides and location, the town is traversed on raised (and often broken) wooden walkways – watch your step! Report to the police station (er, hut) with your *surat jalan* as soon as you arrive. There is nowhere in the Asmat region to change money.

THE ASMAT PEOPLE

The word 'Asmat' comes from either *as akat* ('right man' in the local language) or *osamat* (man from tree), though the Asmat people refer to themselves as *asmat-ow* (real people).

Trees feature heavily in Asmat symbolism, which is not surprising given the immense jungles in the region. The Asmat believe that humans are the image of a tree: their feet are its roots, the torso its trunk, the arms are the branches, and the fruit represents the head. Also, an important element of their belief is that no person – except the very young and the very old – dies for any other reason than through tribal fighting or magic. So, each death of a family member must be 'avenged' if the spirit of the recently deceased can rest in the spiritual world known as *safan*. Not long ago, this 'avenging' took the form of head-hunting raids, and while it is now more ceremonial, 'avenging' is still taken seriously.

The centre of the Asmat people's beliefs is the figure of Fumeripitisj, who first carved wooden figures, thereby 'creating' the Asmat people. Through their carvings, the Asmat remain in contact with their ancestors. Each village appoints a *wow ipits* (woodcarver) based on his skills. Carvings are traditionally made only for use in ceremonies and are then left to rot in the jungle, but these days, inevitably, there is strong tourist demand for these and other specially made carvings.

Funeral ceremonies involve decorated shields which represent and avenge the dead relative, ancestor poles *(bis)* and ancestor figures *(kawe)*. Other ceremonial items include wooden masks, drums made from lizard skins, spears, paddles, and horns that were once used to herald the return of head-hunting raids and to frighten enemies.

Held during the first week of October, the **Asmat Art & Culture Festival** showcases the region's renowned woodcarving, and features traditional dancing.

The **Pusat Asmat & Pusat Pendidikan Asmat** (Asmat Education Centre & Asmat Centre; Jl Yos Sudarso; admission free; ⌚ erratic hours), 400m north of the mosque, is an impressive collection of buildings, primarily of interest for their traditional architecture.

Museum Kebudayaan & Kemajuan (Museum of Culture & Progress; admission 5000Rp; ⌚ about 8am-1pm Mon-Sat), one 'block' behind (south of) the mosque, offers a collection of varied cultural displays; try to recruit an English-speaking guide on your visit, as there are few interpretive signs to explain the exhibits.

SLEEPING & EATING

There are only two hotels in Agats. Guests can preorder meals at either for about 25,000Rp.

Losmen Pada Elo (☎ 31038; Jl Kompas Agats; r 100,000Rp) About 200m northeast of Asmat Inn, this losmen (basic accommodation) offers similar standards, as well as having friendly and helpful service. All rooms have shared *mandis*.

Asmat Inn (☎ 31002; Jl Yos Sudarso; r 125,000-165,000Rp) At the junction opposite the mosque, offers acceptable but unremarkable rooms.

GETTING THERE & AWAY

The tiny Merpati planes fly several times a week between Merauke and Ewer (near Agats), though flights are usually cancelled in the wet season if the grass airfield is waterlogged. The only other air option is the flight three times a week from Merauke to Senggo, from where it's a five-hour boat trip to Agats. Missionary planes can also be chartered from Merauke or Timika for exorbitant sums.

The Pelni liner *Sangiang* comes past Agats twice every two weeks on the route between Merauke (1st/economy class 428,500/128,000Rp) and Timika. Other less comfortable Perintis boats stop every week or so on the way between Merauke and Fak-Fak. The port in Agats is a 10-minute walk north of the police station (and a superb place to watch sunsets).

GETTING AROUND

The airports at Ewer and Senggo are connected to Agats by boat. All passengers on arrival will get a seat on the boat, but to get *to* the airport, you'll have to organise a place on a boat yourself.

Motorboats are the only form of local transport. A sturdy boat with a reputable driver costs about 700,000Rp per day. These boats take between 10 and 15 passengers, but Agats never attracts enough visitors to 'get a group together' to share the cost. Cheaper rates are possible if you ask around Sjuru village, a 10-minute walk south of Agats.

Canoes are a far cheaper alternative, but you obviously can't go very far. They cost about 30,000Rp per hour, plus 15,000Rp per hour for each rower. Ask around Sjuru or at the hotels in Agats.

AROUND THE ASMAT REGION

To explore the region properly, allow plenty of time and plenty of money. In addition to the exorbitant boat hire, add about 150,000Rp per day for a guide and 60,000Rp for a porter or cook. And bring all your own supplies. (Shops in Agats sell basic items.) Alternatively, you can arrange tours from the agencies in Jayapura (p829).

There are no hotels outside of Agats, but in the larger villages, such as **Senggo**, you can sleep at missions or schools (35,000Rp to 50,000Rp per person). Alternatively, bring your own camping gear, although much of the ground is swampy.

Directory

CONTENTS

ACCOMMODATION

Accommodation in Indonesia ranges from a basic box with a mattress to the finest five-star luxury corpulent wallets can buy. Costs vary considerably across the archipelago, but in general Indonesia is one of the cheaper countries in Southeast Asia.

Travellers' centres are superb value for food and accommodation; Bali easily has the best standards but prices for midrange and top-end accommodation are high. Accommodation prices don't necessarily increase in outer and more remote provinces, but less competition often means lower standards.

Some hotels have fixed prices and display them, but prices are often flexible, especially in quiet periods. This applies particularly to midrange and top-end hotels, where discounts of 10% to 50% are readily available.

Accommodation reviews in this book are chosen at the authors' discretion and based solely on merit. Lonely Planet receives no payment and reviews are listed in order of price, starting with budget and winding up with the most expensive option in town. Quoted rates are high season (ie May to September and Christmas/New Year) and may drop by as much as 20% during low season. Budget is anything from 20,000Rp to 150,000Rp per room per night; midrange is 150,000Rp to 500,000Rp and top end above that. 'Budget' often consists of a fan-cooled room in a losmen (simple, family-run hotel) or basic hotel, with a bed and shared *mandis* (Indonesian-type bath), although in the main cities like Jakarta and Yogyakarta rooms often come with a private *mandi*. Midrange accommodation is usually in a hotel and you can expect a private *mandi* or Western bathrooms, more comfortable beds with a modicum of furniture, air-con and TV. Of course standards vary greatly depending on where you are. Top end is generally a more comfortable version of midrange, with newer interiors and satellite TV. Luxury resorts in Bali rival those anywhere in the world. Hotel and resort rooms reviewed in this book include a bathroom unless otherwise stated.

All hotels are required to pay a 10% tax to the government, and this may be passed on to the customer, but most cheap hotels either avoid the tax or absorb it into their room rates. Midrange and top-end hotels

BOOK ACCOMMODATION ONLINE

For more accommodation reviews and recommendations by Lonely Planet authors, check out the online booking service at www.lonelyplanet.com. You'll find the true insider lowdown on the best places to stay. Reviews are thorough and independent. Best of all, you can book online.

PRACTICALITIES

- English-language press includes the *Jakarta Post* and the *Indonesian Observer*. *Kompas* is a respected Indonesian-language daily out of Jakarta. Others include *Pos Kota, Jawa Pos, Suara Pembaruan, Republika, Pikiran Rakyat* and *Media Indonesia*. Popular news and features magazines include *Gatra* and *Tempo*. See also p271 for Bali-specific media.
- Radio Republik Indonesia (RRI) is the national radio station and broadcasts 24 hours a day in Bahasa Indonesia. There are also at least five privately run stations. There is one government TV channel, TVRI, and up to nine commercial channels, depending on your reception and location.
- Videos you buy or watch are based on the PAL system, also used in Australia, New Zealand, the UK and most of Europe. Pirated and genuine DVDs are abundant and most can be played on all-region software, although the picture quality of the former is hit and miss.
- Electricity supply is 220V AC, 50Hz. The sockets accommodate two round prongs, the same as in most European countries. A voltage stabiliser/surge guard is recommended for computers.
- Indonesia uses the international metric system for weights and measures.

have a 21% tax-and-service charge, but not all include it in their advertised tariffs, so ask when checking in to avoid a headache on your way out. Prices in this book include tax unless otherwise stated. Midrange and top-end hotels sometimes 'absorb' the tax if business is slow.

Some useful websites for booking discounted accommodation in Java, Bali and other well-touristed areas:

Asia Rooms (www.asiarooms.com/indonesia)
Bali Hotels (www.balidwipa.com)
Indonesia Hotels Reservations (http://indonesia.hotels-reservations.org)

Camping

Camping grounds are rare, but there are opportunities for back-country camping. It is important that you camp away from civilisation, unless you want spectators all night.

You can probably do without a sleeping bag below 1000m, but at higher elevations you'll certainly need one. Rain is a possibility even in the dry season, especially as you gain altitude, so bring some sort of tent or rain-fly. You'll also want a mosquito net, to guard against insects and other things that crawl and slither in the night.

Hostels

Indonesia doesn't have many hostels, mainly because there are so many inexpensive hotels. One exception is Jakarta, where there are a number of places offering dormitory accommodation. There are a handful of hostels in a few other places, such as Surabaya and Kupang, but it's entirely possible to travel through Indonesia on a tight budget without ever staying in one.

The main thing to be cautious about in hostels is security. Few places provide lockers, and it's not just local thieves you must worry about – foreigners have been known to subsidise their trip by helping themselves to other people's valuables.

If you want to avoid nocturnal visits by rats, don't store food in your room, or at least have it sealed in jars or containers.

Hotels

Hotels in Indonesia come in different grades of price and comfort. At the bottom end of the scale is the *penginapan* or losmen. *Wisma* are slightly more upmarket, but still cheap. Hotels are at the midrange and top of the scale. A *bintang* (star) rating has been adopted by some hotels, but the only real way of knowing if you're getting what you pay for is by checking the rooms yourself.

The real budget hotels are Spartan places with shared Western bathrooms or *mandis*. Many are good, family-run places catering primarily to travellers, while other cheap places can be real rat-holes. Midrange hotel rooms usually come with private bathrooms and five-star hotels can match the best in the West. Top-end hotels often quote prices in US dollars, but most will happily take rupiah if requested.

Staying in Villages

In many places in Indonesia you'll often be welcome to stay in the villages. If the town has no hotel, ask for the *kepala desa* (village head), who is generally very hospitable and friendly, offering you not only a roof over your head in a homestay, but also meals. You may not get a room of your own, just a bed.

Payment is usually expected: about the same price as a cheap losmen as a rule of thumb. The *kepala desa* may suggest an amount, but often it is *terserah* ('up to you'), and you should always offer to pay. While the village head's house sometimes acts as an unofficial hotel, you are a guest and often an honoured one. Elaborate meals may be prepared just for you. It's also a good idea to have a gift or two to offer – cigarettes, photographs or small souvenirs from your country are popular. Homestays and village stays are a great way to socialise with families and neighbours, contribute to the local economy and experience life at a much closer level.

In towns where no accommodation is available, you also may be able to stay with the *camat* (district head) or at the local police station. For more information on cultural considerations when staying at villages see the boxed text on p58.

ACTIVITIES

Indonesia's tumultuous geography lends itself to a range of activities. As a vast archipelago, it encompasses oceans littered with superb diving, snorkelling, swimming and surfing opportunities. Inland, the mountainous peaks, dense jungles and ancient rivers are an adventurer's delight.

Cycling

Cycling in Indonesia is generally a means of transport and as an activity it's limited to a few areas. Yogyakarta and Solo in Java teem with bikes, and hire is possible for around 15,000Rp per day. In Bali there are bicycle tours around Ubud (see p314) and cycling is a popular form of transport around Nusa Lembongan (p346). In Sumatra you can hire bicycles in Danau Toba (p406) for around 25,000Rp per day.

The only place you may be able to purchase a bike in is Java; in Jakarta or Yogyakarta. If you're fit and brave enough to bring your own bike, it's easy enough to carry it on trains and boats when you need to. Buses are another matter however, as they generally don't have sufficient space. See p871 for more information.

Diving & Snorkelling

With so many islands and so much coral, Indonesia presents all sorts of wonderful possibilities for diving. In some areas diving may not be as good during the wet season, from about October to April, as storms tend to reduce visibility.

If diving is beyond your depths, try snorkelling. Many of the dive sites described can also be explored with a snorkel, and there are beautiful coral reefs on almost every coastline in Indonesia. While you can usually buy or rent the gear, it's best to take your own.

Some of Indonesia's best dive sites include:

Bali Padangbai (p334), Nusa Lembongan (p346), Candidasa (p338), Jemeluk (p343) and Tulamben (p344). See also the boxed text on p349.

SAFETY GUIDELINES FOR DIVING

Before embarking on a scuba-diving, skin-diving or snorkelling trip, carefully consider the following points to ensure a safe and enjoyable experience:

- Possess a current diving certification card from a recognised scuba diving instructional agency.
- Be sure you are healthy and feel comfortable diving.
- Obtain reliable information about physical and environmental conditions at the dive site.
- Dive only at sites within your realm of experience and engage the services of a certified dive instructor.
- Check your equipment thoroughly beforehand.
- Be aware that underwater conditions vary significantly from one region, or even site, to another. Seasonal changes can also significantly alter any site and its dive conditions.

RESPONSIBLE DIVING

The popularity of diving puts immense pressure on many sites. Consider the following tips when diving and help preserve the ecology and beauty of reefs:

- Do not use anchors on the reef, and take care not to ground boats on coral.
- Avoid touching living marine organisms with your body or dragging equipment across the reef. Never stand on corals, even if they look solid and robust.
- Be conscious of your fins. The surge from heavy fin strokes near the reef can damage delicate organisms. When treading water in shallow reef areas, take care not to kick up clouds of sand. Settling sand can easily smother delicate reef organisms.
- Practise and maintain proper buoyancy control. Major damage can be done by divers descending too fast and colliding with the reef. Make sure you are correctly weighted and that your weight belt is positioned so that you stay horizontal.
- Resist the temptation to collect corals or shells. The same goes for marine archaeological sites (mainly shipwrecks).
- Ensure that you collect all your rubbish and any litter you find as well. Plastics in particular are a serious threat to marine life. Turtles can mistake plastic for jellyfish and eat it.
- Resist the temptation to feed fish.
- Minimise your disturbance of marine animals. In particular, do not ride on the backs of turtles as this causes them great anxiety.

Java Pulau Seribu (p119), Pulau Kotok (p120), Carita (p125) and Cimaja (near Pelabuhan Ratu, p134).
Kalimantan Pulau Derawan and Pulau Sangalaki (p663).
Maluku Banda Islands (p765) and islands around Tobelo (p789).
Nusa Tenggara Flores (p543), Alor (p575), Komodo and Labuanbajo (see the boxed text, p546), Gili Islands (see the boxed text, p511), Senggigi (p500), Pulau Moyo (p534) and Sumba (p590).
Papua Pulau Biak (p808) and Sorong (p801).
Sulawesi Pantai Bira (p681), Togean Islands (see the boxed text, p726), Tukangbesi Islands (p714), Pulau Bunaken (see the boxed text, p740) and Tanjung Karang (p722).
Sumatra Pulau Weh (p422).

Hiking & Trekking

Despite the fact that Indonesia is littered with superb hiking and jungle-trekking regions, hiking is not well established. Information is lacking, and even the national parks often don't have well-maintained trails.

Where there's a will there's a way though, and where demand exists, local guide services have sprung up. The national parks, such as Gunung Leuser in Sumatra (p392), have good hiking possibilities. In Java, the lack of forest means that hiking is mostly limited to short climbs of volcanoes, or Ujung Kulon National Park – Java's largest wilderness area (p128). Hiking in Bali is similarly restricted mostly to volcanoes, such as Gunung Batur (p358). Gunung Rinjani (p519) on neighbouring Lombok is one of Indonesia's best and most popular hikes (from two to five days). The Baliem Valley in Papua (p816) is one of Indonesia's better-known walking destinations, and Tana Toraja in Sulawesi (p703) is excellent for following the route of traditional villages. In Kalimantan it's possible to trek from the east to west coasts, taking in the Apokayan Highlands (p659) along the way.

Sudden rainstorms are common at high altitudes, and Indonesia is no longer tropical once you get above the 3000m mark. The rain will not only make you wet, but freezing cold. A good rain poncho is essential. Other necessities include warm clothing in layers, proper footwear, sunscreen and a compass. It should go without saying that you must bring sufficient food and water. Don't underestimate your need for water – figure on at least 2L per day, more in extreme heat. It's worth bringing a lightweight kerosene stove (other fuels are less readily available in Indonesia).

GUIDES

A big decision is whether or not you need a guide. Often you do, but be prepared to haggle over the price. A private guide will typically cost around 100,000Rp to 200,000Rp per day, and more through a travel agency.

RESPONSIBLE TREKKING

To help preserve the ecology and beauty of Indonesia, consider the following tips when trekking.

Rubbish

- Carry out *all* your rubbish. Don't overlook easily forgotten items, such as cigarette butts, and make an effort to carry out rubbish left by others.
- Never bury your rubbish: it can take years to decompose and digging encourages erosion. Buried rubbish will likely be dug up by animals, which may be injured or poisoned by it.
- Minimise waste by taking minimal packaging and no more food than you will need. Take reusable containers or stuff sacks.
- Sanitary napkins, tampons, condoms and toilet paper should be carried out despite the inconvenience. They burn and decompose poorly.

Human Waste Disposal

- Contamination of water sources by human faeces can lead to the transmission of all sorts of nasties. Where there is a toilet, please use it. Where there is none, dig a small hole 15cm (6in) deep and at least 100m (320ft) from any watercourse. Cover the waste with soil and a rock.

Washing

- Don't use detergents or toothpaste in or near watercourses, even if they are biodegradable.
- For personal washing, use biodegradable soap and a water container (or even a lightweight, portable basin) at least 50m (160ft) away from any watercourse.
- Wash cooking utensils 50m (160ft) from watercourses using a scourer instead of detergent.

Erosion

- Stick to existing tracks.
- If a track passes through a mud patch, walk through the patch so as not to increase its size.
- Avoid removing the plant life that keeps topsoils in place.

Fires & Low-Impact Cooking

- Don't depend on open fires for cooking. The cutting of wood for fires in popular trekking areas can cause rapid deforestation. Cook on a lightweight kerosene, alcohol or Shellite (white gas) stove and avoid those powered by disposable butane gas canisters.
- Fires may be acceptable below the tree line in areas that get very few visitors. If you light a fire, use an existing fireplace. Use only minimal, dead, fallen wood.
- Ensure that you fully extinguish a fire after use.

Wildlife Conservation

- Do not engage in or encourage hunting. Indonesia is full of endangered critters which need all the help they can get to survive.
- Don't buy items made from endangered species.
- Discourage the presence of wildlife by not leaving food scraps behind you.
- Do not feed the wildlife; it can make them dependent on handouts or seriously ill.

SAFETY GUIDELINES FOR TREKKING

Before embarking on a trekking trip, consider the following points to ensure a safe and enjoyable experience:

- Pay any fees and possess any permits required by local authorities.
- Be sure you are healthy and feel comfortable walking for a sustained period.
- Obtain reliable information about physical and environmental conditions along your intended route (eg from park authorities).
- Be aware of local laws, regulations and etiquette about wildlife and the environment.
- Walk only in regions and on trails/tracks within your realm of experience.
- Be aware that weather conditions and terrain vary significantly from one region, or even from one trail/track, to another. Seasonal changes can significantly alter any trail/track. These differences influence what to wear and what equipment to carry.
- Ask before you set out about the environmental characteristics that can affect your walk and how local, experienced walkers deal with these considerations.

Take some time to talk to your guide to make sure he (Indonesian guides are always male) really understands the route and won't simply help you get lost.

In areas that see a lot of hiker traffic, a system of licensing guides may be in place. If your guide claims to be licensed, ask to see the licence and copy down his name and number. That way, if you encounter some really big problems (eg the guide abandons you on a mountainside), you can report him.

White-Water Rafting

Sulawesi's Sungai Sa'dan (p703) lures adventure junkies to tackle its 20-odd rapids (some up to Class IV). Rafting agents in Rantepao organise trips down its canyon.

Several adventure companies in Ubud organise trips down the infamous and nearby Sungai Ayung (see p314).

In Sumatra dinghies are swapped for tubes on Sungai Bohorok (p393), where navigating the rapids in a truck tyre is all the rage. Guides in Bukit Lawang also organise trekking and rafting tours in the area (see p392).

In Java, white-water rafting is well established on Sungai Citarak (p134), which churns out Class II to IV rapids.

It may not raise the hairs on your neck, but bamboo rafting down South Kalimantan's Sungai Amandit (p643) is a highlight of touring the area. It's easy enough to organise on your own but several companies in Banjarmasin can do the work for you.

There are also a number of un-rafted rivers in Papua, but tackling these will require expedition-style preparations – roads are nonexistent, crocodiles will probably find Western cuisine delightful and there may be unexpected surprises like waterfalls.

BUSINESS HOURS

Government office hours are variable, but are generally 8am to 4pm Monday to Friday (with a break for Friday prayers from 11.30am to 1.30pm), and 8am to noon on Saturday. Go in the morning if you want to get anything done.

Private business offices have staggered hours: 8am to 4pm or 9am to 5pm Monday to Friday, with a lunch break in the middle of the day. Many offices are also open until noon on Saturday.

Banks are usually open from 8am to 4pm Monday to Friday, although they can close as early as 2.30pm. In some places banks open on Saturday until around 11am. Banks in many areas also close during Friday afternoon prayers. The foreign-exchange hours may be more limited and some banks close their foreign-exchange counter at 1pm.

Shops open at around 9am or 10am. Smaller shops may close at 5pm, but in the big cities and in Bali, shopping complexes, supermarkets and department stores stay open until 9pm. Sunday is a public holiday but some shops and airline offices open for at least part of the day.

Restaurants generally open from between 7am and 10am in the morning and remain open until 11pm, or whenever business dries up.

SURF'S UP *Andrew Tudor & Justine Vaisutis*

Indonesia lures surfers from around the globe, many with visions of empty palm-lined beaches, bamboo bungalows and perfect barrels peeling around a coral reef. The good news is that mostly the dreams come true, but just like anywhere else, Indonesia is subject to flat spells, onshore winds and crowding (particularly in Bali). A little research and preparation goes a long way.

WHEN TO GO

The dry season (May to September) is more likely to produce solid ground swell, initiated in the Indian Ocean. Trade winds blow from the east or southeast, which means winds are offshore in Bali, from Kuta to Ulu Watu. During the wet season (October to April), trade winds are west or northwest, and are offshore on the other side of Bali (Sanur to Nusa Dua).

Traditionally June to August provides the most consistent and largest swells – and the largest crowds. Outside the high season, it's still possible to find good waves without drop-ins and jostling.

WHAT TO BRING

On arrival at Denpasar, it pays to carry some Indonesian rupiah as officials sometimes charge a 'surfboard tax' (import duty) for bringing two or more boards into the country – try to refuse to pay.

Indonesia's waves mostly break over shallow reefs and therefore break more sharply. Given this, you'll need to have a few more inches underneath you to avoid getting pitched on the takeoff. Taking a quiver is a good idea. Seven-foot to 7½ft boards are commonly used, but shorter boards are handy for Bali, and you'll need an 8ft board if you're planning on tackling the big swells.

Surfboards can be hired relatively easily on Bali; expect to pay between 30,000Rp and 50,000Rp per day.

INFORMATION & TOURS

Camps and charter cruises catering specifically to surfers lace Indonesia's coastlines and many advertise their wares on the internet. See the regional chapters for details. For health and safety information see the boxed text, p886.

Useful websites:

www.globalsurfers.com Global online forum for surfers.
www.indosurf.com.au Web links and general info.
www.island-aid.org Surfer-run aid organisation.
www.surfaidinternational.org Surfer-run aid organisation.
www.surftravel.com.au Australian outfit with camps, yacht charters, destination information, surfer reviews and more.
www.surftravelonline.com Information on remote Indonesian locations.
www.wannasurf.com Surf reports, current conditions and a message board.

WHERE TO GO

Bali

Bali is touted as a surfing mecca. Though getting to the breaks can be an adventure in itself, the rewards at the end of the road can be well worth it.

Ulu Watu on the west coast (p298) is a true surfers' paradise.

The wave has three left-handers. The Peak is a high-tide wave that handles small and big swells, and is in front of the cave. Racetracks, further down the reef, is a hollow wave that starts to work on the mid-tide and gets better as it runs out. It handles up to about 6ft and is very shallow. On a big swell and a low tide, try Outside Corner for a long ride on a huge face.

In the same vicinity, Dreamland (p298) is the latest discovery.

Kuta and Legian Beaches (p276) are two places where beginners can learn how to surf, although waves can get big and sometimes currents are strong, so take care.

Medewi (p355) in west Bali has a long left-hander over a rock-and-sand bottom. Though a long ride, it's not hollow. Like Canggu (p292), the trade winds are onshore, so early morning on a mid- to high tide is the best time for a surf.

Shipwreck at Nusa Lembongan (p346) is so named because of the rusted hull that pokes out of the reef. It's known for its back-door tubes and fast walling sections.

See the Surfing in Bali boxed text (p282) for hot tips.

Nusa Tenggara

On Sumbawa's west coast, Scar Reef (p530) is a left-hander that breaks over sharp coral and is usually best on the high tide. If it's small at low tide don't despair, the wave often jacks 2ft to 3ft on the incoming tide.

Aptly named Supersuck (p531) turns inside out and is a tube-rider's dream. The steep takeoff funnels into a long sucking bowl over a shallow reef. Unfortunately, Supersuck requires a big swell to turn on, but in its favour the dry-season winds are mostly offshore.

Yo Yo's (p531), a right-hand reef break, is reasonably deep compared with Supersuck, but the end section gets shallow on a mid- to low tide. Early morning surfs are best.

It's possible to surf year-round at Lakey Peak (p536) on the southeastern coast. It's a classic A-frame peak with a left and a right. It's usually better for holding big swells and providing hollow tube sections. Watch out for surfers trying to backdoor the peak.

Sumba and Timor are gaining popularity. Around southwestern Sumba, Rua (p601) is a good place to head. It's a left-hand reef break and the dry-season trade winds are cross-shore to offshore. Tarimbang (p598) on Sumba's central southern coast also has good waves and Baing (p597) has emerged as east Sumba's surf capital.

Lombok

Desert Point (p499) on Lombok's southwest peninsula was recently voted the best wave in the world by one surf-mag poll. A left hollow break of reef and coral this wave reaches 1.5m to 3m on a good day. It's one for experienced surfers.

Kuta (p525) has world-class waves and turquoise water. There are excellent lefts and rights right in front of Kuta's bay as well as the reefs east of Tanjung Aan.

Java

Grajagan (G-Land) at Alas Purwo National Park (p261) on Java's southeastern tip is home to what has become a world-famous surfing break. G-Land is a freight train left-hander that has several takeoff sections, monster barrels and speeding walls. From the camp at Pantai Plengkung, the reef stretches east up around the headland as far as the eye can see and, when a ground swell hits and big tubing left-handers line-up all the way round, it's truly a sight to behold.

In West Java, the beaches near Pelabuhan Ratu (see p134) offer some excellent reef breaks and beachies (waves that break over a sand bank). Batu Karas (p156), near Pandangaran, has one of the coast's best surf beaches and is a good spot to learn.

For hollow waves head to Pulau Panaitan (p129) in Ujung Kulon National Park. The waves here break over super-shallow coral reef and get faster and more hollow towards the end section. This place is for experienced surfers only.

Sumatra

Northern Sumatra's Pulau Nias (p407) is the most-visited surfing destination in the province. The right-hander at Teluk Lagundri is a relatively short wave, but at size is a high and tight tube from takeoff to finish. The outside reef only starts to work on a solid ground swell of about 4ft to 6ft, but holds huge swells and the tubes are perfect. Nearby, Sorake's world-famous right consistently unrolls between June and October (see p410).

An increasing number of surf charters are establishing camps on the Mentawai Islands (p440), which enjoy swells year-round, although they're biggest in the dry season.

CHILDREN

Travelling anywhere with children requires energy and organisation. Most Indonesians adore children, especially cute Western kids; however, children may find the constant attention overwhelming.

Health standards are low in Indonesia compared to the rest of the world, but with proper precautions, children can travel safely. As with adults, contaminated food and water present the most risks, and children are more at risk from sunstroke and dehydration. It depends where and how you travel. Indonesians may have to take their toddlers on gruelling eight-hour journeys in hot, stuffy buses, but you'd be well advised to take a luxury bus or rent a car. And many adults can comfortably sample warung food, but parents with kids will want to be more careful.

If you're travelling only to the main cities and tourist areas, like the resorts of southern Bali, the malaria risk is minuscule, but it's probably not worth the risk to travel to known malarial areas like Papua or Pulau Nias in Sumatra. For detailed information about travelling with children pick up a copy of Lonely Planet's *Travel With Children*.

Practicalities

Kid-friendly facilities such as high chairs in restaurants and cots in hotels are generally limited to Bali, which caters well to holidaying families. Bali has a ready supply of babysitters (often called 'babysisters') and plenty for kids to do. Java doesn't have Bali's mega-tourism industry, so it caters less to children, but its well developed with a range of amenities, transport, hotel and food options. Travel outside cities requires patience, hardiness and experience – for both parents and kids.

Nappy-changing facilities usually consist of the nearest discreet, flat surface. Baby wipes, disposable nappies and baby formula are all readily available in cities and big towns but seldom elsewhere.

Breast feeding in public is acceptable in areas such as Papua and Sumatra but virtually unseen in Maluku, Sulawesi or Kalimantan. In parts of Java it's simply inappropriate. The rule of thumb of course is always to take your cue from local mothers with infants.

Sights & Activities

Travelling in some areas of Indonesia is probably too hard for most people to tackle with small children. Transport and facilities are best in Bali and there are plenty of safe beaches suitable for kids. South Bali has most of the island's family-friendly resorts and there are specific activities to keep little tackers occupied – see p281 for suggestions.

In Java the islands of Karimunjawa (p217) are isolated and some can be difficult to get to but the calm seas and pace make for tranquil family holidays.

The once-heady tourism flux of Sumatra's Danau Toba (p399) has left a legacy of decent infrastructure and families with young kids will find it easy to cope here. It's actually a popular spot for weekend-away expats from Medan and Aceh.

CLIMATE CHARTS

Straddling the equator, Indonesia tends to have a fairly even climate year-round. Rather than four seasons, Indonesia has

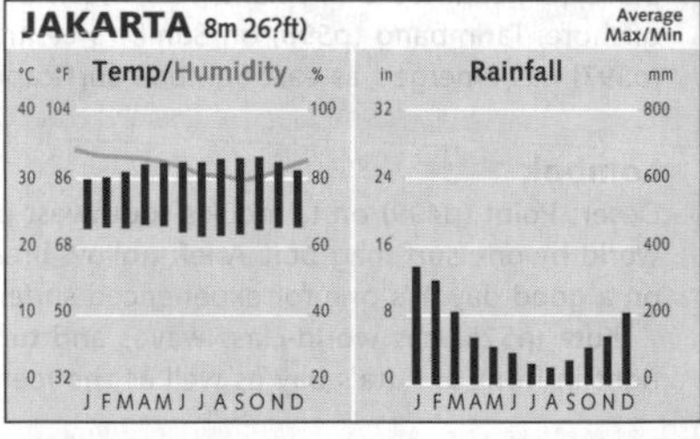

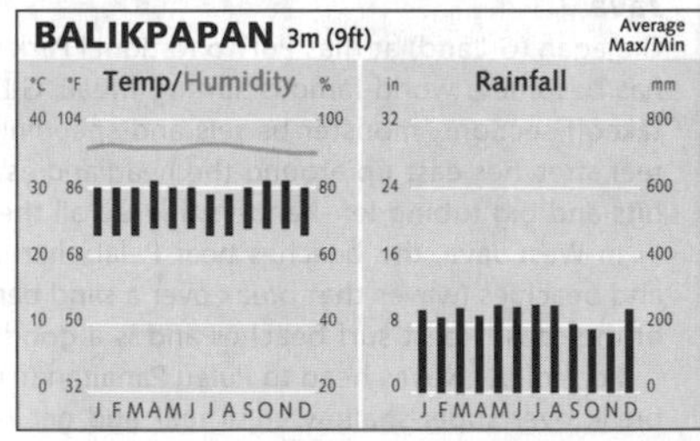

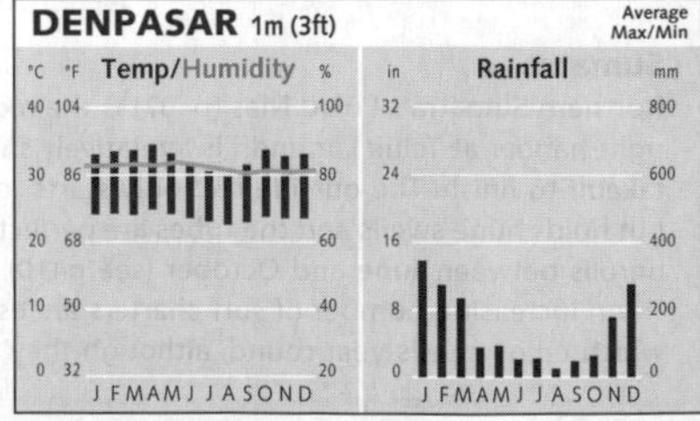

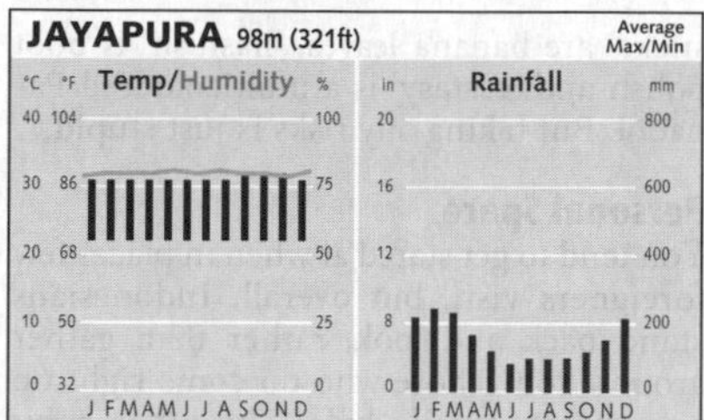

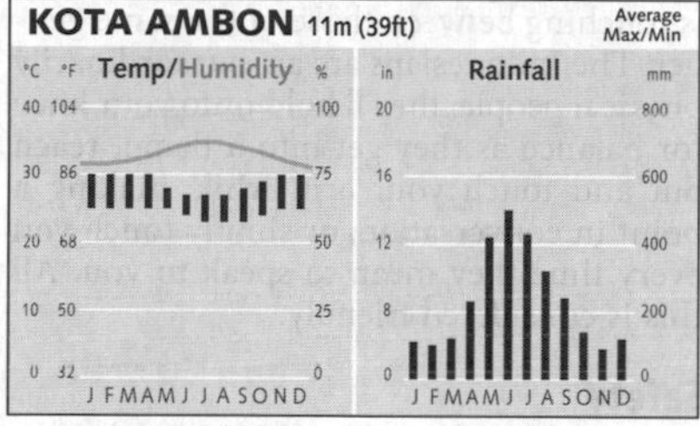

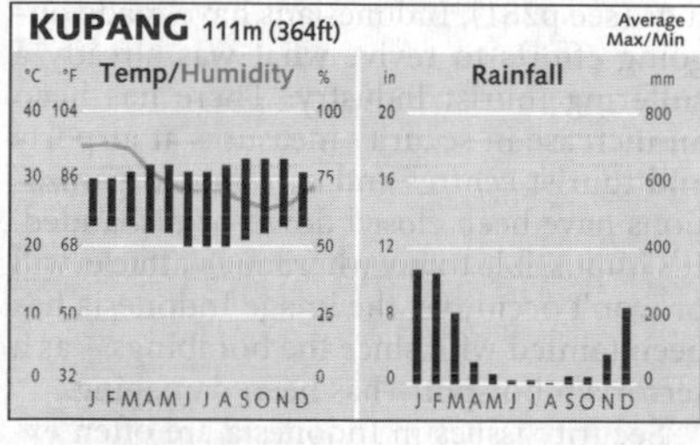

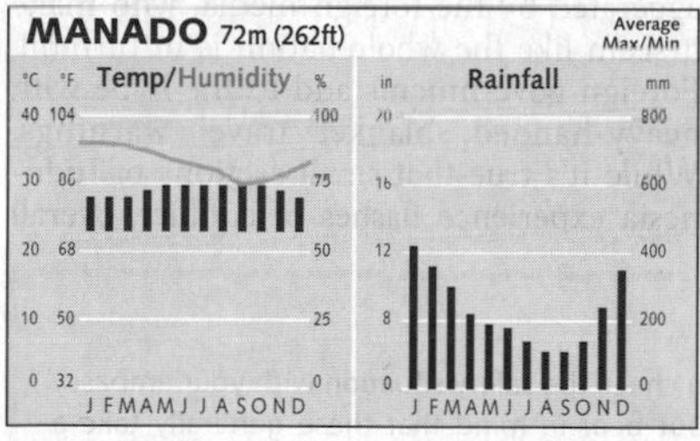

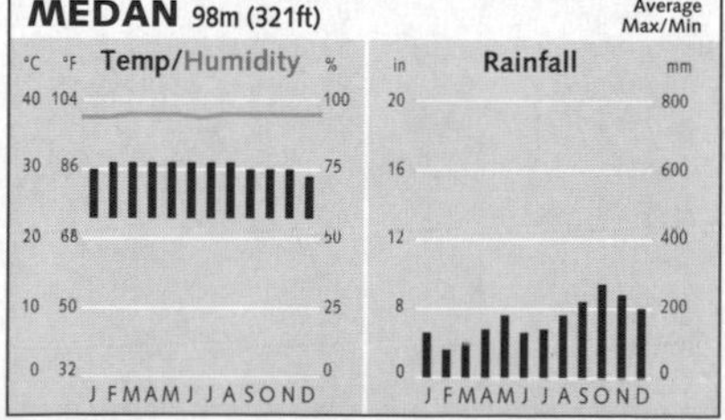

two – wet and dry – and there are no extremes of winter and summer.

COURSES

Many cultural and language courses are available, particularly in the main tourist areas. Once again Bali takes the lead, offering a little something to just about everyone. Ubud is Bali's culinary capital and there are courses to teach the inquisitive gastronome a thing or two; see p87 for details. Look for advertisements at your hotel, enquire at local restaurants and bars, ask fellow travellers and hotel staff, and check out the tourist newspapers and magazines.

Culture junkies and art addicts are also looked after with a host of courses in Ubud teaching pottery, woodcarving, batik, Bahasa Indonesia and more (see p314 for more information). Short batik courses are popular in Yogyakarta (see p177) and in Solo (p198). Also in Java, dance and art classes are held at the Mangun Dhama Art Centre in Candi Jago (p236).

Many students come to Indonesia to study Bahasa Indonesia. The better private courses can charge US$15 or more per hour, though many offer individual tuition. Some of the embassies arrange courses, or have information about teachers and language institutes. Courses are offered in Bandung (p142) and Yogyakarta (p177), both in Java.

CUSTOMS

Customs regulations allow you to bring in a maximum of 1L of alcohol, and 200 cigarettes or 50 cigars or 100g of tobacco.

Prohibited items include narcotics, arms and ammunition, explosives, laser guns, transceivers, cordless telephones and pornography. Film, pre-recorded video tapes, video laser discs or records must be declared and censored. A ban on printed matter in Chinese characters has been lifted, however, customs forms had not been updated at the time of writing. Chinese medicines must be registered with the Indonesian Department of Health in Jakarta.

No restrictions apply on the import/export of foreign currency. You can import/export up to 5,000,000Rp without having to declare it. Amounts between 5,000,000Rp and 10,000,000Rp need to be declared and anything over 10,000,000Rp requires approval from the Central Bank in Jakarta, or from Indonesian representatives abroad.

DANGERS & ANNOYANCES

Drugs

Indonesia has demonstrated its zero-tolerance policy towards drugs with a spate of high-profile arrests and convictions recently. In 2005 Australian Schapelle Corby captured news headlines around the world when she was arrested in Bali for allegedly smuggling 4kg of marijuana into the country. She received a 20-year prison sentence. In the same year five Australians were caught with several kilograms of heroin strapped to their bodies at Denpasar airport. Along with their accomplices they became known (sensationally) as the 'Bali Nine'. Seven received life sentences (later reduced to 20 years) and two were sentenced to death by firing squad.

Indonesia has also become something of an Asian centre for ecstasy, which fuels the local rave scenes in Bali, Jakarta and other big cities. In August 2005, the Indonesian government announced random raids of nightclubs in Jakarta and Bali and mandatory urine tests for anyone found with drugs. Several foreigners have consequently been arrested and convicted. There is no differentiation between 'personal use' and 'distribution' and even one pill is sufficient to land you in jail for many years. Hotel owners are also required by law to report offenders.

In areas where nightclubs are concentrated, such as Bali, you'll still get plenty of offers. More often than not those 'buddha sticks' are banana leaves, 'hashish' is boot polish and 'ecstasy' is a multicoloured Panadol. But taking any risks is just stupid.

Personal Space

You tend to get stared at when in places few foreigners visit, but overall, Indonesians stand back and look, rather than gather around you. Those who do come right up to you are usually kids. The other habit which is altogether ordinary to Indonesians is touching between those of the same gender. The Indonesians are an extraordinarily physical people: they'll hold onto your knee for balance as they get into a bemo, reach out and touch your arm while making a point in conversation, or simply touch you every time they mean to speak to you. All this is considered friendly.

Safety

In the wake of the 2002 and 2005 Bali bombings (see p281), Indonesians have made ongoing efforts to revive what was already a suffering tourist industry. There has been an increase in security measures at airports and tourist centres and extremist organisations have been closed down or disbanded. It's impossible to say where such attacks will or won't occur, yet the image Indonesia has been tainted with since the bombings – as a terrorism hotspot – has been damaging.

Security issues in Indonesia are often exaggerated by the foreign media, who make it seem like the whole nation is in turmoil. Foreign governments add to the hype with heavy-handed, blanket travel warnings. While it's true that small sections of Indonesia experience flashes of conflict, overall

THE BEST ADVICE

If travelling to a potentially risky region of Indonesia check the safety situation with your embassy in Jakarta, or the travel advisory on its website, but bear in mind that these generally take a conservative and overly cautious view.

Government travel advisories:

Australia (☎ 1300 139 281; www.smarttraveller.gov.au)
Canada (☎ 1 800 267 6788; www.voyage.gc.ca)
Germany (☎ 030-5000 2000; www.auswaertiges-amt.de)
Japan (☎ 03-3580 3311; www.anzen.mofa.go.jp)
Netherlands (☎ 070 3486486; www.minbuza.nl)
New Zealand (☎ 04-439 8000; www.mfat.govt.nz)
UK (☎ 0845 850 2829; www.fco.gov.uk/travel)
US (☎ 1-888 407 4747; www.travel.state.gov)

the archipelago is quite safe. Government travel warnings have the potential to protect travellers from risk, but their impact on local tourism industries is decimating. Maluku in particular is experiencing a burst of growth and calm, and travel there is far easier and safer than ever. Yet the province is still on the 'do not travel' list in many travel advisories.

On the other hand, regional and separatist conflicts remain an ongoing problem in Papua. Western mining companies are targeted by frustrated indigenous people here and also in Nusa Tenggara. But most people know the difference between a multinational and a tourist and conflicts rarely affect travellers.

Of course the best ways to ensure your safety are to keep abreast of the news, plan accordingly and apply common sense. Check official travel advisories (see the boxed text, opposite). Monitor local and international media reports and seek the advice of other travellers and locals. Lonely Planet's Thorn Tree (http://thorntree.lonelyplanet.com) is an online travel forum and another excellent source of information.

Scams

As in most poor countries, plenty of people are out to relieve you of your money in one way or another. It's really hard to say when an 'accepted' practice like overcharging becomes an unacceptable rip-off, but plenty of instances of practised deceit occur.

Con artists are always to be found. Usually those smooth talkers are fairly harmless guides seeking to lead you to a shop where they receive a commission. Just beware of instant friends and watch out for excessive commissions. Yogyakarta's batik salespeople fall into this category.

As the main tourist destination, Bali is the home of many scams. Is it possible for a Kuta moneychanger not to short-change you? Then there's the friendly local who discovers a serious problem with your car or motorbike and urgently gets one of his contacts to fix it for you, for an outrageous amount of money.

An invite to visit a traditional Balinese village from an instant friend may end up with a hard-luck story designed to extract money. It is almost always a con. Indonesia is full of heart-wrenching stories of hardship and poverty, and Bali is better off than most provinces. Most Indonesians suffer in silence and would never ask for money; consider giving to aid programmes if you want to help.

Another scam involves being invited to someone's house, then introduced to a card game where you can't lose. Of course, you do lose – big time. These gangs move around.

In Jakarta, police impostors searching foreigners for drugs and trying to extract money have been reported.

Theft

Theft can be a problem. However, if you are mindful of your valuables and take precautions, the chances of being ripped off are small. Most thefts are the result of carelessness or naivety. The chances of theft are highest in crowded places and when travelling on public bemo, buses and trains.

Pickpockets are common, and their crowded bus and train stations are favourite haunts, as are major tourist areas. Compared to most Indonesians, tourists are rich and this attracts thieves. Bali, particularly Kuta, is No 1 in the thievery stakes, closely followed by the other main tourist areas of Yogyakarta and Lombok. The thieves are very skilful and often work in gangs – if you find yourself being hassled and jostled, check your wallet, watch and bag. The Bahasa Indonesia word for thief is *pencuri*. In Kuta, the gangs of small children waving necklaces for sale are notorious pickpockets.

Do not leave your valuables unattended, and in crowded places hold your handbag or day pack closely. A money belt worn under your clothes is the safest way to carry your passport, cash and travellers cheques.

Keep an eye on your luggage if it's stored on the roof of a bus; bag slashing and theft from bags next to you inside the bus are also hazards. Locks on your bags are mandatory – travelling without them is like waving a 'come and get it' banner.

Java and Sumatra are the worst places for theft on buses. Organised gangs board the bus and take the seat behind you. If you fall asleep or put your bag on the floor, they will slash it and be gone with your gear before you know it. The chances of this happening are very slight, but the gangs do target tourists. Economy buses are the worst but travelling deluxe is no guarantee.

Always lock your hotel-room door and windows at night and whenever you go out, even if momentarily. Don't leave valuables, cash or travellers cheques lying around in open view inside your room. It is wise to keep valuables hidden and locked inside your luggage; better hotels have safe storage facilities.

Report any theft to the police, but without witnesses don't expect action. Bus companies and hotels will automatically deny any responsibility. Reported theft is usually termed *kehilangan*, or 'loss' – you lost it and it is your responsibility to prove theft. Police will provide a report, which is necessary for replacement passports and travellers cheques, and for insurance claims.

Be wary and know where your valuables are at all times – but at the same time remember that the overwhelming majority of Indonesians are honest and will go out of their way to look after a visitor. Out in the villages, far removed from the big cities and tourist areas, theft is a foreign concept.

DISABLED TRAVELLERS

Indonesia has very little supportive legislation or special programmes for disabled people, and is a difficult destination for those with limited mobility.

At Indonesian airports, arriving and departing passengers usually have to walk across the tarmac to their planes, and that includes Ngurah Rai airport in Bali. Check with airlines to see what arrangements can be made and if they can provide skychairs. Jakarta airport has direct access and lifts, but not all flights use these facilities. International airlines are usually helpful, but domestic flights are much more problematic.

Building regulations in Indonesia do not specify disabled access, and even international hotels such as the Sheraton, Hyatt and Hilton rarely have facilities. Only top-end and upper-midrange hotels have lifts.

Pavements are a minefield of potholes, loose manholes, parked motorcycles and all sorts of street life, and are very rarely level for long until the next set of steps. Even the able-bodied walk on roads rather than negotiate the hassle of the pavement.

Public transport is also difficult, but cars with a driver can be hired readily at cheap rates and are much more common than self-drive rentals. Minibuses are easily hired but none have wheelchair access. Guides are found readily in the tourist areas and, though not usual, they could be hired as helpers if needed.

Bali, with its wide range of tourist services and facilities, is the most favourable destination for disabled travellers.

For unsighted travellers or those with only limited vision, Indonesia would definitely be a rewarding destination. Music is heard everywhere, Indonesians are always ready to chat, and the exotic smells of incense and tropical fruit linger in the air. With a sighted companion, many places should be reasonably accessible.

There are no Indonesia-specific resources for disabled travellers, however Disability World (www.disabilityworld.org) is a useful website for global trends and progress.

DISCOUNT CARDS

The International Student Identity Card (ISIC) is useful for discounts on domestic flights, although maximum age limits (usually 26) often apply. Some attractions offer student discounts. Click onto www.istc.org for information and details on the application process.

EMBASSIES & CONSULATES

Indonesian Embassies & Consulates

Indonesian embassies and consulates abroad include the following:

Australia Canberra (☎ 02-6250 8600; www.kbri-canberra.org.au; 8 Darwin Ave, Yarralumla, Canberra, ACT 2600) There are also consulates in Adelaide, Darwin, Melbourne, Perth and Sydney.

Canada Ottawa (☎ 613-724 1100; 55 Parkdale Ave, Ottawa, Ontario K1Y 1E5); Toronto (☎ 416-360 4020; 129 Jarvis St); Vancouver (☎ 604-682 8855; 1630 Alberni St)

France Marseilles (☎ 04-9123 0160; 25 Blvd, Carmagnole); Paris (☎ 01-45 03 07 60; 47-49 Rue Cortambert, 75116 Paris)

Germany Berlin (☎ 030-478 070; Lehrter St 16-17, 10557 Berlin); Frankfurt (☎ 69-247 0908; Zeppelin Alle 23); Hamburg (☎ 40-512 071; Bebelalle 14)

Ireland Dublin (☎ 353 852 491; 25 Kilvere Rathfarnham, Dublin)

Japan Fukoka (☎ 092-761 3031; Kyuden Bldg 1-82, Watanabe–Dori–Chome, Chou-Ku, Fukuoka-Shi); Osaka (☎ 83-06 6252 9823; 6th fl, Daiwa Bank Semba Bldg, 4-21 Minami Semba 4-Chome, Chuo-Ku); Sapporo (☎ 011-251 6002; 883-3 Chome 4-Jo, Miyayanomori, Chuo-Ku, Sapporo Shís); Tokyo (☎ 03-3441 4201; 5-2-9 Higashi Gotanda, Shinagawa-ku, Tokyo)

Malaysia Kota Kinabalu (☎ 60-088 218 600; Lorong Kemajuan, Karamunsing); Kuala Lumpur (☎ 03-2145-2011; 233 Jalan Tun Razak, Kuala Lumpur); Kuching (☎ 241734; 111 Jln Tun Abang Hj Openg); Penang (☎ 04-2267 412; 467, Jln Burma)
Netherlands The Hague (☎ 070-310 8100; 8 Tobias Asserlaan, 2517 KC Den Haag)
New Zealand Auckland (☎ 09-300 9000; 2nd fl, 132 Vincent St); Wellington (☎ 04-4758 697; 70 Glen Rd, Kelburn, Wellington)
Papua New Guinea Port Moresby (☎ 675-325 3116; 1+2/410, Kiroki St, Sir John Guise Dr, Waigani, Port Moresby); Vanimo (☎ 675-857 1371; Sandaun province)
Philippines Davao (☎ 63-83 299 2930; Ecoland Subdivision, Davao City); Manila (☎ 02-892 5061; 185 Salcedo St, Legaspi Village, Makati, Manila)
Singapore Singapore (☎ 737 7422; 7 Chatsworth Rd, Singapore)
Thailand Bangkok (☎ 02-252 3135; 600-602 Petchburi Rd, Phyathai, Bangkok)
Timor Leste Dili (☎ 670-312 333; Komplek Pertamina, Pantai Kelapa, Correios, Dili)
UK London (☎ 020-7499 7661; 38 Grosvenor Square, London W1K 2HW)
USA Chicago (☎ 312-345 9300; 72 East Randolph St); Houston (☎ 713-785 1691; 10900 Richmond Ave); Los Angeles (☎ 213-383 5126; 3457 Wilshire Blvd); New York (☎ 212-879 0600; 5 East 68th St); San Francisco (☎ 415-474 9571; 1111 Columbus Ave); Washington DC (☎ 202-775 5200; 2020 Massachusetts Ave NW, Washington DC 20036)

Embassies in Indonesia

It's important to realise what your own embassy can and can't do to help you if you get into trouble. Generally speaking, it won't be much help if whatever trouble you're in is remotely your own fault. Remember that you are bound by the laws of the country you are in. In genuine emergencies you might get some assistance, but only if other channels have been exhausted. If you have all your money and documents stolen, your embassy might assist with getting a new passport, but that's about it.

Most foreign embassies are located in Jakarta and Bali. There are also some in towns close to foreign borders; see regional chapters for details.

BALI

All telephone numbers take the area code ☎ 0361:

Australia (Map pp304-5; ☎ 241118; Jl Hayam Wuruk 88B, Renon, Denpasar) The Australian consulate has a consular-sharing agreement with Canada.
France (Map p293; ☎ 285485; Jl Mertasari, Gang II 8, Sanur)
Germany (Map p293; ☎ 288535; Jl Pantai Karang 17, Batujimbar, Sanur)
Japan (Map pp304-5; ☎ 227628; Jl Raya Puputan 170, Renon, Denpasar)
Netherlands (Map p278; ☎ 761506; Jl Imam Bonjol, Kuta)
Switzerland (Map p278; ☎ 751735; Kuta Galleria, Blok Valet 2, 12, Jl Patih Jelantik, Kuta)
UK (Map p293; ☎ 270601; Jl Tirtanadi 20, Sanur)
USA (Map pp304-5; ☎ 233605; Jl Hayam Wuruk 188, Renon, Denpasar)

JAKARTA

All phone numbers take area code ☎ 021:

Australia (Map pp100-1; ☎ 25505555; Jl HR Rasuna Said Kav 15-16)
Brunei (Map p106; ☎ 31906080; Jl Tanjung Karang 7)
Canada (Map pp100-1; ☎ 25507800; World Trade Centre, 6th fl, Jl Jenderal Sudirman Kav 29-31)
France (Map p106; ☎ 23557600; Jl Thamrin 20)
Germany (Map p106; ☎ 39855000; Jl Thamrin 1)
Japan (Map p106; ☎ 31924308; Jl Thamrin 24)
Malaysia (Map pp100-1; ☎ 5224947; Jl HR Rasuna Said Kav X/6 No 1)
Myanmar (Map p106; ☎ 3140440; Jl Haji Augus Salim 109)
Netherlands (Map pp100-1; ☎ 5248200; Jl HR Rasuna Said Kav S-3)
New Zealand (Map pp100-1; ☎ 5709460; BRI II Bldg, 23rd fl, Jl Jenderal Sudirman Kav 44-46)
Papua New Guinea (Map pp100-1; ☎ 7251218; 6th fl, Panin Bank Centre, Jl Jenderal Sudirman 1)
Philippines (Map p106; ☎ 3100334; phjkt@indo.net.id; Jl Imam Bonjol 6-8)
Singapore (Map pp100-1; ☎ 5201489; Jl HR Rasuna Said, Block X/4 Kav 2)
Thailand (Map p106; ☎ 3904052; Jl Imam Bonjol 74)
UK (Map p106; ☎ 3156264; Jl Thamrin 75)
USA (Map p106; ☎ 34359000; Jl Merdeka Selatan 4-5)
Vietnam (Map p106; ☎ 3100358; Jl Teuku Umar 25)

MEDAN

All phone numbers take area code ☎ 061:

Australia (Map p384; ☎ 4157810; Australia Centre, Jl RA Kartini 32)
Germany (Map p384; ☎ 4568006; Jl Samanhudi 16)
Japan (Map p384; ☎ 4575193; Wisma BII 5, Jl Diponegoro 18)
Malaysia (Map p384; ☎ 4531342; Jl Diponegoro 43)
Netherlands (Map p384; ☎ 4569853; Jl Monginsidi 45T)
Norway (Map p384; ☎ 4570012; Jl Juanda 24)
Denmark & Finland (Map p384; ☎ 4553020; Jl Hang Jebat 2)

FESTIVALS & EVENTS

With such a diversity of people in Indonesia, there are many local holidays, festivals and cultural events.

Regional tourist offices are the best source of information for all national holidays, regional festivals, and many of the music, dance and theatre performances held throughout the year.

Unless otherwise stated, the dates for the following festivals vary from year to year.

January

Tabut (p434) An Islamic festival held in January or February in Pariaman, West Sumatra. Painted effigies, dancing, singing and music.

Gerebeg (p177) Java's three most colourful festivals are held annually at the end of January and April and the beginning of November.

February

Tai Pei Kong festival (p736) In Manado, Kienteng Ban Hian Kong, Eastern Indonesia's oldest Buddhist temple, plays host to this magnificent festival every February.

Pasola (p603) Nusa Tenggara's biggest festival: vividly dressed teams of horsemen engage in mock, though sometimes bloody, battles. Often coincides with Nyale.

Nyale (p525) Huge fishing festival celebrated by the Sasaks of Lombok. Usually February or March.

March

Kirab Pusaka (p198) This festival has been celebrated in Solo on the first day of the Javanese month of Suro (any time from March to May) since 1633.

April

Festival Teluk Kendari (p711) The Kendari Bay Festival turns the capital of Southeast Sulawesi into a frenzy of celebrations with dragon-boat races, traditional music and partying.

Galungan-Kuningan (p271) Ten-day festivals held in Balinese temples during full-moon periods in April to May and September to November.

Gerebeg See entry under January (above).

May

Waisak (p170) Borobudur flourishes with thousands of pilgrims and the saffron hue of Buddhist monks to celebrate the Buddha's birth, enlightenment and reaching of nirvana.

Sekaten (p198) The birth of the Prophet Muhammad is celebrated in the Islamic month of Maurud (from May to July) in Solo, Java. The closing ceremony includes a fair and a huge rice mountain.

June

Yogya Arts festival (p177) Annual festival from 7 June to 7 July, with a wide range of shows and exhibitions.

Bali Arts Festival (p303) Month-long festival starting in mid-June, showcasing traditional Balinese dance, music and crafts.

Danau Toba Festival (p404) Week-long festival held in mid-June with cultural performances and colourful canoe races.

Festival Danau Napabale (p713) Horse combat and kite flying in Latugho, Southeast Sulawesi.

Jakarta Anniversary (p109) Fireworks and the Jakarta Fair kick off Jakarta's birthday, celebrated on 22 June but continuing all the way into mid-July.

Festival of Borobudur (p170) This Borobudur festival features Ramayana-style dance, folk-dancing competitions, handicrafts, white-water rafting and a whole lot more.

July

Tana Toraja funeral festival (p691) A Sulawesi highlight. Held during July and August, Toraja working throughout the country return home for celebrations and funeral rituals.

August

Jayapura Cultural Festival (p829) In the first week of August, dancers and musicians from around the province converge on Jayapura.

Bidar race (p473) Spectacular canoe races held on South Sumatra's Sungai Musi every 17 August (Independence Day) and 16 June (the city's birthday).

Independence Day (p109) Jakarta becomes a spectacle of parades and celebrations every 17 August to mark the country's independence.

Munara Festival (p808) In mid-August, this festival in central Papua's Pulau Biak features fire-walking, traditional dancing and boat races.

Baliem Festival (p826) A celebration of indigenous culture in Papua's Baliem Valley, with mock 'tribal fighting', full traditional regalia, dance and music. Usually 9–14 August.

October

Ubud Writers & Readers Festival (p315) A global festival celebrating the art of writing.

Asmat Art & Culture Festival (p838) Held in the Asmat Region of eastern Papua, this festival showcases renowned woodcarving and traditional dancing. Usually in the first week of October.

November

Gerebeg See entry under January (left).

FOOD

Eating reviews in this book are listed in order of budget, from cheapest to most ex-

RAMADAN

One of the most important months of the Muslim calendar is the fasting month of Ramadan. As a profession of faith and spiritual discipline, Muslims abstain from food, drink, cigarettes and other worldly desires (including sex) from sunrise to sunset. Exemptions from fasting are granted to pregnant women, the ill or infirm, young children and those undertaking extreme physical labour.

Ramadan is often preceded by a cleansing ceremony, Padusan, to prepare for the coming fast (*puasa*). Traditionally, during Ramadan people get up at 3am or 4am to eat (this meal is called *sahur*) and then fast until sunset. Many Muslims visit family graves and royal cemeteries, recite extracts from the Koran, and sprinkle the graves with holy water and flower offerings. Special prayers are said at mosques and at home.

The first day of the 10th month of the Muslim calendar is the end of Ramadan, called Idul Fitri or Lebaran. Mass prayers are held in the early morning, followed by two days of feasting. Extracts from the Koran are read and religious processions take place. During this time of mutual forgiveness, gifts are exchanged and pardon is asked for past wrongdoings. This is the big holiday of the year, a time for rejoicing, and the whole country is on the move as everyone goes home to be with their families.

During Ramadan, many restaurants and warungs are closed in Muslim regions of Indonesia. Those owned by non-Muslims will be open, but in deference to those fasting, they may have covered overhangs or will otherwise appear shut. Ask around for open restaurants. In the big cities, many businesses are open and fasting is less strictly observed. For night owls the cities come alive for the night meal.

Though not all Muslims can keep to the privations of fasting, the overwhelming majority do and you should respect their values. Do not eat, drink or smoke in public or in someone's house. If you must, excuse yourself and go outside.

Ramadan is an interesting time to travel but it can be difficult. Apart from having to hunt down restaurants and abstain from imbibing in public, the first few weeks are not too restrictive, but travel is a real hassle towards the end of Ramadan.

Around a week before and a week after Idul Fitri, transport is chaotic and packed to the gunwales. Don't even consider travelling during this time. You will be better off in non-Muslim areas – eg Bali, east Nusa Tenggara, Maluku or Papua – but even these areas have significant Muslim populations and Idul Fitri is a big national holiday of two days' duration for everyone. Plan well, find yourself an idyllic spot and stay put.

Ramadan and Idul Fitri move back 10 days or so every year, according to the Muslim calendar.

pensive. Prices vary from region to region of course but in most of Indonesia you can tuck into a simple meal at a warung for around 10,000Rp, spend another 10,000Rp or so for a meal at a restaurant and splurge on dinner and a Bintang beer for 30,000Rp and upwards at the finest restaurants.

Indonesia's vast array of culinary delights and regional specialities are explained in detail in the Food & Drink chapter (p81).

GAY & LESBIAN TRAVELLERS

Gay travellers in Indonesia will experience few problems. Physical contact between same-sex couples is quite acceptable, even though a boy and a girl holding hands may be seen as improper. Homosexual behaviour is not illegal, and the age of consent for sexual activity is 16 years. Gay men in Indonesia are referred to as *homo* or *gay;* lesbians are *lesbi.*

Indonesia's community of transvestite/transsexual *waria* – from the words *wanita* (woman) and *pria* (man) – has always had a very public profile. Also known by the less polite term *banci,* they are often extrovert performers as stage entertainers and street-walkers. Islamic groups proscribe homosexuality, but such views are not dominant and there is no queer-bashing or campaigns against gays. It pays to be less overt in some orthodox areas though.

Indonesia has a number of gay and lesbian organisations. The coordinating body is **GAYa Nusantara** (www.gayanusantara.org), which publishes the monthly magazine *GAYa*

Nusantara. In Kuta, **Hanafi** (☎ 756454; www.hanafi.net) is a gay-friendly tour operator who can also organise tours for visitors. **Utopia Asia** (www.utopia-asia.com) also has an extensive list of gay and lesbian venues throughout Indonesia and the rest of Asia.

HOLIDAYS

Public Holidays

Following are the national public holidays in Indonesia. Unless stated, they vary from year to year.

January/February

New Year's Day Celebrated on 1 January.
Muharram (Islamic New Year) Usually late January.
Imlek (Chinese New Year) National holiday in late January to early February.

March/April

Good Friday Late March or early April.
Paskah (Easter) Late March or early April.
Nyepi (Balinese New Year) Balinese businesses close down for one day usually in April, sometimes in March.

April/May

Maulud Nabi Muhammed The birthday of the Prophet Muhammed. Celebrated on one day between late March and early May.
Waisak Day Marks the Buddha's birth, enlightenment and death. Falls in May.
Ascension of Christ May.

August

Hari Proklamasi Kemerdekaan (Independence Day) 17 August. Independence Day is a national public holiday.

September

Isra Miraj Nabi Muhammed Celebration of the ascension of the Prophet Muhammed. Held on one day between late August and mid-September.

October/November

Idul Fitri Also known as Lebaran, this two-day national public holiday marks the end of Ramadan. Held sometime between mid-October and mid-November.

December

Idul Adha Muslim festival held between December and January.
Hari Natal (Christmas Day) Celebrated on 25 December.

School Holidays

Indonesian school holidays vary slightly from province to province but the following should give you a good idea of when they fall. 'Winter holiday' usually falls in the first week of March, 'spring holiday' spans two weeks, usually from late April to early May, 'summer holiday' runs from the very end of June to the first week in September. Then there's a mid-term holiday during the last two weeks of October and lastly Christmas holidays from around December 21 to the first week in January.

INSURANCE

A travel-insurance policy to cover theft, loss and medical problems is essential. There is a wide variety of policies, and your travel agent will have recommendations, but if you're planning to travel to remote areas it's wise to take a policy that will facilitate a speedy evacuation in the event of a medical emergency.

Theft is a potential problem in Indonesia (see p851), so make sure that your policy covers expensive items adequately. Many policies have restrictions on laptop computers and expensive camera gear, and refunds are often for depreciated value, not replacement value.

For information on health insurance, see p879 and for details on car insurance see p876.

INTERNET ACCESS

Internet cafés continue to sprout up across Indonesia, especially in tourist areas and sizable towns. Rates and server speeds vary: expect to pay between 6000Rp and 15,000Rp per hour (more in hotel business centres), and don't be in a hurry. Rural areas are yet to be connected.

In the more developed areas of Bali and Java you may be able to connect your laptop to a phone line if staying in a top-end hotel. Even better is the gradual spread of wireless connection capabilities, which are cropping up in places as far flung as Central Kalimantan. This is useful only if you have your own laptop and it has wireless internet capabilities.

LEGAL MATTERS

Drugs, gambling and pornography are illegal, and it is an offence to engage in paid work or stay in the country for more than 30 days on a tourist visa. Being caught with drugs will result in jail and quite probably a harsh prison sentence (see p850). Generally, you are otherwise unlikely to have any encounters with the police unless you commit a traffic infringement.

Despite claims of reform, corruption is still widespread. Police stop motorists on minor or dubious traffic infringements in the hope of obtaining bribes. Usually there'll be talk about a trip to the police station and lengthy delays, if not court appearances. Don't become impatient or aggressive, or demand your rights. Sit through the lecture and don't offer a bribe – the police may let you off on a warning or will broach the subject after the lecture. If it looks like you will have to go to a station, play the worried tourist and ask if it is possible to pay the fine on the spot. For minor traffic infringements, 50,000Rp is usually plenty, but Balinese police may want more.

In the case of an accident involving serious injury or death, the best advice is to drive straight to the nearest police station, unless you are in an isolated area and can offer assistance. If you hit someone in a village, an angry mob will soon gather. The police may detain you but they will sort it out and you will be safe.

Tourists are unlikely to come across any other problems with officialdom or requests to pay bribes. If you need to report a crime, head to a police station in respectable dress with an Indonesian friend or interpreter in tow. If you find yourself in real trouble with the law contact your embassy or consulate immediately. They will not be able to arrange bail but will be able to provide you with an interpreter and may even be able to suggest legal council.

MAPS

Locally produced maps are often inaccurate. Periplus produces excellent maps of most of the archipelago and includes maps of the major cities. The Nelles Verlag map series covers Indonesia in a number of separate sheets, and they're usually very reliable. Both series are available in Indonesia and overseas.

The Directorate General of Tourism publishes a free, useful information booklet, the *Indonesia Tourist Map,* which includes maps of Java, Bali, Sumatra and Sulawesi, and a good overall map of Indonesia. Maps of major Javanese, Sumatran and Balinese cities are easy enough to come by – ask at a tourist office or try bookshops, airports and major hotels. Elsewhere in Indonesia, maps can be hard to find.

Hikers will have little chance of finding accurate maps of remote areas. It's far more useful (and wise) to employ the services of a local guide, who will be able to navigate seemingly unchartered territory.

MONEY

The unit of currency used in Indonesia is the rupiah (Rp). Denominations of 25, 50, 100 and 500 rupiah are in circulation in both the old silver-coloured coins and the newer bronze-coloured coins. A 1000Rp coin is also minted but rarely seen, and the 25Rp coin has almost vanished. Notes come in 500, 1000, 5000, 10,000, 20,000, 50,000 and 100,000 rupiah denominations.

See this book's inside front cover for exchange rates and p22 for more information about general costs in Indonesia.

There are plenty of options for exchanging money in Indonesia, and it's wise to use all of them: carry some plastic, travellers cheques and some cash.

ATMs

ATMs are increasingly common throughout Indonesia and most now accept Visa, Mastercard, Maestro and Cirrus. Confirm with your bank at home to ensure you can use ATM facilities in Indonesia, and also ask what charges apply.

ATMs in Indonesia have a maximum limit for withdrawals, sometimes it is 2,000,000Rp, but can be as low as 400,000Rp, which is not much in foreign currency terms. Problems can occur if your bank has a minimum withdrawal limit that is higher than the ATM's maximum. In this case your transaction will be refused.

These days, most large towns have banks with ATMs, but as they often experience downtime it's good to keep your options open.

Cash & Travellers Cheques

The US dollar and, to a lesser degree, the euro, are the most widely accepted foreign currencies in Indonesia. Australian, British and Japanese currencies are exchangeable in the most touristed areas of Bali and Java. American Express (Amex) are the most widely accepted travellers cheques. When heading for really remote places, carry stacks of rupiah, as foreign exchange may be limited to US dollars only or simply impossible. Emergency cash in the money belt is a wise stash for Maluku and Papua, where credit cards are rarely accepted anywhere and ATMs are fewer and farther between. Have a mix of notes – breaking even a 20,000Rp note in a warung can be a major hassle out in the villages.

Credit Cards

If you have a credit card, don't leave home without it. If you are travelling on a low budget, credit cards are of limited use for day-to-day travel expenses, as it is only the expensive hotels, restaurants and shops that accept them (and they're virtually useless in places like Papua and Maluku). However, they are very useful for major purchases like airline tickets (though smaller offices in the backblocks may not accept them).

MasterCard and Visa are the most widely accepted credit cards. Amex is a distant third. Cash can be obtained at Amex agents, usually PT Pacto, in major cities only.

Credit cards can be a convenient way to access money, especially if you always keep your account in the black. Cash advances on Visa and MasterCard can be obtained over the counter at many banks (as well as from ATMs), though some charge transaction fees of around 5000Rp – always ask first.

Cash advances are readily obtainable in the main cities, and many regional towns have banks that accept credit cards, but don't rely on them solely. In more remote areas, you're asking for trouble if all you have is a credit card.

Banks often charge transaction fees for the use of credit cards overseas, often much higher than the 1% commission charged on travellers cheques; check this with your bank.

Moneychangers

Moneychangers and banks can be very particular about the condition of cash: torn or marked notes are often refused, as are notes more than five years old. Outside the main cities in Java and Bali, exchanging currencies other than US dollars will require more legwork – first to find a bank that will accept them and second to find one that gives a good rate.

Rates vary, so it pays to shop around. The best rates of exchange are found in Jakarta and Bali. Touristy places have lots of moneychangers as well as banks; banks usually have better exchange rates, though moneychangers may offer the best rates for cash. When changing cash, bigger notes are better – a US$100 note will attract a better exchange rate than a US$20 note.

Moneychangers in Bali offer some of the best rates in Indonesia *if* you don't get short-changed or charged commission. Signboard rates are often a fabrication, and after signing your travellers cheque you may find that a 10% (or higher) commission applies. Be sure to double-check the conversion rate and be aware that some dubious operators even rig their calculators.

Always count your rupiah before you hand over your travellers cheques or foreign currency. Several readers' letters have warned of being short-changed through sleight of hand, particularly in Kuta. A way to avoid this is to count the rupiah in front of the moneychanger. When you are satisfied you have received the correct amount, hand over your currency or travellers cheques. If there are any problems during the transaction, leave with your cash and try another moneychanger.

While the chances of getting short-changed at a bank are perhaps 50 to one, at a Kuta moneychanger the odds are more like 50-50. Moneychangers elsewhere are much less of a problem, but offer lower rates.

PHOTOGRAPHY & VIDEO

Film is cheap and Indonesia is an incredibly photogenic country, so you can easily whip through large quantities of film. Colour print film is preferred; slide film and B&W film are not as readily available. In Jakarta and Bali you can usually find most types of film and video tape. Fuji is by far the most widely available brand for prints and slides.

Developing and printing is cheap. Colour film costs around 35,000Rp for a roll of 36 and slide costs extra, depending on the brand and make. Slide film can be developed in two or three days, and colour print film can be done the same day through photographic shops in major towns all across the archipelago. Try a shop out with one roll before you commit all your holiday snaps. The quality is variable but often good.

Digital cameras are fast replacing film, and facilities for users are following suit. Like anything, it's easiest in Jakarta and Bali to transfer digital images onto a CD. Elsewhere facilities are restricted to large cities. The costs varies wildly.

Indonesia and Indonesians can be very photogenic, but whatever you do, photograph with discretion and manners. It's always polite to ask first, and if the person says no, don't take the photo. A gesture, a smile and a nod are all that is usually necessary. Few subjects expect payment but all will appreciate a copy of the photo or at least a glimpse of its digital form.

Lonely Planet's *Travel Photography* offers helpful tips for capturing the visual splendour of Indonesia on film.

POST

Poste restante is reasonably efficient in Indonesia. Expected mail always seems to arrive at its destination – eventually. Have your letters addressed to you with your surname in underlined capitals, but check for your mail under both your first and family names.

Mail delivered to Australia or the USA usually takes around 10 to 15 days; to Europe it takes up to three weeks. A postcard/letter to the USA costs 5000/10,000Rp; to Australia 7500/15,000Rp; and to the UK 8000/18,000Rp. For anything over 20g, the charge is based on weight. Sending large parcels can be quite expensive. Those weighing a maximum of 7kg can be sent by airmail, or by cheaper sea mail for parcels up to 10kg.

SHOPPING

Indonesia is a great place to buy arts and crafts. The range is amazing and the prices cheap.

Souvenir vendors positively swarm around heavily touristed places. Off the beaten track, shopping is more relaxed. If you're an art collector, you'll find plenty of chances to stock up on unusual items. Wood carvings are on sale everywhere. Batik and ikat (a form of dyed woven cloth; see p70) attract a steady stream of foreign art enthusiasts. Good pottery is available, mostly on Lombok and in Java. See p72 for an overview.

Bali is a shoppers' paradise, with crafts from all over Indonesia. Jl Legian in Kuta (p286) has kilometres of shops selling crafts, antiques, clothes, shoes etc. Sanur, Ubud and other tourist centres are also worthwhile. Yogyakarta (p183) is the best place to shop in Java, where you can purchase hand-crafted batik, silver, puppets and leatherwork. In Sulawesi, silk from Sengkang is some of the finest in Indonesia and can be found alongside Chinese pottery and Makassarese brass work in Makassar (see p678).

Songket, which is silk cloth woven with gold or silver (see p71), is painstakingly

BIZARRE GIFTS FOR AUNTIE

Looking to shock the socks off those removed family members? Indonesia has a couple of quirky curios up its sleeve to satiate daring consumers.

Papua is the leader in this field by way of the penis gourd. Traditionally used by indigenous men in the province's highlands, they are attached to the testicles by a small loop of fibre. Sizes, shapes and colours vary across cultural groups but you can pick one up for around 50,000Rp. This may be a better gift for auntie's new boyfriend and it's bound to add some spice to family reunions. Less risqué gifts from Papua include cassowary-feather head wreaths and bark paintings.

If you actually want to deter annoying family members from reunions then Kalimantan has just the ticket. Once the Dayak weapon of choice for headhunting, the *mandau* is an indigenous machete still slung from the hips of most men in the Kalimantan interior. Today's blades are far plainer and reserved for more domestic purposes, but you can purchase traditional pieces with exquisitely carved wooden handles and bark sheaths. One will set you back around 100,000Rp to 250,000Rp and customs may have a few issues with it, but finding a prominent place to display it at home is worth the effort. Another variety of blade is the kris (see p73), found mainly in Java and Bali.

made into ceremonial sarongs in parts of Sumatra and exquisite examples are up for grabs in Palembang (p474).

Elsewhere in Indonesia you tend to see only locally produced crafts, but of course the price for those items will be much cheaper than in the tourist shops of Bali or Jakarta.

Gastronomes can take some tasty packaged wares home and supermarket chains such as Hero and smaller general stores are well stocked. Look for things that will remind you of your trip such as *sambal* (chilli sauce), *kecap manis* (sweet soy sauce; ABC is a popular brand), sachets of *jamu* (herbal medicine), ready-to-fry *kerupuk* (crackers) and strange-flavoured lollies (candy) such as durian or *asam* (tamarind). A popular treat from the Banda Islands in Maluku is dried nutmeg fruit (see the boxed text, p749). If you can lift it, a *cobek* and *ulek-ulek* (mortar and pestle) is needed for making your own *sambal*. Coconut-shell ladles and handmade wire strainers are other good options. Although big, a rice pot with a built-in colander is another culinary souvenir.

Many foreigners get addicted to Indonesian coffee, which is superb. Both ground coffee and beans can be bought in supermarkets, but the best coffee is bought fresh in markets. Indonesian tea – black, jasmine or green, loose leaf or in bags – is another popular product. And perhaps you'll want to pick up some tea lids to keep your brew warm.

Bali produces a fair amount of alcohol, including rice wine and grape wine, both of which can be found at Denpasar airport as well as local stores.

Bargaining

Many everyday purchases in Indonesia require bargaining. This applies particularly to handicrafts, artwork and any tourist items, but can also apply to almost anything you buy. As a general rule, if prices are displayed, prices are fixed; if not, bargaining may be possible. The exception is tourist shops, especially those selling artwork, where price tags are often absurdly inflated for the unwary – hard bargaining is always required.

When bargaining, it's usually best to ask the seller their price rather than make an initial offer. As a rule of thumb, your starting price could be anything from a third to two-thirds of the asking price – assuming that the asking price is not completely crazy, which it can be in tourist areas. Then with offer and counter-offer you move closer to an acceptable price.

A few rules apply to good bargaining. First of all, it's not a question of life or death, where every rupiah you chisel away makes a difference. Don't pass up something that you really want and that's expensive or unobtainable at home because the seller won't come down a few hundred rupiah. Secondly, when your offer is accepted you have to buy it – don't then change your mind and decide you don't want it after all. Thirdly, while bargaining may seem to have a competitive element to it, try to apply it mostly to shopping. It's a mean victory knocking a poor *becak* (bicycle-rickshaw) driver down from 4000Rp to 3500Rp for a ride.

Don't get hassled by bargaining and don't go around feeling that you're being ripped off all the time – too many travellers do. It is very easy to become obsessed with getting the 'local' price. Even locals don't always get the local price. In Indonesia, if you are rich it is expected that you pay more, and *all* Westerners are rich when compared to the grinding poverty of most Indonesians.

SOLO TRAVELLERS

Solo travellers will receive little attention in Bali and the more heavily populated areas of Java. Outside of these places however, people are simply curious and a single traveller sporting a backpack will always attract wide eyes and 'hello misters'. The more remote the area the greater the focus. Maluku, Papua, Sumatra and Kalimantan encompass vast areas that are virtually untouristed. Be prepared for celebrity status. It's generally harmless and a warm smile will surpass the language barrier and elicit the same in return.

Women travelling on their own in these areas may feel less like a celebrity and more like an enigma. For most rural people, the concept of a woman travelling unaccompanied for no reason other than to travel is somewhat unfathomable. Even if you explain that your husband (real or imagined) is at home/in the next town/on the bus in the next street, it still doesn't explain why you aren't at home rearing children. In Sumatra in particular men are bold and the attention can become more than unwelcome. The best thing to do is simply ignore it and employ common sense. If you've attracted undue attention in daylight don't head out for a beer at night. Be aware of your own personal security. Remote beaches in Papua and Maluku aren't the best places to unwind unless you have a companion in tow. If you're planning a trek into seldom visited territory take the time to research a genuine and reliable guide. See p863 for more information.

TELEPHONE

Telkom, the government-run telecommunications company, has offices *(kantor Telkom)* in many cities and towns. They are usually open 24 hours, and offer telephone and often fax services. These are the cheapest places to make international and long-distance *(inter-lokal)* phone calls, and they often have Home Country Direct phones or allow collect calls.

Telecommunications agencies in Indonesia, either Telkom or privately run, are called wartel, *warpostel* or *warparpostel* and offer the same services. They are often more convenient than Telkom offices, but may be marginally more expensive and usually don't offer a collect-call service.

Domestic calls are charged according to a system of zones – the cost jumps dramatically if phoning other provinces. If making a long-distance phone call inside Indonesia dial the area code (listed beneath town headings in this book) and then the number you want to reach.

Mobile Phones

Indonesia has a number of GSM (global) networks, including Telkomsel, Satelindo, Excelcomindo, Indosat, Lippo Telecom and Telkomobile. All have wide coverage in Java, Bali and the main regional centres. Telkomsel and Excelcomindo have the most extensive networks.

If your phone company offers international roaming for Indonesia, you can use your 'handphone' (as it's called in Indonesia) and home SIM card while there. Mobile calls are cheap in Indonesia, but check the roaming rates charged by your company. Some charge many times higher than Indonesian companies.

Indonesian telephone companies sell SIM cards that you can plug into your phone. This is usually cheaper, especially if you will be making a lot of local calls, and it will give you a local number. Telkomsel's simPATI cards are readily available in the big cities (many Fuji photo shops stock them).

Phone Codes

The country code for Indonesia is ☎ 62. When calling Indonesia from another country dial ☎ 62, then the area code (minus the zero), then the number you want to reach.

To call another country direct from Indonesia dial ☎ 001, then the country code, the area code (minus the initial zero if it has one) and the number you want to reach. All top-end and many midrange hotels offer International Direct Dialling (IDD) on room phones, but their surcharges can be hefty. Calls from a wartel are cheaper.

Phonecards

Most public phones in Indonesia use phonecards. The more common ones use the regular *kartu telepon* (phonecard) with a magnetic strip. The newer ones use a *kartu chip,* which has an electronic chip embedded in it. You can buy phonecards in denominations of 5000Rp, 10,000Rp, 25,000Rp, 50,000Rp and 100,000Rp at wartel, moneychangers, post offices and many shops. An international call from a card phone costs about the same per minute as a call from a wartel.

TIME

There are three time zones in Indonesia. Java, Sumatra, and West and Central Kalimantan are on Western Indonesian Time, which is seven hours ahead of GMT/UTC (Greenwich Mean Time/Universal Time Coordinated). Bali, Nusa Tenggara, South and East Kalimantan, and Sulawesi are on Central Indonesian Time, which is eight hours ahead of GMT/UTC. Papua and Maluku are on Eastern Indonesian Time, nine hours ahead of GMT/UTC. In a country straddling the equator, there is of course no daylight-saving time.

Allowing for variations due to daylight saving, when it is noon in Jakarta it is 9pm the previous day in San Francisco or Los Angeles, midnight in New York, 5am in London, 1pm in Singapore and Makassar,

2pm in Jayapura and 3pm in Melbourne or Sydney.

Strung out along the equator, Indonesia has days and nights that are approximately equal in length, and sunrises and sunsets occur very rapidly with almost no twilight. Sunrise is around 5.30am to 6am and sunset is around 5.30pm to 6pm, varying slightly depending on distance from the equator.

TOILETS & MANDIS

One thing you'll have to learn to deal with is the Indonesian bathroom, which features a large water tank and a plastic scooper. *Kamar mandi* means bathroom and *mandi* means to bathe or wash.

Climbing into the tank is very bad form indeed – it's your water supply and it's also the supply for every other guest that comes after you, so the idea is to keep the water clean. What you're supposed to do is scoop water out of the tank and pour it over yourself. Most of the tourist hotels have showers, and the more expensive ones have hot water and bathtubs.

Indonesian toilets are basically holes in the ground with footrests on either side, although Western-style toilets are becoming more common. To flush the toilet, reach for that plastic scooper, take water from the tank and flush it away.

As for toilet paper, it is seldom supplied in public places, though you can easily buy your own. Indonesians rarely use the stuff and the method is to use the left hand and copious quantities of water – again, keep that scooper handy. Some Westerners easily adapt to this method, but many do not. If you need to use toilet paper, see if there is a wastebasket next to the toilet (that's where the paper should go, not down the toilet). If you plug up a hotel's plumbing with toilet paper, the management is going to get angry.

Kamar kecil is Bahasa Indonesia for toilet, but people usually understand 'way-say' (WC). *Wanita* means women and *pria* means men.

TOURIST INFORMATION

Indonesia's national tourist organisation, the **Directorate General of Tourism** (☎ 021-3838000; www.tourismindonesia.com, www.budpar.go.id; Jl Merdeka Barat 16-19, Jakarta), maintains a head office in Jakarta as well as offices in each province. They produce some literature but are generally not the place to have specific queries answered.

The usefulness of tourist offices varies greatly from place to place. Offices in tourist meccas such as Bali or Yogyakarta provide good maps and information, while offices in the less visited areas may have nothing to offer at all. They'll always try to help, but many offices are a long way out of town and staffed by career bureaucrats with little interest in or idea of tourism, and unfortunately many don't speak English.

VISAS

The following information was correct at the time of writing, but Indonesian visa requirements are prone to wild fluctuations so you need to contact the Indonesian embassy in your home country before you plan your trip.

Study & Work Visas

You can arrange visas for study, short-term research, visiting family and similar purposes if you have a sponsor, such as an educational institution. These social/cultural *(sosial/budaya)* visas must be applied for at an Indonesian embassy or consulate overseas. Normally valid for three months on arrival, they can be extended every month after that for up to six months without leaving the country. Fees apply.

People wishing to study and work in Indonesia must apply directly to the Central Immigration Office in Jakarta (p102) for a Limited-Stay Visa (Kartu Izin Tinggal Terbatas, or Kitas). If you're planning to work in Indonesia get your employer to organise your visa – it's a long and complicated process. Local embassies cannot issue these visas unless, and until, special authorisation is given by the Immigration Office in Indonesia. In the first instance though, call your nearest embassy for the most direct avenue. Those granted limited stay are issued a Kitas card, often referred to as the KIMS card.

The 30-day tourist visa supposedly also covers business travel where the holder is not employed in Indonesia. Visits for conventions or exhibitions are not a problem, but you may be asked a lot of questions if you put 'business' as a reason for travel on your disembarkation card. Inquire at an Indonesian embassy before departure.

Transport

CONTENTS

THINGS CHANGE...

The information in this chapter is particularly vulnerable to change. Check directly with the airline or a travel agent to make sure you understand how a fare (and ticket you may buy) works and be aware of the security requirements for international travel. Shop carefully. The details given in this chapter should be regarded as pointers and are not a substitute for your own careful, up-to-date research.

GETTING THERE & AWAY

ENTERING THE COUNTRY

Entering Indonesia by air is relatively simple and straightforward, particularly if you're eligible for a VOA (visa on arrival); see p862 for important information regarding all visas. Numerous sea ports are similarly easy, and if you're arriving by land you'll have no problems as long as you have a valid visa.

Passport

Check your passport expiry date. Indonesia requires that your passport be valid for six months following your date of arrival. Before passing through immigration you will fill out a disembarkation card, half of which you must keep to give to immigration when you leave the country.

At the time of writing, nationals and passport holders of Israel were not permitted to enter the country unless special authorisation had been granted from the Immigration Office in Indonesia. See p862 for information on visas.

AIR

Indonesia is well connected to the rest of the world by numerous international airlines. Flights from neighbouring countries also stop in several Indonesian cities. Singapore has some of the cheapest flights to Indonesia so it may be cheaper to fly there and then enter Indonesia by air or ship. From Penang in Malaysia, you can take a short flight or ferry to Medan in Sumatra.

Airports & Airlines

The principal gateways for entry to Indonesia are Jakarta's **Soekarno-Hatta international airport** (☎ 021 550 5179; ap2_cgk@angkasapura2.co.id), which sits 35km west of the city centre, and Bali's smaller **Ngurah Rai international airport** (☎ 0361-751011; www.angkasapura1.co.id/eng/location/bali.htm; Jl Raya, Denpasar), which is about 15km south of Denpasar.

Indonesia's national airline, **Garuda** (Garuda Indonesia; ☎ 021-23519999 www.garuda-indonesia.com) flies to various destinations throughout the world.

AIRLINES FLYING TO & FROM INDONESIA

Airlines servicing Indonesia:

Air Asia (airline code AK; ☎ 0361-760116, 0804 1 333333; www.airasia.com)
Air France (airline code AF; ☎ 020-6545720; www.airfrance.com)
Cathay Pacific Airways (airline code CX; ☎ 021-5151747; www.cathaypacific.com)
China Airlines (airline code CI; ☎ 021-2510788; www.chinaairlines.com)

China Southern Airlines (airline code CZ; ☎ 0211-5202980; www.cs-air.com/en)
Continental Airlines (airline code CO; ☎ 021-334417; www.continental.com)
Eva Air (airline code BR; ☎ 021-5205363; www.evaair.com)
Japan Airlines (airline code JL; ☎ 021-5723211; www.jal.co.jp/en/)
KLM (Royal Dutch Airlines; airline code KL; ☎ 021-2526740; www.klm.com)
Korean Air (airline code KE; ☎ 021-5212180; www.koreanair.com)
Lufthansa (airline code LH; ☎ 021-5702005; www.lufthansa.com)
Malaysia Airlines (airline code MH; ☎ 021-5229690; www.mas.com.my)
Philippine Airlines (airline code PR; ☎ 021-5268668; www.philippineairlines.com)
Qantas Airways (airline code QF; ☎ 021-2300277; www.qantas.com.au)
Silk Air (airline code MI; ☎ 0542730800; www.silkair.com)
Singapore Airlines (airline code SQ; ☎ 021-57903747; www.singaporeair.com)
Thai Airways International (airline code TG; ☎ 021-2302552; www.thaiair.com)

Tickets

With a bit of research – ringing around travel agents, checking internet sites, perusing the travel ads in newspapers – you can often get yourself a good travel deal. Generally, there is nothing to be gained by buying a ticket direct from the airline, unless it's via the internet. Many airlines, full-service and no-frills, offer some excellent fares to web surfers. They may sell seats by auction or simply cut prices to reflect the reduced cost of electronic selling.

Generally the cheapest deals for simple one-way and return flights can be found on online travel sites. These booking agencies are best if your dates are fixed and you are unlikely to need any changes. They are, however, no substitute for a travel agent who knows all about special deals, has strategies for avoiding stopovers, can change your dates and times quickly and easily and can offer advice on everything from which airline has the best vegetarian food to the best travel insurance to bundle with your ticket.

Full-time students and people under 26 years (under 30 in some countries) have access to better deals than other travellers. You have to show a document proving your date of birth or a valid International Student Identity Card (ISIC) when buying your ticket.

Reputable online booking agencies:

Airline Consolidator (www.airlineconsolidator.com)
Cheap Flights (www.cheapflights.com) Informative, US-based site.
Cheap Seats (www.cheapseats.com)
Cheapest Flights (www.cheapestflights.co.uk) Cheap worldwide flights from the UK.
Ebookers (www.ebookers.com) Europe and UK-based sites
Expedia (www.expedia.msn.com) Good for flights from the US, Canada, the UK or Europe.
Hotwire (www.hotwire.com) Good site for US and Canadian departures.
Kilroy Travel (www.kilroytravels.com) Specialising in departures from the Netherlands and Nordic countries.
Opodo (www.opodo.com) Reliable company specialising in fares from Europe.
Orbitz (www.orbitz.com) Excellent site for web-only fares.
Priceline (www.priceline.com) Online fares from the US and Canada.
SideStep (www.sidestep.com) Compares a huge range of fares.
STA (www.statravel.com) Prominent in international student travel, but you don't have to be a student; site linked to worldwide STA sites.
Travel.com (www.travel.com) US-based site but with global variations.
Travelocity (www.travelocity.com) US site that allows you to search fares to/from anywhere.
Trip Advisor (www.tripadvisor.com) US-based.
Zuji (www.zuji.com) Excellent site for departures from Australasia and the Pacific.

INTERCONTINENTAL (RTW) TICKETS

Indonesia is a popular stopover on many round-the-world tickets (RTW), which usually include a combination of airlines and permit you to fly anywhere you want on their route systems so long as you do not backtrack. Most tickets are valid for

DEPARTURE TAX

Airport tax on international flights departing from Jakarta and Denpasar is 100,000Rp. At other airports the charge on international flights is 75,000Rp.

For residents of Indonesia, including foreigners on Kitas (one-year temporary stay/work) visas, a *fiskal* tax of 1,000,000Rp is payable when leaving the country.

TRANSPORT

up to one year. Many of the following sites enable you to build your own round-the-world trip from departure points around the world:

Airbrokers (www.airbrokers.com)
Just Fares.com (www.justfares.com) US company.
Roundtheworld.com (www.roundtheworldflights.com)
Travellers Point (www.travellerspoint.com)
Usit (www.usit.ie) Irish company.
Western Air (www.westernair.co.uk) UK company.

Asia

The most popular flight points from Asia to Indonesia include Penang and Kuala Lumpur (Malaysia) to Medan in Sumatra, and Singapore to Jakarta, Denpasar and Balikpapan.

Rough one-way fare estimates including tax are Singapore to Bali US$160, to Jakarta US$116; and Kuala Lumpur to Medan or Penang $180.

Asian-based travel agents:

Jetabout Holidays (☎ 65-6734 1818; www.jetabout.com.sg) In Singapore.
STA Travel Kuala Lumpur (☎ 603-2148 9800; www.statravel.com.my); Singapore (☎ 65-6773 9188; www.statravel.com.sg)

Australia

There are several flights a week from Sydney, plus less frequent services from Melbourne and Perth, to both Bali and Jakarta; Darwin and Brisbane flights go only to Bali. Garuda and Qantas are the main carriers, but Malaysia Airlines also operates competitive flights. It costs around A$900 for a return fare, including taxes, from Sydney to Bali or Jakarta, and from Melbourne to Bali.

The highest demand for flights is during school holidays, especially the Christmas break – book well in advance.

Travel agents are the best places to shop for cheap tickets, but because Bali is such a popular destination, flight discounting is minimal and most agents prefer to sell package holidays. Packages including return airfare with five to 10 days accommodation can cost little more than the price of an airfare alone.

Well-known agencies:

DWI Tour Australia (☎ 02-9211 3383; dwitour@bigpond.com)
Flight Centre (☎ 131600; www.flightcentre.com.au) Specialists for Bali and Indonesian travel.
San Michel Travel (☎ 1800 22 22 44; www.asiatravel.com.au) Southeast Asia specialists.
STA Travel (☎ 1300 360 960; www.statravel.com.au)

Canada

From Canada you'll probably have to fly via Hong Kong or Singapore, or via Europe from the east coast. Return fares including tax from either Vancouver or Toronto to Jakarta or Bali are around C$1500. Canadian discount air-ticket sellers are also known as consolidators and their airfares tend to be about 10% higher than those sold in the USA.

Useful agencies:

Pacesetter Travel (☎ 1800 387 8827, 604 687 3083; www.pacesettertravel.com)
Travel Cuts (☎ 1866-246 9762; www.travelcuts.com) Canada's national student travel agency, with offices in all major cities.

Continental Europe

Generally there is not much variation in airfare prices between the main European cities. The major airlines and travel agents generally have a number of deals on offer, so shop around. Current return fares cost approximately €1250.

Useful agencies:

Barcelo Viajes (☎ 902 116 226; www.barcelo-viajes.es) In Spain.
CTS Viaggi (☎ 840-501 150; www.cts.it) Student & youth specialist company in Italy.
NBBS Reizen (☎ 0900-10 20 300; www.nbbs.nl) Long-standing agent in the Netherlands.
Nouvelles Frontières (☎ 0825 000 747; www.nouvelles-frontieres.fr)
OTU Voyages (☎ 0820 817 817, 0144 41 38 50; www.otu.fr) French network of student travel agencies; supplies discount tickets to travellers of all ages.
STA Travel (www.statravel.com) Offices throughout the region.
Usit Campus (☎ 01805-788 336; www.usitcampus.de) Offices in Germany.
Voyageurs du Monde (☎ 01 40 29 12 22; www.vdm.com) Based in France.
Wereldcontact (☎ 0343 530530; www.wereldcontact.nl) Dutch agency.

New Zealand

There are no direct flights between Indonesia and New Zealand; however, Air New Zealand, Garuda and Qantas connect Auckland with Denpasar via Sydney, Melbourne or Brisbane. The return economy airfare, including tax, from Auckland to

Denpasar is approximately NZ$1800, or NZ$120 more to Jakarta. It's always a good idea to check out deals in the travel section of the *New Zealand Herald*.

Useful travel agents:

Flight Centre (☎ 0800 243 544; www.flightcentre.co.nz) Branches throughout the country.

House of Travel (☎ 0800 367 468; www.houseoftravel.co.nz) Nation-wide travel agency.

STA Travel (☎ 0508 782 872; www.statravel.co.nz)

UK

There are no direct flights to Indonesia from the UK but there are plenty of airlines offering services via Europe, Asia and/or the Middle East. With so much competition, return fare prices to either Jakarta or Denpasar can get as low as £480, but are usually closer to £600 and have a six-month validity.

Discount air travel is big business in London. Advertisements for many agencies appear in the travel pages of weekend broadsheet newspapers, *Time Out*, the *Evening Standard* and the free magazine *TNT*.

There are plenty of travel agencies worth checking for fares:

Apex Travel (☎ 353 1 2418000; www.apextravel.ie) Irish company with cheap online fares and packages.

Flight Centre (☎ 0870 499 0040; www.flightcentre.co.uk)

North South Travel (☎ 01245 608291; www.northsouthtravel.co.uk) English company offering cheap flights; its profits are channelled into grassroots groups in the developing world.

STA Travel (☎ 0870 163 0026; www.statravel.co.uk) Has branches across the country.

Trailfinders (☎ 0845 058 5858; www.trailfinders.com) Highly reputable with offices in the UK and Ireland.

Travel Bag (☎ 0870 607 0620, 44 20 7136 2856; www.travelbag.co.uk) UK company with online sales as well as offices.

USA

There are no direct flights from the USA, but there are plenty of options that involve a stopover in another Asian destination, such as Taiwan, Hong Kong, Singapore or Malaysia. If you are travelling from east coast USA, it's easier to travel via either Frankfurt or Amsterdam.

If you are also visiting other parts of Asia, some good deals can be organised (eg, there are cheap tickets between the US west coast and Singapore with stopovers in Bangkok for very little extra money).

Return airfares to Jakarta or Denpasar start from around US$1100/1600 in the low/high season from the west coast, and around US$1700/2000 from New York. Recent discounts have seen even lower prices and some real bargains, often via Taipei or Seoul.

San Francisco is the discount-ticket capital of America, although some good deals can be found in Los Angeles, New York and other big cities.

The *New York Times, LA Times, Chicago Tribune* and *San Francisco Examiner* all produce weekly travel sections in which you will find any number of travel agency ads.

Airtreks (☎ 1877 247 8735, 1-415-977 7100; www.airtreks.com) Phone and online bookings for flights, tours and packages.

STA Travel (☎ 1800 781 4040; www.statravel.com) Has offices in many major cities.

LAND

Border Crossings

There are three possible land crossings into Indonesia. In all instances you must have obtained a visa before you get to the border; see p862 for visa information.

Regular buses between Pontianak (Kalimantan) and Kuching (Sarawak, eastern Malaysia) pass through the border post at Entikong. They take around 10 hours and if travelling from Pontianak, stop at the border in the wee hours until it opens at 9am. You need to get off the bus and clear immigration on either side. See p614 for specifics.

The border crossing between West and East Timor at Motoain was open at the time of research; a visa is required when travelling from East to West Timor. See the boxed text on p578 for details.

The road from Jayapura or Sentani in Indonesia to Vanimo in Papua New Guinea can be crossed, depending on the current political situation. A visa is required if travelling into Indonesia; see the boxed text, p799.

SEA

There is currently no sea travel between the Philippines and Indonesia.

East Timor

In theory there are two boats a week between Dili in East Timor and Oecussi in West Timor, but they aren't set up for passengers.

Malaysia

Regular and comfortable high-speed ferries run the two-hour journey between Melaka (Malaysia) and Dumai (Sumatra) for around 170,000Rp; see p459 for more information. Similar ferries travel between Penang (Malaysia) and Belawan (Sumatra), taking about five hours and costing from RM140. See p388 for specifics.

There are also boats from Pekanbaru (Sumatra) to Melaka, which cost from 215,000Rp and take around eight hours. See p458 for more information.

From Johor Bahru in southern Malaysia, daily ferries run to Pulau Bintan (see p466) in Sumatra's Riau Islands.

In Borneo there are speedboats every day except Sunday between Tawau in Sabah and Tarakan (150,000Rp) and Nunukan (250,000Rp), both in East Kalimantan. Unless you've got a hankering for small and dusty towns, it's best to bypass Nunukan and head directly to Tarakan.

Papua New Guinea

Daily boats (weather permitting) run between Hamadi Port near Jayapura in Papua, to Vanimo in Papua New Guinea. It's also possible to charter a boat between Jayapura and Vanimo for around 350,000Rp per person. See the boxed text on p799 for more information. A visa is required if travelling into Indonesia.

Singapore

There are frequent, 25-minute ferries between Pulau Batam in Sumatra's Riau Islands and Singapore (see p463). From Batam, speedboats travel through to Pekanbaru on the Sumatran mainland and Pelni ships pass through Batam to and from Belawan (the port for Medan) and Jakarta.

Boats also travel between Pulau Bintan and Singapore (see p467). **Bintan Resort Ferries** (www.brf.com.sg) handles transport between Lagoi and Singapore, with tickets from S$26.

Yachts

It's still possible to hop on yachts around Southeast Asia, but luck is a major factor. Yacht owners frequently need crew members – you'll usually be required to contribute for food too. As for where to look – well, yacht clubs, and anywhere that yachts pass through. People have recently sailed to Indonesia from as far afield as Perth and Hong Kong.

TOURS

Tours will not run while there are security risks. Most tend to be of the standard packaged variety, but some focus on adventure and trekking in places such as Papua, Kalimantan and areas of Java. There are so many tours that it's impossible to list them here.

Prices vary according to the standard of the accommodation. Some try so hard to maximise luxury and minimise hassles that participants are hermetically isolated from the country. Small groups that provide some independence generally also provide a more worthwhile experience.

Imaginative Traveller (☎ 800-316 2717; www.imaginative-traveller.com) UK-based company emphasising sustainable, low-impact tourism.

Intrepid Travel (☎ 1300 360 887, 03-9473 2626; www.intrepidtravel.com.au) Australian-based company with similar focus.

GETTING AROUND

AIR

Airlines in Indonesia

The domestic flight network in Indonesia continues to grow extensively; the schedules are in a constant state of flux and the fares are more competitive than they have ever been. Local carriers servicing small routes tend to operate small and dated aircraft, whereas flights heading to Jakarta, Denpasar or other major cities are usually on larger, newer craft. Prices quoted by airlines and agencies are rarely any different, however visiting a travel agent first can save you time. They know exactly which carrier is flying where and which is the cheapest. Discounting is the exception rather than rule, but a few large travel agents in the main cities may sell tickets at a small discount. Airlines accept credit cards (often with a small surcharge), but don't expect to be able to use them in small offices in the outer islands.

Even if you book on the day of departure, there's a good chance you'll get a seat – but it pays to book as far in advance as possible during Indonesian holiday periods and the

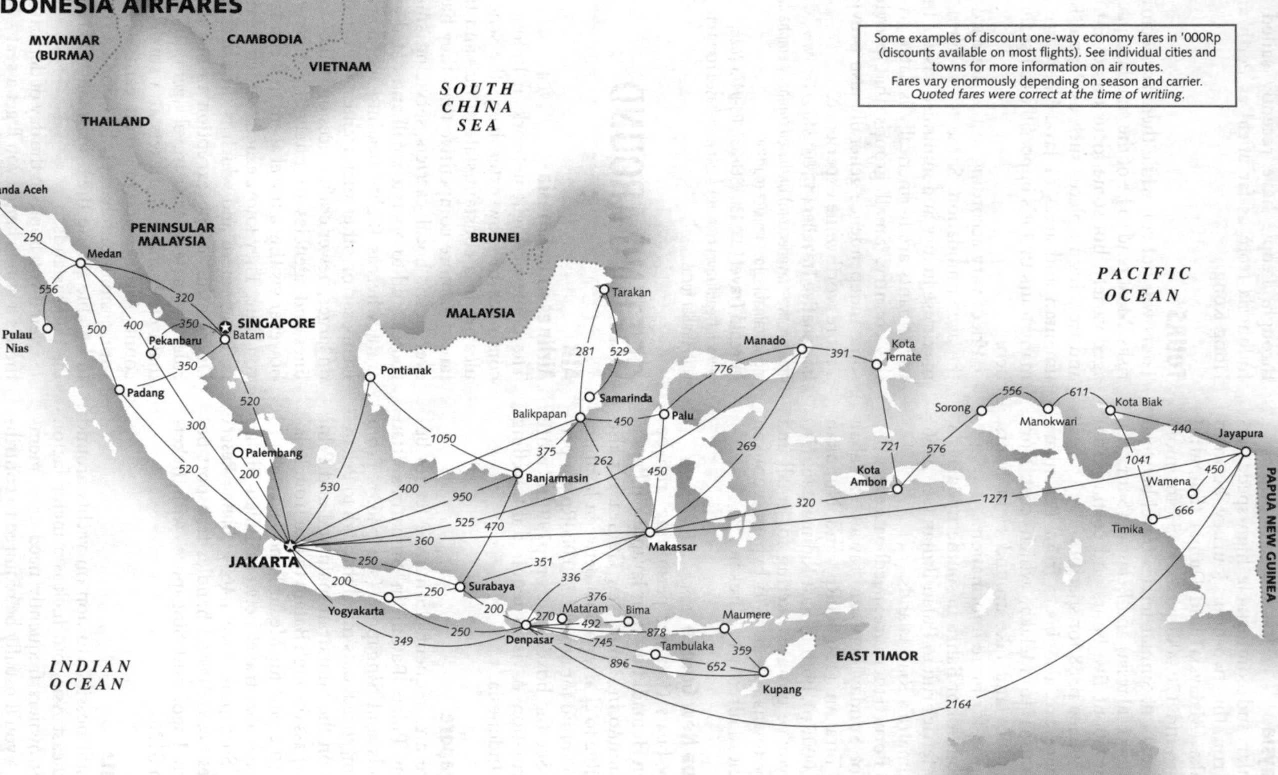
INDONESIA AIRFARES
Some examples of discount one-way economy fares in '000Rp (discounts available on most flights). See individual cities and towns for more information on air routes.
Fares vary enormously depending on season and carrier.
Quoted fares were correct at the time of writiing.
MYANMAR (BURMA)
CAMBODIA
VIETNAM
THAILAND
PENINSULAR MALAYSIA
SOUTH CHINA SEA
BRUNEI
MALAYSIA
PACIFIC OCEAN
INDIAN OCEAN
EAST TIMOR
PAPUA NEW GUINEA
AUSTRALIA
Banda Aceh
Medan
Pulau Nias
Pekanbaru
Padang
SINGAPORE
Batam
Palembang
Pontianak
Tarakan
Samarinda
Balikpapan
Banjarmasin
JAKARTA
Yogyakarta
Surabaya
Denpasar
Mataram
Bima
Tambulaka
Maumere
Kupang
Makassar
Palu
Manado
Kota Ternate
Kota Ambon
Sorong
Manokwari
Kota Biak
Jayapura
Wamena
Timika
250
556
500
400
320
350
350
300
520
520
200
530
1050
400
950
525
470
360
250
200
250
200
349
250
281
529
450
375
262
450
776
269
351
336
376
270
492
878
745
896
359
652
391
721
576
556
611
440
1041
450
666
320
1271
2164

peak season around August. During these times, flights may be booked on the more popular out-of-the-way routes serviced by small aircraft.

It is *essential* to reconfirm. Overbooking is a problem and if you don't reconfirm at least a few days before departure, you may well get bumped. Expect problems in the outer islands, where flights are limited, communications poor and booking procedures haphazard – you should reconfirm and reconfirm again.

Travel agents overseas can usually include discounted domestic flights with an international ticket if you enter Indonesia with Garuda. However, domestic tickets bought overseas are quoted in US dollars and cost around 50% more than if bought in Indonesia in rupiah, so it is usually just as cheap, if not cheaper, to buy them after you arrive.

Depending on the size of the airlines and where they fly, timetables will vary from accurate, national schedules to hand-adjusted printouts of localised areas or provinces on specific islands. Website information is useful for the bigger carriers but nonexistent for the smaller ones. The best option is to check with local airline offices and travel agents (see regional chapters for contact details) to see what's available.

Major airlines flying domestically:

Adam Air (☎ 021-6917540; www.flyadamair.com) Flies to Sulawesi, Kalimantan, Nusa Tenggara, Bali and Java.

Batavia Air (☎ 021-3864338; www.batavia-air.co.id) Flies to Sulawesi, Kalimantan and Java.

Bouraq (☎ 0361-766929) Flies to Sulawesi and Kalimantan.

Garuda (Garuda Indonesia; ☎ 021-23519999 www.garuda-indonesia.com) Operates between major cities on all islands except Nusa Tenggara.

Garuda Citilink (☎ 0807 1 807 807; www.ga-citilink.com) Garuda's little sibling flies to cities in Kalimantan, Bali, Lombok, Java and Sumatra.

Kartika Airlines (☎ 0804 1 101 101; www.kartika-airlines.com) Flies to Kalimantan, Sumatra, Bali and Java.

Lion Air (☎ 0804 1 77 88 99; www.lionair.co.id) Flies to cities Kalimantan, Maluku, Java, Sulawesi and Sumatra.

Mandala (☎ 021 566 5434; www.mandalaair.com) Flies to cities in Sumatra, Kalimantan, Sulawesi, Papua, Java and Bali.

Merpati (Merpati Nusantara Airlines; ☎ 021-6548888; www.merpati.co.id) Flies to major cities on all islands.

Pelita (☎ 0361-762248; www.pelita-air.com) Flies to Bali, Java and Nusa Tenggara.

DOMESTIC DEPARTURE TAX

Domestic departure tax varies from as little as 8000Rp up to 30,000Rp, depending on the airport. On top of the basic fare quoted by airlines, a 10% tax is charged as well as an insurance fee of 2500Rp. Tax and insurance are paid when you buy the ticket, but departure tax is paid at the airport. Baggage allowance is usually 20kg, or only 10kg on the smaller planes, and you may be charged for excess baggage.

Sriwijaya Airlines (☎ 021-6405566; Jl Gunung Sahari) Flies to Java, Sumatra, Sulawesi and Kalimantan.

Airlines with smaller networks include Deraya, Dirgantara Air Service (DAS), Wings Air and Kal-Star. Their routes and contact details are listed in applicable destination chapters.

There are some other intriguing possibilities for flying in Indonesia. The mission air services, which operate in places such as Kalimantan and Papua fly to some really remote parts of the interior of these islands and will take *paying* passengers if seats are available. See the respective chapters for details.

BICYCLE

The main advantage of cycling is the quality of the experience. You can cover many more kilometres by bemo, bus or motorcycle, but you really don't see much on the way. Bicycles also tend to bridge the time gap between the rush of the West and the calm of rural Asia – without the noise of a motorcycle engine you can hear the wind rustling in the rice paddies or gamelan music as you pass a Balinese village.

The main problems with seeing Indonesia by bicycle are the traffic in Java, and the hills and enormous distances you'll find everywhere. Bali is more compact, and seeing it by bicycle is reasonably popular despite the traffic on the roads. There are also bicycle tours offered in some places such as Solo in Java (see p198). At all the main sights in Java there are bicycle parking areas (usually about 1000Rp), where an attendant keeps an eye on your bicycle. See p842 for more information about cycling in Indonesia.

TRANSPORT

BOAT

Sumatra, Java, Bali, Nusa Tenggara and Sulawesi are all connected by regular ferries, and you can use them to island-hop all the way from Sumatra to Timor. These ferries run either daily or several times a week, so there's no need to spend days in sleepy little port towns. Check with shipping companies, the harbour office or travel agents for current schedules and fares.

Going to and between Kalimantan, Maluku and Papua, the main connections are provided by Pelni (below), the government-run passenger line. The increase in competitive airline prices has had a significant impact on many of Pelni's routes and it's difficult to obtain any accurate or solid information about schedules more than a month in advance. Furthermore, Pelni ships generally only operate every two or four weeks, so regular ferries are much more convenient.

Pelni Ships

Pelni is still the biggest shipping line, with services almost everywhere. It has modern, all air-con passenger ships that operate set routes around the islands, either on a fortnightly or monthly schedule. The ships usually stop for four hours in each port, so there's time for a quick look around.

Routes and schedules change every year and the best place to find accurate information is from a Pelni office, but they may only have schedules for the ships that call at their port. At the time of writing the **Pelni website** (www.pelni.com) was four years out of date, but it's useful for details regarding ports and Pelni offices.

Pelni has four cabin classes, followed by economy class, which is the modern version of deck class. It is sometimes possible to book a sleeping place in economy; otherwise, you'll have to find your own empty space. Mattresses can be rented and many boats have a 'tourist deck' upstairs. Even economy class is air-conditioned and it can get pretty cool at night, so bring warm clothes. There are no locker facilities, so you have to keep an eye on your gear.

First class is luxury-plus, with only two beds per cabin. Second class is a notch down in style, with four to a cabin, but still very comfortable. Third class has six beds to a cabin and 4th class has eight. Each of these classes has a restaurant with good food, while in economy you queue up to collect an unappetising meal and then sit down wherever you can to eat it. It pays to bring some other food with you.

Economy class is OK for short trips. Fourth class is the best value for longer hauls, but some ships only offer 1st and 2nd or 3rd class in addition to economy. As a rough approximation, 4th class is 50% more than economy, 3rd class is 100% more, 2nd class is 200% more and 1st class is 400% more.

It's best to book at least a few days in advance, although you can book tickets up to a week ahead. Pelni is not a tourist operation, so don't expect any special service, although there is usually somebody hidden away in the ticket offices who can help foreigners.

As well as its luxury liners, Pelni has Perinitis (Pioneer) ships that visit many of the other ports not covered by the passenger liners. The ships are often beaten-up old crates that primarily carry cargo, but they can get you to just about any of the remote islands, as well as the major ports. They offer deck class only, but you may be able to negotiate a cabin with one of the crew.

Other Ships

There's a whole range of floating tubs you can use to hop between islands, down rivers and across lakes. Just about any sort of vessel can be rented in Indonesia. Fishing boats or other small boats can be chartered to take you to small offshore islands. Some of these boats are *not* reliable and engine trouble can be an occasional problem. Check out the boat before you rent it – it would be nice if it had a two-way radio and a lifeboat, but these are rare.

The longbot (longboat) is a long, narrow boat powered by a couple of outboard motors, with bench seats on either side of the hull for passengers to sit on. They are mainly used in Kalimantan as a standard means of transport.

Outrigger canoes powered by an outboard motor are a standard form of transport for some short inter-island hops, such as the trip out from Manado in northern Sulawesi to the coral reefs surrounding nearby Pulau Bunaken. On Lombok these elegant, brilliantly painted fishing boats,

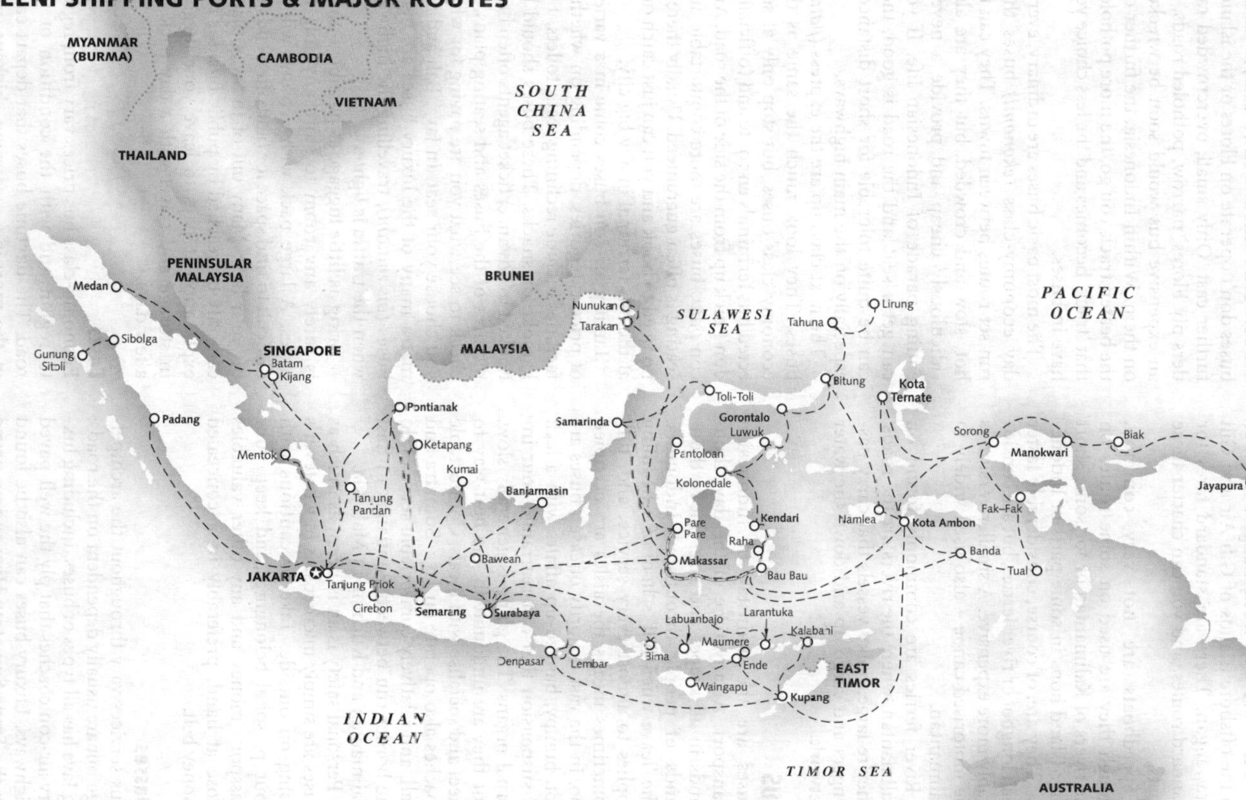
PELNI SHIPPING PORTS & MAJOR ROUTES
MYANMAR (BURMA)
CAMBODIA
VIETNAM
THAILAND
SOUTH CHINA SEA
PENINSULAR MALAYSIA
BRUNEI
MALAYSIA
SINGAPORE
SULAWESI SEA
PACIFIC OCEAN
INDIAN OCEAN
TIMOR SEA
EAST TIMOR
AUSTRALIA
PAPUA NEW GUINEA
Medan
Sibolga
Gunung Sitoli
Batam
Kijang
Padang
Mentok
JAKARTA
Tanjung Priok
Cirebon
Semarang
Tanjung Pandan
Pontianak
Ketapang
Kumai
Bawean
Surabaya
Banjarmasin
Denpasar
Lembar
Bima
Labuanbajo
Samarinda
Nunukan
Tarakan
Toli-Toli
Gorontalo
Luwuk
Pantoloan
Kolonedale
Pare Pare
Makassar
Kendari
Raha
Bau Bau
Larantuka
Maumere
Ende
Waingapu
Kalabahi
Kupang
Tahuna
Lirung
Bitung
Kota Ternate
Namlea
Kota Ambon
Banda
Tual
Fak-Fak
Sorong
Manokwari
Biak
Jayapura

which look like exotic dragonflies, are used for the short hop from Bangsal harbour to the offshore islands of Gili Air and Gili Trawangan. There are standard fares for standard routes, and you can charter these boats.

Speedboats are not very common, though they are used on some routes on the rivers of Kalimantan or for some short inter-island hops in some parts of Indonesia. They are, of course, considerably faster than longbot or river ferries, but are considerably more expensive. A smaller version is the motorised canoe – also used widely in Kalimantan.

River ferries are commonly found on Kalimantan, where the rivers *are* the roads. They're large, bulky vessels that carry passengers and cargo up and down the water network.

BUS

Buses are the mainstay of Indonesian transport. At any time of the day, thousands in all shapes and sizes move thousands of people throughout Indonesia. The 'leave-when-full' school of scheduling applies to almost every service, and 'full' sometimes means the aisles are occupied too. In the vast majority of cases, buses are hot, bumpy, banged-up affairs with a lack of suspension that can rearrange your internal organs. The going is generally slow. But they are undoubtedly the best way to meet and socialise with locals. Comfortable coaches also operate on Java, Sumatra and Bali, and relatively comfortable services do the border run between Pontianak in East Kalimantan and Kuching in Malaysia.

Personal safety is an issue, in as much as buses are simply microcosms of whatever's going on outside. Take precautions with your personal belongings and keep your passport, money and any other valuables close at hand, preferably in a concealed money belt.

Classes

Bus services vary throughout the archipelago but are usually dependent on the roads: eg Java has all types of buses, including luxury air-con coaches that ply the well-paved highways. Luxury buses can also be found on the Trans-Sumatran Hwy and on paved roads in Bali, Lombok and Sumbawa. The 'Wallace Line' for the evolution of buses lies between Sumbawa and Flores, as luxury buses don't operate on Flores or the islands further east. Only small, overcrowded rattlers ply Flores' narrow, potholed roads, as an expensive bus would soon be wrecked on them. Within Indonesia, the further off the beaten track you go, the more potholed that 'track' becomes and the less choice you have in buses.

The most basic buses are ordinary, everyday economy-class *(ekonomi)* buses that run set routes between towns. They can be hot, slow and crowded, but they are also ridiculously cheap and provide a never-ending parade of Indonesian life. If you can get a seat and the road is good, they can be quite tolerable for short distances, especially on the main highways.

The next class up are the express *(patas)* buses. They look much the same as the economy-class buses, but stop only at selected bus terminals en route and (officially) don't pick up from the side of the road. Air-con *patas* buses are more comfortable and seating is often guaranteed. Usually there is no need to book and you can just catch one at the bus terminal in any big city.

Luxury air-con buses come in a variety of price categories, depending on whether facilities include reclining seats, toilets, TV, karaoke or snacks. These buses should be booked in advance; ticket agents often have pictures of the buses and seating plans, so check to see what you are paying for when you choose your seat. In Java, Bali and Sumatra many of the luxury buses are night buses *(bis malam)*, travelling the highways when the traffic is lighter.

Bring as little luggage as possible – there is rarely any room to store anything on buses. A large pack with a frame will be difficult to find space for (and often ends up on your lap). Many out-of-the-way places can only be reached by public bus; for real exploration it pays to leave your luggage in storage and travel with a day pack for a few days.

Costs

Economy-class bus prices vary from region to region and with the condition of the road. The daytime buses that depart early in the morning – carrying chickens, pigs and goats – are usually the cheapest. An

THE PRICE OF PETROL

In recent years the price of petrol has leapt substantially at irregular intervals, with the price of bus fares following suit soon after. Bus fares quoted in this book have taken these increases into account.

eight-hour journey will cost 50,000Rp to 80,000Rp. By way of comparison, an eight-hour journey on a luxurious, overnight bus will cost 140,000Rp to 200,000Rp.

Reservations

Vehicles usually depart throughout the day for shorter routes over good roads; for longer routes, you'll have to get down to the bus terminal early in the morning in order to get a vehicle. On bad roads, there'll be fewer vehicles, so buying a ticket beforehand can be a good idea. In many towns and villages, the bus companies have a ticket/reservations office, or there are shops which act as agents (or own the buses). Often, hotels will act as agents or buy a ticket for you and will arrange for the bus to pick you up at the hotel – they sometimes charge a few hundred rupiah for this service but it's easily worth it.

CAR & MOTORCYCLE

Driving Licence

To drive in Indonesia, you officially need an International Driving Permit (IDP) from your local automobile association. This permit is rarely required as identification when hiring or driving a car in Indonesia, but police may ask to see it. Bring your home licence as well – it's supposed to be carried in conjunction with the IDP. If you also have a motorcycle licence at home, get your IDP endorsed for motorcycles too.

Fuel & Spare Parts

In recent years the price of petrol has leapt substantially at irregular intervals; in 2005 alone it rose by more than 125%. At the time of writing it cost 4500Rp per litre. There are petrol stations around the larger towns, but out in the villages they can be difficult to find. Small roadside shops sell small amounts of petrol; look for signs that read *press ban,* or for crates of bottles with a *bensin* sign. Some of the petrol from these stands is said to be of dubious quality, so it's probably best to refill whenever you see a petrol station *(pompa bensin)*.

Hire

CAR HIRE

The price of car rental will vary according to both location and vehicle. Indonesia has regular car-rental agencies in the large cities such as Jakarta, where a rental costs around US$100 per day. It's generally cheaper to hire a car and driver for 350,000Rp to 500,000Rp per day. Bali is one of the cheapest places to rent a car; a Suzuki 4WD costs around 80,000Rp to 120,000Rp a day, including insurance and unlimited kilometres. In most cases, the price includes unlimited mileage, but you supply the petrol.

If you are travelling in a group, renting a minibus can be a particularly good deal. The minibuses are sturdy, comfortable, go-almost-anywhere vehicles, and can take up to six people plus luggage in comfort. Car or minibus rental, including driver but excluding petrol, costs 250,000Rp to 300,000Rp per day. Bargaining is usually required. It is harder to find a driver for trips lasting longer than a few days. Negotiate a deal covering food and accommodation for your driver; either you provide a hotel room each night and pay a food allowance or negotiate an allowance that covers both (figure on about 60,000Rp per day). It pays to see what your driver is like on a day trip before heading off on a lengthy expedition.

Major car-rental agencies, including **Hertz** (☎ 021-3907282; www.hertz.com) and **Avis** (☎ 021-3142900; www.avis.com) have offices in the main cities, such as Jakarta, Bandung, Yogyakarta, Medan, Surabaya and Denpasar, but they are more expensive than arranging a vehicle through your hotel or a tourist office.

Travel agencies in the travellers' centres are good places to try for minibus rental. Go to the cheap tour operators – agents in the big hotels will charge big prices.

MOTORCYCLE HIRE

You'll find that motorcycles are readily available for hire throughout Indonesia. In the tourist centres they can be rented from around 30,000Rp per day, but in most places the locals rent out their own motorcycles to earn a few extra rupiah. Rental charges vary with the type of bike and the length of hire. The longer the hire period, the lower the rate; the bigger or newer the bike, the higher the rate.

Motorcycles are almost all between 90cc and 125cc, with 100cc the average size. You really don't need anything bigger; the distances are short and the roads are rarely suitable for fast speeds.

Indonesia is not the place to learn how to ride. The main highways are hectic, especially in Java and Bali. Combined with all the normal hazards of motorcycle riding are narrow roads, unexpected potholes, crazy drivers, buses and trucks that claim road ownership, children who dart onto the road, lumbering bullocks, dogs and chickens that run around in circles and unlit traffic at night. Take it slowly and cautiously around curves to avoid hitting oncoming traffic – this may include very large and heavy buses, buffalo, herds of stray goats and children. Keep to the back roads as much as possible, where riding can be pleasurable.

You need to have a licence, especially to satisfy travel insurance in case of an accident, though you'll rarely need to show it.

Some travel insurance policies do not cover you if you are involved in an accident while on a motorcycle. Check the small print.

Insurance

Rental agencies and owners usually insist that the vehicle itself is insured, and minimal insurance should be included in the basic rental deal – often with an excess of as much as US$100 for a motorcycle and US$500 for a car (ie the customer pays the first US$100/500 of any claim). The more formal motorcycle and car rental agencies may offer additional insurance to reduce the level of the excess, and cover damage to other people or their property, ie 'third-party' or 'liability' cover. Your travel insurance may provide some additional protection, although liability for motor accidents is specifically excluded from many policies.

A private owner renting a motorcycle may not offer any insurance at all. Ensure that your personal travel insurance covers injuries incurred while motorcycling. Some policies specifically exclude coverage for motorcycle riding, or have special conditions.

Road Conditions

The relentless traffic congesting every Indonesian city makes driving an activity for the brave alone, unless you hit the open road. Even then, unless you're on a main highway, expect delays due to potholes and congestion. Finding your way around the main tourist sites on any island can be a challenge, as roads are only sometimes signposted and maps are often out of date.

Road Hazards

Aside from the above, avoid driving on rural roads after dusk, when spotting human and other living traffic becomes more difficult.

Road Rules

Indonesians drive on the left of the road (sometimes the right, sometimes the pavement), as in Australia, Japan, the UK and most of Southeast Asia. Indonesia has its fair share of maniacal drivers, including most bus drivers, but there are relatively few accidents. The key is defensive driving. The roads are not just for cars, but also pedestrians, animals, food carts etc.

Driving yourself is not much fun in many parts of Indonesia. It requires enormous amounts of concentration and the legal implications of accidents can be a nightmare – that is if you survive an angry mob should someone be hurt. If you do have an accident, as a foreigner it's *your* fault (see Legal Matters, p856). It is more common and often cheaper to rent a car or minibus with driver.

HITCHING

Hitching is not part of the culture but if you put out your thumb, someone may give you a lift. Confusion may arise as to whether payment is required or not. On the back roads where no public transport exists, hitching may be the only alternative to walking, and passing motorists or trucks are often willing to help.

Bear in mind, however, that hitching is never entirely safe in any country, and we do not recommend it. Travellers who decide to hitch should understand that they are taking a small but potentially serious risk. People who do choose to hitch will be safer if they travel in pairs and let someone know where they are planning to go.

LOCAL TRANSPORT

Bajaj

These machines are noisy, smoke-belching three-wheeled vehicles with a driver who sits at the front, a small motorcycle engine below and seats for two passengers behind. They're a common form of local transport in Jakarta, but you don't see them very often elsewhere.

Becak

These are three-wheeled bicycle-rickshaws. Unlike the version found in India where the driver sits in front of you, or the Filipino version with the driver at the side, in Indonesia the driver sits at the rear, nosing your life ever forwards into the traffic.

Many drivers rent their vehicles, but those who own them add personal touches: brightly painted pictures, bells or whirring metal discs strung across the undercarriage.

The becak is now banned from the main streets of some large cities, but you'll still see them swarming the back streets, moving anyone and anything.

Negotiate your fare *before* you get in; and if there are two passengers, make sure that it covers both people, otherwise you'll be in for an argument when you get to your destination. Becak drivers are hard bargainers – they have to be to survive – but they will usually settle on a reasonable fare, around 2000Rp to 4000Rp per kilometre. Fares vary from city to city and increase with more passengers, luggage, hills and night journeys. Hiring a becak for a period of time or for a round trip often makes good sense if you're planning to cover a lot of ground in one day, particularly in large places like Yogyakarta or Solo.

Bus

Large buses aren't used much as a means of city transport except on Java. There's an extensive system of buses in Jakarta and these are universally cheap, but beware of pickpockets. They usually work in gangs and can empty your pockets faster than you can say '*gado gado*'.

Dokar

A *dokar* is the jingling, horse-drawn cart found throughout the archipelago. The two-wheeled carts are usually brightly coloured with decorative motifs and bells, and the small horses or ponies often have long tassels attached to their bridle. A typical *dokar* has bench seating on either side, which can comfortably fit three or four people. However, their owners try to pack in three or four families plus bags of rice and other paraphernalia. It's a picturesque way of getting around if you don't get upset by the ill-treatment of animals, but generally the ponies are well looked after. The carts often operate on set runs and payment is per person (1500Rp to 2000Rp). Foreigners may have to charter; 10,000Rp to 15,000Rp should get you just about anywhere around town.

In Java you will also see the *andong* or *dilman*, which is a larger horse-drawn wagon designed to carry six people. In some parts of Indonesia, such as Gorontalo and Manado in northern Sulawesi, you also see the *bendi*, which is basically a small *dokar* that carries two passengers.

Ojek

There are various other ways of getting around. *Ojeks* (or *ojegs*) are motorcycle riders who take pillion passengers for a bargainable price. They are found at bus terminals and markets, or just hanging around at crossroads. They will take you around town and go where no other public transport exists, or along roads that are impassable in any other vehicle. They can also be rented by the hour for sightseeing (starting at around 20,000Rp to 30,000Rp).

Taxi

Metered taxis are readily available in major cities, especially in Java and Bali. If a taxi has a meter *(argo)*, make sure it is used. Most drivers will use them without fuss but like anywhere there are a few sharks. Elsewhere, meters don't exist and you will have to bargain for the fare in advance. Non-licensed taxis abound and are sometimes the only option; otherwise, opt for the licensed taxis.

At airports, taxis usually operate on a coupon system, payable at the relevant booth before you board the taxi.

MINIBUS (BEMO)

Public minibuses are used for local transport around cities and towns, short intercity runs, and the furthest reaches of the transport network.

The great minibus ancestor is the bemo, a small three-wheeled pick-up truck with a row of seats down each side, but regular minibuses are more common these days. The word 'bemo' (a contraction of 'becak' – three-wheeled bicycle-rickshaw – and 'motor') is still applied in some cities and certainly universally understood, but you'll encounter a mind-boggling array of names, such as *opelet, mikrolet, angkot, angkudes* and *pete-pete*. Just to make things confusing, they are called taxi in many parts of Papua, Kalimantan and East Java. Often they will be called simply by their brand name, such as Suzuki, Daihatsu or Toyota, but the most popular make by far is the Mitsubishi Colt, therefore 'Colt' is widely used.

Most minibuses operate a standard route, picking up and dropping off people and goods anywhere along the way. This is particularly the case in cities, where one fare applies, regardless of the distance. On longer routes between cities you may have to bargain a bit. Minibus drivers often try to overcharge foreigners and will have no qualms about asking you for triple the amount they just accepted from a local. It's best to ask somebody, such as your hotel staff, about the *harga biasa* (normal price) before you get on; otherwise, see what the other passengers are paying and offer the correct fare.

Beware of getting on an empty minibus – you may end up chartering it! On the other hand, sometimes chartering a bemo is worth considering: if there's a group of you, it can work out cheaper than hiring a motorcycle by the day and much cheaper than hiring a car. Regular bemos carry around 12 people, so multiplying the usual fare by 12 should give you a rough idea of what to pay.

As with all the public transport in Indonesia, the drivers wait until their vehicles are crammed to capacity before they contemplate moving, or they may go *keliling* – driving endlessly around town looking for a full complement of passengers. Often there are people, produce, chickens, baskets and even bicycles hanging out the windows and doors – at times it seems you're in danger of being crushed to death or at least asphyxiated (there's no air-con on any of these vehicles).

Luxurious, express minibuses operate between the main tourist centres in Bali, Lombok and Sumatra.

TOURS

A wide range of tours can be booked from travel agents within Indonesia. Most operate in tourist hotspots. Some of the best 'tours' are with local guides, such as the eco-trips to Halimun National Park in Java with Alwi (p132), or treks to Kalimantan's Apokayan Highlands with Suryadi (p659).

You can be certain that taking a tour will work out to be more expensive than going by yourself, but in remote areas the benefit of local dialects and experience is worth it.

Some recommended agencies:

Bali Adventure Tours (☎ 0361-721480; www.baliadventuretours.com) White-water rafting along Bali's Sungai Ayung river; p314.

Bali Eco and Educational Cycling Tour (☎ 0361-975557) Local company offering mountain biking, cultural and culinary tours around Ubud; p314.

Earthwatch Institute (www.earthwatch.org) US-based company offering eco-sustainable tours and activities and volunteer programmes.

Footprint Adventures (www.footventure.co.uk) UK-based company specialising in small group trekking tours to Sumatra, Kalimantan, Papua and more.

Indosella (☎ 0423-25210; www.sellatours.com) Trekking around Tana Toraja in Sulawesi; p703.

Kartika Trekking (☎ 0274-562016) Local agent specialising in trekking trips to Gunung Merapi; p174.

Mentawai Sanctuary (☎ 0751-767888; www.mentawai.com) Surf charters island and culture tours around Sumatra's Mentawai Islands; p440.

Mesra Tours (☎ 0541-738787; www.mesra.com/tour) Local company offering comprehensive Kalimantan tours including coast-to-coast treks, rafting and river journeys; p649.

Papua Adventure Tours & Travel (☎ 0967-586755; www.papuaadventure.com) Local agency specialising in treks in the Baliem Valley and Asmat region; p829.

TRAIN

Train travel in Indonesia is restricted to Java and Sumatra. In Java, trains are one of the most comfortable and easiest ways to travel. In the east, the railway service connects with the ferry to Bali, and in the west with the ferry to Sumatra. Sumatra's limited rail network runs in the south from Bandarlampung to Lubuklinggau, and in the north from Medan to Tanjung Balai and Rantauparapat.

Health

Dr Trish Batchelor

CONTENTS

Health issues and the quality of medical facilities vary enormously depending on where and how you travel in Indonesia. Many of the major cities are well developed, although travel to rural areas can expose you to a variety of health risks and inadequate medical care.

Travellers tend to worry about contracting infectious diseases when in the tropics, but infections are a rare cause of serious illness or death in travellers. Pre-existing medical conditions such as heart disease, and accidental injury (especially traffic accidents), account for most life-threatening problems. Becoming ill in some way, however, is relatively common. Fortunately most common illnesses can either be prevented with some common-sense behaviour or be treated easily with a well-stocked traveller's medical kit.

The following advice is a general guide only and does not replace the advice of a doctor trained in travel medicine.

BEFORE YOU GO

Pack medications in their original, clearly labelled containers. A signed and dated letter from your physician describing your medical conditions and medications, including generic names, is also a good idea. If you have a heart condition bring a copy of your ECG taken just prior to travelling.

If you take regular medication bring double your needs in case of loss or theft. You can buy many medications over the counter without a doctor's prescription, but it can be difficult to find some of the newer drugs, particularly the latest antidepressant drugs, blood pressure medications and contraceptive pills.

INSURANCE

Even if you are fit and healthy, don't travel without health insurance – accidents do happen. Declare any existing medical conditions you have – the insurance company *will* check if your problem is pre-existing and will not cover you if it is undeclared. If you're uninsured, emergency evacuation is expensive; bills of over US$100,000 are not uncommon.

Find out in advance if your insurance plan will make payments directly to providers or reimburse you later for overseas health expenditures. (In many countries doctors expect payment in cash.) Some policies ask you to call back (reverse charges) to a centre in your home country where an immediate assessment of your problem is made.

VACCINATIONS

Specialised travel-medicine clinics are your best source of information. The doctors will take into account factors such as past vaccination history, the length of your trip, activities you may be undertaking and underlying medical conditions, such as pregnancy.

Most vaccines don't produce immunity until at least two weeks after they're given, so visit a doctor four to eight weeks before departure. Ask your doctor for an International Certificate of Vaccination (otherwise known as the yellow booklet), which will list all the vaccinations you've received.

Recommended Vaccinations

The World Health Organization (WHO) recommends the following vaccinations for travellers to Southeast Asia:

Adult diphtheria and tetanus Single booster recommended if none in the previous 10 years. Side effects include sore arm and fever.

Hepatitis A Provides almost 100% protection for up to a year, a booster after 12 months provides at least another 20 years' protection. Mild side effects such as headache and sore arm occur in 5% to 10% of people.

Hepatitis B Now considered routine for most travellers. Given as three shots over six months. Lifetime protection occurs in 95% of people.

Measles, mumps and rubella Two doses of MMR required unless you have had the diseases. Many young adults require a booster.

Polio Only one booster required as an adult for lifetime protection. Inactivated polio vaccine is safe during pregnancy.

Typhoid Recommended unless your trip is less than a week and only to developed cities. The vaccine offers around 70% protection, lasts for two to three years and comes as a single shot.

Varicella If you haven't had chickenpox, discuss this vaccination with your doctor.

These immunisations are recommended for long-term travellers (more than one month) or those at special risk:

Japanese B Encephalitis Three injections in all. Booster recommended after two years. Sore arm and headache are the most common side effects.

Meningitis Single injection. Recommended for long-term backpackers aged under 25.

Rabies Three injections in all. A booster after one year will then provide 10 years' protection. Side effects are rare – occasionally headache and sore arm.

Tuberculosis Adult long-term travellers are usually recommended to have a TB skin test before and after travel, rather than vaccination. Only one vaccine given in a lifetime.

MEDICAL CHECKLIST

Consider including the following in your medical kit:

- Antibiotics – consider including these if you're travelling well off the beaten track; see your doctor, as they must be prescribed, and carry the prescription with you
- Antifungal cream or powder – for fungal skin infections and thrush
- Antihistamine – for allergies, eg hay fever; to ease the itch from insect bites or stings; and to prevent motion sickness
- Antiseptic (such as povidone-iodine or Betadine) – for cuts and grazes
- Antispasmodic – for stomach cramps, eg Buscopa
- Aspirin or paracetamol (acetaminophen in the USA) – for pain or fever
- Bandages, Band-Aids (plasters) and other wound dressings
- Calamine lotion, sting relief spray or aloe vera – to ease irritation from sunburn and insect bites or stings
- Cold and flu tablets, throat lozenges and nasal decongestant
- Contraceptives
- DEET-based insect repellent
- Ibuprofen or other anti-inflammatory
- Iodine or other water purification tablets
- Loperamide or diphenoxylate – 'blockers' for diarrhoea
- Multivitamins – consider for long trips, when dietary vitamin intake may be inadequate
- Permethrin – to impregnate clothing and mosquito nets
- Prochlorperazine or metoclopramide – for nausea and vomiting
- Rehydration mixture – to prevent dehydration, which may occur, for example, during bouts of diarrhoea; particularly important when travelling with children
- Scissors, tweezers and a thermometer – note that mercury thermometers are prohibited by airlines
- Sterile kit – in case you need injections in a country with medical hygiene problems; discuss with your doctor
- Sunscreen, lip balm and eye drops

HEALTH ADVISORIES

Government travel-health websites:

Australia (www.dfat.gov.au/travel)
Canada (www.hc-sc.gc.ca/english/index.html)
New Zealand (www.mfat.govt.nz/travel)
South Africa (www.dfa.gov.za/travelling)
UK (www.doh.gov.uk/traveladvice)
US (www.cdc.gov/travel)

Required Vaccinations

The only vaccine required by international regulations is yellow fever. Proof of vaccination will only be required if you have visited a country in the yellow-fever zone within the six days prior to entering Indonesia. If you are travelling to Indonesia from Africa or South America you should check to see if you require proof of vaccination.

INTERNET RESOURCES

There is a wealth of travel health advice on the internet. The following are good resources:

Centers for Disease Control and Prevention (CDC; www.cdc.gov) Good general information.
LonelyPlanet.com (www.lonelyplanet.com)
MD Travel Health (www.mdtravelhealth.com) Complete travel health recommendations for every country.
World Health Organization (WHO; www.who.int/ith/) Publishes a superb book called International Travel & Health, revised annually.

FURTHER READING

Lonely Planet's *Healthy Travel – Asia & India* is a handy pocket-size book that is packed with useful information including pretrip planning, emergency first aid, immunisation and disease information and what to do if you get sick on the road. Other recommended references include *Traveller's Health* by Dr Richard Dawood and *Travelling Well* by Dr Deborah Mills – check out the website www.travellingwell.com.au.

IN INDONESIA

AVAILABILITY OF HEALTH CARE

It is difficult to find reliable medical care in rural areas, but most capital cities now have clinics catering specifically to travellers and expats. These clinics are usually more expensive than local medical facilities, but are worth utilising, as they will offer a superior standard of care. Additionally they understand the local system, and are aware of the safest local hospitals and best specialists. They can also liaise with insurance companies should you require evacuation.

If you think you may have a serious disease, especially malaria, do not waste time – travel to the nearest quality facility to receive attention.

Buying medication over the counter is not recommended, as fake medications and poorly stored or out-of-date drugs are common.

Local medical care in general is not yet up to international standards. Foreign doctors are not allowed to work in Indonesia, but some clinics catering to foreigners have 'international advisors'. Almost all Indonesian doctors work at government hospitals during the day and in private practices at night. This means that private hospitals often don't have their best staff available during the day. Serious cases are evacuated to Australia or Singapore.

INFECTIOUS DISEASES

Dengue Fever

As there is no vaccine available for this mosquito-borne disease, it can only be prevented by avoiding bites. The mosquito that carries dengue bites day and night, so use insect avoidance measures at all times. Symptoms include high fever, severe headache and body ache (dengue was previously known as 'breakbone fever'). Some people develop a rash and experience diarrhoea. There is no specific treatment, just rest and paracetamol – do not take aspirin as it increases the likelihood of haemorrhaging. See a doctor to be diagnosed and monitored.

Filariasis

A mosquito-borne disease that is very common in the local population, yet very rare in travellers. Mosquito-avoidance measures are the best way to prevent this disease.

Hepatitis A

A problem throughout the region, this food- and water-borne virus infects the liver, causing jaundice (yellow skin and eyes), nausea and lethargy. There is no specific treatment for hepatitis A; you just need to allow time for the liver to heal. All travellers to Indonesia should be vaccinated against hepatitis A.

Hepatitis B

The only sexually transmitted disease that can be prevented by vaccination, hepatitis B is spread by body fluids, including sexual contact. In some parts of Indonesia up to 15% of the population are carriers of hepatitis B, and usually are unaware of this. The long-term consequences can include liver cancer and cirrhosis.

Hepatitis E

Hepatitis E is transmitted through contaminated food and water and has similar symptoms to hepatitis A, but is far less common. It is a severe problem in pregnant women and can result in the death of both mother and baby. There is currently no vaccine, and prevention is by following safe eating and drinking guidelines.

HIV

Typically, Indonesia has been considered a relatively safe country with respect to HIV/AIDS, with only a few thousand reported infections per year. However, religious and cultural taboos have likely resulted in a systematic underreporting of the problem throughout the country. According to WHO estimates, anywhere from 50,000 to 200,000 are living with HIV in Indonesia. While this is nowhere near as severe a pandemic as in other parts of Southeast Asia, it is high enough for travellers to exercise caution and vigilance.

Japanese B Encephalitis

While this is a rare disease in travellers, many locals are infected each year. This viral disease is transmitted by mosquitoes. Most cases occur in rural areas and vaccination is recommended for travellers spending more than one month outside of cities. There is no treatment, and a third of infected people will die while another third will suffer permanent brain damage.

Malaria

For such a serious and potentially deadly disease, there is an enormous amount of misinformation concerning malaria. Some parts of Indonesia, particularly city and resort areas, have minimal to no risk of malaria, and the risk of side effects from the tablets may outweigh the risk of getting the disease. For most rural areas, however, the risk of contracting the disease far outweighs the risk of any tablet side effects. Remember that malaria can be fatal. Before you travel, seek medical advice on the right medication and dosage for you.

Malaria is caused by a parasite transmitted by the bite of an infected mosquito. The most important symptom of malaria is fever, but general symptoms such as headache, diarrhoea, cough, or chills may also occur. Diagnosis can only be made by taking a blood sample.

Two strategies should be combined to prevent malaria – mosquito avoidance and antimalarial medications. Most people who catch malaria are taking inadequate or no antimalarial medication.

Travellers are advised to prevent mosquito bites by taking these steps:

- Use a DEET-containing insect repellent on exposed skin. Wash this off at night, as long as you are sleeping under a mosquito net. Natural repellents such as citronella can be effective, but must be applied more frequently than products containing DEET.
- Sleep under a mosquito net impregnated with Permethrin.
- Impregnate clothing with Permethrin in high-risk areas.
- Wear long sleeves and trousers in light colours.
- Use mosquito coils.
- Spray your room with insect repellent before going out for your evening meal.

There are a variety of medications available:

Artesunate Derivatives of Artesunate are not suitable as a preventive medication. They are useful treatments under medical supervision.

Chloroquine and Paludrine The effectiveness of this combination is now limited in most of Southeast Asia, including Indonesia. Common side effects include nausea (40% of people) and mouth ulcers. Generally not recommended.

Doxycycline This daily tablet is a broad-spectrum antibiotic that has the added benefit of helping to prevent a variety of tropical diseases, including leptospirosis, tick-borne disease, typhus and meliodosis. The potential side effects include photosensitivity (a tendency to sunburn), thrush in women, indigestion, heartburn, nausea and interference with the contraceptive pill. More serious side effects include ulceration of the oesophagus – you can help prevent this by taking your tablet with a meal and a large glass of water, and never lying down within half an hour of taking it.

Lariam (Mefloquine) Lariam has received much bad press, some of it justified, some not. This weekly tablet suits many people. Serious side effects are rare but include depression, anxiety, psychosis and having fits. Anyone with a history of depression, anxiety, other psychological disorder, or epilepsy should not take Lariam. It is considered safe in the second and third trimesters of pregnancy. It is around 90% effective in most parts of Southeast Asia, including Indonesia.

Malarone This drug is a combination of Atovaquone and Proguanil. Side effects are uncommon and mild, most commonly nausea and headache. It is the best tablet for scuba divers and for those on short trips to high-risk areas.

A final option is to take no preventive medication but to have a supply of emergency medication should you develop the symptoms of malaria. This is less than ideal, and you'll need to get to a good medical facility within 24 hours of developing a fever. If you choose this option the most effective and safest treatment is Malarone (four tablets once daily for three days).

Measles

This highly contagious bacterial infection is spread via coughing and sneezing. Most people born before 1966 are immune as they had the disease in childhood. Measles starts with a high fever and rash and can be complicated by pneumonia and brain disease. There is no specific treatment.

Rabies

This potentially fatal disease is spread by the bite or lick of an infected animal – most commonly a dog or monkey. You should seek medical advice immediately after any animal bite and commence postexposure treatment. Having pretravel vaccination means the postbite treatment is greatly simplified. If an animal bites you, gently wash the wound with soap and water, and apply iodine-based antiseptic. If you are not prevaccinated you will need to receive rabies immunoglobulin as soon as possible.

Schistosomiasis

Schistosomiasis is a tiny parasite that enters your skin after you've been swimming in contaminated water – travellers usually only get a light infection and hence have no symptoms. If you are concerned, you can be tested three months after exposure. On rare occasions, travellers may develop 'Katayama fever'. This occurs some weeks after exposure, as the parasite passes through the lungs and causes an allergic reaction; symptoms are coughing and fever. Schistosomiasis is easily treated with medications.

STDs

Common sexually transmitted diseases include herpes, warts, syphilis, gonorrhoea and chlamydia. People carrying these diseases often have no signs of infection. Condoms will prevent gonorrhoea and chlamydia but not warts or herpes. If after a sexual encounter you develop any rash, lumps, discharge or pain when passing urine seek immediate medical attention. If you have been sexually active during your travels have an STD check on your return home.

Tuberculosis

While rare in travellers, medical and aid workers, and long-term travellers who have significant contact with the local population should take precautions. Vaccination is usually only given to children under the age of five, but adults at risk are recommended pre- and post-travel TB testing. The main symptoms are fever, cough, weight loss, night sweats and tiredness.

Typhoid

This serious bacterial infection is also spread via food and water. It gives a high and slowly progressive fever, headache and may be accompanied by a dry cough and stomach pain. It is diagnosed by blood tests and treated with antibiotics. Vaccination is recommended for all travellers spending more than a week in Indonesia, or travelling outside of the major cities. Be aware that vaccination is not 100% effective so you must still be careful with what you eat and drink.

Typhus

Murine typhus is spread by the bite of a flea whereas scrub typhus is spread via a mite. These diseases are rare in travellers. Symptoms include fever, muscle pains and a rash. You can avoid these diseases by following general insect-avoidance measures. Doxycycline will also prevent them.

TRAVELLER'S DIARRHOEA

Traveller's diarrhoea is by far the most common problem affecting travellers – between 30% and 50% of people will suffer from it within two weeks of starting their trip. In over 80% of cases, traveller's diarrhoea is caused by a bacteria (there are numerous potential culprits), and therefore responds promptly to treatment with antibiotics. Treatment with antibiotics will depend on your situation – how sick you are, how quickly you need to get better, where you are etc.

Traveller's diarrhoea is defined as the passage of more than three watery bowel-actions within 24 hours, plus at least one other symptom such as fever, cramps, nausea, vomiting or feeling generally unwell.

Treatment consists of staying well hydrated; rehydration solutions like Gastrolyte are the best for this. Antibiotics such as Norfloxacin, Ciprofloxacin or Azithromycin will kill the bacteria quickly.

Loperamide is just a 'stopper' and doesn't get to the cause of the problem. It can be helpful, for example if you have to go on a long bus ride. Don't take Loperamide if you have a fever, or blood in your stools. Seek medical attention quickly if you do not respond to an appropriate antibiotic.

Amoebic Dysentery

Amoebic dysentery is very rare in travellers but is often misdiagnosed by local poor quality labs. Symptoms are similar to bacterial diarrhoea, ie fever, bloody diarrhoea and generally feeling unwell. You should always seek reliable medical care if you have blood in your diarrhoea. Treatment involves two drugs; Tinidazole or Metroniadzole to kill the parasite in your gut and then a second drug to kill the cysts. If left untreated complications such as liver or gut abscesses can occur.

Giardiasis

Giardia lamblia is a parasite that is relatively common in travellers. Symptoms include nausea, bloating, excess gas, fatigue and intermittent diarrhoea. 'Eggy' burps are often attributed solely to giardiasis. The parasite will eventually go away if left untreated but this can take months. The treatment of choice is Tinidazole, with Metronidazole being a second-line option.

ENVIRONMENTAL HAZARDS

Air Pollution

Air pollution, particularly vehicle pollution, is an increasing problem in major cities. If you have severe respiratory problems speak with your doctor before travelling to any heavily polluted urban centres. This pollution also causes minor respiratory problems such as sinusitis, dry throat and irritated eyes. If troubled by the pollution leave the city for a few days and get some fresh air.

Diving

Divers and surfers should seek specialised advice before they travel to ensure their medical kit contains treatment for coral cuts and tropical ear infections, as well as the standard problems. Divers should ensure their insurance covers them for decompression illness – get specialised dive insurance through an organisation such as **Divers Alert Network** (DAN; www.danseap.org). Have a dive medical before you leave your home country – there are certain medical conditions that are incompatible with diving and economic considerations may override health considerations for some dive operators.

DRINKING WATER

- Never drink tap water.
- Bottled water is generally safe – check the seal is intact at purchase.
- Avoid ice.
- Avoid fresh juices – they may have been watered down.
- Boiling water is the most efficient method of purifying it.
- The best chemical purifier is iodine. It should not be used by pregnant women or those people who suffer from thyroid problems.
- Water filters should also filter out viruses. Ensure your filter has a chemical barrier such as iodine and a small pore size, eg less than four microns.

HEALTH

Food

Eating in restaurants is the biggest risk factor for contracting traveller's diarrhoea. Ways to avoid it include eating only freshly cooked food, and avoiding shellfish or food that has been sitting around in buffets. Peel all fruit, cook vegetables and soak salads in iodine water for at least 20 minutes. Eat in busy restaurants with a high turnover of customers.

Heat

Many parts of Indonesia are hot and humid throughout the year. For most people it takes at least two weeks to adapt to the hot climate. Swelling of the feet and ankles is common, as are muscle cramps caused by excessive sweating. Prevent these by avoiding dehydration and excessive activity in the heat. Take it easy when you first arrive. Don't eat salt tablets (they aggravate the gut) but drinking rehydration solution or eating salty food helps. Treat cramps by stopping activity, resting, rehydrating with double-strength rehydration solution and gently stretching.

Dehydration is the main contributor to heat exhaustion. Symptoms include feeling weak, headache, irritability, nausea or vomiting, sweaty skin, a fast, weak pulse and a normal or slightly elevated body temperature. Treatment involves getting out of the heat and/or sun, fanning the victim and applying cool wet cloths to the skin, laying the victim flat with their legs raised and rehydrating with water containing ¼ teaspoon of salt per litre. Recovery is usually rapid and it is common to feel weak for some days afterwards.

Heatstroke is a serious medical emergency. Symptoms come on suddenly and include weakness, nausea, a hot dry body with a body temperature of over 41°C, dizziness, confusion, loss of coordination, fits and eventually collapse and loss of consciousness. Seek medical help and commence cooling by getting the person out of the heat, removing their clothes, fanning them and applying cool wet cloths or ice to their body, especially to the groin and armpits.

Prickly heat is a common skin rash in the tropics, caused by sweat being trapped under the skin. The result is an itchy rash of tiny lumps. Treat by moving out of the heat and into an air-conditioned area for a few hours, and by having cool showers. Creams and ointments clog the skin so they should be avoided. Locally bought prickly-heat powder can be helpful.

Tropical fatigue is common in long-term expats based in the tropics. It's rarely due to disease and is caused by the climate, inadequate mental rest, excessive alcohol intake and the demands of daily work in a different culture.

Insect Bites & Stings

Bedbugs don't carry disease but their bites are very itchy. You can treat the itch with an antihistamine. Lice inhabit various parts of your body but most commonly your head and pubic area. Transmission is via close contact with an infected person. They can be difficult to treat and you may need numerous applications of an antilice shampoo such as Permethrin. Pubic lice are usually contracted from sexual contact.

Ticks are contracted after walking in rural areas. Ticks are commonly found behind the ears, on the belly and in armpits. If you have had a tick bite and experience symptoms such as a rash at the site of the bite or elsewhere, fever, or muscle aches you should see a doctor. Doxycycline prevents tick-borne diseases.

Leeches are found in humid rainforest areas. They do not transmit any disease but their bites are often intensely itchy for weeks afterwards and can easily become infected. Apply an iodine-based antiseptic to any leech bite to help prevent infection.

Bee and wasp stings mainly cause problems for people who are allergic to them. Anyone with a serious bee or wasp allergy should carry an injection of adrenaline (eg an Epipen) for emergency treatment. For others pain is the main problem – apply ice to the sting and take painkillers.

Most jellyfish in Indonesian waters are not dangerous, just irritating. First-aid for jellyfish stings involves pouring vinegar onto the affected area to neutralise the poison. Do not rub sand or water onto the stings. Take painkillers, and anyone who feels ill in any way after being stung should seek medical advice. Take local advice on whether there are dangerous jellyfish around and, if so, keep out of the water.

MARINE LIFE TO WATCH OUT FOR

Most venomous fish, including stingrays, stonefish and scorpion fish, are found in salt water. If you do come into contact with these species, it will usually be through stepping on them by accident.

Sea Snakes

These beautiful creatures are found throughout coastal Indonesia. They're often inquisitive, although not aggressive. However, their venom is extremely toxic, so give them a wide berth. Symptoms of poisoning may not appear for several hours, and include anxiety and restlessness, dry throat, nausea and, eventually, paralysis.

Sea Urchins & Other Stingers

Avoid stepping on sea urchins, as their spines can break off and are very difficult to remove. Some species can cause a severe reaction that may result in paralysis and breathing difficulties. Sometimes this results in an itchy skin rash (sea urchin dermatitis) that can last for several months.

Stingrays

These creatures like to lie half-submerged in mud or sand in the shallows. You'll know if you step on one because they whip their tails up in defence. This can cause a nasty ragged wound, but they also have venomous spines which can sometimes be fatal. Shuffle along in the shallows to give stingrays plenty of warning of your approach.

Stonefish & Scorpion Fish

With sharp dorsal fins through which they inject a venom, these species are the most dangerous of all venomous fish. They occur throughout Indonesia.

Stonefish are generally reef dwellers, and as their name suggests, they are masters of disguise and lie half-submerged in sand, mud or coral debris. Their stings are extremely painful and may lead to collapse and coma. There is a stonefish antivenin which should be given as soon as possible after the sting. Scorpion fish are very distinctive and much easier to avoid – the chances of being stung by one are remote. There's no antivenin available.

Treatment

Hot (nonscalding) water can help break down the toxins in fish venom and can be surprisingly effective at relieving pain from stings. The procedure is as follows:

- If any spines are poking out, try to remove them gently (be sure to protect your hands).
- Wash any surface venom off with water.
- Bathe the wound in hot (nonscalding) water for up to 90 minutes or until the pain has gone, or apply hot packs.
- Wash the wound thoroughly. Once the pain is under control, apply a clean dressing.
- Rest with the limb raised.
- Seek medical help for antivenin if necessary, eg for a stonefish sting.

HEALTH

Parasites

Numerous parasites are common in local Indonesian populations; however, most of these are rare in travellers. The two rules to follow if you wish to avoid parasitic infections are to wear shoes and to avoid eating raw food, especially fish, pork and vegetables.

Snakes

Always wear boots and long pants if walking in an area that may have snakes. First aid in the event of a snakebite involves pressure immobilisation via an elastic bandage firmly wrapped around the affected limb, starting at the bite site and working up towards the chest. The bandage should not be so tight that the circulation is cut off, and the fingers or toes should be kept free so the circulation can be checked. Immobilise the limb with a splint and carry the victim to medical attention. Do not use tourniquets or try to suck the venom out. Antivenom is available for most species.

Sunburn

Even on a cloudy day sunburn can occur rapidly. Always use a strong sunscreen (at least factor 30), making sure to reapply after a swim, and always wear a wide-brimmed hat and sunglasses outdoors. Avoid lying in the sun during the hottest part of the day (10am to 2pm). If you become sunburnt stay out of the sun until you have recovered, apply cool compresses and take painkillers for the discomfort. One per cent hydrocortisone cream applied twice daily is also helpful.

WOMEN'S HEALTH

Pregnant women should receive specialised advice before travelling. The ideal time to travel is in the second trimester (between 16 and 28 weeks), when the risk of pregnancy-related problems are at their lowest and pregnant women generally feel at their best. During the first trimester there is a risk of miscarriage and in the third trimester complications such as premature labour and high blood pressure are possible. It's wise to travel with a companion. Always carry a list of quality medical facilities available at your destination and ensure you continue your standard antenatal care at these facilities. Avoid rural travel in areas with poor transportation and medical facilities. Most of all, ensure travel insurance covers all pregnancy-related possibilities, including premature labour.

Malaria is a high-risk disease in pregnancy. WHO recommends that pregnant women do *not* travel to areas with Chloroquine-resistant malaria. None of the more effective antimalarial drugs are completely safe in pregnancy.

Traveller's diarrhoea can quickly lead to dehydration and result in inadequate blood flow to the placenta. Many of the drugs used to treat various diarrhoea bugs are not recommended in pregnancy. Azithromycin is considered safe.

Urinary tract infections can be precipitated by dehydration or long bus journeys without toilet stops; bring suitable antibiotics.

TRADITIONAL MEDICINE

Throughout Southeast Asia, traditional medical systems are widely practised. There is a big difference between these traditional healing systems and 'folk' medicine, which is dubious and should be avoided.

All traditional Asian medical systems identify a vital life force, and see blockage or imbalance as causing disease. Tech niques such as herbal medicines, massage and acupuncture are utilised to bring this vital force back into balance, or to maintain balance. These therapies are best used for treating chronic disease such as chronic fatigue, arthritis, irritable bowel syndrome and some chronic skin conditions. Traditional medicines should be avoided for treating serious acute infections such as malaria.

Be aware that 'natural' doesn't always mean 'safe', and that there can be drug interactions between herbal medicines and Western medicines. If you are utilising both treatment systems ensure that you inform both practitioners what the other has prescribed.

Language

CONTENTS

The 300 plus languages spoken throughout Indonesia, except those of northern Pulau Halmahera (Halmahera Island) and most of Papua (formerly Irian Jaya), belong to the Malay-Polynesian group. Within this group are many different regional languages and dialects. Indonesia's national language is Bahasa Indonesia, which is almost identical to Malay, and most Indonesians speak it just as well as their own regional language.

Like most languages, Indonesian has a simplified colloquial form and a more developed literary form. It's among the easiest of all spoken languages to learn – there are no tenses, plurals or genders and, even better, it's easy to pronounce.

Apart from ease of learning, there's another very good reason for trying to pick up at least a handful of Indonesian words and phrases: few people are as delighted with visitors learning their language as Indonesians. They won't criticise you if you mangle your pronunciation or tangle your grammar and they make you feel like you're an expert even if you only know a dozen or so words. Bargaining also seems a whole lot easier and more natural when you do it in their language.

Written Indonesian can be idiosyncratic, however, and there are often inconsistent spellings of place names. Compound names are written as one word or two, eg Airsanih or Air Sanih, Padangbai or Padang Bai. Words starting with 'Ker' sometimes lose the 'e', as in Kerobokan/Krobokan.

Some Dutch variant spellings also remain in common use. These tend to occur in business names, with 'tj' instead of the modern **c** (as in Tjampuhan/Campuan), and 'oe' instead of the **u** (as in Soekarno/Sukarno).

PRONUNCIATION

Most letters are pronounced more or less the same as their English counterparts. Nearly all the syllables carry equal emphasis, but a good approximation is to stress the second-last syllable. The main exception to the rule is the unstressed **e** in words such as *besar* (big), pronounced 'be-sarr'.

a	as in 'father'
e	as in 'bet' when unstressed, although sometimes it's hardly pronounced at all, as in the greeting *selamat*, which sounds like 'slamat' if said quickly. When stressed, **e** is like the 'a' in 'may', as in *becak* (rickshaw), pronounced 'baycha'. There's no set rule as to when **e** is stressed or unstressed.
i	as in 'unique'
o	as in 'hot'
u	as in 'put'
ai	as in 'Thai'
au	as the 'ow' in 'cow'
ua	as 'w' when at the start of a word, eg *uang* (money), pronounced 'wong'
c	the one most likely to trip up English speakers; always as the 'ch' in 'chair'
g	as in 'get'
ng	as the 'ng' in 'sing'
ngg	as the 'ng' in 'anger'
j	as in 'jet'
r	slightly rolled
h	a little stronger than the 'h' in 'her'; almost silent at the end of a word
k	like English 'k', except at the end of a word when it's like a closing of the throat with no sound released, eg *tidak* (no/not), pronounced 'tee-da'
ny	as the 'ny' in canyon

ACCOMMODATION

I'm looking for a ...	*Saya mencari ...*
campground	*tempat kemah*
guesthouse	*rumah yang disewakan*
hotel	*hotel*
youth hostel	*losmen pemuda*

MAKING A RESERVATION

(for written and phone inquiries)

I'd like to book ...	*Saya mau pesan ...*
in the name of ...	*atas nama ...*
date	*tanggal*
from ... (date)	*dari ...*
to ... (date)	*sampai ...*
credit card	*kartu kredit*
number	*nomor*
expiry date	*masa berlakunya sampai*
Please confirm availability and price.	*Tolong dikonfirmasi mengenai ketersediaan kamar dan harga.*

Where is there a cheap hotel?
Hotel yang murah di mana?
What is the address?
Alamatnya di mana?
Could you write it down, please?
Anda bisa tolong tuliskan?
Do you have any rooms available?
Ada kamar kosong?
How much is it (per day/per person)?
Berapa harganya (sehari/seorang)?
Is breakfast included?
Apakah harganya termasuk makan pagi/sarapan?

one night	*satu malam*
one person	*satu orang*
room	*kamar*
bathroom	*kamar mandi*

I'd like a ...	*Saya cari ...*
bed	*tempat tidur*
single room	*kamar untuk seorang*
double-bed room	*tempat tidur besar satu kamar*
room with two beds	*kamar dengan dua tempat tidur*
room with a bathroom	*kamar dengan kamar mandi*

I'd like to share a dorm.	*Saya mau satu tempat tidur di asrama.*
May I see it?	*Boleh saya lihat?*
Where is the toilet?	*Kamar kecil di mana?*
Where is the bathroom?	*Kamar mandi di mana?*
I'm/we're leaving today.	*Saya/Kami berangkat hari ini.*

CONVERSATION & ESSENTIALS

Be Polite!

Pronouns, particularly 'you', are rarely used in Indonesian. When speaking to an older man (or anyone old enough to be a father), it's common to call them *bapak* (father) or simply *pak*. Similarly, an older woman is *ibu* (mother) or simply *bu*. *Tuan* is a respectful term for a man, like 'sir'. *Nyonya* is the equivalent for a married woman, and *nona* for an unmarried woman. *Anda* is the egalitarian form designed to overcome the plethora of words for the second person.

To indicate negation, *tidak* is used with verbs, adjectives and adverbs; *bukan* with nouns and pronouns.

Welcome.	*Selamat datang.*
Good morning.	*Selamat pagi.* (before 11am)
Good day.	*Selamat siang.* (noon to 2pm)
Good day.	*Selamat sore.* (3pm to 6pm)
Good evening.	*Selamat malam.* (after dark)
Good night.	*Selamat tidur.* (to someone going to bed)
Goodbye.	*Selamat tinggal.* (to one staying)
	Selamat jalan. (to one leaving)
Yes.	*Ya*
No. (not)	*Tidak.*
No. (negative)	*Bukan.*
Maybe.	*Mungkin.*
Please.	*Tolong.* (asking for help)
	Silahkan. (giving permission)
Thank you (very much).	*Terima kasih (banyak).*
You're welcome.	*Kembali.*
Sorry.	*Maaf.*
Excuse me.	*Permisi.*
Just a minute.	*Tunggu sebentar.*
How are you?	*Apa kabar?*
I'm fine.	*Kabar baik.*
What's your name?	*Siapa nama Anda?*
My name is ...	*Nama saya ...*
Where are you from?	*Anda dari mana?*
I'm from ...	*Saya dari ...*
How old are you?	*Berapa umur Anda?*
I'm ... years old.	*Umur saya ... tahun.*
I (don't) like ...	*Saya (tidak) suka ...*
Good.	*Bagus.*
Good, fine, OK.	*Baik.*

DIRECTIONS

Where is ...? *Di mana ...?*
Which way? *Ke mana?*
Go straight ahead. *Jalan terus.*
Turn left/right. *Belok kiri/kanan.*
Stop! *Berhenti!*
at the corner *di sudut*
at the traffic lights *di lampu lalu-lintas*
here/there/over there *di sini/situ/sana*
behind *di belakang*
in front of *di depan*
opposite *di seberang*
far (from) *jauh (dari)*
near (to) *dekat (dengan)*
north *utara*
south *selatan*
east *timur*
west *barat*

SIGNS

Masuk	Entrance
Keluar	Exit
Informasi	Information
Buka	Open
Tutup	Closed
Dilarang	Prohibited
Ada Kamar Kosong	Rooms Available
Polisi	Police
Kamar Kecil/Toilet	Toilets/WC
Pria	Men
Wanita	Women

beach *pantai*
island *pulau*
lake *danau*
main square *alun-alun*
market *pasar*
sea *laut*

HEALTH

I'm ill. *Saya sakit.*
It hurts here. *Sakitnya di sini.*

I'm ... *Saya sakit ...*
asthmatic *asma*
diabetic *kencing manis*
epileptic *epilepsi*

I'm allergic to ... *Saya alergi ...*
antibiotics *antibiotik*
aspirin *aspirin*
penicillin *penisilin*
bees *tawon/kumbang*
nuts *kacang*

EMERGENCIES

Help! *Tolong saya!*
There's been an accident! *Ada kecelakaan!*
I'm lost. *Saya tersesat.*
Leave me alone! *Jangan ganggu saya!*

Call ...! *Panggil ...!*
a doctor *dokter*
the police *polisi*

antiseptic *penangkal infeksi/antiseptik*
condoms *kondom*
contraceptive *kontrasepsi*
diarrhoea *mencret/diare*
medicine *obat*
nausea *mual*
sunblock cream *sunscreen/tabir surya/sunblock*
tampons *tampon*

LANGUAGE DIFFICULTIES

I (don't) understand.
Saya (tidak) mengerti.
Do you speak English?
Bisa berbicara Bahasa Inggris?
Does anyone here speak English?
Ada yang bisa berbicara Bahasa Inggris di sini?
How do you say ... in Indonesian?
Bagaimana mengatakan ... dalam Bahasa Indonesia?
What does ... mean?
Apa artinya ...?
I can only speak a little (Indonesian).
Saya hanya bisa berbicara (Bahasa Indonesia) sedikit.
Please write that word down.
Tolong tuliskan kata itu.
Can you show me (on the map)?
Anda bisa tolong tunjukkan pada saya (di peta)?

NUMBERS

1	*satu*
2	*dua*
3	*tiga*
4	*empat*
5	*lima*
6	*enam*
7	*tujuh*
8	*delapan*
9	*sembilan*
10	*sepuluh*

A half is *setengah*, pronounced 'stenger', eg *setengah kilo* (half a kilo). 'Approximately' is *kira-kira*. After the numbers one to 10, the 'teens' are *belas*, the 'tens' *puluh*, the 'hundreds' *ratus*, the 'thousands' *ribu* and 'millions' *juta*, but as a prefix *satu* (one) becomes *se-*, eg *seratus* (one hundred). Thus:

11	*sebelas*
12	*duabelas*
13	*tigabelas*
20	*duapuluh*
21	*duapuluh satu*
25	*duapuluh lima*
30	*tigapuluh*
99	*sembilanpuluh sembilan*
100	*seratus*
150	*seratus limapuluh*
200	*dua ratus*
888	*delapan ratus delapanpuluh delapan*
1000	*seribu*

PAPERWORK

name	*nama*
nationality	*kebangsaan*
date of birth	*tanggal kelahiran*
place of birth	*tempat kelahiran*
sex/gender	*jenis kelamin*
passport	*paspor*
visa	*visa*

QUESTION WORDS

Who?	*Siapa?*
What is it?	*Apa itu?*
When?	*Kapan?*
Where?	*Di mana?*
Which?	*Yang mana?*
Why?	*Kenapa?*
How?	*Bagaimana?*

SHOPPING & SERVICES

What is this?	*Apa ini?*
How much is it?	*Berapa (harganya)?*
I'd like to buy ...	*Saya mau beli ...*
I don't like it.	*Saya tidak suka.*
May I look at it?	*Boleh saya lihat?*
I'm just looking.	*Saya lihat-lihat saja.*
I'll take it.	*Saya beli.*
this/that	*ini/itu*
big/small	*besar/kecil*
bigger/smaller	*lebih besar/lebih keci*
more/less	*lebih/kurang*
expensive	*mahal*
another/one more	*satu lagi*

Do you accept ...?	*Bisa bayar pakai ...?*
credit cards	*kartu kredit*
travellers cheques	*cek perjalanan*

What time does it open/close?	*Jam berapa buka/tutup?*
May I take photos?	*Boleh saya potret?*

I'm looking for a/the ...	*Saya cari ...*
bank	*bank*
church	*gereja*
city centre	*pusat kota*
... embassy	*kedutaan ...*
food stall	*warung*
hospital	*rumah sakit*
market	*pasar*
museum	*museum*
police	*kantor polisi*
post office	*kantor pos*
public phone	*telepon umum*
public toilet	*WC ('way say') umum*
restaurant	*rumah makan*
telephone centre	*wartel*
tourist office	*kantor pariwisata*

TIME & DATES

What time is it?	*Jam berapa sekarang?*
When?	*Kapan?*
What time?	*Jam berapa?*
7 o'clock	*jam tujuh*
How many hours?	*Berapa jam?*
five hours	*lima jam*
in the morning	*pagi*
in the afternoon	*siang*
in the evening	*malam*
today	*hari ini*
tomorrow	*besok*
yesterday	*kemarin*
hour	*jam*
day	*hari*
week	*minggu*
month	*bulan*
year	*tahun*

Monday	*hari Senin*
Tuesday	*hari Selasa*
Wednesday	*hari Rabu*
Thursday	*hari Kamis*
Friday	*hari Jumat*
Saturday	*hari Sabtu*
Sunday	*hari Minggu*

January	*Januari*
February	*Februari*
March	*Maret*
April	*April*
May	*Mei*
June	*Juni*

July	*Juli*
August	*Agustus*
September	*September*
October	*Oktober*
November	*Nopember*
December	*Desember*

TRANSPORT

Public Transport

What time does the ... leave/arrive?	*Jam berapa ... berangkat/ datang?*
boat/ship	*kapal*
bus	*bis*
plane	*kapal terbang*

I'd like a ... ticket.	*Saya mau tiket ...*
one-way	*sekali jalan*
return	*pulang pergi*
1st class	*kelas satu*
2nd class	*kelas dua*

I want to go to ...	*Saya mau ke ...*
The train has been delayed/cancelled.	*Kereta terlambat/dibatalkan.*

the first	*pertama*
the last	*terakhir*
ticket	*karcis*
ticket office	*loket*
timetable	*jadwal*

Private Transport

Where can I hire a ...?	*Di mana saya bisa sewa ...?*
I'd like to hire a ...	*Saya mau sewa ...*
bicycle	*sepeda*
car	*mobil*
4WD	*gardan ganda*
motorbike	*sepeda motor*

Also available from Lonely Planet: *Indonesian Phrasebook*

ROAD SIGNS

Beri Jalan	Give Way
Bahaya	Danger
Dilarang Parkir	No Parking
Jalan Memutar	Detour
Masuk	Entry
Dilarang Mendahului	No Overtaking
Kurangi Kecepatan	Slow Down
Dilarang Masuk	No Entry
Satu Arah	One Way
Keluar	Exit
Kosongkan	Keep Clear

Is this the road to ...?	*Apakah jalan ini ke ...?*
Where's a service station?	*Di mana pompa bensin?*
Please fill it up.	*Tolong isi sampai penuh.*
I'd like ... litres.	*Minta ... liter bensin.*
diesel	*disel*
leaded petrol	*bensin bertimbal*
unleaded petrol	*bensin tanpa timbal*
I need a mechanic.	*Saya perlu montir.*
The car has broken down at ...	*Mobil mogok di...*
The motorbike won't start.	*Motor tidak bisa jalan.*
I have a flat tyre.	*Ban saya kempes.*
I've run out of petrol.	*Saya kehabisan bensin.*
I had an accident.	*Saya mengalami kecelakaan.*
(How long) Can I park here?	*(Berapa lama) Saya boleh parkir di sini?*
Where do I pay?	*Saya membayar di mana?*

TRAVEL WITH CHILDREN

Is there a/an ...?	*Ada ...?*
I need a ...	*Saya perlu...*
baby change room	*tempat ganti popok kamar*
car baby seat	*kursi anak untuk di mobil*
child-minding service	*tempat penitipan anak*
children's menu	*menu untuk anak-anak*
disposable nappies/diapers	*popok sekali pakai*
formula	*susu kaleng*
(English-speaking) babysitter	*suster (yang bisa berbicara Bahasa Inggris)*
highchair	*kursi anak*
potty	*pispot*
stroller	*kereta anak/dorongan anak*

Are children allowed?	*Boleh bawa anak-anak?*

Glossary

See p89 for food and drink terms.

ABRI – Angkatan Bersenjata Republik Indonesia; the armed forces; now TNI
adat – traditional laws and regulations
air – water
air panas – hot springs
air terjun – waterfall
AMA – Associated Mission Aviation; Catholic missionary air service operating in remote regions of Papua
anak – child
andong – horse-drawn passenger cart
angklung – musical instrument made from different lengths and thicknesses of bamboo suspended in a frame
angkot – or *angkota;* short for *angkutan kota* (city transport); small minibuses covering city routes
angkudes – short for *angkutan pedesaan;* minibuses running to nearby villages from cities, or between villages
anjing – dog
arja – refined operatic form of Balinese theatre
Arjuna – hero of the *Mahabharata* epic and a popular temple gate guardian image

babi rusa – pig deer
bahasa – language; Bahasa Indonesia is the national language
bajaj – motorised three-wheeler taxi found in Jakarta
bale – open-sided Balinese pavilion, house or shelter with steeply pitched roof; meeting place
bandar – harbour, port
bandar udara – often shortened to *bandara;* airport
banjar – area of a Balinese village where community activities are held
bapak – often shortened to *pak;* father; also a polite form of address to any older man
barat – west
Barong – mythical lion-dog creature
batik – cloth made by coating part of the fabric with wax, then dyeing it and melting the wax out
batik cap – stamped batik
batik tulis – hand-painted or literally 'written' batik
becak – bicycle-rickshaw
bemo – minibus
bendi – two-person horse-drawn cart; used in Sulawesi, Sumatra and Maluku
bensin – petrol
benteng – fort
bentor – motorised becak
Betawi – original name of Batavia (now Jakarta); ethnic group indigenous to Jakarta
bis – bus
bouraq – winged horselike creature with the head of a woman
Brahma – the creator; with Shiva and Vishnu part of the trinity of chief Hindu gods
bu – shortened form of *ibu*
bukit – hill
bule – common term for foreigner
bupati – government official in charge of a *kabupaten*

caci – a ceremonial martial art in which participants duel with whips and shields
camat – government official in charge of a *kecamatan* (district)
candi – shrine or temple; usually Hindu or Buddhist of ancient Javanese design
cenderawasih – bird of paradise

dalang – puppeteer and storyteller of *wayang kulit*
danau – lake
dangdut – popular Indonesian music that is characterised by wailing vocals and a strong beat
Departemen Kehutanan – Forest Department
desa – village
dinas pariwisata – tourist office
dokar – two-person, horse-drawn cart
dukun – faith healer and herbal doctor; mystic

Gajah Mada – famous Majapahit prime minister
gamelan – traditional Javanese and Balinese orchestra
gang – alley or footpath
Garuda – mythical man-bird, the vehicle of Vishnu and the modern symbol of Indonesia
gereja – church
gili – islet, atoll
Golkar – Golongan Karya (Functional Groupings) political party
gua – or *goa*; cave
gunung – mountain
gunung api – volcano; literally 'fire mountain'

harga touris – tourist price
hutan – forest, jungle

ibu – often shortened to *bu;* mother; also polite form of address to an older woman
ikat – cloth in which the pattern is produced by dyeing the individual threads before weaving

jadwal – timetable
jalan – abbreviated to Jl; street or road
jalan jalan – to go for a stroll
jalan potong – short cut
jam karet – 'rubber time'; time is flexible
jamu – herbal medicine
jembatan – bridge
jilbab – Muslim head covering worn by women

kabupaten – regency
kain – cloth
kaki lima – mobile food carts; literally 'five feet' (the three feet of the cart and the two of the vendor)
kala – demonic face often seen over temple gateways
kamar kecil – toilet; literally 'small room'; also known as WC (pronounced way-say)
kampung – village, neighbourhood
kantor – office
Kantor Bupati – Governor's Office
karang – coral, coral reef, atoll
kebaya – women's long-sleeved blouse
kepala balai – Dayak village head (Sumatra)
kepala desa – village head
kepulauan – archipelago
ketoprak – popular Javanese folk theatre
Ketuktilu – traditional Sundanese (Java) dance in which professional female dancers perform for male spectators
kijang – a type of deer; also a popular Toyota 4WD vehicle, often used for public transport (Kijang)
KKN – Korupsi, Kolusi, Nepotisme; Corruption, Collusion, Nepotism; buzz word of the post-Soeharto reform era
kora-kora – canoe (Papua)
kramat – shrine
kraton – or *keraton;* walled city palace
kretek – Indonesian clove cigarette
kris – wavy-bladed traditional dagger, often held to have spiritual or magical powers
krisis moneter – or *krismon;* monetary crisis
kulit – leather

ladang – nonirrigated field for dryland crops; often farmed using slash-and-burn agriculture
lapangan – field, square
laut – sea, ocean
Legong – classic Balinese dance performed by young girls; Legong dancer
lontar – type of palm tree; traditional books were written on the dried leaves of the lontar palm
losmen – basic accommodation, usually cheaper than hotels and often family-run

MAF – Mission Aviation Fellowship; Protestant missionary air service that operates in remote regions
Mahabharata – venerated Hindu holy book, telling of the battle between the Pandavas and the Kauravas
Majapahit – last great Javanese Hindu dynasty, pushed out of Java into Bali by the rise of Islamic power
makam – grave
mandau – machete (Kalimantan)
mandi – common Indonesian form of bath, consisting of a large water tank from which water is ladled over the body
marapu – term for all spiritual forces, including gods, spirits and ancestors
mata air panas – hot springs
menara – minaret, tower
meru – multiroofed shrines in Balinese temples; the same roof style also can be seen in ancient Javanese mosques
mesjid – *masjid* in Papua; mosque
mikrolet – small taxi; tiny *opelet*
moko – bronze drum from Alor island (Nusa Tenggara)
muezzin – mosque official who calls the faithful to prayer five times a day

ngadhu – parasol-like thatched roof; ancestor totem of the Ngada people of Flores
nusa – island

Odalan – temple festival held every 210 days (duration of the Balinese year)
ojek – or *ojeg;* motorcycle taxi
oleh-oleh – souvenirs
opelet – small intracity minibus, usually with side benches in the back
OPM – Organisasi Papua Merdeka; Free Papua Movement; main group that opposes Indonesian rule of Papua
ora – Komodo dragon
orang putih – white person, foreigner; *bule* is more commonly used

pak – shortened form of *bapak*
PAN – Partai Amanat Nasional; National Mandate Party
pantai – beach
parkir – parking attendant
pasar – market
pasar malam – night market
pasar terapung – floating market
pasir – beach, sand
patas – express, express bus
patola – ikat motif of a hexagon framing a type of four-pronged star
PDI – Partai Demokrasi Indonesia; Indonesian Democratic Party
PDI–P – Partai Demokrasi Indonesia–Perjuangan; Indonesian Democratic Party for Struggle
peci – Muslim black felt cap

pegunungan – mountain range
pelabuhan – harbour, port, dock
pelan pelan – slowly
pelawangan – gateway
Pelni – Pelayaran Nasional Indonesia; national shipping line with a fleet of passenger ships operating throughout the archipelago
pemangku – temple priest
pencak silat – form of martial arts originally from Sumatra, but now popular throughout Indonesia
pendopo – large, open-sided pavilion that serves as an audience hall; located in front of a Javanese palace
penginapan – simple lodging house
perahu – or *prahu;* boat
perahu lading – longboat
perahu tambing – ferry boat
pesanggrahan – or *pasanggrahan;* lodge for government officials where travellers can usually stay
pete-pete – a type of *mikrolet* or bemo found in Sulawesi
pinang – betel nut
PHKA – Perlindungan Hutan & Konservasi Alam; the Directorate General of Forest Protection & Nature Conservation; manages Indonesia's national parks; formerly PHPA
pinisi – Makassar or Bugis schooner
PKB – Partai Kebangkitan Bangsa; National Awakening Party
pondok – or *pondok wisata;* guesthouse or lodge; hut
PPP – Partai Persatuan Pembangunan; Development Union Party
prasada – shrine or temple; usually Hindu or Buddhist of ancient Javanese design
pulau – island
puputan – warrior's fight to the death; honourable, but suicidal, option when faced with an unbeatable enemy
pura – Balinese temple, shrine
pura dalem – Balinese temple of the dead
pura puseh – Balinese temple of origin
puri – palace
pusaka – sacred heirlooms of a royal family
puskesmas – short for *pusat kesehatan masyarakat;* community health centre

rafflesia – gigantic flower found in Sumatra and Kalimantan, with blooms spreading up to a metre
Ramadan – Muslim month of fasting, when devout Muslims refrain from eating, drinking and smoking during daylight hours
Ramayana – one of the great Hindu holy books; many Balinese and Javanese dances and tales are based on stories from the Ramayana
rangda – witch; evil black magic spirit of Balinese tales and dances
rawa – swamp, marsh, wetlands
rebab – two-stringed bowed lute
reformasi – reform; refers to political reform after the repression of the Soeharto years
RMS – Republik Maluku Selatan; South Maluku Republic; main group that opposed Indonesian rule of southern Maluku
rumah adat – traditional house
rumah makan – restaurant or warung
rumah sakit – hospital, literally 'sick house'

saron – xylophone-like gamelan instrument, with bronze bars that are struck with a wooden mallet
sarong – or *sarung;* all-purpose cloth, often sewn into a tube, and worn by women, men and children
Sasak – native of Lombok
sawah – individual rice field; wet-rice method of cultivation
selat – strait
selatan – south
selimut – blanket
semenanjung – peninsula
sirih – betel nut, chewed as a mild narcotic
songket – silver- or gold-threaded cloth, hand woven using floating-weft technique
suling – bamboo flute
sungai – river
surat jalan – travel permit

taksi – common term for a public minibus; taxi
taman – ornamental garden, park, reserve
taman laut – marine park, marine reserve
taman nasional – national park
tanjung – peninsula, cape
tarling – musical style of the Cirebon (Java) area, featuring guitar, *suling* and voice
taxi sungai – cargo-carrying river ferry with bunks on the upper level
telaga – lake
telepon kartu – telephone card
teluk – bay
timur – east
tirta – water (Bali)
TNI – Tentara Nasional Indonesia; Indonesian armed forces; formerly ABRI
toko (e)mas – gold shop
tomate – Torajan funeral ceremony
tongkonan – traditional Torajan house with towering roof (Sulawesi)
topeng – wooden mask used in dance-dramas and funerary dances

uang – money
ular – snake
utara – north

wali songo – nine saints of Islam, who spread the religion throughout Java
Wallace Line – hypothetical line dividing Bali and Kalimantan from Lombok and Sulawesi; marks the end of Asian and the beginning of Australasian flora and fauna zones
waringin – banyan tree; large, shady tree with drooping branches that root and can produce new trees
warnet – short for *wartel internet;* internet stall or centre
warpostel – or *warpapostel;* wartel that also handles postal services
wartel – short for *warung telekomunikasi;* private telephone office
warung – food stall
wayang kulit – shadow-puppet play
wayang orang – or *wayang wong;* people theatre
wayang topeng – masked dance-drama
Wektu Telu – religion peculiar to Lombok that originated in Bayan and combines many tenets of Islam and aspects of other faiths
wisma – guesthouse or lodge

Behind the Scenes

THIS BOOK

The 1st edition of *Indonesia*, way back in 1986, was the collective work of Alan Samalgaski, Ginny Bruce and Mary Covernton. And cramming this immense, sprawling jewel of an archipelago into one action-packed volume has kept us busy ever since... In subsequent editions we've had 23 different authors travelling the country in search of adventure, enlightenment and ferry timetables.

The previous (7th) edition was the work of Patrick Witton, Matt Warren, Virginia Jealous, Etain O'Carroll, Nick Ray, Alan Tarbell, Mark Elliott and Paul Greenway. (Andrew Tudor and Audra Kunciunas provided expert nous regarding surfing and eating respectively.)

For this 8th edition, coordinating author Justine Vaisutis led a crack team of authors: Patrick Witton (History, the Culture, Indonesian Crafts, Environment, Food & Drink), Neal Bedford (Java), Ryan Ver Berkmoes (Bali), China Williams (Sumatra), Iain Stewart (Nusa Tenggara), Nick Ray (Sulawesi), Mark Elliott (Maluku) and Wendy Yanagihara (Papua). Justine also authored Kalimantan, Destination Indonesia, Getting Started, Itineraries, Snapshot, Directory and Transport. Indonesia expert journalist and author John Martinkus wrote the Indonesia's Separatist Conflicts section in the History chapter. Dr Trish Batchelor wrote the Health chapter.

This guidebook was commissioned in Lonely Planet's Melbourne office, and produced by the following:

Commissioning Editors Marg Toohey, Jessa Boanas-Dewes
Coordinating Editor Nigel Chin
Coordinating Cartographer Kusnandar
Coordinating Layout Designer Wibowo Rusli
Managing Editor Suzannah Shwer
Managing Cartographers Corie Waddell, Julie Sheridan
Assisting Editors Sarah Bailey, Yvonne Byron, Lutie Clark, Louise Clarke, Chris Girdler, Kim Hutchins, Alan Murphy, Maryanne Netto, Rosie Nicholson, Liani Solari, Laura Stansfeld, Simon Williamson
Assisting Cartographers Daniel Fennessy, Jody Whiteoak
Cover Designer Jane Hart
Colour Designer Jacqueline McLeod
Project Managers Eoin Dunlevy, Craig Kilburn
Language Content Coordinator Quentin Frayne
Talk2Us Coordinator Haydn Ellis

Terima kasih banyak Helen Christinis, Sally Darmody, Liz Heynes, Errol Hunt, Virginia Jealous, Helen Koehne, Etain O'Carroll, Susan Paterson, Lauren Rollheiser, Dianne Schallmeiner, Matt Warren, Celia Wood

THANKS

JUSTINE VAISUTIS

The following folk enhanced my journey considerably and I owe them a huge debt of gratitude: Lucas Zwaal at Mesra tours for his tireless efforts and extraordinary knowledge; Suryadi for his expertise, outstanding noodles and engaging conversations; Susan O'Farrell for a fab dinner, excellent tips and lovely company in Berau; Tailah for all things Banjarmasin; Harry and Danson for unforgettable Tanjung Puting; the 12-year-old *ojek* driver who got me to the airport in Ketapang and didn't even overcharge; Alex in Pontianak;

THE LONELY PLANET STORY

The story begins with a classic travel adventure: Tony and Maureen Wheeler's 1972 journey across Europe and Asia to Australia. There was no useful information about the overland trail then, so Tony and Maureen published the first Lonely Planet guidebook to meet a growing need.

From a kitchen table, Lonely Planet has grown to become the largest independent travel publisher in the world, with offices in Melbourne (Australia), Oakland (USA) and London (UK). Today Lonely Planet guidebooks cover the globe. There is an ever-growing list of books and information in a variety of media. Some things haven't changed. The main aim is still to make it possible for adventurous travellers to get out there – to explore and better understand the world.

At Lonely Planet we believe travellers can make a positive contribution to the countries they visit – if they respect their host communities and spend their money wisely. Every year 5% of company profit is donated to charities around the world.

Marion (from France) and Romanic (from Quebec) for laughs, chats and Bintang in Pontianak; and all the gracious locals who patiently interpreted my pidgin Bahasa.

Much kudos, respect and gratitude to my highly talented co-authors; I hope we can do it again sometime. Thanks to Corie Waddell and Marg Toohey for tireless in-house support and to my awesome crew at ACF, particularly Anna, Margie, Katie, Cathy, Josh and Julie.

At home and always thanks to my beautiful sister Aidy for always propping me up when I need it, as well as Mum and Bill for true grace under trying circumstances, Dad for the adventurer genes, Alan for infinite advice, and Bugs for secret languages, nummits and all things wingman.

NEAL BEDFORD

In no order of preference, I'd like to thank: Rebecca and Andrew in Jakarta for getting me off to a flying start; Eddie at Carita for his in-depth knowledge of the west coast; the Jakarta information office for help when needed; Bart of Bugils fame for sharing his thoughts on life in the big city; Daniel Ziv for his insider tips on Jakarta; the domino crowd in Pangandaran for keeping me from my bed and out of the rain; Ana for her impromptu tour of Wonosobo and the chance to see an Indonesian school up close; Atik and Wildan for their precious friendship and healing powers; Jane in Surabaya for taking the time to chat about life; Howie and the Malang crew for retelling the tales of expats and teachers and living it up at L'Amour Fou; and Rene and Rosa for tiger tales and some of the best home-cooked food around. And thank you to friends and family for keeping me sane while on the road. Apologies for anyone I missed out – please take a thank you now.

MARK ELLIOTT

Thank you to the great team of LP authors, editors and cartographers; to Anang for pointers on esoteric Islam; Antonius and Gerson for insights into Kei culture; Farmin in Ambon; Jain in Pelauw; Robert and Isrina Abraham in Sila; Losina Siahaya, Adolf Sahetapy, Yonas Likumafa, Mary and Elen Pasanaya in Itawaka; Coco in Ai; Max Dopeng in Masohi; Ferdy, Udin, Mundix and Dhani in Ternate; Muhlis in Tidore; Alan, Abba, Bahri and Fabienne in Banda; and to Laszlo for help and encouragement the first time round. Most of all eternal thanks to my fabulous parents and wife Dani without whose love and support the whole adventure of life would be so much less fulfilling.

NICK RAY

First and foremost, a big thanks to the good folk of Sulawesi who welcome outsiders with a warm smile wherever they venture. A huge thanks to my wonderful wife, Kulikar Sotho, who continues to encourage my travels, and to my young son, Mr J, who will soon be taking to the road for adventures himself. Your love and support makes it all possible. Also many thanks to my Mum and Dad, who gave me the thirst for adventure from a young age. And a big thanks to good friend John McGeoghan who joined me for some of this trip, making the long bus rides more memorable and the nightlife sections more rounded.

Back in Indonesia, many thanks to Agus Lamba of Indosella, who joined me for some motorbiking around Tana Toraja on this trip. Thanks also to Hernan, who escorted me on some trips in the south. In the north, thanks to many of the dive community, who filled me in on diving around the Manado peninsula and the nightlife of Manado. And, of course, the dive operators of the Togean Islands, who are trying so hard to promote their beautiful home. Oh for more boat services!

IAIN STEWART

Firstly I'd like to thank my wife Fiona and my extended family for keeping it all together back in the UK, and for minding Louis and Monty so well. I was helped by a great many people across Nusa Tenggara, though I'd particularly like to mention Guy and Nadine, Simon of Blue Marlin, Marcus Stevens at Manta Dive, Jo and Marta, my partner-in-crime Sean in Gili T, Christine Barnes and the crew in Gili Air, Barbara and Mel in Senggigi, Made in Kuta, Edo in Sumbawa, Mr Tarsi and Reefseekers in Labuanbajo, Konrardus and Henry in Maumere, Hussein in Alor, Pae Nope in Timor and Mr David in Sumba. Special thanks to Marg Toohey for her patience, the noodles and the tour.

RYAN VER BERKMOES

Many thanks as always to the crew on Bali. Jeremy Allan, Hanafi, Eliot Cohen, Kerry and Milton Turner, Janet de Neefe, Karen McClellan and the wonderful crew of the Ubud Writer's Festival, Jamie James, Kamal Kaul and many more make me feel like I've come home every time I exit the airport into the South Bali hubbub. Special thanks this time to Marg Toohey who proved more partner than shadow both in exploration and when it came time to mix the G&Ts. And thanks as always to Erin Corrigan who lures me home even from places I feel at home.

CHINA WILLIAMS

When you speak Bahasa as poorly as China does, there are a lot of people to thank: Yalta, Lukman and the staff at Kantor Bahasa Provinsi in Jambi; Wendra and Torno in Bukittinggi; Putra in Maninjau; Yu-mee in Padang; Aris in Tuk Tuk; Ton and Marjan in Pulau Weh; Budi, Tim and Alex in Kerinci; Dave Allen, Kate Lewis and the volunteers from UWCSEA in Banda Aceh; Kenneth and Jule in Batam; Ismail in Palembang; and Ichwan and Hermawan in Medan. Thanks to all the sweet chit-chatters on bus and ferry rides, the folks who offered me kindness and smokes, and the travellers (Kris, Lena, Stefan and Sibylle) who shared tips and trips with me. And heaps of thanks to my husband who drove through a blizzard to take me to the airport. Much gratitude to Justine Vaisutis, Marg Toohey and the talented LP production team.

PATRICK WITTON

To Ron Witton, Asti Mulyana and Rachel Blake – many thanks for your generous help and encouragement.

WENDY YANAGIHARA

A mountain of thanks to the many people of Papua who smoothed the path before me – or who didn't – subsequently forcing me to chill out. I am most grateful for the invaluable help and wisdom of Yance Rumaseuw, John Etama, Matheus Rumbarar, Micha Ronsumbre, Benny Lesomar, wonderful Frans of Wasur National Park, lovely Ms Lea in Merauke, Yoris Wanggai, Alex Ferdinand, and Ita Tarigan. *Terima kasih banyak* to Marg for sending me, to Virginia for the leads, and to Justine for keeping tabs. And warm thanks to Kim, Jason, and Eric for putting some fires out and keeping other ones burning.

OUR READERS

Many thanks to the travellers who used the last edition and wrote to us with helpful hints, useful advice and interesting anecdotes:

A Adriano Abbado, Barry Acott, Erik Albrecht, Simone Alesich, Montvazski Anita, Kori Anshor, Lisa Antoine, Claus Ascanius Melvej, Martina Ascherl **B** Allen Bageant, Marleen Bakker, Dieter Balz, Dalk-Ascan Bandilla, Andrew Barber, Miha Barboric, Alexandra Bbrown, Will Beebe, Georgina Benison, Zoe & Shane Bilston, James Bishop, Menno Blom, K Blumenstock, Martin Bode, Frank Booij, Paul Bookallil, Philipp Borgs, Jorma Bosch, Thijs Bosch, Marcel Botman, Rin Boudny, Craig Bradley, Bryan Brandsma, Mark & Cielito Brownbridge, Henry Brownrigg, Nikki Buran **C** H Champion, Helen Chandler, Aswin & Rama Chandrakantan, Deepika Chandrakantan, Anna Cleary, Keith Clemson, Alain & Catherine Cochard, Ruben Coertse, Scott Cole, Alexandra Corradini, Ruth Coxhead, Martin Crichton, Ian Cruickshank **D** Kiki Damayanti, Leon de Borst, Marc De Cotret, Rocco de Giacomo, Arno de Jong, Fedor de Koning, Fedor & Diana de Koning, Marjolein de Quartel, Tineke de Wal, F Demoet, Walter Denzel, Richard Desomme, Jurgen Detienne, Sylvia Deuse, Marie D'haenens, Aprie Dj, Petra Dorn, Paul Dykstra **E** Camille Egger-Foetisch, Philipp Ehrne, Justine Ellis, Elisabeth Elmquist, John Evans **F** Faridah Fauzi, Evan Fearn, Marek Feldman, Claas Feye, Kay Fillingham, Lisa Fleming, Philipp & Mutiara Foerster, David Free, Gerd Fricke, Alexander Fuchs, Tim Fudge, Yuichi Fukumoto **G** Vincent Gaubert, Alex Gazzini, Claudia Gazzini, Daniela Gazzini, Fabian Gerhardt, Erick Gilbert, Jess Glanfield, Maria Goeth, Mark Goniwiecha, Tracey Goodwin, Tiimur Gorshunov, Gina Graham, Thomas Grootueld, Petra Gruber, Barbara Guthrie **H** Arthur Hallett, Thomas Hansson, Teddy Hariyanto, Mariette Harms, Trudi Harper-Smith, Sian Harrison, Mel Hawken, James Hay, Susen Hei, Mary Herman, Stanimir Hilan, Michael Hill, Tamarack Hockin, Robrecht Hoet, Hille Hoogland, Eelko Hooijmaaijers, Aziza Horsham, Randy Horton, David Houliston, Petr Hruska, Michael Huelsmann, Doris Hug, Joyce Huisman, Hans Hulscher **I** Sebastian Imizcoz, Stephen Ireland **J** Eric Jansen, Paul Jansen, Christina Jensen, Jan-Henrik Johnsen, Wally Jones **K** Agnes Kallenberg, Salim Kamaluddin, Haemish Kane, Viktor Kaposi, Catherine Kelly, Wendy Kerr, Esther Killat, James & Kasia Kilvington, Pierre Kintgen, Lothar Kittstein, Michael Kiworr, Frank Klein, Catherine Koch, Deng Koh, Els Koot, Georges Korb, Marieke Krijnen, Hari Kuswanto **L** Sarah Lamigeon, Sienny Lukman Lauw, Edna Lee, Erik Leenders, Bernard Leigh, Aleksandra Liana, Wei Lim, Claudia Linker, Alena Liskova, Jane Lombardo, Michael Lord, Jerry

SEND US YOUR FEEDBACK

We love to hear from travellers – your comments keep us on our toes and help make our books better. Our well-travelled team reads every word on what you loved or loathed about this book. Although we cannot reply individually to postal submissions, we always guarantee that your feedback goes straight to the appropriate authors, in time for the next edition. Each person who sends us information is thanked in the next edition – and the most useful submissions are rewarded with a free book.

To send us your updates – and find out about Lonely Planet events, newsletters and travel news – visit our award-winning website: **www.lonelyplanet.com/contact**.

Note: We may edit, reproduce and incorporate your comments in Lonely Planet products such as guidebooks, websites and digital products, so let us know if you don't want your comments reproduced or your name acknowledged. For a copy of our privacy policy visit www.lonelyplanet.com/privacy.

Low, Roy Low **M** John MacNeil, Paul Macomber, Andrea Magnaghi, Ash Mahajan, Claire Makin, Noriko Manabe, Ukirsari Manggalani, Lee Marsdon, Tim Marshall, Anna Marti, Adrian Martin, Marcello Massoni, Rosslind McHugh, Eric Mein, Claus Melvej, Sander Mieras, Hana Mijovic, Bjarne Milian, Anita Montvajszki, Kathy Morf, Christian Mueck, Lou & Lyn Muench, Bernhard Muerkoester, Sonja Muller, Caroline Murray **N** Dario Nardi, Doug Nareau, Maite Navarrete, Steve Newcomer, Marc Neyt, Dennis Nilsson, Thomas Nilsson, Akane Nishimura, Caren Nitschke, Andreas Nordin, Rachmad Nurdiansyah **O** Sebastian Oergel, Shoko Okahara, Bronwyn O'Malley, Martin Ortner **P** Patrice Parent, Abel Peter, Therese Picado, Lorenzo Pilati, Tracey Polglaze, Maarten Post, Volker Preusser, Ross Pringle, Marcel Put, Bernard Puttaert **Q** Helene Quoidbach **R** Yatinawiah Rasaep, Nicola Reiss, Danielle Rijshouwer, Mandy & Kathrin Ritter, Aldo Rodenhaeuser, Deddy Rosadi, Erik Rovers, Stefano Russiani, Gabriela Rutz **S** Delia Sala, Noel Salazar, Lily Santoso, Martina Sauter, Sean Scannell, Sally Schaffer, Christian Schober, Inge Schrama, Birte Schrein, Amir Schuddebeurs, Penny Secomb, Wolfgang Seel, Fabienne Seydoux, Matt Shanks, David Shannon, Nancy Shneiderman, Geoff Sims, A F Siraa, Casey Smith, Valerie Smith, Sifra Soer, Anwar Soerjomataram, Mara Soplantila, Brian Souter, Federica Spagni, Jan O Staal, Karin Staal, Iren Stanchovska, Yvonne Stephenson **T** Danko Taborosi, Linda Taffijn, Robert Tagg, Anna Tayor, Christine Therrien, Thecla Thielemans, Marloes Tjallema, Rick Tjeerds, Inge Tjeerdsma, Lean Tjioe, Stanley & Christine Tonkins, Roberto Trimarchi, Sean Turner **V** Jarg van Asch, Olaf van der Geest, Remi van der Heiden, Frank van der Most, Kristof van der Schueren, Suzanne van der Velden, Ferre Van Dyck, Monique Van Griensven, Aleid van Hasselt, Jeroen van Hemert, Dennis van Kroonenburg, Jean van Leerdam, Bea van Meel, Inger van Merm, Janine van Noort, Catherine van Ravestyn, Stella van Room, Patrick van Vreeswijk, Peter van Vreeswijk, Arianne Verburg, Kaposi Viktor, Giorgio Vintani, Nienke Vulink **W** Richard Walker, Cynthia Webb, Xuess Wee, Maschal Weeland, Gunter Wehner, Klaus Weiner, David Whitehead, Christopher Whittington, Tamara Wiher, Paul Wilding, Marisa Wilson, Dominique Wirz, Astrid Wortelboer, Wendy Wuijts **Y** Joseph Yin

Index

000 Map pages
000 Photograph pages

000 Map pages
000 Photograph pages

INDEX

000 Map pages
000 Photograph pages

INDEX

N

000 Map pages
000 Photograph pages

INDEX

INDEX

000 Map pages
000 Photograph pages

12am
1am
2am
3am
4am
5am
6am
7am
8am
9am
10am
11am
12pm
Mon
Sun
International Date Line
ARCTIC OCEAN
Queen Elizabeth Is (Can)
Ellesmere Is (Can)
Greenland (Denmark)
GREENLAND SEA
BAFFIN BAY
CHUKCHI SEA
BEAUFORT SEA
Banks Is (Can)
Victoria Is (Can)
NORWEGIAN SEA
Russia
Alaska (US)
Baffin Is (Can)
Iceland
NORTH SEA
HUDSON BAY
BERING SEA
LABRADOR SEA
United Kingdom
Canada
GULF OF ALASKA
Ireland
NORTH ATLANTIC OCEAN
8.30am
Azores (Part)
Spain
Portugal
United States
NORTH PACIFIC OCEAN
Bermuda (UK)
Morocco
Midway Is (US)
Canary Is (Sp)
GULF OF MEXICO
Mexico
The Bahamas
Cuba
Haiti
Hawaii (US)
Eastern Caribbean Islands
Mauritania
Mali
Cape Verde
Guatemala
CARIBBEAN SEA
Nicaragua
Senegal
Burkina Faso
Guinea
Panama
Venezuela
Guyana
Liberia
Ghana
Galapagos Is (Ecuador)
Colombia
Suriname
GULF OF GUINEA
EQUATOR
Ecuador
Kiribati
Ascension (UK)
Samoa
2.30am
Peru
Brazil
Bolivia
Tahiti
French Polynesia (Fr)
Tonga
Cook Is (NZ)
SOUTH ATLANTIC OCEAN
Pitcairn Is (UK)
3.30am
Easter Is (Chile)
Paraguay
Chile
Uruguay
Argentina
Tristan da Cunha (UK)
New Zealand
Gough Is (UK)
12.45am
Chatham Is (NZ)
SOUTH PACIFIC OCEAN
Falkland Is (UK)
South Georgia & South Sandwich Is (UK)
Bouvet Is (Norway)